THE ROUTLEDGE COMPANION TO PHILOSOPHY OF LAW

The Routledge Companion to Philosophy of Law provides a comprehensive, non-technical philosophical treatment of the fundamental questions about the nature of law. Its coverage includes law's relation to morality and the moral obligations to obey the law as well as the main philosophical debates about particular legal areas such as criminal responsibility, property, contracts, family law, law and justice in the international domain, legal paternalism, and the rule of law.

The entirely new content has been written specifically for newcomers to the field, making the volume particularly useful for undergraduate and graduate courses in philosophy of law and related areas. All 39 chapters, written by the world's leading researchers and edited by an internationally distinguished scholar, bring a focused, philosophical perspective to their subjects. *The Routledge Companion to Philosophy of Law* promises to be a valuable and much consulted student resource for many years.

Andrei Marmor is Professor of Philosophy and Maurice Jones Jr. Professor of Law at the University of Southern California.

Routledge Philosophy Companions

Routledge Philosophy Companions offer thorough, high quality surveys and assessments of the major topics and periods in philosophy. Covering key problems, themes and thinkers, all entries are specially commissioned for each volume and written by leading scholars in the field. Clear, accessible and carefully edited and organised, *Routledge Philosophy Companions* are indispensable for anyone coming to a major topic or period in philosophy, as well as for the more advanced reader.

The Routledge Companion to Ancient Philosophy
Edited by Frisbee Sheffield and James Warren

The Routledge Companion to Eighteenth Century Philosophy
Edited by Aaron Garrett

Forthcoming:

The Routledge Companion to Hermeneutics
Edited by Jeff Malpas and Hans-Helmuth Gander

The Routledge Companion to Sixteenth Century Philosophy
Edited by Benjamin Hill and Henrik Lagerlund

The Routledge Companion to Seventeenth Century Philosophy
Edited by Dan Kaufman

The Routledge Companion to Islamic Philosophy
Edited by Richard C. Taylor and Luis Xavier López-Farjeat

The Routledge Companion to Philosophy of Literature
Edited by Noël Carroll and John Gibson

The Routledge Companion to Bioethics
Edited by John Arras, Rebecca Kukla, and Elizabeth Fenton

The Routledge Companion to Medieval Philosophy
Edited by Richard Cross and JT Paasch

The Routledge Companion to Thought Experiments
Edited by James Robert Brown, Yiftach Fehige, and Michael T. Stuart

The Routledge Companion to Philosophy of Race
Edited by Paul C. Taylor, Linda Martín Alcoff, and Luvell Anderson

The Routledge Companion to Virtue Ethics
Edited by Lorraine Besser-Jones and Michael Slote

The Routledge Companion to Environmental Ethics
Edited by Benjamin Hale and Andrew Light

The Routledge Companion to Free Will
Edited by Meghan Griffith, Neil Levy, and Kevin Timpe

The Routledge Companion to Philosophy of Technology
Edited by Joseph Pitt and Ashley Shew Helfin

The Routledge Companion to Feminist Philosophy
Edited by Ann Garry, Serene J. Khader, and Alison Stone

The Routledge Companion to Philosophy of Medicine
Edited by Miriam Solomon, Jeremy R. Simon, and Harold Kincaid

PRAISE FOR THE SERIES

The Routledge Companion to Aesthetics

"This is an immensely useful book that belongs in every college library and on the bookshelves of all serious students of aesthetics."—*Journal of Aesthetics and Art Criticism*

"The succinctness and clarity of the essays will make this a source that individuals not familiar with aesthetics will find extremely helpful."—*The Philosophical Quarterly*

"An outstanding resource in aesthetics . . . this text will not only serve as a handy reference source for students and faculty alike, but it could also be used as a text for a course in the philosophy of art."—*Australasian Journal of Philosophy*

"Attests to the richness of modern aesthetics . . . the essays in central topics—many of which are written by well-known figures—succeed in being informative, balanced and intelligent without being too difficult."—*British Journal of Aesthetics*

"This handsome reference volume . . . belongs in every library."—**CHOICE**

"The *Routledge Companions* to Philosophy have proved to be a useful series of high quality surveys of major philosophical topics and this volume is worthy enough to sit with the others on a reference library shelf."—*Philosophy and Religion*

The Routledge Companion to Philosophy of Religion

" . . . a very valuable resource for libraries and serious scholars."—**CHOICE**

"The work is sure to be an academic standard for years to come . . . I shall heartily recommend *The Routledge Companion to Philosophy of Religion* to my students and colleagues and hope that libraries around the country add it to their collections."—*Philosophia Christi*

The Routledge Companion to Philosophy of Science

A **CHOICE** Outstanding Academic Title 2008

"With a distinguished list of internationally renowned contributors, an excellent choice of topics in the field, and well-written, well-edited essays throughout, this compendium is an excellent resource. Highly recommended."—**CHOICE**

"Highly recommended for history of science and philosophy collections."—*Library Journal*

"This well conceived companion, which brings together an impressive collection of distinguished authors, will be invaluable to novices and experienced readers alike."—*Metascience*

The Routledge Companion to Twentieth Century Philosophy

"To describe this volume as ambitious would be a serious understatement . . . full of scholarly rigor, including detailed notes and bibliographies of interest to professional philosophers. . . . Summing up: Essential."—**CHOICE**

The Routledge Companion to Philosophy and Film

"A fascinating, rich volume offering dazzling insights and incisive commentary on every page . . . Every serious student of film will want this book . . . Summing Up: Highly recommended."—**CHOICE**

The Routledge Companion to Philosophy of Psychology

"This work should serve as the standard reference for those interested in gaining a reliable overview of the burgeoning field of philosophical psychology. Summing Up: Essential."—**CHOICE**

The Routledge Companion to Metaphysics

"The *Routledge Philosophy Companions* series has a deserved reputation for impressive scope and scholarly value. This volume is no exception . . . Summing Up: Highly recommended."—**CHOICE**

The Routledge Companion to Nineteenth Century Philosophy

A **CHOICE** Outstanding Academic Title 2010

"This is a crucial resource for advanced undergraduates and faculty of any discipline who are interested in the 19th-century roots of contemporary philosophical problems. Summing Up: Essential."—**CHOICE**

The Routledge Companion to Ethics

"This fine collection merits a place in every university, college, and high school library for its invaluable articles covering a very broad range of topics in ethics[.] . . . With its remarkable clarity of writing and its very highly qualified contributors, this volume is must reading for anyone interested in the latest developments in these important areas of thought and practice. Summing Up: Highly recommended."—**CHOICE**

The Routledge Companion to Philosophy and Music

"Comprehensive and authoritative . . . readers will discover many excellent articles in this well-organized addition to a growing interdisciplinary field. Summing Up: Highly recommended."—**CHOICE**

" . . . succeeds well in catching the wide-ranging strands of musical theorising and thinking, and performance, and an understanding of the various contexts in which all this takes place."—*Reference Reviews*

The Routledge Companion to Phenomenology

"Sebastian Luft and Søren Overgaard, with the help of over sixty contributors, have captured the excitement of this evolving patchwork named 'phenomenology.' *The Routledge Companion to Phenomenology* will serve as an invaluable reference volume for students, teachers, and scholars of phenomenology, as well as an accessible introduction to phenomenology for philosophers from other specialties or scholars from other disciplines."—*International Journal of Philosophical Studies*

The Routledge Companion to Epistemology

A **CHOICE** Outstanding Academic Title 2011

"As a series, the *Routledge Philosophy Companions* has met with near universal acclaim. The expansive volume not only continues the trend but quite possibly sets a new standard. . . . Indeed, this is a definitive resource that will continue to prove its value for a long time to come. Summing Up: Essential."—**CHOICE**

The Routledge Companion to Philosophy of Language

"This collection presents more than 65 new essays by prominent contemporary figures working in the philosophy of language. Collectively, they represent the cutting edge of philosophical research into issues surrounding the use, understanding, and study of language. . . . the book constitutes an invaluable current resource for students and scholars alike. It will appeal to anyone interested in the current state-of-play within this important area of philosophical research. Summing Up: Highly recommended."—**CHOICE**

The Routledge Companion to Social and Political Philosophy

"This 15th book in the *Routledge Philosophy Companions* series is also the most comprehensive, both chronologically and conceptually. . . . The polish and high quality of the essays provide a multifaceted mirror of the passions and interests of contemporary academic Anglophone philosophy. **Summing Up: Highly recommended."—CHOICE**

THE ROUTLEDGE COMPANION TO PHILOSOPHY OF LAW

Edited by
Andrei Marmor

Routledge
Taylor & Francis Group

NEW YORK AND LONDON

First published in paperback 2015

First published 2012
by Routledge
711 Third Avenue, New York, NY 10017

and by Routledge
2 Park Square, Milton Park, Abingdon, Oxon, OX14 4RN

Routledge is an imprint of the Taylor & Francis Group, an informa business

Library of Congress Cataloging in Publication Data
The Routledge companion to philosophy of law / edited by Andrei Marmor.
    p. cm.—(Routledge philosophy companions)
    Includes bibliographical references.
 1. Law—Philosophy. I. Marmor, Andrei. II. Title: Companion to philosophy of law.
      K235.R68 2011
      340′.1—dc23
      2011038396

ISBN: 978-0-415-87818-0 (hbk)
ISBN: 978-1-138-77623-4 (pbk)
ISBN: 978-0-203-12435-2 (ebk)

Typeset in Goudy
by Swales & Willis Ltd, Exeter, Devon, UK

Printed and bound in Great Britain by
TJ International Ltd, Padstow, Cornwall

CONTENTS

CONTENTS

CONTENTS

CONTENTS

CONTRIBUTORS

Larry Alexander is the Warren Distinguished Professor of Law at the University of San Diego. His principal areas of scholarship are general legal theory, criminal law theory and constitutional theory. He is the author of *Is There a Right of Freedom of Expression?* (2005) and coauthor of *Crime and Culpability: A Theory of Criminal Law* (2009), *Demystifying Legal Reasoning* (2008) and *The Rule of Rules* (2001).

Scott A. Altman is the Virginia S. and Fred H. Bice Professor of Law at the University of Southern California. His main scholarly interests are legal and moral issues arising in family relationships. He has published "A Theory of Child Support" (*International Journal of Law, Policy and the Family*, 2003), "Divorcing Threats and Offers" (*Law and Philosophy*, 1997) and "Should Child Custody Rules be Fair?" (*University of Louisville Journal of Family Law*, 1996).

Daniel Attas is Professor of Philosophy at the Hebrew University of Jerusalem. He works in moral and political philosophy, with special interest in issues concerning equality and property. His publications include *Liberty, Property, and Markets: A Critique of Libertarianism* (2005), "Fragmenting Property" (*Law and Philosophy*, 2006), "The Difference Principle and Time" (*Politics, Philosophy and Economics*, 2008) and "Lockean Justifications of Intellectual Property," in A. Gosseries et al., eds., *Intellectual Property and Theories of Justice* (2009).

Mitchell N. Berman is the Richard Dale Endowed Chair in Law, and Professor of Philosophy, at the University of Texas at Austin. His principal fields of research are the philosophy of criminal law, constitutional theory and the philosophy of sport. His recent publications include "Blackmail" (*Oxford Handbook of Philosophy of Criminal Law*, 2011), "Let 'em Play: A Study in the Jurisprudence of Sport" (*Georgetown Law Journal*, 2011), "Originalism Is Bunk" (*NYU Law Review*, 2009) and "Punishment and Justification" (*Ethics*, 2008).

Michael Blake is Associate Professor of Philosophy and Public Policy and Director of the Program on Values in Society at the University of Washington. His research is on global justice, immigration and the morality of foreign policy. Forthcoming publications include "Coercion and Egalitarian Justice" (*The Monist*) and "Equality Without Documents: Political Justice and the Right to Amnesty" in a special issue of the *Canadian Journal of Philosophy*.

Kimberley Brownlee is Associate Professor of Moral and Legal Philosophy at the University of Warwick. Her topics of research include conscience, conscientious disobedience, practical reason, ideals, rights theory and philosophy of punishment. Her recent publications include "Reasons and Ideals" (*Philosophical Studies*, 2010), "Moral Aspirations and Ideals" (*Utilitas*, 2010) and "Penalizing Public Disobedience" (*Ethics*, 2008). Her book *Conscience and Conviction: The Case for Civil Disobedience* is forthcoming with Oxford University Press.

Thomas Christiano is Professor of Philosophy and Law at the University of Arizona. His main research interests are the foundations of democracy, distributive justice, the legitimacy of international institutions and human rights. He is the author of *The Rule of the Many* (1996) and *The Constitution of Equality* (2008), and editor of the journal *Politics, Philosophy and Economics*.

Meir Dan-Cohen is the Milo Reese Robbins Chair in Legal Ethics at the University of California at Berkeley School of Law. He works in legal and moral philosophy, with a special interest in conceptions of self and criminal law theory. His publications include *Harmful Thoughts: Essays on Law, Self, and Morality* (2002) and *Rights, Persons, and Organizations: A Legal Theory for Bureaucratic Society* (1986).

Judith Wagner DeCew is Professor of Philosophy and Department Chair and Director of the Ethics & Public Policy Concentration at Clark University in Worcester, Mass. Her areas of research are privacy, philosophy of law, ethics, and social and political theory. She is the author of *In Pursuit of Privacy: Law, Ethics, and the Rise of Technology* (1997) and *Unionization in the Academy: Visions and Realities* (2003), and coeditor, with I. Shapiro, of *Theory and Practice* (1995).

Julie Dickson is a Fellow and Senior Law Tutor, Somerville College, Oxford, and Member of the Faculty of Law, University of Oxford. Her research interests are in general jurisprudence, with particular emphasis on the methodology of legal philosophy and the philosophical foundations of European Union law. Her publications include *Evaluation and Legal Theory* (2001), "Methodology in Jurisprudence: A Critical Survey" (*Legal Theory*, 2004), "Is Bad Law Still Law? Is Bad Law Really Law?" in M. Del Mar and Z. Bankowski, eds., *Law as Institutional Normative Order* (2009) and "How Many Legal Systems? Some Puzzles Regarding the Identity Conditions of, and Relations Between, Legal Systems in the European Union" (*Problema*, 2008).

R. A. Duff is a Professor in the Law School, University of Minnesota, and Professor Emeritus in the Department of Philosophy, University of Stirling. He works in philosophy of criminal law, especially on issues concerned with the proper aims and scope of the criminal law, the structures and conditions of criminal liability, and the meaning and justification of the criminal process of trial and punishment. His books include *Trials and Punishments* (1986), *Intention, Agency and Criminal Liability* (1990), *Criminal Attempts* (1996), *Punishment, Communication and Community* (2001) and *Answering for Crime* (2007). He is also a coauthor of *The Trial on Trial* (2007).

Timothy Endicott is the Dean of the Faculty of Law and Professor of Legal Philosophy at the University of Oxford. He writes on general jurisprudence and constitutional and administrative law, with special interests in the role of language in law and in the theory of interpretation. His publications include *Vagueness in Law* (2000) and *Administrative Law* (2nd edition, 2011).

William A. Edmundson is Regents' Professor of Law and of Philosophy at Georgia State University in Atlanta. He specializes in moral, social, political and legal philosophy. He is the author of *Three Anarchical Fallacies* (1998) and *An Introduction to Rights* (2nd edition, 2012), editor of *The Duty to Obey the Law* (1999) and coeditor, with M. P. Golding, of *The Blackwell Guide to the Philosophy of Law and Legal Theory* (2004).

John Finnis is Professor Emeritus of Law and Legal Philosophy, University of Oxford, and Biolchini Family Professor of Law, University of Notre Dame. His books include *Natural Law and Natural Rights* (1980; 2nd edition, 2011), *Fundamentals of Ethics* (1983), *Aquinas: Moral, Political and Legal Theory* (1998) and *The Collected Essays of John Finnis* (five volumes) (2011).

Alon Harel is Phillip P. Mizock & Estelle Mizock Professor of Law, Hebrew University in Jerusalem, and Professor of Law at Boston University Law School. His areas of interest include moral and political philosophy, economic analysis of law and criminal law theory. He is the author of *Why Law Matters* (2014). His recent articles are "Necessity Knows No Law" (*Toronto University Law Journal*, 2011), "The Easy Core Case for Judicial Review" (*Journal of Legal Analysis*, 2010) and "Why Only the State May Inflict Criminal Sanctions: The Case Against Privately Inflicted Sanctions" (*Legal Theory*, 2008).

Scott Hershovitz is Professor of Law and Professor of Philosophy at the University of Michigan. He teaches and writes about jurisprudence and tort law. His publications include "The Role of Authority" (*Philosophers' Imprint*, 2011), "Harry Potter and the Trouble with Tort Theory" (*Stanford Law Review*, 2011) and "Legitimacy, Democracy, and Razian Authority" (*Legal Theory*, 2003).

Douglas Husak is Professor of Philosophy at Rutgers University. He works in philosophy of law, with a special interest in philosophy of criminal law. His recent books are *Philosophy of Criminal Law: Selected Essays* (2011) and *Overcriminalization* (2008).

George Klosko is Henry L. and Grace Doherty Professor of Politics at the University of Virginia. He works in normative political philosophy and the history of political thought. Recent publications include *The Oxford Handbook of the History of Political Philosophy*, which he edited (2011), *The Development of Plato's Political Theory* (2nd edition, 2006) and *Political Obligations* (2005).

Grant Lamond is University Lecturer in Legal Philosophy and Felix Frankfurter Fellow in Law, Balliol College, University of Oxford. His research interests lie in the philosophy of law and in the philosophy of criminal law. His publications include "Coercion and the Nature of Law" (*Legal Theory*, 2001), "Do Precedents Create Rules?" (*Legal Theory*, 2005), "What Is a Crime?" (*Oxford Journal of Legal Studies*, 2007) and "Persuasive Authority in the Law" (*The Harvard Review of Philosophy*, 2010).

Larry Laudan divides his time between the Instituto de Investigaciones Filosóficas at UNAM in Mexico City and the School of Law at the University of Texas at Austin.

His main areas of research are philosophy of science and philosophy of evidence law. His publications include *Truth, Error and Criminal Law* (2006), *Progress and Its Problems* (1977), *Science and Values* (1986) and *Science and Relativism* (1990).

Seth Lazar is a continuing Research Fellow in the School of Philosophy at Australian National University. His research is in ethics and political philosophy, with a focus on the morality of war and killing. His publications include "Responsibility, Risk and Killing in Self-Defense" (*Ethics*, 2009) and "Necessity in Self-Defence and War" (*Philosophy and Public Affairs*, 2012).

Kasper Lippert-Rasmussen works in the Department of Politics, University of Aarhus, Denmark. His main research areas are discrimination, equality, moral responsibility and deontology. His recent publications include "Luck-Egalitarianism: Faults and Collective Choice" (*Economics and Philosophy*, 2011) and "Against Self-Ownership: There Are No Fact-Insensitive Ownership Rights over One's Body" (*Philosophy and Public Affairs*, 2008).

Andrei Marmor is Professor of Philosophy, Maurice Jones Jr. Professor of Law and Director of the Center for Law and Philosophy at the University of Southern California. He is editor in chief of the *Journal of Ethics and Social Philosophy*. His main interests are in philosophy of law and social and political philosophy. His recent books include *The Language of Law* (2014), *Philosophy of Law* (2011) and *Social Conventions: From Language to Law* (2009).

Christopher Morris is Professor of Philosophy at the University of Maryland, College Park. His main interests are in moral, political and legal philosophy, and the theory of practical rationality. He is the author of *An Essay on the Modern State* (1998) and the editor of a volume of essays on the work of Amartya Sen (2011).

Gerald J. Postema is Cary C. Boshamer Professor of Philosophy and Professor of Law at the University of North Carolina at Chapel Hill. His interests are in philosophy of law, political philosophy and the history of both. His books include *Bentham and the Common Law Tradition* (1986), *Philosophy and the Law of Torts* (2001) and *Legal Philosophy in the Twentieth Century: The Common Law World* (2011).

Frederick Schauer is David and Mary Harrison Distinguished Professor of Law at the University of Virginia. He works in constitutional law and theory, freedom of expression, legal reasoning and philosophy of law. He is the author of *Thinking Like a Lawyer: A New Introduction to Legal Reasoning* (2009), *Profiles, Probabilities, and Stereotypes* (2003), *Playing By the Rules: A Philosophical Examination of Rule-Based Decision-Making in Law and in Life* (1991) and *Free Speech: A Philosophical Enquiry* (1982), and the editor of Karl Llewellyn's *The Theory of Rules* (2011).

Seana Valentine Shiffrin is Professor of Philosophy and Pete Kameron Professor of Law and Social Justice at UCLA. She works on philosophical and legal issues surrounding equality and autonomy and their social conditions, with an emphasis on promising, contracts, truth telling and freedom of speech. Her publications include "The Divergence of Contract and Promise" (*Harvard Law Review*, 2007),

"Promising, Conventionalism, and Intimate Relationships" (*Philosophical Review*, 2008) and "Inducing Moral Deliberation" (*Harvard Law Review*, 2010).

A. P. Simester is Professor of Law and Provost's Chair at the National University of Singapore, Honorary Professor at Uppsala University and an Honorary Research Fellow at the University of Cambridge. His interests lie in applied legal philosophy, criminal law, restitution and private law theory. He is the coauthor of *Crimes, Harms, and Wrongs: On the Principles of Criminalisation* (2011) and *Criminal Law: Theory and Doctrine* (2007).

Scott Soames is Distinguished Professor of Philosophy and Director of the School of Philosophy at the University of Southern California. His areas of research include philosophy of language, logic, metaphysics and philosophy of law. He has published many books and numerous articles, most recently *Philosophy of Language* (2010), *What Is Meaning?* (2010) and *Philosophical Essays, Volumes 1 and 2* (2009).

Nicos Stavropoulos is Associate Professor and the University Lecturer in Legal Theory at the University of Oxford. He has written on language and law and the nature of law, and he is the author of *Objectivity in Law* (1996).

Victor Tadros is Professor of Criminal Law and Legal Theory at the University of Warwick. He works on the philosophy of criminal law, just war theory and other issues in moral and political philosophy. His publications include *Criminal Responsibility* (2005) and *The Ends of Harm: The Moral Foundations of Criminal Law* (2011).

John Tasioulas is Quain Professor of Jurisprudence in the Faculty of Laws, University College London. His research interests are in moral, legal and political philosophy. He is the coeditor, with S. Besson, of *The Philosophy of International Law* (2010), and his articles include "Punishment and Repentance" (*Philosophy*, 2006), "The Moral Reality of Human Rights," in T. Pogge, ed., *Freedom from Poverty as a Human Rights Violation* (2007) and "Taking Rights out of Human Rights" (*Ethics*, 2010).

Peter Vallentyne is Florence G. Kline Professor of Philosophy at the University of Missouri. He writes on issues of liberty and equality in the theory of justice—and left-libertarianism in particular. He is an associate editor of *Ethics*.

Jeremy Waldron is University Professor and Professor of Law at New York University, a position he holds in conjunction with his position as Chichele Professor of Social and Political Theory at the University of Oxford. His work is mostly in legal philosophy and political theory, on such issues as constitutionalism, democracy, judicial review, torture, dignity and hate speech. His most recent book is *Torture, Terror, and Trade-Offs: Jurisprudence for the White House* (2010).

Wilfrid J. Waluchow is Professor of Philosophy and Senator William McMaster Chair in Constitutional Studies at McMaster University. He writes in philosophy of law and constitutional theory. His books include *Inclusive Legal Positivism* (1994) and *A Common Law Theory of Judicial Review: The Living Tree* (2007).

Gary Watson is Provost Professor of Philosophy and Law at the University of Southern California. His main areas of research are moral theory, theory of agency, moral psychology, and moral and criminal responsibility. Some of his essays are collected in his book *Agency and Answerability* (2004), and he recently published "Promises, Normative Powers, and Reasons," in D. Sobel and S. Wall, eds., *Reasons for Action* (2009) and "The Trouble with Psychopaths," in R. J. Wallace, S. Freeman and R. Kumar, eds., *Reasons and Recognition: Essays on the Philosophy of T. M. Scanlon* (2011).

Clark Wolf is Director of Bioethics, Professor of Philosophy and Professor of Political Science at Iowa State University. His primary areas of research include bioethics, jurisprudence and political theory. Many of his articles address issues in intergenerational justice, including "Intergenerational Justice and Saving," in J. LaMont, K. Favor and G. Gaus, eds., *Values, Justice, and Economics* (2010), "Do Future Persons Presently Have Alternate Possible Identities?" in M. Roberts and D. Wasserman, eds., *Harming Future Persons: Ethics, Genetics, and the Non-Identity Problem* (2009) and "Intergenerational Justice, Human Needs, and Climate Policy," in A. Gosseries and L. Meyer, eds., *Justice Between Generations* (2009).

Gideon Yaffe is Professor of Law and Professor of Philosophy and Psychology at Yale University. He writes books and articles about the philosophy of action, the philosophy of criminal law, free will and responsibility, and early modern philosophy. His publications include *Attempts* (2011), "Intoxication, Recklessness and Negligence" (*Ohio State Criminal Law Journal*, 2011), "Lowering the Bar for Addicts," in G. Graham and J. Poland, eds., *Addiction and Responsibility* (2011) and "Excusing Mistakes of Law" (*Philosophers' Imprint*, 2009).

Benjamin C. Zipursky is Associate Dean for Research, James H. Quinn '49 Chair in Legal Ethics and Professor of Law at Fordham University School of Law. He works in philosophy of law with special interest in the philosophy of tort law. He is the co-author of a leading casebook, *Torts: Responsibility and Redress* (2nd edition, 2008) and *The Oxford Introduction to Law: Torts* (2010).

PREFACE

Law is one of the most complex, intricate and sophisticated creations of human societies. Modern legal systems regulate almost every aspect of our lives—from individual conduct in our everyday interactions with other individuals to systems of government, commerce and economy, and even relations between nations in the international sphere. It is difficult to imagine human existence in a society without law, and certainly difficult to think of such an existence as anything that would resemble human society as we know it. No wonder, then, that philosophy of law encompasses many topics from myriad perspectives and philosophical concerns. No single volume, even as large as this one, can hope to cover all of the philosophical questions we have about the law and various legal institutions. One aim of this volume is to give readers a sense of how wide ranging the philosophical interest in law is, and how different types of philosophical questions are asked about different aspects of law. Another aim of this book is to demonstrate how philosophical arguments are deployed in contemporary philosophy of law—what is assumed or taken for granted, what is considered problematic and in need of careful examination.

The essays in this *Companion* are not written merely as state-of-the-art reports on particular fields in philosophy of law. The authors present their own views on the topics they discuss, arguing for a particular position they favor. We thought that the best way to introduce readers with different backgrounds to the topics covered in this volume would be to demonstrate how philosophy of law strives to make progress with the issues with which it grapples within a piecemeal and careful examination of the questions that law and legal institutions present. The essays are introductory in nature: they do not presume any prior knowledge of the field, but they also try to advance the ball, making some original contribution to the philosophical debates in their respective areas.

The chapters of the *Companion* are arranged under six headings: theories about the nature of law, legal reasoning and interpretation, theories about particular legal areas (such as criminal law, torts, international law and others), law as a coercive order, the moral obligations we may have toward the law, and rights and equality. These divisions are somewhat arbitrary, of course, and they do not necessarily reflect any differences in philosophical outlooks or methods. As readers will come to realize, philosophy of law is very closely entangled with other philosophical areas, in particular, moral and political philosophy, metaethics, philosophy of action and, in some areas, philosophy of language.

Though we tried to cover a very wide range of issues in philosophy of law, we have not managed to cover them all. In particular, I failed to obtain contributions on law and gender issues, and on moral debates about the economic analysis of law. I hope that these omissions, and no doubt others I have missed, will be included in future editions.

PREFACE

I would like to use this opportunity to express my gratitude to all of the contributors for their wonderful cooperation with this project, and the great effort they have made to present their views in a simple and accessible style without compromising philosophical depth and rigor. I owe a special debt of gratitude to Susan Wampler for handling the logistics of this project and the initial copyediting of the contributions. Without her diligent work, this project would have taken years longer to complete.

Andrei Marmor

Part I

THEORIES ABOUT THE NATURE OF LAW

1

THE NATURE OF LAW

An Introduction

Andrei Marmor

Imagine the following scenario: driving on a California highway, you are pulled over by a police officer, officiously informing you that you have been caught on his radar exceeding the speed limit and are about to be fined. You are in a philosophical mood, and the police officer happens to be very patient and ready to answer your questions. So first you ask him "Officer, have I done anything wrong?" "Of course you have," he tells you. "You have exceeded the legal speed limit." "No, no, that's not what I mean," you clarify. "Have I done something really *wrong*? Morally wrong, for example?" "Well, I don't know that," the officer replies. "I only know that you have violated the law." "And is that necessarily wrong?" you ask. The police officer replies that it is not really for him to tell. He just knows that you violated the law. You realize that this is not leading anywhere, so you try a different tack: "Officer, what makes it the law that the speed limit here is, as you claim, 65 mph?" The officer responds by citing you the relevant section of the California Vehicle Code. "But what makes this code the law?" you ask him. "It is the law in California," he says, "because the code was duly enacted in 1959 by the California Legislature." "But what makes that enactment the law?" you ask. "After all, enactment, as you call it, is just an event that happens somewhere—people gather in a hall, talk, argue, raise their hands, etc.—why is that the law?" Still patient, the police officer explains to you that the California Legislature is an institution created in accordance with the Constitution of California, and granted by it the authority to enact such laws as the California Vehicle Code according to certain prescribed procedures. "Now I see," you reply. "The California Vehicle Code is the law around here because it was enacted by a legislature, and the legislature's authority to make such laws was granted to it by some other law, the Constitution of California. I get it. But what makes the Constitution of California the law around here?" The police officer knows the answer: "The California Constitution is the law because it was duly enacted by the authorization granted to the people of California to have such a constitution by the Constitution of the United States." Still, you are not quite satisfied. "What makes the U.S. Constitution the law?" you ask. "The U.S. Constitution? It is the supreme law of the land!" the officer proudly proclaims. "Yes, yes," you tell him. "I know that it is what people say. But what *makes it* the supreme law of the land?" you ask him again. Not surprisingly at this point the police officer loses his patience, hands you the citation and off he goes.

As a curious philosopher, you remain unsatisfied by this little encounter. The police officer dodged two crucial questions: first, you still do not know whether you have done anything wrong, though you ended up with a hefty fine that you have to pay. Is this all there is to it? Violating the law is just unpleasant, resulting in something bad that happens to you if you are caught? Mustn't the law assume that you deserve to be punished? Second, you still have no idea what makes anything "the law." You have learned that certain actions or events in the world gain the legal significance that they have by way of an authorization granted by some other law; but this chain of authorization comes to an end; at some point we end up with something that amounts to "the supreme law of the land," the kind of law that authorizes the creation of all other laws. But what makes *that* the law? You still have no idea.

Nevertheless, this encounter was not without merits. Although we have not learned much about the answers, at least we know what the questions are. The two main questions that the police officer has dodged are the main questions about the nature of law that have preoccupied philosophers for centuries: one is about the normative character of law; the other is about law's conditions of validity. As we shall see, both of these questions concern, though in different ways, the relations between law and morality. I will take them up in reverse order, starting with the question about the nature of legal validity.

The Conditions of Legal Validity

Whenever one says, "It is the law that X" or, more precisely, "according to legal system S at time *t* it is the law that X," one expresses a proposition that is either true or false (or, perhaps in some cases, it is indeterminate whether it is true or false). The philosophical question here is: what makes it the case that the proposition is true (or false)? What does it *generally* depend on? Notice that it is not a legal answer that we seek here. As we learned from the encounter with the police officer, the legalistic answers are bound to run out. In other words, we are not asking what makes this or that particular requirement a legal one, but what makes anything at all legal to begin with?

Sometimes the best way to understand a philosophical question is by way of looking at the controversies that exist about its answer. The main controversy about the general question of legality is, ultimately, about the possibility of reduction. Can we fully explain the conditions of legality in terms of something else, more foundational in nature? In particular, is it possible to reduce the conditions of legal validity to social (viz., nonnormative) facts, namely facts about people's conduct, beliefs and attitudes? Or is it the case that no such reduction is possible, partly because the content of legal norms, especially their moral content, also bears on the conditions of their validity?

It is the nature of theories, in general, that they try to explain one thing in terms of another. There is, however, a type of theory or explanation we call *reductive*: if there is a clear demarcation of one type of discourse or class of statements, and we can provide a full explanation of that class of statements in terms of some other type or class of statements, then the explanation is reductive. For example, if we could fully explain the realm of our mental life in terms of truths about the physical aspects of the world, we would have provided a reduction of the mental to the physical realm. It is this kind of reduction that we need to consider about the legal case as well. Some legal philosophers have claimed that we can explain what constitutes legality in terms of something else, more foundational in nature. According to this line of thought, in order to answer the question about the conditions of legal validity, we need to have an account of the relevant social facts, concerning the ways in which people behave and the kind of beliefs and attitudes they share about their conduct. Other philosophers, however, deny the possibility of such a reduction. They claim that legality is not fully explicable by social facts, and mostly because legal validity is partly a matter of moral truths. At least in some cases, they claim, truths about morality determine what law actually is.

With one notable exception (Hans Kelsen's "pure theory of law"; see Marmor 2011, ch. 1), the jurisprudential tradition called *legal positivism* (Postema 2012) strove to provide a reductionist account of legal validity. One of the most influential nineteenth-century legal positivists, John Austin, propounded a theory of law that is perhaps the clearest example of a reductionist account of law. According to Austin, law consists in the commands of the political sovereign. A command is defined by Austin as the expression of a wish by one person (or group of persons) that some other person(s) behave in a certain way, backed by a threat of sanction if the addressee does not comply. "Do/don't do this . . . or else . . . ." And then sovereignty is defined sociologically: the sovereign is the person or group of persons who are habitually obeyed by a certain population and are not themselves in a habit of obeying anyone else (Austin 1832).

Thus, according to Austin, the conditions of legal validity are fully reducible to facts of a nonnormative kind: facts about the relevant social reality constituting political sovereignty, identified by habits of obedience, and facts about actual commands issued by (or on behalf of) the sovereign. Though there is something intuitively compelling about Austin's model, later legal positivists have subjected the command model of law to fierce criticism. In particular, H. L. A. Hart, in his seminal work *The Concept of Law* (1961), devoted three or four chapters to a detailed critique of Austin's theory. But a careful reading of Hart should reveal that it is not Austin's reductionist project that Hart objected to, since his own theory of law is just as reductive. Hart's disagreement with Austin is about the main building blocks which are supposed to constitute the foundations.

Austin's main insight has two components: that law always consists of commands (do this . . . or else . . .), and that it always originates with the political sovereign. Hart argued that both theses are fraught with difficulties. To begin with, only a small fraction of law has the structure of a command. The main provisions of a criminal code, or traffic regulations for that matter, do have such a structure: they impose an obligation (do/don't do this . . .), backed by a threat of sanction for failure to comply (or else . . .). However, a great many laws, perhaps even most, do not purport to impose an obligation; they grant legal powers of various kinds, that is, the power to introduce a change in the normative relations that obtain between the relevant parties concerned. Consider, for example, the laws which determine how to form a legally binding contract; such laws do not have the structure of "do this . . . or else." The law is not in the business of telling anyone to form a contract; it is up to the parties whether they want to enter into contractual relations or not. The law only provides a tool here: it designates certain ways in which people can introduce a change in their legal relations, if they want to do so. And this is more typical of most of the areas of private law and many other legal domains. Most of the law is not like the criminal law, where the law imposes an obligation backed by a threat of sanction (Hart 1961, ch. 3; for more details, see Marmor 2011: 36–40).

Furthermore, H. L. A. Hart and other contemporary legal positivists have argued that early positivism exaggerated the centrality of sanctions, and more generally, law's coercive powers, to an understanding of what the law is, and what its main functions in society are. No doubt, the law is a coercive order (Edmundson 2012), and many laws are backed by a threat of sanction for failure to comply. But it is very doubtful that this element of force or law's ability to coerce its subjects is as central to law's main functions in our lives as people tend to assume. In order to see this, consider a thought experiment suggested by Joseph Raz (1990/1975: 158–60): imagine that there is a world inhabited by creatures who are exactly like us, with one important difference, namely, that whatever it is in human nature that requires the law to threaten us with sanctions, those people do not have. They just do not need to be threatened with sanctions in order to comply. Now ask yourself, would this world have need for various norms and institutions that are similar to what we call law in our world? The answer is clearly yes. Even in this world without need for sanctions, people need rules to solve large-scale coordination problems, and rules and institutions to determine what needs to be done when people have reasonable disagreements about their collective endeavors. They would need institutions to determine matters of fact in conflictual situations, and so on and so forth. In short, the law's ability to use force and compel compliance, important as it is, is actually much less important than usually thought. Many of the functions that law serves in our public lives have very little to do with the need for coercion (for some reservations about this argument, see Marmor 2011: 42–44).

Hart's second main disagreement with Austin's reductionism consists in his argument that we cannot explicate the sources of law in terms of political sovereignty because the very idea of sovereignty is a juridical one. Law partly constitutes our conception of sovereignty; it cannot be reduced to it. We can only identify the political sovereign on the basis of the constitutional legal structure that prevails in the relevant community, not the other way around. Austin's idea that habits of obedience are sufficient to constitute political sovereignty, Hart argued, is not a workable idea (Hart 1961, ch. 4).Think, for example, about this question: who is the sovereign in the United States these days? That is, think about the question: Who is the person, or group of persons, that U.S. residents habitually obey, and itself is not in the habit of obeying anyone else? Mind-boggling question, no doubt, but whatever answer you come up with would have to be based on facts that you know about U.S. constitutional law. In short, we just cannot suggest that law is whatever the sovereign commands, because the very identity of the sovereign is law dependent. First, we must have some legal regime in place, then we can come up with some notion of who the sovereign is (that is, at least as long as we seek to identify the sovereign as a source of law).

The failure of Austin's command theory of law does not necessarily doom the reductionist project. In fact, Austin begins with a sound intuition. Even if laws are not necessarily commands, as he thought, they are, by and large, products of deliberate human creation. Laws are created by human agents, enacted by institutions or persons in various institutional roles (Kelsen 1961/1945: 110–11). We need not assume that this is necessarily or always the case; suffice it for now to admit, as one must, that it is typically the case that laws are made, that they are products of an act of will. But of course not everyone who might want to enact a law or change one actually can. My proclamations to the world, wise and commendable as they may be, are not going to have any legal effect whatsoever. I am not in a position to make laws or change existing ones. But then, who is? And more importantly, what makes it the case that anyone is in such a position? Hart's answer boils down to this: certain agents get to make (or modify) the law in a given population in virtue of the fact that most people in the relevant society *regularly behave* in ways which assume that these agents get to do so, *believe* that to be the case, and share certain *critical attitudes* that are in line with this shared belief. In every legal system in place, there are some *social rules* followed by the relevant population determining who gets to make law and how it is to be done. Hart called such rules the *rules of recognition* (1961, ch. 5). The social rules of recognition constitute what we take to be the conditions of legality in the relevant legal system. (So now, if you want to chase down the police officer who got tired of your questions and tell him what makes it the case that the U.S. Constitution is the supreme law of the land in the United States, you could tell him that according to H. L. A. Hart, it is the case simply because most Americans just *take it to be the case*. It is the main rule of recognition we follow around here; certainly the rule that judges, lawyers, legislators and other officials follow, which is what really matters.)

Notice that this is just as reductionist an account of legal validity as Austin's, albeit based on different building blocks. Legality is fully determined, according to Hart, by the social rules of recognition. A social rule consists of actual patterns of conduct accompanied by certain beliefs and attitudes. We have a social rule when there is a regularity of behavior in the relevant population, attended by a complex idea that Hart called "acceptance" of a rule, which consists of (1) a belief shared by most members of the population that the existence of the rule provides them with reasons to comply and (2) a shared attitude of positive endorsement of the rule that is manifest in its use as grounds for exerting pressure on others to comply and criticizing them if they do not (Hart 1961: 82–86).

The reduction is a bit complex here, so let me reiterate the steps: the first step is to realize that there must be some normative framework that determines how law is created or what makes certain actions and events have the legal significance that they do. This normative framework consists in the rules of recognition that prevail in the relevant society. The second step is to realize that these rules of recognition are social rules, actually practiced in the community. Finally, Hart offers a reductive account of social rules, given in terms of people's regularities of behavior, their beliefs and attitudes. Notice that this is also an aggregative account of social rules because it purports to provide an explanation of what social rules are in terms of the conduct, beliefs and attitudes of individual members of the population. If most members of a given population behave in a certain way, and share some beliefs and attitudes with respect to that behavior, then we have "the idea of a social rule," Hart claimed, "without which we cannot hope to elucidate even the most elementary forms of law" (1961: 78).

The kind of reduction Hart offered about the idea of legality has come under a lot of pressure over the years. In particular, it has been argued that no such reduction is possible because moral considerations can sometimes determine what the law is. According to these views, often simply called anti-positivism, the content of the law is partly deduced by moral (and perhaps other types of evaluative) reasoning. We will take a close look at one of the most influential arguments to that effect, propounded by Ronald Dworkin (1977).

First, however, some additional background. Hart clearly recognized that his views about the nature of law entail that the law is bound to run out. It is inevitable, he argued, that cases would come before courts of law that are not settled by the existing law. Because law is mostly created by human agents, such as legislatures and courts, law consists of a finite set of rules and directives, and those rules cannot possibly determine an outcome about every possible case that would need some legal resolution. Since judges rarely have the option of not deciding a legal case they adjudicate, it is inevitable that some cases that they have to decide would require them to create, or at least modify, the law that would settle the case. Therefore, when such an unsettled case comes before a court of law, the decision that judges reach cannot be described as one that *applies* the law, because there is no relevant law to apply. In such unsettled cases, the court's ruling amounts to a modification of the law; it is an act of creating new law, akin to other familiar ways in which law is created or modified by legislatures and other legal authorities (Hart 1961: 121–32). This idea that law is bound to run out—and therefore judges would need to participate in the creation of new law by way of judicial legislation—has been labeled the doctrine of *judicial discretion*.

In a famous article criticizing Hart's theory of law, Dworkin (1977) has argued that the doctrine of judicial discretion is fundamentally flawed. The gist of Dworkin's argument is this: Hart wrongly assumed, Dworkin claimed, that the law consists only of rules. But in addition to legal rules, which are typically enacted by legal authorities (as Hart assumed), there is another type of legal norms, *legal principles*, which do not derive their legal validity from any particular enactment. Legal principles gain their legal validity by a process of reasoning, including moral reasoning, and not by decree.

In order to understand Dworkin's argument, it is essential to realize that there are two main conclusions he wanted to draw from the idea that there are legal principles: first, that the law does not run out, and therefore judges do not have the kind of discretion Hart envisaged; and second, that there is a distinct class of legal norms that cannot derive its legal validity from Hart's rules of recognition. Underlying both of these conclusions is the idea that the legal validity of principles partly, but necessarily, depends on some truths about morality; it is partly a matter of moral truths that some norms are legally valid and form part of the law.

Dworkin begins the argument by suggesting that the distinction between legal rules and legal principles is a categorical one. Rules operate in a kind of "all or nothing" fashion: if a rule applies to the circumstances, it determines a legal outcome; if an outcome is not determined by a rule, then it must be because the rule does not really apply to the case at hand. Contrary to this, principles do not necessarily determine an outcome: if a principle applies to the circumstances, it only provides a reason to decide the case one way or the other, which may weigh more or less under the relevant circumstances, depending on various considerations. To illustrate, consider, for example, our worn-out example of the speed limit on California highways: if you drive on the highway, the rule clearly applies to you, and therefore the outcome is determined; if you exceed the speed limit, you have committed the offense. Now compare such a rule with the legal principle that judges sometimes employ in their decisions (to take one of Dworkin's favorite examples, 1977: 26): a person should not be allowed to profit from his own wrong. This general principle does not quite determine legal outcomes. The law sometimes allows people to profit from a wrong they have committed (a good example is adverse possession in property law). The role of such principles is subtler: to provide judges and other legal agents with reasons to make certain decisions in doubtful or borderline cases. If there is a choice to be made, as it were, and one of the options would allow a person to profit from his own wrong, then the principle counts against allowing such an outcome. But, by itself, the principle does not dictate the outcome—certainly not in every case in which a person may profit from his wrongs.

Whether the distinction between rules and principles is as sharp as Dworkin claims is far from clear (Raz 1984; Marmor 2011: 86), but I will not dwell on this here because the main argument depends on Dworkin's additional thesis pertaining to the ways in which rules and principles gain their legal validity. Legal rules, Dworkin claims, typically gain their validity by an act of enactment, more or less along the lines presumed by Hart and other legal positivists. Legal principles, however, are not enacted: they are deduced by reasoning from certain facts and, crucially, moral considerations. How is that? Suppose, for example, that a court is faced with a problematic case that would seem to be unsettled by the existing legal rules; as far as we can tell, no previously recognized law would settle the case. In such cases judges can, as they often do, reason in the following way: they would look at the legal history of the settled law in the relevant legal area (such as previous precedents, statutes and regulations) and then try to figure out the best moral principles that would justify the bulk of those settled cases. The general principle that forms *the best moral justification* of the relevant body of law *is* the legal principle that would bear on the case at hand. In other words, we conclude that a legal principle forms part of the law by a process of reasoning. We start by observing the relevant legal facts that are established by previous law and then try to reason to the principle that forms the best moral justification of this body of law. The conclusion of this reasoning— which is partly, but essentially, a moral one—is a legal principle, one that forms part of the law (all this is made much clearer in Dworkin 1986, chs. 2 and 7).

So now we can see why Dworkin concludes both that the law never quite runs out and that legal principles are such that they cannot derive their legal validity from anything like the rules of recognition. The law never quite runs out simply because the kind of reasoning that leads to legal principles is one that is always available. Whenever judges might think that existing law does not settle the case they face, the judges can reason their way to the solution by the same process; they can always ask themselves what would be the best moral justification of the relevant body of law and apply the principle that forms the answer to this question to the case at hand. At the very least, it should give the court a reason, a legal reason, to decide the case one way or another. So there is always some law that applies, namely, the general principle that constitutes the best moral justification of previous decisions in the relevant area.

The idea that legal principles are partly deduced by reasoning also shows why these norms cannot gain their legal validity by reference to the rules of recognition in the way Hart had envisaged. Principles do not become part of the law because an authority has decided that they do; their legal validity is partly, but necessarily, a matter of moral truths. A given principle, say P, is part of the law if and only if P actually constitutes the best moral justification of previous legal decisions. P's legal validity, therefore, depends on some truths about what constitutes the best moral justification of previous decisions. Legal validity is thus partly a matter of moral truth.

Dworkin's thesis about legal principles has attracted an enormous amount of attention over the years. Many objections and modifications have been offered, but it has been generally conceded that Dworkin succeeded in showing something of great importance, both about the ways in which judges, especially in the common-law tradition, reason to resolve hard cases, and about the diversity of norms that forms part of our legal landscape. The crucial question, however, is whether what Dworkin describes is really a way in which judges *identify what the law is*, or is better described as a form of judicial reasoning leading judges to *create new* law or at least to modify the existing law, in order to settle new cases (Marmor 2011: 89–92). Even if it is true that whenever judges face a case that would seem to be unsettled by the existing body of law, they reason to the solution in the way Dworkin describes, it would not show that the principle the judges have settled on is one that had been part of the law prior to their decision. An equally plausible option is that the identified principle becomes part of the law because, and only because, of the judicial decision that applies it. Prior to the judicial decision that identifies a certain principle as a legal one, the principle had not actually formed part of the law. It only becomes law when judges say that it is, and only because they say so. And this interpretation would be perfectly in line with Hart's theory of law.

In order to rebut this objection, Dworkin would have had to show that the judicial reasoning that leads to the identification of a certain principle as a legal one is reasoning about what the law had been prior to the decision—that it is a form of reasoning purporting to discover, as it were, what the law is, and not, as I suggest, reasoning about ways in which the law needs to be changed. As far as I can tell, however, the only argument Dworkin presents to support his interpretation is an appeal to judicial rhetoric (1986, ch. 1). When judges apply a legal principle to the cases they adjudicate, they tend *to say* that they just apply a principle that had always been the law, not that they invent a new principle that they favor (morally or otherwise). But this appeal to rhetoric is problematic, and certainly inconclusive; often judges are quite forthcoming in admitting that they create new law, without pretending to apply some preexisting legal principle.

More importantly, as I explained elsewhere (Marmor 2011: 90–92), the view that makes moral truths determine legal validity in some cases faces the problem of rendering a considerable part of the law legally mistaken. Suppose, for example, that the highest courts in a certain legal system *systematically err* on the moral considerations that they rely upon and end up relying on legal principles that are morally off, so to speak; the principles they employ in their decisions do not adequately reflect the correct moral considerations. Dworkin would have to say that in such cases, the courts make a legal mistake: they misidentify the law. But this might lead to the conclusion that a great deal of the law—or, at least, what jurists take to be the law—in a given legal system is legally mistaken. Surely, at some point one would have to doubt whether a theory which allows for a great part of the law to be a legal error is a theory that can actually tell us what the law is.

Needless to say, this is not the end of the debate. Dworkin has modified and extended his views since (Dworkin 1986). His more recent views are grounded on a comprehensive theory about interpretation and the interpretative nature of law. Dworkin's interpretative theory of law strives to show that the identification of legal norms is *always* a matter of evaluative judgments, moral considerations included. Every conclusion about what the law requires in particular cases, Dworkin argues, is a result of some interpretation or other. And interpretation is necessarily the kind of reasoning that relies on evaluative judgments. Therefore, every conclusion about what the law requires is inevitably entangled with evaluative judgments about ways in which the law ought to be from a moral-political point of view. Dworkin's theory of interpretation, and its alleged implications for law, has generated a considerable amount of controversy, and it raises many interesting issues I cannot discuss here (see Marmor 2005 and Stavropoulos 2012).

Additionally, even some contemporary legal positivists have come to argue that the relations between moral considerations and legality are more complex than Hart had originally envisaged, and in his "Postscript" to *The Concept of Law* (1994) published posthumously, Hart seems to have agreed (see, for example, Coleman 1982 and Waluchow 1994; and see Stavropoulos 2012). Others, however, argue that these modifications, allowing moral considerations to determine legality, face the same problems that Dworkin's original theory faces, even if the foundations are different (Raz 1985; Marmor 2011: 92–97). It is, however, time for us to move on, and consider some aspects of the questions about law's normative character and how law might be related to morality in that respect.

The Normativity of Law

The law is, undoubtedly, a normative system; laws are, by and large, prescriptions instructing us, the law's subjects, what to do and what actions to avoid, how to go about achieving some results we might want to achieve in numerous practical domains, and so on and so forth. In short, legal norms purport to guide our conduct. But what kind of conduct guidance is involved here? Suppose, for example, that a law imposes a particular obligation, say, "X is under a legal obligation to φ in circumstances C." Does it mean that X *ought* to φ? And what is the nature of this "ought"? Is it a moral ought? Or does it have nothing to do with morality?

There are, actually, two separate questions involved here, only one of which is relevant to our concerns. One question, discussed by George Klosko in this volume (2012), is about the moral obligation to obey the law: is there a general moral obligation to obey the laws of our legal system? This is quite clearly a moral-political question, one that has to be answered on moral-political grounds. Philosophy of law, however, concerning the nature of law, is interested in *explaining*, not necessarily justifying (or challenging), the ways in which the law purports to guide conduct, and what this guidance consists in.

Once again, the main philosophical question here begins with the possibility of reduction. Can we reduce the idea of a legal obligation to some facts of a nonnormative kind? Austin (1832) clearly thought that the answer is yes. In his view, a statement that expresses the existence of a legal obligation, such as "X is under a legal obligation to φ," is tantamount to a predictive statement that "if X fails to φ, X is very likely to incur some unpleasant consequences." But this is a very questionable approach. It seems to miss the idea that laws aim to guide the conduct of their subjects and mostly in the form of giving them reasons for action. Hart (1961: 80) explained this critique very nicely by giving the example of the order of a robber pointing a gun at his victim, ordering the victim to hand over his money, or else. . . . According to Austin, the only difference between the order of a gunman and the law is that the gunman happens not to be the sovereign. But that seems to be quite wrong. Though there is a sense in which we could say that the victim is obliged to hand over his money to the gunman, surely we do not think that he has an obligation or a duty to do so. On the other hand, it is essential to law's way of guiding conduct that it purports to impose obligations. In short, at least from the perspective of those who regard the law as a binding normative system, law is there to give subjects reasons for action; people regard the law as something that guides their conduct, not mainly a prediction that something bad will happen to them if they do not comply.

Hart expressed this idea in terms of a distinction between what he called the external and the internal points of view: from *an external point of view*, that is, just observing people's conduct from the outside, as it were, there may not be much of a difference between the gunman and the law. However, when we aim to provide a theoretical account of law's normative character, we must take into account *the internal point of view*, the point of view of those who see themselves as cooperative participants in the practice, that is, people who regard the law as something that is there to guide their conduct (Hart 1961: 87).

Unfortunately, Hart's distinction between the external and internal points of view has generated considerable confusion in the literature. Many commentators assumed that its main point is to show why we cannot provide a reductionist account of law's normative character. But a careful reading of Hart's text should reveal that the opposite is the case. True enough, Hart thought that an adequate account of law's normativity must take into account the internal point of view, the point of view of the participants in the practice who regard law's instructions as reason for action. But he also thought that we can provide such an account by describing people's actual beliefs and attitudes: "For the observer may, without accepting the rules himself, assert that the group accepts the rules, and thus may from the outside refer to the way in which they are concerned with them from the internal point of view" (Hart 1961: 87). In short, it is possible, Hart claimed, to provide an adequate account of a normative practice such as law by describing the internal, participants' point of view, in terms of the kind of beliefs and attitudes they have with respect to the rules they follow.

So once again, Hart's objection to Austin's attempt to reduce the normative character of law to nonnormative facts is not about reductionism, per se, but about the details of the reduction. Hart's own account of what law's normativity consists in is also reductive; it aims to explain how law guides conduct by focusing on the relevant beliefs and attitudes of those who *regard* the law as binding. Clearly Hart thought that philosophy of law, distinct from moral-political philosophy, can only point out that wherever there is a functioning legal system in place, most members of the relevant population *regard* the requirements of law, by and large, as binding, that is, as giving them reasons for action. Whether these reasons are moral reasons, and whether they are adequate to the task, are questions for moral philosophers to figure out, and presumably answers will vary with different legal systems in play.

I think that Hart is only partly correct about this issue. Consider the gunman situation again: the crucial difference between the gunman scenario and the law is much better explained by introducing the concept of authority. The gunman is only interested in getting your money. He does not claim—at least there is nothing in the situation to force him to claim—that he is in a position that authorizes him to order you to hand over your money. In other words, the gunman makes no claim to be a legitimate authority or to have a legitimate authoritative claim on your conduct. However, as Joseph Raz (1985) famously argued, it is an essential aspect of law that it always *claims* to be a legitimate authority. When the law makes a claim to your money (by imposing a tax, or a fine, or whatever), it makes this claim as an exercise of its putative legitimate authority. And that is the sense in which legal requirements purport to create obligations: they are requirements based on claims of legitimate political authority. Needless to say, Raz does not suggest that law's claim to be a legitimate authority is generally a sound one, morally or otherwise justified. Whether the law's claim to the legitimacy of its authority is warranted or not—either in particular cases, or wholesale—is a separate, moral-political question, and the answers would vary from case to case. But it is essential to an understanding of what the law is that it always makes this kind of claim—that it claims to be a legitimate political authority. I am not suggesting that Hart's reductionism about the normativity of law necessarily fails. But even if we aim for a reduction of law's normative concepts to social facts, we must acknowledge that law's language, and the kind of claims law has on its subjects, are much closer to morality and moral claims than Hart envisaged (see Marmor 2011, ch. 3).

A Necessary Connection Between Law and Morality?

Since law aims to guide conduct, and it aims to guide conduct for reasons—very often moral reasons—it is natural to think that there must be a necessary or otherwise some essential connection between law and morality. Can we conclude that there is such a necessary connection? It would be a mistake to think that this is one question that can be answered by yes or no. There are various senses in which the answer is clearly yes, others in which the answer is clearly no, and still others in which the answer is problematic and contentious. Very few would deny, for example, that there is something essentially good, perhaps even necessarily so—given certain truths about human society and human nature—about having law in our society. Even wicked legal regimes promote some goods: they provide some services that people need and would be worse off without. So the idea that there is something good about having law seems like a very plausible idea. One might think that political anarchists, at least, are bound to deny this. But they do not have to: anarchists can hold the view that whatever good there is in having law is outweighed by its evils and, therefore, we would be better off without law. Even if you have no anarchist tendencies, you might concede that when a legal regime is totally corrupt and heinous, its subjects might be better off, overall, without it. But all this is compatible with the view that there is something essentially good in having law; that is, having our social lives governed by a legal regime. Perhaps this good is outweighed or undercut in some extreme cases, but to have our social lives governed by law is generally a good thing.

At the other end, yet again, nobody would deny that particular laws are never guaranteed to be morally good. That something is required by a law does not necessarily entail that it is morally required as well, or even that it is morally permitted. In this sense, surely there is *no* necessary connection between law and morality; it is possible, even in a decent and morally legitimate legal regime, to find particular laws that are morally wrong or unjustified. But can laws be totally iniquitous and still be law? Can an entire legal system be totally wicked and still be a legal system? There were times (mostly after World War II, for understandable reasons) when jurists thought that these are difficult questions worthy of serious consideration (Fuller 1958; Hart 1958). There were some jurists and philosophers who thought that morally unacceptable laws cannot count as law at all. Mostly they relied on what they took to be a central tenet of the natural law tradition that laws must meet a certain threshold of moral acceptability to be legally valid. As the famous dictum of St. Augustin has it, *lex inusta non est lex* (unjust law is not law). It is, however, questionable whether the mainstream natural law tradition (viz., the Thomist tradition, named after the thirteenth-century philosopher and theologian Thomas Aquinas) has really maintained this problematic thesis (e.g., John Finnis (1980) has long argued that it has not). The idea that an unjust law, even profoundly and unquestionably unjust, cannot be law, that is, legally valid, seems to fly in the face of reality. There is simply nothing incoherent in saying about a particular legal requirement that it is a profoundly immoral law.

A more serious concern, perhaps, might be about the limits of immorality concerning an entire regime. Suppose we think about a mafia-style regime or form of social control based on sheer terror and oppression. Could that be a legal system? The answer is far from clear. Presumably, in some extreme cases, a regime of sheer terror might have almost nothing to do with law. In most real-life examples, however, even very corrupt regimes have some features that would make them legal—that is, they perform certain functions of law (such as guaranteeing that certain contracts are enforced, or certain harms are remedied, etc.) and others which would make us doubt that they have anything to do with legality. In other words, some forms of governance or social control might be borderline cases of law. As with other borderline cases of vague concepts (see

Soames 2012), there is no saying about such instances whether they are an instance of the relevant concept or not. Borderline cases are just that, borderline cases. I doubt that there is a theoretical payoff in trying to determine whether some borderline cases of legal regimes are really legal or not.

A third sense in which law is necessarily related to morality, and in a way that is hardly controversial, consists in the idea that laws have some essential moral functions in our lives. Part of what laws are there to do, as it were, is to solve some problems in our social lives that have moral significance. In other words, it is quite plausible to maintain that we could not come to understand the functions of law in society without understanding some of the main moral problems we face and ways in which laws aim to solve them.

There are, however, two main areas in which the essential connections between law and morality are controversial. We have already considered one of them in some detail above, with respect to the conditions of legal validity and the question of whether those conditions may depend on moral truths. There is another area, however, in which there might be a necessary connection between law and morality, concerning law's essential purposes and its inherent standards of perfection. As John Finnis explains in his contribution to this volume (2012), there is a long tradition in jurisprudence, going back to ancient Greek philosophy, maintaining that it is an essential feature of law that it aims to promote the *common good* and thus has certain standards of perfection inherent in it. Law is a purposeful institution; it has certain aims which make it the kind of institution that it is. And those aims must have something to do with the good that is common to those whose institution it is.

This view, however, is controversial in two respects: first, in connecting, as this long tradition does, the common good that is essentially law's main purpose with a conception of natural law—or some sense in which law's *telos* or purposes somehow reflect the true nature of things, morally speaking—the thesis has a great deal to say about the nature of morality, perhaps even more than it has to say about law. And of course, views about the nature of morality are philosophically controversial, if anything is.

Second, the idea that the law is necessarily the kind of institution that aims to promote the common good has been challenged from a critical point of view, most notably by the Marxist traditions. Marxists do not doubt that law is manifestly concerned with the "common good"; what they challenge is the true nature of this good, claiming that far from being really good, it is a form of *ideology* or false consciousness, aimed at masking people's true and authentic interests, which are class interests to be free of domination. Some of the contemporary "critical" theories in jurisprudence, including some versions of feminist jurisprudence, make a very similar claim. They argue that the "common good" that law inevitably advances is actually exclusionary in its nature; that is, advancing the common good of the wealthy and powerful segments of the population at the expense of the weak and vulnerable. From a philosophical perspective, the cogency of these kinds of critiques depends on the distinction between critical evaluations of existing practices—no doubt flawed in many ways and in need of reform—from claims about the inevitable, that is, the essential nature of the practices under consideration. Is it really an essential, inevitable, nature of law that it favors the strong over the weak, the wealthy over the poor, etc.? Or is it (if it really is) just the way things have developed over time but could be made to be different? This is a very difficult question and I will not try to answer it here.

References

Austin, J. (1832) *The Province of Jurisprudence Determined*, London: J. Murray.

Coleman, J. (1982) "Negative and Positive Positivism," 11 *Journal of Legal Studies*: 139–64.

Dworkin, R. (1977) *Taking Rights Seriously*, London: Duckworth.

—— (1986) *Law's Empire*, Cambridge, Mass.: The Belknap Press of Harvard University Press.

Edmundson, W. A. (2012) "Coercion," in A. Marmor, ed., *Routledge Companion to Philosophy of Law*, New York: Routledge.

Finnis, J. (1980) *Natural Law and Natural Rights*, New York: Oxford University Press.

—— (2012) "Natural Law Theory: Its Past and Its Present," in A. Marmor, ed., *Routledge Companion to Philosophy of Law*, New York: Routledge.

Fuller, L. (1958) "Positivism and Fidelity to Law: A Reply to Professor Hart," 71 *Harvard Law Review*: 630–72.

Hart, H. L. A. (1958) "Positivism and the Separation of Law and Morals," 71 *Harvard Law Review*: 593–629.

—— (1961) *The Concept of Law*, Oxford: Clarendon Press.

—— (1994) *The Concept of Law*, 2nd edition, P. Bulloch and J. Raz, eds., Oxford: Oxford University Press.

Kelsen, H. (1961/1945) *General Theory of Law and State*, A. Wedberg, trans., New York: Russell and Russell.

Klosko, G. (2012) "The Moral Obligation to Obey the Law," in A. Marmor, ed., *Routledge Companion to Philosophy of Law*, New York: Routledge.

Marmor, A. (2005) *Interpretation and Legal Theory*, revised 2nd edition, Oxford: Hart Publishing.

—— (2011) *Philosophy of Law*, Princeton: Princeton University Press.

Postema, G. J. (2012) "Legal Positivism: Early Foundations," in A. Marmor, ed., *Routledge Companion to Philosophy of Law*, New York: Routledge.

Raz, J. (1984) "Legal Principles and the Limits of Law," in M. Cohen, ed., *Ronald Dworkin and Contemporary Jurisprudence*, Totowa, NJ: Rowman and Littlefield.

—— (1985) "Authority, Law and Morality," 68 *The Monist*: 295.

—— (1990/1975) *Practical Reason and Norms*, Princeton: Princeton University Press.

Soames, S. (2012) "Vagueness and the Law," in A. Marmor, ed., *Routledge Companion to Philosophy of Law*, New York: Routledge.

Stavropoulos, N. (2012) "Obligations, Interpretivism and the Legal Point of View," in A. Marmor, ed., *Routledge Companion to Philosophy of Law*, New York: Routledge.

Waluchow, W. (1994) *Inclusive Legal Positivism*, Oxford: Oxford University Press.

Further Reading

For further reading, see: R. Dworkin (2006) *Justice in Robes*, Cambridge, Mass.: Harvard University Press; H. L. A. Hart (1994) "Postscript," in P. Bulloch and J. Raz, eds., Oxford: Oxford University Press; A. Marmor (2009) *Social Conventions: From Language to Law*, Princeton: Princeton University Press; G. J. Postema (1989) *Bentham and the Common Law Tradition*, Oxford: Oxford University Press; J. Raz (1979) *The Authority of Law*, Oxford: Oxford University Press; and J. Raz (1985) "Authority, Law and Morality," 68 *The Monist*: 295.

2
NATURAL LAW THEORY
Its Past and Its Present
John Finnis

I

The past in which theory of this kind had its origins is notably similar to the present. For this is theory—*practical* theory—which articulates a critique of critiques, and the critiques it criticizes, rejects and replaces have much in common whether one looks at them in their fifth-century BC Hellenic (Sophistic) or their modern (Enlightenment, Nietzschean or postmodern) forms.

In the name of nature or the natural (in some of the many dozens of meanings of those terms), the thinkers whom natural law theory corrects have scathingly criticized conventional conceptions of justice and injustice, of (more generally) right and wrong, and (most generally) of good and bad in human action, affairs and institutions. The conventional conceptions are denounced, or more covertly subverted, as unjustifiable impositions on what is *natural*: a life pursuing passionate satisfactions such as power, sex, and other bodily and emotional interests (today often conceived as psychological or "subconscious" drives or "complexes"). The Sophistic conception of the natural is not naïve; it accommodates some main realities of social existence: typically it counsels compliance with social norms whenever one's detected violation of them would incur sanctions, or other resistance, that would frustrate one's pursuit of one's interests. And it acknowledges that one's interests need not be individualistic; one may find one's satisfactions in one's group's power and prestige, lorded ruthlessly over other groups. The survival and predominance of the fittest, which is the natural goal of existence, is naturally a social matter. It includes winning the support or acquiescence of other members of the group by such stratagems as professing the conventional belief in justice and morality, and making or postulating agreements ("social contracts") to abstain from harming them, to lend them reciprocal assistance and so forth—agreements silently subordinated always to their purpose of advancing the natural priority of one's own purposes and interests in survival, domination, pleasure, etc.

The critique of such theories and forms of life that was carried through by Socrates and Plato ("the Platonic critique") included a purposeful capturing or radical reshaping of the idea of nature, the natural and the naturally fitting. The Platonic critique shares with the Sophists some elements in their critique of the conventional and traditional. For although people who respect traditional norms and standards of evaluating human conduct may well regard these not merely as a social fact but as having directive force for them, and thus a kind of moral truth, nonetheless this attitude of theirs is often—indeed, characteristically—marked by its uncritical marginalizing of the question of truth. For them, the fact that the norms and standards are what they found respected in their society and among their forebears counts in practice as if it were sufficient warrant. The Platonic critique foregrounds the question of the truth or error, the moral reasonableness or unreasonableness, of any and all normative propositions (claims, norms) held out—whether in traditions, dialogue or personal reflection (conscience)—as directive for individuals and groups. It insists on the distinction basic also to the present article: that if there is a natural law that, by reason of the true goodness to which it directs us, is entitled to direct all consciences, it has no past, present or future; only beliefs and theories about it have temporality and a history (Finnis 2011/1980: 24–25).

A central text in this critique of the Sophists' critique is Plato's dialogue *Gorgias*. Here Plato presents, in fictionalized parties to the discourse, a spectrum of Sophistic positions, from the less (Gorgias) to the more radical (Polus) and most thoroughgoing (Callicles). Socrates triumphs dialectically over Callicles while the reader knows that, in real history, politically unprincipled operatives of perhaps Calliclean type worked on a malleable crowd of conventionally minded jurymen fired up about the state's traditions to bring Socrates to his unjust condemnation and execution. The Socratic thesis (*Gorgias* 469b–c, 479c, 489b, 508d–e) that it is better to suffer injustice than to do it is thus given a tacit force and challenge even as Plato tests and vindicates it through a probing discussion of what the criteria of "good" and "better" really are, in reasonable judgment. So, for example, the Calliclean proposals to assimilate the better to the stronger (entitling the strong to rule over the weak regardless of other merits or deservings) is refuted by the consideration that the weak collectively are stronger than the strong, and that a life spent in avoiding this menace to the unscrupulous is a life of servitude to the opinion, interests and whims of the crowd. So if the naturally superior strength of the many entails (as Callicles would have it) that they and their views are better, the Calliclean position breaks down, in a kind of self-refutation:

> *Socrates*: Don't the many [who collectively are stronger] have a rule that says it's just to have an equal share, and a rule that doing what's unjust is more shameful than suffering it? . . . So it isn't merely "as a matter of law" that doing what's unjust is more shameful than suffering wrong, or that justice is a matter of equal shares, but "by nature" too. So you seem to have spoken falsely, earlier, when you challenged me with your claim that *nature* and *law* [instituted by people] are opposites.
>
> (*Gorgias* 488–9, with 483a–b)

The demonstrations that the Calliclean position is incoherent are less important, in the end, than the dialogue's more implicit disclosures of the intelligible goods that are at stake in any dialogue worthy of the name. Dialogue is real, and worth pursuing, only under conditions of knowledge, goodwill and frank free speech among the participants. They, and any audience, can find it worthwhile as a dialogue only if they value both truth and the sharing in discovery and acknowledgement of truth by all concerned. To value and secure this active *sharing* is a further intelligible good, worthy of pursuit alongside the good of *truth and knowledge*. This further good can be called *friendship*.

Each of these intelligible goods is the subject of a normative proposition which naturally—or, more precisely, rationally—even if inexplicitly, comes into play when one is reflecting or deliberating about one's opportunities, and which directs us to be interested in the actualizing of this good and in the avoiding of what negates it (such as ignorance or superstition, or hatred and deception). This normativity or directiveness is not yet "moral," as justice and injustice are. But it soon unfolds into the normativity of the virtuous or vicious (the right and the wrong, if you prefer) because the competition between various worthwhile opportunities (knowledge, friendship, patriotism, marriage, etc.), and between all or any of these and opportunities for gratifying more or less subrational, emotional desires and aversions, calls urgently for adjudication and control by some further and, as controlling, higher principle or source of *order* in one's deliberating, choosing and acting—in one's soul, as Plato puts it. This is the adjudication that only practical reasonableness (Plato's virtue of *phronêsis*) can make, and make actual in one's life and conduct. It is this virtue that enables one to discern, practically, what is just and unjust, courageous and cowardly and rash, and so forth. Its adjudications are, in the last analysis, propositional, and the normativity of these propositions is moral. We have arrived at a new conception of (moral) law, to transcend and replace the directiveness attributed to subrational nature by the Sophists.

The last step in this conceptual reordering is the transfer of the predicate "natural" to this moral "law." The transfer is justified for multiple, distinct reasons. First, one's understanding that truth, friendship, human life itself and the other such possible objects of choice are indeed good—not only as means to other ends but intrinsically—is an understanding achieved readily, non-inferentially and in that sense spontaneously, as an achievement of one's intelligence when attentive to real possibilities and alternatives and free from external distractions or dominantly passionate, subrational factors in one's psychic makeup. It is in these senses a natural understanding, an achievement of natural reason (to be carefully distinguished from data-free intuition). It is available even to children, once they have had sufficient experience of the world to be aware of real possibilities and their alternatives.

Second, the intrinsic and thus basic intelligible goods are understood precisely as pursuit-worthy. So this understanding is practical, concerned not merely with what truly *is*, but also and essentially with what truly *is-to-be* in a sense that is not predictive but directive, normative, articulable from the outset in the language of normativity: should, ought, is-to-be-done. Nonetheless, this practicality of one's understanding of human good in no way entails that the objects of practical understanding and judgment are a matter of invention or creation. Rather, the basic human goods are discovered (as *to-be-brought-into-existence*). In this way, they stand over and against our understanding, and *in this respect* they are like the natural world of objects that are what they are, and have the natural order they have, and follow the natural laws they do, quite independently of human thought, contrivance and action.

Third, life, knowledge, friendship and so forth are understood as basic aspects of *human* flourishing or well-being or fulfillment, actualizable if chosen intelligently and pursued and acted upon. They are understood as good "for me" and anyone like me—and this "like me" soon becomes intelligible securely as: any other being capable, at least radically, of self-conscious flourishing or failure—any human being or person. As aspects of such flourishing, these basic human goods give point, shape, meaning and specific identity to human action. But such actions are always the actualizing of human capacities (powers, potentialities), and capacities in turn are given us by our makeup, our nature, prior to all choice or action of our own. So: to understand the basic aspects of human flourishing is implicitly to understand basic outlines of human nature. Propositions picking out and directing us to the basic human goods can thus be well described as principles of natural normativity, natural rightness or fittingness, and natural law.

Such natural law, though sharply and cleanly distinguishable from laws of nature that govern entities and processes (including many aspects of human reality) independently of any understanding or choices, is factually (that is, ontologically: in the order of being) dependent upon natural reality that we find, not make. But epistemologically (that is, in the order of coming to know), the first principles of natural law are first principles of practical reason and, as such, are not dependent upon a prior adequate knowledge of human nature. Our understanding of them presupposes some knowledge of the factually given structures of possibility, availability, causality and realizability, but adds very significantly to that prior knowledge. In so adding, it makes possible an adequate understanding of human nature via understanding of the human flourishing made possible by human *openness* to ways of acting and living that quite transcend the given—possibilities such as courageous friendship, devotion to justice, humane artistic creativity, holiness of life and so forth. In sum: the *oughts* of the first practical principles (principles of natural right and law) are not inferred from prior knowledge of the *is* of nature. Rather, our *ought*-knowledge of them both presupposes some elements of, and very significantly adds other elements to, the eventual body of such *is*-knowledge.

II

This account has got ahead of Plato's, and fallen behind it. It has fallen behind by omitting, thus far, his critique of the tradition-bound states of mind and culture which the Sophists themselves criticized and delegitimated (even when conforming, by choice, to traditions and conventions). Plato's critique of tradition is presented, explicitly, not so much in the *Gorgias* as in his later, greater work, *The Republic*. And it is a critique not so much of particular customs, perhaps more or less peculiar to one or more societies, but rather of conventional wisdom. But what exactly is that? Plato identifies the object of his critique by exemplifying it. Cephalus, representative of the oldest living generation, the grandparents, defines justice as paying one's debts and telling the truth, and loses interest in the matter when Socrates points out that there are occasions when it is wrong to return what one has borrowed (say, a weapon from a lender who has now gone mad), and wrong to tell the truth (say, to a dangerous maniac) (*Republic* 331b–d). Cephalus's son Polemarchus, host of the whole occasion of the dialogue, is a little closer to the sophistication of the Sophists. He holds that justice is a matter of benefiting one's friends and harming one's enemies, or (under dialectical pressure from Socrates) of benefiting just people and harming the unjust (334). Socrates demonstrates that it is never just to (choose/try to) harm anyone, and Polemarchus has to concede that what he learned about justice from powerful political and financial leaders was unsound (335d–336a). The stage is cleared for the intervention of the radical Sophist, here in the person of Thrasymachus who, like Plato's Callicles, holds that:

> . . . injustice, if it is on a large enough scale [as in the tyrant's efficacious rule over his community], is stronger, freer and more masterly than justice [conventionally conceived] . . . [J]ustice [truly conceived] is what is advantageous to the stronger, while injustice [conventionally conceived] is to one's own profit and advantage.
>
> (344c)

The rest of the dialogue, in effect, is Plato's response, his critique of the Thrasymachean (and Calliclean) critique and rejection of the *conventional* conceptions of injustice.

The Platonic critique takes it as obvious that the large elements of truth in conventional wisdom about (say) giving people their due (335e) must be vindicated against the corrosive Sophistic critique, which sophistically inverts and negates that truth; and obvious too that the vindication will have to be critical and philosophically grounded in ways that conventional wisdom has simply not inquired after or understood. In the terminology of the eventual theory emergent in Plato: natural law and natural right must be vindicated by the theoretical reflections, conceptualizations and arguments that a textbook or companion to philosophy may label *natural law theory*.

Enough has been said in this sketch of some Platonic dialectic to indicate that the conventional or traditional morality which Plato is concerned both to criticize and to (partially) vindicate is not to be understood as merely "positive morality" or "social morality" in the sense proposed by John Austin and H. L. A. Hart. They (especially Hart) spoke as if such a morality were held *as* positive, rather than *as* true. Plato, the more accurate sociologist and philosopher, is clear that even those who hold to a partially untrue morality, and do so without sufficient critical attention to its coherence or its warrant, nonetheless are very unlikely to hold and consider it as simply a fact about their society's beliefs, and equally unlikely to explain it to themselves as warranted precisely and simply because their society or their elders have held them; almost certainly they will hold it rather as a truth (as they suppose) about what is good and bad for people and right and wrong in human action. The problem, as Plato rightly sees it, is that their lack of critical interest in the grounds of their belief—the lack that makes their belief conventional—leaves them (and the conventions) exposed to distortion and error about the truth of, or error in, the belief's moral content.

How is moral error detected and avoided? Implicitly, the answer given by Plato and the whole philosophical tradition which he initiated (the tradition represented by Aristotle and Aquinas) is something like this. A judgment—the affirming or denying of a proposition—is erroneous when it does not cohere with judgments which, even after critical questioning and the test of dialogue and dialectic, one holds to be rationally justified and expects other similarly critical and careful persons, similarly placed, would agree with. In the case of judgments about realities that are what they are independently of anyone's thinking about them, their justification is that they conform/correspond to—fit, and are in line with—those realities; that they so correspond is what is meant in calling them true. These realities, of course, are only known in judgments, but the judgments are based on the data of experience (evidence in all relevant forms), and are justified only on condition that they do not overlook or neglect but rather do rationally account for the data. In the case of judgments about human goods whose realization is dependent on being conceived, considered desirable, opted for, and pursued and achieved or instantiated by action carrying out such choices, the justification of the judgments is again a matter (i) of coherence with other judgments that one thinks all other people would, under ideal epistemic conditions, agree with, and (ii) of correspondence with something that stands over and against one's judgments as their object, something that is affirmed when the judgment is true and misstated or denied when the judgment is false. What is this something, in relation to judgments about what is good and right in human action and achievement? There has been a tendency in the tradition to respond: human nature. But that kind of response overlooks the difference between realities that are what they are affirmed to be, independently of our thought or affirmation (which can thus be called "theoretical" or descriptive reason), and realities that it would be good to achieve by rational choice and action (and as such are the primary subject matter of *practical* reason). A better response is: practical reason's judgments are true when they accurately anticipate—are in anticipatory correspondence to—the human good that can be realized (call it fulfillment or flourishing) by actions in accordance with them (Grisez, Boyle and Finnis 1987: 115–20; Finnis 1998: 99–101).

As with theoretical/descriptive judgments, there is no vantage point outside or prior to practical judgments for assessing this correspondence, and the grandmasters of the natural law tradition did not suppose there was. So the working criterion of truth is coherence with other practical judgments, and capacity to be shared in judgment by other persons in epistemically like cases. The judgments of the Sophists largely fail this test; the Socratic showing of Callicles's self-refutation is only one instance. The Thrasymachean judgments that justice—whether understood as the most reasonable choice for me, or as the "natural order of things"—consists in the rule of the stronger or more deceitfully cunning, and that it is reasonable (because and when advantageous) to practice injustice, have their plausibility only when envisaged as the judgments held and acted upon by a few persons in a community which by and large adheres to the contrary judgments: that promises should generally be kept and debts paid even when a strong or ruthless debtor could get away with reneging on his debt; that lies should not be told (even if false propositions can be defensively articulated to unjust aggressors); that distributions should follow principles of fairness using criteria such as need, desert, function or (by default) equality rather than imperiousness of demand or forcible seizure of the common stock by the strongest or greediest; that one should do to others only what one would be willing to have them do to oneself; and so forth. Similarly, the judgment or thesis that practical reason should look only to the *future* advantage promised by the present choice (whether of the reasoner or of everybody) shows itself false by its incoherence with any reliance on the promised cooperation of others, and with the reasonableness of them contributing (say as one's employees) to one's well-being or other interests in reliance on one's promise. And so forth.

In each case, the Platonic critique lends support to moral positions more or less traditional in his day as in ours. In each case, the critique lends rational support to the positions in several ways. It shows that the counter-positions of the enlightened Sophists tend directly towards a disintegration of social well-being insofar as it depends on taking into account (i) the intelligible relations of present and future to the past (of promises, reliances, undertakings, gifts and gratitude, merit, desert, responsibility of parent for child . . .), (ii) the rational requirement that a judgment of self-interest be subjected to a test of compatibility with others' similar judgments (universalizability, the Golden Rule . . .), (iii) the human goods that depend upon friendly social cooperation extended stably though creatively through time (goods such as science and learning, trust, political compromise and moderation, a rule of law and not of the whims and prejudices of the powerful . . .) and so forth.

It is the intelligible attractiveness of such goods that is the deep source of the critique, and equally of the normativity of the propositions about right and wrong that the critique shows to be warranted and truly worthy of affirmation as the grounded anticipations of human fulfillment and thus as true. The art of the dialogues is the displaying of the sheer *desirability* of these goods, despite the sometimes demanding character of their preconditions. Such desirability is in line with subrational, animal desires or inclinations, but is much more a matter of intelligibility, that is, of a *worth* that only reason understands. Against the self-refuting Calliclean blunder, resumed later by Hume, of supposing that practical reason can only be the slave (ingenious servant) of the passions, Plato already shows that a "practical reason" which has no *reasons* for its proposing of means is not worth calling reason, and that there are indeed intrinsically, intelligently desirable human ends available to give true reason(s) for selection and adoption.

The intelligible beauty, the fineness, worth and excellence of the goods discernible by reason includes the sense of *good* implicit in the *better* of the Socratic "better—more choiceworthy, less shameful—to suffer injustice than to do it" exemplified historically by Socrates, willing (quite without publicity of any kind) to decline participation in an unjust execution (see Plato, *Apology* 32c–e), and unwilling (see Plato, *Crito*) to escape from prison and unjust execution by an act which he judged, for considered reasons (even though we now can judge them less than fully sufficient), to be subversive of his own society and its law, and of proper gratitude. (See also Finnis 1983: 112–20; Finnis 1991: 47–55.)

III

What, then, of the ways in which the foregoing account has got ahead of Plato? After all, his works foretell, at least implicitly, most if not all of the arguments revived or proposed in the Enlightenment that is well under way with Machiavelli and Hobbes, darkens into the chiaroscuro of Benthamite utilitarianism, and after the failed Kantian and post-Kantian resistance reaches full darkness in the overt irrationalities enunciated, verbosely, by Nietzsche and his pragmatist and postmodern epigones. The main anachronisms in our rendering of the Platonic critique are (i) our use of the term "moral(ity)" and (ii) our talk of principles and thus of law rather than right and justice. The two are interrelated. In modern times, morality is thought of as a code (set of rules or standards) of conduct, a code subscribed to or acknowledged by members of a community. And "moral" is understood, accordingly, as a predicate whose proper application is settled by the norms of that or some such code. But even in the work of Aquinas, a pivotal figure in the transition from the ancient to the modern world, "moral" means: pertaining to human conduct as a matter of choice rather than as determined by nature. Moral knowledge or instruction is, accordingly, knowledge of or instruction about the factors that make choices reasonable or unreasonable, good or bad. Of course, the criteria of reasonableness and goodness can and must be able to be stated propositionally, and can thus be articulated in law-like form—that is, as universal propositions directive of choice and action. And therefore there are strong links and even overlaps between the ancient or medieval usage and the modern. But modern morality-talk's focus on rules or norms of law-like form, rather than on the goods that give actions their intelligible objects and thus their appropriate description(s), has some real disadvantages. The modern term "morality" is deeply ambiguous (Gert 2011/2002), above all between a "descriptive" sense in which what is decisive is that the code is subscribed to or acknowledged by some concrete historical community, and a "normative" or "internal" sense in which what is decisive is that the standards referred to are taken to be true and authoritative guides to the predication of virtue or vice, goodness or badness, rightness or wrongness in some (class of) human choices and actions. Discussion, for example, of inclusive legal positivism is hampered if not altogether frustrated by uncertainty about whether what is under discussion as "the relation between law and morality" is a relationship between two sets of standards cognizable as such because *held* by some community or one or more of its judges, or rather a relationship between (on the one hand) a set of (legal) standards so held and (on the other hand) some truths about right and wrong in human choosing and acting.

In any event, what interests Plato in criticizing and transcending the Sophistic is the truth about justice and injustice, and good and bad or superior and inferior in human action. Dispositions to act well, in a humanly superior way, are virtues, and dispositions to act badly, in an inferior way, are vices. The reasonableness or unreasonableness of the relevant kinds of action is what makes them virtuous or vicious. He does not speak, in his own voice, of "natural law," but rather of what is naturally (*physei*; or *kata physin*) superior, reasonable, virtuous, truly choice-worthy, and right.

Still, we are entitled to translate the argumentation and position-taking of Plato into *propositions* justified, implicitly, by higher or deeper justifying *principles*, picking out and directing us all towards goods, and higher and highest goods, and supplying us with criteria of reasonableness in choice and action. And we are entitled to go further. We can distinguish between a first level of principles which pick out and direct us all towards goods such as truth (or knowledge) and life, and a second level of principles. Principles on this second level mediate, so to speak, among the first-level directives, enabling us to discern between reasonable and unreasonable ways of following those first-level directives, calling the reasonable ways just (or rationally tempered) and right and the unreasonable unjust (or cowardly or lust-driven) and wrong. First-level principles can be called (as Aquinas calls them) first principles of natural law, and second-level principles can be called standards or precepts of natural moral law.

Albeit without this terminology, Plato's critique concerns itself with both kinds of principle. We have noticed, in passing, his concern to display the intrinsic goodness of truth (knowledge), and of friendship (including the fellow-feeling of citizens, political friendship). In his critique of sexual immoralities such as fornication, masturbation and same-sex sex acts, the search for an underlying principle leads him to identify, almost explicitly, a further basic human good: marriage (the committed union of man and woman in a procreative or would-be procreative friendship). (See *Laws* VIII: 838e–840e, where Plato's spokesman also speaks of the abuse he expects to get for advancing these arguments and expressing these judgments.) A state law restricting sex acts to marriage is, he affirms, a matter of true reason (835e, 836e) and is *kata physin*, natural (839a)— and this "natural" is not a matter of the nature we share with other animals but rather of reaching standards higher than the animals (840e): reasonableness (*logos*).

No doubt Plato is going too fast in proposing that this standard of practical judgment be also enforced as a coercive state law. But the focus of his thought is on what reasonableness requires of us as individuals, couples and so forth, in our free deliberations and reflections. And his rigorous assimilating of the humanly natural to the reasonable (see Lewis 2009: 79, citing *Laws* 642a, 689b, 690c, 720d, 728d, 733a, 875d, 943a, 966b), and his clear indication that, in the last analysis, an action's reasonableness is the *ground* for calling it natural (not vice versa), are an important phase in the development of the theory we now call natural law theory. The argumentation's conclusion is propositional, law-like; its premises must be, too. But the *force* of the argument, the principles and the conclusions, comes from the goods to which the premises of principle refer, and more precisely from their attractiveness to practical understanding, as goods that we *need* to have as objects of our actions if we are to be fully intelligent and fully masters of our subrational inclinations just insofar as these work to distract us from such full reasonableness, rather than (as they do when our psyche is in good order) supporting and giving fully human weight to our reasonable judgments.

The rendering of ethics (synonymously, morality) and of natural law theory's primary account—an ethics of political society and law—into the form of law-like propositions (principles, norms) is accomplished gradually over the millennium and a half after Plato. Important currents in this are Aristotle's *Ethics* and *Politics* and *Rhetoric*; the Stoics; the Roman publicists and jurists (tightly linking law, right, rights and justice); the Pauline New Testament (pronouncing the revealed moral commandments of the Decalogue to be *also* and equally requirements of humanity's nature and of sound conscience (Romans 2: 14–16); Augustine of Hippo's Platonizing speculations on the directive ideas in the supreme creative intelligence and on "the eternal law" of that creator's ongoing providential ordering and sustaining of every creature; and Thomas Aquinas's synthesis of the whole tradition (despite the unavailability to him of all but a tiny fragment of Plato's works), a synthesis that for the first time penetrates fully to principles and at the same time builds up and builds in a distinct and carefully elaborated theory of human, positive law.

IV

About a century before Plato, the greatest of the pre-Sophistic Greek philosophers, Heraclitus of Ephesus, articulates—albeit *without* the word "natural" or its cognates, and *with* a reference to the divine—the heart of the tradition of natural law theory:

Those who speak with intelligence [*xyn noô*] must hold fast to [or: strengthen themselves with] what is common [*xynô*] to all, as the political community does with the law [*nomô*], and more strongly so. For all human laws [*anthrôpeioi nomoi*] nourish themselves from the one divine [law], which governs as far as it will and suffices (and more than suffices) for all things.
(Diels-Kranz, fragment B114; the wordplay serves, not leads, the thought, which can be taken with fragment B44: "The people should fight for the law [*nomos*] as if for their city-wall.")

Much of Plato's treatment of these matters can be taken as a vast expansion, defense and explication of this. And Plato's greatest pupil makes his clearest statement of the theory, in the unpropitious context of his *Rhetoric*, with a similar appeal to what is common because entitled by its reasonableness and thus its naturalness to be adopted in and by any community:

Justices and injustices, then, have been defined in relation to two kinds of law . . . : I mean, law which is distinctive [*idion*], and law which is common [to everyone] [*koinon*]. Distinctive law is that which a particular group sets down for its own members (it is partly written down, and partly unwritten); law which is common to everyone is that which accords with nature. For there really is, as everyone senses, something just by nature and common to all—and something unjust—even when people have no association or agreement with one another. This for example is what Sophocles's Antigone is plainly referring to, when she says that the burial of Polyneices, although prohibited, is just, meaning that it is just by nature: "Not belonging to today or tomorrow, /It lives eternally: no one knows how it arose."
(Aristotle, *Rhetoric* I.13: 1373b2–15; see also the similar but more difficult passage in his *Nicomachean Ethics* V.7: 1134b18–1135a5)

Sixteen-hundred years later, Aquinas will start to popularize the term "positive law" for what Aristotle had called law distinctive or particular to a particular political group, and will decisively supersede Aristotle's distracting concern with the relatively superficial distinction between written and unwritten, replacing it with a categorization of positive law according to its two modes of derivation from principles that are common to every people precisely because they are reasonable and therefore "natural" (Finnis 2011, vol. IV, essay 7). Where the derivation is by logical specification (as killing or wounding are distinct specifications of harming), that part of the state's positive law can be called natural law or *jus gentium* (law common to all peoples). Where the derivation involves not only rational connection but also a choice between reasonable alternatives, the process of specification is not so much logical as legislative or at least partly creative and optional; Aquinas labels it *determinatio* and indicates that this part of the state's positive law is "positive" in a strict sense—but for its positing by some lawmaker (legislative or judicial), it would have no claim to be part of the state's law. Where such a *determinatio* (strictly: a rule made by such a *determinatio*) is just in its content and procedure, it is *morally binding* (on members of the community to which it applies) *even though it is not* "*part of morality*" but rather is purely positive law and could reasonably have been different in many, many details.

It is of first importance to understand this fully achieved thesis of natural law theory with precision. Any proper example (central case) of legal systems will be *positive law* in its entirety and all its parts, and at the same time will comprise two elements, (i) a set of rules, principles and institutions which are natural and are, or ought to be, common to all other legal systems, and (ii) a set, doubtless much larger, of rules, principles and institutions which are *purely* positive, and more or less distinctive of this particular political community and legal system. The relationship of natural law to the positive law of a particular state (or of the international order) is thus not best thought of as a coexisting of two normative orders. Rather it is a matter of acknowledging (or denying) the validity and legitimacy (not independent of sufficient efficacy and widespread acknowledgement) of that positive law/legal system, while at the same time acknowledging the normative principles which are necessary (though by far not sufficient) to the validating and legitimating of that law and capable of invalidating or delegitimating it.

The preceding sentence refers to both validity and legitimacy because "validity" (and to some extent also "legitimacy") is here ambiguous. Partly, the source of the ambiguity is the permanent tension whereby natural moral law (morality; moral truth about justice . . .) can serve both to make positive law morally binding and to deprive it of moral obligatoriness. But partly, the ambiguity's source is that a main reason for wanting to introduce positive law and the Rule of Law is to resolve disputes within a political community about what justice and the rest of morality requires or authorizes. There is thus good reason to introduce a way of thinking—call it legal or juristic thinking—within which (within undefined but important limits) the sheer fact that a legally ("constitutionally") authorized person or body of persons has pronounced its *determinatio* of some disputed or disputable issue is taken as sufficient ground for affirming the legal validity of the *determinatio* and its propositional product (rule, judgment, etc.). In this way of thinking, issues of the justice or injustice of the *determinatio* are pushed to the margins of the legal domain (though they retain within that domain a kind of underground existence in the form of *juristic* principles or presumptions of interpretation). Only when the moral limits are approached do questions of justice and morality become once again overtly relevant. Thus talk of "validity" can be more or less fully and cleanly reserved to intra-systemic legal (positive-law) discourse, and taken to entail not moral but *legal* obligatoriness (an obligatoriness not to be reduced to liability to penalty or punishment). In such a discourse context, one may choose to use "legitimacy" to signify *moral* relevance, grounding moral obligatoriness. But "legitimacy" too is not free from ambiguity, since some writers in contemporary legal theory seem to treat it, perhaps, as synonymous with (purely legal) validity.

Natural law theory has no quarrel with—indeed, promotes—a bifurcation between *intra-systemic [legal] validity* (and *obligatoriness*) and *legal validity* (and *obligatoriness*) in *the moral sense* (Finnis 2011/1980: 314–20). Indeed, it is not unreasonable to see such a distinction at work in the famous tag "An unjust law is not a law." This is mere self-con-tradiction and nonsense unless "unjust law" here refers to an intra-systemically valid legal rule or order, and "not law" signifies that, moral limits having been transgressed, this same law lacks validity in the moral sense (i.e., legitimacy) and thus, at least pre-sumptively, lacks moral obligatoriness. (Of course, the speaker could alternatively be intending to predicate injustice of certain beliefs and practices—observable as social facts of acknowledgement of certain acts and facts as laws—while not intending to assess legal validity even in a technically and constrained and amoral sense.) That said, it is unfortunately necessary to remark that there is nothing even prima facie self-con-tradictory, nonsensical or paradoxical about the tag. For the idiom is widespread and quite unremarkable: "an insincere friend is not a friend"; "a logically invalid argument is no argument"; "a quack medicine is no medicine"; and so forth.

Shifts of meaning of this kind were studied closely by Aristotle in connection with his accounts of the kinds of equivocation or homonymy, and of what we would now call analogous predication. A word can be said to be analogical when its meaning shifts more or less systematically according to context. The kind of analogy most relevant in the context of human affairs is what Aristotle called *pros hen* homonymy. This is where the various relevant meanings of a word are all relatable to a focal meaning or sense or use, a meaning which picks out a primary or *central* case of the kind of reality or subject matter under consideration—focal and central in some context of discourse or inquiry. The non-focal senses and non-central cases can be thought of as secondary because they are immature or deviant or in some other way watered-down instances or kinds of the reality, at least when regarded from some appropriate viewpoint or for some appropriate theoretical or practical purpose.

One relevant purpose, theoretical but strongly related to the practical, is that of developing an accurate account of human affairs as they have unfolded and are likely to unfold in the existence of manifold human societies of many times and places. Such an account would be highly interesting in its own right, as a matter for contemplation detached from any (other) practical purpose of the reader; but it would also be of practi-cal relevance as a source of accurate information about cause and effect in human affairs. (For all practical reasoning towards choice and action includes, besides its evaluative/normative premise(s), one or more premises about what means are likely to achieve the desired end(s), what are the preconditions for such means, and what the effects and side effects of such means are likely to be.) Aristotle pressed on from achievements of his empirical biological and other natural sciences into the study of human political affairs, his *Politics*; decisive for its method was his decision to select and employ its key terms or concepts by reference to practical reasonableness, human flourishing and the virtues that are both constitutive of and means to human flourishing. Forms of political asso-ciation and action that embody and favor such virtues are central, and the terms that pick out such central forms are therefore employed in their focal sense—focal at least for the purposes of political science. Other forms of political life, however common and "typical," will then be understood as non-central cases, immature or deviant (*parekbaseis*), and will be "polities," "constitutions," "citizenship," "political friendship," "laws," etc., in secondary rather than focal senses of those terms. It is in this scholarly context, resumed in late thirteenth-century Aristotelianizing political science, that Aquinas will take up the old tag about unjust laws not being laws: they are, he prefers to say, not laws *simpliciter*, i.e., without qualification, but rather are laws in a corrupt form ("corrupt form" being his Latinizing of *parekbasis*).

Aristotle's theoretical program was taken up again, in effect if not in intention, by Max Weber in the early twentieth century. On the basis of vastly more extensive historical information, Weber undertook to give an account of human affairs going wider than his title *Economy and Society* (1968/1922). He announced it as value free, purely descriptive-explanatory. But values were involved not only (as he recognized) in his decision to interest himself in all this, but also (as he did not fully acknowledge to himself) in his selection of concepts to provide the explanatory ordering of his whole account and each of its parts. Thus the concepts with which he gives an account of forms of governance are explicitly constructed in terms of greater and less *rationality*. And though his official concept of rationality was quasi-Humeian—the rationality of suitable means to subrationally desired ends—he could not prevent his account from manifesting a more adequate conception of rationality, in which human ends or purposes, too, are ranked for their reasonableness, their coherence with human goods and thus with the flourishing both of individuals and societies with their institutions.

V

The slow process of recovery of political and legal theory from the devastating crudities and impoverishments of Enlightenment social theorizing accelerated somewhat in the later twentieth century. In legal theory, the process was notably advanced by H. L. A. Hart. His project of understanding law, legal concepts and legal systems from "the internal point of view" was, at least implicitly, a return to the perspective of the political/ legal theory that Aristotle put together by developing and redeploying the strategies and elements of Plato's philosophy. For the internal point of view that Hart took as his point of reference is the thinking of persons (citizens, judges or other officials) who in a given political community (or potential community) are in search or (as they suppose) possession of *reasons* for some specific kinds of individual and social choice: the social choice to develop and maintain rules restricting violence, theft and fraud, and individual choices to acknowledge, adhere to and support these rules; the social choice to remedy the defects of such rules by introducing new forms of rule authorizing and regulating the changing and the judicial application of social (now sufficiently articulated to be worthy of the name legal) rules, and individual choices to recognize them in word and deed. This is legal theory done for descriptive/explanatory, rather than justificatory, purposes. But the explanations give the theoretical satisfaction they do precisely by tracking the route that those who accepted the rules as standards for their own and others' conduct do, or reasonably would, follow in order to justify such acceptance to themselves and others. A natural law theory of law follows the same route with an explicitly justificatory purpose. It can do so without loss of descriptive/explanatory coverage or content because it commands the conceptual technique of reference to central and then to secondary cases, employing focal and qualified senses of the terms and concepts it deploys.

Hart thought of his theory, expounded in *The Concept of Law* (1994/1961), as identifying a "minimum content" of positive law, a content he called natural law. But the content he officially included in this minimum was too minimal even to track faithfully the course he had followed in identifying the case for adding secondary to primary rules to yield a legal system. The human goods at stake in these "remedies" for "defects" went beyond the one human good he allowed into his official account: survival. Rather, the defects concerned conditions for living together relatively *well*, responsively to changing circumstances and opportunities and to the demands of efficiency and fairness in resolving disputes about the content and applicability of society's rules. Hart's resiling from acknowledgement of his own theoretical method and achievement went even further in his posthumous "Postscript," when he said:

> Like other forms of positivism my theory makes no claim to identify the point or purpose of law and legal practices as such . . . In fact, I think it quite vain to seek any more specific purpose which law as such serves beyond providing guides to human conduct and standards of criticism of such conduct. This will not of course serve to distinguish laws from other rules or principles with the same general aims; the distinctive features of law are the provision it makes for secondary rules for the modification, change, and enforcement of its standards and the general claim it makes to priority over other standards.
>
> (Hart 1994/1961: 248–49)

That statement is unfaithful to his book itself, which insistently specified the "general aims" of social regulation as aiding survival by restricting violence, fraud, etc., and made its signature contribution to legal theory by specifying the aims of secondary, law-introducing rules in ways that make intelligible and potentially *reasonable* the claim of the new set of rules to be now a *system* and to give reason, in "priority over other standards," for the allegiance of its officials and, in nonpathological cases, of all save criminal citizens. What, then, motivated Hart's recoil from his own method and its achievement? The only plausible answer seems to be that, in face of the questions debated between Plato and the Sophists, his own answers favored the Sophists' denial of moral truth. He thought legal theory could be pursued without confronting or taking a stand on those questions; even the discussions of morality in *The Concept of Law* are framed by him as "seek[ing] to evade these philosophical difficulties" about whether moral principles, so-called, can be anything other than mere "expressions of changing human attitudes, choices, demands, or feelings," in no way matter for discovery (or misidentification) by exercise of reason attaining (or missing) knowledge (168; also 186, 206). But this programmatic agnosticism about good and evil and right and wrong is transgressed, albeit cautiously and with unwarranted restrictions, throughout the legal theory he developed. The transgressions, which give the theory all its substance and worth, are sometimes almost explicit, as when he celebrates the emergence of private powers (and power-conferring rules) as a "step forward as important to society as the invention of the wheel" (42), or vindicates the rectificatory justice of compensation for tortious/delictual injuries (164–65), or treats as decisive for legal theory's selection of concepts the need for clear-sighted confrontation of, and readiness to disobey, "the official abuse of power" (210), or says and repeats that judges "must not" exercise their lawmaking powers arbitrarily but rather "must act as a conscientious legislator would" (273), that is, "relying on his sense of what is best" (275).

Hart's characterization of his work as "positivism" gets its meaning from the implicit contrast: positivism rejects "natural law theory." But the contrast, like the rejection, is a blunder. There is indeed a worthwhile theoretical issue at stake, but it is the one at stake between Plato and Callicles or Thrasymachus or, in real life, Antiphon (see Voegelin 1957 (ii): 312–19): between acceptance and denial that there is *knowledge* of human good and evil and right and wrong. Beyond that, there is really nothing strategic in dispute. A modern natural law theory of law builds on Aquinas's account of positive law, itself a systematization and terminological refinement of the elements in Heraclitus, Plato, Aristotle and the Roman jurists around the turn of the eras. It incorporates without the least strain anything upon which self-styled positiv*ist* accounts of positive law may have shed light, for example the conceptual structure of bilateral, three-term rights, the interrelationships between power, authority and validity, or the legal identity and personality of corporations. It distinguishes intra-systemic from morally predicated legal validity and correlative senses of obligatoriness. A modern natural law theory steadily repudiates all confusion, such as pervades positivist works, between *Is* and *Ought*, for (like Plato, Aristotle and Aquinas, in their basic theorizing) it permits normative predicates only when grounded in, or articulating, principles which are normative all the way to the bottom (where intelligence understands and is directed by goods whose worth is self-evident to anyone with sufficient information about, or experience of, what is possible). Its account of authority builds in the achievements of game theory and other theories of rational choice, without their arbitrary assumptions about the sufficiency of "self-interest" and the commensurability of all goods and transitivity of all preferences. And modern natural law theory is the proper context for reflection and deliberation about human rights, and about the appropriate reach of global as opposed to national or state sovereignty, territorial dominion and law (a question to be approached through the grounds identified by natural law theory for instituting property rights over resources originally common to, and for the benefit of, all human persons).

In modern natural law theory, law (in its central cases) is a modality of authority, available in specifically political communities, a modality responsive in its form to the "procedural" values and justice that (as Fuller 1969/1964 showed in illustrating and systematizing scattered observations of Aquinas) are involved in the Rule of Law, a form of governance which Plato and Aristotle contrasted and, in all but the most exceptional circumstances, preferred to the legally unrestrained rule of a ruler. Its account of deviant forms—abuses—of law is as rich as any positivist's, and richer because its critical understanding of them is unrestrained by fears of over-stepping the bounds of "positivism." For those bounds cannot in the last analysis be other than freely contestable decisions by particular theorists or schools of theorists who have not fully *recovered from the Enlightenment*'s peculiar mixture of unwarranted skepticism with unwarrantable reliance on the models and methods employed in the successful natural sciences—descriptive/explanatory sciences whose subject matter is the nature that *is what it is* regardless of our free choices and thus is radically other than a nature that flourishes only in forms conceived by practical reason and made actual only in and by the free choices which not only shape the course of events but also build up human character as just or unjust, vicious or virtuous. What can be said of human character can be said also of the legal systems that people choose to constitute and maintain in and for their communities.

There is every reason to hope, and some reason to expect, that that recovery will continue and that the future of the philosophy of law will be mainly as a recognizably (even when unlabeled) natural law theory of positive law.

References

Aristotle (1984) *The Complete Works of Aristotle, Volume 2*, J. Barnes, ed., Princeton: Princeton University Press.

Diels, H. and Kranz, W. (1985) *Die Fragmente der Vorsokratiker*, Zurich: Weidmann.

Finnis, J. (1983) *Fundamentals of Ethics*, Washington, D.C.: Georgetown University Press.

—— (1991) *Moral Absolutes: Tradition, Revision, and Truth*, Washington, D.C.: Catholic University of America Press.

—— (1998) *Aquinas: Moral, Political and Legal Theory*, Oxford: Oxford University Press.

—— (2011/1980) *Natural Law and Natural Rights*, 2nd edition, Oxford and New York: Oxford University Press.

—— (2011) *The Collected Essays of John Finnis* (five volumes), Oxford and New York: Oxford University Press.

Fuller, L. L. (1969/1964) *The Morality of Law*, New Haven, CT, and London: Yale University Press.

Gert, B. (2011/2002) "The Definition of Morality," in E. N. Zalta, ed., *The Stanford Encyclopedia of Philosophy*, http://plato.stanford.edu/archives/sum2011/entries/morality-definition.

Grisez, G., Boyle, J. M. and Finnis, J. (1987) "Practical Principles, Moral Truth, and Ultimate Ends," *American Journal of Jurisprudence* 32: 99–151.

Hart, H. L. A. (1994/1961) *The Concept of Law*, 2nd edition, Oxford: Clarendon Press.

Lewis, V. B. (2009) "'Reason Striving to Become Law': Nature and Law in Plato's *Laws*," *American Journal of Jurisprudence* 54: 67–91.

Pakaluk, M., trans. (2010) Aristotle, *Rhetoric* I.13, http://www.nlnrac.org/classical/aristotle/primary-source-documents.

Plato (1997) *Plato: Complete Works*, J. M. Cooper, ed., Indianapolis: Hackett Publishing.

Voegelin, E. (1957) *Order and History, Volume II: The World of the Polis*, Baton Rouge, LA: Louisiana State University Press.

Weber, M. (1968/1922) *Economy and Society*, G. Roth and C. Wittich, eds., New York: Bedminster Press Inc.

Further Reading

In general: J. M. Kelly (1992) *A Short History of Western Legal Theory*, Oxford: Clarendon Press. On the Sophists: E. Voegelin (1957) *Order and History, Volume II: The World of the Polis*, Baton Rouge, LA: Louisiana State University Press (also as *The Collected Works of Eric Voegelin, Volume 15*). On Plato and Aristotle: E. Voegelin (1957) *Order and History, Volume III, Plato and Aristotle*, Baton Rouge, LA: Louisiana State University Press (also as *The Collected Works of Eric Voegelin, Volume 16*). On modern legal theory, especially H. L. A. Hart: J. Finnis (2011) *Philosophy of Law: Collected Essays: Volume IV*, Oxford: Oxford University Press; and J. Finnis (2008) "Natural Law Theories," in E. N. Zalta, ed., *The Stanford Encyclopedia of Philosophy*, http://plato.stanford.edu/entries/natural-law-theories.

3

LEGAL POSITIVISM

Early Foundations

Gerald J. Postema

Legal positivism is a vital and controversial approach to central questions of philosophical jurisprudence. Not only are its core theses contested, but claims about what its core theses are, and what it stands for, have been hotly disputed in recent years. We can get some perspective on these debates if we look to the history of legal theory from which contemporary positivist jurisprudence has emerged. But we should not take any contemporary formulation of the doctrine as canonical, since most such formulations are contested. So, rather than seeking out full-fledged, card-carrying positivist theories in the history of jurisprudence to interrogate, we will explore the articulation and development of a set of themes which arguably have attracted at least some major positivist legal theorists. The aim of this chapter is to set the stage for understanding Hart's neo-positivist theory of law (Hart 1994, first published in 1961), and that of more recent philosophers working in its shadow, by locating their work in the context of positivist themes and arguments that have developed over the long history of philosophical reflection about the nature of law.

Jeremy Bentham and John Austin, thought to have offered classic formulations of positivist doctrine, are central to the plot of the story told here. Both legal theorists, in very different ways, revolutionized jurisprudence, departing dramatically from the developing positivist tradition. Bentham's revolutionary path, for the most part, was not followed or even much considered by subsequent jurisprudence, while Austin's influence was and continues to be great. The nature and scope of their respective reorientations of legal theory are brought into relief in this chapter by sketching first the development of positivist themes beginning with Plato, Epicurus, Aquinas and Marsilius of Padua.

Beginnings

In the course of his classic discussion of the question whether it is better to be ruled by a wise man or wise law, Plato (427–347 BCE) articulated a common-sense understanding of key features of law (Plato 1995). Law, he assumed, is meant to provide rational agents with guidance to right or wise action, but it is addressed in public terms to a public consisting of individuals engaged in complex patterns of social interaction. So it must give its guidance wholesale, i.e., for general circumstances and broad classes of people. But he observed that, as a consequence, law's wisdom can sometimes appear to be folly; law and the right or rational can diverge. Yet, he argued, we are well advised to opt for the rule of law rather than men, since the costs of permitting unregulated official discretion are high.

The Epicurean tradition (third to first century BCE) emphasized even more strongly the adventitious features of law (Long 2007: 122–27). On this view, while pleasure is the greatest good, the greatest pleasure is mental tranquility and the greatest disturbance of such tranquility is fear of harm suffered at the hands of others. Being free of the primary causes of the desire to harm (hatred, envy, low self-esteem), the sage is not inclined to harm others, because he knows that refraining from harming others sacrifices nothing of value. However, he also realizes that if he is known to be unwilling to respond to violence with violence, others who do not appreciate the pointlessness of violence will be emboldened to attack. Thus, Epicurus argued that justice, formally expressed in legal norms, "was never anything *per se*, but a contract regularly arising at some place or other in people's dealings with one another, over not harming or being harmed" (Epicurus 1987: 127) Justice and law are products of a kind of mutual, consensual arrangement; coercive sanctions are added to assure those who are independently motivated to comply with law that advantage will not be taken of them by those who are shortsighted and fail to recognize law's benefits.

Late Medieval Jurisprudence

Epicurean jurisprudence was one form of a more general view of law, common in late ancient and medieval theory, that understood law to be artificial or conventional, in the sense that it is temporally limited and changing, stemming in part from intelligent human activity, and rooted in potentially varying custom or practice, which manifests the "consent" or "consensus" of those subject to the law. Some laws might be made by the prince, on this view, but the bulk of law was planted deeply in the soil of custom, for, as Aristotle (384–322 BCE) wrote, *nomos* [law] has no compelling force beside that of *ethos* [custom] (Aristotle 1996: 49). In the eighteenth century, Hume offered a sophisticated version of the convention-based understanding of law, grounding the formal elements of law in informal social conventions and practices (Hume 2000: 307–45).

However, a more distinctively positivist conception of law is evident in the work of two important late medieval philosophers. I will refer to this as the "thetic" conception—taking the term from the Greek *tithenai*, meaning to put, as in *laid down* or *posited*—to highlight the fact that law, on this conception, is seen to be explicitly and intentionally made and imposed on law-subjects.

Aquinas (1225–1274) took *lex* as opposed to *ius* as the core concept in his discourse on law. The contrast he drew between these two concepts highlights the extent to which he embraced the thetic model of law. According to Aquinas, *ius* is the object of *iustum* (right or justice). It is a condition or state of affairs: the right ordering of the external actions or interactions of members of a community of equals (Aquinas 2002: 158–60). *Ius* is established by nature (*ius naturale*), but it may also be instituted in part by agreement or mutual consent (*ius postiva*) (Aquinas 2002: 161–63, 201). *Lex* is the public expression of *ius*, that is, the rules or measures prescribing right order, publicly expressed and typically reduced to writing (Aquinas 2002: 160). Moreover, *lex* does not merely declare or make public this order, it *makes* or institutes it through this expression, "giving it the force of authority" (Aquinas 2002: 201).

According to Aquinas, *lex* differs from *ius* in nature, source and force. First, *lex* is action-guiding; it consists of rules ("ordinances of reason") addressed to self-directing rational agents, prescribing actions to be performed. It guides action through the agency of another rational being: "Every law proceeds from the reason and will of a legislator" (Aquinas 2002: 153). *Lex* is a dictate of reason that exists first *in* that lawmaker who then "imprints" it on the minds of law-subjects (Aquinas 2002: 110), inducing or restraining ("obliging") their actions (Aquinas 2002: 77). Thus, promulgation is essential to the nature and binding force of *lex* (Aquinas 2002: 82–83). Second, it is essential to *lex* that it originates in and is established by one who has the standing or authority to direct the actions of others. This must be a "public person," one charged with care of the community (Aquinas 2002: 81). Moreover, third, since laws are not merely declared but are imposed on law-subjects (Aquinas 2002: 110), the relationship of lawmaker to law-subject is one of superior to inferior (Aquinas 2002: 58). The appropriate response of the law-subject is obedience, which involves taking the will of the legislator for one's own. "By obedience," Aquinas wrote, "we slay our own will" (Aquinas 2002: 64–65).

Aquinas's model of law is distinctively thetic, but it is not exclusively so, for a directive has the character of law, in Aquinas's view, only if it is in accord with reason, and more specifically, only if it is properly directed to the common good (Aquinas 2002: 78–80). In the view of many, this addition is enough to consign his theory to positivism's rival camp, natural law jurisprudence. But this should not obscure its contributions to the developing understanding of positive law. We should keep in mind that by "character of law" Aquinas does not have in mind the legal validity of some norm, but rather the condition of having the full nature and force of law. So, he means to say that when laws fail to be directed to the common good they fail in an important dimension to be and do what we reasonably expect laws to be and do.

Moreover, Aquinas's account of law is not merely a hybrid of positivist and naturalist elements, for the thetic elements of his account are internally linked to this substantive element. Juridical law is needed, in Aquinas's view, because the common good for a community is in large measure indeterminate both as a goal and with regard to the means needed to achieve it. This makes coordinating our interactions with others especially difficult, for we often do not know what the common good requires of us, and even if we do, we lack adequate assurance that others share our understanding or are sufficiently motivated to comply with its requirements. In view of these conditions, we need publicly accessible, manifestly authoritative, explicitly articulated directives to determine the indeterminate and the difficult to determine, and to assure a sufficient degree of general compliance with the resulting social order that any individual's compliance is reasonable and warranted. This, on Aquinas's view, is precisely what law is designed to offer.

The thetic dimensions of law are even more marked in the work of Marsilius of Padua (ca. 1275–1343). Law, according to Marsilius, seeks to direct actions which are autonomous in nature and transitive in effect (Marsilius 2005: 213–14). Law elicits actions "as a result of [the agent's] empire," i.e., it directs actions which fall within the control, liberty and agency of their agents, and it concerns only actions that have the potential to affect others, especially to harm or injure them. Although we sometimes misleadingly use the term "law" to refer to principles of action to which we are habituated through "disciplines of work," law properly so-called lacks such habituation (Marsilius 2005: 53, 215), and so "lacks a soul and moving principle" (Marsilius 2005: 216). It needs a *maker* to issue the standard, a *judge* to assess acts relative to that standard and a coercive *incentive* to secure compliance. On Marsilius's view, laws are universal judgments of justice and public good which can be viewed in two ways: either as *indications* of what is just or advantageous, or as *imperatives* expressed in a "command . . . which coerces by means of a penalty" (Marsilius 2005: 53). But, strictly speaking, a true judgment of what is just for a community is not yet a law, "unless a coercive command has been given in respect of its observation" (Marsilius 2005: 54, 66). By the same token, although laws can fail as true indications of what is just, a coercive command that does not even pretend to offer an assessment of what is required by justice would have the form of law only but not its proper content, both of which are essential to law.

Marsilius required more of the form of law than that it express a coercive command. Laws, he argued, provide that "without which civil judgments cannot be made in a way that is simply speaking correct" (Marsilius 2005: 56). That is, they are necessarily general and secure a kind of impartiality with respect to particular agents and circumstances. This makes possible a degree of equality or equity among parties governed by it which is essential for the role law plays in social ordering (Marsilius 2005: 56–57). Moreover, following Aristotle, Marsilius insisted that law is prince over all (Marsilius 2005: 61). Law is the form of the prince's exercise of power (Marsilius 2005: 51, 56–57, 61) in the dual sense that it constitutes the office, standing and power of the prince and is the mode of ruling to which the prince is held. The source of law, however, lies not in the prince, according to Marsilius, but in the "human legislator" who holds supreme lawmaking authority and power. This power is located in the community as a whole—the universal body of citizens, or its "prevailing part" (Marsilius 2005: 66–72). It is supreme in a polity because it directs the actions of free individuals, and even more because it defines and constitutes the social order; it is located in the universal body of citizens because it most fundamentally touches their lives. According to Marsilius, law serves three important functions: (1) it defines and confines the exercise of lordship, and in particular warrants and vindicates the exercise of coercive force; (2) it constitutes and structures all fundamental social and political relations; and thereby (3) secures the peace amongst people who, while by nature sociable, are nevertheless prone to passions that drive them into conflicts.

The Command Tradition

In the work of Aquinas and Marsilius we find most of the themes that figure in a tradition of thinking about the nature of law that extends from the thirteenth to the nineteenth century—a tradition in which the idea of command became the central organizing concept or metaphor. Considering only writers in the seventeenth century, we find it not only in the work of Hobbes (1588–1679), but also in Scholastics like Francisco Suarez (1548–1617), Protestant theorists like Samuel Pufendorf (1632–1694) and even classical common-law theorists like Sir Matthew Hale (1609–1676).

The core elements of this tradition, modeled by the concept of command, include the following. First, law is seen as a matter of directives addressed to, and ordering the behavior of, rational, free, self-directing agents. Suarez, for example, wrote, "properly speaking, only those who have the use of intellect and reason are governed by law" (Suarez 1944: 51; see also 22). Similarly, the English jurist, Sir Matthew Hale, wrote that a law is "a rule of moral actions, given to a being endued with understanding and will" British Library Hargrave MS 485, fo. 3; see also Pufendorf 1994: 102, 123). However, law is meant to engage and direct the will, the *executive* faculty of a rational agent (Suarez 1944: 56; Pufendorf 1994: 112). Law presents an agent's will with the product of another agent's deliberation, judgment and will.

Second, the model of command captures the distinctive form of law's normativity: law does not merely point out reasons for action, it imposes binding obligations. Using a trope common throughout the history of legal philosophy, Hobbes wrote, "law in general, is not Counsell, but Command"; "a man may be obliged to do what he is Commanded . . . But he cannot be obliged to do as he is Counselled" (Hobbes 1991: 183, 177). Even the "laws of nature," in his view, are properly regarded only as conclusions or theorems of reason rather than laws, unless they are seen as God's commands (Hobbes 1991: 111). Moreover, third, these new reasons provided by law's commands are tied exclusively to the fact that its directives are *commanded* by one in authority. Pufendorf wrote, "laws are obeyed principally because of their prescriber's will and not because of their content" (Pufendorf 1994: 119). Commands are meant to make conforming behavior nonoptional by *precluding* deliberative consideration of reasons for alternative actions. "Command is, where a man saith, *Doe this*, or *Doe not this*, without expecting other reason than the Will of him that says it" (Hobbes 1991: 176).

Fourth, laws modeled on commands presuppose that the party commanding has the standing or authority to do so. Commands, Hobbes reminded us, are addressed to those antecedently obliged to obey them (Hobbes 1991: 183). And Matthew Hale wrote: a law is "a rule of moral actions, given to a being endued with understanding and will, by him that hath power and authority to give the same and exact obedience thereunto *per modum imperii*" (Hargrave MS 485, fo. 3). Moreover, writers in this tradition uniformly held that the capacity to command presupposes an essential *asymmetry* in the relations between lawgiver and law-subject. Pufendorf, for example, held that "the faculty of enjoining something in the manner of law or precept implies superiority, just as the obligation to obey proves that we are inferior to one who is able to prescribe to us" (Pufendorf 1994: 59; see also Suarez 1944: 127). Making and imposing law was seen as an exercise of *dominion* (Suarez 1944: 67), presupposing the *subordination* of law-subjects to the authority and the coercive power of the lawmakers. Coercive sanctions were typically regarded as logically necessary complements of commands and hence an essential feature of law. The capacity effectively to exact obedience to law is not just a coincidental expression of the lawgiver's dominion, on this view, for it is regarded as essential to manifesting the seriousness, the nonoptional character, of legal obligations and the lawmaker's claim to impose them on the subject. "It is vain to prescribe something that can be neglected with impunity," Pufendorf argued; "one who can be disregarded with impunity rules only by the indulgence of others" (Pufendorf 1994: 59, 126). In this tradition it was thought that the claim of sovereign power made by enacting and imposing laws is in effect withdrawn if violations are known not to be punished.

Hobbes developed this tradition in an important way, arguing for it on explicitly normative grounds. He argued that in the absence of a common authority (that is, in the state of nature), we lack common standards and are forced to make private judgments of good and evil, right and wrong, and mine and thine, as well as judgments of our own best interest and the common interest. Certain demonstrable "laws" of nature and equity are available to the natural reason of each of us, he argued, but they bind only on the condition that we can reasonably expect others to comply with them as well, a condition that is manifestly unmet in the state of nature. We are likely, then, to suffer regular, persistent and disastrous conflicts of interest and principle, which can be avoided, he argued, only by putting full and unlimited authority in the hands of a sovereign. However, to solve the problem posed, the sovereign is charged with minimizing such disastrous conflicts *by* defining for us and enforcing common public standards to govern our interactions. That is, the sovereign is expected to exercise authority *through law*. In his *Dialogue*, Hobbes wrote, "A Law is the Command of him, or them, that have the Soveraign Power, given to those that be his or their Subjects, declaring Publickly, and plainly what every of them may do and what they must forbear to do" (Hobbes 2005: 31). He looked to law to make clear, decisive and determinate standards by which people are expected to govern their actions in the polity. Law is not like philosophy "and other disputable Arts," he argued, but rather is a matter of explicit, public, manifestly authentic commands (Hobbes 2005: 29). This brings to mind Aquinas's view of the primary task of law, except that Hobbes insisted further that for this purpose the standing of a norm as valid and binding must not depend in any way on its judgments of its justice or reasonableness. "It is not Wisdom," he argued, "but Authority [alone] that makes a Law" (Hobbes 2005: 10). Hobbes acknowledged that law is (the expression of) reason, but the reason he had in view is only the fallible, utterly ordinary "natural reason" of the sovereign, which is *deemed* by law-subjects to be *public reason*, i.e., reason that is meant to take the place of their individual, private reason and judgment. To achieve this purpose, the sovereign's commands, the authenticity of which are public and undisputed (Hobbes 1991: 189), must displace the private deliberation and judgment of each citizen. Law, conceived on the command model, is an essential part of the solution to the problem of privacy of judgment which in his view bedevils public life.

Bentham's Revisionist Positivism

Bentham (1748–1832) oriented his thinking to this thetic conception of law and developed the most comprehensive, systematic and sophisticated theory of law in the positivist tradition. Yet his boundless intellectual energy could not be contained within any paradigm and his restless drive to reform legal thought and practice led him to radical revisions of received ideas even as he explicitly endorsed them. Legal theory in general, and the positivist tradition in it, was transformed by his relentless work—or rather, it would have been, had he published the bulk of this work and had the English legal establishment been more receptive to his reform ideas. Rather, it was John Austin's pedestrian account of law and narrow view of the jurisprudential method that defined the career of positivism throughout the nineteenth century and well into the twentieth. Bentham's work (much of it having come to light only in recent decades) represents a positivist road not taken or only recently considered.

Bentham was a tireless and penetrating critic of the practice of English law (see Postema 1986, ch. 8, sec. 2), arguing that its devices, pretenses and modes of thought forced it to lurch unpredictably between absurd rigidity and unconstrained flexibility. This, he charged, made it radically unsuited to the fundamental tasks of law, which are to secure expectations and coordinate the complex interactions characteristic of modern social life (Postema 1986, ch. 5 and references there). Moreover, it signaled a deep incoherence in common-law theory; for if we take common law seriously on terms of its theoretical self-understanding, we can only conclude that "As a System of general rules, Common Law is a thing merely imaginary" (Bentham 2008: 119). Common-law theory is committed to the view that, although judges are empowered to settle particular cases, any formulations of rules justifying their decisions, even those of the deciding judges themselves, are always open to challenge and reformulation. Common law, its partisans maintained, exists not in the case or in judicial opinions, but rather in rules emerging from shared, disciplined judicial practice. This thesis, Bentham charged, is incoherent.

He did not deny that it is possible for lawyers to construct rules from cases, defeasibly but still reliably, by "induction" or "abstraction." Indeed, he thought these general propositions may "appear to be the just expression of the judicial practice in like cases" (Bentham UC 100, 98). Moreover, he allowed, judicial decisions can, "in virtue of the more extensive interpretations which the people are disposed to put upon them, have some what of the effect of general laws" (Bentham 2010: 161). However, he insisted that such rules are merely "inferential entities" (Bentham 2008: 95).

> From a set of *data* like these [namely, a set of judicial decisions] a law is to be extracted by every man who can fancy that he is able: by each man, perhaps a different law; and these, then, are the *monades* which meeting together, constitute the rules . . . of common or customary law.
>
> (Bentham 2010: 195)

Hobbes complained that common law is merely a matter of conjecture and disputation ("philosophy") (Hobbes 2005: 29); Bentham likewise charged that these constructed rules are nothing more than private conjectures, "the idea that *you* have formed of the act in question, the idea that *I* have formed of it, the idea that *Titus* has formed of it," which, if they converge, do so only by accident (UC 69, 151). However, what we demand of law are "common standard[s] which all men acknowledge, and all men are ready to resort to" (UC 69, 188). Private conjectures, no matter how clever, or how accurately they capture the import of a line of cases, cannot serve as law. Law, he assumed (and thought that common-law jurists assumed), is necessarily a matter of common *public* standards and can only perform characteristic tasks of law if it meets the test of publicity. Common-law rules failed as law, not because they did not fit the command model, but because their alleged general and authoritative rules systematically failed the fundamental test of publicity law.

Following Hobbes, Bentham thought that the command model was best suited to the demand of publicity, and he offered a definition of law tailored to this model (UC 69, 69–76; UC 70a, 3–6). However, as soon as he embraced this model he began to sense its limitations. He never officially abandoned the model, but his revisions (begun in a foundational jurisprudential work entitled, *Of the Limits of the Penal Branch of Jurisprudence*) stretched it beyond recognition. First, in the place of mere commands, Bentham developed a theory of "imperation," probably the earliest attempt at a deontic logic, which enabled him to incorporate into the model a range of different types of legal norms beyond mandates and prohibitions (Bentham 2010, § 12 and app. C). Second, he came to recognize that, while coercive sanctions play an important role in law, the relation between coercive penalties and particular laws, even penal laws, is very complex. Primary laws address law-subjects requiring certain actions or omissions, while secondary laws command officials to punish violations of the primary law under certain conditions (and further layers may be in place). Furthermore, penal sanctions are not, in his view, necessary components of every legal rule (UC 70a, 5) and sometimes no sanctions are indicated or needed. Third, even mandatory legal rules, which most comfortably fit the model of a command, do not necessarily impose peremptory demands on law-subjects as the command tradition had insisted. Sovereign commands publicly mark rules as legally authentic and corresponding forms of behavior as to be done, but reasons for behaving in accord with them lie not in the "imperations" themselves. Sovereign commands do not displace the law-subjects' ordinary exercise of their judgment with respect to so acting. Law requires submission of conduct, he insisted, but not submission of judgment (Bentham 2008: 346). Governance by law, in his view, operates not by way of the "influence of will on the will," but rather by influence of "the understanding on the understanding" (UC 126, 1; see also Bentham 1998: 249).

Bentham likewise rejected the assumption of necessary asymmetry or inequality at the heart of the command model. Thus, unlike Austin after him, Bentham recognized constitutional principles, even those that impose limits on the exercise of sovereign power, as integral parts of the law (Bentham 2010: 86–93). He treated these "laws *in principem*" as public commitments of the sovereign modeled on covenants to which the sovereign is held not by formal penal sanctions, but by informal, but no less important, "moral" sanctions of public opinion. The fact that they are self-imposed, or involve commitments to parties who are not the sovereign's superiors, did not stop Bentham from taking this line. This contrasts with typical command tradition doctrine. Pufendorf, for example, held that, while covenants might generate obligations, they could not yield obligations *of law*, precisely because covenants presuppose exchanges among equals (Pufendorf 1994). (See also Hobbes 1998/1642: 14.1–2.) Bentham was even willing to go so far as to say that public opinion "may be considered as a system of law" (Bentham 1983: 36).

Bentham's revisionary analysis of law proceeded on two levels simultaneously. One focused on the logical form of laws, the elemental components of (a system of) law; the other focused on the fundamental social/political tasks of law. The former proceeded from the assumption that the most basic *mode of operation* of law is that of directing the actions of individual rational agents; the latter assumed that law's fundamental task is the ordering or structuring of social and political life, thereby promoting the "security" of every member. Viewed from the former analytic perspective, the *directive* and *coercive* ("penal") aspects of law seem primary, but viewed from the latter perspective it is the *constitutive* aspect of law, defining and putting into coherent order social and political relationships, that are salient. Bentham called this the "distributive" dimension of law, distinguished by two complementary parts: *droit distributive privè* (civil law) and *droit distributive politique* (constitutional law) (UC 99, 34; UC 32, 130). Law not only structures relationships among citizens, enabling coordination of social interaction, but it also structures political power, enabling it to do its governing with a claim to legitimacy, and defining institutions for holding governing power publicly accountable. Thus, from a logical point of view, the "penal" aspects may seem primary and distributive aspects only secondary, handmaidens to the penal; however, viewed more fully, it is the distributive aspect that provides the focus and the penal (especially the coercive-sanctioning) aspect that underwrites and facilitates the primary work of law. "With relation to the civil code," Bentham wrote, "the matter of the penal code is but a means" (Bentham 1838–1843, vol. IX: 12). He was especially keen to analyze and map the constitutive dimension of law, because, on his view, the law's epistemic role, e.g., making publicly known what one's property is or what relationships one bears to others (Bentham 1838–1843, vol. IX: 12), is at least as important as its directive role.

Bentham stretched the command model even further as he explored the necessary *systematic* character of law. Laws must be conceived as commands, but "[a] law . . . is a command," he wrote, only "when it is entire" (Bentham 1838–1843, vol. III: 217). The concept he sought to articulate throughout his career—the focal point of "universal jurisprudence"—was the concept of the law understood as "the sum total of . . . individual laws taken together" (Bentham 2010: 16). The first and most fundamental question of this jurisprudential investigation, therefore, is: what is *a law*—a complete, whole, "entire but single law" (Bentham 2010: 22; UC 70a.5, 8). What he sought was "the logical, the ideal, the intellectual whole, not the physical one: the *law* not the *statute*" (Bentham 1996: 301). Law in this "integral sense" is to statutes as the whole muscle dissected by an anatomist is to the steak cut by a butcher. Invariably, enacted rules are fragmentary, portions of a number of complete laws (Bentham 1838–1843, vol. III: 217). Thus, Bentham's core concept of law is not an empirical, but rather a rational and, in one sense of the word, ideal concept. This is not the idea of *ideal law*, of good or just law, but of law properly understood and articulated, and, in Bentham's view, law properly understood includes not only conditions of validity (marks of authenticity) but also conditions of completeness.

At the core of Bentham's model of a complete law is the idea of a directive for action that includes in it everything necessary for adequate guidance, including all the qualifications, limitations, elaborations that apply to it, and all the institutional and procedural conditions of its implementation and enforcement (Bentham 2010, § 16). Of course, none of this expository, elaborative and qualificative material is uniquely tied to a single (complete) law; indeed, a vast amount of it will be shared by a large number of laws. Laws are like pyramids represented as standing on one base (Bentham 2010: 221–22). A law is complete, then, when all its necessary elements are linked and this is made explicit by "juxtaposition" or "reference" (Bentham 2010: 171–72). Thus, laws are systematically interconnected, not only in their logical relations, but in their shared substance. This implies that the idea of a complete law presupposes the idea of a complete body of law.

> [T]he idea of a law, meaning one single but entire law, is in a manner inseparably connected with that of a compleat body of laws; so that what is a law and what are the contents of a compleat body of the laws are questions of which neither can well be answer'd without the other. A body of laws is a vast and complicated piece of mechanism of which no part can be fully explained without the rest
>
> (Bentham 2010: 21)

To explicate the concept of law, we must explicate the notion of *a* (complete) *law*, but that is not possible without recognizing, and putting at the center of our explication, the *systematic substantive* relationships that inevitably exist among laws. This insight, which structured all of Bentham's vast writings on universal jurisprudence, follows from his conviction that law by its nature directs and informs actions of rational agents and it can do so only if it is public and accessible. Publicity not only demands clear marks of the authenticity of laws, but also that all directives are clearly articulated, and that all the material that qualifies as a simple directive is accessible as well. That puts any given legal directive in a complex network of relations of substance with much if not all of the rest of the laws bearing these same marks of authenticity.

It is evident from this discussion that Bentham had a broad, ecumenical view of the jurisprudential enterprise. His task was to construct a language of analysis and a framework of principles with which to think systematically about law, guided throughout by proximate principles of publicity and security of expectations and ultimately guided by the principle of utility. Although he thought it important to distinguish between expository and censorial jurisprudence, he did not see these as exclusive activities, but rather as partner endeavors in a common enterprise. He was not, as Hart insisted, committed to flatly descriptive, morally neutral analysis of juridical concepts (Hart 1982: 28). His positivist theory was robust, but, like Hobbes's, it rested on a robust, nuanced and complex normative argument (Postema 1986, ch. 9). Moreover, he drew no boundaries around his investigation of the nature of law and legal institutions; no methodological scruples prevented him from raising questions that needed to be raised or using resources from any form of human inquiry needed to answer them. In this respect, as in so many others, John Austin (1790–1859) differed from his intellectual father.

Austin's Analytic Jurisprudence

Austin offered a classic positivist definition of law in his *Province of Jurisprudence Determined*, first published in 1832. He proposed to understand *the law* as an aggregate of *laws* and *a law* as a general command—that is, a rule laid down (posited) for guidance of an intelligent being by another determinate intelligent being having power over the first (Austin 1955: 9–11, 18–19). Necessarily, laws are "set by political superiors to political inferiors" (Austin 1955: 9) and all laws are traceable directly or indirectly to the sovereign, the determinate person or group that holds supreme power in the polity. This power has two dimensions: (a) standing to issue such commands and (b) (some) capacity to execute them to secure compliance. The lawmaker's capacity to command lies in its sovereignty, but this consists not, as Austin's critics sometimes held, in its capacity to compel obedience, but rather on a widespread disposition of subjects to obey. Yet Austin held that to say that laws are commands entails that the lawgiver intends to inflict evil on those who disregard the command (Austin 1955: 14–18). He assumed that the expressed intention to sanction disobedience is the logical consequence of issuing a command and sovereignty is the general standing the lawmaker has to issue such commands. Austin insisted further that this sovereignty cannot be divided or limited by law; indeed, he held that "supreme power limited by positive law, is a flat contradiction in terms" (Austin 1955: 254). (In contrast, Hobbes (1991: 224) argued for the illimitability of sovereignty on distinctly normative grounds.)

There is nothing surprising in this account of law (except the claim that the illimitability of sovereign power is a conceptual necessity, which Bentham (2010: 91–92) roundly criticized). It is a concise statement of the familiar thetic/command conception of law. Hart believed that what was novel in Austin's account was a radically reductionist understanding of the key terms of the definition of law. Hart thought that Austin sought to reduce the normative dimensions of law to simple empirical facts of publicly expressed wishes, probabilities of suffering pain for noncompliance and bare habits or dispositions to comply with expressed wishes, all of which can be fully appreciated from a strictly external, observer's point of view (Hart 1994: 80 and chs. 1–3 passim). But this is a questionable reading of Austin's definition and his intentions in offering it. The "habit" at the foundation of sovereignty, after all, is a habit of *obedience*, which implies that the response to commands involves a complex understanding on the part of the addressee of the normative relationship between the agent and the sovereign, as well as the (normative) nature of the demand expressed in the command. Austin did not obviously suppress these implications of his use of the concept of obedience. Moreover, at several points Austin showed a clear, if not fully articulated, sense of the "internal" aspect of rules of law and morality. He understood, for example, that constitutional constraints on sovereign power might be fully appreciated and regarded as binding by the sovereign. Austin recognized the distinctive "internal aspect" of these rules (Austin 1955: 253–60). They fail to qualify as *legal* limitations, in his view, because they do not (and logically *cannot*) involve subordination of the sovereign to some other party, which is essential to law. They may be regarded as binding, but they are not binding rules *of law* because they are not rules set by a determinate political superior to a political inferior.

What is striking, rather, about Austin's approach is that he opened *Province* with a statement of the command model as a stipulated definition, offering no argument for it, and then used it dogmatically to distinguish law "properly so-called" from other phenomena we are inclined to confuse with it. Further, he deployed this model to demonstrate the systematic separation of law from morality expressed in his familiar dictum: "the existence of law is one thing; its merit or demerit is another" (Austin 1955: 184). This *separation thesis*, showcased by Hart as the core of the classical positivist understanding of law (Hart 1983: 50–56), is conceptually prior to the thetic conception of law, which provides the tool by which law is pried apart and kept distinct from morality: laws are identified solely by linking them to morally neutral facts about the explicit lawmaking activities of a political superior who enjoys a widespread habit of obedience and habitually obeys no one. But, even in this respect, Austin adds nothing to the command tradition that was not already securely established by Hobbes and elaborated by Bentham. Austin's innovation, which has had an enormous impact on Anglophone legal philosophy ever since, was to deploy this separation as a principle of jurisprudential method.

Austin not only embraced what Perry (2001) called "substantive positivism" (the command model and the separation thesis), but also pioneered "methodological positivism." He sought with his thetic definition of law not so much to define the limits of the *domain of law* for those seeking to identify valid and legally binding rules in their social interactions or advice to clients, but rather to determine boundaries of jurisprudence for those undertaking the *study of law*. That is, his aim was neither immediately practical nor abstractly theoretical, but more narrowly pedagogical. Opening *Province*, Austin wrote, "the principal purpose or scope of the six ensuing lectures, is to distinguish positive laws (the appropriate matter of jurisprudence) from [a host of phenomena with which they are regularly confused] . . . they affect to describe the boundary which severs the province of jurisprudence from the regions lying on its confines" (Austin 1955: 2). Indeed, he—or at least subsequent readers and followers of his method—took his work in *Province* not as itself a contribution to jurisprudence, but rather as *prolegomenon to* jurisprudence, as Buckland (1945: 3) pointed out. The task of jurisprudence, on Austin's revolutionary view, was to *analyze* key concepts in the domain defined by his thetic conception. This was to proceed entirely independently of considerations of history, politics, social conditions, morality or metaphysics. One late nineteenth-century reviewer commented that "as a jurist, Austin owes his rank to the fact that he was the first to define the sphere of legal science, by distinguishing [the study of] law from history and ethics" (Rumble 2005: 113). Austin sought a separation not (only) of law from morality, but of jurisprudence from any other form of inquiry into the nature and functioning of law. For this reason, Austin felt no need to defend his definition of law, for it was meant not as a contribution to our understanding of the nature of law and its role in human social and political life, but rather as a means of collecting phenomena, or rather concepts, for this restricted project of analysis. He left the defense of his definition to other, messier modes of inquiry.

This was, of course, a radical departure from earlier, positivist-themed philosophical accounts of law. It would never have occurred to Hobbes or Bentham, let alone Aquinas, Marsilius, Suarez, Pufendorf or Hume, to proceed with the analysis of core legal concepts without locating them in the larger context of an inquiry into the nature of law and its role in human social and political life. Hart may have been right that with Austin the career of positivism as a distinctive legal doctrine was begun, but that doctrine already at its inception was narrow, serving an intellectually and especially philosophically abstemious method of inquiry. Taking Austin as the paradigmatic classical positivist plucks positivist legal theory from the rich and varied soil in which it had thrived until Austin.

Austinian Positivism and Its Critics

Still, Austin shaped the terms and methods of jurisprudential inquiry in the Anglophone world well into the twentieth century. His methodological positivism launched analytical jurisprudence, which dominated English legal theory up to the time of Hart and shaped fundamentally Hart's own understanding of the jurisprudential enterprise. Austin's thetic definition of law also provided the point of departure for most inquiries into the nature of law up to and including Hart's groundbreaking work in the 1960s. We will note here certain key points in the development of positivist thinking about law in the period between Austin and Hart.

The most prominent Austinian legal theorist of the late nineteenth century was T. E. Holland (1835–1926). According to Holland, laws are demands addressed to the will of one rational being by the will of another. Such demands presuppose a determinate authority which is paramount in political society and is empowered both to impose and enforce the demands (Holland 1924: 21–23, 41–42, 53–54). The state alone enjoys this authority and the capacity coercively to enforce these demands. "Every law is a proposition announcing the will of the State" (Holland 1924: 88–89). Thus, he concluded, "until the State is constituted there can be no law" (Holland 1924: 56).

This is classic Austinian doctrine, but Holland departed in a subtle but interesting way from Austinian orthodoxy at one point. Austin treated customs as law only when, and in virtue of the fact that, sovereign-established courts recognized them. Rules of merely positive morality become law, he allowed, only if they were *made law* by the court's acceptance and enforcement of them. Critics argued that this gets the matter backwards, since courts recognize customary rules as legal rather than constituting them as legal through their recognition. Holland answered this criticism, arguing that courts establish customs as law not on a case-by-case basis, but wholesale, as it were, through legislating in advance the conditions that customary rules must meet to be eligible for status as law (Holland 1924: 60–61). Thus, the legal validity of customary rules, on Holland's account, depends on the prior *legislative* activity of the courts. In this way, Holland shifted theoretical attention away from the parliamentary lawmaking activity to the activities of courts, although it still regarded courts in their capacity as deputy legislators.

Oliver Wendell Holmes, Jr. (1841–1935), writing in America in the late nineteenth century, focused his attention exclusively on the courts, but he found their enforcement rather than lawmaking activity to be their most theoretically salient feature. Against Austin, he argued that sovereignty and explicit commands are not necessary for law because power alone is the defining feature of law. The origin of rules is not important; what is important only is the definiteness of the expression of the rules and the certainty of their enforcement (Holmes 1995, vol. I: 215). "The will of the sovereign is law because he has the power to compel obedience and punish disobedience, and for no other reason" (Holmes 1995, vol. I: 294). From this Holmes concluded that for rules of law we should not look to the activities of lawmakers, but to courts which express and exercise the authority and power of the state. Indeed, law just is what courts of sovereign states enforce, a thesis he put provocatively in his essay, "The Path of Law," saying that law just "prophecies of what the courts will do" (Holmes 1995, vol. III: 393). However, he made clear that these prophecies are based on rules and principles that lawyers, in classic common-law fashion, extract from recorded decisions of prior cases. So laws are not merely predictions, but are *rules* which figure in the deliberations of courts—the predictions are norm-based. But we take the rules seriously, and they have the status of law, only when we can count on courts to enforce them. To ensure that lawyers focus on these law-determining matters alone, Holmes proposed as a useful heuristic that they look at the deliberations and decisions of the courts from the point of view of a "bad man" who cares only to learn where the coercive power of the state will impinge on his life and projects (Holmes 1995, vol. III: 392). Viewed from this perspective, he assumed, law will not be confused with legally irrelevant moral, political or other considerations. Thus, Holmes decisively shifted attention of legal theory from the legislative activity of the sovereign to the decision-making, and in particular enforcement activity, of courts. And he proposed yet another technique of separating law from morality, which seemed to be designed largely for lawyers' practice.

Frederick Pollock (1845–1937) sensed in Austinian legal theory generally an uncritical acceptance of something like the "badman" perspective as a fundamental methodological assumption. He argued that the Austinian definition of law reflects the perspective of a member of an advanced political society who, "having acquired a sense of independent power, comes to set the State over against himself as an extraneous agency." This person, informed of his legal duty, asks "'Who bids me do this? In what capacity? And what will happen if I do otherwise?'" (Pollock 1872: 191). He charged that, while this perspective may be useful for highlighting certain features of modern legal systems, nevertheless it mistakes the familiar for the fundamental. Holmesian and Austinian jurisprudential methods were both, in Pollock's view, uncritically narrow, distorting rather than illuminating the nature of law.

The "badman" perspective might also be questioned as a reliable practitioner's tool. It allows practitioners reliably to separate law from legally irrelevant moral (or other) considerations *only if*, in fact, the latter considerations do not figure importantly in judicial decision-making and so cannot contribute to reliable "predictions" of what the court will decide. John Chipman Gray (1839–1915), although he followed Holmes in holding that the law just is what the courts lay down as law, harbored doubts about this reliability. The law, Gray argued (unintentionally echoing Bentham), must be distinguished from this or that law—statutes, constitutions, precedent-making decisions and the like. The latter are not law properly speaking, but rather *sources* of law (Gray 1921: 124). Courts, in the course of adjudicating cases, determine the law based on consideration of these sources. The law is what the courts authoritatively determine, although the sources with which they work are fixed not by the courts themselves, but by those who rule the state (Gray 1921: 121). Counted among these sources, Gray allowed, might be principles of morality, including conventional morality of the community, public policy, justice and matters of the internal integrity of doctrine (Gray 1921: 303). Thus, Gray suggested a possible complexity or ambiguity in the positivist separation doctrine, for if we attend solely to the sources that courts as a matter of fact consider (or are required to consider), we cannot simply rule out the possibility that considerations of morality might, in some legal systems, actually figure as sources of law.

Salmond

The most important contributor to positivist jurisprudence between Austin and Hart was the New Zealander John Salmond (1862–1924). Along with many others, he challenged the command model of law, arguing that it failed adequately to explain the existence of various kinds of laws including permissive laws, laws of procedure, evidence and the like (Salmond 1893: 98–106; 1924: 54). More importantly, it failed to recognize laws providing citizens and officials with capacities and powers to effect changes in the law (Salmond 1893: 103–4). He also challenged Austin's doctrine of the illimitability of the sovereign (Salmond 1893: 137–43; 1924: 527–30) along lines that anticipate Hart's criticisms in chapter 4 of *The Concept of Law*. Among the several criticisms he advanced, one is especially interesting for our purposes. Against Austin's claim that, *necessarily*, sovereignty is illimitable, Salmond argued that the principle according legislative (limited or unlimited) power to some body is a legal principle like any other principle (Salmond 1893: 140); and "a principle is a principle of law . . . [simply] because it is recognised and acted on by the State" (Salmond 1893: 143).

Salmond maintained that law—the body of rules and principles comprised by a community's legal system—is to be identified not by looking to the legislative activity of its sovereign lawmakers (or courts, for that matter), and surely not to the coercive enforcement activity of states' agencies, but rather to the ordinary law-applying practices of its courts. Earlier critics of Austin were right to focus for this purpose on the courts, Salmond argued, for "it is to courts of justice, and to them alone, that we must have recourse if we wish to find out what rules are rules of law and what are not" (Salmond 1924: 57). But the decisive law-constituting facts are facts about the courts' *use* of the rules and principles in their law-applying activities. The law, on his view, is the body of rules and principles recognized, applied and acted upon by courts acting as agents of the state, fulfilling its primary task of administering justice (Salmond 1924: 39–40). These rules are law in virtue of the fact that they are "received and operative" in the courts and "observed in accordance with the established practice of the courts" (Salmond 1924: 40, 57, 528).

Moreover, while principles of law are meant to establish and serve justice in their political community, and thus represent "the wisdom and justice of the organized commonwealth," their status as law, according to Salmond, depends strictly on the fact of their regular use in ordinary law-applying activity. "The validity of a legal principle is entirely independent of its truth. It is a principle of law, not because it is true, but because it is accepted and acted upon by the [courts of the] State as true" (Salmond 1893: 83). The authority of these rules and principles for the courts lies not in their substantive merits, but rather in obligations that judges undertake when they assume their judicial offices (Salmond 1924: 56), and these are not legal obligations, simply because "law is law, not because the courts are under any obligation to observe it, but because they do in fact observe it" (Salmond 1924: 57). The legal status of a principle depends entirely on judicial recognition, and this recognition is strictly a matter of social fact about the ordinary practice of institutions charged with the administration of justice.

But, Salmond hastened to add, we must not make the mistake, made by American legal realists at the time, of concluding that the law just is what the courts happen to say it is. For the recognitional practice of the courts is itself rule-governed. A rule is not merely the regularity of behavior manifest in a practice; it is, rather, "that *reason* to the consistent acceptance and application of which, such a judicial practice is due"

(Salmond 1893: 88, author's emphasis). The court's practice itself yields a hierarchical structure of rules by which its recognitional activities are governed. "The causes or occasions which determine the recognition of new principles of law by the judicature," he argued, "are themselves defined and determined by law" (Salmond 1893: 139). This recognitional practice has a chain-like character: lower-level principles are validated by higher-order principles until the process stops at some ultimate validating principle. Salmond argued that "there must be found in every legal system certain ultimate principles, from which all others are derived, but which are themselves self-existent" (Salmond 1924: 169). The source or grounding of these ultimate principles lies only in the historical fact of regular judicial practice.

Salmond substantially transformed Austinian jurisprudence, and with it positivism, in the twentieth century. In the place of commands, he identified a wide variety of rules and norms, performing functions that include but extend far beyond merely prescribing or proscribing behavior. He (following Holland and Holmes) turned juridical focus to the activities of courts as the key to understanding law, but it was not the lawmaking or law-enforcing aspects of these activities to which he called attention, but rather to their use in deliberation and decision-making of rules and norms of all sorts. He decisively rejected the thetic conception of law that played such an important role in positivist legal theory over the centuries. Yet his is arguably still a recognizably positivist theory because, for all its acknowledgement of the normative character of law, law's ultimate claim to validity is said to bottom out in facts of the practice of the courts. Although we call upon law to serve the polity's aspiration of justice, the existence of law—as determined ultimately by facts of the recognitional practice of the courts—is one thing; its actual justice, wisdom or moral appeal is entirely another thing. It is a small step from Salmond to Hart, although Hart's articulation and defense of these core positivist doctrines achieved a degree of sophistication lacking in Salmond's writings.

Salmond's relationship to Austin's revolution in jurisprudential method was ambiguous. Salmond never systematically defended his account of law. He presented it as the most plausible organizing and explanatory account of law, but he offered little argument to convince the skeptic. However, this may not have been because he believed, following the Austinians, that such further inquiries were beyond the pale of jurisprudence and not relevant to its practice. On the contrary, early on he criticized the view taken by the Austinian school that jurisprudence must be sharply separated from general philosophical reflection on, *inter alia*, the nature of right and wrong and the meaning of obligation. He thought that such separation was impossible, since legal right and moral right, legal justice and natural justice are intertwined in fact and in theory. "To deprive the idea of law of [its] ethical significance . . . [is to deny] one of its most essential elements" (Salmond 1893: 9–10). Nevertheless, Salmond held that the proper work of jurists is not to participate in these more general inquiries, but to draw from them resources needed for their analytical work. General jurisprudence in Salmond's view is ultimately applied moral or practical philosophy—depending on it, but pragmatically separated from it. This attitude of modest pragmatic and nondogmatic separation is a far cry from the methodological abstemiousness of the Austinian approach.

Hart's Theory in a Nutshell

Salmond brings us to the heights overlooking Hart's theory. In Hart's view, law is a complex social fact which typically has normative significance for those who participate in its practices, significance which is intrinsic to the nature and normal functioning of law. To capture these two salient aspects of law, Hart built his theory around his analysis of two fundamental ideas: the concept of practiced social rules and the doctrine of the rule of recognition, a particular kind of "secondary" or legal-system-maintaining rule (Hart 1994: 91–99). The former notion, analyzed in terms of the regularities of behavior and the critical internal attitudes of participants to those regularities (Hart 1994: 55–61, 88–91), was Hart's major contribution to the positivist repertoire; the latter notion, although usually associated exclusively with Hart (Hart 1994, ch. 6), had its roots, as we have seen, in Salmond's work. With these two notions in combination, Hart sought to explain how law is fundamentally a matter of convention, that is, normatively significant social practice (1994: 254–59); how law is an institutionalized system of rules (a "union of primary and secondary rules") (1994: 79–99); how law is a systemic unity that persists through time; how legal rules can be authoritative not in view of their content or merit, but just in virtue of their institutionalized recognition; how legal rules can yield obligations which are not necessarily morally binding; and how the perspective of a law elite can diverge from that of ordinary citizens without law losing its authoritative status (1994: 114–17); and thus how law, which purports to control and guide social interaction normatively, can, without entirely losing its claim to being a legal system, appear to many of those subject to it as an alien coercive machine (1994: 117, 202). This is the core of what we might call Hart's critical positivism (Postema 2011, ch. 7).

Hart's version of what we earlier called substantive positivism can be summed up in two claims: (1) that the validity of legal rules is strictly a function of their recognition by law-applying institutions according to criteria established by the system's rule of recognition; and (2) that the rule of recognition exists, and has its status as a rule, strictly by virtue of the fact that it is practiced by law-applying officials. Law so identified leaves entirely open the question of what moral respect, if any, it is due. Here, Hart followed Salmond's lead, rather than Bentham's, in his challenge to and replacement of Austin's thetic conception of law. Hart also decisively rejected Bentham's and earlier positivists' inclination to ground their understandings of law in part on normative considerations. Rather, Hart embraced a strong methodological positivism, continuous with Austin's, which understands the task of jurisprudence to be strictly descriptive, depending at no critical point on moral considerations, even when what is being described is evaluative or normative.

References

Aristotle (1996) *The Politics and the Constitution of Athens*, S. Everson, ed. and trans., Cambridge: Cambridge University Press.

Aquinas, T. (2002) *Aquinas: Political Writings*, R. W. Dyson, ed. and trans., Cambridge: Cambridge University Press.

Austin, J. (1955/1832) *The Province of Jurisprudence Determined*, H. L. A. Hart, ed., London: Weidenfeld and Nicolson.

Bentham, J., MSS at University College London, box 100, fo. 98.

—— (2010/1780–1782) *Of the Limits of the Penal Branch of Jurisprudence*, P. Schofield, ed., Oxford: Clarendon Press.

—— (2008) *Comment on the Commentaries* and *A Fragment on Government*, J. H. Burns and H. L. A. Hart, eds., Oxford: Clarendon Press.

—— (1998) *Legislator of the World: Writings on Codification, Law and Education*, P. Schofield and J. Harris, eds., Oxford: Clarendon Press.

—— (1996) *An Introduction to the Principles of Morals and Legislation*, J. H. Burns and H. L. A. Hart, eds., Oxford: Clarendon Press.

—— (1983/1830) *Constitutional Code, Volume 1*, F. Rosen and J. H. Burns, eds., Oxford: Clarendon Press.

—— (1838–1843) *The Works of Jeremy Bentham*, J. Bowring, ed., Edinburgh: William Tait.

Buckland, W. W. (1945) *Some Reflections on Jurisprudence*, Cambridge: Cambridge University Press.

Epicurus (1987) *Key Doctrines 33, 32*, in A. A. Long and D. N. Sedley, trans., *The Hellenistic Philosophers*, Cambridge: Cambridge University Press.

Gray, J. C. (1921) *The Nature and Sources of Law*, New York: Macmillan.

Hale, Sir Matthew (n.d.) *Treatise of the Nature of Laws in General and Touching on the Law of Nature*, Hargrave MS 485, British Library.

Hart, H. L. A. (1994) *The Concept of Law*, 2nd edition, P. A. Bullock and J. Raz. eds., Oxford: Clarendon Press.

—— (1983) "Positivism and the Separation of Law and Morals," in H. L. A. Hart, *Essays in Jurisprudence and Philosophy*, Oxford: Clarendon Press.

—— (1982) *Essays on Bentham*, Oxford: Clarendon Press.

Hobbes, T. (2005/1681) *A Dialogue Between a Philosopher and a Student of the Common Laws of England*, A. Cromartie, ed., Oxford: Clarendon Press.

—— (1991/1651) *Leviathan*, R. Tuck, ed., Cambridge: Cambridge University Press.

—— (1998/1642) *On the Citizen*, R. Tuck, ed., M. Silverthorne, trans., Cambridge: Cambridge University Press.

Holland, T. E. (1924/1880) *Elements of Jurisprudence*, Oxford: Clarendon Press.

Holmes, Jr., O. W. (1995) *The Collected Works of Justice Holmes*, S. M. Novick, ed., Chicago: University of Chicago Press.

Hume, D. (2000/1739–1740) *A Treatise of Human Nature*, D. Norton, ed., Oxford: Oxford University Press.

Long, R. T. (2007) "Hellenistic Philosophers of Law," in F. D. Miller, ed., *A Treatise of Legal Philosophy and General Jurisprudence, Volume 6: A History of the Philosophy of Law from the Ancient Greeks to the Scholastics*, Dordrecht: Springer, pp. 111–31.

Marsilius of Padua (2005/1324) *The Defender of the Peace*, A. Brett, ed. and trans., Cambridge: Cambridge University Press.

Perry, S. (2001) "Hart's Methodological Positivism," in J. Coleman, ed., *Hart's Postscript*, Oxford: Oxford University Press, pp. 311–54.

Plato (1995) *The Statesman*, J. Annas, ed. and R. Waterfield, trans., Cambridge: Cambridge University Press.

Pollock, F. (1872) "Law and Command," *Law Magazine and Review*, N.S. 1: 189–205.

Postema, G. J. (1986) *Bentham and the Common Law Tradition*, Oxford: Clarendon Press.

—— (2011) *Legal Philosophy in the Twentieth Century: The Common Law World*, Dordrecht: Springer.

Pufendorf, S. (1994) *The Political Writings of Samuel Pufendorf*, C. L. Carr, ed. and M. Silverthorne, trans., Cambridge: Cambridge University Press.

Rumble, W. E. (2005) *Doing Austin Justice*, New York: Continuum.

Salmond, J. W. (1893) *The First Principles of Jurisprudence*, London: Stevens & Haynes.

—— (1924) *Jurisprudence*, 7th edition, London: Sweet & Maxwell.

Suarez, F. (1944) *On Laws and God the Lawgiver*, G. L. Williams, A. Brown and J. Waldron, trans., Oxford: Oxford University Press.

Further Reading

For further reading, see: M. Lobban (2007) *A History of the Philosophy of Law in the Common Law World, 1600–1900*, Dordrecht: Springer (contains useful discussions of Hale, Bentham, Austin and Holmes); F. D. Miller, ed. (2007) *A History of the Philosophy of Law from the Ancient Greeks to the Scholastics*, Dordrecht: Springer (has a number of important essays on ancient and medieval legal theory); G. J. Postema (2001) "Law as Command: The Model of Command in Modern Jurisprudence," *Philosophical Issues* 11: 470–501 (includes discussion of the "thetic" conception of law); G. J. Postema, ed. (2002) *Bentham: Moral, Political and Legal Philosophy, Volume II*, Aldershot: Dartmouth Publishing Co. (collects several interpretive and critical discussions of Bentham's legal philosophy); and G. J. Postema (2011) *Legal Philosophy in the Twentieth Century: The Common Law World*, Dordrecht: Springer (includes extended discussions of Holland, Salmond, Gray and especially Holmes and Hart).

4

LEGAL POSITIVISM

Contemporary Debates

Julie Dickson

What does contemporary legal positivism seek to tell us about the nature of law, and why might its insights be important? These two questions form the backbone of the present inquiry. In Part I below, I discuss what the term "legal positivism" might mean and which tenets about the nature of law, if any, contemporary proponents of this approach agree upon. However, perhaps the more interesting inquiry is to be found in Part II, where I consider why it might be *important* to focus on, and to have a clear-sighted understanding of, those particular facets of law which contemporary legal positivists wish to draw to our attention. As we shall see, legal positivism highlights only a small subset of truths regarding law's nature, but they are truths which are vitally important for an adequate understanding of law, and which can help shape and direct many other inquiries into various aspects of its character.

I. Contemporary Legal Positivism and the Nature of Law

A. *What Legal Positivism Is Not, and What It May Be*

Above, I posed the question: what does contemporary legal positivism seek to tell us about the nature of law? This, however, may assume something which perhaps ought not to be assumed, namely that "legal positivism" demarcates a specific view or views about the nature of law which a particular group of legal philosophers endorse. Our approach to this issue may depend on whether we are using the term "legal positivism" to denote a broad tradition of thought such as we might discuss in the history of ideas, or whether we take it to demarcate a philosophical position committing its proponents to some distinctive proposition or set of propositions about the nature of law (for this distinction, see also Gardner 2001; Raz 2007). Used in the former sense, the term "legal positivism" is like a kind of jurisprudential "mood music": it sets the tone for the kind of issues and topics which certain theorists find interesting or problematic, but does not denote shared commitment to a specific tenet or set of tenets about the nature of law. It is the latter sense of the term which we are interested in here. The present section of this *Companion* is concerned with theories of the nature of law, so we need to consider which, if any, propositions about the nature of law contemporary legal positivists endorse in common.

Various red herrings are liable to emerge in considering this question. Several of these are identified and ably disposed of by John Gardner in "Legal Positivism: 5½ Myths" (2001) and, for the most part, will not be discussed again here. One myth, however, does merit special mention because of its sheer prevalence in common (mis)understandings of legal positivism and because of its liability seriously to mislead those seeking to further their understanding of that philosophical position, and of contemporary jurisprudential debate more generally.

The myth in question goes by various names, but is perhaps best captured as the "no necessary connection thesis" (Gardner 2001; Raz 2003). According to this thesis, legal positivism is committed to the view that there is no necessary connection between law and morality (for ascription of this myth to legal positivism, see e.g., Davies and Holdcroft 1991: 3). There are (at least) three problems with this thesis, and with its role in contemporary legal philosophy. The first problem is that it is false as a statement about the nature of law. There are many necessary connections between law and morality, from the seemingly obvious and perhaps less significant—such as that, necessarily, law and morality both contain norms; or that, necessarily, legal systems cannot exhibit the personal vice of jealousy—to the potentially more important (and, in some cases, more controversial), such as that, necessarily, law can be subject to moral evaluation; necessarily, law makes moral claims of its subjects (this cannot be explored here, but for an explicit defense of it, see Green 2003 and 2008); or, given the conditions of human existence, necessarily, law regulates some morally important matters in certain ways, for example, in having rules protecting human life and bodily integrity (see, e.g., Hart's discussion of the "minimum content of natural law" in Hart 1994, ch. 9, section 2).

The second problem with the no-necessary-connection thesis is that it is rejected by many contemporary legal positivists, hence characterizing legal positivist thought by reference to it is very misleading, especially for those approaching the subject for the first time (for examples of such rejections see Gardner 2001; Green 2003 and 2008; Raz 2003, 2007 and 2009, ch. 3). The third problem is linked to the second: in addition to being a poor marker of legal positivist thought, the no-necessary-connection thesis does not help us to demarcate important differences between legal philosophical positions more generally. In particular, it does not mark well the divide between legal positivism and natural law. As is noted above, many contemporary legal positivists deny the no-necessary-connection thesis, but, clearly, so do many natural law theorists, for example John Finnis, who espouses the view that: "law is rightly conceived of as *by its nature morally valuable*" (Finnis 2003: 111, emphasis in original). Moreover, the type of necessary connection between law and morality that Finnis has in mind may be very different from the multifarious types of necessary connection which various of those usually classified as legal positivists wish to investigate and/or affirm. We would do well in this to remember H. L. A. Hart's advice: "There are many different types of relation between law and morals and there is nothing which can profitably be singled out for study as *the* relation between them" (Hart 1994: 185). The no-necessary-connection thesis thus also obscures more than it reveals in encouraging us to think in terms of teams of theorists marching under common banners (such as that there is, or is not, a necessary connection between law and morality), which they do not in fact endorse, and which conceal many individually important issues concerning the relationship between law and morality. The better route, then, may be to focus on particular issues as regards the relationship between law and morality—such as whether and, if so, under what conditions there are moral reasons to obey the law, or whether, in virtue of its nature, law has a specific moral task to perform—and then try accurately to attribute views on those particular issues to individual legal theorists before evaluating their truth and explanatory adequacy.

Considerations such as these have led some legal philosophers to wonder whether we should abandon the term "legal positivism" and, more generally, to doubt the value of speaking in terms of broad schools of thought in jurisprudence at all: "In truth, such dichotomies [between legal positivism and natural law] are rarely revealing of any important truth" (MacCormick 2007: 278); "Perhaps it is time not to refute legal positivism, but to forget the label and consider the views of various writers within that tradition on their own terms" (Raz 2007: 35). While these are important cautionary notes to sound, there will be reason to retain the term and its (judicious) use, if, despite the points made above, we *can* find some propositions about the nature of law which are held in common by contemporary legal positivists, and which illuminate something important about the nature of law.

Which views about the nature of law, then, are endorsed by contemporary legal positivists responsible for such diverse and wide-ranging legal philosophical work as are Joseph Raz, Wil Waluchow, Leslie Green, John Gardner, Andrei Marmor, Jules Coleman, Scott Shapiro and Matthew Kramer? (Hugely notable by his absence from this list is, of course, H. L. A. Hart. As we are nearing two decades since Hart's death, I hesitate to include him amongst contemporary legal positivists. However, as his work has had immeasurable influence on most if not all living legal positivists, and as it has remained the subject of many contemporary debates, I will, of course, be making reference to Hart's work in the course of what follows.) I venture to suggest that they are all committed to certain views about *the social nature of law*, and, more particularly, to *the social thesis* as regards the existence and identification of law.

Legal positivists understand law as having a *fundamentally social nature*: it is a human artifact which has been socially constructed. As the term "legal positivism" itself connotes, law exists in virtue of the fact that it has been *posited*: because human beings, and the social institutions they create—such as legislatures, courts and legal officials—have decreed or decided or recognized or practiced or enforced or interacted in some way with a given set of norms (Gardner 2001; Green 2003). Those human social processes bring legal norms into existence, and are also the means by which they are modified and/or extinguished. More specifically, contemporary legal positivists are committed to *the social thesis*. They hold that the existence and content of the law is ultimately to be determined by reference to social facts, in particular by reference to law's social sources, and not by reference to the merits of the legal norms in question. To simplify for the purposes of example: that a bill has been passed by votes in the House of Commons and the House of Lords and has received the Royal Assent—that it has emerged from that series of social facts, has those social and institutional interactions as its source and that legal material emerging from that source is recognized by legal officials in the United Kingdom as constituting valid law—is what makes it into part of the statutory law of the UK. A bill which those social facts has rendered an Act of Parliament is valid law even if it lacks merit to the point where it should never have been introduced to or supported in Parliament in the first place, or recognized or enforced by anyone, and a bill which is meritorious to an admirable degree but which has failed to receive the relevant votes or Royal Assent, and so does not have a social source which counts as a law-constituting source in the UK, is not valid law.

That law has a fundamentally social nature, and that the existence and content of valid legal norms is ultimately to be determined by reference to social sources, and not by reference to the merits of the norms in question, are, in my view, the core tenets to which legal positivism is committed, and are endorsed in the work of all those contemporary legal positivists mentioned above (see, e.g., Raz 2007 and 2009; Waluchow 1994; Green 2003 and 2008; Gardner 2001 and 2007; Marmor 2001 and 2006; Coleman 2001; Shapiro 2000 and 2009; Kramer 1999 and 2004. See also, of course, Hart 1994). Their views stand in stark contrast to those of, for example, Ronald Dworkin, who contends that law must be identified and understood by constructively interpreting it, i.e., by gathering together a community's putative legal and political practices, finding their general justifying value or point, putting them in their best light with regard to that point, and working out which legal rights and duties flow from them thus construed (Dworkin 1986). Dworkin thus rejects the social thesis because he contends that, in trying to identify law and work out what it requires of us—both in the abstract sense in which legal philosophers engage in this task, and the more concrete sense in which judges deciding cases do so (see Dworkin 1986: 90)—we *must* consider and take a stance on the merits of the law, i.e., consider what general justifying value or point underlies the law, how we should understand it in light of that value and how law should go on in a new case in a way which is consonant with that value (for illuminating commentary on Dworkin's interpretivist theory of law, see Stavropoulos 2003).

To return to legal positivism: it should be noted that some have thought that the social thesis lends support to or even entails a version of the no-necessary-connection thesis, i.e., that if law is to be identified ultimately by reference to its social sources rather than by reference to its merits, the law so identified cannot of *necessity* possess any moral qualities. This, however, is a non sequitur which is explicitly rejected by contemporary legal positivists: "The claim that what is law and what is not is purely a matter of social fact still leaves it an open question whether or not those social facts by which we identify the law or determine its existence do or do not endow it with moral merit" (Raz 2009: 38-9); "Legal positivists deny that laws are valid thanks to their moral merits. But they do not deny the converse proposition that laws might be morally meritorious thanks to their validity" (Gardner 2001: 224).

B. *Some Disagreements Around the Agreement*

Although we may have located the shared tenets of legal positivism, they are shared tenets which nonetheless admit of disagreement, for some of the elements they comprise are interpreted differently by various legal theorists. I will mention only a few such disagreements here. The first disagreement pertains to the stringency of the thesis that the existence and content of the law is to be determined by social facts and not by reference to its merits. For those in the so-called "exclusive positivist" or "hard positivist" camp—including Raz, Marmor, Gardner and Shapiro—law is to be identified *solely* by reference to its social sources, whereas for so-called "soft positivists" or "inclusive positivists"—including Hart (at least in the posthumously published "Postscript" to *The Concept of Law* (1994)), Waluchow and Kramer—the merits of a legal norm *may* determine its legal validity and content, but only if, in a given legal system, source-based considerations render those merits relevant to such determinations. So, for example, for soft or inclusive legal positivists, if a norm in a constitution (itself recognized as constituting valid law according to that system's rules of recognition), or a norm forming part of that system's rules of recognition, requires that no statute shall be legally valid unless it is consistent with fairness and equality, then the (moral) values of fairness and equality are thereby included in, or incorporated into, the test for legal validity in that jurisdiction, and the existence and content of the law will be partly dependent on its conformity with merit-based considerations. According to such theorists, their theory remains positivist in character because the merit-based considerations in question are only relevant if, in a given jurisdiction, some social sources implicitly or explicitly make them so, hence maintaining commitment to the social thesis as stated above, that the existence and content of the law is *ultimately* to be determined by reference to social facts (see, e.g., Waluchow 1994 for an extended explanation of the position). Exclusive legal positivists deny that merit-based considerations indicated or referred to by social sources thereby become incorporated into the law, and hence need a different explanation of legal phenomena such as equality or fairness clauses in constitutions or elsewhere in the recognition rules of a given jurisdiction (for one such attempted explanation, see Raz 2004. More generally, for discussion of exclusive vs. inclusive legal positivism, see, e.g., Waluchow 1994; Kramer 2004; Marmor 2001; Raz 1994 and 2004; Green 2003; Shapiro 2000, 2001 and 2009; and Himma 2005).

A second area of controversy surrounds the issue of whether the social facts by means of which law's existence and identity are determined are best understood as social *conventions* of some kind, and, if so, of what kind. Debate on this issue has often been prompted by H. L. A. Hart's version of legal positivism and, in particular, by his contention that the ultimate social fact upon which law's existence and identity depends is acceptance in common by legal officials of a recognition rule specifying criteria of legal validity (Hart 1994). The question has then arisen as to whether, as Hart himself seems to indicate in the "Postscript" (Hart 1994: 256, 267), the common recognition practices of legal officials ought to be regarded as a social convention, i.e., wherein part of the *reason* which each official has for adopting the practice of accepting the recognition rule in question is the fact that her fellow officials so adopt it (for further discussion see Green 1999; Marmor 2001; Shapiro 2002; Dickson 2007).

A third point of contention is whether legal positivism offers a reductive account of legal validity, i.e., whether it attempts to reduce what it is for a norm to be legally valid to a certain combination of social facts. Some of those usually classified as legal positivists vehemently reject such reductivism, and contend that legal validity must be understood in purely normative terms: legal norms are valid in virtue of their relation to other legal norms higher up what are referred to as "chains of validity" of norms (see Kelsen 1967, although Kelsen's work does not feature significantly in the present discussion for the reasons already outlined in relation to H. L. A. Hart). Other positivists, however, do reduce what it is for a norm to be legally valid to a combination of certain facts, e.g., the fact that the norm has been decreed by a sovereign, the fact that it is habitually obeyed by the relevant populace and the likelihood in fact that a sanction will be visited on those failing to comply with that norm (Bentham 1970/1782; Austin 1995/1832). Still others occupy what might be seen as an intermediate and perhaps tricky position, claiming that social facts (such as the fact of acceptance in common by legal officials) identify and constitute the recognition rules which determine legal validity in a given jurisdiction, but also insisting that the recognition rules so constituted must be understood in normative terms, i.e., as creating legal *reasons* for action. On this view, recognition rules must be understood normatively, and not merely as indications that certain facts have occurred or as predictions that they will occur, because that is how those rules are understood and used by the legal officials administering them (Hart 1994, especially his discussion of the "internal point of view" in chs. 5 and 6).

A related issue is that of whether legal positivists accept in common a certain account of legal normativity or of the correct way to understand legal ought-statements such as "according to law, X ought to Φ." Once again, this seems to be an area where disagreement predominates. Some positivists contend that there is a specifically legal sense of "ought" and a specifically legal account of normativity to be had, such that legal ought-statements are to be understood as different in kind and in meaning from moral ought-statements (see, e.g., Hart 1982, chs. VI and X; Harris 1996, offering an interpretation of Kelsen's views). Other legal positivists, however, espouse the view that "ought" has the same meaning in both legal and moral contexts, but that it is possible to make legal ought-statements while not being fully committed to the normative force of those statements (Raz 2009, especially chs. 3, 7 and 8). These "detached normative statements" allow law to be described, and for advice to be given about what law requires, without the speaker being committed to the moral force of the legal statements in question, in the manner of a Roman Catholic advising an orthodox Jewish friend what she ought to do to comply with rabbinical law (Raz 2009, ch. 8).

These complex and somewhat internecine debates can be explored further by referring to those works mentioned in this section. As there is no shared view on them among legal positivists, they do not feature among those core tenets by reference to which that position is characterized here. In any case, the present discussion largely sidesteps these issues in order to devote more attention to what I regard as a more fundamental point as regards contemporary legal positivism, namely why, if at all, are the theses about the nature of law to which it is committed *important*? This will form the topic for discussion in Part II below. Before embarking on that discussion, however, it is important to note a few other things that legal positivism is not.

C. *What Else Legal Positivism Is Not*

Legal positivists are committed to certain views about the nature of law, namely (in the sense explained above) the social thesis regarding the existence and identification of law, and, more broadly, the fundamentally social nature of law. These, however, are but a small subset of purported truths about law's nature: legal positivism marks a commitment to certain views about *some aspects of the nature of law*, but is not, on its own, a comprehensive theory of law nor even a complete account of the nature of law (on this point see also Gardner 2001 and Green 2003). In drawing this last distinction (between a comprehensive theory of law and a complete account of the nature of law), I am alluding to the idea that a full understanding of law's character might include investigation not merely of its nature—that is, of those essential properties which law, at any time, and in any place, must possess in order to be law, and which make law into what it is (for further explanation see Dickson 2001, ch. 1)—but also of some of its contingent properties, such as its propensity to produce certain sorts of social outcomes in certain kinds of societies or among certain social groups. In my view, jurisprudential debate is a very broad church and should welcome many different kinds of inquiries into different aspects of law's character.

Even as regards theories of the nature of law, however, legal positivism cannot be understood as a complete such theory. One reason is because no theory of the nature of law can ever be complete. Part of the reason philosophizing about law can appear to be an endless task is that in a certain sense the task has not remained constant over the time that theorists have engaged in it: those questions and puzzles about law addressed in their theories have changed over time, influenced, for example, by the political, social and intellectual preoccupations of the time and place in which theories of law emerge. The complex and multifaceted character of law allows for a wide variety topics in legal philosophy to come and go, and for our sense of what is difficult or puzzling even with regard to one and the same topic to change over time. This being so, no theory of law could ever give us a completely comprehensive account of the nature of law, because only certain topics and puzzles will emerge and strike a given theorist as sufficiently interesting and important at any given time (these points are discussed at greater length in Dickson 2003).

But even in respect of any given legal positivist's *current* work on the nature of law, her legal positivism does not constitute an attempt to explain all aspects of law's nature as she understands it (indeed Joseph Raz has gone so far as to say that the social thesis "is best viewed not as a 'first-order' thesis but as a constraint on what kind of theory of law is an acceptable theory," in Raz 2009, ch. 3: 39). This is borne out by the many and various views on *other* aspects of the nature of law which feature in the legal philosophical writings of those positivists mentioned above. A commitment to the fundamentally social nature of law, and to the social thesis, leaves open, and leaves room for, a variety of other views and investigations into other aspects of law's nature: whether it necessarily claims and/or possesses moral authority; how we are to understand and justify certain aspects of constitutional adjudication; whether and in what sense law provides reasons for action; whether certain semantic theories can help us make sense of conceptual inquiries into the character of law; and many more. Legal positivism is hence not a complete theory of the nature of law, it is a commitment to a small but (as will be discussed in Part II below) vitally important subset of truths about law's nature.

As legal positivism is an inquiry into certain aspects of the *nature of law*, it should also not be viewed as: a thesis about what qualities it would be morally or politically beneficial for law to possess (see Murphy 2001, but n.b. Murphy 2008 for important modifications to his view); a commendation that legal systems ought to be developed in a way which maximizes the benefits of having clearly identifiable rules which can be applied in a way which minimizes the need for contentious moral judgments (Campbell 1996 and 2004); or a thesis recommending that, if our current concept of law is not positivist in character, then we should alter that concept so that it does have that character (for discussion of this possibility, see Schauer 2005). (Perhaps there is no harm in labeling some of these views as—in some sense—legal positivist in character, as some of their proponents do, so long as we are crystal clear about which view(s) we wish to denote in so doing. But then the term will not be being used in the sense which I have tried to isolate here, to denote a commitment to certain important and significant (see further discussion in Part II) tenets about the nature of law.) Nor does legal positivism offer any explicit or implicit commendation or condemnation of law; give judges or other legal officials moral reasons why they ought or ought not to engage with and uphold the law; or tell judges what theory of interpretation they ought to endorse, and/or how to decide legally underdetermined cases coming before them. Legal positivism comes not to praise, recommend, advise, condone or condemn: it aims to tell it like it is about *some* aspects of the *nature* of law, and so help us better to understand this vitally important and far-reaching social institution with which we are all so familiar, and which plays a significant role in our lives. That law has a nature, aspects of which its philosophers are capable of uncovering, is, of course, a controversial view in itself (for recent criticism, see Leiter 2010). However, it is a view to which legal positivism is implicitly committed in its attempts to illuminate certain aspects of law's nature, and which we must note and understand if we are to grasp that doctrine's aims and character.

II. Legal Positivism: What's Important and Why?

A. *The Importance of Importance*

If there is so much, then, that legal positivism is not, and if what it does denote is a commitment only to a small subset of truths about the nature of law, then why should we care about it, or about what it seeks to convince us of? The first point to note in approaching these issues is that theories of law do not and should not seek to tell us just any old truths they can get their hands on as regards the nature of law; rather, they should try to pick out, illuminate and adequately elucidate features of law which are important and significant to explain.

As I have discussed elsewhere, this need for theorists to be selective, to choose which features of their datum are important to focus on, is a methodological requirement of theories concerning any subject matter whatsoever, and is necessary in order for the work in question actually to be a theoretical explanation, rather than a collection of miscellaneous and unconnected points about some phenomenon. In the case of jurisprudence, however, there are additional factors at work giving shape and direction to the theorist's selection of those facets of law which she seeks to explain. A theory of law, in order to be successful, must appreciate and take to heart the point that the concept of law, and other legal concepts such as the concept of a legal system or the concept of legal obligation, are concepts already used by those living in societies to understand and navigate the course of their lives under law. It is overwhelmingly the case that people living in societies governed by law are aware of law's existence and importance in their lives, and have views about its character, purpose, etc. The concept of law is hence not some esoteric theoretical tool introduced anew by legal philosophers in order to further their research projects: it is already "out there" in people's discourse and thinking about their social and political lives, and is already part of the conceptual currency used by individuals living under law to understand themselves and their social world. In making judgments about which features of law are important and significant to explain, then, the legal theorist must pay attention to and do adequate justice to how those living under law perceive it, and what they regard as important and significant about it. Only by so doing will we explain our subject matter—which includes those attitudes and beliefs held by those living under law—adequately and well, and hence advance our understanding of ourselves, and our lives as members of law-governed polities (for more extended discussion of these points, which are endorsed by many other legal theorists, see Dickson 2001 and 2004).

To return to legal positivism: this theoretical approach involves a commitment not merely to the fundamentally social nature of law and to the social thesis, but also to the view that these facets of law are important and significant to explain. But (and taking into account the points just made above) why, exactly, are they so important? And isn't this rather a banal and obvious point, for surely all legal theorists are committed to the importance and significance of that which they hold to be true about law? We can begin to approach these issues by considering a possible counter-example to the latter point: John Finnis is arguably a legal theorist who accepts legal positivism's truths about the fundamentally social nature of law and the social thesis, but who does not grant those truths the importance and prominence that they warrant.

B. *What's Important #1: The "Social Facticity" and Social Reality of Law*

At certain points in his work on the nature of law, Finnis appears unequivocally to endorse legal positivism's commitments to the fundamentally social nature of law: "human law is artefact and artifice, and not a conclusion from moral premises" (Finnis 1996: 205), and to the social thesis: "'The identification of the existence and content of law does not require resort to any moral argument.' True, for how else could one identify wicked laws"; "why deny that the facts which are referred to as 'human positing'—custom, legislation, judgments—can all be identified by lawyerly historical methods, without 'moral argument'?" (Finnis 1996: 204. See also Finnis 1980: 268–70; and Finnis 2007, Introduction). Finnis claims that natural law thinking, from Aquinas onwards, has recognized and sought to explicate the positivity of human law (see especially Finnis 1996 and 2007). He thus does not regard legal positivism as a rival theoretical position to the form of natural law thinking that he embraces: the latter can and should make adequate room for and explain law's positivity, as well as identifying and explaining its moral purpose and ability to generate genuine reasons for action. In a sense, this should come as no surprise: as was emphasized in Part I, legal positivism is not a complete theory of law, and denotes commitment only to a small subset of truths regarding its nature. This being so, there is no reason why a variety of theorists and theoretical positions should not embrace those truths but then go on to explicate other aspects of law's character—such as law's moral purpose and propensity to generate reasons for action—elsewhere in their theories. So far, so compatibilist. But on closer examination, things are not as straightforward as they seem, and Finnis's "embrace" of the social thesis, and of the fundamentally social nature of law, turns out to be a somewhat remote and chilly one.

Finnis himself would likely deny this. He is on record as saying that it is important and useful in legal philosophy to focus on law's positivity (Finnis 1996), and on social fact-based tests for the intra-systemic validity of law (Finnis 2003). Finnis has also claimed that law's dependence on social facts, and its source-based character, are important elements in enabling law to carry out the specific moral task which he believes it has: to reasonably resolve the coordination problems of a political society and so allow its members, in common, to pursue good and valuable lives (Finnis 2007, section 1. For further discussion of Finnis's view of law's moral task see any of his work in general jurisprudence, e.g., Finnis 1980 and 2003). However, his deeper commitments as regards the importance or otherwise of law's social facticity come to the surface when he discusses how we should understand instances of law which are legally valid according to the relevant social facts tests in a given jurisdiction, but which fail to fulfill law's moral purpose of reasonably resolving societal coordination problems for the common good.

According to Finnis, although there is still a certain sense—a social fact sense—in which such unjust laws can still be accounted as law (Finnis 1980, ch. XII. 4; Finnis 2007), they are also to be regarded—depending on the stridency of Finnis's turn of phrase—as not really law (Finnis 1980: 277–78), less than fully law (Finnis 1980: 279), law only in a secondary, watered-down, non-central or distorted sense (Finnis 2007, section 4) or, simply, not law (Finnis 2003: 114). Moreover, it is this second set of understandings which Finnis regards as being explanatorily more important, as is revealed by a remark he makes in response to a challenge by Joseph Raz as to why law should be regarded as not really or fully law when it is bad, whereas novels or paintings or people still remain novels or paintings or people even when they are bad (for the relevant exchange see Finnis 2003: 114–15 and especially n. 9). Finnis's response goes as follows: "like argument, medicines, and contracts, law has a focused and normative point to which everything else about it is properly to be regarded as subordinate." People, on the other hand, "exist in the natural order as living substances even if they are not functioning adequately or at all in the orders of logic and thought" (Finnis 2003: 114, n. 9). In the case of law, then, its "focused and normative point" or, to put it another way, its moral task of reasonably resolving coordination problems for the common good, is what is regarded as most important about it, and law's other qualities, such as its social nature, and the fact that its existence and content can be ascertained ultimately by reference to social facts, are to be regarded as "subordinate." This being so, although Finnis states that natural law thinking is interested both in law's social facticity and in its moral purpose and propensity to generate reasons for action (Finnis 2007, Introduction), the reality is that he regards the latter, and the explanation of the latter, as primarily important. Those features of law which legal positivism emphasizes as vitally important about it are demoted by Finnis to being subordinate qualities of law, and law which exhibits those qualities, but which does not fulfill law's moral purpose, is seen as a watered-down or secondary kind of law (when it is seen as law at all).

This, however, is a mistake, and understanding why better explains my claim that legal positivism does not merely endorse the social thesis and certain views regarding law's fundamentally social character, but seeks to emphasize the importance and significance of those features of law. Legal systems are institutionalized normative systems in which interrelated norms are created, modified, applied and enforced by social institutions such as legislatures, courts and tribunals, the police and other executive agencies. In any jurisdiction governed by law, some such institutions exist and they and the norms they generate and apply have a deep and pervasive impact on the social reality of those living in the society in question. People fall under the jurisdiction of the legislature, courts and other legal institutions, are subject to their norms, stand liable to have them forcefully applied to them in case of noncompliance, and know and view as important these characteristics of law. Moreover, these features of law, and their impact on the lives of those living under it, persist irrespective of whether law successfully realizes any moral point or objective which it may have (I take no view here on whether it does have any such point). Law and people are hence not disanalogous in the way that Finnis claims: although the social reality of law is very different in character from the biological reality of people, both persist even when those entities fail to live up to those standards which they ought to, and both are properties of sufficient importance such that we should view phenomena exhibiting them as remaining instances of law or people respectively. In the case of law, the importance of those properties stems from the fact that its social and institutional character plays a deep and pervasive role in people's lives irrespective of its moral justification, and from the fact that those living under law regard as important and significant those features of law to which legal positivism draws attention. Law's social facticity—the fact that it is "out there" and has a profound effect upon the social reality of people's lives irrespective of whether it fulfills any moral task it may have—is something significant about law which it is important to foreground and adequately explain in our legal theories. It is not something to be regarded as subordinate or as only determining law's existence in a secondary or watered-down sense (for further discussion of some of these points in a different context, see Dickson 2009).

Moreover, in claiming that those features of law to which legal positivism draws attention must be given adequate place and importance in our theories of law, we do not thereby restrict legal philosophers from also investigating other important features of law such as any specific moral task or purpose which it ought to fulfill. Once again, legal positivism is not a complete theory of law, and hence leaves considerable room for legal theorists to conduct whatever investigations they choose into other aspects of law's character. For example, Joseph Raz shares Finnis's view that law has a specific moral task to perform, and regards the identification and explanation of that task, and its relation to other aspects of law's character, as important for legal theorists to investigate (see Raz 2003, especially section III, and section D below). This view, however, is compatible with not demoting other important properties of law—its fundamentally social nature, and its conformity to the social thesis—to a subordinate status. Legal positivists seek to explain only a small subset of truths about law's nature, but they stand firmly by the importance and significance of those features of law which their theory highlights.

C. *What's Important #2: That Law's Existence Does Not Determine What Ought to Be Done*

An adequate understanding of the social thesis, and of the sense in which law has a fundamentally social character, can also bring to the fore the important point that law's existence does not, without the addition of further premises, determine what anyone ought to do, and, in particular, does not determine whether and under what circumstances legal officials and/or those subject to law ought to follow it.

That this is so should be evident from the discussion so far. Legal positivism is committed to certain views about the nature of law. But the truths it communicates do not, in themselves, give anyone reasons for action. That law has a fundamentally social nature, and that its existence and content are determined, ultimately, by reference to social facts, are facts about the nature of law, not recommendations that anyone ought to do anything. Of course, as several legal positivists point out, if there are already good reasons to engage with law in certain ways, then the social thesis can identify the law with which one is to be engaged. For example, *if* there are good reasons to become a judge in a given jurisdiction, and *if* someone has taken up that role, and acquired the duties that go with it, *then* in order to know which legal norms to apply in a given case, that person will need to know that legal norms are ultimately to be identified by reference to those social sources which count as lawmaking sources in that jurisdiction, and that she must find out what those are and identify law accordingly. But the social thesis, and the official recognition practices which constitute the relevant law-identifying social facts in a given jurisdiction, do not, on their own, and without the addition of further premises, give anyone good reasons to become a judge, or to apply or obey the legal norms which that jurisdiction's recognition practices identify (for further discussion see Gardner 2001, section II; Marmor 2001, chs. 1 and 2, especially: 22, 27–33 and 47–48; Dickson 2007).

Moreover, that law is not something that, simply by existing, determines what ought to be done, is also further underscored by those truths which legal positivism wishes to bring to our attention. Legal positivism emphasizes the man-made and socially constructed character of law. It is familiar to us all that human beings can fall into moral and other error, hence emphasizing law's character as a human artifact reminds us that it may sometimes—perhaps often—be misused and may require of us things which there is no good reason, or insufficient reason, to do (see also Gardner 2007, section III, and: 22). Positivism's social thesis also brings to the fore the point that law's norms exist not in virtue of the fact that they state something meritorious which there is good reason to do, but rather because they have emerged from certain social sources which are counted as law-constituting sources in a given jurisdiction. Human history stands witness to the fact that lawmaking sources such as parliaments and courts can, and have, constituted as law things that were morally repugnant and which ought not to have been so constituted—the nineteenth- and twentieth-century Jim Crow laws in the United States, and many of the apartheid-supporting legal directives of the 1948–1994 South African governments being but two of many possible examples. The realization that law exists in virtue of social sources, and that those same sources can constitute laws with very different moral merits and laws radically lacking in moral merit, further underscores the point that the existence of legal norms does not thereby give us good reason to engage with or follow them.

Why is it so important to emphasize that law is not something which, solely in virtue of its existence, determines what there is good reason to do, or what ought to be done? The features of law and examples noted above point the way to an answer: because a great deal of human misery has been caused by morally misguided and/or abhorrent law, and it is thus important to remind ourselves that when law comes calling, the best response may well not be immediately to jump in line with its demands. In this thought lies the truth of H. L. A. Hart's remark that, "What surely is most needed in order to make men clear-sighted in confronting the official abuse of power, is that they should preserve the sense that the certification of something as legally valid is not conclusive of the question of obedience" (Hart 1994: 210).

Moreover, when law and its makers get things wrong and fall into moral and other error, the consequences for us and for our societies are far more serious than when an individual goes thus astray. Law operates on a mass scale, applying itself compulsorily and with no opt-outs (other than those defined by law itself) to whole population sets at a time. It characteristically comes with the backup of the full panoply of state coercion, which it stands ready to use in cases of noncompliance. Grave errors perpetuated by a social institution on this scale and with this character are likely to be wide-ranging, far-reaching and to have deep and, in some circumstances, catastrophic effects on the life chances of those living under it. None of this is to ignore the fact that law can be, and often is, an instrument of tremendous social and personal good; it is merely to remind ourselves of its—and our—possible darker sides as well.

Legal positivism's truths about the nature of law do not, by themselves, establish all those features and potential downfalls of law mentioned above. But those truths do play an important role in underscoring and bringing to the fore certain aspects of law which, upon further reflection, throw into sharp relief law's potential for moral and other error, and highlight the fact that law's existence does not, of itself, determine what ought to be done.

D. *What's Important #3: The Good and Bad That Law Makes Possible*

As was noted at the beginning of Part II, legal positivists—like all legal theorists— should not seek to tell us just any truths about the nature of law; rather, they should try to pick out, illuminate and adequately elucidate features of law which are important and significant to explain. In carrying out this task, those theorists must be sufficiently sensitive to what is regarded as important and significant about law by those administering and living under it. In previous work, I have also emphasized the point that, sometimes, the reason certain features of law are important to explain, and are understood as such by those subject to and administering the law, is because they bear upon what matters to us and are relevant to our eventual assessments of law as valuable or not, justified or not, and as something we ought or ought not to follow (Dickson 2001, especially ch. 3; Dickson 2004, section IIa). For example, let us grant, for the sake of illustration, that, as many legal theorists contend, law makes a claim to possess legitimate moral authority. This feature of law is arguably an important feature of law to explain because the existence and nature of that claim means that law will hold us to certain standards whether we agree with them or not, and will coercively enforce its edicts against us, perhaps radically curtailing our freedom in certain circumstances if we disobey. This is important because it bears upon what matters to us, e.g., being able to live a fulfilling, autonomous life, and because law's compulsory and potentially coercive nature is relevant to answering questions such as, "Is law morally justified or not?" and "When and under what circumstances, if at all, ought we to obey it?" The relevance of certain features of law to considering and answering those kinds of questions, and to law's capacity for instantiating certain moral and other values, can make those features important to explain. (This idea of the "value-relevance" of certain features of law is also discussed in Waluchow 1994: 19–30.)

As has been noted throughout the present discussion, legal positivism is not a complete theory of law, only a commitment to certain tenets about the nature of law. Moreover, as has also been noted, many of those whose work is classified as legal positivist in tenor are interested in many and various issues regarding the character of law—such as law's claim to authority, the justification conditions of that claim, and which account of constitutional interpretation and adjudication best explains certain aspects of law's operation—which go well beyond those facets of law highlighted by their legal positivism. The point which I want to emphasize in this closing section is that a further reason why legal positivists pick out certain features of law as important to explain is that they regard these features as relevant to law's moral and other evaluation, and as relevant to law's capacity to realize value. Although their legal positivism does not, and cannot, represent certain theorists' more complete theory of law, it does help to shape and direct those further inquiries into other aspects of law's character which they wish to pursue.

That this is so is evident in the recent work of several contemporary legal positivists. For example, Joseph Raz has argued that the social thesis allows law to generate authoritative directives identifiable without reference to those very considerations which the directives are intended to sum up, reflect and replace. He claims that authoritative directives must be identifiable without reference to what he refers to as the "dependent reasons" or considerations that they are there to adjudicate, otherwise authorities will not be capable of performing their central function of mediating between people and the ultimate reasons which apply to them in a way which allows those people better to conform to those reasons than they could if they relied on their own judgment (this long and complex argument features in many of Raz's works. See, e.g., Raz 1994, ch. 10 for one summarized version of it). Law's social nature, and its conformity to the social thesis, hence makes it possible for law to play a valuable role in our lives by the provision of authoritative reasons for action—when certain conditions, given by Raz's normal justification thesis (see, e.g., Raz 1986, especially chs. 3 and 4; Raz 1994, ch. 10) —are met. The social thesis is hence important to focus upon and explain because of the role it plays in allowing law to be capable of realizing certain values. Raz has recently further suggested that law, by its nature, has a specific moral task to perform—namely to facilitate the realization of moral goals which, in a given society, would be unlikely to be realized without law's intervention (Raz 2003: 12). According to Raz, law's moral task is made possible by, and arises out of, the way in which it operates as a structure of authority (Raz 2003). Once again, it can operate as a structure of authority only if its directives are identifiable by reference to social facts and without recourse to those considerations which those directives aim to settle. Raz, hence, does not focus on the social thesis purely for its own sake, or in isolation from these other issues regarding law's character which he views as so important; his focus on the social thesis and on law's social character plays a vital role in his wider account of the nature of law, including those values it can and ought to realize.

However, it should not be supposed, as some legal theorists have done, that the only reason why a given feature of law is important to explain is because it contributes to law's moral value, and that the only way we can know that a given feature of law is important to explain is first of all to work out its contribution to that moral value (see, e.g., Finnis 1980, ch. 1; Finnis 2003; Finnis 2007, section 5). I have argued elsewhere that neither of these points hold good: one can know that a given feature of law is important to explain without yet knowing or taking a stance on whether it is good or bad; and sometimes, the reason why a given feature of law is important to explain is because it contributes in a *negative* way to law's value, i.e., it helps law to realize something which is morally bad or even abhorrent (see Dickson 2001, especially chs. 2–4, where I also discuss some further reasons why certain features of law are important and significant to explain).

Some legal positivist thinkers have been keen to draw our attention to this latter point in recent discussions. John Gardner notes, for example (Gardner 2001, section IIIA), that philosophical anarchists (e.g., Wolff 1970) who contend that legal authority and submission thereto is never legitimate also need to endorse certain aspects of legal positivist thought in support of their position. According to Gardner, "[o]nly if legal norms are posited by someone do they count as exercises of authority" (Gardner 2001: 207). In order to be capable of making the claim to authority which philosophical anarchists find so morally problematic, then, certain legal positivist tenets must be true. Philosophical anarchists, therefore, may want to draw attention to certain legal positivist truths as important because they pick out features of law which enable law to perform what are—according to philosophical anarchists—morally illegitimate functions, e.g., to claim moral authority over people, and attempt to subject them to that authority.

More recently still, Leslie Green has claimed that it is important to focus in our theories of law not merely on the realization of moral value that law makes possible, but also on the *immorality* that law makes possible (Green 2008). Moreover, Green counsels us to explore the idea that specific vices or forms of immorality are made possible in virtue of the *nature* of law, including those aspects of its nature to which legal positivist accounts draw our attention. For example, he contends—following Hart's account of the nature of law—that when law emerges in a given society, we have source-based tests for the validity of legal norms which are constituted by the behavior, attitudes and procedures of legal officials. Those norms, validated according to legal officials' tests, are then implemented and enforced by specialized agencies. That law has this institutional character, and that its norms are created, modified and extinguished by the actions of specialized legal officials, is part of its nature, but precisely because it has that nature, certain kinds of specifically legal vice are made possible. For example, it is possible for law to become alienated from the population whose law it allegedly is precisely because of this division of labor between that population and the legal officials whose behavior and attitudes determine what is recognized as valid law. In this way, some facets of the nature of law to which legal positivist accounts draw our attention are important for Green because they play a role in a wider explanation of "the *immorality* that *law* makes possible" (Green 2008: 1058).

III. Conclusion

Despite harboring some doubts and giving some intellectual health warnings regarding the use of the term "legal positivism" to denote commitment to certain views about the nature of law, I have claimed that two such commitments can be isolated and correctly ascribed to this jurisprudential position: a belief that law is a human artifact and social construct, and a belief that law's existence and content is ultimately to be determined by reference to social facts. What is more significant, however, is not that legal positivism stands committed to these tenets about the nature of law, but that it regards them as important, and *why* it regards them as important. I have discussed three such reasons here: that those truths emphasize the social facticity of law and the impact it has on the lives of those living under it, regardless of whether its justification conditions are met; that they underscore the fact that the existence of law does not, of itself, generate reasons for action and hence remind us to be suitably wary of being too eager to jump when law calls; and that they pick out features of law relevant to its moral and other evaluation—although that evaluation can be both positive and negative—and relevant to further work that legal theorists may wish to pursue regarding other facets of law's character. It may be thought that a somewhat "law-wary" attitude hovers over my discussion of why positivism's truths about law are important and significant. In fact, I am firmly of the view that there is much good that law makes possible, and that to ignore the investigation and explanation of those possibilities in our theories of law would be a mistake. Nonetheless, when dealing with a social institution like law, which operates on a mass scale, applies itself compulsorily to all those falling within its self-defined jurisdiction and comes characteristically armed with the apparatus of state coercion, we would do well to be on our guard, and to remind ourselves of its man-made and morally fallible character, and of the fact that its norms exist in virtue of their sources, not their merits. These facets of law are brought to the fore in legal positivism, which, for this reason at least, deserves to remain part of the rich and varied scene of contemporary jurisprudential debate.

References

Austin, J. (1995/1832) *The Province of Jurisprudence Determined*, W. E. Rumble, ed., Cambridge: Cambridge University Press.

Bentham, J. (1970/1782) *Of Laws in General*, H. L. A. Hart, ed., London: Athlone Press.

Campbell, T. (1996) *The Legal Theory of Ethical Positivism*, Aldershot: Ashgate/Dartmouth.

—— (2004) *Prescriptive Legal Positivism: Law, Rights and Democracy*, London: UCL Press.

Coleman, J. (2001) *The Practice of Principle: In Defence of a Pragmatist Approach to Legal Theory*, Oxford: Oxford University Press.

Davies, H. and Holdcroft, D. (1991) *Jurisprudence: Texts and Commentary*, London: Butterworths.

Dickson, J. (2001) *Evaluation and Legal Theory*, Oxford: Hart Publishing.

—— (2003) "The Central Questions of Legal Philosophy," 56 *Current Legal Problems*: 63.

—— (2004) "Methodology in Jurisprudence: A Critical Survey," 10 *Legal Theory*: 117.

—— (2007) "Is the Rule of Recognition Really a Conventional Rule?" 27 *Oxford Journal of Legal Studies*: 373.

—— (2009) "Is Bad Law Still Law? Is Bad Law Really Law?" in M. Del Mar and Z. Bankowski, eds., *Law as Institutional Normative Order*, Aldershot: Ashgate, pp. 161–86.

Dworkin, R. (1986) *Law's Empire*, London: Fontana Press.

Finnis, J. (1980) *Natural Law and Natural Rights*, Oxford: Clarendon Press.

—— (1996) "The Truth in Legal Positivism," in R. George, ed., *The Autonomy of Law: Essays on Legal Positivism*, Oxford: Oxford University Press, pp. 195–214.

—— (2003) "Law and What I Truly Should Decide," 48 *American Journal of Jurisprudence*: 107.

—— (2007) "Natural Law Theories," in E. N. Zalta, ed., *The Stanford Encyclopedia of Philosophy*, Fall 2008 Edition, http: //plato.stanford.edu/entries/natural-law-theories.

Gardner, J. (2001) "Legal Positivism: 5½ Myths," 46 *American Journal of Jurisprudence*: 199.

—— (2007) "Nearly Natural Law," 52 *American Journal of Jurisprudence*: 1.

Green, L. (1999) "Positivism and Conventionalism," 12 *Canadian Journal of Law and Jurisprudence*: 35.

—— (2003) "Legal Positivism," in E. N. Zalta, ed., *The Stanford Encyclopedia of Philosophy*, Fall 2009 Edition, http: //plato.stanford.edu/entries/legal-positivism.

—— (2008) "Positivism and the Inseparability of Law and Morals," 83 *New York University Law Review*: 1035.

Harris, J. W. (1996) "Kelsen's Pallid Normativity," 9 *Ratio Juris*: 94.

Hart, H. L. A. (1982) *Essays on Bentham*, Oxford: Oxford University Press.

—— (1994) *The Concept of Law*, 2nd edition, Oxford: Clarendon Press.

Himma, K. E. (2005) "Final Authority to Bind with Moral Mistakes: On the Explanatory Potential of Inclusive Legal Positivism," 24 *Law and Philosophy*: 1.

Kelsen, H. (1967) *The Pure Theory of Law*, 2nd edition, M. Knight, trans., Berkeley: University of California Press.

Kramer, M. (1999) *In Defense of Legal Positivism*, Oxford: Oxford University Press.

Kramer, M. (2004) *Where Law and Morality Meet*, Oxford: Oxford University Press.

Leiter, B. (2010) "The Demarcation Problem in Jurisprudence: A New Case for Skepticism," available at SSRN: http: //papers.ssrn.com/sol3/papers.cfm?abstract_id=1599620.

MacCormick, N. (2007) *Institutions of Law: An Essay in Legal Theory*, Oxford: Oxford University Press.

Marmor, A. (2001) *Positive Law and Objective Values*, Oxford: Oxford University Press.

—— (2006) "Legal Positivism: Still Descriptive and Morally Neutral," 26 *Oxford Journal of Legal Studies*: 683.

Murphy, L. (2001) "The Political Question of the Concept of Law," in J. Coleman, ed., *Hart's Postscript: Essays on the Postscript to* The Concept of Law, Oxford: Oxford University Press, pp. 371–409.

—— (2008) "Better to See Law This Way," 83 *New York University Law Review*: 1088.

Raz, J. (1986) *The Morality of Freedom*, Oxford: Clarendon Press.

—— (1994) "Authority, Law, and Morality," in J. Raz, *Ethics in the Public Domain: Essays in the Morality of Law and Politics*, Oxford: Clarendon Press.

—— (2003) "About Morality and the Nature of Law," 48 *American Journal of Jurisprudence*: 1.

—— (2004) "Incorporation by Law," 10 *Legal Theory*: 1.

—— (2007) "The Argument from Justice, or How Not to Reply to Legal Positivism," in G. Pavlakos, ed., *Law, Rights and Discourse: The Legal Philosophy of Robert Alexy*, Oxford: Hart Publishing, pp. 17–36.

—— (2009) *The Authority of Law, Essays on Law and Morality*, 2nd edition, Oxford: Oxford University Press.

Schauer, F. (2005) "The Social Construction of the Concept of Law: A Reply to Julie Dickson," 25 *Oxford Journal of Legal Studies*: 493.

Shapiro, S. (2000) "Law, Morality and the Guidance of Conduct," 6 *Legal Theory*: 127.

—— (2001) "On Hart's Way Out," in J. Coleman, ed., *Hart's Postscript: Essays on the Postscript to* The Concept of Law, Oxford: Oxford University Press, pp. 149–92.

—— (2002) "Law, Plans, and Practical Reason," 8 *Legal Theory*: 387.

—— (2009) "Was Inclusive Legal Positivism Founded on a Mistake?" 22 *Ratio Juris*: 326.

Stavropoulos, N. (2003) "Interpretivist Theories of Law," in E. N. Zalta, ed., *The Stanford Encyclopedia of Philosophy*, Fall 2008 Edition, http: //plato.stanford.edu/entries/law-interpretivist.

Waluchow, W. (1994) *Inclusive Legal Positivism*, Oxford: Oxford University Press.

Wolff, R. P. (1970) *In Defense of Anarchism*, New York: Harper & Row.

Further Reading

For further reading, see: T. Campbell (2004) *Prescriptive Legal Positivism: Law, Rights and Democracy*, London: UCL Press; J. Dickson (2009) "Is Bad Law Still Law? Is Bad Law Really Law?" in M. Del Mar and Z. Bankowski, eds., *Law as Institutional Normative Order*, Aldershot: Ashgate, pp. 161–86; J. Finnis (2007) "Natural Law Theories," in E. N. Zalta, ed., *The Stanford Encyclopedia of Philosophy*, Fall 2008 Edition, http: //plato.stanford.edu/entries/natural-law-theories; J. Gardner (2001) "Legal Positivism: 5½ Myths," 46 *American Journal of Jurisprudence*: 199; L. Green (2008) "Positivism and the Inseparability of Law and Morals," 83 *New York University Law Review*: 1035; A. Marmor (2006) "Legal Positivism: Still Descriptive and Morally Neutral," 26 *Oxford Journal of Legal Studies*: 683; A. Marmor (2011) *Philosophy of Law*, Princeton, Princeton University Press; L. Murphy (2008) "Better to See Law This Way," 83 *New York University Law Review*: 1088; J. Raz (2003) "About Morality and the Nature of Law," 48 *American Journal of Jurisprudence*: 1; S. Shapiro (2000) "Law, Morality and the Guidance of Conduct," 6 *Legal Theory*: 127; and S. Shapiro (2011) *Legality*, Cambridge, Mass.: The Belknap Press of Harvard University Press.

5

THE AUTHORITY OF LAW

Scott Hershovitz

A 30-ton statue looms over the steps that lead to the United States Supreme Court. A seated figure holds a tablet, and just behind that, a sword. The statue is called *Authority of Law*, but it is poorly named. It depicts a view of law's authority most closely associated with the nineteenth-century legal philosopher John Austin (1998: 14–18), who conceived of laws as orders backed by threats. Today, nearly no one holds Austin's view. To be sure, some laws are orders backed by threats, but that is not what is distinctive about law, and it is not what law's authority consists in.

Contrast a gunman who commands "your money or your life" with a police officer who shouts "stop or I'll shoot." Both issue orders backed by threats. But by virtue of her station the police officer's order carries an implication the gunman's does not. The police officer claims the *right* to demand that her subject stop, not just the *power* to make him do it. If the police officer has that right—she might not—her order obligates her subject to do as she says. Not so the gunman: his order does not even purport to obligate. He claims might, not right (Wolff 1998: 4).

Austin's problem was that he understood law on the model of the gunman, rather than on the model of the police officer. And that is the problem with the statue at the Supreme Court too. It depicts law's power. But it does not capture the element that distinguishes law from mere thuggery. It does not capture the fact that legal officials claim the right to issue orders, not just the power to enforce them. Of course, legal officials may not have authority to tell others what to do. They may just be thugs, issuing orders backed by threats. But they claim to be more. This chapter considers the nature of that claim and what we might learn about law from it.

The Paradox of the Just Law

Most philosophers hold that authority (of the practical sort) consists in a right to rule, such that subjects are obligated to obey. However, they disagree about whether the law ever has authority in this sense. Nearly no one thinks that law always has the authority it claims. For instance, almost no one thinks that people in unjust states have an obligation to obey the law, at least not a general one. But a longstanding puzzle known as the *paradox of the just law* aims to establish that there is no such obligation even in reasonably just states, on the ground that a just law could not have a claim on our obedience.

We can use laws that prohibit murder to illustrate the paradox. Murder is wrong quite apart from what the law has to say about it. Moreover, we expect people to refrain from murder because murder is wrong, not because the law prohibits it, and certainly not because the law punishes it. Indeed, it would be perverse to avoid murder on legal rather than moral grounds. This raises the possibility that we do not have an obligation to obey laws that prohibit murder. Perhaps stranger, the reason that we do not have that obligation is that we should *not* obey laws that prohibit murder. Joseph Raz explains the line of reasoning that leads to that conclusion as follows:

> The more just and valuable the law is . . . the more reason one has *to conform to it*, and the less *to obey it*. Since it is just, those considerations which establish its justice should be one's reasons for conforming with it, i.e., for acting as it requires. But in acting for these reasons one would not be obeying the law, one would not be conforming because that is what the law requires.
>
> (1994: 343–44)

If this argument establishes that we should not obey laws that are just, it also establishes that we do not have a general obligation to obey the law even in a reasonably just state. However, the first conclusion is the one of interest here, both because it seems paradoxical and because it poses a serious challenge to law's authority.

Raz (1994: 343) argues that the paradox is "merely apparent." He is willing to accept the conclusion that we do not have an obligation to obey laws that prohibit murder, but he says the paradox is overstated because it does not apply to all just laws. He observes that a legal prohibition may be just even though there is no independent moral prohibition on the conduct proscribed. Consider a city ordinance that restricts parking at certain hours so that streets may be cleaned. If it is important to clean the streets, and it is necessary to coordinate people's behavior to allow cleaning crews access, such a law may be just even though there would be no reason to avoid parking at the prohibited times in absence of the scheme. Here, we cannot say that one ought to avoid parking during restricted hours for the reason that parking at those times is wrong independent of the law. By hypothesis it is not. Yet, the paradox is still present here, at least in mild form, so long as the law is in fact just. Imagine a person who pronounces that, although she understands that she must cooperate if the parking restrictions are to succeed in coordinating behavior, she will avoid parking during restricted hours only because the law requires her to do so, not because doing so will aid the scheme. We would not think this person perverse, but we might think her obtuse. She implies that clean streets have no value, or that she has no role in securing them. But she is wrong, as those are the very considerations we are supposing justify the law. Here again it seems that when faced with a just law, one should act on the reasons that justify it, not simply obey it.

Now it should be obvious that the paradox only gets off the ground if acting on the reasons that justify a law is *not* a way of obeying it. So we must get clear about just what obedience to the law involves. Don Regan explains the standard view as follows:

> I cannot be said to obey a law in the fullest (and philosophically interesting) sense unless I do what I have been told to do *because I have been told to do it*. Consider an example. If a governmental authority commands me to avoid the use of cocaine, and if I subsequently avoid the use of cocaine, but for reasons which make no reference to the authority's command (I might even be a philosophical

anarchist and regard the command, in itself, as a reason *in favor of* using cocaine), then I do not obey the authority in any interesting sense. My behavior [conforms to the law], but I do not "obey."

(1990: 15)

It will help here to borrow a distinction from Raz (1999: 178–79), and stipulate that one *conforms* to an order if one does what it requires, whereas one *complies* with an order if one both conforms to it and takes the order as one's reason for action. Regan, then, tells us that in the fullest sense one obeys an order if, and only if, one complies with it.

If obedience to law means compliance with it—doing what the law requires *and* taking the law as one's reason for action—then there is little to be said in favor of obeying just laws. A morally decent person would no doubt conform her behavior to law on many occasions, but she would rarely if ever obey it. She would certainly not obey the core of the criminal law, and again that seems paradoxical, because one would think that if any laws are deserving of our obedience, it is those that prohibit grave offenses, like murder, rape and mayhem.

We seem to be stuck, but the way out of the paradox is as simple as the way in. The paradox only arises if acting for the reasons that justify the law is not a way of obeying it. The standard view identifies obedience with compliance, so that acting for the reasons that justify a law is not in fact a way of obeying it. But suppose we reject the standard view and identify obedience with conformity—with simply doing as the law requires whatever one's reasons. Then the paradox of the just law disappears. That murder is wrong is a reason not to murder *and* a reason to obey the legal prohibition on murder, for obedience now involves nothing more than not murdering. Indeed, the paradox is flipped on its head—the more justified a law is, the more justified we are in obeying it, which is a much happier state of affairs.

Now we face a choice. There are two ways to understand what obedience involves, one which leads to a paradox and one which does not. That alone might seem reason for preferring the second, but it is a weak reason at best. If the paradox of the just law is genuine, it is what Quine (1976: 1) called a *veridical paradox*—a "conclusion that at first sounds absurd but that has an argument to sustain it." It is not the kind of paradox that involves self-contradiction and therefore cannot be accepted. We should be open to the possibility that just laws have no claim on our obedience, and we should not define obedience down just to conclude otherwise. If we are to reject the paradox on the ground that the conception of obedience that underlies it is too demanding, we must have good reason for preferring a weaker one. Fortunately, we do.

Let us start with an observation: in the normal case one does all that the law requires if one acts as it demands, whatever one's reasons. The law certainly does not regard your behavior as defective if you refrain from murdering for the reason that murder is wrong. No prosecutor will investigate. No charges will be brought. No judge will take you to task for failing to pay proper heed to the law. We would have indeed a puzzle if the law prohibiting murder required that we have the prohibition as our reason for not murdering. Then it would be perverse to discharge the obligation the law purports to impose. But the law does not put us to the choice of failing to conform to its prohibition on murder or acting perversely. It asks only that we not murder, and it leaves the reasons up to us.

This is typical, but there are deviant cases. Sometimes an authority requires that one act as ordered *and* have the demand as one's reason for action. Military orders may have this structure. A sergeant may be keen to have a private do as she says, and for the reason that she said so. She may be justified in making such a demand if the lives of the soldiers in the patrol depend on the private following orders without taking time for reflection. In that situation, it would not be at all perverse for the private to do as the sergeant demands even though doing as the sergeant demands requires taking her demand as the reason for so doing. But situations like this are unusual. Most authoritative orders do not even implicitly specify the reasons for which one must act.

Now we can see the problem with the standard view. If we interpret an authority's right to obedience as a right to compliance, every authoritative order speaks to reasons as well as actions. The result is that many exercises of authority carry a demand which the authority itself has not seen fit to make. But that is bizarre. If the law does not care why people refrain from murder so long as they do, why should we insist that people subject to the law's authority are under an obligation to refrain from murdering for the reason that the law prohibits it? The concept of authority should not demand more than authorities do.

If we identify obedience with conformity, authorities are in the driver's seat. In the rare instance that they want compliance (and are justified in wanting it), they can leverage their right to conformity into a right to compliance. If an authority issues an order that requires subjects to take the order as their reason for action, anyone who conforms with the order will necessarily comply with the part of the order that specifies the action required. Suppose, for example, that a sergeant orders a private to clean a latrine and to do so for the reason that she said so. If the private is under a duty to conform to this order, then he is under a duty to comply with the part of the order that requires him to clean the latrines, as conforming to the entire order requires complying with that part of it. In the far more common case where an authority does not care why its subjects conform so long as they do, an authority can do just what it intends—issue an order that speaks to actions, not reasons.

The bottom line is that authorities are only in control of what they require if they have a right to have subjects conform to their orders. If, instead, they have a right to compliance, their orders will frequently demand more of subjects than intended. That is, I think, as compelling a reason as we could want for interpreting an authority's right to obedience as a right to conformity rather than compliance. It is a happy coincidence that doing so dissolves the paradox of the just law.

The argument to this point, however, might lead us to wonder whether there is a more direct route out of that paradox. Instead of departing from the standard view of obedience, we might depart from the standard analysis of authority. At the start, I said that most philosophers hold that authority consists in a right to rule, such that subjects are obligated to obey. But suppose we dropped obedience from the picture and held that authority consists in a right to rule, such that subjects are obligated to conform. This would have the same consequences as treating obedience as conformity; authorities would have control of the obligations they impose, and we would be free from the paradox. The paradox arises because of the conjunction of two views: (1) that authorities are entitled to obedience; and (2) that obedience entails compliance. So long as we deny one of these propositions, the paradox dissolves.

It does not matter whether we revise our analysis of authority or obedience, at least not for our purposes here. Which route we should take depends on which revision is more easily absorbed into our conceptual scheme, but we do not need to get bogged down with that question. The important point is that it is a mistake to hold both that authorities have a right to obedience and that obedience entails compliance. The conjunction of those views leads to a paradox. But more importantly, it misrepresents what those who assert authority typically claim they are owed.

It is an interesting question why the standard view of obedience is so strongly entrenched, notwithstanding the trouble it invites when joined to the standard analysis of authority. The answer may lie in a phrase which crops up repeatedly in discussions of authority. Let's call it the *because clause*. I've highlighted it here in a passage from Raz:

> Consider the case of two people who refer their dispute to an arbitrator. He has authority to settle the dispute for they have agreed to abide by his decision. . . . [T]he arbitrator's decision is for the disputants a reason for action. They ought to do as he says *because he says so*.
>
> (1990: 121, emphasis added)

Raz's suggestion—that a subject ought to do as an authority says *because the authority says so*—is so familiar a thought that it is easy to overlook the fact that the *because clause* is ambiguous. To see the ambiguity, we need to draw a distinction between the ground of an obligation and its content. The *content* of an obligation is the action (or inaction) that is required to discharge it. The *ground* of an obligation is the state of affairs in virtue of which the obligation exists. If I promise that I will meet you for lunch on Tuesday, the ground of my obligation is my promise, and the content of the obligation is to meet you for lunch on Tuesday. All authoritative obligations exist in virtue of an authoritative order, and hence have the same sort of ground, though they vary in their content.

With this distinction in mind, consider the following claim: " B is obligated not to murder *because the law prohibits it*." This sentence is ambiguous. On one reading it reports that the ground of B's obligation not to murder is that the law prohibits it. On another, it reports the content of B's obligation—B must not murder and B's reason for not murdering must be that the law prohibits it. We know from the discussion above that the law does not in fact impose an obligation to have as one's reason for not murdering the fact that the law prohibits it. So we can only make sense of the claim that B is obligated not to murder because the law prohibits it, if we see it as a report of the ground of B's obligation.

Later, we shall take up the question how the law's prohibition on murder could ground an obligation not to murder. Solving that puzzle will teach us a lot about law. The important point here, however, is that many philosophers flip the *because clause* around. They use it to report the content of the obligation to obey that an authority supposedly imposes, rather than its ground. Robert Paul Wolff writes: "Obedience is not a matter of doing what someone tells you to do. It is a matter of doing what he tells you to do *because he tells you to do it*" (1998: 9). Raz uses the phrase the same way when he says: "[I]n acting for [the reasons that establish that a law is just] one would not be obeying the law, one would not be conforming because that is what the law requires" (1994: 343). Wolff and Raz have good company; most philosophers who write about authority use the *because clause* this way. But this is a mistake. One is obligated to do as an authority says because the authority says so if one is talking about the ground of the obligation. But rarely, if ever, is the content of an authoritative obligation to do as the authority says because the authority says so.

Why is this mistake so common? I do not know, but I have a hypothesis. Often authorities demand more than that their subjects do as told; they demand respect as well. One way of respecting an authority is to act deferentially toward it. Doing as you have been told to do because you have been told to do it may signal trust in an authority, or appreciation for the role that it plays. Doing as an authority demands grudgingly signals just the opposite. The child who says, "I'll do it, but not because you told me to," challenges her parents' authority without defying their order. She could be reprimanded for insolence, but not disobedience.

Because an authority's demand for obedience is often accompanied by a demand for respect, it is easy to run them together and conclude that one only acts as an authority demands if one does what one has been told to do because one has been told to do it. However, there are two reasons to decouple the demand for obedience from the demand for respect, rather than treating them as a single demand for a robust form of obedience. First, not all authorities are owed respect. Good parents are, bad parents are not. To be sure, abusive or neglectful parents surrender their authority. But there is a middle ground. The hapless parent might surrender her claim to have her authority respected before she loses her right to obedience. Second, it is not always appropriate to show respect by acting deferentially. Even if the law is entitled to respect, it would be perverse to show it by refraining from murder for the reason that the law said so.

The fact that authorities are sometimes entitled to respect means that it will sometimes be appropriate to comply with an authority's orders. However, a claim to compliance cannot be constitutive of authority, as many authorities are not entitled to it. The right that is constitutive of authority is a right to have subjects do as one says, not a right to have them do as one says for the reason that one said so.

A Point About the Point of Authority

In the previous section, we deferred a question: how could the fact that the law prohibits murder ground an obligation not to murder? This is tantamount to asking how the law could possibly have the authority it claims. Up to this point, we have been analyzing the structure of authority. We have been trying to figure out what a claim to authority consists in. To explain how the law could ground an obligation not to murder, we need to turn our attention to the question of when a claim to authority is justified or legitimate.

The leading answer is provided by Raz's *normal justification thesis*, which says that one person has authority over another if following her orders would help her subject conform better to reason's requirements than he would if he decided what to do on his own (Raz 1994: 214). On Raz's view, authorities provide a service. They mediate between people and the reasons that apply to them. There are many ways an authority might help a subject conform to reason. An authority might provide epistemic guidance about what people ought to do if it can bring expertise to bear or make decisions free from bias. Or it might render inchoate obligations concrete, in the way that a taxation scheme makes it possible to discharge an obligation to support the provision of public goods. Or it might solve coordination problems, helping people to achieve things with others that they could not on their own (Raz 1986: 75).

I doubt that satisfaction of the normal justification thesis is either necessary or sufficient to establish authority, but I want to put my skepticism on hold for a moment to observe that it has a counterintuitive implication. The core of the criminal law does not reflect an exercise of legitimate authority, at least not with respect to most people subject to it. It is difficult to see how laws prohibiting murder, for example, would help people conform to reason better than they could on their own. They provide little in the way of epistemic guidance; nearly everyone already knows that murder is wrong, perhaps even most murderers. They do not render an inchoate obligation concrete; our obligation not to murder is already concrete. And they do not solve coordination problems; we can refrain from murder whether other people murder or not.

To be sure, laws that prohibit murder encourage people not to murder. After all, they threaten severe punishment, sometimes death. But the penalty does the work, not the prohibition. For the normal justification thesis to be satisfied, the order must provide the service, not the penalty for violating it. This is because the order and the penalty are severable. One could punish murder without prohibiting it (Raz 1994: 345). Even if the penalty helps people to do as they ought to do, it is hard to see how the prohibition does.

I am tempted to say that the conclusion that the law lacks the authority to prohibit murder is *reductio*. But that goes too far. Even if laws that prohibit murder do not give rise to moral obligations not to murder, everyone is already under a moral obligation not to do so. Therefore, even if Raz is right, we are not in a moral free-for-all.

Reductio or not, I think Raz is wrong to imply that the law generally lacks the authority to prohibit murder. To see how Raz goes astray, we need to return for a moment to our analysis of the structure of authority. We spent a lot of time considering the content of a subject's obligation to obey, but we have not analyzed an authority's right to rule, except to say that an authority has a claim on its subjects' obedience. The standard view is that an authority's right to rule consists in a power—not a physical power like a gunman's, but a normative power. Raz, for example, says that authorities have a normative power to change a subject's protected reasons, and by that he means, roughly, a power to obligate subjects to do as instructed (Hershovitz 2011: 10).

Raz is surely right to think that authorities have a normative power to obligate their subjects. However, it is important to see that the converse does not hold—the possession of a normative power to obligate does not entail that one has authority. Consider the following case. A married couple decides to see a financial planner because they do not have the expertise to plan for their retirement. Suppose that the situation is such that each spouse is obligated to the other to do as the financial planner instructs. This entails that the financial planner has a normative power over both members of the couple. His directions will obligate them to do as instructed. But the financial planner does not have authority over the couple because he has no claim on their obedience. He would have no cause for complaint if the wife ignored his instructions and booked a trip to Tahiti rather than increase her retirement savings. She is obligated to her husband, not the financial planner.

The standard analysis of an authority's right to rule as a normative power to obligate is incomplete. There are two ways we might refine it. The simplest solution is to add a qualifier and say that an authority's right to rule consists in a normative power to give others obligations *to oneself*. That would explain why the financial advisor does not have authority. But it seems rather ad hoc. I am inclined to construe the structure of authority differently. I think an authority's normative power to obligate is derivative of its right to rule, not constitutive of it.

On this approach, an authority's right to rule just is its claim on its subjects' obedience. This claim is of course imperfect, as there is nothing to obey until an order is issued. But the fact that it is imperfect explains an authority's power to obligate; the issuance of an order perfects the claim to obedience, giving it content that can be acted on. And it explains why the orders that an authority issues generate obligations that are owed to the authority; they perfect an obligation that is owed to the authority already.

This strikes me as the better rendering of the right to rule, but I will not insist on it here. For our purposes, it doesn't matter which option we choose, so long as we recognize that the end result of an exercise of authority is an obligation *owed to the authority.* Without an obligation so directed, there would be no sense in which an authority would have a claim on its subject's obedience.

Now we are in a position to explain how laws that prohibit murder could be legitimate, notwithstanding the fact that they do not help subjects conform to reason. If the law has authority, and it exercises it to prohibit murder, then the law has a claim on its subjects not to murder, and its subjects in turn owe the law (or, perhaps more idiomatically, the state) an obligation not to murder. The key here is that the moral obligation that the law creates, if it has legitimate authority, is different from the moral obligation not to murder that we have before the law comes on the scene. If that obligation is owed to anyone, it is presumably owed to the people we might harm by murdering—the victim certainly, but also his family and friends, among others. In contrast, the moral obligation the law creates is *owed to the law.*

This is no small thing. When you owe someone an obligation you are accountable to them. The person to whom the obligation is owed typically has the power to demand redress or dispense punishment if you do not discharge it. I said before that the law could punish murder even if it did not prohibit it. That is true, but it is not clear that the law would have the moral standing to do so. There are many moral transgressions that are none of the law's business. In some instances, this is because they lie beyond the proper scope of law's authority. In other cases, it is simply because the law has yet to prohibit them, and thus lacks the standing to respond to them. The point of prohibiting murder may be to confer on the law the moral standing to respond to murder, not to help people conform to their independent obligation not to murder.

I have a more capacious view than Raz of the ways in which authority might be justified. Elsewhere (Hershovitz 2011: 11–16), I have argued that the question whether one person has authority over another depends on whether (1) a morally permissible social practice assigns the first a right to rule and the second an obligation to obey; and either (2) the parties have chosen to participate in the practice; or (3) their participation is morally mandatory and for the authority (but not necessarily the subject) actual. A practice in which the law has the authority to prohibit murder will be valuable if it is desirable that we stand in a relationship of accountability to the state with respect to murder. Whether any actual legal practice is valuable such that participation is mandatory will, of course, be contingent on many facts about the law and the society it is situated in, so it is difficult to draw general conclusions. However, my intuition is that in most developed democracies, laws that prohibit murder reflect legitimate exercises of authority precisely because it is valuable for people to be accountable to one another through the state for serious moral transgressions of that sort.

Positivism and the Point of Authority

What we have learned about law and authority so far will help us evaluate one of the most celebrated arguments in jurisprudence—Joseph Raz's defense of exclusive legal positivism. Exclusive legal positivists hold that the content of the law must be determined exclusively by social facts, not moral facts. In contrast, both inclusive legal positivists and antipositivists think that moral facts may play a role in determining the content of the law. Indeed, some antipositivists take the view that the content is necessarily determined, in part, by facts about what it would be good for the content of the law to be. Raz's argument for exclusive legal positivism is grounded in his theory of authority, so it is a fitting final subject for an inquiry into the authority of law.

Raz (1994: 210–37) starts from the premise that law necessarily claims legitimate authority, whether or not it has it. Next, Raz suggests that the law's claim to authority may be false, but it cannot be conceptually confused. He says that the law must be the kind of thing that could be an authority, given that it claims it. Raz thinks that this entails that the law must have all the nonnormative attributes of authority. However, he builds his argument for positivism around a more modest claim, focusing on a particular attribute he thinks law must have. It must be possible, Raz says, to identify the content of the law without evaluating the reasons to which the law aims to help subjects conform. Were it otherwise, he argues, the law could not help subjects conform to reason better than they could on their own, and that is the role that an authority is supposed to play. Raz concludes from this that law must have only social sources.

Raz illustrates his argument with a story about two people who agree to abide by an arbitrator's decision:

> Suppose that an arbitrator, asked to decide what is fair in a situation, has given a correct decision. That is, suppose there is only one fair outcome and it was picked out by the arbitrator. Suppose that the parties to the dispute are told only that about his decision, i.e., that he gave the only correct decision. They will feel they know little more than they did before. They were given a uniquely identifying description of the decision and yet it is an entirely unhelpful description. If they could agree on what was fair they would not have needed an arbitrator in the first place. A decision is serviceable only if it can be identified by means other than the considerations the weight and outcome of which it was meant to settle.
>
> (1994: 219)

This story drives home Raz's point—an order that leaves one to figure things out for oneself is not particularly helpful. But there is something peculiar about it. The arbitrator does not have authority. He stands in the same relation to the parties that the financial planner did to his clients in the example we just considered. To be sure, his order obligates the parties to do as he says; after all, he is an arbitrator and not a mediator. However, the parties are obligated to each other, not to the arbitrator. The arbitrator has no special standing to reproach the parties or demand redress should they refuse to follow his decision. He has no claim on their obedience.

I do not want to make too much of this. Raz would no doubt disagree, as he views an authority's right to rule as a normative power to obligate, not as a claim on obedience. More importantly, Raz's argument has whatever force it has independent of the example he uses to illustrate it. Indeed, he might redeem the example by substituting a judge for the arbitrator. Still, I raise the issue because Raz's choice of example is instructive.

The trouble with Raz's argument is that he assumes that the point of authority is to provide a service—to help subjects conform to reason. If that were true, an arbitrator would indeed be paradigmatic of authority; when all goes well, an arbitrator helps identify a fair resolution to a dispute. However, in the last section we learned that the ability to help people conform to reason is not sufficient to establish authority. More importantly, we learned that an authority may be legitimate even if it does not help people conform to reason. The key was seeing that the end result of an exercise of authority is an obligation owed to the authority. That raised the possibility that sometimes the point of authority may be to establish that obligation, rather than help subjects conform to reason. If I am right to think that in some cases authority may be justified simply because it is valuable for one person to be able to create a relationship of accountability with another by issuing an order, then Raz's argument for exclusive legal positivism fails. The law may have authority even if it could not possibly help its subjects conform to reason.

Much of what the law does looks mysterious on Raz's picture. The core of the criminal law seems especially odd, as it tells people not to do things they already know they should not do. But some law is even less helpful than that. Often the law directs people to act reasonably but says nothing about what that involves. This would be inexplicable if the point of authority was to help people conform to reason better than they could on their own. But it is easy to understand why legal authorities would issue orders directing subjects to act reasonably. Sometimes it is worthwhile to create a relationship of accountability in respect of what morality already requires, but at the same time it may be unwise to try to pin down exactly what that is. A judge might, for example, order litigants to take reasonable measures to protect privileged information simply to establish that they owe an obligation to do so to the court, thus laying the predicate for contempt proceedings. But she may be reluctant to adjudicate in advance what is reasonable, perhaps because she thinks it will be too hard to anticipate all the relevant factors, or too time consuming, or because she thinks the litigants will come nearer to acting reasonably if her order is terse than they would if she spelled out rules which they could search for loopholes.

I do not doubt that in many circumstances the law aims to help subjects conform to reason. When it does, Raz's argument has some purchase. A law intended to solve a coordination problem had better be clear enough to coordinate action, so it would be unwise to leave the content of such a law contingent on contested claims of morality. But Raz does not aim to show that it must be possible to identify the content of some laws without reference to the reasons they are meant to settle. He argues that all law must meet that condition as a matter of conceptual necessity. Raz is wrong because authority has roles to play beyond helping subjects conform to reason. Morality can play a part in determining the content of the law without undermining law's claim to authority.

Conclusion

At the start, I complained that the statue at the Supreme Court is misnamed. Though it is called *Authority of Law*, it seems a better depiction of law's power than law's authority: the sword behind the tablet seems to invoke Austin's claim that laws are orders backed by threats. Though I think that is the most natural interpretation, the progress we have made toward understanding the nature of law's authority puts us in a position to offer an alternative, which might redeem the name that the statue's sculptor gave it. Instead of seeing the sword as a threat to punish people should they not follow the orders on the tablet, we might see the presence of the tablet as an effort to authorize the state to wield the sword. The statue then illustrates a central lesson of this chapter: often, the point of the law is not to tell people what they must do; rather, it is to render them accountable to the law for failing to do it.

References

Austin, J. (1998/1832) *The Province of Jurisprudence Determined*, Indianapolis: Hackett Publishing Company.

Hershovitz, S. (2011) "The Role of Authority," *Philosophers' Imprint* 11: 7.

Quine, W. V. (1976) *The Ways of Paradox and Other Essays*, Cambridge, Mass.: Harvard University Press.

Raz, J. (1986) *The Morality of Freedom*, Oxford: Oxford University Press.

—— (1990) "Authority and Justification," in J. Raz, ed., *Authority*, New York: New York University Press, pp. 115–41.

—— (1994) *Ethics in the Public Domain*, Oxford: Oxford University Press.

—— (1999) *Practical Reasons and Norms*, 2nd edition, Oxford: Oxford University Press.

Regan, D. (1990) "Reasons, Authority, and the Meaning of 'Obey': Further Thoughts on Raz and Obedience to Law," *Canadian Journal of Law & Jurisprudence* 3: 3–28.

Wolff, R. P. (1998) *In Defense of Anarchism*, Berkeley, CA: University of California Press.

Further Reading

For further reading, see: L. Green (1988) *The Authority of the State*, Oxford: Clarendon Press; D. Regan (1989) "Authority and Value: Reflections on Raz's Morality of Freedom," *Southern California Law Review* 62: 995–1095; J. Raz, ed. (1990) *Authority*, New York: New York University Press; and S. Shapiro (2002) "Authority," in J. Coleman and S. Shapiro, eds., *The Oxford Handbook of Jurisprudence and the Philosophy of Law*, Oxford: Oxford University Press.

6

OBLIGATIONS, INTERPRETIVISM AND THE LEGAL POINT OF VIEW

Nicos Stavropoulos

The Legal Significance of Politics

Some political action is legally relevant: it has an impact on the law, roughly defined as the change in legal rights and obligations (powers, privileges, immunities or liabilities) that obtains, without further political action, as a result of some such action. All legally relevant action taken together constitutes legal practice. Politics plausibly includes much more than action that has an impact on legal rights and obligations, and one of the tasks of legal theory is to specify which kinds of action are legally relevant and what it is, exactly, for such action to have impact on the law. Even if we confine our attention to standard examples—enacting statutes, adopting regulations, deciding cases—some hard philosophical questions arise. What precise aspect of this kind of action is legally relevant? Why so—what gives a given aspect of institutional action legal relevance?

On a version of legal positivism that I shall call the orthodox view, the legally relevant aspects of institutional practice do not include any substantive normative facts such as facts about what is right or good or valuable or what we have reason to do or want or believe. (For convenience, I will call facts other than substantive normative facts "nonnormative." As I will be using those terms, that people ought to have a chance to participate in political decision-making, if true, is a (substantive) normative fact. By contrast, that someone asserts or believes or has some other attitude towards the claim that people ought to participate in that way, or that "democracy" means the rule of the people, are all, if true, examples of nonnormative facts.)

On the orthodox view, institutions shape the law by communication. The fact that a certain statute was enacted and what its text means together explain the impact of its enactment on the law. What the text of a statute says, including what it logically entails, corresponds to one or more new norms that the statute created or determines the extent to which its enactment modified preexisting norms. The law is the set of norms produced in that way (perhaps together with some norms implicitly endorsed by institutions in their settled practice).

On some competing views, institutional communication is only part of the explanation. The law further includes norms that justify institutionally produced norms, or excludes institutionally produced norms that fall below some threshold of decency. On such views, it is not true that history and language alone explain the legal impact of institutional action. Substantive normative considerations, plausibly narrowly moral ones (facts about what we owe to each other), are part of the explanation.

Confining our attention to the way in which these two kinds of view differ, however, is misleading. This is but one way in which the orthodox view contrasts with alternatives regarding the question of whether substantive normative considerations must figure in the explanation of the legal impact of politics. There are other, more fundamental ways. Suppose a theory agrees with the orthodox view that the only thing that matters to the legal impact of an enactment is what the enacted text means, but adds that that is so because government is morally bound to give citizens fair notice of how it plans to treat them. Legal rights and obligations are only those announced by institutions, because government would otherwise wrong its citizens. On this view, the complete explanation of the legal impact of politics includes reference to moral considerations. But the place of those considerations in the explanation is more basic. Morality, on this view, does not directly determine legal impact. It explains why the other, nonnormative, aspects of political action have legal relevance.

The more fundamental controversy brings into play the often overlooked second of the questions identified above, of what gives legal relevance to certain aspects of the practice. It concerns the place, in the complete explanation of the legal impact of politics, of a substantive normative explanation of why certain aspects of the practice should have the relevance that the theory assigns to them. This issue will be my focus in this essay.

The orthodox view has it that the explanation must begin in nonnormative elucidation of what is legally significant in legal practice and why, by the lights of the practice itself. From that "legal point of view" we notice that the practice assigns to some aspects of itself—institutional directives—a certain kind of binding force. The unqualified normative question of why those parts of the practice should have the contemplated role comes last, and concerns whether the law in fact has the force it claims for itself—whether the law so understood ought to be obeyed. Interpretivism, by contrast, begins by rejecting the claim that nonnormative elucidation of the point of view of the practice determines the correct explanation of the legal relevance of institutional practice. Rather, the explanation of how legal practice matters to legal rights and obligations is an ordinary explanation of the normative effects of action by appeal to the substantive normative considerations that give it that role. For interpretivism, the unqualified question of why legal practice matters must come first. If the orthodoxy is right on that matter, interpretivism cannot get started.

The existence of this fundamental controversy undermines the significance of a familiar argument offered in support of the orthodox view and against its competitors. It is a familiar orthodox thesis that the law claims authority. For the law to claim authority is for law-shaping institutional action to have a certain logic, namely to assign to itself the characteristic role of authoritative directive in the practical reasoning of subjects. An authority directs others to take action for the reason that the authority so directed—because it said so. It therefore guides action by means of replacing by authoritative directive the reasons that apply to subjects independently of the directive. Legal institutions claim authority in that they purport to regulate domains of action by their directives, so it must be at least on the cards that their directives might play the practical role just described. But institutional directives wouldn't even be eligible candidates for that role if, of necessity, legal rights and obligations were determined even in part by substantive considerations of the sort that the directives were meant to replace—e.g., by the moral principles that governed the relevant domain of action. So theories that make the identification of law dependent on substantive normative considerations of that kind are untenable because they contradict the very logic of legally relevant institutional action.

This argument from law's claim to authority presupposes that the fundamental controversy between the orthodox approach and interpretivism has been resolved in favor of the orthodoxy. But if it has, it's over for interpretivism. The argument from the claim to authority is redundant.

The Normative Significance of Action: The Formal Approach

The fundamental controversy with which I am concerned also arises in connection with the explanation of some other phenomena, including making a promise, decision or request—actions or attitudes which are generally understood to result in some distinctive obligations or to have some other distinctive normative significance or impact, or at least to be capable of so doing. The relevant theoretical choices are posed particularly clearly in these domains, so I will explore them in some detail in relation to promising.

The first issue, which arises in all these cases, concerns the choice between two approaches to the explanation of how a given kind of normatively significant action produces its distinctive normative effects. On the first, *formal* approach, each kind of such action has its own characteristic logic. Investigation of the logic of the action is nonnormative in character. Taking promising as a familiar example, this investigation tells us how the action looks from the inside. This is not empirical investigation of the psychology of promisors, but conceptual reflection about what it is to take such action, in terms of the attitudes the action implies (which may diverge, at least in certain ways, from those that actually obtain). It explores promising from the perspective of the agent, explaining what it is to occupy that position and to take the action in question. The availability of this perspective allows the theorist to avoid substance. He can set out to describe, not what genuinely matters in the action of promising and therefore what explains why it should normally result in obligations on the part of promisors, but rather, suspending judgment, describe how the action presents itself, including what normative relevance the action, broadly understood to include the attitudes that it implies, assigns to itself. This is not to say that the explanation is merely epistemic, aiming only to describe how promising looks. Rather, it aims to define the subject matter of promising—what promising is and how it works—by appeal to our conceptual scheme, our shared understanding of promising. To do so, it must make explicit the criteria we generally follow, usually unreflectively, in making judgments and drawing inferences that involve the concept of promising; or to articulate the conception that we implicitly possess, which guides such judgments and inferences. This is only a rough characterization of the task. There is much controversy as to what exactly conceptual analysis consists in. Typically, analysis is presented as an explanation of what is implied in saying "I promise to f." But the word "promise" is not essential, and arguably analysis has further tools in addition to reflection about the meaning of characteristic utterances through which one promises, e.g., investigation of common reactions to hypotheticals that involve the concept of promising. (Would we say that an act of assuring others that one will take some action in the future, which failed to induce expectation of performance, binds as a promise? How about an assurance given without an intention to perform? And so on.) One thing seems clear: analysis must aim to derive the complete explanation of its target concept from convergence in the applications, judgments and inferences that competent speakers or thinkers are disposed to make or draw. A theorist who defends some analysis must think that the analysis is made true by these considerations, even though he needn't interrogate actual speakers in order to construct it.

Promising, it is generally agreed, is action that normally results in the promisor being under an obligation to perform another action. The complete explanation of that phenomenon, running from the promising act to the obligation, must include an account of what precise action the promisor becomes obligated to perform; of what it is about the action of promising that has that effect—what is the aspect of the action that is relevant to the production of the obligation; and why—what makes that aspect relevant. You say to your friend Peter: "I will read your draft and send comments by Friday; I promise." Suppose that several things are true at the time. You firmly intend to do what you said you will do and you mean to convey that fact. You also understand that Peter wants assurance that you will read the draft and send the comments, you aim to give him such assurance and you approve of him counting on that assurance in making further plans. All of that matches Peter's understanding of the situation. You also intend that you come to be under an obligation to do what you said you will do regardless of the assurance sought and given, the expectations you believe Peter would be justified in forming and the prospects of his making plans on that basis. You take yourself to have come under an obligation, namely to read the draft and send Peter the comments, just by saying that you will do so. There is a small discrepancy, however, between each party's understanding of what you've committed to do. You take yourself to have committed to sending comments at any time Friday—by midnight, at the latest—whereas he takes you to have conveyed that you commit to send the comments by close of business. This is only a small sample of colorable candidates for some role in the explanation of your coming to be under some determinate obligation by virtue of your speaking as you did. At first sight, any of the candidates might be relevant. Which, if any, are in fact relevant? What makes them relevant?

It is an essential part of the formal approach that nonnormative reflection on the common understanding of the concept of promising can answer all questions such as these to which an answer exists; as for those it can't, they admit of no determinate answer. A prominent example is provided by Raz (1972, 1977, 1978). On Raz's view, conceptual reflection shows that someone who understands what promising is, and acts sincerely, promises when he conveys an intention to undertake, by the very act of conveying that intention, an obligation to perform some other action, namely the action the agent said he will take. This means that the act of promising as such consists in the conveying of the intention just described. Other candidate attitudes or other factors—e.g., the intention to give assurance, the fact that the recipient sought such assurance and so on—may be present in standard examples but are ultimately irrelevant. The key factor, the conveying of an intention to be bound by that very act, entails that the promisor regards his own action, itself, as a new reason for the other action (Raz 1978: 137). It entails that the promisor wants to direct his own future action by his say-so.

This explanation implies a principle to which promisors are tacitly committed, which, if valid, would give the act of promising as explained (conveying the intention just described) the contemplated normative significance (the role of an obligation to perform). (On a social-practice version of this claim, the principle is a social norm that promisors accept and expect others to follow when they promise.) It is important to be clear on the relation between the attitudes and the standard in play, specifically regarding what explains what. The view in discussion is that the attitudes explain the standard, not the other way around. It's not a standard, otherwise constituted, against which a promisor's attitudes are assessed (or else the theory could not confine itself to elucidating others' attitudes, as opposed to critically assessing them). Rather, the standard is what it is in virtue of the attitudes, which therefore cannot correct them. The standard is to be extrapolated from the attitudes. It's because promisors have a certain intention or expectation or consider something or other relevant that they follow a standard on which those considerations are relevant to promissory obligation.

This nonnormative part of the explanation anticipates and shapes the second, normative part. The nonnormative part entails how things must be if an act of communication, assumed to be successful as such, is to achieve its intended normative effects, i.e., if the obligations that it was intended to produce *in the specified way* are actually to obtain. Only at this point are we able to move to the second stage of the complete explanation of promising, where we consider whether things *are* so, and therefore whether promising does impose on promisors the obligations they purport to assume. The second stage is substantively normative in character. We consider at this stage whether promises so understood ought to be kept. To continue with the example, this is to investigate whether the conditions, under which people would get to place themselves under obligations by conveying an intention thereby to do so, actually obtain. In this part, we would be looking to justify the principle to which promisors are tacitly committed. We would do so if we could establish that it is good in some specific way that people should get the power to bind themselves by their say-so under those conditions. It is only at this stage that we consider the question of why promises (understood as the conveying of the intention described earlier) should matter, as a question about their genuine normative relevance.

The formal approach naturally splits the explanation of promising into two parts: the first, nonnormative part concerning what force promisors mean to secure for their action and therefore the conditions under which they might succeed in securing it; and the second, normative part concerning the question of whether they do so succeed. Obviously, success is narrowly defined. Promisors succeed only when, as a result of their action, an obligation to perform comes about in the way they aimed at, as that is explained by the formal part of the account.

This means that the formal approach presents to normative scrutiny a package of candidate obligations, whose existence and content depend only on the considerations identified by nonnormative analysis—on Raz's suggestion, on a promisor's linguistic action alone. Promissory obligations so defined would obtain if substantive normative considerations ratified the package as is. This would be to assign to promisors normative powers to bind themselves by their say-so (Raz 1977). The only other alternative is to reject the package altogether. It is conceivable that promising might never succeed: it might turn out that the normative power it presupposes does not really exist. If so, we would have discovered that promissory obligation does not exist.

This view need not deny that promising may have, perhaps often or even always, *further* normative effects including obligations, by virtue of other considerations that give the act that role (for example, because the act normally induces expectations on the part of promisees that it would be wrong to frustrate). But these effects would be irrelevant side effects, not the effects of promising as such. That may also be the case with someone who uses the language of promising while his actual attitudes fail to conform to the analysis. On this view, analysis presents, as essential to promissory obligation, the specific intention, not merely to come under an obligation but to do so just because of the act of conveying the intention; in other words a claim of a power to bind oneself by one's say-so. Absent the claim, the action would not count as promising and therefore distinctively promissory obligation could not obtain.

The Normative Significance of Action: The Substantive Approach

The other, *substantive* approach, does not expect to find defining conditions in convergent applications, judgments or dispositions to draw inferences. It treats standard examples of promising, understood to include colorable candidates for some role in the explanation of promissory obligation, and intuitions about the act's binding nature, only as a starting point. It then asks a substantive normative question: what is it about these paradigm acts and surrounding attitudes that might make it the case that the acts produce obligations?

Importantly, this approach need not deny that people have intuitions, not only to the effect that promising binds, but also specifically about *how* promising binds (what aspect of promising, broadly understood, is relevant to the explanation of how the act produces obligations and why). However, and even on the assumption that there is a unique pattern of such intuitions shared among competent users of the concept of promising, the approach treats them as hypotheses, which theory checks and may correct, rather than as constraints that theory must respect on pain of changing the subject.

The substantive approach then proceeds by starting at a rough and provisional demarcation of the territory of promising by way of examples and platitudes, and then looks for some normatively interesting feature of that territory that might explain—substantively, rather than from any point of view—why promising should have force. In such an approach, the substantive normative question of why promising should obligate calls the shots: it determines how promising obligates, if it does—what the truly relevant factors are—and therefore the content of the obligation. (If what's relevant is inducing expectations, for example, the promissory obligation as such may not extend to acts that the recipient did not come to expect the promisor to perform.) This is in contrast with the formal approach which, as we already saw, purports to select the relevant factors in the act and therefore the content of the obligation the act is supposed to produce on the basis of our shared conception of how promising works, when it does, and addresses the (substantive) normative question only after matters of relevance and content are settled.

Thomas Scanlon's suggestion, that breaking a promise or making a lying promise is an instance of a familiar moral wrong, is an example of an explanation by appeal to some morally interesting feature of contexts of promising (Scanlon 1998: 296). Broadly understood, Scanlon's suggestion is that a certain moral concern, namely of wronging people by leading them to form expectations that one plans or proceeds to frustrate, is an essential part of the explanation of how promising may create obligations to perform. This concern derives from a fundamental moral constraint on action. Roughly, this requires that actions that might affect the interests of others be brought under principles that are acceptable to them, in some specified sense. This abstract constraint gives general moral relevance to acts of promising. When one promises, this fundamental requirement is triggered. As a consequence, what one may or must now do is governed by certain principles that can be justified to others, and ultimately by the reasons that provide such justification, i.e., the reasons others have to accept them (or not to reject them, provided they aim for principles that are acceptable in that way). Principles so constituted determine why, and how exactly, promising can generate obligations: the principles give certain aspects of promising that kind of normative significance and so explain why those aspects play a particular role in placing the promisor under an obligation.

It's worth noting that Scanlon does not doubt that there exists some conventional promising norm that people accept and expect others to uphold. He thinks that something else—the considerations just sketched—explains promissory obligation regardless. His proposal is *not* that there is some *other* source of obligation that also happens to obtain in much the same circumstances as those governed by the conventional norm.

On Scanlon's account, an intention to become obligated (in *some or other*, or some *particular* way) may normally obtain but is not fundamentally relevant. What matters is that promising normally knowingly creates an expectation in a situation in which the promisor ought to believe that the promisee wants assurance and understands the promisor to be intending to provide it (Scanlon 2004: 244–45).

Procuring Obligations: Two Routes

On Scanlon's substantive account, the reason that results from your telling Peter that you promise to read his draft is given by your circumstances, as these have changed as a result of your action, such that you would now wrong Peter by failing to perform. On Raz's formal account, the reason, if it obtains, is given by the act itself: the fact that you told Peter that you promise to read the draft.

On both accounts, we must appeal to the act of promising in explanation of the existence of the key reason (if it obtains). But, on the former account, the act makes it the case that the reason obtains indirectly, via making it the case that the act changes the promisor's circumstances in normatively important ways, which then constitute the reason to perform. On the latter account, the obtaining of the act directly makes it the case that the reason obtains. This important distinction, due to Greenberg (2011—who develops it in connection with legal obligation), has more general application, allowing us to distinguish between direct and indirect ways in which some normatively significant action makes it the case that a certain normative effect comes into being. An explanation is direct when the obtaining of the action (in this case, saying "I promise to f," or making some equivalent linguistic production), directly explains the obtaining of its effects (in this case, the reason to perform). It is indirect when the act explains something else, which then explains the obtaining of the effect.

The formal approach gives a way to defend explanatory directness. It defends the conclusion that the reason to perform, if it obtains in the right way, i.e., as a result of promising as such, is given by the act of saying "I promise to f" (or equivalent), by citing the fact that we directly infer the existence of the reason from the existence of the act (cf. Raz 1986: 38, on directly inferring the existence of an obligation from the existence of an authoritative directive). The formal approach interprets this as evidence of a commitment, built into the common conception of promising, that the reason to perform is meant to be constituted by the act, so understood, itself. The act implies an intention to bypass any effects the act may have on circumstances (other than the effect of adding itself to the circumstances) and establish an obligation directly. Promisors claim power to create a reason to perform by their say-so. These considerations entail, on this approach, that the act of promising, as such, results in the "right kind" of reason only if the reason is directly explained by the act. The formal approach therefore relies on an inferential link between the act and the reason to establish an explanatory link between them. The substantive approach, on the other hand, is compatible with the existence of certain inferential links, but is not defended on these grounds.

Common Conceptions

We can distinguish three claims about the concept of promising included in the formal account. First, that there exists some common conception of promising. Second, that the common conception includes clauses about how promising works. Third, that the common conception defines the subject matter of promissory obligation.

There are powerful reasons against this combination of claims. To get started, the substantive approach must reject, at a minimum, the combination of the first and third of these claims. It can do so either by denying that a common conception exists; or by denying that a common conception, on the hypothesis that one exists—and whether or not it includes a clause about how promising works—defines the subject matter. This entails that a theory that takes the substantive approach might succeed in spite of con-tradicting the common conception.

How could theory share some subject matter with ordinary thinkers and speakers, even as it purports to correct them individually or even collectively? Wouldn't the revi-sionary character of some theory rather entail that the theory and ordinary folk talk past each other? I will make some brief comments on this profound and highly controversial issue. I will then offer some reasons for rejecting the three claims mentioned above. An adequate treatment is well beyond the limits of this discussion (see Stavropoulos 1996, 2001 and forthcoming for a discussion of some of the main issues in more detail).

It is now a familiar point that sharing a subject matter is *easy*. Two parties can disagree about some object, including its nature, by finding *some* common ground, e.g., by shar-ing some distinguishing properties or examples (those not in dispute). Disagreement is premised on understanding that is good enough for competence, not complete under-standing. But competence is easy. In fact, no truth seems so central to understanding sufficient for competence that no one who understands the sentence that expresses it can coherently reject it—as long as one could offer some exotic theory under which the sentence expresses a falsity (Burge 1991 makes the point in respect of "sofas are pieces of furniture meant for sitting"; Williamson 2007 in respect of "every vixen is a vixen").

In addition, there needn't be any unique conception that tacitly guides talking and thinking about some object. The implicit conceptions that exist need not contain any defining conditions, and might in fact contradict fundamental clauses in such condi-tions. This applies not only to individual tacit conceptions, but even to those that are constructs of (some specification of) communal use. The ancients collectively thought, after all, that stars were holes in the sky and the medievals thought that influenza was a kind of adverse astral influence that affected large numbers of people.

The fact that imperfect understanding and deviant theory are possible implies that the actual record of implicit conceptions will tend to be nonuniform and must anyway be considered unreliable. We couldn't appeal to that record in defense of our account of a concept. Nor could we appeal to the common ground among all such conceptions.

The content of the common ground is arbitrary, contingent on what actual conceptions happen to be around. Besides, different overlapping conceptions will have common ground which, by every conception's lights, misidentifies the phenomenon.

It is sometimes said that what enables different conceptions to lock onto the same objective phenomenon is that they include a tacit provision for deference. Where deference exists, however, it need not be to others, e.g., the experts or the community at large. Experts can also get things wrong—ancient star experts surely did. Must we assume that experts (and through them ordinary thinkers) defer to some future experts such that the current expert conception may lock on to a phenomenon regardless of any mistakes it might contain? If so, what is the theoretical significance of such an assumption? Clearly our crediting someone with a concept does not depend on assuming that he is disposed to defer to anyone (see Peacocke 1998, who credits Newton and Leibniz with the concept of a limit in spite of accepting that these characters were not disposed to defer to anyone and that their own understanding of the concept of a limit, on the assumption that that was the concept they struggled to define, was seriously defective). And experts often disagree with each other—which one of the plausible candidates might I be deferring to, in my no doubt badly flawed thinking about subjects such as justice? And of course the same difficulties appear even if we substitute the entire community for experts. It's more plausible to suppose that implicit conceptions, at least as concerns certain explanatorily interesting concepts, are postulary in character, deferring in a manner of speaking only, albeit to how things really are:

> Thinkers postulate that there is some phenomenon that happens to play (most of) the explanatory roles that interest them, whose nature would be provided by some optimal theory of the phenomenon. After all, we all know that our grip on optimal theories, and the definitions they may provide, is hampered by our accidental evidential relation to the world, and by the difficulties in actually thinking through the demands such a theory might impose.
>
> (Rey 1998: 98)

On this view, thinkers may have individual pet theories about the relevant phenomena. But the fact that they tend to be prepared, at least sometimes, to stand corrected in light of better theories, and to revise their own accordingly, suggests that they hold those theories under a postulary proviso: what thinkers are committed to is the correct explanation, not the one they currently hold to be correct.

All this suggests that, even if we can extrapolate some unique tacit conception of what promises are and, in particular, how they work, from common attitudes, judgments and inferences, the conception is not privileged but instead occupies the same space and competes with substantive normative theories about which aspects of promising are relevant to its role as a source of obligation. If so, there is no space for theory that avoids substance.

Familiar Attitudes and the Correct Explanation

The formal approach to the explanation of promising supposes that there exists some determinate and complete common tacit conception. The version defended by Raz supposes that it includes a clause that discriminates between the action's having such an effect on a promisor's other circumstances that the promisor comes to have an obligation (the indirect route, in the terms introduced above), and the action's being itself the reason to perform (the direct route).

I suggest that such discrimination is too demanding to be part of a common conception of promising. Besides, even if it's not unreasonably demanding, chances are we are likely to find evidence of both sides of the distinction in common reflection—some of us might come out proto-Razians, the rest proto-Scanlonians in our thoughts about promising.

We have already seen that the formal approach appeals to the inference that thinkers tend to make from an act of promising to promissory obligation. We can now see that such inferences are compatible with different explanations. Suppose that ordinary thinkers appeal to the fact of a promise, understood as a linguistic act, in explanation of the promisor being under an obligation to perform. But there is an important distinction between appealing to the linguistic act as an economical way of appealing to the existence of some or other mechanism in which the act figures (after all, one needn't be able readily to produce such an explanation, even as one is confident that some exists), and appealing to it because one thinks that it's the only factor relevant to the obligation it results in. The former implies commitment to the existence of *some* perhaps highly complex mechanism that gives promising its normative effects, analogous to an appeal to the fact that the Fed took action to raise interest rates in explanation of a drop in stock prices. An appeal to the promise, on this alternative, is compatible with thinking e.g., that, once one promised, fairness requires that one perform. The latter kind of appeal, by contrast, entails commitment to a *particular* mechanism. The absence of some agreed upon, complex explanation in ordinary reflection, combined with a shared sense that the linguistic act belongs in the explanatory chain, is not equivalent to a positive judgment that complex alternatives are ineligible. It is compatible with being open minded about how promising works. Other things being equal, promising does result in obligation—recall that on the substantive conception, powerful moral reasons see to it—and this is good enough support of an inference. It may be that the promise is indeed the only relevant factor. But if so, it wouldn't be simply because everyone appealed to it.

One may be convinced, nonetheless, that we all tacitly assume the direct explanation of promissory obligation. It would still not follow that we should continue to do so. Suppose it's part of the common conception that promisors do not merely try to procure an obligation, but that they have a view on how that works, namely that the obligation is directly produced by their action, and they mean to procure it in that way. It would still not follow from the fact that an explanation tracked the common conception that we were not dealing with a case of medieval influenza. The indirect explanation of the sort that Scanlon offers might play the role of modern medicine, allowing us better to understand how promising really works.

In addition, there is another equally fundamental problem with defending the direct route by appeal to our common conception. As I have already suggested, conceptions do not possess, as such, explanatory privilege, and the same holds for the attitudes that may make them up. I earlier stipulated that, when you told Peter that you would read the draft and send comments, you had several distinct attitudes, including one about which of these attitudes counts. You intended that you acquire an obligation to read and send comments by virtue of the act of conveying that intention. Why should it matter that you have that special intention? We would need some theory, defended on grounds other than your attitudes, that showed what role each of your attitudes properly has. We could not refer that issue back to your attitudes, whose relevance is at stake. (A limited version of that argument, regarding the role of different legislative attitudes in statutory interpretation, appears in Dworkin 1986: 313–54; how could an intention that some intention or other attitude count in interpreting a statute settle the question of which if any of these attitudes matters in that way? A general version of this argument, as it concerns the relevance of different candidate aspects of legal practice to the content of the law, appears in Greenberg 2004—who credits Hurley 1989 and traces the fundamental form of the argument to Kripke 1982.)

To be clear, the point is not that the attitudes involved in an act of promising are not relevant. Of course they are. That you intend to bind yourself, if you do, that Peter has reason to expect that you will deliver—that you considered, approved and encouraged him to do so—these are all very plausible candidates for a role in the explanation of how it is that you now have reason to perform. The point is that the attitudes can't determine their own relevance. We must appeal to something outside the nexus of attitudes in order to settle that matter.

The Production of Legal Obligation: The Orthodox View

The formal view of promising asserts that the correct explanation of the production of promissory obligation is implicit in our shared understanding of promising. It asserts that the logic of the promising act determines how the act of promising, as such, may produce an obligation on the part of the agent. The orthodox view of law holds the same for legal obligation. It asserts that the logic of institutional action such as an enactment, as that is revealed in our tacitly shared understanding of law, determines how the enactment, as such, may produce an obligation on the part of others.

On the orthodox account, legal obligation is explained by reference to a set of norms. Norms are rules that mandate or permit some action. According to the most influential account, developed in its strongest form by Joseph Raz, political institutions create a norm that belongs to the set by issuing a directive (Raz 1990). That is an act of communication—typically the production of a text such as a statute that canonically formulates a political decision—which is addressed to certain subjects and meant to direct the subjects' action. When an institution issues a directive, subjects are meant to take the stipulated action because the institution said so. From the perspective of the institution that issued it, a directive always has the force of a binding order that subjects are meant to obey, and brings into existence a norm, namely that subjects ought to take the action the institution said they should take. The fact that the institution issued a directive which it regards as a binding order settles the directive's legal relevance: it matters to the law as an institutionally valid norm. It settles, at the same time, the terms in which the further question of the directive's genuine normative relevance must be posed. This becomes the question of whether the directives work as advertised, i.e., whether they truly create norms—norms that are valid simpliciter, not merely institutionally—and therefore whether subjects do acquire an obligation to take some action because the relevant institution said so.

This brief sketch of the orthodox view contains several related controversial ideas. First, it says that law-shaping institutional action is (at least primarily) communication. Such communication has a distinctive logic, the analysis of which gives us access to the perspective of the institutions whose action shapes the law, and therefore of the law. Examination of the institutional perspective is nonnormative, even as it reveals that, from that perspective, institutional action is normatively significant—that an assembly regards its enactment of a statute as an action that changes people's obligations. We can notice how the action matters in the eyes of the assembly without thereby committing to whether it does matter in that way.

The second central idea is that of institutional validity. Institutional validity of a norm includes the property of its having a source, its having been produced by institutional communication and of its possessing, from the institutional perspective, binding force. A legal obligation exists only in case a norm that imposes it can be traced to institutional communication. A norm can be so traced when its content has been conveyed by an institution's production of an edict. For an institution to regard its edicts as binding norms is for the institution to regard its own action, its having conveyed the content of the norm, as having a certain kind of impact on addressees' (genuine) reasons for action.

It's not enough that institutions regard their own action as having some determinate normative impact, namely that the people to whom their directive is addressed come to have a reason to take the stipulated action. Institutions do not merely purport to direct others' action, i.e., intentionally to change reasons. They could do that by acting to change the addressees' situations in such a way that now, as a result of the action, the addressees come to have a reason to do that which they were directed to do. (In this case the obligation would be *indirectly* explained by institutional action.) Instead, institutions must regard their having directed certain people to take some action to be *itself* the addressees' new reason (therefore regard the obligation as *directly* explained by their action). This means that when an institution issues a directive, it must be understood not merely to convey an intention that subjects come to have a new reason for action—namely a reason to do that which they were directed to do—but rather to convey an intention that subjects acquire *by that very act* a reason to take the action.

A distinction between conveying an intention that others' reasons be changed and conveying an intention thereby to place others under an obligation is central to Raz's thesis that legal institutions claim authority. To claim authority is to claim something stronger than claiming to be in a position to impose obligations deliberately and with justification (which is merely to claim that one can get people to have a reason to act in some way). Institutions ask subjects to submit their action to the institutions' choices, not to the effects of these choices on subjects' circumstances. To claim authority, Raz thinks, is to claim that subjects have reason to submit their action to the putative authority's will.

These results, which the orthodox conception purports to derive through reflection on the logic of institutional communication, set the agenda for the normative part of the account. That consists in investigating whether the conditions, under which legal institutions would possess the claimed powers to change subjects' obligations in the special way mentioned, are met. The justification of legal obligation, therefore, would have to be indirect, relative to the action one is obligated to take: it would be justification of obedience to authority. If obedience were justified, it would follow that one would have reason to take the action that the authority directed one to take, for the reason that the authority so directed.

The third main idea, then, is that the moral problem that law presents is the problem of (legitimate) authority. What makes this the law's characteristic moral problem is the law's claim. (Brute power, understood as control over others' action without the claim, could never lead to the powerful being legitimate.) So the complete orthodox account pairs an explanation of the grounds of legal obligation that appeals to the existence of legal directives with an explanation of the moral problem of the directives' playing the grounding role. But what matters is the order of explanation: the moral problem of authoritative guidance is germane only because analysis of our common conception of law has shown it to be germane.

The Interpretivist Alternative

A hybrid version of interpretivism constitutes one way of being unorthodox. It begins at institutionally valid norms understood in the orthodox way. It then compares that set with a set of genuinely valid norms, namely certain moral principles. It finally adjusts the set of institutional norms to bring its content closer in some specified way to the content of the set of principles, and holds the outcome of the process to be the final set of legally valid norms. This hybrid view is weak for a number of reasons and is not anyway a genuinely interpretivist view (Stavropoulos 2014 explains why it is weak). As we have seen, interpretivism explains the legal relevance of institutional action in terms of its moral relevance. It doesn't take it to be a basic nonnormative fact about law that institutional action has legal relevance (let alone that some nonnormative aspects of such action constitute norms that are to be critically assessed at a later stage).

Plain (non-hybrid) interpretivism proceeds differently. It focuses on a moral concern that makes institutional practice morally relevant in some characteristic way. According to the best known version of interpretivism, the concern is raised by institutions' effective power to use force or otherwise coercively to direct citizens' action (Dworkin 1986).

A general version of this concern is raised by political association, and is familiar from certain conceptions of (socioeconomic) justice (the most prominent example is Rawls 1971; see also Nagel 1991 and 2005 for discussion). This is the relation between members of a political community, roughly defined in terms of coercive control over some population. On this view, certain kinds of action of people so associated are governed by strong egalitarian principles that require that action of that kind be justified in a way that treats everyone's life as equally important. These principles set constraints on the proper design of certain social institutions (for Rawls, those that form the "basic structure").

According to the version of interpretivism in discussion, political association raises another, more specialized concern: this is to do with coercively enforcing demands against individuals. The hypothesis central to this view is that legality is a constraint that regulates such action. It requires that government use its power coercively to enforce a claim against some citizen only when the claim is properly grounded, in some specified sense, in its own past action—in institutional practice. A claim that meets this condition is a lawful claim whose holder is entitled (has a right in law) to ask government to back the claim with its force and those against whom the claim is held must (are under an obligation in law to) conform.

On this view, legality regulates and is a response to a moral concern that arises out of government's ability to use force to get people to do things. Specific interpretivist hypotheses are built on specific explanations of what legality brings to this concern: explanations of why, exactly, tying claims to institutional practice should help make it permissible to enforce them, and of the precise way in which a claim must be thus tied in order that this result be achieved.

Unsurprisingly, specifying in detail what it is for a claim to be properly grounded in past action by way of showing the grounding relation to be dictated by some conception of legality is a complex affair. But for current purposes we needn't do so (see Dworkin 1986 for more detail; cf. Stavropoulos 2014). What matters is that, for the intepretivist, the morality of coercive enforcement gives certain aspects of institutional practice special moral relevance. The fundamental idea is that institutions lay down by their action conditions of enforceability to which they can be held. Government would wrong people if it failed to stand by its own decisions that set out what rights and obligations people have, for reasons of democracy where these apply. It would also wrong people if it frustrated the expectations they were led to form based on its announcements regarding how they are going to be treated, or if it failed to treat like alike in its practice of enforcement. Reasons of various kinds, including reasons of procedural justice (or fairness) and even-handedness, conspire to make how government may use its force now depend on what it said and what it did so far.

Stepping back from the details, for the interpretivist, the role of institutional action as a determinant of legal obligation is explained by some distinctive political virtue that is realized or some purpose that is served by institutional action's having that role. Thus, the legal relevance of institutional practice is derivative from the moral relevance of some of its aspects to the problem of coercive enforcement. Interpretivism is premised, therefore, on the rejection of the view that an explanation of legal obligation must confine itself to the advertised moral relevance of institutional action, as that is specified in some shared conception of law. The explanation that it offers is substantive and indirect.

The Law's Claim to Authority and Source-Based Standards

Raz says that law's characteristic claim to authority shapes—constitutes in part—our concept of authority: authority is the sort of thing that law claims to possess. It follows that law's claim can fail in certain ways only. The law may always fail to have authority, but must be the sort of thing, descriptively understood, that could play the role of authority. Authority guides action by directive, which is communication of one's judgment about how others have reason to act. Authority can only guide action if the existence and content of its directives can be identified by reference to facts alone, without recourse to evaluative considerations, or else the subject would not be guided by the authority's own judgment about what the subject ought to do. The law's claim to authority therefore entails that the law consists of directives that meet this condition (Raz 1994).

There is a way to understand the conclusion that makes the reasoning that precedes it irrelevant. A directive is a linguistic object and its production is an act of communication. Someone issues a directive by making an utterance or producing a text addressed to a given audience. The existence and content of a directive, like any episode of communication, depends on whether some nonnormative facts obtain: whether someone spoke or wrote, and what he thereby said. If it's accepted that the law is constituted by directives, it has been accepted that the law is determined by descriptive facts. What is the point of the argument from the claim to authority?

A somewhat different possibility is that Raz has in mind views on which the law is a composite system of norms. The system includes 1) the norms constituted by directives actually issued by institutions, and 2) the norms (or other sort of standard; I will omit the qualification hereafter) constituted by some hypothetical directives that we must impute to the authority and therefore treat as if they had been so issued. These are directives implied by the actual directives together with some further premises. One example might be hypothetical directives meant to regulate the application of substantive moral clauses in certain actual directives. Another example might be hypothetical directives, whose issuing would be justified, individually or collectively, by the reasons that justify issuing some or all actual directives.

Unlike actual directives, the existence and content of these kinds of hypothetical directive depend in part on substantive normative facts. The first possibility corresponds to an inclusive positivist view. Suppose that a directive stipulates that unfair agreements shall not be enforced. On this view, the actual directive, which includes reference to a moral test, makes considerations of fairness part of the law, and that claim can be represented as the claim that the existence of the original directive entails the existence of a further directive that sets out the substantive moral considerations that make an agreement unfair—and that both directives constitute valid legal norms.

The second possibility corresponds to a hybrid interpretivist view. On this view, the law includes 1) the set of norms constituted by actual directives as well as 2) the set constituted by certain nonactual directives, which simultaneously achieves maximal coherence with the actual set as well as substantive moral merit.

Against such views, it makes sense to argue in the way Raz does. If the law claims authority, we shouldn't enrich the sources of valid norms by adding to actual directives hypothetical directives that the former imply in some specified way. We must think of the law as based on what institutions have actually said, rather than based on what they have said together with what they should or would have said, given what they did say and certain other conditions. Authority can make the difference it's supposed to make only by actually speaking. And that is exactly the way that Raz argues in his article (see in particular Raz 1994, where he explicitly formulates his claims in terms of the reasons that establish that an institution ought to have issued a directive (220); his characterization of inclusive positivism in terms of incorporation, and of interpretivism in terms of coherence (305–15); and his formulation of the dispute as one regarding whether the (source-based) law can be "enriched" by non-source-based standards (296)).

None of this is relevant to the controversy of which interpretivism represents one side. No argument from law's claim to *authority* can engage that view, let alone show it to be flawed. Interpretivism directly contradicts the view that the law makes claims (of authority or anything else) that define the subject matter of legal obligation and therefore denies that the explanation of legal obligation must be such as to make it possible for the claims to be true. The debate must focus on the more fundamental issue: does the law make claims—of authority or anything else—that define the subject matter? If it makes such claims, then it's over for interpretivism.

The Attitudes Implicit in Official Action

Let us consider, then, the thesis that the law claims authority, for the purpose of deciding that fundamental question. Our discussion of promising gives us a preview of how an interpretivist may respond to the thesis.

We often appeal to some specific institutional action, e.g., an Act of Parliament, in explanation of how it is that we are under some legal obligation. This habit may be parlayed by the orthodox view into a tacit conception that includes a disposition to draw direct inferences from a directive to a norm that mandates some action, and therefore includes a clause of direct explanation of legal obligation by the existence of directives. But what we said in respect to promising applies here too. These inferences are compatible with a variety of views as to how institutional action achieves its law-shaping effect, as well as with not having any view on the matter. And even if the inferences uniquely entailed commitment to a certain mechanism, which was thereby built into a common conception of law, it wouldn't follow that that part of the conception were not a flawed hypothesis about how politics works, a hangover from a time when it was thought that the will of kings created reasons by divine delegation (perhaps not coincidentally, a time when influenza was thought to be some astral influence).

It may be said that what matters for philosophical explanation of legal obligation is the attitude of agents who take action in the name of institutions—judges resolving disputes, parliaments enacting statutes—which is implied by their language. That attitude is as a conceptual matter the attitude of authority—the intention to create obligations by their very act—even if, after hours, the agents declare that their action has no moral force, or that its force is explained by factors further to the act's obtaining (e.g., by the fact that the relevant institutions are democratically constituted, or by reasons of fairness) (see Gardner 2012 for discussion).

But what applies to after-hours reflection applies to any attitudes implied in the language of official action. The implication that institutional action has moral force is compatible with a variety of explanations of the source of this force. And even if a specific explanation of that source is uniquely picked out by the implied attitudes of official action, it needn't be the correct one. The attitudes are not privileged. They are finally relevant to the explanation of legal obligation only insofar as, and in the way in which, some consideration other than the attitudes gives them relevance.

Acknowledgments

I was greatly helped by conversations with Mark Greenberg, A. J. Julius, Stephen Neale and David Plunkett on an earlier draft. I am grateful to Andrei Marmor for written comments; to participants at the Philosophy Colloquium, CUNY Graduate Center; and to participants at the Legal Theory Workshop at the UCLA Law School, where David Plunkett gave prepared comments.

References

Burge, T. (1991) "Intellectual Norms and Foundations of Mind," *Journal of Philosophy* 83: 697–720.

Dworkin, R. (1986) *Law's Empire*, Cambridge, Mass.: Harvard University Press.

Gardner, J. (2012) "How Law Claims What Law Claims," in M. Klatt, ed., *Institutional Reason: The Jurisprudence of Robert Alexy*, Oxford: Oxford University Press.

Greenberg, M. (2004) "How Facts Make Law," *Legal Theory* 10: 157–98.

—— (2011) "The Standard Picture and Its Discontents," in L. Green and B. Leiter, eds., *Oxford Studies in Philosophy of Law, Volume 1*, New York: Oxford University Press, pp. 39–106.

Hurley, S. (1989) *Natural Reasons*, New York, Oxford University Press.

Kripke, S. (1982) *Wittgenstein on Rules and Private Language*, Cambridge, Mass.: Harvard University Press.

Nagel, T. (1991) *Equality and Partiality*, Oxford: Oxford University Press.

—— (2005) "The Problem of Global Justice," *Philosophy and Public Affairs* 33: 113–47.

Peacocke, C. (1998) "Implicit Conceptions, Understanding, and Rationality," *Philosophical Issues* 9: 43–88.

Rawls, J. (1971) *A Theory of Justice* (original edition), Cambridge, Mass.: Harvard University Press.

Raz, J. (1972) "Voluntary Obligations and Normative Powers," *Proceedings of the Aristotelian Society, Supplementary Volumes* 46: 79–102.

—— (1977) "Promises and Obligations," in P. M. S. Hacker and J. Raz., eds., *Law, Morality and Society: Essays in Honour of H. L. A. Hart*, Oxford: Clarendon Press.

—— (1978) "Reasons for Action, Decisions, and Norms," in J. Raz, ed., *Practical Reasoning*, Oxford: Oxford University Press.

—— (1986) *The Morality of Freedom*, New York: Oxford University Press.

—— (1990) *Practical Reason and Norms* (reprinted with new postscript), Princeton: Princeton University Press.

—— (1994) "Authority, Law and Morality," in J. Raz, *Ethics in the Public Domain*, Oxford: Clarendon Press.

Rey, G. (1998) "What Implicit Conceptions Are Unlikely to Do," *Philosophical Issues* 9: 93–104.

Scanlon, T. (1998) *What We Owe to Each Other*, Cambridge, Mass.: Harvard University Press.

—— (2004) "Reasons: A Puzzling Duality?" in R. J. Wallace, P. Pettit, S. Scheffler and M. Smith, eds., *Reasons and Value: Themes from the Moral Philosophy of Joseph Raz*, Oxford, Clarendon Press, pp. 231–46.

Stavropoulos, N. (1996) *Objectivity in Law*, Oxford: Clarendon Press.

—— (2001) "Hart's Semantics," in J. Coleman, ed., *Hart's Postscript*, Oxford: Oxford University Press, pp. 59–98.

—— (2014) "Legal Interpretivism," in E. N. Zalta, ed., *The Stanford Encyclopedia of Philosophy* (Summer 2014 edition), http://plato.stanford.edu/archives/sum2014/entries/law-interpretivist

—— (forthcoming) "Kripke and the Law," *Ration Juris*.

Williamson, T. (2007) "Epistemological Conceptions of Analyticity," in T. Williamson, *The Philosophy of Philosophy*, Oxford: Blackwell, pp. 73–133.

Further Reading

For further reading, see: R. Dworkin (2006) *Justice in Robes*, Cambridge, Mass.: Harvard University Press; G. Rey (1983) "Concepts and Stereotypes," *Cognition* 15: 237–62; N. Stavropoulos (2009) "The Relevance of Coercion: Some Preliminaries," *Ratio Juris* 22: 339–58.

Part II

LEGAL REASONING

7

VAGUENESS AND THE LAW

Scott Soames

We all know that much in our thought and language, as well as much in the law, is vague. We are also reasonably good at recognizing cases of vagueness, even though most of us would be hard pressed to say exactly what vagueness is. In recent decades, there has been a flowering of work in the philosophy of logic and language attempting to do just that. Much of this work focuses on what it is for a word or phrase to be vague. The aim of this effort is to clarify what it is for a claim, question, command or promise expressed using such a term to be vague, as well as what it is to reason with such terms. Different logico-linguistic theories have different conceptions of the scope of putative laws of classical logic, including bivalence (which states that every declarative sentence or proposition is either true or false) and excluded middle (which asserts all instances of "A *or* ~A"). In addition to this work in philosophical logic, recent decades have seen a growing interest in vagueness among legal scholars and philosophers of law. Here the focus is not so much on what legal vagueness is, which is generally assumed to be readily recognizable. Rather, it is on the extent and sources of vagueness in the law, the implications of vagueness for interpretation and adjudication, the systemic effects of vagueness and the function—i.e., important positive value—of vagueness in certain areas of the law, as opposed to its disutility in others (Endicott 2000, 2005; Soames 2011).

To date, these two investigations of vagueness—in philosophical logic and the philosophy of law—have been largely independent of one another. This independence gives rise to a natural line of questioning. Can work in one domain contribute to work in the other? Does a commitment to one philosophical theory of what vagueness is carry with it lessons for vagueness in the law? If so, might the need to make good sense of legal vagueness play a role in deciding which philosophical theory of vagueness is correct? Conversely, might one be misled about the pros and cons of vagueness in the law by a faulty conception of what vagueness is? These are the questions to be investigated here. This will be done by comparing two leading philosophical accounts of vagueness and exploring their implications for understanding the value of vagueness in the law and the issues at stake in interpreting vague legal texts.

Vagueness and Borderline Cases

In ordinary life, a remark is often considered vague if the information it provides is insufficiently specific to advance the accepted conversational purpose (especially when the speaker is expected to possess that information). Philosophical logicians have focused on one particularly interesting sub-case—involving the notion of *a borderline case*—of this more general phenomenon. Vague predicates—like "old," "bald," "rich" and "red"—are those for which a range of borderline cases separate things to which the predicate clearly applies from those to which it clearly does not apply. These are cases in which there is no clear answer to the question of whether a predicate is, or is not, true of an object. In such cases, we are pulled in both directions—being inclined to resist definitive verdicts in favor of equivocal remarks like "It sort of is and sort of isn't," "It's not clearly one or the other" or "Call it what you like, but neither choice is definitely correct." In some contexts it may be acceptable to treat the predicate as applying, while in others it may be fine to treat it as not applying. But no investigation into the facts in virtue of which the predicate means what it does could ever identify one of these uses as definitely correct and the other as incorrect. In situations that call for a verdict, this means that a decision is required that is not dictated by knowledge of the nonlinguistic facts under discussion plus the linguistic rules governing vague terms. This is the sense in which "philosophical vagueness"—susceptibility to borderline cases—is an instance of ordinary vagueness: insufficient informativeness (Soames 2011). If a theater director's assistant has been told to cast a bald character and the chief candidate for the role is a borderline case of baldness, the director's request plus the assistant's knowledge of the candidate are insufficiently informative to determine whether or not to offer the role. Some further basis for decision is needed.

Two Philosophical Theories of Vagueness

According to one theory, vague predicates are both partially defined and context sensitive. To say that P is partially defined is to say that it is governed by linguistic rules that provide sufficient conditions for P to apply to an object and sufficient conditions for P not to apply, but no conditions that are both individually sufficient and disjunctively necessary for P to apply or not to apply. Because the conditions are mutually exclusive, but not exhaustive, there are objects not covered by the rules for which P is *undefined*. In the case of vagueness, this, in turn, gives rise to context sensitivity. Since the rules of the common language, plus all relevant nonlinguistic facts, don't determine P-verdicts for every object, speakers using P in certain contexts have the discretion of extending its range to include some initially undefined cases, depending on their conversational purposes. Often they do so by predicating P of an object o, or denying such a predication. When they do, and other conversational participants accommodate their conversational move, the class of things to which P does, or doesn't, apply is contextually adjusted to include o, plus objects similar to o (in certain respects). In such cases, P is (partly) "precisified" by narrowing the range of items for which P is undefined (Tappendon 1993; Soames 1999, ch. 7; Endicott 2000; Shapiro 2006).

Since what counts as a rule of the language (governing the use of a particular predicate) is also vague, higher-order vagueness arises when one considers the predicate ⌐is determinately P⌐, where for o to be determinately *so-and-so* is for the claim that o is *so-and-so* to be a necessary consequence of the rules of the language governing "so-and-so" plus the (relevant) nonlinguistic facts about o. Because of this, the range of application for an ordinary vague predicate P can be divided into five regions as follows:

Table 7.1

P	?	Undefined	?	Not P
$R1_{PDP}$	$R2_{PDP}$	$R3_{PDP}$	$R4_{PDP}$	$R5_{PDP}$

Let "red" be P. Items in $R1_{PDP}$ are determinately red, items in $R3_{PDP}$–$R5_{PDP}$ are not determinately red and it is unsettled whether items in $R_{PDP}2$ are determinately red or undefined for "red." Similar characterizations hold for "not red," working from $R5_{PDP}$ and moving left. Iterating "determinately" doesn't change things (Soames 2003).

Next consider the proposition p expressed by "It's red" relative to an assignment of o as referent of "it" and a context C including a set of standards governing "red." We are *not* here considering the proposition *asserted* by an agent who utters "It's red" in C, referring to o. The issue is semantic (the proposition semantically expressed relative to a context and an assignment), not pragmatic (the proposition asserted by an utterance). If, given C's standards for "red," o is in $R1_{PDP}$ ($R5_{PDP}$), then p is true (not true) in C; if o is in $R3_{PDP}$, p is undefined for truth in C. ("False" and "not true" are interchangeable when applied to propositions.) If o is in $R2_{PDP}$, it is unsettled whether p is true or undefined in C; if o is in $R4_{PDP}$, it is unsettled whether p is not true or undefined. When a proposition p is not true, it is a mistake to assert p, but it may be correct to deny p—i.e., to assert its negation. However, when p is undefined for truth, it is a mistake to either assert or deny p because neither p nor its negation can be *known* to be true (Soames 2010). When it is unsettled whether p is true or undefined it is unsettled whether one who accepts it has made a mistake.

Now consider the related case in which an agent A says "It's red" of o in a context in which the standards governing "red" *prior* to A's utterance place o in regions 2 or 3, but the audience *accommodates* A by adjusting the contextual standards to render A's remark true. In such a case the proposition q that A uses "It's red" to assert is different from the proposition p that the sentence semantically expresses, relative to the context and prior to accommodation (plus an assignment of o as referent of "it"). After accommodation, the partially defined property contributed by "red" to the asserted proposition has o in its region 1. If o was in region 3 originally, A's remark will be *true by stipulation*, in the sense that it is only because A's sentence has been taken to assert q, rather than p, that A's remark counts as true. By contrast, if o had been in region 2 by previous standards, A's remark will again be judged true, but this time it will be unsettled whether it is true *by stipulation*, because it will be unsettled whether the proposition p that A's utterance would have asserted without accommodation is itself true. These instances of smooth accommodation contrast with an attempt to extend the extension of "red" to an item x in region 4 prior to A's remark. In such a case, A's remark will be problematic and may not be accommodated, since prior to A's utterance it was unsettled whether o was undefined for "red" (and so open for inclusion under the predicate) or definitely not red (and so outside the range of legitimate speaker discretion).

That, in a nutshell, is one philosophical theory of vagueness. Another important theory is the epistemic theory, according to which vague predicates are always totally defined, with sharp boundaries separating items to which they apply from those to which they don't—e.g., a single second separating moments when one is young from those when one is not, and a single penny separating one who is rich from one who is not. Borderline cases are those of which we can never *know* the vague predicate P to be true, or to be untrue of a given item. So, whereas the previous theory takes borderline cases to be those for which P is undefined, the epistemic theory takes them to be cases for which one can never know how, in fact, P is defined (Williamson 1994). Here I will be concerned with the standard version of epistemicism, which does not take vague terms to be context sensitive, as opposed to the version in Fara (2000), which does.

According to this theory, bivalence and the law of the excluded middle hold without exception, even for sentences containing vague language. Sorites paradoxes are blocked by denying the major premise of paradoxical arguments like the following:

Minor: A newborn baby is young at the moment of birth.

Major: For every number n, if one who is precisely n seconds old is young, then one who is n + 1 seconds old is also young.

Conclusion: Everyone is young.

Whereas the previous theory of vagueness rejects the major premise while also rejecting its negation (since both are undefined), epistemicism claims the major premise to be false and its negation to be true, which it asserts:

~ Major: There is a number of seconds n such that anyone who is precisely n seconds old is young, but anyone who is n + 1 seconds old is not young.

What epistemicism doesn't do is *identify* any number n as the number in question. Unlike still another theory—supervaluationism about vagueness (Fine 1975)—which also preserves the law of the excluded middle, and asserts (~ Major), epistemicism acknowledges every instance of the quantified major premise to be either true or false, despite the fact that some of the truths are unknowable.

Higher-order vagueness arises for the epistemicist when one considers the predicates ⌜is an object that can be known to be P⌝ and ⌜is an object that can be known not to be P⌝ . When P is vague in the epistemicist's sense, these predicates are also vague. This means that although both predicates are totally defined, and although there are sharp lines separating things to which they apply from things to which they do not, the precise location of these lines is unknowable. Thus, the range of application of P can be divided into four regions as follows:

Table 7.2

P & so knowable	P but unknowable	Not P but not so knowable	Not P & so knowable
$R1_E$	$R2_E$	$R3_E$	$R4_E$

Let "red" be P. Items in $R1_E$ are red and can be known to be so; those in $R2_E$ are also red, but cannot be known to be red. Similarly, items in $R4_E$ are not red, and can be known not to be, while those in $R3_E$ are not red but cannot be so known. Since the norm of assertion is knowledge (Williamson 1996), this means that to assert of an item x in $R2_E$–$R4_E$ that "It is red," as well as to assert of an item y in R_E1–R_E3 that "It is not red" is to violate the norms governing our linguistic practices, and so to make a kind of mistake. Of course, some of these mistakes are worse than others since when x is in $R_E 3$–$R_E 4$, and y is in $R_E 1$–$R_E 2$, what one asserts is also false (in addition to being unknowable). However, all are violations.

This creates a prima facie difficulty. Together, epistemicism plus the view that knowledge is the norm of assertion direct us not to assertively predicate either a vague predicate P, or its negation, of any item in its unknowable range $R2_E$–$R3_E$. In many conversational settings this is unproblematic, since there is often no need to provide definite P-verdicts for particular borderline cases. In some settings, no judgment whatsoever is required, while in others a hedged judgment—e.g., ⌜That may be P⌝, ⌜That is probably P⌝, ⌜That is unlikely to be P⌝—will do. However, if there are situations that do require definite P-verdicts, such hedges will not serve. In these cases, the demand for an unequivocal verdict conflicts with the epistemic theory of vagueness plus the conception of knowledge as the norm of assertion. Since there appear to be legal contexts of this sort, they may provide good test cases for evaluating the dispute between the epistemicism and other theories of vagueness.

Vagueness in the Law

Since vagueness in the law comes in different forms with different consequences, some preliminary distinctions are needed to narrow our focus. Three domains of legal vagueness are particularly important: vagueness in the content of the law, vagueness in the allowable evidence and prescribed procedures used in reaching a legal verdict, and vagueness in the enforcement or effect of the laws. A good example of the latter is the enforcement of the 65 miles per hour speed limit on freeways in southern California. Though the content of the law is precise, the practice of enforcing it includes a range of speeds of roughly 66–70 miles per hour at which whether or not one is stopped is (under normal conditions) a matter of substantial discretion on the part of the highway patrol. The effect is to create a range of borderline cases in which it is vague whether, and to what extent, drivers are in legal jeopardy. This sort of vagueness—which has no effect on the content of the law—is valuable and necessary both to allow law-abiding citizens a reasonable margin for error in their attempts to comply with the law, and to allocate the resources of law enforcement and the judiciary reasonably and efficiently.

Vagueness in allowable evidence and prescribed procedures for reaching legally definitive verdicts is different. The standards "preponderance of evidence" and "guilt beyond a reasonable doubt" used in different types of cases are examples of vagueness encoded in legal language that govern the process of reaching a verdict. The exclusionary rule in the United States—which excludes evidence obtained from an illegal arrest, an unreasonable search or a coercive interrogation (as well as secondary evidence obtained by routes not sufficiently distinguishable from primary evidence so obtained)—is an example of vagueness encoded in authoritative legal texts, including prominent Supreme Court opinions. This type of vagueness can be treated as a sub-case of vagueness of content in which the legal provisions are those governing the conduct of trials and other legal proceedings.

I here assume that the content of a law or set of laws is (to a first approximation) that which the appropriate lawmakers assert, stipulate or prescribe by adopting authoritative legal texts (against the interpretive background provided by already existing laws). I will refer to the contents of these authoritative speech acts as "assertive or stipulative contents," without here going into further detail about the relationship these contents bear to the semantic contents of the sentences used to make the assertions or stipulations (Soames 2009, 2011). Lawmakers are assumed to include legislators enacting statutes, administrative bodies authorized to issue binding rules implementing statutes, ratifiers of constitutions, voters on ballot initiatives and judges issuing precedent-setting opinions. In the sphere of "private law," lawmakers may also include the parties of a contract, those responsible for legislation regulating the general law of contracts, and judges as well as other judicial bodies adjudicating disputes in this area.

Given this conception of legal content, we can discern two different ways in which vagueness in the content of the law may arise. First, and most obviously, a law may be vague because the authoritative text used by lawmakers to enact it contains vague terms. When this is so, the assertive or stipulative contents of the lawmakers' authoritative speech acts will typically be vague, and so will be ripe for interpretation. The need for such interpretation often arises in legal proceedings in which reaching a verdict requires making an unequivocal decision about the application or nonapplication of a vague predicate P, used to express the relevant law or laws, to a borderline case of P.

The second main way in which vagueness of legal content can arise is through the resolution of contradictions generated by different laws, or provisions of the same law, taken in conjunction with the facts of a particular case (Soames 2011). In these cases, contradictory legal conclusions are derivable from the facts of the case plus different but equally authoritative pre-existing legal contents. This glut of legal results is unacceptable, and so produces what is in effect a gap in the law that must be filled by modifying the content of the relevant laws. Often, if there is one way of filling this gap, there are many among which the relevant judicial authority must choose. Although the basis for this choice may vary from one legal system to the next, I will here confine attention to systems governed by the following norm, RJ (Role of the Judiciary):

> RJ. Courts are not to legislate, but to apply the laws adopted by legislative authorities to the facts of particular cases. When the content of the relevant body of laws plus the facts of a case fail to determine a unique legal outcome in situations in which one is required, the task of the judicial authority is (i) to discern the predominant legislative rationales of the lawmaking bodies in adopting the relevant laws and (ii) to fashion the minimal modification of existing legal content that removes the deficiency and allows a decision to be reached that maximizes the fulfillment of those legislative rationales.

Here, in speaking of the rationale of a law or other legal provision we do *not* mean the mix of causally efficacious factors that motivated lawmakers to adopt it, but the chief reasons publicly offered to justify and explain it (Soames 2011, section 7). Though these reasons are often discernable, what counts as "the predominant legislative rationale," "a minimal modification removing the deficiency" and "a modification that maximizes the fulfillment of the discernable legislative rationales" is vague, and so subject to interpretation. Understood in this way, the judicial resolution of legal conflicts can be seen as a sub-case of the precisification of vague language, even though the language in question is not limited to that of the authoritative texts, or to legal language in general.

Vagueness in the Law: The Partial Definition-Context-Sensitive Model

In the simplest case, vagueness in the content of the law arises when lawmakers employ a vague term in adopting an authoritative legal text. On the theory of vagueness under consideration, they may be understood as using the term either with its default content (provided by the rules governing its use in the common language) or with a partially precisified content. In the former case, the application of the law to items for which the term is undefined is left indeterminate, and subject to future precisification by other authorities. In the latter case, lawmakers narrow the range of future interpretation by stipulating in advance how the law is to be applied to certain borderline cases. For example, lawmakers adopting H. L. A. Hart's ordinance (Hart 1958) banning "vehicles" from the parks might respond to lobbying on behalf of the disabled by adding a clause "for the purpose of this ordinance, wheelchairs for the disabled, whether motorized or not, shall *not* count as vehicles." In such cases, the extension of ⌜legally P⌝ is a partial precisification of the ordinary extension of P.

What should be done in interpreting a legal text when it emerges that the verdict in a case crucially depends on whether or not P applies to a given item for which P, as used by the lawmakers, is undefined? In some special cases, it may be possible to send the matter back to them for clarification and precisification. In others, a rule of lenity may dictate favorable verdicts for defendants in situations in which no clear violation is established—where one form of exonerating unclarity involves indeterminacy in the law. But in many cases neither of these exceptions apply, with the result that judges, or other authorities, are expected to fill gaps by precisifying the governing legal provision in a manner not determined, and sometimes not even envisioned, by the lawmaking body. When the relevant judicial decision sets a legal precedent for similar cases, the result is not just an explication, clarification or application of existing law, but an (authorized) modification of the law. Whereas prior to the decision, the law was undefined for, and so silent about, a certain class of cases, it now declares them to have one status or another.

This can be made clearer by considering again the range of a vague predicate P.

Table 7.3

P	?	Undefined	?	Not P
$R1_{PDP}$	$R2_{PDP}$	$R3_{PDP}$	$R4_{PDP}$	$R5_{PDP}$

When the item x on which the outcome of the legal case depends is in $R2_{PDP}$ or $R4_{PDP}$, and there are no other complicating factors, it is relatively easy to specify what the outcome should be. If x is in $R2_{PDP}$, and the judge assigns x a certain legal status L+ on the basis of ruling that x counts as an instance of P, it will be unsettled whether x was already in the extension of P or whether the judge has exercised the minimum possible discretion. By contrast, if the judge rules that x does not count as an instance of P, and thereby assigns x legal status L−, it will be unsettled whether the judge has violated the existing law or whether maximal discretion has been exercised. When there are no extraneous issues pulling in either direction, and including x in the extension of P complies with the rationale of the law, such a decision is clearly called for. This will result in the minimum possible change in the law—a class of things for which it had been legally unsettled whether they were L+ or indeterminate in status, have now become determinately L+. Analogous results hold when x is in $R4_{PDP}$ and is assigned the legal status L−.

When x is in $R3_{PDP}$ the situation is different. Since P is undefined for x, there is a gap in the content of existing law rendering it silent about the status of x. Since the resolution of the case depends on giving it a status, the judge has no alternative but to make new law. Here, our assumption RJ about the role of the judiciary plays an important role. Returning to Hart's no-vehicles-in-the-park example, we may imagine two scenarios providing the rationale for the city ordinance. In scenario 1, the ordinance was passed to preserve the traditional peace and quiet of the park, which had recently been disturbed by cars, motorcycles and motor scooters, and also to reduce air pollution in the city, which had grown worse in recent years. In scenario 2, the ordinance was a response to overcrowding in the park resulting in a number of accidents involving cars, motorcycles and bicycles, all competing for limited space with pedestrians crowding paths, walkways and roads in the park. Although the content of the law passed in these two scenarios is the same—in both cases simply banning vehicles from the park—the implications for future precisification are different. Against the background of scenario 1, judgments that, for purposes of the ordinance, bicycles, skateboards, rollerblades, tricycles and little red wagons are not vehicles, are correct. Against the background of scenario 2, at least some of these judgments are not. This difference has nothing to do with which borderline cases of being a vehicle are more like genuine, known vehicles, and which are more like known non-vehicles. Since, on the view of vagueness under consideration, there simply is no fact of the matter about whether these borderline cases (in $R3_{PDP}$) are, or are not, vehicles, the court's inquiry must be directed toward other matters—which in a legal system featuring RJ is the rationale for the legislation. Once such a precedent-setting judicial decision has been reached, the content of the law will change, bringing its content more fully into line with its original rationale.

It is here that we find the value of vagueness in the contents of laws. In a legal system in which the judiciary operates under a reasonable approximation of RJ, and in which vagueness is understood along the lines of the partial-definition-context-sensitivity model, lawmakers framing legislation with the goal of achieving certain social benefits while avoiding other undesirable results may sometimes rationally prefer a vague law to a more precise one. This will occur when all or most of the following conditions are fulfilled: (i) the vague formulation of the law assigns the clear, non-borderline cases of the term the legal status desired by most lawmakers; (ii) the variety of borderline cases of the term is wide, making them hard to exhaustively anticipate; (iii) the lawmaking body is either divided about the borderline cases or ignorant of the likely consequences of treating some such cases one way rather than another, and so is uncertain about what legal status they should have; and (iv) the lawmakers recognize the value of incremental, case-by-case precisification of the law resulting from adjudication of borderline cases aimed at furthering the law's rationale, in light of the full factual backgrounds uncovered in judicial proceedings. In short, legislation sometimes involves broad agreement about central objectives, combined with disagreement or ignorance at the margins, plus a confidence that those who implement the law and adjudicate disputes arising from it will, through acquaintance with the facts of particular cases and the benefit of an incremental procedure, be in a better position than the lawmakers to further the law's rationale. In such cases, vague language serves the valuable function of delegating rule-making authority to administrative bodies issuing rules implementing the law, to agencies responsible for enforcing the law and to courts adjudicating disputes arising from it.

Here, it is important to distinguish the value of formulating legal rules with borderline cases—in the sense understood by the present philosophical theory of vagueness—

from other values served by the use of words that happen to be vague. It is noteworthy that when vagueness is easily resolvable—e.g., by defining "adult" and "child" in terms of precise ages for particular purposes—the law very often does so, with the result that the vague terms one regularly finds in the law—like "neglect," "well-being," "reasonable," "fair," "unnecessary" and "all deliberate speed"—are often what Timothy Endicott calls "extravagantly vague" (Endicott 2005: 6–7). Unfortunately, this is a bit of a misnomer. Although these terms are usefully vague, their exceptional utility in the law comes from the combination of their vagueness with other semantic features related to, but distinct from, vagueness. It is not that the ratios of borderline to non-borderline cases for Endicott's "extravagantly vague" terms are always so much greater than the ratios of such cases for more garden variety cases of vagueness; the crucial fact is that his terms are, for the most part, highly general, multidimensional and resistant to specific codification—as well as being vague.

Consider, for example, the use of "neglect" in laws regulating the responsibility of parents and other adults for children in their care. In addition to being quite general, this term is multidimensional in the sense that its application is determined by an open-ended combination of factors that includes providing for the satisfaction of children's nutritional, medical, educational, social and emotional needs, in addition to their safety. As a result, judgments about whether particular patterns of behavior constitute neglect tend to be holistic, with lows in one dimension capable of being partially offset by highs in others. Because of this, the variation in behavior exhibited by the range of obvious, non-borderline cases of neglect is enormous and incapable of exhaustive legislative enumeration. Even clear (non-borderline) cases of neglect may sometimes bring together surprising clusters of facts which, though unanticipated by legislators, are obvious when brought to light. This provides a reason for lawmakers to delegate authority for making judgments about individual behaviors to those best able to gather and evaluate the relevant facts—e.g., social agencies and the courts. This delegation is accomplished by using a general, multidimensional term, which, in the nature of things, will also be vague. However the value of its vagueness—in the sense of susceptibility to borderline cases—is analytically distinguishable from the value of its generality and multidimensionality.

Vagueness in the Law: The Epistemic Model

Earlier I mentioned a prima facie difficulty for epistemicism, which characterizes assertive predications of a vague predicate P, or its negation, of any item in its unknowable range $R2_E$–$R3_E$ as violations of the norm of assertion:

Table 7.4

P & so knowable	P but unknowable	Not P but unknowable	Not P & so knowable
$R1_E$	$R2_E$	$R3_E$	$R4_E$

Since adjudicating legal disputes sometimes requires authorities to make such predications, one may wonder whether the epistemicist can accommodate the use of vague legal language. The answer, I think, is that the epistemicist can do so, up to a point, but only at the cost of underestimating the value of vagueness in the law.

Although knowledge is the (default) norm of assertion, not all assertions are held to the same standard. We all recognize circumstances—such as planning future actions in light of well-founded assumptions about future contingencies—in which assertions are acceptable even though that which is asserted isn't known. Of course, not anything goes, even in these cases. When definite (nonconditional) plans must be made in the face of uncertainty, the assertions that occur as parts of those plans are still expected to be justified by a preponderance of evidence. This may not be knowledge, but in some cases, it is close enough.

With this in mind, consider a case the outcome of which depends on applying a vague predicate P to an item x in the extension of P that is barely inside its unknowability range (by virtue of differing very little from items known to be in P's extension, while differing much more from those known not to be in it). This is similar to the case for the previous theory of vagueness in which x is in region $R2_{PDP}$, rendering it unsettled whether P determinately applies to, or is undefined for, x. There, the correct decision was to declare that P applies to x, leaving it unsettled whether the court exercised minimal discretion or no discretion at all. According to the theory in question, a precedent-setting decision to this effect changes the content of the law so that a class of things including x comes to have a determinate legal status which, prior to the decision, it would not have been correct to claim it had. For epistemicism, the outcome of the case is the same, though both the justification and the effect of the decision on the content of the law are different.

Here, the epistemicist may make four reasonable assumptions: (i) for many vague predicates P, elements in the unknowability range for P and its negation ($R2_E$–$R3_E$ above) can be partially ordered along dimensions that determine the applicability of P (e.g., age for "young" / "not young," income and assets for "rich" / "not rich"); (ii) knowledge obtained about where such an item x falls on these dimensions can provide evidence for the claim that P applies, or does not apply, to x; (iii) for many such P, evidence that an item x in R2 is closer along these dimensions to things that are known to be in P's extension than to things known not to be in the extension of P provides justification for the claim that x is in the extension of P; and (iv) a corresponding result holds for evidence that such an item is closer to things known not to be in the extension of P than to any item known to be in it. One need not assume that all vague predicates satisfy these conditions to a robust degree, but surely many do.

When this is so, a legal case that turns on whether P applies to an item x in $R2_E$ that is barely inside its unknowability range should ideally be decided by assertively predicating P of x. After all, judicial decisions should be made on the basis of the best available evidence. If conditions (i)–(iv) are satisfied, and the court is in possession of all relevant evidence, the application of P to x in this case will be mandated. Though no decision made by the judge in this case can (according to the epistemicist) be *known to conform*, or *known not to conform*, to the existing the law, fidelity to the law requires that x be declared to be in the extension of P, since this decision is supported by a preponderance of evidence. If the decision is precedent setting, *the content of the law*—expressed by ⌜Items that are P have legal status L+, while items that are not P have legal status L−⌝—will not change, even though *the effect of the law* will. Something the legal status of which was before unknown will come, with the precedent, to be known. The vague predicate P at the center of this change will not have changed its extension, even though what counts as sufficient, for legal purposes, for being included in its extension will have changed.

Although the disposition of this case is the same for the epistemicist as it was for the theorist who views vagueness as a matter of partial definition and context sensitivity, the different justifications provided by the two theories generalize differently. The key cases are ones in which the partial-definition theory places the crucial item x in the genuine undefined region $R3_{PDP}$ of the range of P, whereas epistemicism places x well into the unknowable section $R2_E$ of the extension of P (closer to $R3_E$ than to $R1_E$). Recall the two scenarios of this sort extending Hart's no-vehicles-in-the-park example. On the non-epistemicist account of vagueness, two different results were reached for some borderline cases of vehicles (e.g., skateboards), based on different rationales the ordinance was intended to serve in the two scenarios. Since the content of the law (as conceived by the non-epistemicist) makes no claim whatsoever about the legal status of x, fidelity to the law requires that the court make its decision on the basis of the rationale the law was intended to serve. Hence the different results in the two scenarios.

Such results cannot be reproduced by the epistemicist for those items x in the unknowability range $R2_E$ of P that are more like things *known to be in the extension of P* than they are like things *known not to be in P's extension*, and hence for which there is discernable (though not overwhelming) evidence supporting the claim that x is in P's extension. In these cases, fidelity to the law requires treating x as being in the extension of P (which it in fact is). Except in cases in which such a decision would produce an absurd result that clearly subverts the law's rationale, this decision is mandated by the norm of adjudication RJ. Things may be otherwise in cases in which the evidence is as weak for the claim that x is in the extension of P as it is for the claim that it isn't—as it may be when x is just barely inside the unknowable boundary line separating things in the extension of P from those not in its extension. In such cases, the epistemicist might reasonably argue that fidelity to the law requires a decision based on the law's rationale. However, on the plausible assumption that such cases constitute a proper subset of the cases for which the partial-definition approach mandates decisions based on the rationale, rather than the content, of the law, we have found a significant difference in the jurisprudential consequences generated by the two philosophical theories of vagueness.

This difference has a material effect on the values the two theories accord to vagueness in the law. As we saw earlier, lawmakers who have achieved general agreement on the rationale for a vaguely worded statute and its treatment of clear, non-borderline cases, may be ignorant of, or unable to achieve consensus on, how best to advance that rationale in many actual and hypothetical borderline cases of the statute's vague terms. If vagueness is understood as partial definition plus context sensitivity, the lawmakers will realize that their vaguely formulated statute is noncommittal about how these items are to be treated. If they are also confident that later administrative or judicial authorities will be guided by fidelity to the law, they will realize that future adjudication of borderline cases will be aimed at how best to advance the rationale that they, the lawmakers, have agreed on. When it is reasonable to expect these authorities to possess important information about how to achieve this goal, which the lawmakers lack, it will be rational for the latter to employ vague language as a way of delegating authority over difficult cases to those in the best epistemic position to advance their goal. Hence, the value of vagueness in the law.

Epistemicism cannot provide a comparable story. The epistemicist will tell you, correctly, that judicial and administrative authorities downstream from the enactment of a statute have no special expertise that the lawmakers lack about where the extension of a (totally defined) vague predicate ends and that of its negation begins. Moreover, since the content of the statute already determines the legal status of every borderline case, the first duty of the downstream authorities is to assign the borderline cases that come before them the legal status those items most probably already have—in situations in which judgments about such relative probabilities can reasonably be made. There may, of course, be items for which such judgments cannot be made, in which case fidelity to the rationale of the statute may then become the basis for adjudication. For this small subset of cases, the two philosophical theories of vagueness can agree on the consequences of legal vagueness, and the basis for adjudicating cases involving it. What the epistemicist cannot do is extend this line of reasoning to the full range of borderline cases for which the proponent of partial definition finds utility in vague legal language. Whereas the latter can properly declare mini bikes, skateboards and children's gravity- or pedal-powered, soapbox derby racers to be *non-vehicles permitted in the park* in scenario 1 of our extension of Hart's example, while properly declaring them to be *vehicles prohibited from the park* in scenario 2, the epistemicist cannot justify arriving at different verdicts in the two scenarios. More precisely, he can't do so on the plausible assumption that he can't reasonably deny that some at least of the examples just mentioned are *more probably vehicles than not* (given his view that each really is a vehicle, or really isn't). In this way, the epistemicist's view of what vagueness really is prevents him from recognizing much of the value that vagueness in the law really has.

Idealization

So far, I have tried to show two things. First, that if legal actors in an idealized system implicitly knew both that vagueness were what the partial-definition-context-sensitivity model says it is, and that adjudication and implementation of the laws were guided by something like the norm RJ of fidelity to the law, then they would correctly and rationally anticipate jurisprudential consequences of the legal use of vague terms of the sort discussed above and rightly assign a high utility to the use of certain vague language in the law. Second, that if they implicitly knew that vagueness was merely epistemic, while also knowing that adjudication and implementation were guided by RJ, then they would correctly and rationally anticipate different jurisprudential consequences (discussed in the previous section), and rightly assign a much lower utility to the use of vague language in the law. To these idealized observations I now explicitly add a further, more empirically based suggestion—namely that the actual jurisprudential consequences of legal vagueness, plus their actual and perceived utility, fit the partial definition model better than they do the epistemic model.

There are several ways of reacting to these claims. A committed epistemicist could accept all of them, except for the final suggestion about the actual value of legally vague language in systems like ours (as well as the suggestions about which adjudications of certain cases are genuinely mandated). Such a theorist would argue from the presumed correctness of epistemic vagueness to revisionary claims about the function, or lack thereof, of vagueness in the law. The point is not hypothetical; an extreme version of this position is taken in Sorenson (2001). A different sort of legal theorist might agree with me about the value of vagueness in our law, while attempting to reconcile epistemicism with this evaluation by challenging the claim that RJ is a governing norm for judicial interpretation. The idea would be to authorize judicial and administrative attempts to further what these authorities take to be the rationale of a law, even in cases in which the weight of evidence indicates that this would result in a revision of its content (which could otherwise be preserved without absurdity). The challenge for this interpretive strategy is to articulate a principled basis for allowing this freedom in cases of vagueness without loosening the constraints on interpretation too far, and so getting undesirable results in cases in which vagueness is not the central issue.

By contrast, one can imagine a committed proponent of partial definition and context-sensitivity who agrees with me about the nature of vagueness, but whose legal scholarship leads him to suspect (a) that relevant actors in our actual legal system *fail* to implicitly recognize that vagueness is what we both take it to be; and (b) that the principles governing adjudication and implementation of the law, as practiced in our legal system, *do not* require very much by way of fidelity to its preexisting content, and are not even approximations of RJ. For this theorist, the job is first to educate our legal actors about what vagueness really is, and then, depending on his normative view about the proper relation between legislation and adjudication, to offer a normative argument that fidelity to the law, in the sense of RJ, is what *should* govern adjudication and implementation.

The main lesson I draw from the discussion in the previous sections is different from, and more straightforward than, any of these. It is based on four suppositions: (i) that relevant actors in our legal system should be credited with implicitly knowing, or at least acting as if they know, what vagueness is; (ii) that legal content is, to a first approximation, the assertive or stipulative content of lawmakers' adoption of authoritative legal texts (against the background of already existing law); (iii) that judicial adjudication and administrative implementation of our laws are, and should be, guided by a principle of fidelity to the law that assigns priority to maintaining existing legal content when possible, while mandating decisions that further legislative rationale when cases cannot rationally be decided on the basis of existing content alone; and (iv) that vague language in our law really does have, and is implicitly perceived to have, roughly the value assigned to it by the partial-definition/context-sensitive model. Given all this, I conclude that whereas the genuine value of vagueness in the law is naturally explainable on the theory that treats vagueness as a matter of partial definition and context sensitivity, it cannot adequately be accommodated by the epistemic theory of vagueness. If I am right, then the special role played by vague language in the law provides us with an argument for one philosophical theory of what vagueness is, and against another.

References

Endicott, T. (2000) *Vagueness in Law*, Oxford: Oxford University Press.
—— (2005) "The Value of Vagueness," in V. K. Bhatia, J. Engberg, M. Gotti and D. Heller, eds., *Vagueness in Normative Texts*, Bern: Peter Lang, pp. 27–48.
Fara, D. G. (2000) "Shifting Sands: An Interest-Relative Theory of Vagueness," *Philosophical Topics* 28: 48–81.
Fine, K. (1975) "Vagueness, Truth, and Logic," *Synthese* 30: 265–300.
Hart, H. L. A. (1958) "Positivism and the Separation of Law and Morals," *Harvard Law Review* 71: 593–629.
Shapiro, S. (2006) *Vagueness in Context*, Oxford: Oxford University Press.
Soames, S. (1999) *Understanding Truth*, New York: Oxford University Press.
—— (2003) "Higher Order Vagueness for Partially Defined Predicates," in J. C. Beall, ed., *Liars and Heaps: New Essays on Paradox*, Oxford: Clarendon Press; reprinted in S. Soames (2009) *Philosophical Essays, Volume 2*, Princeton: Princeton University Press.
—— (2009) "Interpreting Legal Texts: What Is, and What Is Not, Special about the Law," in S. Soames, *Philosophical Essays, Volume 1*, Princeton: Princeton University Press.

SCOTT SOAMES

—— (2010) "The Possibility of Partial Definition," in R. Dietz and S. Moruzzi, eds., *Cuts and Clouds: Vagueness, Its Nature and Its Logic*, Oxford: Oxford University Press; reprinted in S. Soames (2009) *Philosophical Essays, Volume 2*, Princeton: Princeton University Press.

—— (2011) "What Vagueness and Inconsistency Tell Us about Interpretation," in A. Marmor and S. Soames, eds., *The Philosophical Foundations of Language in the Law*, Oxford: Oxford University Press, pp. 31–57.

Sorenson, R. (2001) "Vagueness Has No Function in Law," *Legal Theory* 7: 387–416.

Tappendon, J. (1993) "The Liar and Sorites Paradoxes: Toward a Unified Treatment," *Journal of Philosophy* 90: 551–77.

Williamson, T. (1994) *Vagueness*, London: Routledge.

—— (1996) "Knowing and Asserting," *Philosophical Review* 105: 489–523.

Further Reading

For further reading, see: T. Endicott (2000) *Vagueness in Law*, Oxford: Oxford University Press; T. Endicott (2005) "The Value of Vagueness," in V. K. Bhatia, J. Engberg, M. Gotti and D. Heller, eds., *Vagueness in Normative Texts*, Bern: Peter Lang, pp. 27–48; S. Shapiro (2006) *Vagueness in Context*, Oxford: Oxford University Press; S. Soames (1999) *Understanding Truth*, New York: Oxford University Press, ch. 7; S. Soames (2003) "Higher Order Vagueness for Partially Defined Predicates," in J. C. Beall, ed., *Liars and Heaps: New Essays on Paradox*, Oxford: Clarendon Press, and reprinted in S. Soames (2009) *Philosophical Essays, Volume 2*, Princeton: Princeton University Press; S. Soames (2009) "Interpreting Legal Texts: What Is, and What Is Not, Special about the Law," in *Philosophical Essays, Volume 1*, Princeton: Princeton University Press; S. Soames (2011) "What Vagueness and Inconsistency Tell Us about Interpretation," in A. Marmor and S. Soames, eds., *The Philosophical Foundations of Language in the Law*, Oxford: Oxford University Press, pp. 31–57; R. Sorenson (2001) "Vagueness Has No Function in Law," *Legal Theory* 7: 387–416; and T. Williamson (1994) *Vagueness*, London: Routledge.

8
LEGAL INTERPRETATION
Timothy Endicott

In the Battle of Balaklava in 1854, the Earl of Lucan was in command of British forces facing the valley of death. Russian artillery stood a mile away at the far end, and there were 5,000 Russian cavalrymen in the valley. Russian artillery and thousands of infantry with muskets lined the heights on either side. The Earl received this order:

> Lord Raglan wishes the cavalry to advance rapidly to the front—follow the enemy and try to prevent the enemy carrying away the guns. Troop Horse Artillery may accompany. French cavalry is on your left. R Airey. Immediate.
> (www.nationalarchives.gov.uk/battles/crimea/charge.htm)

The Earl ought to have interpreted the order as referring to captured British guns on the heights, which the Russians were removing. Instead, he won a place in military history by interpreting it as referring to the Russian guns at the end of the valley. He ordered the Light Brigade to charge down the valley in a hopeless attack on the Russian artillery at the end. Of the 673 men, more than 200 (and most of the horses) were killed or wounded.

Interpretation is a creative reasoning process of finding grounds for answering a question as to the meaning of some object. The Earl would have interpreted the order well if he had found good grounds for answering the question he faced (what meaning was to be ascribed to the reference to "the guns"?). But then, if the order had said, "Try to prevent the enemy from carrying away the captured guns on the heights," the question of interpretation would not have arisen. The Light Brigade would not have entered the valley of death.

The disaster should serve as a reminder to lawyers and to lawmakers: that interpretation is a potentially dangerous reasoning process, and that the need to interpret only arises if a person faced with a decision needs to answer a question as to the meaning of some object.

Deciding what is to be done according to law sometimes takes interpretation. But no need for interpretation arises if no question arises as to the meaning of an object. If you approach a red traffic light in your vehicle, you need to know what it means, but the legal rule does not give you the interpreter's task of finding reasons for ascribing one meaning to it rather than another. And where a controversial and difficult question arises as to what is to be done according to law, interpretation may not resolve it. If, on the best interpretation, the law requires you to do what is reasonable, you will need a technique other than interpretation in order to identify the reasons at stake.

Yet it is easy and attractive to think of legal reasoning generally as a matter of interpretation. This mistake means forgetting just how extravagantly the law may leave matters for decision by the parties to a transaction, or by an institution that must resolve a dispute. Conversely, it means forgetting how tightly, transparently and incontrovertibly the law can bind the parties and the institutions.

The mistake is easy to make because of the charm of interpretation. The charm comes from the tantalizing complex of creativity and passivity that interpretation involves (see Finnis 1987: 362–63; Raz 2009, chs. 10 and 12). Judges, instead of claiming authority to invent a resolution to a dispute, have a natural inclination to see what they are doing as interpreting what others have decided (the parties, the legislature, framers of a constitution, states that signed a treaty, previous courts . . .). Conversely, when judges are moved (legitimately or illegitimately) to depart from what others have decided, they have a natural inclination to see what they are doing as interpreting what those others have done. These natural inclinations of judges correspond to the standard techniques of advocates, who do not say, "Please make something up in my client's favor," but "*This* is best interpreted in my client's favor." Advocates do not ordinarily say, "Please exempt my client from this law" but "Properly interpreted, this law does not apply to my client."

The judges' inclinations and the advocates' techniques are related to the best feature of a concern for the rule of law: the determination not to subject the parties and the community to the arbitrary will of an official. But the charm of interpretation can be blinding, and I think that it is healthy to be skeptical about it. So this chapter will be an exercise in skepticism about the importance of interpretation to legal reasoning.

By "legal reasoning," I mean finding rational support for legal conclusions (general or particular—that there is an income tax in English law, that the law requires *me* to drive on the left in *this* country, that *this* defendant is liable to compensate *this* claimant . . .). I do not mean by it merely reasoning that identifies the content of the law, but also reasoning as to what is to be done according to law.

Here are the general propositions concerning interpretation that I will rely on, and I hope you can accept them:

- it is of an object (that is, a good interpretation depends on true propositions that refer to the object); and
- it is creative (that is, an interpretation does not simply state what everyone knows if they are familiar with the object, but ascribes to it a meaning that someone else might dispute); and
- it is rational (there can be reasons for arriving at an interpretation).

And here are two specific propositions that I will rely on concerning *legal* interpretation, which distinguish it from, e.g., literary interpretation or the form of interpretation that is displayed in a performance of a symphony:

- a legal interpretation gives a rule for the application of the law (it is applicative, not generalizing); and
- a legal interpretation is articulate, or propositional (i.e., it can be expressed in propositions).

I will argue that each of the following aspects of legal reasoning need not involve interpretation:

1. Resolving indeterminacies as to the content of the law
2. Working out the requirements of abstract legal provisions

3. Deciding what is just
4. Equitable interference with legal duties or powers or rights
5. Understanding the law

I will see how far I can press the skepticism, for the sake of the exercise. I hope that I will not seem to be making the absurd claim that interpretation is unimportant to legal reasoning. But most legal reasoning is not interpretive. Much of what is commonly called "interpretation" can be done with no interpretation at all.

1. Resolving Indeterminacies as to the Content of the Law

In *Regina v. Monopolies and Mergers Commission, ex parte South Yorkshire Transport* [1993] 1 WLR 23 (House of Lords), two bus companies had merged to provide services in an area of Yorkshire covering less than 2 percent of the area of the United Kingdom, and containing about 3 percent of the British population. The companies challenged the jurisdiction of the competition tribunal to investigate their merger. The legislation required that a merger should affect "a substantial part of the United Kingdom" in order to be subject to investigation. The bus companies asked the court to interpret that provision, to determine that their territory was not a substantial part of the UK and to impose that interpretation on the tribunal.

The Law Lords rejected an interpretation of "substantial" as meaning "more than *de minimis*." They held, on the other hand, that "the court should lean against an interpretation which would give the commission jurisdiction over references of the present kind in only a small minority of cases" (p. 31). They concluded that a substantial part of the UK in the relevant sense was a part of the country "of such size, character and importance as to make it worth consideration for the purposes of the Act" (p. 32). That was all they would do. The Law Lords agreed that it was their task as judges to interpret the legislation to identify "the criterion for a judgment." But:

> the criterion so established may itself be so imprecise that different decision-makers, each acting rationally, might reach differing conclusions when applying it to the facts of a given case. . . . Even after eliminating inappropriate senses of "substantial" one is still left with a meaning broad enough to call for the exercise of judgment . . . the conclusion at which the commission arrived was well within the permissible field of judgment.
>
> (pp. 32–33)

The *South Yorkshire Transport* case shows that there is no general reason to expect interpretation to resolve indeterminacies in the law. Interpreting the legislation meant ascribing a meaning to it, and the meaning that the judges quite rightly chose was itself very vague and did not resolve the question of just how much of the country had to be affected by a merger before it would count as substantial. As this case suggests, the connections between indeterminacy and interpretation are all contingent: there may be conclusive, determinate reason in favor of one interpretation, or there may not. The criterion of judgment yielded by a good interpretation may involve all sorts of indeterminacies in its application, or it may not.

It may seem surprising to say that there is no necessary link between indeterminacy and interpretation. It has often been suggested that interpretation is not necessary if the requirements of the law are determinate, and that it is when they are indeterminate that interpretation comes into play:

> The plain case, where the general terms seem to need no interpretation and where the recognition of instances seems unproblematic or "automatic," are only the familiar ones, constantly recurring in similar contexts, where there is general agreement in judgments as to the applicability of the classifying terms.
>
> (Hart 1994: 126)

> If the formulation of a particular rule is inadequate for purposes of determining a particular result in certain circumstances, then there is nothing more to explain or understand about its meaning; what is required is a new formulation of the rule—one which would remove the doubt—and this is what the term "interpretation" properly designates.
>
> (Marmor 2005: 117)

These views are attractive because there is no room for interpretation if no question arises as to the meaning of the law. There is certainly room for doubt or disagreement if there is room for interpretation. But a doubt or a disagreement may well arise without any indeterminacy. Legal interpretation comes into play when there is a possibility of argument as to the meaning of the law. Interpretation may be needed *in order to work out* what is determinately the best way of understanding the object of interpretation (where, for example, everyone else jumps to a conclusion about how to understand the object, but you can explain why it must be understood differently). There may be a pressing need for interpretation, even where there is only one right answer to the question at issue. At the Battle of Balaklava there was more than one way of interpreting Lord Raglan's order, but there was determinate reason in favor of one particular interpretation. The Earl of Lucan's interpretation was a misinterpretation.

But if no argument can be made, then no interpretation is called for; an "interpretation" arguing the unarguable would not only be a misinterpretation, it would be a pretense, or a failure to interpret, as an irrational argument reflects a failure to argue (Raz 2009: 299 makes the important point that "some interpretations are so bad as to be interpretations no longer").

The British competition legislation did not determine the extent of the competition tribunal's jurisdiction, and interpretation could not make it do so; in fact, the best interpretation of the legislation implies that Parliament had used the vague requirement of substantiality to confer a discretion on the tribunal (subject to control through judicial review) to determine which mergers were important enough for it to investigate. Determining the undetermined is one of the standard functions of adjudication, and it is not an interpretive function.

2. Working Out the Requirements of Abstract Legal Provisions

In April 1999, as part of its response to the Kosovo crisis in the former Yugoslavia, NATO launched a bombing raid on the Serbian capital, Belgrade. A single rocket struck a radio and television station, killing 16 people. The victims' families argued that the European NATO countries had violated the right to life guaranteed in the European Convention on Human Rights (*Bankovic v. Belgium* (52207/99) (2001)). The defendant countries argued that the victims could not assert rights under the Convention because the extra-territorial military operation was not within the countries' jurisdiction for purposes of the Convention.

Article 1 of the Convention provides that "The High Contracting Parties shall secure to everyone within their jurisdiction the rights and freedoms defined in Section I of this Convention." In *Bankovic*, the European Court of Human Rights held that the victims of the Belgrade bombing were not within the jurisdiction of the states under Article 1. The court approached the problem as one of "interpretation" of the jurisdiction provision in Article 1 and set out to decide what "meaning" was to be given to the term "jurisdiction" (*Bankovic*, paras. 53–63).

In fact, the problem before the court in *Bankovic* was not a problem of interpretation. The justices were swayed by the charm of interpretation: they proceeded in their reasoning as if the framers had determined the jurisdiction of states in Article 1, so that the judges' job was to interpret that article to work out what jurisdiction the states had created by adopting the Convention. But the framers had not determined the jurisdiction at all. And by agreeing to secure rights "within their jurisdiction," the state parties did not determine the extent of their jurisdiction.

I do not mean that there is no need for interpretation of Article 1 (indeed, it needs to be interpreted in order to reach the conclusion that it gives judges an open-ended responsibility). We can certainly interpret Article 1 as implying that not all acts of states are subject to the Convention (or the phrase "within their jurisdiction" would be superfluous). And by use of the travaux preparatoires, we can reach the interpretive conclusion that the jurisdiction was not meant to be restricted to residents. But neither the context in which it was used, nor the travaux, determine the extent of the jurisdiction.

The court had to determine whether it extended to an extraterritorial bombing raid, and the judges' role in doing so was not the role of an interpreter. No interpretation —that is, no explanatory account of what the states had done by subscribing to the convention—can answer the question of what the jurisdiction is. The judges seized on the interpretation of Article 1 as a way of relying on the authority of the Convention, by identifying a category of jurisdiction that the framers had prescribed and to which the states had agreed. But that is only deceptive: the courts could not work out the extent of the jurisdiction within which a state must secure the Convention rights by interpreting a provision that they must do so within their jurisdiction.

The case provides a dramatic example of the potential for the charm of interpretation to distort judicial reasoning. If they had faced up to the open-ended nature of the task that the framers and the state parties had handed to them, the judges could have asked the real questions relevant to the issue of how far the jurisdiction ought to be extended —questions concerning the overall purpose of the Convention and the legitimacy of using the remarkable institutional technique of a supranational regional court to control the overseas military operations of the Convention states.

But the judges buried those questions by pretending that the jurisdiction could be determined by "interpreting" Article 1. Their interpretation was that the Convention used the notion of jurisdiction that is used in international law, which is "primarily territorial," with exceptions in special circumstances. There is no single notion of jurisdiction in international law, and no rationale emerges from *Bankovic* for the exceptions to the primarily territorial account of jurisdiction that emerges from the case. This lack of a rationale reflects the attempt to answer a noninterpretive question by interpretation.

The *Bankovic* problem is one instance of another standard function of courts: when lawmakers are not in a position to be specific, the courts very often need to give substance to abstract categorizations. The most famous instances of this problem arise in constitutional and international litigation over fundamental rights. When the courts need to decide what process is due under the United States Bill of Rights, or what counts as showing respect for private life under the European Convention, or what limits on rights can be demonstrably justified in a free and democratic society under the Canadian Charter of Rights, their task seems like one of interpretation. After all, they need to decide the effect of a communicative act that may be understood in various ways. But although interpretive considerations may well constrain their decision in one way or another, we have no general reason to think that interpretation can guide them to a particular conclusion, any more than interpretation can do so when they have to decide whether South Yorkshire is a substantial part of the UK. We have less reason to think it—Article 1 of the European Convention does not even establish a *vague* test of jurisdiction; it requires the court to determine the jurisdiction.

Thanks to the charm of interpretation, "constitutional interpretation" is very widely used as a sort of euphemism for a judicial, constitution-building function that includes a responsibility for the noninterpretive reasoning that is needed to give substance to the community's broad principles in particular areas of life. Those principles include the principle of the separation of powers, which requires courts not to usurp the functions of constitutional framers or legislators.

Constitutional litigation is, of course, only one instance of this sort of judicial function. Much legal reasoning that might seem interpretive is geared to the working out of the requirements of abstract provisions, the use of which may more or less amount (as it did in *Bankovic*) to an allocation of power to a court to do what is just and convenient. And decisions as to what is just and convenient are not generally interpretive either.

3. Deciding What Is Just

When the law confers discretion on a decision-maker by the use of an abstract provision, or expressly requires a decision-maker to act justly, then legal reasoning requires judgments to be made as to what is just. Ronald Dworkin suggested in *Law's Empire* that such judgments are best understood as the result of interpretation, and that disagreements as to what is just reflect competing interpretations: "Justice and other higher-order moral concepts are interpretive concepts" (Dworkin 1986: 424, n. 20; see also 73–76). The idea is defended, broadened and elaborated in his recent work, *Justice for Hedgehogs* (Dworkin 2011). What is the object of interpretation? I think that there is no satisfactory answer to this question.

In Dworkin's "constructive" theory of interpretation, a good interpretation fits its object. But that is not enough; the interpreter must also *justify* the object of interpretation. To find an interpretation that succeeds on the dimensions of fit *and* justification, the interpreter needs to start with two questions: (1) what is it that the interpretation must fit? And (2) what would make that material look good? Dworkin describes two corresponding stages of interpretation (Dworkin 1986: 66), the "preinterpretive" stage and the "interpretive" stage, at which the interpreter answers those two questions. At stage 1 the interpreter identifies the material that an interpretation must fit—the "interpretive data" (Dworkin 2011: 176). At stage 2 the interpreter decides what virtues would make the interpretive data look good.

At stage 3, the "postinterpretive" stage, the interpreter decides what conclusion would best meet the two requirements of fit and justification. An inconsistency with the interpretive data will count against a postinterpretive conclusion, although such a "defect of fit" (Dworkin 1986: 257) will not defeat an interpretation that shows better *overall* fit and justification than an alternative interpretation. Dworkin has sometimes suggested that fit is only a threshold (see, e.g., Dworkin 1993: 111). But if fit were only a threshold, then, in choosing among interpretations that pass the test, an interpreter would stop interpreting and would just choose the most attractive option. *Law's Empire* unequivocally takes the more genuinely interpretive position that, while fit acts as a threshold for *eligible* interpretations, it also acts as a consideration *above* the threshold in deciding which interpretation is best: "even when an interpretation survives the threshold requirement, any infelicities of fit will count against it" (Dworkin 1986: 256).

There are at least two possible accounts of the nature of the interpretive data, which an interpretation must fit.

Interpretation of Practices?

Justice is a quality by which political practices and institutions can be judged. It is their "first virtue," as John Rawls called it (Rawls 1971: 3). But it is not a practice, and it is not an institution. Yet Dworkin, in a turn of phrase that is linked to his interpretive theory, calls justice both a "practice" and an "institution" (Dworkin 1986: 73–75). In any community there are certainly practices of treating this or that as just and unjust, and of arguing about what is just, and so on (practices typically carried on by and within institutions). Dworkin hinted in *Law's Empire* at the view that judgments of justice are interpretations of those practices:

> . . . justice is an institution we interpret. Like courtesy, it has a history; we each join that history when we learn to take the interpretive attitude toward the demands, justifications and excuses we find other people making in the name of justice.
>
> (Dworkin 1986: 73)

In *Justice for Hedgehogs*, this becomes a definite theorem in the theory of justice: the interpretive data are identified as "the practices and paradigms of that concept," "our collective behaviour in using that concept" and "the shared practices of calling institutions, people and actions just and unjust" (Dworkin 2011: 157, 162).

The idea is that the interpretive data consist of the judgments of justice and injustice that members of a community have a practice of making, and also of the sorts of argument that the participants in the practice make in defending their judgments. At the post-interpretive stage, a conclusion as to what justice requires in a particular case will be more attractive if it better fits those facts.

Suppose that evidence emerges that a person imprisoned on conviction for a serious offense was framed, convicted on false evidence, and is patently not guilty of the offense. The release of the prisoner who has been framed (through a process authorized by law) is a paradigm of justice. It is an act that can be used as a standard of comparison in explaining to someone what justice is. Dworkin could agree that the release of the framed prisoner is a paradigm of justice. Now consider the role of such a paradigm in his model of constructive interpretation. First, if some interpretation yields the conclusion that the release of the framed prisoner was just, that will count in favor of the interpretation. Fit with a paradigm is part of an argument in support of an interpretation. Second, however, if a theory of what is just and unjust yields the conclusion that justice does not demand the release of the framed prisoner, that does not rule out the theory. To reject the paradigm-busting interpretation, we need a competing interpretation that shows that the proposition that justice demands the release of the framed prisoner fits other features of the interpretive data and is supported by the principles that justify the other paradigms.

The constructive model is in no danger of saying that actions are just because the members of a community think they are just. It insists that even the unanimous opinion of members of a community does not conclude a question of justice. But it still makes justice relative to the practices being interpreted: an argument about justice will have to seek support *in* those practices.

The practices of a community have a crucial bearing on the demands of justice in all sorts of ways—but not in the respect that a judgment of justice must fit them. The most striking instance of the dependence of justice on practices is, of course, reflected in the fact that justice often demands obedience to the law of a community. The justice of a demand from the government for a percentage of my income may depend (partly but crucially) on mere facts as to whether the legislature has enacted a tax by means that officials happen to recognize as a means of making law. The justice of enforcing a commercial agreement depends, among other things, on whether the agreement was made in a way that the members and the institutions of the community are disposed to treat as a way of making a binding agreement. Justice requires conformity to those practices. In Dworkin's theory, instead, fit with the practices of a community is an ingredient in deciding what justice requires.

Suppose that the English judges are more readily disposed in the 2010s to release prisoners who are shown to have been framed than they were in the 1970s. Imagine that, in the 1970s, they acted fairly consistently on a principle that the good repute of the criminal justice system needed to be protected against disclosure of its mistakes. And imagine that in their sincere judgment it was not unjust to refuse, on the ground of that need, to reopen criminal cases (suppose that they considered that no one has a right to liberty where a release from custody might injure the prestige of such an important institution). Imagine that the practices of other institutions and the practices of citizens in the 1970s supported this judicial approach. Now imagine that the practices have changed in the 2010s, and the judges consistently act on the basis that it is unjust to keep a prisoner in custody in such circumstances, and the practices of the community in general are also in sympathy with that approach. The question is this: do the facts we have imagined weigh in favor of the conclusion that justice demands the release of patently innocent prisoners in the 2010s, or against the conclusion that justice demanded their release in the 1970s? I think that the answer is "no." Those practices are irrelevant to the question of justice. But if judgments of justice interpret the practices of the community, the change in practice we have imagined is a change in the considerations relevant to such a judgment.

If English judges have changed their approach in the way we imagine, the argument in favor of their new approach has gained no added force. The practice of the judges has, in this regard, simply become more just. The practice of a community cannot appeal to itself to find support for the claim that it is just. We have every reason to fit our practices to what is just, but no reason to fit our view of justice to our practices.

Interpretation of Convictions?

But there is also, in *Law's Empire*, an alternative account of the interpretive data for justice:

> . . . if we take justice to be an interpretive concept, we must treat different people's conceptions of justice, while inevitably developed as interpretations of practices in which they themselves participate, as claiming a more global or transcendental authority so that they can serve as the basis for criticizing other people's practices of justice even, or especially, when these are radically different. The leeways of interpretation are accordingly much more relaxed: a theory of justice is not required to provide a good fit with the political or social practices of any particular community, but only with the most abstract and elemental convictions of each interpreter.
>
> (Dworkin 1986: 424–25, n. 20)

If I am seeking to achieve fit with my convictions, and you with yours, we are not giving interpretations of the same thing. So what ground is there for saying that our interpretations genuinely compete with each other, so that we are disagreeing about the same thing? If the interpretive data consist of the interpreter's convictions, then disagreement is inexplicable not only because convictions differ, but for a reason that is related but more basic: I cannot offer, as an interpretive consideration that might persuade *you* to agree with me, the fact that the conclusion I am defending fits *my* convictions.

It is Dworkin who has done more than any other practical philosopher to focus attention on the need to explain how disagreement can be deep, sincere and *genuine*. If a disagreement is interpretive it can only be a genuine disagreement if the disputants are interpreting the same thing. If I am interpreting my convictions, and you yours, we can have no genuine interpretive disagreement and, incidentally, no genuine agreement.

* * * * *

To summarize: an interpretation needs to find support in the object that is interpreted. Judgments of justice cannot find support in the fact that we engage in the practices that we engage in or hold the convictions that we hold. The point is not that true judgments of justice are liable to be completely inconsistent with human practices (though they will be fundamentally inconsistent with many practices). The point is that the considerations in favor of a conclusion about what justice requires do not grow stronger or weaker as that conclusion shows a better or worse fit with what people do or believe. It is not only that people's convictions differ fundamentally, and that communities' practices differ significantly (perhaps that problem can be answered by Dworkin's suggestions that the "leeways" are drawn less tightly around the interpretive data for justice than for law). The problem is that there is no general reason to try to fit judgments of justice to any body of data.

That does not mean that we are bereft of reasons for judgments of justice—far from it. Reasons that pertain to the needs and interests of the framed prisoner, and to the justification of punishment, and to the nature of the judicial office and so on can support a conclusion of justice, but not arguments of fit with our convictions or practices. So disagreements about justice are not disagreements between competing interpretations.

There is a particularly salient value for political philosophy in Dworkin's reminder that not even the unanimous opinion of a community settles a question of justice. But a theory of justice should be more radically critical: it should not portray justice as depending on fit with opinions or practices. Perhaps the best way to interpret the extension of Dworkin's theory of interpretation from law to justice is to treat it as a theoretical metaphor, motivated by his general philosophy of value—that is, by the "unity of value" for which he argues in *Justice for Hedgehogs*. The interpretive theory is attractive to Dworkin insofar as it privileges an intellectual and moral determination to achieve articulate consistency among one's moral principles. For that theory to flourish, it might be best to relinquish the requirement of fit with interpretive data, though, and to propose not that judgments of justice are interpretations, but that they are more appealing insofar as they are part of a unitary theory of value. This is not the place to discuss whether such a theory is sustainable; it needs other grounds than an interpretive theory of justice.

Finally on the topic of justice, we should note that, in spite of everything that has been said above, there *may* be an interpretive task when the law requires justice to be done. For a person giving effect to such a requirement, it *may* be a matter of duty to give effect to whatever conception of justice is held by the authority that has imposed the requirement. Likewise with requirements of reasonableness: they may seem on their face simply to leave a court or other decision-maker to identify reasons as it may, with no constraint from the law. But a responsible court may sometimes need to consider what a lawmaker meant by reasonableness. For example, in deciding what is reasonable for the purpose of the duty of care in negligence, a court in any common-law jurisdiction today will find that it cannot decide what would be reasonable in abstraction from huge bodies of case law; it will need to accord with the reason of the law. A judge might well think that it is unreasonable to impose a duty, and yet hold that it is reasonable *for the purposes of the law* of the jurisdiction. Similarly, if a court is required to make a "just" award of costs of litigation between the parties, it may need to decide what counts as just for the purpose of the law by taking into account (and, perhaps, interpreting) a large body of jurisprudence on the issue. Identifying the reason of the law may involve interpretation. The question is not whether the law uses the term "reasonable" or the term "just," but how, if at all, the law controls decisions as to what is just or reasonable. If it does so through materials that need interpretation, then a court will need to interpret. But to the extent that it does not do so, no issue of interpretation arises.

4. Equitable Interference with Legal Duties or Powers or Rights

Suppose that a town bylaw prohibits vehicles in the park, and an ambulance enters the park to rescue a person who has been injured (and suppose that no institution has acted to authorize ambulances to disregard the bylaw). The driver's behavior may show no disrespect for the rule of law. Is that because the bylaw is *best interpreted* as meaning something like "vehicles are prohibited in the park except in an emergency"? Or is it because of noninterpretive considerations?

The considerations that do not involve interpretation are that driving the ambulance into the park in an emergency is morally justified (in fact, it is required) by a concern for the injured person, and is compatible with due respect for the local authority's jurisdiction to regulate the use of the park, even though the authority has banned vehicles.

But we could describe the question as one of interpretation, of course. You might say that it would be a poor interpretation of the bylaw to treat it as meaning "vehicles are prohibited from entering the park even if it means leaving people to die."

What is the justification for the view that the driver ought to treat himself as exempt from the effect of the bylaw, and the law enforcement officials ought to do so too, and a court as well (if the officials are obtuse enough to try to enforce the bylaw)? We could say:

> The bylaw is best interpreted as being subject to an implicit exception permitting ambulances to respond to emergencies.

Or we could say:

> It would be unconscionable to penalize the driver for an action which was justified by the emergency, and which is compatible with respect for the role of the local authority in regulating the use of the park.

One justification has the form of an interpretation, the other does not. But the *reason* for the law to treat it as permissible for the ambulance to enter the park is, of course, the same either way! For the rationale for reading the implicit exception into the bylaw is that it would be unconscionable to penalize the driver for an action which was justified by the emergency and which is compatible with respect for the role of the local authority in regulating the use of the park. So you do not need interpretation to decide whether it is lawful for the ambulance to enter the park, although you could state your reasoning in the form of an interpretation.

This is actually an *extraordinarily* common phenomenon: there is very often a potential for equivocation between saying that a legal doctrine is supported by the best interpretation of some communicative act, or that it is supported by legal reasons that are not communicated by that act. One important real-life example is the imposition of procedural duties on public authorities carrying out statutory duties. Lord Mustill said in *R v. Home Secretary, ex p Doody* [1994] 1 AC 531, "where an Act of Parliament confers an administrative power there is a presumption that it will be exercised in a manner which is fair in all the circumstances" (p. 560). Is the presumption a technique of interpretation? Or a rule of the common law? It has been a popular view among some academics and judges that the imposition of procedural requirements *must* result from interpretation of the statute, because courts cannot interfere with the legislation (Elliott 2001). But Byles J said, in *Cooper v. Wandsworth Board of Works* (1863) 14 CB(NS) 180, that when a statute does not specify that a power is to be used with due process, "the justice of the common law will supply the omission of legislature" (see p. 108). As Lord Justice Sedley put it in *R (Wooder) v. Feggetter* [2002] EWCA Civ. 554 (para. 44), "The process is not one of discerning implied terms but of adding necessary ones. It has been the engine of modern public law, and there is no reason to believe that its force is spent."

English and American lawyers used to speak of "equitable interpretation" of legislation, equity being a jurisdiction in a court to dispense with the enforcement of legal rights and duties on grounds of conscience. It is a curious sort of idea, which reflects the charm of interpretation: if the courts are exercising a jurisdiction in equity to exempt someone from rules made by legislation, you might say that they are not interpreting anymore, but declining to give effect to the law. The phrase may have passed out of vogue because of the hint that it involves departing from the legislation; these days, judges and lawyers speak of "purposive" interpretation instead. But purposive interpretation is only interpretation if there is something about the object that supports it. What is the consideration that supports the view that it is lawful for the ambulance to enter the park? Nothing about the bylaw, it seems; the support lies in principles that both justify the action and explain why it does not matter that the action is one that the bylaw described as prohibited. The reason for Lord Mustill's presumption is not a fact about the legislature or its enactment: the reason is justice.

5. Understanding the Law

A red traffic light, an income tax, a right to return defective goods under a sales contract—any of these might raise questions of interpretation in particular circumstances, but they need not do so (in fact, they are designed not to do so, and they generally do not do so). The possibility of grasping and following these rules without interpretation reflects a general point about rule-governed behavior. As Wittgenstein said, "there is a way of grasping a rule which is not an interpretation, but which is exhibited in what we call 'obeying the rule' and 'going against it' in actual cases" (Wittgenstein 1967, § 201). This is deeply controversial, but there has been support among some philosophers of law for the idea that not all understanding depends on interpretation (Marmor 2005).

It may seem to be otherwise, because the meaning of any communicative act depends on the context of the communication. And this is a particularly salient feature of *legal* communications, because of the systematic context in which they are made. Even simple legal communications—think of a "NO TRESPASSING" sign—can only be understood in their context. You may understand the words, but to understand the communication requires a capacity to draw the implications that can be drawn from a knowledge of the legal system (and the powers it gives to persons in control of property, and the remedies and sanctions that turn on the exercise of such powers, and the institutional structures that give effect to the remedies and sanctions, and . . .). J. L. Austin said:

> The total speech act in the total situation is the *only actual* phenomenon which, in the last resort, we are engaged in elucidating.
>
> (Austin 1962: 148)

He meant it as a reminder for philosophers, but it is also a maxim for interpreters. And interpretation, you might say, is the task of taking the language we are familiar with and putting it in context. The Earl of Lucan's problem in the Battle of Balaklava was not that he did not understand the word "the" or the word "guns," but that he did not do a successful job of working out how to ascribe a meaning to their use in the circumstances, so as to make a good job of his task of obeying the order that he had received. You might say, as Austin put it, that his task was to elucidate the total speech act in the total situation. Or you might say (I think it amounts to the same) that his task was to *understand Lord Raglan*, by asking what he could conclude about the general's purposes from the fact that he had used *these* words in *these* circumstances. And every communication creates the need to understand the particular communicator, in the total situation in which he or she or it is communicating.

It is quite true that all understanding of communications requires a grasp of context, as well as a grasp of the language being used. The word "interpretation" is certainly flexible enough that you might, if you wish, signal this fact about the understanding of communication by saying that all understanding requires interpretation. Yet sometimes, gaining an understanding requires a creative intellectual process of finding reasons for an answer to a question (which might have been answered differently) as to the meaning of the object. Some understanding does not require that process. The distinction is well signaled by using the term "interpretation" for that process.

A good grasp of the context and the language may mean that there is no question as to how a person is to be understood. The characteristic moment for interpretation arises when an argument can be made that they meant *this*, and an argument can be made that they meant *that*. It is a matter of degree, of course, because there are stronger and weaker arguments. Sometimes only a rather feeble argument can be made that someone is to be understood to mean *this*, and a powerful and convincing argument can be made that they mean *that*. Then it is clear what interpretation you ought to reach. Sometimes no argument at all (or only a sham of an argument) can be made that they mean *this*. And then you do not need to interpret at all.

6. Conclusion

"Adjudication and juristic interpretation resist being taken for the constitutive and legislative moments in the life of the law," as John Finnis wrote, ". . . those moments resist being understood, through and through, as interpretative" (Finnis 1987: 362–63).

Not all reasoning as to what is to be done according to law is interpretive. It is often possible to identify legal duties and rights without needing to interpret. And the law often requires decision-makers to guide their conduct by standards that cannot be identified by interpretation.

References

Austin, J. L. (1962) *How to Do Things with Words*, Cambridge, Mass.: Harvard University Press.
Bankovic v. Belgium (52207/99) (2001) (E.C.H.R.).
Cooper v. Wandsworth Board of Works (1863) 14 CB(NS) 180.
Dworkin, R. (1985) *A Matter of Principle*, Oxford: Clarendon Press.
—— (1986) *Law's Empire*, Cambridge, Mass.: Harvard University Press.
—— (1993) *Life's Dominion*, London: Harper Collins.
—— (2011) *Justice for Hedgehogs*, Cambridge, Mass.: Harvard University Press.
Elliott, M. (2001) *The Constitutional Foundations of Judicial Review*, Oxford: Hart Publishing.
European Convention for the Protection of Human Rights and Fundamental Freedoms, http://www.echr. coe.int/NR/rdonlyres/D5CC24A7-DC13-4318-B457-5C9014916D7A/0/ENG_CONV.pdf.
Finnis, J. (1987) "On Reason and Authority in *Law's Empire*," *Law and Philosophy* 6: 357–80.
Hart, H. L. A. (1994) *The Concept of Law*, 2nd edition, Oxford: Clarendon Press.
Marmor, A. (2005) *Interpretation and Legal Theory*, revised 2nd edition, Oxford: Hart Publishing.
R v. Monopolies and Mergers Commission, ex parte South Yorkshire Transport [1993] 1 WLR 23 (House of Lords).
R v. Home Secretary, ex p Doody [1994] 1 AC 531 (House of Lords).
R (Wooder) v. Feggetter [2002] EWCA Civ. 554 (para. 44).
Rawls, J. (1971) *A Theory of Justice*, Cambridge, Mass.: Harvard University Press.
Raz, J. (2009) *Between Authority and Interpretation*, Oxford: Oxford University Press.
Wittgenstein, L. (1967) *Philosophical Investigations*, 3rd edition, G. E. M. Anscombe, trans., Oxford: Blackwell.

TIMOTHY ENDICOTT

Further reading

For further reading, see: J. Dickson (2010) "Interpretation and Coherence in Legal Reasoning," in E. N. Zalta, ed., *The Stanford Encyclopedia of Philosophy*, Spring 2010 Edition, http://plato.stanford.edu/archives/spr2010/entries/legal-reas-interpret; O. Fiss (1982) "Objectivity and Interpretation," *Stanford Law Review* 34: 739–63; W. J. T. Mitchell, ed. (1983) *The Politics of Interpretation*, Chicago: University of Chicago Press; A. Marmor (1998) *Law and Interpretation: Essays in Legal Philosophy*, Oxford: Oxford University Press; M. Moore (1985) "A Natural Law Theory of Interpretation," *Southern California Law Review* 58: 277–398; J. Raz (1998) "On the Authority and Interpretation of Constitutions: Some Preliminaries," in L. Alexander, ed., *Constitutionalism: Philosophical Foundations*, Cambridge: Cambridge University Press; and N. Stavropoulos (2003) "Interpretivist Theories of Law," in E. N. Zalta, ed., *The Stanford Encyclopedia of Philosophy*, Winter 2003 Edition, http://plato.stanford.edu/archives/win2003/entries/law-interpretivist.

9
PRECEDENT
Frederick Schauer

Introduction

Legal systems, and especially common-law legal systems, claim to place special weight in their decision-making on the constraints of precedent. In law, more than elsewhere, legal decision-makers are expected to follow previous decisions just because of the very existence of those decisions, and thus without regard to the current decision-maker's agreement with or persuasion by the content of those previous decisions. It is the very "pastness" of previous decisions, and not necessarily the current decision-maker's view of the correctness of those previous decisions, that gives the previous decisions their authority. Why this is so, and, more importantly, what it means for it to be so, is the principal topic of this chapter.

It is worth noting at the outset that precedent, although arguably concentrated in, and more important in, law than in other decision-making domains, and more important in, common-law legal systems than in their civil-law counterparts, is by no means unique to legal decision-making. Younger children who demand to be treated just as their older siblings were treated at the same age are relying on arguments from precedent, as are consumers who insist on being given the same prices and terms as those offered to prior customers, as are members of committees and other collective decision-making bodies who treat the very existence of a previous committee decision on some subject as providing a reason to make the same decision on some subsequent occasion.

But although arguments from precedent, as well as the correlative arguments against a proposed course of action for fear of creating a dangerous precedent, appear at times to be ubiquitous, such arguments are alleged to have greater weight in the law, and to be more pervasive in the law as well. Whether these comparative claims of frequency and weight are in fact true is an interesting and important empirical question, but in this chapter I nevertheless assume the truth of the conventional wisdom that a norm of precedent is, descriptively, a more central feature of legal decision-making than it is of decision-making, even good decision-making, generally. Thus, although the analysis presented in this chapter may have some application to any domain in which arguments from precedent have some purchase, it will still be focused almost entirely on the law.

Precedent: The Basic Idea

Precedent is centrally about the (not necessarily conclusive) obligation of a decision-maker to make the same decision that has been made on a previous occasion about the same or similar matters. That seems straightforward enough, but it is nevertheless important to distinguish two different dimensions of precedent. One, which we can label *vertical* precedent, describes the obligation of a court to follow the decision made by a court above it in the judicial hierarchy on the same question, even if that question has arisen in a different case (Schauer 2009: 36–37). When trial courts make decisions on questions of law (as opposed to determining the facts in the particular matter before them), they are expected to follow—to *obey*—the decisions of the appellate courts that sit above them in what can be analogized to the military chain of command, just as the first-stage appellate courts must, in turn, follow the decisions made by courts above *them*. So, in the American federal courts, for example, federal district courts are obliged to follow the decisions of the court of appeals in their circuit, and the courts of appeals are similarly obliged to follow the decisions of the Supreme Court of the United States.

To be contrasted with this sense of vertical precedent is *horizontal* precedent, conventionally referred to as *stare decisis* (typically translated as "stand by what has been decided") (Lee 1999; Wise 1975). Understood horizontally, the obligation of a court is not the obligation to obey a decision from above, but is instead the obligation to follow a decision by the same court (although not necessarily by the same judges) on a previous occasion. And thus the obligation is, by definition, not one of obeying an institution higher in some hierarchy. Rather, the obligation to follow precedent in its horizontal dimension is, in essence, about treating a prior decision as if it came from above, even if it did not, and is accordingly about following an earlier decision solely because it came earlier. Horizontal precedent is about treating temporal priority as sufficient grounds for authoritativeness in its own right.

Thus, both vertical and horizontal precedent are about the authoritative character possessed by, or to be given to, prior decisions. And therefore the authority of a precedent is, as with authority in general, content-independent (Hart 1982). It is the source or status of a precedent that gives it its authority—that provides the reason for a decision—rather than the content of the precedent or the content or persuasiveness of the reasoning it incorporates. For just this reason, the force of precedent is most apparent when the decision-maker in the present case—the *instant* case—disagrees with the result reached in the previous case—the *precedent* case (Schauer 1987). When the decision-maker in the instant case agrees with or is persuaded by the outcome or the reasoning in the precedent case, then an argument from precedent is superfluous. It is only when the decision-maker in the instant case disagrees with the outcome or the reasoning in the precedent case that the content-independent authority of a precedent becomes apparent (Alexander 1989). In such instances, it is most obvious that the decision-maker is under an obligation to follow the precedent because of its source or status, and just because of that source or status, even if the decision-maker in the instant case believes that the decision in the precedent case was mistaken.

Although the force of a norm of precedent is thus most apparent when it compels a decision-maker to do what she would not otherwise have done, it is still important to note that the content-independent reasons supplied by a precedent need not be conclusive. A decision-maker in the instant case who accepts the obligations of precedent, and thus accepts that precedents supply content-independent reasons for decisions, may nevertheless believe that other reasons—legal, moral or prudential, for example—may outweigh the reasons supplied by the content-independent status of the precedent. So although the Supreme Court of the United States professes (whether the court actually behaves in such a way is less certain, as will be discussed in a subsequent section) to operate under a rule of *stare decisis*, such that it believes itself under an obligation to follow its own previous decisions even when a majority of the current court thinks those decisions mistaken, the existence and even the internalization of such a rule is not inconsistent with the current—instant—court, on occasion, overruling or refusing to follow one of its earlier decisions. When, famously, the Supreme Court in *Brown v. Board of Education* ((1954) 347 U.S. 483) in 1954 overruled *Plessy v. Ferguson* ((1896) 163 U.S. 537), which in 1896 had held that officially racially segregated public facilities did not violate the constitutional requirement of equal protection of the laws so long as the racially segregated facilities were physically or nominally equal, the court need not have claimed that the *Plessy* decision had no precedential weight. It could have claimed simply that precedent-based reasons are not conclusive, and that in *Brown* the precedent-based reasons for following the decision in *Plessy* were outweighed by, say, the moral and legal reasons in 1954 for ending official racial segregation in the public schools.

Yet although the content-independent reasons for following a precedent need not be absolute, in a domain in which a rule of precedent is actually operative it would be expected that over a long enough run of cases the reasons supplied by the principle of precedent would on occasion be outcome determinative. That is, we should expect that a court or judge who actually took the reasons supplied by the idea of precedent to provide content-independent reasons for making decisions that it or she otherwise thought mistaken would on occasion follow the precedent in spite of her or its content-based reasons for deciding otherwise. If such subjugation of first-order substantive reasons to the constraints of precedent never or rarely occurred—if a judge or court professed adherence to a norm of precedent but never reached outcomes other than those consistent with her or its content-based and all-things-considered substantive judgment—there would be reason to doubt that the norm of precedent was actually being internalized by the judge or court. This possibility, which is central to the Legal Realist claims about precedent which will be discussed in a subsequent section, should not be discounted, for claims of its empirical plausibility are far from frivolous. Nevertheless, as an initial matter we can still understand what a norm of precedent would do if it were operative, while temporarily delaying considering the extent to which, if at all, such norms are actually operative in various legal decision-making domains.

On Distinguishing Precedent from Analogy

In some of the literature on precedent and on analogy, arguments from precedent are equated with arguments from analogy (Holyoak 2005; Weinreb 2005), but this conflation is a mistake (Schauer 2008), albeit an understandable one. Because arguments from analogy are widespread in law, and because arguments from analogy typically use a previously decided case as the source of the analogy, commentators, especially those external to the legal system, assume that this form of argument is an argument from precedent, but doing so ignores the important differences between the two, and risks misunderstanding or misinterpreting the very idea of precedential constraint.

More specifically, an argument from analogy is ordinarily a form of persuasion and justification, but not of constraint. One making an argument from analogy typically finds an example, called the *source* in the literature on analogical reasoning, and then identifies some conclusion or characteristic about the source that both the user of the analogy and the object of the user's argumentative or justificatory efforts will find appealing, and then calls forth a similarity between the source and the *target*, the current issue that is the subject of the argument from analogy (Gentner, Holyoak and Kokinov 2001; Holyoak and Thagard 1995). If the subject of the argument—those whom someone making an argument seeks to persuade—accepts the similarity, therefore, the subject may be persuaded that the similarity justifies treating the target case in the same way that the source case was treated. When President George H. W. Bush analogized Saddam Hussein to Adolf Hitler in order to justify intervention to prevent an Iraqi takeover of Kuwait, he asked his audience to recognize an important similarity between the two— that both were territory-expanding and highly dangerous dictators—so that someone who recognized the wisdom of stopping Hitler would similarly recognize the wisdom of stopping Saddam Hussein (Spellman and Holyoak 1992). And in law, the same argumentative maneuver is widespread. Consider, for example, *Adams v. New Jersey Steamboat Company* ((1896) 45 NE 369), an 1896 case from the New York Court of Appeals (New York's highest state court) in which the issue, arising out of a burglary on board, was whether a steamboat with passenger compartments was more like a train with sleeping berths, in which case the steamboat owner would be held to normal standards of negligence in determining liability, or more like an inn, in which case the substantially stricter liability standards for innkeepers would apply. In analogizing the steamboat's passenger compartments to the inn and not to the train, the court identified similarities between the two—the presence of lockable doors, for example—and used those similarities to construct an analogy such that the same result reached for innkeepers would be the result reached for the operators of steamboats with passenger cabins.

Although the analogical form of reasoning exemplified by *Adams* is ubiquitous in law, the court's argument was not an argument from precedent in the strict sense. The law relating to an innkeeper's liability did not bind or otherwise constrain the New York court, as would have been the case had there been a previous decision, involving a different steamboat and a different burglary victim, by the very same court holding steamboat owners to the strict standards applied to innkeepers. Precedential constraint is about the obligation of a lower or subsequent court to reach the same result with respect to the same question as had been reached before or above, even if the judge in the instant case believed the previous or higher decision to be mistaken. But no such mechanism was at work in *Adams*. The court in *Adams* used the analogy to justify its chosen result, and not to explain why in fact it had no choice at all, as would have been the case were we talking about precedential constraint. And the advocates in *Adams* presumably each used analogical reasoning to try to persuade the court that the steamboat's passenger cabins were more like rooms in an inn or, on the contrary, more like the open compartments on a train, but neither would have suggested that the court had no choice in the matter, as would have been the case had there been a previous decision on virtually identical facts, or had this been a lower court constrained to follow even those decisions of higher courts with which it disagreed.

Analogical argument, therefore, involves the selection of a source analog (which in legal argument is often but not necessarily a previously decided case) that the maker of the argument believes will be persuasive (Levi 1949), but genuine precedential decision-making is neither about choice nor persuasion. It is about constraint. If there is in fact a case "on point," or "on all fours" (both common legal expressions) from a higher court, or from the same court on a previous occasion, the constrained court has little choice in the matter, and the core idea of precedent, the justifications for which will be considered in a subsequent section, is about the obligation of a court to make decisions, with which it may well disagree as a matter of substance, just because of the existence of the precedent.

That analogical reasoning and precedential constraint are commonly, even if mistakenly, conflated is likely a function of two different causes. First, in legal discourse the source analogs are frequently referred to as "precedents," which in much of law is the umbrella term used to designate any previous decision of any court. It is not a linguistic mistake in legal argument to refer to a decision from another jurisdiction as a precedent, as in saying "there is precedent in Montana for this result" during an argument to a court in New Jersey, which is of course not bound by the Montana decision in any way. And because the word "precedent" is capacious in just this way, it encourages the failure to distinguish genuinely constraining precedents from those previous decisions of various courts that either did not deal with precisely the same question or did not emanate from a court whose decisions are binding on the court deciding the current case.

Perhaps more importantly, cases involving genuine precedential constraint are likely to be underrepresented in appellate decisions, by virtue of what is commonly called the "selection effect" (Priest and Klein 1984; Schauer 1988). Because parties to a dispute would not ordinarily be expected to expend resources to litigate (or appeal) a case in which the law was clearly against them, litigation typically involves disputes where each side, whilst holding mutually exclusive views about the effect of the law on their dispute, believes it has a plausible chance of victory. This can only happen, however, where the law (or, sometimes, the facts) is at least somewhat unclear. And if just this kind of plausible disagreement about the likely outcome is the standard characteristic for litigated cases, and even more so for those litigated cases that are appealed, and more so yet for litigated cases that are appealed to the highest courts of some jurisdiction, then the universe of appellate decisions and opinions is a universe disproportionately populated by hard cases. The corollary of this disproportionate selection of hard cases for litigation and appeal, therefore, is that when there exists a case directly on point from a higher court or from a previous iteration of the same court, the case will likely be an easy one in any decision-making domain in which the norm of precedent operates, and will for that reason be unlikely to wind up in court or on appeal. In other words, the realm of legal disputes in which precedent genuinely constrains will be a realm that remains largely outside of the domain of reported appellate opinions, and conversely, the domain of reported appellate opinions will be those hard cases in which analogical argument but not precedential constraint will dominate.

That analogical argument looms large in appellate decision-making, therefore, should not lead us to overestimate its importance in law generally. And the relative infrequency of reported cases in which precedent is dispositive should similarly not lead us to underestimate the importance of precedent in framing and resolving legal disputes, and in making legal decision-making generally potentially different, as analogical reasoning does not, from those domains in which decision-makers are not expected to subjugate their own best judgment to the judgments of others they believe mistaken.

On Identifying Precedents

It is one thing to observe that precedent is about the obligation of a legal decision-maker to obey those decisions from above or before that constrain the decision-maker in the instant case. It is another to determine which previous decisions actually have, or should have, this force. An important issue that has dominated the literature on precedent, therefore, is the question of what is a precedent—of what makes some previous decision the same as the decision now under consideration (Schauer 2009: 44–60)—and it is to that that we now turn.

Obviously no previous decision from a potential precedent case will be totally identical in all respects to the instant case. At the very least, of course, the parties will be different, and the time—potentially a relevant part of the context—will be different. Still, on numerous occasions those and related differences will be patently inconsequential. In *MacPherson v. Buick Motor Company* ((1916) 111 NE 1050), for example, the New York Court of Appeals, with then-Judge (he was later to become a justice of the United States Supreme Court) Benjamin Cardozo writing the opinion in 1916, held that a purchaser of an automobile could sue the manufacturer of a defective product even though the consumer had bought the product, in this case a Buick automobile, not from the manufacturer but from an independent dealer. Had a subsequent case involving the same question then arisen a year later involving an injury not to Mr. MacPherson but instead to a Ms. Caminetti, and had Ms. Caminetti been injured by a defective Oldsmobile rather than a defective Buick, any attempt to claim that those differences were consequential would ordinarily (we can of course construct unusual hypotheticals challenging this generalization) have been frivolous. Similarly, the United States Supreme Court decided in 1966 in *Miranda v. Arizona* ((1966) 384 U.S. 436) that a suspect held in custody must be advised of his right to remain silent prior to questioning by the police. There is no doubt that the decision, as a matter of genuine precedential constraint, encompassed all felonies and not just the type of felony with which Mr. Miranda had been charged, encompassed all varieties of law-enforcement officials and not just local police officers, and was applicable throughout the United States and not just in Arizona. A judge in South Carolina dealing with a murder or burglary case (Miranda had been charged with kidnapping and rape) would have been obliged as a matter of vertical precedent to apply *Miranda* even if she thought the decision mistaken, and the same would have applied to the Supreme Court itself, as a matter of *stare decisis*, in a hypothetical case decided a year later, an obligation that would have extended even to a new justice who was not on the court when *Miranda* was decided and who believed the *Miranda* decision to be erroneous.

Although the sameness in these cases is obvious, often the question is not so straightforward, and it is just this question of whether some subsequent case is relevantly the same as the most germane precedent case that has generated the literature on just how to determine the scope of the constraint of a precedent case. Consider, for example, the British counterpart to *MacPherson*, the equally famous case of *Donoghue v. Stevenson* ([1932] AC 562 (HL)). That case, decided by the House of Lords in 1932 in litigation initiated in Scotland, involved the same legal question as that in *MacPherson* about the liability of a manufacturer to a consumer who had had no direct dealings with the manufacturer, but in this case that defective product was a bottle of ginger beer which turned out to contain the decomposed remains of a dead snail, producing physical illness and mental distress for the consumer. Putting aside the trivial cases—would the decision in *Donoghue* have applied to the remains of a dead spider, or to a bottle containing lemonade rather than ginger beer—there are still serious and non-frivolous questions about the reach of the precedential constraint of the *Donoghue* judgment. Would the case apply to other food products? Would it apply to food products sold in transparent containers rather than the opaque bottle at issue in *Donoghue*? Would it apply to food products sold at workplaces rather than in public restaurants? And would it apply to consumer products other than food, such as, for example, Buick automobiles?

In answering such questions, it is tempting to say that the holding of the precedent case applies only to *similar* cases, but such a conclusion is merely preliminary, for then the inquiry simply moves to the question of just how we are to determine similarity and difference. Two things may be similar for some purposes but not for others, as when a photographer might treat a black dog and a black pocketbook as similar for the purpose of determining the proper exposure, but not for the purpose of deciding whether or not to bring the pocketbook to the veterinarian if it was in need of repair. Indeed, even those things that would be part of what philosophers would call the same "natural kind" might still be different for legal purposes. Your dog and my dog are both members of the same natural kind—dogs—but in cases of, say, disputed ownership, there is much that matters other than the membership (or not) of something in this or that natural kind.

Because of the fruitlessness of any inquiry into whether things "really" are or are not similar, the traditional answer to the question of similarity for purposes of determining what is a precedent has turned to the question of trying to determine the *ratio decidendi* of the precedent case (Marshall 1997). That is, the question to be asked, so it is said, is just *why* did the precedent court decide the case the way it did? And thus the traditional answer to the question of what is a precedent is that subsequent cases falling within the *ratio decidendi*—or *rationale*—of the precedent case are controlled by that case (Cross and Harris 1991). Under this view, if the House of Lords had allowed liability against the ginger beer manufacturer because of the inability of either the consumer or the retailer to examine the product for defects, then this ruling would apply as well to nonfood products in which again neither the retailer nor the consumer could identify some latent defect, such as, for example, a small crack in the wheel attached to a Buick automobile which would cause the wheel to break under certain, but normal, driving conditions.

Much theoretical ink has been spilled over the question of just how one determines the rationale of some potential precedent case, with some theorists arguing that it is a matter of connecting the facts as found by the court with the outcome, others saying that it must be the connection of *material* facts with outcome and still others believing that it is a matter of actually extracting the argument from the opinion of the first decision (Goodhart 1930; Goodhart 1959; Montrose 1957; Schauer 1991: 181–87; Simpson 1958). All of these approaches, however, seem to founder on the problem of under- determination. That is, with respect to all of these approaches to determining what is a precedent for what, there are multiple rationales that would be consistent with what can be found in the precedent case. A decomposed snail is a nauseating dead animal, but it is also a dead animal, a nauseating substance and simply foreign matter. A Buick is an automobile, but it is also a consumer product, a method of transportation, a potentially dangerous item and a manufactured product whose defects would not be apparent to an ordinary consumer. As among these and numerous other candidates for determining what the precedent case decided, and with reference to what it decided, no description of the facts and the holding, or the material facts and the holding, or even the arguments presented in the case, can uniquely determine the extension of the precise and narrowest holding of the potential precedent case. And if this is so, then except in the trivial and uninteresting ways described above, the very idea of constraint by precedent appears to be illusory, and arguments from precedent turn out to be forms of persuasion used by competing advocates who are free to construct the alleged precedential constraints in largely unconstrained ways (Levi 1949; Stone 1968: 241–57).

As a result of this problem of what we might call illusory constraint, some theorists have recognized that the key to identifying the scope of a precedent is to look at the actual words used by the precedent court to explain and justify its holding (Alexander 1989; Schauer 2009: 53–60). If the House of Lords in *Donoghue v. Stevenson* had *said* that it reached its conclusion because, for example, "any defects in the product could not have been identified by the consumer," then the extension of the case, and the scope of its precedential constraint, would have been to all consumer products whose defects could not be identified by a consumer. But if instead the House of Lords had said that "food products involve special obligations on manufacturers," then the case would have been a precedent for future cases involving food products but not for consumer products other than food, such as Buicks.

For obvious reasons, this model of precedential reach, which relies heavily on the exact words used by the precedent court to solve the indeterminacy problem, has been called the "rule model" of precedent (Alexander 1989; Alexander and Sherwin 2001: 136–56; Alexander and Sherwin 2008: 57–62). Under this model, the exact words used by the first court function in much the same way as a written rule, and in both with reference to a rule and with reference to precedent the scope of the authoritative constraint is both established and circumscribed by the canonical and authoritative words originally employed. Obviously, there will be situations in which the words used in the precedent case will not be clear, but that is true for the rules that appear in statutes, constitutions and regulations as well. The important point is that in order to determine the reach of a precedent one must treat the actual words used by the first court as a rule, and just as the way in which the words of a rule will determine the scope of that rule, so too will the actual words used by the first or higher court determine just what the ruling of the first court will be a precedent for, and just what will lie beyond the constraining force of the first case.

The Value—if Any—of Precedential Constraint

Once we understand that a system of precedent requires legal decision-makers—especially judges—to reach decisions with which they disagree just because some other judge or court has done so previously, the virtues of precedent become more elusive. This may not be the case, of course, with vertical precedent. Lower courts may be obliged to follow the lead of higher courts even in the face of disagreement for the same reason that we expect privates to obey the orders of sergeants and sergeants to obey the orders of lieutenants, for the same reason we expect workplace subordinates to follow the instructions of their supervisors and for the same reason that we expect (and force) people to obey the law even when they disagree with its content. In this respect, vertical authority is a ubiquitous fact of effective human organization, and it should come as no surprise that this fact—or principle—is as applicable to legal decision-making as it is to so many other realms of human organization and cooperation.

With respect to horizontal precedent—*stare decisis*—however, the matter is not so simple. It may well be common to expect privates, workers and citizens to obey orders from above, but we do not typically expect privates, workers, or citizens to behave as their similarly situated predecessors have behaved in the face of belief that their predecessors were mistaken. Nor do we expect presidents and prime ministers to adopt the same policy positions as those who have preceded them just because of temporal priority. Indeed, introductory books on logic and formal and informal reasoning often treat arguments from precedent as fallacies, nasty argumentative habits to be expunged from the minds of hitherto untutored undergraduates. And thus in the normal course of things, a principle of *stare decisis* is, at best, the exception rather than the rule, and accordingly it is hardly obvious why the law appears to place a special burden on legal decision-makers to make what they perceive to be the same mistakes that their predecessors have made. When Justice Oliver Wendell Holmes opined that it was "revolting" that courts should be bound by precedents which "persist . . . for no better reasons than . . . that so it was laid down in the time of Henry IV" (Holmes 1897: 469); when Jeremy Bentham described the constraints of *stare decisis* as "acting without reason, to the declared exclusion of reason, and thereby in opposition to reason" (Bentham 1983); and when Justice Antonin Scalia rejects the constraints of *stare decisis* as inconsistent with his oath to support the Constitution and not what his predecessors have said the Constitution says, observing as well that "[t]he whole function of [*stare decisis*] is to make us say that what is false under proper analysis must nevertheless be held to be true (Scalia 1997: 139), all have noted the peculiar nature of horizontal precedent, and the counterintuitive idea that decision-makers should follow what they believe to be the mistaken decisions of predecessors who are no higher than they are in the legal hierarchy.

Yet although the constraints of horizontal precedent have been prominently excoriated for generations, so too have they been defended. Even more prominent still than the just-quoted denigrations is Justice Louis Brandeis's observation in *Burnet v. Coronado Oil & Gas. Co.* ((1932) 285 U.S. 393, 406) in 1932 that "in most matters it is more important that [the question] be settled than that it be settled right." And thus Justice Brandeis identified what has been one of the most enduring arguments for a system of horizontal—and, indeed, vertical—precedent: the frequent need for stability for stability's sake and predictability for predictability's sake. In large part this is an argument from reliance. The ability to count on some state of affairs or some decision is important in many aspects of life, and often, as Justice Brandeis observed, more important than making sure we are as right as we can be on every occasion. So although there is of course no reason, except in particular cases, to believe that a judge of a particular court will be less able to make the right decision than a prior judge of the same court, and thus no reason to believe that the first judge was more likely correct than the second judge, it still may be true that the positive advantages of consistency will in some domains outweigh the potential advantages of allowing each judge to try to improve on the results reached by his or her predecessor.

Thus, the principal virtues of *stare decisis* are all located in the vicinity of the related ideas of stability, reliance and predictability. And if—a big "if"—we believe, as most common-law systems have apparently believed for a very long time, that stability for stability's sake is more important in the legal system than in other decision-making domains, we can understand why the seemingly peculiar idea of horizontal precedent, an idea that is by no means widespread across all decision-making domains, is especially concentrated in law. The virtues of horizontal precedent in law thus relate to the largest questions about what the law is for, and under some accounts of law's purpose—especially accounts (perhaps like Holmes's) that emphasize law as a tool for social progress and societal change—it is hardly obvious that horizontal precedent need be considered as important as it has been for some time. Interestingly, *stare decisis* is not nearly as old as the common law itself, having little authoritative recognition until the early years of the nineteenth century (Lee 1999; Wise 1975). That *stare decisis* is thus such a comparatively new idea, at least when compared to the age of the common law, to say nothing of the earliest origins of law itself, may indicate that the values of stability for stability's sake, even when coupled with the related values of reliance and predictability, are far more fragile, contingent and context dependent than many of the other values that underlie the legal system.

In addition to the value of stability for stability's sake, *stare decisis* may foster the kind of community-wide cross-temporal integration that Ronald Dworkin has referred to as "integrity" (Dworkin 1986: 225–75). If communities are held together and even defined by shared values and norms, among other things, then requiring consistency across time, which is what a norm of *stare decisis* does, may be a way of making a community cohesive across time, and may even be part of why we can say we are members of the same community as those who are long dead. If the very fact that what has been done in the past is a reason to do it again, a link is forged between the past and the present that may not otherwise have existed.

It is important to note that one of the most common arguments for a system of horizontal precedent turns out to have less purchase than many people have commonly thought. This is the value of "treating like cases alike," and it has been promoted since Aristotle. The problem with this principle, however, as many theorists have noted (Hart 1994: 157–63; Schauer 2003: 199–207; Winston 1974), is that we cannot tell what case is like any other case without having some principle that determines similarity and difference. And thus the determination of likeness and unlikeness is inevitably normative, requiring a determination of the purpose for treating any two technically different items in the same way, or for using some but not other differences to justify treating two items in different ways. It is true that the venerable principle of treating like cases alike would say that once we have determined, with admittedly some external and normative input, that two cases or situations are alike, then a system of precedent would demand that they should be treated the same even if the second decision-maker thinks the first decision-maker was mistaken. But in that case the claim that like cases should be treated alike loses its moral force, and turns into the pragmatic principle of institutional design that Brandeis and the arguments from stability, predictability and reliance have attempted to capture. So it is not so much that the principle of treating like cases alike is wrong. Rather, it is simply that the principle is better understood as restating a conclusion rather than providing an independent argument for that conclusion.

Precedent and Legal Realism

It is one thing to say that a prescriptive norm of precedent does or should exist. But it is very much another thing to say that such a norm is an accurate description of judicial behavior, or of legal behavior more generally. This descriptive question about the actual use of precedent is an important one, in part because of the distinct possibility that norms of precedent are not nearly as strong, in practice, as is commonly believed, and in part because these skeptical inquiries about precedent are such a large part of the challenges to traditional legal reasoning offered by those typically described as Legal Realists (Leiter 1996; Twining 1973).

This chapter is not the appropriate one to describe or analyze Legal Realism in any depth, so a brief and superficial description will have to suffice. But the important idea is that Legal Realism, with its roots in Holmes and various late nineteenth-century European perspectives, is a challenge to the claim that legal rules and legal reasoning are important *causes* of judicial decisions. In the view of exemplary Legal Realists such as Jerome Frank, Joseph Hutcheson, Herman Oliphant, Underhill Moore and, in a more nuanced and qualified way, Karl Llewellyn (Llewellyn 2011), judges behave like lawyers with clients rather than as arbiters who made their decisions only after hearing all of the facts and consulting all of the law. That is, just as the lawyer's position is initially determined by the wishes of her client, so did the Realists believe that, at least in the hard cases that wind up in appellate courts, a judge would first determine how she wanted the case to come out, and would only then marshal legal authorities to support a result reached on grounds other than what might have been dictated by the authorities. For Jerome Frank and others, the initial cause of the outcome preference would be various aspects of the judge's personality, and how those personality attributes intersected with and reacted to the numerous characteristics of the particular litigants and the particular facts of the particular dispute. By contrast, for Llewellyn and similarly policy-oriented Realists, the judge's initial choice of an outcome was more likely based on general policy considerations. But in both instances, and others, the substantial determinant of a legal outcome was, initially, something other than the "paper rules," as Llewellyn referred to the formal law in law books, and was determined prior to, or independent of, consulting the paper rules.

The Realists recognized that legal outcomes reached primarily on such nonlegal grounds could not be described as such, and would have to be justified by reference to standard legal materials such as statutes, constitutional provisions, learned legal treatises and, of course, decided judicial opinions. That is, they believed that references to such materials were not descriptions of the causes of legal decisions, or accounts of the judge's actual reasoning processes. Rather, they were ex post rationalizations or justifications of results reached on other grounds. But the Legal Realists also believed that, especially in an inevitably messy common-law system (and even more so in an especially messy multi-jurisdictional system such as that of the United States), precedents could be found (or described) to support a wide range of results reached on other grounds. For the Realists, therefore, precedents served as ex post rationalizations for decisions reached on other grounds, rather than serving as genuine causes of or constraints on judicial decisions.

The Legal Realist view of precedent—that precedents are neither causal nor constraining, but largely justificatory—is thus an empirical claim, and one that is grounded on the observation that it is often possible to locate a precedent supporting whatever result a judge might otherwise want to reach, coupled with the further observation that even individual judicial decisions are susceptible to such a broad range of interpretations and descriptions that they exercise little, if any, genuine constraint. Moreover, the empirical claim is commonly limited to claims about hard appellate cases, and thus subject to all of the qualifications that emanate out of the selection effect described above.

The Realists, who flourished in the 1930s and 1940s, tended to support their empirical claims with anecdotes and broad observations, rather than with what today would pass muster as serious empirical inquiry. Nevertheless, more contemporary research has tended to provide some support for the Realist views about the effects of precedent, at least in the highest appellate courts. A substantial number of political scientists, for example, over a period of several decades, have examined opinions and decisions of the United States Supreme Court by applying principles of multiple regression to a dataset of case attributes and justice attributes. And this research has provided—for the limited array of cases that reach the Supreme Court, and for an array which because of the political and ideological valence of these cases and in light of the selection effect may well not be fully representative—considerable support for the Realist claims about the effects of formal law in general and precedent in particular (Maveety 2006; Segal and Spaeth 2004). Thus, the research supports the view that nonlegal attitudes and ideologies have more value in explaining the votes of Supreme Court justices, especially but not only in high-salience and high-ideological-valence cases, than do any of the more traditional and formal sources of law. Indeed, the very fact that one of the leading books in this genre is entitled *Stare Indecisis* (Brenner and Spaeth 1995) illustrates the way in which much of the focus of the attitudinal research has been to demonstrate that although the Supreme Court professes to be bound by a norm of *stare decisis*, the actual behavior of the justices suggests that the norm is weaker than is often supposed, and that Supreme Court justices are typically unwilling to subjugate their own best judgment, whether legal or moral or political or pragmatic or policy or otherwise, to the judgments of their predecessors that they believe mistaken (Schauer 2007).

Until recently, there has been much less empirical research about the actual operation of the constraints of precedent in lower courts and in state courts than there has been with respect to the Supreme Court of the United States, although the situation is changing somewhat. And with respect to the empirical question about the effect and weight of precedent in lower courts, the issue of vertical precedent reemerges, because all states' courts and lower federal courts do have a court above them. But the issue of horizontal precedent still exists as well, because state supreme courts typically profess an obligation to follow earlier decisions of their own court, and federal courts of appeals often, albeit with more complications because of the way in which panel decisions (typically of three judges) intersect with decisions *en banc* (by the entire court, which may involve close to 20 members), claim to have a similar obligation to follow earlier decisions within the same circuit. But although it is implausible to suppose that such an internalized obligation has no causal effect whatsoever on outcomes, especially in more routine cases in which judges are unlikely to have strong moral or policy or political preferences, just how great that effect is is a topic for empirical research that no amount of philosophical or jurisprudential analysis of the concept of precedent can resolve. The nature of precedential obligation is assuredly a philosophical and jurisprudential topic, as is the analysis and evaluation of the arguments that might normatively support such an obligation, but the existence—or not—of belief in such an obligation, and the extent to which actual judges and other legal decision-makers behave and decide in accordance with such a belief even if the belief exists, is in the final analysis an empirical question whose answer is likely to vary across jurisdictions, across time, across courts and even across individual judges.

References

Adams v. New Jersey Steamboat Company (1896) 45 NE 369.

Alexander, L. (1989) "Constrained by Precedent," *Southern California Law Review* 63: 1–64.

—— and Sherwin, E. (2001) *The Rule of Rules: Morality, Rules, and the Dilemmas of Law*, Durham, N.C.: Duke University Press.

—— (2008) *Demystifying Legal Reasoning*, New York: Cambridge University Press.

Bentham, J. (1983) "Constitutional Code," in F. Rosen and J. H. Burns, eds., *The Collected Works of Jeremy Bentham*, London: Athlone Press.

Brenner, S. and Spaeth, H. J. (1995) *Stare Indecisis: The Alteration of Precedent on the Supreme Court, 1946–1992*, Cambridge: Cambridge University Press.

Brown v. Board of Education (1954) 347 U.S. 483.

Burnet v. Coronado Oil & Gas. Co. (1932) 285 U.S. 393.

Cross, R. and Harris, J. W. (1991) *Precedent in English Law*, 4th edition, Oxford: Clarendon Press.

Donoghue v. Stevenson [1932] AC 562 (House of Lords).

Dworkin, R. (1986) *Law's Empire*, Cambridge, Mass.: Harvard University Press.

Gentner, D., Holyoak, K. J. and Kokinov, B. N., eds. (2001) *The Analogical Mind: Perspectives from Cognitive Science*, Cambridge: Cambridge University Press.

Goodhart, A. L. (1930) "Determining the Ratio Decidendi of a Case," *Yale Law Journal* 40: 161–83.

—— (1959) "The Ratio Decidendi of a Case," *Modern Law Review* 22: 117–24

Hart, H. L. A. (1982) "Commands and Authoritative Legal Reasons," in *Essays on Bentham: Jurisprudence and Political Theory*, Oxford: Clarendon Press.

—— (1994) *The Concept of Law*, 2nd edition, P. A. Bulloch and J. Raz, eds., Oxford: Clarendon Press.

Holmes, O. W. (1897) "The Path of the Law," *Harvard Law Review* 10: 457–78.

Holyoak, K. J. (2005) "Analogy," in K. J. Holyoak and R. G. Morrison, eds., *The Cambridge Handbook of Thinking and Reasoning*, Cambridge: Cambridge University Press.

—— and Thagard, P. (1995) *Mental Leaps: Analogy in Creative Thought*, Cambridge: Cambridge University Press.

Lee, T. R. (1999) "Stare Decisis in Historical Perspective," *Vanderbilt Law Review* 52: 647–83.

Leiter, B. (1996) "Legal Realism," in D. Patterson, ed., *A Companion to the Philosophy of Law and Legal Theory*, Oxford: Blackwell.

Levi, E. H. (1949) *An Introduction to Legal Reasoning*, Chicago: University of Chicago Press.

Llewellyn, K. N. (2011) *The Theory of Rules*, F. Schauer, ed., Chicago: University of Chicago Press.

MacPherson v. Buick Motor Company (1916) 111 NE 1050.

Marshall, G. (1997) "What Is Binding in a Precedent?" in D. N. MacCormick and R. S. Summers, eds., *Interpreting Precedents: A Comparative Study*, Aldershot: Ashgate/Dartmouth.

Maveety, N., ed. (2006) *The Pioneers of Judicial Behavior*, Ann Arbor: University of Michigan Press.

Miranda v. Arizona (1966) 384 U.S. 436.

Montrose, J. L. (1957) "The Ratio Decidendi of a Case," *Modern Law Review* 20: 587–95.

Plessy v. Ferguson (1896) 163 U.S. 537.

Priest, G. L. and Klein, W. (1984) "The Selection of Disputes for Litigation," *Journal of Legal Studies* 13: 1–23.

Scalia, A. (1997) *A Matter of Interpretation: Federal Courts and the Law*, Princeton: Princeton University Press.

Schauer, F. (1987) "Precedent," *Stanford Law Review* 39: 571–606.

—— (1988) "Judging in a Corner of the Law," *Southern California Law Review* 61: 1717–1733.

—— (1991) *Playing By the Rules: A Philosophical Examination of Rule-Based Decision-Making in Law and in Life*, Oxford: Clarendon Press.

—— (2003) *Profiles, Probabilities, and Stereotypes*, Cambridge, Mass.: Harvard University Press.

—— (2007) "Has Precedent Ever Really Mattered in the Supreme Court?" *Georgia State University Law Review* 24: 381–401.

—— (2008) "Why Precedent in Law (and Elsewhere) Is Not Totally (or Even Substantially) About Analogy," *Perspectives on Psychological Science* 3: 454–60.

—— (2009) *Thinking Like a Lawyer: A New Introduction to Legal Reasoning*, Cambridge, Mass.: Harvard University Press.

Segal, J. J. and Spaeth, H. J. (2004) *The Supreme Court and the Attitudinal Model Revisited*, New York: Cambridge University Press.

Simpson, A. W. B. (1958) "The Ratio Decidendi of a Case," *Modern Law Review* 21, 155–60.

Spellman, B. A. and Holyoak, K. J. (1992) "If Saddam Is Hitler, Then Who Is George Bush?: Analogical Mapping Between Systems of Social Roles," *Journal of Personality & Social Psychology* 62: 913–22.

Stone, J. (1968) *Legal System and Lawyers' Reasonings*, Sydney: Maitland Publications.

Twining, W. (1973) *Karl Llewellyn and the Realist Movement*, London: Weidenfeld and Nicolson.

Weinreb, L. (2005) *Legal Reason: The Use of Analogy in Legal Argument*, Cambridge: Cambridge University Press.

Winston, K. I. (1974) "On Treating Like Cases Alike," *California Law Review* 62: 1–39.

Wise, E. M. (1975) "The Doctrine of Stare Decisis," *Wayne Law Review* 21: 1043–1078.

Further Reading

For further reading, see: L. Alexander (1989) "Constrained By Precedent," *Southern California Law Review* 63: 1–64; L. Goldstein, ed. (1991) *Precedent in Law*, Oxford: Oxford University Press;

G. Lamond (2008) "Precedent and Analogy in Legal Reasoning," in E. N. Zalta, ed., *The Stanford Encyclopedia of Philosophy*, Fall 2008 Edition, http://plato.stanford.edu/archives/fall2008/entries/legal-reas-prec/; G. J. Postema (1991) "On the Moral Presence of Our Past," *McGill Law Journal* 36: 1153–1180; F. Schauer (1987) "Precedent," *Stanford Law Review* 39: 571–602; F. Schauer (2008) "Why Precedent in Law (and Elsewhere) Is Not Totally (or Even Substantially) About Analogy," *Perspectives on Psychological Science* 3: 454–60; and F. Schauer (2009) *Thinking Like a Lawyer: A New Introduction to Legal Reasoning*, Cambridge, Mass.: Harvard University Press, chs. 3, 5.

Part III

THEORIES OF LEGAL AREAS

CRIMINAL LAW

10

THE JUSTIFICATION
OF PUNISHMENT

Mitchell N. Berman

The philosophy of criminal law is a rich and varied domain of legal philosophy, one that both draws upon and contributes to developments in other philosophical subfields ranging from the philosophy of mind and of action to moral and political theory. Among the topics that philosophers of criminal law explore are the character of culpable acts and the relationship between acts and omissions; the nature of intention and its connection to other mental states (and pseudo mental states) such as knowledge and negligence; the metaphysics of causation and the problem of moral luck; the differences between justification and excuse; the moral bearing of insanity and psychopathy; and the principles governing fair ascription of responsibility for acts of others. And this is just a very partial list.

Traditionally, however, one concern has dominated the others: to explain how, if at all, the state is morally justified in subjecting an individual to criminal punishment. Although the precise contours or constituents of criminal punishment are debated, it indisputably involves the intentional infliction of hard treatment or the deprivation of substantial liberties. Because ordinary moral rules dictate that we should not treat one another in such ways, the practice is said to stand in need of justification. And criminal law theorists have long seen the challenge of supplying such justification as their central task. The answers they provide routinely travel under the heading of "theories of punishment," but "justifications for punishment" would be more apt.

This chapter critically reviews the most important justificatory accounts in the literature and offers thoughts regarding where debates over the justification of punishment might profitably turn in the near future. It proceeds in five sections. The first sets the stage by explicating what punishment is—or, as I will argue is the better way to understand the problem, what is meant by "punishment" for purposes of debates regarding its justifiability. Although theorists have proposed and defended a staggering variety of particularistic accounts designed to meet this justificatory challenge, it is conventional to group them into two camps: consequentialism and retributivism. The second section introduces and sketches these two broad schools, while the third notes some recent doubts about this way of classifying proposed justifications for punishment, but explains why the two-part consequentialist/retributivist framework remains generally sound and helpful. The fourth section reviews the dominant challenges to consequentialist and retributivist justifications, along with the predominant responses offered to those challenges. It also shows how consequentialist and retributivist approaches have come close to converging on a desert-constrained pluralism. The final section suggests that, in the face of something approaching a consensus regarding the pluralistic justifiability of punishment, an important philosophical challenge going forward is to explicate and better defend the constraints on punishment that all retributivists and most consequentialists endorse.

What Is Punishment?

Whatever else criminal punishment may be, it is disagreeable to the person punished—far more than usually, if not invariably. But the state does many things to individuals that they find disagreeable: it imposes taxes and quarantines, orders deportation, condemns property and so on. None of these practices is termed "punishment." More importantly, even to the extent that we reasonably question the propriety or permissibility of some of these other practices, we tend to think that the demand that *punishment* be justified is somehow special—more pressing and harder to satisfy. So this practice—punishment—that we aim to justify must be something more or other than the state's imposition of disagreeable consequences upon individuals. Many theorists, therefore, have attempted to identify the necessary and sufficient conditions for an imposition to count as punishment.

For half a century, the dominant view has been that the search for a true definition of punishment is either futile or unnecessary. Accordingly, many commentators follow H. L. A. Hart in focusing instead on the central or standard case, which Hart, building on the work of Anthony Flew and Stanley Benn, identified as consisting of five conditions:

(i) It must involve pain or other consequences normally considered unpleasant.
(ii) It must be for an offense against legal rules.
(iii) It must be of an actual or supposed offender for his offense.
(iv) It must be intentionally administered by human beings other than the offender.
(v) It must be imposed and administered by an authority constituted by a legal system against which the offense is committed.

(Hart 1968: 4–5)

Despite its influence, the Flew–Benn–Hart account is criticized on two basic grounds. Some commentators maintain that it includes too many conditions. For example, conditions (ii) and (v) limit the account to punishment imposed by the state—"legal punishment" or "criminal punishment"—whereas some argue that punishment is a more general concept, one we can better understand by working with a definition that encompasses punishment in extralegal contexts, like the discipline that parents mete out to their children (e.g., Zaibert 2006: 7–37). Other theorists argue that the Flew–Benn–Hart account includes too few conditions. Many follow Joel Feinberg in believing that an additional standard feature of punishment—that it be intended to communicate moral condemnation—is either a necessary condition or at least a marker of the central case (Feinberg 1970).

We can gain a better handle on the definitional debates by recalling the question that brings us here. One possible question arises from a classificatory concern. We observe some practice that appears, pretheoretically, to be a possible or borderline case of punishment—say, imposition of a fine on a corporation, or continued preventive detention of a sex offender after he has served his full sentence—and want to know whether it qualifies as punishment or not. This type of interest might reasonably cause us to ask, "What is the concept of punishment?" If we can answer this question satisfactorily, we will then be much better able to determine whether some possibly borderline case falls within the contours of the concept.

Our concern, however, is not classificatory, but justificatory. That is, we observe, or call to mind, some actual impositions of criminal punishment—say, execution or flogging or incarceration—and ask: "What, if anything, could justify *this?*" We might then generalize our question to "What justifies criminal punishment?" And when we do, we can be led to think that we must identify precisely that which we seek to justify, and thus must answer the classificatory question. That is the mistake I wish to counsel against. Rather, our need is to identify the characteristics of the standard or central case of criminal punishment that are responsible for causing us to think its justifiability significantly in doubt. Put another way, precisely because (or insofar as) we believe that criminal punishment faces a more challenging demand for justification than do other state practices that impose disagreeable consequences on individuals, we want to identify the particular features that render a range of salient legal practices that we customarily term "punishment" in especially demanding need of moral justification.

Once we appreciate the different goals of justificatory and classificatory inquiries, it is easier to see what it is about focal punishment practices that makes them especially worrisome from a moral point of view. Condition (iv) in the Flew–Benn–Hart account of the standard case specifies that punishment must be "intentionally administered." This is potentially ambiguous. It seems probable that any concrete instantiation of punishment—a particular course of floggings or a particular act of imprisonment, say—is administered intentionally, not accidentally. More important is that the authorities who intentionally administer that treatment intend that it cause the subject of that treatment pain or suffering. That is, the practices and actions that forcefully provoke philosophers' worries when they ask "Can punishment be justified?" involve the intentional infliction of hard treatment, or the deprivation of substantial liberties, or both, *because of, and not despite,* the expectation that the person subjected to the treatment would suffer as a result. (Quibbles can and have been raised against this claim. I believe that they can be met, but elaboration would consume more space than is warranted.) One need not fully endorse the doctrine of double effect (a principle that, somewhat simplified, recognizes a firm moral difference between causing harm intentionally and knowingly) to believe that inflicting suffering purposefully is in need of especially strong moral justification, and none of the other practices that also produce suffering has suffering as a goal or aim, whether ultimate or intermediate.

The justificatory question, then, plausibly becomes this: what justifies the state in inflicting hard treatment on people for their supposed or claimed wrongdoing with the intention that that treatment cause the supposed or claimed wrongdoer to suffer? When, for simplicity, we ask what justifies the state in inflicting punishment, the term "punishment," in the question and in proposed answers, is a placeholder for hard treatment intended to cause suffering.

If the difference between classificatory and justificatory enterprises is not yet fully clear, imagine a practice of social discipline in which persons found to have violated the criminal law are flogged with utmost politeness and with conspicuous disavowals of any condemnatory intent. Because the element of moral condemnation is absent, punishment theorists who take themselves to be engaged in a classificatory inquiry might puzzle over whether such treatment counts as punishment. Punishment theorists who are interested in the justificatory inquiry need not be bothered by any uncertainty over the concept: whether or not such a practice is properly deemed punishment, it is properly subjected to a stringent demand for moral justification, and it is the theorists' task either to meet the demand or to show why it cannot be met.

Two Types of Answers: Consequentialism and Retributivism

Although philosophers writing in the Western tradition have endeavored to justify criminal punishment against moral objections since ancient Greece, the dominant contemporary views trace mostly to thinkers from the eighteenth and early nineteenth centuries. Drawing on the work of giants like Bentham and Beccaria, Kant and Hegel, punishment theorists writing in the early years of the twentieth century distinguished among a small handful of proposed justifications, running under such headings as deterrence theory, retribution, annulment theory, denunciation theory, reform and rehabilitation. By mid-century, however, commentators had generally folded this myriad of justifications into a simple dichotomy that more or less persists to this day: consequentialism and retributivism.

Very precise definitions of these alternative, and possibly competing, theories of punishment would beg many important debates. Consequentialist theories of punishment maintain that the intentional infliction of suffering or hard treatment can be justified by the good states of affairs that the practice produces or may reasonably be expected to produce. Retributivists, in contrast, would justify punishment on the grounds that it is deserved or otherwise fitting, right or appropriate, and not in terms of any good consequences that individual acts of punishment or the general practice may cause to be realized. Consequentialist justifications are said to be "forward looking" because they depend upon claims about the states of affairs that are to be produced as a result of punishment. Retributivist justifications are deemed "backward looking" because they depend only upon claims about facts and relationships that exist before punishment is imposed. Both approaches, it bears emphasis, are in-principle justifications: they aim to explain what could justify some forms of punishment under certain circumstances, but not to establish that punishment practices in any actual jurisdiction are in fact morally justified.

Because it is customary to classify moral theories—theories regarding what is morally right, wrong and permissible—as either consequentialist or deontological, it is tempting to suppose that consequentialist theories of punishment must be committed to a consequentialist ethic. The unfortunate habit of many writers to affix the "utilitarian" label to what this chapter, following the more common line, terms consequentialist theories of punishment, strengthens that temptation, for utilitarianism is a familiar comprehensive moral theory. However, the mapping of consequentialist theories of punishment onto consequentialist moral theories is too facile. To be sure, consequentialists about ethics believe, almost inescapably, that punishment, if it can be justified at all, can be justified only by reference to the good it produces. But the converse does not hold. Consequentialism in punishment theory is a view regarding how the intentional infliction of suffering for wrongdoing can be morally justified; it is not a view about value or right action more generally. That is, not only can consequentialists about punishment adopt just about any theory of value, they need not even commit to the core principle of consequentialist ethics that the rightness of any action is determined solely by its consequences (actual or expected). Consequentialists about punishment (what this chapter henceforth means by "consequentialist" and its variants, when unmodified) argue that, in principle, the intentional infliction of suffering can be justified by the net good consequences the practice produces. They need not commit to any more comprehensive theory of rightness. Simply put, it is untrue, as one respected commentator has observed, that consequentialist justifications for punishment "shar[e] with all consequentialist theories the belief that ultimately the only morally significant features of an act are the good and bad consequences produced by it" (Ten 1987: 3).

The heart of consequentialism is sometimes called deterrence theory—the compound claim that credible conditional threats to inflict punishment for specified types of wrongdoing (paradigmatically, acts of antisocial aggression) will reduce their incidence, and that the actual imposition of punishment is (reasonably) necessary to make such threats credible. Insofar as the punishment of one wrongdoer deters other potential offenders from offending, the mechanism is termed "general deterrence"; insofar as the experience of having been punished deters the offender himself from reoffending, the mechanism is "specific deterrence."

Deterrence theory, in both general and specific forms, involves both a view about the good state of affairs that punishment can produce—namely, the state in which there are fewer acts of antisocial violence or rights violations than would otherwise obtain—and a view about the mechanism by which punishment produces that state—namely, by bolstering the credibility of conditional threats. But deterrence is not the only means by which punishment might cause a reduction in antisocial aggression and the like. For one thing, punishment can incapacitate offenders from reoffending, either permanently (say, by execution) or for a time (by incarceration)—though incarceration in practice might do more to shift the incidence of violence and aggression, from the general community to the prison population, than to substantially reduce the total number of harmful or wrongful acts. Also, punishment might in theory reduce violence and aggression by reducing offenders' inclinations to offend, by reforming their character, strengthening their attachment to moral or legal norms and even by providing them with job-related skills. These mechanisms, especially the last, are what people have in mind when they invoke "rehabilitation" as a justification for punishment. (It is worth noting, though, that a wrongdoer does not likely develop socially productive skills as a consequence of punishment itself, but as a consequence of whatever training prison officials can provide auxiliary to an offender's punishment.) Relatedly, if punishment can deter what we might call initiatory aggression, it can also deter retaliatory aggression— aggression by victims and their families against initial offenders—by assuring victims that the wrongs they have suffered will be vindicated.

All the foregoing causal mechanisms that consequentialists frequently endorse— deterrence, incapacitation, reform and discouraging private vengeance—are means to bring about the same general type of good—what we might loosely describe as a reduction in harms. But just as consequentialists can and do emphasize different causal *mechanisms* by which punishment can realize good states of affairs (including the reduction of bad states of affairs), they also focus on disparate *goods* at which punishment should aim.

For example, just as it is good that people enjoy their rights to property and bodily integrity free from interference by others (i.e., it is bad when they suffer "harm"), it is also good, *ceteris paribus*, that their preferences be satisfied. We will see that the core claim of retributivism is that offenders deserve to suffer or to be punished, and therefore that punishment is right, or just, or obligatory. Whether or not this is so, many members of society, not only victims, *believe* it to be true. It follows that punishment could conceivably increase aggregate welfare by satisfying widespread popular preferences that wrongdoers be made to suffer, and its potential to do so can be part of a consequentialist justification. Similarly, the failure to punish might exacerbate widespread feelings of injustice, or breed disrespect for the law. Therefore, and putting matters more positively, punishment can contribute to general moral education and reinforce instrumentally or intrinsically valuable social norms. Or, to take another consequentialist proposal, punishment might be justifiable as a contribution to a certain sort of "republican" freedom—the social freedom "constituted by the enjoyment of certain rights and by the infrastructure of capacity and power which this involves," including the shared knowledge of the rights and their entailments (Braithwaite and Pettit 1990: 9). Terming this freedom "dominion," John Braithwaite and Philip Pettit have argued both that it is the human good that an ideal political community should strive to maximize and that punishment is an important means by which it can do so.

In short, consequentialism as an account of what can justify punishment is capacious enough to embrace diverse states of affairs as valuable, and also to emphasize a variety of causal mechanisms by which state-imposed punishment might plausibly bring about those supposedly valuable states. While the above examples of goods and mechanisms that consequentialists invoke are not exhaustive, they give an adequate flavor of consequentialist theorizing. The core idea, again, is that deterrent, reform and denunciatory, expressive, or educative theories are generally understood today simply as emphasizing different, but not incompatible, mechanisms by which punishment can realize a variety of desirable consequences. While some individual consequentialists may be value monists, consequentialism as a family of approaches to justifying punishment is value pluralist.

Notwithstanding the diversity internal to consequentialism, its core idea is reasonably easy to express, and is readily comprehensible (which is not to take a position on whether it is ultimately persuasive). Retributivism is harder to encapsulate. Indeed, writers have identified so many diverse theories that have been called "retributivist" by either their proponents or detractors (e.g., Cottingham 1979; Walker 1999) that some have advocated that "retributivism" be renamed "non-consequentialism"—much as many philosophers prefer "non-consequentialism" to "deontology" as the antipode to "consequentialism" in moral theory.

This picture of retributivism as a hopelessly sprawling collection of views that shares nothing in common beyond being non-consequentialist is overdrawn. To start, some theories labeled retributivist—such as those that emphasize the good of satisfying popular retributivist impulses, and others that emphasize communication and moral education—are more accurately classified as consequentialist. Others, albeit seemingly non-consequentialist, have few if any present-day adherents. This may be true, for example, of Hegel's theory that punishment "annuls" or cancels out the criminal wrong (Hegel 1967: 66–73). It is hard to find a punishment theorist, even among the self-described retributivists, who finds such claims informative rather than either question-begging or unhelpfully metaphorical.

The central retributivist claim is that punishment is justified "in terms of the desert of the offender" (Ten 1987: 46). Anti-retributivists have long objected that attempts to justify punishment in terms of desert are vacuous: to assert that offenders deserve to be punished, and to add that justice simply consists in giving people what they deserve, is wholly uninformative. This is a fair objection if desert-centered retributivist arguments proceed on just those terms. But few retributivist arguments are quite so compact. A more common view maintains that offenders deserve to suffer, and that the state has adequate reasons to bring that suffering about. Of course, retributivists owe accounts of why wrongdoers deserve to suffer, and why it is the proper business of the state to bring such suffering about. But if those details can be filled in, then the retributivist view is a true *argument*, and not a bare *assertion*.

To be sure, not all retributivists focus on desert. Among the more notable alternative retributivist views is Herbert Morris's once-popular "fair play" account, according to which the criminal law promotes the interests of all by enjoining each member of the community not to interfere in specified ways with others' pursuit of their own goods. Lawbreakers enjoy the benefits of the system, in terms of self-restraint exercised by others, without paying their fair share of the costs in terms of their own self-restraint. Punishment is justified, then, as a way to remove the unfair advantage the offender has thus secured (Morris 1968). But this account meets many objections, the most pronounced being that it seems to mischaracterize the wrongness involved in violating the criminal law. It seems bizarre to suppose that the wrongness of, say, raping a child is grounded in the rapist's gaining any unfair advantage over his fellows who refrain from criminal wrongdoing.

Of course, much more could be said about the fair play account and about other views that have been termed retributivist. The bottom line, though, is that contemporary retributivism is overwhelmingly centered on an offender's ill-desert. One commentator's observation from over 30 years ago still captures dominant opinion: "Retributivism without *desert*—the concept of punishment as something deserved by whoever is rightly made liable to it—is like Hamlet without the Prince of Denmark" (Bedau 1978: 608). The core claim of retributivism remains that the state's infliction of hard treatment with the intention of causing suffering can be morally justified in terms of the offender's supposed ill-desert without regard for any further and contingent good consequences.

Reconsidering the Consequentialist/Retributivist Dichotomy

Despite its longstanding currency, the consequentialist/retributivist classificatory framework has met increasing resistance in recent years. I am not now speaking of challenges to the particular theories—i.e., of arguments that either consequentialist or retributivist justifications for punishment are unsound. We will address some such criticisms in the next section. I am speaking here of challenges to this way of classifying theories into either of two categories. There are two types of challenge: that the division between consequentialist and retributivist theories is *false* because some approaches are both consequentialist and retributivist; and that the classification is *incomplete* because other viable justifications are neither consequentialist nor retributivist.

The worry that opposing consequentialism and retributivism might be false is most pronounced in the case of what some have called teleological retributivism (Moore 1997, ch. 4) or consequentialist retributivism (Berman 2011). As we will see, there is considerable uncertainty regarding what it would mean for an offender to deserve to suffer or to be punished. One view holds that it is equivalent (or nearly so) to his suffering being intrinsically good or valuable. A putative retributivist who holds this understanding of ill-desert might view punishment as a means to bring about the good of deserved suffering.

We can construe the relevant concepts—*punishment, consequentialism* and *retributivism*—in such a way as to make "teleological retributivism" a justification of punishment that is both consequentialist and retributivist. This would be so were *punishment* just the intentional infliction of hard treatment on supposed or claimed wrongdoers, *consequentialism* the claim that hard treatment is justified by its consequences, and *retributivism* the claim that hard treatment is justified by reference to, or in terms of, the desert of the wrongdoer. In fact, these are common understandings of the relevant concepts or common definitions of those terms and theories.

But things look different once we conceive of punishment, for purposes of investigations into its justifiability, as the infliction of hard treatment on supposed or claimed wrongdoers with the intent or purpose that they thereby be made to suffer. When punishment is thus defined, consequentialism naturally emerges as the theory that such a practice or activity can be justified by the *further* good consequences produced as a result of the (supposed or claimed) wrongdoer's suffering, while retributivism is the theory that such a practice can be justified by reference to the fact that such suffering is deserved, without regard for any other consequences that may or may not be produced. On this picture, teleological retributivism is indeed a retributivist justification for punishment—it is a version that, perhaps unlike other types of retributivism, grounds the rightness or permissibility of punishment in the goodness of the state of affairs it produces—but it is not a consequentialist justification. Accordingly, it does not challenge the consequentialist/retributivist binary.

While the possibility of teleological retributivism threatens to collapse a two-part distinction into one (with a possible further consequence that the one would splinter into a multiplicity of theories, depending on the good states of affairs at which punishment aims, or the mechanism by which punishment causes those states of affairs), other theories could be read as seeking to expand the menu. Indeed, two of the most prominent trends in punishment theory over recent decades—the growing embrace of communicative or expressive theories, and the emergence of the restorative justice movement—are sometimes understood in just this way. (In addition, some commentators might be moved to add mixed theories that combine consequentialist and retributivist elements. But it is preferable to address such accounts in the next section.)

One of the most striking trends in recent punishment theory is the turn toward a family of theories loosely classed as communicative or expressive. Although discrete accounts differ in detail, they commonly justify punishment as a means to communicate deserved censure to the offender and (often) the broader community. Whatever the virtues of such theories may be, however, the present question is whether they are truly alternatives to, rather than subclasses within, retributivist and consequentialist approaches. Observing that censure and condemnation can be communicated through symbolic means, like verbal reprimands and solemn pronouncements, critics wonder what is supposed to justify the state in choosing to communicate its censure by means of hard treatment. Obviously, insofar as the claim is that hard treatment is (reasonably) necessary to communicate the message of censure adequately, the justification seems comfortably consequentialist. In response, Antony Duff, a leading advocate of communicative justification, takes pains to characterize punishment as a kind of secular penance (Duff 2001). But, again, many observers doubt that this conception grounds an alternative to the standard approaches, capacious as they are. If penance is a means to the offender's own moral reform, we seem to remain in consequentialist terrain. Insofar as penance is deemed valuable all by itself, then it seems perilously close to a recharacterization (if possibly an illuminating one) of the core retributivist notion of deserved suffering.

Most communicative theories justify punishment in terms of the intended and expected uptake by the wrongdoer, or others, of a message of condemnation or censure. To the extent that a theory maintains that the state has reason (adequate to justify punishment) to express such a message without regard to whether anyone receives or understands it, the account is more aptly termed "expressivist." Because such a theory does not depend upon any downstream and contingent consequences of the expressive act, it is not consequentialist. And if the theory maintains that our reason (or duty) to express condemnation through punishment does not depend upon the rightness or goodness of the offender being made to suffer, it might not be retributivist either. So it is easier to understand how expressivist theories of punishment, unlike their communicative relatives, would, if plausible, constitute a genuine potential alternative to both consequentialism and retributivism. The problem is that the plausibility of such theories seems extremely doubtful, for they must explain why the state's interest in simply expressing (rather than communicating) a commitment to correct values is sufficiently weighty, or of the right sort, to justify intentionally inflicting hard treatment on persons with the intent that they suffer. Indeed, it is difficult even to identify a clear defender of an expressivist justification, though Robert Nozick's effort to justify punishment as a means to "connect" offenders to right values is sometimes said to come close (Nozick 1981: 363–80).

In any event, to accommodate the possibility of expressivist justifications, one might find it preferable to distinguish consequentialist from non-consequentialist justifications and to count retributivist theories as a family—by far the most important family—of non-consequentialist approaches. Alternatively, we could just understand that the familiar classificatory framework that recognizes only consequentialism and retributivism is more typologic than taxonomic, which is to say that it disavows any pretense to in-principle exhaustiveness.

No more monolithic than the growing communicative/expressivist camp is the restorative justice movement. Its central theme is that crime provokes a need for the wrongdoer to repair the harm he has done and a need for the community to help restore relationships—paradigmatically but not exclusively between the wrongdoer and his victim—that the crime has disrupted. Repair and restoration can be accomplished through a variety of means including victim–offender mediation and community repentance rituals (e.g., Braithwaite 2002).

Whatever may be the value of mediation and reconciliation enterprises, however, restorative justice is better understood not as a competing *justification for* punishment, but as a vision of proper social response to crime that would be an *alternative to* punishment. Recall that we are conceiving of punishment as the infliction of hard treatment with the intent to cause suffering or pain or the like. Most restorative justice proponents wish to displace practices of this sort (either fully or partially), not to justify them. Individual advocates of restorative justice may or may not believe that customary punishment practices are justifiable for certain types of offenses for which the responses they prefer are unlikely to be either useful or appropriate, or as a backstop when restorative justice interventions fail to accomplish their goals. Those who believe that such practices are not justifiable in any of these circumstances are abolitionists; those who believe that such practices are justifiable in some such circumstances must then appeal to consequentialist or retributivist rationales.

Challenges and Near-Convergence

If the consequentialist/retributivist distinction, albeit not watertight, is still a useful way to organize the complex terrain of punishment theories, it remains now to examine how each approach fares against challenges advanced by critics.

For much of the twentieth century, the philosophical tide was strongly consequentialist, and retributivism roundly condemned as barbaric. But consequentialism was criticized on two principal grounds: that it violates the Kantian mandate to "always treat humanity, whether in your own person or in the person of any other, never simply as a means, but always at the same time as an end" (Kant 1998: 429); and because it justifies inflicting harm on one to serve the good of others, that it tolerates scapegoating—the practice of punishing persons known by the authorities to be innocent when doing so would achieve net social benefits.

Consequentialist rejoinders to the first objection naturally fall into two broad categories: denial that punishment, when consequentially justified, violates the best understanding of Kant; and denial, insofar as such punishment does run afoul of Kant, that the Kantian maxim is sound. To appreciate the first route, note that the precise meaning of this particular formulation of the Kantian categorical imperative—"the humanity formula"—is famously controversial. Accordingly, a first, common, consequentialist rejoinder stresses that the formula prohibits, not the use of *individuals* as means, but the use of the *humanity* in persons merely as means. And, the argument continues, whatever use is made of an offender when the state punishes him for the community's greater good (as through general deterrence) is a usage that respects his humanity insofar as he has exercised his rational capacity when committing his wrong. Moreover, there are many routes to the conclusion that punishment, even to the extent that it treats an offender (or his humanity) as a means, treats him as an end as well. For example, an offender is not *only* an offender, but also a potential victim of other offenders. So to punish him to achieve general deterrence treats him as a means (*qua* punishee) but also as an end (*qua* potential victim).

The second consequentialist rejoinder to the first objection is even more straightforward. Although consequentialists about punishment *need not* be consequentialists about ethics, of course many are. So insofar as the humanity formula is best construed, as a matter of Kant exegesis, in a way that would condemn consequentialist rationales for punishment, these consequentialists can respond with a shrug: so much the worse for Kant, they say.

The second and more frequently pressed objection to consequentialism has provoked several responses. Two can be put aside quickly. First, some have argued that scapegoating is a logical impossibility because punishment is properly *defined* as infliction of hard treatment *on a wrongdoer*. This is a transparently unacceptable way to sidestep the problem—Hart rightly disparaged it as a "definitional stop"—and we have preempted it by defining the sort of practice that we are interested in as the imposition of hard treatment (with intent to produce suffering) on a supposed *or claimed* wrongdoer. Second, some few theorists bite the bullet, agreeing that consequentialism might justify scapegoating *in theory*, while emphasizing reasons to disbelieve that scapegoating would ever be welfare enhancing, and thus justifiable, *in practice*.

H. L. A. Hart furnished the most important and influential response to the scapego-ating challenge when (broadly following a path blazed separately by both Quinton and Rawls) he urged that what most theorists had treated as a single justificatory question should be reconceived as three separate questions: "What justifies the general practice of punishment? To whom may punishment be applied? How severely may we punish?" His answer to the first question was squarely consequentialist (in fact utilitarian), but his answer to the second was, he thought, retributivist: "punishment should be only of an offender for an offense." Thus, by recasting the challenge of justifying punish-ment in this way, Hart believed that consequentialist justifications could escape even an in-principle acceptance of scapegoating while retributivism would also get its due (Hart 1968: 1–27).

Hart's view was ambiguous. In places, he seemed to justify his proposed principle of "Retribution in Distribution"—the notion that punishment should only be imposed on "offenders for an offense"—as a means to provide members of the community with the welfarist benefits that come from being able to plan their affairs knowing the circum-stances that would potentially make them liable to criminal punishment. It is hard to see how this essentially utilitarian justification for Retribution in Distribution could be anything more than a presumption, potentially defeasible in any given case. Elsewhere, however, Hart described his principle that punishment must be limited to offenders as a dictate of justice or fairness. Whatever Hart's own considered view might have been, his marriage of a consequentialist "General Justifying Aim" to "Retribution in Distribution" is commonly seen as the intellectual forebear of the widespread current view that the reasons to punish are consequentialist while pursuit of consequentialist goals must be constrained by a principle that forbids the knowing infliction of punishment on persons who lack ill-desert or in excess of their ill-desert. Often called "negative" or "limiting" retributivism, such a position is perhaps more felicitously conceived of as a side-con-strained consequentialism (Duff 2001: 11), where the constraint is constituted by indi-vidual desert. In principle, "mixed" or "hybrid" justifications for punishment that seek to combine consequentialist and retributivist elements could take many forms (Wood 2002). But by far the most common mixed justification for punishment—indeed, prob-ably the most commonly endorsed justification for punishment, mixed or otherwise—is desert-constrained consequentialism.

Despite its prevalence, critics object that desert-constrained consequentialism is untenable, that no such constraints can be reconciled with the core consequentialist justification. This objection seems mistaken. While consequentialists about punish-ment who are also consequentialists about ethics would face a steep uphill climb should they wish to defend desert-based constraints, there is nothing about consequentialism about punishment per se that prevents its proponents from recognizing that people have rights in general or that such rights include those not to be punished absent, or in excess of, their ill-desert. We might even go further: it is not obvious that consequentialists face any greater difficulty in embracing desert-based constraints on punishment than do most retributivists.

This latter claim is undeniably heterodox, for theorists overwhelmingly assume that retributivism necessarily incorporates desert-based constraints on punishment. Put another way, "positive retributivism"—i.e., retributivism as what Hart called the "Gen-eral Justifying Aim" of punishment—is almost universally thought to entail "negative retributivism"—i.e., the claim that punishment absent or in excess of ill-desert is imper-missible. Admittedly, this entailment does hold true so long as we *define* retributivism as the view that punishment can be justified as a response to deserved suffering and only as a response to deserved suffering. The important point, however, is that the affirmative claim (roughly, that an offender's ill-desert produced in virtue of his blameworthy wrongdoing is *sufficient* to justify criminal punishment) does not itself entail the negative claim (roughly, that such ill-desert is *necessary* to justify criminal punishment). There is logical space for a view that would justify punishment in terms of an offender's desert, but that is not committed to the proposition that punishment can be justified *only* in such terms. Clarity might therefore be advanced by calling a view of this sort "retributivist," even while observing that most retributivists, as a matter of fact, are also anti-consequentialists. Whatever arguments retributivists (in this nonexclusive sense) have to support their anti-consequentialism might then turn out to be arguments that desert-constrained consequentialists may also adopt to support their desert-based constraints.

While the endorsement, by consequentialists, of desert-based constraints has helped to make their justifications for punishment more palatable, the more interesting developments in punishment theory over the past twenty-odd years have involved a rebirth of retributivism.

For a long time, anti-retributivists have targeted the retributivist notion of ill-desert. Some anti-retributivists are skeptical of the very notion of natural or pre-institutional desert. More commonly, they argue that, even if people can deserve various goods, to maintain that anyone could ever deserve to suffer, or to experience punishment, is pure barbarism. In response, retributivists have long resorted to intuition-pumping thought experiments. Consider two worlds identical in all respects except that actors who had engaged in atrocious wrongdoing (say, Nazi war criminals) live happily ever after in one and suffer on account of their actions in the other. If you believe that the second world is better than the first (while keeping in mind that the two worlds do not differ in respect of any downstream effects that may obtain as a consequence of the facts that the criminals do or do not suffer) then you have reason to conclude that a wrongdoer's suffering as he deserves is inherently good or valuable. And your attraction to retributivist desert might be further strengthened by reflecting on the guilt you would yourself experience, and your corresponding judgment that you ought to be punished, were you the wrongdoer (Moore 1997, ch. 3).

Many people find retributivist thought experiments along these lines persuasive. Others do not. But if anti-retributivists bemoan that retributivists rely overmuch on intuition on this score, not argument, they cannot wholly escape the same charge. It is notoriously hard to develop arguments that are not highly intuition-dependent for or against different views about the states of affairs that are or are not intrinsically good. Accordingly, anti-retributivists increasingly emphasize a different argument: even assuming arguendo that wrongdoers deserve to suffer (or something like this), they say, the state has no reason, or inadequate reason, to bring about that deserved suffering. Indeed, some argue further that endeavoring to inflict suffering violates the punishee's rights even if his suffering is deserved.

Retributivists have many responses to the strong objection that punishment violates the punishee's rights even when he deserves to suffer (or even when he deserves to be punished). Some argue that any rights of the wrongdoer claimed to be violated are waived or forfeited by his wrongdoing. Others contend that the rights at issue are secondary or derivative from a more fundamental right to be treated with respect as a person, and that punishment does not deny him the respect to which he is entitled, for we respect a person's nature as a morally responsible agent by providing what he deserves by virtue of the exercise of his will (Berman 2008: 277–81). In any event, the argument that punishment violates individual rights seems unpromising as an argument against retributivism for it cuts too broadly: it cuts against consequentialist justifications too and therefore can be maintained by abolitionists, but not by mere anti-retributivists.

More intriguing is the weaker anti-retributivist argument that retributivists have not yet established, as they must, that the state has adequate reason to bring about suffering, even if deserved. The supposition that the state has *no* reason to bring about deserved suffering seems overblown. Whatever else it might mean for suffering to be deserved, at a minimum it probably means that such suffering is good, and that provides the state some reason to bring it about. Some retributivists have argued that we have a duty to inflict deserved suffering—a position standardly, if controversially, attributed to Kant. But regardless of what Kant's own views might have been, few if any criminal law theorists today believe that the state has an *absolute* duty to punish wrongdoers. So the language of duty should not distract us. The key point, anti-retributivists contend, is that even if wrongdoers deserve to suffer for their wrongdoing and even if the state has some reason—even some "duty"—to cause that suffering to obtain, retributivists are committed to the implausible claim that the state's interest in bringing about deserved suffering is sufficiently strong all by itself to justify punishment in the face of the great many costs it incurs, including (without limitation) its tremendous expense, the inevitability of punishing innocent defendants and the suffering predictably experienced by offenders' loved ones and dependents.

To understand the retributivists' response to this charge, we must attend to the dialectical logic of demanding and supplying justification. We can distinguish two different types of justification, what we may call "all things considered" and "tailored" (Berman 2008: 262–66). An all-things-considered justification of an act or a practice is just what it sounds like: it establishes that the act or practice is morally justified, or permissible, in light of all considerations. A tailored justification, in contrast, establishes the permissibility of the challenged act or practice against one or more particular grounds for doubt, what we may term "demand bases." It shows that the particular grounds explicitly invoked (or implicitly relied upon) for thinking the act or practice unjustifiable lack force or are overridden.

As we have seen, punishment is said to stand in need of justification because it involves the intentional infliction of suffering. Hart, agreeing with Stanley Benn, noted that it is "the deliberate imposition of suffering which is the feature needing justification" (Hart 1968: 2, n. 3). As another commentator rightly emphasized, "The moral problem that the having of a legal institution of punishment presents can be stated in one sentence: It involves the deliberate and intentional infliction of suffering" (Burgh 1982: 193). Because it is the fact that punishment involves the intentional infliction of suffering on the punishee that particularly demands justification, philosophers of punishment have understood their core task to be explaining how punishment can be justified in light of, or against, *this* objection. In other words, they have sought a justification of punishment tailored to meet this concern, even if other (subsidiary) objections to punishment—e.g., that it is costly—might remain to be addressed to establish the all-things-considered justifiability of punishment.

If retributivism is best understood as offering a tailored justification for punishment, then contemporary retributivism and consequentialism are less far apart than has traditionally been believed. While nose-counting is hazardous, is seems likely that most contemporary consequentialists (about punishment) accept desert-based constraints on the state's pursuit of consequentialist goals. Moreover, despite periodic doubts, there do not appear to be any insuperable bars to their doing so. Meanwhile, most retributivists probably recognize that some among the downstream goods and mechanisms typically invoked by consequentialists—from deterrence and incapacitation to moral education and communication—must be relied upon in order to justify punishment, all things considered.

Going Forward: Scrutinizing Desert-Based Constraints

Some theorists—the abolitionists—believe that none of the extant proposed justifications succeeds, and that no satisfactory justifications are waiting in the wings. More commonly embraced is the nearly polar judgment that punishment can be adequately justified on myriad grounds, even though different grounds would have different implications for concrete punishment practices (e.g., Davis 1983). For example, a consequentialist who emphasizes deterrence need not deny that communicating censure is also valuable. And a retributivist need not deny that the consequences that punishment produces could also justify. Again, many retributivists do deny this. My point is only that a retributivist justification does not by itself entail the unsatisfactoriness of a consequentialist justification too.

Given this growing pluralism about the justifiability of punishment, what is yet to be done? What are the more promising and productive lines of inquiry for persons interested in the justification of punishment? One possibility is to scrutinize desert-based constraints or limits. The principal constraints are two: it is widely thought impermissible (1) to intentionally inflict suffering on one known to be innocent, or to lack ill-desert, and (2) to intentionally inflict suffering in excess of an offender's ill-desert. While both constraints are intuitive, neither is without difficulty.

Difficulties with the second constraint, often dubbed the requirement of "proportionality," are well known. To start, it is unclear how we could possibly determine how much suffering (or punishment) is deserved in virtue of varying degrees of wrongdoing or blameworthiness. And the problem is not merely epistemic: it is unclear how magnitudes of deserved suffering are fixed metaphysically. A common approach, associated most closely with Andrew von Hirsch, is to array desert and punishment on scales of severity, and to ensure that no offender be assigned a punishment that ranks higher on the punishment scale than his desert ranks on the desert scale (von Hirsch 1976, 1993). But as von Hirsch acknowledges, this approach seems to promise *ordinal* proportionality at best; it is consistent with the imposition of vastly different actual punishments for the same offense (or of offenders with the same ill-desert) depending entirely on how severe is the most severe punishment on the scale.

Beyond all this, the normative grounding of principle (2) is questionable. Defenders of the principle often claim that any punishment meted out to an actual wrongdoer in excess of what he deserves is tantamount to the infliction of punishment on an innocent. But this is not obviously true: because the wrongdoer has, by hypothesis, voluntarily offended, we might think he has assumed the risk of being punished more than his wrongdoing deserves. That, of course, is not to say that the state faces no limits on the amount of punishment it may inflict. It is to say only that moral limits on the severity of punishment might be grounded in a different source than whatever grounds the moral prohibition on knowingly punishing the morally innocent.

And what are we to say about that, seemingly more basic, moral prohibition? We have seen that it is very widely accepted, by most consequentialists and virtually all retributivists. It is worth noting, then, that persons who lack ill-desert are punished all the time, either because the system convicts legally innocent defendants or because the relevant legal doctrines fail to ensure that all persons who are legally guilty are morally blameworthy too. (Many theorists believe this latter defect is true, for example, of rules that attach liability in cases of strict liability and even negligence, not to mention rules denying the defense of reasonable ignorance or mistake of law.) Of course, theorists who endorse this prohibition are free to reject the rules and practices that predictably result in the punishment of undeserving persons. But not all do, and the cost would often be high: indeed, the only way to ensure that *no* legally innocent persons are punished is to abolish criminal punishment entirely. So any theorist who maintains an absolute ban on intentionally inflicting punishment on persons known (or believed) not to deserve it must insist on a very strong moral difference between the duties we owe to specifically known individuals and the duties we owe to what are sometimes termed "statistical" persons. That such a difference exists is assumed by much moral theorizing. Yet compelling arguments for such a difference are, at present, surprisingly underdeveloped.

References

Bedau, H. A. (1978) "Retribution and the Theory of Punishment," *Journal of Philosophy* 75: 601–20.

Berman, M. N. (2008) "Punishment and Justification," *Ethics* 118: 258–90.

____ (2011) "Two Kinds of Retributivism," in R. A. Duff and S. Green, eds., *Philosophical Foundations of Criminal Law*, Oxford: Oxford University Press, pp. 433–60.

Braithwaite, J. and Pettit, P. (1990) *Not Just Deserts: A Republican Theory of Criminal Justice*, Oxford: Oxford University Press.

Braithwaite, J. (2002) *Restorative Justice and Responsive Regulation*, Oxford: Oxford University Press.

Burgh, R. W. (1982) "Do the Guilty Deserve Punishment?" *Journal of Philosophy* 79: 193–210.

Cottingham, J. (1979) "Varieties of Retribution," *Philosophical Quarterly* 29: 238–46.

Davis, M. (1983) "How to Make the Punishment Fit the Crime," *Ethics* 93: 726–52.

Duff, R. A. (2001) *Punishment, Communication, and Community*, New York: Oxford University Press.

Feinberg, J. (1970) "The Expressive Function of Punishment," in *Doing and Deserving*, Princeton: Princeton University Press, pp. 95–118.

Hart, H. L. A. (1968) *Punishment and Responsibility*, Oxford: Oxford University Press.

Hegel, G. W. F. (1967/1821) *The Philosophy of Right*, T. M. Knox, trans., Oxford: Oxford University Press.

Kant, I. (1998/1785) *Groundwork of the Metaphysics of Morals*, M. Gregor, trans., Cambridge: Cambridge University Press.

Moore, M. S. (1997) *Placing Blame: A Theory of Criminal Law*, Oxford: Oxford University Press.

Morris, H. (1968) "Persons and Punishment," *The Monist* 52: 475–501.

Nozick, R. (1981) *Philosophical Explanations*, Oxford: Oxford University Press.

Ten, C. L. (1987) *Crime, Guilt, and Punishment*, Oxford: Oxford University Press.

von Hirsch, A. (1976) *Doing Justice: The Choice of Punishments*, New York: Hill and Wang.

____ (1993) *Censure and Sanctions*, Oxford: Oxford University Press.

Walker, N. (1999) "Even More Varieties of Retribution," *Philosophy* 74: 595–605.

Wood, D. (2002) "Retribution, Crime Reduction and the Justification of Punishment," *Oxford Journal of Legal Studies* 22: 301–21.

Zaibert, L. (2006) *Punishment and Retribution*, Aldershot, Hants, UK: Ashgate.

Further Reading

For further reading, see: D. Boonin (2008) *The Problem of Punishment*, Cambridge: Cambridge University Press (defense of the rarely developed abolitionist position; also useful for its critical review of justificatory theories); R. A. Duff (2001) *Punishment, Communication, and Community*, New York: Oxford University

Press (sophisticated presentation of a communicative theory); H. L. A. Hart (1968) *Punishment and Responsibility*, Oxford: Oxford University Press (immensely influential mid-century development of mixed justification); and M. S. Moore (1997) *Placing Blame: A Theory of Criminal Law*, Oxford: Oxford University Press (collection of essays by the foremost contemporary desert-based retributivist).

11
WRONGNESS AND CRIMINALIZATION

Victor Tadros

No one would deny that there is some important relationship between moral wrongness and the appropriate content of the criminal law. Many criminal offenses, including the most familiar offenses such as rape and murder, are also moral wrongs. And it is difficult to believe that their wrong-making features do not also sometimes provide reasons to criminalize them. This idea commits us only to a very weak view of the relationship between moral wrongness and the content of the criminal law. For example, it is consistent with the view that harm is central to the justification of criminalization. Some conduct may be wrong in virtue of its being harmful. And that characteristic of the conduct provides a reason to criminalize it. But the view leaves open the possibility that it is permissible to criminalize conduct that is not wrong if that conduct is harmful, and also the possibility that there is some wrongful conduct, namely non-harmful wrongful conduct, that there is no reason to criminalize.

For example, assault may be wrong in virtue of the harm that it causes. Those who believe that the criminal law is justified only because it prevents harm might justify criminalization of assault in virtue of the harm that it causes, and not because it is wrong. If this is true, harm explains the wrongness of assault and also justifies criminalizing it. In contrast, writing racist books in private may be wrong but not harmful. It may be wrong in that it expresses, through action, contempt for others. But if it is not harmful, writing racist books in private may not be criminalized. The mere fact that the conduct is wrong, defenders of this view might suggest, provides us with no reason at all to criminalize it.

Many people believe in a closer relationship between wrongness and criminalization than this. Here are two ideas. One is that moral wrongness is a constraint on criminalization decisions. On this view, *only* morally wrongful conduct can be criminalized. A stronger version of this idea claims that conduct may be criminalized only if that conduct is morally wrong independently of the creation of the criminal law (Duff 2010a). This view rules out what we might call "pure *mala prohibita* offenses." Pure *mala prohibita* offenses are offenses which criminalize conduct that is wrong only in virtue of its having been *criminalized*. It is consistent with this view that it is permissible to criminalize conduct which becomes wrong in virtue of having been regulated in some other way.

The latter possibility is essential to the plausibility of the strong view. For example, it is implausible to rule out criminalizing driving on the wrong side of the road. But driving cannot *be* on the wrong side without some formal or informal regulation governing driving. Defenders of the strong view can explain this as follows. We are permitted to create regulations governing driving. That renders some kinds of driving wrongful. In virtue of that fact the conduct may be criminalized. The strong view only excludes the criminalization of conduct that is rendered wrong only by being criminalized.

A weaker version of the view that wrongness is a constraint on criminalization holds that it is permissible to criminalize some conduct only if the conduct, once criminalized, is wrong (Husak 2008: 72–77). On a strict reading, *all tokens* of the conduct prohibited must be wrong. This view admits the possibility of pure *mala prohibita* offenses. It may nevertheless be a significant constraint on criminalization. For we may be tempted to criminalize some conduct in order to pursue a social goal even if some tokens of the conduct are not wrong even after it has been criminalized.

For example, prohibiting sexual intercourse with a person below the age of 16 may be the most effective way of protecting vulnerable young people from sexual exploitation. But perhaps not all of the conduct prohibited by a criminal law of that kind is wrong even after the conduct has been criminalized, for example if the defendant is a young person himself or herself and his or her partner was a particularly mature 15-year-old. It depends on whether the defendant has a moral obligation to obey a law prohibiting this conduct once it is created. If he does, defenders of the weaker version of the view, unlike defenders of the stronger version, have no objection to its being criminalized. If he does not, defenders of the weaker version of the view will regard the criminalization of the conduct as troubling.

A second idea is that moral wrongness always creates a reason *in favor* of criminalization. Michael Moore endorses this "legal moralist" view (Moore 1997, ch. 16). It extends the very weak view that I outlined in the introduction to all cases of wrongness. It holds that any characteristic in virtue of which something is wrong provides a reason to criminalize that thing. This view is consistent with a range of constraints on criminalization. It may be that it is permissible to criminalize conduct only if that conduct is harmful. We might justify this on the grounds that the enforcement of the criminal law inevitably causes harm, and the harm that it causes must be outweighed by prevention of harm. But harm, on this view, may only play the role of defeating reasons against criminalization. Wrongness is a reason in favor of criminalizing all conduct. But a further constraint imposed by the harm principle must not be breached to justify criminalizing the conduct all things considered. This bears some similarity to Joseph Raz's account of the harm principle within his perfectionist liberal political philosophy (Raz 1986; see also Moore 1997, ch. 18).

Here are some principles that reflect these views.

1) The *Wrongness Justification*. It is always a reason in favor of criminalization of some conduct that the conduct is wrong.
2) The *Strong Wrongness Constraint*. It is permissible to criminalize some conduct only if that conduct is wrong independently of its being criminalized.
3) The *Weak Wrongness Constraint*. It is permissible to criminalize some conduct only if that conduct is wrong either independently of its being criminalized or as a result of its being criminalized.

My aim in this essay is to evaluate the first two principles. I leave consideration of the third principle for another occasion.

Before proceeding further, it is worth clarifying the ambiguous idea of wrongness. Wrongness, in this discussion, might be thought to refer either to prima facie wrongness, or wrongness all things considered. We might evaluate the principles as applied to either kind of wrongness. I will assume that the principles refer to wrongness all things considered. Providing defendants with a justification defense provides a way of decriminalizing conduct that is prima facie wrong but justified all things considered. So, for example, if killing in self-defense is prima facie wrong, but justified all things considered in morality, killing in self-defense can be decriminalized by making self-defense available as a defense to murder.

This invites reflection on a further question—what is the role of excuses? Typically, excused conduct is understood to be wrong *all things considered*, but the defendant is not blameworthy of perpetrating it. We might object to the *Wrongness Justification* on these grounds—there is no reason to criminalize conduct that is fully excused. We can respond to this trivial objection by amendment:

> The *Wrongness Justification* (as amended). It is always a reason in favor of criminalization of some conduct that the conduct is both wrong and blameworthy.

This is the version of the *Wrongness Justification* that I will evaluate.

The Wrongness Justification

The *Wrongness Justification* is false if there are some things that are wrong that there is no reason to criminalize. Antony Duff and Sandra Marshall have developed an increasingly influential view that holds that there are such things (Marshall and Duff 1998; Duff 2007; Duff and Marshall 2010; see also Husak 2008: 135–37). On their view, there is good reason to criminalize all and only those things that are *publicly* wrong. Public wrongdoing is a restricted class of wrongdoing. It includes only those wrongs that the public ought to be concerned with in their role as members of a political community.

Here is how they develop this view. One component of understanding what it means for a person to be responsible for committing some wrong involves considering *to whom* one is responsible for committing that wrong. A public wrong is a wrong which an agent is responsible to the public for committing. The public is constituted by shared membership of a political community. The idea that an agent is responsible to the public for wrongdoing is to be understood as the agent having a duty to answer to the public for that wrongdoing. It follows that if an agent does not have a duty to answer for a certain kind of wrongdoing to the public, there is no reason for the state to criminalize that wrongdoing.

One further specification of this view is important in helping us to evaluate it. In Duff and Marshall's most recent account of it, the idea of public wrongdoing is not intended to provide an account of *criminal* wrongs. It is intended as an account of wrongs that the state can regulate, where the criminal law is one among a number of potential state responses to that wrongdoing (Duff and Marshall 2010). This evades a concern that I have previously expressed about their account (Tadros 2010): that their view seems to justify incorporating civil wrongs within the criminal law. In their recent development of the idea of public wrongdoing, they suggest that whether some public wrong ought to be criminalized depends on alternative methods for dealing with the conduct. On this account, though, the idea of public wrongs is not really an account of the criminal law at all, but an account of the kind of wrongdoing that the state in general is concerned with.

Reasons Against Criminalization: Practice and Principle

On Duff and Marshall's view, a person may lack a duty to answer for some public wrong-doing *all things considered*. For example, suppose that the police entrap me to commit theft. I may have a prima facie duty to answer for theft. Theft is a public wrong. But in *this case* I don't have a duty to answer to the state for my theft, for the state lacks standing to demand that I answer to it (for more discussion of standing see G. A. Cohen 2006; Duff et al. 2007; Tadros 2009; Duff 2010b). Similarly, I may lack an all things considered duty to answer for theft because requiring me to answer would seriously interfere with my health, or the health of another, or because doing so would be too costly. These considerations do not undermine the idea that theft is a public wrong. It is a public wrong as a *type* of conduct even though it is not true that each *token* of theft results in an all things considered duty to answer for the conduct.

What if there is some conduct which cannot be criminalized *by type* for the reason that it will *typically* be the case that requiring a person to answer for that conduct will be too burdensome or costly? Consider dropping litter. It may be that in *every* case of litter-dropping there is no duty to answer to the state for dropping litter because requiring a person to answer to the state for dropping litter is always too costly. Let's work on the supposition that this is true. My question is—on the Duff/Marshall view, what are we to say about this kind of case? Does the fact that there is never a duty to answer to the state for dropping litter imply that dropping litter is not publicly wrongful and hence that there is no reason to criminalize it?

This question could be answered in the negative, though as I will suggest in a moment, this is not what I take Duff and Marshall's view to be. If it is, the following argument might be given:

1) Dropping litter is wrong in virtue of the nuisance that it causes to members of the public.
2) That provides a reason to consider it a public wrong.
3) The fact that demanding citizens to answer for it would always be too costly defeats this reason to consider it a public wrong.
4) Hence it is not a public wrong. And hence there is no reason to criminalize it.

The difficulty with this argument is that it adds unnecessary complications to an argument available to friends of the *Wrongness Justification*. Friends of the *Wrongness Justification* argue as follows:

1) Dropping litter is wrong in virtue of the nuisance that it causes to members of the public.
2) That provides a reason to criminalize it.
3) The fact that demanding citizens to answer for it would always be too costly defeats this reason to criminalize it.

It is not obvious what the extra complications in the first argument add to the second. If we object to the *Wrongness Justification* only because of the extra steps added by the first argument, the objection is trivial. In contrasting their view with Michael Moore's legal moralism, Duff and Marshall think that we should distinguish between wrongs that we should leave the parties merely to sort out between themselves and wrongs which the state should intervene in (Duff and Marshall 2010). But Moore could respond that it is consistent with his view that we should leave it to people to sort out litter-dropping between themselves and 3) is the reason why.

The better interpretation of Duff and Marshall's view, the one that I suppose they intend for this kind of case, suggests that dropping litter *is* a public wrong *even if* it cannot be criminalized. They may argue as follows:

1) Dropping litter is wrong in virtue of the nuisance that it causes to members of the public.
2) This renders it publicly wrongful.
3) That provides a reason to criminalize it.
4) The fact that demanding citizens to answer for it would always be too costly defeats this reason to criminalize it.

This argument implies that the costs of criminalizing conduct are independent of whether the wrong is public. It also implies that there is a difference in kind between the considerations that determine whether some wrongful conduct is publicly wrongful and the considerations that determine whether a public wrong ought to be criminalized. To demonstrate that the *Wrongness Justification* is false, the quality of these special considerations needs to be clarified.

The natural way to do this is to show that there are practical considerations, such as cost, that may render the criminalization of some public wrongs unwarranted that are distinct from the principled considerations that render some wrongs nonpublic. We require a robust way of distinguishing between these "in principle" and "in practice" considerations. This way of understanding Duff and Marshall's view is clearly implied in Duff and Marshall (2010). In that piece they explore alternative methods of dealing with some conduct that they believe is publicly wrongful. The principles that distinguish public wrongs from the more general class of wrongs remain elusive, however. If *all* of the considerations that determine whether a wrong is public are of the same kind as the consideration of cost in the example of litter-dropping, there is no important difference between Duff and Marshall's view and legal moralism.

It is by no means easy to make a case for principled restrictions on criminalization. Take Duff's favorite example of adultery (Duff 2007: 144–45). Adultery may reasonably be thought at least sometimes to be wrong—it is a breach of a legitimate expectation of fidelity created by marriage. But is it publicly wrong? Duff tends to think not (though he is not completely unequivocal about it). But we might think that the reason why we should not criminalize adultery is because doing so would tend to result in unhelpful intrusions into relationships, or because it is very difficult to determine whether adultery is wrong in any particular case. These do not seem different in kind from considerations of cost. So why not conclude that adultery is publicly wrongful?

In *Answering for Crime*, Duff does provide an account—though one that I think is not fully developed—of what might do the work here. When he discusses public wrongs, he indicates that there are some wrongs which also violate the values of the political community, and it is this fact that renders those wrongs public. He writes:

> A justification of criminalization will need to begin by specifying some value(s) that can be claimed to be public, as part of the polity's self-definition; show how the conduct in question violates that value or threatens the goods that it

protects; and argue that that violation or threat is such as to require or demand public condemnation.

(Duff 2007: 143)

He then indicates that examples must be discussed on a case-by-case basis. This view seems to depend on the idea that there are some values that render conduct wrong, but as they are not values of the political community, the conduct cannot be criminalized in virtue of those values.

One difficulty with this idea is in identifying the values of the political community. Obviously, the account must be normative—we are concerned not with the values that the political community actually endorses, but rather with the values that it ought to endorse. The fact that the political community values things that it ought not to value cannot provide it with reasons to criminalize things that appear wrong to it in the light of those values. And the fact that the political community *fails* to value things that it ought to value cannot provide it with a reason against criminalizing things that are wrong in the light of those values.

Perhaps there is a more modest relativism in Duff's account whereby the values that a political community ought to endorse depend to some extent on its particular features. That leaves open the possibility that there are values that some people rightly endorse and conduct can be wrong in the light of those values. But as the political community lacks a reason to endorse that value, it also lacks a reason to criminalize that wrongful conduct. I am not sure that this idea can be made compelling.

The core of my concern relates to the idea that we should begin with the polity's "self-definition." I am not sure what a polity's "self-definition" is, or what it means to claim that a value is public as a part of it. Take property rights. The state ought to protect property rights. As theft violates those rights there is good reason to criminalize theft. But I am not sure how the value of property rights or the goods that it protects form part of the state's self-definition. What advance does the idea of self-definition make over specifying the legitimate functions of the state?

Furthermore, I am not clear that the polity's self-definition, insofar as it is distinct from the proper functions of the state, can be established prior to the criminalization of conduct. There is a whiff of circularity about Duff's suggestion. What a state criminalizes seems to determine its self-definition, but its self-definition is supposed to govern what it criminalizes. Perhaps we need some clear examples of things that are wrong in virtue of some value that is not a value of the political community. I doubt that adultery is a good example, as it is difficult to see why the state has no interest in the value of people abiding by the legitimate expectation of fidelity that they create through marriage. There are many reasons not to criminalize adultery, but I doubt this is one of them.

Public Reason and Wrongness

Perhaps there are adequate responses to these concerns, which can give a polity's self-definition an appropriate role in determining the scope of public wrongs. I want to explore a different way of distinguishing between the practical considerations that defeat reasons against criminalizing some conduct and the principled considerations that might render some wrongs beyond the business of the state. This draws on the idea that the state must remain neutral about more comprehensive conceptions of the good. For example, the state must not reflect a particular religious view, nor a comprehensive liberal view such as the kinds of liberal view that Kant or Mill defended, which make specific judgments about why it is right or good that persons are free to live their lives as they wish.

The idea is that there is some conduct which is wrongful, but because the state has an obligation to remain neutral about the good it cannot declare that conduct to be wrongful. Hence that conduct, whilst wrong, is not publicly wrong. For example, it may be wrong not to attempt to realize the potential that human beings have in virtue of their special capacities. This is true on some versions of moral perfectionism. But this is not something that the state, through its institutions, can assert in virtue of the demand that the state must not endorse a particular conception of the good that others may reasonably reject. I will be able to do no more here than sketch out the terrain and indicate how it might help to bolster the idea of public wrongs.

Legal moralists believe that there is always a reason for the state to promote the good and to prevent the bad. Suffering of wrongdoers is, for Moore, a good. And it is a good that the state always has reason to promote. Legal moralists may be liberals of a kind, for they may think that autonomy or freedom is very important (Raz 1986; Hurka 1993, part 3), and Moore is liberal in this way (Moore 1997, ch. 18). But this kind of liberalism is distinct from the liberal idea of neutrality, an idea that has more recent origins. Let us call neutralists "political liberals" following John Rawls's well-known defense of that view in his book *Political Liberalism* (Rawls 1993).

Political liberals believe that there are goods that the state may not promote, and wrongs that it may not prevent. Typically they believe this for the following reason: the state must treat each of its citizens with respect. Respecting citizens involves ensuring that the basic institutions are shaped in a way that can publicly be justified to each citizen. An institutional arrangement that conflicts with a citizen's reasonable conception of the good cannot publicly be justified to that citizen. Hence, public institutions must be capable of being justified to citizens with a reasonable conception of the good. Under liberal conditions, there will inevitably be a range of different conceptions of the good that citizens endorse. Hence, public institutions must be capable of being justified in the light of a range of conceptions of the good.

If the state fails to meet this demand, it will govern citizens by institutions that they cannot accept in the light of their comprehensive views. This threatens a particularly valuable kind of stability—the kind of stability that is generated when each citizen in a political community can endorse its political institutions despite the reasonable and intractable differences between them that are the inevitable product of living in a liberal society.

There is a disagreement between political liberals about the implications of this view. Does it restrict only the basic political institutions and constitutional essentials of society, what Rawls calls the "basic structure of society," or does it restrict the reasons that citizens can appeal to in particular public debates on policy issues? Rawls used the idea only with respect to the former issue (Rawls 1993). That would still provide some restraint on criminalizing wrongful conduct in that there would be some restrictions in basic constitutional principles on such criminalization, but the restrictions would be much greater if the latter is true.

On the latter view, there are certain restrictions on what can count as reasons offered in favor of any policy in the public sphere. Only certain kinds of reasons can count as "public reasons" and only public reasons can be offered in the course of democratic deliberation. And this implies that the reasons that can be offered in a democratic polity in favor of criminalization are limited. Joshua Cohen, a well-known defender of this view, puts it the following way:

> Democracy is not simply a matter of living together but also, ideally at least, a society of equals, whose members decide together how to live together. People who disagree fundamentally, however, have trouble occupying a common ground in which they can justify to one another those joint decisions.
>
> One response to this trouble is to try to characterize such a common ground of political justification. I will call this "democracy's public reason." Democracy's public reason is a terrain of political reflection and judgment that equal persons, drawn to conflicting doctrines, can reasonably be expected to occupy and endorse as a basis for addressing public issues. The essential point here is that common ground, if it is available at all, requires that the content of public reason is restricted relative to the doctrines endorsed by members.
>
> (Cohen 2009: 353–54)

If this is the right view, it might also rule out some kinds of wrong from the sphere of criminalization. There may be things that are wrong but which cannot be shown to be wrong through public reason because their wrongness depends on endorsing some particular comprehensive moral doctrine that other reasonable citizens in the polity do not share (see, further, J. Cohen 2009; Quong 2011, ch. 9). For example, some people will believe that blasphemy is wrong simply in virtue of being an affront to God, rather than because it is offensive. On this view even private blasphemous conduct is wrong. But whilst it may be possible to show, in a public forum, that acting in a way that is offensive to others is wrong, it will not be possible to show that private blasphemous conduct is wrong without endorsing a particular and controversial religious view. If such conduct is wrong, it will nevertheless be impossible to argue publicly for criminalizing it.

If this view can be convincingly developed, it would also show that there are some things that there is no reason to criminalize. It would do so for the highly principled reason that no reason can be *offered* in the public domain in an attempt to argue for the criminalization of some wrongful conduct. It is worth noting here that Rawls is permissive about introducing reasons for some political rule based on comprehensive doctrines as long as public reasons can also be offered in due course.

If an argument in favor of criminalization of some wrongful conduct depends on endorsing a controversial comprehensive doctrine about the good that may reasonably be rejected by other citizens as members of a liberal polity, no argument may be given for the criminalization of the wrongful conduct without violating the respect that is owed to one's fellow citizens. And we can conclude from the idea that no reason can be offered in favor of the criminalization of such conduct that there *is* no reason in favor of the state criminalizing the conduct. The restriction on the reasons that can be offered in favor of some state policy is also a restriction on the reasons that can motivate state actions. It follows that if this version of political liberalism is right, the *Wrongness Justification* is false, and in a nontrivial way.

Political liberalism is, of course, highly controversial (see, for example, Raz 1994). It is not obvious whether any plausible conception of public reason—a conception that could nevertheless appropriately guide detailed policy decisions, such as decisions about whether to criminalize conduct—can be developed. And even if it could, it might be argued that restricting the rights of people to offer arguments based on their considered moral views in the public sphere is not a proper way to respect them (see Dworkin 2006, ch. 3).

Defending the idea of public wrongs, I should say, does not depend on political liberalism as such. It does not depend on showing that the state must be neutral about the good. It does depend, I think, on showing that there are principled restrictions on the reasons that can be offered in favor of state decisions. Duff must defend the view that there are wrongs that ground reasons for individuals to condemn them, but those reasons cannot be offered in favor of condemnation by the state. Duff is, in this respect, in the same camp as political liberals.

Furthermore, political liberalism is, to my knowledge at least, the only well-developed view that attempts to demonstrate that public reason is constrained in this way. It is grounded in something that is plausibly morally significant: it aims to foster and build respect between people in spite of the deep moral disagreements that inevitably emerge between them when they live in liberal societies. It is less clear on Duff's own views about political philosophy what motivates the restriction on state condemnation when compared with private condemnation. Defending any substantive position on this question is well beyond the scope of this paper. I point only to the kind of work that must be done to improve our understanding of how meaningful the disagreement between Duff and Moore is, and who is right.

The Strong Wrongness Constraint

Let us turn to the *Strong Wrongness Constraint*. This constraint has many defenders. It may seem that we can offer a fairly simple defense of it. Two of the central functions of criminal law are condemnation and punishment of offenders. But condemnation and punishment are justified only if the person has done wrong. Therefore, it is wrong to criminalize conduct that is not wrong. To do so would be to warrant condemnation and punishment of conduct that is not wrong.

Criminalization and Assurance

Whilst this argument seems appealing, it is unsatisfactory. Let us focus on punishment. It does seem wrong to break the tie between wrongdoing and punishment, or the tie between punishment and desert. It is false, as Doug Husak notes, that punishment is deserved for *all* wrongful conduct on any sensible account of punishment. Punishment is not deserved, Husak suggests, if the conduct is excused, for example, or (more controversially) if the wrong is private rather than public (Husak 2008: 82–83). But it may be true that punishment is *only* deserved for wrongful conduct. Hence, the idea that only those who have done something wrong deserve punishment might help to vindicate the *Strong Wrongness Constraint*.

But whilst many people will agree that, in some sense, punishment is warranted only if it is deserved, many people will doubt that the idea of desert is always (or indeed ever) basic in determining what can be criminalized. The retributivist idea of desert is the controversial idea that the suffering of wrongdoers is morally good. The state, on their view, has a duty to bring this good about. The moral goodness of their suffering can be established independently of the criminal law that they violate, and hence what wrongdoers deserve is "pre-institutional."

We also use the term "desert" to apply to cases where a person breaches a legitimate rule of a game, where the rule is created simply to further a legitimate purpose. For example, we can say about a football player who deliberately handles the ball that he deserved to be sent off. Desert, here, is appropriately used simply because the player violated a legitimate rule of football where an appropriate sanction was attached. And the rule is legitimate because the game of football is enhanced by a rule, accompanied by a sanction, prohibiting handling the ball.

On this second idea of desert, what is deserved is set by the institutional practice of football, and is not prior to it. Prior to the creation of football, we cannot say that any-one deserves anything that football matches then pick out and punish. There are norms governing the development of the rules of football. Rules are legitimate if they tend to enhance the value of the game—say by making it more entertaining, competitive and so on. Once these rules are in place, though, breach of them is wrongful.

Perhaps something similar is true in the case of the criminal law. Consider the devel-opment of a regulated market. We aim to ensure that the market achieves a set of social goals: growth, the development of creative opportunities and so on. Setting up the market in this way involves the creation of a set of regulations, some of which are criminal. Regulations are made criminal if the goals that we set for this practice are properly achieved through the threat of punishment and execution of the threat in case of breach of the regulations. If some individual breaches the criminal law that regulates those markets, we might say that the person deserves punishment. But prior to the cre-ation of the regulated market, there is no wrongful conduct to pick out and condemn.

Against this, it might be argued that the idea of desert that underpins criminal justice must be retributivist desert. That *may* be so, but it needs demonstrating. My suspicion is that the retributivist idea of desert is wholly misguided (Tadros 2011, ch. 4). But even were it acceptable as an idea, it is difficult to believe that it is essential to the justifi-cation of punishment in all cases. Why should we not punish in cases where there is a very important social goal that we wish to pursue, and criminalization is essential to the pursuit of that social goal? Why must we *always* be required to pick out some con-duct that is wrongful independently of our criminalization decisions in order to justify criminalization?

Of course, in many cases, the fact that a person's conduct sets back our ambitions to pursue our social goals also renders that conduct wrongful. But the relevant conduct may not always be wrong prior to the creation of the rule of the criminal law. Rather, the creation of a criminal law may be legitimate even though it is only this fact—the fact that the conduct has been criminalized—that renders the conduct wrong. If this is so, the *Wrongness Constraint* is false. What we are pointing to, in other words, is that there may be legitimate, pure cases of *mala prohibita*. What I mean by this is that there may be cases where it is legitimate to create a criminal law that renders non-wrongful conduct wrongful.

These cases are to be distinguished from the standard cases that are often thought to be *mala prohibita*. Many of the crimes that are typically called *mala prohibita* are not pure, for many of these crimes prohibit conduct that is wrong independently of the criminal law. Take the most familiar case—breach of specific driving regulations. Suppose that a person drives on the right-hand side of the road in the UK, where driving on the right is prohibited. This conduct is wrong. But it is not wrong in virtue of the fact that driv-ing on the right side of the road is prohibited by the criminal law. It would be enough to render the conduct wrong that most other people drive on the left. And a mere convention or noncriminal regulation would be sufficient to ensure that most other people did this. Were others to follow the convention and drive on the left, driving on the right would then be dangerous, and that is enough to render the conduct wrong. In virtue of this, it is permissible to criminalize driving on the right without conflict with the *Strong Wrongness Constraint*.

It is worth noting, at this point, that demonstrating the falsity of the *Strong Wrongness Constraint* does nothing to attack the *Weak Wrongness Constraint*. Doug Husak, for example, suggests that penal liability is warranted only for those who have done wrong. This, he argues, provides a constraint on the scope of the criminal law (Husak 2008: 72–77). This idea is consistent with the existence of legitimate pure *mala prohibita*. The wrongness of conduct need not, on this view, be a necessary condition for criminalizing the conduct. But punishment would be unjustified if the conduct, once criminal, were not wrong.

Whilst Husak only endorses the *Weak Wrongness Constraint*, he is puzzled by pure *mala prohibita* and so is tempted by the *Strong Wrongness Constraint*. According to Husak, no one has shown that punishment is warranted for *mala prohibita* offenses. If he is right, we should be troubled. For it is difficult to believe that it is always wrong to create pure *mala prohibita* offenses.

We can demonstrate the attractions of pure *mala prohibita* offenses with the following abstract argument. Suppose that there is some important social goal g. To secure g, each person in a state must do an action, v. Each act of $v$ing will then make a necessary contribution to the achievement of g. If each person vs, the burden on each person will be very modest. If anyone fails to v, there is no value in anyone else $v$ing. Hence if anyone vs and the others do not, the costs to the person of $v$ing are not compensated by any benefit to anyone. Only the threat of state punishment will ensure that each person vs. If failing to v is criminalized, the law will be reasonably certain and easy to adhere to, and no one will breach it.

In this case, refraining from $v$ing cannot be wrong unless state punishment is threatened for failing to v. To do this, a law is created requiring citizens to v, and if they refrain from $v$ing they will be punished. Creating such a law criminalizes failing to v. Refraining from $v$ing is rendered wrong in this case only by the criminalization of the failure to v. But it is difficult to believe that, for all cases of v, criminalizing the failure to v is wrong. If there are *any* such cases, the *Strong Wrongness Constraint* is false.

Some Objections

Against this argument it might be claimed that although failure to v would not be wrong independently of the criminal law in these circumstances, the proper conclusion to draw is that it is wrong to criminalize failure to v. In deciding whether to criminalize some conduct, we are not permitted simply to think of the social goals that we wish to pursue. We may criminalize only the conduct that we have already identified as requiring condemnation and punishment.

That seems to me a radical and unwarranted conclusion. Suppose that g was *very* important—say the saving of several lives. Would it really be wrong to criminalize failure to v? Through the law, we would demand each citizen to bear some modest cost, fairly distributed, for the sake of saving one million lives. We would back up our demand with the threat of punishment. Each citizen could avoid punishment easily though— simply by $v$ing. Each citizen would benefit from criminalization of the conduct. And

VICTOR TADROS

once the criminal law was in place, anyone who refrained from $v$ing would have done wrong, indeed a very serious wrong. They would have violated their duty to save several lives at minimal cost to themselves. Hence, were we to create such a law, there would be no question that we were threatening to punish those who did not deserve it. It is difficult to believe that it is wrong to criminalize failure to v in these circumstances.

A second objection is that there are no cases that are like the one that I described— where complete compliance with a rule is required to render breach of the rule by any person wrong. As I will suggest in a moment, even if this is true, the case can be adjusted to accommodate this idea. But perhaps there are cases where complete compliance with a rule is required to render breach of the rule wrong.

For example, it may be wrong for a spy to report certain security information only if every other spy who knows the information refrains from leaking the information into the public domain. Refraining from reporting the information is valueless where others have reported it already. Now, suppose that I am a spy. If all spies keep quiet for the rest of the year, 100 lives will be saved. If I leak the information now, one life will be saved, a life that no one else can save.

If I have good reason to believe that everyone will keep quiet until the end of the year, I ought not to leak the information now. If I have good reason to believe that someone else will certainly leak the information before the end of the year even if I keep silent, I ought to leak the information now. Were I to fail to do that the life that I could have saved would be lost, and no one else would be saved. Whether those who leak are punished affects what I have reason to believe the other spies will do. I may have good reason to believe that others will not leak the information before the end of the year only if leaking is criminalized with severe sanctions. Hence, whether leaking the information is criminalized determines what I ought to do.

A third objection is that it is wrong to suppose that the threat of punishment can secure complete compliance with the law in typical cases. This is true, but its truth does not undermine the argument against the *Strong Wrongness Constraint*. We can easily adjust the argument to accommodate this fact. Suppose that g could be achieved only if *enough* people v, say 75%. If we regulate failure to v without the threat of punishment <75% of people will v. If we criminalize failure to v 75% of people will v. It follows that failure to v would not be wrong unless $v$ing were criminalized.

Perhaps it might be argued that any person who fails to v in these circumstances does not do wrong *even once failure to v is criminalized*. For the actions of any individual will not set back the achievement of g. Even if this were true, I doubt that it would be sufficiently important to render the criminalization for failure to v unjustified. Perhaps we should simply drop the demand that only wrongdoers can be punished. But it would be nice if we could retain the intuitive idea that punishment can only be imposed on wrongdoers.

One idea is that if failure to v is criminalized, anyone who fails to v will be a free-rider; they will unfairly benefit from the conformity of others to the rule prohibiting failure to v. Notice here that the threat of punishment is required in order to make the argument from fair play go through. Without the threat of punishment, there would *be* no advantage from which noncompliers could unfairly benefit.

Husak argues against the use of free-rider arguments in this context. The main argument that he might propose against the view defended here is as follows. (Some of his other arguments against the free-rider view advanced in Green (1997) may be valid. Green's argument is more general than the one proposed here.) Prosecution and

168

punishment for *mala prohibita* is inevitably selective and discretionary. As a result, only some people who fail to *v* will be prosecuted and punished. Hence, we should doubt that prohibition of the failure to *v* enhances fairness, for the burdens on compliers and noncompliers would not be distributed equally (Husak 2008: 118).

This argument lacks force, in this context at least. Each of the noncompliers in the example above would benefit from the compliance of others with the criminal law. They would each be advantaged unfairly when compared with compliers. If some, but not all, of these noncompliers were punished, they could hardly complain that they have been treated unfairly on the grounds that other noncompliers were not made to bear the same cost. If some noncompliers are picked out on the wrong grounds, say because of race, clearly there would be unfairness. But if resources are scarce, so that it is possible to prosecute and punish only some members of the group, and wrongdoers are selected randomly, no one is treated unfairly. Of course, other things being equal it would be fairer to distribute punishment equally amongst the group of noncompliers. But where this is impracticable or too costly, there is nothing per se unfair about selective punishment.

There is admittedly much more to say to defend the role of fair play in this context. But even if this fair-play argument is unsuccessful, there may be other reasons why failing to comply with the law is wrong where failure to *v* is criminalized. It may be that any person who fails to *v* in such circumstances runs an unwarranted risk that she may tip the balance from securing *g* to failing to secure *g*. Even if the risk that each person creates is small, if the goal to be secured is very important and the costs of *v*ing are insignificant, it may be wrong to refrain from *v*ing. Any person who violates the prohibition, in this case, risks serious harm to others (for a related argument, see Parfit 1986: 73–75).

Furthermore, there may be related cases where this objection does not apply. There may be cases where criminalization of some conduct renders that conduct wrong not because participation of others is required to achieve an important goal, but rather because the costs of the conduct will only be sufficiently modest if it is criminalized. If the conduct is not criminalized, the costs of refraining from doing it may be too high to render it wrong all things considered. Criminalization is required to render the conduct unjustified all things considered.

Here is an example. Possession of a knife in a public place may be wrong. But it may be wrong only if enough other people comply with the prohibition on knife possession. Were many people to carry knives, possession of a knife in a public place would be justified to enhance personal security. The appropriate security threshold that renders knife possession wrongful may be reached only if knife possession is criminalized. Mere regulation of knife possession, where the regulation is not backed up by a threat of punishment, may be insufficient to render public knife possession wrong. Once enough people comply with the law prohibiting public knife possession, it becomes wrong to possess a knife. The dangers that public knife possession imposes on others, as well as the fear that knife possession may cause harm to citizens would, in that case, outweigh any benefits to the person who possesses the knife.

It is difficult to believe that it is necessarily wrong to criminalize knife possession if this set of facts obtains. Everyone benefits from the criminalization of public knife possession. Criminalization, in such circumstances, can save many lives. Everyone's security is advanced, and at no great cost, if the criminal law is adhered to. It is true that some people will breach the prohibition and will be punished. But this should not be thought to render the criminal law unjust, and for three reasons. First, knives kill, and it is better to be punished than dead. Second, it is easy for all citizens to avoid punishment. They can do so simply by abiding by the criminal law. We should be less concerned that the criminal law makes people liable to be punished, if punishment is easily avoidable (see Tadros 2011, chs. 3 and 14, for further discussion). And third, knife possession would, under these circumstances, be publicly wrong, and hence may be condemned by the criminal law.

It is sometimes argued that there is no conflict between *mala prohibita* and the *Strong Wrongness Constraint*. For the conduct that is prohibited by a *malum prohibitum* offense could have been prohibited by a mere regulation. Breaching the regulation would be wrong. And that wrongdoing warrants punishment. In fact, this would suggest that there is typically a *duty* to criminalize breaches of the regulations (Duff 2010a: 111). The arguments that I have been developing suggest that this view is unsound. There are some regulations that we are not obliged to follow unless we are assured that sufficient numbers will follow them. We can be assured that sufficient numbers will follow them only if they are backed up by a threat of punishment. And yet it is implausible to think that criminalization is always unwarranted in all of these cases.

Perhaps some might still argue that the cases that I have developed create the illusion that failing to *v* is not wrong independently of the creation of the criminal law. Here is an argument that might be given to bolster this view. Return to the case where *g* is an important social goal that can be achieved only if >75% of people *v*. If *g* is important, and we can achieve *g* by *v*ing, we are obliged to form and execute an agreement that we each *v*. We are required to do so simply in virtue of our obligation to pursue very impor-tant social goals if we can do so at minimal cost to ourselves. If we have created such an agreement, anyone who violates that agreement does wrong. We could then criminalize failure to *v* on the grounds that each person who violates the agreement would have done wrong independently of the decision to criminalize failure to *v*.

This argument is misguided. Suppose that, recognizing that *g* is important, we form an agreement that we each *v*. If <75% of people *v*, no progress towards *g* will be made. I know that the mere agreement that each of us must *v* will result in <75% of people *v*ing. There is now no point in me *v*ing. My *v*ing will do nothing to achieve *g*. And in that case there can be no obligation for me or anyone else to form an agreement that each of us will *v*. Forming an agreement that we each will *v* will be a waste of time. In fact, we can make a stronger claim. It would be *wrong* for us to form an agreement that each of us *v*s. Any such agreement would involve demanding that each person *v*s knowing that any person who *v*s will be wasting her time. It is wrong to demand of people that they waste their time.

Perhaps it might be argued that people who fail to *v* will be free-riders in this case. But this is false. For as <75% of people will comply with the regulation, *g* will not be achieved, and there will then be no benefit that anyone will have secured for free. Free-riders need moving vehicles, and without criminalization the buses remain parked.

We can see this even more clearly where the costs to others of a person *v*ing where insufficient others *v* are high. Suppose that if *g* is achieved, each instance of *v*ing is non-harmful, but if *g* is not achieved each instance of *v*ing will harm others signifi-cantly. We form an agreement that each of us will *v* to achieve *g*. I know that, as our agreement is not backed up by the threat of punishment, <75% of people will *v*. What should I do? If I *v* I will significantly harm others. Surely, in that case, I ought to refrain from *v*ing. If I *v* I will harm others for no good reason. So I ought to *v* only if punishment is threatened for failure to *v*.

Perhaps it might be argued that a regulation with a threat of punishment does not constitute a criminal law. Something else is required. I doubt that something else is required, but suppose that it is. Suppose that to create a criminal law it is not only required that we threaten punishment for breach of the law, but also that we warrant condemnation for the breach. This would not rescue the *Strong Wrongness Constraint*. We could simply adjust the example above to accommodate this idea.

Suppose that it is insufficient to threaten punishment to motivate enough people to *v*. We also need to condemn people. It would still be implausible that we could not warrant criminalizing the failure to *v* in these circumstances. Warranting condemnation for failure to *v* would be a bit like a benign version of a self-fulfilling prophecy. Through warranting condemnation for failure to *v* we would ensure that failure to *v* deserved to be condemned. But there is no problem in doing this. It is normally wrong to condemn that which is not wrong, but it is not necessarily wrong to condemn that which becomes wrong only in virtue of our practices of condemnation. It is worth remembering here that self-fulfilling prophecies are true. Whether we ought to articulate self-fulfilling prophecies depends on the goods that we might advance or hamper in doing so. They cannot be objected to on grounds of their falsity.

Now return to the concern that, in practice, there are no cases like the ones that I have been outlining above. I very much doubt that this is true. For example, I suspect that my account of knife possession is fairly realistic for at least some communities. I also suspect that, in some cases at least, tax avoidance is wrong only on condition that sufficient other people pay their taxes. If I pay my taxes and others do not do so, not only is my absolute level of wealth reduced for the sake of some goal, my *comparative* level of wealth is reduced. The value of the money that I have depends on how much others have. Their bargaining position becomes stronger if they have more than I, and that will increase the burden that I bear by paying taxes. For this reason it is often wrong to demand that citizens pay taxes unless sufficient assurance is given that others will pay. The threat of punishment is probably a necessary condition of ensuring that enough people pay their taxes to render all cases of tax evasion wrong. If that is true, it may well be wrong to refrain from paying at least some taxes only if tax evasion is criminalized.

But even if there are no real-world cases where the argument that I have mounted has application, the argument is nevertheless significant, and for two reasons. First, it has theoretical importance. It demonstrates that we should reject influential retributivist accounts of criminalization. Retributivist accounts of criminalization claim that the wrongness of some conduct prior to its criminalization provides the only reason for criminalizing it. They believe this because they think that punishment is justified only in order to ensure that wrongdoers get the suffering they deserve.

The argument that I have developed, if it is sound, demonstrates that this view is false. It would be very odd indeed to criminalize conduct *in order to make it wrong*. So retributivists would have no reason to criminalize conduct on the basis of the argument developed here. Retributivists believe that the suffering of wrongdoers is good in itself. But surely they don't believe that its goodness can motivate us to bring about more wrongdoing so that we can pursue more of this good. The view that I have outlined suggests that we can criminalize conduct simply in order to achieve important social goals. That may render the conduct that has been criminalized wrong, but its wrongness does not provide the reason for which we criminalize it. Arguments of this kind are incompatible with retributivism.

Secondly, the view would retain practical importance of a different kind. Its practical importance would be in the kinds of argument that decision-makers are entitled to rely on when justifying the decision to criminalize something. When considering whether to criminalize conduct, decision-makers may consider the following three things: a) the importance of the social goal that they are pursuing; b) the extent to which the goal can be pursued only through criminalization; and c) the burdens that the decision to criminalize would have on citizens. Perhaps they also need to show that the conduct, once criminalized, will be wrongful. But they need not show that it is wrong for citizens not to pursue that goal independently of the creation of the criminal law.

Conclusions

If the *Strong Wrongness Constraint* is false, as I think it is, we must evaluate the *Weak Wrongness Constraint*. Though a full evaluation of that principle is beyond the scope of this essay, in favor of this weak constraint is as follows: the criminal law condemns and punishes, but condemning and punishing can only appropriately be done to wrongdoers. Hence, we should endorse the *Weak Wrongness Constraint*.

This simple argument is again inconclusive. Whilst it is true that we must condemn only wrongdoers, it is not so obvious that we may punish only wrongdoers. When we condemn a person, we imply that the person is a wrongdoer. In all but the most unusual circumstances, the state ought to imply this about a person only if it is true. Hence, we cannot warrant condemning those who have done nothing wrong.

It is sometimes thought that the same thing is true about punishment: that punishment necessarily has an expressive quality—it expresses the wrongfulness of the conduct punished (Feinberg 1970). But this is less obviously true than the idea that condemnation implies wrongdoing. Punishment might simply involve harming a person in response to their conduct in order to deter others from acting in the same way. For example, when gangland bosses punish people for ratting on them, they may not imply that those punished are wrongdoers. They punish rats simply to deter others from ratting.

Of course, this case of punishment is unjustified. But perhaps punishment of non-wrongdoers is sometimes warranted. We might have good reason to deter some non-wrongful conduct, and perhaps we can do that by punishing non-wrongful conduct. So perhaps we have good reason to punish some non-wrongdoers. If that were true, it might be permissible to criminalize some conduct that is not even rendered wrong by the act of criminalizing it simply in order to deter it. Were this justified, we would have to find a way of ensuring that those punished were not implicitly condemned at the same time. This is difficult, but perhaps not impossible, to achieve.

Rejecting the *Weak Wrongness Constraint* is much more controversial than rejecting the *Strong Wrongness Constraint*, though. I suspect that the *Weak Wrongness Constraint* is a valid principle. But its implications are also less radical. It admits that forward-looking considerations may, within some limits, be decisive in the decision of what to criminalize.

References

Cohen, G. A. (2006) "Casting the First Stone: Who Can, and Who Can't, Condemn the Terrorists?" *Royal Institute of Philosophy Supplement* 58: 113–36.

Cohen, J. (2009) *Philosophy, Politics, Democracy: Selected Essays*, Cambridge, Mass.: Harvard University Press.

Duff, R. A. (2007) *Answering for Crime: Responsibility and Liability in the Criminal Law*, Oxford: Hart Publishing.

—— (2010a) "Perversions and Subversions of Criminal Law," in R. A. Duff, L. Farmer, S. E. Marshall, M. Renzo and V. Tadros, eds., *The Boundaries of the Criminal Law*, Oxford: Oxford University Press, pp. 88–112.

—— (2010b) "Blame, Moral Standing and the Legitimacy of the Criminal Trial," *Ratio* 23: 123–40.

Duff, R. A., Farmer, L., Marshall, S. E. and Tadros, V., eds. (2007) *The Trial on Trial, Volume 3: Towards a Normative Theory of the Criminal Trial*, Oxford: Hart Publishing.

Duff, R. A. and Marshall, S. E. (2010) "Public and Private Wrongs," in J. Chalmers, F. Leverick and L. Farmer, eds., *Essays in Criminal Law in Honour of Gerald Gordon*, Edinburgh: Edinburgh University Press.

Dworkin, R. (2006) *Is Democracy Possible Here?: Principles for a New Political Debate*, Princeton: Princeton University Press.

Feinberg, J. (1970) "The Expressive Function of Punishment," in J. Feinberg, *Doing and Deserving*, Princeton: Princeton University Press, pp. 95–118.

Green, S. P. (1997) "Why It's a Crime to Tear the Tag Off a Mattress: Overcriminalization and the Moral Content of Regulatory Offenses," 46 *Emory Law Journal*: 1533.

Hurka, T. (1993) *Perfectionism*, Oxford: Oxford University Press.

Husak, D. (2008) *Overcriminalization*, Oxford: Oxford University Press.

Marshall, S. E. and Duff, R. A. (1998) "Criminalization and Sharing Wrongs," 11 *Canadian Journal of Law and Jurisprudence*: 7–22.

Moore, M. (1997) *Placing Blame*, Oxford: Oxford University Press.

Parfit, D. (1986) *Reasons and Persons*, Oxford: Oxford University Press.

Quong, J. (2011) *Liberalism without Perfection*, Oxford: Oxford University Press.

Rawls, J. (1993) *Political Liberalism*, New York: Columbia University Press.

Raz, J. (1986) *The Morality of Freedom*, Oxford: Oxford University Press.

—— (1994) "Facing Diversity: The Case of Epistemic Abstinence," in J. Raz, *Ethics in the Public Domain: Essays in the Morality of Law and Politics*, Oxford: Oxford University Press.

Tadros, V. (2009) "Poverty and Criminal Responsibility," 43 *Journal of Value Inquiry*: 391–413.

—— (2010) "Criminalization and Regulation," in R. A. Duff, L. Farmer, S. E. Marshall, M. Renzo and V. Tadros, eds., *The Boundaries of the Criminal Law*, Oxford: Oxford University Press, pp. 163–90.

—— (2011) *The Ends of Harm: The Moral Foundations of Criminal Law*, Oxford: Oxford University Press.

Further Reading

For further reading on criminalization, see: R. A. Duff, L. Farmer, S. E. Marshall, M. Renzo and V. Tadros, eds. (2010) *The Boundaries of the Criminal Law*, Oxford: Oxford University Press; and (forthcoming) *The Structures of the Criminal Law*, Oxford: Oxford University Press; J. Feinberg (1984) *The Moral Limits of the Criminal Law, Volume 1: Harm to Others*, New York: Oxford University Press; J. Feinberg (1985) *The Moral Limits of the Criminal Law, Volume 2: Offense to Others*, New York: Oxford University Press; J. Feinberg (1986) *The Moral Limits of the Criminal Law, Volume 3: Harm to Self*, New York: Oxford University Press; J. Feinberg (1988) *The Moral Limits of the Criminal Law, Volume 4: Harmless Wrongdoing*, New York: Oxford University Press; D. Husak (2008) *Overcriminalization*, Oxford: Oxford University Press; and J. Schonscheck (1994) *On Criminalization: An Essay in the Philosophy of the Criminal Law*, Dordrecht: Kluwer.

12

THE VOLUNTARY ACT REQUIREMENT

Gideon Yaffe

Introduction

It is abhorrent to punish someone for something he did not do. This feeling motivated Illinois Governor George Ryan in 2000 to commute the sentences of many defendants awaiting execution. The idea that the state should not just *punish* someone, but *execute* him, for something he did not do was more than Ryan could bear. It is rarely recognized, however, that there are two different ways to be punished for something one did not do. In the first kind of case, which is the sort that was on Ryan's mind, there is a doing, a genuine action, performed by *someone*—a murder, for instance—and worthy of punishment; the trouble is that the person being punished is not the very one who performed the awful act. In the second kind of case, there is no mistake of identity, but there is also no genuine action; the punished person is not punished for something he *did*, but, instead, for merely being a certain way—for "appearing" drunk on the highway after the police carried him bodily from his home to the highway before arresting him, as in *Martin v. State* (31 Ala. App. 334 (1944)). In such cases, someone is punished for something that cannot be attributed to his agency, something with respect to which he is passive. If it's wrong to punish in the first kind of case, isn't it just as wrong to punish in the second? In both, the punished person did not *do* anything prohibited.

Laws that enact the presumption of innocence are aimed at preventing conviction of people different from those who actually committed the relevant crime. Such laws enshrine our abhorrence of punishment of the innocent, the kind of abhorrence that motivated Ryan. The criminal law's Voluntary Act Requirement (VAR) is often seen as enshrining in law the injustice of punishment in the second class of cases where there is no genuine action by the defendant on which to predicate criminal liability. The requirement is statutorily codified in many jurisdictions (cf. *Model Penal Code* § 2.01(1), critically discussed in Husak 2007) and accepted as a foundational principle of law in jurisdictions in which it is not written into a statute. The VAR should be understood as follows:

> A conviction of a defendant for crime C is justified only if (1) There is a voluntary act, the performance of which is necessary for C's occurrence (given the statutory definition of C) and (2) the defendant has been shown (typically, beyond a reasonable doubt) to have performed such a voluntary act.

Under the VAR, we cannot criminalize in the first place, and so cannot legally punish, the meeting of a set of conditions that can be met without the performance of a voluntary act.

The VAR is a legal representation of a legitimate moral idea. There is something morally objectionable about violating it, as it would have been violated had the trial court's conviction of Martin for appearing drunk in public not been overturned. The question is what, exactly, the underlying moral idea is. As we will see, many of the valid moral principles that one might take the VAR to legally enshrine fail to capture important aspects of it. Further, it will be argued that, perhaps surprisingly, the moral idea that in fact justifies the VAR is the familiar one that what qualifies wrongful conduct for criminal punishment is the way in which that conduct manifests the defendant's objectionable mental states, such as bad intentions.

Section 1 explains some of the features of the VAR that need to be accounted for by a moral rationale for it. Section 2 discusses several attractive rationales and argues that each falls short of providing a fully satisfactory account. Section 3 offers an alternative, drawing on an appealing picture of the morally relevant relationship between criminal conduct and the mental states of the criminal, a relationship which, it is argued, is at risk of being absent when the VAR is violated.

The Legal Doctrine

Although it is rarely made explicit, the law uses a definition of the term "voluntary act" that departs in significant respects from the ordinary concept. For legal purposes, a voluntary act is a *willed bodily movement*. To will, in the sense of relevance to the VAR, is not merely to mentally represent the bodily movement and for that bodily movement to be guided by that representation. If the mental state that guides the bodily movement is not "conscious"—a term explicitly used in the law—then that mental state is not a *willing*, or a *volition*, and the bodily movements it guides are therefore not voluntary actions. So the law provides two significant limitations in its definition of a voluntary act: only bodily movements count, and, of those, only bodily movements guided by *conscious* mental representations count. There are thus (at least) two kinds of voluntary action, in the ordinary sense, that do not count as voluntary actions in the law's sense: (1) voluntary thoughts (e.g., voluntarily thinking about a problem); and (2) bodily movements guided by unconscious mental representations of them.

The first of these two departures from the ordinary notion of a voluntary act is easily explained. There is something objectionable about criminalizing thoughts alone. Prohibitions on thoughts are intrusive violations of privacy, efforts at mind control, and inconsistent with the goals and role of a liberal state. This idea gains legal expression in the idea that crimes consist of *both mens rea* elements *and actus reus* elements. The *mens rea* elements of the crime are mental states, thoughts, that the defendant must be shown to have had for guilt—an intention to kill, for instance. But mature legal systems do not allow guilt merely on the strength of adequate proof of mental states. *Actus reus* elements—further facts distinct from the mental states of the defendant—must also be shown for guilt: that somebody died, and that the defendant caused that death, for instance. It is because the VAR is a restriction on the *actus reus* (among the *actus reus* elements must be a voluntary act) that the law defines the term "voluntary act" so as to exclude voluntary thoughts. The thoughts that are relevant to criminal liability are part of the crime's *mens rea* (and, in fact, none of them need to be shown to be voluntary). So, the fact that the VAR cannot be satisfied by proof that the defendant had a voluntary thought is merely an artifact of the formal structure of crimes—the division between *mens rea* and *actus reus*—that is, itself, a legal mechanism for barring crimes of pure thought.

The second departure from the ordinary notion of a voluntary act—the exclusion from the category of bodily movements guided by nonconscious mental representations of them—is more puzzling and in need of independent explanation. To see that this second category includes behaviors that we would ordinarily characterize as voluntary, consider the case of *People v. Newton* (87 Cal. Rptr. 394 (1970)). After a traffic stop and an altercation with police, Newton was shot in the gut. Immediately following, he shot and killed one of the police officers and fled the scene, arriving shortly afterwards at a hospital. Later he claimed not to remember the shooting, or traveling to the hospital, and claimed to have been unconscious for the crucial period of time beginning from the moment at which he was shot. Medical testimony supported the contention: a doctor testified that people suffering from traumatic injuries often engage in complex, motivated bodily movements in the absence of consciousness. Newton was convicted at trial, but his conviction was overturned on the grounds that the mental states that guided his bodily movements—the finger movements on the trigger, for instance—were not conscious and so were not willings; but if they were not willings, then the relevant bodily movements were not voluntary, and so it would be a violation of the VAR to punish Newton for the officer's death. Newton's finger movements on the trigger were not likely to be purely reflexive; they were clearly goal-directed. Newton seems to have been *aiming* the gun at the officer, and so must have been mentally representing a particular goal, namely to shoot the officer, a mental representation that was involved in guiding his bodily movements. Many people would take such considerations to show that the relevant bodily movements were voluntary actions in the ordinary sense, but they were not voluntary in the law's sense.

Morally justifying the VAR requires explaining what justifies the exclusion of behaviors that we would ordinarily classify as voluntary acts. In addition, however, there are events that we would probably *not* classify as voluntary actions—in fact, they may not even meet *the law's* definition—but that the law treats as though they were. This is true, in particular, of omissions—failures to act—and of habitual actions. If a defendant is shown to have omitted a bodily movement (under certain conditions), or shown to have engaged in a habitual bodily movement, then that's good enough to comply with the restriction imposed by the VAR.

This is not as peculiar as it might seem. In many places in the law we find that X, which is different from Y, is treated for legal purposes as though it were Y. Under, for instance, the doctrine of transferred intent in homicide, a person who intends to kill one person and, acting on that intention, kills another instead, is treated *as though* he intended to kill the person he killed. The law does not make the mistake of holding that the defendant in such a case *really* intends to kill the person he kills; everyone recognizes that the death in such a case was, in a sense, an accident. Rather, it is that the defendant is treated *as though* he had that intention since, it is thought, his actual intention was just as bad (or worse) than the one the law actually takes to be an element of an intentional homicide (namely, an intention to kill the person who was killed). Similarly, the law treats both omissions and habitual, often reflexive, acts *as though* they were voluntary acts for the purposes of the VAR, even though they may not be in fact.

Consider the case of omission first. There is an open question in the philosophy of action as to whether omissions are to be identified with willed bodily movements. Consider a mother who sits idly by while someone seriously injures her infant and makes no effort to stop the beating. Is her omission—the one we refer to when we say, "She failed to protect her own child"—to be identified with the bodily movement in which she *did* engage, the bodily movement, for instance, associated with sitting idly and watching? Perhaps. Or perhaps not. Perhaps the action referred to by such a sentence consists only in *the absence* of the act of protecting her child, rather than that positive bodily movement that occurred in its stead. (For discussion and further references, see Bach 2010.) But whatever the outcome of this debate, a defendant in an omission case such as this need not *be shown beyond a reasonable doubt* to have willed the bodily movements in which she is engaging when she ought to have been protecting her child. And there's surely a good reason for this. Unless it speaks to the question of her capacity to protect her child, it would seem to miss the moral point of the VAR to acquit a defendant on the grounds that at the moment when she could have been protecting her child she was instead simply sitting idly, a bodily movement that she did not will. Precisely what seems morally salient is what *she did not do or will*, not whether or not she willed that in which she was, instead, engaged. The result is that the VAR is to be interpreted as allowing criminal liability in the absence of a voluntary action in the case of omissions meeting appropriate conditions. Like the exclusion by the VAR of criminal liability in cases where bodily movements are guided by unconscious mental states, the *inclusion* of criminal liability for the case of omissions must also be explained by an adequate account of the moral rationale of the requirement.

A word about habitual actions is also in order. Consider a defendant who has been trained by the military to spin around and fire immediately, and without thinking, on a threat behind him. This behavior has become, thanks to his training, habitual. Is he to be held guilty of a crime when, at the local firing range, he spins and fires on a person behind him who yells something threatening? Or would such a verdict violate the VAR? The bodily movements in cases such as this are routinely taken to provide an acceptable basis for criminal liability (cf. *Model Penal Code* § 2.01(2)(d)). Noting that the defendant spun and fired only thanks to his military training will not serve to undermine the case against him through appeal to the VAR, although it might support a claim that he lacked some further mental state, such as an intention to kill, relevant to his degree of criminal liability. As suggested above, the law does not take this stance because it is believed that habitual actions are, in fact, *willed*. Nobody tasked with making legally binding decisions knows whether such actions are willed or not, or even whether some types are and some are not. It is an empirical question that would require careful investigation by psychologists and neuroscientists. Normally, our ignorance about a feature of pertinence to criminal liability is enough to supply reasonable doubt, and thus enough to support an acquittal. But not in habitual action cases. If there is reasonable doubt about whether the defendant's bodily movement was voluntary *deriving from the fact that it is habitual*, that reasonable doubt fails to undermine the case for guilt. We treat habitual bodily movements, that is, *as though* they were voluntary acts in the legal sense, even though we have no idea whether they are in fact. This fact, also, about the VAR should be explained, ideally, by a moral justification of it.

To summarize, then, there are three features of the law's application of the VAR that should be accounted for by a justification of it: (1) there's no criminal liability for goal-directed bodily movements guided by nonconscious mental representations;

(2) there is criminal liability for some omissions; and (3) there is criminal liability for habitual bodily movements even though there is reasonable doubt as to whether they are willed. An adequate rationale of the VAR will, first and foremost, explain why a voluntary action is necessary for justified criminal liability. But, ideally, the explanation will also entail (1), (2) and (3).

Insufficient Rationales for the VAR

Broadly speaking, there are two different kinds of moral rationale that can be given for a criminal law doctrine that draws distinctions among defendants and then predicates differences in criminal punishment on the distinctions that it draws. Under the first kind of rationale, the doctrine is shown to draw a distinction on the basis of a property that makes a difference to desert of punishment. For instance, many offenses are graded by the mental states of the defendant. We punish more heavily someone who intentionally burns a neighbor's barn out of spite than someone who negligently burns it by forgetting to put out a campfire. This doctrine is explained by the fact that intentional wrongdoing is morally worse than negligent wrongdoing.

The second kind of rationale appeals to a moral norm governing the behavior of those who are to inflict punishment. Ordinarily, for instance, we think it wrong to punish someone whom we lack good reason to think deserving of punishment *even if he is deserving of punishment*. To punish someone deserving without knowing for sure that he is deserving is not to give someone something other than what he deserves—if he's deserving, he's deserving—but it is to nonetheless do something wrong; it is to violate a norm governing the conduct of punishers. This moral norm—do not punish unless *you know* the punished is deserving—explains, for instance, some criminal law doctrines pertaining to evidence: we often punish only one of two equally deserving defendants when one, but not the other, has been proven to be guilty by the admissible evidence.

Two of the possible rationales for the VAR discussed in this section—called here the "Evidentialist" and "Actual Invasion" rationales—are of the second sort: they identify moral norms governing punishers and claim that those norms would be violated were the state to fail to follow the dictates of the VAR. The other two—what will be called the "PAP" and "Reasons–Responsiveness" rationales—are of the first sort: they identify features on the basis of which the VAR distinguishes among defendants that speak to a difference in desert of punishment.

The Evidentialist Rationale

An adequate philosophy of mind will explain the fact that there is something private about our mental lives. We are wrong more than we like to admit about what's going on between our ears, but we nonetheless have access to it in a way that others do not. Despite this privacy, however, desert of punishment for wrongdoing turns crucially on the mental states of the wrongdoer. If we are to give punishment to only and all those who deserve it, we must somehow overcome the privacy of the mental in our assessments of who deserves to be punished. We have tools for doing this, perhaps most importantly the very same tools that we use to overcome the barrier of privacy in virtually every interaction that we have with any other human being: in the criminal law, that is, we exercise the very same tools for "reading minds" that we use when we make eye contact with a stranger in the elevator. But when there is a great deal at stake in our judgments about what others are thinking—as there is when we inquire in order to decide whether and how to punish—we need a greater degree of certainty than we need in most human interactions. We need extremely good evidence of what is going on in the minds of those whom we might punish. And one might think that we necessarily lack that kind of evidence in the absence of some voluntary act that evidences the private mental states that we need to know about in order to know what kind of punishment is deserved. On this view, it is because morality requires punishers to have adequate evidence of facts that are difficult to evidence—namely mental states—that the VAR is justified. Call this the "Evidentialist Rationale" for the VAR.

The Evidentialist Rationale provides a satisfactory explanation for our allowance of criminal liability for omissions, even if they fall short of voluntary actions. What a person does *not* do sometimes tells us all we need to know about his desert-relevant mental states. It should be no surprise that the *absence* of sufficient concern for others, for instance, could be properly evidenced by the *absence* of action, at least in some circumstances; there are things that people who are sufficiently concerned would *do*, and so the failure to do them can evidence the absence of sufficient concern.

However, precisely what makes it possible to explain the law's treatment of omissions under the Evidentialist Rationale undermines the case for thinking that that rationale captures the relevant moral principle enshrined by the VAR. Omissions can provide satisfactory evidence of desert-relevant mental states *even if omissions are not voluntary acts*. In fact, there are many sources of adequate evidence of such mental states other than voluntary acts. Involuntary actions tell us a great deal about mental state—think of blushing. In fact, because it is much harder to prevent involuntary manifestations of mental state than voluntary manifestations, involuntary actions sometimes provide *significantly better* evidence of mental state than do voluntary actions. Arguably, this is the rationale for the admissibility in court of "excited utterances" which would otherwise be inadmissible as hearsay (Federal Rules of Evidence, Article VIII, Rule 803(2)). Because the excited utterance is involuntary, it is more likely to be expressive of what the speaker actually believes than an unexcited utterance would be. If the VAR were supposed to ensure that the government does not violate the norm against punishment in the absence of adequately supported belief in guilt, the requirement would be at best an inept effort to conform the state's conduct to moral principle.

The Actual Invasion Rationale

Sometimes we should neither censure nor punish conduct deserving of such a response because we lack standing to do so. Intuitively, the wrongdoing in question is none of our business. You hear a stranger say something sexist to his wife at a nearby restaurant table. His conduct is wrongful and he would deserve to be reprimanded. But you ought not reprimand him, or demand that he apologize. In fact, not just the man, but the person he insulted with his comments, would have grounds for complaint were you to get involved. It's simply none of your business.

Broadly speaking, when it comes to criminal law, the state's business is with invasions of the legally protected interests of citizens; anything else is not its business. Add that only voluntary acts actually invade the legally protected interests of others, and we reach the conclusion that for the state to punish in the absence of a voluntary act would be for the state to violate the norm against punishing in the absence of standing to punish. Call this the "Actual Invasion Rationale" for the VAR.

To explain the fact that faultless, involuntary behaviors are excluded from criminal punishment by the VAR, the Actual Invasion Rationale must be coupled with a particular conception of a legally protected interest. Imagine that D, who has no history of seizures, has one while driving and injures V. Has V's legally protected interest in bodily security been invaded? Under some conceptions of a legally protected interest, it has. But we might think that the legally protected interest with which the criminal law concerns itself is the interest in not being *wronged*, and not just the interest in not being *harmed*. V in this example has been harmed, but since D was in no way at fault for the harm that he caused, V has not been wronged.

Even when "invasions" are understood as "wrongings," the Actual Invasion Rationale falters with respect to two features of the law identified in section 1, namely, the exclusion from criminal liability of behaviors guided by nonconscious mental representations, and the inclusion of habitual acts. First, there is no reason to think that a victim is wronged by a harmful bodily movement only if the mental state guiding it is conscious. The officer Newton killed was wronged by the killing. If we hesitate to accept that conclusion, it is because we have doubts about the mental state that accompanied Newton's bodily movements when he pulled the trigger. We wonder, for instance, whether he really intended to kill given his state of shock following his injury. But to take such intuitions to support the claim that the officer was not wronged is to fail to distinguish a lower grade of wrongdoing from its absence. Perhaps the officer was less badly wronged if Newton killed him with some mental attitude falling short of intention, or as a result of provocation or emotional disturbance. These considerations point to differences in degrees of wrongdoing that the laws against homicide take into consideration in grading the crime. But it is to succumb to confusion to suggest that no matter what Newton's nonconscious mental state, the officer was not wronged since Newton was not conscious. The bodily movements in which Newton engaged are *potentially* wronging; they would wrong the officer were they accompanied by objectionable mental states, and so they cannot be excluded, wholesale, from criminal liability under the Actual Invasion Rationale. They *did* actually invade the officer's legally protected interest, even if it is unclear how bad the invasion was.

On the flipside, without knowing whether habitual actions are either willed or result from prior fault, we are lacking any grounds on which to insist that those who are harmed by them are wronged. If to be injured by a habitual action is no different, substantively, from being injured by a falling tree limb broken by the wind, there is no sense in which such injuries wrong their victims. The result is that to allow criminal liability in such cases, in the absence of any showing to the effect that there is either a willing that issued in the bodily movement or prior fault of some sort, is to fail to conform to the moral principle that is taken to be crucial by the advocate of the Actual Invasion Rationale.

The PAP Rationale

One might think that to punish in the absence of a voluntary action is to punish where the agent could not have done otherwise, or was not free. Add that the ability to do otherwise is necessary to be justifiably held responsible, and it seems that the VAR has a natural rationale. To pursue this line is to take the VAR to be the law's way of concretizing an appealing moral principle, sometimes called the "Principle of Alternate Possibilities" (PAP), according to which *a person is morally responsible for his conduct only if he could have done otherwise.* Call this the "PAP Rationale" for the VAR.

PAP itself has come under attack since Harry Frankfurt's important paper offering counterexamples to it (Frankfurt 1988). Frankfurt constructed examples of people who seem unable to do otherwise because of something that would block them from doing otherwise *were they to try to*, but never try to. Since the people in the examples just act badly for their own reasons, without ever trying and failing to do otherwise, they seem to be responsible for their bad behavior. If PAP is false, then that would indeed undermine its power to justify a legal practice that aims to induce legal actors to comply with it. However, even if we grant the truth of PAP, the PAP Rationale is inadequate. Note, first, that defendants who engage in voluntary actions need not be shown to have had the ability to do otherwise in order to be held guilty. This point would not in itself impugn the PAP Rationale were showing that a person acted voluntarily sufficient for showing that he had the ability to do otherwise. But it is not. As has long been recognized, voluntariness, while necessary for freedom, is not sufficient for it. John Locke offered a convincing counterexample to the sufficiency claim in his *Essay Concerning Human Understanding* in the late seventeenth century:

> [S]uppose a Man be carried, whilst fast asleep, into a Room, where is a Person he longs to see and speak with; and be there locked fast in, beyond his Power to get out: he awakes, and is glad to find himself in so desirable Company, which he stays willingly in, *i.e.* preferrs his stay to going away. I ask, Is not this stay voluntary? I think, no Body will doubt it: and yet being locked fast in, 'tis evident he is not at liberty not to stay, he has not freedom to be gone.
>
> (Locke 1979, II.xxxi.10: 172)

Imagine that the man in the example lacks permission to stay and so is trespassing, which is a crime. While we can argue over whether it is just to punish him for staying, the VAR *itself* does not provide us with reason to object. The man engaged in a voluntary act; his bodily movement, in staying in the room, was willed. There would be nothing objectionable by the standards of the VAR about a statute that defined a crime in such a way that this man's conduct met the definition, as statutes prohibiting trespassing do.

A response to this concern can be made through noting that cases of voluntariness without the ability to do otherwise are rare. But this amounts to the assertion that it is rare under the VAR to punish someone who is unworthy of punishment. If the ability to do otherwise is what we really require for criminal liability, then wrongful conviction would be even rarer were we to write PAP into law.

The PAP Rationale also yields the wrong results about habitual action. Do those who engage in habitual actions have the ability to do otherwise? Under one construal, habitual actions are simply "triggered" by perception of the environment. It is because he hears something threatening behind him that the soldier, in the earlier hypothetical, spins and fires. But given that it is not in his control that he should hear the threat, it is not under his control that he should spin and fire on the person who issued it. Were the PAP Rationale correct, we would have good reason to exclude habitual actions from criminal liability, rather than include them, as we do.

The Reasons–Responsiveness Rationale

Those who accept the arguments against PAP, and so hold that it is possible to be fully morally responsible for one's conduct even in the absence of the ability to do otherwise,

181

might nonetheless hold that there is a necessary condition of responsible conduct that is not met when the agent being assessed has not performed a voluntary act. According to John Fischer's position, a person is morally responsible for his behavior only if it issued from a "reasons–responsive" mechanism. (See, for instance, the essays collected in Fischer 2006.) While the full set of conditions that must be satisfied for a mechanism giving rise to behavior to count as reasons–responsive, in Fischer's sense, is complex, the basic idea is this: *responsibility requires that the agent would have recognized and responded to reasons to do otherwise had there been such reasons.* It is possible to be responsive to reasons for alternatives even while lacking the ability to pursue them: imagine that the man in the locked room would have tried to leave were he offered a sum of money; he would have responded to reasons to leave, but still would have stayed. Since reasons–responsiveness and the ability to do otherwise pull apart, Fischer's condition on responsibility is distinct from PAP.

Fischer's idea suggests an alternative rationale for the VAR: when an agent's behavior is not voluntary, by the law's standards, it arises from a process, or a mechanism, that is not reasons–responsive. Therefore, if reasons–responsiveness is necessary for responsibility, and responsibility is necessary for desert of punishment, the Voluntary Act Requirement helps the law conform to moral principle. Call this the "Reasons–Responsiveness Rationale."

This rationale succeeds in accounting for many aspects of the VAR. Martin, who was dropped on the highway by the police and then arrested for appearing there, did not appear on the highway as a result of his own reasons–responsive mechanism; no matter what reasons he had and recognized for not appearing on the highway, he was going to appear there given the police's determination that he should. A defendant who flails his arms while in the grips of a seizure, for the same reasons, does not engage in bodily movements that have their source in a reasons–responsive mechanism; the electrical activity that gives rise to the relevant bodily movements would not alter in the face of reasons not to move the body in that way. And the Reasons–Responsiveness Rationale does well in accounting for the fact that omissions are as good as voluntary acts for legal purposes: a person who omits to aid her child, for instance, might very well fail to do so as a result of the workings of a mechanism such that, had she had certain reasons for helping her child, she would have recognized and responded to them. Maybe, for instance, she would have done so had someone offered her crack in exchange. If so, then that fact, on Fischer's view, would show that she omitted through a reasons–responsive mechanism (Fischer and Ravizza 1998, ch. 5).

The Reasons–Responsiveness Rationale does substantially less well at explaining some other aspects of the VAR. First, consider the law's exclusion of bodily movements guided by nonconscious mental states from the category of the voluntary. There is no reason to suppose that consciousness is required for reasons–responsiveness. Newton, for instance, seemed to be acting from a reasons–responsive mechanism when he ran from the scene of the shooting to the hospital: had he thought the hospital was elsewhere, he would have run there instead. And yet he is not to be held criminally liable for his bodily movements. Either this is an error on the law's part, or else the Reasons–Responsiveness Rationale falls short of identifying the moral principle underlying the VAR.

Further, consider the fact that habitual actions are to be treated as though they were voluntary actions. Willed or not, such bodily movements do not arise from a reasons–responsive mechanism. Consider again the soldier whose habitual reflexes lead him to shoot someone at a firing range whose threatening conduct warrants a much less aggressive response, if any at all. The circumstances that "trigger" the defendant's bodily movement—the victim shouting an obscenity towards him—would trigger that bodily movement no matter what reasons the defendant had not to squeeze the trigger. In fact, he had plenty such reasons and failed to respond to them. The mechanism in this case simply does not respond to reasons in the way that one might take to be necessary for moral responsibility.

Some will be drawn to the idea that the soldier, in the hypothetical just offered, ought not to be going to the firing range knowing, as he does, of his conditioned, reflexive habits. That is, some will be attracted to the possibility of assigning some kind of responsibility in this case through appeal to prior fault—in this case prior voluntary action that placed the agent in a situation where he would be at risk of encountering a "trigger" of his habit of shooting at threats behind him in circumstances in which he would be armed. However, the law does not inquire in habitual action cases about prior fault. The defendant in a case like this would need not be shown to have been at fault for being in the circumstances in which he found himself, nor would the behaviors that got him there need to be shown to have been voluntary. The mere fact, rather, that the relevant bodily movements were the product of a habit is sufficient to show there to be compliance with the VAR in assigning a guilty verdict. For instance: imagine that the defendant believed, and had every reason to believe, when he went to the firing range that he would handle only unloaded weapons. In that case, he could not be guilty of the crime through appeal to his earlier voluntary acts leading to his presence at the firing range; at the time of those bodily movements, he had no reason to believe that he was even risking harm to anyone else of the sort that he eventually caused. However, under the criminal law, the case would need to be made that he did not know he was risking harm to anyone *at the time of the habitual bodily movements*; his earlier mental state would be relevant only in so far as it provided evidence of his later mental state. In stipulating that habitual bodily movements are to be treated as voluntary actions, the criminal law is not pursuing the kind of prior fault analysis to which an advocate of the Reasons–Responsiveness Rationale might be attracted.

Enacting the Requirement of Correspondence

When a defendant is shown to be guilty of a crime, he is shown to have performed certain acts with certain results in certain circumstances—he is shown, for instance, to have lit a fire (an act) that burned a piece of property (a result) that was not his own (a circumstance). And he is shown to have been in certain mental states—he is shown, for instance, to have intended to light the fire, to have been aware of a substantial and unjustifiable risk that property would burn as a result, and to have known that the property in question was not his own. But, in fact, there is an additional requirement that is so rarely at issue as to go unmentioned most of the time: the defendant's actions must correspond with his mental states. The fact that the defendant once long ago intended to light the fire matters not at all if he didn't intend to light the fire that he lit *when he lit it* or if he didn't light it *as a result of* that very intention. The mental states that matter must be linked to ("concur with," "correspond to") the acts that form the basis of criminal liability. Call this the "Requirement of Correspondence."

Under what conditions do the act and mental state "correspond"? Criminal law students are taught that the needed correspondence is present when the act and the mental states take place at the same time. Teaching the Requirement of Correspondence this way may serve pedagogical purposes, but it misses the point of the requirement. We can illustrate this with examples in which an agent has two intentions at a particular time, but is only acting on one of them. D and V go hunting. D intends to kill V when the moment is right, but intends to hunt deer until then. When he fires towards both a deer and V, and hits V, killing him, is there appropriate correspondence between his intention to kill V and his act? There is not, if at that moment he was acting on his intention to kill the deer and merely accidentally killed V. Of course, such a defendant has an uphill battle to convince a jury that he was not acting on his intention to kill V. But in fighting it he is trying to show that the Requirement of Correspondence was not met. The Requirement of Correspondence does not merely bar liability when the act and mental state are not simultaneous. Rather, it bars liability when the act is not *the manifestation* or *the product* of the mental state. In fact, there is an intuitively appealing moral principle here: *a person's mental states contribute to his responsibility for his act only if the act is the manifestation (in an intuitive but not yet defined sense) of those mental states.* If this is right, then a person is morally responsible for a package consisting of mental states and conduct only if the mental states in question are manifested in the conduct. The parts of the package must be glued together, as it were, for there to be responsibility for the package.

It is a foundational principle of criminal law that part of what justifies punishing a defendant are the objectionable mental states that he was shown to have had. Further, when we grade a crime on the basis of mental state—giving, for instance, a lower penalty for a negligent than for an intentional homicide—we assume that the moral quality of the act is a function in part of the mental state that gave rise to it. However, if the moral principle about correspondence is correct, then mental states contribute to the defendant's responsibility only if they are manifested in action. The homicide, for instance, deserves to be classified as intentional, rather than negligent, that is, only if the intention to kill was manifested in the act of killing. But, for reasons to be explained in this section, mental states are manifested in action (at least in the paradigm case) only if the defendant performed a voluntary act. Hence, the VAR is justified because failure to comply with it would involve failure to comply with the moral principle concerned with correspondence. Voluntary acts matter to criminal liability, on this view, because without them we lack the link between objectionable mental states and objectionable acts that is required to be justified in punishing for the package of mental states and conduct that crimes, in fact, consist in. There is *mens rea* and there is *actus reus*; but without a voluntary act, there is not the link between the two that is required for desert of punishment for the conjunction.

Call this the "Manifestation of Mens Rea Rationale" for the VAR. Under it, the VAR is a byproduct of the idea that *mens rea* is an essential part of criminal liability. It is because we already think that people should not be punished in the absence of a showing of *mens rea*, under the rationale, that we are barred, for moral reasons, from punishing them in the absence of a voluntary act. *Mens rea* is essential, but it isn't relevant unless it's manifested. And it isn't manifested unless there's a voluntary act. To punish, then, in the absence of a voluntary act is morally no different from punishing in the absence of *mens rea*, and that is unacceptable. The rest of this section will be spent defending this rationale for the VAR.

To see why a voluntary act is required for there to be correspondence with mental state and conduct, consider, first, the paradigm case: at t1, D decides to kill V and forms an intention to do so; at t2, acting on that intention, D squeezes the trigger of a gun and V is killed. In this description of the case, the crucial phrase is "acting on that intention." To say that is to say that the Requirement of Correspondence has been met. But what does that phrase mean? Under what conditions is a person acting on a particular intention? Consider the following possible answer:

> At t2, D acts on his intention to kill V if and only if the intention causes D's bodily movement (the movement of his finger on the trigger) at t2.

As attractive as this simple theory is, it will not do. The problem is well known to philosophers of action: if the causal route from intention to bodily movement is "deviant" then the right side of the biconditional will be satisfied, but not the left. For instance, say that at t2 D is at the firing range and notices that V is passing between him and the target at which he is pointing. Recalling that he earlier formed an intention to kill V, D becomes very nervous—"My God," he thinks, "I might actually go through with this!"—and his nervousness causes his hands to shake violently, resulting in the bodily movement of his finger pulling the trigger. In such a case, the bodily movement is not the manifestation of the intention of the sort that is required for correspondence, or, as we say, for it to be the case that D is "acting on the intention. " In that case, although the intention causes the bodily movement—the causal sequence is intention–nervousness–finger movement—the bodily movement is not the manifestation of the intention in the sense that matters for responsibility.

We can't solve the problem by insisting that there be no causal intermediaries between intention and later bodily movement when someone acts on an intention. After all, there are causal intermediaries between the intention and the relevant bodily movement in paradigm cases of acting on an intention. You intend to go to the baseball game next weekend and so buy tickets. You have no plans about how you will get from your house to the stadium. When the time comes, you walk. In walking you are acting on the intention to go to the game. But that intention did not represent those bodily movements; you had not decided how you would get to the stadium when you formed the intention. Still, *something* must have represented those bodily movements. In fact, we know what that something is: an intention to get to the stadium by walking. *That* later intention is a causal intermediary between your intention to go to the game and your bodily movements.

This reflection on the paradigm case, however, makes evident an important difference between the case in which the intention misfires, as in the case in which it makes D so nervous that he squeezes the trigger of the gun, and the case in which it does not, such as the case of going to the game by walking there. There is a difference between the causal intermediaries between intention and bodily movement in the two cases. In particular, in the game case the causal intermediary is itself a representation of the act it causes: you intend *to walk* and this results in your walking. The intermediary has representational content that turns out to match the world when it causes walking. By contrast, in the misfire case the causal intermediary is just nervousness, which may represent no act at all, much less the act of squeezing the trigger. That state of nervousness could have caused D's eye to twitch rather than his finger without there having been any apparent mismatch between the mental state and the world.

Notice that, in the game case, we can also look for causal intermediaries between the intention *to walk* and the bodily movement it causes. And, in fact, we find some:

when you decide to walk, you haven't decided whether to start with your left foot or your right. When you begin with your right, that bodily motion is a paradigm instance of acting on the intention to walk. *Something* must have represented that bodily movement. But it wasn't the intention to walk. So, there must have been some intermediary between the intention to walk and the movement of your right foot which represented that movement. What intermediary? Probably an intention to move your *right* foot. And we can extend the point further. When you formed the intention to start with your right foot, you didn't decide that you would step with that foot *over* the puddle in the yard rather than into it. But *something* must have represented that longer-than-normal bodily movement. What? Answer: an intention to step a longer-than-normal distance with your right foot. In the paradigm case of acting on an intention—that is, in principle, between *any* intention and the bodily movement it causes—there is some other representational state, perhaps some other intention, that represents features of that bodily movement that are not represented by the previous intention in the sequence. There is a causal sequence of intentions, that is, that are increasingly specific, or fine-grained, in their content. The first, in this case, is the intention to go to the game; later there is the intention to walk; and later still there is the intention to take an extra-long step with the right foot. It is thanks to the fact that there is this sequence ending with the movement of the foot itself that that movement is an instance of acting on the first intention in the sequence, namely the intention to go to the game.

Of course, at some point this search for causal intermediaries that represent features of the bodily movement not represented by the most recent intention we've identified will give out. Your foot lands exactly .4 inches past the edge of the puddle. But no mental state represented *that* feature of the bodily movement; it is not as though you would have failed to do as intended had your foot landed .5 inches past the puddle's edge instead. So, at some point, the mental state that serves as intermediary in the paradigm case will be as fine-grained in its content as it gets. It is an empirical question how fine-grained such representations are. Still, at least in the paradigm case, there must be causal intermediaries with remarkably fine-grained content: in stepping over the puddle—in stepping three feet rather than merely two—you are acting on your intention *to go to the game*, and so there must be some mental state, caused by the intention to go to the game (among other things, such as a belief that the puddle is in the way), that represents a longer-than-normal bodily movement and thus causes it to be the case that you engage in one. Let's give the name "volition" to the mental state that is as fine-grained in content as it gets and which we find in the paradigm case of acting on an intention. (John Searle uses the term "intention-in-action" to refer to this mental state. See Searle 1983, ch. 3.)

The central point here is, perhaps, already clear: if all cases were paradigm cases, then whenever there is appropriate correspondence between intention and later bodily movement—correspondence of the sort that is needed for the bodily movement to be the manifestation of the intention in the sense that matters for responsibility for the intention-action package—the bodily movement would have to be caused by a representation of it, which is part of what is needed under the VAR. In paradigm cases of legal importance, the relevant intention is not the trivial intention to move the body in a certain way. It is, instead, an intention that is not nearly so fine-grained in its content, such as an intention to kill, or an intention to remain somewhere that you have no right to remain, or the intention to deface public property. What we need to know is whether the bodily movements that then cause a death (in homicide), or cause someone to remain where they shouldn't (in criminal trespass), or cause public property to be defaced (in destruction of public property) were manifestations of these objectionable intentions. In the paradigm case, these bodily movements were not such manifestations if they weren't guided, at the time, by mental representations of them, volitions, in the sense just defined. And so, since we care about the Requirement of Correspondence, we need to care about guidance of bodily movement by volition.

What has been said so far, then, explains the defining feature of the VAR, namely that, putting aside exceptions, there is no criminal liability in the absence of a bodily movement that is immediately guided by a mental representation of it. But can appeal to the Manifestation of Mens Rea Rationale explain the features of the VAR identified in section 1? Yes.

First, consider the law's refusal to allow bodily movements guided by nonconscious representations to count as voluntary acts for the purposes of the VAR. To see that this can be explained, first consider the *Model Penal Code*'s definition of an intention (or "purpose") to act or bring about a result:

> A person acts purposely . . . if . . . it is his conscious object to engage in conduct of that nature or to cause such a result.
>
> (MPC § 2.02(2)(a))

By requiring that a legally relevant intention be *conscious*, as specified here, the *Model Penal Code* sets the rule that we never impose criminal liability for unconscious intentions. The framers of the *Code* may be concerned to exclude conviction for purposeful crimes through appeal to Freudian explanations. The accidental killing of the defendant's father, for instance, can be made to appear to be a purposeful killing through assignment to the defendant of a subconscious intention to kill his father; add an Oedipal diagnosis and a jury could be led to a very draconian verdict. If we think the requirement that the intention be conscious is a good one, the question then is whether, in the paradigm case, the causal intermediaries between conscious intention and bodily movement can be *un*conscious when the bodily movement is a manifestation of the intention. If the volition were unconscious, that would at least provide reasonable doubt as to whether the act was really the manifestation of the conscious intention in the way that matters for criminal responsibility. The sufferer from the Oedipal complex, who has managed to bring his intention to kill his father into consciousness, might nonetheless repress into subconsciousness the mental states through which he executes that conscious intention. To convict in such a case for intentional homicide on proof of the intention to kill would be no different, in the end, from convicting for intentional homicide when the intention to kill itself is subconscious. Therefore: it is because we require conscious intention that we require conscious volition under the VAR. Without consciousness of volition, conscious intention would not be properly manifested in action. In a case like *Newton*, then, there are really two reasons not to ascribe Newton with criminal responsibility for the killing: his intention to kill (if he had one) was unconscious, and so were the mental states through which that intention became manifested in the bodily movements that caused the death.

Second, consider the rule that a certain class of omissions can suffice for the VAR. This practice too admits of an explanation under the Manifestation of Mens Rea Rationale: what we *do not do* often manifests our objectionable mental states just as much as what we *do do* even if there is no volition present. The mental state of disregarding one's child's welfare is manifested by *the failure* to do that which the child's welfare requires that one do. However, in such cases, there need be no volition to serve as causal intermediary between the morally and criminally relevant mental state—in the imagined case the state of "disregard"—and the failure to do as one ought. While that failure may need to be caused by the prior objectionable mental state for the failure to manifest it in the morally relevant way, such causation does not require volitional intermediaries.

And third, consider the case of habitual actions. The rationale for treating convictions for habitual actions as complying with the VAR is, roughly, that we have reason to believe that, like some omissions, some habitual actions can be manifestations of objectionable mental states in the sense that matters to morality, even if they are not guided by conscious volitions. One benefit of a habit is that it produces conduct for which there are reasons without the agent taking the time to reflect on and weigh those reasons; the habit of rolling through a stop sign on the way to work allows D to shave a few seconds off his commute while, at the same time, not interrupting his musings about how to handle his boss that day. However, a byproduct of this valuable feature of habits is that they override our tendencies to withhold action in the face of reasons to do so. Since D has a habit of rolling through the stop sign, he does so on a particular occasion even though consciously aware of a much greater danger on that occasion than usual. In this case, the mental state of recklessness manifests itself in the bodily movement *thanks to* the fact that the bodily movement is habitual. Normal agents find themselves in objectionable mental states all the time; most of us override the impulses to conduct that those mental states supply. Failure to override is one way in which such mental states can be manifested in behavior, and this is found in at least some habitual actions. Hence to exclude them on the grounds of involuntariness would be to miss the point of the VAR. It is because that requirement helps us to be sure to comply with the Requirement of Correspondence that habitual actions, also, serve for criminal liability.

One objection to the Manifestation of Mens Rea Rationale arises from reflection on cases of "strict liability": cases in which guilt can be established despite the absence of a showing of any particular culpable mental state with respect to crucial elements of the crime's *actus reus*. Consider the case of *State v. Kremer* (262 Minn. 190, 114 N.W. 2d 88 (1962)). Kremer's brakes failed, without any prior warning, and he ran through a flashing red light, in violation of a city ordinance. To be guilty of the crime, a defendant need not be shown to have been even negligent with respect to the fact that he was running the light. There is guilt even if, for instance, the light were covered from view by a tree branch, so that even a reasonable person exercising due care would not have known that he was running the light. Kremer appealed his conviction on the grounds that it was in violation of the VAR. The question before the court, then, was whether the VAR applies even when the offense is strict liability.

The Manifestation of Mens Rea Rationale might appear to imply that when the crime is strict liability, as in *Kremer*, the VAR is irrelevant: if no mental state is required for guilt, then it seems that a requirement meant to assure that culpable mental states *be manifested* does not apply. However, the court in that case went the other way, quashing Kremer's conviction on the grounds that it was in violation of the VAR. Indeed, this is settled law. However, it is only through a mistaken conception of strict liability that one can reach the objection to the Manifestation of Mens Rea Rationale just offered. There are two ways to construe strict liability crimes: (1) the crime has no *mens rea* requirements; or (2) the crime has *mens rea* requirements but any mental state on the part of the defendant meets them. To conceive of strict liability in the first way is to see strict liability crimes as involving a major departure from fundamental axioms of criminal law, particularly the principle according to which acts are never worthy of punishment in the absence of accompaniment by culpable mental states. While there is good reason to think this is the wrong way to construe strict liability, if it were the right way to construe it, then it would follow that the court in *Kremer* made a mistake: the VAR would not apply. It is hard to see how someone willing to accept strict liability on these grounds could object to this conclusion. If we are ready to overturn fundamental principles of the morality of criminal law for the sake of social order, why not the VAR too?

Under the second construal of strict liability, however, the *Kremer* court made the right decision, but for reasons that are compatible with the Manifestation of Mens Rea Rationale. Under that construal, running a flashing red light is punishable only if it manifests a culpable mental state; but, as it happens, *any* mental state would be culpable. Hence, the behavior is punishable only if it manifests *some* mental state. The trouble with convicting Kremer, however, is that his act manifested *no mental state at all*. Under the second construal of strict liability, that is, the Requirement of Correspondence still needs to be met. And so the VAR still needs to be met, under the Manifestation of Mens Rea Rationale for it.

Conclusion

The Manifestation of Mens Rea Rationale explains central features of the legal doctrines involved in the VAR that are either inexplicable, or explicable inelegantly, through appeal to alternative rationales. What this suggests is that the central point of the VAR is to enshrine in law a common-sense moral requirement: we are not morally responsible for a package of objectionable mental states and harmful conduct unless the conduct is the manifestation of the mental states. This is a condition that is not met *in the paradigm case* in the absence of a voluntary act. And when the case differs from the paradigm case and the condition is nonetheless met, as in some cases of omission and habitual action, the VAR allows criminal liability in the absence of a voluntary act.

So, insofar as criminal punishment should be applied only to the morally deserving, we ought to conform, as we do, to the VAR. The VAR enshrines in law a maxim of morality as fundamental as the maxim against punishing someone other than the perpetrator of the crime. The maxim that underlies it is as fundamental—in fact, as has been argued here, *exactly* as fundamental—as the maxim against punishing in the absence of a showing of mental state. It is because the criminal's mind matters to his responsibility that we punish him only if it has been manifested in his conduct.

References

Bach, K. (2010) "Refraining, Omitting, and Negative Acts," in T. O'Connor and C. Sandis, eds., *A Companion to the Philosophy of Action*, Oxford: Wiley-Blackwell.

Fischer, J. (2006) *My Way: Essays on Moral Responsibility*, Oxford: Oxford University Press.

—— and Ravizza, M. (1998) *Responsibility and Control: A Theory of Moral Responsibility*, Cambridge: Cambridge University Press.

Frankfurt, H. (1988) "Alternate Possibilities and Moral Responsibility," in H. Frankfurt, *The Importance of What We Care About*, Cambridge: Cambridge University Press.

Husak, D. (2007) "Rethinking the Act Requirement," 28 *Cardozo Law Review*: 2437–2460.

Locke, J. (1979) *An Essay Concerning Human Understanding*, P. H. Nidditch, ed., Oxford: Clarendon Press.

Searle, J. (1983) *Intentionality*, Cambridge: Cambridge University Press.

Further Reading

For further reading, see: M. Bratman (1994) "Moore on Intention and Volition," *University of Pennsylvania Law Review* 142, 5: 1705–1718; V. Chiao (2009) "Action and Agency in the Criminal Law," *Legal Theory* 15: 1–23; R. A. Duff (2007) *Answering for Crime: Responsibility and Liability in the Criminal Law*, Oxford: Hart Publishing; D. Husak (2010) "Does Criminal Liability Require an Act?" in D. Husak, *The Philosophy of Criminal Law: Selected Essays*, Oxford: Oxford University Press; M. Moore (1993) *Act and Crime*, Oxford: Oxford University Press; and M. Moore (1997) *Placing Blame*, Oxford: Oxford University Press.

13

CRIMINAL ATTEMPTS

R. A. *Duff*

Initial Questions

Many criminal offenses are so defined that their commission requires the occurrence of the primary mischief or harm with which the law is concerned. The mischief with which offenses of homicide are primarily concerned is the death, or unlawful killing, of a human being; murder and other species of criminal homicide are so defined that they are committed only when someone is killed. The primary mischief with which the offense of criminal damage is concerned is the nonconsensual destruction of or damage to property; the offense is so defined that it is committed only if such destruction or damage actually occurs. We can call such offenses "consummate" (see Husak 1995): their commission involves the consummation of the mischief at which the law is aimed.

Systems of criminal law typically also criminalize attempts to commit consummate offenses: alongside the range of specific consummate offenses, there is a general offense of attempting to commit any such offense (above a minimal level of seriousness). If I try to kill someone, without justification or excuse, I am guilty of murder if I succeed, and of attempted murder if I fail; if I try unlawfully to destroy another's property, I am guilty of criminal damage if I succeed, and of attempted criminal damage if I fail. Criminal attempts form one category of "nonconsummate" offenses. An offense is non-consummate if the conduct that constitutes it is criminalized because of its relationship to some primary harm or mischief, but the commission of the offense need not involve the occurrence of that primary harm or mischief: attempts are criminalized because the conduct that constitutes a criminal attempt is related to a primary harm or mischief (as an attempt to cause it); but the commission of an attempt does not require the occurrence of that primary harm or mischief. Other general nonconsummate offenses are incitement and conspiracy: it is an offense to incite another to commit, or to agree with another to commit, a consummate offense, even if that offense is not actually committed (see Simester and Sullivan 2010: 285–328). But we will focus here on criminal attempts.

Three initial questions arise about criminal attempts. Why should we criminalize attempts to commit crimes? How should a criminal attempt be defined? How (how severely) should criminal attempts be punished? Each of these questions has occupied theorists of criminal law, and leads into larger issues in philosophy of action and moral philosophy; each generates further questions, which will emerge more clearly if we look initially at the question of definition.

Defining Attempts

We cannot assume that in defining offenses the criminal law will or should always use terms in their precise extralegal meaning: the law's proper purposes might be better served by creating a legal definition of attempt which does not precisely match our extralegal concept. But we can assume that there must be (or have been) at least some quite close relationship between legal and extralegal conceptions, and a brief examination of the extralegal concept will bring out some of the further questions raised by the law of attempts.

Two aspects of the extralegal concept are particularly important for present purposes. First, attempts require intention: I attempt or try to Φ only if I intend to Φ. Furthermore, the intention must be a "direct" intention: it is not enough that I act with what Bentham (unhelpfully) called "oblique" intention (Bentham 1781: ch. VIII.vi; 2000: 70), consisting in the certain belief that my action would bring about the relevant result; it must be at least part of my purpose to bring that result about, even if I intend to bring it about only as a means to a further end.

(We should note two complications here. One is that the distinction between intended results and foreseen side effects comes under pressure when the connection between what is intended and what is foreseen is so close that they seem inseparable: if I intend to blow up an aircraft, I must surely also be taken to intend the deaths of those whom I know to be on board, even if my aim is only to destroy the aircraft; if I fail in my endeavor, I have surely attempted to kill them. What makes such cases plausible as cases of intention, however, is not the mere fact of certain foresight, but the way in which the foreseen effect is part, rather than a further consequence, of what is intended: if I intend to explode the aircraft, I intend to destroy the whole thing—which includes its (human) contents. Whatever my further purpose, my intended means encompass that destruction (see, generally, Yaffe 2010: 119–24; Simester 1996). The other complication concerns what must be intended when the consummate offense includes circumstantial elements that are essential to its wrongful character. A person commits rape when he sexually penetrates another person without that person's consent, and is reckless as to whether the other person consents; he need not intend the penetration to be nonconsensual, or know that it is nonconsensual. But what if he tries but fails to sexually penetrate the other, non-consenting, person? For this to constitute attempted rape he must at least intend that penetration, but must he also intend that penetration to be nonconsensual, or at least know that it is not? Or is it enough that he is reckless as to whether it is consensual? It seems plausible to hold that the attempt should not require intention as to that aspect of the consummate offense: he attempts rape if the other person is actually non-consenting and he is at least reckless as to that possibility. We could then say that whilst an attempt requires intention as to the central consequential aspects of the consummate offense, it does not require intention as to every aspect. However, we then face the challenge of distinguishing those aspects of the consummate offense as to which intention is required from those as to which it is not—a challenge that we cannot take up here (but see Duff 1996, ch. 1; Yaffe 2010, chs. 4–5).)

Second, attempts require conduct that comes quite close (at least as the agent envisages it) to the completion of the intended enterprise. I might form the intention to rob a bank, make detailed plans for the robbery, recruit colleagues to help me, buy the necessary equipment and watch the bank to see when and how I can best carry out my plans: I am preparing to rob the bank, but not yet attempting to rob it. Even when I steal the car we will use, and turn on the engine, I am still preparing rather than attempting the robbery: I am attempting to rob the bank only once I move beyond preparation to the actual execution of the intended robbery, though the boundary between preparation and execution is far from sharp or clear. On the other hand, the extralegal concept of attempt reaches further than "complete" or "last-act" attempts in which the agent has done the last thing there is for him to do to complete the action: as I enter the bank with a drawn gun, shouting "This is a holdup," I am attempting to rob the bank, although there is still more that I must do to complete the robbery. If a would-be assassin is captured as he aims his gun but before he actually pulls the trigger (which would be the "last act"), it is still true that he attempted to kill his target.

(I can be attempting to Φ even if what I am doing is in fact remote from actually Φ-ing: if I put sugar in your cocoa, believing it to be arsenic and intending to poison you, I am attempting to kill you, even though putting sugar in someone's cocoa is not close to the actual commission of murder. This counts as an attempt because, if the facts had been as I believe them to be, I would have been executing my plan to kill you. It is not clear, however, whether the agent's beliefs are always conclusive. If I fire at what is in fact a tree stump, believing it to be the person I want to kill (who is actually miles away), is it true that I am attempting to kill him? Such examples raise the question of whether attempts must have some actual connection to the real world, rather than merely what the agent believes to be a connection (see, further, Duff 1996: 219–32).)

Attempting to Φ therefore involves action that constitutes the execution of an intention to Φ. Some philosophers have portrayed trying or attempting as a kind of identifiable (usually mental) occurrence: trying to Φ is a distinct activity by means of which I hope to bring it about that I Φ (see, e.g., O'Shaughnessy 1973; Armstrong 1973). All action can then be analyzed into a "trying" and such further effects as that trying produces. But this is not what we mean when we talk about "trying" or "attempting": rather than picking out some distinctive element of an action, such talk constitutes an adverbial, contextualizing qualification of the action verb that it modifies. To say that A is trying to Φ, that is, is to set A's conduct in a certain context. It might be to connect what A is doing to the Φ-ing that forms its aim: we explain why A is running so fast down the road by saying that she is trying to catch a train; the trying does not involve anything more or other than the running for that purpose. But talk of trying also sets the action in a context of failure, doubt or difficulty: if A has been unsuccessful in executing her intention to Φ, or we are not sure that she will successfully execute it, or its execution is arduous or difficult, we say that she is trying to Φ rather than that she is Φ-ing (see Heath and Winch 1971; Duff 1996, ch. 10).

Once we recognize these aspects of trying in the ordinary extralegal meaning of the concept, our initial three questions about criminal attempts multiply into a larger set of questions.

Further Questions

If we start with the category of consummate offenses, which actually bring about the primary harm or mischief at which the law is aimed, our first question must be why we should extend the criminal law any more widely than that. To avoid begging too many questions, we can put this question in the language not of attempts, but of nonconsummate crimes, whose commission does not require the occurrence of the primary mischief at which the law is aimed. Attempts constitute just one kind of nonconsummate crime;

others will be noted below. We criminalize consummate crimes such as homicide and criminal damage: why should we also criminalize nonconsummate versions of those crimes, such as failed attempts to kill or to damage another's property? Such attempts can of course cause other kinds of mischief that properly concern the criminal law: they can, if known, cause fear or anxiety, or disrupt social order (see Becker 1974). But that gives us no reason to criminalize attempts that are not noticed at the time, and does not seem to capture the wrongfulness of attempts. When we convict and punish someone for attempted theft, we are surely not simply convicting and punishing her for the fear, anxiety or disruption that her failed attempt might have caused.

Our further questions arise when we ask why, if we are going to criminalize nonconsummate crimes, we should do so through a law of attempts, and whether such a law should use "attempt" in its ordinary extralegal meaning.

One question is why we should extend the law as widely as the concept of attempt suggests. The most modest extension of the law's scope beyond consummate offenses would capture only complete or "last-act" attempts, when the agent has done all that there is for her to do to complete the crime. As we saw, the extralegal concept of attempt is broader than that, but why should the criminal law go so far? Why should it not cover only last-act attempts (apart from the difficulty, in some cases, of identifying a "last act" that does not actually complete the crime)? One important consideration, to which we will return later, is that until she has completed her attempt the agent still has a chance to abandon her criminal enterprise voluntarily—a "locus poenitentiae." So why should she be criminally liable before she has definitively and irrevocably committed herself to the commission of the crime (see Alexander and Ferzan 2009, ch. VI)?

If we can justify extending the reach of the criminal law beyond consummate offenses, and even beyond "last-act" attempts, further questions arise about why we should not extend it further than is suggested by the extralegal concept of attempt (and further than our existing laws extend it). Why should we not also criminalize other kinds of nonconsummate offense that are related to a primary mischief but that do not amount to what extralegal usage would count as an attempt? Our existing laws include a range of other types of nonconsummate offense, three of which are worth noting here.

First, our attempt laws typically follow extralegal usage in requiring an intention to commit the complete crime (although intention is sometimes interpreted to include "oblique" intention). They also criminalize some kinds of reckless endangerment: conduct that is not intended to cause harm, but that creates an unjustified risk of harm and whose agent acts recklessly as to that risk. Some such offenses are relatively specific as to the type of risk whose creation is criminalized: they criminalize risk-creation in the course of particularly dangerous activities, or by agents with particular responsibilities, or that threaten particularly vulnerable kinds of potential victim (see Smith 1983; Duff 2007: 161–64). Others are relatively general: the American Model Penal Code, for instance, criminalizes conduct that "recklessly endanger[s] another person" by creating a risk of death or serious injury, or that creates a risk of a "catastrophe" that would affect "the safety or property" of many (§§ 211.2, 220.2(2)). But none are as general as the law of attempts: whilst it is an offense to attempt to commit (almost) any consummate crime, it is not similarly an offense to take a reckless risk of causing any result whose actual causation would be criminal. I commit criminal damage if I damage another's property either intentionally or recklessly—if I throw a stone that breaks my neighbor's window, whether I intended to break it or recklessly took the risk that I would do so. If my brick misses the window, I am guilty of criminal attempt if I threw it with the intention of breaking the window, but have committed no offense if my throwing was merely reckless as to the risk that it would break the window. This is puzzling. We convict both the deliberate and the reckless stone-thrower of the same offense if they actually cause damage, and convict the deliberate thrower if his stone misses: but whatever our grounds for convicting him, whether they are that he is no less culpable than one whose stone hits its target, or that he shows himself to be as dangerous, or that we want to deter people from such dangerous actions, similar reasons seem to warrant criminalizing the reckless agent whose stone misses. If we are to have a general nonconsummate crime, why should it be a crime of "attempt," requiring intention, rather than a broader crime consisting in conduct that comes sufficiently close to the consummate offense, and a "fault element" identical to that required for the consummate offense? If criminal damage requires conduct that damages another's property, and either an intention to cause such damage or recklessness as to the risk of causing it, why should we not define "nonconsummate criminal damage" as consisting in conduct that comes sufficiently close to damaging another's property, done with the intention or the recklessness that would make the agent guilty of criminal damage if he actually caused damage?

Second, although attempts do not require a "last act," they do (in extralegal usage) require conduct that constitutes execution of the intended action, rather than merely preparation for it. Some attempt laws preserve this feature of extralegal usage: English law requires conduct that is "more than merely preparatory to the commission" of the intended offense (Criminal Attempts Act 1981, s. 1), which courts have interpreted to require that the agent have "embarked on," or be "in the process of committing" the offense (*Gullefer* [1990] 1 WLR 1063). Other laws are wider: under the American Model Penal Code, an attempt requires conduct that constitutes a "substantial step" towards the commission of the crime, conduct that is "strongly corroborative" of the agent's criminal purpose (§ 5.01). This is intended to encompass conduct falling well short of what extralegal usage would count as an attempt. But once we extend the law of attempts this far beyond the ordinary extralegal meaning of the term, why should we stop there, rather than extending criminal liability to cover any conduct that is intended to culminate in or lead to the commission of a consummate offense? In the early stages of the development of the law of attempts, courts flirted with a "first-act" test. "So long as an act rests in bare intention, it is not punishable . . .: but immediately when an act is done, the law judges, not only of the act done, but of the intent with which it is done," and the act is criminal "if it is coupled with an unlawful and malicious intent" (Lord Mansfield in *Scofield* [1784] Cald. 397, 403). Now such a "first-act" test was never really part of the law of attempts, but our laws do contain specific offenses that criminalize preparatory or preliminary actions that fall a very long way short of attempts. It is, for instance, an offense in English law to have in one's possession anything that is intended to be used to damage another's property (Criminal Damage Act 1971, s. 3(a)), or "for a purpose connected with the commission, preparation or instigation of an act of terrorism" (Terrorism Act 2000, s. 57). Now those who are preparing to commit consummate offenses are presumably guilty of wrongdoing as soon as they embark on their criminal enterprises, and pose a danger to others. So why should we criminalize their conduct only once it progresses far enough to count as an attempt, or a "substantial step"?

Third, our laws contain some nonconsummate offenses that reach even further than this, to encompass conduct that is not intended to lead to the commission of a consummate offense, and that poses no direct risk to a legally protected interest (a "direct" risk is one whose actualization does not depend on further action), but that might facilitate the commission of a crime or make the occurrence of a criminal harm more likely. It is an offense to possess "information of a kind likely to be useful to a person committing or preparing an act of terrorism, without a reasonable excuse" (Terrorism Act 2000 s. 58); or to possess, without official authorization, any of a range of weapons (Firearms Act 1968, s. 5). Why then should we not extend the law more generally to capture such potentially dangerous types of conduct? Why should our general nonconsummate offense be one of "attempt," which captures only conduct that is intended to do criminal mischief and that has advanced a considerable way towards doing it?

The point of raising these questions is not to suggest that we should have a vastly extensive general law of nonconsummate offenses; indeed, existing laws that criminalize conduct "remote" from any primary mischief are often far too broad, capturing conduct that should not be criminal (see von Hirsch 1996; Dubber 2001; Husak 2007). But by considering these extensive types of nonconsummate offense we can focus more sharply on the questions that we must ask about the law of attempts. Why should we have a general law of nonconsummate offenses which reaches as far as our attempt laws do (beyond both consummate crimes and "last-act" attempts), but no further? If we are to have a law of attempt, how should "attempt" be defined in the criminal law: how should we specify the types of conduct that should be criminalized in this way?

But we have not yet finished with questions. We have so far taken for granted that attempts should be distinguished from consummate crimes—that the person who tries but fails to commit a consummate crime should be convicted of a distinct offense of "attempt." One reason for such a distinction would be that failed attempts should be punished less severely than would have been appropriate had they succeeded, which is what usually happens under our existing laws; another reason would be that attempts and successes are significantly different as offenses, and that for reasons of "fair labeling" the law should mark them as such. But the first reason is notoriously controversial, which will also cast doubt on the second.

In punishing attempts less severely than they would have been punished had they succeeded, the law offers a penal discount for failure: but what justifies that discount? It is true that attempts do not cause the primary harm or mischief that a consummate crime involves (though they might cause such "secondary" harms as fear or anxiety). Were we looking through the lens of civil law, when the central question is typically who should pay to repair or compensate for harm that has been caused, the difference between success and failure would therefore be crucial: if the attempt fails there is no, or less, harm to be repaired. But that is not the criminal law's focus, and whether we think of punishment in, for instance, retributive, or deterrent, or reformative, or incapacitative terms it is hard to see why failure should make a difference to the would-be criminal's penal fate. The main focus of philosophical discussion has been on the issue of retribution and desert, which is bound up with the problem of "moral luck" (see Nagel 1976; Williams 1976; Ashworth 1988; Duff 1996, ch. 12; Enoch and Marmor 2007). If we are going to justify differential punishments for failure and for success, we must, from this perspective, be able to argue that a person whose attempt fails therefore deserves a lighter sentence than he would have deserved had it succeeded—either that failure reduces penal desert or that success increases it. Now the difference between success and failure is typically a matter of luck: either it is a matter of luck that my attempt failed (or succeeded), or it would have been a matter of luck had it succeeded (or failed). But we surely cannot say that desert depends on luck: penal desert should depend on culpability, since that is what is within the agent's control. Luck, by contrast, is precisely what lies outside one's control, so what is a matter of luck cannot affect culpability, and should not affect penal desert.

We will return to this familiar argument below, but should notice here two ways in which it can be extended to raise further questions about the law of attempts.

First, arguments about the punishment of attempts do not typically question the law's formal distinction between success and failure—the different labels that are attached to them at the stage of conviction—but perhaps that should be questioned. Existing laws sometimes define offenses in "the inchoate mode" (see Ashworth 1987a), so that their commission does not require the actual occurrence of the primary mischief with which the law is presumably concerned. The mischief that justifies criminalizing fraud is presumably people suffering financial loss through deception, but English law defines criminal fraud simply as dishonestly making a false representation with intent to cause loss or gain (Fraud Act 2006, s. 2): no one need be deceived, no loss or gain need ensue. The complete offense of fraud covers both successful frauds and failed attempts at fraud. The primary mischief that concerns the law of perjury is, presumably, courts being deceived by witnesses' false evidence, and the outcomes of cases being unjustly affected. But the complete offense of perjury does not require any such result: it is committed by anyone who, as a sworn witness, makes a statement on oath that he does not believe to be true (Perjury Act 1911, s. 1); he need not actually deceive the court, nor need his statement actually be false. This way of defining offenses implies that there is no significant difference that should be formally marked between success and failure. Why then should we not apply that suggestion more generally? If a criminal actor deserves the same punishment, displays the same culpability, whether her attempt succeeds or fails, why could we not say that she commits the same wrong, and should be convicted of the same offense, in either case—that all crimes should be defined "in the inchoate mode"? Instead of having separate offenses of murder and attempted murder, we would have just one offense, of "murderous conduct," of which both the successful and the failed murderer would be guilty.

Second, the same issue arises about offenses that consist in endangerment rather than an attempt to cause harm: it is a matter of luck that my reckless action causes harm (or that it does not cause it). Why should that matter of luck make a difference both to the offense of which I am then liable to be convicted, and to the punishment I am then liable to suffer? Why should the law distinguish, as English law does, dangerous driving from causing death by dangerous driving, as distinct offenses (Road Traffic Act 1991, s. 1), the latter of which attracts a heavier punishment? Why should we not define all endangerment offenses in the inchoate mode?

Finally, we have seen that many consummate offenses are so defined that either intention or recklessness suffices as the "fault element," and have raised the question of why the nonconsummate offenses related to them should not retain just the same fault element: why we should convict of the same offense the person who causes damage intentionally and the person who causes damage recklessly, but not convict someone whose reckless action luckily causes no damage of the same nonconsummate offense as one who tries but fails to cause damage (indeed, under existing law the former might be guilty of no offense at all). If all offenses should be defined in the inchoate mode, which makes the actual occurrence or nonoccurrence of the primary mischief irrelevant to the agent's guilt, we need not give intention the status that our law of attempts accords it: we can retain the same fault elements as are currently required for consummate offenses, and simply remove the requirement that the relevant harm or mischief actually be caused. The new offense of "criminal damage," as defined in the inchoate mode, would thus consist in action that is either intended to damage another's property or reckless as to the risk of causing such damage, and that comes close enough to causing such damage. (For a more radical version of this suggestion, see Alexander and Ferzan 2009; they would also make recklessness the only type of fault.)

I do not suggest that we should go down this route. But these questions and these imaginable reforms to our existing law remind us that we cannot simply take the existing shape of our law for granted: these are the questions that we must answer, and the challenges we must meet, if we are to make normative sense of anything like our existing law of criminal attempts.

To answer these questions, and to work out what kind of law of nonconsummate offenses (if any) we could justify, we must inquire more deeply into the proper aims of the criminal law and the proper grounds or principles of criminal liability.

Working Towards Some Answers

If we take a purely consequentialist view of the proper aims of a system of criminal law, for instance that its purpose is to prevent (as cost-effectively as possible) various kinds of harm by reducing the incidence of various kinds of conduct that cause such harm, the question of what kinds of law of nonconsummate crimes we should have becomes an empirical question. We will see reason to criminalize conduct that does not actually cause harm. That should be an efficient way of deterring actually harmful conduct: for people who are not otherwise sufficiently mindful of others' interests are more likely to be deterred from acting dangerously if they know that they will be liable to punishment even if they do not actually cause harm. It might also enable us more efficiently to identify dangerous agents whom we could subject to incapacitative or reformative measures: for the fortuitous fact that a dangerous action causes no harm does not show its agent to be any less dangerous. If we attend to wider issues of social peace and stability, we will also see reason to criminalize manifestly dangerous or threatening conduct that is socially disturbing or disruptive even if it does not cause the kinds of harm with which the criminal law is primarily concerned. These points, however, do not help us to decide just which kinds of nonconsummate conduct we should criminalize: whether, for instance, we should define some or all offenses in the inchoate mode; whether the criminal law should distinguish attempts (defined in terms of an intention to harm) from endangerments; how far back from completed, consummate crimes the criminal law should reach, by way of a general nonconsummate offense or by way of a range of more specific offenses; and so on. All these decisions would require large and complex empirical inquiries, which we cannot pursue here, into the likely costs and benefits of different provisions.

However, a purely consequentialist approach to criminal law is not especially plausible: we must surely believe that the criminal law (like all political institutions) is subject to the demands of justice, which cannot be understood in purely consequentialist terms. Even those who reject a "positive retributivism," according to which the primary point of criminal law and punishment is to ensure that wrongdoers receive their just deserts, often accept a "negative retributivism" which sets constraints of justice on the scope and operations of the criminal law (see Dolinko 1991: 539–43). Two familiar constraints are that only the guilty should be punished, and that they should not be punished more severely than they deserve for their crimes. If these constraints are to do real work, they must apply to the substantive criminal law as well as to criminal punishment: the law must criminalize only kinds of conduct that do deserve to be punished, and its classifications and definitions of offenses must reflect appropriate judgments of the relative seriousness of the kinds of conduct that are criminalized. If we accept such constraints, we must therefore ask whether and why those whose conduct is related to a primary mischief, but does not actually bring about the mischief, deserve criminal liability; and what kinds of discrimination the criminal law should make between consummate and nonconsummate offenses, and among nonconsummate offenses, if it is to mark relevant differences between the various types of offense.

This will not help us make progress without an account of the proper basis of penal desert: in virtue of what do we deserve criminal conviction and punishment? How we answer this question will make a crucial difference to how we can understand the grounds for criminalizing inchoate conduct, and the scope and structure of the law of nonconsummate offenses.

Suppose we say, for instance, that penal desert must, as a matter of justice, be determined by (and only by) culpability, and that culpability is determined by choice: I deserve conviction and punishment only for that for which I am culpable, and only to the extent of my culpability; I am culpable only for that which lies within my control; and I have control only over my choices, not over their actual efficacy or outcomes (see, e.g., Ashworth 1987b; Ferzan 2001). We will then have reason to criminalize consummate crimes; last-act attempts in which the agent does all that there was for him to do to commit the crime; and complete instances of endangerment, when the agent creates a direct risk to others, whose actualization no longer depends on him. In all these cases the agent has definitively and irrevocably chosen to cause or to risk causing harm. We will, indeed, have no reason to distinguish consummate from nonconsummate crimes here: the choice is the same, and as culpable, whether harm ensues or not. (Whether we will distinguish attempts from endangerments will depend on whether we can see any intrinsically significant difference between a harmful choice that consists in a direct intention to harm and one that consists in the acceptance of harm as a foreseen side effect of one's action.) Some argue from this perspective that we have no reason to criminalize conduct that falls short of a "last act," since until that point the agent has not irrevocably chosen to cause harm—she could still abandon her action and avoid unleashing the risk on others (Alexander and Ferzan 2009). Now we will see that the availability of a *locus poenitentiae* is significant, but it is surely not *that* significant: one who embarks on a criminal enterprise, whether of attempt or endangerment, has made culpable choices well before her last act. We can put this point in the language of reasons (see Yaffe 2010, ch. 1). One who completes a crime has made a culpable choice which is either guided by wrong reasons or not guided by right reasons: but the choices of one who embarks on what will become a consummate crime if she completes her enterprise as she expects or intends are in the same way not properly responsive to right reasons; they too are culpable. If I embark on a fraud, I am making culpable choices well before the last act: as I complete the insurance claim form with a false account of my supposed loss, I am doing wrong. If I leave the bar, knowing I am drunk, and fully intending to drive my car home, I am making culpable choices before I begin to drive. One who does not complete her enterprise might be less culpable than she would have been had she completed it, since she did not make the final, irrevocable choice to do wrong—and we might, as we will see, have reason not to criminalize the early stages of a criminal enterprise. But if our focus should be on culpable choices, we have reason to criminalize even the very early stages. This perspective, therefore, cannot make norma-tive sense of the way that our laws distinguish consummate crimes from complete but still nonconsummate attempts or endangerments (to which its proponents will of course reply—so much the worse for our laws), nor does it give us any positive reason to limit the laws of nonconsummate crimes to anything narrower than a "first act."

Suppose that we instead ground penal desert in character rather than in choice: what makes an agent criminally culpable is not his criminal choice as such, but the defective character trait that his choice reveals—a trait that might also be revealed in unchosen conduct (see e.g., Bayles 1982; Huigens 1995; Tadros 2005). From this perspective, we also have just the same reason to criminalize both consummate crimes and "last-act" attempts or endangerments: for the fortuitous occurrence or nonoccurrence of the rele-vant harm makes no difference to what is displayed by way of a defective character trait. We also have reason to criminalize conduct falling well short of a last act, since one who embarks on (what will become) a criminal enterprise already displays a defect of charac-ter. As to whether someone who has not yet completed their enterprise is less culpable than she would be if she completed it, a character theorist's answer must depend on the extent to which action should be taken to be constitutive of character. If we attend only to what the person actually does, in the course of committing an incomplete noncon-summate offense, we cannot ascribe as firmly a defective character trait to one who does not get as far as the last act. If she desists voluntarily, her character is shown not to be as defective as it would have been shown to be had she not desisted. Even if she is prevented, rather than desisting voluntarily, if the only evidence that we may consider is what she did or did not do, we cannot be sure that she would not have desisted voluntarily, and therefore cannot be sure that her action flowed from the kind of unqualifiedly defective character trait that a completed nonconsummate offense reveals. But why should we, or the court that tries the defendant, attend only to the evidence provided by the person's criminal conduct? Why may we not also look to other kinds of evidence of character, on the basis of which we might be able to judge whether she would have continued had she not been prevented? One answer to this question appeals to values external to the character account: to the dangers of error, to the intrusiveness of the investigation that a search for other kinds of evidence would involve. This would be to accept that one whose enterprise is incomplete might in fact be as culpable as one who completes his enterprise, but it also would be to argue that we should treat him *as if* he is less culpable since we lack the only kind of admissible evidence—the enterprise's completion—that would prove full culpability. Another kind of answer, however, makes action more integral to the determination of character. Action is the best mark of character, on this view, because it partly constitutes character: one who has not completed his attempt at fraud, for what-ever reason, does not yet have the fully defined character of a fraudster; he constitutes himself as a fraudster only if he completes his attempt. From this perspective, someone whose nonconsummate crime is incomplete is not (yet) as culpable as he would be if he completed it (whereas on the former view we simply lack admissible evidence of whether he is or is not as culpable), in which case, if we are to criminalize his conduct, it should be as a lesser offense. (One problem for this view is that whilst it maybe plausible for first-time offenders, it is less plausible for repeat offenders—for someone who constituted himself as a fraudster by his past completed frauds or attempted frauds. We cannot pursue this issue here, although it raises some important questions: about why, for a character theorist, action should be necessary for criminal liability; about whether or when the prosecution should be allowed to use prior convictions as evidence of present guilt.)

Suppose, finally, that we ground criminal liability and penal desert neither in choice taken by itself, nor in character as something beyond and underlying action, but in action: what makes me criminally liable is not merely what I choose to do, nor the character traits that my action might reveal, but what I actually do—the wrongs that I actually and culpably commit (see Duff 2007, ch. 5). From this point of view we have reason to criminalize nonconsummate kinds of conduct, whether complete or incomplete, but also to distinguish both consummate from nonconsummate crimes, and complete from incomplete nonconsummate crimes. More precisely, we have such reasons if we understand action, as it bears upon moral or criminal responsibility, to include the actual impact that one's agency has on the world. Only then can we properly say that one whose attempt at criminal damage succeeds commits a different action from one whose attempt fails, or that a reckless driver who actually causes death commits a different action from one who luckily does not cause death. It is obvious that in ordinary parlance they do perform different actions: the former damages property, the latter (only) tries to; the former kills, the latter (only) endangers. But we cannot simply assume that our ordinary language, which has many other uses than that of marking out moral categories, is used in this context to mark some significant moral distinction. The difference between an actual killing and a failed attempt to kill is significant in many ways. Those who deny that the criminal law should distinguish completed crimes from failed attempts agree that it matters from other perspectives whether an attempt succeeds or fails. To meet their argument, we must show, rather than just assume, that the ordinary distinctions between success and failure match a significant moral distinction in kind or degree of culpable responsibility.

The way in which the criminal law distinguishes, in the context of nonconsummate offenses, kinds of conduct that it does not separate in the context of consummate crime is also exemplified in ordinary language. If I damage your property, either intentionally or recklessly, you might say, in accusatory rather than merely descriptive tones, "You damaged my car." The fact that I caused the damage recklessly rather than intentionally would not require you to qualify that ascription of responsible agency. If I actually cause no damage, but acted in a way that was intended to do so, you might properly accuse me of attempting to damage your car, but no such accusation would be possible if I merely took a reckless but unactualized risk of damaging your car. The most you could then say would be something like "You could have damaged my car"—a locution that sets me further away as an agent from actual damage than does "You tried . . ." Here again, however, ordinary language is at best suggestive, rather than dispositive: we must explain why, rather than simply assuming that, it reflects a significant moral difference in culpable responsibility.

Two lines of argument might help to meet these challenges (see Duff 1996, ch. 13). First, to see why the criminal law should distinguish consummate from nonconsummate crimes, we could look to a communicative conception of criminal conviction and punishment as a process which seeks to bring offenders to confront what they have done. An offender's conviction says in part, "Look what you have done!", and his punishment should fill out and reinforce that message. But what should we want the offender to recognize? If he has actually done the mischief with which the criminal law is concerned, either intentionally or recklessly, that mischief must be salient in his attention: "Look at the mischief you have done!" We may also want to distinguish intentional from reckless mischief-doers, but what will be most salient is the mischief itself. If that mischief does not ensue, however, we will want to convey a different message, one that includes relief:

the relief that we feel, and that the offender should come to feel, that ("thank God") the mischief was not done. The offender must still realize that he has done wrong by attacking or endangering others, which is why we have reason to criminalize nonconsummate crimes: but the relief that is appropriate when the mischief does not ensue can make sense of the "discount for failure," as a way of communicating that appropriate relief.

If we ask why the law should then define some offenses, as English law defines fraud, "in the inchoate mode," one reply might be that it should not do so. Another reply would be to suggest that it should do so when the, or a, primary mischief is wrought by the attempt itself, whether it succeeds or fails: that, for instance, the primary mischief wrought by both successful and failed frauds is the damage that they do to trust in our financial dealings.

Second, by thinking about the difference between attack and endangerment, we can see why the criminal law might distinguish them more sharply when the contemplated mischief does not ensue than when it does. Attacks are actions undertaken with the (direct) intention of harming an interest, which actually come reasonably close to harming it (we cannot pursue here the question of what counts as "reasonably close"). Endangerments are actions that create a risk of harm to an interest—a harm that might be foreseen as certain, probable or possible, or be unforeseen. Some would say (from a consequentialist perspective) that this distinction is morally significant only to the extent that it marks a difference in the likelihood that the harm will ensue: attacks are morally distinctive, and morally worse, only if and insofar as they are more likely to cause harm than are endangerments—because the attack itself is more likely to do so, or because the attacker is more likely to try again if a first attempt fails. But we might instead find an intrinsic moral significance in the distinction, as a distinction between actions that are directed (that manifest active hostility) against a protected interest, and actions that at worst display a lack of regard for the interests that they endanger. That difference might not be of great importance when the harm actually ensues: what matters centrally in our response to both an attacker and a culpable endangerer is that they recognize the harm they have culpably caused. But the difference can become more salient if the contemplated harm does not ensue, since an attack connects the agent more closely to that harm than does an endangerment, and thus gives us stronger reason to criminalize her conduct even if the harm does not ensue. (One could also argue that, if the distinction is morally significant, the criminal law should distinguish attacks from endangerments in the context of consummate crimes too—that it should formally distinguish, for instance, intentional from reckless criminal damage.)

None of this helps us to determine how far our laws of nonconsummate crime should reach. One who embarks on a criminal enterprise is acting wrongly from the start; why then should we not criminalize "first-act" criminal enterprises? Part of the answer is that the costs of enforcing so extensive a law of inchoate crimes would be astronomical, and there are more urgent demands on public resources. But part of the answer is a matter of principle, concerning responsibility. We noted the significance of the *locus poenitentiae*—the space between embarking on a criminal venture and completing it, in which the agent can still change her mind and desist. If we are to treat each other as responsible agents, we must take this *locus* seriously, and recognize that to deprive someone of it is a nontrivial matter: not because it is actually likely that she will avail herself of it (we might have good reason to believe that she will not), but because to see her as a responsible agent is to see her as someone who could change her mind and should be given the chance to do so. This gives us reason to limit the law of nonconsummate offenses

202

to "last-act" cases, in which the agent has spurned the last available *locus poenitentiae*, but not conclusive reason, since we must weigh against it the need to enable criminal enterprises to be interrupted before they are completed, in order to protect (materially and symbolically) the interests that are attacked or endangered. Any tolerable law of nonconsummate offenses must mark a compromise between these two kinds of value.

I do not pretend to have offered persuasive answers to the various questions that are raised by our laws of attempt, and of other kinds of nonconsummate crime. The most I can hope to have done is to clarify the range of questions that are raised, to show why they are both important and difficult, and to sketch some possible ways of trying to answer them.

References

Alexander, L. and Ferzan, K. K. (2009) *Crime and Culpability: A Theory of Criminal Law*, Cambridge: Cambridge University Press.

American Law Institute (1962) Model Penal Code.

Armstrong, D. (1973) "Acting and Trying," *Philosophical Papers* 2: 1.

Ashworth, A. J. (1987a) "Defining Criminal Offenses Without Harm," in P. Smith, ed., *Criminal Law: Essays in Honour of J. C. Smith*, London: Butterworths, p. 7.

—— (1987b) "Belief, Intent and Criminal Liability," in J. Eekelaar and J. Bell, eds., *Oxford Essays in Jurisprudence*, 3rd Series, Oxford: Oxford University Press, p. 1.

—— (1988) "Criminal Attempts and the Role of Resulting Harm Under the Code, and in the Common Law," *Rutgers Law Journal* 19: 725.

Bayles, M. (1982) "Character, Purpose, and Criminal Responsibility," *Law and Philosophy* 1: 5.

Becker, L. (1974) "Criminal Attempts and the Theory of the Law of Crimes," *Philosophy and Public Affairs* 3: 262.

Bentham, J. (2000/1781) *An Introduction to the Principles of Morals and Legislation*, Kitchener, Ontario: Batoche Books.

Criminal Damage Act 1971 (c. 48), United Kingdom.

Dolinko, D. (1991) "Some Thoughts about Retributivism," *Ethics* 101: 537.

Dubber, M. D. (2001) "Policing Possession: The War on Crime and the End of Criminal Law," *Journal of Criminal Law and Criminology* 91: 829.

Duff, R. A. (1996) *Criminal Attempts*, Oxford: Oxford University Press.

—— (2007) *Answering for Crime: Responsibility and Liability in the Criminal Law*, Oxford: Hart Publishing.

Enoch, D. and Marmor, A. (2007) "The Case against Moral Luck," *Law and Philosophy* 26: 405.

Ferzan, K. K. (2001) "Opaque Recklessness," *Journal of Criminal Law and Criminology* 91: 597.

Firearms Act 1968 (c. 27), United Kingdom.

Fraud Act 2006 (c. 35), United Kingdom.

Heath, P. and Winch, P. (1971) "Trying and Attempting," *Proceedings of the Aristotelian Society, Supplementary Volumes* 45: 193.

Huigens, K. (1995) "Virtue and Inculpation," *Harvard Law Review* 108: 1423.

Husak, D. (1995) "The Nature and Justifiability of Nonconsummate Offenses," *Arizona Law Review* 37: 151.

—— (2007) *Overcriminalization: The Limits of the Criminal Law*, Oxford: Oxford University Press.

Nagel, T. (1976) "Moral Luck," *Proceedings of the Aristotelian Society, Supplementary Volumes* 50: 137.

O'Shaughnessy, B. (1973) "Trying (As the Mental 'Pineal Gland')," *Journal of Philosophy* 70: 365.

Perjury Act 1911 (c. 6), United Kingdom.

Road Traffic Act 1991 (c. 40), United Kingdom.

R. v. Gullefer [1990] 1 WLR 1063.

R. v. Scofield [1784] Cald. 397.

Simester, A. P. (1996) "Why Distinguish Intention from Foresight?" in A. P. Simester and A. T. H. Smith, eds., *Harm and Culpability*, Oxford: Oxford University Press, p. 71.

—— and Sullivan, G. R. (2010) *Criminal Law: Theory and Doctrine*, 4th edition, Oxford: Hart Publishing.

Smith, K. J. M. (1983) "Liability for Endangerment: English Ad Hoc Pragmatism and American Innovation," *Criminal Law Review*: 127–36.

Tadros, V. (2005) *Criminal Responsibility*, Oxford: Oxford University Press.

Terrorism Act 2000 (c. 11), United Kingdom.

von Hirsch, A. (1996) "Extending the Harm Principle: 'Remote' Harms and Fair Imputation," in A. P. Simester and A. T. H. Smith, eds., *Harm and Culpability*, Oxford: Oxford University Press, p. 259.

Williams, B. (1976) "Moral Luck," *Proceedings of the Aristotelian Society, Supplementary Volumes* 50: 115.

Yaffe, G. (2010) *Attempts: In the Philosophy of Action and the Criminal Law*, Oxford: Oxford University Press.

Further Reading

For further reading, see: L. Alexander and K. K. Ferzan (2009) *Crime and Culpability: A Theory of Criminal Law*, Cambridge: Cambridge University Press; A. J. Ashworth (1988) "Criminal Attempts and the Role of Resulting Harm Under the Code, and in the Common Law," *Rutgers Law Journal* 19: 725; R. A. Duff (1996) *Criminal Attempts*, Oxford: Oxford University Press; D. Husak (1995) "The Nature and Justifiability of Nonconsummate Offenses," *Arizona Law Review* 37: 151; and G. Yaffe (2010) *Attempts: In the Philosophy of Action and the Criminal Law*, Oxford: Oxford University Press.

14

THE INSANITY DEFENSE

Gary Watson

My lords, in some sense, every crime proceeds from insanity. All cruelty, all
brutality, all revenge, all injustice, is insanity. . . . My lords, the opinion is right
in philosophy, but dangerous in judicature.

R. v. Ferrers, 1760 (Walker 1968: 63)

Introduction

The significance of the insanity defense as a topic for philosophy and jurisprudence
lies not in the frequency with which it is raised in practice, but, I shall argue, in what it
reveals about the enterprise of criminal law itself. A finding of insanity marks a defendant as one whose incapacities make criminal conviction meaningless or inapt. To the
extent to which the requisite capacities remain obscure, so do the aims and meaning of
criminal law itself.

Criminal defenses attempt to show that the meaning and purpose of the criminal
law cannot be served by convicting the defendant in question of a crime. The theory
of defenses is therefore fraught with all of the controversies of criminal law. The theory
and practice of the insanity defense has been especially contentious, however. This
is due partly to special conceptual and evidential difficulties concerning the notions
of insanity, mental "disorder" and the like. One ongoing issue is the extent to which
criminal law should follow the lead of those disciplines concerned with defining and
identifying "mental disorders"—psychiatry, psychology and, these days, neuroscience.
But the sources of contention, I believe, run deeper than this. Failures to articulate a
sensible and useful insanity defense cast doubt on the competence of the criminal law
to sort out "the mad from the bad" in a principled way.

These doubts explain the atmosphere of anxiety that has surrounded this subject
from the start. This anxiety is evident in some of the earliest recorded cases in Eng-
lish law and in the increasingly severe circumscription of the insanity defense in most
Anglo-American legal systems in recent times. Consider *Rex v. Arnold* (1724), in which
Edward Arnold is charged with attempting to murder Lord Onslow (a capital offense).
(My discussion in what follows of the early history of the insanity defense leans heavily
on the invaluable study, Walker 1968. The trials are recorded in Howell 1816–1828.)
The defense argued that Arnold suffered from the delusion that he was the victim of
Onslow's persecution and bewitchment, which caused "imps" to dance in his bed all

night. "I can't be easy," Arnold reported; "he plagues me day and night. I can't eat or drink; if I eat anything, it comes out of my body. I am . . . as if they pumped the breath out of my body" (Howell, vol. 16: 721).

The prosecution insisted that Arnold was not a "madman" but a "wicked man." True, according to testimony, the prisoner was "very much out of the common way of men," for example, "morose and ill-natured," keeping to himself, given to outbursts of unprovoked laughter and cursing. "Though he acted like a wicked man, void of reason, you will have little reason to think he acted like a madman." That the family did not, despite their testimony, regard Arnold as a madman, the prosecution argued, was shown by their frequent appeals to him to improve his life and his relations with others. You don't try to "reason with" someone you take to be mad (Howell, vol. 16: 724).

Justice Tracy's instructions to the jury regarding the legal standards for insanity (or "madness") strongly support the prosecution's line of argument:

> [P]unishment is intended for example, and to deter other persons from wicked designs; but the punishment of a madman, a person that hath no design, can have no example. . . . [I]t is not every kind of frantic humour or something unaccountable in a man's actions that points him out to be such a madman as is to be exempted from punishment: it must be a man that is totally deprived of his understanding and memory, and doth not know what he is doing, no more than an infant, than a brute, or a wild beast; such a one is never the object of punishment; therefore, I must leave it to your consideration, whether [the defendant] . . . knew what he was doing and whether he was able to distinguish whether he was doing good or evil.
>
> (Howell, vol. 16: 764–65)

Unsurprisingly, on these standards, Arnold was found guilty as charged.

Arnold was reprieved by King George II from the death sentence and was instead incarcerated the rest of his life. Prior to the establishment of an official plea of insanity, this sort of reprieve was not uncommon. This tendency is noteworthy because it evidently reflected recognition of something that the law was loath to codify, that malice is insufficient for (full) criminal responsibility.

Tracy's famous instructions are remarkable in several respects. The conception of madness as complete deprivation of the capacities for "understanding" or for "designs" is absurdly stringent; no historical candidates for a defense on these grounds lack these capacities altogether. Indeed, the standards fail to exempt four-year-old children or even dogs, who obviously pursue goals in view of some understanding of their environment. From their anxiety to punish the wicked, Tracey's standards simply evade the difficult questions posed by defendants like Arnold, who surely have some sort of capacity to reason and plan. The problem with these defendants is rather that those very capacities are seriously compromised by mental disorder. To contrast malice to madness is to sidestep the question of how to think about cases in which the malice is itself a piece of madness.

Note that Tracy also invokes the age-old standard that, to be competent, a defendant must be "able to distinguish whether he was doing good or evil" (765), as though that were more or less equivalent to the standard of total deprivation. Surely it is not. Many an "infant" with a capacity for some level of reasoning and planning falls short of anything we should call the capacity to distinguish "good from evil." We will return to this point later.

The trial of James Hadfield in 1800 had an instructively different outcome. Hadfield had the notion that the Second Coming depended on his being executed by England, and for this reason, he took a shot at George III. Thomas Erskine, Hadfield's defense counsel, boldly challenged the narrow doctrine of *Arnold*, arguing that the standard of "total deprivation" has no meaningful application to those who come before the law as mad. Hadfield was not in his right mind, but he was not mindless. Erskine defended a broader view of madness, in which "reason is not driven from her seat, but distraction sits down upon it with her, holds her, trembling upon it and frightens her from her propriety" (Walker 1968: 77). In other words, reason is not destroyed by insanity but distorted and driven by it. By this reasoning, Arnold too should have been acquitted.

Hadfield was in several ways a more appealing figure than Arnold. His madness was almost certainly due to the visible brain injuries he suffered while fighting for his country. And his attempt to shoot the king was not animated by hostility. Arnold was in contrast a surly loner who long harbored animosity toward his victim. These differences must have played some role in the verdicts. In any case, these trials employed two very different conceptions of the bearing of mental disorder on criminal responsibility. The total deprivation view is far too severe to do justice to the claims of madness. The argument in *Hadfield* makes more sense, but it fails to enunciate a broader standard of exculpation.

Subsequent criminal law has attempted to do better but, as we'll see, to little or no avail. Depending on the temperaments of the juries, both Arnold and Hadfield could well be found guilty under the standards that prevail in 2011 in most English-speaking jurisdictions. What does this tell us about the criminal law?

The Meaning and Purposes of Criminal Law

The insanity defense is an incompetence defense: a claim that the defendant lacks the capacities that are necessary to make his or her criminal conviction just or even intelligible. An account of what those capacities are should fall out of an account of what criminal law is about. Criminal law is the paradigmatic application of coercive political power, and we need to explain why that is a legitimate use of public authority.

Three different kinds of question arise here, one conceptual and two moral. A substantive question of political morality is: what sort of conduct should be criminalized? This depends on two other questions: what does it mean to criminalize conduct (what is it to make something a *crime*?), and why should we want to do that? These latter questions are important for this essay, because the rationale of criminal defenses, and hence of the insanity defense, depends on how we answer them.

At a minimum, to declare a kind of conduct a crime is to declare that it warrants an official adverse public response. I do not assume that criminalization is conceptually linked to liability to *punishment*. There are nonpunitive ways of holding people accountable for violations. Further, as some have suggested, conviction itself can be regarded as a limiting case of punishment (Gardner 1953: 193). Clearly to prohibit by law is not merely to publicly proclaim a system of proscriptive norms. Criminalization is a declaration that certain behavior is not to be tolerated, and this implies the liability of violators to coercive responses of some sort. Whatever liability entails, exactly, our question is why successful defenses, and pleas of insanity in particular, show such liability to be inappropriate.

Two sorts of answer to this question have dominated the theory of criminal law. One appeals to protection and deterrence; the other appeals to condemnation (or retribution). As I will argue, a third answer—that defenses are required by criminal law as a system of fair prohibitions—deserves to be taken seriously as well.

Criminal Law as a System of Deterrence

The first answer builds on an undeniable principle of political morality: that the political community is entitled, indeed obligated, to protect its members from certain dangers to security and liberty. Call this the protective aim. On a very common view, this aim is the overriding rationale of criminal law. Societies might try to pursue this aim without codes of crime and punishment. They might seek to protect their members by systems of moral or religious training or, more ominously, by preemptively incapacitating and manipulating potentially dangerous actors. On the protective view, criminal law is justified if and only if it is a more effective means than alternative practices for achieving our protective aims. Criminal defenses such as the insanity defense are thus to be explained by their contribution to this protective aim.

This is an unsatisfactory explanation of the phenomenon. Defendants who are acquitted of murder on grounds of insanity are typically subject to further protective custody in response to the dangers their disorders are thought to pose. Civil commitment and criminal conviction are thus alternative responses to individuals who are determined to be a threat to security. The judgment that the dangerous mentally disordered defendant is an inapt candidate for criminal incarceration implies that criminal conviction is more than a means to protection.

The protective theory of criminal law is standardly put in terms of deterrence, and in that form the theory is often endorsed by the courts. Those who qualify for the insanity defense are said not to be deterrable; hence they are not rightly subject to the criminal law, in which case we might rely on civil procedures. In *R. v. Porter* ((1933) 55 CLR 182), Judge Dixon declares that criminal punishment's "prime purpose is to preserve society from the depredations of dangerous and vicious people" (186). The judge then asks, rhetorically, "What is the utility of punishing people if they be beyond the control of the law for reasons of mental health?" (187). Judge Dixon's mistake here is to confuse individual with general deterrence; punishing a non-deterrable offender might well have some kind of a discouraging effect on lawbreaking in the general population. (This mistake is (first?) identified in Hart 2008. Note that the same mistake is made by Tracy in the passage quoted above from *Arnold*.) Furthermore, Dixon's declaration ignores the fact that deterrability is a matter of degree. It is doubtful that those for whom an insanity defense is appropriate are altogether beyond the reach of deterrent incentives, and once this is acknowledged the implications of the deterrent theory appear less straightforward. How deterrable does an individual have to be?

We can also expose the weakness of Dixon's explanation by noting that his rhetorical question has no particular force for the defense of insanity. Want of "mental health" is not the only trait that renders offenders relatively undeterrable. "What is the utility of punishing people," we can ask, "if they be beyond the control of the law for reasons of hardened criminality, or want of prudence and virtue?" The law adamantly rejects these factors as reasons not to punish. So the deterrability theory leaves out something crucial. (Of course, our conclusion so far is consistent with more complex consequentialist explanations, in which "what is left out" of the simple deterrent theory has indirect protective functions. Condemnation, for example, has its uses.)

Despite its evident shortcomings, this doctrine continues its hold on legal practice. Significantly, the deterrent theory fits smoothly with the wild beast test. Brutishness consists in virtual imperviousness to the threat of punishment; that is what "total deprivation" must mean for legal purposes. As we see in Judge Tracy's instructions, this unresponsiveness is taken as the measure of the capacity to know "good from evil." The implicit identification of these capacities was also central to William Blackstone's teachings about the age of criminal liability. Blackstone writes, in the eighteenth century:

> A girl of 13 has been burnt for killing her mistress; and one boy of 10, and another of 9 years old, who had killed their companions, have been sentenced to death, and he of 10 years actually hanged; because it appeared upon their trials, that the one hid himself, and the other hid the body he had killed; which hiding manifested a consciousness of guilt, and a discretion to discern between good and evil.
>
> (Blackstone 1766)

Here the capacity to know good from evil is treated as tantamount to the awareness of one's liability to sanctions, as revealed in efforts to conceal what one has done—tantamount, in a word, to deterrability. This equation is of course absurd, but on the deterrence theory, it is the only interpretation that can capture the traditional standard of "knowing good from evil."

This peculiar conflation is not just a relic of archaic legal doctrine but persists in important contemporary legal decisions as well. For instance, in *Arizona v. Clark* (548 U.S. 735 (2006)), the defendant argued that his psychosis, which included the belief that "aliens" pretending to be police officers were out to get him and could only be stopped by bullets, deprived him of the capacity to know that his conduct was wrong.

> In rebuttal, a psychiatrist for the State gave his opinion that Clark's paranoid schizophrenia did not keep him from appreciating the wrongfulness of his conduct, as shown by his actions before and after the shooting (such as circling the residential block with music blaring as if to lure the police to intervene, evading the police after the shooting, and hiding the gun).
>
> (745)

This rebuttal was evidently dispositive, since the state's argument prevailed.

This reasoning harks back to the wild beast test. Clark was not "devoid of reason" (the capacity to know right from wrong) because he was in principle deterrable, as manifested by his attempts at concealment. The persistence of this astonishing inference goes a long way to confirm the thesis that the law has advanced very little beyond *Arnold* in its account of criminal competence.

Let's turn now to the second prominent answer to the question of why mental disorders should be a defense against criminal conviction.

GARY WATSON

Criminal Conviction as Condemnation

A conspicuous feature of the criminal law is that it speaks the language not (merely) of danger but of culpability, good and evil, right and wrong. This is a textbook common-place, but it puts its finger on something central to the self-understanding of criminal law and is implicit in the aspiration to distinguish the mad from the wicked. As the court says in *Holloway v. United States* ((1945) 80 U.S. App. D.C. 3, 4, 148 F.2d 665): "Our collective conscience does not allow punishment where it cannot impose blame" (666). In the same vein, *State v. Guido* ((1993) 40 N.J. 191, A.2d) cites the stigmatizing role of criminal conviction: "The postulate is that some wrongdoers are sick while others are bad, and that it is against good morals to stigmatize the sick" (45).

Of course, if we take wickedness to be entailed by the fact that a deterrable offender was undeterred, then this second answer reduces to the first. But the theory of criminal conviction as condemnation asserts something more than this. The Model Penal Code of the American Law Institute endorses this theory in its commentary on the insanity defense. The commentary asserts that the line between criminal law and other modes of coercive constraint is the "line between the use of public agencies and force (1) to condemn the offender by conviction, with resulting sanctions in which the ingredient of reprobation is present no matter how constructive one may seek to make the sentence and the process of correction, and (2) modes of disposition in which the condemnatory element is absent, even though restraint may be involved" (American Law Institute 1985: 164). Criminal conviction expresses "reprobation" or "condemnation" of the offender. It is a form of public blame for conduct that has been prohibited by public authority. On this view, convicted criminals are regarded as wrongdoers to whom it is therefore appropriate to respond in these ways. The theory of excuses and exemptions, including the insanity defense, specifies conditions in which those who violate criminal laws nonetheless do not warrant condemnation.

This conception is broadly retributivist in the sense that conviction and sanctions are considered to be intrinsically fitting responses to wrongdoing. Conviction marks off the offender as a citizen in less than good standing, as one who warrants the distinctive form of blame that punishment constitutes. Retributivism is often more narrowly defined as the view that the suffering of the wrongdoer from just punishment is good in itself. In this form, retributivism strikes many people as an unattractive normative position. It is in any case questionable whether aiming at such a putative good is a legitimate function of coercive political power. It is important, therefore, to note that retributivism in the broad sense need not take this form. On a weaker view, the expression of hard feelings by the criminal law is a demand for recognition by the offender of his or her wrongdo-ing, as well as an affirmation of the rights of the victims. The expression and enforce-ment of this demand is said to be valuable independently of whatever suffering, if any, it might induce. (For the best worked-out version of weak retributivism, see Duff 2001. For strong retributivism, see Moore 1987. The defense by Ripstein 2009 of a Kantian interpretation of retributivism is more difficult to categorize.)

Criminal Law as a System of Fair Prohibitions

Since the foregoing account locates the distinct character of criminal law in its blam-ing stance toward wrongdoing, I shall refer to it as "moralism." Moralism compares favorably with deterrence theory in its ability to explain why we would want to have an

210

insanity defense. On moralist theories, excuses mark the conditions in which violators are nonetheless not blameworthy, and therefore not appropriate targets of criminal condemnation. This explains why civil commitment is a very different protective response from criminal conviction. But it is important to see that there is an attractive non-moralist alternative to the protective/deterrent theory.

On the view I have in mind, it is no accident that criminal convictions are typically stigmatizing, but that's not criminal law's primary business. Political community is conceived as a system of reciprocal rights and duties that define the terms of fair, cooperative association. The political community has a fundamental interest in and entitlement to protect its members against various forms of aggression and fraud that are inconsistent with the basic terms of social cooperation. (That's part of its raison d'être.) The function of the criminal law is to identify and define these terms in the form of general prohibitions or requirements. It thereby puts citizens on notice that violations will be subject to procedures and sanctions meant to deter and hold accountable those who would otherwise ignore the sanction-independent moral reasons against such violations.

The legitimacy of pursuing this protective interest in this way requires procedures and safeguards that aim to ensure that only responsible violators are charged and punished. Criminal prohibitions are addressed to citizens as free and responsible agents, and to be justifiable, conviction and sanctions must be constrained by various conditions that ensure that citizens have a fair opportunity to comply with the law. Citizens who run afoul of criminal prohibitions in ignorance or under duress, or due to agential incapacities for which they are not responsible (such as age-based immaturity and insanity), are not fairly held liable. Thus, criminal law aims to codify and enforce a system of reciprocal rights and duties by which it is fair to demand that free and equal citizens guide their interpersonal lives.

On the assumption that the criminal law is procedurally and substantively just, violators will in general be wrongdoers who are open to blame. But the application of sanctions is once again primarily a matter of procedural justice in the service of a fair system of collective protection, not an expression of collective blame or of retributive sentiments. As a legal offender, I am punished not under the heading of moral wrongdoer but as a warranted application of legitimate principles which citizens have generally decisive reason to endorse.

At a different level, however, the fact that I am a wrongdoer does come into the account, for the right of the political community to criminalize certain conduct depends on the rights to security and liberty of its members. Although the fair-protection account is not, in the sense defined earlier, moralist, core crimes, at least, will naturally engage sentiments of blame, guilt and shame. In central cases, criminal conviction signifies that one has culpably fallen short of the standards of good citizenship, and that distinction is important to our sense of ourselves and others as citizens. (This exposition of the fair-protection theory is inspired by Hart 2008, Rawls 1971, Quinn 1985 and Scanlon 2003. Rawls claims to be following Hart: "punishment is [not] primarily retributive or denunciatory" (Rawls 1971: 241). But he points to a moral foundation of criminal law that seems to me neglected by Hart: "[T]he purpose of the criminal law is to uphold basic natural duties, those which forbid us to injure other persons in their life and limb, or to deprive them of their liberty and property, and punishments are to serve this end" (Rawls 1971: 314).)

A rationale for an insanity defense follows fairly straightforwardly from the theory just described. Criminal law as a codification of reciprocal rights and duties presumes that the citizens to whom it is addressed are capable of governing themselves by this system. This presumption is defeated by the developmental immaturity of younger children but also by the mental disorders of many adults. Small children and those declared insane are in different ways incompetent to bear the burdens of citizenship, at least here and now, and in such and such respects.

The deterrability theory lacks an adequate foundation, I have argued, since it cannot by itself explain why we should want to pursue our protective aims by a system of criminal law, with its concern for responsibility, rather than by some other means of social control. The assumption that it is uniquely effective as a system of protection is merely gratuitous. In the remainder of this essay, therefore, we shall assume that either the fair-protection theory or some version of moralism is correct. For our purposes, we need not choose between them.

Insanity as an Affirmative Defense

Mental disorder bears on criminal liability in three different ways. Due to mental disorder, a defendant may prove to have been incapable of satisfying the definition of a crime. For example, due to a psychotic episode one may be incapable of forming the intention or having the knowledge required for the crime of theft or murder. In that case, the appropriate plea is that the defendant has not committed or has not been proven to have committed the crime of which she was accused. Such pleas are variously called "negative" or "failure of proof" defenses (the latter terminology is due to Robinson 1984). A second way in which mental disorder can affect criminal liability is by mitigation. The accused indeed committed the crime of theft but in her circumstances she is thought to merit a reduced sentence. The insanity defense illustrates a third way in which mental disorder is relevant to liability. This defense concedes that the defendant's conduct satisfied the definition of the crime (thus it is an "affirmative defense"), but it argues that her disorder makes it inappropriate to convict her. A successful affirmative defense results in acquittal, not mitigation.

Affirmative defenses attempt to break the presumptive connection between legal violation and legal culpability. Three other defenses in this category are involuntary intoxication, duress and mistake. Affirmative excuses of this kind *exculpate* without negating any specific definitional conditions of the crime. (Some affirmative defenses are nonexculpatory. These include technical or administrative bars to conviction, such as diplomatic immunity or statutes of limitation.)

There are importantly different ways of explaining the force of affirmative exculpating defenses. On one explanation, they are all impairment defenses; they assert respects in which the defendants' capacity to comply with the law is substantially impaired in a way that makes them non-responsible. But arguably the rationale for the insanity defense (and of involuntary intoxication) differs significantly from the excuses of duress and mistake. For instance, duress exculpates not because it renders offenders non-responsible but because it puts them in circumstances in which even responsible agents of "reasonable firmness" are likely to go astray (American Law Institute 1985). Their position as law-abiding citizens is not impugned. In contrast, mental disorders (or intoxication) exculpate because they render defendants incompetent (non-responsible) to answer to the criminal law. (Recent writers who underscore this contrast include Dressler 1987–1988, Gardner 2008, Horder 2004 and Kadish 1987.)

The McNaughtan Rules and Their Critics

The McNaughtan Rules are the most familiar of modern attempts to specify the incompetence in question. As measured by longevity and influence, these rules must be counted a great success. The M-rules (for short) were formulated by the English House of Lords in 1843 in response to the unpopular acquittal of Daniel McNaughtan in a murder trial that same year. (The spelling here follows Moran 1981: xi, who argues convincingly that this was the family spelling.) In one variation or another, the M-rules have prevailed in most jurisdictions in the English-speaking world. Their persistence, though, is due not to their self-evident ability to do justice to disordered offenders but to a lack of agreement on anything better.

A defense under the M-rules turns on three main points. Offenders must have been prevented (1) by "disease of the mind" either (2) from knowing the "nature and quality" of their act or (3) from knowing that their act was wrong. Each of these clauses has given rise to interpretive and substantive problems, but two sorts of dissatisfaction have been especially pressing. One is that the rules' understanding of the way mental disease affects responsibility is too "cognitive." The second dissatisfaction concerns the interpretation of "wrong" in the third clause. If *legal* wrong is sufficient, then the rules are in this respect too narrow. On the other hand, if *moral* wrong is required, the rules are arguably too broad.

The earliest systematic critique of the M-rules was by James Fitzjames Stephen, whose commentary still stands as one of the most astute contributions to the theory of criminal insanity. In Stephen's hands, the objection that the rules are "too cognitive" comes to this: that they regard insanity as significant only as a source of innocent ignorance or mistake. As Stephen critically put it, "The origin of the mistake can have no other effect than that of making the mistake itself innocent. Its effect as a mistake would be precisely the same whether it arose from disease of the brain or from false information . . . [I]n a word, the prisoner is treated as a sane person under a mistake of fact for which he is not to blame" (Stephen 1883: 157). By locating the significance of mental disease not in the madness itself, but in some independently exculpating cognitive condition such as a delusive belief, the rules amount to a mistake defense rather than an incompetence defense. Stephen argues that this is a serious misunderstanding of what is at stake. Delusion is significant not as an epistemic state of an otherwise competent mind, but as a "symptom" of a general impairment of the individual's capacity to respond to the world as required by law and morality. This seems to me a profound insight.

Stephen supposes instead that "a delusion of the kind [presented by candidates for the insanity defense] never, or hardly ever, stands alone, but is in all cases the result of a disease of the brain, which interferes more or less with every function of the mind, which falsifies all the emotions, alters in an unaccountable way the natural weight of motives of conduct" (157). Stephen's alternative holistic hypothesis is that mental disorders at least sometimes work by "affecting a man's whole view of the world in which he lived, falsifying his senses, rendering him inaccessible to reasoning of the simplest kind, and incapacitating him from performing the commonest and most conclusive experiments" (161). The M-rules are adequate only if madness is never like this, and to Stephen this position would be "so surprising, and would, if strictly enforced, have such monstrous consequences, that something more than an implied assertion of it seems necessary before it is admitted to be part of the law of England" (159).

One "monstrous" consequence, in Stephen's view, is that Hadfield should not have been acquitted. For Hadfield's very aim was to commit a capital offense. By a bit of sophistical moral casuistry, he reasoned that since suicide is a sin, his death must not be by his own hand but by decree of the Crown. The M-rules suppose that his mad delusion sits alongside "the same power of controlling his conduct and regulating his feelings as a sane man" (160), whereas Stephen sees defendants such as Hadfield as unable to attend to the obvious reasons why their conduct was wrong. They are in this way similar to those who commit crimes in states of extreme intoxicated agitation or psychedelic reverie.

In short, delusion is relevant not because it is a source of innocent ignorance or such that if it were true, deluded agents would be justified, but because it is symptomatic of the agents' incapacity to respond to the norms to which the law would hold them accountable. They may well be aware that their conduct violates the law. But knowledge "has its degrees like everything else and implies something more real and more closely connected with conduct than the half knowledge retained in dreams" (166).

Stephen proposed to capture the relevance of mental disease to the criminal law by this formula:

> if it is not, it ought to be the law of England that no act is a crime if the person who does it is at the time when it is done prevented either by defective mental power or by any disease affecting his mind from controlling his own conduct, unless the absence of the power of control has been produced by his own default.
>
> (168)

Stephen would be content for the law to work in practice with a "knowledge that an act is wrong" test, just so long as this phrase is glossed along the lines he suggests (171). His "control" test is not meant to privilege the volitional over the cognitive: "It is as true that a man who cannot control himself does not know the nature of his acts as that a man who does not know the nature of his acts is incapable of self-control" (171).

Like the first clause of the M-rules, Stephen's proposal requires that the defendant's impairment be the result of mental "disease" or "defect." The meaning of these terms has been much debated, but we should ask why they are even needed. Why not simply delete them from Stephen's formula, or from the M-rules? What matters for criminal responsibility is that defendants be impaired as specified by the formula, provided they are not responsible for this impairment. It seems unprincipled to restrict the defense to any specific etiology. As Stephen notes, one's cognitive/volitional competence can be impaired by things other than "disease," such as involuntary intoxication.

To be sure, in this generic form, the defense would not be, specifically, an *insanity* defense; mental disease is just one kind of explanation of the competence in question. A generic defense would have the conceptual advantage of emphasizing what is crucial. The origins of the impairment might indeed be relevant to the disposition of the defendant upon acquittal (for example, to whether civil commitment is warranted because the condition is persistent and untreatable), but not to the question of acquittal itself.

This proposal leads to a worry, however. A generic incompetence defense would seem to commit the law to entertaining any argument that an offender's competence is impaired by factors for which he or she is not responsible. This might leave an opening for pleas that an offender's competence was impaired by unfortunate early socialization or by "psychopathy" (or "moral insanity" as it was called in Stephen's day). This challenge puts pressure on the competence condition. What is common to madness and extreme intoxication, as Stephen convincingly illustrates, is that the agents are in an obvious sense "out of their minds"; certainly that's an inapt description of the condition of those who lack "moral sense" but are otherwise intact. The challenge is to say why being "out of one's mind" in this manner is not just one of a number of different ways of lacking the relevant normative competence. Restricting the defense to mental disease (and intoxication) is convenient but, again, unprincipled. If what is crucial to the impairment of such defendants as Hadfield is "the power of passing rational judgment on the moral character of the act which he meant to do" (as Stephen sometimes puts it, 163), there is a strong case to be made that what is now called "psychopathy" entails the kind of incompetence required by criminal law. (For arguments to this effect, see Duff 1977, Fingarette 1967, Fine and Kennett 2004, and Watson 2011.)

Stephen has a response to this worry. He does not dismiss out of hand the possible relevance of moral insanity to criminal responsibility, but he is skeptical, since he does not think it affects knowledge of right and wrong in the way madness does (Stephen 1883: 185). His conclusion rests on a peculiar understanding of moral knowledge. It is worth setting this out, because this understanding has been employed by a number of courts. To know that a type of conduct is morally wrong, Stephen argues, is simply to know that it will be subject to "blame and hatred" by the general community. Even those who lack moral sense know this sort of thing, "just as an atheist would know that most Englishmen are Christians" (Stephen 1883: 167). In contrast, Hadfield's madness prevented "anything like a calm judgment" about the moral characteristics (so understood) of his conduct. So while Stephen insists that criminal responsibility requires more than the capacity to know that one's conduct is illegal (in contrast to some narrower interpretations of the M-rules that hold sway today), knowing that something is wrong does not on his account require an exercise of moral capacities of one's own. Rather, simple cognizance of the fact that crimes are generally the object of moral opprobrium by one's fellow citizens will suffice. This construal of moral knowledge defuses the worry about moral insanity and the potential hazards of a generic incompetence defense. But as we'll see, it otherwise lacks philosophical, moral or legal motivation.

Interpreting the "Knowing That an Act Is Wrong" Clause

The third clause of the M-rules—the requirement that one know that one's act was wrong—has been interpreted in law in three importantly different ways. The weakest interpretation is that the capacity for right and wrong is the capacity to know that one's conduct is contrary to prevailing law. This is the standard laid down in *R. v. Windle* ([1952] 2 QB 826), which held that "the word 'wrong' in the M'Naghten Rules means contrary to law and does not have some vague meaning which may vary according to the opinion of different persons whether a particular act might not be justified." *Windle* is now the governing interpretation in English law. Call this interpretation *Law of the Land*.

The *Windle* court strongly opposed what we can call a *Community Moral Standards* interpretation such as that proposed by Stephen, on the grounds that it provides indeterminate or inconsistent guidance. What would invite moral opprobrium might have been sufficiently definite in Victorian England, but that question leads to perplexity in any moderately pluralistic culture. For instance, the crime under consideration in *Windle* was an alleged instance of euthanasia. Plausibly, a sizable percentage of the population in mid-twentieth-century England viewed such killings as, at least sometimes, morally permissible. Probably *Law of the Land* and *Community Moral Standards* deliver more or less the same verdicts in core cases, but in heterogeneous societies they will often diverge beyond that range. So the *Windle* court has a legitimate concern.

However, *Community Moral Standards* is affirmed over *Law of the Land* in some United States jurisdictions, for example by the Supreme Court of Colorado in *People v. Serravo* ((1992) 823 P.2d 128 (Colo.)): "the phrase 'incapable of distinguishing right from wrong' refers to a cognitive inability to distinguish right from wrong under existing societal standards of morality" (139). The *Serravo* court criticized the *Windle* interpretation on the same grounds as those pressed by Stephen, that:

> it injects a formalistic legalism into the insanity equation . . . A person in an extremely psychotic state, for example, might be aware that an act is prohibited by law, but due to the overbearing effect of the psychosis may be utterly without the capacity to comprehend that the act is inherently immoral. . . . A standard of legal wrong would render such a person legally responsible and subject to imprisonment for the conduct in question notwithstanding the patent injustice of such a disposition.
>
> (134)

The *Serravo* court agreed with Stephen that it would be "patently unjust" to punish a psychotic lawbreaker just because he or she knew she was breaking the law. What the court fails to see is that *Community Moral Standards* is no corrective to this implication of *Law of the Land*. Ironically, that standard is open to the same objection the court makes against *Windle*: a highly psychotic person might be quite aware that his conduct is contrary to societal standards but rendered quite unable to "comprehend that the act is inherently immoral." Hence, the reasons for being dissatisfied with *Law of the Land* also tell against *Community Moral Standards*. Indeed, community standards, independently of legal or moral status, provide no reasons for compliance whatever.

We have reached the following dialectical situation. There are compelling reasons for rejecting *Law of the Land*; it is incapable of doing justice to defendants such as Hadfield. *Community Moral Standards* goes beyond *Law of the Land*, but it provides no stable stopping place. One could possess the knowledge it requires without being in a position to assess its practical relevance. The problem with these two standards, it seems, is that they attempt to reduce normative understanding to understanding of facts about legal and social norms. This diagnosis suggests that the impairment at issue in the insanity defense is not just an impairment of sociological understanding of the local laws and mores but rather is more essentially normative.

Such a normative interpretation is advanced, implicitly at least, in some court opinions and some statutory revisions of the M-rules. In the Australian case of *R. v. Porter* ((1933) 55 CLR 182), the court is fairly explicit. The governing question for an insanity defense under *McNaughtan*, it argues, is this:

> Was it the case that through disorder of the mind [the accused] could not think rationally of the reasons which to ordinary people make that act right or wrong? If through the disordered condition of the mind he could not reason about the matter with a moderate degree of sense and composure it may be said that he could not know that what he was doing was wrong. What is meant by 'wrong'? What

is meant by wrong is wrong having regard to the everyday standards of reasonable people. (189–90. The *Porter* standard is codified in the Australian Criminal Code Act 1995 (Cth), Section 7.3 (1), as quoted in Fine and Kennett 2004: 427.)

As I read it, *Porter*'s reference to the "everyday standards of reasonable people" is to an essentially normative perspective that calls not for a factual judgment about the prevailing social morality but for a judgment about how one is reasonably to conduct oneself in the circumstances. Call this the *Reasonable Person* interpretation of the "knowledge" clause.

In contrast to *Community Moral Standards*, *Reasonable Person* is a plausible corrective to the limitations of *Law of the Land*; the grounds for dissatisfaction with the latter are grounds for shifting to such a normative interpretation. This shift invites something like the objection in *Windle* that *Reasonable Person* is indeterminate. But the law is already committed to using reasonable-person standards in many domains. More significant, perhaps, is that *Reasonable Person* returns us to the issue about moral impairments such as psychopathy.

Recall that it was *Community Moral Standards* that enabled Stephen to give that issue such short shrift. Those who lack "moral sense" are in some obvious sense incompetent to reasonably assess the normative import of the considerations they encounter in practical life. *Reasonable Person* has to exempt such agents from criminal responsibility or to explain why not. The inclusion of psychopathy in a generic incompetence test will have little practical import by itself, since it is a rare condition. But the slopes are treacherously slippery here. If psychopaths are exempted, why not those whose moral viciousness is due to bad socialization, for which people are not, for the most part, responsible? We have to tell a story here and it is not clear how that story goes. (To appeal to "free will," as courts and commentators sometimes do at this point, is to provide not a story but a placeholder for a story yet to be told.)

In sum, the inadequacies of nonnormative interpretations seem to support something like *Reasonable Person*, but that interpretation raises unsettling questions about the criminal competence of many defendants who are paragons of the wicked. No doubt this explains, without justifying, the anxious retreat to something like *Law of the Land*. In the words of *R. v. Ferrers* (quoted in our epigraph), our conclusion seems "right in philosophy, but dangerous in judicature."

Alternatives to the M-Rules

Dissatisfaction with the M-rules led to significant turmoil in twentieth-century criminal law, especially in the United States. Some reactions were modest, others were breathtakingly bold.

The most influential of these was proposed by the American Law Institute in its Model Penal Code (MPC), Section 4.01. (These liberalizing provisions led to the adoption of the MPC test by over half of the states and by all of the federal appellate courts in the United States. See Bonnie et al. 2008: 18.) The section states in part:

A person is not responsible for criminal conduct if at the time of such conduct as a result of mental disease or defect he lacks *substantial* capacity either to *appreciate* the criminality [wrongfulness] of his conduct or to *conform* his conduct to the requirements of law.

(emphases added)

The code's first revision of the M-rules is signaled by the word "substantial"; the incapacities in question need not be total. The second change is introduced by the substitution of the word "appreciate" for "know," which acknowledges that the capacity for "mere cognizance" of illegality might not be enough for criminal liability. Finally, the MPC allows explicitly for the possibility of a defendant with full "appreciation" of the requirements of law who is nevertheless substantially incapable of compliance. This last amendment is now known as the "volitional prong" of the test. The second two revisions respond in different ways to the idea that the M-rules are too "cognitive." Among other things, the term "appreciate" implies a sort of normative understanding that is not required by *Law of the Land*.

The MPC rule is a significant but modest revision of the M-rules, but other critics have proposed abandoning the *McNaughtan* framework altogether. A common theme of these criticisms is that it is a mistake to attempt to articulate the specific symptoms or incapacities required for an insanity defense. Thus in *Durham v. United States* ((1954) 214 F.2d 862 (D.C. Cir.)), the District of Columbia Circuit Court rejected *McNaughtan* in favor of a "product test," according to which "an accused is not criminally responsible if his unlawful act was the product of mental disease or mental defect" (874–75). The thought here was that mental disease or defect by its nature rendered one *non compos mentis*, and that it is fruitless to define this condition by "particular symptoms which medical science has long recognized do not necessarily, or even typically, accompany even the most serious mental disorder" (875).

The *Durham* test puts all the pressure on the terms "mental disease" and "product"; in the ordinary sense, it is simply not true that those whose conduct in some way "results" from mental disorder are necessarily incapacitated for the purposes of criminal law. Consequently, *Durham* inadvertently invited an overreliance on psychiatric expertise and gave rise to intractable disputes about what the legally pertinent senses of these terms might be. For these reasons, in *United States v. Brawner* ((1972) 471 F.2d 969 (D.C. Cir.)), the District Court replaced *Durham* with MPC 4.01. The most striking part of this opinion was the strong dissent of Chief Judge Bazelon, who had himself authored the *Durham* opinion. Bazelon agreed that *Durham* should be scrapped, but in his dissent he argued for an even more open-ended test than *Durham*: "Our instruction to the jury should provide that a defendant is not responsible if at the time of his unlawful conduct his mental or emotional processes or behavior controls were impaired to such an extent that he cannot justly be held responsible for his act" (1032). Like *Durham*, this proposal gives up on the project of articulating the nature of the specific competence that is impaired in the mentally disordered defendant. But unlike *Durham*, it drops all technical terms like "mental disease" and simply asks for a judgment about whether someone in the defendant's condition at the time of action is rightly held responsible. This provides no guidance whatever, but at least it asks a clear and legally relevant question that a jury might understand and be able to answer. To what extent we should be confident that a jury is likely to answer it correctly is another matter.

Obviously the MPC rule is much less open ended, but notice that it has already taken a couple of steps down the path recommended by Bazelon (as Bazelon himself points out—1034). Arguably, insofar as this rule improves upon *McNaughtan*, it does so by passing the burden of normative judgment to juries via the words "substantial" and "appreciate." That is to say: "substantial" incapacity means sufficient incapacity to warrant acquittal from criminal responsibility; lack of "appreciation" is deficiency in the sort of understanding that is required for reasonably holding offenders criminally responsible. The impression that MPC 4.01 provides much more guidance than Bazelon's instructions is arguably illusory.

Unsurprisingly, Bazelon's proposal has not been taken seriously, though a number of academic writers have attacked the M-rules in the same spirit. Stephen Morse proposes basically the same test as Bazelon's, though in more vernacular terms: "A defendant is not guilty by reason of insanity if, at the time of the offense, the defendant was so extremely crazy and the craziness so substantially affected the criminal behavior that the defendant does not deserve to be punished" (Morse 1985: 820). Fingarette 1972, Duff 1984 and Moore 1985 also reject a *McNaughtan*-style "knowledge of wrong" test, but they go beyond Bazelon by explicitly identifying criminal responsibility with the capacity for practical rationality. The jury is not simply to judge whether defendants' impairments render them nonresponsible, but whether their practical irrationality renders them nonresponsible.

Michael Moore puts it this way:

> Insanity betokens a difference so fundamental that we deny moral agency to those afflicted with it. The insane, like young infants, lack one of the essential attributes of personhood—rationality. For this reason, human beings who are insane are no more the proper subjects of moral evaluation than are young infants, animals, or even stones.
>
> (Moore 1985: 1137)

It seems right to see criminal competence in terms of practical rationality, but Moore's formulation harks back to the "total deprivation" standard of *Arnold*. Once again, no candidate for the insanity defense "lacks rationality" full stop. (Nor should we simply deny the criminally insane the status of persons.) Hadfield took relevant means to kill the king, and Clark took intelligible steps to avoid capture. The insane reason, but sometimes madly, and sometimes from mad premises or with mad ends.

Conclusion: Retreat and Abolition

None of these proposals to improve upon or replace the M-rules has prevailed. Between the first attempt by *McNaughtan* in 1843 to articulate a sensible standard for the responsibility of the mentally disordered and the decision in *Brawner* in 1973, there looked to be momentum for substantial revision and refinement of the earliest legal doctrines. The last quarter century, however, has been a period of severe reaction and retrenchment. What Andrew Ashworth says about the "narrow and antiquated defence of insanity" in England, which is so "rarely invoked" ("about 20 cases a year") as to be virtually abolished (Ashworth 2006: 279), can be said as well about the practice in the United States. The defense has been so sharply circumscribed in most jurisdictions, and even outright abolished in a few, that in many ways we have returned to the beginning.

The modest liberalization introduced by the MPC rule was short lived. Partly in the wake of the moral panic set off by John Hinckley's insanity acquittal for the attempted assassination of President Reagan (see Bonnie et al. 2008), stricter forms of the M-rules replaced the MPC rule in federal law and in many state jurisdictions. As in England, *Law of the Land* has, more or less, become the law of the land. That is so even though we know that the present practice fails to articulate a defensible standard of criminal responsibility. This is surely a scandal for criminal law.

We should add that the insanity defense is seldom sought not only because the increasingly narrow criteria are so difficult to meet, but because the rare successful plea is liable to result in indefinite civil commitments that are often worse for defendants than a conviction would have been. The present practice invites a pernicious abuse of civil authority, since post-acquittal commitments seem to be used punitively, rather than with realistic concern for the well-being or dangerousness of the individuals who are committed. We still cannot resist treating the mad retributively (Robinson 2001; Silver 1995). In this context, that may be a moral argument for complete abolition (for defenses and criticisms of abolitionism, see Morris 1982, Slobogin 2000 and Morse 1985). Meanwhile, these chronic confusions about the insanity defense should prompt us to rethink the project of criminal law altogether. It looks as though we do not know what we're doing.

References

American Law Institute (1985) Model Penal Code.

Arizona v. Clark (2006) 548 U.S. 735.

Ashworth, A. (2006) *Principles of Criminal Law*, 5th edition, Oxford: Oxford University Press.

Blackstone, W. (1766) *Commentaries on the Laws of England*, bk. IV, ch. 2.

Bonnie, R. J., Jeffries, J. C. and Low, P. W. (2008) *A Case Study in the Insanity Defense: The Trial of John W. Hinckley, Jr.*, 3rd edition, New York: Thompson/Foundation Press.

Dressler, J. (1987–1988) "Reflections on Excusing Wrongdoers: Moral Theory, New Excuses, and the Model Penal Code," 19 *Rutgers Law Journal*: 671.

Duff, R. A. (1977) "Psychopathy and Moral Understanding," *American Philosophical Quarterly*, 14: 189–200.

____ (1984) "Mental Disorder and Criminal Responsibility," in R. A. Duff and N. E. Simmonds, eds., *Philosophy and the Criminal Law*, Wiesbaden: Franz Steiner Verlag, pp. 31–48.

____ (2001) *Punishment, Communication, and Community*, Oxford: Oxford University Press.

Durham v. United States (1954) 214 F.2d 862 (D.C. Cir.).

Fine, C. and Kennett, J. (2004) "Mental Impairment, Moral Understanding, and the Purposes of Punishment," *International Journal of Law and Psychiatry* 27: 425–43.

Fingarette, H. (1967) *On Responsibility*, New York: Basic Books.

____ (1972) *The Meaning of Criminal Insanity*, Berkeley: University of California Press.

Gardner, G. (1953) "*Dailey v. Richardson* and the Constitution of the United States," *Boston University Law Review* 176: 193.

Gardner, J. (2008) *Offences and Defences: Selected Essays in the Philosophy of Criminal Law*, Oxford: Oxford University Press.

Hart, H. L. A. (2008) "Prolegomenon to the Principles of Punishment," in H. L. A. Hart, *Punishment and Responsibility*, J. Gardner, ed., Oxford: Oxford University Press.

Holloway v. United States (1945) 80 U.S. App. D.C. 3, 4, 148 F.2d 665.

Horder, J. (2004) *Excusing Crime*, Oxford: Oxford University Press.

Howell, T. B., ed. (1816–1828) *Howell's State Trials*, London.

Kadish, S. (1987) "Excusing Crime," 75 *California Law Review*: 257.

Moore, M. (1985) "Causation and the Excuses," *California Law Review* 73: 1091–1149.

____ (1987) "The Moral Worth of Retribution," in F. Schoeman, ed., *Responsibility, Character, and the Emotions: New Essays in Moral Psychology*, Cambridge: Cambridge University Press, pp. 179–219.

Moran, R. (1981) *Knowing Right from Wrong: The Insanity Defense of Daniel McNaughtan*, New York: The Free Press, Macmillan Publishing Co.

Morris, N. (1982) *Madness and the Criminal Law*, Chicago: University of Chicago Press.

Morse, S. (1985) "Excusing the Crazy: The Insanity Defense Reconsidered," 58 *Southern California Law Review*: 777.

People v. Serravo (1992) 823 P.2d 128 (Colo.).

Quinn, W. (1985) "The Right to Punish and the Right to Threaten," *Philosophy and Public Affairs* 14: 327–73.

R. v. Porter (1933) 55 CLR 182.

R. v. Windle [1952] 2 QB 826.

Rawls, J. (1971) *A Theory of Justice*, Cambridge, Mass.: Harvard University Press.

Ripstein, A. (2009) *Force and Freedom*, Cambridge, Mass.: Harvard University Press.

Robinson, P. (1984) *Criminal Law Defenses*, St. Paul, MN: West Publishing.

____ (2001) "Punishing Dangerousness: Cloaking Preventive Detention as Criminal Justice," 114 *Harvard Law Review* 5: 1429.

Scanlon, T. M. (2003) "Punishment and the Rule of Law," in T. M. Scanlon, *The Difficulty of Tolerance*, Cambridge, Mass.: Harvard University Press.

Silver, E. (1995) "Punishment or Treatment?: Comparing the Lengths of Confinement of Successful and Unsuccessful Insanity Defendants," *Law and Human Behavior* 19: 375–88.

Slobogin, C. (2000) "An End to Insanity: Recasting the Role of Mental Disability in Criminal Cases," 86 *Virginia Law Review* 6: 1199–1247.

State v. Guido (1993) 40 N.J. 191, A.2d.

Stephen, J. F. (1883) *A History of the Criminal Laws of England*, London: Macmillan.

United States v. Brawner (1972) 471 F.2d 969 (D.C. Cir.) (Bazelon, D., dissenting).

Walker, N. (1968) *Crime and Insanity in England, Volume 1*, Edinburgh: Edinburgh University Press.

Watson, G. (2011) "The Trouble with Psychopaths," in R. J. Wallace, S. Freeman and R. Kumar, eds., *Reasons and Recognition: Essays on the Philosophy of T. M. Scanlon*, Oxford: Oxford University Press.

Further Reading

For further reading, see: R. Bonnie (1984) "Morality, Equality and Expertise: Renegotiating the Relationship Between Psychiatry and the Criminal Law," 12 *Bulletin of the American Academy of Psychiatry and Law*: 5–20; A. Duff (2008) "Theories of Criminal Law," in E. N. Zalta, ed., *The Stanford Encyclopedia of Philosophy*, http:// plato.stanford.edu/archives/fall2008/entries/criminal-law; H. Fingarette (1972) "Insanity and Responsibility," *Inquiry* 15: 6–29; H. L. A. Hart (2008) "Punishment and the Elimination of Responsibility," in H. L. A. Hart, *Punishment and Responsibility: Essays in the Philosophy of Law*, Oxford: Oxford University Press, pp. 158–85; M. Moore (1984) *Law and Psychiatry: Rethinking the Relationship*, New York: Cambridge University Press; J. Murphy (1972) "Moral Death: A Kantian Essay on Psychopathy," *Ethics* 82: 284–98; T. M. Scanlon (1998) *What We Owe to Each Other*, Cambridge, Mass.: Harvard University Press; and R. Schopp (1991) *Automatism, Insanity and the Psychology of Criminal Responsibility: A Philosophical Inquiry*, New York: Cambridge University Press.

15

SELF-DEFENSE

Larry Alexander

Theories of self-defense are numerous and quite varied. Most take as their master hypothetical an Attacker and a Victim and then ask when the Victim is *justified* in preventing the Attacker's threatened attack by employing *force*. (From now on I shall assume that the Victim is employing deadly force, and that, unless otherwise noted, the harm Victim fears at the hands of Attacker is death or serious bodily injury.) Usually, theorists only vary the master hypothetical by varying the extent to which Attacker is *culpable* for the threatened attack.

I believe that most of the extant theories of self-defense are deficient and are so because the master hypothetical is far too simple to represent the complexity of self-defense. For example, there is considerable disagreement over whether Victim's mistaken but "reasonable" perception of an imminent attack renders his defensive use of force *justifiable* or only *excused*. But his mistake can only be exposed by reference to a different perspective on the events—God's, a trial court's or jury's, or a Third Party's. And note that the perspective of the trial court, jury or Third Party can itself be mistaken relative to that of God.

I believe that by focusing on the permissibility of Victim's response, these theories overlook the value of beginning the analysis from the perspective not of Victim, but of a Third Party who is willing to intervene to prevent the attack. Moreover, I believe that instead of seeking to pigeonhole responses as either justified or excused, we should ask whether a response is culpable or nonculpable. I hope that the utility of emphasizing the Third-Party perspective and culpability will become apparent.

Third-Party Defense

So let us assume Third Party perceives what he believes is likely an impending attack on Victim (with deadly force) by Attacker. Third Party believes he can prevent the attack by using deadly force against Attacker. Will Third Party—who is not a member of Victim's family and has no duty to defend Victim—be culpable for using deadly force against Attacker?

To answer that question requires a theory that tells us when such a use of defense-of-others force is culpable or nonculpable. What elements should go into such a theory?

The Array of Possible Attackers

First, the theory should account for the different kinds of Attackers that Third Party might perceive. Who are they?

(1) The Culpable Attacker (CA)

CAs come in different stripes. There is (i) the CA who intends to kill Victim. There is (ii) the CA who intends to impose a risk of death on Victim (for example, by playing involuntary Russian roulette on Victim). There is (iii) the CA who is intending to do something that he knows will impose a risk of death on Victim, though he might wish it did not (for example, the CA intends to detonate explosives in the vicinity of Victim, or to drive 100 miles per hour within inches of Victim).

(2) The Innocent Attacker (IA)

Like CAs, IAs come in different stripes. There is (i) the IA who mistakenly believes Victim is a CA out to kill *him* or out to kill someone else who is not culpably threatening Victim. There are (ii) IAs who are not morally responsible agents— the young, the insane and the senile. And there is (iii) the IA who is nonculpably unaware that his conduct threatens Victim (for example, an IA who does not realize that the use of his cell phone will detonate a bomb in Victim's house).

(3) The Anticipated Culpable Aggressor

Some persons are not yet CAs in that they are not contemplating attacking Victim. However, Third Party may predict that one who is not yet a CA will become one in the future, when it may be impossible to protect Victim. So suppose Third Party sees Anticipated Culpable Attacker (ACA) about to enter ACA's office. Third Party knows that Victim is in ACA's office, awaiting ACA for a business conference. Third Party knows that ACA carries a loaded gun; knows that ACA is murderously jealous; knows the ACA's wife has left a voicemail message on ACA's office answering machine confessing an affair with Victim; and knows that ACA always listens to his voicemail as soon as he enters his office, even when there is someone else present waiting to speak with him. So Third Party anticipates that once in his office, ACA will become a CA before Victim can leave the office. The question a theory of self-defense must answer is whether Third Party may nonculpably use deadly force against an ACA who is not yet a CA. (Assume Third Party does not believe he has a nonlethal method available that would be equally as effective as deadly force for averting the threat to Victim—though whether Third Party must use nonlethal force when it is available and effective is an issue I will raise when I take up proportionality, necessity and retreat.)

(4) The Anticipated Innocent Aggressor

Some persons are not yet contemplating attacking Victim. However, as with ACAs, Third Party may predict that such persons will become aggressors in the future when it may be impossible to protect Victim. However, unlike ACAs, such persons will be IAs. For example, suppose CIA agents have positioned themselves just outside Enemy Nation's missile silo. They have been informed that Enemy Nation's president has just ordered a missile launch against America. They also have been informed that the order is inside the silo on the control computer, awaiting the new shift of soldiers who man the silo. Finally, they know that the soldiers are quite likely to carry out such an order when they read it, although because they believe in the rectitude of their president and the propaganda to which they have been subjected, they will be nonculpable for doing so. And once they are inside the silo and read the order, the CIA agents will be powerless to stop the launch. They believe that to avert the missile launch, they must kill the approaching shift of soldiers before they get inside the silo and read the order—that is, before they form the intent to aggress. (Assume delaying the launch will give America time to take actions that will avert future launches.) Those soldiers are Anticipated Innocent Aggressors or AIAs.

(5) Culpable Persons (who are not CAs)

Another category of persons against whom Third Party might be tempted to use deadly force are persons who are in some way culpable but who are not presently attacking Victim. For example, suppose two people attack Victim with deadly force—in this case, guns—but CA1 has run out of ammunition. CA2 is continuing the attack on Victim, but Third Party's ability to protect Victim by using deadly force against CA2 is thwarted by the fact that CA1—now just a culpable person (CP)—is in the way of a clean shot. (He currently has his foot caught in something; he is *not* intentionally shielding CA2, an act that would make him a CA through complicity.) May Third Party nonculpably use deadly force against CA1, the CP, in order to then use deadly force against CA2 and save Victim? Notice that CPs, whose presence is unintentionally preventing defense of Victim, can, like CAs, come in a variety of types. There are CPs (i) who, as in the example above, have just finished attacking Victim; (ii) who attacked Victim in the more distant past (but were not punished for this); (iii) who attacked, not Victim, but someone else on a prior occasion (and were not punished); or (iv) who were culpable to a lesser extent than a deadly CA (and were not punished). A good theory of self-defense should tell us whether Third Party may nonculpably use deadly force against any or all of these CPs to protect Victim.

Finally, there are CPs who are accessories to attacks by CAs. Some of these accessories are actually CAs, as their present participation is instrumental to the success of CA's attack. But others are persons whose participation in CA's attack is over—the crime boss who ordered CA's "hit," for example, or the accessory who gave CA the gun. If for some reason Third Party can avert CA's attack by using deadly force against these accessories—perhaps the hit man CA will call off his attack if he learns that his crime boss has been killed—may Third Party use deadly force against the accessory CP rather than against the CA?

(6) Culpable Fakers

There is one category of culpable actors against whom the use of force by Third Party will generally be culpable. Suppose someone fakes a deadly attack on Victim as a (bad) practical joke. We can assume that person has acted culpably in frightening Victim. He is a Culpable Faker (CF). If Third Party knows CF is in fact a CF, then Third Party cannot use deadly force against CF, for that would be unnecessary for Victim's defense. (Victim needs no defending from a fake attack.) On the other hand, Victim may be acting nonculpably in using deadly force against CF. (Victim will be an IA vis-à-vis CF by virtue of Victim's innocent mistake.) What should Third Party do in such a case? It should be clear that he should not use deadly force against Victim, despite Victim's mistake. If anyone should bear the risk of death here, it should be CF. (The same is also true of someone who was at one time a CA and who has changed his mind but cannot signal Victim of this change of mind; he is not a CF, but like a CF, he is culpable for creating Victim's belief that he is a CA.) So Third Party should not intervene to protect CF if that requires him to use deadly force against Victim. And if CF, who is now a potential victim of a deadly attack from an IA (Victim), seeks to defend himself against Victim with a real gun, Third Party should either not intervene or intervene on the side of Victim, the IA.

CF, though not initially an attacker, is culpable for having created the incident. His life should not be preferred to that of Victim.

Such is the array of possible persons against whom Third Party might be tempted to employ deadly force to protect Victim. My own view is that, other factors to be discussed put aside, Third Party may nonculpably use deadly force against all categories of CA and against CPs who are unintentionally shielding CAs and have culpably risked Victim's or others' deaths and have not been punished. ACAs are a more difficult case because they are not yet culpable. They raise the question of just how far preemptive strikes can go without being culpable. (All defensive force is preemptive, a point discussed more fully below; however, ACAs raise the issue of preempting not just an attack but the attacker's culpability.)

IAs, on the other hand, cannot ordinarily be attacked nonculpably. There is no reason why Third Party should prefer Victim's life to an IA's. Both are innocent. There are various accounts of self-defense that suggest Victim's life should be preferred to IA's, but these are unpersuasive because they are usually advanced from Victim's rather than Third Party's impartial perspective. From the latter perspective, IA and Victim are equally innocent, and their confrontation is equally tragic no matter who survives it. The fact that IA initiates the attack does not alter this verdict. For if Victim may employ deadly force to protect himself from IA, he is as much a threat to IA as IA is to him.

On the other hand, if the numbers count, or if there are other reasons to intervene (for example, Victim—or IA—is on the verge of finding a cancer cure), then Third Party may nonculpably use deadly force on the preferred side of the conflict. There may be two or more IAs and only one Victim. Likewise, there may be more than one Victim and only one IA. If two deaths are worse than one, then Third Party may nonculpably use deadly force to save the greater number, even if those against whom the force is used are innocent. (The situation is similar to the famous trolley hypothetical, where one can save five trapped workers by diverting a runaway trolley from the track on which the five are trapped to a siding on which one is trapped. The numbers favor the diversion, and the body, labor or talents of the one are not necessary to bring about the saving of the five (the one is not "used"). The same is true in a Victim–IA confrontation where the numbers support intervening on one side or the other.)

Riskiness of the Attack

Third Party, in deciding whether to intervene to defend Victim, must consider not only the status of Attacker—culpable or innocent—but also the risks that Attacker will impose on Victim if Third Party does not intervene. Those risks that Third Party perceives may be different from the risks Attacker perceives or intends. If Third Party but not Attacker knows Attacker's gun is unloaded, then Third Party will perceive the risk to Victim as far less than the risk Attacker perceives. Or if Third Party but not Attacker knows that Attacker's cell phone is rigged to set off a bomb in Victim's house, Third Party will perceive a grave risk to Victim even though Attacker perceives none.

Even in a simple case, such as that of a CA who intends to kill Victim by firing a gun, Third Party's assessment of the risks of death and injury to Victim will be complex. It will be based, first, on Third Party's estimate that CA will indeed carry through on his present intention and actually fire the shot (a point I take up below). But even if it is 100 percent certain that CA will fire the shot, the risk of death to Victim will be a function of the condition of CA's gun (is it loaded? Is it jammed?); CA's marksmanship; the orientation of Victim's body; Victim's apparel (is it bulletproof?); and Victim's physical condition.

Risks not only vary in degree, depending on the epistemic vantage of the person estimating the risk, but also in kind. A risk of death usually is accompanied by a greater risk of bodily injury. And a risk of bodily injury usually carries with it a somewhat lesser risk of death. And frequently risks of death or injury are accompanied by risks to property and to emotional well-being.

Here, as stated earlier, I shall assume that the risk at issue is the death of Victim. Third Party may perceive that risk as high, moderate, small or nonexistent. But again, Third Party's assessment may differ radically from Attacker's.

Likelihood of Attack

Theorists of self-defense frequently overlook its perhaps most significant aspect, namely, that it is preemptive in nature—a "preemptive strike," if you will. Even the CA who at present intends to kill Victim may change his mind and abort the attack. Indeed, even if CA has already fired a shot at Victim, Third Party's *defensive* intervention, as opposed to a punitive or vengeful one, will always be aimed at averting the next shot, and the CA can always decide not to fire the next shot. The same is true of all the CAs and IAs. They may change their minds. Or they may be prevented from carrying out the attack by a change in circumstances between the time at which Third Party considers intervening and the feared attack.

One can perhaps think more clearly about these two risks—the risk that there will be an attack, and the risk that the attack, if it occurs, will produce various harms—by considering the following two scenarios, each of which makes one of these two risks a matter of virtual certainty. In Scenario One, Third Party sees CA about to play involuntary Russian roulette on Victim. CA holds a gun to Victim's head, a gun into which CA has put one live bullet and then spun the chambers. Third Party is certain CA will pull the trigger if Third Party does not shoot CA first. How many empty chambers must the gun have before we will say Third Party should not be permitted to shoot CA? Five, as with a six-shooter? Nine? Twenty? Fifty?

In Scenario Two, CA is again pointing a gun at Victim's head, but this time Third Party believes that the gun is fully loaded (and is not jammed or otherwise defective, nor is Victim's head protected by a bulletproof shield, etc.). In other words, Third Party believes that *if* CA pulls the trigger, Victim will certainly die. However, Third Party is not at all certain CA will pull the trigger. He could be bluffing (a CF). He could intend to do so but lose his nerve. And so on. In this scenario, how confident must Third Party be that CA will pull the trigger in order for shooting CA to be permissible? Will *any* chance that CA will pull the trigger be sufficient, given that CA is culpable? Or must that chance be above some threshold, and if so, what? If, on the other hand, the person with the gun is an IA rather than a CA—he's a child, a lunatic or someone who mistakenly believes he is justified in killing Victim—then if Third Party for whatever reason may favor Victim's life over IA's, what probability that IA *will* pull the trigger will permit Third Party to shoot IA? These are important questions that theorists of self-defense virtually never ask, much less answer.

So there are two "risks" that Third Party must consider. There is the risk that, if he does not intervene, Attacker will indeed attack. And there is the risk that, if Attacker does attack, Victim will be harmed. A theorist may believe that those two risks should be treated together as factors in an overall risk to Victim. On that view, a perceived 90 percent probability of an attack with a perceived 90 percent chance of killing Victim should be considered as a single perceived risk of 81 percent of Victim's death. On the other hand, because one risk is that of a human choice while the other is one of natural events, a theorist may believe they should be disaggregated and treated separately.

Finally, suppose Third Party has 100 percent confidence in his judgment about the status of Attacker—whether Attacker is a CA, a CP, an ACA, a CF or an IA. But suppose, further, that Third Party does not have 100 percent confidence in his judgment about whether there will be an attack and, if there is, how much harm it will cause Victim. In such a case, should Third Party's estimate of the likely harm (likelihood of attack times, likelihood of various harms if an attack) that renders his defensive force justifiable vary according to whether he believes Attacker is a CA, CP, ACA, CF or IA? In other words, may Third Party use deadly force against Attacker based on a lower estimate of the risk posed by Attacker if Third Party believes Attacker is a CA, say, rather than an IA?

Timing of the Feared Attack

Some theorists of self-defense believe the length of time remaining until the anticipated attack is expected to occur is an independently significant factor in assessing the culpability of Third Party's intervention. Traditionally, criminal law doctrine concurred and required that the feared attack be "imminent" before either Third Party or Victim could employ defensive force.

The Model Penal Code changed the timing focus from the imminence of the feared attack to the necessity of employing the defensive force at the time it is employed. An attack that may not be imminent might nonetheless be one that it is possible to avert only by acting now. On this view, the time of the feared attack is relevant only as it bears on the risk that it will indeed occur if not averted. Attacker may change his mind. Or other things may occur that will thwart the attack. But taking all these things into consideration, if the perceived likelihood of the attack is still high enough, and waiting will only increase the dangers to Victim, then Third-Party intervention is nonculpable on this view.

Third Party's Confidence Level

Thus far I have adduced several factors that Third Party must consider in deciding whether to intervene: the status of Attacker (as a CA or IA); the risks to Victim that Third Party thinks the attack will impose; and the perceived likelihood that Attacker will indeed attack if Third Party does not intervene. (I have expressed my doubts about whether the timing of the anticipated attack is material to the permissible use of defensive force independently of its effect on the likelihood of the attack.) But notice that Third Party may not be certain of any of these factors. He may believe that Attacker is a CA, but only with a "slightly more likely than not" level of confidence. And he may likewise have varying degrees of confidence in his estimates of the risks of various harms and the likelihood of the attack.

Now Third Party's degree of confidence in the latter two estimates of risk—or, if they should be treated together, the overall risks of harms to Victim—is probably already accounted for in Third Party's estimate of the risks Victim faces. For if Third Party believes at a 51 percent level of confidence that Victim faces an overall risk of death of 10 percent, and believes at a 49 percent level of confidence that Victim faces a 5 percent risk of death, Third Party then can be said to believe at a 100 percent level of confidence that Victim faces slightly less than a 7.5 percent risk of death.

On the other hand, Third Party's confidence level in his assessment of the Attacker's status—as a CA, IA or, if he is not attacking but shielding, a CP—is independently significant. For suppose Third Party thinks Attacker is a CA with a 40 percent degree of confidence—must he then act as if Attacker *is* an IA? Theorists of self-defense tend to stipulate that Attacker is a CA or an IA. But in the real world, Third Party will believe Attacker is a CA or IA (or CP) with a level of confidence greater than zero but less than 100 percent.

Consider this example. Third Party knows that two sets of twins are out to kill Victim. One set, Pixie and Trixie, are classic IAs. Perhaps they've been told by a (to them) credible source that Victim is a terrorist and must be killed on sight to avert a disaster. Or perhaps they're insane.

The other set of twins, Dina and Dana, are classic CAs. They just hate Victim and wish to do her in.

Suppose Third Party knows all this but does not know what the twins look like. He sees a pair approaching Victim with guns drawn. If they are Pixie and Trixie—IAs— then arguably it will be culpable for Third Party to kill them in order to save Victim, no matter how high Third Party assesses the likelihood to be that if he does not intervene, Victim will be killed. For there is no obvious reason for Third Party to prefer the life of one Victim over two IAs. On the other hand, if the twins are the CAs, Dina and Dana, killing them will not be culpable. Now suppose Third Party considers this and concludes that it is 50 percent likely that the twins are Pixie and Trixie and 50 percent likely that they are Dina and Dana. Third Party's only options are to shoot the twins or abstain. Abstention is permissible but will result in Victim's death, or so Third Party believes. Would shooting the twins also be permissible given Third Party's belief that it is 50 percent likely that they are IAs? Would *any* chance that they are IAs require Third Party to treat them as if they are IAs, in which case, because there is *always* a chance that an apparent CA is really an IA, Third Party—and Victim as well—would always have to act on the assumption that an Attacker is an IA? The question is one of the required confidence level in the material facts, and it is a question on which almost every self-defense theorist has been completely silent.

The same confidence level problem comes up when Third Party sees Victim apparently threatened, not by a CA who *intends* to kill Victim, but by a reckless CA. That would be the case if the apparent CA is, for example, playing Russian roulette on Victim. CA might be insane. But it is also the case when Third Party sees apparent CA driving very fast on a narrow road that Victim is on, and Third Party can only protect Victim by shooting CA or shooting his tires (which will likely kill him by causing his car to go out of control and careen off the road and over a cliff). Apparent CA might be culpably reckless and thus an actual CA. But he also may not be a CA at all, as would be true if he has a very ill passenger he is rushing to the hospital, making the risks he is imposing on Victim justifiable.

Collateral Damage (of Shields and Bystanders)

Thus far, the only personae in my playlets have been Third Party, Attacker and Victim. However, any defensive force employed by Third Party against Attacker could create risks of various types and magnitudes to otherwise noninvolved persons.

Although some might wish to divide this group into those who are nonculpably shielding attacker from Third Party—so-called "innocent shields"—and those who are merely in Attacker's vicinity—bystanders—the division seems pointless. Innocent shields are merely bystanders in a spatial relation to Attacker and Third Party that render them more likely to be harmed by Third Party's defensive force than other bystanders. So all bystanders and innocent shields should be considered the same regarding the magnitude of risk (as perceived by Third Party) to which they may be nonculpably subjected. (Culpable shields—those who, for bad reasons, such as support of Attacker's attack, try to shield an Attacker who is otherwise a legitimate target of defense—should be regarded as CAs; Third-Party defensive force against them should be analyzed the same way as Third-Party defensive force against other CAs insofar as assessments of risks and confidence in their status as CAs are concerned.)

Now if Third Party's defensive force against Attacker is otherwise nonculpable, it is not rendered culpable merely by the fact that Third Party perceives that his use of force is creating risks to innocent bystanders. Those perceived risks count against his use of force, but they can be outweighed by the perceived risks to Victim if Third Party abstains. In other words, innocent bystanders are no less but also no more legitimate objects of Third-Party concern than is Victim. They complicate Third Party's calculus but do not fundamentally alter it.

(Third Party cannot, of course, *use* a bystander to defend Victim. He cannot, for example, shove a bystander into Attacker's line of fire, even to save multiple Victims. But risking is not the same as using. On the other hand, if the bystander is not innocent but instead a CP, such as an accessory whose aid has already been given to the Attacker, might "using" such a CP as a shield be justifiable?)

Proportionality/Necessity/Retreat

I shall take up this trio of doctrines—namely, (1) that defensive force should be proportional to the harm threatened, (2) that the level of defensive force should be no greater than that necessary to avert the harm and (3) that retreat rather than defensive force is preferable where feasible—when I turn to Victim's use of defensive force. I take it up there because I consider this trio of doctrines to be, in reality, only one doctrine, and because the third aspect of this doctrine—retreat—has no application to Third Party defensive force. When I analyze the doctrine in the context of Victim's use of defensive force, I shall note the implications of that analysis for Third Party's use of defensive force.

* * * * *

I began my analysis of self-defense by focusing, not on self-defense itself, but on Third-Party defense of others. I did so because many of the issues that bear on the culpability of Third-Party defense bear as well on the culpability of Victim's self-defense. Put simply, whenever Third Party will be acting nonculpably in defending Victim, Victim will be acting nonculpably in defending himself. However, as we shall see, it is not the case that whenever Third Party will be acting *culpably* in defending Victim, Victim will be acting culpably in defending himself. For there are various circumstances that will render self-defense but not other-defense nonculpable. And it is those I shall emphasize in the next section.

I have also focused on culpability and not justification and excuse. I gave my reason for doing so at the outset. The controversy over when defensive force is justified or is only excused arises when a defender has made a mistake over whether he is being attacked, whether the attack might be lethal or (for some) whether the attacker is a CA or an IA. Those who wish to extend the label "justified" to those who make such mistakes argue that given their beliefs, these defenders acted in ways we would want them to act or at least not condemn them for acting. For we cannot be guided in acting by things as they really are but only by things as they appear to us to be. On the other hand, the "excuse" camp points out that where the defender is mistaken, third parties, aware of the mistake, cannot assist him in his defense—and the ability of anyone to assist conduct is the mark of that conduct being justified.

My temptation is to act like the proverbial rabbi and pronounce both positions "right." If Third Party's beliefs, were they true, would make his defending Victim against Attacker impermissible, Third Party would be culpable if he defends Victim—even though Victim's different beliefs, were *they* true, would make *his* defensive force permissible and hence nonculpable. But Third Party's perspective is just that—a perspective. Third Party's belief that Victim is not being attacked could be mistaken, not Victim's belief that he is being attacked. From a Fourth Party's perspective, a nonculpable Victim or nonculpable Third Party, preparing to use defensive force against Attacker, might be just a mistaken IA. And even the trial court, post hoc, has only its perspective on the facts, which also could be in error. So finite perspectives, not God's-eye ones, are all we have, which lends credence to the justification position on mistaken defensive force. On the other hand, the excuse position reflects the fact that what our beliefs aim at is the truth of the matter: we care about what *is* true, not what we believe to be true. We want our defensive force to *be* justified from a God's-eye perspective, not merely *appear* justified to us.

The culpability approach recognizes that we are all prisoners of our perspectives and the beliefs we form because of them. We always act from a position of less than absolute certainty. Although the culpability analysis implies what would be the case if one were 100 percent certain of the facts, it more usefully has something to say about how to proceed when one lacks 100 percent certainty, which is the situation in which any defender, Third Party or Victim, will find himself.

Notice also that I have spoken only of culpability and not about results. If Third Party would be culpable for acting in a given situation because of how he perceives that situation, it does not matter whether he injures or kills anyone. His culpability attaches to what he tries to do and the risks he believes he is imposing, regardless of whether he succeeds or whether those risks turn out to be nonexistent. The same is also true of Victim acting in self-defense.

Self-Defense

I now turn to Victim's defense of himself. (What is true of Victim's self-defense can also be true of one's defense of his family. From here on when I analyze self-defense, I mean to include as well Third-Party defense of *Third Party's* family.)

The first point is one I mentioned above: whenever, on Third Party's view of the facts, Third Party can nonculpably defend Victim against Attacker, Victim, if he has the same view of the facts, can nonculpably defend himself. Thus, whatever level of confidence in Attacker's status as a CA, whatever estimate of the likelihood that he will attack and whatever estimate of the likelihood of the various harms that will result if he does attack render Third Party nonculpable for using defensive force, the same confidence and likelihood levels will render Victim nonculpable for doing so. So the analysis in the first section of this essay of when Third Party can act nonculpably is equally applicable to Victim's self-defense.

Innocent Aggressors and Self-Defense

Recall that I argued that Third Party should not be able to use deadly force against Attacker if he believes Attacker is an IA. For, from Third Party's perspective, both IA and Victim are innocents who unfortunately find themselves in a deadly confrontation. Unless there are special circumstances that make saving Victim's life preferable to saving IA's—there are several Victims and few IAs, or perhaps Victim is on the verge of finding a cancer cure and IA is not so socially valuable—then Third Party must abstain from employing deadly force against IA.

However, the fact that use of deadly force against an IA would be a culpable act for Third Party does not necessarily make it a culpable act for Victim. For both morality and the law might grant Victim a privilege to save himself or his family from death or serious injury against an IA or even multiple IAs, even though, from an impartial standpoint, the IA's life and limb are equally worthy of protection. In other words, morality and the law may not require Victim to be as impartial as they require Third Party to be.

Now if this is true, we might deem the Victim's nonculpable use of deadly force against an IA "excused." Or we might describe it as "personally but not socially justified." What is important is that it is nonculpable.

The Limits of Nonculpable Defensive Force Against IAs

(1) Probabilities of harm

Even if we are going to permit Victim but not Third Party to use deadly force against IAs and not just CAs, there are limits beyond which Victim will be culpable that do not apply to defense against CAs. One limit might well concern Victim's estimates of the probabilities of IA's attack and, if it comes, its consequences. When Victim has the requisite level of confidence that Attacker is a CA, we might deem Victim's (or Third Party's) use of defensive force nonculpable even if his estimate of the likelihood of attack and the likelihood of death or serious injury given an attack is fairly low. (Recall the case of the CA playing involuntary Russian roulette, where there is some chance the CA will change his mind and not pull the trigger, and a greater chance that if he does, the chamber will be empty.) On the other hand, where Victim believes Attacker is an IA, we may think that he should endure a higher risk before employing deadly force. After all, we all face some risks of death and serious injury from innocent others every day, as, for instance, when we drive or walk close to a road. We would surely be culpable were we to gun down other drivers to protect ourselves from the finite but small risk that they will lose control of their vehicles and injure or kill us. The same restriction should apply to Victim when facing an IA. His assessment of the likelihood of attack and harm should be above—perhaps well above—the level at which defense against a CA would be warranted.

(2) Multiple IAs

If Victim is not culpable for defending himself against IAs even though Third Party would be culpable for defending Victim, is Victim's "excuse" limited if he must kill multiple IAs? Suppose, for example, five small children are threatening Victim with loaded guns left out by their parents, guns that they think are toys. May Victim nonculpably defend himself against five IAs? Ten IAs? Or consider the proverbial one worker stuck on the trolley siding. He sees IA nonculpably about to throw the switch that will send the trolley toward him. He not only knows that the person about to throw the switch is an IA, but he knows why he is, namely, that there are five workers stuck on the main track. May this one worker—Victim—nonculpably (excusably) defend his life at the cost of the one IA and the five workers? (Obviously, if Victim is nonculpable, because excused or "personally justified," in endangering many to save himself or his family, he is nonculpable irrespective of whether those he endangers are IAs, innocent bystanders, or those, like the five trapped workers, who would otherwise be saved by the IA.)

(3) Defense of IAs against Victim

Because IAs are innocents, Victim's permission to defend himself against IAs, which I have characterized as more in the nature of an excuse that is personal to Victim than a justification that weighs everyone's interests impartially, raises the question of what an IA may do to defend himself against Victim should Victim employ self-defense. Assuming the IA cannot prudently retreat—see the discussion of retreat below—or is insane, a child or convinced Victim is a CA, then IA should regard Victim as an IA. IA should have the same permission to defend himself against Victim as Victim has to defend himself against IA. (This applies as well to Culpable Faker (CF), whom Victim mistakenly sees as a CA; if Victim attacks CF, he is, to CF, an IA; but if CF defends himself, his excuse does not eliminate his initial culpability.) And unless the numbers favor IA or Victim—as when there are multiple IAs and fewer Victims, or vice versa—or some other qualitative factor does so, Third Party should not be permitted to intervene in defense of either party. (This last point demonstrates the error of current defense-of-others doctrine, which allows Third Party to defend Victim whenever, given what Third Party believes about the situation, Victim would be entitled to protect himself. For if Attacker is an IA, Victim is, under current doctrine, entitled to employ defensive force, even if lethal. However, there is no reason to permit Third Party to use such force against an Attacker whom Third Party believes to be an IA.)

(4) Defense of CAs and CFs against Victim

What if the clash is not between an IA and Victim but between a CA or CF and Victim? Suppose, for example, that when Victim goes to defend himself, CA decides to abandon his attack but cannot communicate credibly his change of mind to Victim or otherwise avoid the confrontation—say, by retreating. May CA defend himself against Victim? And similarly for CF, whom Victim takes to be a CA: If CF cannot safely retreat and cannot credibly communicate to Victim that he was merely pretending to be a CA, may CF defend himself against Victim? Put differently for both CA and CF, what difference does their initial culpability make to their ability to defend themselves against Victim?

I have already said that Third Party should, if he decides to intervene, intervene on Victim's side, not the side of CAs or CFs, even if they outnumber Victim. But what holds for Third Party may not hold for CAs or CFs. For them, one must distinguish between their culpability in creating this confrontation, the risk of which is a major determinant of the level of their culpability, and what they may now do to defend themselves. Their culpability is permanently on their moral ledger, and they can be punished for it no matter what happens subsequently—that is, even if they manage to avoid injurious or deadly consequences. On the other hand, if they have now abandoned their culpable intentions but find themselves in a confrontation that is a consequence of their prior culpable acts, it is a separate question whether they may *nonculpably* defend themselves against Victim. Compare their position vis-à-vis Victim with one who violates the rights of an innocent person because he was threatened with harm by another if he did not do so. The latter is a candidate for the defense of duress despite the innocence of his victim. I have argued that the logic of the excuse of duress should extend it beyond responses to unlawful threats to responses to natural threats and to human threats that are *lawful*. For the excuse does not turn on the victim's liability to attack—which is absent—but on the difficulty of the attacker's resisting attacking the victim in the face of a threat to which a "person of reasonable firmness" could not resist succumbing. And from that perspective, it is immaterial whether the threat is unlawful or lawful, human or natural.

The logic of the excuse of duress is the basis for concluding that Victim acts nonculpably in defending himself from IAs even when he knows they are IAs, and even when they outnumber him. (If there were more Victims than IAs, then Victims would not need an excuse: killing the IAs would be justifiable as the choice of a lesser evil, just as it would be if Third Party killed the IAs.) That same logic should lead us to conclude that a CA or CF may nonculpably defend himself against Victim, who is, from their perspective, an IA. The CA or CF's culpability for creating the situation remains. But that does not entail that their defensive acts of self-preservation are culpable. If, from the perspective of the CA or CF, Victim is an IA, the CA or CF too is now a Victim. His culpability for employing defensive force should parallel that of any Victim against any IA.

(5) Using innocent bystanders

Third Party cannot "use" a bystander to protect Victim. He cannot place a bystander in a position that shields Victim from Attacker, just as he may not protect the five workers in Trolley by pushing a fat man into the trolley's path. On the other hand, we have said that Victim might be excused if he defends himself against an IA and even multiple IAs, even if Third Party could not defend Victim against them. What if Victim uses a bystander as a shield, however? (Similarly, what if the one worker in Trolley can throw a fat man into the trolley's path and save both himself and the five workers?) If there is a deontological constraint against using others as means that prevents Third Party from being nonculpable in doing so, does that constraint also prevent Victim from being *excused* and hence nonculpable for doing so and saving himself and perhaps multiple IAs whom he might otherwise be excused from killing? Why would Victim be more culpable for violating a deontological constraint against using a bystander than he would be for defending himself or a loved one against multiple IAs?

(6) Proportionality, necessity and retreat

Proportionality, necessity and retreat are typically regarded by both the doctrine and by theorists as three separate conditions limiting the permission to use defensive force. *Proportionality* is understood to require that the level of force employed defensively be roughly proportionate to the harm that the defender seeks to avert. Thus, deadly defensive force can only be used to avert death, serious bodily injury, rape and other similarly grave harms.

The *necessity* condition requires that the level of defensive force be no greater than that necessary to avert the threatened harm. Thus, if Victim can ward off a deadly attack with his fists, he cannot use a gun. The *retreat* condition requires that if Victim can safely retreat from the threat, he must do so rather than use defensive force.

When properly analyzed, these three requirements turn out to be only one require-ment—proportionality. To see this, consider that the proportionality requirement is really a requirement that Victim must sacrifice lesser interests of his to avoid sacrificing greater interests of Attacker. Thus, if a wife can avoid getting slapped around by her husband only by using deadly force—she is not strong enough to avert the slapping by nonlethal means—then she must endure the slapping rather than take her husband's life.

The necessity requirement amounts to the same thing. Suppose Victim can avert a lethal attack by using a gun (deadly force) or by wrestling Attacker to the ground. The latter defense will be effective, but it will require Victim to expend great amounts of energy and to endure cuts and bruises. Using the gun requires little energy and will not injure Victim in the slightest. If the necessity requirement rules out use of the gun, then it amounts to a requirement that Victim sacrifice lesser interests of his—avoiding expenditure of great amounts of energy, avoiding cuts and bruises—in order to spare Attacker's greater interest (his life).

Note that there is another aspect to necessity that is neglected by theorists. Con-sider that Victim might have defensive options, but they may differ in likely effec-tiveness. Suppose Victim could use his fists against an IA, which would be unlikely to kill or seriously injure IA, and avert a lethal outcome (for Victim) with a 25 percent likelihood. Or he could use a baseball bat, which would be more likely to kill or seriously injure IA, and avert a lethal outcome with a 60 percent likelihood. Or he could fire a gun, which would be extremely likely to kill or seriously injure IA, and avert a lethal outcome with a 90 percent likelihood. Finally, he could throw a hand grenade at IA, which would kill IA and save Victim with almost a 100 percent likelihood. What force is *necessary* in such a case?

It is now easy to see how the retreat requirement also fits with proportionality. For it again requires Victim to sacrifice a lesser interest—namely, to be in a place where he has a right to be—in order to avoid sacrificing Attacker's greater interest in his life. Only some jurisdictions have a retreat doctrine; nevertheless, it is a logi-cal corollary of the more universal proportionality and necessity doctrines. (Query: How does or should one distinguish a requirement of retreat from a requirement that one not venture out on pain of forfeiting nonculpable self-defense—that one not go "looking for trouble"? And when is the requirement of retreat triggered? When the train carrying the killers arrives at the station? When the killers' shadows show them to be near the street where one is standing? When they are on that street but beyond gun range? Retreat must occur before it is too late to do so. But short of that, when is it premature?)

Typically, criminal law doctrine imposes these requirements in all instances where defensive deadly force might be employed. But it is a fair question whether, if Attacker is a CA, these requirements are warranted. For why should Victim be required to sacrifice *any* legitimate interest when faced with an Attacker who is culpable? (Notice that if Victim violates the proportionality, necessity and retreat requirements, he becomes a CA vis-à-vis Attacker.) Consider the example above of

234

one who faces being slapped around (but not seriously injured or killed) by a culpable assailant against whom she has no other defense than a lethal one. Why should she sacrifice her interest in bodily integrity and the avoidance of pain to spare the life of one who is culpably attacking her?

In other contexts, we can make committing even property crimes extremely dangerous for those who are culpable. With appropriate warnings we can protect our belongings with electric fences, razor wire, vicious dogs, deep moats and other mechanisms that render theft dangerous to the thief's life and limb. Presumably, we are permitted to do things which would escalate another's minor culpable act into a quite dangerous one that would entitle us to use deadly force to defend ourselves (for example, Victim could lie down on a path on his property that a trespasser drives on, escalating the CA's trespassing into a threat to Victim's life and permitting Victim to use deadly force if CA does not stop his vehicle). If this is correct, why is the case different when CA is threatening Victim with a minor rights violation, such as the infliction of pain, and Victim has no opportunity to escalate CA's offense into a more dangerous one, as in the preceding example (perhaps by attaching a bomb to her body that would detonate if she is slapped)? In general, why should not Victim be able to avoid pain from a CA by a credible threat of lethal response? Theorists of self-defense need to answer this question.

It may be the case that this is another place where it is important to distinguish CAs from IAs. Proportionality and its corollaries, necessity and retreat, seem appropriate when Attacker is an IA. If Victim is excused for privileging his life over the life of an IA, that excuse should be a limited one and should not apply when Victim can, at a lesser cost than loss of *his* life, spare the life of the IA. And perhaps he should be quite confident that Attacker is a CA and not an IA before he can use disproportionate or unnecessary force or stand his ground rather than retreat. Indeed, perhaps the proportionality/necessity/retreat doctrine can be justified in *all* cases on the grounds that Victim can never know for certain that Attacker is a CA rather than an IA. Still, if there is a level of confidence that Attacker is a CA that is sufficiently high, in theory at least, Victim perhaps should not have to limit his response to one that is proportional and necessary. (Nor should Third Party for that matter.)

(If Victim must retreat rather than kill an IA, what does this imply for soldiers resisting an unjustly aggressing army? If the enemy soldiers are mostly IAs—they are conscripts, dupes of their government's propaganda and so on—must the resisting soldiers retreat rather than kill? If retreating is tantamount to surrendering, and surrendering will lead to genocide, harsh oppression or further aggression, then resistance is nonculpable even if most of the enemy soldiers are IAs.)

(7) The provoking victim

If Victim has culpably created fear in an IA, then we have said that, as a CA or CF, Victim must attempt to communicate his present lack of an aggressive intention before IA can be converted into a CA and Victim can be justified (as opposed to excused) in defending himself. But suppose Victim has provoked a culpable overreaction by a CA, perhaps realizing there was a good chance the CA would overreact, or perhaps for the purpose of getting the CA to overreact. (Think of Charles Bronson in *Death Wish*, posing as a vulnerable target walking through Central Park at night, hoping that he gets attacked in a way that would make deadly defensive force justifiable. Or think of Jack Palance in *Shane*, insulting a hotheaded farmer in order to provoke him to draw his gun so that Palance can kill him in self-defense.) Should Victim be deemed nonculpable for defending himself against an overreaction to his provocation if his provocation anticipated, or even was meant to induce, that overreaction?

Conclusion

In this essay I have set forth what I believe are the significant building blocks of a theory of self-defense, and I have elaborated on why I believe they are the significant building blocks. I have not produced a complete theory of self-defense, but I have taken a stand on several of the components of such a theory.

Theories of self-defense currently on offer are inadequate because they fail to deal with, even if they recognize, the fact that self-defense and defense of others are always preemptive. They occur prior to the feared attack. Therefore, defenders must operate on the basis of their estimates of various probabilities—the probability that Attacker is a CA or an IA; the probability that unless prevented by defensive force, Attacker will indeed decide to launch the attack; and the probabilities of various harms if the attack is launched. Moreover, Victim's perspective and thus his estimate of those probabilities can differ from Third Party's perspective and estimate, which can differ from Fourth Party's, etc., and, post hoc, from a court's. Self-defense theory must come to grips with those realities of preemptive strikes, as well as with the significance of Attacker's culpability or innocence.

On the other hand, I believe self-defense theory should concern itself with culpability. It should be irrelevant that a culpable attack—say, by Third Party against someone he believes to be an IA—fails to inflict harm. Results should not matter, morally or legally.

Also, I have discussed beliefs, but I have nowhere discussed the *culpability* of those beliefs. That is because I do not think beliefs can themselves be culpable—or, put differently, that a person can be culpable for believing what he does. One can be culpable for acting on his beliefs if his beliefs, if true, do not justify his act. But that does not entail culpability for beliefs. And my rejection of culpability for beliefs entails that so-called negligence—failure to advert to risks which the "reasonable person" would have recognized—is *not* a form of culpability. That is why my discussion of the various beliefs about status and risk does not contain a discussion of reasonable (nonculpable) beliefs. All beliefs are "reasonable" from the believer's point of view, and only actions, not beliefs, are culpable.

Appendix 15.1: Chart of the Elements of a Successful Theory of Self-Defense

Perspectives:

Third Party
Victim
IA

Statuses:

CA
ACA

CP
CF
IA
AIA
Bystander

Perceived probabilities:

Re: Status
Re: Will Attack
Re: Attack's Consequences

Other factors:

The Numbers
Proportionality/Necessity/Retreat
Using Bystanders

Further Reading

For further reading, see: L. Alexander (1993) "Self-Defense, Justification, and Excuse," *Philosophy and Public Affairs* 22, 1: 53–66; L. Alexander and K. K. Ferzan (with S. J. Morse) (2009) *Crime and Culpability: A Theory of Criminal Law*, Cambridge: Cambridge University Press, ch. 4; L. Alexander and K. K. Ferzan (forthcoming 2012) "Danger: The Ethics of Preemptive Action," *Ohio State Journal of Criminal Law*; Y. Benbaji (2005) "Culpable Bystanders, Innocent Threats and the Ethics of Self-Defense," *Canadian Journal of Philosophy* 35: 623–40; K. Draper (2009) "Defense," *Philosophical Studies* 145(1): 69–88; K. K. Ferzan (2005) "Justifying Self-Defense," *Law and Philosophy* 24: 711–49; K. K. Ferzan (forthcoming 2012) "Culpable Aggression: The Basis for Moral Liability to Defensive Killing," *Ohio State Journal of Criminal Law*; C. Finkelstein (1996) "Self-Defense as a Rational Excuse," *University of Pittsburgh Law Review* 57: 621–49; H. Frowe (2010) "A Practical Account of Self-Defense," *Law and Philosophy* 29(3): 245–72; F. M. Kamm (2004) "Failures of Just War Theory: Terror, Harm, and Justice," *Ethics* 114(4): 650–92; M. Kamm (2005) "Terror and Collateral Damage: Are They Permissible?" *Journal of Ethics* 9(3–4): 381–401; F. Leverick (2006) *Killing in Self-Defense*, Oxford: Oxford University Press; J. McMahan (2002) *The Ethics of Killing: Problems at the Margins of Life*, New York: Oxford University Press; J. McMahan (2005) "The Basis of Moral Liability to Defensive Killing," *Philosophical Issues* 15(1): 386–405; J. McMahan (2005) "Self-Defense and Culpability," *Law and Philosophy* 24(6): 751–74; P. Montague (1981) "Self-Defense and Choosing Among Lives," *Philosophical Studies* 40(2): 207–19; P. Montague (1989) "The Morality of Self-Defense: A Reply to Wasserman," *Philosophy and Public Affairs* 18(1): 81–89; P. Montague (2000) "Self-Defense and Innocence: Aggressors and Active Threats," *Utilitas* 12(1): 62–78; M. Otsuka (1994) "Killing the Innocent in Self-Defense," *Philosophy and Public Affairs* 23(1): 74–94; M. Raymond (2010) "Looking for Trouble: Framing and the Dignitary Interest in the Law of Self-Defense," *Ohio State Law Journal* 71: 287–340; U. Steinhoff (2006) "Torture—The Case for Dirty Harry and Against Alan Dershowitz," *Journal of Applied Philosophy* 23: 337–53; J. J. Thomson (1991) "Self-Defense," *Philosophy and Public Affairs* 20(4): 283–310; S. Uniacke (1994) *Permissible Killing: The Self-Defence Justification of Homicide*, Cambridge: Cambridge University Press; and D. Wasserman (1987) "Justifying Self-Defense," *Philosophy and Public Affairs* 16(4): 356–78.

(ii)

CONTRACT

16

IS A CONTRACT A PROMISE?

Seana Valentine Shiffrin

Introduction: Some of What Is at Stake

Many, perhaps most, lawyers, theorists and lay people in the United States consider contracts to be "legally enforceable promises" (Fried 1981; Markovits 2004; Markovits 2011: 296, 314–18; Murphy 2007; Shiffrin 2007; Wilkinson-Ryan and Baron 2009: 420–23). That description seems initially confirmed by examples like the following: suppose that I promise to paint your house if you promise to pay me $3,000 for doing so. By exchanging these promises, we have formed a contract and each of us is both morally and legally obliged to perform. If one of us fails to perform, contract law empowers the other party to obtain a legal judgment and a remedy for the other's failure to keep her promise.

Associated with this description of a contract as a legally binding promise is the theoretical ambition to use the moral, common-sense features of promises as starting material to fashion a plausible legal theory of contracts. The thought is that if contracts have, at their foundations, the same moral relations that we describe as promises in our everyday social relations, that fact might provide the seedlings both of a justification for contract law and of a guide to the principles it should follow.

For example, on the justification front, this description may encourage the view that contract law exists to buttress the moral institution of promising, whether by facilitating the social benefits we glean from that institution; by vindicating and protecting the rights promisors transfer to promisees; by providing support and recognition for a valuable social relationship; or, on still other moral theories, by protecting promisees' reasonable expectations of legitimate public concern.

On the guidance front, such justifications may suggest that a contract's doctrinal principles should be designed in ways that support and enhance the moral practice of promising, that protect promisees' legitimate interests and/or, more weakly, in ways and for reasons that moral agents could accept while retaining their moral integrity and their stance of fidelity toward their promises (Shiffrin 2007: 713–18). From this perspective, lawyers, judges and scholars devising principles of contract law may have a great deal to gain by considering carefully what promises are, and why they are valuable to promisors, promisees and society at large. Of course, even on this view, the legal treatment of promises and the moral treatment of promises may vary substantially because our legitimate legal purposes may be both broader and narrower than our moral purposes. For instance, the law typically involves vindications of interests by outside parties (whereas that is rarer in moral life). But, while law's sweep is broader than morality's in that sense, it is narrower in another: in liberal societies at least, the law's interest in enforcing moral behavior *as such* is limited and has a circumference limited to what facilitates shared *social* and *political* life (Shiffrin 2007: 740–46). So, contract may be devoted to the enforcement of promises and that understanding may inform the proper design of contract doctrine, yet the distinctively *legal* interests at stake may, in some cases, entail that the legal enforcement of promises differs from the form taken by their moral enforcement and vindication.

The "promissory" characterization of contracts also suggests some challenges that contract theorists would need to confront, including how the legal and moral interests in promissory fidelity differ, whether and why *some* promises should be legally enforceable but not others, as well as what sorts of reasons might be offered to explain and justify why the legal treatment of legally enforceable promises should differ, if at all, from the analogous moral treatment of promises.

But, although viewing contracts as types of promises might prove theoretically rewarding (Fried 1981 and 2011; Markovits 2004; Shiffrin 2007), some theorists regard this perspective as misguided (DeMoor 1987; Penner 1996; Schwartz and Scott 2003; Pratt 2007; Craswell 2011). They believe that some or all contracts are better described as legally binding agreements or commitments that need not be *promissory* agreements or commitments (Penner 1996; Pratt 2007: 532). On their view, some contracts are also promises, but not all contracts are promises.

Indeed, a redescription of our initial example might cast doubt upon the immediate plausibility of the idea that contracts involve promises. Suppose that instead of *promising* to paint your house for $3,000, I *agree* to paint your house if, in return, you *agree* to pay me $3,000. "Agreement theorists" believe that in so doing, we would have created a contract, but without having *promised* to engage in these activities. For many agreement theorists, our agreements in this case would not necessarily carry with them the *moral* duties associated with promises, although we would be legally obliged to discharge them.

For these thinkers, the justifications for contract law and its particular doctrines need not bear any close relation to the moral structure of promises; nor is it evident for them that contract theorists should be attentive to questions about whether and how the institution of contract supports or detracts from moral agency or the moral practice of promising. Thus, although the separation of contracts from promises might deprive contract theory of what appears to be a natural resource to draw upon for justification and guidance, that separation may also be liberating. If contracts are not promises, then we may be freer to structure contract law in ways that allow us to achieve important purposes that we might not be empowered to achieve if contracts were promises. (Some critics take this stance only with respect to particular sorts of contracts or contracting parties, e.g., contracts between business firms or intimates (Schwartz and Scott 2003; Bagchi 2011).)

For example, if contracts are agreements but not inherently promises, then perhaps the law may *legitimately* authorize (and even encourage) contractors to break these agreements intentionally and pay their disappointed contractual partners a price (say the financial amount that performance would have been worth to the partner) if breaching the contract would allow one party to take advantage of a remarkable and more profitable opportunity that has unexpectedly arisen (Craswell 2001: 21–25; Craswell 2011: 11–20). Permitting such flexible arrangements might serve our overall economic welfare. It may encourage parties to make agreements (and thereby to make mutually advantageous exchanges) that they might otherwise be shy to forge if they thought they would be more inflexibly bound to perform.

On the other hand, if contracts are promises and contract law enforces promises in order to provide official recognition and support to the moral institution of promising, we may feel less comfortable with the idea of officially authorizing or encouraging parties to break their promises, at least not for the mere reason that it would be financially advantageous for them to do so. It is an important moral aspect of a promise that you commit to doing what you have promised, even when a better opportunity comes along, unless your promisee releases you from your commitment. Your promisee may, therefore, count on you to do what you said you would do; he may also count on you to be settled and focused on doing what you said you'd do, rather than scouting for better opportunities. Although being paid the financial value of the performance one expected might mitigate the sting of an intentional breach of a promise, most promisees will understandably not feel as though a promise was satisfied or taken seriously if they are paid a price by a promisor who simply no longer feels like performing. Promises are valued in part for the commitment by the promisor not to reconsider; what was promised is no longer up for grabs, but rather is a settled matter. If the promisor wishes to change course, she should seek the promisee's permission. Indeed, if promises are conceived as transfers of decision-making power (Owens 2006: 71–75), then a promisee may still legitimately feel wronged if a promisor pays him money while breaking his promise. The promisee may feel as though a decision that was his to make, namely whether to require or to waive performance, has been wrested from him without consultation; the promisor unilaterally treating payment as an unexceptionally satisfactory alternative pays no heed to the disrespect done to the distribution of decision-making authority established by the promise (Shiffrin 2007, 2008 and 2009).

So, if that analysis is right (and, of course, not everyone agrees), you can see why it might matter whether a contract is a promise or not. If it is a promise, then that fact may help us see how contract law should be structured, but we may have to investigate what function(s) promises serve, what is required of a promisor once she has made a promise, as well as what sorts of rules support and what sorts of rules disrespect, undermine or are in tension with the institution of promising. If a contract is not a promise, then some of these constraints will not confine how we construct the rules of contract. On the downside, however, it may then be less clear why we should enforce contracts and we may have to turn elsewhere for guidance about what justifications contract doctrines should answer to.

Assuming it does matter whether a contract is a promise or not—is it? Both the answer and the methodology of arriving at an answer are contested.

How We Characterize Contracts and Promises

Ordinary and Legal Language

A natural place to begin might be to characterize what promises are and then examine how we, and the law, characterize the relationship between contracts and promises. Unfortunately, it is difficult to identify a clear characterization of a promise around which a consensus has formed; indeed, some of the controversy about the relation between contracts and promises may well trace to disagreements about what is essential to promises. Still, to start somewhere, consider the rough, abbreviated idea that a promise is a voluntary commitment to perform (or to omit) an action the promisor has the authority to perform, a commitment qualified (sometimes explicitly) by apt conditions of performance, that works by transferring some form of the promisor's right to decide whether or not to perform that action to the promisee. In light of this transfer, the promisee has a right to expect (and often to demand) performance and has the concomitant power to use her transferred power or decision to waive or excuse the promisor's obligation of performance.

On this view of promise (and on many others), the idea that contracts are composed of promises seems, at first, like a plausible idea for a couple of reasons. First, legal authorities commonly describe contracts as "legally enforceable promises." The Restatement of Contracts, for example, defines a contract as "a promise or set of promises for the breach of which the law gives as a remedy, or the performance of which the law in some way recognizes as a duty" (American Law Institute 1981, § 1; see also § 75). Contract cases are saturated with references to promises that the parties made to one another and frequently refer to the parties as "promisors" and "promisees."

Second, making a promise (whether through the explicit language of "promise" or through other communicative means) is how contracts are fashioned. Of course, not all promises are legally binding. Under U.S. law, a promise must either be supported by some offering by the other party in return (whether a promise or a performance or through the other party's active and reasonable reliance). But, interestingly, in the U.S., a promise need not be made with the specific, positive intention to be legally binding; just by promising, without an eye to the legal consequences, one may make a legally binding contract (ibid., § 21).

Third, upon making a promise, contracts have the same elemental features of promises. The recipient of a contractual commitment has a right to expect performance and if performance is not forthcoming (and no valid justification or excuse pertains), this suffices to show breach, just as it would with a promise. Further, just as with a promise, the recipient of a contractual commitment has the power to waive or excuse performance. These practices provide some support for the view that contracts are constituted by promises and for the working hypothesis that contract law is an institution meant to support promissory relationships and trust, to encourage promissory fidelity, to react to promissory infidelity and to protect those whose trust was induced by others' promises.

A Challenge to the Ordinary-Language Argument

One may object that this appeal to our linguistic practices and the law's own perspective on promises does not yield conclusive results. We and the law may *call* the sorts of commitments contract law recognizes "promises" but that semantic institutional practice may not settle the matter. It may just amount to convenient shorthand or the coining of a legal term of art, one that confusingly overlaps with, but is not identical to, a common lay term. (This is not unheard of. For example, the commonplace meaning of "assault" differs from its legal meaning. In common parlance, an assault involves unconsensual physical contact, and is usually understood to be violent, whereas, in law, an assault need not involve physical contact but may be accomplished just through a *threat* that causes the victim to apprehend the possibility of violence. "Burglary" too has a technical legal meaning that resembles, but differs from, the common meaning; commonly, burglary is thought to just involve breaking and entering, but in legal contexts, burglary often requires a further intent to commit a felony.)

Indeed, with respect to "contract" and "promise," other practices suggest that at least some legal contracts reasonably fail to carry with them the moral significance of promises; this may lend support to the hypothesis that the use of "promise" in legal contexts is more a term of art. As Michael Pratt has argued, one can make sense of the following question: "It's a contract, sure. But is it also a promise?" Moreover, the following exchange (a variation on an example of Pratt's) seems entirely sensible and possible: Meg asks Peter to build her a bookcase for $1,000. Peter says, "I'll happily *contract* with you to do so, but I only wish to be legally bound. I don't care to be *morally* bound to a friend over a business matter. So, I won't *promise* to build the bookcase but I will place myself legally on the hook." The sensible possibility of a stance like Peter's, Pratt concludes, shows that contracts need not be promises and that one could create a contract without thereby promising (Pratt 2008: 807–9).

To elaborate: Pratt's interpretation is that a contract often involves a concomitant (morally tinged) promise but it does not do so necessarily. Peter's distinction clarifies the separation between the two commitments. This distinction may seem reinforced by the fact that different remedies are available for breach of promise, morally, and for breach of contract, legally. The moral remedy for failing to perform a promise without excuse would generally be to perform; failing that, the moral consequences for breaching a moral promise may include others' disapproval, reputational damage, guilt and other forms of recrimination, as well as some sort of compensation to the promisee where appropriate. For unexcused breach of contract, the legal remedy is, typically, the (required) provision of expectation damages, that is, an amount of financial compensation meant to give the promisee the financial equivalent of the position she would have been in had the contract been performed. Punitive damages, the law's standard civil remedy that expresses disapprobation, are generally disallowed for garden-variety breach of contract. When Peter denies he is making a promise but affirms that he is making a contract, he may be thought to be clarifying that, should he fail to perform, he would appropriately be susceptible to demands for expectation damages but not appropriately castigated, blamed or otherwise regarded as having acted wrongly from a moral point of view.

Answering Pratt's Challenge

A different interpretation of this exchange is possible, however, that avoids the counterintuitive, even "oxymoronic" (Kimel 2010: 220), conclusion that a contract has been made without a promissory commitment or that a contract and some kind of commitment have been made, yet without moral significance. Instead of interpreting the example as Pratt does, we might instead think that, through his clarification, Peter does not successfully rebuff a promissory commitment so much as clarify and constrain the promissory terms to which he commits himself.

That is, one may insist that contracts are, in fact, promissory commitments, whatever protestations or silent reservations contractors may make to the contrary. Peter's effort to distinguish between a promise and a contract and to attest that he is making only the latter misdescribes what he achieves. Counter to his own description, he has specified the terms of his promise in a way that departs from the standard promissory terms that would be presumed absent explicit clarification; he has not evaded making a promise, but rather has altered (or clarified) the terms of the promise he makes when he forms the contract.

245

He may have clarified in one (or both) of two ways. First, in my variation on Pratt's example, the fact that the parties are friends about to enter into a business relationship may contribute significantly to the hypothetical's intelligibility. Peter may be clarifying that he regards this promissory commitment as more on the model of a promise between strangers than one between friends. The moral impact of most promises between friends encompasses more than just the promissory commitment as such to performance. The moral connotation of promising to perform a service for a friend usually involves a larger commitment to care for the underlying interests of one's friend that are promoted by that service (see also Shiffrin 2011: 170–72; Dannenberg 2010). The duty to promote those interests is less concrete and specific than the promissory core (namely to perform (or omit) a specified activity or activities); this subsidiary obligation is usually limited to reasonable efforts proportionate to the effort envisioned in the promised performance. But, still, between friends, although one needn't make a promise, once one does, one often implicitly assumes some obligation that ranges beyond the particular performance promised. In Kantian lingo, one assumes a perfect duty to perform what is promised and, also, alongside the promise, a more open-ended, imperfect obligation of care toward the friend's underlying interest. In less Kantian jargon, we might say that one *has* to do what one has committed to do through the promise, even when other tempting opportunities arise, but that the relation of friendship tends to add, on the occasion of the promise, a looser obligation to try to promote the underlying interest. For this secondary obligation, by contrast with the promissory obligation, the occasions of satisfaction may be more flexibly identified and may more readily give way if there are competing considerations to act otherwise.

For example, suppose you ask me to promise to take you to the airport. I know you ask not because you lack funds for a cab, but because you are nervous before a flight and want company so you are not alone mulling over your potentially imminent demise. Suppose after taking you, we discover that your flight is delayed for two hours. Then, if I am free, there may be a reasonable moral presumption that I will continue to keep you company because the underlying aim promoted by the promise has not been satisfied, even though the promised performance has been rendered. Or, if I promise to help you to build five bookshelves and we understand that the reason you want them is to tidy the unholy mess your office has become, then when we discover that five is not enough and you need six, then I may have a loose obligation to help with the sixth. This further duty is not part of the promise, per se, but may be a presumed concomitant responsibility between friends.

When friends do business with one another, however, it may be rather unclear whether the presumptions of friendship apply or whether the promise's penumbra extends strictly only to the specified performance. Peter's clarification may underscore that his promise to build does not carry with it the further duties often implicated through undertaking a project for a friend. By saying he "contracts but does not promise," he may be taken to convey that he is only promising to build the shelves but nothing more; that his promise covers only the moral territory typically associated with promises between strangers rather than that traversed through promises between friends.

Peter may also, or in the alternative, be clarifying the terms of his promise in another way. Typically, when one contracts to paint a house, one makes a promise *to paint a house*. But, in this case, Peter may be understood to clarify that all he is promising to do is either to perform or to pay the monetary equivalent of performance—expectation damages—which is typically all that the law would enforce were he to fail to paint. That is, he is not promising to perform, in particular, but rather only promising to do exactly what the law would require him to do by virtue of making the contract, namely either to perform or to pay its monetary equivalent. Controversially, some theorists even take the view that this disjunctive is *always* the default, standard content of the promise between contractors, or at least between contracting businesspeople (Macaulay 1963: 61; Markovits and Schwartz 2011; but see Macaulay 1963: 63; Bernstein 2001: 1762–88; Wilkinson-Ryan 2010: 637). Less controversially, most agree that it is *possible* to make such a disjunctive promise, especially if one's eye is fixed upon the law's reaction to failed performance, although some regard this as a rather shabby sort of promise, of a sort that should not be made a habit and preferably should not be articulated so opaquely.

Thus, Peter's remarks might be understood to amount to the clarification that this is a business deal only, without the further benefits associated with promises between friends, or the even starker clarification that he is not committing to perform per se but only to "perform or pay." Either way, he has not evaded promissory commitment, but merely shifted its terms from what they would otherwise naturally be assumed to be. Both of these interpretative possibilities emanate from the fact that, as a default, what morality expects of a promisor often exceeds what the law would expect or enforce of a promisor through the law of contract. Although morality presumes a more robust commitment than the law enforces, it is possible for a promisor, through explicit clarification, to rebut that presumption and to forge a more limited and defined moral commitment that more closely tracks the law's minimal expectations.

Contract Without Promise or Contract as Promise?

Which interpretation is better? Pratt's interpretation that legal commitment may be hived off from promissory commitment; or the alternative interpretation that recasts Peter's self-representation as an indirect way of clarifying the limits of his promissory commitment?

On one hand, Pratt's interpretation may seem more charitable because it represents Peter as having self-knowledge and as accurately reporting his status: legally but not morally bound. The alternative interpretation involves attributing some sort of inaccuracy to Peter. On the other hand, Pratt's interpretation also involves a reconfiguration of contract law's ubiquitous self-description that it enforces *promises*, and the attribution to the contract law of a term of art that it does not treat as one. So, neither interpretation can avoid, it seems, some sort of attribution of error and consequent redescription. Principles of charitable interpretation will not settle the question.

One further consideration may speak on behalf of the "contracts are promises" interpretation, that is, the one that insists that Peter has, through contracting, promised *something*. At this point in the dialectic, both positions share as common ground that Peter's formation of a contract and his speech surrounding it may entail that he need not feel morally compelled to ensure Meg's study is neat and that her every book has found a home; and, further, that given his clarification, Peter need not even feel morally compelled to build the shelves, that he needn't feel guilty if he does not, and that Meg cannot legitimately form *moral* expectations that Peter will actually build them rather than compensate her if he does not. Okay. Now let's suppose he does not build the shelves simply because he does not feel like it and not because he has any strong reason or excuse for omitting carpentry. Isn't he *morally* bound without prompting to pay Meg expectation damages, i.e., compensation for his chosen failure to perform? If hiring another replacement carpenter would be more expensive, shouldn't Peter be (and feel) *morally* obliged to compensate Meg for the extra expense she incurs due to Peter's agreement and subsequent breach? Wouldn't we find it *morally* outrageous if Peter did not pay and if, instead, he declared, "All my agreement with you does is to render me legitimately legally vulnerable to a suit, so go ahead and sue me. I predict you will win"? If he doesn't make that thought explicit, but ducks his head and quietly acts on this rationale, it would seem morally objectionable all the same. Whether Peter was a friend or a stranger, such behavior would be morally wrong in light of Peter's commitment. This suggests that it is not true that Peter has made merely a *legal* commitment, but rather that he has also made a minimal *moral* commitment: to perform or pay damages. If that is true, then it seems we should conclude that he has made a promise (to build the shelves or pay damages) by making a contract, albeit one with unusual, disjunctive terms.

In response, Pratt might concede that, in this elaborated scenario, Peter behaves immorally, not because he breaks a promise but because he fails voluntarily to discharge a clear legal obligation and instead requires Meg to litigate and to deploy the coercive arm of the state. That is, Pratt may suggest that the moral wrong emanates from Peter's alienated, desultory posture to his legal duty to Meg rather than from his breach of a *promise* to her. Perhaps. Or, perhaps, Peter morally wrongs Meg *both* by breaking his promise and by shirking his legal duty. Imagine that after he was scheduled to build the shelves, the legal system changed its position and decided that expectation damages were no longer available in contract, but only restitution, or that contracts for relatively small amounts of money no longer gave rise to legal liability. If Peter then were to refuse to pay anything to Meg because his legal duty had altered, would it really seem that he did nothing at all that was morally untoward? That seems hard to swallow and suggests that the source of his moral commitment is not reducible to the content of his enforceable legal obligation. Even so, Pratt might challenge whether the residual moral commitment emanated from a promise or, maybe, from the force of the expectations Peter cultivated in Meg at the time of contracting.

Although we might pursue the matter even further, perhaps we've wrung most of the heuristic value from this somewhat strange hypothetical example. Rather than further attempts to nail down which characterization of Peter's immoral behavior is more apt and whether there is a clear semantic answer to the question of whether a contract is a promise, we might instead switch gears and think more directly about what is normatively appropriate or preferable.

Do Contract Doctrines Settle the Question?

How else might we approach the question of whether contracts are promises? One approach, deployed by some critics, is to ask whether contract law consistently treats promises as contracts and whether contract law treats contracts the same way morality treats promises. Similarities are thought to support the thesis that contracts are promises and, more often, dissimilarities are thought to undermine that thesis. Penner, for instance, argues that contracts are not promises because under the consideration doctrine in Anglo-American law, unilateral promises, by which I mean promises offered without a reciprocal promise or performance in return, are true promises but do not suffice as contracts, which require some form of joint agreement (Penner 1996: 328–30). Promissory estoppel aside, that's true enough, but it only undermines the claim that all promises can be contracts, a stronger claim than the one under consideration. More generally, these points beg the question against those contract as promise theorists who claim that contract law has not fully faced the implications of contracts being promises. The consideration doctrine, for instance, which Penner cites as evidence of the nonidentity of contract and promise, is exactly what Charles Fried cites as the shortcoming of contract law and the suggested target of reform; to Fried, the consideration doctrine does not disprove that contracts are promises but rather that contract law has not, so to speak, fully internalized the significance of contracts being promises (Fried 1981: 28–39; Fried 2011).

That chicken and egg problem is likely to recur with respect to other examples involving particular doctrines, e.g., contract law's relative insensitivity to subjective intent in formation (Barnett 2011) or to objective intent in performance or breach (Kimel 2010: 225–27). Critics of the contract as promise view will see divergent doctrines as counterexamples, whereas proponents of the claim will 1) dispute the critic's underlying view of promise (e.g., thinking promises also involve objective intent in their formation); or 2) regard these doctrines as targets of criticism; or 3) take these divergent doctrines to be explained by reasons distinctive to features of legal enforcement or regulation that render it sensible for the legal treatment of such promises to differ from their moral treatment (Shiffrin 2007: 719–39). Mid-level doctrinal points, then, are unlikely to do much to resolve the dispute, because whether doctrinal similarity or dissimilarity is revealing depends ultimately on the underlying normative arguments about whether and how contract and promise should be strongly, if complexly, tied to one another.

Should Contracts Be Built on Promises?

It seems that we have to address the larger question of whether we should endorse a conception of contract built upon the foundation of promises or whether we should rather endorse a division, understanding contracts to bear only a loose connection to promises. An interlocutor might concede that contemporary institutions of contract (and ordinary language) correctly regard promises as foundational and necessary elements of contracts, but still question whether we *should* craft the legal institution in that way. Perhaps we *should* have a "law of agreements" understood to be distinct from, though sometimes overlapping, the moral practice of promising. How exactly would these legally cognizable agreements differ from promises? The suggestion might be first, that they, in themselves, have no moral force directly, but only insofar as they generate legal duties, whereas moral promises have direct moral force. Second, the legal significance of these agreements, as we would construct it, need not be influenced by or predictably connected to the moral significance of their promissory counterparts.

A proponent of contract as promise might question whether this suggestion is truly conceivable, specifically whether there could be legitimate agreements (as opposed to illegitimate agreements, e.g., between criminals to rob a bank) that produced legal duties but no direct moral duties. Is it really possible to declare that one will make a commitment to another person (or organization) but—just by fiat—successfully declare that it will not have the moral power of a promise? That's a valid concern, but for our purposes, let's put it to the side. Supposing it were possible to create a legal institution that enforced "agreements," and that by its own understanding, these agreements were distinct from promises and that promissory norms would have no influence, direct or indirect, on the legal treatment of these agreements. Would this division be wise?

As was canvassed at the outset, having parallel institutions of contract and promise may offer contract (and maybe promise) a source of justification and a source of guidance (perhaps only partial) about what shape its legal norms should take (Shiffrin 2007: 717–22; but see Craswell 1989: 490, 508–16). It may also render the institution more familiar and predictable to ordinary, non-lawyer citizens. On the other hand, a divisionist approach may permit innovation and flexibility in contract that the parallel approach does not.

Of course, in thinking about the normatively preferable institutional arrangement, our thinking should not be confined to the effect on contract law. We should also consider the impact on the moral relationships and on our moral culture of promising (Shiffrin 2007; Murphy 2007).

Moral Arguments for the Division of Contract and Promise

Some argue that it behooves the moral culture if promising and contracting, and the norms associated with them, are kept distinct. On the one hand, some find the norms of promising too intimate and beneficent to extend to relations between strangers, mere business associates or impersonal organizations; having a distinctive relation of contract supports the development of limited and constrained relations of trust between strangers without inappropriately forcing on them the closer relations and stronger duties associated with promissory partners (cf. Kimel 2003: 78–80).

Others worry that an overly tight connection between promise and contract threatens some of the values realized within the moral practice of promising. For example, if contract law were to enforce familial promises or promises without consideration, some worry that the background threat of enforcement might alter the meaning of such promises and their fulfillment; the motives for promissory compliance might become mixed or become perceived as mixed by recipients, and thereby deprive participants in such promises of the opportunity to use them and their fulfillment to express affection, voluntary beneficence and/or promissory fidelity clearly (cf. Eisenberg 1997: 847–49; Kimel 2003: 27–29; Bartrum 2011: 225, 234–35; Bagchi 2011).

Is Contract as Promise Too Morally Demanding?

The first argument—that, in essence, contract as promise renders contracts too morally demanding and generates closer relationships than contractual parties reasonably seek—seems misguided. First, the treatment of contracts as promises need not involve imposing legal duties that would transform all contractual promises into the tighter bonds associated with promissory relations between intimates. Many of those tighter bonds of care and concern for the aims and goals of one's promissory partner, as I argued earlier, are closely associated with promising, but usually, strictly speaking, are not encompassed within the promissory commitment itself. True, taking contracts as promises seriously might entail some legal change that would be more demanding on promisors. Contract law might, in some cases of intentional and opportunistic breach, better reflect that contracts are promises by resorting, at least on some occasions, to stronger remedies than it does now, e.g., a more liberal use of specific performance, disgorgement or punitive damages. Even if it were to do so, however, that would not amount to creating fiduciary duties between contractual partners or requiring contractors to show care and concern for one another. Treating contract as promise consistently, even if it would amount to some legal reforms that render enforcement of contracts more rigorous, is not tantamount to requiring contractors to show deep care and concern, to form close relationships or otherwise to treat each other as intimates.

Moreover, it isn't morally obvious that we should promote the sort of extreme version of an arm's-length relation between contractors imagined by this objection. Why should the law *aim* to encourage parties to negotiate the distribution and exchange of socially important resources but to do so within relationships featuring only thin, almost alienated, (perceived) moral bonds to each other? Some proponents of this objection celebrate, for example, the efficient breach which, when performed opportunistically, involves unilaterally reneging on a commitment to one party merely in order to take advantage of a better, late-appearing opportunity with another. *That* sort of disdain for the reasonable and cultivated interests and expectations of one's contractual partner in performance as such, or even in participating in a decision to modify the arrangement in light of later-appearing opportunities and needs, does not seem intrinsically worth protecting or encouraging; we need not protect that sort of relation of indifference to one contracting party's perspective on how the matter should be resolved in order to generate a contrast that will make the character of intimate relations meaningful. Cultivating an alienated stance toward others outside one's closest circle may fuel one sort of market efficiency, but does so at the risk of some troubling moral, relational and social costs. Some worry that it flirts with, and even spills over into, the sort of uninvolved, commodifying, exploitative and deeply self-interested stance toward one's neighbors that, in the long run, is incompatible with a fulfilling life and a sustainable community.

Even if that distant stance could be restricted or compartmentalized to mere business relations, that compartment is not discrete, small or insignificant. Business relations, in aggregate and often in the particular, involve transfers of important resources, major expenditures of time and large amounts of human contact and interaction (as in the employment market, for example). With respect to such significant interactions, it seems perverse to suggest as an ethical *ideal* that participants should proceed at the degree of arm's-length distance that suggests the other party smells. While, of course, the law is not the only important social and moral mechanism by which to resist the deterioration of social relations, at the same time, the law is an important social institution whose pronouncements and reasons sometimes exert normative force, sociologically. Further, the law aspires to represent our joint collective reason. Hence, whether or not it legitimately falls within the law's sphere of responsibility to prevent drastically alienated relations or not, it seems appropriate to insist that the law not regard alienation as an end around which to design doctrines and decide cases.

Does Contract as Promise Dilute the Moral Significance of Promises?

Hence, the second argument, the one about dilution or adulteration of the moral practice, seems like the more serious one. Two related concerns may be at issue: first, that the background of contractual enforcement may alter the motives of promisors in undesirable ways and second, that the minimal requirements of contract may substitute for the norms of promising, transmogrifying what should be the legal floor into a moral ceiling. Meeting minimal legal requirements may come to seem morally sufficient and thereby dilute (in perception) morality's richer demands, whereas, if the two practices were kept conceptually distinct, the law's treatment of contract could not threaten to contaminate the moral practice of promising. Although there are real hazards here, I suspect these concerns are not dispositive.

These concerns about adulteration and dilution sometimes take an expressive cast and sometimes an empirical cast. We might worry that by creating a legal institution of contract, we are expressing or suggesting that contractors' motives for performance should be driven by the law's decrees and by the law's reactions to nonperformance (Bagchi 2011). Consequently, we might then care to distinguish between contract and promise because it is important to the moral values of promise that they be achieved through voluntary performance, from some sort of respect for the promisee's rights or concern for his interests.

Or, in the (nonexclusive) alternative, we might worry that whether or not the existence of the legal institution of contract suggests that legal reasons should dominate the motives of contractors, that empirically, legal recognition and legal remedies have just that effect; they come to dominate contractors' motives and so, if contract and promise are identified with one another, legal motives for compliance will displace, or "crowd out," moral motives and thereby strip some important moral practices of their full meaning.

Floating somewhere in between the expressive claim and the empirical claim is the concern that the identification of contract with promise may give promisees some reason, whether or not it is a decisive or accurate reason, to suspect promisors of complying with their promissory commitments from fear of legal repercussions. Promisors who transact against the backdrop of the prospect of this anxiety, in turn, lose the opportunity to express their promissory fidelity purely, without the suspicion that their motives are more self-interested than other-regarding. Let's call that concern the worry that contract rules "cloud out" clear moral and affective forms of expression.

Does Contract Law Aim to Figure in Promisors' Motives for Compliance?

The expressive version of this concern seems strained. It reflects an implausibly narrow view of what legal institutions express to the public about the activity they recognize and regulate. That is, the existence of a legal institution is not well interpreted to convey any collective desire that contractors' motives be dominated by responsiveness to the legal institution and its decrees. We might adopt an institution of contract as a form of recognition of and support for the value of promising: among other things, to provide blueprints to the parties for how to handle hard or unforeseen circumstances as well a way to render promises official and recognizable to third parties. Rather than communicating something about ideal motives for compliance to potential contractors, the legal institution may aim to empower promisors by providing them with the stamp of certification or even approval. It may be used to identify or qualify participants for other resources (like marital benefits, ownership upon dissolution of a partnership, creditor's rights in case of bankruptcy, etc.) or induce third parties to proffer other opportunities (e.g., other contracts such as loans) to one party given that she or he has already secured other recognized contractual partners. This is, for example, how many understand the legal institution of marriage, a particular form of legal recognition for both a relationship and particular promises within it; scant few, not even the critics of marriage, believe that the expressive point of the legal institution of marriage is to convey that marital partners should participate in marital activities in deference to the legal institution's recognition and interest in marriage. Quite the contrary.

In the case of marriage and in the case of other contracts, we might also adopt a legal institution of contract to provide a backstop of security and assurance of protection for contractors in case standard practices of compliance falter or encounter obstacles; providing a backstop in no way conveys that we hope or aim for contractors to substitute legal-regarding motives for performance for the correct relational and moral motives. This backstop function should also be familiar from the case of torts and criminal law. Although the aim of a backstop may be to provide additional and failsafe reasons for compliance for the tempted or the improperly motivated, no one believes that civil and criminal prohibitions on assault and remedies for noncompliance are intended to *substitute* among generally compliant citizens for the more powerful reasons for respecting others' rights to security and bodily autonomy. So, why take it that the expressive aim of contract law, in particular, is to displace the foundational moral motives for making and keeping contracts?

To be sure, legal institutions do often aim to generate reasons for action even for compliant citizens, whether through the mechanism of direct regulation or through mechanisms like subsidies. Where, prior to the law, citizens (whether as a collective or as individuals) do not otherwise have a reason or a decisive reason to perform an action, the law may provide such reasons. Laws identifying what side of the road to drive on, what form to use to fill out one's tax return, where to mail one's return, where to dispose of recyclables, or laws subsidizing particular modes of environmentally sustainable transport, etc., aim to give citizens a reason to do something on the very grounds that that action is legally specified or encouraged; the prior moral reasons to act either did not decisively point in that direction or would direct otherwise unless there were official direction or security that others would have a decisive reason to act in coordination. But although the law does, on occasion, aim to provide leading reasons for actions, there is little reason to suppose that the case of contract has *that* expressive meaning with respect to promissory fidelity, given that there is already sufficient moral reason to perform.

Could Contract as Promise Exert a Poor Influence on Promisors' Motives?

Even if the expressive concern can be answered, is there more cause for alarm that, empirically, the institution of contract as promise will encourage people to substitute legal-regarding motives for moral motives? Or, that in worrying that others will do so, important forms of moral expression will be sufficiently ambiguated or eclipsed? These possibilities are, in principle, important ones, but without further evidence, it isn't clear that they represent significant threats. To merit serious concern, it seems that at least three further things would have to be shown. First, that crowding out and clouding out are more serious risks for contract than for tort or criminal law, serious enough to suggest a conceptual division between contract and promise. In the case of tort, there is little serious concern that legal regulations on bodily contact have come to dominate the motives of citizens or that citizens believe their safe passage across the streets is generally a matter attributable to law and not to basic civic decency. Why should we worry more about the case of contract law's infiltrating and tainting moral citizens' primary motives of promissory fidelity and trustworthiness, rather than its working as a form of official recognition and source of backstop assurance? Second, it would need to be shown that to the extent that these concerns are serious, they resist effective management through institutional design, clarification and public communication. To avoid crowding out moral motives, it may be important that the purpose and rationale for legal regulations and reactions be clarified—that they be presented as guidance measures, backstop measures and as the community's remedial reaction to wrongdoing, rather than their presentation remaining open to the interpretation that they are prices for the alternative behavior of breach or enforcement measures reflecting distrust in citizens' moral virtue or fidelity. It is unclear that the law would crowd out moral motives where the law's purpose was clearly designed and explained as aiming to express, supplement and buttress a normative expectation, rather than as aiming to replace the moral culture with a pricing scheme or with legal-regarding motives (Bowles and Polania Reyes 2009: 20–21; Bowles 2011: 57–65, 72–74). Further, in many of the documented cases of external incentives or regulations crowding out self-regulation or self-regulatory moral motives, specifically delineated fines, quotas or financial incentives were presented as reactions to particular choices (Gneezy and Rustichini 2000; Bowles 2008); this specificity may encourage the view that they are prices for behavior, suggesting that the behavior was discretionary if the agent were willing to pay. This may provide a further argument for remedial design based on standards of proportionality and fairness, which are both explicitly normative in content but somewhat uncertain in application, rather than upon remedial design measures emphasizing precise and predictable rules, formulas, multipliers or caps (Shiffrin 2010: 1240–45).

Might Divisionist Approaches Dilute Moral Expectations?

Indeed, the empirical concern about contract diluting moral culture may run in the other direction, operating as a criticism of divisionist approaches. Even if we could conceive of contracts as entirely distinct from (and not building upon the foundation of) promises, we might worry. Given the similarities between agreements that are contracts and agreements that are promises, an official division between the two domains (manifested by an authorized practice of looser fidelity with respect to contract, for instance) might yield potential inadvertent seepage from contract to promise. Because the law often establishes (and deliberately expresses) a baseline of *minimally* morally permissible behavior, a posture of encouraging an instrumental approach to fidelity with respect to agreements that are contracts might transmit misleading blueprints and potentially corrosive habits toward agreements as a general matter, that could, in turn, infect our moral habits and intuitions about agreements that are promises. We might try to clarify that contracts and promises are distinct entities, to thereby enable people to make a moral distinction between their appropriate treatments. But an effective and tight compartmentalization between the two may not take root in the soil of a basically artificial, contrived distinction. Unless we can point to larger, more fundamental differences between the agreements that make up contracts and the agreements that make up promises other than just that a division instrumentally suits our convenience, the strong similarities between them may encourage interchangeable treatment. If we begin to rely on what passes as minimal respect for one sort of agreement, that practice and habit may risk that, operationally, we will lower the felt baseline for what is expected and counts as minimal respect for the other. Of course, this empirical counter-concern, like the other empirical claims so far discussed, would require further investigation and evidence to merit any strong conclusions.

Does Contract's Proximity to Promise Affect the Meaning of Promissory Practices?

Finally, turning to the "clouding out" concern, to regard it as serious we would want a reason to think that individual and social efforts at clarification could not succeed to disambiguate individual motives (as they seem to in the case of most people's observable reasons for refraining from intentional torts). In the case of gift promises, for example, if they were legally enforceable even absent detrimental reliance, their serving as expressions of personal care (rather than as legal duties) might be ascertainable from the fact that they were voluntarily offered and from the evident spirit with which they were carried out—whether from a continuing spirit of affection or from the compulsion of duty. Promisees truly anxious about the meaning of the performance could also generate clarification by explicitly waiving the legal duty to perform and then observing whether the promisor acts nonetheless.

Two further points might be made about the clouding-out concern. Although the backdrop of legal enforcement may risk ambiguating the expressive meaning of voluntary performance, it also provides a distinctive expressive opportunity. It allows a gift promisor, for example, to indicate that her desire to make a gift is serious enough that she is willing to express it in ways that render her legally accountable; although, if the concern bears out that the prospect of legal enforcement eclipses the clarity and transparency of moral action, that expressive opportunity probably pales in comparison. More importantly, if the institution of contract does ambiguate moral performance in certain pockets of promissory life like those involving gift promises, the contract as promise approach has the resources to acknowledge this. If the purpose of legal enforcement of promises is to buttress the moral culture of promising, but if with respect to certain promises, legal enforcement overly complicates, confuses or contaminates the moral culture, then that provides a legally distinctive reason for abstaining from enforcement in that domain; the contract as promise approach need not treat all promises as contracts. Its exemption of some promises from contractual enforcement on grounds relating to the purposes of law (e.g., enforcing only those promises that are demonstrable to third parties) or to the health of the moral culture resonate consistently with a general approach that aims to take promises seriously.

Thus, I doubt whether concerns about the effects of (a well-designed) contract law on our moral culture provide substantial reasons to treat contract and promise as entirely distinct domains (assuming it is possible to do so), and I believe the contrary conclusion is more apt.

A Final Moral Argument for Contract as Promise

A concluding consideration both about the meaning of the divisionist proposal and its fairness: although the expressive meaning of the law is not always simple to divine, as I have explored, one might worry about the expressive significance of the divisionist proposal. It would intentionally and deliberately hive contract from promise and, thereby, deliberately endorse a legal regime that provides no legal enforcement and no direct and general public recognition of promises as such. We often intend the law and our legal practices to convey, and they often are understood to convey, messages and patterns of what constitutes morally minimally acceptable (if not, as discussed above, optimal) activity. Against the backdrop of a legal system that includes a system of tort, a system of property recognition and enforcement, and a system of recognition of enforcement of individual rights, this omission might seem to convey that promises, bonds of trust and their breach matter less than these other goods and wrongs the system does recognize. On its face, it is hard to justify that hierarchy from a political point of view, given the tremendous significance of practices of fidelity and trust to a flourishing social system (Bowles 2011: 47; Shiffrin 2007: 714). Why should we think that suffering breach of trust does not rate public concern but that minor property damage or injury to reputation does? It would be hard for a moral agent to accept this hierarchy as a reasonable public rationale, even if its implementation might provide greater economic benefits in the aggregate and for particular promisors and promisees.

References

American Law Institute (1981) Restatement of the Law, Second, Contracts, §§ 1, 21 and 75.

Bagchi, A. (2011) "Separating Contract and Promise," *Florida State University Law Review* 38: 709–58.

Barnett, R. E. (2011) "Contract Is Not Promise; Contract Is Consent," *Suffolk University Law Review* 45: 647–65.

Bartrum, I. (2011) "Thoughts on the Divergence of Contract and Promise," *Canadian Journal of Law and Jurisprudence* 24: 225–38.

Bernstein, L. (2001) "Private Commercial Law in the Cotton Industry: Creating Cooperation Through Rules, Norms, and Institutions," *Michigan Law Review* 99: 1724–1790.

Bowles, S. (2008) "Policies Designed for Self-Interested Citizens May Undermine 'The Moral Sentiments': Evidence from Economic Experiments," *Science* 320: 1605–1609.

—— (2011) "Is Liberal Society a Parasite on Tradition?" *Philosophy and Public Affairs* 39: 46–81.

—— and Polania Reyes, S. (forthcoming 2012) "Economic Incentives and Social Preferences: Substitutes or Complements?" *Journal of Economic Literature*.

Craswell, R. (1989) "Contract Law, Default Rules, and the Philosophy of Promising," *Michigan Law Review* 88: 489–529.

—— (2001) "Two Economic Theories of Enforcing Promises," in P. Benson, ed., *Theory of Contract Law*, New York: Cambridge University Press, pp. 19–44.

—— (2011) "Promises and Prices," *Suffolk University Law Review* 45: 735–76.

Dannenberg, J. I. (2010) "Promising as Valuing," in *Promising as Paradigm* (Ph.D. diss., University of California Los Angeles).

De Moor, A. (1987) "Are Contracts Promises?" in J. Eekelaar and J. Bell, eds., *Oxford Essays in Jurisprudence*, Oxford: Clarendon Press, pp. 103–24.

Eisenberg, M. (1997) "The World of Promising and the World of Gifts," *California Law Review* 87: 821–66.

Fried, C. (1981) *Contract as Promise*, Cambridge, Mass.: Harvard University Press.

—— (2011) "*Contract as Promise* Thirty Years On," *Suffolk University Law Review* 45: 961–78.

Gneezy, U. and Rustichini, A. (2000) "A Fine Is a Price," *Journal of Legal Studies* 29: 1–18.

Kimel, D. (2003) *From Promise to Contract*, Oxford: Hart Publishing.

—— (2010) "The Morality of Contract and Moral Culpability in Breach," *King's Law Journal*, 21: 213–31.

Macaulay, S. (1963) "Non-Contractual Relations in Business: A Preliminary Study," *American Sociological Review* 28: 55–67.

Markovits, D. (2004) "Contract and Collaboration," *Yale Law Journal* 113: 1417–1518.

—— (2011) "Promise as an Arm's-Length Relation," in H. Sheinman, ed., *Promises and Agreements*, New York: Oxford University Press, pp. 295–326.

—— and Schwartz, A. (2011) "The Myth of Efficient Breach: New Defenses of the Expectation Interest," *Virginia Law Review* 97: 1939–2008.

Murphy, L. (2007) "Contract and Promise," *Harvard Law Review Forum*, http://www.harvardlawreview.org/issues/120/january07/forum_467.php.

Owens, D. (2006) "A Simple Theory of Promising," *The Philosophical Review* 115: 51–77.

Penner, J. E. (1996) "Voluntary Obligations and the Scope of the Law of Contract," *Legal Theory* 2: 325–57.

Pratt, M. G. (2007) "Promises, Contracts and Voluntary Obligations," *Law and Philosophy* 26: 531–74.

—— (2008) "Contract: Not Promise," *Florida State University Law Review* 35: 801–16.

Schwartz, A. and Scott, R. (2003) "Contract Theory and the Limits of Contract Law," *Yale Law Journal* 113: 541–620.

Shiffrin, S. V. (2007) "The Divergence of Contract and Promise," *Harvard Law Review* 120: 708–53.

—— (2008) "Promising, Intimate Relationships, and Conventionalism," *Philosophical Review* 117: 481–524.

—— (2009) "Could Breach of Contract Be Immoral?" *Michigan Law Review* 107: 1551–1568.

—— (2010) "Inducing Moral Deliberation: On the Occasional Virtues of Fog," *Harvard Law Review* 123: 1214–1247.

—— (2011) "Immoral, Conflicting and Redundant Promises," in S. Freeman et al., eds., *Reasons and Recognition: Essays in Honor of Thomas Scanlon*, Oxford: Oxford University Press, pp. 155–78.

Wilkinson-Ryan, T. (2010) "Do Liquidated Damages Encourage Breach? A Psychological Experiment," *Michigan Law Review* 108: 634–72.

—— and Baron, J. (2009) "Moral Judgment and Moral Heuristics in Breach of Contract," *Journal of Empirical Legal Studies* 6: 405–24.

Further Reading

For further reading, see: P. S. Atiyah (1979) *The Rise and Fall of Freedom of Contract*, Oxford: Clarendon Press; P. S. Atiyah (1981) *Promises, Morals, and Law*, Oxford: Clarendon Press; P. S. Atiyah (1981) "Book Review: Charles Fried, *Contract as Promise*: A Theory of Contractual Obligation," *Harvard Law Review* 95: 509–28; R. Barnett (1992) "The Sound of Silence: Default Rules and Contractual Consent," *Virginia Law Review* 78: 821–911; R. Barnett (1986) "A Consent Theory of Contract," *Columbia Law Review* 86: 269–321; A. Bellia (2002) "Promises, Trust, and Contract Law," *American Journal of Jurisprudence* 47: 25–40; L. Bernstein (1992) "Opting Out of the Legal System: Extralegal Contractual Relations in the Diamond Industry," *Journal of Legal Studies* 21: 115–57; C. Bridgeman (2009) "Contracts as Plans," *University of Illinois Law Review* 2009 (2): 341–402; R. Brooks (2006) "The Efficient Performance Hypothesis," *Yale Law Journal* 116: 568–97; B. H. Fried (2007) "What's Morality Got To Do With It?" *Harvard Law Review Forum*, http://www.harvardlawreview.org/issues/120/january07/forum_447.php; C. Fried (2007) "The Convergence of Contract and Promise," *Harvard Law Review Forum*, http://www.harvardlawreview.org/issues/120/january07/forum_457.php; G. Klass (2012) "Promises Etc." *Suffolk University Law Review* 45: 695–717; J. S. Kraus (2009) "The Correspondence of Contract and Promise," *Columbia Law Review*, 109: 1603–1649; N. MacCormick (1972) "Voluntary Obligations and Normative Powers," *Proceedings of the Aristotelian Society, Supplementary Volumes*, 46: 59–78; J. Raz (1972) "Voluntary Obligations and Normative Powers," *Proceedings of the Aristotelian Society, Supplementary Volumes* 46: 79–102; J. Raz (1977) "Promises and Obligations," in P. M. S. Hacker and J. Raz, eds., *Law, Morality and Society*, Oxford: Clarendon Press, pp. 210–28; J. Raz (1982) "Promises in Morality and Law," *Harvard Law Review* 95: 916–38; J. Raz (1986) *The Morality of Freedom*, New York: Oxford University Press, pp. 173–76; T. M. Scanlon (2003) "Promises and Contracts," in T. M. Scanlon, *The Difficulty of Tolerance*, Cambridge: Cambridge University Press, pp. 234–69; H. Sheinman, ed. (2011) *Promises and Agreements*, New York: Oxford University Press; S. Shiffrin (2000) "Paternalism, Unconscionability Doctrine, and Accommodation," *Philosophy and Public Affairs* 29: 205–51; S. Smith (2004) *Contract Theory*, Oxford: Clarendon Press; Symposium (2012) "*Contract as Promise* at 30: The Future of Contract Theory," *Suffolk University Law Review* 45: 601–978.

(iii)

TORTS

17

PROXIMATE CAUSE IN THE LAW OF TORTS

Benjamin C. Zipursky

The Problem of Proximate Cause

The term "tort law" names the branch of common law concerning who shall prevail against whom in a private lawsuit not based on contract. Like criminal law, and unlike the law of property or contract, there are distinct and discernable wrongs that, as a collective, comprise the subject. Just as burglary, rape, narcotics distribution, arson and homicide are distinct crimes, so battery, trespass, libel and medical malpractice are distinct torts.

The most common tort today is the tort of "negligence," which is short for "negligent infliction of harm." The basic idea of a negligence claim is that if one person's careless conduct causes another person a physical injury, the injured person is allowed to sue the careless person and thereby to recover an award of monetary damages to compensate him or her for the injury that was inflicted. Quite straightforwardly, one can understand the injured person (the plaintiff) as someone who comes to court demanding to have the putative injurer (the defendant) held responsible for having inflicted an injury upon him or her. In a wide variety of cases, courts will accede to such a demand by permitting an injured person to exact damages from a defendant who negligently inflicted the injury upon the victim.

Frequently, a defendant who is willing to concede for the purposes of argument that he or she acted negligently and that the plaintiff suffered a genuine harm nevertheless maintains that there should be no liability for the harm for which the plaintiff seeks compensation. Of the reasons defendants use to support such a position, there is one, above all, that has fascinated legal scholars, judges and lawyers. It is the argument that *proximate cause* is an essential component of a negligence claim and that it is missing in the particular fact pattern before the court. This chapter aims to explain what "proximate cause" means, why it is typically deemed essential to a negligence claim and why its content has eluded easy formulation. It also sets forth what are regarded as the most promising analytical approaches to interpreting and justifying the proximate-cause requirement.

The Wagon Mound is one of the classic proximate cause cases in Anglo-American law (*Overseas Tankship (UK), Ltd. v. Morts Dock & Eng'g Co. (The Wagon Mound No. 1)* [1961] 1 All E.R. 404 (Privy Council Austl.)). The defendant shipper leaked a large quantity of oil into a harbor whose shoreline property was owned by a variety of commercial enterprises, including the plaintiff. One of the plaintiff's employees was welding and a spark flew from the welding iron onto the harbor, where it ignited a piece of floating debris. The debris was soaked in the oil that had leaked, and so, engulfed in flames, the debris lit the whole surface of the harbor on fire. As a result, the plaintiff's pier was destroyed and its shorefront property was severely damaged by the fire. The plaintiff sued the shipper on the ground that its negligent oil leakage was the cause of plaintiff's expensive property damage. The defendant shipper argued that even if one conceded negligence in the oil spill and one conceded that the plaintiff had suffered real property damage, there should be no liability because proximate cause was missing. The court agreed and the plaintiff lost the case.

What is most striking about difficult proximate cause cases is that there is a straightforward sense in which the defendant's conduct *did* cause the plaintiff's injury. Negligence law famously utilizes a necessary-condition criterion, or "but-for" test, for actual causation: the question is whether *but for the defendant's conduct, the plaintiff would not have been injured.* In *Wagon Mound*, we see that the defendant's negligent conduct plainly qualifies as a cause of the plaintiff's injury under the but-for test, leading one to the question of whether the defect in the plaintiff's suit in that case (assuming there was a defect) could really be a defect falling within the rubric of "causation."

The concept of proximate cause specifically targets that aspect of the concept of causation that is not captured by the but-for test. The standard lawyer or judge feels in a case like *Wagon Mound* that there may be something *too attenuated about the connection* between the tortious conduct and the injury. In this way, the proximate-cause requirement seems to presuppose a conception of a normal or standard causal connection, as opposed to one that is too attenuated or freakish. Courts commonly say that the harm for which plaintiff seeks compensation must be a "natural and probable" result of the negligent conduct. Yet it has long been evident that this phrase is not particularly helpful, for it is clearly *not* a necessary condition that the causal process leading to the injury be *natural* in the sense of being *unmediated by additional human agency*, and it is just as clearly *not* a necessary condition that negligent conduct rendered the injury *probable* in the sense of being *more likely than not to occur.* The degree of intervening human agency and the degree of probability are typically probative of the intuitive notion of proximate cause, and lawyers and judges certainly bring these factors into consideration when making a proximate-cause determination. However, this only deepens the puzzle, because we are led to wonder what the concept is that makes these considerations seem so clearly relevant.

Proposed Approaches

Over the past century, two "tests" for proximate cause have vied for top position: a foreseeability test and a directness test. *Wagon Mound* is the leading case that adopts a foreseeability test. The court in that case ruled that—assuming it was unforeseeable that an oil leakage would lead to a massive harbor fire destroying piers and other shoreline property—the negligent leakage of the oil was not a proximate cause of that damage. More to the point, the court argued that it would be wrong to extend liability for injuries that were unforeseeable. One reason for this conclusion is that liability imposition is unfair if it lacks a sort of proportionality to the wrongfulness of the conduct, and foreseeability is aimed in part at establishing that connection. A second is that there is a sort of irrationality in requiring the defendant to pay for injuries different in character than those which it supposedly was negligent in failing to guard against. But if the injury for which plaintiff seeks recovery was unforeseeable, then a fortiori, she was not negligent in failing to guard against it.

The classic "directness" case is *Polemis* (*In re Arbitration Between Polemis and Furness, Withy & Co., Ltd.* [1921] 3 K.B. 560). Plaintiff chartered a ship to defendant (a company). Stevedores hired by the defendant were loading cargo through a hold in the boat when one of them negligently caused a plank of wood to fall into the hold. When the dropped plank landed on something in the hold below, the friction between the two pieces of wood generated a spark. The spark ignited benzene gas that had leaked out into the hold, and a fire ensued, destroying the entire ship. The ship-owner plaintiff argued that the negligent dropping of the plank caused the fire and that the defendant should therefore be held liable for the ensuing damages. The defendant responded that this sequence of events was unforeseeable and therefore proximate cause was missing. The court sided with the plaintiff, reasoning that the linkage between the harm and the negligent act was actually quite direct, and that directness was the touchstone of proximate cause.

A third approach to proximate cause—the risk rule—has achieved less recognition among judges but has proved quite attractive to academics. The facts of *Larrimore v. American Nat'l Ins. Co.* nicely illustrate the idea ((1939) 89 P.2d 340 (Okla.)). A defendant landlord had left a can of rat poison in the kitchen area of the commercial tenant's space. The rat poison, which was flammable, exploded because of the heat of the stove in the kitchen, causing serious injury. The plaintiff argued that it was negligent to leave rat poison in a kitchen, where food was prepared, and that this negligent conduct caused the injury. The defendant, in turn, argued that regardless of the imprudence of leaving rat poison in the kitchen, there was no liability unless it was foreseeable that rat poison was explosive. Otherwise, the causal chain is too attenuated. The court agreed with the defendant, couching its decision in the language of foreseeability. Subsequent commentators have pointed out a different feature of *Larrimore*—the absence of a nexus between the risk that made it negligent to leave rat poison in the kitchen—poisoning—and the harmful event that actually occurred—an explosion. The risk rule, first articulated as such by Harvard Law Professor Robert Keeton, says that proximate cause fails unless the injury for which the plaintiff seeks to impose liability is a realization of the risk that the defendant negligently took (Keeton 1963).

Andrews's *Palsgraf* Dissent and the Reductionistic Challenge

A practicing lawyer asked to remember a proximate cause case from law school will typically recall the famous case of *Palsgraf v. Long Island Railroad* ((1928) 162 N.E. 99 (N.Y.)). *Palsgraf*'s notoriety as a proximate cause case is ironic, to say the least, given that Chief Judge Benjamin Cardozo's majority opinion expressly disclaims all reliance on causation in overturning the plaintiff's verdict ("[t]he law of causation, remote or proximate, is thus foreign to the case before us"). It is, in part, the eloquent dissenting opinion in *Palsgraf* that has led to its fame as a proximate cause case. And it is in great part the remarkable facts of the case that have left an indelible impression upon those who have studied it. A quick overview of those facts will help us focus on our topic.

In *Palsgraf*, the defendant's employees witnessed a passenger leaping onto a train just as it began to leave the platform, and they pushed him or nudged him so that he would land securely on the train. In the process of doing so, the guards caused the leaping passenger to drop a package wrapped in newspaper. The package was fireworks, which exploded when they hit the track. The fireworks caused a large explosion in the train station, which in turn caused a metal balance scale at the end of the platform to fall down on the head and neck of the plaintiff, Mrs. Palsgraf. Mrs. Palsgraf apparently suffered some neurological damage from this event, and afterwards had great difficulty speaking. She sued the railroad company on the theory that its employees' negligent conduct (the careless manner in which they pushed the leaping passenger onto the train, leading his package to fall) had caused her physical injury. A jury returned a damages verdict for Mrs. Palsgraf, which Chief Judge Cardozo, writing for a 4–3 majority, reversed. In a dissenting opinion, Judge William Andrews famously expressed a quite skeptical view:

> As we have said, we cannot trace the effect of an act to the end, if end there is. Again, however we may trace it part of the way. A murder at Serajavo may be the necessary antecedent to an assassination in London twenty years hence. An overturned lantern may burn all Chicago. We may follow the fire from the shed to the last building. We rightly say the fire started by the lantern caused its destruction.
>
> A cause, but not the proximate cause. What we do mean by the word "proximate" is, that because of convenience, of public policy, of a rough sense of justice, the law arbitrarily declines to trace a series of events beyond a certain point. This is not logic. It is practical politics.
>
> (352 (Andrews, J., dissenting))

As Andrews points out, the need for a proximate cause requirement seems quite obvious: it is simply that but-for causation alone would yield far too much liability, and so courts must draw a line and then give a name to their line-drawing activity. Yet Andrews's pragmatic and reductive approach appears to be inadequate *for legal scholars* in three respects. One is that it provides far too little guidance to trial judges, lawyers and legal actors, such as insurance companies, who must be able to estimate potential liabilities. A second, as we will see, is that pragmatic line drawing is really very different from what courts seem to be saying and doing. And a third is that most students, judges and lawyers actually come to believe that there is something which the idea of proximate cause is trying to get at—that there are cases that should qualify and cases that should not.

For all of these reasons, legal scholars have been engaged by the enterprise of trying to figure out a nonreductive analytical approach to proximate cause that is justifiable from a normative point of view. Such an analytical explanation appears important if one is to justify the proximate cause restriction, if one is to select a particular concept or concepts for elucidating and applying the restriction, and if one is to fend off the legal realist attack generated by Andrews. Incidentally, Cardozo himself analyzed the legal issues in *Palsgraf* in a way that did not require him to tangle with proximate cause, and ultimately led him to deny recovery (he reasoned that even if one assumes the conductors were negligent, their negligence did not involve any want of care in relation to Mrs. Palsgraf, and therefore did not constitute any breach of a duty owed to her, and therefore could not support a tort claim by her).

In what follows, I briefly survey the rationales that have been offered for each of the three leading approaches and the problems faced by each.

Foreseeability

Proportionality

Two justifications are typically offered for limiting liability to the foreseeable consequences of negligent conduct. The first draws from the idea of proportionality. As Viscount Simonds wrote in *Wagon Mound*, "it does not seem consonant with current ideas of justice or morality that, for an act of negligence, however slight or venial, which results in some trivial foreseeable damage, the actor should be liable for all consequences, however unforeseeable and however grave, so long as they can be said to be 'direct'" (422). The general idea would appear to be that norms of justice do not simply govern *whether* an actor shall be subjected to sanction or to liability, but also *what magnitude of sanction or liability* is appropriate. Relatively greater liability may be imposed for relatively greater fault, but if the fault is relatively lesser, then the liability must not be too great. Broadly speaking, this is a cousin of the principle that the punishment must fit the crime.

There are three problems with the proportionality account of foreseeability in proximate cause. The first is that it is plainly untenable if intended to serve as part of an explanation of the positive law of torts, because it is beyond question that tort law does in fact impose liability in a manner that is grossly disproportionate to fault. A generally careful driver who takes his eyes off the road for just a moment to switch the radio station will be liable for tens of millions of dollars in damages if his negligent glance leads him to crash into a car carrying a precious sculpture that is destroyed (Waldron 1995). A would-be assassin who fires at and strikes his intended victim, and believes he has killed his intended victim, faces no tort liability if unbeknownst to him, the intended victim had died minutes earlier of a massive stroke. (He will, however, face prosecution for attempted murder.) Miniscule fault—or sometimes no fault at all—can lead to massive tort liability, while willful viciousness can lead to none. It would be odd if proximate cause were principally a device for ensuring proportional liability, given that the common law of torts is, in its basic operation, otherwise so indifferent to proportionality.

A second problem is that the principle of proportionality, as we usually understand it, concerns punishment for crime, not liability for injury. A proportionality norm for punishment is keyed to the idea that a sanction for a crime should approximate what a criminal deserves by way of punishment, and what the criminal deserves turns on how wrongful her or his act was. Insofar as tort law concerns desert, it is to a great degree about what the victim of the injury deserves, in light of what was wrongfully done to her. It is not clear why, in tort law, we should be moved by the degree of wrongfulness associated with the tortfeasor's actions.

The third problem is the most basic, in some ways. It is that *even if we assume that proportionality is an important norm of liability imposition*, it is not clear why foreseeability of injury should track the degree of fault associated with the defendant's conduct. Return to the *Larrimore* case. Even if it were not foreseeable that rat poison would cause a kitchen explosion, it is foreseeable that rat poison might inadvertently kill all the customers of the restaurant, if it were mistakenly used to season the food. In such case, there would be massive and arguably disproportionate liability, yet no proximate cause problem for any of the claimants.

Responsibility

The most powerful normative account of why liability should be limited by foreseeability is rooted in the notion of responsibility. On Stephen Perry's account, it is unfair to impose liability upon someone for some loss unless the one upon whom liability is imposed can be understood as *responsible* for having brought about that loss (Perry 2001). Even if their conduct was in fact a necessary condition for the loss having occurred, that is not sufficient to deem them responsible for the loss. If we are to hold an actor responsible for bringing about an outcome, we must view him or her as having been able to avoid bringing about that outcome. It therefore must be that we can understand him as having been able to choose to act in a manner that avoided the risk of bringing about this injurious outcome. This will not be the case if the outcome was not a reasonably foreseeable consequence of the action.

Perry's account is appealing on a number of levels. It is straightforward; it hews to the language of responsibility, which lies on the face of tort law and proximate cause decisions; and it captures much of what courts have said. Nevertheless, the responsibility account of foreseeability in proximate cause faces many obstacles.

The problem with Perry's account lies more in the interpretive than the moral domain, at least in the first instance. The positive law of torts contains a very well-established principle called "the eggshell skull rule." According to this rule, a defendant who acts in a manner that risks physical injury to the plaintiff and thereby causes the plaintiff physical injury will be held liable for the entire cost of the injury *even if the injury fortuitously turns out to be far greater than anyone would have foreseen.* If a fender-bender in a parking lot causes the plaintiff to bump her head, and the head bump turns into a major neurologic disease because of an underlying idiosyncratic proclivity to such disease, then defendant will be held liable for the costs of compensating plaintiff for the disease.

Again, in the interpretive domain, there are innumerable cases where proximate cause fails but foreseeability does not really seem to be the core of the problem. A manufacturer sells a kind of fertilizer that it knows is highly combustible. Indeed, the manufacturer has been in the business of selling this kind of fertilizer long enough to know that criminals and terrorists sometimes use fertilizer to create makeshift bombs (*Port Authority of New York and New Jersey v. Arcadian Corp.* (1999) 189 F.3d 305 (3rd Cir.)). Victims of bombings that utilized fertilizer will typically not be able to recover from the fertilizer manufacturer, even if it can be shown that another design for the fertilizer would have reduced its usefulness for bomb making, and even though use in bombing was foreseeable. While it is true that the rejection of proximate cause in this case may have something to do with attribution of responsibility, it has nothing to do with foreseeability. And this result seems both doctrinally and morally correct. As we will see below, there is an aspect of directness to at least some proximate-cause thinking, which the foreseeability idea does not capture.

Finally, it is not quite so clear how morally compelling the responsibility/foreseeability account really is, for it appears to rely quite heavily upon the intuition that it is unfair to impose liability upon someone for a loss for which they are not responsible. The most powerful response to this intuition is, "unfair compared to what?" The most common alternative to imposing liability upon the one causing the injury is simply to leave the plaintiff's loss where it initially fell, upon the plaintiff. If the plaintiff is entirely innocent, forcing him or her to bear the burden of this injury seems unfair, too. Consider the famous case of *Smith v. Leech Brain & Co., Ltd.* ([1962] 2 Q.B. 405).

The plaintiff's husband worked a crane that dipped various objects into molten lead. Because the workplace lacked basic safety features that a careful employer would have provided, molten lead splattered onto his lip, burning it. Subsequently, the plaintiff's husband developed a fatal form of cancer, which initially presented at the precise spot of the burn, leaving the plaintiff a widow. The argument that the company could not have foreseen death from the molten lead splattering is a good one, and it does indeed seem to attenuate the company's responsibility for the husband's death (as opposed to the initial burn). But the argument that fairness demands nonliability is more questionable, because it is plausibly more unfair to require the innocent widow to bear the entire cost of her husband's premature demise, given that the evidence strongly suggested that the death was caused by the defendant's careless operation of the workplace. This leads quite easily to a further objection to the foreseeability/responsibility account. Perhaps it is artificial to suppose that there is a prelegal answer to the question of whether the company is responsible for the employee's demise. Tort law, arguably, is in the business of *deciding who shall be held responsible* for which losses, as a normative matter, not *ascertaining who is responsible* and then imposing liability.

Directness

The appeal of directness as a test for proximate cause is best understood by looking at its converse: indirectness as a ground for no proximate cause. In this vein, the most important cases involve third parties whose conduct interrupts the linkage between the initial tortfeasor's negligent action and the plaintiff's injury. These cases are typically referred to as "superseding cause" cases.

The fertilizer case discussed above would count as a superseding cause case. A terrorist's decision to create a bomb by utilizing fertilizer is an act that occurred temporally between the marketing of fertilizer and the explosion terrorist attack. Most courts would say that it is the terrorists who have caused the destruction, not the fertilizer manufacturer. It is the terrorists who are responsible for this loss. Cases of this sort are legion. The driver of an oil tanker carelessly spills oil in a town and a terrible fire ensues. A third party takes the opportunity of the oil spill to satisfy his urge to commit arson, and throws a lit match on the oil, resulting in massive property damage. Most courts would decline to impose liability on the driver and the oil company. There would be no liability because his intentional action would block the assignment of liability under the proximate cause test.

As suggested by cases such as these, there are ways in which "directness" works better than "foreseeability" as a gloss on the words "proximate cause," but it also does quite well conceptually and normatively and, to use perhaps too grand a term, metaphysically. Part of the idea of proximate cause is that an actor's act being a necessary condition of an event's occurrence is not enough for the actor's act to count as having brought about the occurrence of the event. Whether the defendant's conduct brought about the plaintiff's injury has typically been understood through a hindsight analysis of the sequence of events between defendant's conduct and plaintiff's injury. The sequence of events can be so skewed or another person's conduct can be so significant that it is really a stretch to say that defendant *caused* the plaintiff's injury. The concept of causation, it seems, is being pushed too hard.

A Texas decision, *Union Pump Co. v. Allbritton*, provides a good illustration ((1995) 898 S.W.2d 773 (Tex.)). The defendant manufactured an industrial pump whose valve was allegedly defective. A fire began at the plaintiff's workplace (an industrial plant), allegedly due to the defective pump valve. The fire caused some damages, but eventually water sprinklers and hoses were used to put it out. Hours after the fire was put out, the plaintiff and her supervisor at the plant crossed the factory working area in order to examine the valve. Because of the route selected by the supervisor and the wetness of the surfaces upon which the plaintiff crossed the factory, the plaintiff slipped and fell, injuring herself. She sued the pump manufacturer, arguing that the wet surface on which she slipped would not have been wet had the defective valve not caused a fire. The Texas Supreme Court rejected her suit on the ground that proximate cause was missing. The defective valve was a *mere* condition of the injury occurring, but not a cause of it, the court reasoned. Although *Allbritton* was not expressly decided on a "directness" basis, it nicely illustrates the metaphysical idea that supports the directness test. Simply because tortious conduct caused an event that was a necessary condition for an injury occurring, it does not follow that the tortuous conduct caused the injury. If the sequence of events linking the conduct and the injury is too attenuated or indirect, it is untenable to conceive of the negligent conduct as causing the injury.

The rationale for a directness test is therefore in some ways the most straightforward: the defendant's conduct has not actually caused the injury, notwithstanding the ability of the plaintiff to pass the but-for test. Whether it be responsibility or efficient cost allocation or compensation policy or deterrence, almost every normative approach to tort theory seems to answer the question: why should defendants be held liable for the injuries they have caused through negligent conduct? If it turns out that defendants in cases that are too indirect have not really caused the injury, each of these tort theories by its own terms will favor denying liability.

Notwithstanding its considerable strength from a conceptual point of view, the directness account presents serious problems at operational, doctrinal and normative levels. Operationally, it is quite unhelpful precisely because the notion of directness misleadingly evokes notions of spatial and temporal proximity. There is simply no question that a defendant drunk driver who causes a collision on the roadway with a dozen domino effects can in some cases be subject to liability for the eleventh and twelfth car crashes. There is no question that injuries occurring decades after exposure to negligently transmitted toxins can satisfy proximate cause, and no question that injuries caused thousands of miles from the scene of the careless conduct are perfectly actionable. Directness sounds like it calls for examination of proximity but it does not, and therefore it is far from clear what examining directness would amount to.

With respect to intervening acts, there are many in which a third party's independent, intervening wrongful acts—even criminal acts—do not suffice to defeat the victim's claim on proximate-cause grounds. In *Kline v. 1500 Mass Ave.* ((1970) 439 F.2d 477 (D.C. Cir.)), for example, a landlord who negligently failed to provide locks and lighting for the public lobby of his apartment building was held liable for the injuries inflicted on his tenant when assaulted in the lobby by an unknown assailant.

The largest problem with directness is that courts seem prepared to allow heightened foreseeability to defeat a no-proximate-cause argument based on indirectness. This is not simply a doctrinal problem, however, but a normative one, too. If a defendant can and should anticipate a sequence of actions and events by others as a result of which the defendant's negligent conduct will in fact lead to the plaintiff's injury, it seems entirely cogent to demand that the defendant take account of those foreseeable occurrences and alter its conduct accordingly. If it then fails to do so and injury foreseeably results, there seems to be nothing objectionable, from a normative point of view, in holding the defendant at least partially responsible for those injuries.

To take a hot-button issue in tort law, consider a person rendered quadriplegic by a drunk driver who leaves a tavern that knowingly served him 15 shots of whiskey, with full awareness that the patron would be driving himself home in his own car, parked in the tavern parking lot. Now imagine that the tavern was sued by the quadriplegic plaintiff for negligently rendering the plaintiff too drunk to drive safely, when it knew the bar patron was driving after drinking. The bar would seem to have an excellent no-proximate-cause argument based on an indirectness argument (imagine, if this helps, that the driver stops at a McDonald's and a 7–11 and permits a couple of hours to elapse before resuming driving and causing the accident). Nonetheless, the fact that automobile accidents by bar patrons who have consumed far too much alcohol are foreseeable would seem to provide a good reason to deem the bar at least partially responsible for the accidents that are caused by the drivers to whom the bar has served excessive alcohol.

The Scope-of-the-Risk Test

The scope-of-the-risk test, or the "risk rule," is the most elegant of the three approaches, in at least two respects. First, it offers the most nuanced set of judgments about which fact patterns are well-formed proximate-cause cases and which are not. Second, it provides a definition of the test that—while openly normative—links the normative judgments of proximate cause to the normative judgments made in the underlying determination of whether the defendant's acts or failures to act were negligent. These two points are best explained by reference to an analogous area of negligence law: liability for breach of statutory duties.

In *Matteo v. Livingstone* ((1996) 666 N.E.2d 1309, 1312 (Mass. Ct. App.)), the plaintiff became quadriplegic when he rode his mountain bike off the porch of the defendant's store. A local ordinance required buildings that were elevated by more than 30 inches to have railings, which this building did not. The plaintiff argued that the defendant had violated the ordinance and therefore was liable under the doctrine of negligence per se (which directs that violations of statutes or ordinances under certain circumstances will constitute per se negligence by the defendant). Well-established principles of negligence law dictate, however, that the court must first determine whether a plaintiff belonged to the class of persons that the statute or ordinance was intended to protect and whether the injury suffered was the type of injury the ordinance was aimed to protect against. The court quite correctly ascertained that the ordinance was intended to protect people who were standing on a porch or elevated building against injuries from falling, *not to protect those on a vehicle who drove off of it*. This does not mean, of course, that the court could not find the defendant negligent, but rather that the breach of an ordinance cannot be used to do so.

Now let's return to negligence claims that do not involve statutory or regulatory violations. The risk rule calls for an analogous approach to that displayed in the mountain bike example above: the key question for understanding proximate cause is whether the injury of which the plaintiff complains is of a kind that would underlie a determination that the defendant acted negligently. A familiar example involves a father who hands his child a loaded gun. The child drops the gun on the bare foot of a third person, breaking his toe. If the plaintiff sues the father for negligence and predicates his showing of carelessness on the claim that it is negligent to give a child a loaded gun, the plaintiff will have trouble when it comes to proximate cause. The risk that would underlie a determination that it was negligent to hand the child the loaded gun was the risk that the child would accidentally cause the gun to fire, injuring someone with a bullet wound. That is not the risk that was realized in this hypothetical. The lack of a nexus between the injury negligently risked and the injury that actually occurred severs the proximate-causal connection. As in the mountain bike case, there is a judgment of required care that underlies the norm of conduct, and that judgment is based on a certain kind of peril. The proximate-cause requirement looks to the normative grounds of the judgment to determine what shall count as having been proximately caused. The defendant's negligent conduct may have been a necessary condition of the accident occurring, but it will only be permitted to serve as the basis of tort liability for those injuries that involved an actualization of the risks that rendered that conduct negligent.

Harvard Law Professor Warren Seavey used an early version of the risk rule more than half a century ago to offer what is in essence a third opinion in *Palsgraf* (i.e., one distinct from both Cardozo's and Andrews's) (Seavey 1939). What made it negligent for the conductors to push the passenger on the train as they did was the risk of physical injury to the man they were pushing and the risk of property damage to him, in light of the package that might have been (and was) jostled. The injury of which Mrs. Palsgraf complained was not a realization of that risk; indeed, the risk to her was so unforesee-able and tangential that it was not negligent to fail to take steps to guard against it. Because there was no nexus between the negligently taken risk and the actual injury, there was no proximate cause. Andrews was right that it should have been decided as a proximate-cause case, but Cardozo was right that the defendant should win.

What has been most elusive to scholars about the risk rule is not its intuitive appeal but its justification. Why *should* courts use the risk rule for their proximate-cause deter-minations? The short answer seems superficial: it is that the reasons for having liability at all should determine the limits of the liability. In what follows, we shall try to dig beneath this platitude.

The best normative defenses of the risk rule have derived from Guido Calabresi (1975) and Arthur Ripstein (1999). Despite their very different foundations (Calabresi in an economic analysis of the law, Ripstein in a Rawls/Kant version of corrective jus-tice), the two accounts have a common structure. Calabresi sees tort law as allocating the costs of accidents to the cheapest cost avoider (the person or entity best situated to make judgments about how accidents of this sort are most efficiently reduced). For every risk of injury, there is some potential actor or actors to whom the system should charge this potential cost. Drivers are the cheapest avoiders of car accidents, manufacturers of product-liability problems, newspapers of reputational attacks and so on. Now once the system decides that, from an efficiency point of view, *the job of avoiding the risk* should be assigned to a particular actor, it must stay true to the allocation by imposing *the cost of the loss* on the actor to whom the risk was assigned. To put it differently, the system counts as placing the risk of a certain loss on a certain actor when that risked loss is one that the defendant will be required to pay for if and when it occurs. Permitting liability for a *kind of loss* is for that reason treating the risk of *a loss of that kind* as something the defendant is held responsible for avoiding.

Ripstein's view from *Equality, Responsibility, and the Law* (1999) runs parallel to Cala-bresi's. Negligence law, in effect, specifies *who owns which risks*. It is an allocation of var-ious risks of loss based on an overall framework that reconciles liberty with security in a manner that treats persons as equals. Saying that there is a responsibility to take care to avoid a certain kind of loss is, in effect, saying that if that loss occurs, the defendant owns it (will have to pay for it). To say, as in *Larrimore*, that it is negligent to store rat poison in a kitchen is in part to say that one who does so is taking an unjustifiable risk that patrons will be poisoned; if a person does so, he owns the risk of those poisonings. Once one understands this, one sees that there is no basis for inferring liability for the explosion-related harms from the riskiness of the poisoning. Of course, it is possible that the risk of explosion in the kitchen presented by keeping rat poison in the kitchen is sufficiently great that the law should treat that risk as one the defendant owns, as beyond the risks she has a liberty to take without owning the consequences. But if the plaintiff is to show this, she must show that the risk of explosion was one that it was negligent to have taken. Showing the unjustifiably high level of the other risk (the risk of poisoning) is not sufficient for generating liability for the explosion.

In very different ways, Calabresi and Ripstein thus get beneath the platitude that the reason for deeming the conduct wrongful should limit the scope of liability. The essence of the concept of wrongfulness utilized is such that it begins with the idea that actors are responsible for certain of the losses their conduct brings about. Their respective normative accounts must explain both how this concept of responsibility works, and how it can be telescoped back into an account of the breach, or unreasonable risking, element of the negligence claim.

Although the risk rule has generally gained great support among academics in recent years—being selected as the preferred analysis by the American Law Institute Reporters for the Restatement (Third) of Torts—some commentators have been highly critical of it. Heidi Hurd and Michael Moore have constructed a forceful critique of the risk rule along various lines (Hurd and Moore 2002). Two are especially important. First, they have argued that the risk rule is incoherent because it falsely presupposes that there is a single risk or category of risk in light of which the reasonableness of a course of conduct is to be judged. To take the example of the loaded gun handed to the child, it is not clear why we should say that *the* reason that handing a child a loaded gun is negligent is that the child might accidentally cause the gun to discharge. It would be better to say that this risk is *a reason* or *one of the reasons* or even *the principal reason*. However, it is still an open possibility that there are other risks, and those other risks contribute to its being negligent. More generally, whether a course of conduct is negligent is a function of both the burden of taking certain precautions and the magnitude of all the risks that are altered by those precautions, and their potential costs to others. In other words, it is unlikely that there is any such thing as "the" risk rendering the conduct negligent.

Secondly, even if one were to assume that the risk rule could be cogently stated and applied, Hurd and Moore are skeptical about its justifiability. The problem is similar to the one we saw in connection with foreseeability. If one is faced with a tortfeasor who has caused an injury to a wholly innocent plaintiff, why should the plaintiff be the one to bear the cost of the injury? From the point of view of the principal functions that tort law allegedly serves—compensation of the injured and deterrence of socially harmful conduct—liability makes more sense than leaving the cost on the plaintiff's shoulders. This is also the case if one is considering which is fairer; as the argument goes: between an innocent victim and a careless actor whose carelessness has caused the victim harm in an admittedly haphazard, odd or unpredictable way, it is fairer to make the careless actor bear the loss.

I would add to the problems faced by an account like Calabresi's or Ripstein's the phenomenon of the eggshell skull rule. As we saw above, defendants are, by virtue of this rule, sometimes held responsible for injuries far beyond those which a prudent person would have foreseen. Perhaps the eggshell skull rule ought to be rejected from a normative point of view, or perhaps it is an ad hoc appendage to the structure of tort law, but from an interpretive point of view, it presents a significant problem for their respective views.

Concluding Questions

Faced with this barrage of analytic proposals and substantial objections, a scholar or student might respond in a number of different ways. The most straightforward kind of response is simply to stick with one of these approaches and work to fend off the criticisms. The opposite would be to adopt a kind of anti-intellectual skepticism, of the sort articulated by Judge Andrews (although on my view, this would need its own defense, and faces even more serious problems). A third would be to hope for some kind of integration, in which one approach could plug the gaps in the other, and so on. Relatedly, one might decide that the proximate cause problem is not one but several, and that each of the parts of the problem has an approach that is suitable to it; the job is to show how such an integrative account is possible. Finally, one might decide that all of these approaches are unpromising, and that a new approach is needed.

Whichever of these directions one might take, a number of larger questions will need to be addressed. First, is "proximate cause" really an aspect of *causation* or is the placement of "cause" in the phrase actually a misnomer; is proximate cause really just about how much liability there should be?

Second, when courts are trying to decide proximate cause questions, they are clearly trying to do so, in part, because they must ascertain the extent of liability. The language used frequently slides onto the question of whether the defendant can be held *responsible* for certain harms. It thus often appears that courts are really trying to ascertain *legal liability* for certain injuries by reference to *moral responsibility* for those injuries, and that proximate cause is really a conceptual tool for thinking about moral responsibility. Is this really what is happening? Is proximate cause really about moral responsibility for outcomes? If so, what do foreseeability, directness and the risk rule tell us about moral responsibility? If not, why does the language of responsibility loom so large in this area?

Third, in most of the difficult proximate cause cases we have examined, the defendant has clearly done something wrong and an innocent plaintiff is stuck with a serious injury that she would not have suffered but for the defendant's wrongful conduct. Some theorists maintain that fairness requires that the cost of the injury be shifted to the wrongdoing defendant, regardless of foreseeability or directness. Yet our legal system does not do this. Although some scholars have maintained that the resistance to such cost shifting is based on fears of too much litigation and other functional problems, and although this is clearly part of what is going on, scholars overwhelmingly perceive that considerations of principle are part of the law's reasons for declining to impose liability in all such cases. *What sorts of justifications—short of practicality—can really justify these limitations, given that an innocent person ends up bearing the cost of her own loss?*

Fourth, there are some cases in which the intervening conduct of others—such as the conduct of the terrorists in the fertilizer case—stands in the way of imposing liability upon a defendant. Yet in others—consider liability for landlords of buildings with poor security, or even the simpler cases of multiple-vehicle accidents or dangerous pharmaceutical products that are administered by careless doctors and nurses—the intermediating conduct of third parties does not stand as an obstacle to liability imposition. Why does intervening human conduct sometimes break the causal link, and sometimes not? How is one person's responsibility altered by what others choose to do?

Finally, who within our legal system should apply the concept of proximate cause? American tort law typically gives judges an oversight role on proximate cause; a weak enough proximate cause case will lead a judge to say that there is no point in sending the case to the jury, because no reasonable jury could find proximate cause. There are differences in how aggressively judges exercise this form of oversight. But, in every other common-law system that uses "proximate cause," juries play no role whatsoever; it is judges who decide. If proximate cause is ultimately based on an intuitive judgment call, who should make that call, and why?

References

American Law Institute (2010) Restatement (Third) of Torts: Liability for Physical and Emotional Harm, § 29.

Calabresi, G. (1975) "Concerning Cause and the Law of Torts: An Essay for Harry Kalven, Jr.," 43 *University of Chicago Law Review*: 69–108.

Hurd, H. M. and Moore, M. S. (2002) "Negligence in the Air," 3 *Theoretical Inquiries in Law*: 333.

In re Arbitration Between Polemis and Furness, Withy & Co., Ltd. [1921] 3 K.B. 560.

Keeton, R. E. (1963) *Legal Cause in the Law of Torts*, Columbus, OH: Ohio State University Press.

Kline v. 1500 Mass Ave. (1970) 439 F.2d 477 (D.C. Cir.).

Larrimore v. American Nat'l Ins. Co. (1939) 89 P.2d 340 (Okla.).

Matteo v. Livingstone (1996) 666 N.E.2d 1309, 1312 (Mass. Ct. App.).

Overseas Tankship (UK), Ltd. v. Morts Dock & Eng'g Co. (The Wagon Mound No. 1) [1961] A.C. 388 (Privy Council Austl.).

Palsgraf v. Long Island R.R. Co. (1928) 162 N.E. 99 (N.Y.).

Perry, S. R. (2001) "Responsibility for Outcomes, Risk, and the Law of Torts," in G. Postema, ed., *Philosophy and the Law of Torts*, Cambridge: Cambridge University Press, pp. 72–130.

Port Authority of New York and New Jersey v. Arcadian Corp. (1999) 189 F.3d 305 (3rd Cir.).

Ripstein, A. R. (1999) *Equality, Responsibility, and the Law*, Cambridge: Cambridge University Press.

Seavey, W. A. (1939) "Mr. Justice Cardozo and the Law of Torts," *Yale Law Journal* 48: 390–425.

Smith v. Leech Brain & Co., Ltd. [1962] 2 Q.B. 405.

Union Pump Co. v. Allbritton (1995) 898 S.W.2d 773 (Tex.).

Waldron, J. (1995) "Moments of Carelessness and Massive Loss," in D. Owen, ed., *Philosophical Foundations of Tort Law*, Oxford: Clarendon Press.

Further Reading

For further reading, see: J. C. P. Goldberg and B. C. Zipursky (2009) "Intervening Wrongdoing in Tort: The *Restatement* (Third)'s Unfortunate Embrace of Negligent Enabling," 44 *Wake Forest Law Review*: 1211–1246; L. Green (1927) *The Rationale of Proximate Cause*, Kansas City, MO: Vernon Law Book Company; H. L. A. Hart and T. Honoré (1985) *Causation in the Law*, 2nd edition, New York: Oxford University Press; P. Kelley (1991) "Proximate Cause in Negligence Law: History, Theory and the Present Darkness," 69 *Washington University Law Quarterly*: 49; B. C. Zipursky (2009) "Foreseeability in Breach, Duty, and Proximate Cause," 44 *Wake Forest Law Review*: 1247–1275; and B. C. Zipursky (1998) "Rights, Wrongs, and Recourse in the Law of Torts," 51 *Vanderbilt Law Review*: 1.

(iv)

PROPERTY

18

PRIVATE PROPERTY

Daniel Attas

What is the right to private property? What are its grounds? What is its scope and extent? In particular, do government regulation and taxation, as such, violate private property? These are contentious issues. At one end, for libertarians, property is itself foundational, hardly in need of any justification at all. Self-ownership, a property in one's own body and mind, is considered the basis of all rights. At the other end, some claim that all property is theft; there can be no grounds that would justify the exclusive rights of some over resources that everyone could conceivably enjoy. In between, liberal egalitarians recognize a right to hold personal property. But what exactly such a right amounts to remains vague, if not in legal practice, at least in theory. To the question of whether taxation violates ownership, some respond simply "yes" (Nozick 1974; Epstein 1985), others simply "no" (Murphy and Nagel 2002) and yet others "no," but it takes them a great deal of intellectual acrobatics to show that it doesn't (Waldron 1988; Christman 1994; Fried 1995; cf. Attas 2006).

In what follows, I aim to trace two historical strands of development of thought about property. Though both strands set out to justify property, and though they were always in dialogue with each other, they discuss two distinct concepts, and accordingly, the kind of justification they provide is markedly different. That they were, and still are, using the same terms, is obviously not very helpful for clarifying the important issue of the meaning, grounds and limits of whatever it is we wish to call property. So one purpose of this essay is to set these apart as two distinct concepts: on the one hand, the *regime view* of property as a system regulating the control of assets, and on the other the *entitlement view* of property as an individual (natural) right. These have separate sorts of justification, distinct foundational values they are aimed to advance and different compositions.

It is not unusual to see property as a bundle of liberties, claims, powers and immunities one holds with respect to certain assets. When so describing property, one often refers to Honoré's noted list of incidents. This comprises 13 kinds of claims, powers and immunities often included in the notion of private property (Honoré 1987). Notwithstanding the air of haphazardness conveyed by this list, the items therein can be arranged in a more regimented form. These include control rights (possession, use, management), income rights (to the fruits, profit and rent), transferability (the power to alienate, transmit by inheritance, liability to repayment of debt) and continuity (security, residuary character, absence of term) (Attas 2006).

Many writers on property, primarily (but not only) libertarians, seek to justify what is sometimes called "full liberal ownership." That is, the most extensive set of incidents associated with the concept of property—the full rights of control, income and transfer. Yet, as I aim to show, the sort of justification provided for either a natural property right or a property regime quite clearly fails to establish this sort of all-inclusive property. A justification of property may seem to endorse full liberal ownership only when one equivocates the two views.

The structure of this chapter is as follows. Section 1 expounds on the regime view of property and the limited conception of property it can justify. Section 2 does the same for the entitlement view. Section 3 investigates the possibility that the best regime in terms of valuable social goals happens to be such that respects a conception close enough to full liberal ownership. Section 4 describes the failed attempt to justify full liberal ownership by fusing together the regime and entitlement views.

1. Property as Regime

There is an important tradition of property discourse that focuses on justifying a property *regime*. In effect this sort of justification boils down to an explanation of the function of such a regime, the social values it tends to promote. Beginning in the seventeenth century and up to our present age, I shall indicate how thinkers in this tradition point to the values of *peace or stability, prosperity, equity or fairness* to justify a regime of rights assigning exclusive control of assets to individuals.

According to Samuel Pufendorf, the original God-given state of the world is one of a perfect liberty of all to use and consume. Such an original state does not necessitate instituting property. To see why, Pufendorf directs our attention to the behavior of animals. Like humans, animals too are free to use and consume, yet they are incapable of such dominion as property requires. Though some animals might respect physical possession, property requires the recognition of continued entitlement even when the asset is not under one's physical control. Since this goes beyond what we might expect from animals, it goes to show that property does not necessarily follow from the original state.

Nevertheless, a state of perfect liberty is bound to lead to conflict; yet God gave no instructions as to how humankind ought to regulate such free use by all. "But it was left to Reason of Men to determine, what Measures should be taken to prevent any Discord that might arise amongst them from the exercise of this right" (Pufendorf 1672: 320–22). Reason may advise "property" as a means to settle conflict, but there are still a lot of details to be worked out about the precise form such property must take before it can be made at all practical, and these can only be resolved by mutual agreement. Still, whatever form will be agreed upon will be justified "according as the Peace of Human Society seem'd to require" (ibid.). So it is not any special relationship between individual and object that justifies property rights or their extent, but a society-wide interest in preserving peace that justifies rules for the assignments of rights over objects.

David Hume echoes a similar concern. Society provides man with many benefits required to overcome his natural incapacity to deal with the challenges and threats that confront him in his solitary state. Joining forces with other men amplifies their power, a division of labor generates superior ability and mutual support provides greater security. To counter the natural partiality of man that endangers the peace and stability of society, and with it all the advantages society affords, the artifice of justice and property is established by convention (Hume 1986/1739–1740: 539ff). Rules setting out exactly what kind of control individuals may expect to have over objects will reduce misunderstanding and conflict.

John Stuart Mill also argues that the original function of the institution of private property was not utility but the preservation of peace (Mill 1994/1848: 7). Once established however, the institution of private property receives its justification from the greater utility it engenders in comparison to alternative regimes of common ownership. Moreover, the precise form property will take—for example, the extent of the right of capital to a share of the product, laws regulating inheritance and property in land, and so on—are to be determined primarily by their tendency to promote utility.

Inquiring about whether the individualistic regime of private property should be superseded, by comparing it to a socialistic regime of communal property and equality of income, another utilitarian, Henry Sidgwick, concludes that "there is no principle of abstract equity" that morally requires private property. Moreover, were a socialistic system feasible without too much loss, present inequalities due to the capitalist system would surely be unjust. Difficulties of transition from one system to the other would be no more serious than those involved in the abolition of slavery (yet, presumably, no one would deny the injustice of the latter on that account). Therefore, the case in favor of a private property regime can only be settled on the basis of economic (i.e., utilitarian) considerations. That is to say, the justification of private property must be sought in its greater efficiency and tendency to increase utility (Sidgwick 1903/1883, chs. 6–7).

Contemporary liberal theories of justice provide a further example of the regime view of property. For John Rawls, the choice of political-economic regime is determined according to how well its institutions may be designed to achieve our conception of justice. He promptly rejects the three regimes of laissez-faire capitalism, welfare-state capitalism and state socialism as incompatible with the principles of justice. The first of these is a system that respects full liberal ownership. Such a system, Rawls argues, secures merely formal freedom and is thus incompatible with fair value of equal political liberties and fair equality of opportunity. The second regime, that of welfare capitalism, embodies a more restricted form of property, but only for the sake of providing a decent minimum to cover basic needs. It is rejected on the basis of the great inequalities "in the ownership of real property (productive assets and natural resources)" it permits. The third regime, that of state socialism, recognizing no property in productive assets, is discarded only because it violates the principle of equal liberty. Thus the first three types of regime are rejected by Rawls without any regard to how well they embody private property. Indeed, the two regimes compatible with the principles of justice that Rawls proceeds to examine—a property-owning democracy (the means of production are controlled mostly by private individuals) and liberal socialism (the means of production are socially controlled)—are assessed, and the choice among these ultimately determined, by how well they enable the basic structure to uphold the principles of justice, regardless of whatever special relationships may be thought to exist between certain individuals and specific objects (Rawls 2001: 135–40. See also Clark and Gintis 1978: 302–25; Krouse and McPherson 1986: 119–38).

From Pufendorf to Rawls, the primary question this sort of justification addresses is *why should anyone own anything at all?* We assign spheres of control and entitlements to income according to certain rules insofar as these are a necessary condition of peace, or a means of maximizing prosperity or welfare, or of achieving equity or fairness. Only derivatively can it be asserted that an individual P should own a particular asset X. This follows merely because these are the rules of the regime that best promote this particular favored social function. The kind of entitlement thus justified, its extent and scope, are also determined by its instrumentality in achieving the goal.

The first quality required of such rights, so that they may serve the justifying function, is clarity. The boundaries of individual entitlements must be clearly demarcated so as to minimize conflict and allow efficient use. Perhaps also such entitlements must be exclusive, or else a clear division of powers with respect to the asset must be defined. Thus if it is unclear with respect to a certain resource who has powers of decision over it, who is to benefit from its improvement and how secure that benefit will be, many potential sources of conflict remain and perhaps also proliferate. Moreover, some clear incentives to improve the asset and to produce welfare to the benefit of all will be removed. Beyond that, however, the determinations of property remain an open question. How much one is to benefit from improvements to owned resources, and how secure these benefits must be, depend on how much is needed to motivate the average individual to put their assets into socially beneficial use. Thus taxes may be seen not as a limitation of ownership, but as an element in the complete account of individual entitlements (Murphy and Nagel 2002). Restrictions on use (zoning laws, conservation, safety and hygiene and so on), or on transfer (estate taxes, gift taxes, entailment, laws against self-enslavement), designed to increase stability, aggregate utility or fairness, collectively define the precise contours of property rights. Generally speaking, any bundle of clearly defined restrictions on control, income and transfer may be considered property rights, in the full unproblematic sense, when they follow from the social values the regime is intent to promote. In particular, nothing in this view of property, focusing as it does on the social values promoted by the regime, obliges us to espouse the notion of full liberal ownership as the only possible justifiable conception of private property.

2. Property as Entitlement

A second tradition of property discourse focuses on justifying property as an entitlement or *natural right*. In effect this sort of justification sets out to provide reasons for the recognition of such a *right*, to point out the individual values it tends to protect or enhance for the owner. As I did in the previous section for the regime view, I shall now indicate how various thinkers in justifying property have appealed to several individual (rather than social) values. Focusing on the owner, these can be the guarantee of subsistence or needs; the promotion of individual welfare; enhancing autonomy or enabling unobstructed project pursuit; permitting the development of personality; and so on.

According to Hugo Grotius, when the world is held in common by all humankind, as it originally must have been, individuals can seize from the common stock for their own use and consumption. Depriving them of whatever they so took was considered an injustice. At this early stage of common use there is effectively present a regime of "natural equity." However, this state can no longer continue once human society loses its simplicity in terms of lifestyle, goodwill and mutual forbearance. The development of elaborate forms of consumption intensifies conflict and requires clearly demarcated spheres of dominion or exclusive control (Grotius 1625, book II, ch. 2). At this point, reached long ago, private property becomes necessary to allow unhindered individual use and to promote welfare. It becomes "inconvenient" to persist in common ownership. Hence tacit consent is given that first occupancy establishes not merely a liberty to consume but a full-fledged individual entitlement. Individuals need this because some forms of consumption stretch over time—some things they want to save for later use, or they may have plans for these things to interact with other objects at different points of time to allow more complex interrelated forms of management and use. Nevertheless, these entitlements always remain subject to the original principles of natural equity, so that in cases of extreme necessity the rationale of self-preservation may override these individual property rights (ibid.: 91f).

John Locke's discussion of property begins by noting that both reason and revelation concur that man has a right to self-preservation and therefore also to the natural resources necessary to the "support and comfort of their being." Yet before they can be of any use or at all beneficial to any particular individual, he must first appropriate these resources. Thus Locke appears to be saying that private property in a natural resource is a necessary condition for beneficial use. Consequently, there must be a morally acceptable method to unilaterally acquire parts of the natural world and to make them one's own. Famously, Locke bases the method of acquisition on the investment of labor, and restricts its scope by the proviso that enough and as good is left for others (Locke 1988/1689: 285ff). But whatever the means of original appropriation, Grotius and Locke similarly maintain that the real justification of property is its necessity for the beneficial use for whichever individual initiated a sort of relationship with the object, whether by laboring or by mere occupancy. That is to say, the benefit to the owner.

The justification of property might extend beyond the provision of subsistence, needs or moderate contribution to welfare. According to Loren Lomasky, persons "have a natural interest in having things." Neo-Lockeans (libertarians of all stripes and colors) such as Lomasky insist that this interest amounts to the ability to employ the object in the furtherance of one's project, perhaps in the pursuit of long-term life plans. Since control of such objects is a necessary condition of being able to pursue one's projects, there is an interest not merely in having objects but also in being accorded property rights with respect to them (Lomasky 1987: 120–21).

G. W. F. Hegel's justification of property, though more complex, is briefly stated: "The person must give himself an external *sphere of freedom* in order to have being as idea" (Hegel 1991/1822, § 41). "To have being as idea" is, according to Hegel, the end and purpose of all human striving. Such an achievement involves being a self-consciousness; that is to say, being aware of one's own subjecthood and freedom. But a necessary step in the achievement of self-consciousness is being recognized as such by other self-consciousnesses, by other persons. Now, to be recognized as a self-consciousness one must expose one's internal free will to the full view of others. One must make it observable, perceptible, salvage it from its mere subjective internality, and to externalize it into something objective: "an external sphere of freedom." A thing, completely unfree, fully under my control, might be a manifestation of my free will, open to the view of others. It is this end that property is designed to promote. In taking possession of an unowned thing, in using it and ultimately alienating it, one manifests one's free will residing in the object. Consequently, it exposes one's will to full view, allowing recognition, and by these means comes the achievement of self consciousness. Hence, property draws its value from *owning* rather than from the thing owned. It is not advantages, such as the satisfaction of needs, increased welfare or greater freedom of control, that the thing owned confer on the owner, that justify property. It is the "superseding of mere subjectivity" enabled by the recognition of an external sphere of control. In this sense Hegel's account is very different from that of Grotius, Locke or modern-day neo-Lockeans.

From Grotius to Hegel, the primary question this sort of justification addresses is why an individual P should own a particular asset X. The reason is that by incorporating it in a project, or investing it with one's personhood, X is made necessary for the promotion of values such as need, welfare or the realization of self-consciousness *for P*. Spheres of control are determined by individuals taking possession of unowned parts of the world, by occupying, laboring, using or placing their will in objects, thereby gaining entitlements to control the object and to the income it generates to the necessary extent. Only derivatively can it be asserted that there should be such an institution at all. The property regime that ensues is justified merely as a consequence of respecting the sort of entitlements that best promote these particular individual values.

What scope and extent of property does this conception require? In particular, does the full list of incidents follow from such a justification? Evidently, the first quality of such rights is continuity. That is to say, an indefinite duration of the right and an immunity against expropriation. As Locke put it, the nature of property is "that without a Man's own consent it cannot be taken from him" (Locke 1988/1689: 395). Whatever rights we have, we must be sure that they remain ours until we voluntarily abandon or dispossess them (or "alienate," in the word often used by classical philosophers). But this is perhaps more relevant for a Hegelian justification than for Locke or Grotius. If needs and welfare ground such a right, then surely the right persists only as long as it remains beneficial, and it is hard to see what claim one would retain to it when it no longer generates the kind of value that grounded it. The neo-Lockean idea of incorporating it in a project may go further when we hold an expansive view of what might count as a project and by what means objects are incorporated into it.

In order to survive, people must eat and drink, perhaps wear protective clothing and inhabit a dwelling. The sort of entitlements in objects justified in this strand of thought obviously require the primary incidents of *possession and use rights*. But this is still not quite what we set out to justify. In some cases nothing like property follows. Though it seems reasonable that food and drink must exclude others in the process of their consumption, it is far from clear that this implies a property right in any interesting sense. For a property right includes not merely use, but also control, management and the right to transfer. Yet these incidents do not apply in Locke's paradigmatic case of a chewed, swallowed and digested apple, for example.

Use rights grounded on subsistence needs are quite limited in scope. If what I am permitted to take from nature is what I need to eat and drink, then I may do just that. Of course, in a slightly more advanced economy I may want to specialize in apples, say, and trade them for your eggs. Exclusive property rights are certainly required to allow a division of labor to develop and for the possibility of trade, but it does not follow that these are necessary for subsistence. Rights to clothing and shelter, insofar as they are justified as necessary means of subsistence, may not be used in any way other than that. This allows such little discretion regarding how these assets may be used that it is hardly plausible to call whatever rights one may have in respect of these "property rights." Nevertheless, whatever rights these are, they would need to be exclusive if even a minimal degree of privacy is to be secured.

Moreover, for use rights justified on needs or welfare grounds it is not necessary that they be exclusive. In some cases *joint use rights* or a mere *liberty to use* may be sufficient to satisfy the needs or guarantee the welfare that justifies them. Tools and machinery for the production of subsistence needs do not necessarily need to be our exclusive property. These can sometimes be used more efficiently when shared rather than privately owned. It is even less plausible that land for recreation requires exclusivity for its effective use, though it might need a rationing mechanism for its most efficient use. The same goes for some material consumption goods such as books or DVDs. Sharing through public libraries might be, in an intuitive sense, more effective than private possession in satisfying most of these individual values.

Management rights (the power to permit others to use the asset) also seem unnecessary on either benefit/welfare grounds or on personhood grounds. As far as the Hegelian justification is concerned, it is not clear how one's will may be externalized, open to view, when another is using or in possession of the asset. Surely, it is more difficult to recognize the owner's will when someone else is controlling it, even if this was only possible with the owner's permission. In terms of benefit and the Grotius/Locke sort of justification, my interest may indeed be served by allowing the plumber to mend my water pipes. But this sort of management seems markedly different from renting out my land for a fee. Not that I can't benefit from the pay, but this raises the question of why I should be the one to reap this sort of benefit. Similarly, income rights are unnecessary. If an asset is no longer beneficial, or if I wish to remove my will from it, I can simply leave it—why require and protect payment? Nor are transfer rights necessary: though there'll be an immunity against expropriation, there need be no restriction on taxing income, inheritance and so on.

Not only is property based on these individual values limited in scope in the various ways just mentioned, but it is also limited in its extent. That is to say, how much property must be owned for these purposes? In principle, property seems to set no limits. As long as the asset is acquired by legitimate means, originally or by voluntary transfer, it is justifiably owned. Hegelian rights, the aim of which is achieved by making the will recognizable in the object, do necessitate exclusive possession and use. However, it is unclear why this would require anything more than token ownership, sizeable enough to allow the will to be recognized, but nothing beyond that. Rights based on needs or welfare, on the other hand, would permit greater ownership, but these would be limited by the extent that can be made useful and beneficial. Locke recognizes as much with his non-spoilage proviso (ibid.: 290)—that one may appropriate only as much as one can make beneficial use of before it spoils (a condition he dubiously argues to have been superseded by the introduction of money). "Incorporating in a project" allows for a wider range of more elaborate goods. Land or diamonds, food or mansions, can be part of a project. At least insofar as we are considering objects as a means to the pursuit of happiness, anything can be such that necessitates exclusive control. Arguably, however, such unlimited extension robs the idea of property based on individual values of the urgency it initially seemed to address.

To recap: the kind of entitlements that follow from the justification of natural property rights based on individual values such as need, welfare or the achievement of self-consciousness act as constraints on any kind of regime a society may consider. This is the sort of justification appealed to by writers such as Grotius, Locke and Hegel, and continues to rally support in contemporary thought. Yet, what I hope to have established in this section is that there are some serious challenges to the view that anything like full liberal ownership must follow from such a justification.

3. The Problem of Redistribution: Is It Possible That the Best Regime Is One of (Almost) Full Liberal Ownership?

Treating the regime view, so far, I have pointed out that a regime justified on the basis of how well it promotes certain social values such as stability, efficiency and equity, is not directly concerned with the kind of individual interests that property tends to advance for the owner. It is thus of no consequence for the regime view how well full liberal ownership may enhance these individual interests. Could it be, however, the case that full liberal ownership, or something close to it, would do better to promote the social goals that such regimes explicitly aim to advance than a more restricted form of ownership? I do not mean to provide a full assessment in response to this question. What I shall do instead is to draw very roughly the form of reasoning such an assessment should take. This should demonstrate the difficulty in attempting to substantiate the claim that the promotion of social values that justify a property regime would be best served by instituting rights that amount to full liberal ownership, or something close enough. Let me focus on one central feature of property. For this purpose any feature would do, since full liberal ownership includes the complete list of unrestricted incidents. However, I direct the reader's attention to the incident of transmissibility: the full discretionary power of the owner to transfer their title to any individual of their choice (subject only to the transferee's consent).

A few words on the significance of transmissibility and why I choose to focus on it are in order. This feature may be regarded as the most distinctive of property and at any rate the most contentious. If a case can be made on the basis of the social values of stability, efficiency or equity for a robust right to transfer title, then this could be a significant result of full liberal ownership.

Property can obviously serve the material interests of the owner, whether or not these interests are those that grounded the right. Still, whoever happens to be the owner is not the only one who could benefit in a similar way from the object. If it is food, clothing, shelter or any other consumer goods and services, there are many persons who could benefit as much as the owner, and some could benefit even more. A once-and-for-all allocation is bound to become an impediment on the realization of interests (some of which it may have been designed to advance). When reciprocal transfers can improve the situation of both parties to the exchange, without harming anyone else, the distribution is inefficient. Efficiency of this sort requires a system of redistribution. A mechanism for the recurrent transfers of these rights must be available. This mechanism can be anything on the continuum between consensual transfer—whereby the power of transfer lies in the hands of the owner alone—on the one end, and socially governed transfers—the power of transfer is held exclusively by the state—on the other. The former is a system of property rights in the narrow or strict sense, the latter is not, or it is a property system in what I shall call the wide or loose sense only.

I'm proposing here a distinction between property in the strict sense that, whatever other incidents it may include, includes also the power of the owner to alienate or transfer the right in its entirety to another. If full liberal ownership consists of the *complete* list of incidents, then the conception of strict ownership falls short of this ideal. However, it is, in an important respect, close enough. Any conception of property would probably have to include, at a minimum, the primary control incidents of possession and use. In addition to that, the power of transfer, by making use of it conditionally, will effectively guarantee a right to obtain income in return. Property in the more relaxed or wide sense merely applies to rules of assignment to individuals of *some* control over objects, the question of who has the power to transfer remaining open.

To rephrase the question at issue: does the promotion of certain social values such as stability, prosperity or fairness require the establishment of a regime of property in the strict sense? On the spectrum of possible regimes of property we can identify three fixed points of reference:

(a) collectivist regime. At one end, a centralized system where all transfers are governed and imposed by some collective agency. Such an agency would aim to achieve Pareto improvements once the original distribution has outgrown itself. Other than that, the regime may be geared to achieve whatever social values are thought to ground property (in the wide sense). For this it uses the one remedial tool of redistribution.

(b) libertarian regime. At the other end of the spectrum, individuals enjoy strict property rights that include the power to transfer the right, if not the complete list of incidents that comprise full liberal ownership. All redistribution is decentralized, all and only voluntary exchanges being permitted. It can be assumed that all transfers would constitute Pareto improvements. Though the regime may still be planned to achieve various additional social goals, its only means is the design of the conception of property rights—the sort of restrictions on possession, use and management that are thought to be most conducive to whatever values the system aims to attain. What must remain unregulated and decentralized for the regime to be considered in this sense libertarian is the transfer of property rights.

(c) a liberal-egalitarian regime. Somewhere in between these two end points lies a mixed system whereby individuals enjoy property rights (in the wide sense) comprised of some, perhaps most, incidents of property, including a right to alienate and transfer these rights. Yet, all these incidents are subject to whatever restrictions seem required to achieve the social goal of the regime. In particular, these rights are vulnerable to redistribution by the collective agency. Thus the system utilizes two kinds of tools to achieve Pareto improvements as well as the realization of other social values: the design of property rights and redistributive taxation. What is aimed at are clearly marked boundaries of possession of objects, their use and the extraction of income, including explicit conditions under which the boundaries will be transgressed (e.g., by taxes), and some, no less explicit, freedom to avoid these conditions (e.g., by earning less).

Each of these regimes is at least minimally adequate insofar as boundaries are clearly demarcated, and assuming they enjoy wide legitimacy, they would enable peace and stability. Other than that, these regimes widely differ. Choice among them would be informed by our evaluations of the following questions:

i. Which of these regimes is likely to be more productive, generating greater prosperity?
ii. Which is more just or more conducive to establishing justice or equity?
iii. Which best balances considerations of justice/equity and efficiency with individual values such as "project pursuit"?

A collectivist regime is generally thought to be less productive. This is so mainly for problems of information and self-interested behavior: the collective agency will need to absorb all relevant information, to analyze it, and to issue effective directives, compliance with which will result in greater productivity. There is some doubt that such an agency could do a better job at this than the impersonal workings of the market that require merely voluntary transfers and exchanges led purely by self-interest. Whatever costs in terms of productivity such a system entails may be balanced by considerations of justice and equity that the system seems better designed to achieve. Setting aside problems of trust and competence of bureaucratic agents, the collective agency seems well placed and empowered to impose a more equitable distribution. It should be noted however, that if the conception of equity imposed by the central agency is at odds with most people's ideas, then this regime is unlikely to command the kind of support necessary for the stability and peace of society. Moreover, when this equivocal accomplishment in terms of efficiency and equity is assessed against individuals' capacity to pursue long-term projects, some of which may extend beyond a lifetime, the collectivist regime appears to be, all things considered, an inferior arrangement.

A libertarian regime is unlikely to achieve any kind of equitable distribution. This is perhaps not surprising since it is not at all among the aims of the regime to do this. The resulting distribution of such a system is unpatterned (Nozick 1974), purely a consequence of uncoordinated, contingent, individual transfers. It traces no kind of consideration that may inform distributive justice. On the contrary, such a system will have the consequence of reflecting differences in (arguably undeserved) marketable skills and capabilities, and amplifying them over generations through inherited wealth. But a libertarian regime is also no guarantee of productivity and welfare. Though it may do better than collectivist planning, insofar as it may benefit from the advantages that markets possess in the transmission of information and incentive structure, it will not be able to provide public goods (from street lighting to reliable commercial advertising) and to correct the many failures generated by an unregulated market. Again, this may not come as a huge surprise since productivity is not the direct concern of such a system and any benefits of welfare that may ensue are a mere windfall. Of course, a libertarian regime will excel in facilitating project pursuit for those fortunate enough to enjoy the benefits of private possessions. From the point of view of social value, a property regime is chosen and justified insofar as it optimizes and balances values of stability, productivity, equity and autonomous project pursuit. There is no reason at all to be so optimistic as to believe that libertarian regimes barring all centralized transfers would outclass, in these terms, the kind of regimes that calculatedly redistribute to achieve just this end.

A liberal-egalitarian regime embodies a compromise in terms of productivity and equity, but arguably does a better job at both than the libertarian regime and, at least in terms of productivity, better also than the collectivist regime. Recognizing as it does private property that includes the power of transfer, it can take advantage of the Pareto optimizing tendencies of free exchange and the incentive structure and information-transmission mechanism that come with it, but also concomitantly holding on to the prerogative of imposing taxes and regulating the exercise of these rights for the sake of increasing efficiency as well as for the promotion of social goals such as equity and stability by instituting arrangements and distributions that would tend to generate their own support. Though project pursuit may be thus constrained, such a system will nevertheless allow a significant degree of autonomous choice, while also extending its scope, allowing more individuals to materially enrich their lives. Arguably, a liberal-egalitarian regime at some ideal point on the spectrum of regimes will do a better job generating wealth, establishing justice, achieving stability and allowing personal freedom and project pursuit. It appears therefore implausible that a property regime justified by any assortment of social goals will comprise of full liberal ownership, or any conception of property, in the strict sense, that is close enough insofar as it includes full powers of transfer.

4. Full Liberal Ownership and the Uneasy Fusion of Both Justifications

On the *regime view*, property is a haphazard, contingent, almost accidental bundle of incidents and incident-fractions, pieced together so as to promote at a society level some valued social goals. I have argued that it is highly improbable that full liberal ownership, or a conception sufficiently similar, would be found justified on this basis. The functions of the justified regime allow for a much more finely tuned design of property (in the wide sense), and can allow for further considerations such as equity. On the *entitlement view*, property comprises several incidents exhibiting an internal coherence and integrity, designed to protect certain individual values for the owner. Such a conception acts as a constraint that must be respected by any kind of property regime. The extent and scope of property may be wider or narrower depending on the values intended to be protected. By extent I mean the incidents included and their degree of stringency; by scope I mean the kind of assets that may be owned. As I have shown, the extent and scope of property justified on the basis of the kind of individual values typically appealed to will be, in all likelihood, less than full liberal ownership. The sort of purposes that individual rights of ownership are meant to advance can be fully accomplished with a lesser conception. Thus the ideal of full liberal ownership cannot be justified either as an individual entitlement nor as a social regime.

Could we, however, justify full liberal ownership by combining the entitlement and the regime view of property? Might it be the case, given the constraints imposed by a weaker conception of property justified by the entitlement view, that the best we could do in terms of prosperity, for example, would be to increase the extent and scope of these individual entitlements? The idea is that since these weaker entitlements may not be infringed even for the sake of greater efficiency, the remaining range of maneuvers permitted for government regulation of property is too narrow to make any considerable and favorable difference for wealth creation. This goal may be better approached by increasing the extent and scope of entitlements to a level sufficiently close to full liberal ownership, than by managing and regulating whatever remains beyond individual entitlements.

It is very difficult to evaluate such a claim, though it seems very unlikely that the state of affairs described by this argument is necessarily the case. That is to say that it follows from conceptual considerations and the rationale of human behavior that the best we could do in terms of productivity is simply to assign full liberal ownership of increased extent and scope, or at least full discretionary power of transfer to the owner. This is unlikely, because all the concerns raised against the libertarian regime and the need to undo market failures, externalities and the provision of public goods continue to hold after individuals are granted entitlements of control and some income. Arguably, these concerns are the product of exactly the exclusive and full power of transfer now proposed to be added to gain the extra productivity and efficiency.

Moreover, there are other social goals that the entitlement view cannot easily address. The social value of justice or equity, for instance, is inescapable. Libertarians typically endorse a historical conception of justified holdings. If everyone holds only what they legitimately acquired, mostly by voluntary exchange, then there can be no complaint by any third parties to whatever distribution ensues. Thus we are freed from excessive preoccupation with distribution. But it is precisely this supposed legitimacy of the power of transfer involved in voluntary exchange that we are at this point questioning.

Taking a step back: the grounds of entitlement are worthy individual values that merit protection and promotion—such as need, welfare, project pursuit—yet are shared by many. That is to say, the freedom or welfare provided to the owner by the control of certain assets may be provided to virtually anyone other than the owner; yet due to the exclusive entitlement it is denied to everyone but the owner. The justification that a person P should own an item X must be supplemented by further reasons connecting the particular person to the individual asset. Yet these justifications revert to such flimsy grounds as first occupancy, first to labor on, or first to integrate the asset in a personal project. Fundamentally, they are grounded on the wholly arbitrary feature of being first. Most writers of this school seem at least implicitly aware of the shaky grounds they're on, which may explain the prominence of the "Lockean Proviso" in contemporary neo-Lockean thought. This proviso, in its various formulations, requires that no one be made worse off, relative to some baseline, by an original appropriation. Now such a proviso is open to several interpretations regarding the time at which others shouldn't be made worse off, who these others might be, the terms in which they should not be made worse off, and obviously, the baseline in comparison to which they shouldn't be made any worse off (Attas 2003).

It is at this point that the uneasy fusion of regime justification and entitlement is introduced. We may ask what exactly is the event or circumstance that according to the proviso should not make others worse off. The most natural answer is that an individual P's ownership of a particular resource X should not make any other individual R's situation worse. Yet this may be too stringent, since ownership does restrict everyone's liberty (and opportunity to appropriate) and, by itself, does not create any counterbalancing benefits. Such an interpretation of the proviso would make all and any appropriation impermissible. Perhaps it is not the ownership that ought not make others worse off (because it certainly does) but what's done with one's assets in the act of appropriation. If the owner works to improve the resource, making it more valuable, then this might result in benefits for all. So only when some act makes X more valuable to the degree that would counterbalance the loss of liberty will the appropriation of X be justified. Now, this sets severe limits on what can be appropriated and how. Mere designating cannot count as appropriation; instead there must be a value-adding trait to the act of appropriation. The amount appropriated is also limited by the requirement of counterbalancing gains. Moreover, even if the act of appropriation improves what then becomes one's property, the asset or parts of it must be made available for others to use, at a price they would be willing to pay, so that they too may gain from the enhancement of value. I doubt that such a requirement is consistent with full ownership of a resource.

At this point a libertarian may be tempted to get around the problem, as Nozick does, by appealing to the counterbalancing values of the regime:

> Is the situation of persons who are unable to appropriate (there being no more accessible and useful unowned objects) worsened *by a system* allowing appropriation and permanent property?
>
> (Nozick 1974: 177)

Perhaps a capitalist system of private property would be favored by its superior efficiency in raising everyone's standard of living. The whole system of property is now to be considered the counterbalancing factor in cases of original acquisition. This is where, it seems to me, the uneasy fusion of entitlement and regime justifications is introduced. The proviso is a requirement of *particular* appropriations. Particular appropriations have to involve counterbalancing gains in order to be justified. Since clearly not all appropriations have this effect, we get rid of the proviso on *particular* appropriations, replacing it with a promise of increased benefits of the *general* system. Once we allow the regime to be the counterbalancing feature permitting private appropriations, we can establish individual entitlements. But then we may question the efficiency of this particular regime (a capitalist system of full liberal ownership) not merely in comparison to the absence of *any kind* of property regime, but also in comparison to the many kinds of conceivable regimes of property (in the wide sense) that may do better in terms of efficiency. Moreover, if we allow considerations of prosperity to counterbalance losses due to individual entitlements, then why not also considerations of equity? Could we not appeal directly to inequalities produced by individual entitlements as restrictions on appropriations? Finally, the social values of peace and stability might be jeopardized by full liberal ownership. Though drawing clearly marked boundaries is necessary to avoid conflict, the extent of inequalities in principle permitted by full liberal ownership, and likely in practice to develop, may turn out to be too much of a challenge. Absent all regulation and redistributive taxation, a regime respecting full liberal ownership will arguably fail to generate the support of those living under it.

5. Conclusion

I have traced two lines of thought, justification and discourse about property. The *regime view* effectively sets out to explain the function of a property regime in terms of the social values, such as stability, prosperity or fairness, it tends to promote. The *entitlement view* specifies reasons for the recognition of a property right in terms of the individual interests, such as need, welfare or project pursuit, it protects and enhances for the owner. Neither of these views taken separately, nor a combination of them both, unproblematically justifies the complete set of incidents that make up full liberal ownership, or even a lesser conception that includes the unrestricted power of transfer (what I have called property in the strict sense).

In practice, never and nowhere is full liberal ownership respected. Property is regularly subjected to various restrictions such as zoning, labor regulations, environmental protection and, most significantly, taxes of all kind and manner. Yet to many it seems that this is a sort of compromise. On this common view, full liberal ownership is an ideal, a natural right or entitlement that follows from whatever it is that, in terms of individual values, it tends to promote, even if regularly outweighed by other interests or practical considerations. Thus, it is often thought that government regulation and taxes may be a justifiable infringement of property, but an infringement nevertheless. In this respect there is something regrettable about such regulation. The package of full ownership and public spending strike a balance between competing ideals. As I hope to have shown, full liberal ownership is no ideal. Restricting it is no compromise at all.

References

Attas, D. (2003) "The Negative Principle of Just Appropriation," 33 *Canadian Journal of Philosophy*: 343–72.
—— (2006) "Fragmenting Property," 25 *Law and Philosophy*: 119–49.
Christman, J. (1994) *The Myth of Property*, New York: Oxford University Press.
Clark, B. and Gintis, H. (1978) "Rawlsian Justice and Economic Systems," 7 *Philosophy and Public Affairs*: 302–25.
Epstein, R. (1985) *Takings: Private Property and the Power of Eminent Domain*, Cambridge, Mass.: Harvard University Press.
Fried, B. (1995) "Wilt Chamberlain Revisited: Nozick's Justice in Transfer and the Problem of Market-Based Distribution," 24 *Philosophy and Public Affairs*: 226–45.
Grotius, H. (1901/1625) *The Rights of War and Peace: Including the Law of Nature and Nations*, New York: Walter Dunne Publishers.
Hegel, G. W. F. (1991/1822) *Elements of the Philosophy of Right*, Cambridge: Cambridge University Press.
Honoré, T. (1987) "Ownership," in T. Honoré, *Making Law Bind: Essays Legal and Philosophical*, Oxford: Clarendon Press.

Hume, D. (1986/1739–1740) *A Treatise of Human Nature*, Harmondsworth: Penguin Classics.

Krouse, R. and McPherson, M. (1986) "A 'Mixed'-Property Regime: Equality and Liberty in a Market Economy," 97 *Ethics*: 119–38.

Locke, J. (1988/1689) *Two Treatises of Government*, Cambridge: Cambridge University Press.

Lomasky, L. (1987) *Persons, Rights, and the Moral Community*, New York: Oxford University Press.

Mill, J. S. (1994/1848) *Principles of Political Economy*, Oxford: Oxford University Press.

Murphy, L. and Nagel, T. (2002) *The Myth of Ownership: Taxes and Justice*, New York: Oxford University Press.

Nozick, R. (1974) *Anarchy, State and Utopia*, New York: Basic Books.

Pufendorf, S. (1672) *Of the Laws of Nature and of Nations*.

Rawls, J. (2001) *Justice as Fairness: A Restatement*, Cambridge, Mass.: Harvard University Press.

Sidgwick, H. (1903/1883) *The Principles of Political Economy*, London: Macmillan.

Waldron, J. (1988) *The Right to Private Property*, Oxford: Oxford University Press.

Further Reading

For further reading, see: J. Harris (1996) *Property and Justice*, Oxford: Oxford University Press; S. Munzer (1990) *A Theory of Property*, Cambridge: Cambridge University Press; L. Murphy and T. Nagel (2002) *The Myth of Ownership: Taxes and Justice*, New York: Oxford University Press; and J. Waldron (1988) *The Right to Private Property*, Oxford: Oxford University Press.

19
TAXATION, REDISTRIBUTION AND PROPERTY RIGHTS

Peter Vallentyne

What kinds of taxation, if any, are just, relative to a given set of property rights? To answer this question, we first need to clarify what taxation is, what justice is and what property rights are. We shall see that full moral ownership of a resource is indeed incompatible with just taxation for the use or ownership of that resource, but various forms of near-full ownership are compatible.

Taxation and Justice

Our topic is the justice of taxation relative to a given set of moral property rights. Let us start by clarifying the notions of taxation and justice.

A *tax*, roughly speaking, is a financial charge made by a state upon an entity (e.g., individual or corporation) for the support of state operations and programs and subject to forcible extraction and perhaps penalty if not paid. For accounting or legal purposes, taxes are often distinguished from: (1) compulsory payments for social insurance (e.g., unemployment insurance, health insurance or pension plans), (2) user fees for state-provided services (e.g., for using parks, sewage disposal or roads), and (3) miscellaneous other revenue (e.g., fines). I shall, however, understand taxes broadly to include all of these. Moreover, I shall also include state-required provisions of services (e.g., military service, or use of one's car or land) or goods (e.g., crops) as taxes as well (even though they need not require the payment of any specified financial value). In this broad sense, taxes include all state-required provisions of goods (including money) or services to the state. For simplicity, I shall not address state-required provisions of goods or services to others (e.g., state-required payments of car or health insurance premiums to a private company), but these can raise similar issues.

Our main question concerns the justice of taxation, but what is justice? Unfortunately, the term "justice" is used in different ways by different authors: (1) as moral permissibility for basic social structures, (2) as distributive fairness (e.g., net benefits in accordance with comparative desert), (3) as the fulfillment of all duties owed to someone (i.e., as wronging no one) and (4) as fulfilling all enforceable duties, where an enforceable duty is one for which someone is permitted to forcibly ensure compliance (e.g., the duty not to kill, but not the duty to keep your promise to your mother).

I shall here use "justice" in the sense of the fulfillment of all interpersonal duties (duties owed to someone). Just actions in this sense are actions that wrong no one in the sense of infringing no one's rights. As long as rights are understood broadly to include choice-protecting and interest-protecting rights, as being either pro tanto or conclusive, and as sometimes being highly conditional, the topic of justice in this sense is very broad. It includes all moral duties except impersonal moral duties (duties owed to no one; i.e., a duty to X that applies even when all autonomous agents have validly consented to not-X and when not-Xing benefits all entities with moral standing).

It is important to keep in mind that my arguments do not automatically apply to the other concepts of justice above. If, however, one holds, as I do, that all and only duties owed to someone are enforceable (in principle), then the arguments will also apply to the concept of justice as fulfilling all enforceable duties (the fourth concept above).

Property Rights and Ownership

Ownership of a thing is a certain kind of bundle of rights over it. Throughout, we will focus on moral ownership (a certain kind of bundle of moral rights) as opposed to legal ownership (a certain kind of bundle of legal rights). We shall see that it does, if the individual *fully* owns the resource, but it need not do so where the ownership is less than full.

The classic analysis of ownership is that given by Honoré (1961), who identifies 11 elements of full (or liberal) ownership. This list, I believe, can be radically simplified to the following three kinds of right, where *use* of an object is understood broadly to include all the ways that persons can physically impact upon an object:

1. Rights to *control use* of the object: for example, the rights to possess, use, consume, waste, modify and destroy the object, and the right to manage (decide how others may use) the object;
2. Rights to *transfer* the rights to others (by sale, rental, gift or loan): for example, the right to alienate (transfer) the rights, and the lack of restrictions on transmissibility (e.g., all rights held can be transferred to others who may then transfer them to others *ad infinitum*);
3. Immunity to loss of these rights, except perhaps as a result of a rights infringement, and immunity to the loss of other rights for the mere possession or exercise of these rights: for example, the right to security (immunity from expropriation), absence of term (no loss after mere passage of time) and the absence of any conditionality on the provision of goods or services (e.g., rent).

Honoré has three elements that are not included in the above list, but they seem out of place: (1) prohibition of harmful use, (2) revisionary character (rules governing lapsed ownership rights) and (3) the right to income (e.g., rents and profits for allowing others to use it). The first element is not necessary, since the liberty right to use one's property is only a liberty right to use the object *as such*, in the sense that no one else's permission is needed for the mere use of the object. Property rights do not give the owners a liberty right to use the object in any way that they please. The full owner of a baseball bat has no liberty right to smash your car with it. Hence, there is no need to include a prohibition of harmful use. That prohibition comes from the rights of others (e.g., your rights over your car).

The second element, revisionary character, concerns rules governing lapsed ownership rights. Such rules are indeed important, but they are not needed for a specification of full ownership, since they are about how one can *acquire* rights over a thing that someone else has abandoned or otherwise lost.

The third element is the right to income (fruits, rents, profits) from the object. Somewhat controversially, I believe that this element is not part of the rights of full ownership. The core idea of this right is that the owner of an object (e.g., a movie theater) who grants permission to others to use it for a fee (or rents it out or sells it) has a right to the income (or other resources) that this generates. I do not question that the owner has a right to this income; I merely question that this flows from her full ownership of the thing generating the income. To make this point clear, let us assume that I fully own a movie theater, the admission fee is $10, you fully own $10 and you have paid me this amount for admission. I now own the $10, but this is so because you fully owned the $10 before, and your full ownership included the full right to transfer it to me with my consent. I would still fully own the $10 if you simply gave it to me as a gift and I accepted it. My ownership of the movie theater causally enabled me to get you to transfer $10 to me, but it did not include a right to the full income. That flows from your full ownership of the $10 and our mutual consent to a transfer.

There are two further property rights that Honoré mentions as accompanying remedies, but does not list separately:

4. Rights to compensation against another, if he/she uses the object without your permission and this harms you.
5. Rights of enforcement to prevent or rectify (e.g., extract compensation) use of the objection without one's permission.

Full ownership of a thing is a maximally strong bundle of property rights of the above five sorts. More exactly, it is a maximally strong bundle of such rights over a given thing compatible with someone else having the *same rights* over everything else in the world (except for the agent and the space the thing is occupying). Full ownership thus includes full rights to control the use of the object and full rights to transfer it to others. As I shall explain, however, there is indeterminacy with respect to the immunity to loss and the rights to compensation and enforcement.

The concept of full ownership, I claim, is indeterminate with respect to how strong the following three elements are: immunity to loss, rights to compensation and enforcement rights. This is because the stronger one person's compensation or enforcement rights are, the weaker another person's immunity to loss is. At one extreme (radical enforcement rights), the compensation and enforcement rights might be so strong that a person loses all his ownership rights if he infringes the rights of the former. At the other extreme, there might be no compensation or enforcement rights: individuals would have an unconditional immunity to loss of their ownership rights. Neither extreme view is plausible, but the point here is simply that there is a logical tension between (1) the compensation and enforcement rights and (2) the immunity to loss. As a result, the notion of full ownership is indeterminate with respect to these elements. This leaves, however, a determinate core of full ownership that consists of the full rights to control use, the full rights to transfer the rights to others and full immunity to loss if one has not infringed the rights of others. (For further discussion of this issue, see Vallen-tyne, Steiner and Otsuka 2005.)

Let us now turn to our main question: whether just taxation is compatible with ownership.

Just Taxation and Ownership

Suppose that you *legally fully* own certain apples. Is that compatible with the legal per-missibility of the state extracting an annual property tax on the value of your apples? It is not. Full legal ownership of a thing precludes the legal permissibility of taxation of the use of the thing or the possession or exercise of those rights. Our topic, however, is justice, and that is a moral, not a legal, issue. It concerns moral rights, not legal rights. The fact that you legally fully own something tells us little about what moral rights you have to it. Those who legally owned other people as involuntary slaves did not have any moral ownership of those individuals. If we are to assess the justice of taxation, we must focus on what *moral* rights of ownership people have.

Let us start by dismissing a radical challenge from Murphy and Nagel (2002). They claim that it is "logically impossible that people should have any kind of [moral] enti-tlement to all of their pretax income" (32). They defend this view by claiming that pre-tax income presupposes a market, which presupposes a government, which presupposes taxes (32). Thus, they conclude, "the idea of a prima facie property right in one's pre-tax income—an income that could not exist without a tax-supported government—is meaningless" (36). This is not correct. The mistaken claim here is that a market presup-poses a government. There is nothing incoherent in the idea of people having property rights in things (e.g., the apples and oranges that they grow) and their trading them in the absence of any government. Indeed, something like this takes place in primitive societies. Obviously, governments typically play a significant role in supporting mar-kets, but that is not enough to support their radical claim that it is logically impossible for there to be markets without governments.

In the above passages, Murphy and Nagel overstate their case. Their real point is that moral property rights to external things are *justice-determined* rather than justice-deter-mining (10). Moral property rights are, they claim, whatever rights suitably promote a just distribution of benefits and burdens (44–45, 75, 175). For example, on an egalitarian view, moral property rights might be whatever system of conventional property rights best promotes the relevant equality. This is a perfectly respectable view, but it does not show that prelegal moral property rights are logically impossible or meaningless. At best, it shows that they do not in fact exist. Moreover, even if moral property rights are justice-determined, this does not show that there are no *prelegal* property rights. What the law is is one thing, and what the just distribution of conventional property rights is is another. Egalitarians can, for example, claim that the disadvantaged in unjust inegal-itarian states have a moral property right to more resources than the law acknowledges.

Let us return, then, to the question of whether moral ownership of a resource pre-cludes taxation. Suppose that you *morally fully* own certain apples, and the state imposes an annual property tax on the value of your apples and takes possession of some of your apples accordingly. Does your full moral ownership establish that such a tax is unjust? It does indeed. If you fully own a thing, then you have an immunity against loss of any of those rights, as long as you are not infringing the rights of others. If the state takes pos-session of some of your apples, it infringes your moral property rights over the apples and hence is unjust. More generally, moral full ownership of a thing precludes any taxation based on owners' mere possession or exercise of the ownership rights.

This point is compatible with property rights being justice-determined rather than justice-determining. The claim is only that, *if* someone has full moral ownership of a resource, then various kinds of taxation are unjust. We here leave open whether anyone has full moral ownership of anything (a claim that most people would deny). Moreover, just taxation is compatible with "almost" full ownership of a thing. One could have all the rights of full ownership except that one was liable to certain kinds of taxation. Full ownership is a bundle of rights and there is no conceptual reason why one must have either all of them or none of them. The core issue is thus the substantive issue of determining what property rights individuals have and what kinds of taxation, if any, that they allow.

Let us note two related points. First, even if taxation of a certain sort (e.g., income tax) is just, it doesn't follow that all kinds of taxation (e.g., head tax or wealth tax) are just. It depends on what is allowed by the form of moral ownership that individuals have. Second, even if a certain kind of taxation is just in principle, it does not follow that it is just in any particular case. It depends on how the tax revenues will be used. For example, if they will be used simply to enrich corrupt dictators and their associates, they will not be just.

For what purposes must tax revenues be used in order for them to be just? This is a controversial moral issue, but the least controversial use of tax revenues is providing solutions to problems of *market failure* (where the free market fails to operate efficiently). Three of the main sources of market failure are *imperfect competition* (where buyers or sellers can influence market price, e.g., monopolies and monopsonies), *externalities* (where costs or benefits are imposed on individuals without their consent, e.g., pollution) and *non-excludable goods* (where no one can be effectively excluded from using the good if it is provided to someone, e.g., national defense). In such cases, taxes can be used to provide disincentives for negative externalities or for subsidies for the provision of underprovided goods. Of course, the mere fact that there is a market failure does not guarantee that such government intervention is just. Sometimes there is *government failure*, where state intervention makes things less efficient than nonintervention (even if nonintervention involves market failure).

Two other, more controversial, purposes of taxation are paternalism and redistribution. *Paternalistic taxation* is taxation for the benefit of the person taxed. It might be an excise tax (e.g., on cigarette sales or casino winnings) intended to decrease use of certain goods or services, or it might be a required payment to provide certain goods or services (e.g., required payment to unemployment insurance, health care insurance or pension plan). Paternalistic taxation is controversial because some people believe that the state should not be paternalistic. *Redistributive taxation* is taxation to transfer income or wealth from some to others, typically from those with more to those with less. Although some moral views (e.g., radical right-libertarianism) reject all redistributive taxation, most views accept the justice of such taxation, at least in the case of taxing the very well off to help those who are very poorly off through no fault of their own (e.g., financing basic nutrition, health care and education of young children). More demanding forms of redistribution—to achieve some kind of equality of distribution of wealth or income, for example—are, however, highly controversial.

In short, full moral ownership of something precludes the justness of taxing the mere possession or exercise of the ownership rights. Nonetheless, such taxation is compatible with near-full moral ownership of the thing. The ownership rights just have to be weakened enough to allow the taxation, and the taxation revenues have to be used for a morally suitable purpose. The core debate about the justice of taxation is thus about the exact content of our moral property rights. The mere existence of moral property rights does not settle the issue.

In the final section, we shall consider certain property-rights arguments against taxation.

Property-Rights Arguments Against Taxation

Although we shall not consider all possible arguments against taxation, it will be instructive to consider three influential libertarian arguments on the topic made by Robert Nozick (1974). (For general discussion of Nozick's theory of justice, see Vallentyne 2011. For discussion of the justice of taxation according to various versions of libertarianism, see Vallentyne 2012.)

To start, there is Nozick's famous Wilt Chamberlain example (160–64), which is intended to show that theories of justice that require specified distributive patterns of goods involve unacceptable continual interference with people's lives. We shall focus on it as an argument against redistributive taxation.

Suppose that everyone starts with a just initial set of holdings (on one's preferred theory of justice, say equality of some sort). Now suppose that Wilt Chamberlain, a famous basketball player, agrees to play basketball in return for 25 cents from each spectator and the spectators voluntarily agree. Suppose that, over the course of the season, a million fans voluntarily purchase tickets and there are no other financial transactions. Chamberlain now has (at least) $250,000 more than each of the fans. Whatever distributive pattern was invoked for the initial holdings (egalitarianism, desert theory, etc.), it would only be by accident if it were still satisfied. Thus, if justice is to be maintained, there must be continual redistribution among individuals. This, Nozick claims, is implausible. Given that the distribution arose from the voluntary choices that individuals had with respect to resources that they were, by assumption, entitled to control, how could the result be unjust? Moreover, such redistribution involves continual interference with people's lives, and it seems implausible that justice would require this. Nozick concludes that principles of justice do not impose distributive patterns.

Do theories of justice that are not purely procedural necessarily require continual interferences with people's lives in some empirical (nonmoral) sense? They do require at least some occasional interference, but the real question is whether nonprocedural theories require *significant* continual interference with people's lives. Some certainly do. For example, a theory that requires equal wealth *at all times* would be continually adjusting people's wealth levels, sometimes in significant ways. Nonprocedural theories, however, need not (as Nozick recognized: 164) be concerned with *difficult to achieve* states (such as maximal equality) *at each time*. Consider a principle that holds that justice requires that each person have *enough annual income for basic subsistence*. Under moderate abundance, if people start with a just share, this will not require frequent significant adjustments to the distribution.

Moreover, even Nozick's favored libertarian theory involves continual interference with people's lives. Those who are not entitled to given resources are threatened with force if they use them without permission, are often forcibly prevented from attempting to use them and are often forced to compensate the victims if they do so. The real issue for Nozick, I think, is, not interference with people's lives but rather, the idea that, if one has certain (e.g., initial) rights over certain resources and one exercises them in a way that respects the rights of others, then the result must be just (and interference unjust). Let us explore that issue.

Nozick implicitly assumes that, in the Wilt Chamberlain example, the individuals have *full* ownership of their initial resources, but this need not be so. The correct theory of justice may only give them partial ownership. Individuals may have full rights to control the use of their property and to transfer those rights, but those rights may be conditional upon making certain payments to others (e.g., taxes). In the Wilt Chamberlain example, the correct theory of justice may say that initial and subsequent ownership of resources is conditional upon the payment of certain taxes on wealth levels above $100,000 (where tax revenues are used to finance public goods and to provide equality of opportunity for young children). If the initial rights are so conditional, then there is nothing unjust about extraction of those payments. It all depends on how strong those initial rights are. Nozick's argument works only if one assumes full ownership of the initial allocation of resources.

Let us now consider a second argument of Nozick's (169–72) against taxation. He claims that "[t]axation of earnings from labor is on a par with forced labor." The issue here only concerns income taxation, and only concerns labor income as opposed to capital income (e.g., interest, rents and profits) and natural resource income (e.g., rents on natural resources). In a footnote, Nozick states that he leaves open whether "on a par with forced labor" is to be understood as "is one kind of forced labor" or as something like "has the same moral problems as forced labor." Labor-income taxation, however, is, pace Nozick, clearly not a kind of forced labor, since it does not force anyone to labor in the relevant sense. It only requires one to pay a tax if one chooses to labor. Those who are independently wealthy need not labor at all. Still, most people will need to generate labor income in order to survive, and these people will need to work additional hours in order to meet their basic needs. Unlike paradigm cases of forced labor, however, they are typically free to choose when, where, how and how much to labor. Moreover, no one is physically forcing them to labor. Hence, it seems to be a mistake to equate labor-income taxation with forced labor.

Even if labor-income taxation is morally equivalent to forced labor, this does not refute labor-income taxation. They may both be morally justified under certain conditions. Suppose that you have a morally enforceable obligation to repay the loan I made to you. If you have no external assets, and the only way of getting you to pay off your debt to me is to force you to labor with some of your wages going to me, it may be just to do so. Likewise, for taxation, if you have an enforceable duty to pay a labor-income tax, and you labor and refuse to pay the tax, then the state may have a liberty right to confiscate some of your assets. If you have insufficient assets, the state may have a liberty right to force you to labor in order to pay your fair share. Of course, there may be reasons against the state imposing forced labor, but it's far from clear that it is inappropriate in principle when it is the only way of getting someone to discharge an enforceable duty. If so, then both forced labor and labor-income taxation may be just under certain conditions. The key question is whether the individual has an enforceable duty to make the specified payments (e.g., taxes).

Let us now consider a third argument by Nozick against income taxation in particular and taxation in general. He writes that "[w]hether it is done through taxation on wages or on wages over a certain amount, or through seizure of profits . . . patterned principles of distributive justice involve appropriating the actions of other persons. . . . These principles involve a shift from the classical liberal principle of self-ownership to a notion of (partial) property rights in *other* people" (172). I fully agree that an enforceable duty to provide labor is incompatible with full self-ownership. The question is whether this is also true of the taxation of labor income or other kinds of taxation. I shall argue that it is not.

Suppose that you and I fully own ourselves and that you fully own $100 except that it is subject to, say, 50% taxation if you transfer it to someone else (as a gift or as a payment for something). Such taxation is, I claim, fully compatible with our respective full self-ownership. We each have, for example, full rights of control of our bodies, and we each have the full moral power to transfer these rights to others. Our full self-ownership precludes the justice of forced labor, a wealth tax on personal internal endowments (natural talents), a tax on the use of one's body and the tax on the transfer of rights of self-ownership (e.g., sale of a kidney). Our full self-ownership does not, however, preclude the justice of a tax on the transfer of *external* resources (e.g., money from you to me). The full ownership of those external resources, by contrast, does preclude such a tax. (The point here is similar to that made above with respect to whether full ownership, of a movie theater for example, includes a right to income.)

Nozick believes, however, that full self-ownership leads to full ownership of certain external resources, and hence that taxation on the possession or exercise of those rights is unjust. Let us consider that argument (225–26), which I reproduce verbatim except for the material between square brackets.

1. People are entitled to their natural assets.
2. If people are entitled to something, they are entitled to whatever flows from it (via specified types of processes).
3. People's holdings flow from their natural assets [via the specified types of process].

Therefore,

4. People are entitled to their holdings.
5. If people are entitled to something, then they ought to have it (and this overrides any presumption of equality there may be about holdings).

The crucial conclusion is 4. Conclusion 5 merely makes clear that the entitlement is conclusive and not merely pro tanto.

Conclusion 4 and the supporting Premise 3, however, are clearly too strong. The history of the world is the history of theft and violence. It is thus implausible that the holdings that people happen to have flow from their natural assets via the specified entitlement-generating types of process (Premise 3) and implausible that people are entitled to the holdings that they happen to have (Conclusion 4). Nozick, of course, was aware of this, and he must here have intended merely to give an argument for the claim that it is *possible* for people to be entitled to their holdings. For our purposes, then, we should drop Premise 3 and weaken Conclusion 4 to:

> (4*) If people's holdings flow from their natural assets (via the specified types of process), then they are entitled to their holdings.

This is the core conclusion of the argument that is relevant to our purposes. Let us, then, examine the two supporting premises. Throughout, I shall interpret Nozick's references to entitlement as reference to full ownership (which is I what I believe he intended).

The first premise is just an assertion of initial full self-ownership (natural talents are one's initial, personal internal endowments). Although this would be rejected by most, I shall not question it here. My goal is to show that taxation of external resources does not infringe full self-ownership.

The second premise asserts that someone who fully owns something fully owns the results of applying specified processes to it. This presupposes that the determination of moral ownership is purely procedural (purely historically based) and not sensitive to consequence-based (future-regarding) considerations. Many would reject this, but even if it is granted, there are still problems with the argument. The key issue concerns the content of the specified processes. Nozick is not entirely clear on this, but his appeal, just prior to the above argument, to Lockean rights (225; see also: 150–53, 174) suggests that there are three generic kinds of processes: (1) appropriation: a process by which one acquires private property over resources that were previously unowned, (2) transfer: a process by which one person transfers some of her rights to another and (3) prevention and rectification: a process by which a person acquires certain rights in virtue of another infringing his or someone's rights. For the sake of argument, let us accept these three generic processes and ask whether they support the second premise. For simplicity, let us focus on the appropriation process. Similar points apply to the other two.

Clearly, it is *conceptually possible* for morality to be such that certain appropriation processes give one full ownership of the unowned resources. The relevant issue, how-ever, is whether the *correct* principles of morality recognize such processes. Nozick is thinking that something like the following is a valid moral principle:

Unrestricted Appropriation

If one fully owns oneself, one stakes a claim to (and/or mixes one's labor with) unowned resources and one compensates anyone who would be disadvantaged by one's appropriation of those resources, then one fully owns those resources.

This does support Premise 2, but it is a principle that few would accept. Moreover, a slight variation on the principle casts doubt on the premise. Consider:

Restricted Appropriation

If one fully owns oneself, one stakes a claim to (and/or mixes one's labor with) unowned resources and one compensates anyone who would be disadvantaged by one's appropriation of those resources, then one fully owns those resources, *except that those rights are subject to expropriation if certain taxes are not paid.*

Like the unrestricted version, this is a purely procedural principle, but it does not confer full ownership. It confers all the rights of full ownership except that the immunity to loss is weakened to allow expropriation for nonpayment of certain taxes. (A version of left-libertarianism endorses this principle with taxes equal to the competitive value of the claimed rights over natural resources and the funds used to promote equality of opportunity. See, for example, Vallentyne, Steiner and Otsuka 2005 and Vallen-tyne 2012.) This principle does not support the second premise, since the specified process does not confer full ownership of what flows from full ownership via the process. It confers the rights to control use and the right to transfer the rights to others, but the immunity to loss is conditional on the payment of certain taxes. There is, that is, nothing about procedural processes as such that guarantees the truth of Premise 2.

This, of course, does not establish that Premise 2 is false. It merely shows that it is far from obvious that it is true. Indeed, it is true only on a specific, purely procedural conception of justice that is rejected by most (even left-libertarians). Still, it is enough to cast doubt on Nozick's claims that income taxation in particular, and taxation in general, is incompatible with full self-ownership.

Conclusion

We have addressed the question of what kinds of taxation, if any, are just relative to a given set of property rights. Throughout, justice was understood as the fulfillment of all interpersonal duties (duties owed to someone, as opposed to impersonal duties), although much of the argument extends to justice understood as fulfillment of all enforceable duties.

Full moral ownership of a resource is incompatible with the justice of taxing the owner's exercise or possession of those ownership rights. Full ownership of a resource is the logically strongest set of property rights over that resource that is compatible with someone else having the same set of rights over everything else in the world (except for the agent and the space he is occupying). Full ownership thus includes full rights to control the use of the object, full rights to transfer it to others, a full immunity to loss of these rights as long as the rights of others are not infringed and a full immunity to the loss of other rights for the mere possession or exercise of these rights. The immunities preclude just taxation for mere possession or exercise of the rights.

Ownership, however, is a bundle of rights and is not all or nothing. Near-full ownership of a thing is compatible with just taxation for mere possession or exercise of those rights, as long as the ownership rights do not include an immunity to such taxation. Moreover, full moral self-ownership does not preclude other kinds of taxation. It is compatible with use, income, wealth or transfer taxation of rights over external resources (e.g., natural resources).

Of course, if certain right-libertarian arguments are correct, then individuals can have full ownership of themselves, artifacts and natural resources. If this view is correct, then effectively all taxation may be unjust. I have argued, however, that Nozick's generic arguments against the justice of taxation are extremely weak without the supporting libertarian infrastructure.

References

Honoré, A. M. (1961) "Ownership," in A. G. Guest, ed., *Oxford Essays in Jurisprudence*, Oxford: Clarendon Press, pp. 107–47. Reprinted in A. M. Honoré (1987) *Making Law Bind*, Oxford: Clarendon Press.

Murphy, L. and Nagel, T. (2002) *The Myth of Ownership: Tax and Justice*, Oxford: Oxford University Press.

Nozick, R. (1974) *Anarchy, State, and Utopia*, New York: Basic Books.

Vallentyne, P. (2011) "Nozick's Libertarian Theory of Justice," in R. Bader and J. Meadowcroft, eds., *Anarchy, State, and Utopia—A Reappraisal*, Cambridge: Cambridge University Press.

____ (forthcoming 2012) "Libertarianism and Taxation," in M. O'Neill and S. Orr, eds., *Taxation and Political Philosophy*, Oxford: Oxford University Press.

____, Steiner, H. and Otsuka, M. (2005) "Why Left-Libertarianism Isn't Incoherent, Indeterminate, or Irrelevant: A Reply to Fried," *Philosophy and Public Affairs* 33: 201–15.

Further Reading

For further reading, see: D. Attas (2005) *Liberty, Property, and Markets: A Critique of Libertarianism*, Burlington, VT: Ashgate Publishing Company (a detailed analysis of the concept of property and a criticism of libertarian arguments for full private property); L. Becker (1977) *Property Rights: Philosophical Foundations*, Boston: Routledge & Kegan Paul (an introduction to the main arguments for and against private property); and J. Waldron (1988) *The Right to Private Property*, New York: Oxford University Press (a detailed analysis of the main arguments for and against private property).

Related Topics

The Right to Private Property, International Law and Global Justice, Human Rights, Coercion, The Nature of Rights, Welfare & Economic Rights

FAMILY

20
THE PURSUIT OF INTIMACY AND PARENTAL RIGHTS

Scott A. Altman

Though not usually listed among our fundamental rights, we value the right to pursue intimacy—the right to form and sustain intimate relationships. Intimate relationships shape identity, life plans and happiness. Among the most important is the relationship between parents and children. The right to form and sustain the parent–child relationship is the subject of this chapter. In it, I explore whether parents' interests in forming and maintaining intimate relationships justify parental rights.

Before advancing an argument for parental rights based on a right to intimacy, I should clarify three preliminary issues. First, equating the parent–child relationship with forms of adult intimacy might seem unusual. Friendships begin with mutual consent, usually exhibit equality and symmetry, and most often include more than emotional components—we talk with our friends in addition to having strong feelings toward them. For parents of infants most of this is reversed. Relationships begin without the child's consent and lack equality or symmetry. Children are dependent and eventually subordinate. And relationships with infants rely on emotional bonds but not shared ideas. Despite these early differences, parent–child relationships have something in common with friendships—the value people find in them.

Second, the characteristics of intimacy might be thought obvious. Intimate relationships are particular. My connection to another person is intimate if we do not regard each other as fungible—another friend or lover would not be as good. Intimacy also includes trust, vulnerability, companionship, emotional connection, affection, and mutual support and concern. But intimacy is actually a contested ideal. Some people understand intimacy in mundane psychological terms; others embrace spiritual accounts equating intimacy with communion. This variation is understandable in a diverse society. Indeed it may be desirable; autonomous individuals come to understand for themselves the value of intimacy and then create that sort of intimacy as best they can. I remain agnostic about which characteristics are most important for intimacy.

Third, describing intimacy as a right might seem odd. Intimacy is a feature of voluntary relationships, an achievement that can no more be guaranteed than can being graceful or satisfied. I do not propose to assert a right to intimacy but a right to seek intimacy and to be provided with background institutions that make success reasonably likely.

A right of intimate association has been discussed extensively in American constitutional law, particularly after an influential article by Ken Karst (1980). And though many intimate relationships have since then been protected with rights, parental-rights claims have fallen into disfavor. Parental rights are acknowledged, if at all, as derivative—usually as legal entitlements created to protect children's interests (and therefore as limited by those interests) or as bribes necessary to induce parents to care for children. Such derivative justifications, while certainly capturing facets of family life, also ignore important reasons to treat parental rights as independent: intimate relationships are a core part of a life well lived. Autonomous individuals exercise some control over these relationships by, for example, selecting intimates and shaping relationships.

A nonderivative right to establish and maintain intimate relationships raises more questions than it solves. Certainly it shows why shunning or isolating people is a prima facie wrong—extended isolation makes intimacy almost impossible. But a right to intimacy does not alone explain which relationships or potential relationships must be respected, what support such relationships are due (from laws or from specific individuals) or what other interests justify institutions that undermine intimacy.

The specific questions I consider include whether parents are morally entitled to live with their children and to deny others access to those children. I do not limit this inquiry to genetic parents; similar claims to association are raised by stepparents, grandparents and intentional parents, by which I mean both adoptive parents and individuals who contribute to the creation of a child by, for example, hiring a surrogate mother or securing sperm for artificial insemination. I inquire first about a right to establish relationships not yet formed, in contexts such as a father seeking future access to an unborn or recently born child. Having considered a right to establish intimacy, I next consider disputes about the ability to maintain intimacy in established relationships, such as conflicts over relocation by one parent, or a parent's effort to deny continued contact to a stepparent, grandparent or other caretaker.

I conclude that the pursuit of intimacy provides an important basis for some parental rights but that other elements traditionally associated with parental rights are justified, if at all, by other interests. I explore one alternative interest briefly at the end of this essay.

The Right to Establish Intimacy

Consider first potential relationships. A right to seek intimate relationships consists partly in not having the group of potential intimates unduly restricted. Being held in complete isolation deprives people of this right. So too does declaring off limits anyone in a large group of people, especially if the off-limits group includes all those with whom a person seeks intimacy. Legal bans and social taboos against gay people engaging in public affection or private sex acts or marriage inhibit intimacy in this way.

But unduly restricting the class of potential intimates is not the only (or even main) restriction on potential intimates that matters. Some rules or customs deny access to a specific person as a potential intimate without dramatically limiting the class of potential intimates. For example, traditional rules (no longer universally enforced) prevent donors of sperm and ova, and parents placing children for adoption, from knowing where their genetic children are being raised—in part to prevent them from having relationships with these children (78 ALR 4th 1990 218; 83 ALR 4th 1991 295). These rules were designed to inhibit formation of specific relationships. Similar are rules declaring that a child's biological father has no parental rights if the child's mother was married to another man (*Michael H. v. Gerald D.* (1989) 491 U.S. 110), or rules permitting an unmarried mother to place a child for adoption without the father's consent if he has not come forward rapidly enough to establish a relationship with the child (*Lehr v. Robertson* (1983) 463 U.S. 248).

Some of these rules make sense—both because they advance important goals and because any interest in forming a specific relationship is voluntarily waived (at least from the parent's perspective). Should we be concerned about the others? So long as a person can form other intimate relationships, why object to declaring off limits one specific (not-yet-formed) relationship? Surely my rights are not violated if Kobe Bryant refuses to be my friend or if Julia Roberts declines when I ask her on a date. Not only do their associational rights require this outcome, we rightly think that I can find friendship and love by looking among those who are willing. We could take a similar attitude toward children: I should not be able to insist on forming a relationship with any particular child so long as I have ample opportunity to become a parent to a different child.

Consider an example: Monsey and David conceive a child, perhaps through birth control failure or after unprotected sex. Monsey has arranged for adoption, either by a couple seeking an infant or by her new life partner. David does not learn about the pregnancy until after the child is born. He learns about the adoption shortly before (or shortly after) it is finalized and then seeks to be declared the child's father.

The legal question—should someone like David be able to rear the child or prevent its adoption by another—arises frequently, sometimes eliciting great controversy (*In Re Baby Girl Clausen* (1993) 502 N.W. 2d 649). Outcomes vary depending on whether the mother was married when the child was conceived, how rapidly the father comes forward to seek the child and whether he acts responsibly toward the child from the start. The moral question—on what basis should we evaluate his claim—is no less contested. Arguments for parental rights over infants usually rely on outdated interpretations of children as property (or property-like claims based on causation) or derive parental rights from children's needs (Austin 2005; Scott and Scott 1995; Buss 2000).

David's interest in intimacy cannot easily support his rights claim because David has so many alternatives. Just as my interest in forming a friendship with Kobe Bryant is reduced by the large pool of other potential friends, David's need to care for this infant is undermined by other actual or potential children. To succeed, the argument from intimacy to parental rights must show how infants differ from potential friends.

Infants differ from potential friends in at least one key respect: parents have duties toward infants. If I have a duty (or believe myself to have a duty) to form a close relationship with a specific child, my opportunities to care for other children would not undermine my reason for establishing this relationship.

Why would someone have a duty to establish a relationship with a specific child? Procreating causes a child to exist and to have predictable needs, including stable, loving relationships with adult caretakers. Society could arrange to provide children with such relationships in many ways, some no doubt better than others. But in most actual societies, even in those that assign caretaking duties to servants or that forego long-term cohabitation (kibbutzim or boarding schools), parents are expected be the focal point of, and to reciprocate, a child's love. Given the widespread expectation that a parent will fulfill this basic need, and the parental role in creating this need, most parents reasonably regard meeting the need as a prima facie duty.

Not all duties, however, need to be fulfilled personally. Parents who place children in adoptive homes fulfill their duties indirectly by providing their children with loving parents. Why then should a genetic father whose child is adopted have any further duty to fulfill?

Perhaps the duty to provide children a loving home cannot be delegated so easily. Parents who believe they must personally rear their genetic children offer varied reasons—ranging from a desire to continue a family name or tradition (which they might understand as a religious duty, or as a duty to ancestors, or as a duty to provide the child with a connection to the past), to a recognition that a child placed for adoption may feel herself abandoned no matter how loving her eventual home, to a simple understanding of the caretaking duty as inalienable.

Not everyone believes the duty to rear their children is nondelegable. And even those who regard the duty as better fulfilled personally do not always think it wrong to place children for adoption. Disagreement concerns both moral and factual issues: not everyone feels a strong commitment to provide their genetic children a connection to family line, or believes that loss associated with abandonment is serious.

Such moral and factual disagreements do not necessarily preclude judgment or regulation. But delegating parental responsibility is a question about which reasonable people can disagree. More importantly, it is a question at the core of individual identity for many people: what are my obligations as a parent and how ought I best fulfill them? For this reason, states should hesitate about preventing people from fulfilling parental duties personally.

Three objections to this account are likely apparent. First, even if this explanation is correct, it makes parental rights derivative of children's interests because the duty relies on a child's interest in being cared for by a loving parent. Second, even if the right is not derivative, it relies not on intimacy but on duty. Third, even if people have a right to fulfill their duties, they do not have a right to fulfill alleged duties that they mistakenly believe they have.

According to the first objection, my argument makes parental rights derivative of children's interests. A parent's right to associate with an infant is based on his interest in forming an intimate association. His duty explains why his interest in intimacy cannot be adequately satisfied elsewhere. But the duty element seems to rely on children's needs. This objection, I think, misunderstands my argument. Children may indeed have interests in being reared by a genetic parent. But the argument from parental duty to parental rights does not rely on children's interests. Rather it is the parent's interest in fulfilling his duty by creating an intimate association, rather than the child's interest in the association, that justifies the right.

The suspicion that my argument relies on children's interests is understandable. I claim that a parent is entitled to fulfill duties owed to children—duties that provide for children's basic needs. Surely this argument derives parental rights from children's interests. But I do not think this connection necessary. Consider some examples. You save a stranger's life, and he insists on showing you gratitude in ways he regards as morally obligatory. Even though you do not want to receive this expression of gratitude, he might have a prima facie right that you do so. In this case the right of the person rescued to repay the rescuer depends on a duty but does not derive from the rescuer's interests. Or consider a father who seeks to care for his biological child. His duty, as he sees it, stems from an obligation to honor his ancestors. Here too, if one accepts a right to fulfill a duty, the basis for this right does not derive from the immediate beneficiary's interests.

Or consider someone who accepts an honor-based code of conduct. She promises to repay a loan. The lender is so wealthy that he tells her not to bother; the money makes no difference to him. If she plausibly has a right to repay him nonetheless, her right does not depend on repayment advancing the lender's welfare.

The second objection has more merit. My argument, that parents have a right to form relationships with children when they (believe themselves to) have a duty to do so, does not depend on a right to pursue intimacy. Even if a right to seek intimacy did not exist, or a parent did not want intimacy, the parent might still assert his right to fulfill a duty. In the example above, we might add that David has no desire to spend time with his children. He wants only to be a scholar who studies religious texts, mostly in isolation from others. But he believes it his religious obligation to rear his genetic child in his faith, and to teach the child, personally, about its main texts. He thus plans to revise his life aims and to devote time each day to his child's education. Perhaps he will come to value the intimacy of this relationship. But establishing such intimacy holds no attraction to him now and is not the basis for his claim to access. If his perceived duty justifies access, then apparently intimacy plays no role in my core argument.

I acknowledge that a right of access might be persuasive absent any claim to intimacy. But this need not undermine my claim. Perhaps intimacy is not necessary to justify a right to form a relationship with an infant. But for people who do value intimacy as their reason for establishing a relationship with a child, the argument from duty becomes an interest in establishing a relationship with *this* child. The interest in intimacy is not derivative—it is an independent right—but its application in this context does depend on another right.

The third objection is serious. Perhaps people have a right to fulfill actual duties. Moral arguments usually presume that *ought* implies *can*: if I am obligated to X, then I must be permitted to X (or else be released from my obligation). But it does not follow that if I *think* I am obligated to X, I must be permitted to X. After all, I might think I am obligated to become president of the university or king of California. My sincere belief does not create a right.

Liberalism might warrant recognizing a right to fulfill some alleged duties. In any society there will be individuals who sincerely claim duties (whether religious or based on nonreligious conceptions of the good) that are neither broadly accepted as true nor appropriately discarded as mistaken. Conceptions of the good typically include fulfilling one's obligations; they differ in specifying what obligations people have. In these disputed cases, alleged duties should sometimes be accommodated with rights (Waldron 1981).

This argument from liberal accommodation might seem overbroad. On most liberal accounts, I should be free to do anything I like (whether I believe I am obligated to do so or merely wish to do so) unless my actions harm another. Why should liberal accommodation for varied conceptions of the good owe more deference to actions based on an alleged duty than to actions strongly desired for other reasons?

Alleged duties often deserve special accommodation. Fulfilling duties can be central in people's life plans, and in their perceptions of themselves as aiming for good ends. People act wrongfully in their own estimation if they cannot fulfill duties they embrace. So compelling people to act against such norms violates individual conscience (or personal integrity), much like coercing confessions, mandating religious oaths or sending conscientious objectors to war. Alleged duties thus deserve special accommodation because mandated violations of conscience interfere more deeply with basic autonomy interests than do more mundane barriers to achieving goals.

Arguing for the special importance of alleged duties may seem odd. But I do not think the argument strays far from common intuitions. Often we take more seriously the need to accommodate individual choices by people who understand their actions as duties. For example, in disputes over religious accommodations, added weight has sometimes been given to claims that a rule not only makes religious practice more difficult but also impedes fulfilling a religious duty (Greenawalt 2006: 202–14). Special accommodations are also sometimes made when charitable giving is regarded as a duty—such as tithing (Kang 2002). Or consider how the Family Medical Leave Act creates rights for employees who care for a sick family member but not for those who care for a sick friend. Although all of these examples might be interpreted in other ways—the state might simply be accommodating aims it favors or drawing simple lines—they plausibly illustrate deference to asserted duties.

Rights to Sustain Intimacy Through Continued Association

Intimacy does not require proximity or daily contact. But distance and irregular communication hinder relationships, especially relationships with children. Rules separating intimates are sometimes obviously unjust, such as when families are separated by national borders and inflexible migration rules. But most impediments to intimacy raise hard moral and practical questions. Examples include grandparent visitation, stepparent visitation and relocation after divorce. Grandparents can encounter difficulty visiting grandchildren if their own child is dead or in prison and the grandchildren's other parent has remarried (69 ALR 5th 1999; 71 ALR 5th 1999). Stepparents who do not adopt children often cannot visit after separation or divorce (1 ALR 4th 1980). Relocation disputes arise when a couple separates and the custodial parent seeks to move, perhaps for a new relationship or a new job, or to be closer to her own family. This makes regular visitation difficult for the now-distant parent.

In all these cases, parents opposing continued contact have their own interests in nonassociation or travel, or their own particular knowledge about why continued contact might harm the children. And of course children have strong stakes in maintaining these relationships (or sometimes in resisting them). These disputes require a choice between conflicting interests, only some of which depend on a right to intimacy. Nonetheless, intimacy might be important to how we analyze the conflicts.

Ongoing relationships differ from new relationships. In new relationships, the potential for alternative relationships posed a challenge to anyone asserting that intimacy justified access to a specific person. Few people could meet that challenge—primarily genetic or intentional parents. In ongoing relationships, genetic connection and alternatives play a lesser role. Lost intimacy can be painful even for those who lack genetic connection and who had no right to establish the relationship from the start.

Family law scholars advance two conflicting arguments, assumption of risk and reasonable reliance, to explain which adult should prevail in continued-association disputes. Assumption-of-risk arguments favor custodial parents who oppose contact rights for grandparents or stepparents, or who seek to relocate after separation. According to this argument, vulnerability to loss is inherent in intimacy—both because intimacy makes us vulnerable and because making oneself vulnerable may be necessary to establish intimacy. Because this vulnerability is well known, becoming attached to another person should always be interpreted as accepting the risk that the relationship will end.

Reasonable reliance arguments favor those sympathetic to maintaining relationships. Vulnerability accompanies intimacy; loss is always possible, through untimely death or rejection by the other person. But this well-known vulnerability does not mean that people who become intimate accept all risks of loss. Vulnerability is equally well known to those who allow others to establish relationships with them, or with their children, as is the fact that adults who form such relationships will be harmed if the relationship ends. This knowledge imposes a burden of protection on people who permit (and often benefit from) these relationships.

These two perspectives on voluntary vulnerability—that people who make themselves vulnerable assume risks of loss, or that people who knowingly accept another's vulnerability owe duties not unreasonably to disappoint those who rely on them—are pervasive in both legal and moral relationships. The appropriate choice between perspectives has itself been the subject of intense debates. Some people think the answer depends on whether the specific sort of vulnerability ought to be encouraged (perhaps because vulnerability is necessary to some desirable institution). Others think it depends on whether one party can better take precautions to mitigate the harms of loss. Still others think our rules or customs should encourage contractual allocations of risk.

In the case of intimate relationships, I do not think any simple choice between assumed risk and reasonable reliance can solve the problem, for the simple reason that both sides in these cases are vulnerable to each other (depending on what background norm we assume). Consider an example: Molly and Dan have twin children. Shortly after the kids are born, Dan leaves the house (either he dies or he and Molly divorce). After a time, Molly falls in love with Stephen, who moves in and helps care for the twins. Dan's parents visit frequently, often watching the children after school while Molly and Stephen are at work. When the twins are 10, Molly becomes angry with Stephen and with Dan's parents. She learns that they have been doing something she finds unforgivable—perhaps supporting a political cause she detests, or exposing the twins to violent sports, or using drugs. She decides to end her relationship with Stephen and to cut off all contact between the twins and Stephen and the grandparents.

We could say that Stephen and the grandparents assumed a risk that Molly would refuse to allow them access to the twins. Or we could conclude that Molly assumed a duty not to cut Stephen and the grandparents off (absent strong reasons) when she allowed them to start spending time with her children and thus to rely on an ongoing relationship.

Some people have no difficulty choosing a perspective. Treating intimacy as assumption of risk seems callous. Siding with Molly in the hypothetical favors selfish unconcern and rigid parental prerogatives over human feeling. But dismissing Molly's position like this ignores at least two complexities. First, even if Molly seems cruel on these facts, most people accept the assumption-of-risk argument in appropriate cases. For example, Molly might fire a nanny who has grown attached to the twins. Caretakers predictably form attachments to children. But because parents might hesitate to allow contact with babysitters if they could not later end these relationships, and because customary parental rights in this case are widely known, assumption of risk seems a far more natural interpretation.

Second, siding with Stephen and the grandparents—perhaps protecting their relationship with legal rights to visit or seek custody—reverses the vulnerability, creating a mirror image of the reliance and assumption of risk arguments. By presuming that ongoing relationships deserve protection, we treat Molly's decision to allow Stephen and the grandparents to form bonds with the twins as assuming the risk of unwanted intrusions into her life (and potentially control over where she lives if we extend this analysis to relocation cases). Seen in this way, the real interpretive choice is about allocation of risk. Either Molly assumed a risk that she would cede control over her own associations, or Stephen and the grandparents assumed a risk of lost intimacy. These are not identical risks. But they are both serious enough that neither interpretation should be dismissed as obviously callous.

How then can we distinguish intimacy as assumed risk from intimacy as reasonable reliance on continuity? Laws or customs sometimes help sort this out. If everyone knows that stepparents have no enforceable rights of access to their spouse's children, then perhaps it seems fair to regard the decision to enter this family relationship as assuming a risk of later loss. But this resolution is not always plausible. Do grandparents really choose to grow close to their grandchildren knowing what law applies to later disputes? More importantly, this analysis offers no guidance on what laws or customs are desirable.

Choosing a side in these disputes might turn on a difficult comparison of harms. If stepparents like Stephen are entitled to visit the twins, or even seek custody, then Molly's decision to allow Stephen into her life meant risking regular forced association with him for a decade or more, and perhaps significantly less control over her residence and schedule than she might otherwise expect. If Stephen has no such rights, then affection for these children and concern for their lives all developed with an implicit understanding that it could be cut off unilaterally by Molly. Which of these seems appropriate might depend on which loss—intimacy or nonassociation and control—seems greater under the circumstances. Or perhaps we will find both harms roughly equivalent, and resolve disputes on another basis, such as the child's welfare or fairness to adults (Altman 1996).

Alternatively, one might try to resolve this case based on protecting the parent–child relationship. Parents necessarily have some authority over children if they are to carry out core functions of protecting children and making important decisions. Is the ability to cut off contact with grandparents or stepparents not presumed by parental status?

I do not think that one can solve problems of grandparent or stepparent access so easily. The appropriate scope of parental authority needs justification. The fact that some decisions need to be made by parents does not show which decisions must be so made or what constraints are appropriately placed on parental decisions. Whether exclusionary rights are necessary to the parental relationship—necessary either to sustain parent–child intimacy, or for some other purpose—is the topic addressed next.

The Right to Preserve Intimacy by Exclusion

Parents often regard themselves as having property-like rights over children—not only a right of unfettered access to the child, but also a right to exclude others from such access. No doubt this sentiment owes something to the property analogy, at least historically: parents produce and sustain children (much as they do crops) and naturally feel themselves entitled to control children. But almost everyone now rejects the property analogy. Other accounts of parental authority (both to exclude and more broadly to control a child's upbringing) derive parental rights from children's needs. Because children need protection and guidance (and because parents usually care about their children and are in a good position to have information about dangers), parents are entitled to broad decisional authority.

I do not dispute that some parental authority can be derived from children's interests. But the derivative account has difficulty explaining moral (rather than legal) rights of exclusion. Consider the example of Molly. Perhaps the law rightly allows Molly very broad discretion to exclude Stephen and the grandparents. She thinks they exposed the children to violent activities. Allowing her to make this choice, without having to prove her fears justified in court, may best protect the children. But evidentiary concerns need not constrain moral inquiry. Is Molly morally entitled to cut off Stephen and the grandparents without strong justification? What if the violent sport they allowed the children to see was football? A broad parental right of exclusion, derived perhaps from a larger parental right to direct a child's upbringing, is often thought to include a right to make idiosyncratic decisions about child welfare and in so doing to impose harms on others without having to offer good reasons.

Might a nonderivative parental right based on intimacy justify a right to exclude? Intimacy requires some seclusion—close friends and lovers need time apart from others. But this commonplace observation cannot justify a broad right to exclude. One does not need a right to bar others from access in order to have sufficient private time needed to sustain intimacy. Only inappropriately obsessive friends and lovers demand the right to veto all one's other friendships.

Perhaps the analogy with adult intimacy misses a crucial element: the parent–child relationship does not begin (as do ideal relationships among adults) with equality or consent. The intimacy between parents and young children does not arise from symmetrical reciprocity, but from caregiving and authority.

How might intrusions on parental authority undermine parent–child intimacy? Some psychologists think that parent–child bonding requires children to view their parents as authorities. Perhaps bonding also requires parents to view themselves as authorities. Even so, it seems unlikely that parent–child bonds demand absolute dominion. No one imagines that police should be forbidden from giving parking tickets to parents in front of their children. Likely, teachers should refrain from criticizing parents in front of children—calling into question a parent's skills as a parent. Which analogy—parking tickets or humiliating lectures—most resembles compelling parents to allow grandparent or stepparent visitation? Unlike traffic stops, visiting over parental objection calls into question a parent's authority as a parent. But unlike acts that humiliate a parent in front of a child, it stems from general laws applicable to all. Whether intimacy is sturdy enough to withstand public enforcement of visitation rights is an empirical question. But since we already force visitation for noncustodial parents, I suspect the addition of grandparents and stepparents would not further undermine intimacy.

I expect there are strong reasons, both moral and practical, for allowing parents authority over who has access to children and generally how children are reared. But I do not think these are justified by a parental right to intimate association.

A more promising argument for parental authority—to exclude and to direct a child's upbringing—is worth exploring. Intimacy is a core reason that people become parents; it plays a crucial role in human flourishing. It is not, however, the only important reason for becoming a parent. Parenting is also an act of creation. Those who choose to become parents seek an ongoing relationship, comparable in some ways to friendship and romantic love. They also seek an opportunity to shape another person, influencing her values, exposing her to ideas (and sheltering her from others), and supporting and perhaps directing her interests, religious commitments and character. In short, parenting is not only intimacy, it is also creation (Page 1984).

In identifying parents as creators, I mean to compare them with artists, writers and artisans (not with God the creator) who bring something into being and shape its features. Comparing parents with artists might seem like a return to treating children as property. But I think it avoids the most problematic elements of property-based theories. First, on most understandings, an artist's claim to control her creation comes to an end at some specific point—the core claim to control is based on the integrity of the process, not on having been the causal creator of the work. Puzzles over children as property often arise when critics ask why children cease being property at adulthood, and indeed why they are not owned by their grandparents, who—after all—plausibly own the parents. The analogy to artist allows us to see why parental rights fade. As children grow older, parents' ability to shape them fades, and of course they come to have rights of their own—not coincidentally, rights to shape themselves.

I do not mean to valorize the delusional and destructive approach to parenting in which adults seek to live through their children's accomplishments or measure success through their children. I mean only to notice that parenting makes sense to most people as a creative project. The longevity and demands of this project, and its centrality to a life well lived for those who choose it, suggest that the element of shaping another person deserves as much attention as the basis for parental rights as does the pursuit of intimacy.

Indeed, intimacy and creativity may merge in the project of rearing children. Parents no doubt have more in mind, as they try to mold children, than simply creating friends for themselves. But it is through intimacy that parents and children shape each other. Just as most artists regard the act of creation as intimate, so too intimacy and creativity likely merge with parents and children.

References

Altman, S. (1996) "Should Child Custody Rules Be Fair?" 35 *Journal of Family Law*: 325–54.
Austin, M. (2005) "The Failure of Biological Accounts of Parenthood," 38 *Journal of Value Inquiry*: 499–510.
Buss, E. (2000) *Adrift in the Middle: Parental Rights After* Troxel v. Granville, *Supreme Court Review*: 279–324.
Grandparents' Visitation Rights Where Child's Parents Are Deceased, or Where Status of Parents Is Unspecified (1999) 69 ALR 5th 1.
Grandparents' Visitation Rights Where Child's Parents Are Living (1999) 71 ALR 5th 99.
Greenawalt, K. (2006) *Religion and the Constitution: Volume I: Free Exercise and Fairness*, Princeton: Princeton University Press, pp. 202–14.
In Re Baby Girl Clausen (1993) 502 N.W. 2d 649.
Kang, J. N. (2002) "Tithing: A Fraudulent Transfer or a Moral Obligation?" 18 *Bankruptcy Developments Journal*: 399.
Karst, K. L. (1980) "The Freedom of Intimate Association," 89 *Yale Law Journal*: 624–92.
Lehr v. Robertson (1983) 463 U.S. 248.
Michael H. v. Gerald D. (1998) 491 U.S. 110.
Page, E. (1984) "Parental Rights," 1 *Journal of Applied Philosophy*: 187.
Post Adoption Visitation by Natural Parents (1990) 78 ALR 4th 218.
Rights and Obligations Resulting from Human Artificial Insemination (1991) 83 ALR 4th 295.
Scott, E. and Scott, R. (1995) "Parents as Fiduciaries," 81 *Virginia Law Review*: 2401.
Visitation Rights of Persons Other than Natural Parents or Grandparents (1980) 1 ALR 4th 1270.
Waldron, J. (1981) "A Right to Do Wrong," 92 *Ethics*: 21–39.

Further Reading

For further reading, see: A. Gutmann (1980) "Children, Paternalism, and Education: A Liberal Argument," 9 *Philosophy & Public Affairs*: 338–58; and F. Schoeman (1980) "Rights of Children, Rights of Parents, and the Moral Basis of the Family," 91 *Ethics*: 6–19.

EVIDENCE

21

IS IT FINALLY TIME TO PUT "PROOF BEYOND A REASONABLE DOUBT" OUT TO PASTURE?

Larry Laudan

I find it rather unsettling that we are using a formulation [of the standard of proof] that we believe will become less clear the more we explain it.

Judge Jon Newman (1993: 984)

Introduction

There would appear to be no element in a trial, whether criminal or civil, more important than the standard of proof. Essentially, the standard provides a decision rule to the triers of fact, a rule that informs them when a guilty verdict or a finding for the plaintiff should be rendered. Without such a decision rule, jurors (or judges, depending on the judicial system in question) would be left without direction concerning the most important decision in a trial. This, in turn, would seem an open invitation to arbitrary variability from one trial to the next and would constitute a massive obstacle to assuring fairness between trials.

In a criminal trial, which will be our focus here, the standard of proof takes the generic form: "Provided that condition X has been satisfied, you should convict the defendant; otherwise, he must be acquitted." In most of the Anglo-Saxon world, and increasingly elsewhere (e.g., Chile and Italy), X is glossed as "the defendant's guilt has been proved beyond a reasonable doubt." In other countries, X may be "the trier-of-fact has an intimate conviction about the guilt of the defendant" (among others, France), "the judge has a full proof of the guilt of the defendant" (Mexico), or "the rules of sound reasoning clearly indicate the guilt of the defendant" (Argentina). My focus in the early sections of this paper will be with the notion of proof beyond a reasonable doubt (hereafter: BARD), but very similar arguments to those marshaled here apply indifferently to virtually all the commonly utilized standards of proof.

Despite the importance of a standard of proof, it can be said unequivocally that virtually *all* existing criminal standards of proof are vague, ill defined (if defined at all) and provide precious little information to jurors or judges about what kind(s) of proof they should be looking for in reaching their decision about guilt or innocence. Consider, in particular, the case of proof BARD. While jurors are instructed that they must acquit the defendant unless his guilt has been proved beyond a reasonable doubt, no effort is spared to discourage judges from telling jurors how to distinguish between reasonable doubts and unreasonable ones. Indeed, the U.S. Supreme Court is on record multiple times as urging judges not to attempt to define what a reasonable doubt is, not even when (as commonly occurs) jurors explicitly request the judge to clarify the meaning of this key notion (see Laudan 2006, esp. ch. 2). If judges give any responses to jurors' requests for clarification, they tend to be empty bromides of the sort: "Well, a reasonable doubt is not an unreasonable doubt." In a classic case in 1894, the U.S. Supreme Court found this tautologous response to be a perfectly appropriate reply to one jury's request for clarification of "reasonable doubt" (*Dunbar v. U.S.* (1895) 156 U.S. 185). The court has even gone so far as to say that a doubt can qualify as a "reasonable doubt" (thereby requiring acquittal) even if the juror holding that doubt can give no reason whatever for it! (". . . it is not essential that a juror who has a reasonable doubt be able to give 'some proper reason for entertaining it'; it may exist without his being able to formulate any reason for it" (*State v. Dauphinee* (1936) 121 Pa. Super.: 590.) How the hapless juror is to determine whether a doubt for which he can give no reasons might nonetheless be a reasonable doubt is deliberately enshrouded in mystery.

Officially, the court's rationale for this policy of refusing to explain what "reasonable doubt" means hinges on its holding that BARD's meaning is self-evident and that any attempt to define it would only obscure jurors' preexisting comprehension of the difference between reasonable and unreasonable doubts (one can perhaps be forgiven for thinking that the fact that jurors frequently ask for clarification of BARD gives the lie to the idea that its meaning is self-evident). What is more likely to be the real reason that American courts discourage judges from defining BARD is that trial judges have sometimes botched the explanation badly and created a situation where appellate courts have felt bound to overturn a conviction because the judge defined reasonable doubt in a way that higher courts found to be insufficiently demanding. In some jurisdictions (Oklahoma for instance), any effort by the judge to define BARD is regarded as a basis for throwing out the verdict. The case establishing that, in Oklahoma, any explanation of "reasonable doubt" is a reversible error is *Pannell v. Oklahoma* (1982) 640 P.2d: 568. For Wyoming's similar rule, see *Cosco v. Wyoming* (1974) 521 P.2d: 1345. Jurors, then, are left to their own devices to figure out what the standard of proof means. That poses two acute puzzles: a) do different jurors and juries understand it more or less the same way? and b) does such consensus as jurors are able to arrive at reflect a sound grasp of how robust and exacting the court expects a proof leading to a conviction should be?

The problem, then, is not only one of fairness between trials. If jurors in a particular case bring into the jury room very disparate conceptions of the rigorousness of BARD, we might well expect that 12 jurors—confronted with the same evidence—might fail to reach unanimity about whether guilt has been proved. In some jurisdictions (e.g., California), mistrials—due chiefly to lack of juror unanimity—occur in about 12 percent of the cases that go to trial (in certain California counties (Alameda and San Francisco), the three-year average for hung juries is higher than 20 percent (Hannaford-Agor et al. 2002: 7, table 1.1)). If one in every seven trials ends in a hung jury, we are faced with formidable economic and emotional inefficiencies, not only for the defendant but also for the state.

An abundance of empirical studies of mock jurors shows that jurors' understanding of BARD ranges from "guilt must be more probable than not" to "defendant can be convicted only if his guilt has been proved conclusively." (For this one example among many studies that have found enormous variations in how jurors construe "reasonable doubt," see Kramer and Koenig 1990.) If jurors can be this confused about what BARD demands, how confident can society be that one randomly selected set of 12 jurors will arrive at the same verdict that a second set would have reached? Should a criminal trial be such a crapshoot that its outcome depends on whether a defendant is landed with jurors who think that p(guilt) >0.5 is sufficient or those who think that nothing less than p(guilt) = 1.0 will do?

Under such circumstances, it seems difficult to escape the conclusion that a standard of proof exists in name only. BARD is the nominal standard and the phrase "proof beyond a reasonable doubt" is repeated by the judge on multiple occasions in every criminal trial, but its meaning is left entirely to the triers of fact to decipher for themselves. One might conjecture that the presumption of innocence could be called into play in stressing the idea that an acquittal should be the default verdict, absent a robust proof of guilt. Yet this remedy is to little avail, absent informing jurors what sort of proof is required to defeat the presumption of innocence. It is specifically the standard of proof that should identify when that presumption has been defeated. Clearly, BARD—given its failure to clearly differentiate between reasonable doubts and unreasonable ones—does little to ameliorate this conundrum. The presumption of innocence merely says that a defendant should be acquitted unless his guilt has been proved to the relevant standard; it entails nothing whatever about what constitutes such a proof nor even about whether such a proof need be strong or weak.

Clearly, given the centrality of the standard of proof to reaching a just verdict, it seems that we should try to put this situation right by formulating a standard of proof that, unlike BARD, is clear, capable of being explained to, and understood by, jurors and justified (in the sense of capturing our value judgments about the respective costs of errors). The English, who first conceived BARD as a legal standard of proof in the late eighteenth century, have already abandoned it; the bad news is that they have replaced it by an equally unclear standard: "being sure of the guilt of a defendant." This suffers from all of the arbitrariness of BARD and at least part of the latter's ambiguity, since it leaves wholly unspecified how sure is "sure."

Still, in dwelling on the lack of a bright line of separation between having reasonable doubts and having unreasonable ones (which is the most obvious problem with current jurisprudence about the standard of proof), we run the risk of ignoring an even more egregious problem with BARD. I refer to the high degree of *subjectivity and inferential laissez-faire* associated with current criminal standards of proof. Even if we had a clear way of distinguishing doubts as between reasonable and unreasonable ones, it would remain the case that the BARD standard gives jurors no instruction as to the kinds of inferences that could legitimately sustain a finding of guilt. The brute psychological fact that a juror has no lingering, rational doubts about a defendant's guilt may or may not indicate that the hypothesis of the latter's guilt has passed epistemic tests that would warrant a well-founded belief that the defendant committed the crime in question. Since U.S. courts generally offer jurors no instructions about the kinds of inferences that could make that guilt highly probable, jurors are left wholly to their own inferential devices in reasoning from the evidence they have seen to a conclusion about guilt. (Virtually all extant standards of proof in criminal law across the globe share this same feature of "free proof," which in this case simply means a refusal to say anything to the trier of fact about the character of the inferences that are appropriate to warrant a guilty verdict.) The jury is given full latitude to engage in whatever inferences it regards as suitable, subject only to the constraint that, once all those inferences have been made, jurors must have no serious, lingering doubts about the conclusion they have reached, if that conclusion is a guilty verdict.

The BARD rule is preposterous as a standard of proof because of this subjectivity. Imagine saying to a mathematician that he has proved a certain theorem so long as he has no lingering doubts about it or saying to a scientist that he has proven a certain hypothesis so long as he is convinced that it is highly probable. Such advice would properly be considered a joke in very poor taste. Both the mathematician and the scientist must show their peers that their results have been derived using widely recognized and demanding deductive or inductive proof procedures. The fact that someone has "proved" something to his own satisfaction and that she has no lingering doubts about it leaves wholly open the question whether her "proofs" are legitimate. Similarly, the fact that a juror is strongly persuaded that a defendant committed the crime should impress none of her fellow jurors unless we know something about the kinds of inferences that juror used in arriving at that inculpatory conclusion.

In many legal systems, the trier of fact is expected to submit a written opinion in which she lays out precisely the inferences that led her from the evidence presented in the case to her verdict. All the world (and especially the appellate courts) can see for themselves whether the reasoning was cogent. In Anglo-Saxon trials, by contrast, the jurors are neither informed beforehand about what sorts of inferences they should use nor expected after the fact to articulate their reasoning. All they must attest to, in the case of a conviction, is that they have no lingering "reasonable doubts."

If this sort of wholesale subjectivity is to be minimized and if we are to avoid a situation in which a juror can report that he has no reasonable doubts even when he has reasoned badly, it would be preferable to have a standard of proof that provided something more concrete by way of describing or exhibiting the features that a legitimate inference to guilt should exhibit. In the next section, I will describe two distinct proposals that have been made recently for informing jurors about the kinds of inference that would legitimately sustain a guilty verdict. Each aims to replace BARD by a standard of proof that focuses on the structure of the arguments jurors need to construct to arrive legitimately at a guilty verdict rather than, as BARD does, on the subjective confidence that jurors should have.

Rethinking the Standard of Proof

One interesting proposal for replacing BARD comes from evidence scholars Ronald Allen and Michael Pardo (see esp. Allen and Pardo 2008). They would have us imagine a trial—whether civil or criminal—as a process in which two rival stories or narratives are elaborated. Such narratives attempt to tie together the pieces of evidence in a way that makes them credible and coherent. The task of the criminal jury, Allen and Pardo conjecture, is to assess the coherence of the stories produced by the prosecution and the defense. A necessary but not sufficient condition for a conviction is that the prosecution's narrative must provide a highly plausible account of the defendant's guilt, capturing the salient pieces of inculpatory evidence as pegs on which the narrative hangs. A sufficient condition for an acquittal, according to Allen and Pardo, occurs when the defense can offer a minimally plausible narrative about the evidence that is compatible with the defendant's innocence. If both parties fail to present plausible stories, an acquittal is called for. For a conviction to occur, the prosecution's narrative must be plausible while the defendant's story lacks such credibility. Of course, the key notions involved here have to be fleshed out more than I have done. We want to know more about the conditions of plausibility and their link to coherence. Still, the basic ideas have two virtues: a) most jurors have plenty of prior experience hearing stories or narratives and judging whether they cohere convincingly (anyone who has ever suspected that he is being lied to has had experience judging a prima facie implausible story); and b) the test of internal and external coherence implicit in this proposed standard points jurors in the direction of the sorts of inferential tests to which they should submit the stories offered by the parties to the trial.

A second suggestion for a standard of proof was proposed by the author in his book *Truth, Error, and Criminal Law* (2006, see esp. ch. 3). It rests on the insight emerging from statistics and the philosophy of science that a powerful test of the truth of any empirical hypothesis, H, is its ability to account for apparent facts or data that would seem utterly unintelligible if H were false. Applied to the legal context, the idea would be that the prosecution's claim that the defendant is guilty acquires high plausibility just to the extent that some pertinent evidence has been established as prima facie true that can be readily accounted for if the defendant is guilty but that would be highly unexpected if the defendant were innocent. If some of the important features of the case that the guilt hypothesis can make sense of are likewise compatible with a hypothesis of innocence, then the prosecution's case is insufficiently strong to warrant a conviction. Likewise, if there are any pertinent facts that make sense only on the hypothesis of innocence, then an acquittal is called for. In short, this proposed standard demands that a conviction is warranted if and only if a) the hypothesis of guilt can explain most of the salient facts of the case; and b) the innocence hypothesis can account for no important evidence that is inexplicable on the guilt hypothesis. Just as we say that a scientific hypothesis that makes no surprising, corroborated predictions—unanticipated by its rivals—is not very credible, so a guilt hypothesis not backed up by very surprising evidence in its favor lacks the strong empirical support that should be a sine qua non for a conviction.

While BARD is agnostic about the kinds of inferences necessary for a conviction, American legal practice has often toyed with jury instructions for filling that gap. For instance, until half a century ago, when the court abandoned its time-honored distinction between direct proof and circumstantial proof, jurors in cases involving circumstantial evidence often received this instruction:

> However, a finding of guilt as to any crime may not be based on circumstantial evidence unless the proved circumstances are not only (1) consistent with the theory that the defendant is guilty of the crime, but (2) cannot be reconciled with any other rational conclusion. . . . Also, if the circumstantial evidence permits two reasonable interpretations, one of which points to the defendant's guilt and the other to innocence, you must adopt that interpretation that points to the defendant's innocence, and reject that interpretation that points to guilt.
>
> (CALJIC 2.01)

Arguably, this instruction would be as appropriate for noncircumstantial cases as for circumstantial ones.

As these few examples show, it is not a Herculean task to come up with a standard of proof that is reasonably clear, readily understood and one that instructs jurors about some key logical attributes that a warranted inference to guilt must satisfy. Still, even if this roadblock can be overcome, serious conceptual challenges face those of us concerned with fixing the standard of proof.

The Distributionist Conundrum

The hardest of those challenges emerges as soon as we realize that—apart from clarity and a focus on exemplary patterns of inference—there is a third crucial constraint in play in the design of an acceptable *criminal* standard of proof; to wit, the standard must reflect our normative beliefs about the respective costs of the two mistakes that might result (that is, false convictions and false acquittals). Other things being equal, the less demanding we make the standard of proof, the more likely a false conviction becomes. Contrariwise, the more demanding the standard, the more likely we are to see a spate of false acquittals. It is the conventional wisdom, of course, that false convictions are much more costly than false acquittals. This suggests that we want a standard that is well above p(guilt) = 0.5. On the other hand, false acquittals are not minor mistakes; among other things, they involve setting free a guilty defendant who may well commit further crimes rather than passing his days incapacitated in prison. It is a challenging puzzle to figure out how these two types of error weigh off against one another. But doing so appears to be a prerequisite to the task of articulating a defensible standard of proof.

As already indicated, it is the conventional wisdom that false convictions are much worse and more costly than false acquittals. Given that (sound) belief, it has traditionally been assumed that a key role for the standard of proof is to *distribute* the errors in such a way that false acquittals are much more likely than false convictions. Obviously, in adopting a demanding standard of proof, we give an important probative advantage to the defendant. The tricky question, of course, is how much of an advantage to give him. For more than two centuries since the English jurist Lord Blackstone first suggested that "It is better that ten guilty persons escape punishment than that one innocent suffer" (Blackstone 1765–1769: 358), there has been a broad consensus that the standard of proof should be set so that the ratio of errors at trial is precisely an order of magnitude. This consensus often assumes the role of an unquestioned dogma, as when Carleton Allen confidently insists that, "We must never forget that . . . the acquittal of ten guilty persons is exactly ten times as great a failure of justice as the conviction of one innocent person" (Allen 1931: 286–87).

While it is entirely reasonable to believe that false convictions are more egregious than false acquittals, it is—contrary to Allen's insistence—not at all obvious that what is often called "Blackstone's ratio" (defined as the ratio of false acquittals to false convictions over a long run of criminal trials) should be targeted at anything like a value of 10:1. A normatively reasonable value for this ratio depends on empirical questions about the respective costs of these two sorts of error and on the respective benefits of true verdicts (a factor commonly and inexplicably ignored in most discussions of the standard of proof). Whatever society finally fixes on as an acceptable value of the Blackstone ratio, it seems to me much more likely that it will be closer to 2:1 (which was originally the value proposed for this ratio by Voltaire—"'Tis much more Prudence to acquit two Persons, tho' actually guilty, than to pass Sentence of Condemnation on one that is virtuous and innocent" (1974/1749)—than to Blackstone's own proposal of 10:1.

If we had the luxury of building a legal system from scratch, there would be a strong case for proceeding as follows:

1. determine acceptable ratios of errors and successes, taking into account the utilities and disutilities of the four possible outcomes at trial;
2. use that ratio (or, better, that utility profile) to define a standard of proof that would make us indifferent as to whether a trial ended in a conviction or an acquittal; and
3. adopt rules of evidence and procedure that aimed not at distributing error (since that problem would already be accommodated in the standard of proof) but at minimizing error by admitting relevant evidence and excluding irrelevant evidence.

Such a division of labor between error reduction and error distribution would enable us both a) to fine tune the standard of proof so that it satisfies our distributionist values; and b) to make the rules of trial epistemically robust in the sense of maximizing the likelihood that the triers of fact would have an optimal evidence base for their decision (see Laudan 2006).

Unfortunately, however, we aren't building a trial system from scratch. We already have in place numerous rules of evidence and procedure that are not party neutral and that, de facto, tend to make false convictions much less likely than false acquittals. Consider a small subset of such rules:

*   jurors are strictly instructed to attach no probative value to defendant's refusal to testify;
*   evidence of the defendant's prior convictions, however relevant, is usually excluded;
*   the defendant can prevent from testifying those with knowledge of his situation if they fall into certain "privileged" categories (psychologists, social workers, physicians, priests and so on);
*   the prosecutor is prevented from presenting evidence of the defendant's character, unless the defendant himself introduces character evidence; and
*   the defendant's corroborated confession, offered without threats or coercion from the police, will nonetheless be excluded if the defendant was not "Mirandized" when arrested.

Every one of these rules, whether it excludes relevant evidence or precludes plausible inferences by jurors, makes it harder to convict the guilty and, in that sense, has the same de facto result as raising the standard of proof would have.

Because we have a system of trials in which both the standard of proof and many rules of evidence and procedure impinge on the ways in which trial errors are distributed, it is impossible to specify in advance precisely how much distributional work we need the standard of proof to do for us. That means, in turn, that we have no reasonable mechanism for specifying how demanding a new standard of proof should be, even if we were able to reach consensus on an acceptable version of Blackstone's ratio of errors. The only practicable solution to this conundrum involves taking a more global view. We must consider the error-distributing tendencies of the trial *as a whole*, including the standard of proof, the rules of evidence and the rules of procedure. If we want a system of trial that reflects our judgments about the appropriate ratio of errors, we must attend not only to its component parts but to the functioning of the whole apparatus, since the current system refuses to localize distributional effects to their logical source (the standard of proof).

To see how closely intertwined the rules of evidence are with the distributionist aim of the standard of proof, one has only to consider the fact that every rule of evidence that excludes relevant, inculpatory evidence (and that is precisely what most rules of evidence do) has the same effect as raising the standard of proof would have: it makes a false acquittal more likely. Every rule that excludes exculpatory evidence in effect lowers the standard of proof, thereby enhancing the prospects of a false conviction. Accordingly, if we are working within a system that already has literally dozens of mechanisms—apart from the standard of proof—for jiggering with the frequency of the two sorts of error, then we have no choice but to look at the error-prone tendencies of the entire system rather than trying to fix the distribution of error by adjustments to the standard alone. I'm not particularly happy with this state of affairs (partly for its inelegance, partly because of its murkiness) but, short of redesigning trials in wholesale fashion, we have to think of the trial itself rather than the standard of proof as the mechanism whose error propensities we need to study and understand.

While that might sound like a very difficult task, it is not so complex as one might think. It is not out of the question that we could collect evidence for any given system of trial rules, R, and ascertain how frequently such a system leads to false acquittals and false convictions. If the overall frequency of trial errors fell within an acceptable range, and if those errors distributed themselves in a way that political morality tells us is acceptable, then we could have significant confidence that the system was working more or less as we wanted it to. On the other hand, if either the overall frequency of errors or the pattern of distribution of errors fell outside the acceptable band, we would have to come up with adjustments designed to prod the error frequencies in the desired direction. This would be an inevitably clumsy process of trial and error, requiring constant monitoring and frequent adjustments but it is, in my judgment, the only possible, well-conceived way of figuring out whether criminal trials are sufficiently reliable instruments for discovering the truth, and the only way to inspire confidence that they are well engineered and adequately serving their purposes.

One of the ironies of the current legal system is that, until very recently, *no* serious efforts were made to find out how often trial verdicts were false. In science, medicine and engineering, it has been a core axiom for more than a century that the use of any instrument or technology requires one to learn something about how error prone the technique is. The frequency of mistakes and the kinds of mistakes are routinely investigated and widely known in most forms of empirical inquiry. Not so, however, with criminal trials. Until recently, we have placed enormous confidence in our legal system (whose decisions can be devastating for those who have to live with their consequences) without having the slightest idea how reliable trials are as instruments of empirical investigation. It is more than mildly ironic that courts now routinely insist—in line with the requirements of *Daubert* (1993)—that those offering expert testimony must be able to provide information about the error rates associated with their methods of inquiry before such testimony can be admitted. Self-servingly, however, the justice system has never encouraged, let alone insisted, that this sensible expectation be brought to bear in judging the reliability of "knowledge" generated by judicial inquiry.

It is time that all that changed, and that the legal system began to study in earnest its own mistakes in order to form an idea about both their frequency and about how to correct them. One might think that this is already the primary function of appellate review. Such optimism would be unfounded. Most appeals are founded on supposed procedural irregularities; that is, one party (almost invariably a convicted defendant) alleges that the rules of evidence or procedure failed to be scrupulously followed in his trial. While higher courts routinely adjudicate such claims, those courts are usually determining whether the existing rules of evidence and procedure were followed. Such determinations tell us nothing about whether the rules themselves conduce to the discovery of the truth about a crime. Their focus is on the *procedural* integrity of the trial rather than on the veracity of the verdict. Accordingly, appellate review is an extraordinarily inefficient instrument for learning much about the epistemic efficacy of trials. Fortunately, however, the circumstances for changing this appalling situation look fairly auspicious.

Some Estimates of the Error Profile in American Criminal Adjudication

Thanks in no small measure to the commendable work of a variety of so-called Innocence Projects and the empirical labors of a small group of academic lawyers, we have come to learn quite a lot about how often false convictions occur. While our empirical information about false acquittals is much less robust, it too enables us to make some probably reliable ballpark estimates. Aggregating that data, we can also draw reasonably confident inferences about how often trials issue false verdicts. Although I have been speaking of the error profile of a criminal *trial*, it is crucial to extend our analysis of errors beyond the walls of the courtroom itself. Most convictions (more than 90 percent) do not emerge as verdicts from a judge or jury but as confessions in the form of plea bargains negotiated between the defendant and the prosecutor. Likewise, most "acquittals" (more than 80 percent) are not findings of a jury but the result of decisions by prosecutors or judges to drop charges against persons that the police believe have committed a crime.

Even though most of these events do not result from trials, it is entirely appropriate to consider them in the context of a discussion of the rules of trial. This is because the parameters governing the plea negotiation and the decision to drop charges are principally the standard of proof and the rules of evidence and procedure at trial. The typical guilty defendant will not accept a plea unless he believes that the evidence the state can produce at trial will persuade a jury to convict him. Likewise, a prosecutor will not drop charges lightly unless he believes either that the evidence produced by the police is weak or that its provenance is sufficiently suspicious that it will probably not be admissible. For such reasons, it is important, in assessing the errors of the system, to take into account not only erroneous verdicts from juries (and judges in bench trials) but false confessions in plea bargains and dismissals of charges against defendants who are probably guilty. Accordingly, when I say hereafter that a "false conviction" has occurred, I will be referring either to a false verdict of guilty or a false guilty plea. When I refer to a "false acquittal," I shall mean either a false verdict of guilt not proven or the dropping of charges by a judge or prosecutor against someone whom the police correctly charged with a crime.

False Convictions

For a variety of reasons, we have much more ample and robust data about the frequency of false convictions than we have for false acquittals. Roughly, the evidence for false convictions is of two types: judge–jury disagreements (where the judge would have acquitted but the jury convicted) and exoneration studies, where post-trial evidence emerges that strongly suggests that someone convicted of a crime, or who confessed to a crime, was in fact innocent of it. Without going into further details here, it can be reported that the rate of false conviction at trial is in the neighborhood of 5 percent (or less) while the rate of false confessions in pleas is approximately 0.5 percent. Since pleas are roughly 10 times more likely than trials, the aggregate false positive rate appears to be approximately 0.75 percent. (For the three most compelling studies of false conviction rates, see Gross et al. 2005: 532, n. 21; Risinger 2007: 761; and Kalven and Zeisel 1966. It should be stressed that these studies generally focus on false-conviction rates at trial rather than via plea.)

False Acquittals

If a defendant's case goes so far as a jury trial and he is acquitted, we can use judge–jury disagreements as a rough-and-ready index of the frequency of false acquittals at trial. In the famous large-scale study of Kalven and Zeisel, one finds two separate stabs at identifying the false acquittal rate. Judges disagreed with jury acquittals about 58 percent of the time and found acquittal to be wholly "without merit" in about one-in-four cases (Kalven and Zeisel 1966: 429–31, n. 17). In a much later study sponsored by the National Center for State Courts, judges were reported to be "not at all satisfied" with 20 percent of the acquittals and "very dissatisfied" with 12 percent of the acquittals (Givelber 2005). Where the data are much sparser is in the more important (because much more frequent) case of arrested defendants against whom charges are subsequently dropped or dismissed before trial.

Here, accordingly, our surmises must be highly tentative and based simply on plausibilities. The one serious study of this issue by Hans Zeisel suggests that prosecutors report that, among the cases where they drop charges, the reason for not pursuing the case has to do with evidential weakness in about half the cases (Zeisel 1982). Supposing that prosecutors are reasonably reliable judges of the strength of a case, this means about half of dismissals involve innocent defendants. This fits with what we might surmise about the broad ranges of likely error. Specifically, we know that a defendant can be charged with a crime only if the police or grand jury are satisfied that there is probable cause to believe that the defendant committed the crime. If the prosecutor drops the charges, it is usually (but not invariably) because he is persuaded that the evidence he possesses which is admissible fails to come close to satisfying the demands of BARD. In short, we are dealing here with defendants whose apparent probability of guilt lies between 0.5 and something like 0.9. It is reasonable to suppose that a sizable proportion of persons with an apparent guilt in that range are, in fact, guilty, even if their apparent guilt fails to approach the threshold defined by BARD. By the same token, a sizeable proportion of them are probably innocent. Fixing the proportion more finely than Zeisel's 50/50 estimate would require data that should have been collected and analyzed long ago but in general have simply not been explored. Until it is available, this remains a huge lacuna in our knowledge about the error rates committed by the legal system.

These figures—even with all their penumbras of error—nonetheless permit us to draw some intriguing conclusions about how well the justice system is functioning (leaving aside that system's striking nonfunctionality in terms of appallingly low apprehension rates for most crimes). Let us return for a moment to the question of Blackstone's ratio. Among those who actually stand trial, there is roughly an equal number of false acquittals and false convictions. (Among 100 arrestees, five will go to trial, with four convictions and one acquittal. Seventy will accept a plea bargain and 25 will have the charges dropped. Supposing the false-conviction rate is 5 percent, this equals 0.2 false convictions. Supposing further, with Kalven and Zeisel, that the false acquittal rate at trial is 20 percent, there will be 0.2 false acquittals.) This suggests that the de facto Blackstone ratio at trial is about 1:1. Indeed, an innocent defendant who makes it to the trial phase is significantly more likely to be falsely convicted than a guilty defendant who goes to trial is likely to be falsely acquitted. One's initial reaction to such numbers is likely to be that the legal system is not doing enough to protect the innocent defendant. But that would be a misleading reading of a complex situation. Recall, first, that it is probable that the vast majority of truly innocent, arrested defendants never make it to the trial phase. Given that 95 percent of acquittals and convictions are settled without going to trial, the actual Blackstone ratio at trial becomes largely irrelevant.

What is not irrelevant is what we can conclude by looking at how the cases of those actually charged with a crime are resolved overall. Assuming for the sake of argument that half of those against whom charges are dropped are genuinely innocent, most innocent persons charged with a crime (95 percent) are acquitted while most guilty defendants (85 percent) are convicted. (These figures are arrived at by assuming a 5 percent false-conviction rate at trial, a 0.5 percent false-conviction rate in pleas, a 20 percent false-acquittal rate at trial and a 50 percent false-acquittal rate in dismissals. These four figures are all described and referenced elsewhere in the text.) Whether such numbers are acceptable in terms of political morality is doubtless a subject about which there can be much dispute. But this much seems uncontroversial: any remedies to the system, and proposed changes to the standard of proof or the other rules of trial, have to be judged against this rough-and-ready benchmark. Unless such modifications promise to improve the current error rate, they should be rejected.

There is a prominent school of thought that argues that false convictions are so egregious in comparison with false acquittals that we should be ready to implement changes in the system even if they increase the overall error rate, provided that they offer additional protection to innocent defendants. In my view, such recommendations—which can be found abundantly in well-intentioned articles in virtually every journal dealing with criminal law—fail to acknowledge the very serious costs associated with false acquittals. Still, even if one accepts as definitive the unargued, a priori stipulation that Blackstone's ratio should be about 10:1, it is compatible with everything we now know to say that we are currently falsely acquitting about 14 guilty defendants for every innocent defendant falsely convicted (this assumes for the sake of argument that half of those against whom charges are dropped are guilty). Even by Blackstone's lights, such a ratio is higher than political morality requires. Even within the framework of the Blackstone proposal, therefore, we could contemplate modifications to the system that would reduce the likelihood of false acquittal of the guilty without running afoul of Blackstonian intuitions.

Still, it would be a serious mistake to suppose that general error reduction will emerge from significant revisions of the criminal standard of proof. While changes of the standard may reduce errors of false conviction (or false acquittal), they will generally increase the corresponding errors of false acquittal (or false conviction). For such reasons, serious overall error reduction is not likely to come from new and cleverer formulations of BARD. There are three primary ways to lower overall error rates: 1) improving the inferential sagacity of jurors (for instance, by giving them empirical information about the error rates of eyewitnesses and expert witnesses); 2) admitting much of the relevant evidence that is now available but excluded (including eliminating privileged witnesses, permitting inferences from a defendant's silence, permitting the state to present character evidence, etc.); and 3) discovering new forensic techniques (e.g., DNA testing) capable of producing reliable and relevant evidence.

Different Standards?

As in most other countries, it is a given in American legal theory that the same standard of proof—whether BARD or some other—should apply uniformly across the board to all crime types and to all categories of defendants. The case that established BARD as the constitutionally mandated standard, In re Winship ((1970) 397 U.S. 358), held that due process demanded that even juvenile court cases should be governed by this standard. The logic of this ruling, however, is more than a little curious in that the court's general argument for a demanding standard across the board was predicated on the idea that the costs of a false acquittal are substantially less than the costs of a false conviction. If, as that notion suggests, the demandingness of the standard of proof should reflect our considered judgment about the respective costs of errors, then whether the standard should be uniform across crimes and cases and defendants makes sense only if the error profiles are the same across those three categories. This hypothesis is, I believe, wildly implausible.

Consider just a few of the variables that are in play. Crimes vary in seriousness and gravity. (Even the same crime, say homicide or rape, may reflect varying degrees of moral culpability and social disapprobation. Is violent rape the same sort of thing as sex with someone who is too drunk to give their assent?) Moreover, defendants come to trial with radically different prior histories. Guilty first-time offenders, if acquitted, are substantially less likely to commit subsequent crimes than guilty but acquitted serial offenders are. Such differences arguably impact the cost profiles of the kinds of mistakes that can be made at trial. Falsely acquitting a serial offender generally poses much greater danger to society than acquitting a guilty, first-time offender does. Falsely convicting someone of a charge of shoplifting is much less costly than falsely convicting them of kidnapping.

Without any doubt, the most obvious example of nonstandard error ratios is provided by cases involving capital crimes. There, a false conviction is an unspeakably costly mistake. Because it is, it would be reasonable to hold that capital murder trials should involve a higher standard of proof than that used in cases of noncapital homicide, where the mistakes of a false conviction are clearly less costly and, in principle, indefinitely correctable.

There is another consideration that should be brought into play here. Some crimes are much harder to successfully prosecute than others. In the U.S. during the 1960s and 1970s, most cases of rape either never made it to trial or resulted in acquittals. While it was not usually difficult to prove that intercourse had occurred (provided suitable forensic tests were made in a timely fashion), it was fiendishly difficult to prove beyond a reasonable doubt the absence of consent. Since most rapes went unwitnessed (except by the victim), these cases often boiled down to "he said/she said" standoffs. Because prior convictions of the defendant were often excluded while the prior sexual history of the alleged victim was always fair game, many guilty rapists probably won acquittals. In short, the situation was ripe for lowering the standard of proof in such cases. Instead, during the 1980s and 1990s, steps were taken by most states to remedy this situation not by lowering the standard of proof but by ad hoc changes in the evidence rules that applied to rape cases. (Specifically, the defendant's prior convictions for sexual crimes were automatically admitted, while the victim's prior sexual history was put off-limits.)

Juvenile cases are arguably another place where the error cost profiles are so different from an ordinary trial that a different standard would be appropriate. Since juvenile sentences for serious crimes are dramatically shorter than sentences for comparable crimes committed by adults, since juvenile records are generally confidential and don't form a part of one's criminal history, and since the conditions of juvenile incarceration are usually much less harsh than ordinary prisons, it seems clear—In re Winship notwithstanding—that sending an innocent 17-year-old to a reformatory for a year is a less costly mistake than sending the same innocent person a year later to a multi-year incarceration in prison.

The idea that a one-size-fits-all standard of proof is a constitutional requirement ignores the fact that, as the court itself has repeatedly recognized, the standard must reflect our considered judgments about the acceptable ratio of errors. If the ratio of costs and benefits varies from one crime to another and from one type of defendant to another (as it surely does), then we should contemplate moving to a much more nuanced system, where the standard in play and the resulting profiles of error reflect accurately the striking differences between crimes, punishments and defendant histories.

Concluding Philosophical Postscript

I have suggested that the current criminal standard of proof is vague, ill understood, profoundly subjectivist and inappropriately universalized (in that its constancy ignores the vagaries in the costs of mistakes from one situation to another). One might conclude, if all or most of that is true, that it is well past time to revisit the question, with a view to producing a better standard (or better standards if more than one is to be utilized). Such a proposal butts directly up against a claim—widely accepted among numerous philosophical theorists of the law—that a criminal defendant not only has a constitutional right to be judged against the BARD standard but also a *moral* right to be so judged. Ronald Dworkin, prominently among many others, has argued that because a false conviction inflicts an egregious moral harm on an innocent defendant, morality itself requires the maintenance of BARD. Specifically, Dworkin insists that, while BARD will lead to more false acquittals than a less demanding standard would do, its use is essential to "guard against a mistake [a false conviction] that involves greater moral harm than a mistake in the other direction" (see Dworkin 1985: 80ff. This passage in particular can be found at 89).

Dworkin's is a curious argument since its conclusion—one has a moral right to be tried according to BARD—patently does not follow from the sound premise that false convictions are worse than false acquittals. If that premise entails anything about the standard of proof, it requires that the latter must be more demanding than p(guilt) > 0.5. The problem is that there are obviously many possible standards (of which BARD is but one) that are more exacting than the preponderance of the evidence. Consider, for instance, the familiar standard of proof by clear and convincing evidence; although generally considered as weaker than BARD, it clearly gives a strong probative advantage to defendants, thereby satisfying Dworkin's demand that an acceptable standard must recognize that false convictions are more egregious than false acquittals. If all that a deontological political morality requires is that the standard must reflect our intuition/belief that false acquittals are less harmful than false convictions, then the fixing of a specific standard—as opposed to delineating a very broad range of morally acceptable standards—seems beyond the conceptual resources of moral philosophy.

LARRY LAUDAN

Several legal theorists sympathetic to Dworkin's view have attempted to justify the claim that BARD is the only morally acceptable standard by insisting that BARD represents the *best* effort that the state can make to insure that innocent defendants are not convicted. On this analysis, a defendant is entitled to insist that the state take every precaution against falsely convicting innocent defendants. The use of BARD, they say, represents the best that the state can do to minimize that possibility. While we cannot demand that defendants can be convicted only if we are absolutely certain that they are guilty, the best realistic and viable protection that we can offer is that they must be acquitted unless their guilt has been proven BARD. For such reasons, these theorists would find the proposals of this essay—to wit, that BARD should be replaced by a clearer, less subjective standard and possibly by a multiplicity of them—morally unacceptable. Perhaps the best known advocate of the view that we must expend our best efforts to protect innocent defendants from conviction is the evidence scholar Alex Stein, who holds that:

> A legal system may justifiably convict a person *only if it did its best in protecting that person from the risk of erroneous conviction* and if it does not provide better protection to other individuals.
>
> (2005: 175, my italics)

For Stein, one key part of a legal system "doing its best," according to this analysis, is its adoption of BARD as the criminal standard of proof. Rinat Kitai puts the thesis succinctly:

> The duty imposed on the state [by the social contract] . . . gives rise to the individual's absolute and inalienable right . . . not to be convicted unless her guilt has been proven beyond all reasonable doubt.
>
> (2003: 1175)

Three decades ago, Laurence Tribe stressed the same theme:

> The [criminal justice] system does *not* in fact authorize the imposition of criminal punishment when the trier recognizes a quantifiable doubt as to the defendant's guilt. Instead, the system . . . insists upon as close an approximation to certainty as seems humanly attainable in the circumstances.
>
> (1971: 1818)

(Can Tribe really believe that if the trier of fact is persuaded that the likelihood of a defendant's guilt is 99.999 percent, an acquittal is required? The fact that a doubt is quantifiable has nothing to do with whether it is reasonable or unreasonable.) Given the enormous variability of meanings that jurors assign to BARD (as shown by numerous studies of mock jurors), the refusal of the court to say clearly what BARD means, and the absence of any argument that BARD incorporates an accurate reflection of the respective costs of false acquittals and false convictions, we haven't the slightest idea whether this standard represents the best possible effort that the state could take to protect innocent defendants from false convictions. (Put differently, for precisely those reasons, we can reasonably infer that BARD isn't the best possible protection for innocent defendants.)

Supposing for the sake of argument that the overriding consideration was the minimization of false convictions (with no attention whatever given to the costs of false acquittals), there are indefinitely many ways in which the state could do more than it now does to protect innocent defendants from false conviction. Consider just a few examples: a) increasing jury size while maintaining the requirement of unanimity would inevitably lead to fewer convictions, including fewer false convictions; b) requiring concurrence of the judge in the jury's verdict would lead to the same result; c) excluding all retracted confessions would lead to significantly fewer confessions, some of which are doubtless false; and d) jurors could be required to proffer written verdicts, documenting their reasoning, which would enable appellate courts to detect some invalid convictions now missed because the court lacks any real clue about how the jury arrived at its verdict.

The point is that there is literally no limit to the additional measures that a state might take to reduce the possibility of false convictions if, as Dworkin, Tribe and Stein (among others) suggest, that were the overriding moral consideration. But of course, minimizing false convictions is by no means the only moral variable in play. Justice White, writing for the majority in *Patterson*, got it right when he noted that:

> Due process does not require that every conceivable step be taken, at whatever cost, to eliminate the possibility of convicting an innocent person. Punishment of those found guilty by a jury, for example, is not forbidden merely because there is a remote possibility in some instances that an innocent person might go to jail.
>
> (*Patterson v. New York* (1977) 432 U.S. 197: 208)

To be fair, Dworkin acknowledges this point with respect to the rules of legal procedure. He is very clear that, while the laws of criminal procedure should "be structured to achieve a margin of safety in decisions, so that the process is not biased strongly against the conviction of the innocent" (1985: 197), that does *not* entail that defendants "have a right to the most accurate possible procedures for testing the charges against them" (92). For some unexplained reason, he denies the applicability of this sensible point to the standard of proof.

I have argued here that morality does not require, any more than due process does, that innocent defendants be given every conceivable probatory concession so as to avert a false conviction. For such reasons, BARD, a whimsical creation of late-Enlightenment jurists, is *not* a requirement of political morality. And it would not be so even if it represented the utmost that humans could do to prevent a false conviction. If we combine that conclusion with an acknowledgement of BARD's unclarity and subjectivity, then it seems time to initiate a serious discussion about what an adequate standard of proof would look like.

References

Allen, C. K. (1931) *Legal Duties and Other Essays in Jurisprudence*, Oxford: Oxford University Press.

Allen, R. and Pardo, M. (2008) "Juridical Proof and the Best Explanation," 27 *Law & Philosophy*: 223–68.

Blackstone, W. (1765–1769) *Commentaries on the Laws of England*.

Criminal California Council of California Advisory Committee on Criminal Jury Instructions (2011) "California Jury Instructions—Criminal" Westlaw: rule 2.01.

Cosco v. Wyoming (1974) 521 P.2d: 1345.

Daubert v. Merrell Dow Pharmaceuticals, Inc. (1993) 509 U.S. 579.

Dunbar v. U.S. (1895) 156 U.S. 185.

Dworkin, R. (1985) *A Matter of Principle*, Oxford: Clarendon Press.

Givelber, D. (2005) "Lost Innocence: Speculation and Data about the Acquitted," 42 *American Criminal Law Review*.

Gross, S. R. et al. (2005) "Exonerations in the United States, 1989 through 2003," 95 *Journal of Criminal Law and Criminology* 2.

Hannaford-Agor, P. L. et al. (2002) "Are Hung Juries a Problem?" National Center for State Courts.

In re Winship (1970) 397 U.S. 358.

Kalven, H. and Zeisel, H. (1966) *The American Jury*, New York: Little, Brown.

Kitai, R. (2003) "Protecting the Guilty," 6 *Buffalo Criminal Law Review*: 1169–1170.

Kramer, G. and Koenig, D. (1990) "Do Jurors Understand Criminal Jury Instructions?" *University of Michigan Journal of Law Reform* 23: 401–37.

Laudan, L. (2006) *Truth, Error, and Criminal Law: An Essay in Legal Epistemology*, Cambridge: Cambridge University Press.

Newman, J. O. (1993) "Beyond 'Reasonable Doubt,'" 68 *New York University Law Review*: 979.

Pannell v. Oklahoma (1982) 640 P.2d: 568.

Patterson v. New York (1977) 432 U.S. 197.

Risinger, D. M. (2007) "Innocents Convicted: An Empirically Justified Wrongful Conviction Rate," 97 *Journal of Criminal Law and Criminology* 3.

State v. Dauphinee (1936) 121 Pa. Super.: 565.

Stein, A. (2005) *Foundations of Evidence Law*, New York: Oxford University Press.

Tribe, L. H. (1971) "The Continuing Debate over Mathematics in the Law of Evidence: A Further Critique of Mathematical Proof," 84 *Harvard Law Review* 8: 1810–1820.

Voltaire (1974/1749) *Zadig*, photo reprint.

Zeisel, H. (1982) *The Limits of Law Enforcement*, Chicago: University of Chicago Press.

Further Reading

The principal recent works dealing with the themes explored here are A. Stein (2005) *Foundations of Evidence Law*, New York: Oxford University Press; L. Laudan (2006) *Truth, Error and Criminal Law*, Cambridge: Cambridge University Press; and H. H. Lai (2008) *A Philosophy of Evidence Law*, Oxford: Oxford University Press.

INTERNATIONAL LAW

22
INTERNATIONAL LAW AND GLOBAL JUSTICE

Michael Blake

What is the relationship between international law and distributive justice? Domestic legal systems are frequently thought to give rise to distinct duties of distributive justice; those who share liability to a domestic state, on such accounts, share a distinct set of duties to one another, including some duties of distributive justice. The creation of the legal apparatus of the domestic state transforms the duties of those within that state's territory, giving rise to novel duties of distributive justice (Blake 2001). The question this essay will examine is whether or not the international legal system also gives rise to novel egalitarian duties of justice. Does the creation of the international legal system similarly bring about a distinct set of egalitarian duties?

My answer to this question will be negative; sharing the institutions of international law does not itself give rise to new duties of distributive egalitarianism. This is not to say that no duties of distributive justice exist between states right now. It is to say, instead, that such duties are not dependent upon the existence of international law; we would have these duties regardless of whether or not we share the network of norms constitutive of international law. I will not, at present, attempt a full theory of what these duties might be. I will, instead, simply argue that these duties must be applicable to states qua states, regardless of what legal instruments bind states together. International legal institutions may make some difference in how we fulfill these duties; they may make compliance with our duties more or less easy, for example, or specify a particular method by which our duties might be discharged. The duties themselves, however, are not dependent upon the legal system's existence, and this fact marks a significant difference between the domestic and international legal systems.

I will try to justify this assertion below, by examining three ways in which international law might be thought to be the source of distinct duties of egalitarian justice. Before I do this, however, a few clarifications are in order. The first is that I am here dealing only with the norms and practices of public international law, rather than with the related but distinct field of private international law or with those parts of domestic legal systems dealing with conflict of laws. I am here referring to public international law as defined with reference to its sources—namely, international conventions, international custom and the general principles of law recognized by civilized nations (Aust 2010: 1–12). The second clarification is that I will, in what follows, be dealing only with

MICHAEL BLAKE

distributive justice, rather than with justice more generally. The latter has many aspects that do not reduce to distribution—I assume, for example, that there is a strong relationship between democratic legitimacy and justice, and that this fact would have to be part of any complete discussion of the justice of international law. I will, in the present context, focus on distributive justice. The third clarification is that I will assume, throughout this paper, that international law will for the foreseeable future have the same relationship to coercive power that it currently does. International law, at present, serves as a means by which states justify their actions towards one another, including such coercive actions as military interventions; it does not, however, involve the creation of a particular collective agent with adequate power to coerce all the states of the world. International law is invoked in justification of what I call *horizontal* coercion, in which states deploy its norms in the justification of their coercive actions towards one another; in this, it contrasts with the *vertical* coercive structure of domestic law, which involves the creation and justification of a central authority with adequate power to coerce all those within the jurisdiction of that authority (Blake 2011). I assume that, in the short to medium term, we are able to change the *content* of international law, but not its foundational *structure* as a creation of state agency (Goldsmith and Posner 2005). The final clarification I want to make follows on from this third one: I will assume that, in the short to medium term, states will have significantly different abilities to make, interpret and break the norms of international law. Powerful states such as the United States are frequently able to ignore unwelcome norms and contrary judgments with something very much like impunity, whereas more marginal states are unable to do the same. The United States was, for example, able to effectively ignore contrary judgments of the International Court of Justice in the case of the mining of the harbors of Nicaragua, and the United Nations in the case of the invasion of Iraq (Gwertzman 1984; Hirsch 2010). For the moment, I want simply to assume that something like this inequality of power will be true for the foreseeable future. I do this not to make the case that this inequality would be true in an ideally just world—I cannot imagine that it would— but simply to accept that this fact is part of the world in which our theorizing must apply; ignoring this inequality, or assuming it away, does nothing to help us in the here and now.

With these ideas in mind, we can proceed to specifying the question that will be the subject of this essay. The relationship between distributive justice and international law might give rise to at least two distinct questions:

1. What duties exist between agents who share liability to the international legal system which do not exist between agents who do not share that liability? We may call this the *question of creation*: it asks us what duties are created by the fact of the legal system itself.
2. What must the legal system look like for it to do justice to all those agents within its jurisdiction? We may call this the *question of fulfillment*: it asks us what the legal system would look like for it to adequately ensure that those subject to it fulfill their duties of justice, whatever those duties might be.

These questions are distinct. We might imagine, for example, someone who believes that individuals have strong egalitarian duties simply in virtue of sharing the status of human, so that the international legal system ought to be reorganized in an egalitarian manner, even though this system is not itself the source of these egalitarian

336

duties (Caney 2011). My own purpose in this essay is to focus on the question of creation, although I will have the opportunity to make some brief remarks on the question
of fulfillment.

I will try to make my argument by comparing the world we have now with what I
take to be the nearest possible world without institutions of international law. In such
a world, we would still have, I think, collective agents with territorial jurisdiction
and coercive force over the inhabitants of that jurisdiction; we would have, in other
words, states. Their relationships, however, would not be mediated by the norms
of international law. We might imagine, instead, that whatever relationships they
derived would be up to the states in question. We can imagine that such states are
able to enter into relationships, make contracts, and have a moral nature sufficient
to regard these contracts as having at least some moral force. The only difference
would be that each of these relationships would have to be, as it were, *sui generis*; the
norms governing any given set of states would have to be ultimately agreed upon by
those states, with reference to their own interests, desires and moral ideals. I think
that such a world without an *international* legal system is a great deal more palatable
than a world without *domestic* legal systems. A world in which there are no domestic
governments at all seems, to most of us, as a bad—or at least very dangerous—place to
live. The space between that world and our own is quite large. The domestic state is a
powerful force, to which agency and duties of justice are properly ascribed. The existence of this state seems to transform what the inhabitants of this state's territory can
expect; it also transforms what those individuals owe to one another. A world without
law mediating the relationships between states, however, seems less obviously distinct
from the world in which we currently live.

This project might be thought impossible, for at least two reasons. Someone might
insist, first, that the very fact of states is impossible except through international law;
what counts as a state is itself a matter of recognition through international legal
norms, particularly the Montevideo Convention of 1933. If this response is right, then
the closest possible world I imagine is, in fact, impossible. States cannot live without
international law, because they do not exist until international law creates them.
This response is mistaken, though. International law defines the criteria states ought
to use in their decision-making about which states shall be recognized; it is a mistake
to think that, in the absence of these criteria, states would themselves cease to exist.
The existence or absence of distinct territorial units, each with a rough monopoly on
the use of coercive force within that territory, is a matter of fact, rather than a matter
of law. The widespread refusal to recognize Taiwan as a sovereign nation, for example,
has hardly caused the country to cease to have the functional apparatus of a domestic
state. To think otherwise is to confuse a legal set of criteria with a set of existing social
institutions. In the world we are examining here, we can assume that states exist as
we know them in our own world; the relationships between these states are distinct,
in that there are no standing legal institutions to which these states can refer in their
interaction, but the existence of these states does not depend itself upon such legal
institutions.

It might be asserted, instead, that the world I have described does in fact contain a
legal order, insofar as the states in question are able to make and keep promises. Much
international law, after all, results from the agreements states make with one another.
Indeed, a foundational norm of international law is that agreements shall only be made
in good faith—as noted in Article 26 of the Vienna Convention of 1969. Is it not,

then, impossible to imagine that we could have a world in which states make promises, without that fact itself implying the existence of some legal order, however primitive or weak? The answer, I think, is no—so long as one is able to imagine that we might be able to make promises, and bind ourselves morally, in the absence of any particular set of social institutions or norms. Tim Scanlon, on this note, imagines the possibility of a chance meeting between two members of different tribes, who are able to come to an agreement with one another through gestures and broad indicators of what they each decide (Scanlon 1990). It would seem foolish to think that these two tribesmen have thereby created an institution, in the sense demanded by the objection described here. The agency of these tribesmen is their own: they have each indicated a willingness to bind themselves to a certain course of action, and this willingness exists simply in virtue of their status as agents. They neither create nor require any separate institutional set as a part of this endeavor. Similarly, I think it is entirely possible for groups of individuals, or their representatives, to understand themselves as agents with this ability, without thereby demanding that we give rise to something akin to international law. The world I am imagining demands only that states have the ability to communicate and to enter into agreements; nothing in this, I think, demands or constitutes a distinctively legal set of institutions.

With this in mind, we can examine three distinct forms of argument, each of which might be invoked to defend the idea that the international legal institutions we see right now create distinct distributive duties between states. The first argument looks to the international legal order as itself a causal reason for the poverty and underdevelopment of much of the world. We members of well-off states have duties to redistribute wealth, on this account, because we—through a legal order we have set up in our own interests—are causally responsible for this poverty. We may call this the argument from *causation*. The second argument instead looks towards the complex network of agreements that have come into existence between societies, and argues that these agreements themselves constitute a site of justice. On this argument—it can be called, without too much distortion, the argument from *conversation*—the states of the world have distributive duties of justice because they have created complex administrative institutions with substantial degrees of independence from their creating states. Therefore, on this argument, these institutions are themselves subject to the norms of justice, insofar as they are bound to create the conditions under which all agents affected are able to speak and be heard by those institutions. The final argument involves a simple analogy between the domestic and international legal systems, and argues that they are both examples of a common type of norm-governed institution. The *cooperation* argument argues that the international legal system, like the domestic, is a primary site of justice in virtue of its ability to define individual material holdings and affect the lives of all individuals within its reach.

None of these arguments, I suggest, is ultimately successful as an attempt to derive distributive duties from international law. I do not mean by this that these arguments are utterly mistaken; I mean, instead, to argue that none of them is successful at differentiating between the world of international law and our imagined world without international law. What this means, I suggest, is that our duties to the less developed nations of the world may in fact be quite strong—for reasons closely related to the reasons discussed here—but that these duties do not have international legal institutions as part of their justifying stories.

The Argument from Causation

The argument from causation is not a new one; it finds expression as far back as the earliest writers in the dependency theory tradition, which argued that the persistent underdevelopment of the global South could be ascribed to decisions and practices taken by the global North (Roberts and Hite 2007). What is common in those who make this argument is the idea that the wastage of human life endemic in the underdeveloped world is neither inevitable nor the fault of domestic mismanagement and corruption. Rather, this underdevelopment stems from a set of global institutions that are imposed on the poor by the rich, for the benefit of the rich. The result is that those who are benefitting from this injustice have a special duty to overcome it—by first ceasing to be the beneficiaries of injustice, and then in working to create an alternative, justified global order.

These ideas have found their most prominent modern advocate in the recent work of Thomas Pogge, who has articulated a view on which the inhabitants of modern Western societies are guilty of collectively imposing a set of institutions on the global poor which is causally responsible for an enormous quantity of avoidable death and misery (Pogge 2002). There are several strands of Pogge's argument that are worth noting in this context. The first is that the basis of Pogge's claim is the international legal practice of state recognition. The legal practices of recognition consist of any set of persons who are able to effectively control a state's territory, and who give incentives to individuals to take over the political apparatus of states. The group, no matter how vicious or nonrepresentative, obtains the right to speak internationally in the name of the people. The most serious problem emerges when these patterns of recognition are combined with the international borrowing privilege, by which these individuals are able to bind the people of their society by incurring debt in their name, and the resource privilege, by which the natural resources of that society may be sold without any regard for the interests of the population. The conclusion of all these issues is that the international legal system is directly causally responsible for the poverty and death faced by the global poor (Pogge 2010). The global wealthy have, on this account, a distinct set of duties to alleviate the poverty created by international law; they are responsible for the law's creation of poverty, and therefore responsible for overcoming this historic evil.

I will not, in this context, discuss what has proven to be Pogge's most controversial idea—that our system of international norms is actually harming the poor, rather than simply failing to adequately help them (Risse 2005). I will, instead, simply assume that he is right about that, and that he is right about the causal story he tells about the origin of poverty and underdevelopment. The question we must ask, though, is what this tells us about international law. Pogge interprets the facts described above as sufficient to tell us that international law is responsible for the poverty and underdevelopment of the global poor. My own response is to think that these facts tell us something quite different: that the powerful states of the world are violating the rights of the global poor, and citing international law as an unsuccessful method of justifying these violations. The two are not the same, and should be distinguished from one another. If the international system itself is—in whole or part—responsible for the poverty of the underdeveloped world, then the system itself must count as an agent, so much so that it can itself be the bearer of duties and rights. I think this way of speaking is natural in the domestic context, in which the vertical coercion we set up naturally leads us to think that the state—through its legal system—can be ascribed intentions and desires, obligations and entitlements. But it seems a mistake to take this language and apply it in the international context. The only agents to whom these moral concepts properly apply seem to be states, rather than the norms cited by states in justifying their acts.

To see this, look only to the core idea of state recognition identified by Pogge as a key part of the legal system's wrongness. States offer one another recognition, or fail to offer one another recognition, and they use the tools of international law in justifying how they do so. Their patterns of recognition do not accord perfectly with the norms of international law; the above-mentioned example of Taiwan demonstrates that much. But the entities doing the recognizing—and thereby demonstrating a willingness to enter into trade—are states themselves. If these states were in a lawless international world, would they face a substantially different set of moral duties? I do not see how they could; they would still have to face the moral question of which states are entitled to recognition, and they would still have the same strong moral reasons adduced by Pogge to avoid granting recognition to morally illegitimate claimants. We should distinguish, I think, between the act of recognition itself and a given pattern of argument about when such recognition is appropriate. The latter is the realm of international law, but the former is distinctively the realm of states. Recognition, after all, is the precursor to more specific forms of relationship such as trade, and the willingness to trade with despots is a presumptively immoral act even if there is no standing norm prohibiting such trade. If this is right, though, then states have the obligation to avoid causal complicity in the sorts of evils described by Pogge as a matter of course under all circumstances. These duties are not brought into being by international legal instruments, and they are not dependent upon their continued existence.

States are blameworthy, then, if they engage in actions that have the effect of encouraging or abetting theft and tyranny in the underdeveloped world; so much I am accepting, here, for the purposes of our argument. My contention is that they would have the same duties even under anarchic circumstances. States always have an obligation to avoid lending comfort and material support to tyrannical regimes. If what I have said is correct, then this burden falls on all states in all circumstances.

What, then, does international law change, if it is not the source of our duties? For this, I think we can return to the idea that international law can be used to make our duties more or less easy to fulfill, even if this law is not itself the source of the duties. This is, of course, to move from the question of causation to the question of fulfillment. International law, as I have described it above, is at least part of a backdrop of normative argument that can be invoked by states in the defense of their international agency. As such, international law might be fruitfully changed so as to make the legal standards for recognition more in tune with our moral duties as described above. Allen Buchanan has come up with a promising plan by which such legal reform might be undertaken (Buchanan 2003). It might be possible for international law to be used to make it more difficult—if only through moral suasion—for states to do business with kleptocracies and corrupt regimes. The moral duties of states, though, persist even if such legal reform is not undertaken. Indeed, I think it might be plausible that those states that have the most ability to violate the terms of international law—such as, notably, the United States—are the most blameworthy for refusing to do so in the cause of justice. I will not, however, pursue this thought any further in the present context. I will say, instead, only that even if Pogge is right about the causal analysis of international poverty, it does not follow that the duties held by Western states are ultimately produced by international law. These duties are, instead, held by states more generally; they affect what international law should be, but do not themselves depend upon the existence of international legal institutions.

The Argument from Conversation

The view that justice has some relationship with discourse—and, therefore, with some appropriate set of norms for mutually respectful discourse—is not a new one. It is a key aspect of John Rawls's political liberalism, although the appeal of this view is by no means limited to this context (Rawls 1993). The idea is applied to international justice, however, by Josh Cohen and Charles Sabel, who have articulated a particular view of how the modern web of international institutions that states have created gives rise to a distinct set of international duties of justice (Cohen and Sabel 2005, 2006). Their argument is developed in response to Thomas Nagel, who has argued that outside the state there is no justice—or, more precisely, that outside the state there are no relationships to which duties of justice apply (Nagel 2005). Cohen and Sabel respond to this by noting the complex web of governance set up by transnational institutions such as the World Trade Organization (WTO) and the International Labor Organization (ILO). Acceptance into these organizations is, in practical terms, a necessary precursor to entry into the international marketplace. These organizations are, moreover, to some degree independent in their operations, set up as adjudicative entities able to resolve disputes between member states. These facts, collectively, mean that novel norms are created by these institutions; states who join the WTO acquire duties towards other member states which are best described as duties of justice, and which do not exist between states generally. Cohen and Sabel describe these duties in terms substantially similar to the duties ascribed to domestic citizens in Rawls's political liberalism: states have duties to justify their actions to one another through reasons that are derived from the public political culture of the shared institutional set. In this, states acquire a distinct set of duties of justice, in virtue of their shared membership in international legal institutions. Although Cohen and Sabel do not emphasize the point, it is surely right that this methodology could be used to defend duties of distributive justice between states. If justice applies to states in virtue of their shared membership in a set of institutions, then they might be thought to have duties to ensure equal standing before that set of institutions, potentially including some guarantees of material equality.

I do not want to defend Nagel against Cohen and Sabel; unlike Nagel, I think international justice exists, and that it binds states even in the absence of a global sovereign. I want, instead, to dispute the idea that the norms identified by Cohen and Sabel are genuinely novel norms, created by the institutions in which states are situated. Even if Cohen and Sabel are right about the substance of the duties held by states, that is, they are wrong to think of these duties as being dependent upon the existence of shared social institutions. These duties are, instead, one specific form taken by a more general duty to avoid certain forms of illegitimate exploitation of impoverished and marginal states. To see this, I think we might note that there are at least two different ways in which we might think that the norms of reason-giving as described here are obligatory upon us. In the domestic case, the citizens who create a coercive state give themselves genuinely novel duties towards one another. These citizens are all subject to the coercive power of the state, and this new normative fact gives rise to duties that would not exist but for that state. In the case described by Cohen and Sabel, however, we might think that states have a standing duty to avoid certain sorts of behavior. A wealthy state might be constrained, for example, not to exploit the fact that some other state is sufficiently vulnerable that it can be effectively threatened into full compliance with terms favorable to the wealthy nation. This general duty, however, could be made more specific by some set of principles that demand the giving of reasons sufficient to justify the actions taken by this wealthy state towards the weaker state. Given that—on my view—there is no novel agent created internationally that has coercive power over all states as the state does over all citizens, it seems better to think of the duty to engage in reason-giving identified by Cohen and Sabel as being a means by which violations of this general duty might be avoided.

To see this, we might examine two distinct sorts of hegemonic relationship. Imagine that the United States is able to effectively insist that other, more vulnerable states cease their agricultural subsidies, while continuing itself to subsidize agricultural production (Watkins and Fowler 2004). We might assume that this is unjust, although of course a full theory about why it is unjust cannot be provided here. For the moment, the idea that some forms of exploitation are unjust might stand in for this full theory. In one case, the United States codifies this unequal relationship in a set of institutions, which it imposes as contracts of adhesion upon all states that wish to engage in trading relationships with the United States. In the second case, the United States does not do anything so grandiose; it does not set up a multilateral treaty, or describe its wishes in terms of a standing set of institutions. Instead, it simply makes contracts with all these vulnerable states, obliging each one to accept unjust terms as a precondition for entering into relationships of trade. Is there a significant moral difference between these two cases? I fail to see one; it seems as if the conduct of the two states is likely to fail the tests of basic justice for the same reason. If this is right, then I think Cohen and Sabel are wrong to think that the duty to engage in the process of political justification is itself a product of the legal system. Instead, it seems that this duty precedes the legal institutions discussed here, and constrains all states regardless of whether or not such institutions exist.

Cohen and Sabel might, of course, insist upon the novelty of such institutions; they rightly point out that these institutions are rather unlike a series of bilateral treaties. The institutions are denser and more administratively complex, for one thing. Perhaps more importantly, in this context, they operate with some degree of independence from the wishes of the parties that set them up. This latter fact, in particular, seems relevant, insofar as it seems to hold out the possibility that transnational institutions of this form might represent a genuinely novel form of international institution. Does this difference not lead to an analysis more akin to that found in the domestic state, in which the creation of a new agent gives rise to the creation of new duties?

The response here, I think, is to accept the argument, but deny the premise. If it is true that these institutions can operate in genuine independence, and are not beholden to the wealthy states of the world for their continued survival, then it may be that the case I have described here cannot be made. I believe, however, that this is likely not so for most transnational institutions, including the WTO and ILO. Different states are differentially vulnerable to these institutions; the wealthiest states of the world can, in principle, simply abandon these institutions should their policies prove too costly. This is, I think, one reason why the terms of trade adopted by the WTO have proven to be so favorable to the interests of the wealthier Western powers. The greater power of exit available to these states provides them with greater voice than more marginal states, and therefore with more power to insist upon their own interests being given priority.

If this is right, then I think the best description of the WTO and its ilk is not that they are institutions binding upon all states who are members, but rather that they are a set of rules imposed by the strong upon the weak. This does not imply that there is no need for rules of international justice—if anything, it should emphasize the reason such rules are needed. It does, however, imply that the way these rules are understood internationally should not be akin to the manner in which they are understood domestically. The WTO is morally significant not as an independent site of political discourse, but because it represents—at its worst—a simple threat made by the rich against the poor.

We can return, now, to the discursive duties described by Cohen and Sabel. Despite the criticism I am making here, I think these duties are not implausible; for the purposes of this article, I simply accept that they might be the best description of the duties that states have. I simply want to question their status as genuinely novel duties, created by the legal institutions described here. Again, I think this difference is due to the fact that the domestic state is able to act as a coercive agent in its own right, whereas these legal institutions are better understood as justifying individual coercive actions on the part of states; the former alters the moral relations of citizens at a foundational level, whereas the latter does not do the same as regards the relations of states. The duties of states not to exploit vulnerability, however, might be regarded as a rather broad and abstract set of duties. The best explanation of the egalitarian duties described by Cohen and Sabel might be that these duties are one particular specification of general duties, made more concrete through an insistence upon a particular method of discharging them. One way of demonstrating that we are not engaging in unjustified coercion or exploitation, after all, is the giving of reasons that we can legitimately expect will motivate the other side in the dispute. The duties ascribed to states by Cohen and Sabel are plausible precisely because they seem to give us a means by which this task of reason-giving might be made more operational. The best explanation of these duties, that is, regards them as one particular instantiation of the more general duties applicable to state agents. This means, I think, that even if Cohen and Sabel have specified an attractive vision of international justice, they have not made the case that genuinely novel norms are brought into being by international law.

I would close this section by returning to a distinction made at the start of the chapter, between the question of creation and the question of fulfillment. I have here been discussing only the question of creation, and insisting that international law does not itself give rise to novel duties of justice. I would reiterate, however, that nothing I have said here argues that international law cannot be helpful in the pursuit of justice. If Cohen and Sabel are right, then the international bodies we have set up—if reinterpreted to embody a more egalitarian ethos—might be very useful indeed in the pursuit of justice. This possibility remains open, even if my argument that these institutions create no novel norms of justice is accepted.

The Argument from Cooperation

Very little in the preceding section focused directly upon distributive justice. Our focus was, instead, on justice and its relationship to international law more generally, with distributive justice as one particular implication that might be derived from this analysis. This will change, I think, when we start to look at the argument from cooperation. This argument is, at its heart, an argument about the distribution of material goods. It makes the case that, where we have complex rule-governed activities of a specified sort, we have an obligation to equalize some form of material holdings between the members of that activity. The argument comes in at least two varieties: the first, and historically most prevalent, is an interpretation of Rawls's basic structure; the second is a more general argument that institutions such as a legal system give rise to egalitarian duties of distributive justice. I will examine these arguments in turn.

The first, Rawlsian version of the argument was prominent in analyses of global justice that emerged after the introduction of Rawls's *A Theory of Justice*. Rawls's concept of the basic structure—the "way in which the major social institutions distribute fundamental rights and duties and determine the advantages from social cooperation" (Rawls 1971: 7)—seemed well poised to offer an analysis that demonstrated the importance of global egalitarianism (Beitz 1979; Pogge 1989). Two related points buttressed this argument: the first is that the international system of legal and economic norms seems to count as a particularly powerful distributive mechanism, and what it distributes is indeed comprehensible as the advantages brought about by economic cooperation both between and within states. The second point is that Rawls insists that the basic structure is the primary subject of justice because its effects are so powerful and present from the start of any human life. If this is true, and if international markets are as influential on life chances as they undoubtedly are, how can the international rules not count as a basic structure?

The second point can be dealt with first: from the fact that the international system is powerful and unavoidable, it does not follow that it is a basic structure. This seems to be a misreading of Rawls, but an unfortunately common one. The best understanding of Rawls's argument, I think, makes it clear that he is thinking of the basic structure as an independently defined entity and only then describing its attributes; he is not saying that any institutional framework with these attributes is therefore a basic structure. Rawls's understanding of the basic structure, as is made clear in both *A Theory of Justice* and (especially) his later writings, involves the major social institutions as enmeshed in the coercive network of a constitutional state. Rawls's refusal to regard the international system as a basic structure for purposes of international justice stems not from insufficient boldness, but from a consistent recognition that the basic structure of the state—which involves the creation of a coercive agent distinct from any found internationally—is a morally distinctive entity, giving rise to novel duties among those who share it. The response to the first point, then, is to simply note the difference between the international realm and the domestic state: while both involve the distribution of benefits from cooperation, only the domestic state involves the creation of a coercive sovereign with effective power over all those agents to whom duties of justice will apply. Not every case of cooperation, even those with profound effects upon human happiness, gives rise to duties of distributive justice. Ideals of beauty, for example, are obviously linked with human happiness; we are likely to do better in our search for love and happiness, all else being equal, when we are beautiful. But it does not follow from this that we have any duty to redistribute beauty, or money as compensation for its lack. Beauty is simply not part of the basic structure as defined through the legal and political system of society. Beauty can, of course, become an avenue through which legal and political injustice occurs: if the non-beautiful are discriminated against in employment, it becomes a legitimate part of the Rawlsian analysis. But beauty itself, however influential, is not part of the basic structure as Rawls understands it.

The more general point, however, remains. Even if the use of Rawls to justify international egalitarianism fails, might we not simply say that wherever there is a cooperative enterprise, there is some normative pressure towards material equality? Darrel Moellendorf has recently articulated such an argument, and his argument might well be used to defend the proposition that international law gives rise to novel duties of egalitarianism:

> The idea is that duties of social justice exist between persons who have a moral duty of equal respect to one another if those persons are co-members in an association that is (1) relatively strong, (2) largely non-voluntary, (3) constitutive of a significant part of the background rules for the various relationships of their public lives, and (4) governed by norms that can be subject to human control.
>
> (Moellendorf 2011)

I do not think Moellendorf's vision of cooperative justice is an altogether attractive one; I do not think that all of the various varieties of cooperative enterprise that might fall under this description give rise to egalitarian duties in the manner described. More to the point for our present purposes, though, is that we might accept that something like Moellendorf's view might be right, but then ask whether or not the existence of international legal institutions is actually a prerequisite for the application of his egalitarian norms. If the answer is no, then we have at least some reason to think that international law does not give rise to a novel set of norms among those states subject to it.

To see this, imagine again the two versions of the hegemonic United States discussed above. In one world, the United States sets up an inegalitarian system of rules and norms for international trade; it understands this system as an indivisible normative system, which it imposes upon more marginal states as a contract of adhesion. In the second world, the United States does the same, but doesn't refer to anything so grandiose as a legal system—there is no set of rules, or procedures, or anything as law-like as that. The United States simply throws its weight around, and relies upon the greater vulnerability of other states to gain concessions and favorable terms of trade. How do these two worlds differ, in normative terms? I think they cannot differ much; if the United States acts unjustly in the first world, it seems to be acting equally unjustly in the second. Whatever justice-based principles are incumbent upon the former are also incumbent upon the latter. If this is true, then it is not that the creation of any set of legal institutions gives rise to distinct duties of justice; these duties exist prior to any legal relationship, and simply condemn certain forms of state interaction. Whatever duties we have, or fail to have, seem utterly unaffected by the legal or nonlegal status of the norms that states act upon in their dealings with others.

This conclusion might not bother Moellendorf very much, since he understands his argument as defending international justice wherever there is cooperative association between states, rather than wherever there is law. But if someone wished to use Moellendorf to defend the proposition that transnational institutions give rise to novel duties, they would have to insist that state action and international law are so linked that the actions of our hypothetical United States are, in fact, creating a legal order through its actions. This seems, however, rather unpromising as a response. It would seem to assert, first, that any action, however isolated, can be redescribed as an institution or association—which would seem to push very hard indeed upon this concept. Even if we were to accept that such acts create an association, though, I think it would still be true that the association is simply not of the right *type* to ground duties of distributive justice. The domestic system of law creates a novel coercive agent, and thereby creates novel duties of justice. The international acts described here, even if they could be understood to create associations or institutions, seem to involve no similar creation, and so seem to give rise to no equivalent duties of distributive justice.

Nothing in what I have said justifies these hegemonic actions; they are, I believe, morally wrong. The point, though, is that the wrong is not created by the legal system. Whether or not the actions are given force in law, the hegemonic power used in a non-symmetrical form is the basis of the objection. Law does not create, here, a system of vertical coercion. There is no novel agent that is itself the subject of moral evaluation, whose acts can be ascribed to it. Internationally, states act; sometimes they cite law, sometimes they do not. These states, however, are the agents to whom the acts are ascribable, and it is their actions that ought to be judged as just or unjust. We confuse the issues unnecessarily by thinking that it is the international *system*—of law, economics or anything else—that is at the heart of our moral evaluations.

If all this is right, then I think we have some reason to think that the first question—the question of creation—ought to be answered with a no. Whatever else we think about international justice, we should not believe that it involves novel duties created by international law. I should note, here, that this does not in any way impugn the character of international law. It is emphatically *not* to say that international law is irrelevant. The second question—the question of fulfillment—matters, and matters enormously. Even if international law does not create our duties of justice, it might make fulfilling those duties more or less easy; it might make certain actions more or less costly, if only by creating the normative language to condemn or approve of those states proposing to do them. We are accustomed, in ordinary life, to thinking of illegal actions as normatively special—marked out by a need for special justification. Illegal international actions seem to give rise to similar normative stories. In the words of Thomas Franck:

> Laws, including the U.N. Charter, are written to govern the general conduct of states in light of historic experience and the requisites of good order. If, in a particular instance, a general law inhibits doing justice, then it is up to each member of the community to decide whether to disobey that law. If some so choose, however, their best strategy is not to ridicule, let alone change the law; it is to proffer the most expiating explanation of the special circumstances that ordained their moral choice.
>
> (Franck 1999: 118)

States, in short, do not like to be seen as breaking the law.

This means, I think, that international norms that more closely approximate our actual duties will make acting for justice easier—and, perhaps, more likely. We should not overestimate the power of international laws; it is a mistake to think of them as more than a single tool in the struggle for global justice. But they have some force, and we ought to think of them as revisable. My conclusion is that we should neither ignore international law, nor fetishize it. It does not originate our duties of justice, nor can it easily help us fulfill them, but it may be able to help us gradually come closer to our objectives. Such slow and imperfect steps, in a world like this one, may be the steps we have the most reason to prize.

References

Aust, A. (2010) *Handbook of International Law*, 2nd edition, Cambridge: Cambridge University Press.

Beitz, C. (1979) *Political Theory and International Relations*, Princeton: Princeton University Press.

Blake, M. (2001) "Coercion, Distributive Justice, and Autonomy," 30 *Philosophy and Public Affairs*: 257–96.

—— (2011) "Coercion and Egalitarian Justice," *The Monist* 94(4).

Buchanan, A. (2003) *Justice, Legitimacy, and Self-Determination: Moral Foundations for International Law*, Oxford: Oxford University Press.

Caney, S. (2011) "Humanity, Associations, and Global Justice," *The Monist* 94(4): 506–34.

Cohen, J. and Sabel, C. (2005) "Global Democracy?" 37 *International Law and Politics* 4: 763–97.

—— (2006) "Extra Rempublicam Nulla Justitia?" 34 *Philosophy and Public Affairs*: 147–75.

Franck, T. M. (1999) "Break It, Don't Fake It," 78 *Foreign Affairs*: 116–18.

Goldsmith, J. and Posner, E. (2005) *The Limits of International Law*, Oxford: Oxford University Press.

Gwertzman, B. (1984) "U.S. Voids Role of World Court on Latin Policy," *The New York Times*, April 9, 1984: A1.

Hirsch, A. (2010) "Iraq Invasion Violated International Law, Dutch Inquiry Finds," *The Guardian*, January 12, 2010.

Moellendorf, D. (2011) "Cosmopolitanism and Compatriot Duties," *The Monist* 94(4).

Nagel, T. (2005) "The Problem of Global Justice," 33 *Philosophy and Public Affairs*: 113–47.

Pogge, T. (1989) *Realizing Rawls*, Ithaca, NY: Cornell University Press.

—— (2002) *World Poverty and Human Rights*, New York: Polity.

—— (2010) "The Role of International Law in Reproducing Massive Poverty," in S. Besson and J. Tasioulas, eds., *The Philosophy of International Law*, Oxford: Oxford University Press, pp. 417–36.

Rawls, J. (1971) *A Theory of Justice*, Cambridge, Mass.: Harvard University Press.

—— (1993) *Political Liberalism*, New York: Columbia University Press.

Risse, M. (2005) "Do We Owe the Global Poor Assistance or Rectification?" 19 *Ethics and International Affairs*: 9–18.

Roberts, J. T. and Hite, A. B., eds. (2007) *The Globalization and Dependency Reader: Perspectives on Development and Global Change*, Malden, Mass.: Blackwell Publishing.

Scanlon, T. M. (1990) "Promises and Practices," 19 *Philosophy and Public Affairs*: 199–226.

Watkins, K. and Fowler, P. (2004) *Rigged Rules and Double Standards: Trade, Globalisation and the Fight Against Poverty*, Oxford: Oxfam.

Further Reading

For further reading, see: A. Buchanan (2011) *Human Rights, Legitimacy, and the Use of Force*, Oxford: Oxford University Press; L. Cabrera (2004) *Political Theory of Global Justice*, London: Routledge; O. A. Hathaway (2011) "Do Human Rights Treaties Make a Difference?" 111 *Yale Law Journal*; L. May (2011) *Global Justice and Due Process*, Cambridge: Cambridge University Press; R. Miller (2010) *Globalizing Justice: The Ethics of Poverty and Power*, Oxford: Oxford University Press; and J. Rawls (2001) *The Law of Peoples*, Cambridge, Mass.: Harvard University Press.

23

HUMAN RIGHTS

John Tasioulas

1. Orthodox and Political Conceptions

Over the past decade or so, after a long period of comparative neglect, philosophers have increasingly turned their attention to human rights. Such rights are generally construed in normative rather than positive terms. They are not the standards actually enshrined in what we call the "human rights" texts and practices of law and politics, but independent moral standards that such texts and practices are characteristically intended to recognize and implement. Of course, when philosophers attend to any subject matter, it is usually in the mode of disagreement. But human rights provoke disagreements well beyond the philosophy seminar room, and these are not confined to the familiar legal-political disputes about their identification, implications or enforcement. There are also deep divisions among historians regarding the origins of our concept of a human right. In a recent book, Samuel Moyn contends that the concept only emerged as a significant historical force in the 1970s, some decades after the Universal Declaration of Human Rights of 1948 (UDHR) (Moyn 2010). At the other extreme, Brian Tierney interprets our concept of human rights as strongly continuous with the natural rights tradition—a tradition that, he contends, originates in the humanistic jurisprudence of the twelfth century (Tierney 1997).

Other historians reject Tierney's thesis, associating the birth of natural rights with late medieval or early modern thinkers such as Ockham, Grotius and Locke. Nevertheless, the orthodox view about the concept of a human right, at least among philosophers, has long been that it is broadly equivalent to that of a natural right. First, they are both moral rights possessed by all human beings simply in virtue of their humanity. Moral rights are here to be understood primarily as claim rights, associated with duties on others that are owed to the right-holder. Duties, in turn, are moral reasons for action that apply to their bearers independently of how the latter are motivated and which enjoy a special force or weight as against some countervailing reasons. Their violation, without justification or excuse, properly renders one subject to blame and sometimes punishment. Human rights are distinguished from other moral rights because we possess them not due to any personal achievement, social status or transaction, nor because they are conferred upon us by a positive legal order, but simply in virtue of our standing as human beings. And the second dimension along which human rights resemble natural rights is that we discover these rights by the use of ordinary moral reasoning, or "natural reason" in a venerable locution, rather than through "artificial" (e.g., legal) reasoning or divine revelation (exponents of the orthodox view include O'Neill 1996; Griffin 2008; Wolterstorff 2008; Finnis 2011. See also Tasioulas 2011).

On this orthodox conception, human rights are universal moral rights. This is perfectly compatible with their having important political implications, e.g., for the legitimacy of states or the permissibility of international intervention. Indeed, it may even be the case that certain of these political implications are necessary truths. Given the nature of states and the nature of human rights, for example, it may be a necessary truth that states should respect human rights. However, the orthodox conception does not explain the essential nature of human rights—what one needs to grasp in order to have an adequate mastery of the concept of a human right—in terms of any such political role, beyond perhaps the rather minimalist idea that human rights are the subset of universal moral rights that may be, in principle, socially (or, more substantively, legally) enforced.

That human rights are universal moral rights does not entail that they are possessed by all human beings throughout human history. Instead, a proponent of the orthodox view may coherently refer to the "human rights" possessed only by all human beings within a certain historical period, such as that of modernity (Tasioulas 2007). This is one way to read the UDHR, which includes many rights (e.g., the rights to nationality, a fair trial, an adequate standard of living) that cannot easily be ascribed to humans, such as Stone Age cave-dwellers, who inhabited epochs in which the fulfillment of the counterpart duties was unfeasible given limitations in available institutional capacities, material resources or technological capabilities. To this extent, human rights are not to be identified with "natural rights," if this means moral rights that are meaningfully possessed even in a state of nature (Beitz 2009, ch. III). But this is just one historically formative, but hardly canonical, strand within the natural rights tradition (Tierney 1997: 70).

What other reasons might historians such as Moyn have for treating human rights as discontinuous with natural rights? One reason is that they regard human rights as norms that justify subjecting states to certain constraints with an international institutional dimension, an idea whose prevalence they take to be of recent vintage. This sort of rationale has been recently elaborated by philosophers, mostly influenced by John Rawls, who advance what might be called a political conception of human rights. Its adherents claim that the first limb of the orthodox conception, according to which human rights are universal moral rights, ignores the political functions that are integral to the concept of a human right and which distinguish such rights from natural rights. Different advocates of the political conception specify these political functions in diverse ways and in varying combinations.

One idea is that human rights are primarily claims on states or political institutions that assert a right to rule backed up by the threat of coercion (Pogge 2002: ch. 7, subsequently recanted in the second, 2007 edition; possibly also Beitz 2009). On one version of this view, a "human rights" violation only exists when some failure on the part of officials is present. Hence, we cannot automatically infer from the fact that A has tortured B simply for the pleasure that the former derives from doing so that B's human rights have been violated. A may well have violated a right of B's not to be tortured, even a universal moral right. But the act of torture will only be a *human rights* violation if A is an official of the state or his conduct is suitably connected to a coercive institutional order inhabited by A and B. One form of connection, stressed by Thomas Pogge (2002), emerges from an affirmative answer to the question of whether the act of torture is a foreseeable and reasonably avoidable upshot of the imposition of that order. However, many will question whether it is worth countenancing a dualism of human rights and universal moral rights of this sort unless the former notion is given some additional, and more specific, political dimension.

We should therefore turn to two other political roles in terms of which human rights have been characterized. Internally, human rights are interpreted as at least necessary conditions for the legitimacy of a state or comparable institution, constraining its right to rule. Unless a state complies with them, its laws will not impose obligations of obedience on its putative subjects. Externally, human rights operate as standards whose violation, if extensive and persistent, triggers a defeasible case for some form of international action (e.g., military intervention, economic sanctions, etc.) against the guilty state.

The characterization of human rights as *both* conditions of internal legitimacy and limitations on immunity from external interference is a prominent theme in the work of John Rawls and Joshua Cohen (Rawls 1999; Cohen 2004, 2006). This dual political function is taken to distinguish human rights both from universal moral rights and from the more expansive set of rights properly upheld in liberal democratic societies. But this analysis of human rights confronts the objection that it is internally conflicted. There appears to be a discrepancy between the conditions of internal legitimacy and those of international intervention, such that the self-same list of rights is incapable of discharging both functions. Whether a state possesses legitimacy depends on the morality of its actions in relation to its putative subjects. But whether it is liable, even in principle, to external interference depends on other considerations, including the value of political self-determination and facts about the geopolitical environment, such as the incidence of predatory behavior among states. In consequence, the mere fact that a state acts beyond the scope of its legitimate authority does not give rise to a reason, in any circumstances, for interference by other states, just as not every personal wrongdoing is justifiably prevented or punished by others (Raz 2010a: 330).

Subscribers to the dual-function view might respond by specifying more precisely how human rights operate as *defeasible* triggers for external intervention, rather than all-things-considered justifications. But there remains a problem with characterizing human rights *either* in terms of legitimacy or intervention, which is that both analyses threaten to issue in a severely truncated list of human rights. This threat is notoriously realized by Rawls's theory, which results in the following parsimonious list:

> [the] right to life (to the means of subsistence and security); to liberty (to freedom from slavery, serfdom, and forced occupation, and to a sufficient measure of liberty of conscience to ensure freedom of religion and thought); to property (personal property); and to formal equality as expressed by the rules of natural justice (that is, that similar cases be treated similarly).
>
> (Rawls 1999: 65)

Notable omissions from Rawls's list that figure in standard international human rights documents include: rights to nondiscrimination on the grounds of sex, race and religion; rights to freedom of opinion, speech, movement and political participation; rights to education, work and an adequate standard of living; and so on. Indeed, Rawls asserts that only articles 3 to 18 of the UDHR contain human rights proper; the rest are only "liberal aspirations" (Rawls 1999: 80, n. 23).

Now, this heavily revisionist upshot is a major drawback of Rawls's account for anyone who takes it to be a key desideratum of a theory of human rights that it makes (charitable) sense of existing human rights practice. A determined Rawlsian might reply that such fidelity to existing practice is not an important metatheoretical desideratum, as compared with spelling out the implications of Rawls's political liberalism for the foreign policy of liberal societies. Or that even if it is, Rawls's meager schedule of human rights reflects how fidelity must be compromised in light of a competing metatheoretical desideratum of great weight, i.e., the need to arrive at a conception of human rights that is suitably nonparochial, so that human rights are not simply liberal constitutional rights projected globally.

However, a more moderate line is taken by advocates of the political conception who diagnose the problem of fidelity with Rawls's theory as stemming from the specific kind of international response that he makes criterial for human rights. In effect, Rawls holds that a human right is distinguished by its capacity to justify *military* intervention when violated gravely and extensively. Naturally, there are other ways of implementing human rights short of military intervention, such as economic sanctions or diplomatic censure. But for Rawls it seems to be their ability to sustain a pro tanto case for military intervention that distinguishes human rights from other rights. However, a more generous list can be secured if we broaden the criterial notion of intervention to include nonmilitary and noncoercive forms of international response otherwise prohibited by norms of state sovereignty (see Raz 2010a). Or, alternatively, if we conceptually tie human rights not exclusively to intervention, but to the wider remedial response of "international concern," of which the multifarious forms of intervention are just one species (see Beitz 2009: 33–42).

It is not obvious that either maneuver meets the concern about fidelity. (For an alternative approach that focuses on human rights as conditions of legitimacy, see Dworkin 2011, discussed in section 2). Core norms appealed to in the wider human rights culture, such as those prohibiting discrimination on the grounds of sex or affirming a right to an adequate standard of living, might still face an uphill struggle (see Beitz 2009, ch. 7). But supposing this worry could be allayed, one might still be puzzled by the more general idea, implicit in the political conception, that human rights are "revisionist appurtenances of a global political order composed of independent states" (Beitz 2009: 197). Consider anarchists, who reject the state in all its forms, or advocates of cosmopolitan government, who wish to transcend the state system altogether in favor of a unitary world government. Both routinely appeal to human rights to justify their positions, but this would hardly be a coherent strategy if human rights are inherently bound up with the state or the state system. Even if anarchism and cosmopolitanism are not, in the end, compelling doctrines, it seems extremely uncharitable to portray their advocates as victims of a conceptual confusion about human rights.

The line of thought so far recommends adopting the first limb of the orthodox conception, leaving it as a further, substantive question to what extent human rights have any specifically political functions. Such a view is not very remote from forms of the political conception that treat human rights as a proper subset of the universal moral rights picked out by the orthodox conception (e.g., Raz 2010a and b). However, a deeper disagreement would persist with versions of the political conception that resist the subset approach, regarding human rights as sui generis with respect to the broader category of (universal) moral rights. But this sui generis approach seems incapable of adequately capturing the characteristic *moral* significance of human rights. Charles Beitz (2009), for example, describes human rights as norms protecting certain "urgent interests" against standard threats posed to them by one's government. But even the most urgent interests can be impaired in all sorts of ways without any moral wrongdoing, and it is questionable whether the distinctive significance of these interests in human rights discourse can be grasped without introducing the idea that they are protected by individual rights that impose obligations on others.

There is another, more subterranean explanation for Moyn's thesis of a discontinuity between natural and human rights thought. It seems to be part of a commonly accepted ideal of professional objectivity that historians' explanations should not turn on the truth or falsity of moral propositions. This prevents them from seriously entertaining the hypothesis that the rise and gathering momentum of the human rights movement is to be explained in part by the fact that it is inspired by fundamentally correct moral principles. But this dislodges an important motivation for treating human rights as continuous with natural rights: namely, the belief that both terms have been used to designate some objective truths of human morality, truths which have been formulated and implemented in different ways, and with varying degrees of insight and success, in diverse historical epochs.

Now, this arms-length relation to the moral truth also finds a parallel in contemporary philosophy. John Rawls, again, has led the way in arguing that human rights are categorically distinct from natural rights because, contrary to the second limb of the orthodox conception, they are not grounded in ordinary moral reasoning (Rawls 1999). For Rawls, people inevitably disagree about whether and how moral truth is discerned and about which moral propositions are true. But human rights, with their claim to regulate coercive intervention across international boundaries, must be justifiable to others despite their persistent ideological disagreements. So, Rawls claims, unlike natural rights, they must be grounded in a form of "public reason" that is discontinuous with ordinary moral reasoning, levitating above the fray of interminable philosophical and religious quarrels about morality, human nature and divinity:

> [Human rights] do not depend on any particular comprehensive religious doctrine or philosophical doctrine about human nature. The Law of Peoples does not say, for example, that human beings are moral persons and have equal worth in the eyes of God; or that they have certain moral and intellectual powers that entitle them to those rights. To argue in these ways would involve religious or philosophical doctrines that many decent hierarchical peoples might reject as liberal or democratic, or as in some way distinctive of Western political tradition and prejudicial to other cultures. Still, the Law of Peoples does not deny these doctrines.
>
> (Rawls 1999: 68)

This is a deeper sense in which one might hold a "political" view of human rights: they are political not only in their defining subject matter (e.g., political legitimacy, international intervention), but in the genre of reasoning that grounds them. For Rawls, the justification of human rights is modeled by a social contract at two levels. At the first level, liberal democratic societies agree to principles to govern their relations—a Law of Peoples, including its truncated list of human rights. At the second level, "decent" hierarchical societies are shown to be able to endorse the same principles from their own, nonliberal outlook. The fact that they can attract the allegiance of nonliberal societies is supposed to exonerate those principles from the charge of parochialism.

But how can the charge of parochialism be avoided unless human rights are grounded in ordinary moral reasoning, itself understood to embody an aspiration to objective correctness, i.e., correctness that is independent of the beliefs and attitudes that prevail in any given society? The alternative is to rely on standards that, in some sense, people actually share. So, for example, Rawls's starting point in deriving human rights is the values implicit in liberal democratic culture. But that leaves us with the problem of what to say to those who do not share those values, including "outlaw states" that would be the potential targets of military intervention in a Rawlsian global dispensation. Of course, Rawls stresses that some nonliberal, but decent, societies may endorse, for their own moral reasons, his schedule of human rights. But that very schedule is only a candidate for their endorsement because it has been previously validated within an exclusively liberal perspective, one from which decent societies receive the backhanded compliment of being "not fully unreasonable" (Rawls 1999: 74). And even for members of liberal societies, is it enough to say that human rights flow from values deeply embedded in their political culture, absent an independent vindication of those values? Without an objective grounding the human rights project risks becoming just another fundamentalist commitment, as so many of its critics allege (Tasioulas 2010a: 107–8).

There are doubtless other ways of elaborating the idea of public reason, in opposition to ordinary moral reasoning, that do not lapse into parochialism of Rawlsian proportions. One line of thought begins not from public reason understood as ideas implicit in liberal democratic culture, but rather from a global public reason (see Cohen 2004, 2006; Nussbaum 2000, ch. 1; Sen 2009, part IV). These views, however, remain at a fairly embryonic stage of development. Pending their fuller elaboration, the default position may be to accept the second limb of the orthodox conception and embark on the task of discovering which moral rights are indeed possessed by all human beings simply in virtue of their humanity. Of course, once these rights have been identified, it would not automatically follow that they should be enshrined in international law or enforced by international action (see section 3, below). Nor would it necessarily follow that there is a single best institutional model, whether American or European in inspiration, for implementing those rights. To this extent, legitimate concerns about parochialism and intolerance can be addressed without abandoning the orthodox idea that human rights need to be grounded in ordinary, truth-oriented, moral reasoning.

2. Human Dignity and the Foundations of Human Rights

What form should an objective justification of human rights assume? Jacques Maritain famously remarked about the UDHR, "We agree about the human rights, provided no one asks us why." Today, however, many people answer the "why" question by appealing to the value of human dignity. Indeed, the link between human rights and human dignity already surfaces in the UDHR, although only in the 1966 Covenants on Civil and Political Rights and Economic, Social and Cultural Rights is it explicitly stated that "these rights derive from the inherent dignity of the human person." The basis of human rights in human dignity was powerfully reaffirmed by the UN General Assembly in 1986 (GA Res 41/120), and the concept has become a near-ubiquitous presence in both international and regional human rights instruments (see McCrudden 2008). But is the rather amorphous notion of human dignity doing any real justificatory work, or is it just a placeholder for a justification that the speaker vaguely implies exists but has done nothing to specify?

As one might expect, approaches to the justification of human rights span pretty much the entire gamut of orientations in moral philosophy, including natural law theory (e.g., Finnis 2011), Kantian deontology (e.g., Gewirth 1996) and consequentialism (e.g., Talbott 2005), all the way through to withering skepticism about the availability of any such justification (MacIntyre 2007: 69). However, a notable trend in recent years has been the tendency of philosophers to reflect the broader human rights culture by invoking (human) dignity as the master grounding value. In this section, we shall critically survey two important accounts of this kind elaborated by Ronald Dworkin and James Griffin (Dworkin 2011; Griffin 2008; see also Habermas 2010 and Kateb 2010).

Ronald Dworkin's is a political view of human rights that abandons the first, but not the second, tenet of orthodoxy. Human rights are construed as belonging to the more general class of political rights, i.e., claims primarily against one's own political community that confer on their individual holders trumps over what would otherwise be adequate justifications for government action. Justice in general demands that a government respect the dignity of all its members—their fundamental right to equal concern and respect. Dignity, so construed, has two components. First, a community must treat its members' fates as equally objectively important; second, it must respect their personal responsibility for defining what counts as success in their own lives. This fundamental right is the source of other, more specific political rights.

Human rights, however, are picked out within the class of political rights by reference to an even more abstract and fundamental right, one that bears on the legitimacy (and not only on the justice) of a government's rule. This is the basic human right to a certain *attitude* of good faith on the part of one's political community: "a right to be treated *as a human being whose dignity fundamentally matters*" (Dworkin 2011: 333). Although governments inevitably make *mistakes* regarding what dignity requires, and to that extent act unjustly, human rights violations are committed only when these mistakes manifest *contempt* for the dignity of some or all of its members. The touchstone of good faith, and so of the absence of contempt, is one of *intelligibility* rather than correctness. Human rights are respected "only when a government's overall behavior is defensible under an intelligible, even if unconvincing, conception of what [the] two principles of dignity require" (ibid.: 335–36).

Dworkin admits that drawing the line between error and contempt can be controversial in individual cases; it is an "interpretative" matter, one not settled by a government's (sincere) protestations of good faith. But some cases he takes to be obvious human rights violations. The first principle of dignity, for example, is violated in this way when a political community acts out of the belief that some of its members, e.g., infidels, Semites, blacks, are of "inferior stock" or "condones humiliation or torture for amusement" (ibid.: 336). Policies that are human rights violations under the second principle, according to Dworkin, include those that forbid the exercise of any religion other than the officially approved one, or that punish heresy or blasphemy, or that deny, in principle, freedom of speech and the press.

Some may doubt that mere good faith always suffices to underwrite the legitimacy of a government's rule. If a government wields coercion in the service of a deeply flawed, albeit intelligible, conception of dignity, why should its laws morally bind its subjects? But let us focus on the problems with this test as a criterion for identifying human rights rather than legitimate rule. One set of problems comes under the heading of fidelity, a consideration Dworkin himself invokes against interventionist accounts of human rights. First of all, the theory appears seriously to compromise the presumed universality of human rights. This is because it requires that interpretative judgments as to the existence of "good faith" be sensitive to variations in local political, economic and cultural conditions. As a result, a "health or education policy that would show good faith effort in a poor country would show contempt in a rich one" (ibid.: 338). This threatens seriously to dilute the idea that human rights require access to the self-same object—e.g., a substantive level of health care—for all human beings. It leaves open the disquieting possibility that IVF treatment, or even some forms of cosmetic surgery, are human rights entitlements in developed societies, while people in poor countries are only entitled to rudimentary levels of health care. Given that legitimacy essentially consists in the obtaining of a certain kind of relationship between a particular government and members of a particular political community, any theory that makes compliance with human rights anything like a sufficient condition of legitimacy will arguably confront similar difficulties in capturing their universality.

Quite apart from this concern about universality, the "good faith" test is rather indeterminate, given the difficulty in identifying just when the flouting of dignity crosses over into contempt. But to the extent that it constitutes a determinate standard, it seems overly lax. For it looks as if many political ideologies that sponsor paradigmatic human rights violations are plausibly interpreted as offering *intelligible* conceptions of equal concern and respect. For example, Dworkin rather optimistically asserts that "in our age, laws that forbid property, profession, or political power to women cannot be reconciled with women's responsibility for their own decisions" (ibid.: 337). Yet it is hardly obvious that deep-rooted ideologies that exclude women from certain public or religious offices, on the basis of a supposedly divinely ordained division of labor among the sexes, fail to embody even *intelligible* (as opposed to just radically mistaken) conceptions of women's dignity. If this were so, we should be hard pressed to explain the persistence of such ideologies in the present age, even among members of Western societies.

But perhaps the deepest problem with Dworkin's theory is the heavy emphasis it places on equality and freedom to generate a recognizably complete schedule of human rights, a problem it shares with James Griffin's structurally similar dignity-based theory. Griffin subscribes to both limbs of the orthodox conception, and grounds human rights in the value of possessing, and being able reasonably effectively to exercise, the capacity for personhood or normative agency. Personhood distinguishes us from nonhuman animals, and Griffin offers it as a salient and historically resonant interpretation of human dignity (Griffin 2008: 36). The idea of personhood is broken down into three components. The first is autonomy, which involves choosing one's conception of a worthwhile life from a range of eligible alternatives without being dominated or controlled by others. The second is liberty, which is the ability to pursue one's choices free from the forcible interference of others. And finally, there is minimum provision, since one can make real choices, and effectively pursue them, only if one has certain minimum resources and capabilities. (ibid.: 32–33). In addition to personhood, Griffin also appeals to a norm of basic human equality—one that encompasses all human beings above a certain threshold of normative agency—but he regards equality as at the root of interpersonal morality in general, and so not a distinctive ground of human rights.

For Griffin, the values of personhood are teleological: they are components of human well-being, so that "the exercise of personhood is an end the realization of which enhances the value of life" (ibid.: 57). This contrasts with Dworkin's interpretation of the second principle of dignity as a moral constraint. Griffin recognizes other human interests besides autonomy and liberty, such as enjoyment, achievement and deep personal relations. However, it is only the values of personhood that play a direct role in grounding human rights; the other values have at best an indirect significance, insofar as they influence our assessments of what counts as a worthwhile conception of a good life that is an intelligible object of autonomous choice. Personhood values play this grounding role in conjunction with "practicalities," which are a diverse set of historically invariant facts relating to human nature and social life. By giving substance to the maxim "'ought' implies 'can,'" practicalities enable personhood values to generate "effective, socially manageable claim[s] on others" (ibid.: 38). Indeed, Griffin believes that the personhood theory is able to "generate most of the conventional list of human rights" (ibid.: 33).

Now, one might suppose that Griffin's personhood theory endows human dignity with a richer rights-generative content than its Dworkinian cousin, and that it does so precisely by construing it as an element of human well-being. But there is a serious question about whether the personhood theory remains unduly restrictive, still not going far enough in giving well-being its full role in the grounds of human rights. One manifestation of this is that the theory issues in needlessly roundabout and precarious justifications of paradigmatic human rights. For example, Griffin contends that torture is a human rights violation because of the way it attacks our capacity to reach a decision or stick to it (ibid.: 52). Certainly, this must be part of the story. But there are many other ways of subverting people's wills, such as injecting them with mind-altering drugs. Part of what makes torture a graver human rights violation is that it achieves its purpose through the infliction of severe pain, and the avoidance of severe pain is surely another universal interest, along with the interest in normative agency. The human right not to be tortured appears to draw its force from a number of interests that are impaired by torture, not just personhood. This point generalizes to other familiar human rights, e.g., the rights to education, work and leisure, which are most naturally taken to reflect the importance of knowledge, achievement and play, respectively, in addition to personhood.

However, Griffin believes that the pluralist grounding of human rights just bruited connives at the "debasement" of human[s] rights discourse, exacerbating the very problem of the radical indeterminacy of sense of the phrase "human right" that his theory is designed to address. Now, even someone who doesn't share Griffin's scathing assessment of contemporary human rights discourse as having rendered the notion of a "human right" "nearly criterionless" (ibid.: 52) should resonate to his call for determinacy. But why suppose that the pluralist approach, which invokes human interests in addition to those of personhood, is incapable of securing it? It does not license us to say that there is a human right to X wherever we find a universal human interest in X, no more than Griffin is committed to the existence of a human right whenever personhood values are at stake. Instead, we have to ask whether, for each and every human being, that interest generates a duty with the same content, and in asking that question we must surmount the obstacles on the way from dignity and interests to universal moral rights. If these obstacles, which Griffin refers to as "practicalities," can suitably discharge this role in the case of rights generated by personhood values, what prevents them from doing the same for the rights-generative significance of other elements of the human good?

The objectivity and universality of the underlying grounding values, the constraints imposed by the threshold requirements, and the necessity for the self-same duty to be owed to each and every human being may be enough to instill the requisite intellectual discipline in human rights discourse. If so, there will be no need for an additional *ex ante* restriction on the kinds of interests that may ground human rights. Indeed, it is not clear that Griffin himself always abides by his self-imposed restriction, given the way that non-personhood goods are seemingly implicated in some of his arguments for particular human rights, such as his case for a human right to same-sex marriage, which turns in part on the value of deep personal relations (for criticism of Griffin's theory along these general lines, see Tasioulas 2010b: 658–66. For more pluralistic accounts of the grounds of human rights, see Finnis 2011, ch. 8; Nickel 2007, chs. 4–5; Buchanan 2010, part I).

The line of thought pursued so far is that claims about the foundational role of human dignity—whether construed in Dworkin's or Griffin's terms—are over-ambitious. We need to appeal to more in our grounding of human rights than human equality and the significance of freedom, whether the latter is construed as a moral principle or a component of well-being or both. This pluralistic approach to the grounds of human rights encourages us to shift our attention to the threshold question of the conditions under which the plurality of individualistic considerations—equality, dignity and universal interests—generate universal moral rights. As we have seen, Dworkin's appeal to a "good faith" as a threshold faces serious problems of infidelity and indeterminacy. But as Dworkin himself points out, Griffin's invocation of "practicalities" is overly sketchy. It is plausible, however, that there are at least two obstacles that have to be surmounted on the road, from considerations of dignity (equality and/or freedom) and interests, on the one hand, to the derivation of duties with broadly identical content owed to all human beings.

At the first threshold, we ask whether, in the case of all human beings, it is possible to secure the underlying values (dignity and interests) through a duty with the proposed content. Sometimes the impossibility is *logical*: there can be no duty to ensure both one's existence and nonexistence twenty years after one's birth. Other impossibilities are *metaphysical or physical*: there can be no right of all human beings, including males, to give birth. Some are mundanely *contingent*: there is no human right to a Rodeo Drive lifestyle given the lack of resources, now and in any realistically attainable future, to secure such a lavish standard of material resources for everyone on the face of the earth.

Some failures to cross the first threshold are rather more subtle, involving what might be called directly *evaluative* impossibilities. Who can deny, for example, that romantic love is one of the most life-enhancing aspects of human existence? But does it follow from this that anyone is under a duty to love anyone else, that there is a right to be loved romantically? Such a right seems to be ruled out at the first threshold: the very nature of romantic love is at odds with the existence of a positive duty to love others in this way. It is not merely that romantic feelings are not suitably under the control of their subjects. After all, a modern-day equivalent of Puck's potion in *A Midsummer Night's Dream* might be invented. Rather, the idea is that the way romantic love enhances our lives is inconsistent with anyone bearing a duty to give it. Romantic love is valuable as a freely bestowed gift, a spontaneous expression of the lover's own deepest desires, rather than something one is obligated to deliver and blamable for failing to do so. In making love an object of duty, violence is done to its nature: the supposed right-holder stands to receive only the pitiful simulacra of such love rather than the genuine article.

But even if the right to love passes this first threshold, it surely comes to grief at a second threshold, one relating to *burdensomeness*. Here we register the costs imposed by the putative right on the bearers of the counterpart duty and on our ability to realize other values that have a normative claim on us, including other human rights. Even if, *contra* the argument just rehearsed, conferring romantic love could in principle be a matter of duty, we may reasonably conclude that no such duty exists, because the burden it imposes on potential duty-bearers in terms of autonomy, spontaneity and the strains of psychological self-policing are excessive.

The putative human right to romantic love is admittedly an exotic case; but, arguably the same line of argument that rules it out also invalidates the claims of some items in leading human rights instruments to reflect genuine requirements of human rights morality. For example, on any literal interpretation, the right to the highest attainable standard of health (article 25, UDHR), fails to cross both thresholds. First, it is not possible for the highest attainable standard of health to be an object of duty. One's level of health depends upon one's own decisions in a way that prevents it from being a duty of others to secure for you. But even if we adjusted the right's content so that it refers to the provision of the highest attainable standard of health *care*, rather than health itself, it would likely stumble at the threshold of burdensomeness, since it would entail excessive costs, including unacceptable sacrifices in our capacity to fulfill other human rights (see Raz 2010b: 44–46 and Nickel 2007, chs. 4–5).

So far we have been considering a moderate line of criticism of dignity-based accounts of human rights, according to which human dignity does not exhaust the foundations of human rights. A more radical objection, however, denies it any foundational role. This objection is inspired by a certain literal reading of the first limb of the orthodox conception, i.e., the idea that human rights are moral rights possessed by all human beings simply in virtue of their humanity. But not all human beings, i.e., members of the species *Homo sapiens*, possess the capacity for rational self-determination that is central to Dworkin's account of responsibility and Griffin's account of personhood. Nonetheless, many would regard it as a flagrant human rights violation to torture someone in the advanced stages of senile dementia simply for the sadistic pleasure one derives from doing so. Considerations such as these motivate Nicholas Wolterstorff's theistic justification of human rights (2008). Of course, some theistic accounts of human rights are also dignitarian: they interpret the dignity of human beings as consisting in some quality—free will, rationality, etc.—whereby they resemble God (*imago Dei*). But these accounts face the same problem of restricted scope that affects their secular counterparts. By contrast, Wolterstorff's claim is that all human beings possess all human rights not because of some special value inhering in them, but because they are the objects of God's love. Moreover, since God loves us all equally, even the most disabled human being has exactly the same human rights as the most gifted members of the species.

Leaving aside the nontrivial matter of the assumption of God's existence, by Wolterstorff's own reckoning this argument vindicates so few human rights—even fewer than Rawls's theory—that there is a real question about whether he is even addressing the same subject as the mainstream human rights culture. And then there is a version of the familiar difficulty that plagues theistic accounts of moral concepts: doesn't God need a reason to make humans, and not earthworms, the special object of his love, for otherwise his love would be entirely capricious? And surely this reason must relate to valuable qualities possessed by humans but not earthworms. In which case, why can't those qualities directly ground human rights, without reference to God's love? Perhaps the answer is that they are not sufficiently impressive, by themselves, to confer the great protection afforded by human rights. But then there is a deeper question about whether this is a justification of the right kind. Human rights are supposed to pay tribute to the value of each individual human being, but on this account, they are ultimately ways of respecting God. Human beings are, in consequence, radically decentered within human rights morality.

We may tentatively conclude that an adequate justification of paradigmatic human rights will dispense with the literal interpretation of the first limb of the orthodox conception, whereby all human rights are possessed by all human beings, where a "human being" is any member of the species *Homo sapiens*. However, accounts of the grounding of human rights that do not exclusively appeal to dignity may be better equipped to accord at least some human rights to human beings that are not normative agents, thereby addressing some of the worries of under-inclusiveness that motivated Wolterstorff's theistic account (for Griffin's attempt to address the problem posed by nonnormative agents, see Griffin 2008, ch. 4).

3. From Human Rights Morality to Human Rights Law

Even if we have established to our satisfaction the existence of a schedule of human rights, i.e., universal moral rights that are in principle eligible for social or legal enforcement, it is a further question to what extent, if any, they should be established as legal rights conferred on all human beings. The relationship that should obtain at any given time between the morality and law of human rights will seldom if ever resolve into a simple, one-to-one isomorphism. Sometimes there are conclusive reasons for not incorporating into law a norm with matching content, as when doing so would be counterproductive. Conversely, there can be conclusive reasons for establishing a legal human right that does not correspond to an independent moral human right. For example, perhaps there is no human right not to be subject to the death penalty under any circumstances. However, given the susceptibility to grave error and abuse endemic to the institution of capital punishment, there may be a decisive case for creating such a right in law. The reasons for doing so will consist in the ways in which the legal right serves various other values, including moral human rights to life and against unjust punishment, that do not match it in content.

Now, human rights morality may find expression in domestic, regional and international legal orders. In this section, I shall focus on international human rights law (IHRL). An essential feature of a legal order is the claim to legitimate authority it asserts over a group of putative subjects. It claims to impose a moral obligation of obedience on them quite apart from whatever independent reasons they already had to do what the law requires. Although the nature and justification of legal authority is the subject of a voluminous jurisprudential literature in recent years, philosophers have only recently started to give serious attention to the special problems arising for the legitimacy of international law, including its human rights component (see Buchanan 2010, parts I–II; Besson and Tasioulas 2010, chs. 3–6). IHRL is chiefly generated by treaties and customary international law (including *jus cogens* norms which purport to be binding on states irrespective of their consent). To what extent does such law enjoy legitimate authority over its putative subjects, which are predominantly states?

There are various accounts of the ultimate standard of legitimacy, among them consent and democratic theories. Theories of these kinds face problems in the domestic context which, if anything, are magnified when we shift our focus to international law (this is so whether we interpret them as requiring the consent or democratic participation of individuals or, less ambitiously, of states) (see Buchanan 2010, part II). However, one justly influential account of legitimate authority that seems generally applicable is the service conception of authority developed by Joseph Raz. It holds that the ultimate standard of legitimate authority is the Normal Justification Condition (NJC), according to which: "A has legitimate authority over B if the latter would better conform with reasons that apply to him if he intends to be guided by A's directives than if he does not" (Raz 2006: 1014). In the rest of this section, some aspects of the legitimacy of IHRL are explored by reference to the NJC.

The extension of the NJC to IHRL is not straightforward because, in the international sphere, no unified legislature exists comparable to those prevalent within domestic legal systems. Nonetheless, norms governing the formation of customary international law may be thought of as constituting an institutional process whereby the activities of various agents—predominantly, but not exclusively, states—combine to produce law that lays claim to authority. The application of the NJC to treaty law is yet more problematic, since treaties are more readily subsumed under the category of promise-based obligations. However, even here the NJC retains a twofold, albeit indirect, relevance. First, it can provide individual states with some guidance as to which treaties they should ratify. Second, multilateral treaties, in particular, often play an important role in the formation of customary international law itself, so that obligations originally specified in treaties come to bind non-states parties.

One recurrent challenge to the legitimacy of IHRL is that it is not binding on all states because it embodies a parochial, distinctively Western, moral outlook that non-Western societies do not have any compelling reason to adopt. Although this objection is often advanced on the basis of a general skepticism about reasons, one that would comprehensively undermine the possibility of the NJC ever being satisfied, it is probably not best defended in this radical way. Instead, it is best seen as reflecting an underlying ethical pluralism, according to which, although the norms of IHRL may exemplify one in-principle acceptable selection and ordering of values, there are also other such selections and orderings. If so, societies subjected to purportedly universally binding norms of IHRL that reflect orderings they do not endorse might properly complain that those norms unjustifiably impose an alien perspective on them at the expense of the no-less-valuable forms of life sustained by their own cultures. To that extent, the NJC is not satisfied, at least with respect to them, because they do not better conform with the independent reasons that apply to them through obedience to IHRL (Tasioulas 2010a).

Allen Buchanan has offered the most comprehensive response to various specific manifestations of this parochialism objection, taking into consideration factors such as the content of key IHRL norms and the quality of the processes through which they are generated and implemented. He contends that, if properly designed, IHRL institutions can provide vital epistemic assistance regarding the identification of moral norms of human rights and the most effective ways of enhancing compliance with them. Among the ways they can do so are by: (a) accessing and utilizing reliable factual information crucial to the justification and/or specification of human rights norms; (b) achieving a more inclusive representation of interests and viewpoints than is available at the domestic level, thereby mitigating the risk of culturally biased assessments in determining the content of human rights norms and of the best institutional means of implementing them; and (c) providing authoritative specifications of human rights when there is a range of reasonable alternative specifications (Buchanan 2010: 91).

Buchanan's argument is restricted to the case of "properly designed" institutions, and it is a very much open question whether real-world IHRL institutions meet that exacting specification. But, even if they do, it is important to note that the sorts of epistemic advantages described by Buchanan could not, by themselves, constitute a sufficient basis for the legitimacy of IHRL. The epistemic virtues of A can typically only establish that A is an epistemic authority, i.e., someone whose judgment on a given topic provides others with reasons to *believe* what he says. They will not show that A is a practical authority, i.e., someone regarding whom there is an obligation to *act* in conformity with their directives, unless further conditions are satisfied. Classically, among the further conditions relevant under the NJC are considerations of *efficacy*, i.e., the power to secure compliance with one's directives. So, for example, one source of the authority of the state is its power to resolve problems of collective action in achieving a common goal by laying down standards that its putative subjective have reason to comply with because, inter alia, those standards are likely to be obeyed. This is why the actual traffic code in the UK has practical authority over inhabitants of that country, whereas the radically different, yet "ideal" code produced by an academic expert on traffic regulation does not.

However, some critics of the legitimacy of IHRL identify its Achilles heel precisely at this point. International law, unlike most domestic legal systems, generally lacks the capacity to deploy effective sanctions against noncompliance. And IHRL faces special efficacy-undermining burdens. Compared to many other forms of international law, it derives limited benefits from the logic of reciprocity. The failure of a state to respect human rights law in its treatment of its own people does not, of itself, harm other states, nor can the latter meaningfully retaliate by failing to respect their own citizens' rights. This leads to a serious collective-action problem for the international implementation of IHRL, one exacerbated by the difficulty of securing international consensus on which kinds and levels of human rights violations warrant which forms of international response, such as military intervention or economic sanctions.

Invoking problems of this sort, Eric Posner has claimed that the international human rights treaty regime "has either had no effect on the behavior of states or very little" (Posner 2009: 186). However, arguably the most comprehensive and rigorous recent empirical study of the consequences of human rights treaty ratification contradicts this sweeping skepticism. Beth Simmons has argued that human rights treaties play a "crucial constraining role" in shaping the behavior of the states that ratify them. The public commitment to be legally bound by human rights norms that is expressed by treaty ratification influences various agents' expectations regarding how ratifying states will behave. Subsequent shortfalls in state behavior trigger political demands for compliance, mainly from domestic constituencies, but also internationally. Simmons focuses on the role of three domestic mechanisms through which such demands are channeled: elite-initiated agendas, litigation and popular mobilization (Simmons 2010). As she rightly cautions, we cannot readily extrapolate her conclusions to nontreaty law. However, as we have already noted, treaties often play an important role in the crystallization of norms of customary international law, so to that extent her findings have an indirect bearing on the efficacy of the latter.

The legitimacy of IHRL under the NJC, therefore, is clearly hostage to geopolitical realities relating to its efficacy. We should, however, register a more principled limitation on the legitimacy of IHRL. The NJC is generally subject to an Independence Condition (IC), according to which "the matters regarding which [it] is met are such that with respect to them it is better to conform to reason than to decide for oneself, unaided by authority" (Raz 2006: 1104). Even if, for example, I would fare significantly better in my personal relationships by heeding the directives of government experts, I am not bound by their directives, because these are matters regarding which I have conclusive reasons of autonomy to arrive at my own assessment of the balance of reasons.

It is an important question to what extent IC-relevant considerations of freedom arise in the case of states. Certainly, states lack the kind of ultimate moral significance we attribute to the individual human beings who are their members. Nonetheless, states arguably have reasons to make and pursue their own choices within certain domains, and to respect and protect the similar freedom of other states. Some of these reasons are instrumental: if a state chooses and acts freely, it may be more likely to conform with other reasons that apply to it, including reasons of human rights morality. More controversially, some of these reasons are intrinsic, grounded in the value of free choice and action, as such, independent of their consequences. Here the idea is that there is intrinsic value to the exercise of self-determination by political communities associated with states, a value that extends to some nondemocratic states. In addition, the freedom of a state may be relevant under the IC even in cases in which the state itself does not have reason to decide and act freely. This would be so, for example, if interference with the state's freedom is likely to have massively destabilizing geopolitical consequences. These considerations of freedom are what properly shape an acceptable norm of state sovereignty under international law.

If the foregoing approach is on the right lines, it suggests that the sovereignty of states may constrain the legitimacy of IHRL in complex and varying ways, depending on the content of the relevant law and its means of enforcement. In the most extreme imaginable cases, respect for sovereignty is incompatible with the exercise of any legitimate authority on a given topic. Then there is a middle range of cases in which legitimate laws may be enacted, but their content is subject to significant constraints. Finally, there are the less extreme cases in which what is ruled out is the legitimacy of enforcing otherwise legitimate laws in some particular fashion, e.g., through the use of coercive mechanisms. Whether considerations of state freedom have a trumping effect in any of these ways is a matter for substantive argument. But on the picture that has emerged, one cannot just assume that any moral human right can be established in international law without unjustifiably encroaching upon state sovereignty. Existing international law already reflects this conclusion, insofar as it confers on states a limited power to make reservations even to multilateral human rights conventions or to escape being bound by customary norms of human rights (those that are not properly accorded *jus cogens* status). To this extent, we can capture an insight that underpins some versions of the political view of human rights discussed earlier, i.e., that the orthodox view does not by itself furnish a complete normative theory of IHRL. But that is something that the proponent of the orthodox view should not only accept, but insist on: the road from human rights morality to human rights law is often long and winding.

References

Beitz, C. (2009) *The Idea of Human Rights*, Oxford: Oxford University Press.
Besson, S. and Tasioulas, J. (2010) *The Philosophy of International Law*, Oxford: Oxford University Press.
Buchanan, A. (2010) *Human Rights, Legitimacy, and the Use of Force*, Oxford: Oxford University Press.
Cohen, J. (2004) "Minimalism About Human Rights: The Most We Can Hope For?" *Journal of Political Philosophy* 12: 190–213.
—— (2006) "Is There a Human Right to Democracy?" in C. Sypnowich, ed., *The Egalitarian Conscience: Essays in Honour of G. A. Cohen*, Oxford: Oxford University Press, pp. 226–48.
Dworkin, R. M. (2011) *Justice for Hedgehogs*, Cambridge, Mass.: Harvard University Press.
Finnis, J. M. (2011) *Natural Law and Natural Rights*, 2nd edition, Oxford: Oxford University Press.
Gewirth, A. (1996) *The Community of Rights*, Chicago: University of Chicago Press.
Griffin, J. (2008) *On Human Rights*, Oxford: Oxford University Press.
Habermas, J. (2010) "The Concept of Human Dignity and the Realistic Utopia of Human Rights," *Metaphilosophy* 41: 464–80.

International Convention on Civil and Political Rights, 16 December 1966, 999 *UNTS* 171.

International Convention on Economic, Social and Cultural Rights, 16 December 1966, 993 *UNTS* 3.

Kateb, G. (2010) *Human Dignity*, Cambridge, Mass.: Harvard University Press.

MacIntyre, A. C. (2007) *After Virtue: A Study in Moral Theory*, 3rd edition, Notre Dame, IN: University of Notre Dame Press.

McCrudden, C. (2008) "Human Dignity and Judicial Interpretation of Human Rights," *European Journal of International Law* 19: 655–724.

Moyn, S. (2010) *The Last Utopia: Human Rights in History*, Cambridge, Mass.: Harvard University Press.

Nickel, J. (2007) *Making Sense of Human Rights*, 2nd edition, Oxford: Blackwell Publishing.

Nussbaum, M. C. (2000) *Women and Human Development: The Capabilities Approach*, Oxford: Oxford University Press.

O'Neill, O. (1996) *Towards Justice and Virtue: A Constructive Account of Practical Reasoning*, Cambridge: Cambridge University Press.

Pogge, T. (2002) *World Poverty and Human Rights*, Cambridge: Polity Press.

Posner, E. (2009) *The Perils of Global Legalism*, Chicago: University of Chicago Press.

Rawls, J. (1999) *The Law of Peoples with "The Idea of Public Reason Revisited,"* Cambridge, Mass.: Harvard University Press.

Raz, J. (2006) "The Problem of Authority: Revisiting the Service Conception," *Minnesota Law Review* 90: 1003–1044.

—— (2010a) "Human Rights without Foundations," in S. Besson and J. Tasioulas, eds., *The Philosophy of International Law*, Oxford: Oxford University Press, pp. 321–38.

—— (2010b) "Human Rights in the Emerging World Order," *Transnational Legal Theory* 1: 31–47.

Sen, A. (2009) *The Idea of Justice*, Cambridge, Mass.: The Belknap Press of Harvard University Press.

Simmons, B. (2010) *Mobilizing for Human Rights*, Oxford: Oxford University Press.

Talbott, W. (2005) *Which Rights Should Be Universal?*, Oxford: Oxford University Press.

Tasioulas, J. (2007) "The Moral Reality of Human Rights," in T. Pogge, ed., *Freedom from Poverty as a Human Right: Who Owes What to the Very Poor*, Oxford: Oxford University Press, pp. 75–101.

—— (2010a) "The Legitimacy of International Law," in S. Besson and J. Tasioulas, eds., *The Philosophy of International Law*, Oxford: Oxford University Press, pp. 97–118.

—— (2010b) "Taking Rights Out of Human Rights," *Ethics* 120: 647–78.

—— (2011) "On the Nature of Human Rights," in G. Ernst and J. C. Heilinger, eds., *The Philosophy of Human Rights: Contemporary Controversies*, Berlin: de Gruyter, pp. 17–60.

Tierney, B. (1997) *The Idea of Natural Rights: Studies on Natural Rights, Natural Law, and Church Law 1150–1625*, Grand Rapids, MI: William B. Eerdmans Publishing Company.

United Nations General Assembly (1948) Universal Declaration of Human Rights, 10 December 1948, 217 A (III).

—— (1986) Resolution on Setting Standards in the Field of Human Rights, 4 December 1984, 41/120.

Wolterstorff, N. (2008) *Justice: Rights and Wrongs*, Princeton: Princeton University Press.

Further Reading

Instructive historical accounts of the postwar human rights movement are given in J. Morsink (1999) *The Universal Declaration of Human Rights: Origins, Drafting and Intent*, Philadelphia: University of Pennsylvania Press; M. A. Glendon (2001) *A World Made New: Eleanor Roosevelt and the Universal Declaration of Human Rights*, New York: Random House; and S. Moyn (2010) *The Last Utopia: Human Rights in History*, Cambridge, Mass.: Harvard University Press. An excellent philosophical introduction to human rights is J. Nickel (2007) *Making Sense of Human Rights*, 2nd edition, Oxford: Blackwell Publishing, which addresses a range of issues beyond those covered in this entry. Two significant recent philosophical monographs on human rights are J. Griffin (2008) *On Human Rights*, Oxford: Oxford University Press (which is the subject of a symposium issue of *Ethics* 120 (2010)) and C. Beitz (2009) *The Idea of Human Rights*, Oxford: Oxford University Press. Allen Buchanan's important essays on human rights and the legitimacy of international (human rights) law are collected in his (2010) *Human Rights, Legitimacy, and the Use of Force*, Oxford: Oxford University Press. There are also useful essays on these topics in S. Besson and J. Tasioulas, eds. (2010) *The Philosophy of International Law*, Oxford: Oxford University Press, chs. 3–6, 15–17. There is now a growing literature on particular human rights: see, for example, T. Pogge, ed. (2007) *Freedom from Poverty as a Human Right: Who Owes What to the Very Poor?* Oxford: Oxford University Press.

24

THE MORALITY AND LAW OF WAR

Seth Lazar

Introduction

This paper explores the relationship between the morality of war and the law of war. The focus is on permissible conduct in war, specifically the principle of noncombatant immunity, which confines belligerents to targeting only military objectives (see article 48 of the first Additional Protocol (API) to the Geneva Conventions, Roberts and Guelff 2000: 447), and the legal equality of combatants, which grants soldiers the same permissions and holds them to the same prohibitions irrespective of the justice or injustice of their cause (preamble to API: 422–23).

Call soldiers whose side satisfied *jus ad bellum*—the principles governing justified resort to war—j-combatants, and those whose side did not satisfy those principles u-combatants (for unjustified). The dominant figure in late twentieth-century just war theory, Michael Walzer, argued that all combatants enjoy equal permissions to target one another, grounded in the threat that they pose to each other's lives (Walzer 2006: 42–45). In virtue of that threat, u-combatants and j-combatants alike lose their rights against lethal attack, so are not wronged when their adversaries kill them. By contrast, noncombatants, unthreatening by definition, retain those same rights, so are not permissible targets. Noncombatant immunity and combatant equality, then, are grounded in a single argument: one may permissibly target only those who have lost their rights against lethal attack; all combatants have lost that right; all noncombatants retain it.

Walzer's position has developed into a conventional orthodoxy, bolstered by its consonance with international law. In recent years, however, many philosophers have become increasingly dissatisfied with his arguments. In particular, these revisionist critics have discredited his account of how one loses the right to life, showing its inconsistency with other plausible beliefs about permissible harming (see especially Coady 2008; Fabre 2010; McMahan 1994, 2004; McPherson 2004; Rodin 2002). Against Walzer, they argue that the morality of harming is almost always asymmetrical—a person who defends himself against unjustified attack does not become liable to be harmed by his attacker, simply by now posing a threat. To become liable to be killed, the threat one poses must be unjustified. Moreover, posing an unjustified threat is neither necessary nor sufficient for liability. A politician who sends a u-combatant to fight an unjustified war might be liable, despite not posing any threats himself; a child soldier, out of his mind on drugs and with a gun to his head, might not be liable, despite posing a threat. Walzer's critics have concluded that what matters for liability is (1) responsibility for

(2) contributing to threats of (3) unjustified harm (Coady 2008; Fabre 2010; McMahan 2004; Rodin 2008).

Though their criticisms of Walzer are shared, revisionists diverge in how they combine these three elements. How much and what kind of responsibility? What degree of contribution? Must the threatened harm be pro tanto or all things considered unjustified? Their views' practical implications depend on the answers to these questions, which determine where the liability bar is set; and revisionist though they are in theory, most of these critics endorse quite conservative practical conclusions. Though they reject the moral equality of combatants, they endorse conventional views, such as noncombatant immunity, and the rejection of pacifism (that is, they reject the view that warfare can never be justified). Insofar as they endorse these commonsense conclusions, however, they each face the same problem. If a significant number of u-noncombatants and u-combatants, in any given conflict, are responsible to just the same degree, for just the same quantum of contribution to the same unjustified threats, we cannot retain both noncombatant immunity and the rejection of pacifism.

Distinguish between micro-threats to specific lives and the macro-threat posed by a state. Many u-combatants neither pose micro-threats themselves, nor contribute to those posed by their comrades, while their contribution to the macro-threat posed by their state is negligible (Lazar 2010). By definition, u-noncombatants do not pose micro-threats, but many of them contribute to micro-threats, for example by producing the goods (military and nonmilitary) that sustain their armed forces' ability to fight (Fabre 2010). This also contributes to the macro-threat, which they also further through their taxes, popular support and, in a democracy, their vote. Moreover, many u-combatants— both those who contribute to micro- and macro-threats and those who do not—are guiltless for their actions, fighting either from duress or under a reasonable belief that their cause is justified. Meanwhile, many u-noncombatants will make their contributions without duress and without the nonculpable ignorance excuse. They will be culpable.

The liability theorists face a dilemma. If they endorse a low threshold of responsibility for liability—say, minimal responsibility for some small contribution to micro- or macro-threats—they will render too many noncombatants permissible targets (and their criterion of liability may also be independently implausible: Lazar 2009). If they endorse a high threshold—requiring a significant contribution to micro- and macro-threats, a significant degree of responsibility or both—they will struggle to justify the killing inevitable in justified wars, because too many u-combatants will not be liable to be killed, and j-combatants cannot discriminate between liable and nonliable u-combatants. This is the "responsibility dilemma" for the liability view (Lazar 2010). The first horn leads to permitting the justified side to target too many noncombatants; the second leads to contingent pacifism—the view that although wars can hypothetically be permissible, in all feasible cases we should not fight, for fear of violating our enemies' rights. If the liability theorists aspire to less controversial practical conclusions than these, their view needs additional support.

Some find this support in the distinction between the morality and law of war. They argue that the contingent pacifist and noncombatant immunity objections might be good reasons not to implement their view in the laws of war, but do not undermine their account of war's underlying morality (Fabre 2010: 39; Frowe 2011; Hurka 2005; McMahan 1994, 2004, 2008, 2009, 2010). The following sections first set out the most fully developed version of this argument, then criticize it, before asking just what the relationship between war's law and its morality should be.

The Appeal to Law

The appeal to law is quite simple. People often act wrongfully. Sometimes they choose to do so; other times they do so by mistake or accident, for example because they lack important information. How should this predictable wrongdoing impact our morality, and our laws? One response is that the predictable failure to act rightly should not alter what the right is, but might be relevant to choosing our laws. In war, two causes of predictable noncompliance are particularly troubling. First, combatants' lack of important information: whether their side satisfied *jus ad bellum*, whether this operation proportionately conduces to that just cause and whether their targets are liable are all very complex and urgent questions whose answers depend on often ambiguous or unavailable information. Second, voluntary noncompliance: of course, in one sense this is endemic to warfare, since without some voluntary wrongdoing, it is unlikely there would be any conflict in the first place. But especially salient here is the tendency of u-combatants to arrogate to themselves any permissions that are made available to j-combatants. Even if the injustice of their cause should be clear to them, they are likely to affirm themselves to be j-combatants, and so entitled to the relevant schedule of permissions.

Revisionists deny that this predictable noncompliance is relevant to the morality of war. The epistemic shortfall might make acting morally difficult, but that is to be expected: doing the right thing is often hard (McMahan 2005: 770). If we ought to X if we had full information, then we ought to X even when our information is incomplete (though we might be excused for failing to do so). Likewise, that others will abuse our principles is no argument against them, qua principles. However, these are both appropriate worries when devising the law. If people will routinely disregard a law, or if it makes unachievable demands, then the law will be regarded as irrelevant, unfair and unrealistic, and will lose its capacity to guide action. If the laws of war have any value or purpose (McMahan, for example, argues that they can be used to minimize wrongful suffering—2008: 28) then we must guard against this outcome.

Morality and law, the argument goes, should therefore come apart (McMahan 2008: 32; 2010: 506). Though combatant equality and noncombatant immunity lack substantial foundations in moral principle, they might nonetheless be justified as laws. If the laws of war enforced combatant asymmetry they would be unworkable, because uncertainty over who is liable to be killed would render them impossible to enforce (Fabre 2010: 57; McMahan 2008: 32). Moreover, any permissions granted to the justified side would be abused by the unjustified side as well. Similarly, noncombatant immunity must be retained in law because extending the permission to kill noncombatants to j-combatants would mean its abuse both by them and by u-combatants.

This approach enables the following response to the responsibility dilemma. Perhaps it does identify salient pragmatic concerns, and the liability view would be difficult to implement. But these pragmatic concerns are irrelevant to the moral principles that govern warfare. That a principle is hard to follow, or abused by some, does not make it false. The contingent pacifist objection worries that the liability view will deny states and people the moral option of fighting justified wars. But in practice, soldiers and states need not worry about killing only the liable, since they can instead adhere to the laws of war, which permit them to kill enemy combatants and noncombatants who are directly participating in hostilities. The noncombatant immunity objection worries that the liability view renders too many noncombatants permissible targets—but the laws of war will retain noncombatant immunity, so this worry is misplaced.

Why Should We Obey the Laws of War?

Although the appeal to law raises interesting questions, it does not resolve the problems with the revisionist position. We can begin with two general worries before turning to specifics.

How should soldiers respond when legal and moral injunctions diverge? Though the appeal to law is often made, this vital topic has scarcely been discussed. If legal reasons always trump moral reasons, then the revisionist morality of war would be redundant in practice. If moral reasons always trump legal reasons, then the appeal to law would be equally pointless. For the appeal to law to work, moral reasons must sometimes trump legal ones, and vice versa. Most will agree that moral reasons can override legal ones; the reverse ordering is much harder to explain. First, because it requires an account of the duty to obey the law of armed conflict (LOAC), and it is notoriously difficult to ground a duty to obey any law—especially one that explicitly diverges from our other moral reasons. Second, even if we can produce some such account, if we ought to obey the law when it clashes with morality, then the law in this case describes what we ought to do, and the "morality of war" can be no more than a subset of the relevant moral reasons.

The second general worry is that the appeal to law cannot resolve the contingent pacifist and noncombatant immunity objections, it can only deflect them. To resolve the contingent pacifist objection, it must show that soldiers (at least j-combatants) may obey their legal permission to kill enemy combatants, even when morally prohibited from doing so because their adversary is not liable. But if our most fundamental moral prohibitions—against killing the nonliable—can be overridden by a mere legal permission, then the morality of war truly is irrelevant, and we should simply focus on the laws of war. Where noncombatant immunity is concerned, even if the law does reduce the targeting of noncombatants, that does not answer the objection that with a low liability threshold too many noncombatants will be liable. The appeal to law would then look like the utilitarian's response to the slavery objection—enslaving some will never in fact maximize utility. Even if this were true, it would not adequately resolve the objection, which is that people's freedom should not be vulnerable in this way to calculations of overall utility. Similarly, even if, given these laws, noncombatants will not often be targeted in practice, we can object that they should not, in principle, be morally vulnerable to attack.

Turning to specifics: McMahan (2008: 37–38) helpfully distinguishes between moral and legal permissions, prohibitions and positive requirements, then argues that when morality requires what law permits or prohibits, and when morality prohibits what the law permits, soldiers should obey their moral reasons. But when the law prohibits what morality permits, combatants should adhere to the law. He says little about clashes between legal requirements and moral permissions and prohibitions, since he thinks the law rarely requires positive action. This is an important oversight, since the additional protocols do require, for example, combatants to observe a duty of constant care toward civilians (article 57—see Roberts and Guelff 2000: 452–53). Moreover, soldiers are required by their own military law (often backed up by an oath of allegiance) to obey lawful orders. However, let us set that aside to concentrate on the orderings McMahan does defend.

For the appeal to law to have any purchase against the noncombatant immunity objection, we must first show that j-combatants are morally permitted, not required, to kill liable u-noncombatants, and then that legal prohibitions trump moral permissions. Neither is easy to do. Combatants generally have strong positive moral reasons for action—they have natural duties to protect their comrades and their country, and contractual duties grounded in their roles and the oaths they took. If they can save their comrades or advance their just cause by killing liable u-noncombatants, then one could readily argue that they are required to do so. Since moral requirements trump legal prohibitions, the appeal to law would not resolve the noncombatant immunity objection.

Even if j-combatants are merely permitted, not required, to kill liable u-noncombatants, we can justify denying them this option only if we have a strong argument for a duty to obey the law. Again, despite the frequency with which the appeal to law is made, discussions of this crucial point are scarce and brief. McMahan adumbrates two relevant arguments. The first sees the fact that X is against the law as a reason not to consider other reasons for X-ing. He argues that "combatants should be reluctant to give their individual judgment priority over the law, for the law has been designed in part precisely to obviate the need for resort to individual moral judgment in conditions that are highly unconducive to rational reflection" (McMahan 2008: 41). This presupposes a particular conception of law's authority, according to which law gives us "protected reasons," which preempt the need to appeal to our own judgment (Raz 1979). The second sees the fact that X is against the law as providing an additional reason not to X—it argues for a pro tanto duty to obey the law, grounded in the fact that disobedience will lead to further breaches by others (McMahan 2008: 38).

The first argument fails: the laws of armed conflict do not provide protected reasons. If they did, then adherence would be required without exception, since if other moral reasons could justify disobedience to the law, then we would have to consult those reasons in any situation to determine whether it is exceptional. The law would not, therefore, obviate the appeal to our own judgment. Since McMahan thinks (plausibly) that some moral reasons do override legal reasons, the protected-reasons logic is unavailable.

Could revisionists make the narrower argument that the law governing noncombatant immunity, at least, grounds protected reasons? They might argue that few u-noncombatants will in fact be liable to be killed, while even j-combatants with the best intentions will likely inflate the permissions available to them, and so end up mistakenly killing nonliable u-noncombatants. Adherence to the laws of war will then better enable them to comply with their reasons not to kill nonliable noncombatants, since their own judgment will be excessively permissive.

There are at least two problems with this argument. First, if j-combatants are indeed sometimes morally required to kill the liable u-noncombatants, then they ought to disobey the law. They cannot therefore defer to the law's authority: they must assess each case on its merits, against the full range of moral reasons. Second, the argument presupposes a high liability threshold, given the premise that few u-noncombatants will be liable. With a low liability threshold, j-combatants could plausibly argue that restricting their attacks to adult u-noncombatants is discriminating enough. Raising the liability threshold to ensure few noncombatants cross it must also mean rendering more u-combatants non-liable (those who make no significant contribution to micro- and macro-threats, and on some accounts those who are only minimally responsible for their contributions). This puts us squarely back at the contingent pacifist objection.

The second argument mooted by McMahan is that combatants have a duty to obey LOAC, since even morally permissible breaches will encourage others to impermissibly breach it. Evidently this applies only if and when disobedience will actually lead to further disobedience by others. Breaking the law in secret, or when one's adversary lacks the capacity to retaliate, would still be permissible. But even when the empirical speculation holds, we still need more argument, which would have to be developed along these lines: if some soldiers kill liable noncombatants, other soldiers will likely end up killing nonliable noncombatants. The original soldiers are partly responsible for this outcome, and so are morally required to forego killing liable noncombatants even when it is otherwise permissible.

This argument's weakness is the idea that combatants are responsible for their adversaries' unjustified actions and retaliations, and should forego options that might save their lives and those of their comrades, as well as advance their just cause, to avoid bearing that responsibility. Elsewhere in most versions of the revisionist view (Fabre is an exception), our responsibility for our own wrongdoing is thought far greater than for the wrongful acts of others that we fail to prevent. And yet here we expect j-combatants to sacrifice their lives, and the opportunity to contribute to a just cause, because of speculative claims about how their conduct might connect with the voluntary wrongful actions of other combatants in the future. On the one hand this seems to demand too much of j-combatants. *Mala prohibita* in domestic society tend to impose small costs on us—driving at the speed limit, for example—not to remove options that can literally be the difference between life and death. On the other hand, if this principle goes through, then the appeal to law is not really an appeal to law but an appeal to an additional moral principle—that soldiers should sacrifice themselves if otherwise permissible self-defense might lead to others' predictable noncompliance. The argument works identically without any reference to the law.

Of course, if j-combatants never confronted situations wherein they can save lives or advance a just cause by harming noncombatants more than the laws of war allow, then this might be a purely theoretical worry. Unfortunately, this is not the case. In contemporary urban warfare, noncombatants can contribute to threats to combatants without directly participating in hostilities—for example, by (knowingly or unwittingly) revealing their position to enemy combatants, or by concealing information about potential threats. Moreover, the law not only prevents combatants from targeting liable u-noncombatants, it also demands that they minimize harm to noncombatants that is incidental to attacking their military objectives. This imperative often removes options that would reduce risks to j-combatants, to protect liable u-noncombatants. If the u-noncombatants are in fact liable to be killed, then, like liable u-combatants, harms to them should not need to be minimized, and j-combatants should be able to reduce their risks in these ways. We can also readily conceive of conflicts that could be won through air power alone, without the use of ground forces, which, despite minimizing friendly casualties, would be ruled out by the laws of war either for intentionally threatening u-noncombatants, or for exposing them to excessive risks of harm, but would be permissible under the morality of war, if enough of those u-noncombatants are liable to be harmed.

Especially in contemporary warfare, combatants must often choose between accepting additional risks to themselves, and either intentionally targeting noncombatants or disregarding foreseeable but unintended harms to them. If the morality of war says that they are entitled to shift these risks to liable u-noncombatants, but the laws of war deny them that option, then the laws of war deny them morally permissible means to protect their own lives and those of their comrades. It can do so only if we have a plausible argument for a strong duty to obey LOAC, such as has not yet been offered by the revisionist camp.

SETH LAZAR

Perhaps other arguments could be advanced, derived from the familiar debate over the duty to obey the law within states. It could be a requirement of fair play (Klosko 1987; McDermott 2004), or grounded in soldiers' actual or hypothetical consent to obey the law (Simmons 1979), or perhaps in some sort of associative obligation (Horton 2007) or identification with the law (Raz 1979: 259). However, even in an ideal state with perfect liberal institutions, deploying these arguments is not straightforward (Simmons 1979). International institutions lack capacity and legitimacy; the laws are vague and, on this account, diverge from our actual moral reasons. There is arguably no global community that could ground an associative obligation to obey the law, or give soldiers a sense that this is their law, one that they identify with and for which they must show respect. The fair-play argument presupposes that we are engaged in a shared and just project for mutual benefit—which is hardly how one would describe the belligerents in war. Perhaps the relevant project is adherence to the war convention, but this works to the participants' mutual benefit only on the assumption that they cannot increase their chances of military success by abandoning it—an assumption that often will not hold. Some soldiers do consent to obey only lawful orders, and so might derivatively be said to consent to international law, but that is only a subset; plus they can hardly be held to that consent when their adversaries refuse to comply. It is hard to see how a compelling argument could be advanced for a duty to obey LOAC; at the very least, the appeal to law remains inadequate until the revisionists have filled in this gap.

Applied Moral Principles

To set up the next line of critique, it will help to distinguish moral principles along an axis that extends from abstract at one end to applied at the other. Abstract principles are devised and/or defended in abstraction from important but extrinsic moral and nonmoral facts. Applied principles tend to arise by combining our abstract principles with other moral and nonmoral facts to yield action-guiding conclusions. All abstract principles are probably to some extent also applied, and vice versa—these classifications are neither precise nor mutually exclusive. In this section I make three closely related objections against the appeal to law. First, it wrongly dichotomizes normativity into abstract moral principles and laws, omitting applied moral principles. Second, the applied principles entailed by the revisionist view (though inadequately discussed by it) should be rejected. Third, since we should reject the applied principles entailed by the combination of their abstract principles and facts on the ground, then we ought to reject or modify those abstract principles as well, at least until the facts change.

The first point should be obvious. We must not confine our moral enquiry about a given practice to scenarios that abstract from all the complications endemic to that practice, and then seek guidance from the law when the complications are fed back in. This would imply that real-world complications render moral principles irrelevant, and the law exhausts our normative resources. But this seems obviously false. It clearly makes sense to ask, when the law prohibits me from X-ing in real-life situation Y, whether I morally ought not to X in Y; likewise, when the law permits or requires, there is always a further moral question to answer. The notion that we can confine ourselves to elaborating on the one hand an abstract morality of war and on the other hand more pragmatic laws of war, occludes and omits a fundamental component of our theory.

370

The revisionist critics of conventional just war theory must defend an applied morality of war. They cannot confine themselves to working out principles that abstract from the causes of predictable noncompliance in wartime. The question, then, is whether the applied morality that can be inferred from their fundamental principles is sustainable in light of the causes of non-compliance, in particular the uncertainty endemic to war. Citizens, commanders and combatants are regularly uncertain whether their side satisfied *jus ad bellum* at the outset, and whether continuing the conflict is *ad bellum* justified now (this point is conceded by revisionists, e.g., Fabre 2010: 57; McMahan 2008: 32). I have also argued, here and elsewhere, that unless the liability bar is set low enough to render large numbers of noncombatants liable to be killed, a significant proportion of u-combatants will also not be liable. Evidently, distinguishing between liable and nonliable u-combatants will be nigh on impossible.

It follows that, if some u-combatants will not be liable to be killed, and if j-combatants may intentionally kill only liable targets, then if j-combatants cannot discriminate between liable and nonliable u-combatants, they will intentionally kill some nonliable u-combatants. In which case, fighting can be justified only if some other reasons override the rights of the nonliable combatants whom they kill. Since, with one exception (Fabre, who reserves judgment), the revisionists all think that intentional violations of the right to life cannot be justified except to avert a rare and momentous catastrophe (Coady 2002; McMahan 2008: 38; Rodin 2011: 461), this means the revisionist view cannot justify fighting in these circumstances. The applied morality of war that derives from the revisionist position, then, is that we should endorse pacifism. This is why revisionists make such efforts to show that all u-combatants will be liable to be killed: they have no other resources on which to draw, should some u-combatants prove nonliable. The problem is that as they lower the requirements for liability to be killed, they expand the liability net to include noncombatants who should not be permissible targets.

Even if we could somehow arrive at a Goldilocks criterion of liability—one that perfectly encompassed all the u-combatants we will intentionally kill, while concurrently excluding all the noncombatants from liability who warrant that immunity—there would still be problems for the revisionist version of the applied morality of war. As already noted, in any given conflict there will be considerable uncertainty both over whether our side initially satisfied *jus ad bellum* and whether the campaign is at present justified by those *ad bellum* standards. This uncertainty ranges over both moral and nonmoral propositions: we do not know what the principles of *jus ad bellum* should be; moreover the nonmoral facts in any given case—for example, "who started it"—are often also extraordinarily difficult to ascertain definitively and depend on information that is either inherently ambiguous or is unavailable to key participants in the conflict, such as citizens and combatants.

It is very hard, then, to know whether fighting was justified in the first place, and whether we are now justified in continuing to fight. Citizens, combatants and commanders who wish to implement the liability view must ask themselves what to do given this uncertainty. Even if it were true that, should they turn out to be in the right, they could fight without intentionally killing nonliable u-combatants, they still face a serious risk that if they turn out to lack *ad bellum* justification, they will engage in massive, outrageously wrongful rights violations. Of course, there will usually be good reasons against appeasement and submission, but these pale in comparison with the wrongdoing involved in fighting unjustifiably—particularly for adherents to the liability view, who think that our responsibility for rights violations that we commit is considerably greater than any responsibility to prevent rights violations by others. The question, then, is how high the probability must be that we are j-combatants, and how strong the reasons in favor of fighting, for us to be justified in risking even a small probability of participating in the spectacularly objectionable wrongdoing involved in fighting an *ad bellum* unjustified war. The answers must surely be very high, and very strong, and we can reasonably ask whether real wars are likely to be sufficiently clear-cut to be justifiable on this account. When commanders, combatants and citizens are not all but certain that they enjoy *ad bellum* justification, they ought not to fight. The magnitude of the wrongdoing involved in an unjustified war is so spectacular that even a small chance that the war is unjust would render it impermissible from this *ex ante* perspective. In practice, the uncertainty endemic to war means that there is always a good chance that our side is in the wrong, such that fighting simply involves running too serious a risk. Applied to real-life scenarios, the liability view again compels us toward pacifism.

No account of the morality of war is complete until it shows how its fundamental principles should be applied in the messy reality of war. That messy reality cannot be fobbed off onto the laws of war—especially if we lack any viable account of why soldiers should obey the law instead of the relevant moral principles. In my view, the reality of war is that we will inevitably intentionally kill people who have rights not to be killed. The alternative to this is, I think, wishful thinking—a fanciful idea of a morally pure war. If this is right, then in practice the liability view leads us inexorably toward pacifism because it cannot justify violating the fundamental rights of some, even to save others from having their rights violated. But even if this is wrong, and a morally pure war could be fought, the uncertainty that surrounds *ad bellum* justification—both in starting the war and in its operations and phases as it continues—means that the decision to fight involves taking a serious risk of committing unforgivable wrongs. From the *ex ante* perspective, citizens, commanders and combatants applying the liability view ought to appease and submit, rather than risk engaging in such spectacular wrongdoing. Even if all u-combatants were liable to be killed, then, the chance that we are ourselves u-combatants, combined with the unmatched evil of killing the nonliable, should be enough to direct us toward pacifism if we endorse the liability view.

Of course, one response to this would be to simply endorse contingent pacifism as the consequence of applying our abstract morality of war to real-life situations. If that conclusion is untenable, however—if we think that we can permissibly fight some real-life wars—then we should question the abstract principles that underpin the applied principles discussed here. In particular, we should ask whether the revisionists' powerful emphasis on the moral significance of individual rights, and their restrictive attitude to lesser-evil justifications, can really be sustained. If endorsing a more permissive attitude to lesser-evil justifications is what it takes to avoid pacifism in realistic war situations, then it would seem a price worth paying.

What Should the Relationship Be Between Morality and Law in War?

This penultimate section of the paper turns away from the revisionist critique of conventional just war theory, and asks instead what the proper relationship between war's law and its morality should be. Before presenting my own views, I briefly consider two contrasting accounts of that relationship. Each calls for a closer connection between the morality and law of war than that advocated by McMahan, though in quite different ways. Henry Shue (2008) argues that the laws of war should be coextensive with the morally justified rules for war, and these should exhaust the morality of war. David Rodin (2011) argues that the laws of war should implement (his version of) the liability view precisely.

Shue contends that the laws of war should track the morally best rules for war. Insofar as they do not, we should change them to remedy this (Shue 2008: 95). These rules, Shue thinks, are quite different from the morally justified rules that govern ordinary life, since war as a practice presupposes a level of violent contention with no parallels outside of war. If there are to be rules for war—if we are not simply to outlaw it altogether—those rules must be quite different from the rules that apply to conduct in ordinary life. We cannot (and perhaps ought not) eradicate the practice of warfare (Shue 2010: 516). We should instead endorse rules that minimize the suffering it causes (Shue 2010: 515). Those rules, Shue asserts, include the legal equality of combatants and the principle of noncombatant immunity (and the other constraints of *jus in bello*). They exhaust the morality of war: besides them, there is nothing else.

Shue's argument includes two important propositions. First, that the morally best laws for war should aim to minimize the suffering that war causes. Second, these laws exhaust the morality of war. Each of these claims, taken on its own, is quite controversial. But their conjunction is surely false. A u-combatant fighting a war of territorial aggression, who realizes that he is fighting unjustifiably, should not continue to fight in accordance with the laws of *jus in bello*; if he realizes he is killing unjustifiably, he should simply stop (Shue in fact admits this at Shue 2008: 109). Shue's argument for the rules regulating war taking the minimization of suffering as their aim presupposes the practice of war: since we cannot eradicate war, the argument goes, the best rules should seek to minimize its calamitous implications. Individuals are not, however, entitled to justify their own wrongdoing on the grounds that it is inevitable, and so must be regulated, not proscribed. The laws of war are addressed to people in the third person, and on Shue's account they run like this: "Since people will unjustifiably fight, the moral imperative is to limit the damage they do." If we formulate this argument in the first person, however, we see how it cannot exhaust the morality of war: "Since I will unjustifiably fight, the moral imperative is to limit the damage I do." On Shue's account, the laws of *jus in bello* are justified in the third person, so they cannot exhaust the morality of war: we need a first-person account as well.

David Rodin agrees with Shue's second proposition, but denies the first, arguing instead that the morally best laws for war should be the precepts of the liability view, and that we should therefore reject the traditional *jus in bello* in favor of laws that permit combatants to kill only those who are liable to be killed (though Rodin thinks that the liability view might be able to support noncombatant immunity). He mounts two main objections against the first proposition. First, that it is based on unsubstantiated speculation about consequences (Rodin 2011: 453). And second, that it wrongfully instrumentalizes the rights of nonliable j-combatants.

The second objection starts by observing that j-combatants are not liable to be killed. Granting u-combatants the right to kill them, then, amounts to endorsing their violation of j-combatants' rights to life. Granting this right in order to minimize overall suffering amounts to treating their rights to life as a resource that can be sacrificed in the pursuit of better overall outcomes (Rodin 2011: 461). He drives home his point with an example. Imagine a society in which an ethnic minority is victimized, culminating in the annual sacrifice of one member of the group. The authorities have tried to prevent the sacrifice, but in the years when they succeed, the minority suffers still worse abuse, including more murders. Should the authorities then legalize the annual sacrifice, in order to minimize the suffering caused by this ineradicable practice of minority victimization (Rodin 2011: 456)?

The example certainly pumps some strong intuitions; such a law would be clearly unjustified, and the analogy does appear appropriate. Nonetheless, there are two ways to challenge the analogy, and so defend the Shue/McMahan account of the purposes of legal equality.

The first important disanalogy is that in the scapegoating example, it is predictable who will be the victims, and who the perpetrators. In war, we cannot tell in advance who will end up on the unjustified side. Since we don't know this when we establish the symmetrical *jus in bello*, perhaps we could argue that it is in soldiers' *ex ante* interests that the law should be symmetrical. This is salient, but it doesn't seem decisive. After all, the ritual-sacrifice law could be justified on *ex ante* grounds to the members of the despised minority, but that does not seem sufficient to justify it all things considered. Plus, the argument does nothing to cater for combatants who join up only in order to fight justified wars.

The second disanalogy is that there are some obviously aggravating features of the ritual sacrifice that seem not to be salient for killing j-combatants. A vulnerable, defenseless, innocent person is usurped by an overwhelming force, to be sacrificed to the racist hatred of the majority. This is an egregiously wrongful form of killing. Even if killing j-combatants does violate their rights to life, we must surely distinguish between different violations of this right according to the degree of wrongfulness involved. Rodin himself concedes that there can be aggravating features of rights violations. Killing the defenseless and unthreatening, for the purpose of satisfying a loathsome hatred, is especially wrongful—mobilizing the whole power of the state against that one individual exacerbates matters. J-combatants are not defenseless, and are often killed when they pose immediate threats. They have chosen to place themselves in harm's way, and to occupy an institutional role defined by that choice. Even if these features are not sufficient to deny j-combatants the protection of their rights to life, it does seem likely that wrongfully killing a nonliable j-combatant is not as wrongful as the scapegoat killing. If it is less wrongful, then it might be easier to justify granting u-combatants a legal right to kill, in order to thereby minimize the calamities of war.

These disanalogies are important, but the key weakness of Rodin's case is not his critique of the Shue/McMahan account of the purposes of legal equality. That might actually go through. Instead, the real problem is the viability of his alternative to their position. Rodin assumes that the alternative to symmetry is asymmetry: j-combatants get the right to kill u-combatants, to whom the reciprocal right is denied. But if the arguments of this paper are correct, not only will it often be very difficult to determine who are the j-combatants and who the u-combatants, but some j-combatants will be liable to be killed, while some u-combatants will not. We cannot simply infer from their side having apparently satisfied *jus ad bellum*, that they will be liable to be killed. To endorse simple asymmetry, then, is to instrumentalize the rights of the nonliable u-combatants in order to grant j-combatants the possibility of pursuing their cause. Instead, if the laws of war should mirror the liability view, then they must be not merely asymmetrical, but completely individuated—both to the agent and to the specific act. The laws of war would then be either extraordinarily complex, and therefore obviously not justiciable, or they would be too broad and vague to have any critical purchase.

Either they would specify each instance of permissible killing, or they would simply say to combatants: intentionally kill only those who are liable to be killed.

Given the arguments of this paper, the resulting laws would evidently lead us straight into the contingent pacifist objection. The only way for soldiers and states to ensure compliance with LOAC would be to endorse pacifism: if they cannot be sure that they are in the right (and when can they be?) then the risk of wrongdoing is exponential; even if they are in the right, they will inevitably end up intentionally killing many nonliable people—which the proposed laws of war will not allow. The laws of war would therefore make it impossible to fight a justified war (while respecting those laws). And perhaps that is the big disanalogy with the scapegoating example. By outlawing the sacrifice, we do not thereby deter others from the justified use of force to defend things of real value. But implementing the liability view in the laws of war would outlaw war. If there are justified uses of force, then this is a serious problem—and the intuition supporting political communities' right to use lethal force to defend themselves against some sorts of attack is as robust as the intuition grounding individual rights, on which Rodin's argument rests. But even if there are no justified uses of force, it is entirely unrealistic to expect states and soldiers to adhere to laws of war that in practice mandate pacifism. If the laws of war were based on the liability view, they would be universally disregarded.

Rodin might counter that it is better to have laws of war that map onto the moral truth, but are disregarded, than to buy states' and soldiers' conformity to the law by sacrificing the rights of the nonliable. We can see clearly here how Rodin's position is the mirror opposite of that of Shue. Where Shue argues that the third-person morality of rules of war is all there is to the morality of war, Rodin reduces it to his account of first-person morality. Each believes that our account of the morality of war cannot accommodate these two distinct perspectives. I think this is a mistake.

Both Rodin and Shue seek greater congruence between the laws and morality of war than seems viable. Shue allows predictable wrongdoing too great a role in determining war's morality, while Rodin is too indifferent to the epistemic difficulties of war, and too rigidly committed to respecting rights, even ultimately at the cost of endorsing pacifism. McMahan is surely right that laws, as institutions, depend on third-person moral arguments that should take some forms of noncompliance as parametric in ways that our first-personal moral reasons should not. The laws of war cannot track morality directly—either by bending our moral reasons to match the laws or shaping the laws to exactly follow our moral reasons. But I would defend greater congruence than does McMahan between these two sources of normative principles. Specifically, I think legal equality sometimes reflects moral equality (though it is also often a necessary compromise). And I think noncombatant immunity has principled foundations. More generally, unlike McMahan and the other revisionists, I think that both the morality and laws of *jus in bello* can be satisfied by both justified and unjustified combatants.

The legal equality of combatants is in part grounded in moral equality, because your side having satisfied or failed to satisfy *jus ad bellum* is not determinative of whether you are a justified combatant—whether you can justifiably use lethal force. I have argued throughout this paper and elsewhere that some u-combatants will not be liable to be killed, and some j-combatants will be liable. That alone suggests that the j-combatants who kill nonliable u-combatants might not be justified, while the u-combatants who kill liable j-combatants might be justified. More importantly, though, it indicates that if warfare as a whole is ever justified, it is as a lesser evil—all wars will involve wrongdoing, which can only be justified if some stronger countervailing reasons override it. Whether you have sufficiently strong countervailing reasons is not determined by whether your side went to war justly. Some u-combatants, for example, will fight only to protect their fellow citizens (both combatants and noncombatants), and they might be justified in doing so. Some j-combatants, by contrast, will not have sufficient justification to violate the rights they will inevitably violate by fighting—though admittedly it is more likely that j-combatants will be justified combatants than that u-combatants will be. The key point here is that a strict moral or legal inequality of combatants, according to which u-combatants are considered unjustified combatants, and j-combatants considered justified combatants, is morally untenable.

If the laws were to track morality directly, then, they would be differentiated to identify justified combatants and unjustified combatants, regardless of the side they are on. Identifying which soldiers are justified and which unjustified would require a level of detailed information about individuals' reasons that is clearly beyond the reach of international law. Moreover, the matter is shrouded in considerable epistemic uncertainty, as argued above. The laws of war cannot be sufficiently subtle to distinguish justified from unjustified combatants, and even if they could be adequately specified, applying them would be impossible in virtue of this epistemic uncertainty. We are driven to endorse some form of equality between j-combatants and u-combatants. This could be captured with a universal prohibition on fighting, but the law should not prohibit justified combatants from fighting—not only because it would be disregarded, but because it is a greater wrong to outlaw justified fighting than to fail to criminalize unjustified fighting.

That last point is crucial. The laws of war should be neutral between j-combatants and u-combatants. But this does not mean we should enshrine, in international law, a right for all combatants to fight—as we see, for example, in articles 43 and 44 of the first Additional Protocol, and in the British *Manual of the Law of Armed Conflict* (UK Ministry of Defence 1994). Rodin is probably correct to argue that the law should not grant people the right to kill unjustifiably. The law should simply be silent on that question, neither granting nor denying combatants the right to fight. This would not need too radical a change in the laws of war as they currently stand—at present, the principal purpose of granting all combatants equal rights to fight is to guarantee their immunity from prosecution by their adversaries. But immunity from prosecution can be justified on its own terms; it need not be grounded in a right to fight.

Combatant legal equality, then, is partly grounded in moral principle and partly in practicality. What about noncombatant immunity? McMahan claims that all we need here is a legal doctrine of noncombatant immunity that can be justified in consequentialist terms. I reject the idea that noncombatant immunity is a purely legal artifact, for two reasons. First, the intuitions that underpin it are as strong and deeply rooted as any on which participants in this debate have drawn. Second, as argued above, if their moral reasons permit or require soldiers to kill noncombatants, but law prohibits it, they are either permitted or required to disregard the law, so legally protecting noncombatants is not enough. Of course, these two points are not sufficient to justify the principle of noncombatant immunity—they merely motivate the search for an adequate defense.

Fortunately, I think a solid defense of noncombatant immunity is available. First, I think the threshold for liability to be killed should be high, requiring some degree of culpability for a significant contribution to an unjustified threat. At that level, most ordinary civilians in a modern state will not be liable to be killed. That is the first bulwark of noncombatant immunity, and an important one. Of course, it means many combatants will not be liable either. The challenge, then, is not to explain noncombatant immunity, but to explain combatant non-immunity. Combatants can be permissible targets, on my account, because killing nonliable combatants is less wrongful along a variety of axes than killing nonliable noncombatants. The two key axes, I think, are that combatants have consented to put themselves in harm's way—indeed, it is part of their profession to do so—while noncombatants have not, and that noncombatants are vulnerable and defenseless, while combatants are not. Killing nonliable people who have put themselves in harm's way is, other things equal, less wrongful than killing nonliable people who have not done so; killing nonliable people who are vulnerable and defenseless is, other things equal, more wrongful than killing nonliable people who are not. I develop these and other ideas in depth elsewhere (Lazar forthcoming); the point of mentioning them here is simply to show that morality's resources for justifying noncombatant immunity are profound and rich.

One final observation is warranted. One reason for McMahan, Rodin, Hurka and others denying that the legal equality of combatants can have moral foundations is that they think u-combatants cannot satisfy *jus in bello*. They cannot fight discriminately, insofar as discrimination requires killing only the liable. Nor can they satisfy the criteria of necessity and proportionality that are usually also built into *jus in bello*—each seems predicated on their use of force achieving some good, which if they are u-combatants is impossible. These philosophers share two mistakes. The first is to think that the principle of distinction mandates killing only the liable. As we have seen, if it did, then it would enjoin pacifism. Instead, the principle of distinction is genuinely a principle of noncombatant immunity, justified on the terms just summarized. Second, they mistakenly interpret the principles of *jus in bello* as specifying necessary and sufficient conditions for justified killing in war. Combatants who target only combatants, and who use the minimum force required to achieve their objectives, and cause only collateral damage that is not excessive in relation to the advantage they secure, are not thereby assured of fighting justifiably. These are necessary conditions of justified war fighting, but they are not sufficient. The laws of *jus in bello*—and the underlying moral principles—specify constraints which any combatant must satisfy in order to fight justifiably. But they must also have sufficient reason for the havoc they wreak, and the laws of war are silent on that. U-combatants and j-combatants can equally well adhere to these constraints. Otherwise unjustified combatants who adhere to these constraints do not thereby become justified—though they fight less wrongfully than they otherwise would. Otherwise justified combatants who fail to meet these constraints are to that extent unjustified.

Conclusion

The revisionist critique of conventional just war theory has undoubtedly scored some important victories. Walzer's elegantly unified defense of combatant legal equality and noncombatant immunity has been seriously undermined. This critical success has not, however, been matched by positive arguments, which when applied to the messy reality of war would deprive states and soldiers of the permission to fight wars that are plausibly thought to be justified. The appeal to law sought to resolve this objection by casting it as a pragmatic worry about implementation, which while germane to debates over the laws of war, need not undermine the fundamental principles the revisionists advocate.

This response is inadequate. Revisionists have not shown that soldiers should obey the laws of war, in practice, when they conflict with their other moral reasons—our worries about application remain intact. Moreover, a theory of war that offers only an account of the laws of war, and a set of fundamental principles developed in abstraction from feasibility constraints, is radically incomplete. We need to know how to apply those fundamental principles, and whether, when applied, they lead to defensible conclusions. Only two options seem to remain. Perhaps the revisionists' arguments for their chosen fundamental principles are sufficiently compelling that we should stick with them, and accept their troubling conclusions—in other words, accept pacifism. Alternatively, we need to revise our fundamental principles so that when applied they yield conclusions that we can more confidently endorse.

Though it does not save the revisionist view from the responsibility dilemma and cognate objections, the appeal to law does raise an important, and previously inadequately theorized, question—or, rather, resurrects a neglected topic, discussed in depth by historical just war theorists such as Grotius and Vattel. There are good grounds for distinguishing the laws of war from the morality of war, and for adjusting the former to accommodate predictable noncompliance, that should not impact on our account of the latter. Nonetheless, I have argued that there are some profound moral insights underlying both combatant legal equality and noncombatant immunity: specifically, we cannot infer from a combatant's side having not satisfied *jus ad bellum* that he may not justifiably use lethal force; and other things equal, it is more wrongful to harm a nonliable noncombatant than to harm a nonliable combatant.

References

Coady, C. A. J. (2002) "Terrorism, Just War, and Supreme Emergency," in T. Coady and M. O'Keefe, eds., *Terrorism and Justice: Moral Argument in a Threatened World*, Carlton: Melbourne University Press, pp. 8–21.

—— (2008) "The Status of Combatants," in D. Rodin and H. Shue, eds., *Just and Unjust Warriors: The Moral and Legal Status of Soldiers*, Oxford: Oxford University Press, pp. 153–75.

Fabre, C. (2010) "Guns, Food, and Liability to Attack in War," *Ethics* 120: 36–63.

Frowe, H. (2011) "Self-Defense and the Principle of Non-Combatant Immunity," *Journal of Moral Philosophy* 8(4): 530–46.

Horton, J. (2007) "In Defense of Associative Political Obligations: Part Two," *Political Studies* 55: 1–19.

Hurka, T. (2005) "Proportionality in the Morality of War," *Philosophy & Public Affairs* 33: 34–66.

Klosko, G. (1987) "Presumptive Benefit, Fairness, and Political Obligation," *Philosophy & Public Affairs* 16: 241–59.

Lazar, S. (2009) "Responsibility, Risk, and Killing in Self-Defense," *Ethics* 119: 699–728.

—— (2010) "The Responsibility Dilemma for Killing in War," *Philosophy & Public Affairs* 38: 180–213.

—— (forthcoming) *War and Associative Duties*, Oxford: Oxford University Press.

McDermott, D. (2004) "Fair-Play Obligations," *Political Studies* 52: 216–32.

McMahan, J. (1994) "Innocence, Self-Defense and Killing in War," *Journal of Political Philosophy* 2: 193–221.

—— (2004) "The Ethics of Killing in War," *Ethics* 114: 693–732.

—— (2005) "Self-Defense and Culpability," *Law and Philosophy* 24: 751–74.

—— (2008) "The Morality of War and the Law of War," in D. Rodin and H. Shue, eds., *Just and Unjust Warriors: The Moral and Legal Status of Soldiers*, Oxford: Oxford University Press, pp. 19–43.

—— (2009) *Killing in War*, Oxford: Oxford University Press.

—— (2010) "Laws of War," in S. Besson and J. Tasioulas, eds., *The Philosophy of International Law*, New York: Oxford University Press, pp. 493–510.

McPherson, L. (2004) "Innocence and Responsibility in War," *Canadian Journal of Philosophy* 34: 485–506.

Raz, J. (1979) *The Authority of Law: Essays on Law and Morality*, Oxford: Clarendon Press.

Roberts, A. and Guelff, R. (2000) *Documents on the Laws of War*, 3rd edition, Oxford: Oxford University Press.

Rodin, D. (2002) *War and Self-Defense*, Oxford: Clarendon Press.

—— (2008) "The Moral Inequality of Soldiers: Why *jus in bello* Asymmetry Is Half Right," in D. Rodin and H. Shue, eds., *Just and Unjust Warriors: The Moral and Legal Status of Soldiers*, Oxford: Oxford University Press, pp. 44–68.

—— (2011) "Morality and Law in War," in H. Strachan and S. Scheipers, eds., *The Changing Character of War*, Oxford: Oxford University Press, pp. 446–63.

Shue, H. (2008) "Do We Need a Morality of War?" in D. Rodin and H. Shue, eds., *Just and Unjust Warriors: The Moral and Legal Status of Soldiers*, Oxford: Oxford University Press, pp. 87–111.

—— (2010) "Laws of War," in S. Besson and J. Tasioulas, eds., *The Philosophy of International Law*, New York: Oxford University Press, pp. 511–30.

Simmons, J. A. (1979) *Moral Principles and Political Obligations*, Princeton: Princeton University Press.

United Kingdom Ministry of Defence (1994) *The Manual of the Law of Armed Conflict*, Oxford: Oxford University Press.

Walzer, M. (2006) *Just and Unjust Wars: A Moral Argument with Historical Illustrations*, 4th edition, New York: Basic Books.

Further Reading

For further reading, see: Y. Benbaji (2008) "A Defense of the Traditional War Convention," *Ethics* 118 (3): 464–95; A. Buchanan (2006) "Institutionalizing the Just War," *Philosophy & Public Affairs* 34 (1): 2–38; F. M. Kamm (2011) *Ethics for Enemies*, Oxford: Oxford University Press; C. Kutz (2005) "The Difference Uniforms Make: Collective Violence in Criminal Law and War," *Philosophy & Public Affairs* 33 (2): 148–80; D. Luban (1980) "Just War and Human Rights," *Philosophy & Public Affairs* 9 (2): 160–81; D. Rodin (2002) *War and Self-Defense*, Oxford: Clarendon Press; and D. Rodin and H. Shue, eds. (2008) *Just and Unjust Warriors: The Moral and Legal Status of Soldiers*, Oxford: Oxford University Press.

25
THE LEGITIMACY OF INTERNATIONAL INSTITUTIONS

Thomas Christiano

The Challenge for an Account of Legitimacy

The analysis of legitimacy of international institutions presents a distinct challenge because we do not yet have an entirely clear picture of the nature of international society and the position of international institutions within that society. The institutions are not very much like state institutions or voluntary associations. At the same time international society shares features of both of these kinds of association. This is an important observation because these are the classical kinds of association to which ideas of legitimacy have traditionally been applied. And so the notion of legitimacy that we apply in the case of international law and institutions will have some features of both of these.

It is worth our while to have some further observations about the international system before we proceed. One, we need to have on the table the list of entities that are relevant to the characterization of international society. First, the most important entities are the states that make up the international system. Second are the international institutions that states have created but that in some cases exhibit some independence from the states that have created them. We will discuss these in some detail. Third are nongovernmental organizations that play a role in international society. Fourth are multinational corporations. Fifth are individual persons. All five of these elements are directed by international law and institutions, although states are still the principal subjects. Individuals are only marginally directly subjected to international law; mostly they are indirectly subjected to it.

Two, the system is highly fragmentary. Distinct institutions govern functionally distinct as well as regionally distinct activities. There are regional economic organizations such as the European Union. The World Trade Organization has a kind of legislative function over its members' trade relations. Global environmental treaties such as the Montreal Protocol are designed to regulate some specific global environmental matters. The United Nations Security Council has assumed some quasi-legislative functions since the end of the Cold War, but these are still fairly limited (Szasz 2002). The Security Council also exercises a kind of enforcement authority by permitting states to act against other states that threaten international peace and security. Other institutions exercise a kind of administrative authority. They make rules within the framework of a treaty that establishes the institution and that mostly help implement the more general treaty law. The Montreal Protocol has provisions for rule making and rule alteration that are along these lines (Kingsbury 2007). Some international institutions exercise judicial authority as well. The dispute-settlement mechanism of the World Trade Organization has the authority to settle disputes between states when a member state complains that another member state has violated its agreements. The International Court of Justice adjudicates as well but only for those states that accept jurisdiction in the case at hand. And there are international lending agencies, which are lenders of last resort to states in economic crisis.

In addition, there are a variety of institutions that create what is called "soft law." This is law that is not binding on the state parties, though there can be pressure on states to conform to this law. Declarations and other acts of the United Nations General Assembly are generally construed as nonbinding. The rule making of many different institutions also has soft-law status.

What can make these institutions legitimate? That is, how might these institutions have the powers to create binding obligations for states and/or individuals? The traditional answer to this question is that international law is binding on states primarily because and only because states consent to it. The *Statute of the International Court of Justice* lists in addition that the sources of international law include custom, the general principles of international law and the opinions of eminent jurists. But the two main materials are treaties and customary international law.

In this essay, I will attempt to lay out the idea of state consent as the ground of the legitimacy of international institutions, its bases and its limits, as well as some proposed ideas about how to extend and modify it. In the end I will argue that state consent, suitably modified, must play a central role within a larger system of international decision-making. I will start with some observations about legitimacy and some of the reasons for which consent has been taken seriously as a basis of legitimacy. I will then articulate the doctrine of state consent. Then I will go through a series of objections to the doctrine that can be met by the doctrine, in some cases only with important modifications. Finally, I will discuss a series of objections that can only be met by supplementing state consent with two other important requirements on the system of international decision-making: a constitutional system with enabling and limiting components and a set of internal standards for particular international institutions.

Legitimacy

Let us start with some of the elements of the idea of legitimate authority. I will understand legitimate authority as involving at least a moral power to impose a set of rules by which the others must regulate their conduct. These rules can be straightforward duties, they can be power-conferring rules (or rules that specify how persons may bind themselves and others) and they can be rules conferring permissions. Usually legitimate authority involves the power to impose all three of these rules but the imposition of duties on others is the most central case and the hardest case of legitimate authority because it involves the imposition of burdens on persons or groups. Possession of a moral power is a minimal sense in which a person or group can be said to have a right to rule. It is not the only thing that can be meant by this; sometimes the right to rule involves in addition a claim on the part of the ruler to the obedience of the ruled so that the obedience is owed to the ruler. Though this latter relation holds in some important cases, it is not necessary for legitimate authority.

The exercise of the moral power grounds the duty in the subject. In this way the subject has a content-independent reason for complying with the directive of the ruler. He has the reason to comply because the ruler has exercised the moral power. Hence he has a reason to obey.

The moral function of legitimacy is to have a public moral standard for making decisions when there is considerable disagreement among the subjects. Subjects have moral reasons to go along with the legitimate authority even when they disagree with it. This enables societies to pursue basic moral purposes in a coordinated fashion.

How does a person or group of persons acquire such a power? There are, in contemporary thought, three main types of answer to this question. They needn't be mutually exclusive. The first answer is that a person or group of persons acquires a moral power to impose duties on others only if the others have consented to the group possessing the moral power. The consenters thereby acquire content-independent reasons to go along with the directives. The second answer is that the moral power is somehow possessed collectively by a democratic assembly, in which case the subjects must comply with the democratically made decisions. The third kind of reason is an instrumental one. If a purported authority is reasonably just and its directives enable subjects to act better in accordance with reason, then the purported authority has a moral power to impose rules on its subjects.

The consent and democratic conceptions of legitimacy are distinctive in two ways. One, they establish, in addition to a moral power in the decision-maker, a claim right in persons to whom the compliance is owed. Consent establishes a claim right either in the power holder or in other persons subjected to the power holder (as in the case of classical consent theory) to the compliance of the consenter. The democratic conception establishes a claim right in the democratic assembly to the compliance of every member in the society. Two, the consent and democratic conceptions are distinctively public standards of legitimacy in the sense that each of these standards is one that subjects can see to be in effect for the most part. In this respect the instrumental basis of authority is a weaker basis. It cannot serve the public function of legitimacy as well as the consent or democratic principles, since the authority is based in the quality of the outcomes, which are precisely the subject of disagreement among the members. For this reason, it is worthwhile trying to figure out whether institutions that purport to have authority can have it on the basis of consent or democratic principles. These will be the focus of this essay, though I do not wish to suggest that the instrumental conception of authority is of no significance. One last remark: I will not focus here on ideas about global democracy because I do not think that we are even close to realizing the kinds of institutions that would be necessary for global democracy (Christiano 2010). Instead, we will see how democratic ideas can inform and modify the traditional idea of legitimacy in international institutions: through state consent.

Consent

Consent gives a fairly straightforward answer to the question, how does one person acquire the moral power to impose duties on another? Consent does this in part by having the person impose the duty on himself, with the concurrence of the power holder, as one does with a promise. The latter is a fairly uncontroversial form of imposition of duty. Furthermore, it involves a duty of the right type. When I promise to do x, I have a duty to do x merely on the ground that I have promised. The promise is a content-independent reason for doing x. And if I promise to obey a ruler, that gives me a content-independent reason to comply with the ruler's directives (Simmons 2001).

Usually consent must be given voluntarily and the person or group to whom consent has been given must not have defrauded the consenter. Furthermore, consent must be accompanied by some additional conditions under which the consent creates the moral power. For example, the consent must be given by a minimally competent person and it must not be given to obviously and seriously immoral commands. We shall consider some other conditions in what follows.

There are three traditional grounds for consent as a requirement on legitimate authority. The first is that normally a person is morally at liberty to do or not to do the kinds of things that eventually come under the scope of an authority. She may do it or not and act on the basis of her own moral judgment about the quality of the actions at issue. Consent to the authority is what suspends the moral liberty in the sense that the consenter must now comply with the authority's directives, merely because the authority has said so. Consent suspends this moral liberty in a way that is compatible with the freedom of the consenter. Hence the requirement of consent protects the freedom of persons. The second ground is that the requirement of consent protects the moral equality among persons. Unlike the relation between parent and child, the relation between two adults is normally a relation among equals, which only consent can change. But consent does this by preserving the basic equality. Finally, the requirement of consent and the possibility of refusal as well as of terminating consent creates a relationship of accountability between the purported authority and the subject, since the subject can change the relationship at will. In sum, the requirement of and power to consent enable me to advance my interests and concerns as a free and equal person by binding myself to others.

The most straightforward application of the consent basis for legitimate authority is voluntary association. When I join a club, I thereby acquire a reason to go along with its rules and I accept the normative power of the duly constituted authority in that group to change the rules. When my consent to this authority is required and I am able to consent, my freedom and equality are preserved even when I bind myself to the voluntary association.

Some have argued that consent is the basis of the legitimate authority of the state (Locke 1986/1690), but this is a weakly grounded application of the consent idea. The reason why the requirement of consent is not very strongly grounded in this context is that it doesn't protect the moral liberty of action or the equality of persons, nor does it secure the accountability of power to the consenter. Possession of the moral liberty usually involves the permission to act in a certain way or not and it involves the permission to act in accordance with one's own judgment about how to act. These permissions clearly hold in the normal case in one's relations to voluntary associations. Furthermore, the fact that I must consent to membership in the club and can exit it makes the club accountable to me to some extent.

But the permissions associated with moral liberty do not hold so clearly in the case of a reasonably just state. Here, in order to coordinate with others on a reasonably just course of action, one must follow the directives of the state officials—so moral liberty seems not to be very extensive with respect to the directives of the state. Thus the requirement of consent that is grounded in the protection of these permissions seems not to be present to any great degree (Raz 1986). Furthermore, consenting and refusal of consent seem to make for little accountability of the state to the person, except in unusual cases. My consent or lack of consent communicate very little to the state about my attitudes towards the state and impose little or no penalty on the state. Finally, in a democratic state, my equality with others is preserved in the democratic process of collective decision-making. I do not say that consent can play no role here; I want to say that in the case of a reasonably just state, consent is at best required only at the margins.

State Consent and Legitimacy

As I noted above, international institutions are neither state-like institutions nor voluntary associations, so the application of the consent idea to them poses distinct challenges. State consent is a large part of the traditional account of the legal obligations of international law. The *Statute of the International Court of Justice* lists treaties, custom and the general principles of law as the principal sources of international law (United Nations 1945, Article 38). The obligation of a treaty is grounded in the consent of the state parties to the treaty. The interpretations of treaties are usually based on the negotiations that preceded the treaty as well as the subsequent behaviors and statements of the state parties to the treaty. Furthermore, the Vienna Convention on the Law of Treaties asserts conditions for the validity of state consent that are very much like the usual conditions on valid individual consent to contracts (United Nations 1969, Articles 48–52). Most treaties, in addition, specify that it is permissible to exit the treaty in question (Helfer 2005). And states may tailor the provisions of a treaty to their particular interests by attaching reservations and understandings to their ratification of the treaty. Finally, treaties are agreed to one by one in a relatively fragmentary system. These features suggest a fair degree of accountability of international law to states through the process of state consent. And states have been traditionally conceived as morally at liberty to choose whether to join a treaty or not.

To be sure, I have been speaking in the previous paragraph of legal obligation, but given the power of promising to create obligations, it is reasonable to think that the consent of states under the right conditions and within reasonable moral bounds morally obligates the states.

There are four serious objections to the idea that state consent can ground obligations to international law.

Democratic State Consent

The first objection is that, while in the past international law may have mainly directed the actions of states, now international law directs the actions of individuals directly or indirectly. International law does hold individuals accountable for the violation of human rights in wartime as well as large-scale human rights violations in peacetime. But international law also directs individual action indirectly by requiring that states impose requirements on individuals. International trade law and international environmental law both impose requirements on states to alter their legal systems in various ways that direct the actions of individuals. But this suggests that the consent of states may not be sufficient for legitimacy since it is individuals who are directed (Bodansky 1999). A conception of the legitimacy of international institutions must somehow reach down to individuals who have content-independent reasons for action.

This is an important objection but it can be mostly met with an important modification to the idea of state consent. We might modify it by conjoining a democratic conception of political legitimacy with the consent theory. If we regard democratic states as having legitimacy with respect to their citizens, then we might think that the consent of democratic states to treaties could conceivably reach down to individuals, providing them with content-independent reasons to go along. Democracy has been thought to be a basis of legitimacy of states on the ground that to obey the decisions of a democratic assembly (within certain morally defined limits) is necessary to treating one's fellow citizens with equal respect, which we are duty bound to do (Christiano 2008). If we combine the state-consent doctrine with the idea of the democratic legitimacy of democratic states, we have a hybrid conception of the legitimacy of international institutions.

The inclusion of democracy as a condition for the validity of state consent greatly strengthens the moral grounds of the state-consent doctrine of legitimacy. We enlist the most powerful and most successful institution we know of for accommodating the interests of large numbers of people in a way that is accountable to those people in order to make international law and institutions accountable to persons. And we enlist an institution on which there is very widespread support within the international system (Franck 1996).

To be sure, this response to the objection leaves us with a difficult dilemma. We must discount the consent of nondemocratic states on the grounds that the consent merely reflects the interests and concerns of the elites ruling the society. Alternatively, we could count societies in some way partially accountable to their people on a scale, as in the case of the scales of democratization. This latter is a hazardous enterprise but at least it might take some account of the interests of the persons subjected to these societies.

Fairness and State Consent

A second important objection to the state-consent doctrine is that the consent of states is often gotten under conditions of unfair advantage taking. Unfair advantage taking requires its own analysis and I cannot hope to provide that here. But we might think that some exchanges entered into voluntarily and knowingly by individuals might still be morally quite defective. The usual conditions of unfair advantage taking in exchange involve two properly related elements. The first element is that the benefits of the exchange are quite disproportionately distributed when measured on some objective basis. The second is that the exchange occurs under conditions in which one of the parties has much greater bargaining power than the other. In the standard case this occurs because one of the parties can withdraw from the proposed arrangement only at great risk to his or her fundamental interests while the other party can take or leave the arrangement without much loss. The standard illustration is one in which a medical doctor comes upon a person who needs fairly rudimentary first aid to stop a life-threatening blood loss. The bleeding person cannot make it to a hospital on time and no one else is around. The doctor then asks a price that is much greater than the usual price for such treatment. The doctor can leave without much problem, but the bleeding individual must get the aid or face a highly likely prospect of death. Here we see the two elements together. It is crucial of course that the asymmetrical bargaining power explain the highly disproportionate distribution of benefits. Finally, it is crucial that the equitable distribution of benefits from exchange be itself Pareto superior to no exchange. When these three conditions are met, it is usually thought that there is something morally defective about the exchange. In some cases, exchange under these conditions defeats the generation of any obligation from it (Gordley 2001).

Many have contended that some of the major international institutions have been brought about in just this kind of way. The World Trade Organization was created by the United States and the European Union offering to continue with the liberalized trade regime of the General Agreement on Tariffs and Trade with other countries only on condition that they accept the Trade Related Intellectual Property regime, a watered-down commitment to lowering barriers to agricultural trade and a strong Dispute Settlement Mechanism whose decentralized enforcement strongly favors large, wealthy countries. The relative market shares of the United States and the European Union ensured that they had much less to lose than smaller, poorer countries if the regime just fell apart. So the poor countries agreed (Steinberg 2002). But they have never ceased to complain of the evident unfairness of the arrangement and the legitimacy of the World Trade Organization has suffered greatly, at least in the eyes of the developing world (Narlikar 2009).

We need some notion of fair negotiation that goes beyond mere voluntariness and nondeception if we are to capture what is going on in the frequent criticisms of the World Trade Organization and others. But here, too, we face a difficult dilemma. If the negotiations have displayed substantial unfair advantage taking, does this imply that the agreements reached are not binding and that the institutions created do not have legitimate authority? In many respects, this is an attractive idea—but it does have a downside. Poor countries enter into these agreements because they desperately need the agreements. But wealthy states may refuse to enter agreements that are less advantageous to them for a variety of reasons, including, for example, the political power of agricultural producers. And agreements that are not binding or agreements that have more equitable distributions of the goods exchanged may be spurned in favor of other agreements. Then we will have equity but greater poverty. With the World Trade Organization, we have some improvement in the situations of the world's poorest countries, even though it is inequitable.

The Independence of International Institutions

A third objection to the idea that state consent is the ground of legitimacy is that international institutions have a certain degree of independence from the states that have created them. This can come in a variety of forms. Some international institutions, such as the World Trade Organization, have independent judicial bodies that judge the complaints of members against other members on the basis of the agreements they have entered into and that authorize limited retaliatory action by one member against another that has been found in violation of an agreement. Some institutions, such as the Montreal Protocol, include modest rule-making committees that can bind states. And some institutions, such as the United Nations Security Council, have power to authorize military force and economic sanctions as means of enforcing basic rules of international security. Here the enforcement activity is carried out by the member states in accordance with the mandate given to them by the Security Council.

This objection can be understood in a number of ways. One, it may simply be asserting that there is some independence of the institutions from the states. But this does not by itself show that these institutions are not the voluntary products of states and that they do not have their binding force from the voluntary acts of creation or joining by states. We see voluntary organizations in ordinary domestic societies with partially independent decision-making bodies and this fact does not undermine the idea that they obligate only those who have joined.

Two, some of these institutions involve modest delegations of powers to highly specialized and expert bodies. And one might think that these bodies have become unaccountable to the people in the states that have created these bodies. But it is hard to know how to take this objection. The problem of delegation to independent, specialized bodies is one that exists in contemporary democratic states. This problem has not been solved entirely but there are mechanisms of accountability in those states that work more or less well (Lupia and McCubbins 1998). It is unclear why this couldn't be done in the case of international institutions that are the products of democratic states.

Customary International Law

The fourth objection to the state-consent approach starts from the observation that not all international law is created through treaties. A significant part of international law consists in customary international law. And customary international law is only weakly based on the consent of states. A rule of custom becomes binding on a state only if the state has not asserted persistent objections to it. If it has asserted such objections, the rule is not binding on it. If it has not asserted persistent objections, then the rule binds. This looks very much like a doctrine of tacit consent, but without the problems that have beset the Lockean idea of tacit consent to the state. First, the problem of how to interpret the lack of persistent objections is solved because states understand the persistent-objector rule. Second, the law has no authority over the persistent objector before it objects.

One problem with customary international law from the standpoint of the state-consent view is that there appears to be no way unilaterally to exit customary international law, unlike most treaty law. To be sure, the law can be modified, particularly through the making of treaties. But this cannot be done unilaterally. To this extent there are limits to the voluntariness of adherence to customary international law. But those limits are more serious than this, because subsequent generations also do not have a unilateral power to exit customary international law. So, from the point of view of a state-consent doctrine that is supposed to be grounded in individuals, this implies a serious limitation to the individualistic version of state consent. To my knowledge, this problem has never been properly addressed.

The Basic Constraints on State Consent

Another serious problem with customary international law from the standpoint of the state-consent view is that there are some parts of customary international law that are binding on states and persons regardless of their consent. *Jus cogens* norms are norms of international law that arise through custom but acquire a peremptory status such that every state is bound by the norms and no state can create a treaty that violates one of these norms. *Jus cogens* norms include norms against aggressive war, against slavery, against genocide, against piracy and against torture. The basis of these norms as legal norms is much contested, though there seems to be less and less skepticism about their existence. This kind of norm is described in the Vienna Convention on the Law of

Treaties as a ". . . norm accepted and recognized by the international community of States as a whole as a norm from which no derogation is permitted and which can be modified only by a subsequent norm of general international law having the same character" (United Nations 1969, Article 53). Some have argued that these norms suggest the truth of a natural law approach to international law.

In addition to what are normally described as *jus cogens* norms, there are other, nearly equally important norms in the international system, such as the norm of *pacta sunt servanda* (that pacts must be performed). This too is a norm that has not been, until recently, embodied in treaty law.

These objections suggest that important modifications must be made to the state-consent approach to the bindingness of international law and the legitimacy of international institutions. They imply that there are deep constraints on what arrangements states may voluntarily enter into or exit. And these constraints appear to have a legal character. In some respects many of these constraints may have the character of constitutional norms, which in effect are beyond the ordinary processes of lawmaking in international law, just as constitutional norms are beyond the ordinary processes of lawmaking in domestic systems of law. And just to push the analogy a bit further, they have the character of an unwritten constitution of the sort we see in the British constitutional system.

If we assimilate the *jus cogens* norms and the norm of *pacta sunt servanda* to something like constitutional norms of the international system as a whole, then the state-consent model can be seen as the basic model of ordinary lawmaking for an international system that is bound by certain constitutional norms.

From a moral standpoint, we can think of the state-consent account of legitimacy as a morally bounded system of voluntary association among peoples. The boundaries of that system reflect the commitment to the fundamental interests of persons that no system of voluntary association may violate.

Morally Mandatory Aims and State Consent

There is another related and difficult issue to face for such a system. The global community is currently facing some fundamental moral challenges, which can be recognized as such on virtually any scheme of morality. The aims of the preservation of international security and the protection of persons against serious and widespread violations of human rights are already recognized in Article 1 of the Charter of the United Nations, which lays out the purposes of the United Nations. In addition, there are aims of equally great moral importance that must be pursued by the international system. First, it must pursue the avoidance of global environmental catastrophe. Second, it must pursue the alleviation of severe global poverty. And third, it must establish a decent system of international trade. These challenges will require significant cooperation from most of the world's states at least.

The morally mandatory character of the aims and the necessity of general cooperation in the pursuit of the aims imply that there are certain tasks that are morally mandatory for states to participate in. This suggests a set of moral imperatives that are not the usual context for voluntary association. The usual context of voluntary association is that persons are morally at liberty whether to join or not and even if some associations do pursue morally important aims, there are enough of them that one may pick and choose among them without moral cost.

There may still be room for the moral liberty that state consent protects in such a society but it must be heavily bound by constraints. The justification for the state-consent requirement may be grounded in the fact that, though we are morally required to cooperate in solving these fundamental moral problems, there is a great deal of uncertainty as to how these problems can be solved. Though there is general agreement among scientists that the earth is warming due to human activity, there is disagreement as to how much this is happening and how quickly. There is also substantial disagreement about how to mitigate global warming and what a fair and efficient distribution of costs might be. The same uncertainties attend thinking about how to alleviate global poverty, how to create a decent system of international trade and how to protect persons from widespread human rights abuses.

This kind of uncertainty provides a reason for supporting a system of state consent with freedom to enter and exit arrangements because it supports a system which allows for a significant amount of experimentation in how to solve the problems. Experimentation within different regional associations as well as within competing global arrangements may be the best way to try to solve the problems we are facing. And democratic states are the ideal agents for this kind of experimentation because of their high degrees of accountability and transparency.

But the system of state consent must be heavily bounded given the morally mandatory need for cooperation. In the usual case of treaties, refusal of entry and exit are permissible and require no explanation. In the cases of any treaty that attempts to realize a system of cooperation that is morally mandatory, the exit from or the refusal to enter it would require an acceptable explanation that lays out the reasons for thinking that the treaty would not contribute to solving the problem and that some alternative might be superior. Exit or withdrawal is permissible but only with an adequate explanation. By "adequate explanation" I mean an explanation that is not irrational, unscrupulous or morally self-defeating and that displays a good-faith effort to solve the problem at hand. The explanation must be in terms of the morally mandatory aims or in terms of a crushing or severely unfair cost of cooperation. The explanation need only be adequate, in the sense that it need not be the correct explanation, but it falls within the scope of what reasonable people can disagree on. An irrational explanation goes against the vast majority of scientific opinion. An unscrupulous explanation free rides on others' contributions to morally mandatory aims or it refuses to shoulder any share in a morally mandatory pursuit. A morally self-defeating explanation is one that insists on a different coordination solution, defeating a coordination solution that in the circumstance advances everyone's aims.

One possible example of unscrupulous nonconsent might be the unwillingness of the United States and the European Union to lower their barriers to trade in agricultural goods with developing countries. It seems clearly unscrupulous since these societies have spared nothing in advocating for the benefits of free international trade. They simply refuse to do so when that would involve setting back certain domestic interests. Another more contentious possible example of problematic refusal to participate would be the United States' refusal to participate in the Kyoto Protocol. A complete defense of these claims would require a lot more study and discussion than I have space for here, but they are potential candidates.

When a state refuses to participate in a cooperative venture for the pursuit of morally mandatory aims and has no adequate explanation, it may be subjected to some kind of sanction or coercion. States would be within their rights to contemplate noncooperation or even more coercive responses to those states that refuse to participate for unscrupulous, irrational or morally self-defeating motives. Hence there are severe limits to the moral liberty of states when it comes to morally mandatory aims.

This is, I think, the farthest one can take the system of state consent. It contemplates a heavily bounded system of consent and exit. It is bounded on the one hand by *jus cogens* norms and the underlying principles of voluntarily incurred obligation. It is also bounded by the moral imperative on every state to pursue certain basic moral goods. In these respects one can see how international institutions and law occupy some kind of middle ground between voluntary associations and state-like political institutions.

Beyond State Consent

Now that we have a view of the highly constrained process of state consent, we can see some ways in which the system must be supplemented by other ideas. One worry is that the system has little in the way of resources to constrain the power of the most powerful states. Though I have suggested that states may be coerced if they fail to offer an adequate reason for nonparticipation in a regime designed to pursue one of the morally mandatory aims, this can provide a check on the most powerful states only in certain circumstances, e.g., when there are a number of other powerful states willing to put pressure on the recalcitrant state. The consequences of this are that weaker states are constrained while the most powerful state or states are not. This is the most serious institutional-design problem confronting any normative approach to international institutions. At this point, it has not been solved.

A second worry is that the scheme is too conservative. It requires states to agree. If a powerful state does not agree and its agreement is essential to the successful cooperation among states, generally the chosen arrangement will not work. This is especially an issue for the mitigation of global warming, which will require some kind of global solution. It will be hard to move beyond the status quo because powerful states, which prefer the status quo, will be favored.

A third related worry is that the scheme is unwieldy. Requiring states to consent to major changes to international law makes for a slow process of making law and may have very serious transaction costs (Buchanan and Tullock 1962). The worry is that the needs for coordination and for adjustments to coordination are too great to allow it to be the case that all decisions are made by state consent.

To be sure, states do set up on occasion more streamlined mechanisms for collective decision-making. As noted above, there are parts of international law that have some modest independence from states. Some parts require some kind of majoritarian decision-making, some involve modestly independent judicial institutions and some constitute committees that are empowered to make proposals. But the question is whether this shouldn't be required as part of a system of international lawmaking, particularly when dealing with issues of such moral weight and urgency as the prevention of global warming and the alleviation of global poverty, which may require very timely decision-making.

John Locke argued that when a group of persons comes together to form a political body they implicitly agree to make subsequent decisions by some non-unanimity method. His grounds for this were that unanimous agreement would be hard to come by when there is a lot of disagreement and that every person who joins knows that this would make the political society ineffectual (Locke 1986/1690, § 95–96). This has mostly not been the case for the associations that contemporary states have entered into; they remain heavily committed, with a few exceptions, to state consent being the basis of further obligations. The fear of external costs imposed by other states seems to outweigh the concern that consensual decision-making is very slow and cumbersome and threatens to undermine the capacity of international organizations to solve major problems.

For institutions to be legitimate, they must have at least a moderate capacity to pursue the aims that are morally mandatory or at least not block the pursuit of morally mandatory aims. Hence if the state-consent requirement is too unwieldy for the pursuit of the morally mandatory aims it must be in some way replaced or supplemented by other requirements. These internal constraints would be broadly constraints of effectiveness and fairness to the affected parties.

We might then envision a three-stage conception of legitimacy for international institutions, along broadly Lockean lines. The three stages are a constitutional stage of *jus cogens* norms and other general principles of law, a heavily bounded system of fair voluntary association among democratic states and some internal principles for the design of international institutions. Legitimate international institutions must be created through a constitutionally constrained and heavily bounded process of state consent and they must satisfy certain other, more internal constraints, which enable them effectively to pursue the aims in a broadly egalitarian way.

It is in this spirit that we should look at the proposal offered by Allen Buchanan and Robert Keohane, which they call the "complex standard" of legitimacy for global governance institutions. This standard has three elements: one, the ongoing consent of democratic states; two, minimal moral acceptability (in the sense of nonviolation of basic human rights), comparative benefit (relative to other feasible institutions) and institutional integrity (the institution is pursuing the goals to which it is committed); and three, epistemic virtues that enable the participants in the institutions and the stakeholders to determine whether the standards are being met and enable them to contest and revise the standards and goals of the institutions (Buchanan and Keohane 2006: 432).

The second part asserts some basic outcome benchmarks for the institutions. The third part of the standard involves some partially democratic norms for the manner in which the goals are pursued.

My account above gives the rationale and the limits to the state-consent part. It can supply the rationale and some substance to the second standard in terms of the *jus cogens* norms, but it also supplies an essential supplement to their account by asserting the necessity of pursuing the morally mandatory aims. The third part of the standard is designed to introduce a democratic element in the independent decision-making institutions of the organization. What it lacks, however, is a firm conception of fairness in the internal structure of international institutions.

Devising fair internal standards for institutions is one of the most difficult problems in thinking about international institutions. There are legislative, administrative, enforcement and judicial institutions and there are also lending agencies. The norms of fairness vary significantly from one type of institution to another. Each must arise through the bounded process of state consent. Legislative institutions ought to have a more democratic character, though the exact character will depend on the relative stakes and shares of the stakeholders. In contrast, judicial institutions must be judged on the basis of the quality of the statutes that they apply in adjudication, the impartiality and fairness with which they assess liability, the impartiality with which they determine remedies and the impartiality of the processes by which those remedies are imposed. For example, the Dispute Settlement Mechanism of the World Trade Organization usually receives high marks on the second and third parts of the criterion but since enforcement is up to each aggrieved state, poor and weak states do not even bother bringing cases against wealthy states. Administrative rulemaking bodies must be judged by the quality of the mandate they are trying to implement, the openness of the process of rulemaking, the competence of the experts and their faithfulness to the mandates. Lending agencies that are lenders of last resort to desperate countries must ensure that those countries have adequate voice in the process of structuring the loans. These are just some examples of the very distinct internal standards that must be realized by legitimate institutions.

To be sure, our conception of these internal standards must be quite abstract because we want states to have significant latitude to experiment with creating and modifying international institutions.

Remarks on Method

This essay sheds harsh light on the current international system. The aim has been to define a conception of legitimacy based on consent and democracy that can be realized in the international system as we know it and as we expect it to be for the medium-term future. To this end, I have developed an ideal theory that draws on the best resources actually available in the international system. The basic facts of the system we have been dealing with are: the primacy of states as players in the international system, the high degree of disagreement and uncertainty we currently face in trying to solve the most important problems, and the need for institutions that are capable of timely decision-making. The focus on consent and democratic grounds of legitimacy will imply that the ideas sketched have an important element of ideal theory in them. While no model of legitimate institutions will correspond to the way the world actually works, a model is illuminating to the extent that it helps us articulate and shed light on the major problems that the current system faces and that it defends standards against which one can reasonably evaluate the current system.

Conclusion

I have argued that state consent has an important role to play within a multistage conception of how international law and institutions must be constructed. The first stage is the quasi-constitutional stage of *jus cogens* norms and basic norms of lawmaking, such as *pacta sunt servanda*, as well as the central role of morally mandatory aims in thinking about the justification of international law and institutions. The second stage is the heavily bounded process of fair democratic state consent. The third stage is a set of principles for ensuring that international institutions that pursue morally mandatory aims are reasonably effective and fair in their internal structure.

References

Bodansky, D. (1999) "The Legitimacy of International Governance: A Coming Challenge for International Environmental Law?" *The American Journal of International Law* 93: 596–624.

Buchanan, A. and Keohane, R. (2006) "The Legitimacy of Global Governance Institutions," *Ethics and International Affairs* 20: 405–37.

Buchanan, J. and Tullock, G. (1962) *The Calculus of Consent: Logical Foundations of Constitutional Democracy*, Ann Arbor, MI: University of Michigan Press.

Christiano, T. (2008) *The Constitution of Equality: Democratic Authority and Its Limits*, Oxford: Oxford University Press.

—— (2010) "Democratic Legitimacy and International Institutions," in S. Besson and J. Tasioulas, eds., *The Philosophy of International Law*, Oxford: Oxford University Press, pp. 119–38.

Franck, T. (1996) *Fairness in International Law and Institutions*, Oxford: Oxford University Press.

Gordley, J. (2001) "Contract Law in the Aristotelian Tradition," in P. Benson, ed., *The Theory of Contract Law: New Essays*, Cambridge: Cambridge University Press, pp. 265–334.

Helfer, L. (2005) "Exiting Treaties," *Virginia Law Review* 91: 1579–1648.

Kingsbury, B. (2007) "Global Environmental Governance as Administration: Implications for International Law," in D. Bodansky, J. Brunnee and E. Hey, eds., *The Oxford Handbook of International Environmental Law*, Oxford: Oxford University Press, pp. 64–84.

Locke, J. (1986/1690) *Second Treatise on Civil Government*, Buffalo, NY: Prometheus Books.

Lupia, A. and McCubbins, M. (1998) *The Democratic Dilemma: Can Citizens Learn What They Need to Know?*, Cambridge: Cambridge University Press.

Narlikar, A. (2009) "Law and Legitimacy: The World Trade Organization," in D. Armstrong, ed., *The Routledge Handbook of International Law*, Abingdon, UK: Routledge, pp. 294–302.

Raz, J. (1986) *The Morality of Freedom*, Oxford: Oxford University Press.

Simmons, A. J. (2001) *Justification and Legitimacy: Essays on Rights and Obligations*, Cambridge: Cambridge University Press.

Steinberg, R. (2002) "In the Shadow of Law or Power? Consensus-Based Bargaining and Outcomes in the GATT/WTO," *International Organization* 56: 339–74.

Szasz, P. (2002) "The Security Council Starts Legislating," *American Journal of International Law* 96: 901–5.

United Nations (1945) *Statute of the International Court of Justice*, 3 Bevans 1179; 59 Stat. 1031; T.S. 993; 39 *AJIL* Supp. 215.

—— (1969) Vienna Convention on the Law of Treaties, 1155 UNTS 331; 8 ILM 679; 63 *AJIL* 875.

Further Reading

For further reading, see: R. Dahl (1999) "Can International Institutions Be Democratic? A Sceptic's View," in I. Shapiro and C. Hacker-Cordon, eds., *Democracy's Edges*, Cambridge: Cambridge University Press, pp. 19–36; M. Doyle (2009) "The UN Charter—A Global Constitution?" in J. L. Dunoff and J. P. Trachtman, eds., *Ruling the World?: Constitutionalism, International Law, and Global Governance*, Cambridge: Cambridge University Press, pp. 113–32; H. Grotius (2005) *The Rights of War and Peace*, R. Tuck, ed. and trans., Indianapolis: Liberty Fund; R. Howse (2001) "The Legitimacy of the World Trade Organization," in J. M. Coicaud and V. Heiskanen, eds., *The Legitimacy of International Organizations*, Tokyo: United Nations University Press, pp. 355–407; G. Klosko (2004) *The Principle of Fairness and Political Obligation*, 2nd edition, Lanham, MD: Rowman and Littlefield; D. Moellendorf (2008) *Global Inequality Matters*, London: Palgrave-Macmillan; T. Pogge (2002) *World Poverty and Human Rights*, Malden, MA: Polity Press; S. C. Schlesinger (2003) *Act of Creation: The Founding of the United Nations*, Boulder, CO: Westview Press; and E. Vattel (2008/1758) *The Law of Nations*, B. Kapossy and R. Whatmore, eds., Indianapolis: Liberty Fund.

(viii)

ENVIRONMENTAL LAW

26

ENVIRONMENTAL ETHICS, FUTURE GENERATIONS AND ENVIRONMENTAL LAW

Clark Wolf

I. Harms to Persons or Harms to the Environment? Justifying Environmental Law

According to a popular theory of legislation, usually associated with the work of John Stuart Mill, laws that limit people's liberty are justifiable only if their effect is to prevent *harm to others* (Mill 1982/1859). On this liberal view, which has recently been given careful examination and qualified defense by Joel Feinberg (1984–1988), it is unjustifiable *legal moralism* to employ the coercive powers of the state simply to compel people to do what others regard to be good or right. Those who accept this account of the moral limits of law may find themselves challenged to provide adequate justification for environmental regulations. While some environmental laws are clearly designed to protect people from harm, others focus on the environment itself as the object to be protected. This raises the question of whether many environmental laws may be an expression of an illiberal and possibly unjustifiable *moralism* on the part of those who enact and implement them. I will use the term *liberal environmentalism* to refer to the Millian view that environmental regulations are justifiable only when they prevent harm to others. *Environmental moralism*, by contrast, is the view that environmental regulations may be justified when they provide effective protection for the environment, whether or not this protection is necessary to prevent harm to human beings.

Those who hope to explain and justify environmental laws might seriously consider alternatives to liberal environmentalism, since other theories will permit a broader range of justificatory reasons for liberty-limiting legislation. Environmental moralism provides a simpler justification for regulations that protect environmental systems and species that may seem unconnected with human rights and interests. Many people believe that we have a moral obligation to protect the environment and that fulfillment of this obligation is sufficient justification for environmental-protection law. Environmentalists who find legal moralism unpalatable might instead argue that environmental laws are appropriate and effective as a means to protect people from harm. Thus Shrader-Frechette

(2005, 2010) documents the use of environmental legislation to protect people from negligently inflicted health hazards and other injustices associated with pollution and environmental destruction.

However, some present environmental damage might be presently harmless, and the activities that cause this damage may even provide net benefits for present and proximate generations of human beings. Such damage might nonetheless constitute a serious threat to the interests of more distant future generations. Writing in 1977, Toby Page cites a fictional example:

> You are the director of the Office of Management and Budget. A proposal reaches your desk about a riskless project which will extract energy from the sun at an increased rate for 200 years. New production processes could use the energy to triple our GNP every year until 2180. Total project costs are negligible with one exception. The sun will explode [because of the project] and end life in 2180.
>
> (Page 1977: 250)

Even though the people who would be harmed by this project are people who don't presently exist, it is still plausible to think that we have an obligation not to adopt present policies that doom them (along with all other living creatures) to an untimely demise. One might urge that policies that doom the distant future, or which are negligent or reckless with respect to the risks they impose in the distant future, are inappropriate and unjust because they will cause harm to *future* people, even though they may provide benefits for people who presently exist. While Page's scenario is fanciful, the essential elements are similar to contemporary arguments to mitigate the effects of global climate change by reducing the level of greenhouse-gas emissions: while current and proximate generations might benefit from present consumption of fossil fuels, the associated emissions may cause terrible human and environmental damage in the more distant future (IPCC 2007). Climate policy is often presented as a trade-off in which members of the present generation are asked to forego benefits for the sake of preventing harms to future generations (Gardiner 2011; Wolf 2009a). Thus a third strategy employed to support environmental regulations urges that such regulations are a necessary or appropriate way to protect the interests of distant future persons.

This article will begin in section II with a brief discussion of the status of future generations in environmental ethics and environmental law. Sections III and IV discuss two central grounds for skepticism concerning the possibility that future generations can have rights, and articulate several different strategies to address such skepticism. Section V very briefly considers whether liberal environmentalists who accept Mill's harm principle (or a close relative of Mill's principle) can accept liberty-limiting environmental legislation that aims to protect the rights and interests of distant future people. Then Sections VI and VII examine the status of future persons in contemporary theories of justice, with special attention in section VII to the work of John Rawls. Because Rawls's work focuses on needs, and on the ability of institutions to provide stable intergenerational protections for needs, section VIII evaluates several different conceptions of intergenerational sustainability, and the relationship between need, sustainability and intergenerational justice. Finally, sections IX and X consider the status of future generations in positive law, and prospects for future environmental legislation designed to guarantee just treatment for the members of distant future generations.

II. Future Generations, Environmental Ethics and Environmental Law

It is perhaps surprising that environmental ethicists have not given more careful attention to environmental obligations to future generations. Perhaps this is partly explained by the way the field of environmental ethics is often distinguished from other fields: some ethicists define the field of environmental ethics around the distinction between "anthropocentric" and "non-anthropocentric" theories. Anthropocentric theories of ethics are those theories that hold that all our obligations are, in the final analysis, obligations to other *persons*. Non-anthropocentric theories, by contrast, hold that we can have obligations that are not directed at persons, and that our obligation to preserve and protect environmental systems are best understood as obligations to promote the intrinsic or noninstrumental value these systems possess. Thus quite a lot of discussion in the field of environmental ethics has involved explication of the concept of intrinsic value and the development of arguments to show that environmental systems have this kind of value.

When environmental ethics is *identified* as the study of non-anthropocentric value systems, then consideration of our environmental obligations to future generations is excluded from consideration as a topic in environmental ethics. But many of our most important environmental obligations involve the pursuit of multiple objectives: if we pursue efforts to regulate mountaintop removal as a method of coal mining, we may, at the same time, hope to preserve mountaintop ecosystems, protect rural communities, ensure the safety of mine workers, prevent stream runoff, maintain biodiversity and promote alternative methods of energy production. Some of these objectives may be non-anthropocentric, but these will at most be a subset of the total set of motives and interests that need to be taken into account in the articulation of an appropriate policy. Even if we do have fundamental and irreducible obligations to nature (or to natural systems), and even if one holds that these obligations are based on the intrinsic value of the subject to which they are directed, we need to place these values alongside other values and other kinds of values before we can properly understand the way in which they contribute to justifying environmental laws and policies. As many contemporary environmental ethicists recognize, the fields of environmental ethics and environmental-policy analysis must address this broader range of concerns and objectives.

One salient reason for implementing policies for environmental protection is that these policies are necessary, or would be an effective way to protect the interests and perhaps to secure the rights of future people or future generations of people. But some people find it odd to think that we have obligations to people who don't yet exist, or that their future rights might constrain present liberties. The next sections will consider key challenges to the idea that present enforceable obligations might be linked to future claimants or to future rights.

III. Skepticism About Future Rights and Present Obligations

One view of legal rights is that they serve to secure or guarantee protection for moral rights. On this model, people have natural or moral rights—for example, rights against assault or theft—and the function of legal regulations is that they provide an enforcement mechanism that ensures that the possessors of moral rights get the treatment they have a right to receive. While many people profess skepticism about natural or moral rights, it is plausible to think that we have some obligations to others even when legal institutions do not enforce them. Moral rights may simply be identified with these obligations and the corresponding claims of those to whom they are owed. Another function of legal rights is that they can *create* claims and liabilities where no prior claims existed. Thus Thomas Jefferson, author of the first U.S. patent law, argued that there is no natural or moral right to intellectual property, but held that it is perfectly legitimate for a legal right to be created (Jefferson 1977/1813). In considering the status of the moral and legal rights of future persons, it will be important to consider each of these possibilities.

Because future persons do not presently exist, some writers are skeptical about the idea that they might have rights or that present persons might have obligations to them. Different grounds have been expressed for such skepticism. For example, Beckerman and Pasek write:

> [P]roperties, such as being green or wealthy or having rights, can be predicated only of some subject that exists. Outside the realm of mythological or fictional creatures or hypothetical discourse, if there is no subject then there is nothing to which any property can be ascribed. Propositions such as "X is Y" or "X has Z" or "X prefers A to B" make sense only if there is an X. If there is no X then all such propositions are meaningless.
>
> (2001: 15)

If one wishes to respond to this argument in defense of the rights of future persons, there are three principal strategies one might pursue: first, one could argue, *pace* Beckerman, that future persons do in fact have present rights. Second, one might argue that legislation may create legal rights for future persons, even though these rights would not be associated with any antecedent moral rights. Third, one might argue that present actions can be wrong because they violate *future* rights—the rights that future people *will* possess when they come to exist.

In support of the first strategy, it should be noted that the present nonexistence of future people does not make them imaginary like fictional people: they do not exist in an alternative possible world, but in a future state of our own world. In some contexts, we refer to future individuals by the properties they will or may come to possess, as when as-yet-nonexistent children are accommodated in a will. Further, possession of a right is not like current ownership or like the possession of a property. To say that A has a right against B is simply to describe a moral relation that holds between A and B. But perhaps relations can hold between individuals who exist at different times: for example, the "prior to" relation would seem to hold wherever A exists *prior to* B, and present persons exist *prior to* future ones. If the existence of a normative relation between present and future people is more like the existence of a *relation* between them, then it will not follow that future persons cannot have rights merely because they suffer the temporary present embarrassment of nonexistence. While this argument does not show that future persons have present rights, it may be sufficient to undermine Beckerman and Pasek's argument against the possibility that they could.

A second strategy would be to urge that these rights can appropriately be created through a kind of legal fiction. There is no conceptual problem with the creation of legal rights in this way, though it might be difficult to know how they should be enforced, if the goal is to promote the interests of future people and prevent present actions that could mar their lives. In some cases we may have a clear understanding of the interests of future generations—we can confidently predict that they will be worse off if earlier generations leave a toxic environment behind. But in other contexts it is more difficult to know what future people will need, and we might reasonably be skeptical of those who claim to speak for future interests. The legal enforcement of such rights might also raise concerns: if future people have only *legal* rights, then liberty-limiting legislation designed to promote these rights would seem moralistic, and inconsistent with Mill's harm principle.

A third strategy, consistent with the other two, and perhaps sufficient in itself, focuses on the rights that future people will have when they come to exist. On this view, present actions may be wrong and appropriately prohibited when they are likely to violate the legal or moral rights that people will come to possess in the future (Davison 2008; Feinberg 1986). In other legal contexts, such a view concerning future rights is relatively uncontroversial. For example, consider the following:

> *Scheme for future theft*
> Before Beth's birth, Alph works to set in place a scheme to steal money that would otherwise come to Beth as an entitlement when she reaches a certain age. As a result of Alph's scheme, Beth's money is later untraceably transferred to the account of Alph's children. Many years later, long after Alph himself has died, Alph's children innocently enjoy this windfall, unaware that it has been stolen.

It is plausible to think that Alph's wrongful action violated some of Beth's present rights, by changing her prospects. But it is also plausible to think that Alph's action results in the later violation of additional rights that Beth acquires when she comes of age. If someone noticed Alph's scheme and intervened to set things right, Alph would still have violated the earlier rights but the later rights would not have been violated at all. Obviously, legal measures that prohibit actions like these are fully justified by a legitimate interest to protect the rights that people will come to possess.

It is a short and highly plausible step to urge that present actions may be similarly wrongful when they lead to the violation of the future rights that people come to possess, even if the people who will possess these violated rights don't exist when the wrongful actions take place. On this view, legal prohibition of such wrongful actions would be justified by the need to prevent future rights violations and their associated harms. While the present enforcement of future rights might seem hypothetical, courts have sometimes found ways to accomplish it. For example, the Philippine Constitution asserts in Article II, section 16 that, "The state shall protect and advance the right of the people to a balanced and healthful ecology in accord with the rhythm and harmony of nature." The Philippine Supreme Court ruled in 1993, in a case to be discussed at further length in section IX, that this right belongs to future as well as present generations of Philippine citizens. The court found that timber contracts that threatened destruction of the nation's forests were accordingly unconstitutional (*Minors Oposa v. Secretary of the Department of Environment and Natural Resources (DENR)* (1993) 33 I. L.M. 173). The courts of other nations have not, for the most part, found ways to follow this road, but there is no reason *in principle* why similar constitutional provisions or similar legislation could not be crafted to accomplish the same thing.

IV. The Nonidentity Problem

There is another well-known argument that is regarded by many people to call into question the idea that future persons may have rights, and even the more modest view that presently existing people may have obligations to the members of future generations. According to the *nonidentity problem*, present actions do not simply change the circumstances of life for future generations, they also change the *constituency* of future generations (Parfit 1984, ch. 16). That is, different people will exist, depending on our present choices. Any large-scale social policy will cause subtle changes in many people's lives, and as a consequence different people will meet and different children will be born. Over time, small changes create more and more differences between the actual world and the world as it would have been if the policy had not been put in place. Eventually, it is claimed, entirely different people will exist from those who would have existed otherwise. This argument is sometimes taken to undermine the view that present actions could violate distant future rights: can one be harmed by an action without which one would not have existed at all? For the same reason, this *nonidentity* argument is sometimes thought to undermine the view that present actions could set back future interests.

Some people find this argument persuasive (Heyd 1992). But as a reason for skepticism about rights or obligations, it is peculiar. Typically our obligations to other people accrue to them not because of their unique genetic identities but, as Annette Baier puts it, "because of the roles they fill, roles that relate to others. For example, children, *qua* children have obligations to and rights against parents *qua* parents. My obligations as a teacher are owed to my students whoever they may be" (Baier 1981: 173). Analogously, the obligation not to roll boulders down a mountain is owed to anyone who might be passing on the path below, and do not in any way depend on the specific identities or the genetic makeup of the persons who might be harmed by such an action (Wolf 2009b: 108). To set a boulder rolling is to set in motion a causal chain of events that may cause harm. Even if the boulder roller is lucky and no one is harmed, the act is wrong because it recklessly creates a risk of harm.

Policies that purchase present benefits at the cost of distant future harms are wrong in the same sense: they are like intergenerational "boulders" that threaten harm to people who will live in the distant future, and they are similarly wrong because of the effect they will have on the lives they may blight. In explaining why such actions are wrong, and in justifying legislation to prohibit them, we do not in any way need to refer to the identities of the people who might be on the path and whose rights might be violated if the boulder lands on them, or the people whose lives are blighted by our present environmental destruction. The relation that stands between present wrongful actions that result in harms to distant future persons, and the harms those actions cause, are relevantly similar. The future people whose lives might be blighted by our present pollution are wronged, and the wrong done to them does not in any way depend on their contingent identities. It rather depends on the relationship that holds between our present policies and the suffering these policies may cause. If we are reckless or negligent, failing to take future costs into account, we may properly be held responsible for our failing.

One might still ask, however, whether such laws benefit the people whose interests they aim to protect. If the passage of such a law is identity-determining for the human population of the earth, then those who come to exist are different people from the people whose interests would have been set back or flattened if we had adopted a different policy. In response to this worry, however, we should carefully examine the conception of "identity" involved. If the identities of the people involved are a function of the characteristics these people possess and the circumstances of life they experience, then it is up to us to determine whether they are "the same people" or "different people" in the relevant sense. Since future people don't have present identities at all, there are no facts of the matter concerning the identities they will come to have other than these characteristics they possess. In this context, the appropriate conception of "identity" may be one that simply identifies future persons as "the people who will live in the future, and whose lives will not overlap our own." This definite description picks people out as the relevant object of our present obligations and the potential victims of present wrongs. Because we can identify the victims in this way, it is simply a mistake to use the nonidentity problem as an excuse to avoid thinking about the consequences of our present choices (Wolf 2009b). As long as there will *be* future people, this definite description will appropriately identify the aspects of their identities that are relevant from the moral point of view, and as a matter of policy and law.

V. Liberal Environmentalism and Future Harms

How might present legislation or legal action protect future interests? It is not likely that harms to future persons would, in many circumstances, constitute a cause of action to support a lawsuit. However, present legislation and present policies might be put in place to protect future interests. Indeed, one important reason for statutes that protect environmental resources is that these resources should be preserved for the benefit of future generations. Liberal environmentalists accept Mill's harm principle as an appropriate constraint on legislative actions that limit individual liberty. Such environmentalists will regard environmental regulations to be unjustified if they are not necessary to prevent personal harms, but should not distinguish, in this respect, between present harms and future harms. Future harms may be less certain than more proximate harms, but to discount them according to their uncertainty is not the same as discounting them because of the time when they will occur. This distinction between the degree of uncertainty associated with a threat, and the time at which the threatened harm might occur, is well accommodated in other legal contexts, and should not create any special problem in the case of distant future harms. The arguments above provide some support for the view that present actions may be wrong, and may appropriately be made illegal, when they set back the interests or violate the rights of future persons. But to specify the content of obligations to future generations, we would need to fit these obligations into a broader theory of justice.

VI. Intergenerational Justice: Rights, Community, Contract and Cooperation

Not all theories of justice can easily accommodate the notion that norms of justice apply between people who are members of different and distant generations. While it may be easy to explain how we can have obligations of justice to people whose lives overlap, and who can therefore cooperate and interact, distant future generations cannot cooperate, and reciprocity between their members is impossible. Most contemporary theories of justice can be identified as one of three different general types: libertarian, liberal, and communitarian. This section will briefly introduce each of them, considering the problems the different kinds of theories face in the case of intergenerational justice.

Libertarian theories hold that justice essentially involves the protection of negative rights, and that political institutions exceed their legitimate authority when they enforce positive rights. Negative rights include claims against force and fraud but do not include any requirement of positive action to aid others who may be in need. For example, Alph's right to be free from violent assault is a negative right because it requires other people not to engage in violent assaults on Alph. Libertarians typically include property rights among the negative rights, since Beth's obligation not to take or interfere with Alph's property is similar, in many respects, to Beth's obligation not to interfere with Alph's person. Positive rights, by contrast, oblige action on the part of others. A child's right to an education, a disabled person's right to subsistence or a broader right to basic health care would all qualify as positive rights, since other people need to *provide* education, subsistence or health care in order to secure such positive rights.

Perhaps libertarians have a problem with intergenerational justice: the obligation to save resources for the future, for example, would seem to be a positive obligation. The view that this is an obligation of justice would imply, therefore, that future people have a positive right to the resources we might save for them. If the requirements of justice include no positive obligations, this would imply that members of the present generation cannot have an obligation to save resources for the future. Some libertarians do not regard this to be an objection. Perhaps libertarians should simply accept that future generations are not protected by norms of justice. But those who regard it to be a problem might adopt one of three different strategies to incorporate provision for the future. First, one might argue that we have obligations to future generations that are based on negative rights: perhaps we have an obligation not to use up resources they will need, and to avoid creating hazards that will undermine their well-being. One might argue that our obligation not to use up or destroy such resources is a *negative* obligation, since it involves a requirement *not* to act rather than a positive obligation to provide benefits. Perhaps such obligations are similar to the obligation not to assault future people by planting a time bomb scheduled to go off many generations hence. Second, one might argue that the market institutions that libertarians favor will adequately provide for the needs and interests of future generations even if they do not have rights and are not covered by a theory of justice. Indeed, many libertarians urge that market institutions are the institutions most likely to protect future interests, since they provide incentives for productive activities that will benefit the future (Nozick 1974; Beckerman and Pasek 2001; Cowen 2007). A third way favored by some libertarians is to argue that there are limitations implicit in property rights themselves, which prohibit us from acquiring rights that would leave others destitute. Thus in the Second Treatise of Government, Locke includes a proviso specifying that the appropriation of resources must leave "enough and as good" for others who must also have their chance to appropriate goods from the common (Locke 1963/1714). Several "left libertarian" arguments have been offered that base the claims of future generations on libertarian restrictions concerning the initial appropriation of resources (Wolf 1995; Steiner and Vallentyne 2009).

Communitarian theories are pluralistic and sometimes have few characteristics in common (Sandel 1982; de-Shalit 1995). But all of them emphasize the significance of particular relationships and the norms that bind people together in communities. Some communitarians hold that obligations are *restricted* to communities, and that the idea of an abstract theory of justice that is not based on community values must be too empty to command the allegiance of community members. Thus Avner de-Shalit (1995) argues that our commitment to future generations is based on our understanding that we and they are members of the same transgenerational community. But more distant future generations may be very different from us, and it is not at all obvious that they are members of our community. Since the effects of our present actions may influence people's lives for tens of thousands of years, it is worth asking whether we can rightly consider the people who will live then to be part of a transgenerational community that includes us. To test this, it may be sufficient to compare the present international community with the trans-historical community that includes people who are equally distant in the past. When we go back far enough, however, perhaps we will find that our community bonds with present people in distant lands are stronger and more significant than our bonds to our most ancient ancestors. Community bonds dwindle and become thin as they stretch across long periods of time and over generations. This might make it difficult for a communitarian theory to account for any significant obligations to distant future generations. On the other hand, communitarians might incorporate the idea that we are an *intergenerational* community, and might incorporate concern for future generations in the interest that communities have to perpetuate themselves through time.

Liberal theories of justice, like their libertarian cousins, place a high value on individual liberties, but also include a role for positive rights, often to ensure that people are *equal* in some specified respect. Thus Rawls (1971) argues that the principles of justice should articulate fair terms for cooperation, and that these principles will protect fundamental rights and liberties (the "equal liberty principle"), and ensure fair equality of opportunity ("open offices principle"). Where it can be done without sacrificing rights or undermining fair equality of opportunity, social institutions are to be adjusted so that they are maximally beneficial for the worst-off members of society ("difference principle"). These principles are to be applied in an ordered hierarchy, with the principle of equal opportunity prior to the difference principle, and the equal liberty principle prior to both of the others. Because Rawls's view is both influential and controversial, it will be discussed further in the next section.

VII. Rawls on Intergenerational Justice

Rawls argues that the principles of justice embody fair terms of cooperation among different members of a pluralistic society, and that the appropriate principles are the ones we would adopt from an initial position which is intended to eliminate bias. This strategy, developing a theory of justice from an ideal of unbiased or impartial choice, has been employed by a number of different theorists including Harsanyi (1955), Vickrey (1960) and Mueller (1974), but is most famously associated with the work of Rawls (1971). In order to guarantee that the principles of justice will reflect the interests of every member of society, Rawls asks that we imagine the choice of principles of justice to take place among individuals who are blind to their identities. While they know general features of society, they do not know who they are or what their particular characteristics will be. This makes it impossible to select principles of justice on the basis of special advantages one might enjoy, or disadvantages one might suffer depending upon one's arbitrary characteristics. As Rawls argues, from this *original position* one would not select principles that are racist or sexist, because one must be aware of the possibility that one will be a member of the disadvantaged group. For the case of justice among contemporaries, Rawls posits that it would be rational to select two principles: the *equal liberty principle* specifies that every member of society is to enjoy the same fundamental liberties consistent with equal liberty for everyone. The *principle of tolerable inequality* has two parts: the first part, the *open offices requirement*, specifies that positions of advantage in society must be open to all under conditions of equal opportunity. The second part, the *difference principle*, limits the range of acceptable social inequalities: inequalities are justified only if they are maximally beneficial to the least advantaged members of society.

Rawls argues that the difference principle is inappropriate as a principle of justice between generations. If we were to adopt the principle that generational inequalities are unjust unless they are maximally beneficial to the worst-off generation, he urges, then it would be impossible for one generation to *save* resources in order to ensure that their descendants would be better off. Generational saving, as Rawls sees it, improves the prospects of later generations relative to those of earlier generations. Since no generation benefits from its own intergenerational saving, on Rawls's view, earlier generations would be the worst off, and an intergenerational difference principle would forbid sacrifices by earlier generations to benefit subsequent generations.

This argument is questionable at best: intergenerational saving can indeed benefit the savers, when generations overlap over long periods of time (Heath 1997). And where generations overlap, it is sometimes possible for the members of different generations to develop a cooperative system that will benefit *all* generations, including the first one (Wolf 2010). The ability to do this will depend, among other things, on the rate at which saved resources grow from period to period and between one generation and the next. If this is so, then Rawls may have abandoned the intergenerational difference principle for the wrong reasons.

The view Rawls articulates, however, is independently plausible and interesting in its own right (1971, 1999a–b): he specifies a two-stage process whereby earlier generations save so that later generations will be able to implement more effective protections for fundamental rights and liberties. Such saving is appropriate when an earlier generation is not sufficiently wealthy to ensure the possibility for "a worthwhile life" for all citizens. In a relatively late work, Rawls writes:

> The purpose of a just (real) savings principle is to establish (reasonably) just institutions for a free constitutional democratic society (or any well-ordered society) and to secure a social world that makes possible a worthwhile life for all its citizens. Accordingly, savings may stop once just (or decent) basic institutions have been established. At this point, real saving may fall to zero; and existing stock only needs to be maintained or replaced, and nonrenewable resources carefully husbanded for future use as appropriate.
>
> (1999b: 107)

Rawls does not specify the amount that one generation should save for the next, but he does represent saving as a sacrifice for the earlier generations, to be undertaken for the benefit of those who come later. The saving rate cannot ask an unreasonable amount from the present generation, but should balance the claims of the present against those of the future. It is clear in Rawls's discussion that he regards intergenerational *dissaving* to be unjustifiable: the earlier generations may not consume so much that they leave *less* for subsequent generations than they themselves enjoyed.

In the spirit of Rawls's project, we might ask whether this two-stage scheme is fair to members of the earlier generation, who must save for the sake of their relatively wealthier descendants. It may be necessary to consider the question of saving from both the *intra*generational and *inter*generational perspectives: presumably the members of the earlier generation who are required to save are those who are relatively well off. Of course, contributing their resources to *saving* rather than to the improvement of the situation of their worst-off contemporaries does mean that the worst-off members of the earlier generation will not be as well off as they would have been in the absence of any intergenerational saving at all. But if the goal for these resources is to mitigate the disadvantage of those who are worse off, that goal may sometimes be better served by devoting resources to *future* people who would be disadvantaged, rather than to those who are presently worst off. In that case, we might consider the complaint of the worst-off members of the present generation to their better-off contemporaries: "You could have done better for us," they might urge, "therefore your choice to save for later generations is unfair!" When intergenerational saving is just, perhaps the better off have an adequate reply to this complaint: "While it's true that you're worse off than you would have been," they might reply, "the people who are benefited by this saving are also badly off. We made the choice to benefit them rather than benefiting you, but by saving we can reduce the number of people who will have a legitimate complaint."

Is this response satisfactory? Rawls seems to have in mind the case where the saving of earlier generations enables subsequent generations to achieve a more perfectly just society. There is no guarantee, however, that the present people whose claims are overridden will not be still worse off than those in later generations who benefit from intergenerational saving. In this sense, the trade-off involved looks like just the kind of regressive move that Rawls usually prohibits.

There are at least two salient ways in which a Rawlsian might respond to this objection. First, note that the problem arises only when those who benefit from intergenerational saving are better off than the worst-off members of the present generation. This will not always be the case. Where imperfectly just institutions are passed from one generation to the next, the worst-off members of one generation may frequently be no better off, or even worse off, than the present worst-off group. While Rawls does not seem to have considered the details of this problem, it is possible that he might have specified that intergenerational saving is *only* just where those who benefit from it would otherwise be worse off than the worst-off members of the present generation. That move would be consistent with Rawls's overall theory and the conception of reciprocity he carefully develops. But in some circumstances the resultant account of intergenerational saving would permit the perpetuation of unjust (or imperfectly just) institutions from one generation to the next, which is a result Rawls clearly hopes to avoid.

A second possible response would permit some regressive intergenerational transfers for the sake of improving institutions over time. In several places in his later works, Rawls allows that one might articulate a *needs* principle, and make this principle lexically prior to the other principles of justice:

> . . . the first principle covering the equal basic rights and liberties may easily
> be preceded by a lexically prior principle requiring that citizens' basic needs be
> met, at least insofar as their being met is necessary for citizens to understand
> and to be able fruitfully to exercise [their] rights and liberties. Certainly any
> such principle must be assumed in applying the first principle.
>
> (1993: 7)

This passage considers a major change in Rawls's theory. But the spirit of this proposal is quite in line with other things Rawls writes in his discussion of intergenerational justice: the purpose of intergenerational saving, he says in the passage quoted earlier, is to secure just institutions that make possible "a worthwhile life for all citizens" (1999b: 107). Since the satisfaction of basic needs might be identified as necessary for a worthwhile life, this sounds very much like a requirement that basic needs should be met.

VIII. Intergenerational Needs, Sustainability and the Environment

There are several different reasons why one might regard meeting basic needs as a high-priority requirement of justice. First, a society that fails to meet citizens' needs might not be defensible to all of its members, but people may have no reason to respect institutions that cannot be justified to them. People whose needs are unmet may have no good reason to respect other people's property rights, for example. So if institutions of government are supposed, among other things, to provide a scheme of cooperation that supports justifiable property rights, it had better provide for basic needs. Second, satisfaction of basic needs is necessary for the meaningful exercise of the rights and liberties that justice protects. Rights to free speech and movement, for example, may be irrelevant to a person whose fundamental needs are unmet.

There are different ways to formulate a needs principle, and to connect such a principle to a theory of intergenerational justice. One might, for example, prioritize the claims of those who are worst off up to the point where needs are met. A concern with such a prioritarian view is that it might require overlooking the needs of many if there are a few people whose needs are very difficult to meet. Alternately, one might adopt a principle to minimize the number of people whose basic needs are unmet. The latter principle would allow *triage* decisions whereby the needs of those who are worst off might receive lower priority than those of people who may more easily be brought above the minimal level of need provision.

Intergenerationally, the view that meeting needs is a first priority of justice implies a sustainability requirement. The 1987 report of the World Commission on Environment and Development (WCED) specifies a conception of sustainable development that focuses on needs as a first priority. According to this report, usually called the Brundtland Report, sustainable development is development that "meets the needs of the present generation without compromising the ability of future generations to meet their needs" (WCED 1987: 43). This famous phrase can be formulated as a general criterion of sustainability:

Brundtland sustainability
Institutions are sustainable when they meet the needs of the present generation without compromising the ability of future generations to meet their needs.

More simply and generally, one might formulate this as a conception of *human* sustainability, which focuses on the ability of human institutions to continue to meet human needs:

Human sustainability
Institutions are humanly sustainable only if their operation does not leave later generations worse equipped to meet their needs than members of earlier generations.

While the requirement of human sustainability may be a plausible first principle of intergenerational justice, it may not be entirely adequate as a principle for environmental law or policy. While the goal to meet human needs and the goal of environmental preservation are often coincident, ensuring human sustainability will not always guarantee appropriate environmental protections. For example, one way to assure that future needs will not go unmet would be to take steps to prevent the *existence* of future generations, or to take steps to diminish their number. In that case, the requirements of human need might diminish over time, and preservation of the environment might be *unnecessary* for the satisfaction of human needs.

If we have an independent interest in environmental preservation, it might be necessary to articulate that need in an independent principle of *environmental* sustainability, as opposed to human sustainability. As before, this conception will focus on human institutions and their effect on the environmental systems in which they exist:

> *Environmental sustainability*
> Institutions are environmentally sustainable when their operation leaves the environmental systems with which they interact or on which they depend no more damaged in successive generations than they were in earlier generations.

Application of this principle would require the development of a principle of environmental *damage*. This concept will itself be controversial, since one might articulate such a concept in terms of human interests, or in terms that are more directly non-anthropocentric.

Norms of justice apply between *persons*, and thus may simply be inadequate to account for our obligations concerning the natural world. Nonetheless, in many circumstances, environmental sustainability will also be a requirement of justice: we have every reason to believe that future generations will be worse off, and that many of their members will be unable to meet basic needs, if earlier generations destroy the natural systems of the world. But what should we conclude when we find cases for which human and environmental sustainability diverge? If environmental sustainability is not a principle of justice, will this imply that it must be a *low*-priority objective? Mill's Harm Principle implies that it is wrong to limit people's liberty for the sake of environmental sustainability. Noting this, fundamentalist Millian libertarians must conclude that the objective to promote environmental sustainability will not justify coercive legislation. Others may take this implication as sufficient reason to reject Mill's harm principle, counting the protection of the environment as a sufficient ground for the limitation of at least *some* liberties, even where this is not necessary to prevent human harms.

IX. Future Generations in Environmental Law

Legislators often refer to the interests of distant future generations when proposing and defending environmental legislation. But legal action expressly in defense of distant future interests is extremely uncommon. Some advocates urge that appropriate legal reform would include stronger protections for distant future interests, and some have urged constitutional reforms aimed at providing protection for fundamental rights of future people (Weston and Bach 2009). There have, however, been a few valiant attempts to incorporate protections for future generations into international and domestic legal regimes.

In a recent noteworthy case, briefly mentioned in section III above, the Supreme Court of the Philippines agreed to hear a suit in which the plaintiffs claimed to represent not only their own interests, but the interests of future generations of Philippine citizens. The Philippine Constitution expressly includes guarantees for the right to a "balanced and healthful ecology," and in *Minors Oposa v. DENR* (1993) the court asserts that this right provides present protection for the interests of unborn generations of Filipinos. The court voided existing timber-harvesting licenses on the ground that the proposed harvests would irreparably damage the environmental interests of present and future citizens.

Another noteworthy attempt to provide legal protection for future generations took place in 1893, when Britain and the United States conducted negotiations concerning the slaughter of fur seals. During the negotiations, United States representatives asked that the discussion should be governed by two underlying principles:

> First, no possessor of property, whether an individual man, or a nation, has absolute title to it. His title is coupled with a trust for the benefit of all mankind.
>
> Second, the title is further limited. The things themselves are not given him, but only the usufruct or increase. He is but the custodian of the stock, or principle thing, holding it in trust for the present and future generations of man.
>
> (Carter 1893: 59; Weston 2008: 416)

Rights "in usufruct" are rights to the *increase* of a sustainable stock, but require that the stock itself be undiminished by the harvest of this increase. The view that human property rights are rights in usufruct is the view that owners may use resources at a sustainable rate, but may not consume them faster than they regenerate. The purpose of the Fur Seal Arbitration was to develop legislation that would regulate the slaughter of seals and protect fur-bearing animal populations from overexploitation. The U.S. representatives went on to assert as a principle of positive international law that:

> . . . the title which nature bestows upon man to her gifts is of the usufruct only, is . . . but a corollary . . . for in saying that the gift is not to this nation or that, but to mankind, all generations, future as well as present, are intended. The earth was designed as the permanent abode of man through ceaseless generations. Each generation, as it appears upon the scene, is entitled only to use the fair inheritance. It is against the law of nature that any waste should be committed to the disadvantage of the succeeding tenants. . . . That one generation may not only consume or destroy the natural increase of the products of the earth, but the stock also, thus leaving an inadequate provision for the multitude of successors which it brings into life, is a notion so repugnant to reason as scarcely to need formal refutation.
>
> (Carter 1893: 65–66; Weston 2008: 417)

This theory of property and resource use was revolutionary, and might have had far-reaching consequences had it been accepted as proposed, as a principle of positive international law. Burns Weston writes, "Regrettably, but perhaps understandably from an 1893 perspective, the arbitrators did not accept this argument. It was a 'novel' argument, they said, insufficiently grounded in international law" (2008: 417). But as

Weston notes, the arbitrators did not reject the proposed principles as the foundation for a theory of intergenerational justice and resource use, but only the more contentious claim that this conception of intergenerational equity was a settled principle of positive international law. The constituents of international law are often taken from precedent set by earlier negotiations, so if the Fur Seal Arbitration negotiators had accepted this view in 1893, it might very substantively have improved the resources available to present international arbitrators negotiating terms for environmental protection.

Relevantly similar negotiations are perpetually under way to govern the protection of the world's oceans, the atmosphere, global protection of endangered species and greenhouse gas emissions. Because national interests frequently conflict, international environmental laws will always be controversial, and it may not be reasonable to expect international agreements to include actionable protections for distant future interests. In the context of domestic environmental law, where community interests are more likely to converge, the prospects might seem better. Smaller communities often have a direct interest in the protection of local environmental resources, and have sometimes been able to enact rules to protect these interests. It must be noted, however, that local communities are not always effective guardians of environmental interests and resources. Some communities regularly lobby *against* local environmental protections, when community members believe their economic interests to be at odds with their interest in preserving the natural world.

X. Conclusion

It is not likely that international or domestic environmental law will soon be reorganized around the values of human and environmental sustainability or the protection of the rights and interests of distant future generations. But legislative proposals for environmental legislation are often defended as protecting environmental systems from damage, and sometimes defended in terms of the interests or rights of future people. There is every reason to expect that our obligation to preserve environmental systems and valuable resources for future generations will continue to be an important motive for environmental legislation, and that the rhetoric of intergenerational justice may gain increasing legal significance as we gain a more articulate understanding of the influence of present actions and policies on the lives of people who will inherit the earth after the present generations have passed it on. If our obligation to preserve resources and environmental systems for future generations is not mere rhetoric, but a genuine requirement of justice, then we may hope that such regulations will be crafted to protect future rights and interests.

References

Baier, A. (1981) "The Rights of Past and Future Persons," in E. Partridge, ed., *Responsibilities to Future Generations*, Buffalo, NY: Prometheus Press, pp. 171–83.

Beckerman, W. and J. Pasek (2001) *Justice, Posterity, and the Environment*, New York: Oxford University Press.

Carter, J. C. (1893) "Fur Seal Arbitration: Argument of the United States," in *Fur Seal Arbitration: Proceedings of the Tribunal of Arbitration*, Washington, D.C.: U.S. Government Printing Office.

Constitution of the Republic of the Philippines (1987) Article II, section 16.

Cowen, T. (2007) "Caring about the Distant Future: Why It Matters and What It Means," *University of Chicago Law Review* 74: 5–40.

Davidson, M. (2008) "Wrongful Harm to Future Generations: The Case of Climate Change," *Environmental Values* 17: 471–88.

de-Shalit, A. (1995) *Why Posterity Matters*, New York: Routledge.

Feinberg, J. (1984–1988) *The Moral Limits of the Criminal Law, Vols. 1–4*, New York: Oxford University Press.

—— (1986) "Wrongful Life and the Counterfactual Element in Harming," *Philosophy and Social Policy*, 4: 145–78.

Gardiner, S. (2011) *A Perfect Moral Storm*, New York: Oxford University Press.

Harsanyi, J. (1955) "Cardinal Welfare, Individualistic Ethics, and Interpersonal Comparisons of Utility," *Journal of Political Economy*, 63: 309–21.

Heath, J. (1997) "Intergenerational Cooperation and Distributive Justice," *Canadian Journal of Philosophy*, 27: 361–76.

Heyd, D. (1992) *Genethics*, Berkeley, CA: University of California Press.

Intergovernmental Panel on Climate Change (IPCC) (2007) *Climate Change 2007: Climate Change Impacts, Adaption, and Vulnerability*, Cambridge: Cambridge University Press.

Jefferson, T. (1977/1813) "Letter to Isaac McPherson," in M. Peterson, ed., *The Portable Thomas Jefferson*, New York: Penguin Books, pp. 525–32.

Locke, J. (1963/1714) *Second Treatise of Government*, New York: Cambridge University Press.

Mill, J. S. (1982/1859) *On Liberty*, Cambridge: Hackett Publishing Co.

Minors Oposa v. Secretary of the Department of Environment and Natural Resources (1993) 33 I.L.M. 173 (1994) Philippines Supreme Court.

Mueller, D. (1974) "Intergenerational Justice and the Social Discount Rate," *Theory and Decision* 5: 263–73.

Nozick, R. (1974) *Anarchy, State, and Utopia*, New York: Basic Books.

Page, T. (1977) *Conservation and Economic Efficiency*, Baltimore, MD: Resources for the Future.

Parfit, D. (1984) *Reasons and Persons*, Oxford: Oxford University Press.

Rawls, J. (1971) *A Theory of Justice*, Cambridge, Mass.: Harvard University Press.

—— (1993) *Political Liberalism*, New York: Columbia University Press.

—— (1999a) *A Theory of Justice*, revised edition, Cambridge, Mass.: Harvard University Press.

—— (1999b) *The Law of Peoples*, Cambridge, Mass.: Harvard University Press.

Sandel, M. (1982) *Liberalism and the Limits of Justice*, New York: Cambridge University Press.

Shrader-Frechette, K. (2005) *Environmental Justice*, New York: Oxford University Press.

—— (2010) *Taking Action, Saving Lives: Our Duties to Protect Environmental and Public Health*, New York: Oxford University Press.

Steiner, H. and Vallentyne, P. (2009) "Libertarian Theories of Intergenerational Justice," in A. Gosseries and L. Meyer, eds., *Intergenerational Justice*, New York: Oxford University Press, pp. 50–76.

Vickrey, W. (1960) "Utility, Strategy, and Social Decision Rules," *Quarterly Journal of Economics* 74: 507–35.

Weston, B. H. (2008) "Climate Change and Intergenerational Justice," *Vermont Journal of Environmental Law* 9: 375–430.

—— and Bach, T. (2009) "Recalibrating the Law of Humans with the Laws of Nature: Climate Change, Human Rights, and Intergenerational Justice," working paper, Vermont Law School, University of Iowa, http://www.vermontlaw.edu/Documents/CLI%20Policy%20Paper/CLI_Policy_Paper.pdf.

Wolf, C. (1995) "Contemporary Property Rights, Lockean Provisos, and the Interests of Future Generations," *Ethics* 105: 791–818.

—— (2009a) "Intergenerational Justice, Human Needs, and Climate Policy," in A. Gosseries and L. Meyer, eds., *Intergenerational Justice*, New York: Oxford University Press, pp. 347–76.

—— (2009b) "Do Future Persons Presently Have Alternate Possible Identities?" in M. Roberts and D. Wasserman, eds., *Harming Future Persons*, Dordrecht: Springer, pp. 93–114.

—— (2010) "Intergenerational Justice and Saving," in J. Lamont, G. Gaus and K. Favor, eds., *Values, Justice, and Economics*, Palo Alto, CA: Stanford University Press.

World Commission on Environment and Development (WCED) (1987) *Our Common Future*, New York: Oxford University Press.

Further Reading

For further reading, see: A. Gosseries and L. Meyer, eds. (2009) *Intergenerational Justice*, New York: Oxford University Press; T. Mulgan (2006) *Future People*, New York: Oxford University Press; D. Parfit (1984) *Reasons and Persons*, New York: Oxford University Press; M. Roberts and D. Wasserman, eds. (2009) *Harming Future Persons*, New York: Springer; J. Thompson (2009) *Intergenerational Justice*, New York: Routledge; E. Weis (1989) *In Fairness to Future Generations*, Tokyo: United Nations University Press; D. Gauthier (1986) *Morals by Agreement*, New York: Oxford University Press; and A. Leopold (1949) *A Sand County Almanac*, New York: Oxford University Press.

(ix)

CONSTITUTIONALISM

27

CONSTITUTIONAL INTERPRETATION

Wilfrid J. Waluchow

Vexing Questions

Constitutional interpretation is a highly controversial practice. It raises a host of questions concerning its nature, its limits and its legitimacy or justification. These questions have consumed much time and energy among constitutional theorists, lawyers, legal scholars and philosophers of law. But the ensuing debates have not been confined to the academy. On the contrary, they often emerge into public view, and engage the interest of journalists, commentators and sometimes the general population, when highly controversial issues of constitutional law are decided in landmark cases. Critics of a court's decision sometimes complain that the judges have become far too "activist" by failing to restrict themselves to the task of interpreting the constitution, preferring instead to substitute their own views on the relevant moral and political issues for those expressly endorsed in the constitution—all under the guise of interpretation. Controversies arise, no less forcefully, when candidates are being considered for appointment to a court empowered to decide important constitutional issues. Serious questions concerning his approach to constitutional interpretation were front and center during the long, contentious process surrounding Robert Bork's potential appointment to the U.S. Supreme Court. Opposition revolved around two principal concerns: first, Bork's controversial moral views concerning hot-button issues like abortion and women's reproductive freedom; and second, his espousal of a very robust, and in the view of many, naive version of "originalism," the view (to be explored more fully below) that constitutional provisions are to interpreted solely in terms of "original understandings." So constitutional interpretation is not an arcane subject confined to the often-arid landscape of academic disputation. It is an issue of great public and political interest—and, of course, controversy. Here are some of the more salient questions that arise when the subject of constitutional interpretation comes to the fore.

Is constitutional interpretation at all like interpretation in disciplines like literary studies or history, or perhaps even the natural and social sciences where investigators are sometimes said to interpret the available data? Some think so, viewing interpretation itself as a kind of generic social practice of which literary criticism, historical analysis and constitutional interpretation are species (Dworkin 1986; Fish 1989). Dworkin develops a very general theory of interpretation, focusing on what he calls "constructive interpretation," from which it follows that the interpretation of a novel, or a series of decisions concerning the requirements of a written constitution, always represents an attempt to make the object of interpretation "the best it/they can be." Of course interpretation can sometimes be of a form quite different from the shape it takes when one interprets a text or string of words, where one attempts to reveal or exhibit the meaning of one set of words by way of a second set of words. We often talk of historians interpreting historical trends, actors interpreting plays and even musicians interpreting musical scores. Thus, a further question one might ask, should one seek to derive a theory of constitutional interpretation from a more general theory, is the following: is constitutional interpretation similar in any important and relevant ways to historical interpretation or to what we might call "interpretive performances," such as an interpretation, by the Berlin Philharmonic, of Beethoven's Ninth? The latter, of course, is an interpretive performance we might, in turn, be led to describe (in our own written interpretation of that interpretive performance) as a tour de force, displaying aspects of Beethoven's creative masterpiece that had hitherto lain underappreciated or undiscovered.

This strategy of generating a theory of constitutional interpretation from a very general theory of interpretation, though perhaps interesting and promising in some contexts, is not one that is generally pursued by constitutional scholars. Instead, the focus is on explaining how constitutional interpretation relates to other forms of legal interpretation. And that is the course we will pursue in this entry. Narrowing our focus, then, we might begin by asking this important question: to what extent is constitutional interpretation like the interpretation of ordinary statutes? Perhaps the answer depends on whether the constitution consists entirely, partly or even at all, of written instruments, such as the Basic Law for the Federal Republic of Germany or Canada's Constitution Act, 1982. There is, of course, no necessity that constitutional law includes, let alone exclusively, written instruments. A state's constitution might consist almost entirely of important common-law rules, customs and conventions, as was often said of the United Kingdom for centuries. But this is not the norm. Usually a state's constitution includes at least one central written instrument. Yet another point to bear in mind is that constitutional *law* may be different from *the constitution*, where the latter is meant to refer to a historical document like the United States Constitution. It can, as just noted, include various rules, customs and conventions, as well as years worth of interpretive decisions originating in court decisions revolving around the requirements of the relevant written instrument(s). One might argue that the constitution, properly construed, includes these interpretive decisions. This is the view of David Strauss, who distinguishes, for purposes of United States law, between the written U.S. Constitution and the "small- c constitution: the constitution as it actually operates, in practice" (Strauss 2010: 35). The "living constitution," he suggests, is the two combined. Whether this is true, or whether such decisions are better classified as part of constitutional law (not the constitution itself) is an interesting question with which we needn't be concerned. The point remains that discussions of constitutional interpretation almost invariably focus on the interpretation of written constitutional instruments—and it is on the interpretation of these that we will focus.

To what extent, then, is the interpretation of a constitutional instrument like the United States Constitution similar to the interpretation of an ordinary penal statute passed by Congress? It is tempting to answer that interpretation must be roughly the same in both contexts. After all, in each case what takes place is the interpretation of a canonical string of words, normally put together, adopted and ceremoniously proclaimed by way of special acts of special persons with the authority to create that particular kind of legal norm. But that answer would be far from correct. Interpreting the

United States Constitution is a decidedly different enterprise from interpreting the U.S. Copyright Act of 1976. The fact that the former is *the constitution* and the latter an ordinary Act of Congress marks a significant difference between the two activities, a difference largely dependent on special features of constitutions and the role(s) they play in law, politics and social life, differences to which we will return below. That there are these crucial differences suggests a decidedly different approach to the interpretation of a constitution. This is particularly so when a case turns on how we are to interpret those provisions that deal with abstract civil rights (e.g., the right to due process of law or to equality) over which there is so much controversy and upon which we will focus in this entry. What exactly that different approach is, or ought to be, in the case of constitutional interpretation, is the subject of intense controversy among legal practitioners and theorists. Views range from those who espouse originalism to those who reject this approach as either politically and morally unattractive, impossible to implement in practice or largely or entirely incoherent. As we shall see, these stark differences of view are usually rooted in very different views on either the proper role of a constitution or on the appropriate role of a judge within constitutional democracies.

A further, central issue that figures prominently in discussions about constitutional interpretation is this: is that practice, when pursued properly—i.e., as an exercise of *interpretation*, not something else masquerading as interpretation—exclusively a matter of attempting to retrieve, so as to conserve and apply, existing meaning(s)? If so, in what do such existing meanings consist? Is an attempt to interpret a constitutional text perhaps an attempt to discern the intentions of its authors? If this is the route one must take, then yet another question immediately arises: who precisely are to count as the constitution's authors? Those who wrote it up? Those who approved it at a special constitutional convention? Those, e.g., individual state governments, who later ratified what the authors had earlier created, as occurred in the United States? These last two answers assume, however, forms of constitutional creation that are not always present. Constitutions sometimes come into existence in the absence of an originating convention, and often do so without anything remotely like a formal process of ratification. Sometimes constitutions come about through the normal activities of legislative bodies like Parliament or the Bundestag. At other times, they are simply imposed by one political regime and taken up later by a new regime, or eventually accepted by a population which may initially have struggled against the original imposition but now accepts both the legitimacy of the imposing regime and its constitution. This latter scenario might be thought to raise yet another possibility: that the true authors of a constitution are, in reality, "the people" whose constitution it is. This, however, stretches the idea of authorship beyond the bounds of intelligibility. "The people" may reasonably be said to have accepted, or perhaps even consented to or adopted, the constitution, and these facts may serve a crucial role in determining a constitution's legitimacy. But this is a far cry from saying that the constitution belongs to them as the creative product of their authorship.

Let's assume that the constitution did have specific authors and that we know their identities. If interpreting the constitution is in some way tied to the intentions of these authors, then yet another question immediately arises: which of the possibly many intentions they might have had are we to attempt to discern for purposes of constitutional interpretation? Are we, perhaps, to focus exclusively on the intention to create fundamental laws understood according to the usual conventions of understanding prevalent within the relevant community at the time of authorship? It is this intention, but applied to conventions existing *at the time of interpretation*, that Joseph Raz (1996) claims must, of necessity, govern all attempts to interpret the existing meaning of enacted law. Whether other kinds of intentions can count is, for Raz, dependent on a number of factors which may vary from one situation to the next. In any event, if we accept some such convention-based answer to our question, a further question now emerges: what is the relevant community whose conventions count in determining constitutional meaning? The population at large? The community of prominent political actors whose views and actions were in some way instrumental in the constitution's creation? Lawyers? Constitutional lawyers? One reason we might want to identify the relevant community with one of the latter two groups is that legal meanings often diverge from the ways in which terms are widely understood within the general population. In some jurisdictions the legal meaning of the word "assault" (the threat of violence) is quite different from the meaning of the word "battery" (actual physical violence) whereas in general parlance, assault is understood to involve the latter. There is little reason to believe that similar divergences of meaning do not exist at the constitutional level, where phrases like "due process of law" and "freedom of speech" often take on meanings that diverge considerably from ordinary meanings.

So the identity of the relevant community of understanding can be crucial. Yet another question that emerges, once we begin to focus on authorial intentions, is this: should we sometimes, or perhaps even always, count the purposes the authors sought to achieve by enacting what they did? But which purposes and at which level of generality? In some very general sense, the purpose of every constitutional provision is to effect the realization of justice, or at least a reasonable balance of all the relevant values and principles at play in creating a constitution. But presumably this is not much help in settling difficult interpretive questions. So perhaps we must look for something more specific, e.g., the goal of fostering a vibrant democracy, which arguably is one of the central purposes behind free-expression guarantees? But is this specific enough? Or must we look for something even more concrete? Must we also count as relevant the particular applications the authors intended their words to cover—the specific kinds of things they intended to protect, prohibit or permit, e.g., the freedom to express a political opinion in a newspaper? If intended applications don't count, then we'll need to know why. If they do count, then we're faced with further questions: what if we have very good evidence that the authors were actually very poor draftsmen, selecting words whose conventional understandings may lead to applications that would thwart or hinder achievement of the very goals and purposes they intended or hoped to realize? How are constitutional interpreters to deal with these conflicting intentions? And finally, how does one interpret when, as is all too often the case, we have inconclusive evidence as to what the relevant authors' intentions might have been? Perhaps some of the authors intended X, while others intended Y.

Our discussion thus far has assumed that constitutional interpretation consists exclusively of a retrieval exercise, that is, an exercise of retrieving so as to conserve and apply already existing meaning(s). But is there sometimes, usually or perhaps even always, a decidedly creative or innovative aspect to constitutional interpretation, at least in some contexts? In other words, does constitutional interpretation sometimes alter, develop or replace existing meanings, that is, consist in what we will call " *innovative interpretation*"? The thought that it does, indeed must, has an air of plausibility, if only because many constitutional provisions, e.g., those upon which we are focusing, namely those we find in bills or charters of rights, are expressed in highly abstract moral terms like "equality," "due process" or "the principles of fundamental justice." As such, their interpretations seem ripe for alteration, development and supplementation, in much the same way that our nonlegal interpretations of abstract moral principles often change as we come to better (or at the very least different) understandings of morality's many demands. As recognized in *Edwards* ([1930] A.C. 124), now commonly referred to as "The Persons Case," there is a very real and important sense in which moral equality meant something decidedly different in 1930 than it did in the nineteenth century, before women were considered "persons" for purposes of common law. It may even be the case that it meant something different in the United States immediately after the Supreme Court's denouncement of racial segregation in *Brown* ((1954) 347 U.S. 483) than it did immediately before that landmark decision. But if this is true, then we are faced with another, equally difficult question: if constitutional meanings can or must change by way of innovative interpretation, what is to be done if new, current meanings contradict, say, the meanings the authors can be presumed to have intended, had in mind or presupposed when they did what they did—i.e., enact such and such a string of words with these particular meanings? This, as suggested above, is a distinct possibility. It is highly plausible to suppose, e.g., that the authors of the Fourteenth Amendment to the United States Constitution understood "equal protection of the laws" in ways that did not authorize courts to declare separate but equal facilities unconstitutional. Yet the current understanding of that phrase, both within the United States and elsewhere, is such as to render such facilities clearly unconstitutional. If this is so, and if these changes are considered well within the boundaries of justified constitutional development brought about through innovative constitutional interpretation, then what sense can we make of the idea of *constitutional authorship* and the authority seemingly tied up with this practice? Can such steps be taken and yet the practice of constitutional interpretation remain genuinely *interpretative*? Does constitutional interpretation become nothing more than making constitutional texts mean whatever we want them to mean?

So perhaps allowing for so-called innovative interpretation actually results in a type of activity essentially different from what we can meaningfully call "constitutional interpretation." That is, maybe what we have in such cases is not constitutional *interpretation* but *revision, amendment* or *construction*. In all such cases of so-called innovative constitutional interpretation, the existing constitution will simply have been replaced, in part, with something else newly created by the act(s) of the interpreter(s). Those who begin to feel uneasy about such a prospect—i.e., the prospect that innovative judicial interpreters are actually changing the constitution while purporting to interpret it—have at least three options. One is simply to declare such innovative interpretations out of bounds for the judiciary, an option taken by many originalists. But this is not a strategy open only to such theorists. It is also, somewhat paradoxically, a view endorsed by Ronald Dworkin, one of originalism's most forceful critics. Dworkin's distinction between "concepts" and "conceptions" (1977) and his claim that constitutional authors (often) intend to enact provisions embodying the former but not the latter, allows him, he believes, to claim that the meanings of the rights provisions of a constitution—i.e., the abstract concepts or principles of political morality it embodies—have not changed, despite the radically different constructive interpretations of those abstract concepts and principles endorsed by constitutional interpreters over time. On this view, an innovative interpretation is one that introduces a new interpretation of an unchanged abstract principle embodied in a constitution whose authorial meaning remains unaltered.

A second option for those worried over the prospect that innovative interpretation actually changes the constitution is to find some way to make sense of the idea that changed meaning does not have this result. More concretely, one might try to explain the idea that the Fourteenth Amendment to the United States Constitution has not changed even though its (unchanged) guarantee of equal protection of the laws once meant that separate but equal schools are constitutionally permissible and now means that this institutional arrangement stands as an unqualified repudiation of that protection. The prospects of success here seem dim, however, unless one identifies a constitution with nothing more than the particular string of words—the marks on paper—included within the written instrument. Now, it is true that innovative constitutional interpretations do not affect the actual string of words included within the written constitution. The phrase "equal protection of the laws" was introduced in 1868 and remains there to this day, despite the new understandings of its meaning developed and endorsed over the years. So constitutional interpretation, even when it results in a radically new understanding, is clearly different from the process of formal constitutional amendment, where new words are added or old ones are eliminated and possibly replaced with new ones. But this difference between formal amendment and innovative constitutional interpretation, significant though it may be, is not going to alleviate the concerns of those worried about the latter. And the reason is simple: it would be a serious mistake to view laws, and hence constitutional laws, as nothing more than strings of words. They are the *norms* expressed by those strings of words within a particular context (of utterance, use or understanding). They are, if you like, the meanings of the relevant string of words found within the written document, its actual content. And so the identity of the constitution created by an act of constitutional authorship is partly a function of the meaning of the string of words chosen, however that meaning is identified. If this is right, then when constitutional meaning changes, the constitution changes right along with it. And we are once again left to face the serious moral and political questions that result.

So the idea that the constitution remains unchanged, albeit with new meanings ascribed to it, seems an unpromising way to alleviate the concerns of those worried about innovative constitutional interpretations. A third way of responding is simply to bite the bullet and accept that the constitution does change along with whatever new meanings are ascribed to it. The United States Constitution that sanctioned separate but equal schools is not the same constitution that now condemns it. If this is the route one proposes to take, then new, equally thorny questions emerge, most urgently this one: by what authority do those who effect such changes—almost inevitably judges who decide constitutional cases—do so? Can their taking such a step be reconciled with the role a constitution is supposed to play in law and politics? More importantly, can it be reconciled with the demands of democracy? After all, in most systems the judges whose role it would be/is to offer these new, contentious interpretations of their constitution are neither elected by nor accountable to the population whose constitution they interpret. They are most certainly not accountable in the various ways in which elected officials are directly accountable, e.g., by threat of future electoral defeat. By what possible authority could such unaccountable individuals substitute their new meanings—in effect, new constitutional laws—for those set in place by those duly authorized to do so at earlier times?

Suppose that one could answer whatever qualms there might be over the legitimacy of a form of innovative constitutional interpretation that either results in a changed constitution, or leaves the constitution unchanged but with a new and different understanding attached. And suppose it made sense to continue to call this "constitutional interpretation." One will then have to answer further questions of equal significance and difficulty, questions like this: when should judges engage in such innovative interpretation and when should they stick to the task of retrieving and applying existing meanings? Are there any limits, rational, conventional, moral or otherwise, to innovative interpretation, assuming that we could, in principle, justify that practice? Or is it just a matter of judicial interpreters doing what they think best in the circumstances? If it's the latter, then in what sense can the constitution count as binding law? If it's the former, then what exactly are these limits and how are they to be observed in practice? Will we ever be able to identify a valid innovative interpretation? If not, what are the implications for our understanding of law—and, perhaps most importantly, for the practice of holding people accountable for breaching its requirements?

In what follows I will consider some of the above questions—which constitute, I hasten to add, a mere sampling of the broader range of questions in dispute. I will do so by discussing one of the liveliest and most contentious debates to have arisen in constitutional scholarship during the past several decades: the debate between originalists and their non-originalist opponents over interpretation of abstract moral provisions of constitutions, such as section 7 of the Canadian Charter of Rights and Freedoms, which "guarantees the right to life, liberty and security of the person and the right not to be deprived thereof except in accordance with the principles of fundamental justice." In very broad terms, the dispute between originalists and their opponents is between, on the one side, those who would restrict interpreters (or at least judicial interpreters) of such constitutional provisions to the retrieval of "original understandings." Originalists view anything more than an attempt to retrieve, so as to enforce and preserve, such original understandings as illegitimate constitutional revision masquerading as the interpretation of an unchanged original. On the other side, we have those who endorse what we will call "living tree constitutionalism" (henceforth LT theory). Proponents of this latter family of positions (Kavanagh 2003; Waluchow 2007; Strauss 2010) view originalism as a reactionary theory serving only to tie a community to the "dead hand of the past." Originalists, their LT opponents claim, render us incapable of responding rationally and responsibly to changing social circumstances and improved moral views about the requirements of the abstract principles articulated in a constitution. LT theorists, the originalist claims, recommend practices that threaten a number of cherished values, among them the rule of law and the separation of powers. In effect, they are happy to place the constitution in the hands of contemporary judges who are licensed, under the guise of interpreting it, to change it to suit their fancy or the whims of the day. But this, originalists claim, only serves to thwart cherished values secured by having a constitution, and may render all talk of genuine constitutional constraint meaningless.

Some Key Features of Constitutions and Constitutionalism

If the above discussion reveals anything at all, it is that a theory of constitutional interpretation must be sensitive to a number of key facts. Among these is the fact that those engaged in constitutional interpretation (bearing in mind that our focus is exclusively on the interpretation of the abstract moral provisions of *written* constitutions) are not only interpreting laws, and are not only interpreting laws that take written form. They are engaged in the interpretation of a *constitution*, the most fundamental of all the written laws governing their political community. In order fully to understand constitutional interpretation, and just what is at stake in contemporary debates over its nature and legitimacy, it is therefore helpful to consider first some of the distinctive features of written constitutions, and of the general idea associated with their use, "constitutionalism."

In one very basic sense of the term, a constitution consists of a set of fundamental norms constituting or creating government powers and authority. Understood in this way, all states have constitutions and all states are constitutional states. Anything recognizable as a state must have some acknowledged means of constituting the three standard forms of government power: legislative power (making new laws), executive power (implementing laws) and judicial power (adjudicating disputes under laws). When scholars talk of constitutionalism and a constitutional state, however, they normally mean something more than this. They mean not only that there are norms creating legislative, executive and judicial powers, but that these (or related) norms shape and impose limits on those powers. Often these limitations are in the form of individual or group rights against government, rights to things like free expression, association, equality and due process of law. But it is important to be clear that constitutional limits can come in a variety of forms. They can also concern the *scope* of authority and the *mechanisms* used in exercising the relevant power. To have a constitution in this sense is not only to have an instrument that empowers government, it is to have an instrument which at the same time limits those powers in significant ways. It is also to insist that government officials, bodies and agencies observe the specified limits, and that the authority of their/its actions depends on observance of them. The most contentious issues of constitutional interpretation concern the interpretation of those abstract civil rights provisions in which the limits imposed are of a decidedly moral nature. Their decidedly moral nature no doubt explains why there is so much controversy surrounding them.

So constitutions, in the sense of the term that will concern us here, serve not only to create but also to shape and limit the various powers of government. A further, characteristic feature of constitutions, so understood, is that they are typically designed to last a long time. As Joseph Raz puts it, a constitution "is meant to serve as a stable framework for the political and legal institutions of the country, to be adjusted and amended from time to time, but basically to preserve stability and continuity in the legal and political structure, and the basic principles that guide its institutions" (Raz 1998: 153). Raz sums up this *first* feature by saying that a constitution is "*stable*, at least in aspiration."

A *second* characteristic feature of constitutions is one to which we have already paid some attention: they take canonical form in one or more written documents. These written documents serve as the primary focus of constitutional interpretation, and their abstract civil rights provisions are often seen to embody and express a community's most fundamental moral and political commitments. Because of this, a constitution often takes on a special symbolic role: it serves as the focal point for discussions surrounding the moral and political identity of the community whose deepest fundamental commitments it is normally taken to express.

A *third* characteristic feature of constitutions is that they constitute *superior law*. That is, when an ordinary law is declared by a superior court to be incompatible with the constitution, the latter in some way takes precedence. What exactly results from such a finding of incompatibility can vary from one jurisdiction to the next. In some systems, such a finding renders the ordinary law invalid and hence inoperative. If the law takes statutory form, it will be as if it had been repealed, or perhaps never adopted, by the responsible legislature. In other systems, with weaker forms of judicial review, a judicial declaration of incompatibility does not mean that the ordinary law ceases to have force and effect. In the UK, with its relatively new Human Rights Act, the ordinary law remains operative until such time, if such a time ever comes about, that the legislature responds so as to amend or repeal the offending law. Of course, any legislature that fails to take such a step runs the risk that it will be perceived as being prepared to run roughshod over the constitution. Few legislatures in healthy democracies are prepared to assume this risk.

A *fourth*, crucial feature of constitutions is that, for the sake of facilitating continuity and stability, they tend to be *entrenched*. What this means is that those whose powers are constitutionally limited—i.e., the organs of government—are not legally empowered to change or expunge those limits using whatever standard procedures are normally used for the introduction, amendment and repeal of laws. Most written constitutions contain amending formulae requiring things like constitutional assemblies, super-majority votes, referenda or the agreement of not only the national government in a federal system but also some number or percentage of the sub-national governments or regional units within the federation. The result is that most constitutions are not easily changed. It is very difficult, if not in many cases well nigh impossible, to muster the political will and resources required to change or replace a constitution using one or more of these methods. This, as we shall see, has significant consequences for debates about the nature and legitimacy of constitutional interpretation. The fact that constitutions tend to be heavily entrenched seems to imply that one group of people—those who were responsible for its introduction—can in effect tie the hands of other groups of people, sometimes living decades or centuries later. These latter groups can end up being severely restrained by constitutional limitations they find unacceptable but in practice unalterable. Whether this feature of constitutions can be reconciled with the democratic ideal of *ongoing* self-government is a question which divides constitutional authors, and which has led many to embrace the LT option.

A *fifth* characteristic feature of constitutions is that some of their provisions tend to be framed in very abstract, moral terms, while others, for example those which establish the terms of government offices, employ terms that are very concrete and nonmoral. Consider the Fourteenth Amendment of the United States Constitution, which prohibits a state government from denying "to any person within its jurisdiction the equal protection of the laws." Compare this with the provisions of that same constitution specifying the terms of qualification for the office of U.S. President. Section 1 declares that "He shall hold his Office during the Term of four Years." This latter provision is very rule-like, specific and does not include anything remotely like a moral term. And though its interpretation can fall prey to the kinds of indeterminacy and vagueness to which all laws are susceptible, difficult interpretive questions seldom arise. On matters with which such provisions deal, it is presumably thought important that there be clear ground rules, leaving little room for dispute and controversy within the rough and tumble of everyday politics. So specific rules are chosen which provide a more or less stable, noncontentious framework. As for the equal protection clause, or the Eighth Amendment's ban on "cruel and unusual punishment," it is not so clear that the dominant goals are continuity and stability. That the authors of the United States Constitution chose to prohibit activities described in these very abstract moral terms, instead of providing far more concrete nonmoral descriptions (they could, e.g., have barred drawing and quartering and other concretely specified forms of punishment), strongly suggests that something else is at play here, something more, or other, than the need to provide a stable framework of a kind facilitated by a phrase like "shall hold his Office during the Term of four Years." And it is this something else that divides originalists from their opponents.

Originalism

Originalism comes in a wide variety of forms (Bork 1990; Scalia 1997; Whittington 1999; Barnett 2004; Solum 2008). Some originalists believe that their view follows necessarily from a more general theory of interpretation: to interpret is necessarily to retrieve something that existed at the time of authorship—an original object. Others are happy to acknowledge that interpretation can also include innovative interpretation that in some way changes the original. But these originalists go on to argue, on moral and political grounds having to do with, e.g., the principles of democracy, the rule of law and values underlying the separation of powers, that innovative interpretations should never be pursued by constitutional interpreters. Other originalists are content to leave a little leeway here, suggesting something like the following: though there is a presumption, perhaps a very heavy one, in favor of interpretation as retrieval, it is one which can, on very rare occasions, be overcome. For example, an originalist might say that the presumption in favor of retrieval can be defeated when there is a discernible and profound sea change in popular views on some important issue of political morality. This was arguably the case in the United States with respect to slavery and equal protection. Yet another concession, in this case one that is characteristic of originalists, concerns the force and effect of authoritative court interpretations of the constitution. Many originalists believe that *Roe v. Wade* ((1973) 410 U.S. 113) rested on a mistaken interpretation of the United States Constitution, one that flew in the face of original meanings and intentions; but virtually no one denies that any contemporary interpretation of the First, Fourth, Fifth, Ninth and Fourteenth Amendments is justified only if it can be reconciled with that decision. Whether this concession is in fact consistent with the spirit of originalism is, however, highly questionable. Such "faint-hearted originalism" (Strauss 2010) seems to reduce, in the end, to a form of LT theory. Indeed, as we shall see in the next section, the role of judicial interpretations of abstract constitutional provisions is central to a prominent form of LT theory which views constitutional interpretation as largely a matter of common-law reasoning.

Another way in which originalists split is over the identity of the original object of interpretation. Some originalists focus on the retrieval of original intentions of constitutional authors, while others claim that the focus should be on original meanings or understandings. But intentions still seem to matter for the latter group because, in their view, among the intentions of constitutional authors is the intention to enact provisions that mean what they were generally understood to mean at the time of adoption, understood presumably in terms of conventions of interpretation which existed at that time. On the other hand, original meaning necessarily matters for those whose focus is original intentions. The primary means of conveying one's intentions in the context of legal enactment are the words actually chosen. And those words cannot convey one's intentions unless some standard meaning is assumed, a standard meaning to which both authors and readers have access and in terms of which the latter can, and are expected, to understand the meaning the authors intended to convey. But that meaning cannot be anything other than the original one because authors do not have crystal balls and therefore have no access to future meanings. An originalist who in this way focuses on intention may not, however, wish to restrict interpreters to original meanings and understandings. Should it turn out, for instance, that original understanding leads to unforeseen applications that we have good historical evidence to believe the authors did not intend to include, or would not have wished to include had they known what we now know, an originalist might allow these further intentions to override original understanding. The authors, and their intentions, are still being respected in such cases.

Among the ways in which one might be able to determine that constitutional authors did not intend, or would not have wished to endorse, a particular application suggested by original meaning is by appeal to the general purposes we have reason to believe they intended to achieve by enacting what they did. Sometimes these goals and purposes are explicitly expressed in the preamble to a constitution, as is often true in the case of ordinary statutes. But such statements of purpose in constitutions tend to be very broad and are therefore of very limited use in dealing with the more specific questions that arise under particular constitutional provisions. So appeal is sometimes made to official (and unofficial) debates and discussions surrounding the drafting, adoption or ratification of the constitution or the particular provision in question. Sometimes appeal is even made to widely held beliefs at the time on the relevant issue. Capital punishment, for example, was widely held in eighteenth-century America to be a perfectly acceptable response to murder and treason. Thus one might have very good historical reason to believe that it could not have been among the purposes of the Eighth Amendment to ban such a practice. An original understanding of that amendment that is sensitive to this fact might therefore support the constitutionality of capital punishment.

But perhaps things are not quite this simple. Suppose we agreed that the goal of the Eighth Amendment's authors was to ban cruel and unusual punishments, and that they believed that capital punishment did not fall within the extension of that phrase. If so, and if one believes that capital punishment is *in actual fact* cruel and unusual, then one might fashion an argument of the following sort, one which has, at least superficially, an originalist flavor. Respecting the intentions of the authors—to ban cruel and unusual punishment—actually *requires* that capital punishment be deemed unconstitutional, even though the authors would have disagreed. This, in effect, is the argument made by Dworkin, who submits that what he calls the "semantic intentions" of the authors of the Eighth Amendment—what it is they intended to say—was that an abstract, partly moral standard banning cruel and unusual punishment is to be observed by governments. This was, as it were, their (semantic) purpose in framing the Eighth Amendment in the way that they did. Respecting their intention, therefore, requires holding as unconstitutional whatever truly does come under the extension of that phrase, that is, whatever truly does constitute cruel and unusual punishment. Imagine, one might construe Dworkin as suggesting, that one could bring an author of the Eighth Amendment to life and that one could convince him, via good empirical and moral argument, that capital punishment is in actual fact cruel and unusual. How might he respond to the claim that the only way to respect his intentions is to continue to accept, as constitutional, the practice of capital punishment? His likely response would be to say: "We meant to ban cruel and unusual punishment, not what I can now see we incorrectly understood that ban to entail. If we had wanted to ban capital punishment specifically, we would have said so!" Whether appeal to semantic intentions in this way is enough to render one an originalist—if only a fainthearted one—is highly questionable, however.

Such an appeal seems to render one's theory of constitutional interpretation a form of LT theory, one which can easily ascribe a role to "semantic intentions."

In any event, originalists differ on the role, in constitutional interpretation, of goals and purposes, sometimes referred to as "further intentions." Some are prepared to allow some further intentions to override original meanings or understandings in some cases, while others reject the use of these intentions altogether. One reason is that the historical evidence concerning the existence and content of such intentions tends to be highly unreliable or inaccessible to later interpreters. One of the essential functions of law is the guidance of behavior. Yet one cannot be guided by a law unless one knows what it means. And if its meaning depends on factors about which there is great dispute, or which are largely inaccessible, as is more often than not true when it comes to the intentions of long-dead authors, then one cannot be guided by the law. Hence, rule-of-law arguments are sometimes used to justify precluding (significant) appeal to authors' intentions (further or otherwise) in all but exceptional cases. A second reason for rejecting appeal to further intentions is the fact that there is an important difference between what a constitution actually says or means and what those who created it might have wanted or intended to achieve in creating it. Interpretation is an attempt to retrieve so as to conserve or enforce the former, not the latter.

So originalism comes in a wide variety of forms. But the main divisions concern the object of interpretation (original intentions versus original understandings) and the theoretical grounding of that interpretive theory (interpretation is by its very nature the retrieval of an existing object—an original—and cannot therefore be innovative; or interpretation, though it can be innovative, should not be so, at least usually). Despite these important differences, originalism, as a general family of theories which ties constitutional interpreters to original understandings and/or intentions, is subject to a number of objections. For example, original intentions and understandings are often very unclear, if not largely indeterminate, leaving the interpreter with the need to appeal to other factors. Sometimes the only things upon which joint authors can agree are the words actually chosen. The intentions and understanding lying behind their agreement vary significantly. Let's consider intentions. They can range from the very general to the highly specific. At one end of the spectrum are the various and sometimes conflicting *purposes* the authors of a provision might have intended their creation to achieve (say, justice). At the other end are the very specific *applications* they might have had in mind when they agreed to the particular words upon which they settled (say, drawing and quartering). Different authors might have "intended" all, none or some of these purposes and applications when they agreed upon the Eighth Amendment. And there is considerable room for inconsistency and conflict. Constitutional authors, no less than legislators, union activists or the members of a church synod, can have different purposes and applications in mind *and yet settle on the same set of words*. Analogous things can be said of original understandings if these are to be our focus. These too can vary, often depending on the particular moral and political views of the person in question. One author or one segment of the public might have understood "equal protection of the laws" so as to preclude separate but equal facilities, while another might have understood that phrase in a way that entails the exact opposite. In light of these facts, it is usually unhelpful to rely on original intentions or understandings when interpreting a constitution.

Yet another serious difficulty faced by originalism is one to which attention was drawn above: contemporary life is often very different from the life contemplated by the authors of a constitution. As a result, many applications suggested by original intentions and understandings may now seem absurd or highly undesirable in light of new scientific and social developments and improved moral understanding. Modern life includes countless situations that the authors of a constitution could not possibly have contemplated, let alone meant to be dealt with in any particular way. The right to free speech that found its way into many constitutions in the early modern period could not possibly have been understood by its defenders to encompass, e.g., pornography on the Internet. In response to such difficulties, an originalist might appeal to what we might call "hypothetical intent." The basic idea is that an interpreter should always consider, in cases involving new, unforeseen circumstances, the hypothetical question of what the original authors *would have intended* to be done in the case at hand had they known what we now know to be true. We are, on this view, to put ourselves imaginatively in the authors' shoes and determine, perhaps in light of their intended purposes, and perhaps by way of analogy with whatever clearly intended applications we have reason to believe they had in mind, what they would have wanted done in the new circumstances. But this move is highly problematic. First, it presupposes that we can single out one consistent set of purposes and applications attributable to the authors. Yet as we have already seen, the authors of a constitution invariably have different things in mind when they agree on a constitutional text. Second, even if we could single out, at some appropriate level of generality, a single set of purposes and applications from which our hypothetical inquiry could proceed, it is unlikely that there will always be a uniquely correct answer to the counterfactual question of what the authors would have wanted or intended to be done in light of these factors. What would an eighteenth-century founder, firmly in favor of freedom of speech, have thought about pornography on the Internet in the circumstances in which we find ourselves in the twenty-first century? Thirdly, and perhaps most importantly, we are left with the question of why it much matters what a long-dead group of individuals might have intended or wanted done were they apprised of what we now know. The main appeal of originalism is that it appears to tie constitutional interpretation to facts about *historical decisions actually made* by individuals with the legitimate authority to answer questions concerning the proper shape and limits of government powers. If we are now to consider, not what they *did* decide, but what they *might have decided* had they existed today and knew what we now know, then the question naturally arises: why not just forget this theoretically suspect, counterfactual exercise and make the decisions ourselves? Why attempt to rely on the authority of the constitution's authors in such cases? Do we really want to perpetuate their possibly misguided views about the appropriate moral limits to government powers? Think back to Dworkin's imagined conversation with an author of the United States Constitution. Unless we reject completely the idea that there might be moral progress, or demand that any such progress must always be sacrificed for the sake of the stability and continuity allegedly guaranteed by rigid adherence to original understandings, there seems little reason to believe that we should be so tied. To think otherwise really would be to allow the dead hand of the past to govern the affairs of today in a way that cannot possibly be justified. And there is reason to believe that the authors of the constitution's abstract moral provisions would not have disagreed with this assessment. If they did, would they not have chosen their terms differently?

But if we are not to be tied to the dead hand of the past when we engage in constitutional interpretation, how are we to proceed? The dominant alternative, one that takes its inspiration from the difficulties in originalism detected in the preceding paragraph, is that family of views, alluded to earlier, which construes a constitution—or at least those parts of it that incorporate abstract moral principles—as a living tree whose limitations are sometimes open to revisiting and revision in light of those changing times and (one hopes) improved moral/political understandings that tend to cause originalists so much trouble.

Living Tree Interpretation

Whatever else might be said of law, this much is undeniably true: where law exists, various forms of conduct are rendered, or put forward as being, nonoptional. In other words, law by its very nature is intended to restrict behavior, often in significant ways. A law can also, of course, protect or empower us. But when it does, it typically does so by restricting the behavior of *someone else*, e.g., the person who is legally prevented from assaulting me or from entering my property. But in many instances, these restrictions can be removed or changed, as when a common-law precedent is overturned, or a statute repealed or amended because it no longer serves useful purposes. Not so with constitutions. As we saw above, they tend to be heavily entrenched. They are also meant to be long lasting, so as to serve the values of securing continuity and stability in the basic framework within which the often contentious affairs of law and politics are conducted. And, finally, they tend to include very abstract, moral provisions limiting the powers of government bodies in significant ways. Consider, for example, the First Amendment of the United States Constitution, according to which "Congress shall make no law respecting an establishment of religion, or prohibiting the free exercise thereof; or abridging the freedom of speech, or of the press; or the right of the people peaceably to assemble, and to petition the Government for a redress of grievances." These special features of constitutions give rise to a fundamental question, one that causes the originalist so much trouble and to which living tree constitutional interpretation provides a better answer: how can one group of people legitimately place entrenched constitutional impediments of a decidedly moral nature in the way of a second group of people who might live in radically different circumstances and perhaps with radically different moral views? How, in short, can one generation legitimately bind the behavior and moral choices of another? The answer to this intergenerational problem, living tree theorists contend, revolves around four basic claims:

(a) a constitution is the kind of thing whose abstract provisions can grow and adapt to its ever-changing environment without losing its identity and its guidance function;
(b) a constitution's abstract provisions should be allowed to grow and adapt to its (or their) environment;
(c) this process can take place via genuine constitutional interpretation, not formal amendment; and
(d) it can do so legitimately.

In defending this particular view of constitutions and their interpretation, LT theorists are of course focused on those abstract moral provisions upon which we have been concentrating: e.g., the Eighth Amendment of the U.S. Constitution or section 3(1) of the German Basic Law which proclaims that "All persons shall be equal before the law." According to the LT theorist, the meanings of these entrenched provisions consist in the rights or principles of political morality they express, not what those rights or principles were taken to require by those who chose them for inclusion in the constitution. Recall, again, our imaginary conversation between Dworkin and an American constitutional author. The choice to employ abstract moral terms, instead of using more concrete, nonmoral terms, is presumably made in recognition of at least four crucial facts: (1) it's important that governments not violate certain important rights of political morality; (2) constitutional authors cannot anticipate the future and the many cases in which these important rights will be in some way relevant; (3) constitutional authors do not always agree on what concretely is required in the many cases in which those rights are, or will later be seen to be, relevant; and (4) even when they do agree on what those rights concretely require, and are comfortable binding *themselves* to those understandings, they are not particularly comfortable doing so in respect of future generations who will live in very different times and may think very differently. And so the decision is made to express constitutional commitments in very abstract terms, leaving it to later generations, at later times, to substitute their possibly different concrete understandings for those of the authors (or perhaps more broadly those who lived at the time of authorship). The result is that as understandings of entrenched constitutional-rights provisions change, the results warranted by these provisions can legitimately change right along with them. And, importantly for the LT theorist who does not wish to surrender to the charge that she counsels infidelity to the constitution, these changes can occur without either the constitution or its meaning having changed, as would be true were a process of formal amendment successfully invoked.

Despite its undoubted appeal, LT theory faces a number of significant objections. Perhaps the most prominent ones are these: (a) the theory, it might be said, renders all talk of constitutional interpretation, properly understood as a retrieval exercise, utterly meaningless—constitutional interpretation becomes nothing more than unconstrained, constitutional creation masquerading as innovative interpretation; (b) LT theory might be said to rob the constitution of its ability to serve its guidance function—how can a party be guided by a constitution whose application to its conduct and choices will be determined by the unconstrained views of later "interpreters?"; and (c) LT theory is often charged with violating the separation-of-powers doctrine—if the constitution and its limits become whatever contemporary interpreters take them to mean, and if those interpreters tend to be found in courts, then democratically unaccountable judges end up deciding what the proper limits of government power shall be, a task for which they are eminently unqualified and which ought to be reserved for individuals democratically chosen to serve that function. Hence the appeal of originalism.

LT theorists have fashioned a number of responses to these objections. For instance, some claim that LT constitutional interpretation is by no means the unconstrained, arbitrary exercise its opponents often portray it to be. David Strauss (2010) and Wil Waluchow (2007) suggest that the ongoing interpretation of a constitution's abstract rights provisions is a process much like the process by which judges develop equally abstract common-law notions like negligence and the reasonable use of force. According to Strauss, the U.S. constitutional system "has become a common law system, one in which precedent and past practices are, in their own way as important as the written U.S. Constitution itself . . . [I]t is not one that judges (or anyone else) can simply manipulate to fit their own ideas" (Strauss 2010: 3). On this view, constitutional interpretation must accommodate itself to previous attempts to interpret and apply the rights provisions expressed in the constitution's text. And just as the traditional rules of precedent combine Burkean respect for the (albeit limited) wisdom and authority of previous decision makers with an awareness of the need to allow innovation in the face

431

of changing circumstances and views, so too must constitutional interpreters respect the wisdom and authority of previous interpreters, while allowing the constitution to adapt so as to respond to changing moral views, especially within the community. LT constitutional interpretation, though flexible, is no less constrained than reasoning under common law.

Another response open to LT theorists is to deny that their theory of constitutional interpretation ignores the special role played by a constitutional text and its authors. The text plays a key role insofar as any constitutional interpretation, innovative as it may be, must be consistent with that text, until such time as it is formally changed via some acknowledged process of constitutional amendment. That, as Strauss suggests, "is an essential part of our constitutional culture" (Strauss 2010: 103). There is also no reason to deny that original understandings of a constitution's abstract provisions can be relevant to later interpretations. This is especially so for interpretations that occur shortly after the constitution's adoption, when worries about binding future generations are not in play. Original understandings simply cannot be dispositive, at least not in perpetuity. In the end, the relative importance of factors like text, original understandings, later interpretations and intended purposes, is, as Raz (1996: 176–91) notes, a fundamentally moral question which cannot be answered in the abstract and without considering what it is that justifies, at that particular moment of interpretation, having an entrenched constitution at all, let alone one with such and such particular content. Sometimes, retrieval of existing meaning will be required, especially when the constitution is in its infancy and was partly meant to settle a range of concrete moral questions as to the proper limits of government power, *at least for a while*. But if an interpreter has good reason to believe that this settlement function has been overtaken by other more pressing concerns, perhaps the need to adapt in light of dramatically changed circumstances or much better moral understanding, then innovative interpretation may be called for. And once again, to say that constitutional interpreters must sometimes be innovative is not to say that a constitution can be interpreted to mean whatever the interpreter wants it to mean.

Acknowledgments

I wish to thank Fabio Shecaira and Andrei Marmor for very helpful comments on earlier drafts of this essay.

References

Barnett, R. E. (2004) *Restoring the Lost Constitution: The Presumption of Liberty*, Princeton: Princeton University Press.

Bork, R. (1990) *The Tempting of America: The Political Seduction of the Law*, New York: Simon and Schuster.

Brown v. Board of Education (1954) 347 U.S. 483.

Canadian Legal Information Institute, The Constitution Act, 1982, http://www.canlii.org/en/ca/const/const1982.html.

Copyright Act of 1976, Pub. L. No. 94–553, 90 Stat. 2541.

Dworkin, R. (1977) *Taking Rights Seriously*, Cambridge, Mass.: Harvard University Press.

—— (1986) *Law's Empire*, Cambridge, Mass.: The Belknap Press of Harvard University Press.

Edwards v. Canada (Attorney General) [1930] A.C. 124.

Fish, S. (1989) *Doing What Comes Naturally: Change, Rhetoric, and the Practice of Theory in Literary and Legal Studies*, Durham, NC: Duke University Press.

Human Rights Act 1998, c. 42.

Inter Nationes (1998) *Basic Law for the Federal Republic of Germany*, http://www.iuscomp.org/gla/statutes/ GG.htm.

Kavanagh, A. (2003) "The Idea of a Living Constitution," 16 *Canadian Journal of Law and Jurisprudence*: 55–89.

Raz, J. (1996) "Intention in Interpretation," in R. George, ed., *The Autonomy of Law: Essays on Legal Positivism*, Oxford: Clarendon Press, pp. 249–86.

—— (1998) "On the Authority and Interpretation of Constitutions: Some Preliminaries," in L. Alexander, ed., *Constitutionalism: Philosophical Foundations*, Cambridge: Cambridge University Press, pp. 152–93.

Roe v. Wade (1973) 410 U.S. 113.

Scalia, A. (1997) A *Matter of Interpretation: Federal Courts and the Law*, Princeton: Princeton University Press.

Solum, L. B. (2008) "Semantic Originalism," Illinois Public Law Research Paper No. 07–24, available at SSRN, http://ssrn.com/abstract=1120244.

Strauss, D. (2010) *The Living Constitution*, New York: Oxford University Press.

U.S. Constitution Online, The Constitution of the United States, http://www.usconstitution.net/const. html.

Waluchow, W. (2007) A *Common Law Theory of Judicial Review: The Living Tree*, Cambridge: Cambridge University Press.

Whittington, K. (1999) *Constitutional Interpretation: Textual Meaning, Original Intent, and Judicial Review*, Lawrence, KS: University Press of Kansas.

Further Reading

For further reading, see: L. Alexander, ed. (1998) *Constitutionalism: Philosophical Foundations*, Cambridge: Cambridge University Press; S. Barber and J. Fleming (2007) *Constitutional Interpretation: The Basic Questions*, New York: Oxford University Press; M. Berman (2009) "Originalism Is Bunk," 96 *New York University Law Review*: 1–96; R. Dworkin (1996) "Bork: The Senate's Responsibility" in R. Dworkin, *Freedom's Law: The Moral Reading of the American Constitution*, Cambridge, Mass.: Harvard University Press; R. Dworkin (1997) "Comment," in A. Scalia, A *Matter of Interpretation: Federal Courts and the Law*, Princeton: Princeton University Press, pp. 115–27; J. Ely (1980) *Democracy and Distrust*, Cambridge, Mass.: Harvard University Press; G. Goldsworthy (2000) "Dworkin as Originalist," *Constitutional Commentary* 17: 49–78; G. Goldsworthy (2009) "Constitutional Interpretation: Originalism," *Philosophy Compass* 4(4): 682–702; A. Marmor (1995) *Law and Interpretation: Essays in Legal Philosophy*, Oxford: Clarendon Press; A. Marmor (2005) *Interpretation and Legal Theory*, revised 2nd edition, Oxford: Hart Publishing; L. B. Solum (2010) *Legal Theory Lexicon 019: Originalism*, http://lsolum.typepad.com/legal_theory_lexicon/2004/01/legal_theory_le_1.html; W. Waluchow (2008) "Constitutionalism," in E. N. Zalta, ed., *The Stanford Encyclopedia of Philosophy*, Fall 2008 Edition, http://plato.stanford.edu/archives/fall2008/entries/ constitutionalism; and K. Whittington (2001) *Constitutional Construction: Divided Powers and Constitutional Meaning*, Cambridge, Mass.: Harvard University Press.

28

JUDICIAL REVIEW OF LEGISLATION

Jeremy Waldron

Sometimes, in order to frame an issue in legal or political philosophy, it is good to begin with some facts. Our topic is judicial review of legislation—a practice that, like many in this subject area, can be justified or disputed in the abstract or considered in light of our experience of how it actually operates. There will be plenty of abstract argument in this essay, in the second and subsequent sections. But I want to begin with our historical experience of judicial review in the history of the United States.

A Disgraceful History

Between 1880 and 1935, more than 170 statutes—state and federal—dealing with labor matters (health and safety, working hours, child labor, unionization) were struck down by American courts. The best known is *Lochner v. New York* ((1905) 198 U.S. 45), in which the United States Supreme Court held that a New York statute limiting working hours for bakers to 10 hours a day was an "unreasonable, unnecessary and arbitrary interference with the right and liberty of the individual to contract." This period is often called "the *Lochner* era," but it is important to understand how many years it lasted and how much legislation was overthrown. It was enough to demoralize two generations of labor legislators and their supporters (Forbath 1991).

In the United States, a decision of this kind by a court is a big deal. An individual or an organization aggrieved by a statute comes before a court to challenge its constitutionality. The constitutionality is almost always a matter of dispute, in part because the provisions of the U.S. Constitution are so vague. But the courts have the last word on the validity of the statute. It matters not that people have gone to the trouble to secure a majority in both houses or that they have gotten the consent of the governor of the state or, in the case of federal legislation, the consent of the president. It matters not that the legislators have formed their own judgments of the measure's constitutionality during the several stages of its passage. A court can decline to enforce the legislation, in effect striking it from the statute book. And it can do so by a simple majority decision (five votes to four in the U.S. Supreme Court)—in contrast to the elaborate bicameral and super-majoritarian procedures required in most legislatures. When a majority of judges votes to strike down the statute, all the legislators can do is try to assemble their coalitions and majorities again to pass another bill in somewhat different terms, hoping that this time it will satisfy the scrutiny of the courts. But the courts may well strike it down again, as it struck down statute after statute in the *Lochner* era. In some circles this is referred to as the "dialogue" theory of constitutional review (Hogg and Bushell 1997).

In other countries, the courts have somewhat weaker powers in respect of legislation. The United Kingdom operates what is sometimes called a system of "weak-form judicial review" under the Human Rights Act 1998, whereby legislation is scrutinized by judges who may issue a formal "Declaration of Incompatibility" between the statute and the provisions of the European Convention of Human Rights. But the British judiciary may not decline to apply legislation that they judge incompatible. The legislation remains on the statute book. What the Declaration does is open the possibility of fast-track amendment in Parliament; but still it is for Parliament ultimately to decide the fate of the statute (Kavanagh 2009; Tushnet 2003; Gardbaum 2001). This seems to me to be an admirable system. It combines ultimate parliamentary responsibility with a "canary in the coalmine" function for the judiciary, exercising whatever expertise they may have in matters of rights to alert the polity formally and publicly to the dangers posed by certain pieces of legislation. Experience shows that these alerts are taken seriously, but this is achieved without undermining the authority of the elected branches of government (Hiebert 2006). In this essay, however, I shall concentrate on the American example. This is because the practice of "strong-form" judicial review that we find in the United States remains normative for many constitutionalists around the world (see Barak 2006 and Dworkin 1990); the British system is sometimes disparaged as a "half-measure." The strong form of the practice shows most clearly the advantages and the difficulties of empowering judges in this matter.

Let us return to the *Lochner* era. Why was it thought a good idea to give judges, most of whom were unelected and democratically unaccountable, the right to strike down statutes enacted by a representative legislature? One cynical answer is that those who gave the judges this right were afraid that if the common people were enfranchised they might use their legislative power to attack the system of property, wage labor and capitalist exploitation. This has been a perennial apprehension. Since the time of the ancient Romans and the land reforms of Tiberius Gracchus, it is has often been thought that popular rule will endanger the property of the rich, and that therefore those who set up the framework of a new society have a responsibility to guard against this in their constitutional designs. Certainly the threat to property and the sanctity of contract was a theme at the time of the American founding (Nedelsky 1990) and the *Lochner* era may be seen as playing out this familiar anti-populist trope. Scholars associated with the Critical Studies Movement often lament the fact that today liberal defenders of judicial review seem to have forgotten all about this (Kennedy 1997). They have forgotten how brutally and for how long judicial power was used in America to defeat and demoralize working people and their political leaders. The modern defenders of judicial review tend to represent *Lochner v. New York* as nothing more than a regrettable mistake perpetrated way back in 1908 (Dworkin 1985: 58)—they seldom pay attention to the length and scope of the *Lochner* era—and they believe it should not be used to discredit the whole institution of judicial review of legislation, which they think is a necessary and valuable part of a modern constitutional democracy.

They say that the real point of judicial review is to protect everyone—rich or poor—against the worst human-rights abuses. Defenders of the practice worry that democracy is always liable to degenerate into the tyranny of the majority, imposing on members of vulnerable minorities the worst effects of majoritarian oppression and greed. But if this is the point of judicial review, then we have to say it has by and large failed in the United

States. The worst rights abuses in the history of the country were bound up with the persistence of chattel slavery for the first 80 years of the republic's existence. But judicial authority was *never* mobilized against slavery; on the contrary, judicial review was used many times to strike down legislative efforts to mitigate its worst effects. For example, in *Prigg v. Pennsylvania* ((1842) 41 U.S. 539), the U.S. Supreme Court struck down a Pennsylvania statute that sought to protect African-Americans from slave-catchers in a free state. And in *Scott v. Sanford* ((1857) 60 U.S. 393), known popularly as "the *Dred Scott* case," the Court struck down congressional legislation (the Missouri Compromise) that prohibited slavery in the territories, and held that Congress was not competent to make a black man a citizen. Almost 30 years later, in the 1883 *Civil Rights Cases* ((1883) 109 U.S. 3), when the matter of citizenship had finally been settled by war, by executive proclamation and by constitutional amendment, the Supreme Court struck down the Civil Rights Act of 1875, which purported to guarantee access to public accommodations for everyone, regardless of race, color or previous condition of servitude, and the Court also limited the effects of the 1871 Civil Rights Act, which tried to protect African-Americans in the South from racial terror.

Those were some of the Court's sins of commission—cases where strong-form judicial review made things worse or blocked any attempt to make things better. There were also sins of omission, for example, in *Korematsu v. United States* ((1944) 323 U.S. 214) where the Court decided that citizens of Japanese ancestry were not entitled to protection from internment in concentration camps in the American interior during World War II, or *Plessy v. Ferguson* ((1896) 163 U.S. 537), where the Court upheld segregation laws. It was not until 1954, 89 years after the passage of the Fourteenth Amendment, and 163 years after the enactment of the original Bill of Rights, that the Court acted against segregation, and even then its action was hesitant, controversial and bitterly resisted. Its decision, in *Brown v. Board of Education of Topeka* ((1954) 347 U.S. 483), has been held up as an icon by defenders of judicial review ever since. Cases like *Brown*, along with the decision that secured reproductive rights for women in the U.S., *Roe v. Wade* ((1973) 410 U.S. 113), are often presented as the poster children of judicial review. They are cited because they are supposed to illustrate how valuable the institution is for us. But I have taken the liberty here of reversing the order of presentation, beginning with the darker side of the Supreme Court's decision-making to illuminate front and center what are usually hidden away in shady and embarrassed footnotes.

The cases I have mentioned are cases on which I think there is widespread agreement that the institution of judicial review has not served us well. Quite apart from the objections one might make against its nondemocratic character (objections I shall explore in the second half of this essay), these are simply bad outcomes—outcomes that would have been better if the courts' power to review legislation had been weaker or nonexistent. Defenders of the practice may say that we should blame the text of the Constitution for these outcomes, not judicial review. They say, for example, that it was the Fugitive Slave Clause of the Constitution that compelled the decision in *Prigg v. Pennsylvania* and the Contracts Clause that led to *Lochner v. New York*. But this really won't do. Without judicial review to amplify their effects and focus them onto sharp-edged political decision-making by the judiciary, such unfortunate provisions in the Constitution might have faded into desuetude, dismissed at the outset as merely admonitory (which is how many Northern legislators actually regarded the Fugitive Slave Clause) and treated as less and less relevant for the purposes of modern politics. We say that a constitution needs judicial review or it will not be enforced; but if judicial review is to be present among us as an active enforcement mechanism we had better pray that we have the right constitutional provisions, because it is difficult if not impossible to change them once judicial authority reveals the actual impact of the clauses. Not only that but in some cases, such as the *Dred Scott* case, the Court was not simply mapping a clear piece of constitutional text onto the vexed issue of Mr. Scott's citizenship. The Court went out of its way to dredge the constitutional record for scraps of authority to justify its conclusion that blacks are "beings of an inferior order, and altogether unfit to associate with the white race, either in social or political relations." With that as a precedent, we must pray not only that we have the right constitution but that our judges bring to their task the right ideology of personhood, dignity and rights.

Certainly the cases I have cited give the lie to any claim that legislators are incapable of addressing responsibly the rights that (it is said) we need courts to protect. In the first three of the race cases I mentioned—*Prigg, Dred Scott* and the *Civil Rights Cases* of 1883—the legislatures had done their work; it was the courts that set about undoing it. We trumpet the achievement in *Brown*, such as it was. But eventually it was Congress that enacted the Civil Rights Act of 1964 and secured whatever we have in the way of racial and sexual equality. And the same is true of all those cases in the *Lochner* era: it was legislatures that had discerned the need for certain minimal social and economic rights; it was the legislatures that worked hard to secure them; and it was legislatures that had to do that work all over again after 1935 when the judiciary finally backed down in the face of President Franklin D. Roosevelt's exasperated threat to pack the Court with justices who would not obstruct the New Deal.

Disagreement on Watershed Issues

So much by way of background. I have set all this out because I believe we should begin our evaluation of judicial review by noting that, like other political institutions, it does not have an unblemished record. Any institution of government may work for good or for ill. This is true of democracy and elective institutions—as the defenders of judicial review have always emphasized—and it is true of judicial institutions as well. Now, the record I have spoken of is uniquely American. Other practices of judicial review around the world have not done the damage that the U.S. Supreme Court did to the rights of labor, the campaign against slavery and the early stages of the enforcement of civil rights. This is partly because the American system of judicial review is much older than the equivalent institutions in Europe and elsewhere. It is partly because other constitutional systems do not empower their courts to do so much damage: I have mentioned weak-form judicial review in the United Kingdom, for example. But even those countries that have strong-form judicial review seem to have used it wisely and helpfully: this appears to be true of Germany, Canada and South Africa, for example, in the modern era, and—though it is a slightly different case—it is true by and large of the way in which the European Court of Human Rights has exercised its powers.

Nevertheless, what is emphatically true of the way in which all these institutions now exercise their powers—the U.S. Supreme Court included—is that they intervene to decide matters on which the polities in question are deeply divided. There is a range of issues that confront every modern democracy, and in every modern democracy that has judicial review they come up for decision by the courts from time to time. Besides the cases about race and social and economic rights that I mentioned already in the first part of this paper, these issues include: abortion, affirmative action, capital punishment, the

437

boundary between church and state, the conditions of imprisonment, the rights of criminal suspects, defamation, the treatment of detainees in the war on terrorism, the disenfranchisement of prisoners, flag burning, gay rights (including same-sex marriage), gun control, hate speech, language rights, military service, minority cultural rights, policies on obscenity and pornography, police powers to "stop and search," privacy, the precise limits of the free exercise of religion, the regulation of speech and spending in electoral campaigns, and so on. Some of these are more important than others and systems vary in the extent to which certain of them are live issues available for judicial decision: for example, for the most part, legislative control over people's access to firearms is not a subject for judicial review in Europe, and also some issues (like capital punishment) are settled there even though they are not settled in the United States. But with some variations, the list I have given comprises a set of what I have called elsewhere "watershed issues," which every modern democracy has to face (Waldron 2002 and 2006).

These watershed issues define major choices that any modern society must face, choices that are reasonably well understood in each society. As things stand, the choices they pose will be settled finally by legislative decision-making in countries that have weak-form judicial review or no judicial review of legislation, and they will be settled finally by courts in countries that have strong-form judicial review. I don't mean that, in strong-form systems, legislative settlements are never allowed to stand. The first moves on these issues are almost always made by legislators. But even when their decision-making turns out to be final, it is so only on sufferance of the courts. The courts could have struck down the statute; the statute prevails only because it was not subject to challenge before the judiciary or because, even if it was challenged, the judiciary allowed it to stand. As Ronald Dworkin (1996: 74) has put it—and he is a *defender* of judicial review—on "intractable, controversial, and profound questions of political morality that philosophers, statesmen, and citizens have debated for many centuries," the people and their representatives simply have to "accept the deliverances of a majority of the justices, whose insight into these great issues is not spectacularly special."

The choices involved are likely to have a very significant impact on the lives of many people and on the tenor of the society as a whole. So why do some societies let their judges rather than their legislators have the final say on issues like these? Two theories suggest themselves. One is that the watershed issues define important moral as well as political choices, and moral choices are thought to be particularly appropriate for judges to make. Some view them as issues of natural law or natural rights (Moore 2001 and Fleming 2001). But not everyone is comfortable with that language and many prefer to speak, less tendentiously, about moral principles and moral rights. Whatever the detail, these watershed issues are patently issues of principle, not the issues of preference and strategy that—it is said—legislatures are set up to deal with. They engage values such as freedom, autonomy, dignity, equality and the value of human life as well as the more familiar currency of public policy—efficiency, prosperity and security. To the extent that they also involve empirical, economic and strategic issues, which many of them do, those issues are thoroughly entangled with moral conundrums as well. (Think of the debates about capital punishment: the value of life entangled with a policy debate about the best way to fight crime. Or think of affirmative action: the importance of racial and sex equality entangled with a policy debate about the best way to achieve it.) The other theory, better known (though it is not incompatible with the first), is that the choices in question are governed by the constitution of the society in question or some bill of rights that has equivalent authority, and are therefore to be determined as a matter of law, not as a matter of legislative choice. I say the two theories are compatible. The first may explain the second: the constitution or the bill of rights may be framed specifically to cover the moral issues of principle that are likely to arise.

But neither explanation is satisfactory or complete as it stands. We can accept that the issues define moral questions as well as strategic ones, questions of principle—like the meaning of human dignity and the relation between freedom and equality—as well as calculations of policy and strategy. But it is wrong to suggest either that legislatures are inept at dealing with moral choices or that courts are invariably reliable when moral issues are at stake. In systems of weak-form judicial review or no judicial review at all, legislatures deal well and straightforwardly with moral issues: the record of legislative reforms on capital punishment, abortion and the decriminalization of homosexuality in countries like the United Kingdom and New Zealand in the 1960s and '70s attests to that. And the American history we explored in the first section of this chapter shows that courts are by no means trustworthy on matters of morality such as the wrongness of slavery or the need to protect the rights of workers. What we reviewed in that section was legislatures making moral moves on moral grounds and having to back down in the face of hardheaded obstruction by the courts.

We have to say at least this: the choices at issue, moral or nonmoral, are all highly controversial. There is an immense amount of disagreement about them; there was disagreement in nineteenth- and twentieth-century America about the issues we set out in the first section and there is ferocious disagreement about all of these watershed issues I have mentioned in this section. This is moral disagreement—not just disagreement between one set of people taking a moral stance and another set of people taking their stand on some other nonmoral ground like economic efficiency. Though it is hard for partisans on each side to see this, both sides on every one of these issues holds to a strong and well-thought-through moral position. They disagree about what values are important, what their priorities are, what trade-offs to allow and how to weigh and balance competing moral considerations; and they disagree about how to map the values onto the complex tangles of fact and speculation in each of the issues in question. These disagreements are not surprising, nor is there any reason to blame them exclusively on ignorance, bias, superstition or self-interest. As John Rawls (1993) argued in relation to debates about comprehensive values, disagreement is best explained by "the burdens of judgment"—the difficulty of the subject matter, together with the different perspectives and experiences people inevitably bring to the debates.

Elsewhere I have made the case that these disagreements are just colloquial versions of the disagreements one finds among philosophers (Waldron 1993). We philosophers argue about rights, principles and ultimate values in our hallways, seminars and published symposia. And ordinary people argue about them in roughly similar terms at home, at church, on the streets and in their political activity. We find these disagreements throughout society in every institution and at every level of political decision-making. Voters disagree about them. The legislators they elect disagree about them. And it is no surprise to find disagreement about them on the judiciary too, since the judges are drawn (albeit not on a representative basis) from the society that is wracked with these disputes. Like citizens and legislators (though using cruder procedures) the judges too have to vote and decide by majority rule when they are figuring out which legislative decisions really respect the rights that people have.

Nor are the disagreements likely to disappear. Academic disagreements about rights show no sign of diminishing or being put to rest by philosophers' expertise, and the same is true of the public and political disagreements. Of course, each philosopher may think that he has the right answer, and he will insist (quite rightly) that his academic opponent's denial of this doesn't make him wrong. But his opponent across the hall will take exactly the same stance. And so will the citizens, legislators and judges in society. Few of them are moral skeptics—they think there is a truth of the matter and some of them think they have got it. The trouble is they are not all on the same side. For even if there is an objective moral truth, it does not disclose itself to us on Earth in ways that belie our disagreements. As I have argued elsewhere, moral objectivity is not the issue (Waldron 1992 and 1998a). On some issues on which we disagree, we have the good fortune not to need a common answer: we don't have to agree about the Holy Trinity or the causes of the First World War. But the watershed issues I have mentioned are not like that. They are issues of public policy on which some position has to be taken in the name of us all, and on which few of us are indifferent about which position we want our name associated with. The question we have to ask, then, in evaluating the practice of judicial review of legislation, is not whether there are right answers, but what is the best or—if this is different—the fairest way to make a decision in the name of the whole society?

Besides the moral character of these disagreements, the other characteristic that is cited in favor of their being decided by courts is their legal character. Legislative decisions will become law but, in ordinary cases, the decisions are not governed by law prior to or at the time of enactment. But—it is said—this is not true of our watershed cases. Those are not issues on which the legislature is supposed to have a free hand. The choices the legislature faces are governed by the provisions of the constitution or bill of rights that a given society has already committed itself to.

We have to be careful with this argument. As I have noted several times, some societies have bills of rights but do not empower judges to make final decisions about the issues they define. A case can perhaps be made that the Rule of Law requires that the legislature must regard itself as bound by the norms of the constitution. But whether this "being bound" requires enforcement by a court is open to question. On the one hand, there is the position of the American Supreme Court since *Marbury v. Madison* ((1803) 5 U.S. 137), that a court has no choice but to refuse to enforce a statute once the court has determined that the statute is at odds with the Constitution that defines the legislature's authority. But a bill of rights need not be part of the Constitution: societies face a choice as to whether to entrench their rights commitments into a constitutional document that would leave courts no option but to strike down legislation that was incompatible with it—some do it and some don't—and the considerations canvassed in this essay are relevant to that choice. In recent years, a number of American jurists have started to talk about constitutional populism (Kramer 2005; Tushnet 2000; Parker 1998), emphasizing that legislators and popular majorities are capable of making constitutional judgments too and that the framers of the U.S. Constitution did not envisage such judgments as the exclusive province of the judiciary. A system of constitutional law is not necessarily a system of judicial supremacy.

Then there is the fact of disagreement, as stubborn in the constitutional realm as it is in the moral realm. People disagree about the bearing of these constitutional and bill of rights positions on the watershed issues. In the United States, for example, on each of the issues I have mentioned, it is indisputable both (1) that the provisions of the Bill of Rights have a bearing on how the issue is to be resolved and (2) that the provisions of the Bill of Rights do not themselves determine a resolution of the issue that is beyond reasonable dispute (Waldron 2006). The rights provisions are almost always vague and abstract in their formulations; their abstraction means that people who disagree about concrete moral issues can commit themselves to the formulations nonetheless: both opponents and defenders of capital punishment can agree not to allow punishments that are cruel and unusual; both opponents and defenders of affirmative action can agree not to deny anyone the equal protection of the laws, and so on. Disagreement does not prevent the enactment of a bill of rights. But the disagreements on the watershed issues remain unresolved, leaving us in a situation in which—when a question about a piece of legislation arises—it is beyond dispute that a bill of rights provision bears on the matter. But what its bearing is and whether it prohibits (or should limit the application of) the legislative provision that is called into question remains a matter of dispute among reasonable people.

The abstraction of our rights provisions is not an aberration. As Ronald Dworkin (1996) has argued, it is not inappropriate to phrase rights guarantees in general terms, because we cannot foresee the exact form in which issues will arise. If our constitutional provisions were more specific, we might have to admit that they have no application to new and unforeseen cases or that their application depends on analogy, which would be equally controversial. Also our rights provisions are sometimes not just generalizations but *moral* generalizations, using predicates like "cruel" or "reasonable" because any more empirical predicate would sell short the principles we are trying to represent (Dworkin 1996). There is a school of jurisprudential thought that maintains that this sort of indeterminacy arises only around the margins of natural language predicates: we agree, for example, on central cases of cruelty but we do not agree on cases in that concept's "penumbra" (Hart 1994). But this model is mistaken. Disagreements are often on central cases—one way of putting this is that the concept is "essentially," not just peripherally, contested (Gallie 1955–1956 and Dworkin 1977)—and these disagreements seem to flourish without throwing the conceptual debate into unproductive confusion. The general point here is that both parties to the dispute can reasonably claim that they take the underlying constitutional provision seriously. And as we have seen, to the extent that the constitutional provision embodies a moral principle, they can reasonably claim to be taking that seriously as well.

This is not to deny that arguments can be made that seem conclusive—at least to those who make them—as to the bearing of the rights provisions on the watershed issue in question. If judicial review is set up in the society, then lawyers will argue about these issues using both the text and the gravitational force (Dworkin 1977) of the text of the bill of rights. Each side to each of the disagreements will claim that its position can be read into the bland commitments of the bill of rights if only those texts are read generously or narrowly enough. And as a matter of political strategy, neither will be prepared to acknowledge what I am assuming right now will be obvious: that the bland rhetoric of the bill of rights simply finesses the real and reasonable disagreements that are inevitable among people who take rights seriously for long enough to see such a bill of rights enacted.

None of this shows conclusively that decision-making by courts is inappropriate. Courts often have to make decisions on which the law is deeply contestable. But it helps undermine some of the sillier arguments that are put forward in favor of judicial review.

One such argument is that the constitutional or rights provisions represent *precommitments* by the society and that the courts, when they decide them, are simply enforcing something to which the society has already committed itself (Freeman 1990). The idea is that, like Ulysses choosing to be bound to the mats so that he can hear but not respond to the Sirens, so a polity may bind itself with a constitutional commitment so that it may hear but not respond to the siren call of rights violations. But the model of precommitment simply doesn't work in the context of the extent of disagreement we are talking about (Elster 2000). Though the society may have been wholehearted in its embrace of the original commitment to some provision about rights, it is utterly divided about whether a present piece of legislation represents the danger that the rights provision was supposed to guard against (Waldron 1998b and 1999). If someone insists nevertheless that society has committed itself to a particular view about the right in question and that the judges, by voting among themselves, are able somehow to ascertain that precommitment or even construct it on society's behalf (Waluchow 2005), then it is not clear why the precommitment should hold given that an alternative understanding of the right is in play. The Ulysses model works only when the precommitment guards against various aberrations of choice, not when it prevents changes of mind in relation to genuine disagreement as to what a reasonable outcome would be (Schelling 1984, ch. 4).

Outcomes and Methodologies

None of this talk about disagreement makes the underlying issues go away. Society does need to take a stand on each of these watershed issues. Is abortion to be treated as homicide or is it to be left to the choice of women and their doctors? Is affirmative action to be permitted as a strategy for equality or is it to be forbidden as itself a form of invidious discrimination? Is capital punishment to be made available as a punishment for particularly heinous offenses or is it to be taken out of our penal repertoire? Choices on these matters cannot indefinitely be postponed. So I return now to the question I posed a little while ago. These matters could be settled by legislatures—by elected representatives of the people deciding through complicated majoritarian and super-majoritarian processes—or they could be taken ultimately by unelected judges deciding by simple majority voting in a supreme court whether to approve or disapprove of the legislative decision. Both institutional practices are fallible, as we saw in the first section of this chapter. But which is the better or—if this is different—which is the fairer way to decide?

Some philosophers maintain that the only proper basis for answering this question looks to the likelihood that one or the other procedure will come up with the right answer. According to Raz, "[a] natural way to proceed is to assume that the enforcement of fundamental rights should be entrusted to whichever political decision-procedure is, in the circumstances of the time and place, most likely to enforce them well, with the fewest adverse side effects" (1998: 45).

That sounds reasonable. After all, everyone agrees that the stakes in these decisions are high: they are issues of right and justice and we want to get the correct outcomes in as many of these cases as possible. On the other hand, there are also reasons that bear on our question that are not purely outcome related. Consider for example, the principle of self-determination: we believe, for any given society, that the watershed issues I have identified should be settled by decision procedures *within* that society rather than imposed on it by diktat from outside (e.g., by a neighboring government or a former colonial power). I don't mean that societies have nothing to learn from one another, but what they do learn is fed back into their own autonomous political processes (Waldron 2011). Of course, strong-form judicial review and democratic legislative decision-making both satisfy this requirement. But there may be other similar reasons of a non-outcome-related kind that distinguish between the two decision procedures. We should not neglect these issues of process and fairness just because of the importance of getting to the right outcome.

The contrast between outcome-related and process-related considerations is a complicated one. Since we disagree about what counts as the right outcomes, we are hardly likely to agree as a society on a decision procedure based directly on outcome-related considerations. If you think the pro-life alternative is the right outcome on abortion you may favor legislative decision-making in the United States, whereas your pro-choice opponents—equally convinced of their view about outcomes—may favor judicial review. True, there are some outcomes on which we all now agree, such as the wrongness of slavery. But as we have seen, that outcome-related consideration does not settle anything in favor of judicial authority.

If we are going to settle this in an outcome-related way, we will have to adopt a less direct approach, focusing on aspects of procedure that seem to us more likely to lead to good outcomes even when we disagree about what those outcomes are. As Aileen Kavanagh puts it:

> [W]e do not need a precise account of what rights we have and how they should be interpreted in order to make some instrumentalist [i.e., outcome-related] claims. Many instrumentalist arguments are . . . based on general institutional considerations about the way in which legislatures make decisions in comparison to judges, the factors which influence their decision and the ways in which individuals can bring their claims in either forum.
>
> (2003: 466)

Unfortunately, reasons of this kind also seem to point in both directions: we quickly encounter antinomy upon antinomy. On the one hand, many say that it counts in favor of judicial decision-making that judges are insulated from the interests and emotions of popular majorities. Undistracted by majority interests, they are better able to form an impartial view of the matter. On the other hand, if the question is about the moral attention due to the interests of vulnerable people, we may affirmatively value the fact that legislatures enable decisions to be made by representatives of the persons whose lives will be affected by the legislation in question, particularly in circumstances where those people do not have any other sort of social, economic or political power. As Raz puts it, "[s]ometimes one may be unable to appreciate the plight of classes of people unless one belongs to the same class oneself, and therefore rather than entrusting the decision to those not affected by it, it should be given to those who are so affected" (1998: 46). This seems to have been true of the issues that faced America during the *Lochner* era: the legislative decisions were sensitive to the interests of working people, whereas the judges, being selected by nonrepresentative means from among the higher ranks of the wealthy professional classes, were less able to apprehend what could be said in favor of legislation of this kind.

It is also sometimes said that the duty of judges to cite reasons for their decisions counts in favor of judicial review. Legislators may be politically more accountable, but they are not accountable in this particular way, which seems to go to the heart of responsible and reasoned decision-making. Courts give reasons for their decisions, we are told, and this is a guarantee that they are taking seriously the moral considerations that are at stake, whereas legislatures often do not. In fact, this is a false contrast. Legislators give reasons for their votes just as judges do. The reasons are given in what we call debate and they are published in *Hansard* or the *Congressional Record*. The difference is that lawyers are trained to close study of the reasons that judges give; they are not trained to close study of legislative reasoning (though they will occasionally ransack it for interpretive purposes).

Perhaps this argument is not really about the presence or absence of reason giving, but rather about its quality. In my view, however, the reasons that courts tend to give when they are exercising powers of judicial review of legislation are seldom the reasons that would be canvassed in a full deliberative discussion, and the process of searching for, citing, assessing and comparing the weight of such reasons is quite different for courts than for an ideal political deliberator. If one examines an American judicial opinion, one will find plenty of discussion of interpretive theories, as the judges struggle to find a way to map very general eighteenth-century prose onto a quite specific twenty-first-century problem. And one will find plenty of reference to and discussion of earlier cases, in which the judges try to present a plausible analogy between what they are doing in the instant case with what other judges, exercising similar powers have done in the past. All this is no doubt of great juridical interest, but it does not necessarily capture the important moral reasons that are at stake. Indeed, often in American judicial opinions, interpretive and precedential issues crowd out any discussion of the substantive merits of the case.

In the Supreme Court's 50-page opinion on abortion in *Roe v. Wade* ((1973) 410 U.S. 113), for example, there are no more than a couple of paragraphs dealing with the moral importance of reproductive rights in relation to privacy, and the few paragraphs addressed to the other moral issue at stake—the rights status of the fetus—are mostly taken up with showing the diversity of opinions on the issue. The outcome of the case may be appealing to pro-choice advocates, but from a moral point of view the "reasoning" is threadbare. In contrast, it is striking how rich the reasoning tends to be in legislative debates on such issues in countries without judicial review. I recently read through the House of Commons debates on the Medical Termination of Pregnancy Bill from 1966, a bill proposing to liberalize abortion law in Britain (see Waldron 2006: 1384–85). The second debate on that bill is as fine an example of a political institution grappling with moral reasons as you could hope to find. It is a sustained debate—about 100 pages in *Hansard*—and it involved pro-life Labour people and pro-choice Labour people, pro-life Conservatives and pro-choice Conservatives, talking through and focusing on all of the questions that need to be addressed when abortion is being debated. They debated the questions passionately, but also thoroughly and honorably, with attention to the rights, principles and pragmatic issues on both sides. It was a debate that in the end the supporters of the bill won; the pro-choice faction prevailed. American judicial reasoning on the issue was mostly concerned with interpretation, doctrine and history. But in the British legislature, responsible lawmakers were able to focus steadfastly on the issue of abortion itself and what it entailed—on the ethical status of the fetus; on the predicament of pregnant women and the importance of their choices, their freedom and their privacy; on the moral conflicts and difficulties that all this involves; and on the pragmatic issues about the role that law should play in regard to private moral questions. Those are the issues that surely need to be debated when society is deciding about abortion rights, and those are the issues that are given most time in the legislative debates and least time in the judicial deliberations.

Maybe these instances are aberrations; in other cases, the roles may be reversed. But it is pretty clear that indirect, outcome-related reasons of this kind do not establish a decisive advantage in favor of strong-form judicial review.

Objections Based on Political Equality

What then of procedural reasons that are not outcome related? The most important of such reasons have to do with democracy—the array of institutional practices that seek to establish control by the people, i.e., by all the individuals in society over the fundamental conditions of their association, on roughly equal terms. For a political philosopher, it is one of the many delights of the debate about judicial review that it takes us back to the first principles of democratic theory. Philosophers who support judicial review sometimes write as though this idea of democracy were a complete innovation (Alexander 2007): who is supposed to be enfranchised, they ask, and on what issues, and how are agendas to be set and questions posed? They write as though the very idea of democratic decision-making on important matters of principle were preposterous—a reflection, perhaps, of the ancient grudge that philosophy has had against democracy since the time of Socrates. On the other hand, some of the recent books on democratic theory that bear on this issue happen to be among the best yet written on the justification (and the limits) of democratic decision-making (e.g., Christiano 1996 and 2008; Estlund 2008).

There is no space here to rehearse a general theory of democracy. But I do want to emphasize one thing. In the argument about judicial review, the democratic argument does not suppose that there is some entity called "the people" whose decisions are entitled to prevail, or some group called "the majority" which is entitled to rule. We can eschew all such reifications. There are just individual persons, millions of them, with views and interests of their own, who live their lives together in a community, and individually and occasionally in factions and parties want their views to have influence in the corridors of power. They accept that in the circumstances of disagreement that we have outlined, no individual can be guaranteed that his or her view will prevail. An individual may often have to submit to decisions on the watershed issues we have been discussing which he or she thinks are wrong or unjust or misconceive the rights that people have. This is so under a system of judicial rule and it is also true under a system of democratic decision-making. The difference is that in a system of strong-form judicial review, those who make the final decisions act as though the views they happen to hold—which of course they think are right—are entitled to a great deal more respect than the views that I happen to hold or any one of my millions of fellow citizens happen to hold. In other words, the issue comes down to fairness and the principle of political equality.

It is worth dwelling on the basis of the affront to political equality that judicial review involves (Waldron 1993). People fought long and hard for the vote and for democratic representation. They wanted the right to govern themselves, not just on mundane issues of policy, but also on the high matters of principle that are represented in the watershed issues I have been discussing. They rejected the Platonic view that ordinary people are incapable of thinking through issues of justice. Consider the struggles there have been, in Britain, Europe and America—first, for the abolition of property qualifications; second, for the extension of the franchise to women; and third, for bringing the legacy of civil rights denials to an end in the context of American racism. In all those struggles, people have paid tribute to the democratic aspiration to self-governance, without any sense at all that it should confine itself to the interstitial quibbles of policy that remain to be settled after some lawyerly elite have decided the main issues of principle.

The relevant disparity of power is between citizens and judges. In most polities, judges are not elected to their office and they are not accountable publicly for their decisions. Citizens do not have the opportunity to choose or review their judges in a process that treats them (the citizens) as equals. In most countries judges who exercise powers of judicial review are appointed by elected politicians and in some countries confirmed by elective assemblies. But they operate at one or two removes from direct popular accountability. I say "in most countries." In a few American states, though not at the federal level, high judicial office *is* elective. But this tends to raise more problems than it solves (Nagel 1973). Defenders of judicial review sometimes ask me if I would lessen my opposition to the practice if all judges were elected. The question is usually disingenuous; those who ask it have no intention of pressing for such a change. And quite rightly: in the states where they exist, elective judicial arrangements are marred by the absence of any respectable theory about the appropriate relation between election and accountability on the one hand and the proper basis of judicial decision-making on the other, which could possibly guide the way in which judges campaign and respond to popular influence.

Legislators, by contrast, are elected, and electoral systems are designed to ensure that the system of elections gives something approximating an equal say to each enfranchised citizen in the choice of those who will exercise legislative power. What is more, in the case of legislators we do have a well-worked-out theory of representation—which we do not have for elective judges—relating the conditions of campaigning, election and subsequent electoral accountability to the character of the deliberation and decision-making in which representatives participate. The theory is not perfect—we oscillate in an attempt to find a balance between Burkean representation, constituency representation, party representation and the representation of interests (Pitkin 1972)—but it is immeasurably better thought through than the equivalent theorizing about the way in which elected judges ought to behave. The practice is not perfect either. Controversies about electoral systems continue and improvements are slow in coming. We have not yet succeeded in presenting the political equality of all citizens as a sure function of the equality of legislators voting in their chambers together with the equality of electors voting in their constituencies (Buchanan and Tullock 1967, ch. 15).

But we are certainly far enough advanced both in theory and practice to be able to say this: judicial review is a massive violation of the principle of political equality, which is fundamental to democracy. In matters of which the people of a society disagree in good faith, matters important to their lives and to their life together, strong-form judicial review gives immeasurably greater weight to the views of appointed judges than it gives to ordinary citizens. Defenders of the practice, sensitive to this charge, will respond that legislative decision-making also gives immeasurably greater weight to the views of legislators than to the views of ordinary citizens. But the difference is that, in the case of legislators, there is an electoral system that enables the system of representation to act as an approximation to the principle of political equality—a shabby approximation sometimes, as I have acknowledged, but an immeasurably closer approximation in the case of legislators than in the case of judges. Legislators are accountable to ordinary people; legislative representation is designed in part to allow the channeling of opinion from ordinary people to their lawmakers in roughly equal terms; and the legislative system is designed so that no substantial interest in the community will be neglected, even when they are interests of the (otherwise) powerless and vulnerable. All these factors mean that there is a substantially greater amount of political fairness in the way decisions are made in a system of legislative supremacy than there is in a system of strong-form judicial review.

I do not deny that there is a modicum of democratic legitimacy in the way judges are appointed and confirmed (more so in some countries than in others), nor that judges may find it difficult in the long term to run in the face of popular opinion (Friedman 2009), nor that judicial review offers a kind of access for citizens to the sinews of power. But our question is a comparative one: which mode of decision-making is fairer? Which mode of decision-making defines a *more* equal process? It seems to me that when the question is focused in that way, the advantage of legislative supremacy is undeniable.

Of course the fact that legislative decision-making is fairer is not conclusive. Some may give greater weight to the outcome-related dimension and they may have a more sanguine view about the prospects for good judicial decision-making than I have. Charles Beitz (1989) has argued that the principle of political equality requires us to take substantive as well as procedural factors into account. And Ronald Dworkin (1996) has argued that the principle of political equality gets no purchase unless we are sure that people are already being respected in their fundamental rights. We should not underestimate the willingness or ability of the defenders of judicial review to add epicycle after epicycle to the debate. Nor should we doubt the ability of its opponents to make their case at any level of complexity chosen by the defenders of this practice.

References

Alexander, L. (2007) "Judicial Review and Moral Rights," *Queen's Law Journal* 33: 463–81.
Barak, A. (2006) *The Judge in a Democracy*, Princeton: Princeton University Press.
Beitz, C. (1989) *Political Equality: An Essay in Democratic Theory*, Princeton: Princeton University Press.
Brown v. Board of Education of Topeka (1954) 347 U.S. 483.
Buchanan, J. M. and Tullock, G. (1967) *The Calculus of Consent: Logical Foundations of Constitutional Democracy*, Ann Arbor, MI: University of Michigan Press.
Christiano, T. (1996) *The Rule of the Many: Fundamental Issues in Democratic Theory*, Boulder, CO: Westview Press.
—— (2008) *The Constitution of Equality: Democratic Authority and Its Limits*, Oxford: Oxford University Press.
Civil Rights Act 1871 (United States).
Civil Rights Act 1875 (United States).
Civil Rights Act 1964 (United States).
Civil Rights Cases (1883) 109 U.S. 3.
Dworkin, R. (1977) *Taking Rights Seriously*, Cambridge, Mass.: Harvard University Press.
—— (1985) *A Matter of Principle*, Cambridge, Mass.: Harvard University Press.
—— (1990) *A Bill of Rights for Britain*, London: Chatto and Windus.
——(1996) *Freedom's Law: The Moral Reading of the American Constitution*, Cambridge, Mass.: Harvard University Press.
Elster, J. (2000) *Ulysses Unbound: Studies in Rationality, Precommitment, and Constraints*, Cambridge: Cambridge University Press.
Estlund, D. (2008) *Democratic Authority: A Philosophical Framework*, Princeton: Princeton University Press.
Forbath, W. (1991) *Law and the Shaping of the American Labor Movement*, Cambridge, Mass.: Harvard University Press.
Fleming, J. E. (2001) "The Natural Rights-Based Justification for Judicial Review," *Fordham Law Review* 69: 2119–2130.
Freeman, S. (1990) "Constitutional Democracy and the Legitimacy of Judicial Review," *Law and Philosophy* 9: 327–70.
Friedman, B. (2009) *The Will of the People: How Public Opinion Has Influenced the Supreme Court and Shaped the Meaning of the Constitution*, New York: Farrar, Straus and Giroux.
Gallie, W.B. (1955–1956) "Essentially Contested Concepts," *Proceedings of the Aristotelian Society* 56: 167–98.
Gardbaum, S. (2001) "The New Commonwealth Model of Constitutionalism," *American Journal of Comparative Law* 49: 707–60.
Hart, H. L. A. (1994) *The Concept of Law*, revised edition, Oxford: Oxford University Press.
Hiebert, J. (2006) "Parliament and the Human Rights Act," *International Journal of Constitutional Law* 4: 1–38.
Hogg, P. W. and Bushell, A. A. (1997) "The Charter Dialogue Between Courts and Legislatures (or Perhaps the Charter of Rights Isn't Such a Bad Thing After All)," *Osgoode Hall Law Journal* 35: 75–124.
Human Rights Act 1998 (United Kingdom).
Kavanagh, A. (2003) "Participation and Judicial Review: A Reply to Jeremy Waldron," *Law and Philosophy* 22: 451–86.
—— (2009) *Constitutional Review under the UK Human Rights Act*, Cambridge: Cambridge University Press.
Kennedy, D. (1997) *A Critique of Adjudication*, Cambridge, Mass.: Harvard University Press.

Korematsu v. United States (1944) 323 U.S. 214.

Kramer, L. D. (2005) *The People Themselves: Popular Constitutionalism and Judicial Review*, New York: Oxford University Press.

Lochner v. New York (1905) 198 U.S. 45.

Marbury v. Madison (1803) 5 U.S. 137.

Moore, M. S. (2001). "Justifying the Natural Law Theory of Constitutional Interpretation," *Fordham Law Review* 69: 2087–117.

Nagel, S. S. (1973) *Comparing Elected and Appointed Judicial Systems*, Thousand Oaks, CA: SAGE Publications.

Nedelsky, J. (1990) *Private Property and the Limits of American Constitutionalism: The Madisonian Framework and Its Legacy*, Chicago: University of Chicago Press.

Parker, R. (1998) *Here, the People Rule: A Constitutional Populist Manifesto*, Cambridge, Mass.: Harvard University Press.

Parliamentary Debates (House of Commons), 5th Series, vol. 732, pp. 1067–1166 (Hansard).

Pitkin, H. F. (1972) *The Concept of Representation*, Berkeley: University of California Press.

Plessy v. Ferguson (1896) 163 U.S. 537.

Prigg v. Pennsylvania (1842) 41 U.S. 539.

Rawls, J. (1993) *Political Liberalism*, New York: Columbia University Press.

Raz, J. (1998) "Disagreement in Politics," *American Journal of Jurisprudence* 43: 25–52.

Roe v. Wade (1973) 410 U.S. 113.

Schelling, T. C. (1984) *Choice and Consequences: Perspectives of an Errant Economist*, Cambridge, Mass.: Harvard University Press.

Scott v. Sanford (1857) 60 U.S. 393.

Tushnet, M. (2000) *Taking the Constitution Away from the Courts*, Princeton: Princeton University Press.

—— (2003) "Alternative Forms of Judicial Review," *Michigan Law Review* 101: 2781–2802.

Waldron, J. (1992) "The Irrelevance of Moral Objectivity," in R. George, ed., *Natural Law Theory: Contemporary Essays*, Oxford: Oxford University Press, pp. 158–87.

—— (1993) "A Right-Based Critique of Constitutional Rights," *Oxford Journal of Legal Studies* 13: 18–51.

—— (1998a) "Moral Truth and Judicial Review," *American Journal of Jurisprudence* 43: 75–97.

—— (1998b) "Precommitment and Disagreement," in L. Alexander, ed., *Constitutionalism: Philosophical Foundations*, Cambridge: Cambridge University Press, pp. 271–99.

—— (1999) *Law and Disagreement*, Oxford: Oxford University Press.

—— (2002) "Judicial Power and Popular Sovereignty," in M. Graber and M. Perhac, eds., *Marbury versus Madison: Documents and Commentary*, Washington, D.C.: Congressional Quarterly Press, pp. 181–202.

—— (2006) "The Core of the Case Against Judicial Review," *Yale Law Journal* 115: 1346–1406.

—— (2011) "Rights and the Citation of Foreign Law," in T. Campbell, K. D. Ewing and A. Tomkins, eds., *The Legal Protection of Human Rights: Sceptical Essays*, Oxford: Oxford University Press, pp. 410–27.

Waluchow, W. (2005) "Constitutions as Living Trees: An Idiot Defends," *The Canadian Journal of Law and Jurisprudence* 18: 207–47.

Further Reading

For further reading, see: B. Ackerman (1991) *We the People: 1. Foundations*, Cambridge, Mass.: Harvard University Press; A. Bickel (1986) *The Least Dangerous Branch: The Supreme Court at the Bar of Politics*, 2nd edition, New Haven: Yale University Press; C. Eisgruber (2001) *Constitutional Self-Government*, Cambridge, Mass.: Harvard University Press; J. Hart Ely (1980) *Democracy and Distrust: A Theory of Judicial Review*, Cambridge, Mass.: Harvard University Press; R. George, ed. (2000) *Great Cases in Constitutional Law*, Princeton: Princeton University Press; S. Holmes (1995) *Passions and Constraint: On the Theory of Liberal Democracy*, Chicago: University of Chicago Press; F. I. Michelman (1999) *Brennan and Democracy*, Princeton: Princeton University Press; G. N. Rosenberg (1991) *The Hollow Hope: Can Courts Bring about Social Change?*, Chicago: University of Chicago Press; A. de Tocqueville (1994/1835) *Democracy in America*, New York: Alfred A. Knopf; and M. J. C. Vile (1998) *Constitutionalism and the Separation of Powers*, 2nd edition, Indianapolis: Liberty Fund.

Part IV

LAW AS A
COERCIVE ORDER

29

COERCION

William A. Edmundson

The concept of coercion figures in the philosophy of law in two main ways.

The first way casts coercion as an essential, defining element of *law*, or of *a law*, or of a *system* of laws or some combination of the three. I will call this first way the explanatory use or the explanatory sense of the concept of coercion. When I refer to the explanatory use or sense of the concept I mean to include uses intending not as much to explain as to describe or mark off law from other phenomena, or a law or legal system from another. Although coercion is a concept that figures into a variety of specific doctrines within the law—e.g., in criminal law: the duress defense, the offense of extortion; in contract law: to negate elements of formation and modification—this chapter will not discuss them.

The second main way seeks not to explain or to describe law but is concerned with the need to *justify* the coerciveness of law, laws or legal systems, once it is assumed or concluded that coercion is either a necessary feature of law, laws or legal systems, or that it is a contingent but pervasive feature of laws or legal systems. (I assume here that the nature of law itself has no contingent features, but only necessary ones.) The second way encompasses challenges to the justification or legitimacy of laws and legal systems as well as efforts to meet such challenges. (The nature of a thing, such as law, cannot stand in need of or receive a justification—unless its nature requires that it be actualized. The concept of law is not necessarily instantiated, for the world might have existed and may yet exist without containing any laws or legal systems or anything else answering to the concept of law.) I will call this second way the normative use or sense of the concept of coercion.

The Explanatory Use of the Concept of Coercion

The explanatory uses of the concept of coercion that I will discuss cast it as an essential, defining element of law, a law, or a legal system or some combination of the three. One might say that no social phenomenon can count as a legal system unless it employs coercion. One might say that no rule can count as a legal rule unless it is connected to some coercive sanction against violations. One might say that no theory of law can be adequate unless it explains how law and coercion are related. One might deny all of these three things (cf. Schauer 2011: 610–21); or one might say any one of these three things and deny the other two, for they are logically independent. One might say, for example, that an adequate theory of law will have to say something about the relation between law and coercion, while denying that a legal system necessarily employs coercion, and also denying that every law of a legal system carries a coercive sanction. Or one might say that law itself can be understood without relying on the notion of coercion, and that laws need not carry coercive sanctions, but go on to deny that legal systems can be individuated one from another without taking account of their respective coercive reaches or purported reaches. Or one might say that no rule can be a legal rule unless it is connected with an authorization to use coercion if the rule is not followed, but go on to say that coercion has nothing further to add about the unity of legal systems or the nature of law.

Consider law itself, laws and legal systems as three distinct foci of concern. Coercion may and has been used as an explanatory notion with respect to any or all of these in any combination, and so combined with (or perhaps without) logical consistency. Hans Kelsen, the preeminent legal theorist of the twentieth century, held that norms are legal norms only if they are coercive (Kelsen 1945/1961: 19). By this he meant that a scientific account of the content of a legal system would necessarily consist of a set of statements of the following hypothetical form. The antecedent of each such hypothetical will specify a condition, and the consequent a coercive sanction that is authorized or required in case the antecedent condition is met. Such a statement, or *rechtsatz*, could take this form: "If anyone murders another, then that person ought to be executed." Execution is the coercive sanction. The norm of law described by jurisprudence—the science of law—need not be of hypothetical form, and need make no reference to a coercive sanction. If the norm is expressed in a statute, it might simply state: "The penalty for murder is death." The legal norm is not to be confused with the scientific statement of the content of the law. The latter makes essential reference to coercion, or so Kelsen believed, while the former need not. Legal theory, whose task is not to inventory the legal norms of any given system of law, but to explain how those norms are both valid and a unitary system, has no further use of the concept of coercion. So, to summarize (while oversimplifying) Kelsen's view, coercion is an essential element in the scientific statement of the content of a legal system, and in that sense a legal system is necessarily coercive. A legal norm itself need not employ the idea of coercion. But no norm is a legal norm unless it is both valid—that is, authorized by some superior norm—and a condition of a coercive sanction.

Kelsen's account of law employs a conception of coercion that is roughly equivalent to the idea of compulsion. This usage sets him apart from recent Anglophone theorists, who distinguish between coercion and compulsion (but cf. Anderson 2008). Coercion, according to the currently dominant view, is properly understood as involving a threat, or an expression of some undesired consequence to be brought about if, but only if, the addressee fails to do as commanded. Coercion differs from altering another's behavior by issuing a warning, in that the coercer at least pretends to have control over the occurrence of the undesired outcome (Nozick 1969). John Austin's (nineteenth-century) account of law was founded on the concept of coercion as a threat—law was properly defined as a set of orders from a sovereign, given under threat of sanction, to subjects who habitually obey (Austin 1954/1832). Both Kelsen and Austin are key figures in the history of legal positivism. Both believed that coercion had an essential role in what we call law. But they had different ideas of what coercion is, and where it figures in.

For Kelsen, a statement of law describes a condition, a "delict," the occurrence of which requires, or authorizes, some official to compel the delinquent (or someone suitably related to the delinquent) to do something or undergo something. The legal norm described by a true legal statement need not be addressed to the potential delinquent at all—although frequently legal norms have and are meant to have that effect. For Austin, on the other hand, a law is just an order backed by a threat. (The threat might be a threat to use force to compel conformity, but it need not be: it might be a threat to bring about some unpleasant consequence.) If Rex, the sovereign, merely authorizes some subordinate to apply force to a subject should the subject behave in a certain way, then what all that amounts to is not a law, at least not in the strict, proper and primary sense. Obviously, if Rex's subordinates conspicuously apply force with some regularity to a certain type of behavior, his subjects are likely to come to regard themselves as ordered not to behave in that way. Austin could consistently count that situation as adding up to an order backed by a threat, and hence a law. But Austin viewed the order backed by a threat as the "positing" of law, whereas Kelsen saw the legal norm to be accurately describable without reference to coercion in Austin's sense. Duly authorized compulsion was enough.

Which conception of coercion better explains what law is: Austin's notion of coercion as threat, or Kelsen's notion of coercion as compulsion? This essay will not take a position on that, but it is worth noting that more recent legal theorists have been more of Austin's mind than Kelsen's on this point. Lon Fuller, a natural law theorist, insisted that making law involves more than merely authorizing force. Law, in Fuller's view, is essentially a public direction to all citizens subject to law, and is therefore not in essence duly authorized compulsion (Fuller 1964). H. L. A. Hart, a critic of both Austin and Kelsen, conceived of law as in essence a matter of rules, and of rules, in turn, as human practices, organized in a distinctive way, having both an internal and an external aspect (Hart 1961). A rule can be said to exist only if someone views it as a standard of behavior, such that lapses from that standard are subject to criticism. But not everyone subject to a rule need view it that way. Distinctively legal rules, however, are backed by authorizations to apply "serious social pressure" to assure conformity. By social pressure, Hart did not mean to confine law to the application of force, at least not proximately. Law takes hold in a society when a certain set of rules of conduct are recognized and insisted upon as binding, in the sense that nonconformity may be met with serious social pressure to conform. The greater the degree to which "physical sanctions are prominent and usual," the more inclined one will be to regard the rules as forming a "primitive or rudimentary" legal system, even though these sanctions be "neither closely defined nor administered by officials." But a legal system and laws, in a robust sense, depend upon the presence of "secondary" meta-rules identifying the rules of conduct that are enforceable by serious pressure, providing for the introduction and retirement of rules so sanctioned, and—most importantly—rules governing the resolution of disputes involving the "primary" rules of conduct. It is this (distinctively organized) serious social pressure antecedent to the unwanted conduct that marks the existence of a legal rule, and that rule's membership in a legal system.

For Hart, it is a mistake to think that coercion, in either Austin's threat sense or in Kelsen's compulsion sense, is essential to any particular rule or norm or command counting as a law. A rule may for example empower private parties to make binding agreements, or may disable a legislative body from regulations in some field, without failing to be law. But Hart agreed that coercion, at least in the sense of serious social pressure (forms of which may be culturally various, and need not include what we would describe as physical compulsion) was an essential part of any legal system and, to that degree, an essential part of an adequate theory of law.

WILLIAM A. EDMUNDSON

The Normative Sense of the Concept of Coercion

It is important not to confuse the explanatory enterprise of showing law to be more than and distinct from mere coercion from the normative enterprise of redeeming the apparent coerciveness, or coercive element or dimension, of law. That law is coercive as a straightforward matter of descriptive fact is a commonplace view (Lamond 2000: 39). The coerciveness of law as a descriptive matter is often invoked as a way of introducing or of framing the question whether the state—regarded as a legal system effective in some territory—can be morally justified, and the (separate) question of whether law imposes a moral obligation of obedience. As John Rawls put it, "political power is always coercive power [and] this raises the question of the legitimacy of the general structure of authority" (Rawls 1993: 136–37). In particular, the assumed coerciveness of law, as a descriptive fact, is often taken to frame the questions of justification and legitimacy in a way that casts a burden of proof upon the defender or apologist for the state. Hart, for example, wrote, "We are committed . . . to the general critical principle that the use of legal coercion by any society calls for justification as something prima facie objectionable" (Hart 1963: 20–21). The rhetorical significance of casting the burden of proof upon the state is that the issues of justification and legitimacy are to be decided against the state, in case the argument in favor is inconclusive or contestable. The defender of the legitimacy of legal authority thus bears a "risk of non-persuasion" (Gaskins 1992) that the skeptic does not. Moreover, even if the apologist for the state succeeds in carrying this burden, many will maintain that the "objectionable feature that attaches to each instance of coercion persists even after a demonstration that the particular deprivation of freedom is justified [for it] is simply *outweighed* in such cases" (Husak 1983: 355, emphasis in original; see also G. Dworkin 1968).

The thought that the defense of the state has to bear a burden of proof has also influenced the kind of justification that political philosophers have believed to be required. In particular, many prominent twentieth-century philosophers have believed that the inherent coerciveness of law entails that any adequate defense of the state must command unanimous assent, at least at some level. The clearest statement of this unanimity requirement is put forward by Thomas Nagel: "In view of the coercive character of the state, the requirement [of unanimity as at least to some "higher-order principle"] becomes a condition of political legitimacy" (Nagel 1991: 150–51). But a similar stringency can be located in the work of Rawls, and Jeremy Waldron finds common to a wide range of liberal, libertarian and socialist theories the "requirement that all aspects of the social world should either be made acceptable or be capable of being made acceptable to every last individual" (Waldron 1993: 36–37). It is perhaps worth noting also a curious way of running this requirement in reverse: legal theorist Ronald Dworkin identifies the law of certain legal systems (i.e., those of most English-speaking countries) with whatever would justify—at least to an ideally perspicacious mind—their past applications of coercion. Whatever at a given time "figures in or follows from" the most attractive account of the legal history and practices of a given polity is identical with its law at that time (R. Dworkin 1986: 225). From this idealized judicial perspective, the law of modern Anglophone nations (if it exists at all) is necessarily coercive, but also necessarily justifiably and legitimately so.

What is it about coercion and, particularly, state coercion, that is "prima facie objectionable" (Hart) and such as to demand of it a special justification not required of run-of-the-mill human activity? This question—a foundational one for political philosophy of the Rawlsian era—was the focus of Robert Nozick's attention in a 1969 paper, titled simply, "Coercion." This is the seminal article in the field, and the diligent reader might wish to put this chapter to one side until she has read and digested what Nozick had to say. The paper was intended as "a preliminary to a longer study of liberty, whose major concerns will be the reasons which justify making someone unfree to perform an action, and the reason why making someone unfree to perform an action needs justifying" (Nozick 1969: 440). That "longer study" was *Anarchy, State, and Utopia* (1974). It did not address the question "why making someone unfree to perform an action needs justifying," but instead assumed that "the anarchist claim that in the course of maintaining its monopoly on the use of force . . . the state must violate individuals' rights and hence is intrinsically immoral" (Nozick 1974: xi) was sufficiently compelling to serve as a premise.

Analyzing the Concept of Coercion

Assessing the normative sense that the concept of coercion has been assigned must wait upon further analysis of the concept itself. This analysis can best proceed by concentrating on a canonical form of the *coercion claim*, and the contexts in which such a claim might be asserted or rejected. A coercion claim is any statement approximately equivalent to one of the form:

By φing, person A coerces or attempts to coerce person B into ψing.

The φing by A will typically involve a declaration or threat of conditional form, which can be termed the *coercive proposal*. "Proposal" is meant to be a morally neutral term. Some writers have thought it important to distinguish threats from offers, and to analyze coercion claims in terms of threats; but the more promising approaches have avoided being drawn into disputes about where and how the line between threats and offers is to be drawn. Coercion claims—including statements that someone has been coerced or subjected to coercion—can occur in one or more of three distinct kinds of context. Coercion claims in these types of contexts at least potentially raise questions about justification. The three can be called, respectively, *justification-supplying, justification-defeating* and *justification-demanding* contexts.

A coercion claim occurs in a justification-supplying context if the claim is offered in order to satisfy a demand for justification of another action that need not itself be coercive, but could be. "I was coerced!" is a representative coercion claim made in a justification-supplying context: it functions as an excuse more often than as a straightforward justification. An affirmative defense of duress raised to avoid criminal liability creates this kind of context. The proper dimensions of the duress defense in criminal law are a matter of controversy; and it might be argued that a coercion claim can never, in and of itself, supply a justification for wrongdoing, as opposed to a mere excuse (a distinction whose import is, itself, a matter of dispute).

A coercion claim occurs in a justification-defeating context if the claim is made in order to negate a justification of consent to what would otherwise be wrongful. If, for example, an alleged rapist protests that his victim consented, then a coercion claim by or on behalf of the victim may be made in order to defeat that justification. The justification-defeating use of coercion claims is not unfamiliar to political philosophy: it is a standard rejoinder to consent theories of political obligation. In law and morals generally, consent is ineffective if coerced. Opponents of the Lockean idea that the

WILLIAM A. EDMUNDSON

governed at least tacitly consent to obey the state's authority are quick to point out that most citizens have no real alternative to those actions said to betoken consent, such as remaining in the territory of one's birth, or receipt of benefits such as a stable currency, public rights-of-way and defense from foreign invaders. Nothing more will be said here about coercion claims in justification-defeating contexts, for the central importance of the concept of coercion has to do with coercion claims in justification-demanding contexts, to which I now turn.

A vivid sense of a justification-demanding context of a coercion claim can be gotten by considering hypothetical cases such as the following:

Highway Robbery
Gunman stops Traveler on the highway and threatens to shoot Traveler if Traveler does not surrender Traveler's wallet. Gunman's proposal is *coercive*. Traveler gives up the wallet. Traveler has been *coerced*.

In a case such as Highway Robbery it should be clear that the coercion claims are true, and that Gunman's conduct stands in need of justification. Moreover, it seems obvious that precisely the same features that make Gunman's conduct coercive ground the demand for a justification. Compare the following case:

Tax Statute
A state enacts a statute providing that anyone who fails to pay taxes duly assessed is guilty of a felony punishable by a term of imprisonment. The initial intuition registered by many is that the statute is a *coercive* proposal, and that those who pay are *coerced*.

The analogy between Highway Robbery and Tax Statute is imperfect, but is widely believed to be close enough to support the commonplace belief that the claim that the state is coercive is both true and sufficient to ground a demand for a justification. Normally the state can provide a justification, most would be quick to add, if the taxes are assessed fairly and go to benefit the payor. Gunman, on the other hand, normally cannot provide a justification but, in unusual circumstances, might be able to: if for example Gunman was hoping to foil a terrorist plot in which Traveler was an unwitting accomplice. A good justification would not, however, alter the fact that, in both the Highway Robbery case and the Tax Statute case, coercion was involved.

The fact that coercion claims can create, or occur in, each of the three types of context does not in itself foreclose the possibility of a univocal semantic analysis of the concept of coercion (but see Berman 2002). Following on some of Nozick's suggestions, and drawing upon a body of legal examples, political philosopher Alan Wertheimer has offered an influential "two-prong" account, which (as modified below) will be the focus of much of the discussion here:

A coerces B to φ if and only if A makes a proposal to B which (1) creates a choice situation for B such that B has no reasonable alternative but to φ and which (2) is pro tanto wrongful of A to make.

One immediate objection to this analysis is that it unduly restricts coercion to circumstances in which a proposal is involved. Mitchell Berman, admitting that most cases involve proposals, i.e., conditional threats, nonetheless finds this feature inessential. He poses a case in which person A wants to make sure that another person, B, is not in B's office at 2:00 pm. A therefore plants a bomb at B's house set to detonate at 3:00 pm, leaves town, then calls B with instructions on how to defuse the bomb in time. *Pace* Nozick, A, in calling, does not make a proposal, for A has no further control over the bomb. But A has coerced B, because "A's course of conduct seems functionally and morally equivalent to [the paradigmatic] case of a [wrongfully coercive] conditional proposal" (Berman 2002: 51–52). On Nozick's behalf, one might insist that there is both a functional and moral difference: in the example, A lacks further control. In cases of coercion, the coercer exercises continuing control (Yaffe 2003). Coercion involves the coercer's declaration that his will is to prevail, or else. Trickery and manipulation, though objectionable and usable to achieve the same ends, do not involve one actor humbling another in a contest of wills.

More widely voiced objections go to other aspects of Wertheimer's schema. For convenience, I adopt Wertheimer's terminology and refer to condition (1) as the "choice" prong and to condition (2) as the "proposal" prong. The choice prong reflects the commonsense idea that one cannot be coerced, properly speaking, unless one's range of options has been constrained in a significant way. If, in the Highway Robbery example, Gunman had proposed to pinch, rather than to shoot, Traveler, the case would not count as one of coercion even though it is wrongful of Gunman to propose either.

The "proposal" prong is more controversial. Its inclusion makes the analysis a conspicuously "moralized" one (although determining the reasonableness of alternatives, under the "choice" prong, may call for moral judgment as well). A moralized analysis is what one would expect of coercion claims that have a justification-demanding sense, and it is consistent with intuition. As Hans Oberdiek writes:

> Coercion is a *moral notion*. [L]ike deception, wantonness, [and] bribery . . . coercion embodies a moral assessment: insofar as an act or institution is coercive, it is morally unjustified and therefore stands in need of a moral defense or excuse. At the same time, coercion is an incomplete moral notion, since truly describing an act or institution as coercive does not conclusively settle its moral unjustifiability, though it does place a definite *onus probandi* on anyone who wishes to defend or excuse the act or institution.
>
> (Oberdiek 1975: 80, emphasis original)

The correctness of moralized analyses of coercion has been a matter of extensive debate (see, e.g., Frankfurt 1973; Ryan 1980; Zimmerman 1981 and 2002; Murphy 1981; Alexander 1983). Before exploring this issue, it must be clarified that normally what makes a proposal wrongful is the wrongfulness of what Vinit Haksar has usefully called the coercer's "declared unilateral plan" (Haksar 1976: 68). In the Highway Robbery example, Gunman's proposal is to shoot unless given the wallet, and the declared unilateral plan is to shoot unless put in possession of the wallet. It is wrongful to shoot, and therefore wrongful to propose to shoot unless put in possession of the wallet. Under this description, the wrongness of making the proposal derives straightforwardly from the wrongness of shooting. But in other cases the wrongness of the proposal does not derive from or depend upon the wrongness of the declared unilateral plan. Blackmail is an example. Blackmail consists in a coercive proposal to publish embarrassing information unless some condition is met, usually a payment of money. But publishing embarrassing information need not, itself, be wrongful, and in some circumstances might be laudable or even a duty. Nonetheless, blackmail is classified as coercive.

Thus, although the quality of the declared unilateral plan often determines whether or not a proposal is pro tanto wrongful, this is not always the case, and the critical issue is whether the proposal (i.e., the proposing, the act of making the proposal) is pro tanto wrongful. This suggests a vivid way of evaluating the proposal. Compare the proposee's pre-proposal to his post-proposal situation: if it is pro tanto wrongful of the proposer to move the proposee away from the proposee's pre-proposal baseline, the proposal is pro tanto wrongful. The usefulness of this framework is plain when it becomes necessary to distinguish coercion from hard choices one must make because of unwelcome proposals by others. Many, though not everyone, will register the distinction. To bring it into relief, consider whether the following case is one of coercion:

Hard Bargain
A learns that B, whose train has derailed, is about to miss a steamship connection that is essential to B's avoiding a huge monetary loss. A proposes to carry B to portside on A's elephant, but only on condition that B buy the elephant for a large sum. B agrees.

The first, or "choice" condition, of the two-prong analysis is satisfied. But the second, or "proposal" condition, is perhaps not. One's intuition about the coerciveness *vel non* of A's proposal in Hard Bargain might be affected by comparing:

Easy Rescue
A, while boating, discovers B drowning in the water. A offers to rescue B, but only on condition that B buy the boat for a large sum of money. B agrees.

Many would classify Easy Rescue as a case of coercion, but not Hard Bargain. Some writers might disagree, at least in the more common case of capitalist wage offers (Hale 1923; Zimmerman 1981; Murphy 1981; Cohen 1983); but whatever one's classification of the two, the crux on a moralized account is whether B's baseline included A's performing the service A proposes to render only on the onerous stated condition. If one believes that B is entitled to be rescued, B's moral baseline includes the rescue, and B is made worse off by A's proposal, and, on Wertheimer's analysis, should be classified as a case of coercion. On the other hand, if one denies that B is entitled to easy rescue, then B's moral baseline does not include it, and A's proposal does not make B worse off with respect to it, and, accordingly, A's proposal is not coercive.

The "baseline" metaphor was original with Nozick; but Nozick's analysis formulated the "choice" prong in terms not of wrongness but in terms of making the proposee worse off with respect to either of two baselines. One baseline was the moral baseline which Wertheimer adopted. The other was a "normal and expected," non-moralized baseline, which Wertheimer decided against including. The two baselines gave different results, as appears vividly in a hypothetical case:

Nozick's "Slave Case"
A owns slaves, among whom is B. A routinely flogs his slaves, and B has been flogged daily for years. One day, A proposes not to flog B if B will do some deed that B would much rather not do. B agrees, and performs the deed.

Nozick acknowledged that the case seems to be one of coercion even though the proposal makes B better off, not worse, in terms of the normal and expected. B's "normal and expected" baseline includes being flogged; but B's moral baseline does not. B has a moral right not to be flogged, and if that is the relevant baseline, A's proposal makes B worse off with respect to it, and A's proposal is thus coercive.

In Nozick's view, the Slave Case was not conclusive. This was because, in other cases where the two baselines diverge, intuition favors the result directed by the "normal and expected" one, and not the moralized one. Consider:

Nozick's "Addict Case"
A regularly sells illegal, highly addictive drugs to B. B has no other source of supply, as A knows. One day, A tells B the supply will cease unless B performs some deed which B would much rather not perform. B performs the deed.

In this case, one's intuition is likely to be that B is coerced because in the normal and expected course of events B pays only the going black-market price. The moral baseline, however, is one in which A does not sell drugs to B, so A's proposal does not make B worse off with respect to that. Nozick concluded that the intuitions in both the Slave and the Addict cases were sound enough, and thus that making the proposee worse off with respect to either would suffice to render a proposal coercive (assuming that B had no reasonable alternative). To track intuitions across cases faithfully, Nozick appeared to endorse a kind of "dual-baseline" analysis, with the following observations:

> The relevant difference between these cases seems to be that the slave himself would prefer the morally expected rather than the normal course of events whereas the addict prefers the normal to the morally expected. . . . It may be that when the normal and the morally expected . . . diverge, the one of these which is to be used . . . is the course of events that the [proposee] prefers.
> (Nozick 1974: 450)

This suggestion could be characterized as a "dual baseline with a preference tiebreaker" analysis. Nozick was evidently not fully satisfied with it, and it is reasonable to suspect that he perceived—but chose not to pursue—the difficulties that arise if the coercion judgment is hostage to the structure and history of the proposee's preferences. For example, in Nozick's Addict Case, the coercion judgment hinges upon whether the addict would prefer to continue to use drugs. The preference tiebreaker would classify the unwilling addict as not coerced, the willing addict as coerced. (Those lacking a preference function, such as the ambivalent, and those having incomparable or intransitive preferences, would presumably be unclassifiable.) These discriminations seem not to correspond to intuition, and to that extent Nozick's effort to "save the phenomena" is in difficulty even before confronting further complications, such as the question of whether the proposee's preferences are to be taken as given, or are rather to be assessed with reference to what, counterfactually, the proposee would prefer given better information, or freed from bias, self-deception and addiction.

Is Law Coercive in the Justification-Demanding Sense?

Legal theorists have generally been drawn to the idea that law, laws and legal systems are coercive in a descriptive sense that has an explanatory significance; but, as noted in the first section, there has not been wide agreement about what coercion is, about where it comes into the depiction of law, laws and legal systems, or about its normative implications. By contrast, political philosophers across the spectrum from libertarians to egalitarian liberals to Marxists have tended to take the coerciveness of legal systems as a descriptive fact having far-reaching normative implications. Nozick, almost alone among recent political philosophers writing in English (an exception is Felix Oppenheim 1961), took up the task of analyzing the concept of coercion, and in so doing noticed the tendency of that analysis to undercut the descriptive assumption that states and legal systems are by their very nature coercive. If locating coercion in the world involves a preliminary drawing of moral baselines, then coerciveness in the justification-demanding sense can no longer be viewed as a cold and neutral descriptive attribute of the state. As Wertheimer puts it, "entire political theor[ies] may rest on a theory of coercion" that leads straight on to "a theory of coercion [that] rests on a moral and political theory—in particular, on a theory which allows us to set moral baselines" (Wertheimer 1987: 220–21). The presumptive wrongness of the state and its activities can no longer be taken as given by its descriptive coerciveness. Moreover, depending upon what emerges as the best theory of moral baselines, it may turn out that the rule of law is not coercive, and thus not pro tanto wrongful (Haksar 1976: 73 and 74, n. 11; Edmundson 1998: 73–124).

Some regard this tendency of moralized analyses as self-refuting (Cohen 1983: 3–4), and dismiss them without further argument. But there are numerous cases in which attention to a moralized baseline does seem to correct an initial intuition about coerciveness. Consider this case:

Ninety-Eight-Pound Weakling

Weakling, a man of modest build, is taunted by Nemesis, who is more muscular. In particular, Nemesis kicks sand in Weakling's face at the beach. To put an end to this, Weakling joins a health club and bulks up. Weakling, thus conspicuously enlarged and empowered, returns to the beach. As Weakling hopes and intends, Nemesis stops the teasing.

Has Weakling coerced Nemesis? It would seem not, and this intuition survives if the case is altered by substituting the course of prior taunting with Weakling's anxiety that it might begin. Although, discussing a similar case, Zimmerman (2002: 579) dismisses the "not coercive" verdict as "absurd," the very fact that intuitions about the presence of coercion are, for many at least, responsive to the pre-proposal distribution of rights and permissions lends some support to the moralized form of analysis. Alter the 98-Pound Weakling case so that Weakling, instead of going to the gym, asks his friend Big Buddy to go to the beach with him. Again, it does not appear that Nemesis is coerced and, analogously, it would not appear that the state, through its legal machinery, coerces Nemesis either.

Nozick (1969: 451–52) sought to avoid the counterintuitive conclusion that law and the state are not inherently coercive in the justification-demanding sense. He argued that the relevant pre-proposal situation is not one in which the state punishes stealing generally. Rather, the relevant baseline is one in which the state does not punish a particular act of stealing, though it otherwise punishes stealing generally. Against this as the normal and expected baseline (which the thief can be assumed to prefer to the moralized alternative), the state's proposal to punish this act of stealing makes the thief worse off, and thus coerced. Nozick's "token-subtractive" technique, though ingenious, cannot plausibly be employed elsewhere (cf., Zimmerman 1981: 121, 142). It would, for example, entail that anyone who unfavorably affects the consequences of anyone else's doing anything acts, ipso facto, coercively, no matter how far from the "normal and expected" (or the morally tolerable) the putative coercee's preferred, pre-proposal outcome might be.

Non-Moralized Accounts

David Zimmerman warns that without access to non-moralized conceptions of coercion and related concepts, classical and neo-liberal, libertarian and (one should add) liberal Marxist political philosophies lack the "normative Archidemean point" (2002: 602) needed to give them leverage against competing visions of the social and political world: "[E]ssential moralization renders the very content of liberty and coercion [unable to] do any foundational work in a deontological moral theory" (2002: 600). Hoping to avoid this result, Zimmerman and others have proposed alternative, non-moralized analyses. On some of these accounts, given sufficiently great pressure upon B to accept, A coerces B in case B prefers that A had not made the relevant proposal at all (Gunderson 1989; Gorr 1986). Another non-moralized approach looks beyond the proposal situation, and holds that A coerces B when A actively frustrates B's preferred, feasible, pre-proposal outcome (Zimmerman 1981).

Non-Moralized "Pressure" Theory

A "pressure theory" holds that coercion is at heart a matter of psychological pressure, pure and simple, and that any action that creates or exploits such pressure is pro tanto wrongful. Identifying instances of coercion, then, is primarily a matter of attending to the degree of pressure a suspected coercer brings to bear upon another (Yankah 2008). One difficulty with this approach is that of specifying a threshold at which noncoercive pressure becomes coercive. The alternative, to say that any degree of pressure suffices, unacceptably counts as coercive what most users of language would regard as not pro tanto wrongful. One person's "Good morning" to another will normally call for an acknowledgement of some kind, but it would be extravagant to say that it was coercive. A threshold must be set, but where? If it is set above zero but still too low, it will count as coercive a vast range of everyday dealings that intuition will not be prepared to regard as coercive in the justification-demanding sense. For example, an employee may be offered a promotion that she, though free to refuse, might find irresistible. Surely the offer is not pro tanto wrongful.

Non-Moralized, Preference-Baseline Accounts

To avoid the difficulty affecting a straightforward pressure theory, some have offered preference-baseline accounts. On such an account, intentionally bringing great psychological pressure to bear upon another is coercive (in the justification-demanding sense) just in case the person under pressure would prefer that the action creating the pressure not have been performed at all. Thus, an offer "too good to refuse" is coercive in the justification-demanding sense just in case it creates a kind or such a degree of pressure that the offeree would prefer it not have been made at all. This and similar

461

preference-baseline approaches are open to numerous objections, many of which are noted by Wertheimer. One objection is that the coerciveness of a proposal or other conduct, because it so depends upon the vagaries of the psychology of the putative coercee, will have to be relativized to an unacceptable degree. Moreover, the account is insensitive to the way the offeree's preferences have been formed. Non-moralized accounts, as noted above, must normalize the concept of pressure they employ, and for similar reasons the concept of preference seems to demand to be normalized as well. Extensive normalization could be taken to indicate that moralization has already begun to infect avowedly non-moralized baseline approaches (Yankah 2008: 1219).

Even if some non-moralized account were able to overcome the objections gathered above, whether it could count law and the state as coercive in the justification-demanding sense is questionable. Coerciveness would seem to have been relativized to the psychology and circumstances of each putative coercee, at least within the normal range. And those of a generally law-abiding disposition could not be said to be coerced at all, except in exceptional cases. For parallel reasons, coerciveness would have to be further relativized to particular legal requirements. But law is only seldom felt as pressure. Those laws backed by heavy penalties typically forbid what morality forbids anyway, such as murder, assault and larceny. The remaining body of mandatory law is, arguably, morally obligatory by operation of a moral principle of fairness, given widespread legal compliance by others (Edmundson 1998: 113–17; Hart 1955). As indicated above, it is a disputed question whether proportionate penalties for violation of such laws is even pro tanto wrongful (Haksar 1976). Moreover, laws backed by lighter penalties, or by heavy ones for which the likelihood of sanction is small, appear incapable of bringing to bear sufficient rational pressure to reach the aforementioned threshold. Where the perception of pressure has been dulled by a course of habituation or indoctrination there may yet be reason to count the state's posture as coercive (Anderson 2008: 419); but that fact would only shift the focus of argument to earlier points in the supposed chronology. The objectionableness of coercion may remain despite the coercee's habituation; but whether the putative coercee's earlier condition involved coercion in the justification-demanding sense must still be shown.

If pressure to comply with a given directive is not counted as coercive unless it is high enough to alter an individual's behavior, the prevalence of legal coercion falls significantly short of the expectation that political philosophers may have excited. But if coercion were pressure plus something else—a non-moralized something else—that the state invariably exhibits, then the pressure threshold might be lowered even as the prevalence of recognized legal coercion were expanded. Recent contributions to the literature shed light on what that further, non-moralized factor might be.

A Non-Moralized, Coercer-Intention Account

A non-moralized account might acknowledge that unwelcome pressure, even great pressure, taken alone, does not capture what is pro tanto wrongful about coercion. The crucial additional element might be the intention with which that pressure is applied. Grant Lamond suggests such a position:

> Why should it be thought that action-inducing coercion is prima facie impermissible in *every* instance? In the face of physical compulsion the answer is clear: it is because it involves a physical interference with another person.

Rational compulsion, on the other hand, is *prima facie* impermissible because it involves the threat *deliberately* to bring about an unwelcome consequence—some disadvantage—if the other person does not comply with a demand: thus it involves the proposal *deliberately* to set back their interests or deprive them of some expectation if they are uncooperative.

(Lamond 2000: 49, emphasis added)

It is undeniable that intentional physical interference is often at least pro tanto wrongful, and likewise undeniable that rational compulsion is often at least pro tanto wrongful. Do these facts establish that action-inducing coercion is pro tanto wrongful? With respect to intentional physical interference, the key notion of interference is ambiguous. If it is a purely spatial concept, like physical displacement, there are many instances in which intentional physical interference is not even pro tanto wrongful. If, for example, I stand on the summit of a hitherto unclimbed peak, with the intention of preventing your doing so first, I do not wrong you even a little bit. If I take the best seat in the house for the sole purpose of depriving you of it, I may disappoint you, but I do not wrong you—not even a little—unless you can claim some entitlement (cf. Ripstein 2004). Unless you have a ticket giving you that right, you have none. Or is it pro tanto wrongful intentionally to spite others? To say that it is would, I think, be to confuse two importantly distinct categories: the pro tanto wrongful and what Julia Driver (1992) has called the "suberogatory." What is pro tanto wrongful is wrongful unless redeemed by important justifying reasons. What is suberogatory is what is permissible though less than the best, or less than one's best. The suberogatory is to the wrongful as the supererogatory is to the morally required. I may be small-minded in depriving you of the distinction of being the first to summit Peak X, or of the pleasure of the best seat in the house. But what I do is not pro tanto wrongful unless one supposes that you had more than an interest or an expectation. Once that "more" is built into the case—a protected interest, or a legitimate expectation—we will have already introduced morally evaluative elements. A parallel argument applies to the case of rational compulsion.

A Not-Necessarily Moralized Account Keyed to Compliance-Tracking

Gideon Yaffe is another recent writer to have sought an explanation of the distinctive wrongness of coercion. Yaffe's focus is the intermediate idea of a reduction in freedom. Constraints of all kinds reduce freedom in some sense, but we intuitively regard the constraints imposed by coercers as diminishing our freedom in a distinctive way. This way is not a matter of mere effects, as can be seen by considering the difference between losing $10 to an armed robber and losing $10 to a sudden gust of wind. The former, coercive loss is felt to represent a diminution in freedom while the latter is not, despite the fact that the monetary loss is the same. If this is correct, then on the further assumptions that a loss of freedom is a harm and that harming another is pro tanto wrongful, the conclusion could be drawn that law is coercive in the justification-demanding sense because it diminishes freedom, or diminishes it in a harm-constituting way.

The crux is to explain how coercion diminishes freedom in a way that mere bad luck does not, even where the effect on the agent's options is identical. Yaffe's proposal is this:

The key to the explanation for the freedom-undermining force of coercion is that, as a general rule, coercers don't merely produce, but also track, the compliance of their victims. . . . The coercer tailors his threat to the features of the mechanism for response to reasons that the victim possesses.

(2003: 351)

Assuming this is correct, the characterization of the coercer bears only a distant resemblance to the modern state; and this distance renders unlikely the prospect of bolstering the assumption that political society is inescapably tainted by the pro tanto wrongness of its essential and central mode of operation. The state ordinarily does not closely monitor the compliance of its citizens. The panoptic dystopias familiar from twentieth-century literature should indeed be thought to track citizens' conduct in a way inimical to freedom. But those caricatures cannot fairly be extended to modern (post-) industrial democracies. Yaffe does not suggest, and we cannot assume, that the rule of law is, by its very nature, a coercer in the requisite sense. Indeed, Yaffe (breaking ranks with non-moralized approaches) adds that manipulation whose effect is to keep the manipulated on the track of rightful conduct does not diminish freedom, and thus is not coercive in the justification-demanding sense (2003: 349).

A General Difficulty for Non-Moralized Approaches

Non-moralized analyses of coercion in its justification-demanding sense assume that a logical passage from non-moralized factual description to a moral judgment of pro tanto wrongness can be made. The familiar "is–ought" objection is bound to come up. It should not be assumed that the objection is decisive, here or elsewhere; but, in the matter of the law's alleged coerciveness, it might serve as a reminder that the burden of justification that political philosophy has routinely assigned to the state and its defenders stands, itself, in need of justification.

Summary

Coercion is often assumed to be an essential feature of law, both in an explanatory sense and in a justification-demanding sense. Explanations of law have cast coercion in a variety of roles, and the conception of coercion fitted into these roles has been variously understood. Some, like Kelsen, equate coercion with physical compulsion, but the currently dominant view is that coercion essentially involves the wills of at least two persons. One person, a coercer, communicates to the other, the coercee, a proposal to alter the coercee's situation in an unwelcome way unless the coercee performs some specified act. Typically, the coercer makes it understood that the unwelcome alteration will not occur if the coercee complies with the coercer's demand.

Some philosophers argue that the coercer's role in this type of entanglement of wills is pro tanto wrongful, without further description or with no further description than what will assure that the psychological pressure brought to bear upon the coercee is objectively nontrivial. Others, perhaps the greater number at this writing, argue that these conditions are not coercive without what will amount to a further stipulation that the coercer's proposal was wrongful to make. No matter which of these two views is correct, the commonplace view that law, laws and legal institutions are essentially coercive in a justification-demanding sense can no longer be taken for granted.

References

Alexander, L. (1983) "Zimmerman on Coercive Wage Offers," *Philosophy & Public Affairs* 12: 158–64.

Anderson, S. (2008) "Of Theories of Coercion, Two Axes, and the Importance of the Coercer," *Journal of Moral Philosophy* 5: 394–422.

Austin, J. (1954/1832) *The Province of Jurisprudence Determined*, H. L. A. Hart, ed., London: Weidenfeld & Nicholson.

Berman, M. (2002) "The Normative Functions of Coercion Claims," *Legal Theory* 8: 45–89.

Cohen, G. A. (1983) "The Structure of Proletarian Unfreedom," *Philosophy & Public Affairs* 12: 3–33.

Driver, J. (1992) "The Suberogatory," *Australasian Journal of Philosophy* 70: 286–95.

Dworkin, G. (1968) "Compulsion and Moral Concepts," *Ethics* 78: 227–33.

Dworkin, R. (1986) *Law's Empire*, Cambridge, Mass.: The Belknap Press of Harvard University Press.

Edmundson, W. (1998) *Three Anarchical Fallacies: An Essay on Political Authority*, Cambridge: Cambridge University Press.

Frankfurt, H. (1973) "Coercion and Moral Responsibility," in T. Honderich, ed., *Essays on Freedom of Action*, London: Routledge and Kegan Paul. Reprinted in Frankfurt, H. (1988) *The Importance of What We Care About: Philosophical Essays*, Cambridge: Cambridge University Press.

Fuller, L. (1964) *The Morality of Law*, New Haven: Yale University Press.

Gaskins, R. (1992) *Burdens of Proof in Modern Discourse*, New Haven: Yale University Press.

Gorr, M. (1986) "Toward a Theory of Coercion," *Canadian Journal of Philosophy* 16: 383–406.

Gunderson, M. (1989) "Threats and Coercion," *Canadian Journal of Philosophy* 9: 247–59.

Haksar, V. (1976) "Coercive Proposals," *Political Theory* 4: 65–79.

Hale, R. (1923) "Coercion and Distribution in a Supposedly Non-Coercive State," 38 *Political Science Quarterly* 38: 470–78.

Hart, H. L. A. (1955) "Are There Any Natural Rights?" *Philosophical Review* 64: 175–91. Reprinted in J. Waldron, ed. (1984) *Theories of Rights*, Oxford: Oxford University Press.

—— (1961) *The Concept of Law*, Oxford: Clarendon Press.

—— (1963) *Law, Liberty, and Morality*, Stanford: Stanford University Press.

Husak, D. (1983) "The Presumption of Freedom," *Noûs* 17: 345–62.

Kelsen, H. (1961/1945) *General Theory of Law and State*, A. Wedberg, trans., New York: Russell & Russell.

Lamond, G. (2000) "The Coerciveness of Law," *Oxford Journal of Legal Studies* 20: 39–62.

Murphy, J. (1981) "Consent, Coercion, and Hard Choices," *Virginia Law Review* 67: 79–95.

Nagel, T. (1991) *Equality and Partiality*, Oxford: Oxford University Press.

Nozick, R. (1969) "Coercion," in S. Morgenbesser, P. Suppes and M. White, eds., *Philosophy, Science, and Method: Essays in Honor of Ernest Nagel*, New York: St. Martin's Press, pp. 440–72. Reprinted in Nozick, R. (1997) *Socratic Puzzles*, Cambridge, Mass.: Harvard University Press, pp. 15–44.

—— (1974) *Anarchy, State, and Utopia*, New York: Basic Books, Inc.

Oberdiek, H. (1975) "The Role of Sanctions and Coercion in Understanding Law and Legal Systems," *American Journal of Jurisprudence* 75: 71–94.

Oppenheim, F. (1961) *Dimensions of Freedom*, New York: St. Martin's.

Rawls, J. (1993) *Political Liberalism*, New York: Columbia University Press.

Ripstein, A. (2004) "Authority and Coercion," *Philosophy & Public Affairs* 32: 2–35.

Ryan, C. (1980) "The Normative Concept of Coercion," *Mind* 89: 481–98.

Schauer, F. (2011) "The Best Laid Plans," *Yale Law Journal* 120: 586–621.

Waldron, J. (1993) *Liberal Rights: Collected Papers 1981–91*, Cambridge: Cambridge University Press.

Wertheimer, A. (1987) *Coercion*, Princeton: Princeton University Press.

Yaffe, G. (2003) "Indoctrination, Coercion, and Freedom of the Will," *Philosophy and Phenomenological Research* 67: 335–56.

Yankah, E. (2008) "The Force of Law: The Role of Coercion in Legal Norms," *Richmond Law Review* 42: 1195–1255.

Zimmerman, D. (1981) "Coercive Wage Offers," *Philosophy & Public Affairs* 10: 121–45.

—— (2002) "Taking Liberties: The Perils of 'Moralizing' Liberty and Coercion in Social Theory and Practice," *Social Theory and Practice* 28: 577–610.

WILLIAM A. EDMUNDSON

Further Reading

R. Nozick (1969) "Coercion," in S. Morgenbesser, P. Suppes and M. White, eds., *Philosophy, Science, and Method: Essays in Honor of Ernest Nagel*, New York: St. Martin's Press, pp. 440–72. Reprinted in Nozick, R. (1997) *Socratic Puzzles*, Cambridge, Mass.: Harvard University Press, pp. 15–44 (the chief landmark in the literature); F. Oppenheim (1961) *Dimensions of Freedom*, New York: St. Martin's (combines lucid analysis with an effort to locate coercion in a wider conceptual terrain); A. Wertheimer (1987) *Coercion*, Princeton: Princeton University Press (is both a thorough discussion of the literature up to that date and a systematic defense of the moralized approach); and S. Anderson (2006) "Coercion," in E. N. Zalta, ed., *The Stanford Encyclopedia of Philosophy*, Winter 2011 Edition, http://plato.stanford.edu/archives/win2011/entries/coercion (a valuable later discussion of the state of the literature, and appends an extensive bibliography).

30

PATERNALISM

Douglas Husak

I assume that most of the controversy about the topic of paternalism involves the question of whether and under what circumstances it is justified. An answer must address two preliminary matters: what paternalism *is*, and what would qualify as a *justification* for it. Since each of these background issues could consume an entire essay, I will attempt to say as little as possible about them in order to move directly to what I hope is more central. But these matters cannot be avoided altogether. I further assume that legal philosophers are less likely to be interested in paternalism per se than in paternalism in the domain of law. Thus I will concentrate on the special problems that arise in justifying legal paternalism. As we will see, these problems are formidable. Little of the progress that moral philosophers have achieved in justifying paternalism in personal relations is readily adaptable to legal contexts.

What Paternalism Is and What Counts as a Justification for It

On most occasions in which A is justified in not allowing B to act according to his preferences, A's objective is to protect persons who might be harmed by B's behavior. When A treats B paternalistically, however, B is prevented from acting because of the adverse effects on B himself. As a very rough approximation, A treats B paternalistically when A interferes with B's freedom for B's own good—to protect or promote B's health, safety, economic interests or moral well-being.

When philosophers attempt to be more precise about the nature of paternalism, however, the details of their definitions vary considerably (Archer 1990). They debate whether particular examples that deviate from the foregoing approximation do or do not qualify as genuine instances of paternalism. I will mention two (of many) such debates briefly. Still, for reasons that will become clear, I avoid commitment about how paternalism should ultimately be defined.

First, some philosophers point out that paternalism need not involve two parties. In some examples, only one party is needed. Suppose that Jane understands her proclivity to gain weight, so she locks her refrigerator at night. Is her act of making food inaccessible an instance of paternalism in which Jane plays the role of both A (her present self) and B (her later self whose preferences she disregards)? In other examples, three or more parties are involved. Suppose that parent A forbids his oldest son C from sharing cigarettes with his youngest son B on the grounds that tobacco is bad for B's health. This case is unlike a typical situation in which A coerces C to prevent him from harming B, since B may be eager to engage in the proscribed transaction. In this case, we again are invited to conclude, A treats B paternalistically. Paternalism in this case is said to be *impure* or *indirect* (Dworkin 1972), since A interferes directly with the liberty of C, and only indirectly with that of B, the intended beneficiary.

A second debate about the nature of paternalism stems from the claim that the paternalist need not *interfere* in anyone's freedom (Gert and Culver 1976). Suppose, for example, that doctors in an emergency room are presented with an unconscious victim whose life can be saved only by surgery. Since the patient remains unconscious throughout the procedure, it is hard to conclude that the surgery interferes with her liberty. Still, it seems apparent that the doctor treats the patient paternalistically.

So-called *libertarian paternalism* poses a possible counter example to the claim that paternalists interfere with liberty (Sunstein 2006). Libertarian paternalism works primarily by designing default rules to correct for well-known cognitive biases and volitional lapses, thereby minimizing the likelihood that persons will make decisions that are contrary to their own interest (Trout 2005). Consider the following two examples. Rather than explicitly choosing to participate in an efficient company health plan, employees might be enrolled automatically unless they opt out. Seat belts might be constructed to buckle immediately upon closing a car door, although occupants could unbuckle them if they choose. Are these provisions really paternalistic? As long as persons can change these default rules, no *interference* with choice has occurred. Notice that individuals "can" alter the default rule in two senses. First, persons face no penalty if they elect not to comply. Second, opting out is not onerous, requiring a mere stroke of the pen or push of a button. When these two conditions are satisfied, it seems more accurate to construe these rules as designed to *influence* persons to pursue their self-interest.

Are these two kinds of nonstandard cases genuine counter examples to my rough approximation, requiring that my definition be modified? Probably. But I am skeptical that a "right answer" to such questions can be defended. That is, I am unsure that we can decide whether each nonstandard case is or is not a "real" instance of paternalism. I suspect that some cases are simply *better* or *worse* examples than others. We should not expect decisive reasons for or against categorizing an example as an instance of paternalism. Ultimately, a philosopher who insists on a yes-or-no answer to the question of whether a given case is an instance of paternalism must resort to stipulation. The more important issue, I submit, is whether the behavior of A (or the default rule in question) is justified in the foregoing examples. Generalizations about whether and under what circumstances paradigmatic cases of paternalism are justified may or may not be defensible when applied to nonstandard situations.

Whatever else paternalism is taken to be, I suggest it should be understood as a *reason* or *motivation* for acting (Grill 2007). An interference with liberty should not be construed as paternalistic in virtue of its *effects*. Consider two kinds of case in which effect and motivation diverge. Suppose that A somehow succeeds in advancing B's interests even though A's reason for interfering in B's freedom is to enrich himself. Or suppose that A fails to advance B's interests despite A's best efforts to do so. I believe that the latter but not the former case should be categorized as an instance of paternalism. This categorization follows from defining paternalism in terms of the motives that lead A to interfere with B, rather than by how A's interference actually affects B's welfare. Although consequences may be important in deciding whether paternalism is *justified*, I believe they are unimportant in understanding what paternalism *is*. The decision to construe paternalism as a reason or motivation has several important implications that I will later discuss, with special emphasis on the law.

It may be helpful to present a concrete, ordinary case from which to generalize about the nature and justifiability of paternalism as well as to highlight the difficulties of defending it in the legal domain. The best examples are drawn from personal relations. When asked about his preference, four-year-old Bobby objects to taking his oral flu vaccine. His father has tried to persuade him, but Bobby is unmoved. I stipulate that the father's only reason for wanting Bobby to take his vaccine is to safeguard his child's health. It seems reasonable for his father not to permit Bobby to eat ice cream, his favorite dessert, unless he takes the vaccine. This example not only describes a situation in which Bobby is treated paternalistically, but also represents a relatively clear case in which the treatment is justified. In any event, I make these two assumptions about this case.

Five criteria conspire to make this example a relatively clear case of justified paternalism. *First*, the intrusion involves a minor interference in Bobby's liberty. Bobby is not beaten or deprived of something of great significance to induce him to change his behavior. *Second*, the objective sought by his father is obviously valuable. No one contests the importance of health and the ill effects of contracting flu. *Third*, the means chosen are likely to promote this end. The vaccine is effective, and Bobby is likely to agree to take the vaccine if his desire for ice cream is strong. *Fourth*, Bobby himself is not in a favorable position to make the right decision. Children have notorious cognitive and volitional deficiencies relative to competent adults that prevent them from recognizing their best interests or from acting appropriately when they do. *Fifth*, his father stands in an ideal relationship to Bobby to treat him paternalistically. Parents have special duties to protect and enhance the welfare of their children. My example satisfies each of these five criteria, and the easiest cases of justified paternalism do so as well. I do not insist that any of these conditions is necessary to justify paternalism. I simply allege that particular examples will prove more difficult to justify as they deviate from this paradigm.

Can Laws Be Paternalistic?

If paternalism is construed as a particular reason for failing to regard the preference of a person as decisive, disagreements about whether a given law is or is not paternalistic may be misguided and futile. *Laws* do not seem to be the kinds of things that *can* be paternalistic; only *reasons* can be paternalistic. Still, claims that a law is paternalistic are frequently voiced by philosophers and should not be dismissed as confusions (Goldman and Goldman 1990). How should these claims be understood? Perhaps a law should be categorized as paternalistic when it exists for paternalistic reasons.

Several difficulties plague this attempt to understand how a law can be paternalistic. What does it mean to "exist for paternalistic reasons"? Many of these difficulties are familiar to legal philosophers who defend theories of statutory or constitutional interpretation that attach significance to legislative intent. The first kind of problem arises even when a legislator is a single individual, like a monarch. A legislator is not generally required to disclose his motivation for enacting legislation. In most cases, his reason must be inferred from various sources, many of which can be ambiguous or even contradictory. In addition, a legislator may have no single reason to favor a given law; he may have several distinct purposes in mind. The second kind of problem arises in a modern democracy in which laws are enacted by a number of representatives. How can we combine the separate motives of several individuals into the purpose of a group?

Should we count only those legislators who voted in favor of the law, or should we also consider the reasons of those who opposed it? Even if we agree about which legislators should count, these persons are bound to have diverse reasons for enacting the statute. One legislator may vote in favor of a bill for paternalistic reasons, another may vote for the bill even though he rejects this paternalistic reason, while yet a third may support the bill for reasons having nothing to do with its merits. How can we possibly decide whether to classify such a law as paternalistic? Finally, the *persistence* of law complicates endeavors to categorize it. All of the legislators who passed a statute may be dead. Suppose that most of the legislators who enacted a law did so for paternalistic reasons, but this rationale is now widely discredited and legislators have non-paternalistic reasons for not repealing the law. Since the law persists for altogether different reasons than those that led to its enactment, should we continue to classify the law according to the original motivation of those who created it? In light of these (and other) difficulties, we might despair of any prospects of identifying "the reason" for a law.

Problems in categorizing laws as paternalistic arise whenever particular examples are discussed. Consider a statute forbidding child labor. Presumably, many legislators favored such a law in order to protect the welfare of children. An additional reason for the statute, of course, is to preserve the jobs and wages of adults who otherwise would be forced to compete with underage workers. As far as I can tell, there simply is no definitive answer to the question of whether such a law is or is not paternalistic. I suspect that every actual law that anyone has ever been inclined to categorize as paternalistic resembles the example of child labor in this respect. Here, then, is the first of many difficulties that arise in attempts to apply philosophical insights about paternalism in personal relationships to legal contexts. Admittedly, on some occasions, the motivations for interference can be complicated and unclear even in personal relationships. Flu vaccines, for example, help to prevent other persons from contracting the disease. I assume, however, that Bobby's father may be confident about his reason for requiring his son to take the vaccine. The difficulties in classifying a given interference as paternalistic are seldom as formidable in personal relationships as in legal contexts.

This fact will become important when we turn to whether and under what circumstances paternalism is justified. Most philosophers, it is fair to say, have relatively strong intuitions against the justifiability of paternalism, at least when it is imposed on sane adults. Suppose that a philosopher becomes persuaded of a theory according to which paternalism is never justified, or is justified only under narrowly specified conditions. Of what value is his theory in assessing legislation in the real world? It is hard to see how his theory could be used to condemn any existing law. That is, he cannot demand that any particular law must be repealed because he is convinced that his theory is correct. All that he is entitled to conclude is that such a law is unjustified insofar as it exists for paternalistic reasons.

Nonetheless, a theory about the conditions under which paternalism is justified would have some limited relevance in legal contexts. Such a theory might constrain the considerations to which legislators are allowed to appeal in their deliberations about whether to support a given piece of legislation. That is, a legislator may be persuaded that some kinds of reasons he might otherwise cite in support of a proposed law should not be permitted to count in its favor. Alternatively, such a theory might constrain the considerations to which citizens are allowed to appeal in making judgments about whether a law is justified (Waldron 1993). After all, citizens in a democracy should be encouraged to make their own judgments about whether laws are good or bad. A theory about the conditions under which paternalism is acceptable as a rationale could be useful for these purposes.

Despite these enormous obstacles, I remain hopeful that the label "paternalistic" can meaningfully be applied to given laws, and that a theory of when paternalism is justified in personal relations is relevant to the issue of whether such laws are justified. Perhaps the most promising proposal for interpreting the claim that a given law is paternalistic is that "the most plausible rationale" or "the best rationale" in favor of the law is to limit the freedom of persons for their own good. According to this proposal, a law can be paternalistic even though no one, past or present, ever thought to defend it on paternalistic grounds. "The best rationale" of a law can be something other than the reasons that actually led anyone to support it. Of course, commentators are bound to disagree about whether one rationale is more plausible than another. But those who conclude that the best reason in favor of a given law is paternalistic are committed to categorizing it as paternalistic. Even though I tend to favor this approach, we should remain cautious and tentative when we attach the label "paternalistic" to a given law.

Thus far, I have pointed out some of the difficulties in applying a definition of paternalism to particular laws. In addition, our understanding of what paternalism *is* becomes less clear as we move from nonlegal to legal contexts. My central basis for this claim is that laws are necessarily general and applicable to groups of persons whose circumstances differ widely. The fact that a law is applicable to a group of persons—whereas a paradigm case of paternalism in a personal relationship is applicable only to a single individual—gives rise to many of the perplexities in understanding the nature and justification of legal paternalism. Suppose we (somehow) decide that legislators have enacted a given law to limit the freedom of persons for their own good. Even so, we are likely to find that the law does not disregard the preferences of each and every person whose liberty is restricted. Some limitations of liberty are best construed as devices that *enable* persons to attain their antecedent objective. I am doubtful that we should deem a rationale as paternalistic when it enables a person to achieve an objective that he recognizes as desirable but is unlikely to attain in the absence of the legislation that limits his liberty (Dworkin 1972).

A good example of this phenomenon is a statute that requires persons to contribute to a social security plan. Consider Smith, who does not want to spend all of his income in the present, but is well aware of his inability to save the amount of money for the future that he realizes is optimal. Although he grumbles occasionally, he usually approves of legislation that prevents him from succumbing to his own weakness. If the legislator who enacted this statute believes that everyone resembles Smith in these respects, I would be hesitant to categorize his motivation as paternalistic. The legislator is not disregarding Smith's preference, but helping him to attain the end he prefers or judges to be best. Complications arise, of course, because legislators know that many of the persons to whom the law applies will *not* resemble Smith. Consider Jones, who, like Smith, is made to contribute to the retirement plan. Unlike Smith, however, Jones would prefer to spend all of his income in the present. The law does not regard Jones's preference as decisive, and he is certain to perceive the law as a paternalistic interference in his freedom. How should the law be categorized when legislators realize that the liberty of both Smith and Jones will be restricted? When the preferences of many but not all of the persons whose liberty is restricted are regarded as decisive, I see no basis for identifying a "right answer" to the question of whether the rationale of the law is paternalistic.

DOUGLAS HUSAK

How Not to Justify Legal Paternalism

In order to decide whether given laws are justified, we need criteria of justification applicable to the legal domain. Obviously, this task is incredibly difficult, dividing political philosophers for eons. Suppose, however, that we invoke a simple justificatory theory: utilitarianism. The foregoing problems of categorization do not arise under this theory, since the very same justificatory criteria apply whether or not the law in question qualifies as paternalistic. Although John Stuart Mill famously argued that no paternalistic laws could pass the test of utility, his reasoning seems curiously *a priori* and unwilling to address empirical realities (Shafer-Landau 2005). Mill's reservations aside, I see no reason to be confident that laws we are inclined to classify as paternalistic *cannot* produce more good than bad overall.

Whether or not they adhere to some version of utilitarianism, it is fair to generalize that most moral and political philosophers have expressed strong objections to paternalism, tolerating it under very narrow conditions. As I have indicated, examples involving personal relationships typically have been used to develop theories about whether and under what circumstances paternalism is acceptable. In this section I will argue that the progress that has been made in this direction is of little or no use in efforts to justify paternalism in legal contexts. Two examples support my position and indicate that a fresh start is needed.

First, the contrast between *hard* and *soft* paternalism is the single most important distinction that has been introduced in attempts to justify paternalism in personal relationships (Feinberg 1986). According to soft paternalists, A may treat B paternalistically only when B's conduct is *nonvoluntary*. According to *hard* paternalists, A sometimes may treat B paternalistically even though B's conduct is *voluntary*. Although some philosophers contend that a few instances of hard paternalism can be justified (Kleinig 1984; Scoccia 2008), the appeal of soft paternalism is evident. The soft paternalist favors intervention in B's choice for his own good only when it seems that B's choice is not really his own. If B's conduct is fully voluntary and expresses his will, soft paternalists insist that no interference for B's own good is warranted.

Clearly, the significance of the distinction between hard and soft paternalism depends on a theory of what choices are truly ours—on an account of the voluntary. The contrast between hard and soft paternalism has proved difficult to draw (Pope 2004). According to a sensible proposal by Joel Feinberg (1986), voluntariness should be conceptualized as a matter of degree. He develops a model of a *perfectly voluntary choice* in which the agent is fully informed of all the relevant facts and contingencies and makes a decision in the absence of any manipulation or coercive pressure. Perhaps no choice in the real world corresponds to Feinberg's ideal; particular choices are relatively nonvoluntary to the extent that they deviate from it. Inevitably, troublesome borderline cases on this continuum will arise in which we are unsure whether a choice is sufficiently voluntary to render paternalistic interference unjustifiable (according to the soft paternalist). For example, philosophers often struggle to decide when consent to medical treatment is sufficiently voluntary (Buchanan 1989).

But the distinction between hard and soft paternalism, potentially helpful in identifying the conditions under which paternalism is justified in personal relationships, is much less valuable in identifying the conditions under which legislators are justified in enacting laws for paternalistic reasons. This lack of relevance is largely a product of a phenomenon I have already noted: law is necessarily general and applicable to large numbers of persons whose circumstances vary.

Perhaps the most obvious variable in the circumstances of the persons who are subject to law is their differing motivations for wanting to engage in the conduct the law would prohibit. Suppose that a legislator who accepts soft but not hard paternalism deliberates about whether to proscribe a potentially harmful but pleasurable drug (Husak 1989). He finds that a great many actual and prospective users are misinformed about the health hazards of their decisions. Other existing users are addicts. If ignorance and/or addiction undermine voluntariness, the legislator may infer that the choices of these persons are not sufficiently voluntary. Hence he will tend to favor proscription on soft-paternalist grounds. But suppose that this legislator also finds that large numbers of actual and prospective users are neither addicted nor misinformed about the risks of the substance. Like many persons who elect to eat fast food rather than nutritious meals, these users have decided that the benefits of pleasure outweigh the risks to health. Since this legislator finds that the preferences of these latter persons are sufficiently voluntary, he will tend to allow the drug to be used.

What conclusion, then, should this legislator reach about whether or not to enact the law? The proscription seems justified in its application to those persons whose choices are nonvoluntary, but unjustified in its application to those persons whose choices are voluntary. Ideally, the legislator will search for a solution that manages to treat each person individually, so that the drug is permitted for those persons whose decisions are voluntary, but is banned otherwise. The drug might be distributed under a system of licensure, so that it would be available only to those adults who demonstrate their ability to quit and their knowledge of the relevant risks. But this ideal solution encounters both pragmatic and principled difficulties; licensing is extraordinarily cumbersome, inefficient and subject to error and abuse. Since the state cannot be expected to successfully adjust its approach to the distinct circumstances of each person, it needs a default position (Kennedy 1982). The legislator must engage in *trade-offs*; that is, he must balance his judgment about the merits of soft paternalism against the demerits of hard paternalism. The principles that govern these trade-offs—that govern the application of a theory of justified paternalism to legal contexts—are highly controversial. If the default position results in drug prohibition, many persons will be subjected to hard paternalism.

This legislator will find additional important differences in the circumstances of the persons in his jurisdiction. Some prospective users of the drug are adolescents, while others are adults. Everyone agrees that paternalistic intervention in the preferences of adolescents is justified more easily than in the preferences of competent adults. How should this legislator take account of this fact in his deliberations? The obvious solution is to permit the drug for users over a given age, typically 18 or 21. But this solution is problematic. Whenever a substance is made available to adults, "leakage" to adolescents is bound to occur. In other words, greater numbers of adolescents will succeed in using the drug illegally if it is permitted for adults than would manage to do so if it were prohibited for persons of all ages. Thus, this legislator will be tempted to proscribe the drug altogether if he is greatly concerned about its deleterious effects on adolescents. Again, such a legislator must engage in trade-offs. On this occasion, he somehow must balance the freedom of adults against the welfare of adolescents.

To this point, I have described various kinds of differences in the circumstances of the persons whose preferences are disregarded by a given law, and how these differences complicate attempts to apply to the domain of law a theory of justified paternalism derived from personal relationships. The differences I have mentioned thus far are all (roughly) psychological—law applies to persons of different degrees of sanity and maturity, with disparate motivations and distinct levels of knowledge about the consequences of engaging in the activity in question. But purely physical differences between persons may be important as well. Because of physical dissimilarities between individuals, a given law may protect the welfare of some while jeopardizing that of others. Air bags in automobiles illustrate this phenomenon. The deployment of an air bag reduces the severity of injuries for the vast majority of drivers involved in automobile accidents. In some kinds of collisions, however, persons who are very short are more likely to be injured by the deployment of the air bag than by the crash itself. Ideally, of course, air bags should be constructed to benefit *all* occupants of cars. But engineers may be unable to design an air bag to realize this ideal. If a legislator decides to require air bags to protect the safety of persons involved in automobile accidents, he necessarily trades a reduction in injuries to some drivers for an increase in injuries to others. Alternatively, engineers may be able to design an air bag to benefit all occupants, but only at an exorbitant cost. A legislator who declines to require this expensive but optimal air bag necessarily balances the value of money against the desirability of reducing injuries.

The foregoing phenomenon provides an occasion to return to some of the difficulties in defining paternalism with which I began. Suppose that a legislator must vote for or against a regulation mandating that automobiles contain air bags. He is inclined to support the regulation because he believes that occupants of cars should be protected from injuries. But he also is aware that this regulation will actually decrease the safety of a minority of drivers. If he ultimately supports the law, should we categorize his motivation as paternalistic? That is, should we describe his reason *as paternalistic* even though he knows he will jeopardize the welfare of some persons because he also knows he will promote the welfare of many of the persons in the group of those whose liberty is restricted? This question lacks a straightforward answer.

The second prominent effort to justify paternalism in personal relations is similarly hard to apply to legal domains. This effort attempts to justify paternalism by reference to *consent*. Of course, the beneficiaries do not consent at the moment the interference takes place. According to Gerald Dworkin's pioneering article, however, "future-oriented consent" is the key to justifying paternalism. Dworkin construes paternalism "as a wager by the parent on the child's subsequent recognition of the wisdom of the restrictions. There is an emphasis on what could be called future-oriented consent—on what the child will come to welcome rather than on what he does welcome" (Dworkin 1972). Return to my example of Bobby. Dworkin's proposal, as I understand it, entails that his father's paternalistic intervention is justified if and only if Bobby subsequently comes to appreciate it. If Dworkin is correct, my stipulation that the father is justified in withholding ice cream entails that Bobby eventually will consent to the restriction.

Elsewhere, I have contended that this rationale fails for three reasons (Husak 2009). First, I doubt that Dworkin is really talking about consent at all. It is unlikely that consent *can* be retrospective (but see Chwang 2009). Clearly, I do not consent to everything I subsequently come to welcome. Often I am in a better position to assess how events affect my welfare long after they occur, but this superior perspective should not be mistaken for consent because I later come to realize that the treatment I disliked at the time operated to my benefit. Second, criteria are needed to justify paternalism *ex ante*, when the parent must decide whether to impose it. We do not offer helpful advice to Bobby's father if we inform him that no one can tell whether his proposed interference is justified until some moment in the future. Finally, which of several possible future moments should we privilege? Bobby may *vacillate*, changing his mind throughout his lifetime (Kasachkoff 1994). He might resent the interference for a short while, welcome it subsequently, only to object to it again later. As this possibility suggests, the fundamental problem with Dworkin's proposal is that Bobby's *ex post* opinion is irrelevant to whether his father is justified—even if we could accurately predict what Bobby would come to welcome. We should not conclude that his father is unjustified in treating Bobby paternalistically simply because actual consent is never given. Bobby may fail to appreciate the wisdom of the restriction because he grows up to be stubborn, stupid or—in the most extreme case—does not grow up at all. The decision is justified *whatever* may happen to Bobby at a later time.

Consent may be utterly irrelevant to the justification of paternalism (Husak 2009). Still, I am less interested in assessing this proposed justification in the context in which it was developed (viz., the parent–child relation) than to assess its potential application to law. The obvious difficulty in implementing a principle of future-oriented consent in the legal domain is the overwhelming likelihood that some but not all of the persons whose liberty is restricted will eventually come to appreciate the wisdom of any given interference. Apparently, such a law would be justified with respect to those who subsequently welcome it, but not with respect to those who do not. This conclusion, however, is not especially helpful. We still need to know: Is the law justified or not? I conclude that at least two of the principles that philosophers have believed to play a central role in attempts to justify paternalism in the context of personal relationships are problematic when applied to the domain of law.

A Possible Justification of Legal Paternalism

If neither nonvoluntariness nor consent ("future-oriented" or otherwise) is helpful to show why his father is justified in treating Bobby paternalistically, what is? To answer this question, it is instructive to identify the general kinds of deontological objections philosophers tend to raise against the justifiability of paternalism in personal relations. The most familiar such attempts invoke a conception of *autonomy* with which paternalistic interferences are said to be incompatible. Three difficulties surround these objections. One must (a) specify the nature of autonomy; (b) show why it is valuable; and (c) weigh its value against the value of reducing whatever harm is prevented by the paternalistic restriction. Each of these three difficulties is formidable.

Any philosopher who objects to some (or all) paternalistic interferences because they infringe on autonomy must specify the conception of autonomy on which he relies. The supposed incompatibility between paternalism and autonomy must be defended rather than presupposed (Husak 1980). Of course, autonomy might be *defined* so that its incompatibility with paternalism is guaranteed; one might characterize autonomy as the freedom to do what one wants. According to this conception, respect for autonomy always requires deference to personal preferences. I think, however, that this conception of autonomy is implausible. A preferable alternative, however, is likely to be compatible with some instances of paternalism. I will not endeavor to support this claim in any detail; too many different conceptions of autonomy have been proposed (May 1994). But even if we conclude that paternalism is incompatible with our favored conception of autonomy, we should not condemn all instances of paternalism unless we are persuaded that autonomy, as so construed, has value. Indeed, autonomy must have *enough* value to outweigh whatever good the instance of paternalism promotes. It seems unlikely that the value of autonomy can be sufficiently great to outweigh *all* competing considerations that might lead a state to enact paternalistic legislation.

Efforts to preserve autonomy need not lead to anti-paternalism. I propose that the concept of *personal* autonomy, which has figured so prominently in philosophical endeavors to object to paternalism in personal relations (Feinberg 1986) might actually provide the key to justifying some instances of paternalism in law. Suppose we construe persons to be autonomous when they make or author their own lives (Raz 1986). Philosophers have offered very different kinds of accounts of how someone may succeed in "making his own life." On any explication, however, this conception of autonomy provides a reason to oppose instances of legal paternalism. The ability of persons to author their own lives is diminished whenever they are subject to a legal interference for any reason—paternalistic or otherwise. At the same time, however, this conception of autonomy provides a reason to *favor* some instances of legal paternalism. Many restrictions on liberty improve the opportunities of persons to make their own lives by enhancing what might be called the *conditions* of autonomy—the conditions under which persons are likely to develop into autonomous agents who succeed in authoring their own lives. These conditions contribute to autonomy regardless of the details of what one happens to value in life. For example, laws that limit the number and severity of physical injuries help to preserve opportunities for persons to lead the lives they choose. A motorcyclist whose skull is fractured in an accident in which he failed to wear a helmet has lost a significant part of his ability to make his own life. Since the value of autonomy gives us a reason to create the conditions in which these accidents are less likely to occur, we have a basis for enacting a law that requires motorcyclists to wear helmets. Thus we have both a reason to oppose this law and a countervailing reason to support it—each of which is derived from the value of personal autonomy. Whether one ultimately accepts or rejects this example (as well as other examples) of legal paternalism depends largely on how one weighs these conflicting reasons.

Many factors will enter into this difficult balancing; no precise formula can be provided. Two matters, however, are of special significance. First, we must weigh the value of the liberty with which we interfere. Of course, it is hard to defend criteria to weigh the value of various freedoms. I assume, however, that the liberty to drive a car without a seatbelt does not rank especially high on anyone's list of precious freedoms. The experience of driving while belted is not drastically unlike the experience of driving while unbelted. Although controversial, such judgments about the value of given liberties must be made if a theorist hopes to decide when legal paternalism is justified. A second important matter that enters into a viable balancing test is the means by which the paternalistic law is enforced—an issue to which I return in the final section of this essay.

One might attempt to bolster my defense of legal paternalism by appeals to *hypothetical* consent—to the agreements that a rational person would make under idealized circumstances (Rawls 1972). This strategy, of course, moves far beyond endeavors to justify an interference with liberty by reference to the actual consent of the person treated paternalistically. It seems plausible to suppose that rational persons who value personal autonomy would consent to subject themselves to instances of legal paternalism that contribute to the conditions of autonomy and thereby increase the probability that they will succeed in leading autonomous lives (but see Valdman 2010).

I suggest, then, that the key to developing a theory of justified paternalism in legal contexts is to understand how various laws enacted for paternalistic reasons affect the

476

conditions of autonomy—that is, how these laws enhance or undermine the ability of persons to make or author their own lives. More specifically, attempts to evaluate instances of legal paternalism require, first, a set of principles about the value of different liberties; second, a theory about how given interferences affect the conditions under which persons are able to make their own lives; and third, some means to balance these (hopefully commensurable) values against one another. Small wonder that judgments about legal paternalism remain so controversial!

Paternalism in Various Domains of Law

Up to this point, I have talked indiscriminately about paternalistic laws, with no indication of what *kind* of law is involved. But distinctions between kinds of law are tremendously important in endeavors to justify legal paternalism by applying the theory I sketched above. In particular, paternalistic laws enforced by the *criminal* sanction are much harder to justify than those in the civil domain.

The criteria I invoked to justify the decision of the father to induce his son Bobby to take his vaccine help to show why criminal paternalism is so difficult to justify. Consider the first condition. A paternalistic interference becomes harder to defend when the means required to attain its objective involve a greater hardship or deprivation of liberty. The criminal law, by definition, subjects persons to *punishment*. If the state must resort to punishing persons in order to protect their interests and well-being, we should suspect that the cure is worse than the disease. It may be bad for persons to smoke tobacco, for example, but it might be even worse to punish them to try to get them to stop. When punishments are severe, their gains typically will not be worth their costs for the persons on whom they are inflicted (Bayles 1974). But when punishments are not severe, they rarely will create adequate incentives for compliance and thus will fail to improve the behavior of the persons coerced. An acceptable set of constraints to limit the imposition of the criminal sanction will require that criminal laws be reasonably effective in attaining their objectives (Husak 2008). A criminal law motivated by a paternalistic end that does not succeed in altering conduct will fail to satisfy this condition. I doubt that paternalistic reasons will justify state punishment in more than a handful of cases.

In addition, most proposals to treat competent adults paternalistically are rendered problematic by the fourth criterion I described. Susceptibility to the flu may be no less unhealthy for middle-age individuals than for Bobby, but sane adults rarely suffer from the deficiencies of typical four-year-olds. Of course, age is simply a crude proxy for what is relevant: the set of cognitive and volitional capacities characteristic of sane adults. An adult who is cognitively and volitionally comparable to a child would seem to be an equally plausible candidate for paternalistic intervention. Although some such persons exist, the paternalistic treatment of adults is less often justified.

The following example helps to explain my reservations about paternalism as a rationale for criminal legislation. Suppose that some activity—boxing, for example—risks substantial injuries to persons who engage in it. Suppose also that some adults are foolishly inclined to perform this activity, perhaps because it is exciting, euphoric or profitable. Why not protect these persons from their own foolishness by enacting a statute to punish boxing (Dixon 2001)? My answer is simple. A criminal law merely proscribes behavior, but cannot always prevent it. In a world of perfect compliance, no instances of the proscribed activity would occur. Total deterrence, of course, is unrealistic.

477

The threat of criminal punishment may succeed in reducing the incidence of boxing, but some persons will persist in it, whatever the law may say. Suppose that Rocky is one such person. What should be done to Rocky if he is detected? Presumably, he must be punished unless the state does not mean what it says in classifying the statute as criminal.

How might Rocky's punishment be justified? Two answers might be given. First, Rocky's punishment might be justified in order to preserve the efficacy of the criminal law as a deterrent. But punishing Rocky in order to deter others from following his foolish example can hardly be thought to promote the interests of Rocky himself. In other words, the state does not treat Rocky paternalistically when he is punished to deter others. If the law purports to treat Rocky paternalistically, punishment must be thought to be in *his* interest. This second answer, however, seems implausible. How can punishment be in Rocky's interest? Is Rocky really better off if he were punished than if he were free to box? The answer probably depends on further details about *how* he is punished. A small monetary fine would not seriously undermine Rocky's ability to make his own life. If the threat of further fines persuades him to stop boxing, the law will have succeeded in protecting the conditions of his autonomy. The difficulty, of course, is that Rocky may continue to box even though he pays the fine. Suppose, then, that Rocky is imprisoned. This mode of punishment has (perhaps!) a greater probability of successfully preventing him from continuing to box. But it is hard to believe that imprisonment is really in Rocky's interest. Can a legislator sincerely believe that Rocky is better off not boxing in jail than boxing out of jail? If the answer to this question is negative, Rocky's punishment cannot be justified paternalistically. Almost no conduct that sane adults are voluntarily inclined to perform is so destructive of their autonomy that they are worse off if allowed to continue than severely punished.

Perhaps a few counterexamples to this generalization can be found (Hurd 2009). Suppose that large sums of money induce impoverished persons to engage in gladiatorial contests to the death. I concede that the punishment of potential combatants would probably enhance their welfare. Few examples in the real world, however, are analogous. Since paternalists should be unwilling to impose a "cure" that is worse than a "disease," they should be reluctant to back paternalistic laws with the criminal sanction. Criminal paternalism may be easier to justify, however, when it is indirect and imposed on a third party. In the gladiator example, the state might punish promoters who profit by paying others to fight. Clearly, punishment would be designed to benefit the combatants, not the promoters. In such a case, it seems plausible to conclude that the state can succeed in furthering the conditions of autonomy of numerous persons by punishing a single individual. When paternalism is direct, however, the criminal sanction should rarely be used.

Since criminal paternalism rarely is justified, especially when it is direct, many of the more interesting questions about legal paternalism are not questions about the criminal law. Instead, they are questions about other legal domains. Sometimes paternalistic rationales for law give rise to little dispute, as when states create and support social institutions to encourage persons to take better care of themselves. Health and safety regulations may be enacted, such as requirements that water contain fluoride. States can sponsor advertisements to steer citizens toward healthy lifestyles. Taxes may be used to dissuade persons from consuming dangerous products such as tobacco. These sorts of state actions are not enforced through criminal penalties, and only occasionally give rise to objections from philosophers who purport to dislike paternalism. The reluctance of these philosophers to complain about such examples probably indicates that they do not oppose legal paternalism altogether, but only direct legal paternalism enforced by the criminal sanction. On my view, these noncriminal modes of law are more easily justified because they can be effective in promoting the personal autonomy of the individuals who are subject to them.

Paternalistic rationales are more defensible in civil than in criminal contexts. In contract law, such rationales are often invoked against the enforcement of given kinds of agreements. Of course, agreements are not enforced unless the parties are competent, thereby protecting the incompetent from their own commitments (Wikler 1978). Some agreements are unenforceable, however, even when made by parties whose competence is unquestioned. Agreements about given kinds of subject matter—involving the sale of body organs, for example—are unenforceable. Other agreements involve legitimate subject matter, but contain terms or conditions that are unenforceable because they are unconscionable. This controversial doctrine authorizes a judge to refuse to enforce agreements that are one-sided, overreaching or exploitive. In addition, some terms in agreements cannot be waived, and thus are imposed as a matter of law. For example, a consumer cannot voluntarily relinquish his statutory right to be paid a minimum wage, or to repay a loan at more than the rate of usury. Nor can a consumer waive his statutory right to a "cooling-off" period in a door-to-door sale. Seemingly, each of these aspects of contract law is supported largely by a paternalistic rationale (but see Shiffrin 2000).

Paternalism also plays an important role in tort law—and has contributed to a blurring of the line between contract and tort. Critics of contemporary tort law frequently allege that its rules erode individual responsibility—the duty to take adequate care of oneself. The transition across the country from contributory to comparative negligence, for example, allows plaintiffs to recover some of their accident costs even when they are partly at fault for causing their own injuries. Moreover, the doctrine of assumption of risk is invoked much less often today than in the past (Sugarman 1997). Consumers often are unable to trade decreases in safety for lower prices. Some courts, for example, have allowed drivers of an automobile to recover compensatory damages for injuries that would not have occurred had their car been equipped with an air bag—even though the drivers seemingly had assumed the risk of injury by electing not to buy a safer but more expensive automobile. The gradual disappearance of this defense in tort law might be explained by a growing acceptance of paternalism among the judiciary. If my reasoning is cogent, paternalism is less objectionable in civil contexts than in the criminal domain because it more often enhances than undermines the conditions under which persons are able to lead autonomous lives.

References

Archer, D. (1990) "Paternalism Defined," 50 Analysis: 36.

Bayles, M. (1974) "Criminal Paternalism," in J. R. Pennock and J. W. Chapman, eds., Nomos XV: The Limits of Law, New York: Lieber-Atherton: 174.

Buchanan, A. (1989) Deciding for Others: The Ethics of Surrogate Decision Making, New York: Cambridge University Press.

Chwang, E. (2009) "A Defense of Subsequent Consent," 40 Journal of Social Philosophy 117.

Dixon, N. (2001) "Boxing, Paternalism, and Legal Moralism," 27 Social Theory and Practice: 323.

Dworkin, G. (1972) "Paternalism," 56 The Monist: 64.

Feinberg, J. (1986) Harm to Self, New York: Oxford University Press.

Gert, B. and Culver, G. (1976) "Paternalistic Behavior," 6 Philosophy & Public Affairs: 45–57.

Goldman, M. and Goldman, A. (1990) "Paternalistic Laws," 18 Philosophical Topics: 65.

Grill, K. (2007) "The Normative Core of Paternalism," 13 *Res Publica*: 441.

Hurd, H. M. (2009) "Paternalism on Pain of Punishment," 28 *Criminal Justice Ethics*: 49.

Husak, D. (1980) "Paternalism and Autonomy," 10 *Philosophy & Public Affairs*: 27.

—— (1989) "Recreational Drugs and Paternalism," 8 *Law and Philosophy*: 353.

—— (2008) *Overcriminalization*, New York: Oxford University Press.

—— (2009) "Paternalism and Consent," in F. G. Miller and A. Wertheimer, eds., *The Ethics of Consent*, Oxford: Oxford University Press, pp. 107–30.

Kasachkoff, T. (1994) "Paternalism: Does Gratitude Make it Okay?" 20 *Social Theory and Practice* 1.

Kennedy, D. (1982) "Distributive and Paternalist Motives in Contract and Tort Law," 41 *Maryland Law Review*: 563.

Kleinig, J. (1984) *Paternalism*, Totowa, NJ: Rowman & Allanheld.

May, T. (1994) "The Concept of Autonomy," 31 *American Philosophical Quarterly*: 133.

Mill, J. S. (1859) *On Liberty*, London: Parker and Son.

Pope, T. M. (2004) "Counting the Dragon's Teeth and Claws: The Definition of Hard Paternalism," 20 *Georgia State Law Review*: 659.

Rawls, J. (1972) *A Theory of Justice*, Cambridge, Mass.: Harvard University Press.

Raz, J. (1986) *The Morality of Freedom*, Oxford: Clarendon Press.

Scoccia, D. (2008) "In Defense of Hard Paternalism," 27 *Law and Philosophy*: 351.

Shafer-Landau, R. (2005) "Liberalism and Paternalism," 11 *Legal Theory*: 169.

Shiffrin, S. (2000) "Paternalism, Unconscionability, and Accommodation," 29 *Philosophy & Public Affairs*: 206.

Sugarman, S. (1997) "Assumption of Risk," 31 *Valparaiso University Law Review*: 833.

Sunstein, C. R. (2006) "Preferences, Paternalism, and Liberty," 59 *Royal Institute of Philosophy Supplement*: 233–64.

Trout, J. D. (2005) "Paternalism and Cognitive Bias," 24 *Law and Philosophy*: 393.

Valdman, M. (2010) "Outsourcing Self-Government," *Ethics* 120: 761–90.

Waldron, J. (1993) "Legislation and Moral Neutrality," in J. Waldron, *Liberal Rights: Collected Papers*, Cambridge: Cambridge University Press.

Wikler, D. (1978) "Paternalism and the Mildly Retarded," 8 *Philosophy & Public Affairs*: 377.

Further Reading

For further reading, see: G. Dworkin (1972) "Paternalism," 56 *The Monist*: 64; J. Feinberg (1986) *Harm to Self*, New York: Oxford University Press; J. Feinberg (1985) *Harm to Others*, New York: Oxford University Press; D. Husak (2003) "Legal Paternalism," in Hugh LaFollette, ed., *The Oxford Handbook of Practical Ethics*, Oxford: Oxford University Press, pp. 387–412; J. Kleinig (1984) *Paternalism*, Totowa, NJ: Rowman & Allanheld; R. Sartorius, ed. (1983) *Paternalism*, Minneapolis: University of Minnesota Press; S. Shiffrin (2000) "Paternalism, Unconscionability Doctrine, and Accommodation," 29 *Philosophy & Public Affairs*: 205–50; H. Thaler and C. R. Sunstein (2008) *Nudge: Improving Decisions About Health, Wealth, and Happiness*, New Haven: Yale University Press; and D. Van DeVeer (1986) *Paternalistic Intervention*, Princeton: Princeton University Press.

31
ENFORCING MORALITY

A. P. Simester

Introduction

Suppose that we are considering whether an action is immoral. Its harmfulness is sometimes, but not always, our starting point. Some actions, such as murder and attempted murder, are wrongs because of the harm to which they conduce. Others are not. Actions such as rape, perjury and blackmail are wrongs prior to any consequences they cause. Their wrongfulness originates elsewhere. It may spring from the means by which the agent does something: not in *where* you go, as it were, but in how you get there—notably, how you treat people along the way. (Did you deceive her?) In special cases, it may be motive-based, resting on *why* a person does something. (Was it a warning or threat? An offer or blackmail?) These kinds of action involve what might be termed nonderivative wrongs, in as much as their basic wrongfulness is not dependent upon an outcome. If asked, "Which comes first, the wrong or the harm?" We can only say: it depends.

When deciding whether to prohibit such actions, however, a parallel question may not receive the same reply. Famously, for Mill (1859, ch. 1), "the only purpose for which power can rightfully be exercised over any member of a civilised community against his will is to prevent harm to others." Perhaps, like Feinberg (1984: 34–36), we might require that the harm *also* be wrongful, but part of the point of the Harm Principle is to focus attention on the harm—and to reject immorality, or wrongfulness *per se*, as a ground of prohibition. On the other hand, Patrick Devlin (1965: 12–13) controversially asserted that "it is not possible to set theoretical limits to the power of the State to legislate against immorality . . . or to define inflexibly areas of morality into which the law is in no circumstances allowed to enter." Indeed, according to a school of thought known as Legal Moralism, an action can warrant proscription simply on the ground of its moral wrongfulness.

Ultimately, these approaches are incompatible. But they share common ground, and Devlin's challenge helpfully focuses our attention on the requirements of the Harm Principle itself. There is nothing special, or objectionable, about confining prohibitions to morally wrongful actions, i.e., actions that one ought not to do. Those are exactly the sorts of action that prohibitions should address. As we shall see, it is certainly arguable that there are harm-based constraints on state intervention to regulate wrongs. If so, however, they complement rather than displace the wrongfulness requirement. Indeed, a concentration on harm may divert attention from the more general inquiry whether, and if ever when, we should prohibit *wrongful* conduct.

What Counts as Immoral?

Depending on one's views about the scope of morality, it is possible to narrow the gap. Michael Moore (1997: 662), for example, rejects the thought that morality has anything to say about consensual sexual practices. Hence, even on his retributivist view, the state has no basis to criminalize such activities. More generally, if one thinks of morality as an antidote to selfishness (cf. Mackie 1977, ch. 5), reasons may be "moral" ones when they address how we should treat each other. On that view, the legal moralist's claim to enforce morality will tend to converge with the Harm Principle's focus on conduct that, directly or indirectly, affects other people's lives.

But that would artificially truncate our inquiry. Devlin's skepticism about limiting state enforcement of morality finds its strongest expression if we take it that an action is "immoral" whenever it is morally wrongful; and that it is morally wrongful whenever, all things considered, one ought not to do it. In turn, one ought not to do an action whenever the reasons favoring its performance are, all things considered, defeated by the reasons against. For an action to be immoral, therefore, does not require that it is seriously or profoundly wrong, that it be evil or wicked; only that it should not be done. Most wrongful conduct is venial.

On this view, practical morality is concerned not merely with how one should treat others but with the question, what should one do? Thus no categorical distinction is drawn here between "moral" and other kinds of reasons, such as prudential ones. There are, of course, many distinctions that we *can* draw, in particular between guiding reasons (which in fact apply to an action—Raz 1990: 16ff) and explanatory reasons (by which the agent is, subjectively, motivated). The present essay is concerned with guiding reasons—that is, with the reasons why we ought, or ought not, to do something. Yet within that realm, reasons, whether prudential, altruistic or of some other character, are either good—i.e., valid—reasons for doing something, or they are not. Those narrower labels are meaningful, but they are not foundational to the moral question, what ought one to do? Obviously, different kinds of reasons may have differing weights and priorities; what we tend to call "moral" reasons, especially concerning the interests of others, often have relatively greater importance. Yet a reason that is, say, prudential in character can still be a good reason for doing something. Imprudence can be a vice too. Imagine the case of a successful, patriotic businessman, who decides to kill himself should the UK do badly in the next Eurovision Song Contest. He may justly be criticized morally by his friends for resolving to "throw away" his life on such a foolish basis.

We do need, however, to distinguish an action's wrongfulness, or immorality, from its being *a wrong*. In the usage I adopt here, an action is a wrong when it breaches a duty or violates a right. On occasion, it may be permissible—not wrongful—to perpetrate a wrong, as when D breaks into V's house in order to call an ambulance to the accident on the road outside. Our main concern in this essay is with the converse issue: whether, as Jeremy Waldron (1981) would put it, one has a right to act wrongfully.

Three Theses Concerning Immorality

Taking moral wrongfulness as a starting point may seem counterintuitive. It is often said that the law should not be in the business of prohibiting immoral behavior, and at least one version of that claim is surely right. But we need to be careful about what is meant by the claim, and about how convincing it really is. Clarification is required. Here are three possible interpretations:

1. That φing is immoral is insufficient to justify its criminalization (Insufficiency Thesis).
2. That φing is immoral is necessary to justify its criminalization (Necessity Thesis).
3. That φing is immoral is insufficient to establish even a pro tanto ground for its criminalization (Non-qualifying Thesis).

(For convenience, I will focus primarily on enforcement through criminal law. As we see below, however, similar principles apply to coercion through the civil law.) The first thesis, that moral wrongfulness is insufficient to justify criminalization, seems uncontroversial. Even Devlin could embrace it. Suppose that φing ought not to be done. Accept too, for the moment, that this generates a reason to prohibit it. It does not follow that, *all things considered*, we should prohibit φing, because the reason favoring prohibition may be defeated by other considerations.

One set of counter-considerations is operational. Even if a prima facie case can be made for prohibition, and φing lies within the range of conduct that there is reason to criminalize, that case must still overcome various negative constraints that militate against criminalization generally. At the very least, to make an all-things-considered case for criminalization, we need to show that the criminal law offers an appropriate method of controlling φing, and is preferable to other methods of legal regulation available to the state. Recall the disastrous attempt by many western governments in the twentieth century to regulate alcohol using criminal prohibitions, which created a black market ripe for extortion and racketeering. Rightly, alcohol licensing and taxation laws are now preferred. Other constraints include the practical challenges of crafting an offense definition in terms that are effective, enforceable and which meet rule of law and other concerns (Simester and Sullivan 2007, § 16.5–7). It may be, if these demands cannot be met, that the state ought not to prohibit φing despite the prima facie case for doing so.

The in-principle case must also be weighed up against the burdens of prohibition itself, most notably in terms of freedom and lost opportunities (Feinberg 1984: 216). No doubt extramarital affairs constitute wrongful betrayals. But perhaps they should not be criminalized because of the extensive intrusions that their prohibition would involve. For all of these reasons, we should concede the Insufficiency Thesis. But we can do so without concern. For it is a long step from that thesis to concluding (i) that immorality is *unnecessary* to justify criminalization, or (ii) that even an in-principle case for criminalizing φing requires *more* than that φing is immoral.

The Need for Moral Wrongfulness

A very long step. Indeed, conclusion (i) would be a misstep, because the truth is the other way around. Preventing immorality is an *indispensable* condition of criminalization. It is the Necessity Thesis, not an "un-necessity" thesis, to which we should subscribe: any prohibition of φing can be justified only when φing is morally wrongful action.

Within the criminal sphere, the Necessity Thesis is most easily defended by reference to the distinctive nature of criminal law, which punishes, and censures, the offender for having done wrong. The criminal law is a blaming institution, and one cannot blame a person unless that person does something morally wrong; that is, unless she does something that, all things considered, she ought not to do. One can, of course, also judge people morally for their good deeds: yet such judgments are not blaming judgments. Blame lies only for conduct that, all things considered, one should not do.

As it happens, while that argument is adequate for the criminal law, a version of the Necessity Thesis holds also for the civil law; and, indeed, for all of us. No moral agent should act wrongfully. And the state is, like the rest of us, subject to the requirements of morality. It too should act in accordance with undefeated, all-things-considered reasons. Where it fails to do so, it acts wrongly, just like the rest of us.

This matters because if, all things considered, D has undefeated reason to φ, it generally follows that no one, including the state, should stop D from φing. Notwithstanding that D's reasons to φ may be personal to D, the existence of those reasons is itself a general matter (cf. Gardner 2007: 131). That D has reason to φ, therefore, is something that commands our allegiance too. This is not so much because D herself is entitled to respect—since respect for another human being does not imply that we must always respect the reasons for which that person acts. Rather, it is because the reasons themselves are entitled to respect—that is, because they are (good) reasons.

(In passing, we should allow some provisos to this claim. On occasion, the existence of reasons may depend on the status of the agent; thus it is possible that some reasons for individuals to φ may be excluded in the hands of certain other agents, such as the state, and vice versa. More on this possibility later. Neither do I suggest that we should all care *just as much* about reasons that are personal to others as we should about those personal to us.)

Legally Created Wrongs?

But what about regulatory laws? It is a commonplace that the state frequently prohibits conduct that is not pre-legally wrong. Indeed such offenses, which Anglo-American lawyers call *mala prohibita*, form the major part of the criminal canon. They vastly outnumber *mala in se* proscriptions of conduct that is pre-legally wrong. Yet, if φing is not morally wrongful, how can we justify its prohibition and subsequent punishment? Is the Necessity Thesis incompatible with *mala prohibita* offenses? This worry has concerned many writers. As Douglas Husak (2007: 112) complains, "I fail to understand why persons behave wrongfully when their conduct is *malum prohibitum* but not *malum in se*." While accepting that some *mala prohibita* prohibitions may give substantive content to underlying, preexisting wrongs, Husak doubts that many modern offenses do specify such pre-legal wrongs.

This line of thought is partly right and partly misleading. It is right in so far as it reflects the truth—and it *is* a truth—that φing does not become morally wrong just because the state declares it so. But it is misleading in that it doesn't sufficiently distinguish prohibition, which is forward looking, from punishment, which is retrospective and *ex post*. The justification of an act of criminalization is not the same as the justification of an act of punishment. They are different acts. The former can play a role in justifying the latter.

How so? Because the state sometimes *creates* specific moral reasons. Moreover, it can do so in a variety of ways (e.g., Honoré 1993; Finnis 1980: 284ff). Indeed, that power is not restricted to the state. When the soccer referee shows a player a red card, the player thereupon has a reason, indeed a duty, to leave the pitch. Any moral agent in a position of authority can create reasons: the power to do so is part of the very idea of authority (cf. Raz 1979, ch. 1). Prior to law, there is no reason to drive on any particular side of the road, but one arises as soon as the state stipulates on which side the citizens should drive. If the state rules that we must drive on the right, it thereby creates a post-legal reason so to do.

Admittedly, this involves a contingency: that the authority is not merely legitimate but effective, so that there is a reasonable expectation of conformity with the rules it creates. But this does not seem too much to require, since effectiveness is a general condition of the instrumental reasons underpinning a state's authority. In one sense, the law's role here is to generate authoritative conventions. At the same time, the rule is not mere convention. Imagine that (as sometimes occurs in certain countries) one arrives at a road being unsure what is the local driving practice. One knows the legal rule—drive on the left, say—but not whether it is observed. Other things being equal, one should drive on the left. Slowly.

Many standard examples of successful norm creation involve conventions, typically as coordinating rules or as content-determinations of some more abstract, pre-conventional norm. How many players to field on a soccer team? How should we return the ball into play? What side to drive on? The answers to these questions may be to some extent arbitrary, even suboptimal; yet the very existence of an authoritative answer is itself valuable. Now we can have an organized game. Now we can drive with more safety. And so on. The precise content of these coordinating rules may be less important than the purpose they serve. Even a rule about the age of consent in underage sexual intercourse, which most people would regard as a *mala in se* offense, is partially conventional. It varies widely across jurisdictions and history. But the rule is valuable—morally valuable—in virtue of helping to articulate one boundary of permissible sexual activity, benefiting potential offenders as well as potential victims by its clarity.

In all these kinds of cases, the state has good *ex ante* reason for passing the relevant law. In effect, the state acts as a conduit, crystallizing those *ex ante* reasons into a more particular, practicable form—the moral force of which derives not from the enactment itself, but from its function. Generally speaking, the wrongfulness of a rule-violation depends on the moral force of the rule. For a *malum prohibitum* rule, the moral force comes from its instrumental value, which depends, in turn, on the reasons the rule serves and how well it serves them.

Of course, not all prohibitions are justified. They are neither self-justifying nor do they automatically justify the punishment of violations. The point here is that there is a normative gap between prohibition and punishment. Husak insists that punishment is appropriate only if φing is wrongful. I agree. But it need not be wrongful independently. Whether φing is wrongful depends on whether it is, all things considered, wrong to φ; and at the stage of punishment, the reasons not to φ are to be assessed *post-legally*, not pre-legally.

What's the difference? When does the state succeed in creating reasons not to do something that, pre-legally, was morally permissible? What counts is whether the authoritative agent creates those reasons *for good reasons*. More precisely, what counts is whether the agent's legislative act is justified. In the driving case, the reason we now have is created as a particular determination of the more general reasons we have to drive safely. Even though the content of the rule is arbitrary, it acquires moral force in virtue of its purpose. Here, the particular crystallizes the abstract; but notice that it is the abstract which gives the particular its moral force. Even here, the state should do what morality gives it *ex ante* reason to do. Even authorities need a basis for their actions.

Authorities do not always have to be right. They just have to generate reasons. The referee who makes an error still creates a duty for the player to leave the pitch. On the other hand, those reasons have to be sufficient, and that depends on why and how they were created. The hard cases are the marginal ones, where the state has pressing need to regulate µing but cannot practically do so without also regulating φing. Speed limits, drunk-driving limits and age-of-sexual-consent rules are examples where a prohibition is unavoidably *overinclusive*, capturing both pre-legally immoral and pre-legally permissible instances of their perpetration. A prohibition is overinclusive when it proscribes a wider range of conduct than is required by the reasons motivating the prohibition. For example, a prohibition on driving above a certain speed limit may criminalize both safe and unsafe instances of such conduct, even though it is only the unsafe instances that motivate the prohibition. Since driving above the speed limit is not always dangerous, and the actor may know this is the case, Husak questions:

> In these circumstances—when a defendant commits a hybrid offense by engaging in conduct that is *malum prohibitum* although not simultaneously *malum in se*—how can punishment be justified within a theory of criminalization that includes the wrongfulness constraint? . . . In the circumstances I have just described, how can punishment be justified at all?
>
> (2007: 107)

To my mind, we should flip Husak's question around. The primary issue is not whether punishment of φing is justified but whether the state is justified in prohibiting it. If the restriction is justified, we don't need supplementary grounds to show why φing is then wrongful. We don't need, in other words, to look for some supervening vice to explain why it is wrong for D then to φ. (Husak himself rejects such explanations: 108ff; although they may be relevant to judgments of culpability.) If the state's exercise of authority was justified, then φing is already immoral. Post-legally, D ought not to φ.

Mere Immorality?

So, I think, the Necessity Thesis is right too. But what about the third claim, that the in-principle case for criminalizing φing requires more than that φing is immoral? This is a much stronger version of the Insufficiency Thesis. According to the Non-qualifying Thesis, immorality per se does not generate even a pro tanto case for prohibition. Only certain kinds of immorality qualify. Something extra is needed. The Non-qualifying Thesis really does stand opposed to Patrick Devlin's view (1965: 12–13) that "it is not possible to set theoretical limits to the power of the State to legislate against immorality." Devlin's verdict finds modern resonance in decisions such as *1568 Montgomery Hwy. v. City of Hoover* ((2010) 45 So. 3d 319), where the Alabama Supreme Court upheld a provision of the Alabama Code making it a crime to sell devices "for the stimulation of human genital organs." The court ruled that public morality could supply a rational basis for the legislation.

For those who reject Devlin's position, the challenge is to identify what else is needed to justify the additional criteria that state intervention requires. Most secular responses to that challenge are consequential, holding that conduct is eligible for criminalization only when it involves further effects. Depending on the version, qualifying effects may be restricted to those impacting adversely upon people and their lives, or may be extended to other kinds of victims, such as other sentient creatures. This should be no surprise, since (secular) authority does not exist, and is not granted, for its own sake—it exists for instrumental reasons, as a means to promote the quality of people's lives, perhaps the lives of other creatures, etc. Thus, according to the Harm Principle (Feinberg 1984), what counts in the justification of state intervention is the impact of conduct upon other human lives. Conduct becomes eligible for prohibition when it adversely affects the interests that serve another person's well-being, the opportunities that she has (or may have) to pursue and enjoy a good life.

How much constraint does the Harm Principle add? Certainly, the Principle is nowhere near as restrictive as it might seem. Conduct may prima facie qualify for proscription without actually harming people, either directly or necessarily. Sometimes indirect risks will do (cf. von Hirsch 1996). Moreover, there is nothing in the Harm Principle to rule out the protection of things of intrinsic value, provided those things have implications for our lives. For example, the state might legitimately impose export restrictions, backed up by coercive laws, in order to conserve the nation's art heritage; as under the UK Export Control Act 2002.

However, the Principle does restrict doing so *for the art's own sake*. Suppose that a work of art can be preserved in such a way that no one will ever be able to see or experience it. Even the knowledge of its existence will be lost. In such a case, its protection falls outside the scope of the Principle, which constrains intervention to the sorts of events that in some manner affect people's lives.

Even if indirectly, then, there must be harm—some negative effect on people and their lives.

Yet this, too, seems a tenuous constraint, since in at least one sense the effect need not be negative. Seemingly, it is permissible within most versions of the Harm Principle for the state to enact coercive laws for the sake of *improving* peoples' lives. The case for enforcing contractual promises supplies an example. The regime of contract law facilitates well-being by empowering us to bind ourselves within exchange transactions. Without state intervention, systems of contract would be ineffective, resulting in lost opportunities for the kinds of welfare gains that can be secured from coordinated economic activity. State enforcement of contractual promises is warranted, therefore, by reason of the *benefits* to people thereby secured. And there is nothing in principle to stop a suitably contumelious breach from being criminalized.

(Contrast Husak 2007: 135–37, who regards contractual wrongs as "private" in nature. But a breach of contract is at least as "public" as a domestic assault, in as much as it involves other-affecting behavior—indeed, it may be legitimately criminalized if done fraudulently. While typical cases of breach of contract are insufficiently serious to warrant criminal regulation, it is hard to see any conceptual distinction that rules them outside the reach of the criminal law *tout court*.)

Notice that, although I have focused on criminal law as the standard means for coercively enforcing morality, the same issue arises for coercion through the civil law. Mill's articulation of the Harm Principle was not specific to the criminal law: it applied to any exercise by the state of coercive power over its citizens (cf. Smith 2000). Hence the state ought not to give effect to a regime of contract, even through the civil law, unless to do so is consonant with the Harm Principle.

A similar analysis holds for the regime of property law. Strictly speaking, even property wrongs are *mala prohibita*, in the sense that, for most modern societies, property rights are not pre-legal (Simester and Sullivan 2005). The allocation of proprietary interests is itself a matter of legal rules. I don't need the law to know that this arm is mine; I do need the law to know who owns that table. To invoke the Harm Principle successfully, therefore, we must demonstrate that the use of coercive laws to protect property rests on values other than protecting property rights for their own sake—otherwise the state's claim to be protecting property owners from harm would be self-justifying. This challenge is met by reference to the value of having a *regime* of property law. The law of property facilitates the creation of forms of welfare and human flourishing that only the peaceful ownership and possession of property can deliver. Assuming minimum standards of just distribution of property, the regime itself is a public good. It provides a reliable means by which we can pursue a good life, through the voluntary acquisition, use, and exchange of resources. Having such a system may promote our well-being even if the particular form of the regime is imperfect (Coleman 1992: 350–54), provided that members of the community benefit by having a predictable, reliable, set of rules with which to organize their lives.

In the criminal law, the securement of benefits finds its best known expression through the law of omissions, which sometimes imposes positive duties to act for the sake of others, e.g. by rescuing someone who has fallen into danger, or by sending one's child to school. Such cases are controversial because of their potential onerousness, but not because of their *ineligibility* under the Harm Principle. If my child does not attend school, he will be worse off (in the long run). He will lack an adequate preparation for adult life in a developed economy, being denied many of the employment and other opportunities to advance his welfare that others will typically have.

So there is nothing in the Harm Principle, or in the requirement of immorality, that draws a sharp line between the promotion of value and the prevention of disvalue. Sometimes, even frequently, there may be associated differences in the kinds of interests affected by acts and omissions (e.g., Honoré 1991), but those differences enter the criminalization analysis later, affecting the strength of the case for regulation rather than its eligibility. Sometimes, one may be morally obliged to act for the benefit of another, sometimes to refrain from acting to another's detriment. Neither the Necessity Thesis nor the Harm Principle precludes this.

What else, then, can we say in favor of the Non-qualifying Thesis? There are two lines of argument that might be adopted.

A Red Herring

But first, let's clear out one inconclusive argument. Defenders of the Harm Principle accept that the principle does not restrict criminalization only to actions that directly cause harm. Indirect harm will suffice. Some writers object, however, that this move results in overbreadth. They suggest that it hopelessly undermines the ability of the principle to restrict criminalization, since it allows the proscription of otherwise harmless conduct on the basis of how that conduct is perceived by others; e.g., because it leads those other persons to experience anxiety and fear (Stewart 2010: esp. 26ff).

Now, the Harm Principle would certainly be problematic if it allowed the criminalization of conduct merely because of the distressed reactions of other people. But that truth doesn't refute the Harm Principle. It just shows that we would need to refine it, so that only certain kinds of indirect harm qualify. Moreover, if one accepts the Necessity Thesis, it follows that the Harm Principle must be compatible with criminalizing only wrongful behavior. Its supporters cannot, and indeed do not, argue that harm, whether direct or indirect, suffices in itself for criminalization. *And conduct does not become wrongful by reason of the manner in which other persons respond to it* (Simester and von Hirsch 2002). A properly articulated Harm Principle is therefore likely to be immune from this objection of overbreadth.

Reasons for Strangers, and the Role of the State

There are also problematic arguments in favor of the Non-qualifying Thesis. The challenge for Legal Moralism is to get from the proposition, φing is wrongful, to the proposition that the state may use coercion to prevent people from φing. It may be thought that the major barrier to navigation lies in a kind of agent-relativism about reasons: the objection that the state has no interest in reasons that don't involve other persons. Without more (say, harm to others), the objection goes, that φing is wrongful supplies *no reason at all* for the state to intervene.

There is something in this argument, but we need to be careful how we formulate it. One might seek to put the point more generally: that third parties (strangers) have no interest in purely self-regarding reasons, i.e., reasons that don't involve other persons. That seems too strong. Earlier, I suggested that, where a person has reason to φ, that reason is entitled to our respect. Similarly, the reasons she has *not* to φ also command our allegiance. If that's right, even "private" wrongfulness is capable of generating reasons for other persons. Suppose that D's φing is morally valuable or good. Then third parties have reason to promote, support or facilitate its occurrence. Conversely, that φing is bad supplies reason to avoid its occurrence. This isn't controversial; or, at any rate, it shouldn't be, since it is inherent in the very idea of morality. *Any* agent ought to do good and avoid bad. And the state is an agent too. We should not be indifferent to moral reasons just because they don't concern us. To be sure, the claim here is only that there is *some* reason, not that it is sufficient or even that third parties have standing to act upon it (without which it is, as Raz would say, excluded), let alone that they should use coercion. Sometimes—frequently—others should not intervene. But that doesn't mean that there is no reason in play for them *at all*.

To see this, consider paternalistic interventions (Husak 2011). Sometimes, all things considered, they are morally desirable. Indeed, someone who sees another pedestrian about to step off the curb in front of an oncoming car *should* physically restrain that person (cf. Raz 1986: 378). It would be wrong not to. If we accept this, it follows that even conduct which is not other-affecting can generate reasons for third parties. Indeed, it is this possibility that creates the moral space for justifying *any* form of paternalistic coercion, even via the civil law.

Why not, then, intervene to prevent immorality more generally? One line of argument depends on how one conceives of the role of the state; a conception that affects its standing to intervene. Suppose that we take the state to be a straightforwardly instrumental actor, an artificial creation that exists in order to advance the welfare of its subjects. On this view, the state has no interest in regulating conduct that does not affect people's lives. Pure moral wrongs fall outside its remit. That still leaves the Necessity Thesis untouched. Moral wrongfulness is indispensible to coercive intervention. But it is not sufficient. Ultimately, the point of intervention lies in its consequences for human beings (and, perhaps, the needs of other creatures to whom humanity owes duties). The state has an interest only in regulating conduct that affects peoples' lives.

Obviously, that conception is not shared by all. One might think of the state's primary aim in terms of doing justice (of some kind); or indeed of ensuring that events transpire—and citizens behave—as morality demands. These ways of thinking about the law have particular resonance when we imagine the legal system in terms of what happens in a courtroom, and in terms of the criminal law. The operation of the courts in this context tends to be retrospective. At the moment of trial, the law operates *ex post*. The deed is done. Or, rather: we have to decide whether it was done and, if so, whether it was done culpably; and, if so, how much to penalize it.

]The difficulty with this approach is that the civil law can be coercive too: yet no-one suggests that the civil law's coercive rules are driven by punitive motives. Consequently, the retributive analysis implies a deep separation between criminal and civil law.

Yet coercion is always forward looking. Just like the law's role in creating reasons, it operates *ex ante* in both types of law. It is the threat of future legal consequences, not the consequences themselves, that guides the behavior of citizens. On this *ex ante* view, there is no fundamental distinction between crimes and other branches of law that impose sanctions. The criminal law is simply a special kind of regulatory tool in the state's toolbox for influencing behavior—the morally loaded tool. The criminal law has a communicative function which the civil law does not. It speaks with a distinctively moral voice, one that the civil law lacks. Beyond that difference in mechanisms, however, the ultimate aims of criminal law are no different from those of the civil law, which is why Mill was quite right to extend the Harm Principle to civil-law coercion too.

This analysis generates convergence between the reasons that underpin the state's involvement in legal regulation through both criminal and civil law. Such reasons engage the principal reasons for the state's existence, as an institution for helping to secure and improve the lives of its citizens. There are various means of going about those aims. One is by generating public goods such as education, roads, hospitals, and the like. Another is by setting certain basic rules of engagement, or terms of interaction, among citizens. Those rules can be criminal or civil.

Coercion

Suppose, however, that we reject the constraint that state intervention should be designed to improve the quality of people's lives, to promote the goods of human welfare. Even without such benefits, minimizing wrongful conduct is surely a good thing, something desirable in principle. Perhaps, then, we can justifiably *interfere*, and seek to minimize immorality, say by creating a better social and economic environment, thereby giving citizens a range of preferable options.

But coercion *destroys* options. Even if the remaining options are valuable (or indeed beneficial), they are imposed rather than voluntary. In principle, this objection applies to strangers who intervene as well as to the state. But the state's interventions are recurrent in nature: this feature is characteristic of legal rules, which tend to apply generally rather than occasionally. In this respect, the case of a coercive law is unlike that of intervening to restrain someone about to step in front of an oncoming car. On that specific occasion, intervention may be the right thing to do. But laws are not concerned with *ad hoc* scenarios. They regulate activities systematically.

Here we have the second line of reasoning in favor of the Non-qualifying Thesis and against enforcing morality: that coercion is a prima facie wrong. It may sometimes be justified. But not, the argument goes, for the sake of suppressing merely wrongful conduct. This is not to deny that merely wrongful acts warrant censure *ex post*. But it is to claim that something more is required to justify the *ex ante* step of criminal prohibition. That your φing would be wrongful doesn't entitle me to coerce you not to do it.

Coercion is a prima facie wrong on two of the three grounds identified at the start of this essay. It can lead to harm. And it treats people badly.

One source of harmfulness rests in the fact that coercive prohibitions can significantly affect people's lives. They foreclose options that some individuals may value, and which (even if themselves wrongful) may form part of a valuable way of life. Indeed, because of their general nature, they tend in practice to be overinclusive, even ruling out instances of the proscribed conduct that are not wrongful at all. It is hard to see how these effects of coercion can be justified when that conduct has no adverse effects on anyone's well-being.

Prohibitions take options away from people—they are meant to. Accepting the general case for proscribing mere immorality will, inevitably, lead to restrictions of autonomy, especially because the law is rather coarse-grained, so that its rules are typically framed in broad rather than narrow terms. Given the diversity of human needs and preferences, criminal prohibitions will inevitably deprive some individuals of freedoms that are valuable to them. For such persons, the very existence of the prohibition will mean that their lives go less well: they will, in effect, be harmed by the prohibitions. The strongest cases for depriving people of opportunities in this way arise where D's activity is likely to diminish the opportunities for others to live good lives. In these cases, a condition of D's well-being (her autonomy) is weighed against a condition of V's well-being: like is compared with like. In these cases, if you like, the state has a role as arbiter, since there is a real trade-off of competing human interests that needs to be made. But, in these very cases, D's conduct is by definition harmful. Where, by contrast, the conduct is merely immoral, the interests of persons (such as D) are being weighed only against abstract judgments of morality. There is no well-being or autonomy-based reason *for* criminalization, only against: like is not being compared with like. In a liberal society, the interests of persons should take priority at this point. Thus mere wrongfulness is, by itself, insufficient for criminalization.

The other way of putting the matter is as a concern about means. Even if the end may be valuable, there are norms governing how we should treat people in the pursuit of those ends. Perhaps we can agree that the state is entitled to foster valuable rather than valueless options; yet it does not follow that we can short-cut individual choices in order to promote those options. A meaningful right of self-determination must include a right to make bad decisions, at least when those decisions do not adversely affect other people. People have a right to be treated as self-determining creatures. This is a right of respect, or human dignity. And it is violated by coercive measures, which attack D's right to choose whenever they make intervention contingent on the choice being a good one.

Self-determination is backed by welfare interests. We have noted that coercion reduces options. But it also interferes with the process by which they are *self*-chosen. Well-being depends not only upon the successful pursuit of the goals that make one's life worthwhile; it depends additionally upon those goals' being one's own. When choices, even valuable choices, are imposed rather than self-determined, their imposition undermines the individual's ability to shape and direct her own life, a life framed by loyalty to and engagement with her own commitments.

This is not to claim that consent, or a voluntary choice, prevents an action from being wrongful. Choices don't become valuable just because they are freely made. Freely chosen, self-oriented acts are capable of satisfying the first condition of criminalization: that the conduct ought not to be done. Of course, what morality requires (if anything) is often hard to ascertain, especially in the context of self-regarding conduct, which itself supplies a reason why the state should hesitate to intervene (Moore 1997: 662–63). Nonetheless the argument here accepts that, in principle, the state can be alive to immorality. Noncoercive measures, including public information initiatives, may be appropriate. But coercive responses are not. To this extent, we have a right to act wrongfully.

Harmless Wrongs to Others?

It does not follow that we have a right to *wrong others*. Indeed, that conclusion doesn't follow even when the wrong is harmless.

In the context of the Harm Principle, the victim's involvement is not voluntary and, consequently, the state's involvement is not entirely voluntary either. Where conduct affects the interests of other persons, the potential for conflict between individuals tends to place the state in a position of arbitration, negotiating the boundaries of permissible social interaction. It cannot simply decline to intervene, since—in a situation of conflicting actions and interests—that establishes a rule too. Rather, it has to weigh up the effects and risks at stake, accommodating the likely extent and severity of the problem that an act is likely to generate.

Even though, in cases of harmless wrongs to others, there is no such balancing of consequences, much the same still holds true about the state's role. Consider the Offense Principle. Insulting or exhibitionist behavior, for example, is offensive because it wrongs other people by treating them with a certain lack of consideration and respect (Simester and von Hirsch 2002). Even when no harm occurs, the existence of a (right-violating) wrong creates normative space for arguments in favor of coercive intervention, where those arguments do not rely just on the immorality of the conduct but respond to the fact that D has attacked V's right to be treated as an equal qua self-determined, morally responsible, human being.

The point is that, unlike pure immorality, D's conduct is not merely wrongful *in abstracto*: it too is other-affecting. D's wrong generates a conflict between V's right to be treated with respect and D's interest in being able to express herself freely. That tension is not an abstract one: typically, D's attack has real, unpleasant, effects in virtue of the affront it causes to V. Moreover, where there is conflict between individuals in a community, regulating the terms of their engagement is exactly the sort of function that the state exists to perform. At least where that conflict is sufficiently serious (e.g., because D's behavior causes widespread offense across a society), the state is surely an appropriate referee. It has a prima facie reason to intervene, bearing in mind the state's role in setting the terms of interaction between individuals in a society. At the same time, since D's conduct is *ex hypothesi* a wrong, there is no reason for the state to support D's liberty to behave in that manner, save in so far as is necessary to protect the conditions of D's well-being. Hence, to the extent that the state has good reason to intervene, it may be thought that V's rights should be preferred.

So the case for regulating wrongs to others is different from, and stronger than, the case for regulating mere immorality. The argument for intervention still gives priority to people and not simply to morality. Hence, it contains and does not eschew the central advantage that the Harm Principle has over legal moralism.

It remains unclear, however, whether this possibility really does generate harm-independent cases of justified state coercion. Recognizing that rape is a non-derivative wrong, a wrong prior to any harm it may cause, some writers have suggested that the case for its criminalization is a counter-example to the Harm Principle (e.g., Stewart 2010). But one of the reasons why rape is so serious a wrong is because of the great harm that it typically causes. It is very hard, perhaps impossible outside the realm of philosophy, to imagine rape as a harmless wrong. It certainly wouldn't be rape as we know it. And perhaps the case for criminalization would be weaker. Further, even if the case remained just as strong, there are very few rights that don't depend for their justification on the welfare interests they serve. Certainly not property rights. Normally, harm is in the background.

Acknowledgments

Many thanks to audiences who commented on versions of this essay presented at the Universities of Frankfurt and Auckland in 2007–08; also to Andrew Halpin for comments on a later draft. This essay forms part of a larger project on criminalization undertaken with Andreas von Hirsch, who invented the Eurovision Song Contest example.

References

1568 Montgomery Hwy. v. City of Hoover (2010) 45 So. 3d 319 (Alabama Supreme Court).

Coleman, J. (1992) Risks and Wrongs, New York: Cambridge University Press.

Devlin, P. (1965) The Enforcement of Morals, Oxford: Oxford University Press.

Export Control Act 2002 (UK).

Feinberg, J. (1984) Harm to Others, New York: Oxford University Press.

Finnis, J. (1980) Natural Law and Natural Rights, Oxford: Oxford University Press.

Gardner, J. (2007) "Complicity and Causality," 1 Criminal Law and Philosophy: 127.

Honoré, A. M. (1991) "Are Omissions Less Culpable?" in P. Cane and J. Stapleton, eds., Essays for Patrick Atiyah, Oxford: Oxford University Press, p. 31.

—— (1993) "The Dependence of Morality on Law," 13 Oxford Journal of Legal Studies: 1.

Husak, D. (2007) Overcriminalization, Oxford: Oxford University Press.

—— (2012) "Paternalism," in A. Marmor, ed., Routledge Companion to Philosophy of Law, New York: Routledge, pp. 467–80.

Mackie, J. L. (1977) Ethics: Inventing Right and Wrong, London: Penguin Books.

Mill, J. S. (1859) On Liberty, London: Parker and Son.

Moore, M. S. (1997) Placing Blame: A Theory of Criminal Law, Oxford: Clarendon Press.

Raz, J. (1979) The Authority of Law, Oxford: Oxford University Press.

—— (1986) The Morality of Freedom, Oxford: Oxford University Press.

—— (1990) Practical Reason and Norms, 2nd edition, Princeton: Princeton University Press.

Simester, A. P. and Sullivan, G. R. (2005) "The Nature and Rationale of Property Offences," in R. A. Duff and S. Green, eds., Defining Crimes: Essays on the Criminal Law's Special Part, Oxford: Oxford University Press, p. 168.

—— (2007) Criminal Law: Theory and Doctrine, 3rd edition, Oxford: Hart Publishing.

Simester, A. P. and von Hirsch, A. (2002) "Rethinking the Offense Principle," 8 Legal Theory: 269.

Smith, S. (2000) "Towards a Theory of Contract," in J. Horder, ed., Oxford Essays in Jurisprudence, Fourth Series, Oxford: Oxford University Press, p. 107.

Stewart, H. (2010) "The Limits of the Harm Principle," 4 Criminal Law and Philosophy: 17.

von Hirsch, A. (1996) "Extending the Harm Principle: 'Remote' Harms and Fair Imputation," in A. P. Simester and A. T. H. Smith, eds., Harm and Culpability Oxford: Oxford University Press, p. 259.

Waldron, J. (1981) "A Right to Do Wrong," 92 Ethics: 21.

Further Reading

For further reading, see: R. Dworkin (1985) A Matter of Principle, Cambridge, Mass.: Harvard University Press; R. Dworkin (1986) Law's Empire, Cambridge, Mass.: Harvard University Press; J. Feinberg (1988)

Harmless Wrongdoing, New York: Oxford University Press; L. L. Fuller (1969) *The Morality of Law*, New Haven: Yale University Press; R. P. George (1993) *Making Men Moral: Civil Liberties and Public Morality*, Oxford: Clarendon Press; R. P. George (1999) *In Defense of Natural Law*, Oxford: Clarendon Press; H. Grotius (1925/1625) *On the Law of War and Peace*, F. W. Kelsey, trans., Oxford: Oxford University Press; J. R. Lucas (1966) *The Principles of Politics*, Oxford: Clarendon Press; A. Marmor (2001) *Positive Law and Objective Values*, Oxford: Clarendon Press; M. S. Moore (2000) *Educating Oneself in Public: Critical Essays in Jurisprudence*, Oxford: Oxford University Press; T. Nagel (1987) "Moral Conflict and Political Legitimacy," 16 *Philosophy and Public Affairs*: 215; H. Oberdiek (2001) *Tolerance: Between Forbearance and Acceptance*, Lanham: Rowman & Littlefield; S. Pufendorf (1934/1673) *On the Law of Nature and of Nations*, C. H. and W. A. Oldfather, trans., Oxford: Oxford University Press; and J. Raz (1995) *Ethics in the Public Domain: Essays in the Morality of Law and Politics*, Oxford: Oxford University Press.

32

THE RULE OF LAW

Grant Lamond

Introduction

The "Rule of Law" is an ideal that features prominently in contemporary political discourse. Departures from the Rule of Law are regarded as flaws or failings in a legal system, or at best regrettable necessities that carry a significant burden of justification. The Rule of Law is often considered to be the distinctive virtue of legal systems, and a prerequisite for the existence of a good or decent system of law. But while all (or almost all) agree that the Rule of Law is an indispensable aspect of a worthwhile legal system, there is less agreement on the content and scope of the ideal. It is normally thought to include such elements as official conformity to the law; the independence of the judiciary; laws being clear, prospective and public; and the ability to challenge the applicability of a law in a fair hearing (see Jowell 2007). Nonetheless, lawyers and theorists debate the merits of "formal" or "thin" accounts of the Rule of Law over "substantive" or "thick" accounts, without agreeing among themselves about the details of these accounts (see Tamanaha 2004, chs. 7–8). Formal and thin accounts of the Rule of Law focus on various formal and procedural features of the law, whereas substantive and thick accounts add some requirements of substantive justice, or human rights, or democratic processes.

In this article I will defend a restricted conception of the Rule of Law that is not limited to formal or procedural features, but does not embrace the general protection of human rights or substantive justice or democracy. So the account is neither thick nor thin, neither substantive nor formal, but something in between. The account is grounded in the fundamental idea that the Rule of Law serves to promote and protect governance by law under non-ideal conditions. I will begin by considering Lon Fuller's and Joseph Raz's highly influential analyses of the Rule of Law, and the limitations of those accounts. I will go on to propose an analysis of the Rule of Law that is broader than theirs and yet still narrower than "thick" or "substantive" accounts. Finally, I will argue that the value of the Rule of Law ultimately depends upon the overall moral merits of a legal system—not because the Rule of Law has only instrumental value, but because it is an inherently mixed-value good.

Fuller and Raz on the Rule of Law

There are two particularly influential philosophical accounts of the Rule of Law: those provided by Fuller (1969) and Raz (2009: 210–29). Both take a narrow view of the Rule of Law whilst regarding it as an important legal ideal. What is distinctive about the two accounts is that they suggest two (very different) ways in which the requirements of the

Rule of Law might be unified. There is a great deal to be learned from both the accounts themselves and from their limitations.

Fuller's account of legality is best known for the claim that it constitutes an "internal morality" (or "inner morality") of law (1969, ch. 2). He points out, plausibly enough, that a legal system could not exist if all of its laws lacked any one of the following eight features (or "desiderata"), which could be described as: (1) generality; (2) publicity; (3) prospectiveness; (4) clarity; (5) non-contradiction with other laws; (6) the possibility of conformity to the law; (7) constancy through time; and, finally, (8) congruence between the announced laws and their administration. These represent the principles of legality that a legal system should aspire to satisfy (1969: 41–44. For two illuminating discussions of the desiderata see Marmor 2007 and Kramer 2007, ch. 2). What makes these principles an "internal morality" is a more elusive matter. Fuller's key thought seems to be that law is the enterprise of subjecting human conduct to the governance of rules (1969: 46, 49, 162). In order to succeed in this enterprise the eight principles must be respected. In particular, principle (8)—faithful application of the existing law—is necessary if there is to be any point in citizens obeying the law (1969: 209–10). In effect the state is undertaking (a) that it will be possible for the citizen to know and obey the law and (b) that if the citizen obeys the law then the state will abide by it too (1969: 39–40). Consequently, it is an affront to the citizen's dignity as a responsible agent to depart from the principles (1969: 162).

On the other hand, Fuller recognizes that the principles have only a *pro tanto* force, i.e., that they can be outweighed by other considerations (including conflicts within the principles themselves, 1969: 45). Thus it can be acceptable to use retroactive legislation to correct a failure of publicity (1969: 53–54). Other illustrations of the *pro tanto* force of the principles might be the permissibility of some laws bestowing a welcome status on named individuals (e.g., the original membership of a newly formed court) and some cases of selective enforcement of the criminal law. It is also widely thought that the objective standard of care in negligence law is acceptable even though it renders some "short-comers" (i.e., those incapable of satisfying the standard) liable (Honoré 1999). So the importance of Fuller's principles of legality lies in the value of (a) being able to conform to the law and (b) knowing the consequences of conformity and nonconformity. One limitation of this analysis lies in the fact that these values are always susceptible to being outweighed by some competing value that can be better achieved by departures from the principles. The Rule of Law, on Fuller's approach, no longer seems to impose quite as strong a normative constraint on the law as it is often thought to do.

The more fundamental limitation of Fuller's account, however, is simply that it omits so much that is central to our ordinary conception of the Rule of Law, such as the independence of the judiciary, the effective ability of citizens to challenge the legality of state actions in the courts and the observance of due process in civil litigation and criminal prosecutions. Fuller's principles are quite simply those that are *necessary* for subjecting human conduct to the governance of rules. But they say nothing about the other conditions that must prevail if the law is to govern a community. (Indeed it may be that Fuller did not envisage his principles of legality as being coextensive with the "Rule of Law," a term he first uses in the "Reply to Critics" in the revised edition of his work (1969: 187–242).)

So let us turn to Raz's alternative analysis of the Rule of Law. Raz rejects the idea that the Rule of Law represents an "inner morality" of law (2009: 223–24). He sees it instead as premised on the assumption that people should obey the law and be ruled by it (2009:

212). The "basic intuition" of the Rule of Law is that if the law is to be obeyed it must be *capable of guiding* the behavior of those to whom it applies (2009: 214). The Rule of Law itself is constituted by those features of the law that are necessary for it to be capable of guiding behavior. This rationale is applicable to Fuller's desiderata of the Rule of Law, though Raz himself places more emphasis on institutional features that are important for ensuring consistent application of the law and supervising conformity to the Rule of Law itself. He suggests the following (non-exhaustive) list of principles (2009: 214–19):

(1) all laws should be prospective, open and clear;
(2) laws should be relatively stable;
(3) the making of particular laws (particular legal orders) should be guided by open, stable, clear and general rules;
(4) the independence of the judiciary must be guaranteed;
(5) the principles of natural justice must be observed;
(6) the courts should have review powers over the implementation of the other principles;
(7) the courts should be easily accessible; and
(8) the discretion of the crime-preventing agencies should not be allowed to pervert the law.

Raz ultimately sees the Rule of Law as an inherent virtue of the law, because a legal system that better conforms to the Rule of Law is better able to achieve the function of guiding human behavior. He emphasizes, however, that this is not a *moral* virtue, but rather an *instrumental* virtue, i.e., the virtue of efficiency (2009: 226). In his well-known image, the specific function of knives is to cut, and thus the sharpness of a knife is one of its inherent virtues, but a knife can be put to both morally desirable and morally deplorable uses. So too with the uses to which the law can be put. A legal system that conforms to the Rule of Law, is a "good" one, but only in the sense of being well-suited to the specific function of law (2009: 223–26).

On the other hand, Raz does attribute other (moral) value to the Rule of Law, such as (a) reducing the scope for arbitrary power, (b) facilitating individual planning and (c) serving the value of human dignity by reducing uncertainty over the future and reducing frustrated or disappointed expectations (2009: 219–23). But he sees the Rule of Law as a purely *negative* virtue, because its value lies in lowering the risks that are created by the law's existence in the first place. It is like the duty not to deceive in communicating with others. Absent the ability to communicate we could not deceive. But the value of communication does not lie in failing to deceive others—it lies in the positive goods that can be achieved through communication (2009: 224, 228).

Raz's account is forceful, but it has three important limitations. The first concerns the way in which it frames the conception of the Rule of Law in terms of the guidance functions of *the law*. The Rule of Law is normally thought to be particularly relevant to how the *state* acts, directing it to govern through (and be governed by) law. The reason for this is obvious enough: the state has many possible means at its disposal to alter the behavior of its subjects and bring about various ends. The state can "guide" conduct by (a) intentionally bringing about that conduct, or, more specifically, (b) intentionally bringing about that conduct by laying down standards to be followed. The behavior of the general public can be altered in many ways other than by laying down standards, e.g., by persuasion (health campaigns, propaganda), or by providing services and resources (roads, hospitals, art galleries, public parks), or by changing the circumstances of choice (e.g., by expanding or contracting the money supply, buying and selling assets, deploying more police on the beat). In the case of these sorts of measures, there is no reason to think that they will be more effective in guiding behavior if they are legally authorized than if the state or its officials simply act without authorization.

The Rule of Law, however, *does* require the state to have legal authorization for the use of its resources and personnel. It is not simply that the state and its officials should obey the general law: there should also be legal controls over how it acts *within* the general law. This aspect of the Rule of Law is ignored by Raz because he sees the matter in terms of the relationship of the law to the *government* (2009: 212–13). For Raz, to say that the government should be subject to the law is tautologous, since an action unauthorized by law cannot be an action by the government as a government (2009: 212). The only alternative Raz sees to this "legalistic" conception of government is government in a "political sense," i.e., government in the sense of where "real power" is located in a community (e.g., with big business, or trade unions, etc.). But it is more common to think that the problem of the Rule of Law is a particularly pressing one for the state, and the "state" in the political sense of a system of institutions which have characteristic social functions and which make characteristic claims about the justification for those functions. The state is not necessarily the location of "real power" within a community: it is instead an entity with a special legal and political status within society (and, very often, considerable social power). It would be misleading to think of unauthorized actions of the state as being of no greater significance than the unlawful actions of other social actors. The state is intimately connected to the law, and there is a heightened concern that it be subject to the law.

Secondly, even on its own terms the instrumental view of the Rule of Law contains a significant inherent limitation, as Raz himself recognizes (2009: 225). Even where the legal standards are used to guide behavior, it is not the case that the ends pursued by the state will be more effectively pursued through conformity to the Rule of Law. There is an important reason for this. The state often pursues some end *indirectly* through the law: it makes doing X legally required in order to promote or bring about Y (Raz 2009: 224–25; see also 167–68). So the state may require vehicles to be inspected and registered with a central authority. But ordinarily the aim of such measures will not be inspection or registration for its own sake. Inspection and registration are normally desirable because they promote the goal of road safety by ensuring that more vehicles are roadworthy than they would be without these measures. Now whether that indirect goal will be better served by, e.g., a very clear and precise set of criteria (conforming to the desiderata of clarity), or by an extremely vague standard, seems to be a contingent question. Perhaps more car-users will err on the side of higher quality if the standard is extremely vague, leading to greater road safety. Otherwise they will settle for nothing more than barely passing the precise criteria. Equally, perhaps the most effective way of dealing with the phenomenon of "designer drugs" (where the molecular structure of a chemical is modified to escape the definitional scope of current prohibitions, while preserving the effect of the substance) would be to criminalize and punish them retroactively, thereby deterring others but violating the Rule of Law requirement of prospectiveness. Similarly, the widespread official toleration of certain unlawful methods of evidence-gathering (such as maintaining an unlawful database of people's DNA, or using intrusive surveillance) might be more effective in reducing some types of criminal wrongdoing than the scrupulous use of legal methods.

These examples indicate that it is only the performance of the very conduct specified in the standard that is made easier by conformity to the desiderata of the Rule of Law. The underlying aim of the standard, i.e., the goal that the introduction of the standard was designed to promote, might be better achieved by departures from the Rule of Law. So it is misleading to think that adherence to the Rule of Law is straightforwardly underwritten by considerations of instrumental effectiveness. The use of clear, or prospective, or public, standards is not an inherently superior method of achieving some ends than the use of standards that lack these features, or to the use of some other means altogether. It is only inherently conducive to enabling those to whom the standards are directed to do the very thing that the standard requires: i.e., it is only inherently conducive to enabling the *standard itself* to be followed. So it all depends on the nature of the goal in question whether the most effective method of pursuing it is via a standard that conforms to the Rule of Law.

Finally, Raz extends Fuller's parsimonious list of conditions for the Rule of Law by including a range of institutional arrangements (independence of the judiciary, accessibility of courts, due process) that are designed to help ensure that the law is applied faithfully by the state (2009: 216–19). This takes his account of the Rule of Law closer to a traditional understanding, but has a paradoxical potential. Rather than supporting a very narrow (or "formal"—2009: 214) conception of the Rule of Law, it seems to invite a very broad conception. For it is not only institutional arrangements that help ensure that the law is faithfully followed and applied. A democratic political system, freedom of the press and freedom of association also serve this goal. It is also served by people having access to legal advice, and having a level of education and resources to be able to gain access to the courts easily. If all of the political and social conditions that help to ensure the law is faithfully followed and applied are part and parcel of the Rule of Law, then it is a very extensive ideal. Raz excludes these further conditions by restricting the Rule of Law to actions of the state (2009: 218–19), but: (a) some of the conditions such as legal protection of freedom of the press and democratic accountability *are* actions of the state; (b) the restriction to state actions does not flow from the "basic intuition" that the law must be capable of guiding behavior; and (c) the restriction excludes some conditions (such as an independent legal profession) that are quite plausible candidates for even a narrow conception of the Rule of Law.

The instrumental conception, then, has a number of difficulties in accounting for standard features of the Rule of Law. The focus on what the law must be like to be *capable* of guiding behavior does not explain what must be the case for the law to *succeed* in governing a community.

Governance by Law

The basic idea of the Rule of Law, obviously enough, is that it exists when a community is ruled, or governed, by law. There is a longstanding conception of a law-governed community as one that avoids the alternative evils of tyranny and anarchy (or at least tyranny and what might be called "Hobbesian anarchy," i.e., where chaos and violence prevails). In the case of tyranny, it is an individual or group of individuals who rule a community, irrespective of any requirements of the law, whereas in the case of anarchy there is no effective governance or law at all. By contrast, a law-governed community is one where although there are rulers, both rulers and ruled are subject to law, and the law is effective in governing the community. This points to three fundamental elements of the Rule of Law: (1) that the legal system is effective; (2) that the state is governed by law and governs through law; and (3) that individual laws can be (severally and jointly) obeyed. Let me consider each one in turn:

1. The Law Is Effective

For the Rule of Law to prevail in a community, the law must be effective in guiding its subjects. To be effective, there must, obviously, be a legal system, viz., a set of institutions that are constituted by and apply legal standards and that have whatever other attributes are involved in its being a legal system (on these attributes compare, e.g., Raz 2009, chs. 5–6 with Simmonds 2007, ch. 2, and Waldron 2008). The law must also be followed and applied (to a sufficient degree). The Rule of Law does not obtain when some other powerful societal actor, such as a drug cartel or a group of rebels or insurgents, takes over effective control from the legal system and rules in its place (entirely, or in some region). Nor does the Rule of Law exist in a state where legal institutions are so cowed or corrupt that those with the relevant type of influence can generally succeed in acting contrary to the law. Nor, finally, does it prevail if the law is widely disregarded by the general population (as it is, apparently, in Yap, Micronesia, despite the existence of a functioning legal system. See Tamanaha 1997: 136–37). It is not enough that there is a recognizable legal system in place if the laws of that system do not play a significant role in guiding the behavior of the general population.

The law must also be effective in the sense that it can be used by those to whom it applies. There is no point having various legal rights and remedies if there are no legal avenues through which these can be asserted against those who deny or violate them. Similarly, there is no point having such access if the officials do not conscientiously apply the law according to its terms. So for the law to be effective, there must be sufficient conformity to the law by the general population, and there must also be a set of officials who are available (and able) to apply the law either when called upon or at their own initiative.

2. The State Is Governed by Law and Governs Through Law

That the legal system is effective, in the sense of being followed and prevailing over non-state competitors, does not in itself guarantee that the agencies of the state will themselves be subject to the law. A state could reserve the right to act extralegally when it judged it appropriate, whilst allowing many matters to be settled by existing legal regulation. It could also exempt its own internal workings and decision-making from legal regulation. The subjection of the state and its instrumentalities to the law imposes an additional level of legal governance to the community. (This should not be equated with a general requirement for judicial review: a state's processes can be regulated by law even if disputes over those processes are nonjusticiable.)

This element is not a purely formal one, for it requires more than simple conformity to existing law. It would not be satisfied if all state officials enjoyed a clear, prospective and promulgated legal exemption from liability under any law of the system. This is not because such an exemption for some officials could never be justified (as it may be in the analogous case of diplomatic immunity). But *prima facie*, exemptions from laws that would otherwise apply if a person were not an official must be necessary for those officials to carry out their particular functions (inspection, arrest, adjudication, repossession). Blanket exemptions of officials from otherwise applicable laws would mean that the state was not effectively under legal governance.

3. *That Individual Laws Can Be (Jointly and Severally) Obeyed*

To be governed by law, the law must be such that it is possible to obey it, i.e., to conform to it and be guided by it. Whether the law is directed to agencies of the state or members of the community (or both), it can only govern if it can be obeyed. This is the element given great prominence in formal accounts of the Rule of Law, as it points to the desirability of clarity, prospectiveness and non-contradiction of standards. But the other two elements are equally important for the Rule of Law. There is generally no point in obeying the law if it is ineffective. Nor does the ability to obey the law help, unless one's behavior will later be assessed according to the law that one obeyed. In fact, the three elements are mutually supportive: it must be possible to obey the law if it is to be effective (i.e., followed) and if it is to be able to guide the state and its officials.

These three elements account well for Fuller's desiderata, as well as going beyond them, but they still leave out some central features of our ordinary conception of the Rule of Law such as the independence of the judiciary and due process. Why is this? Fuller's list of requirements seeks to identify those conditions that must be satisfied (at least to some extent) for a system of law to exist at all (1969: 55). But the focus of the Rule of Law is not on the *existence* of law (important as that is) but on *governance* by law. The latter requires there to be law, but requires more besides. The three elements above constitute the minimum conditions for the law to govern. But in addition to these, there are other factors that are highly conducive to the maintenance of those conditions. It is into this category that requirements such as judicial independence, access to the courts and the principles of natural justice (due process) fall.

This does not mean, on the other hand, that *every* condition that is conducive to maintaining a law-governed community should be regarded as part of the Rule of Law. As noted above, many factors play an important role in indirectly supporting governance by law. But they are *indirect* factors inasmuch as serving the Rule of Law is not the principal or primary reason for their establishment and maintenance. The core of the Rule of Law—the subjection of the state to law, the formal features of law and laws, the institutional and procedural demands on the legal system—are those conditions that are sought *because* they serve the goal of governance by law. The principal reason for establishing these conditions is that they serve that end. Many other conditions can serve and promote the Rule of Law, but the main rationale for seeking these conditions is not that they serve the Rule of Law: instead, it is that they promote other goods, such as respect for human rights and human dignity or the good of political participation. That they are conducive to the Rule of Law is a further reason in favor of bringing them about, but they would still be worth pursuing in the absence of their service to that good. It is worth maintaining a distinction between factors that are simply conducive to governance by law and those whose principal rationale lies in promoting that end.

So this implies a fourth element of the Rule of Law:

4. *Those Legal and Social Arrangements Whose Primary Rationale Lies in Their Being Highly Conducive to the Existence of Elements 1–3*

This element, for example, supports the existence of an independent legal profession as an aspect of the Rule of Law, since one of the main rationales for such a body is to maintain governance by law. It also supports a degree of arm's-length separation between administrative agencies and the government. As the example of an independent legal profession illustrates, the fourth element is not necessarily limited to institutional processes and arrangements within the legal system itself. There may well be other social conditions whose main rationale is to serve governance by law, in which case they too are rightly regarded as forming part of the Rule of Law. Indeed, even some of Fuller's original desiderata, such as publicity and stability, are best understood as falling partly under (4) as well as (3). To guide behavior, for instance, it is often unnecessary for anyone, other than those to whom a law applies, to be aware of it (Marmor 2007: 17). Publicity on the other hand—*general* knowledge of the existence of a legal standard—serves to open the law to scrutiny of its compliance with other elements of the Rule of Law, such as congruence of official action to law (Kramer 2007: 153 and Marmor 2007: 18). Similarly, a degree of stability may be necessary for discharging some duties, since it may take time and effort to be in a position to do so. But it also makes it easier for the law to be known if it has a degree of constancy through time, and easier for those seeking to conform to the law to do so.

It would be wrong to think that because the fourth element serves the other three, it is simply "ancillary" or "peripheral," and thus less important to the Rule of Law. The Rule of Law is an ideal for law-governance in an imperfect world, i.e., under non-ideal circumstances where people are fallible (and worse). Conditions such as the independence of the judiciary are just as crucial to governance by law under these circumstances as are the other elements. The same is true of the central procedural requirements of the Rule of Law, such as access to a hearing by an impartial and competent adjudicator, and the opportunity to make submissions over the content of the applicable law. For the law to govern, there must be processes to resolve disputed questions *of law* in a principled way, as well as processes for determining whether the conditions for the application of the law have been satisfied. (On the importance of the procedural dimensions of the Rule of Law, see Waldron 2008 and 2011.)

What can make these further conditions seem less central to the Rule of Law is that the form that some of them take will be dependent upon the particular political and legal culture of each country. How best to secure an independent judiciary—through a career judiciary or through the appointment of experienced lawyers to the bench—may simply depend upon the history of a particular legal culture, and how well its practices have served that goal.

This leads to a further question. Why is upholding the Rule of Law ordinarily regarded as a particular responsibility of the *state*? Why is it that departures from the Rule of Law by the state are especially criticized? One answer, of course, lies in the threat that the state poses to the Rule of Law. The legal system is ultimately part of the state, and the legal system relies upon the willingness of other state instrumentalities to obey its decisions, since it does not have the resources to physically compel compliance. On the other hand, the state is not the only societal actor that can pose a threat to the Rule of Law. Protest movements, political parties, trade unions and large business conglomerates can also threaten the Rule of Law if they have sufficient social power, as can the general population if it fails to be significantly guided by the law. So why single out the state—both in the sense of the government and state officials? Because the degree of control the state enjoys over the legal system and the content and operation of the law means that it is uniquely placed to support and promote (as well as threaten) the Rule of Law. Consequently, a special responsibility falls upon it to scrupulously uphold the ideal, and to set an example by doing so.

The preceding discussion explains the reasons for adopting a restricted conception of the Rule of Law, one which does not extend it to the general protection of human rights, or to democracy, or other human goods. The restricted conception best captures the idea that the point of the Rule of Law is to provide the conditions for the law to govern the community, and that upholding the Rule of Law is a special responsibility of the state. But it also makes sense of the inclination to extend the Rule of Law to all of those other conditions that are conducive to governance by law. In the end, however, it is worth distinguishing those conditions which are justified *because* they serve governance by law from those that are valuable for other important reasons and whose main *raison d'être* is not the maintenance of legal governance. To say that this is a *restricted* conception, on the other hand, is not to say that it is limited to formal or procedural features of law and legal institutions. Some aspects, such as the application of the law to officials, or the independence of the judiciary, are neither. It is simply to indicate that it does not encompass all of those other conditions that are conducive to governance by law.

The Value of the Rule of Law

Why is the Rule of Law normally regarded as both a legal and a moral ideal? What is valuable about the Rule of Law? Two questions need to be separated here: (a) what is the basic rationale or justification for the Rule of Law, and (b) what values are served by the observance of the Rule of Law? While the values that justify the Rule of Law are served by its observance, it does not follow that all of the values served by the Rule of Law are part of its underlying justification. Observance of the Rule of Law requirement on publicity, for instance, may facilitate criticism of the merits of various laws (Fuller 1969: 51; Marmor 2007: 18; Kramer 2007: 151), but the point of publicity is to facilitate conformity to the law and conformity to the Rule of Law itself. It is an additional virtue that it enables the law to be criticized on its merits.

The most common value associated with the Rule of Law is human dignity, in the sense of people's capacity for rational agency and autonomous choice (for a variety of alternatives, see Fuller 1969: 162–67; Raz 2009: 221–23; Finnis 1980: 270–73; MacCormick 1992: 123; Waldron 2008: 26–28). This is based on the fact that the Rule of Law operates to make the application of the law (fairly) predictable and to ensure that those to whom the law applies are able to conform to it. But there are reasons to question the primacy of this rationale for the Rule of Law.

First of all, the value of human dignity and rational agency is clearly not a sufficient rationale for the full scope of the Rule of Law. Much of constitutional law, for instance, deals with the processes of decision-making within the state—which person or body is authorized to take which decision and in what way. Similarly, much of the law regulates how people should be treated *by* officials (e.g., in having their interests considered in making a decision, or in being arrested). In a liberal society this is commonly done in a way that respects people's dignity and agency. But nothing in the Rule of Law requires people to be treated in this way. That the law must be capable of being followed by officials in their roles is not generally understood in terms of serving the rational agency of *officials*. It is instead designed to put processes in place for which officials can be accountable, and to ensure that officials do not misuse their position. Nor does the Rule of Law provide very much in the way of other protections for human dignity and rational agency. The law may infringe upon these values in a wide variety of ways: it may limit people's freedom of movement, their employment, the practice of their religion, whom (and whether) they can marry, whether they can have (or care for) children, with whom they can associate or communicate. It can regulate their access to reading matter, art and music, their appearance (clothing, hair, use of makeup, head-covering, tattoos, piercings) and their dwellings. None of these encroachments are *per se* incompatible with the Rule of Law.

Second, the Rule of Law does not require (or even create a presumption) that the behavior of non-officials be guided exclusively by the laying down of standards for them to follow. As noted earlier, the law can influence behavior by authorizing other methods to promote desirable ends, such as education campaigns, soup kitchens, mobile libraries, art galleries and public parks. The provision of services and resources can be the best method of promoting some ends. What matters from the perspective of the Rule of Law is not that non-officials always be guided by standards, but that the measures taken to influence behavior are authorized by law, i.e., that the actions of officials are subject to the law.

Finally, while the dimension of the Rule of Law that requires it to be possible to obey the law clearly does serve human dignity and rational agency by enabling people to conform to the law (and know the consequences of their actions), it also serves to ensure governance through law. The point is that the state does not govern through law if it uses standards that are *so* vague that it is simply up to the discretion of officials how these standards apply, or if it changes the standards retrospectively whenever it wants to, or if the standards are unknown to those to whom they apply, or if its officials are inconsistent in how they enforce the law. In all these cases, the state is not really governing through law—instead it is taking advantage of its control over the content and application of the law to act at its own discretion. It is only if the standards that it is going to apply are known, prospective, relatively clear, non-contradictory and applied consistently that the state is subjecting itself to governing through law. Similarly, to demand what is *literally* impossible is simply an abuse of form: it implies that liability to certain official measures is conditional on conformity when in fact it is simply being unconditionally created. It is a desirable consequence of the demands on legal governance that it makes it possible for people to conform to those laws that require them to do something. In many cases this will reduce the risks of falling foul of the law and enable people to take advantage of opportunities created by the law. Legal governance thus *presupposes* that its subjects are rational agents and capable of being guided by standards. But in the end the law's promotion of human dignity and rational agency depends upon the *content* of the laws of a particular legal system, not simply the observance of the Rule of Law.

These three points suggest that while the Rule of Law serves human dignity and rational agency, its underlying justification rests instead on the value of having a law-governed community. What is it that governance by law brings to a community? Clearly it does not guarantee that the law will pursue desirable ends, or that the community will be an admirable one. There have been (and are) many states committed to the Rule of Law in which serious injustices have been (and are) perpetrated and supported by law. On the other hand, it does seem that part of what makes an admirable community admirable is its observance of the Rule of Law. Why is this? For a start, such a community not only has good laws, it has a law-abiding population, where those laws are followed by those to whom they apply. Second, such a community is one in which the state and its officials operate through legal processes and according to legal demands. Why is this so important? Because the power and influence that the state and its officials have over the content and the application of the law create a standing risk of corrupt and self-interested actions. Whatever worthwhile ends the state may pursue through the law, these will be compromised by a state apparatus that lacks fidelity to the law. Moreover, the greater the departures from fidelity to law, the more that the pursuit of those ends will be compromised. Maintaining the integrity of the state and its processes is indispensable to the pursuit of valuable goals through the law, including the goals of respecting and promoting human dignity and autonomy. Nor is it feasible to have a law-abiding general community in the midst of official corruption. If people do not believe they will be treated according to the existing law, their reasons for obedience are much reduced. So the Rule of Law is a necessary condition for a flourishing community (or, at least, for communities like ours that possess a state). This is not because it is simply a *means* to achieving valuable ends, since the attainment of some ends is made more difficult by adherence to the Rule of Law. Rather, it is because the Rule of Law manages to provide a method of pursuing ends with built-in safeguards against the abuse and misuse of those methods. They are not always the most efficient methods, but they are likely to ensure the integrity of the agents charged with carrying them out.

What light does this throw on the question of whether an "evil" regime—a regime which does not simply perpetrate serious injustices, but is exclusively concerned with its own interests (and the interests of its supporters), at the expense of the interests of the community at large—would have any reason to conform to the Rule of Law (Finnis 1980: 273–76)? An evil regime would clearly have some reasons for conformity, e.g., to guide the population effectively, to provide incentives for conforming to the law, and to coordinate the activities of the state's officials (Kramer 1999: 66–71). And whether or not it would have more reason than a benign regime to depart from the Rule of Law depends upon the circumstances (under normal conditions it arguably would have more reason to depart: Simmonds 2007: 76–99; contrast Kramer 2004). But what distinguishes an evil regime is its attitude to the Rule of Law. A benign regime is committed to pursuing its ends through law, and accepts that this is a constraint on its actions. An evil regime does not. Of course, were conformity to the Rule of Law the most effective means to pursue *any* end, an evil regime could see it as a *rational* requirement on its actions. But as we saw above, all that the Rule of Law necessarily facilitates is conformity to the law itself, not the attainment of any further aim. At times the law, especially laws that comply with the Rule of Law, will not be the most effective means of achieving an aim. So an evil regime will have reasons to conform to the Rule of Law, but it will also have reasons to depart from the Rule of Law whenever there is a more effective method of achieving its aims. Whether it will have more reason to observe the Rule of Law in any particular case will depend on the balance of reasons, including the collateral effects (if any) of departures from the Rule of Law (such as the effects on its reputation for conformity to the Rule of Law). A benign regime, by contrast, will not see the observance of the Rule of Law in this way. It values maintaining governance *by* and *through* law because of the goods that such governance serves, not just as a means to an end. It will only depart from the constraints of the Rule of Law where there is some important good that cannot be achieved at an acceptable cost through conformity. Whether it will depart depends upon the seriousness of the departures and the urgency and importance of the value that would otherwise have to be sacrificed. In short, an evil regime will be unable to *comply* with the Rule of Law, even when it conforms to it, because such a regime does not value governance by law in itself, but simply as a means to its ends.

Finally, is the observance of the Rule of Law *always* morally valuable? To the extent that it serves values such as state integrity and human dignity this must be so. Moreover, as the threats to these values are created by the existence of the state, not simply the existence of the law, their reduction is not simply a negative value (as Raz suggests, 2009: 224). To say that the Rule of Law always has some value is not, of course, to say that every legal system which observes the Rule of Law is, all things considered, worthwhile. That depends, naturally, on the merits of the laws in the system. What is not generally recognized is that the same is true of the Rule of Law itself: it also is not always worthwhile, all things considered. This is because the Rule of Law is (in our imperfect world) a double-edged virtue. The fundamental requirement that the state and its officials scrupulously and consistently apply the law entails that all laws, whatever their merits, be applied. The goods achieved by the Rule of Law depend upon officials consistently applying the law rather than doing so selectively. One of the central components of the Rule of Law is official conformity to the law. In the light of our various moral limitations (such as our fallibility, our susceptibility to self-preference, our weak will), coupled with the great goods that a reliable and stable legal system may bring to community life, there is much to be said for this position. (Or at least, there is much to be said for the idea that officials always have a strong reason to follow the law, though there may be circumstances where officials should not conform.) But it is not an unalloyed good, since it inevitably comes at the moral cost of following and applying even unmeritorious laws. In order to deliver the goods that the Rule of Law can bring, officials must follow and apply laws, including those that are morally unjustified. But where the content of a legal system is sufficiently unmeritorious *overall*, the goods achieved by general conformity to the law may not be worth the price. Ultimately, then, the value of the Rule of Law itself is dependent upon the merits of the legal system as a whole—not because it is simply a means to whatever ends the law pursues, but because it is, inherently, a mixed-value good.

It is this that helps explain our ambivalent attitude towards the Rule of Law in unjust regimes such as apartheid South Africa. The observance of the Rule of Law under apartheid (to the extent that it occurred: Abel 1999) clearly had some value in restricting arbitrary official action and creating some space for actions opposing the regime. But the Rule of Law also involved a body of officials helping to maintain that regime through their consistent use and application of the law. Under these conditions, a wholehearted commitment to the Rule of Law would have been misguided. Instead, the forms of legality had a value in assisting resistance and, ultimately, in assisting the transition to a system of democratic majority rule under law.

Conclusion

The Rule of Law is the ideal of a law-governed community. Many conditions must be satisfied for that ideal to be realized, going well beyond the formal features of laws and official conformity to the law. For the Rule of Law is not simply an ideal of a law-governed community: it is an ideal of a law-governed community in a non-ideal world. It is constituted by those conditions that are highly conducive to, and are justified by, their contribution to governance by law. Other conditions, such as respect for human rights and democratic accountability, can also be conducive to the Rule of Law, just as the Rule of Law itself is an important condition for the effective protection of human rights and democratic processes. But it is worth maintaining a distinction between these different ideals, despite their mutual supportiveness, in terms of the main rationale for their existence. Hence the idea that this is a restricted conception of the Rule of Law, i.e., one that is neither thick nor thin, neither substantive nor formal, but something in between.

The Rule of Law serves many values, but its fundamental rationale lies in its promotion of state legality, i.e., in the subjection of the state itself to effective legal regulation, and the adherence of the state to governing through law. The Rule of Law is not an ultimate end, since it alone cannot guarantee that the legal system will be a meritorious one. Instead, its value lies in the fact that a meritorious legal system is one that partly consists in, and cannot be achieved without, the Rule of Law.

Acknowledgments

I would like to thank Pavlos Eleftheriadis, John Gardner and Wayne Sumner for their discussion of an early draft of this paper. I am particularly grateful to John Stanton-Ife and Andrei Marmor for their helpful comments on this paper.

References

Abel, R. (1999) "Legality Without a Constitution: South Africa in the 1980s," in D. Dyzenhaus, ed., *Recrafting the Rule of Law: The Limits of Legal Order*, Oxford: Hart Publishing, pp. 66–80.

Finnis, J. (1980) *Natural Law and Natural Rights*, Oxford: Oxford University Press.

Fuller, L. (1969) *The Morality of Law*, revised edition, New Haven: Yale University Press.

Honoré, T. (1999) "Responsibility and Luck: The Moral Basis of Strict Liability," in T. Honoré, *Responsibility and Fault*, Oxford: Hart Publishing, pp. 14–40.

Jowell, J. (2007) "The Rule of Law and Its Underlying Values," in J. Jowell and D. Oliver, eds., *The Changing Constitution*, 6th edition, Oxford: Oxford University Press.

Kramer, M. (1999) *In Defense of Legal Positivism*, Oxford: Oxford University Press.

—— (2004) "On the Moral Status of the Rule of Law," in M. Kramer, *Where Law and Morality Meet*, Oxford: Oxford University Press, pp. 172–222.

—— (2007) *Objectivity and the Rule of Law*, New York: Cambridge University Press.

MacCormick, N. (1992) "Natural Law and the Separation of Law and Morals," in R. George, ed., *Natural Law Theory*, Oxford: Oxford University Press, pp. 105–33.

Marmor, A. (2007) "The Rule of Law and Its Limits," in A. Marmor, *Law in the Age of Pluralism*, New York: Oxford University Press, pp. 3–38.

Raz, J. (2009) *The Authority of Law*, 2nd edition, Oxford: Oxford University Press.

Simmonds, N. (2007) *Law as a Moral Idea*, Oxford: Oxford University Press.

Tamanaha, B. (1997) *Realistic Socio-Legal Theory*, Oxford: Oxford University Press.

—— (2004) *On the Rule of Law: History, Politics, Theory*, Cambridge: Cambridge University Press.

Waldron, J. (2008) "The Concept and the Rule of Law," *Georgia Law Review* 43: 1.

—— (2011) "The Rule of Law and the Importance of Procedure," in J. Fleming, ed., *Getting to the Rule of Law: Nomos L*, New York: New York University Press.

Further Reading

For further reading, see: T. R. S. Allan (2001) *Constitutional Justice: A Liberal Theory of the Rule of Law*, Oxford: Oxford University Press (study of the Rule of Law in the common law from a constitutional perspective); R. M. Dworkin (1985) "Political Judges and the Rule of Law," in *A Matter of Principle*, Oxford: Oxford University Press (classic defense of a substantive account of the Rule of Law); R. M. Dworkin (2006) "Hart's Postscript and the Point of Political Philosophy," in *Justice in Robes*, Cambridge, Mass.: Harvard University Press (arguing that legality is an interpretive concept and fundamental to the nature of law); D. Dyzenhaus, ed. (1999) *Recrafting the Rule of Law: The Limits of Legal Order*, Oxford: Hart Publishing (wide-ranging collection of essays with case studies and analysis of the Rule of Law); and C. Sampford (2006) *Retrospectivity and the Rule of Law*, Oxford: Oxford University Press (a detailed study assessing the Rule of Law arguments against retrospective laws).

Part V

MORAL OBLIGATIONS TO LAW

33

THE MORAL OBLIGATION TO OBEY THE LAW

George Klosko

The moral obligation to obey the law, or as it is generally called, political obligation, is a moral requirement to obey the laws of one's country. Traditionally, this has been viewed as a requirement of a certain kind, to obey the law for the "content-independent" reason that it is the law, as opposed to the content of particular laws. In characterizing this as a moral requirement, theorists distinguish political obligation from legal obligation. All legal systems claim to bind people subject to them; part of what we mean by a valid law is that the relevant population is required to obey it. This requirement is generally supported by coercion, while those who do not obey are subject to sanctions. But these aspects of legal obligation leave open more ultimate questions about the state's justification for imposing such requirements. Unless citizens have moral requirements to obey the law, they may be forced to do so, but in compelling obedience, the state is acting unjustly and impinging on their freedom.

As H. L. A. Hart argues, the distinctive thrust of political obligations can be seen in the contrast between being obliged to do p and having an obligation to do it (Hart 1961: 80–88). If a gunman holds Smith up and threatens to shoot her unless she turns over $50, she is likely *obliged* to surrender this sum. But by this locution, we mean no more than that the alternatives to complying are significantly unpleasant, which gives her a strong reason to comply. According to Hart, obligation adds to this an internal dimension. While Smith's being obliged to do p is analyzed in terms of her assessment of the consequences of obeying or not obeying, her having an obligation to do p adds to these concerns the moral legitimacy of what she is compelled to do. If Smith is a citizen of a legitimate state that requires she pay $50 in taxes, once again she could well be forced to comply; the consequences of noncompliance could be unacceptable to her. But in this case, it is *right* that she surrender the money. If she recognizes the obligation, she will believe it is the right thing to do—although we should note that this is a prima facie moral requirement, capable of being overridden by additional moral considerations.

At the present time, no theory of political obligations is generally accepted. All accounts are subject to vigorous controversy. Absence of consensus on moral reasons is accompanied by more basic disagreements about the nature of political obligations themselves and whether a satisfactory account is possible. At the present time the dominant position in the literature may well be that there are no political obligations in the traditional sense. But this contention too is disputed by scholars from numerous directions.

According to standard analysis, an obligation is a moral requirement that an individual imposes on himself or herself (Brandt 1964; Hart 1958; Simmons 1979, ch. 1). For instance, if A promises B to do p, the moral requirement to do p is generated by the act of promising and would not otherwise exist. But in spite of the label "political obligation," most scholars argue that moral requirements to obey the law need not be grounded in requirements of this kind (an exception is Pateman 1979). In spite of other disagreements, scholars largely agree about a few basic criteria that a successful theory of political obligation should satisfy (Simmons 1979, ch. 2; Klosko 2005, ch. 1). First, the theory should be general; that is, it should explain the obligations of all or almost all citizens. It should also explain their requirements to obey the laws of their own country. This criterion is generally referred to as "particularity" (Simmons 1979: 31–35). It should be comprehensive, i.e., explain requirements to obey all or almost all laws. Finally, as indicated above, in keeping with the general thrust of liberal political theory, the moral requirements in question should be of only limited force. They should bind citizens as a rule, but, as prima facie obligations, able to be overridden by conflicting moral requirements (see Klosko 1992: 12–14). Other features are discussed in the literature. But these should be adequate for this essay. Putting these four features together, we may say that a successful theory of political obligation explains the requirements of all or almost all citizens to obey all or almost all laws of their own countries, with these requirements of limited force.

In the literature, scholars have attempted to justify political obligations on a variety of grounds. In the liberal tradition, arguments from voluntary consent are traditionally most central. Until relatively recently, the history of political obligation has been a history of consent (Klosko 2011b). Additional approaches that will be discussed in this essay are consequentialist arguments, based on the effects of obedience or disobedience, arguments based on the principle of fairness (or fair play), which turn on receipt of benefits from the state, and arguments based on a principle of membership or association, and a natural duty of justice. I will examine the strengths and weaknesses of these different approaches and recent developments that have called into question central features of political obligations as traditionally understood.

Consent Theory

Although elements of a consent theory of political obligation are present in earlier thinkers, the view receives its classic statement in John Locke's *Second Treatise of Government* (1988/1690). Locke argues that people are naturally free in the state of nature. Although the state of nature is governed by natural law, in the absence of an authority to enforce this, Locke subscribes to the "strange Doctrine" (§ 13) that all men have the right to enforce it for themselves. However, general self-enforcement leads to conflict, and so people are willing to surrender their enforcement powers. They do this in two stages—erecting a community, which then places its powers in a legislative authority. Because people surrender only certain of their rights, the legislative power is able to act only in these areas. But in these areas, individuals agree "to submit to the determination of the majority, and to be concluded by it" (§ 97). Because Locke's overall purpose in the *Second Treatise* is to justify revolution, he is deeply concerned with limitations on authority. Although he does not use the word "contract," he argues that legitimate political authority is held in trust. When the limitations are violated, people have strong rights of resistance, including resistance by single individuals when they believe "the Cause of sufficient moment" (§ 168). However, Locke argues that this right will not lead to disorder, as individuals will realize the futility of acting alone (§ 208).

Locke holds that, because people are naturally free, only their own consent can place them under political authority (e.g., § 95). It follows that one is not bound by the consent of one's father, or by an original contract made at the foundation of society (§ 116–18). However, although "express consent" establishes clear political bonds, Locke recognizes that few people actually consent in this way. Thus he turns to "tacit consent," which is able to bind most or all inhabitants of a given country. As a result, his theory of political obligations based on consent is for all intents and purposes a theory of tacit consent.

Locke's account of the actions that constitute tacit consent is expansive:

> And to this I say that every Man, that hath any Possession, or Enjoyment of any part of the Dominions of any Government, doth thereby give his tacit Consent, and is as far forth obliged to Obedience to the Laws of that Government, during such Enjoyment, as any one under it; whether this his Possession be of Land, to him and his Heirs for ever, or a Lodging only for a Week; or whether it be barely traveling freely on the Highway; and in Effect, it reaches as far as the very being of any one within the Territories of that Government.
>
> (§ 119)

By reducing consent to, in effect, simply being within a given territory, Locke is able to argue that all or virtually all people have consented. But this raises a problem of its own. In making consent all but unavoidable, Locke deprives it of its moral significance. According to Hanah Pitkin: "we are likely to feel cheated by Locke's argument; . . . why go through the whole social contract argument if it turns out in the end that everyone is automatically obligated?" (Pitkin 1965: 995). In spite of this and other problems, Locke's view of consent is probably the standard account in the literature and—directly or indirectly—has influenced how many people think about political obligations.

Locke's view of tacit consent was classically criticized by David Hume, in the latter's essay, "Of the Original Contract" (Hume 1985). Hume agrees with Locke's fundamental claims concerning the ability of consent to bind and the limited nature of political power. But he rejects the existence of an actual historical contract into which people entered, because of the lack of evidence this ever occurred. He agrees with Locke that most people have not consented expressly to government. If they had done so, they would remember this but do not. He also breaks with Locke in regard to tacit consent, claiming that, because of the nature of existing societies, most people should not be viewed as having consented. We will return to this subject below.

Variations on Consent

Theorists have attempted to preserve consent theory in different ways. Certain theorists have attempted to identify widely performed actions that constitute tacit consent. One possibility is voting. If Jones votes in an election, one could argue that he has agreed to be governed by the winners, and so to obey the law (Plamenatz 1968: 168–71). Other similar actions could be suggested, e.g., saying the Pledge of Allegiance or taking the appropriate oath upon joining the armed forces. But if we examine the conditions necessary for an act of consent to create a moral requirement to obey the laws, it can be seen that these and similar acts fall short.

As A. John Simmons notes, when people talk about "consenting" to one's government, they often mean something much looser than voluntarily accepting a moral requirement to obey the law. Rather, they employ an "attitudinal" sense of consent. When Smith says that she consents to her government, what she frequently means is that she approves of it (Simmons 1979: 93–94). Perhaps, as indicated below, she would consent if given the opportunity, but this does not mean that she has actually bound herself to obey its laws through an act of consent.

Although a full account of the conditions necessary for effective consent cannot be presented in this context, for our purposes, three are especially important. First, the consenter must not be forced to consent—that is, reasonable means of refusing to consent must be available to her; she must be aware of what she is consenting to; and she must be competent to do so. Circumstances that do not satisfy these conditions may be described as "defeating conditions" and prevent acts of consent from generating moral obligations (Beran 1987, ch. 1).

These conditions cause problems for acts that have been purported to constitute tacit consent. Consider voting. Although it may seem that someone who votes is among other things expressing support for the political system, this is not enough for voting to ground political obligations. To use a distinction of Simmons's, we may say that voting is "consent implying" (Simmons 1979: 88–95). It does not make much sense to vote if one does not support the political system. But this is different from saying that the act of voting actually constitutes consent. It is unlikely that many people vote with the idea that, by doing so, they are agreeing to obey the laws of their countries, and that if they did not vote, they would not have moral requirements to do so. If voting is to generate a moral requirement analogous to what is created by a promise, something along these lines would have to be true. There are similar problems with other actions that have been taken to constitute consent. For instance, although the oath one takes upon entering the armed forces does appear to generate moral requirements in regard to the oath's contents, it ordinarily binds only as long as one is serving. When one leaves the armed forces, such oaths ordinarily expire.

The most plausible action—or lack thereof—that may be taken to constitute tacit consent is staying in one's country. There is a certain plausibility to this position. Most people are probably aware that if they remain in a given country, they will be required to obey its laws, while this requirement will no longer obtain if they leave. However, the requirement referred to in the last sentence is legal—likely backed up by coercion—rather than moral. If staying in one's country is to ground moral requirements to obey the law, in this case lack of action must constitute consent. As Simmons argues, failure to act may communicate consent; tacit consent differs from express consent not because it is not communicated but in the manner through which it is communicated. But additional conditions must be satisfied. Potential consenters must not only know that consent is called for, but they must also know how it is communicated, and the period of time during which they may consent or not consent (Simmons 1979: 80–81). In addition and most important, as noted above, the mode of indicating dissent must be "reasonable and reasonably easily performed." In order for consent to be voluntary, the consequences of dissent must not be extremely harmful or detrimental to the potential consenter (81). Accordingly, hanging over this form of tacit consent is the criticism of Hume, who rejects claims that residence constitutes tacit consent, because the means of expressing lack of consent are not ordinarily available:

> Can we seriously say that a poor peasant or artizan has a free choice to leave his country, when he knows no foreign language or manners, and lives from day to day, by the small wages which he acquires? We may as well assert, that a man, by remaining in a vessel, freely consents to the dominion of the master, though he was carried on board while asleep, and must leap into the ocean, and perish, the moment he leaves her.
>
> (1985: 475)

Clearly, if one is prevented from leaving a given territory, remaining in it cannot constitute consent.

Two centuries later, conditions have changed in certain respects. With greater affluence and improved transportation it is easier for many people to travel. But one can move to another country only if another is willing to take one in. Moreover, as Simmons argues, much of what is precious in life cannot be taken with one: family, friends, a particular culture (1979: 99). Therefore, choice of either consenting or leaving could well be viewed as coercive.

In response to the difficulties of tacit consent, theorists have worked out other variants of consent. One possibility is that the consent in question need not be actual consent. Rather, if conditions in one's country are such that one would consent to obey the laws if given the opportunity, then this hypothetical consent could ground moral requirements to obey the law. This approach traces back to Immanuel Kant, who argues that government's power is limited by the requirement that the legislator should "frame his laws in such a way that they could have been produced by the united will of a whole nation" (Kant 1970: 79; see Waldron 1987). However, "hypothetical consent" is immediately vulnerable. To use the words of Ronald Dworkin: "A hypothetical contract is not simply a pale form of an actual contract; it is no contract at all" (Dworkin 1977: 151). Hypothetical consent is useful in shifting attention away from actions performed or supposedly performed by the obligee to aspects of the political system that would justify consenting to it—along the lines of the attitudinal sense of consent mentioned above. But because it is not able to establish obligations on its own, if it is to ground political obligations, hypothetical consent must be supplemented by additional moral principles.

An alternative means to establish political obligations based on consent is to devise political institutions that provide opportunities for more individuals freely to consent. A possible mechanism would allow citizens to consent when they reach a certain age. Various political systems have had such mechanisms, among them ancient Greek cities (see Kraut 1984: 154–57). A "reformist consent" mechanism that could be set up in the United States would require individuals to apply for formal citizenship at the age of 18, the age at which men are presently required to register for military service. An oath of allegiance to the government and/or Constitution could be part of the process. In his defense of consent theory, Harry Beran proposes that individuals who do not consent be given the option of emigrating to a "dissenters' territory" (Beran 1987: 31–32, 37–42).

However, the obvious flaw with these proposals concerns what happens to individuals who refuse to consent. They could be required to leave the territory. But if such a choice is viewed as coercive as an alternative to tacit consent, it is unlikely to pass muster here. Thus Beran's proposal is unlikely to be acceptable, as it not only forces individuals to emigrate but has the additional disadvantage of forcing them to live in a dissenter's territory. The situation is not improved if individuals are allowed to stay in their countries (see Walzer 1970). The main benefits provided by the state are public goods and so available to all inhabitants of a territory whether or not they have consented. Non-consenters who stay in the territory will continue to receive these benefits without being required to support the institutional mechanisms that provide them. This would not only be unfair to consenters, whose efforts produce the benefits in question, but it could well make non-consent more attractive and so lead increasing numbers of people to refuse to consent (Klosko 1991). As fewer people consented, the costs of providing basic public goods would rise, encouraging additional people not to consent, and so leading to possible social collapse.

Consequentialism

Along with his rejection of political obligations based on consent, Hume developed an alternative view based on social utility. His argument is in accord with common sense. Government is required for the good of society and so should be obeyed, as long as it promotes this end. If it ceases to be useful, it loses its reason for being and also its authority. However, because it is so costly to change governments, this is justified only if governments become egregiously tyrannical (*Treatise of Human Nature*, III, ii: 9). In central respects, Hume's conclusions are similar to those of Locke. But Hume believes he is able to establish these without the fictions of an original state of nature, individual consent and social contracts.

Hume's basic position was developed by subsequent theorists in the utilitarian tradition, e.g., Bentham (1988/1776, ch. 1). In departing from the voluntarism of consent theory, this position has the considerable advantage of being able to bind most or all citizens, regardless of actions they may or may not have performed. However, consequentialism faces a central difficulty in grounding requirements for given individuals to obey the law.

The problems with consequentialism, like those with consent, stem from conflict with the facts of society. Under certain circumstances, it is actually more beneficial to society if a given individual disobeys. Whether or not other people are complying with some social norm, it is in a given individual's interest not to comply (see Taylor 1987; Klosko 1990). Important cases involve actions that are beneficial to the agent, while causing small or undetectable harms. But if performed by large numbers, these actions become extremely harmful (Harrod 1936: 148). An example is Brown's contributing to air pollution by not fixing the catalytic converter on her car. Sensitive scientific instruments would be unlikely to detect the difference in air quality caused by her conduct. If the large majority of her fellow citizens do comply with anti-pollution laws, air quality will be acceptable, and so, on consequentialist grounds, it is not clear why it is wrong for Brown not to comply. Since we may stipulate that fixing the catalytic converter would be expensive, her noncompliance affords Brown additional money to spend, which could contribute to her happiness or that of her family and friends. Thus in this case, it is actually more beneficial for society—as of course for Brown herself—if she breaks the law rather than complies. Something similar holds for laws requiring Brown to pay her taxes or to serve in the military. If her society is large, encompassing many millions of people, it is likely that, on consequentialist grounds, her disobeying these laws would also be better for society. However, in these and similar cases, the consequences of general disobedience could well be disastrous.

The difficulties here are well known, and consequentialist theorists have tried a number of ways to get around them. This essay is not the place for a full examination of this problem. But very briefly, unlike "act-utilitarians," who argue that the rightness or wrongness of an action depend on its consequences alone, "rule-utilitarians" apply the consequence test to moral rules rather than to specific actions falling under the rules. Thus rather than assessing the rightness or wrongness of fixing one's catalytic converter according to the consequences of that specific act, rule-utilitarians assess the consequences of following general rules of obeying air-pollution laws or not obeying them. If this test were applied to Brown's situation, the result would be that it would be wrong not to fix the catalytic converter. The consequences of general rules not to pollute the air, to pay taxes and to provide military service are obviously superior to those of general rules of not doing these things.

However, rule-utilitarianism has been criticized by scholars. For instance, according to J. J. C. Smart, for a utilitarian, it does not make sense to require Brown to obey a given rule, when, as we have seen, society is actually better off if she breaks it. To require her to obey is "superstitious rule worship." Smart believes the only defensible form of rule-utilitarianism consists of one rule: "maximize utility" (Smart 1967: 177; 1973: 9–12). This of course would not solve the problem of requiring Brown to fix her catalytic converter. Alternatively, it is widely held that, when rule-utilitarianism is worked out, it can be seen to be extensionally equivalent to act-utilitarianism. The difficulty concerns the exact rule that should be complied with under particular circumstances. According to rule-utilitarianism, this should be the rule that is most beneficial to society. As just noted, society is much better off if this requires non-pollution than pollution. However, society will be even better off if the rule in question is crafted to require general avoidance of pollution but to allow Brown not to fix her car. Additional exceptions must be built into the rule to accommodate the immediate gains from additional noncompliance. As a result, rule-utilitarianism collapses into act-utilitarianism. Consequentialist theorists have attempted to get around this difficulty in other ways. Their efforts raise formidable technical questions in regard to the consequences of particular actions. For instance, Derek Parfit argues that acts with small or undetectable consequences may be wrong when they are parts of sets of acts that are clearly harmful (Parfit 1984, ch. 3). This principle would explain the harmfulness of contributing to air pollution. But it has proved difficult for consequentialist theorists to provide the "moral mathematics" to support this position (Gruzalski 1986; Parfit 1986; Klosko 1990).

The Principle of Fairness

The difficulties with consequentialism indicate the advantages of arguments from the principle of fairness (or fair play). Return to the pollution case. As we have seen, because general but not universal adherence to anti-pollution laws is necessary, it is actually better for society, as of course for Brown herself, if she disobeys them. But one could ask why Brown rather than other citizens should gain the benefit of noncompliance. Is it fair that she simply assumes this advantage, while most or all other citizens would presumably also prefer not to comply? Underlying the principle of fairness is the intuition that in situations along these lines, advantages of noncompliance should be distributed fairly. It is unfair for a given individual who benefits from the sacrifices of her fellow citizens simply to assume for herself the additional benefits of noncompliance.

The principle was first clearly formulated by Hart in 1955 (exposition here draws on Klosko 1992 and other works):

> [W]hen a number of persons conduct any joint enterprise according to rules and thus restrict their liberty, those who have submitted to these restrictions when required have a right to a similar submission from those who have benefited by their submission.
>
> (Hart 1955: 185)

The moral basis of the principle is mutuality of restrictions. Under specified conditions, the sacrifices made by members of a cooperative scheme in order to produce benefits also benefit noncooperators, who do not make similar sacrifices. According to the principle, this situation is unfair, and it is intended to justify the obligations of noncooperators. The underlying moral principle at work in such cases is described as "the just distribution of benefits and burdens" (Lyons 1965: 164).

In certain cases, concerning supply of "excludable" goods, the principle's workings are clear. Assume that three neighbors dig a well. For a fourth, who refused to share their labors, to take water from it would be a clear case of free-riding. In such cases, recipients of the scheme's benefits have the option of whether or not to receive them, and it seems clear that they must accept or otherwise seek out the benefits, if they are to incur obligations. But the principle is of greater interest as it concerns the supply of non-excludable or public goods, which, because of their nature, cannot be sought out or even accepted. Such goods must be generally available to the population of a given territory if they are supplied to only certain members. The most important examples are public goods produced by the cooperative efforts of large numbers of people that are vital to people's lives. Included in this class are public goods bearing on physical security, most notably national defense and law and order. Because provision of such goods requires that people's activities be coordinated by the state, theorists contend that the principle of fairness grounds moral requirements to obey the state in regard to the relevant cooperative schemes. However, because the benefits in question are public goods, it must be explained how individuals who have not accepted them incur obligations. Important theorists argue that recipients must accept benefits in order to incur obligations, and so that the principle of fairness does not bind recipients of public goods (Rawls 1971: 113–16; Dworkin 1986: 192–93).

This position is supported by a famous example of Robert Nozick's. Assume that Jones's neighborhood organizes a public-address system to provide music and other programs, and each neighbor takes a turn running the system for a day. If Jones has enjoyed listening to the system, must he give up a day when his turn comes? What if he prefers not to? Nozick argues that Jones does not have a requirement to participate. The principle of fairness does not eliminate "the need for other person's *consenting* to cooperate and limit their activities" (Nozick 1974: 93–95, his emphasis). Important scholars agree that, under these circumstances, Jones does not have an obligation to comply. But they draw various conclusions in regard to exactly how the example works and what it means for the principle of fairness. For instance, according to Simmons, the reason Jones does not incur an obligation is that he is simply a bystander in regard to the public-address scheme. It has been built up around him, with no input from him. In order for him to have obligations to do his part in running it, he must be a *participant* in the scheme (Simmons 1979: 120–21). To be a participant, he must have particular attitudes in regard to benefits it provides. He must believe the benefits are worth their costs, and he must receive them "willingly and knowingly." This last condition requires that he know that the benefits in question *are* products of a cooperative scheme, a condition that Simmons believes is not generally satisfied (Simmons 1979, ch. 5).

Other scholars believe that argument along these lines can be countered. Richard Dagger argues that state benefits are in fact widely accepted. In many of their activities, citizens take advantage of facilities the state provides. They make use of roads and communication facilities, and do so voluntarily. Although theses facilities cannot be avoided, they are used "voluntarily," taking "voluntarily" in a wider sense as meaning "not under constraint or duress" (Dagger 1997: 75). Although a given citizen may not perform a particular action that constitutes acceptance of state benefits, the latter are central to their lives. Because there is a clear sense in which they have voluntarily accepted these benefits, it would be wrong for recipients not to do their part in providing them (Dagger 1997: 77).

Other theorists argue that voluntary acceptance is not necessary. I believe Nozick's example appears to work because of the trivial nature of the benefits in question. But if we consider cooperative schemes that provide much more important benefits, conclusions are different. I characterize goods that are indispensable, necessary for acceptable lives, as "presumptively beneficial." Included in this class are public goods necessary for national defense, law and order, and protection from deadly diseases and natural disasters. Because of the great importance of these goods, it can be presumed that almost all recipients *would* accept them, if given the opportunity. Clearly, if placed in a neutral choice situation such as Rawls's original position and given the choice whether to accept these goods at the required price, virtually all citizens would do so. But obligations under the principle of fairness do not turn on hypothetical consent, that people would accept them, but on the fact that they actually receive the benefits (Klosko 1992, ch. 2). That we all need the public goods in question regardless of whatever else we need is a fundamental assumption of liberal political theory. It is notable that liberal theorists generally view providing them as central purposes of the state.

On this interpretation, the principle of fairness overcomes the generality problem that besets consent, as the benefits in question are received by all or virtually all citizens, who require them for acceptable lives. In addition, while consequentialist theories are plagued by difficulties concerning the miniscule or undetectable consequences of single acts of not obeying the law, the principle of fairness does not require that disobedience cause actual harms (cf. Smith 1973: 956–58). In the cases under consideration, regardless of actual consequences, disobedience is unfair to one's fellow citizens and wrong for that reason.

At the present time, the principle of fairness is widely viewed as the most promising avenue for justifying political obligations (Green 2002: 530; Soper 2002: 103), but problems remain. For instance, in response to the contention that citizens accept benefits such as defense and law and order, one may ask whether they have a choice. As noted above, it could be said that citizens accept them in the sense that they make use of them in planning their activities. But once again, because the benefits pervade the environments in which they live and cannot be avoided, does this actually constitute acceptance in a meaningful sense? As noted above, Dagger construes "voluntarily" in an extended sense, as "not under constraint or duress." In response, one may ask whether "acceptance" in this sense—what Simmons characterizes as "mere receipt"—is sufficient to generate obligations. According to Simmons: "Certainly, it would be peculiar if a man, who by simply going about his business in a normal fashion benefited unavoidably from some cooperative scheme, were told that he had voluntarily accepted benefits," and so incurred obligations to support the scheme (Simmons 1979: 131).

Against a view that does not depend on an extended sense of "voluntary," there are numerous lines of attack. Even if we grant that the principle of fairness is able to ground moral requirements to do one's part in cooperative schemes that provide essential public goods, the state does much more than this. Central tasks of governments generally include building roads, educating children, preserving the environment, providing museums and recreational facilities, and much more. Are all these tasks essential for acceptable lives? If not, does this mean that citizens are not required to obey the laws that pertain to them (see Klosko 1992, ch. 4)? Alternatively, what if citizens genuinely do not want the benefits provided by government? As Simmons argues: "Goods are only benefits to persons on balance if their costs and the manner in which they are provided are not sufficiently disvalued by those persons" (Simmons 1993: 258). Suffice it to say that, at the present time, debate about the principle of fairness is ongoing.

Association Theories

Theories of obligation based on association or membership are supported by common-sensical belief that we should obey the laws of our societies because we belong to them. An example often invoked is the family. It is commonly held that family members have special moral requirements towards one another, simply because they belong to the same family. Transferring this contention to the political sphere, theorists explain connections between membership and requirements to obey the laws in different ways, according to different accounts of "association" or "membership." For instance, Margaret Gilbert focuses on a variant of tacit consent. Through certain kinds of association, people acquire attitudes and commitments towards one another that make them "plural subjects" (Gilbert 2006). Jointly engaging in various activities—e.g., going for a walk together—is able to generate certain obligations. Even though subjects may not explicitly articulate the substance of their joint undertaking, this is communicated through other means and jointly understood. Gilbert construes the understanding of citizens along similar lines, arguing that such common sentiments imply requirements to obey the law.

A very different view is presented by John Horton in perhaps the most sophisticated association theory. Horton too appeals to feelings of shared political identity and collective political responsibility that are common features of political life. But he argues that the binding force of association requires no independent justification: "My claim is that a polity is, like the family, a relationship into which we are mostly born; and that the obligations which are constitutive of the relationship do not stand in need of moral justification in terms of a set of basic moral principles or some comprehensive moral theory" (Horton 1992: 150–51).

Like other theories of obligation, association views have been strongly criticized. An important criticism concerns certain association theories' lack of sustained argument. In response to Horton, saying that no explanation is necessary does not constitute an explanation. We still require an account of why the fact that an individual has certain feelings in regard to a particular community in itself entails particular moral requirements towards it. In perhaps the most important critical account, Simmons presents this criticism and others (Simmons 1996). Most notable is what Simmons refers to as the argument from "normative independence." Very briefly, Simmons claims that feelings that we should abide by the rules of certain associations are grounded in the value of the associations, rather than in independent principles of association. Clearly, an association that pursues evil purposes will not generate obligations, as, according to general beliefs, these characteristics preclude obligations. But imagine an association that is absolutely neutral in regard to moral worth. In Simmons's words: "To the extent that a practice seems morally pointless . . . to that extent it seems very hard to imagine anyone insisting that the associative obligations it assigns have any genuine moral weight. Even mildly beneficial, harmlessly silly practices seem unable to impose any genuine obligations on non-consenters assigned roles within them" (1996: 269–70). Theorists of association have responded to these and other criticisms (see esp. Horton, 2006–2007). On this subject as with many others, discussion is ongoing.

Natural Duty of Justice

Serious attention to a theory of political obligation based on a natural duty of justice began with John Rawls's A Theory of Justice (Rawls 1971). According to Rawls, the natural duties of justice apply directly to individuals, unlike the principles of justice, which apply to institutions. But they are like the principles of justice in that they are justified by being chosen in the original position. For instance, a duty of mutual aid, i.e., a duty to help others when they are in need or distress, would be chosen because it's likely that its benefits would outweigh its costs (1971: 338). Relevant to political obligations is a natural duty "to comply with and to do our share in just institutions when they exist and apply to us" (334; and, similarly, 115). We may refer to this as "the natural political duty." Rawls does not view requirements established by the natural duties as obligations; he reserves that term for moral requirements that are self-imposed, e.g., by making promises. But requirements established by the natural political duty are functionally equivalent to political obligations.

An important advantage of these requirements is their generality. Their ability to bind all members of society, as opposed to requirements established by the principle of fairness, which, he believes, depend on acceptance of benefits, was Rawls's reason for abandoning a position based on fairness, which he had previously held (Rawls 1964; Rawls 1971: 113–14). In A Theory of Justice, Rawls discusses the natural political duty in reference to its ability to require obedience to unjust laws, as long as the overall political system is tolerably just. But although he did not develop other aspects of an overall theory of political obligation, his discussion has had considerable influence, and natural-duty theories are now prominent in the literature.

Although Rawls establishes his particular natural duty through the device of the original position, other scholars generally view a natural political duty as intuitively clear in its own right. Among the most influential discussions are articles by Jeremy Waldron (1993) and Christopher Wellman (2001). Following a discussion of Kant in The Metaphysical Elements of Justice, Waldron views the state as a construction into which people enter to resolve conflicts and to secure property. In order for these functions to be fulfilled, people must leave the state of nature and enter into the state. A natural duty to comply with the laws of one's state follows, as it will not be able to function effectively unless its commands are obeyed. In Waldron's words: "Our cooperation in establishing and sustaining political institutions that promote justice is morally required" (1993: 29).

Wellman argues according to a principle along the lines of Rawls's duty of mutual aid, which he calls "samaritanism." Given the familiar idea that people have strong moral requirements to come to the aid of others who are in peril or in dire need, we can rescue others from the state of nature only by supporting the state. And so citizens may justifiably be forced to obey the law. Wellman supports this claim with examples according to which the rights of a given person may be violated in order to rescue someone else. In his words: "coercion is permissible because the peril of others generates weightier moral reasons than the presumption in favor of each individual's dominion over her own affairs" (2001: 746).

Considerations of space rule out discussion of possible criticisms of these theories in this essay (a valuable and devastating critique is presented by Simmons, in Wellman and Simmons 2005). Probably the most important criticism of a natural-duty position turns on the requirement of "particularity" (see Simmons 1979, ch. 6). As noted above, to satisfy this requirement, a theory of political obligation should explain the close ties people have to their own states. But on Rawls's position, it is not clear why we should support the institutions of one state rather than another. If England has just institutions, why should we support the institutions of the state in which we live rather than of England? According to Rawls, we are to support the state that "applies" to us. But he does not explain what this means. As argued by Simmons, clear ways for a state to "apply" to a given individual include her consenting to or receiving benefits from it. If this is what Rawls has in mind, then the problem is that relationships with one's state such as these appear to be able to generate obligations to obey its laws on their own, without reference to the natural duty. At the present time, the problem of "particularity" is widely viewed as a severe impediment to natural-duty theories of political obligation.

Philosophical Anarchism

In recent years, a prominent trend in the literature—perhaps the most prominent—has been denial of the existence of political obligations. Scholars present skeptical arguments of two main types: conceptual, and what we may characterize as "empirical." Supporters of these positions, so-called "philosophical anarchists," differ from radical political anarchists such as Mikhail Bakunin, in not entirely rejecting the state.

The most prominent conceptual approach was developed by Robert Paul Wolff, in his brief, polemical book, *In Defense of Anarchism* (R. P. Wolff 1970). Wolff claims a fundamental conflict between authority and autonomy. Because people's "primary obligation" is preserving their autonomy, they must assume responsibility for their actions and obey only rules that they impose upon themselves. This means that they cannot submit to state authority, which, according to Wolff, means obeying laws "*simply because they are the laws*" (18, his emphasis). "If all men had a continuing obligation to achieve the highest degree of autonomy possible, there would appear to be no state whose subjects have a moral obligation to obey its commands" (19). Wolff allows an exception, a "unanimous direct democracy," in which all citizens are authors of all laws (1970, ch. 2). In addition, unlike traditional anarchists, he recognizes the value of certain state activities, and holds that those that the subject views as valuable should be supported. But unlike a general requirement to submit to the laws, Wolff believes the state's commands "must be judged and evaluated in each instance before they are obeyed" (71). He believes that voluntary compliance with state directives will be sufficient to allow achievement of its legitimate ends (80).

Most scholars reject Wolff's argument. They criticize his belief in an "obligation" to pursue autonomy (e.g., Simmons 1987: 269, n. 2) and his view of autonomy's exaggerated strength, that it always overrides conflicting values. This would denigrate other moral requirements, e.g., promises, as well as the overall requirement to act justly. Moreover, Wolff recognizes circumstances under which autonomy should be subordinated to other concerns. For instance: "when I place myself in the hands of my doctor, I commit myself to *whatever* course of treatment he prescribes" (1970: 15, my emphasis). If it is allowable to submit to the judgment of another person for reasons of health, it is not clear why it is wrong to do so in order to achieve crucial ends that the state pursues.

The empirical approach is straightforward. A series of scholars have argued against the existence of political obligations by criticizing the theories that have been put forth to explain them. I use the term "empirical" because this position is based on experience, which has shown that no theory works satisfactorily. Many arguments taken from practitioners of this approach are drawn on in the above discussion. So successful have the efforts of these scholars been that there is wide belief in a "skeptical consensus" in the literature (Morris 1998: 214; Buchanan 2002: 696). For instance, in the best-known example of this genre, Simmons criticizes in turn theories of political obligations based on consent, fairness, gratitude and a natural duty of justice. Other theorists who pursue similar strategies include Leslie Green (1988), Joseph Raz (1979, ch. 12), William Edmundson (1998) and M. B. E. Smith (1973)—although, it should be noted that not all of these theorists identify themselves as philosophical anarchists.

The philosophical anarchists' response to this situation is of great theoretical importance. Although they believe themselves to have refuted the idea that there is a single reason to obey all laws, they do not believe all laws should be disobeyed. Rather, as R. P. Wolff suggests, laws should be assessed on a case-by-case basis and obeyed if the moral facts support this. As Simmons argues (1979, ch. 7), confronted by a particular law, the subject should take all moral consideration into account. Although there is no presumption that laws should be obeyed, in many cases there are good reasons to behave in accordance with specific laws, generally so as not to hurt or inconvenience other people. Moreover, under these conditions individuals would have rights—indeed, would be morally required—to punish other people who violate the moral law, while the state would possess similar rights. For example, if it is wrong to commit murder and Smith would be acting morally if she prevented Black from murdering Brown, or punished him if he did so, then the state too would be acting morally if it acted against Black. The implication is that people should behave in accordance with many laws, even though they do not have obligations to obey them simply as laws.

Practical Implications

A notable implication of the philosophical anarchists' approach is rejection of the traditional view that political obligations are "content independent," that laws should be obeyed simply *because they are laws* (see Klosko 2011a). Belief that laws are content independent is supported by the "self-image of the state" (Green 1988, ch. 3). According to Leslie Green, the state views itself as a "duty imposer," able to bind its subjects by making laws, regardless of the content of the laws (1988: 86). This view was pioneered especially by Hart (1958; 1982), and is widely subscribed to. According to Green, content independence could not be abandoned "without abandoning part of any satisfactory analysis of political authority" (1988: 239).

One consideration that supports this view is an analogy between laws and promises. If A promises B to do p, the obligation to do p does not arise from the nature of the promised action but from the promise itself. Similarly, according to traditional views of political obligation, if Grey has an obligation to obey the law, this too is content independent. He is required to obey law L because the state has made it the law, rather than because of its content. However, this analogy breaks down. In the case of promises, the content of each specific promise is determined by the obligee, who renders it obligatory through the act of promising. In contrast, (a) the contents of specific laws are determined by state authorities rather than directly by the obligee, and (b) the obligee himself does not attach obligating force to the content of each law; rather, this is done by state authorities. Because the subject does not have a direct role in either choosing the content of a given law or in affixing normative force to its particular content, in order for a law to generate normative force for a particular content, the basis of the state's right to bind its subjects in this way must be explained. As traditionally interpreted, the problem of political obligation is to identify the relevant features of the relationship between individuals and the state that give the state this right. And so scholars have attempted to develop theories of obligation such as those discussed above (see Klosko 2011a).

What we are left with if we reject content independence is a view according to which moral reasons to obey the law depend on considerations that bear on each particular law, assessed on a case-by-case basis. Such a view agrees with philosophical anarchists about the nature of moral requirements to obey the law. However, philosophical anarchists do not recognize the practical implications of their view. If we believe that most laws of legitimate states fulfill justifiable purposes, the results of this mode of inquiry will be moral requirements to obey virtually all laws. Thus, in spite of the theoretical importance of the philosophical anarchists' critique of traditional views of political obligation, their critique lacks significant practical implications. It leaves intact the traditional beliefs that we have moral requirements to behave in accordance with all defensible laws.

This discussion of philosophical anarchism is predicated on acceptance of their claim to have successfully refuted the traditional theories of obligation. Obviously, a ready way to overturn their position is to develop a theory of obligation that resists their criticisms. In recent years, the main theories of political obligation have found renewed defenses (most notably, for consent, see Beran 1987; for fairness, Arneson 1982 and Klosko 1992 and 2005; for gratitude, Walker 1988; for natural duty, Waldron 1993 and Wellman 2001; for association, Horton 1992 and 2006–2007). But none of these should be viewed as clearly overcoming all problems.

However, it is important to recognize how critiques of these theories have been developed. Skeptical scholars have generally approached the traditional theories of obligation from a particular perspective, criticizing them *seriatim*, one after another. When a particular theory is found not to satisfy all conditions, the theorist moves on to the next. Simmons proceeds this way, as do the other scholars I have mentioned. What this strategy overlooks is the possibility that general reasons to obey the law can be established by combining different principles, thereby overcoming the weaknesses of a theory based on a single principle (J. Wolff 2000; Klosko 2005, ch. 5).

A moment's reflection reveals that examining theories of political obligation one at a time defies common sense. As the philosophical anarchists argue, a range of moral considerations is relevant to whether or not specific laws should be obeyed. It is possible that, by combining two (or more) theories of obligation, the result will be a position that is stronger than either of the original theories on its own. Many political obligations are clearly overdetermined, while there is also an element of truth in many different theories. Even if a theory based on a single principle—e.g., consent or fairness—is not able to overcome all difficulties, this does not mean it is not able to account for at least some requirements to obey the law. While the overlap of different principles complicates the task of laying out a satisfactory theory, moral requirements to obey the full range of laws could well stem from the crosshatch of different principles.

Principles may interact in different ways. Different principles may cover different services provided by the state, and so by combining principles, a larger range of services may be accounted for. Alternatively, in regard to certain state functions, if a given principle on its own cannot justify compliance, the problem could possibly be overcome by more than one principle working in tandem. By combining moral principles in these and other ways, it may be possible to develop moral reasons to obey all or virtually all laws, thereby accomplishing the traditional practical aim of theories of political obligation, explaining why all citizens have moral requirements to obey all or virtually all laws.

References

Arneson, R. (1982) "The Principle of Fairness and Free-Rider Problems," *Ethics* 92: 616–33.

Bentham, J. (1988/1776) *A Fragment of Government*, R. Harrison, ed., Cambridge: Cambridge University Press.

Beran, H. (1987) *The Consent Theory of Political Obligation*, London: Croom Helm.

Brandt, R. B. (1964) "The Concepts of Obligation and Duty," *Mind* 73: 374–93.

Buchanan, A. (2002) "Political Legitimacy and Democracy," *Ethics* 112: 689–719.

Dagger, R. (1997) *Civic Virtues*, Oxford: Oxford University Press.

Dworkin, R. (1977) *Taking Rights Seriously*, Cambridge, Mass.: Harvard University Press.

—— (1986) *Law's Empire*, Cambridge, Mass.: Harvard University Press.

Edmundson, W. (1998) *Three Anarchical Fallacies*, Cambridge: Cambridge University Press.

Gilbert, M. (2006) *A Theory of Political Obligation*, Oxford: Oxford University Press.

Green, L. (1988) *The Authority of the State*, Oxford: Oxford University Press.

—— (2002) "Law and Obligations," in J. Coleman and S. Shapiro, eds., *The Oxford Handbook of Jurisprudence and Philosophy of Law*, Oxford: Oxford University Press, pp. 514–47.

Gruzalski, B. (1986) "Parfit's Impact on Utilitarianism," *Ethics* 96: 760–83.

Harrod, R. F. (1936) "Utilitarianism Revised," *Mind* 45: 137–56.

Hart, H. L. A. (1955) "Are There Any Natural Rights?" *Philosophical Review* 64: 175–91.

—— (1958) "Legal and Moral Obligation," in A. I. Melden, ed., *Essays in Moral Philosophy*, Seattle: University of Washington Press.

—— (1961) *The Concept of Law*, Oxford: Oxford University Press.

—— (1982) "Commands and Authoritative Legal Reasons," in *Essays on Bentham: Jurisprudence and Political Theory*, Oxford: Oxford University Press.

Horton, J. (1992) *Political Obligation*, London: Macmillan.

—— (2006–2007) "In Defence of Associative Political Obligations, Part One" *Political Studies* 54: 427–33.

Hume, D. (1969/1739) *A Treatise of Human Nature*, E. Mossner, ed., Harmondsworth: Penguin Books.

—— (1985) *Essays: Moral, Political and Literary*, E. Miller, ed., revised edition, Indianapolis: Liberty Fund.

Kant, I. (1970) *Kant's Political Writings*, H. Reiss, ed. and H. Nisbet, trans., Cambridge: Cambridge University Press.

Klosko, G. (1990) "Parfit's Moral Arithmetic and the Obligation to Obey the Law," *Canadian Journal of Philosophy* 20: 191–213.

—— (1991) "Reformist Consent and Political Obligation," *Political Studies* 39: 676–90.

—— (1992) *The Principle of Fairness and Political Obligation*, Savage, Md.: Rowman and Littlefield.

—— (2005) *Political Obligations*, Oxford: Oxford University Press.

—— (2011a) "Are Political Obligations Content Independent?" *Political Theory* 39(4): 498–523.

—— (2011b) "Political Obligation," in G. Klosko, ed., *The Oxford Handbook of the History of Political Philosophy*, Oxford: Oxford University Press.

Kraut, R. (1984) *Socrates and the State*, Princeton: Princeton University Press.

Locke, J. (1988/1690) *Two Treatises of Government*, P. Laslett, ed., Cambridge: Cambridge University Press.

Lyons, D. (1965) *Forms and Limits of Utilitarianism*, Oxford: Oxford University Press.

Morris, C. (1998) *An Essay on the Modern State*, Cambridge: Cambridge University Press.

Nozick, R. (1974) *Anarchy, State, and Utopia*, New York: Basic Books.

Parfit, D. (1984) *Reasons and Persons*, Oxford: Oxford University Press.

—— (1986) "Comments," *Ethics* 96: 832–72.

Pateman, C. (1979) *The Problem of Political Obligation: A Critique of Liberal Theory*, Berkeley: University of California Press.

Pitkin, H. (1965) "Obligation and Consent–I," *The American Political Science Review* 59: 990–99.

Plamenatz, J. (1968) *Consent, Freedom, and Political Obligation*, 2nd edition, Oxford: Oxford University Press.

Rawls, J. (1964) "Legal Obligation and the Duty of Fair Play," in *Law and Philosophy*, S. Hook, ed., New York: NYU Press.

—— (1971) *A Theory of Justice*, Cambridge, Mass.: Harvard University Press.

Raz, J. (1979) *The Authority of Law*, Oxford: Oxford University Press.

Simmons, A. J. (1979) *Moral Principles and Political Obligations*, Princeton: Princeton University Press.

—— (1987) "The Anarchist Position: A Reply to Klosko and Senor," *Philosophy and Public Affairs* 16: 269–279.

—— (1993) *On the Edge of Anarchy*, Princeton: Princeton University Press.

—— (1996) "Associative Political Obligations," *Ethics* 106: 247–73.

—— (2005) "The Duty to Obey and Our Natural Moral Duties," in C. H. Wellman and A. J. Simmons, eds., *Is There a Duty to Obey the Law?*, Cambridge: Cambridge University Press, section II.

Smart, J. J. C. (1967) "Extreme and Restricted Utilitarianism," in *Theories of Ethics*, P. Foot, ed., Oxford: Oxford University Press.

—— (1973) "An Outline of a System of Utilitarian Ethics," in J. J. C. Smart and B. Williams, *Utilitarianism: For and Against*, Cambridge: Cambridge University Press.

Smith, M. B. E. (1973) "Is There a Prima Facie Obligation to Obey the Law?" *Yale Law Journal* 82: 950–76.

Soper, P. (2002) *The Ethics of Deference*, Cambridge: Cambridge University Press.

Taylor, M. (1987) *The Possibility of Cooperation*, Cambridge: Cambridge University Press, 1987.

Waldron, J. (1987) "Theoretical Foundations of Liberalism," *Philosophical Quarterly* 37: 127–50.

—— (1993) "Special Ties and Natural Duties," *Philosophy and Public Affairs* 22: 3–30.

Walker, A. D. M. (1988) "Political Obligation and the Argument from Gratitude," *Philosophy and Public Affairs* 17: 191–211.

Walzer, M. (1970) "Political Alienation and Military Service," in *Obligations: Essays on Disobedience, War, and Citizenship*, Cambridge, Mass: Harvard University Press, pp. 99–119.

Wellman, C. H. (2001) "Toward a Liberal Theory of Political Obligation," *Ethics* 111: 735–59.

—— (2005) "Samaritanism and the Duty to Obey the Law," in C. H. Wellman and A. J. Simmons, eds., *Is There a Duty to Obey the Law?*, Cambridge: Cambridge University Press, section I.

Wolff, J. (2000) "Political Obligation: A Pluralistic Approach," in M. Baghramian and A. Ingram, eds., *Pluralism: The Philosophy and Politics of Diversity*, London: Routledge, pp. 179–96.

Wolff, R. P. (1970) *In Defense of Anarchism*, New York: Harper and Row.

Further Reading

For further reading, see: H. Beran (1987) *The Consent Theory of Political Obligation*, London: Croom Helm; L. Green (1988) *The Authority of the State*, Oxford: Oxford University Press; L. Green (2002) "Law and Obligations," in J. Coleman and S. Shapiro, eds., *The Oxford Handbook of Jurisprudence and Philosophy of Law*, Oxford: Oxford University Press, pp. 514–47; J. Horton (1992) *Political Obligation*, London: Macmillan; G. Klosko (1992) *The Principle of Fairness and Political Obligations*, Savage, Md.: Rowman and Littlefield; G. Klosko (2005) *Political Obligations*, Oxford: Oxford University Press; A. J. Simmons (2000) *Justification and Legitimacy: Essays on Rights and Obligations*, Cambridge: Cambridge University Press; and A. J. Simmons (1979) *Principles and Political Obligations*, Princeton: Princeton University Press.

34

CONSCIENTIOUS OBJECTION AND CIVIL DISOBEDIENCE

Kimberley Brownlee

Introduction

Dissent and disobedience are ancient practices that can excite reverence and resentment in seemingly equal measure. They are undoubtedly valued practices, but often they seem to be valued more in the abstract or in retrospect than in the moment. On the one hand, praise is generally lavished on that unnamed hero—the dissenter—who shows her humanity in her independent-minded, faithful counsel and conduct. Poet Archibald MacLeish (1956), for one, writes, "the dissenter is every human being at those moments of his life when he resigns momentarily from the herd and thinks for himself." More fulsomely, John Stuart Mill (1859) observes that, "In this age, the mere example of non-conformity, the mere refusal to bend the knee to custom, is itself a service." And George Bernard Shaw's Jack Tanner writes in "Maxims for Revolutionists" (1903) that "disobedience [is] the rarest and most courageous of the virtues." Praise is also sometimes lavished on named dissenters. For instance, Albert Einstein says of Mahatma Gandhi that "generations to come, it may be, will scarce believe that such a one as this ever in flesh and blood walked upon this earth" (1950: 240). And similar tributes have been paid to such historical and literary dissenters as Socrates; Sophocles's Antigone; Aristophanes's Lysistrata; Jesus; Galileo Galilei; Thomas More; the colonial participants in the Boston Tea Party; and the suffragettes.

On the other hand, however, there is also no shortage of resistance against, and demonization of, people who dissent or disobey. The personal histories of some of the figures just listed and of other icons, such as Emmeline Pankhurst, Martin Luther King Jr., Nelson Mandela, Aung San Suu Kyi and Liu Xiaobo, highlight the majority's tendency to shoot the dissenter in the act and to celebrate her only much later, if at all. Historian J. B. Bury (1913) observes simplistically, though perhaps not inaccurately, that, wherever prevails the belief that the welfare of a state depends upon rigid stability, "novel opinions are felt to be dangerous as well as annoying, and any one who asks inconvenient questions about the why and the wherefore of accepted principles is considered a pestilent person." In addition to the patterns of negative reaction to dissent and disobedience, there is a host of familiar aphorisms and catchphrases that warn us against nonconformity. Some are injunctions: "Don't rock the boat," "Mind your Ps and

Qs," "Respect your elders," "Don't upset the apple cart." Some are declarations of fact: "A chain is only as strong as its weakest link," "A house divided against itself cannot stand." And, some are thinly veiled condemnations of behavior: "He wants taking down a peg," "She's going against the grain."

Perhaps such content-insensitive distrust of dissent is more a reaction to the threat of disobedience of formal norms than an intolerance of contrary positions as such. Perhaps it is when dissent manifests itself in a breach of law or a direct refusal to adhere to lawful requests that the specter of righteous indignation tends to arise and expose the strength of the conformist pressures that we can and do exert upon each other. Yet, as Mill notes, sometimes social pressures, not legal pressures, can be the most stringent:

> Society can and does execute its own mandates: and if it issues wrong mandates instead of right, or any mandates at all in things with which it ought not to meddle, it practises a social tyranny more formidable than many kinds of political oppression, since, though not usually upheld by such extreme penalties, it leaves fewer means of escape, penetrating much more deeply into the details of life, and enslaving the soul itself. Protection, therefore, against the tyranny of the magistrate is not enough; there needs protection also against the tyranny of the prevailing opinion and feeling; against the tendency of society to impose, by other means than civil penalties, its own ideas and practices as rules of conduct on those who dissent from them; to fetter the development, and, if possible, prevent the formation, of any individuality not in harmony with its ways, and compel all characters to fashion themselves upon the model of its own.
>
> (1859, ch. 1)

The force of such conformist pressures, whatever their source, may explain in part how a general reverence for celebrated dissenters can arise concomitantly with a revilement of the actual dissenter on our street or in our office, who tests our patience and threatens social harmony.

The purpose of this chapter is to consider two types of dissent that are generally described as *conscientious*, namely, civil disobedience and conscientious objection, both of which raise pressing normative questions not only about the proper parameters of dissenters' rights and duties within a reasonably good society, but also about both the scope of legitimate toleration of assertions of conscientiousness and the appropriate legal and political responses to conscientious disobedience. In what follows, I begin by outlining the conceptual territory of *civil disobedience* and *conscientious objection*. I then offer a qualified endorsement of the moral justifiability of these two practices before examining both the scope and legitimacy of their status as moral rights and their grounds for legal defensibility. Among other things, I challenge the dominant liberal position that, in relation to both moral rights and legal defenses, a more compelling case can be made on behalf of private conscientious objection than on behalf of civil disobedience.

Conceptions of Civil Disobedience and Conscientious Objection

Civil Disobedience

Henry David Thoreau coined the term "civil disobedience" in an 1849 essay to describe his refusal to pay the state poll tax, which he did to protest against the Mexican War (1846–1848) and the Fugitive Slave Law. In defense of his law breaking, Thoreau maintained that it was imperative that he not lend himself to the wrong he condemns. In his view, only a very few people—heroes, martyrs, patriots, reformers in the best sense—serve their society with their consciences in this way, and necessarily resist society for the most part, and often are treated by it as enemies. Numerous subsequent dissenters have proudly identified their own deliberate, communicative, cause-driven breaches of law as acts of civil disobedience, paying the legal and social price for nonconformity while often acting as catalysts for social change through their condemnation of existing laws or policies. Whether these dissenters may credibly apply the generally laudatory label of "civil disobedience" to their breaches of law is a further question that depends in part upon how narrowly we specify the concept of civil disobedience.

John Rawls defines "civil disobedience" very narrowly as a public, nonviolent, conscientious yet political breach of law typically done with the aim of bringing about a change in laws or government policies (1971: 364ff). For Rawls, the *public* nature of civil disobedience takes a distinctive *ex ante* form. Civil disobedience is never done covertly or secretively, but only openly in public, and only ever with advance notice to legal authorities. In Rawls's view, such publicity is one mark of disobedients' civility and willingness to deal fairly with authorities. Another mark of their civility is their nonviolence. Rawls states that violent acts likely to injure are incompatible with civil disobedience as a mode of address: "any interference with the civil liberties of others tends to obscure the civilly disobedient quality of one's act." A third mark of civility is disobedients' willingness to accept the legal consequences of their actions, including punishment. In Rawls's view, these features together show that, unlike revolutionary actors or militant protesters, civil disobedients have a fidelity to law at the outer edge thereof. Their disobedience is a political act, but it is a conscientious and sincere one that invokes the commonly shared conception of justice that underlies the political order, which in the case of Rawls's just or nearly just society is a conception that centers on his two principles of justice.

One detraction of Rawls's conception of civil disobedience is that it implicitly excludes many acts that commonsensically are seen as civil disobedience such as the nonviolent protests of Gandhi, who had no fidelity to British rule in India. Yet, the worry that Rawls's conception cannot accommodate a case such as Gandhi may be allayed somewhat by the fact that Rawls did not develop his account for an imperialistic political order such as British India, but for his ideal, just or nearly just society, in which fidelity to law might be more credible. The cost, though, of confining the analysis to this ideal context is that it leaves unsettled whether Rawls's account of civil disobedience could be applied without radical alteration to less just, and more realistic, societies.

Another difficulty concerns Rawls's overly restrictive conditions of publicity and nonviolence as signifiers of civility. Publicity can detract from or undermine persons' attempts to communicate through civil disobedience since announcing an intention to break the law provides both political opponents and legal authorities with an opportunity to abort those communicative efforts, which does no favors to the dissenter's cause even though that cause may be a just one (Smart 1991: 206). For this reason, unannounced or (initially) covert disobedience can be preferable. Disobedience carried out covertly in the first instance to ensure that the act is successful may nonetheless be taken to be open and communicative when followed by an acknowledgment of the act and the reasons for taking it (Raz 1979).

Turning to violence, the presumed incivility of violence is problematic for several reasons. First, a commonsense conception of *violence*—as the likelihood or actuality of a person or group causing injury to someone or damage to something—will include not only a range of acts and events, major and minor, intended and unintended, that *cause* damage or injury, but also a range of acts and events that *risk* but do not necessarily *cause* damage or injury, such as catapulting stuffed animals at the police or shooting into the sky. Given that a range of elements can be counted as violence, it is implausible to hold that any instance of violence in the course of disobedience, however modest or noninjurious it may be, is, by definition, uncivil. Second, focusing attention upon violence draws attention away from the presumptively more salient issue of harm. As Joseph Raz notes, many nonviolent acts and many legal acts can cause more harm to other persons than do violent breaches of law (1979: 267). His example is that of a legal strike by ambulance workers, which will in all likelihood do far greater harm than, say, a minor act of vandalism. Moreover, sometimes the wrong or harm done by a law or policy is so iniquitous that it may be legitimate to use violence to root it out. Raz observes that such violence may be necessary to preserve or to reestablish the rights and civil liberties that coercive practices seek to suspend. Such observations about harm and violence are consistent with the view that nonviolent dissent is generally preferable because it does not encourage violence in other situations where violence would be wrong, something that an otherwise legitimate use of violence may do. Moreover, as a matter of prudence, nonviolence does not carry the same risk of antagonizing potential allies or of cementing opponents' antipathy, or of distracting the public's attention, or of providing authorities with an excuse to use harsh countermeasures against disobedients.

The above objections to Rawls's conception coalesce around a more general concern that it anticipates the normative evaluation of civil disobedience. By restricting civil disobedience to nonviolent, public breaches of law taken by persons who have a fidelity to the legal system and are willing to accept its punishments, Rawls leads us too easily to the conclusion that most, if not all, civil disobedience is morally justifiable (Brownlee 2004). The evaluation of civil disobedience as a deliberate, communicative breach of law carried out in both liberal and illiberal regimes requires careful, impartial reflection that does not predetermine its moral status through overly idealistic stipulations that are at odds with practical realities.

A broader conception of civil disobedience, offered by Raz, characterizes it as any "politically motivated breach of law designed either to contribute directly to a change of a law or of a public policy or to express one's protest against, and dissociation from, a law or a public policy" (Raz 1979: 263). This conception does not rule out the possibility of either violent or covert civil disobedience, and it does not anticipate the normative evaluation of this practice. It also acknowledges more explicitly and consistently than Rawls's conception does that civil disobedience can be either direct or indirect. Direct disobedience is the breach of the law that is actually opposed. Indirect disobedience is the breach of a law that is not opposed in order to communicate one's objection against the law, rule, norm or policy that is opposed. Trespassing onto a U.S. military base with a spray-paint can and carrying out acts of vandalism in order to protest against an ongoing war is an example of indirect civil disobedience.

However, Raz's conception may be faulted since, first, it excludes from the class of civilly disobedient acts those breaches of law that protest against the decisions of nongovernmental agencies such as trade unions, banks and private universities (1979: 264). This exclusion is arbitrary because the policies and practices of nongovernmental institutions—such as the University of Mississippi's initial refusal to admit African American student James Meredith—are matters of law as the lawfully accepted practices of legally recognized institutions. In condemning such policies and practices, civil disobedients challenge, among other things, the legal framework that accepts these policies and practices as lawful.

A second objection to Raz's definition is that it misrepresents civil disobedience by describing it in terms of *expression* of protest and not *communication* of protest. Whereas expression need not be directed toward other people, communication is necessarily an other-directed activity that involves the engagement of a "speaker" with a "hearer" to bring about the hearer's understanding of what the speaker conveys. Civil disobedience is an intentional breach of law that aims to *communicate* to a relevantly placed audience, usually society or the government, in ways that typically have both forward-looking and backward-looking aims. The backward-looking aims are to communicate both a disavowal of, and dissociation from, a given law or policy and the reasons for that disavowal. The forward-looking aims are to draw attention to the issue and to the reasons for the protest so as to persuade the relevant audience to accept the disobedient's position and, thereby, to instigate a lasting change in law or policy. A parallel may be drawn between the communicative aspects of civil disobedience and the communicative aspects of lawful punishment by the state since, like civil disobedience, the state's use of lawful punishment is associated with a backward-looking aim to communicate condemnation of certain conduct as well as a forward-looking aim to bring about a lasting change in that conduct (Brownlee 2004).

There is much that can be said for civil disobedience as a vehicle for communication. It can often better engage with society and the state than legal protest can since the added sensationalism of civil disobedience, even when suitably constrained and modest in form, tends to garner greater publicity than do lawful defenses of minority views. Sometimes civil disobedience serves principally to educate the public about an issue. Other times, it confronts the defenders of established policies with the costs of retaining those policies in the face of concerted, ongoing opposition to them.

A final criticism of Raz's conception of civil disobedience is that it identifies no particular features that could signify or explain the *civility* of this practice. In my own view, the civility of civil disobedience lies in the conscientious motivations of its practitioners. Civil disobedience involves not just a communicative breach, but a conscientious communicative breach of law motivated by steadfast, sincere and serious (though possibly erroneous) moral convictions. This combination of conscientiousness and forward- and backward-looking communicativeness places constraints upon how a civil disobedient may promote her cause because, to bring about a lasting positive change in law and to be true to the sincerity of her convictions as a reasoned position, she must avoid being overly radical in her communication. That is, she has reasons to seek rationally to persuade others of the merits of her view rather than merely to coerce them to make changes, partly because the appeal of her communication may be lost if it is drowned out by overly coercive tactics, and partly because the appeal rests upon treating her audience as interlocutors with whom she can engage in a rational and moral discussion. Thus, it is in such self-restraint and reason-based sincerity that we find the civility of civil disobedience, although this does not entail that civil disobedience can never be violent or partially covert, or revolutionary, or partly coercive. It can be provided that such properties are adequately constrained by, and consistent with, backward- and forward-looking communicative conscientiousness.

Conscientious Objection

The second practice under consideration here is conscientious objection. The term came into common usage first in the late 1890s and then during the First World War to describe pacifist resistance to military conscription. Although the term is sometimes still associated with pacifism, it applies more generally now to any person's principled refusal to follow an injunction, directive or law on grounds of a declared steadfast personal conviction. Contemporary contexts in which such refusals occur, in addition to military service, include healthcare provision, civil service, retail work, criminal justice, family law, education and personal attire in public. Common cases include the pharmacist who refuses to prescribe an emergency contraceptive pill; the religious patient who refuses a blood transfusion or an inoculation; the religious parents who refuse to take their child to see a doctor for a life-threatening but curable disease; the civil servant who refuses to perform same-sex civil-partnership ceremonies; the religious grocery store employee who refuses to shelve or process the sale of alcohol; the doctor or nurse who refuses to participate in the provision of abortions; the judge who refuses to hear gay couples' applications for adoption; and the religious person who refuses to wear or not to wear legally regulated clothing or ornaments in public, at work or at school.

This conception of conscientious objection as a principled refusal to follow an injunction, directive or law on grounds of personal conviction contrasts with some other conceptions in the literature. Conscientious objection is sometimes conceived of more narrowly as necessarily a violation of the *law* motivated by the dissenter's belief that she is morally prohibited to follow the law because the law is either bad or wrong, totally or in part (Raz 1979: 276). The conscientious objector may believe that the general character of a law is morally wrong (as an absolute pacifist would believe of conscription) or that the law extends to certain cases that it should not cover (an orthodox Christian would regard euthanasia as murder) (ibid.: 263). In Raz's view, "Conscientious objection is a private act, designed to protect the agent from interference by public authority . . . [The conscientious objector is] an individual asserting his immunity from public interference with matters he regards as private to himself" (ibid.: 276). In one sense, this definition is too narrow since it does not acknowledge that acts of conscientious objection need not be breaches of law.

A slightly less narrow conception of conscientious objection is given by Rawls, who views it as an act of conscientious refusal or noncompliance with a more or less direct legal injunction or administrative order, such as Jehovah's Witnesses' refusal to salute the flag (Rawls 1971: 368). In Rawls's view, *conscientious refusal* is distinct from a related species of conscientious objection, namely, *conscientious evasion*. When people conscientiously refuse, they operate on the assumption that authorities are aware of their nonconformity with a given law, order or injunction. When they engage in conscientious evasion, they act on the assumption that their conduct is covert, such as the devout person continuing to practice her banned religion in secret.

Like "civil disobedience," the term "conscientious objection" has a conventionally laudatory connotation; it identifies a sphere of personal conviction around which a liberal society and its laws tend to tread with some care. There is considerable overlap between these two practices in that both are forms of sincere and serious dissent that involve some kind of principle-governed nonconformity or disobedience. Indeed, in some cases, a single act can be described as both civil disobedience and conscientious objection, such as the selective, communicative objection—draft dodging—engaged in by many U.S. National Guard members during the Iraq War.

However, despite the overlap between these practices, their paradigmatic forms do differ. First, whereas civil disobedience is paradigmatically a deliberate breach of law, conscientious objection is not. It may not be a breach of law at all. It may instead be a breach of a directive, order or norm that falls short of law. In the case of military conscription, for instance, some legal systems regard conscientious objection as a legally legitimate ground for avoiding frontline military service. And, in the context of healthcare, civil service and retail, there is a growing number of legal accommodations for persons who refuse to perform parts of their job on grounds of personal (religious) conviction. Moreover, even when conscientious objection is a breach of law, it is not necessarily deliberately so; it may be only incidentally illegal.

Second, whereas civil disobedience can be either direct or indirect, conscientious objection can only be direct. It is necessarily a direct refusal to carry out all or part of a given order, injunction or law.

Third, whereas paradigmatic examples of civil disobedience can be either individual or collective, paradigmatic examples of conscientious objection are individual. The grounds for the conscientious objection may be collective when they are based in the individual's familial or religious community commitments, but the conscientious objection itself is usually an individual act.

Fourth, although *conscientiousness* is an important notion for both civil disobedience and conscientious objection—partly because it identifies one conceptual and evaluative difference between these practices and ordinary acts of offending (when conscientious objection is illegal), which are not motivated by deep conviction—conscientiousness nevertheless takes a different form in each of these two practices. As noted above, the conscientiousness of civil disobedience takes a communicative form. Disobedients aim not only to communicate to others their concerns about perceived injustices in law or policy, but also to dissociate themselves, and to be seen to dissociate themselves, from the law or policy they condemn. By contrast, although conscientious objectors also distance themselves from the law or rule that they regard as wrong, they do not do it with an eye to remedying that perceived wrong through engagement with their society. Rather, they merely wish to act without interference in ways they take to be consistent with their own convictions. To the extent that they do communicate, or seek to communicate, at all, they communicate that the law should not interfere with them in this domain. Such communication is incidental or secondary to their purposes, though it does indicate that, to some extent, their act is a *political* act of asserting their immunity from certain laws of their community (Brownlee forthcoming). A conscientious objector may, of course, see her nonconformity as a measure of last resort, to which she must turn if the law or directive is not legally abolished, and if legal exemption is not granted to her. The question then is whether she has sought to play any role in society's deliberations about the law at issue; if she has, then her efforts may be better characterized in terms of civil disobedience.

The differences between the aims and motivations of communicative and non-communicative disobedients reveal a difference in the quality of their conscientiousness. The civil disobedient alone may claim to recognize that when we judge some conduct to be seriously wrong we must not only avoid such conduct ourselves to the best extent that we are able, but also judge such conduct in others to be wrong and *ceteris paribus* be willing to communicate this judgment (Brownlee forthcoming). As Antony Duff has noted in a different context, to remain silent can cast doubt on the sincerity of our conviction (2001: 28). This implication of the difference in motivation leads us into the evaluation of the respective moral merits of these two practices.

Moral Justifiability

Examination of the moral justifiability of civil disobedience and conscientious objection often proceeds against the background assumption that, in a broadly liberal regime, there is either a general pro tanto moral obligation to follow the law or at least a general presumption in favor of following the law. Within this framework, the conditions for the justifiability of civil disobedience tend to include both a content-sensitive constraint on the moral merits of the dissenter's cause and consequence-oriented constraints aimed at limiting the negative effects of the disobedience. The latter constraints include the following. The disobedience must be undertaken, first, as a last resort only when lawful efforts have repeatedly shown the majority to be immovable or apathetic to the dissenter's efforts; second, in coordination with other minority groups to ensure a general regulation of overall dissent that lessens the likelihood of self-defeat (Rawls 1971: 374ff); third, nonviolently (as explored above); and fourth, with a high probability of producing positive change through the disobedience. Only this can justify exposing others to both the divisiveness of civil disobedience and the risks of it encouraging either copycats or a general disrespect for the law.

Although plausible at first glance, many of these conditions can ultimately be rejected. Concerning coordination, there will be occasions in which there is no time or opportunity to coordinate with other minority groups or, even if there is, those groups will be unable or unwilling to coordinate, which would give other minorities a veto over the moral quality of a dissenter's civil disobedience if coordination were required for justifiability. Concerning harm, the empirical claims that civil disobedience is necessarily divisive and encourages more disobedience can be doubted. But even if those claims were credible, it would not follow that it is inexorably a bad thing if civil disobedience had these consequences. Finally, concerning the likelihood of success, intuitively, civil disobedience is most justifiable when the minority's situation is most desperate and the government refuses to attend to more conventional forms of protest. Even when general success seems unlikely, civil disobedience may be defended for any reprieve from harm that it brings to victims of a bad law or policy (Brownlee 2007).

As these comments indicate, the general presumption in favor of following the law is impervious to the context-sensitive, broadly non-codifiable nature of persons' genuine moral obligations. Certainly there are ordinary moral reasons to follow the law in a reasonably just society and there are moral obligations to follow those particular laws that track genuine moral prescriptions against murder, robbery, rape, etc., but in general the moral merits of actions lie in their character and consequences, not their legality. It is by these measures that civil disobedience and conscientious objection are to be assessed.

The gap between codified law and non-codifiable morality is easily discerned in difficult situations where conformity to formal norms rightly elicits condemnation. For example, in a recent case, two British police community support officers (CSOs) endeavored to save a child drowning in a pond not by attempting a rescue, but by radioing for a trained emergency crew to come to the scene. In the intervening time, the child died. The officers were praised by their superior for following proper procedure, but censured by both the community and government officials, one of whom stated that, "What was appropriate in this circumstance for a uniformed officer would be appropriate for CSOs as human beings, never mind the job" (BBC 2007). Similar condemnation may rightly be elicited when judges sentence convicted offenders to death, or when police or intelligence officers use extreme interrogation techniques, or when doctors oversee executions by lethal injection, even though in each of these cases the law may well have demanded the conduct. As Joel Feinberg observes, what morality requires of a person in morally difficult circumstances is not something to be mechanically determined by an examination of the person's office or position. An individual must on some occasions have the courage to rise above all that and obey the dictates of (good) conscience (2003: 16). And this truth is not restricted to lower-level officials or ordinary citizens. Raz rightly observes that, "Sometimes courts ought to decide cases not according to the law but against it. Civil disobedience, for example, may be the only morally acceptable course of action for the courts" (Raz 1994: 328).

The point here is not simply that a reasonably just or liberal society should make provision for persons to excuse themselves from adhering to formal demands that are especially onerous for them. Certainly, in many cases, it should do that. Rather, the point is that society should strive as well as it can to avoid setting up institutional frameworks to address important concerns which place overly weighty moral burdens on any would-be occupants of those institutions. For instance, in states such as California, doctors have justifiably refused to carry out the function of overseeing executions by lethal injection because their assigned function is not just to reduce the condemned person's suffering, but to intervene to facilitate death if the person wakes up. This task deeply conflicts with doctors' responsibilities as healers and carers to promote people's well-being. As a result of doctors' refusal to perform this function, a moratorium was imposed on capital punishment in California (Gels 2006). A similar objection can be raised against prison doctors' function of treating offenders in high-security prisons whose conditions are often marked by brutality, degradation and deprivation, thereby requiring doctors to oversee punishments highly detrimental to offenders' well-being.

It does not follow from these observations that a society may never ask its members to engage in morally problematic conduct. A society may legitimately ask a civil registrar to conduct civil partnerships for homosexual couples irrespective of her personal convictions in order to ensure nondiscriminatory provision of a secular alternative to religious marriage. Similarly, a society may legitimately ask its medical professionals to provide adequate, nondiscriminatory healthcare services irrespective of their convictions about the moral merits of lawful procedures and medications. And, in those rare times of genuine crisis, a society may legitimately call upon its citizens to go to war. The general principle behind these cases is that society must pay close attention both to the institutional structures that it sets up to address important community concerns and to the specification of the offices that comprise those institutions, so as to minimize the genuine moral burdens that it imposes upon its members, and thereby to reduce the occasions in which nonconformity is the only morally acceptable course of action (Brownlee 2010).

Even though, in the three cases just given of healthcare, civil service and war, refusal of performance is *ceteris paribus* not morally legitimate, there is the further possibility that such refusals are protected by a moral right of conscientious disobedience. The question is: when a person mistakenly believes that a law or directive is morally wrong, should her refusal to adhere to it be regarded as an exercise of a moral right of conscientious disobedience? And, if so, what implications does this have for how her act should be viewed by the law?

Moral Rights and Legal Defenses

Often political philosophers explore the idea of a moral right to civil disobedience separately from a moral right to conscientious objection on the grounds that these practices are sufficiently disparate that, if they are protected by moral rights, they are protected by different moral rights. One by-product of this approach is the proposal that the moral right to civil disobedience is regime sensitive. The claim here is that, while there may well be a moral right to civil disobedience in illiberal regimes, there is no such moral right in liberal regimes because in such regimes there is adequate protection for ordinary forms of political participation and, thus, the only forms of illegal protest that the society must be expected to tolerate are those that are defensible on their merits (Raz 1979; Green 2003). Where there is fair access to participation, there is no right to civil disobedience. In response to this view, it may be argued that, even in liberal regimes, persistent and vulnerable minorities are, by nature, less able than majorities to make their views heard before decisions are taken and laws are made. There is inherent comparative unfairness in the imbalance of political power between majorities and vulnerable minorities and, therefore, the scope for participation should accommodate some suitably constrained civil disobedience by vulnerable minorities, as this rectifies the imbalance in meaningful avenues for political participation (Lefkowitz 2007).

Putting aside this debate about the scope for participation in different regimes, there are reasons to consider civil disobedience and conscientious objection together in the debate about moral rights. Given both their intersection and their respective assertions of conscientiousness, these practices are most fruitfully considered in relation to a single proposed right to conscientious disobedience (where *disobedience* is construed broadly since not all conscientious objection is in breach of law) to determine which, if either, practice has the best case for claiming protection as a right.

The most compelling ground for a moral right to conscientious disobedience is society's duty to honor human dignity. The principle is one of humanism, that is, respect for the conscientious dissenter's deep conviction and the overly burdensome pressure that the law places upon her when it coerces her to act against those convictions. Thinkers such as Raz (1979: 286) and Jeremy Horder (2004) maintain that this humanistic principle lends modest protection to private conscientious objection. Taking the case of fighting in war as an example, Raz argues that the killing and subjugation of other peoples must never be viewed lightly, even in unfortunate cases when such acts are necessary and justified. "Whatever the justification, undeniably the readiness to kill or to participate in oppression have profound significance for the one who carries out such acts. Hence, the right to conscientious objection to such acts takes precedence over the legal obligation to take part in them" (Raz 2003). In a similar spirit, Horder argues that a plausible legal defense on the grounds of personal conviction arises from an appreciation that disproportionate emphasis is placed on law abidance when society insists that a person always sacrifice her beliefs in order to comply with legal demands no matter how trivial those demands may be. Horder argues that accommodation must be made for individuals' private moral commitments and nonmoral goals and projects that are constitutive of their identity. When these commitments clash with the demands of the law, these offenders can show that they had reason to believe they had undefeated reasons to act as they did.

In opposition to Raz and Horder, I maintain that the humanistic principle lends modest protection principally to civil disobedience for the reason outlined above, that, unlike private "conscientious" objectors, civil disobedients are willing to risk being seen, and thus held to account, for their conscientious disobedience. As such, their acts do not raise the specter of doubt that conscientious objectors' acts can raise that their conviction is too shaky to accept the risks of communication. In my view, the draft dodger is most plausibly protected by a right of conscientious disobedience not when he is out to seek a personal exemption or keep his own hands clean, but when he is willing to be seen to dissociate himself from the order to go to war, and to bear the risks of communicating and defending that decision to his society.

The opponents of my view stress that civil disobedience is a strategic and political act, but conscientious objection is not. The claim is that, although civil disobedients often act from deep moral conviction, their motives are at least partly political and strategic; they challenge the democratic legislature's supreme right to take strategic decisions for the whole community. Hence, their conduct falls outside the scope of the humanistic principle. By contrast, the private conscientious objector does not seek to challenge the state's right, through law, to take decisions on behalf of the entire community. She does not choose (for purely strategic reasons) the laws to be disobeyed (Horder 2004: 224).

This strategic-action objection has some force against indirect civil disobedience because the person breaches a law that she does not oppose and, hence, acts strategically. Yet sometimes it is not so much strategy as necessity that forces dissenters to engage in indirect civil disobedience. Indirect action can be more justifiable than direct action when it causes less harm or, in addition, is a more efficacious way to redress perceived injustices.

The strategic-action objection is not forceful against direct civil disobedience because this objection under-appreciates the importance of reasoned communication for conscientiousness. Paradigmatically, civil disobedience involves principled disobedience undertaken by persons who appreciate the importance for integrity and self-respect of communicating their views in certain contexts. And the objection assumes, mistakenly, that politics and strategy do not figure into conscientious objection. Breaches carried out in secret with the aim of remaining secret are strategic acts, especially when the acts are chosen with calculation to preserve liberty from coercive interference from the law. For these reasons, civil disobedience should not be ruled out from the humanistic principle on the basis of motivation.

The strategic-action argument might be represented as a concern that modest protection of civil disobedience would provide a (strategic) reason for other would-be protestors, whether or not like minded, to engage in the lawbreaking conduct to further their political aims. This would undermine the authenticity of the claim to legal defensibility and may give rise to further unwelcome follow-on threats to common goods, such as a greater willingness among protest movements at large to forego a preference for law-abiding protest in favor of rights violations (Horder 2004: 224). In reply, when dissenters use suitably constrained civil disobedience, they have not necessarily foregone a preference for law-abiding protest in favor of rights violations because it is not inevitable that civil disobedience violates rights, and their acts may often serve to secure or restore rights that the government is abusing or neglecting. Moreover, the worry that a legal defense would create a strategic reason for nonconscientious would-be protestors to break the law appeals to a mistaken slippery slope since the protection would not be available to those who engaged in more radical forms of protest. And burdening conscientious agents in order to deter widespread dissent uses those agents merely as a means to prevent other types of conduct, which, unlike their own conduct, are not suitably constrained and conscientiously motivated. Punishing civil disobedients in order to restore deterrence levels disrespects civil disobedients as autonomous persons who contribute to collective decision-making in tolerable ways.

Another argument against limited protection of civil disobedience turns on the idea that, in a liberal democracy, the legislature is better placed than individual citizens to account for all of the reasons that bear upon the right guidance to follow (Horder 2004: 224). This assertion is dubious on empirical grounds. It is doubtful that legislatures are invariably better placed than, say, environmentalists or soldiers to account for all of the reasons whether and how to protect the environment or to go to war, particularly when legislatures must contend with well-funded lobbying groups with opposing views. Moreover, even if the legislature were best placed in all cases to assess the relevant reasons, it could still benefit from pointed minority opposition to ensure that it remains alive to all of the salient reasons for and against a given policy.

There is a distinctive social value in conscientious dissent and disobedience. These practices contribute centrally to the democratic exchange of ideas by forcing the champions of dominant opinion to reflect upon and defend their views. Following Mill, it may well be that, if there are persons willing to contest a received opinion, we should thank them for it, open our minds to listen to them and rejoice that there is someone to do for us what we otherwise ought to do ourselves (Mill 1859, ch. 2). And when their causes are well founded and their actions justified, these dissenters serve society not only by questioning, but by inhibiting departures from justice and correcting departures when they occur, thereby acting as a stabilizing force within society (cf. Rawls 1971: 383). In performing such services, society's dissenters and disobedients may prove to exemplify truly responsible citizenship and civic virtue. Richard Dagger argues that:

> To be virtuous . . . is to perform well a socially necessary or important role. This does not mean that the virtuous person must always go along with the prevailing views or attitudes. On the contrary, Socrates and John Stuart Mill have persuaded many people to believe that questioning and challenging the prevailing views are among the highest forms of virtue.
>
> (1997: 14)

It is in this spirit that we should understand the best of conscientious dissent and disobedience (Brownlee forthcoming).

References

BBC News (2007) "Blunkett Criticises Pond Officers," September 22, http://news.bbc.co.uk/2/hi/uk_news/england/manchester/7008077.stm.
Brownlee, K. (2004) "Features of a Paradigm Case of Civil Disobedience," *Res Publica* 10: 337–51.
—— (2007) "Civil Disobedience," in E. N. Zalta, ed., *The Stanford Encyclopedia of Philosophy*, http://plato.stanford.edu/entries/civil-disobedience.
—— (2010) "Responsibilities of Criminal Justice Officials," *Journal of Applied Philosophy* 27: 123–39.
—— (forthcoming) *Conscience and Conviction: The Case for Civil Disobedience*, Oxford: Oxford University Press.
Bury, J. B. (1913) *A History of Freedom of Thought*, The Gutenberg Project, http://www.gutenberg.org/files/10684/10684-h/10684-h.htm.
Dagger, R. (1997) *Civic Virtues*, New York: Oxford University Press.
Duff, A. (2001) *Punishment, Communication, and Community*, Oxford: Oxford University Press.

Einstein, A. (1950) *Out of My Later Years*, London: Thames and Hudson.

Feinberg, J. (2003) *Problems at the Roots of Law*, Oxford: Oxford University Press.

Gels, S. (2006) "California Puts Execution Off After Doctors Refuse to Help," *Washington Post*, February 22.

Green, L. (2003) "Civil Disobedience and Academic Freedom," *Osgoode Hall Law Journal*: 41: 381–405.

Horder, J. (2004) *Excusing Crime*, Oxford: Oxford University Press.

Lefkowitz, D. (2007) "On a Moral Right to Civil Disobedience," *Ethics* 117: 202–33.

MacLeish, A. (1956) "In Praise of Dissent," *The New York Times*, December 16.

Mill, J. S. (1859) *On Liberty*.

Rawls, J. (1971) *A Theory of Justice*, Cambridge, Mass.: Harvard University Press.

Raz, J. (1979) *The Authority of Law: Essays on Law and Morality*, Oxford: Clarendon Press.

—— (1994) *Ethics in the Public Domain*, Oxford: Oxford University Press.

—— (2003) "Bound by Their Conscience," *Haaretz*, December 31.

Shaw, G. B. (1903) "Maxims for Revolutionists," in G. B. Shaw, *Man and Superman*, Cambridge, Mass.: The University Press.

Smart, B. (1991) "Defining Civil Disobedience," in H. A. Bedau, ed., *Civil Disobedience in Focus*, London: Routledge.

Thoreau, H. D. (1849) "Resistance to Civil Government"; republished posthumously (1866) as "Civil Disobedience"; (1991) "Civil Disobedience," in H. A. Bedau, ed., *Civil Disobedience in Focus*, London: Routledge.

Further Reading

For further reading, see: H. A. Bedau, ed. (1991) *Civil Disobedience in Focus*, London: Routledge (reproduces several seminal pieces on civil disobedience); R. Dworkin (1977) *Taking Rights Seriously*, London: Duckworth (outlines a theory of compliance with the law that, among other things, addresses theoretical questions about civil disobedience); K. Greenawalt (1987) *Conflicts of Law and Morality*, Oxford: Clarendon Press (analyzes the conflicts between the foundations of law and morality and the challenges they raise for lawmakers and potential lawbreakers); B. Medina and D. Weisburd, eds. (2002) *Refusals to Serve—Political Dissent in the Israel Defense Force*, special issue, *Israel Law Review*, 36 (3) (examines the theoretical issues that underpin the debate over refusals to serve in the Israeli Defense Force); A. J. Simmons (2003) "Civil Disobedience and the Duty to Obey the Law," in R. G. Frey and C. H. Wellman, eds., *Blackwell Companion to Applied Ethics*, Oxford: Blackwell (provides an overview of the conceptual and normative issues surrounding civil disobedience and legal obligation); and C. Sunstein (2003) *Why Societies Need Dissent*, Cambridge, Mass.: Harvard University Press (an accessible examination of psychology studies of group behavior and cases of conformity and group polarization in American politics, law and society).

35

LAW, LOYALTY AND CITIZENSHIP

Meir Dan-Cohen

"to thine own self be true"

William Shakespeare, *Hamlet*

The Political Question

It is commonly believed that countries, their governments and their laws make at least a prima facie normative claim on citizens. For the most part people conduct their lives as though they owed a measure of loyalty to their country, their government had a modicum of authority over them, and the law was at least somewhat binding. To be sure, attitudes to one's country, its government and its law may diverge, and each raises some distinctive philosophical issues of its own. Under the heading of patriotism, philosophers explore the general, mostly affective attitude to the country; political philosophers tend to focus on the question of the government's authority; and legal philosophy is centrally concerned with the duty to obey the law. But though separable, these issues are closely related. Ordinarily, a vital aspect of allegiance to one's country is acknowledging its government's authority, and law is by far the most significant medium through which that authority is exercised. The divergent issues that arise in this area have a common core: we are expected to pay some heed to our country's interests by, in part, accepting its government's authority, an acceptance manifested in part in a disposition to obey the law. What grip, if any, does this composite claim have on us? Call this *the political question*.

In one form or another, the political question has occasioned over time mountains of writings. Under these mountains, however, is buried a simple if dispiriting truth: we are no closer to a satisfactory answer than we have ever been before. Philosophers who till these fields have their employment secure. In these circumstances, adding yet another molehill to the landscape may seem foolhardy or worse. We can nonetheless engage with these issues in a different spirit. Though existing approaches provide a useful and inescapable foil, the aim is not to offer a better answer, since the aim is not to provide an answer at all. It is rather to use this question as the focal point for an imaginative reconstruction, partial and simplified, of a certain segment of the human condition. In this process, the question itself and the terms used to pose it get reformulated and transformed. The results are the rudiments of a theory, designed to add to a cumulative stock, which is itself part of the subject matter under investigation; an attempted contribution to the fund of ideas that inform and so shape that segment of the human condition, even when cast as a commentary on it. The guiding principle of the present inquiry is an old insight that goes back at least as far as Plato: that social and political arrangements are refracted in, and are a refraction of, the structure of the human self; to study the one is to study the other.

Two preliminary points. First, the political question arises with particular acuity with respect to an unjust state. "My country, right or wrong" is a well-known, for many notorious, sentiment. But we must also query allegiance to a just state. Our obligations to our own political system are supposedly different from our obligations to others, no matter how just these others may be. The fact that any given country, government or law is just does not by itself bind us to it in the way in which we are supposed to be bound to our own.

Second, the political question is a quest for justification. Such a quest does not arise in a void. Justification usually proceeds as an attempt to silence some qualms or reply to putative or actual opponents. Allegiance to the state, political authority and law's bindingness need to be justified. Why? A common answer fixes on the state's coerciveness, since coercion by itself is presumptively bad. But coercion is not my primary concern. In focusing on normativity, I mean to attend to an aspect of the state, its government and law, that is independent of coercion, and if anything is antithetical to it. The state's and so the law's normativity consist in an appeal to voluntary allegiance and compliance. The political question is an invitation to assess this appeal quite apart from the fact that the state is in a position to enforce it. What challenge other than coercion gives rise to the political question and guides the efforts to answer it?

It is instructive that there are in fact two prominent challenges, diametrically opposed: one associated with an individual, self-regarding standpoint, the other with a universal, other-regarding standpoint. Seen from the individual's standpoint the question is, why should I assume the burdens the state seeks to impose on me and accept the setback to my own interests it often demands? From the other end of the spectrum the question arises, why do my political community's claims get priority over similar claims of other people or humanity as a whole? Each of the two opposing perspectives is commonly tied to a normative orientation of its own: individual self-interest is subject to considerations of prudence, whereas the universal concerns are the turf of morality. The political question accordingly arises between the prudential and the moral, and is answerable to both.

That the challenges to the state's normative claims come from two opposing directions is sometimes obscured by the fact that the same idiom, of autonomy, is used to express both challenges: being subjected to the state's authority and deferring to its demands is allegedly inimical to one's autonomy. But here the polarity is hidden by an ambiguity in these claims between *personal* and *moral* autonomy. Roughly, personal autonomy concerns a person's ability to carry out her wishes and desires and so advance her interests. Moral autonomy, at least as interpreted by Kant, is a matter of acting on universally valid principles one endorses. The charge that political authority and the law threaten autonomy can accordingly amount either to the claim that they restrict people's capacity to pursue their own goals, or that they displace the universal principles that as moral agents people otherwise endorse (Dworkin 1988; Hill 1989; Raz 1988).

Given the two polar challenges, it is not surprising that answers to the political question should often consist in efforts to account for the state's normative claims either by showing that these claims arise out of self-regarding individual concerns and are congruent with them, or else that they are the implications of a universal morality and part of it. This is not the place to canvass the voluminous literature, other than to comment that the very volume and endurance of the two contrasting lines of thought raises some doubt that either is fully satisfactory. In any case, there is a prima facie phenomenological objection to both reductionist accounts, as unable to capture the experience of the political domain as a *distinctive* site of normative considerations, marked precisely by their failure to neatly align with the self-regarding/other-regarding divide. For example, some people pay their taxes resentfully, betraying a conflict between their self-regarding wish to keep the money and the state's demands. The same people may feel personally offended and outraged when their country's embassy is attacked or flag burnt. The state's claims seem in this way to belong to a large and variegated category of what appear to be *intermediate* interests (values, attitudes) and their associated reasons and norms, which cannot be classified clearly and stably either as one's own or as those of others. Although a satisfactory answer to the political question would have to meet both the prudential and the moral challenges to the state's normative claims, the answer needs also account for the perceived distinctiveness of these claims, rather than collapsing them into one pole or the other.

I have mentioned that the twin challenges to the state's normative claims are sometimes phrased in the idiom of autonomy, either moral or personal. Here too, the apparently intermediate location of the political between the individual and the universal can be observed, confounding the binary division. Autonomy is self-government, and a state's sovereignty is the realization of a people governing itself. Who, however, is the referent of this reflexive expression? It may appear that I have already answered the question in the course of posing it by designating "the people" for that role. But the history of political philosophy is in part the record of pursuing two radically different interpretations of this answer and of coping, inconclusively, with the difficulties to which each of them leads. "The people" either labels an aggregate of individuals, or a single entity, existing over and above, as the saying goes, the group of individual members. Both answers, however, create a rift between the self-government of the state and the autonomy of its individual members. Each individual is governed by a group of other individuals in the one case, or by some independent entity in the other. In neither case does the reflexive subject of self-government coincide with the individual self. But here too familiar facts appear to belie this picture. In the name of national self-determination, people often favor a more oppressive regime of their own over a more benign foreign rule. In doing so, they experience themselves as promoting their own autonomy rather than that of some third party, be it other individuals or an impersonally perceived collective entity.

It is possible, of course, to dismiss all such attitudes that people exhibit toward their country as deluded and wrongheaded. But even if this is one's verdict, it would make better sense to reach it on normative rather than conceptual grounds. We should be hesitant to diagnose large segments of human history as displaying a *conceptual* error. The reluctance stems in part from the explanatory paucity of such an account. Given how pervasive the attitudes in question are, an adequate account, even if not upholding them, should tell us something about what prompts and sustains them. Ascribing to people a conceptual error that renders their attitudes senseless or incoherent is unlikely to meet this goal. It would be more fruitful to try to maintain conceptual room for political autonomy, seen as a genuine and distinct possibility, even if we denounce on normative grounds its supposed realizations.

The Moral Question

When the political question is raised, and the state's normative claims are brought before the court of morality, this court's jurisdiction is for the most part taken for granted. That the political question arises between two contrasting poles—of prudence and morality—reminds us, however, of the challenge the self-interested individual poses not just to the state and its law but to morality as well. For this individual, keen to advance her interests and satisfy her desires, morality presumes to stand in the way. Why would the individual care? How are we to understand morality's grip in possible derogation of our own interests and desires? In Kant's well-known formulation, how is morality possible? Call this *the moral question*. Clearly, our answer to the political question must be linked to our answer to the moral question.

Adding the moral question to the political question, while compounding difficulties, also provides a clue. Both questions must respond to the same challenge, posed by the self-regarding individual. Given the similarity between the two questions and the common challenge they face, strategies for coping with the moral question may be employed in coping with the political question too. One response to the moral question—of which Kant's own moral theory is a prime example—resorts to abstraction. Since morality purports to speak in a single voice to or on behalf of individuals whose interests and desires potentially conflict, it presumably requires a unitary standpoint, occupied by every human being; abstraction paves the way. By abstracting from actual, concrete individuals, their interests and desires, we efface differences and construct a single platform on which they all stand. In Kant's case this feat is accomplished by means of the noumenal self, characterized exclusively by the possession of a rational will, and by the uplifting image of a Kingdom of Ends, a forum in which abstractly conceived noumenal selves spell out the practical implications of their shared humanity (Kant 1964/1785, ch. 2).

The most influential recent engagement with the political question, that of John Rawls, does indeed purport to follow Kant in this regard. Since Rawls considers justice to be the primary virtue of political institutions, his response to the political question takes the form of a procedure for constructing a society's constitution, laws and institutions that embody sound principles of justice. In doing so, Rawls explicitly models his procedure on Kant's approach to the moral question. The participants in the original position, a forum Rawls analogizes to the Kingdom of Ends, are abstracted from actual human beings by means of the veil of ignorance, and so reach principles of justice in their shared capacity as citizens, oblivious to distinguishing characteristics and conflicting ends that keep them apart (Rawls 1971).

On a closer look, however, Rawls's use of abstraction turns out to be at once too timorous and excessive in ways that help reveal some of the broader issues involved. To appreciate the first weakness, we need to compare Rawls's theory to Kant's. Despite their similarity, the approaches are fundamentally different, exposing a crucial ambiguity in the notion of abstraction and its relationship to the self. In employing abstraction, Kant is making a metaphysical claim. His moral theory is grounded in a bifurcated metaphysics which distinguishes between the world of appearances—that is the world as it appears to creatures with the particular perceptual and cognitive capacities that human beings happen to possess—and the world as it exists apart from humans' perception of it, the world of things-in-themselves. People belong to both domains. As phenomenal selves, we belong to the world of appearances, in which psychological *inclinations* participate in the same system of perceptual and cognitive capacities by means of which all of human reality is constructed. Qua noumenal selves, however, we belong to the domain of things-in-themselves, to which ex hypothesi we have no experiential access. We can, however, use our philosophical imagination to project on this blank screen the features of our moral experience which the phenomenal self cannot by itself accommodate. Specifically, we can view moral reasons as applying to us as noumenal selves and motivating us in this capacity (Kant 1964/1785, ch. 3).

Much of post-Kantian philosophy, however, is averse to this bifurcated metaphysics, and at any rate Rawls abjures it. Cut off from such metaphysical moorings, Rawls's abstraction differs radically from Kant's. Unlike the Kingdom of Ends and its noumenal inhabitants, the original position is a *hypothetical* meeting of *imaginary* representatives, whose characteristics purport to be nothing more than theoretical stipulation. The original position and its abstract inhabitants accordingly play a much more attenuated role in answering the political question than the Kingdom of Ends and the noumenal self play in answering the moral. The normative force of the principles of justice and of the laws and institutions they generate comes from outside the theoretical devices Rawls employs. He appeals from the start to people who are assumed to possess a sense of justice; the original position serves only as a heuristic device designed to instruct them about what justice, to which they are in general already independently committed, requires (Rawls 1971: 12, 16, 21, 120). But appealing in this way to a sense of justice is unsatisfactory. If we are puzzled about the source of our alleged obligation toward the state, even a just one, positing a sense of justice is too ad hoc, and has little explanatory power.

Rawls's abstraction is also excessive for the task he undertakes. Depriving the participants in the original position of all individuating characteristics is designed to replicate Kant's subject of morality, the noumenal self. But what would stop such an abstract self from assuming a universal perspective? Why would its interest in justice and the scope of the principles it adopts be confined to domestic institutions and apply only to citizens of a single state? This indeed is the gist of the critique that communitarians launch against Rawls. On the communitarian view, only a "situated" self, thickly constituted by communal norms and practices, can sustain the burdens of communal life and exhibit the other-regarding concerns that justice mandates (Sandel 1998).

But this communitarian critique of Rawls's position, and the alternative it presents to liberalism's abstract strain, raises difficulties of its own. First, by privileging the community and its norms, the communitarian position militates against a universal morality, and weighs instead in favor of moral relativism that many, including some communitarians, find unappealing. Second, when the communitarian trains her critique on Kantian abstraction, she tends to downplay the individualist challenge to which the political question must also respond. After all, the communitarian's situated self isn't quite the concrete, prudential self either. The integration of the individual into the community denoted by the "situated" conception of self risks displacing not only the universal standpoint of morality but also the unique standpoint of the individual and its normative significance. I consider these next.

The Question of Prudence

In contemplating both the moral and the political question, the self-regarding individual provides the natural, taken-for-granted point of departure, posing a seemingly obvious challenge with which morality and law must contend. The claims of morality and of law are commonly perceived as *demands* made on the individual, and so her responding to them is deemed in need of explanation in a way that her pursuing her own interests is not. Removing your hand from a burning stove is easily explained in terms that don't seem to apply to your pulling someone else's hand from harm's way. Nothing corresponding to the heavy machinery of morality or law that comes into play in the latter case seems to be involved in the former. Your own sharp pain does all the motivating as well as explanatory work.

But even this simple example reveals a difficulty in the notion of the self-interested individual and in the kind of normative challenge it is taken to present. To act in a self-interested manner is not the same as to act on impulse, instinct or whim. Much as you're inclined to escape an occurrent pain, prudence might require that you endure it, say, for medical reasons. Removing one's hand from the fire is explained by the fact that the fire hurts. But when you refrain from doing so on account of prospects of greater future pain, we need an altogether different account, since unlike occurrent pain, future pain does not hurt. Why would you resist present desires or assume burdens on behalf of a future self? Call this *the question of prudence* (Sidgwick 1981/1874: 382, 386, 404; Nagel 1970: 58, 99–100).

This question too can be posed in the idiom of autonomy. I have earlier mentioned the distinction between personal and moral autonomy, and suggested that political autonomy represents a distinctive category intermediate between the two. But what does personal autonomy amount to, and what does it have in common with moral autonomy? A possible answer invokes Kant's distinction between psychological inclinations and rationality. Just as moral autonomy is a matter of subjecting psychological promptings to the discipline and oversight of a universal standpoint that encompasses humanity as a whole, personal autonomy requires subjecting those same promptings to similar control from a standpoint representing one's life as a whole (Sidgwick 1981/1874: 382, 386, 404; Nagel 1970: 58, 99–100). Juxtaposing the alleviation of one's own occurrent pain to that of someone else's conflates two different issues: the self-regarding as against the other-regarding, and inclination as against rationality. To exhibit personal autonomy requires that one submit one's psychological inclinations, even when self-regarding, to a regime of prudence that resembles in this respect the regime that governs other-regarding concerns as well. The addict, for example, has cravings for narcotic drugs, and yet, to be autonomous, he must comply with prudential considerations which mandate that these cravings be resisted and ignored (compare R. S. Taylor 2011). How are we to understand this regime and the autonomy it enables?

Not only are these serious puzzles, but they resemble the ones raised by law and morality. When considering the political question and the moral question, we saw how abstraction can provide the requisite unitary perspective, universal in one case, communal in the other. Abstraction from what? The natural answer presumes a concrete individual, whose properties are fully determinate and given. But reflection on the problem of prudence reminds us that no such individual exists. A temporally perduring and unified individual must be *constructed* in light of some template, idea or plan. Here too unity must be *imposed* on an endless experiential manifold and an equally unruly menu of potential responses and acts. And here too, abstraction, in the form of highly selective attention to facts and their organization in light of some master plan, can be seen as the route to the unity we seek.

Take a trivial example: a decision to go to the movies. While generally endorsing the plan, prudence may recommend that rather than watching the Bergman movie I'm

MEIR DAN-COHEN

eager to see I should go to a thriller to better relax, and that instead of choosing a front-row seat from which I enjoy movies best I take a back-row seat to avoid a headache. But prudence also demands that I disregard myriad other details that are inevitably involved in this venture, about myself (e.g., my shoe size) and about external circumstances (such as the usher's name). We commonly exercise such selective attention as a matter of course, in response to what we take to be obvious canons of *relevance*. This, however, does not make such selectivity trivial, but rather attests to how rational, up to a point, we are, and how adept at these kinds of abstraction. And it is only in light of some such overall selective schema, a veil of ignorance if you like, that a unitary subject that goes to the movies and does a host of other related things can be constructed.

We can draw two lessons from these remarks. One is about the crucial role that abstraction plays, even at the level of the individual and indeed in constituting one. The second is that even if abstraction can thus provide an answer to the question of prudence, it will not be *the same* abstraction employed in the case of either morality or law. Prudence may require that we introduce yet another abstract conception of the self, but this conception would now be in competition with the universal abstraction of the noumenal self or the communal abstraction of the situated self.

The Abstract Self

It is time to take stock. An adequate answer to the political question must do more than assess the claims of the state in moral and prudential terms, since these two perspectives are themselves under a similar shadow of doubt. At the start of inquiry, prudence, law and morality are all up in the air. We cannot confidently answer any one of the three practical questions in terms of the others, but must try to answer them all in one fell swoop. An answer to the political question must be part of a more general account that encompasses morality and prudence as well. In seeking such an answer we need not commit ourselves in advance to the state's legitimacy or to the validity of law's normative claims. We do, however, want to explore the (ideal) conditions for this legitimacy and validity to obtain, whether or not these conditions are in fact ever satisfied. One difficulty that such a unified account faces, however, is the seeming exclusivity each of these normative systems appears to claim. Morality, law and prudence are all *comprehensive*, in the sense that they claim authority over human life as a whole, at least in the sense of being in charge of defining over which issues they each have a final say. This suggests an inescapable conflict that a unified account would be hard put to resolve.

We have so far focused on attempts to meet these practical challenges in terms of variously abstract conceptions of self. But two difficulties arise. The first concerns the competition among these conceptions. To align each of the various normative standpoints (universal, communal, individual) and their correlative normative orientations (morality, law, prudence) with a suitable conception of self is to replay the tension among the normative systems as a conflict among conceptions of self. The second difficulty concerns the relationship between abstraction and the self. A conception of an object is a representation. And only representations can be more or less abstract, not the objects themselves. A drawing or description of an elephant may render it in various degrees of resolution and detail, and so be more or less abstract. But it makes no sense to talk about a more or less abstract version of Jumbo itself. Now if abstraction relates to human beings as to elephants, then human beings cannot be any more abstract than Jumbo can. On this view, and as the discussion of Rawls illustrates, abstraction can yield only hypothetical representations of human beings, thereby creating a gap between the unitary normative standpoint that abstraction is expected to create and the actual, concrete individuals that are supposed to occupy it.

Removing these obstacles requires a more capacious conception of self than any of the contending candidates, and one that relates abstraction to self differently than in the elephant's case. To meet these ends, instead of a competition among variously abstract conceptions of self, let me introduce a single conception of self *as abstract*. On this conception, abstraction pertains to the actual self, rather than being a property of its representations, and different levels of abstraction are all internal to the self, rather than being alternative representations of it.

Meaning and Self

Many thinkers have alternately spoken of the self in dramaturgical, literary, hermeneutical or more broadly semiotic terms (see, for example, Goffman 1961; Schechtman 1989; and Wiley 1994, respectively). What conception of self lurks amidst these metaphors and imageries and makes them seem appropriate? A related and partially overlapping body of thought considers the self to be socially constructed (e.g., Mead 1934). What kind of thing is the self assumed to be if construction by society is to be a significant option?

We can answer these questions by recognizing in these various approaches to the self a common thread, regarding the self's intelligibility: like plays and novels, human beings are constituted by meaning and are subject to interpretation; in neither case is there a fixed or canonical level of detail independent of these interpretive articulations. To view the self as a concatenation of meanings that are embodied, or enacted, or conveyed by a particular organism is to insist on an ontological gulf that separates human beings from animals (e.g., Baker 2000). Occurrences at the level of the organism are attributable to a self, or give rise to one, only insofar as they assume a semantic dimension so that a syntax/semantics distinction becomes applicable. This is easiest to see in regard to phenomena that are distinctly human, most notably speech. Physiological and acoustic productions that involve such organs as the tongue, the mouth and the larynges assume their human significance by virtue of possessing semantic content associated with language and speaking.

The same point can be extended to human actions more generally. Ignoring many qualifications and refinements, think of actions as intentional bodily movements. As such they can be conceived as determinate physical events, describable at indefinite levels of detail concerning the physiological, neurological, biochemical and other physical processes involved. But this is not how we ordinarily refer to actions at all. Rather, in describing an action we commonly articulate the intention that prompts the action and makes it the action it is. However, in articulating an intention, unlike describing a physical object or process, we are not faced with a fixed bit of reality. Rather, through interrogation and reflection we (and that includes the agent herself) can arrive at ever more expansive, detailed and far-reaching articulations of the relevant intention. Such articulations are at once expansions of the intention and expansions of our understanding of it. Similar remarks apply to emotions. An emotion is what it is by virtue of the content or meaning that attaches to what otherwise would be an inchoate and inscrutable sensation or feeling. This content or meaning can be expanded through elaboration or contracted through synopsis without there being any independently available stable benchmark relative to which these variations can be assessed (C. Taylor 1985).

547

Finally, not just actions and emotions, but even more rudimentary phenomena that may appear exhausted by their biological properties, and that humans and animals seem to share, are also constituted by meaning. There is a state of the cat's organism which corresponds to the state of my organism when both of us are hungry. Only in my case, however, but not the cat's, is the hunger attributable to a self. Why? It is inherent to my hunger that it appears as *my* sensation; it shows up as an awareness that can be articulated as "I am hungry" or "I feel like having some food." Hunger serves as a determinant in decisions and behavior because of this synonymy between the sensation and such verbal cognates. This is not to say that in order for hunger to influence one's practical reasoning it must be first verbalized; to the contrary, the sensation itself is ordinarily acted upon or resisted. But the mode in which this influence is exerted is not just causal or mechanical; hunger participates in the domain of reasons, and in order to do that, it must participate in its capacity as a carrier of meaning, a capacity it has in common with the equivalent verbal expressions.

The self is not just a random aggregate of meanings, however. To form a self these meanings must be organized in some fashion; the literary and dramaturgical imageries suggest recognizable templates in light of which the organization of discrete meanings into a unified self can be understood. On a literary conception, "a life story" is not a story *about* a person's life; rather, this expression is meant to depict life itself as an unfolding narrative. Similarly, the dramaturgical imagery presents social roles as constituents of human identity. To be a physician, a teacher, a carpenter or a nurse, a son or a daughter, a wife or a husband is to follow a script, and that in turn amounts to the enactment or expression of a bit of meaning or content in which this script consists.

Levels of Abstraction

Such literary and dramaturgical analogies also suggest a different model of the way abstraction relates to human beings. We saw that in the case of physical objects there is a clear distinction between the object and its representation, e.g., Jumbo and a drawing or description of it. In the case of literary objects, this distinction is effaced. The point can be made succinctly in terms of the two different uses of the verb "tell," transitive and intransitive. In telling me *about* a physical object, an elephant or a car, you provide a description of the object or an account of it. The description or the account is external to the object: in describing the car you don't give me the car or any part of it. But when it comes to literary objects, *tell* can be used transitively. To tell a story or a joke is not to describe but to *transcribe* it; it is to convey to the listener the very story or joke that is the subject matter of the telling.

The telling of the story, its transcription, can be performed at various levels of abstraction or detail. Suppose that I ask you to tell me the story of *Macbeth*, and you oblige with a synopsis. This may be fully responsive to my request. Whether the level of abstraction of your narrative is adequate will depend on such contextual considerations as the degree of my curiosity or whether I am in a rush, and such considerations may call for greater abstraction as much as for more detail. Just as interpretation can add detail to a story without changing it, a synopsis gives us a shortened version of it. Different renditions of a story that vary in level of abstraction are equally *versions* of the story itself. In addition to such "vertical" differences among versions in level of abstraction, versions can also diverge "horizontally," when they differ in some of their detail, e.g., the story of *Faust* as rendered by Marlowe, Goethe, Lessing, Heine and Mamet. In what sense are they all, despite their differences, versions of a single story? Here too the answer lies in abstraction. Since increased abstraction effaces differences among the versions, at a higher level of abstraction, the different versions merge into a single story, whereas at lower levels of abstraction (or higher levels of resolution), the differences among the versions appear.

If we think of the self in such literary terms as a cluster of meanings, we are thinking of it *as abstract*; abstraction is internal to it rather than a property of its representation. Moreover, the content or meaning constitutive of the self can range over various levels of abstraction. Distinguishing characteristics that appear at lower levels of abstraction are effaced at higher levels, and so interpersonal commonalities and unities appear.

The point can also be made in terms of the dramaturgical imagery. Many of the roles constitutive of our identities are nested: *dermatologist* and *cardiologist* are both subcategories of *physician*. If I am a cardiologist and you a dermatologist, we are both physicians. In what sense do we occupy different roles, and in what sense one and the same? As in the case of the versions of a story, roles too can differ at lower levels of abstraction and converge at a higher level.

Now if we think of selves along such narrative or dramaturgical lines, and further ascend the ladder of abstraction, we reach the idea of a *person* understood in terms of the convergent abstract content of all human lives. To be an individual is on this view to enact and thus realize at high levels of specificity, and therefore in vastly ramified and divergent ways, a singular meaning or content that pertains to all persons as such.

Person and *individual* thus label the two polar extremes on a spectrum of abstraction over which the self ranges. This spectrum contains innumerable intermediate levels, such as those occupied by the role of cardiologist or physician just mentioned. But here we need draw a further distinction. Both person and individual are *comprehensive* terms in that at their respective levels of abstraction they each pertain to a human being as a whole, whereas cardiologist and physician are partial, pertaining to some aspects of a physician's life and identity but not to others. In addition to terms referring to partial roles, however, there is logical room for a comprehensive term that applies to a human being as a whole at an intermediate level of abstraction. *Citizen* can serve as such a term (compare Conover 1955). To be French in this sense is to be constituted by a concatenation of meanings that at a suitable level of abstraction defines a common identity of being French. These three terms—individual, citizen, person—accordingly designate the same human being conceived at different levels of abstraction: *individual* alludes to a cluster of meanings unique to her; *French* to meanings she shares with the other French people; whereas *person* alludes to the abstract content that every human being shares.

Answering the Questions

As this picture suggests, the three subdivisions of ethics we have distinguished—prudence, law and morality—apply to us in the same *kind* of way, by engaging with and constituting aspects of our identity. Morality defines in important part what a person is, thereby helping constitute the common identity of all human beings; law defines in important part what a citizen is, thereby helping constitute the common identity of, say, the Brazilians or the French; and prudence defines in important part what each individual is, thereby helping constitute each individual's unique identity. Since the three branches of ethics correspond to the distinction within the self between different levels of abstraction, they represent points on a continuum rather than standing for a disjunction or an opposition. Even so, they can be each loosely associated with a different value or goal. Applying to people at the highest level of abstraction, morality upholds *dignity*, the value all persons have as such. Law spells out the more specific requirements of *justice* among the members of a political community. Prudence, operating at an even greater level of specificity, at which each individual's particular experiences come into view and take pride of place, is oriented toward the individual's *happiness*. Acting in one's capacity as an individual, a citizen and a person, one acts, respectively, prudently, legally and morally, and so one pursues happiness, realizes justice and respects dignity.

To see morality, law and prudence as operating at various levels of abstraction explains how each of them can be comprehensive in the sense mentioned earlier, that is apply to one's life as a whole, without being in necessary conflict with the others. Since they are each other's abstractions, or in reverse order, each other's elaborations, they can each claim exclusive dominion over the self's corresponding level of abstraction, consistent with recognizing the others' exclusivity at other levels.

Within this picture, the pressure is relieved to divide all interests, reasons, attitudes and the like into self-regarding and other-regarding. This binary division is replaced by a continuum of increasing abstraction and correspondingly greater convergence of content, a continuum of which the unique individual and humanity as a whole are the two extreme poles. Political reasons (attitudes, etc.) pertain to intermediate levels of abstraction, which create smaller clusters of partial convergences of content, and hence more limited pockets of solidarity than the entire human race.

The tripartite division of autonomy into personal, political and moral also finds its place. Autonomy at all three levels involves subjecting impulse to norm. The norm must be internal, though, rather than externally imposed. But to be internal it need not be, indeed it cannot be, invented by the agent or pulled out of thin air. Rather, a norm is internal insofar as it fits, at a suitable level of abstraction, within the structure of meanings that defines the agent as an individual, a citizen and a person, or, to put the same point differently, insofar as the agent identifies with it, or endorses it, as an element within the overall structure of meanings she enacts. Within this picture, the subject of the self-government exercised by the state, and hence of political autonomy, is not an aggregate of individuals, nor is it an impersonal collective entity, but rather each citizen, abstractly conceived.

Ideal and Reality

The preceding account of citizenship, and relatedly of law and the state, is highly idealized, in two senses. First, in the Weberian sense of an ideal type. By highlighting certain salient features of a segment of our experience, we get a simplified, but for this reason potentially illuminating, schematic representation, a model, that exhibits what is arguably an inner logic that connects various aspects of that experience. Such a model can serve as a methodological baseline or template in light of which the relevant range of real-life phenomena can be studied and assessed. But this account also presents an ideal in a more substantive sense, as something attractive and appealing. It does so in two related ways. One is to show that some conflicts and trade-offs we experience among various normative claims made on us are not necessary. We might, in an ideal world, have certain cakes and eat them too. The other is a promise, held out in such a world, of a harmony within the self in the form of a narrative unity among various levels of abstraction that merges the demands of humanity, community and individuality into a coherent whole.

Such utopian ruminations are not, however, best treated as goals to guide our aspirations, but rather as reminders of how far we fall short. Clarifying an ideal, and so increasing awareness of how remote it is, may serve as a caveat against delusion and as a bulwark against wishful thinking. Given the human propensity to mix reality with fantasy, we should remain ever vigilant in drawing the line between the two. One way of doing so is to retain a robust grasp on reality. But another is to spell out the fantasy. In either way we improve our capacity to tell which is which. In this concluding section I accordingly indicate some of the idealizations the previous account indulges, and the way they affect where we stand relative to this account.

To begin with, in posing the political question I have followed a common usage by associating it with talk of a political community. But such talk is not innocuous. The term *community*, no matter how broadly and loosely used, does not designate the entire array of social formations, and contrasts with other collective terms such as *bureaucracy* and *organization* (Dan-Cohen 1994). Formulating the political question in the idiom of community accordingly loads the dice from the start in favor of certain values and ideas—concerning bonds of culture, tradition, history and language among citizens— that do not apply in the case of many states. It is in light of such "thick" bonds that citizenship can plausibly designate a *comprehensive* identity. When such factors are missing or fractured, citizenship is no longer a sufficiently significant source of meaning to unify the citizens and secure their solidarity.

But even relatively homogenous countries do not entirely fit the image of community. We often encounter the state as a vast bureaucracy or, perhaps more accurately, as a conglomerate of bureaucracies—formal, impersonal and instrumental. Such social formations exhibit a mechanical, functional unity that is a far cry from the enactment of shared communal meanings. Even when governmental organizations are harnessed in the service of communal goals, they have well-documented and partially understood tendencies to depart from those goals, develop their own interests, and become self-aggrandizing and self-perpetuating. We tend to experience our interactions with them as external and remote. They create a very different environment, and call for a different set of attitudes, than those suggested by the idiom of community.

These differences bear directly on another cardinal idealization in the account I have proposed. It concerns our supposed identification with our role as citizens. Identification labels the integration of the role within the self, and so is crucial to the location of the norms governing the role as internal to us and consistent with our autonomy. But not all social roles are integrated in this way. Some are enacted in a detached, impersonal and strategic manner; we engage in them only due to some external inducement, a threat or a reward, but otherwise maintain them outside the scope of our identifications and on the periphery of the self. When citizenship is conceived in the context of the state's bureaucratic persona, it becomes such a detached role; we enact it in interaction with alien, impersonal forces, and we respond in kind.

This finally brings us to the most radical idealization in my account. I have formulated the political question as an inquiry into the state's normativity, leaving coercion aside. The state's normativity consists in part in an appeal to its citizens that they obey its laws. Some believe that this appeal must be always resisted; autonomy requires no less (Wolff 1970). I have tried to show that under some conditions, allegiance to the state and a disposition to obey its laws may be an expression of political autonomy, on a par and compatible with one's personal and moral autonomy. But the state is a quintessentially coercive agency. Its normative appeal is backed by sanctions. This fact, too, militates against identification with the citizen role, and introduces a rift between obedience and autonomy. The real enemy of autonomy is not the state's demand for loyalty, nor the law's demand for obedience, but the enforcement of these demands by coercive means (Dan-Cohen 2002).

Two aspects of coercive enforcement are of critical importance here, its logic and its scope. The logic of coercion is somewhat disguised by the fact that enforcement is never fully effective, and so leaves room for people's discretionary behavior. But this state of affairs counts as an imperfection and a failure, or else the product of various exogenous constraints on the exercise of coercion, such as the retributive considerations that ordinarily delimit the permissible severity of criminal sanctions. The logic of coercion in terms of which its performance is assessed does not by itself allow for such leeway. By using coercive threats, government does not merely seek to provide its subjects with an additional reason for compliance. To be coercive, the avowed purpose of the threat must be to bring about the commanded behavior independently of the agent's own values and desires. The scope of coercion may also mislead, by appearing more limited than it is, e.g., only those who violate the law are actually put in jail. But this impression too misses the point. The main strategy of legal enforcement is deterrence, i.e., coercive threats. And these are neither discriminatory nor selective; they address everyone, the good and the bad, with the same invidious message: obey, or else.

These features of coercion bear directly on the nature of citizenship. Inviting someone's voluntary obedience, as the normative face of law purportedly does, only to back up this invitation with coercive threats designed to secure compliance irrespective, renders the initial appeal disingenuous. Relatedly, the state's pretense to respect its citizens' autonomy is to this extent a sham. By supplying a wholesale, decisive, external motivation for carrying out citizenship's obligations, a motivation that bypasses or overrides the agent's own will (informed as her will may be by this very same role's script), coercion acts as an alienating factor, disrupts identification, and casts the citizen's role as pro tanto distant and detached.

Coercion is here to stay. At least in the world as we know or think we know it, law must be backed by sanctions. Political and legal philosophy commonly begin, soundly enough, by marking the state's coerciveness as a potential evil, and then struggle to redeem it through one or another justification. The tacit belief is that a satisfactory justification will solve the problem of coercion, so that at least within the parameters defined by the favored account the exercise of coercion ought no longer trouble the collective conscience or disturb the good citizen's sleep. Focusing instead on the question of law's normativity, the approach I have sketched takes us in a different direction. The violence perpetrated in the name of the law is never fully rectified by the practical imperatives that may necessitate it. A lesser evil is still an evil. The result is to sunder full identification with the citizen role, and render a certain ideal of citizenship and its location within the self practically unattainable.

This is for the most part a negative conclusion; but we can also glimpse its more positive, if somewhat paradoxical, complement. When state coercion crosses a certain threshold and registers as oppression, it may evoke the subversive display of a community spirit, a common enactment of a suitably abstract self, guided by what is sometimes referred to as "higher law." Such public reaction is designed to drain the existing government's pronouncements of their putative authority, and instead expose or perhaps rather constitute them as mere "positive law" backed by brute force. Counterposed to the detached or alienated citizenship of ordinary times we find at such moments the realization of a kind of citizenship that comes closer to unifying loyalty to the political community with loyalty to oneself, and gives fuller expression to an ideal of political autonomy than is otherwise the case. This is possibly one reason why despite great individual hardships, such times of upheaval can present their protagonists with some of their finer moments.

Two further conclusions follow. One is to somewhat chill enthusiasm toward an idea, favored by some, of world citizenship supposedly tied to a global government. Since such a government is bound to be both bureaucratic and coercive, the previous considerations alert us to the danger that it would tend to fracture our humanity and alienate us from it and so from morality. A similar conclusion applies to the other end of the spectrum of abstraction where individuality is at stake. At issue are paternalistic laws, such as those seeking to regiment people's dietary or sexual practices for, say, health-related reasons. These laws amount to the enforcement of prudence, and so pose the corresponding danger of fracturing our individuality and distancing or alienating us from segments of it as well.

References

Baker, L. R. (2000) *Persons and Bodies: A Constitution View*, Cambridge: Cambridge University Press.

Conover, P. J. (1955) "Citizen Identities and Conceptions of the Self," *Journal of Political Philosophy* 3: 133–65.

Dan-Cohen, M. (1994) "Between Selves and Collectivities: Toward a Jurisprudence of Identity," 61 *University of Chicago Law Review*: 1213.

—— (2002) "In Defense of Defiance," in M. Dan-Cohen, *Harmful Thoughts: Essays on Law, Self, and Morality*, Princeton: Princeton University Press, pp. 94–121.

Dworkin, G. (1988) *The Theory and Practice of Autonomy*, New York: Cambridge University Press.

Goffman, E. (1961) *Encounters*, Indianapolis: Bobbs-Merril.

Hill, T. (1989) "The Kantian Conception of Autonomy," in J. Christman, ed., *The Inner Citadel: Essays on Individual Autonomy*, New York: Oxford University Press, pp. 91–105.

Kant, I. (1964/1785) *Groundwork of the Metaphysic of Morals*, H. J. Paton, trans., New York: Harper.

Mead, G. H. (1934) *Mind, Self, and Society*, Chicago: University of Chicago Press.

Nagel, T. (1970) *The Possibility of Altruism*, Princeton: Princeton University Press.

Rawls, J. (1971) *A Theory of Justice*. Cambridge, Mass.: Harvard University Press.

Raz, J. (1988) *The Morality of Freedom*, Oxford: Oxford University Press, ch. 14.

Sandel, M. (1998) *Liberalism and the Limits of Justice*, 2nd edition, Cambridge: Cambridge University Press.

Schechtman, M. (1989) *The Constitution of Selves*, Ithaca, NY: Cornell University Press.

Sidgwick, J. (1981/1874) *The Methods of Ethics*, Indianapolis: Hackett Publishing Company.

Taylor, C. (1985) "Self-Interpreting Animals," in C. Taylor, *Human Agency and Language: Philosophical Papers 1*, Cambridge: Cambridge University Press, p. 45.

Taylor, R. S. (2011) *Reconstructing Rawls: The Kantian Foundations of Justice as Fairness*, University Park, PA: The Pennsylvania State University Press, ch. 2.

Wiley, N. (1994) *The Semiotic Self*, Chicago: University of Chicago Press.

Wolff, R. P. (1970) *In Defense of Anarchism*, New York: Harper and Row.

Further Reading

For further reading, see: R. Dworkin (2011) *Justice for Hedgehogs*, Cambridge, Mass.: Harvard University Press; G. Fletcher (1993) *Loyalty*, New York: Oxford University Press; C. Korsgaard (1996) *The Sources of Normativity*, Cambridge: Cambridge University Press; D. Miller (2000) *Citizenship and National Identity*, Cambridge: Polity Press; and M. Nussbaum (1996) *For Love of Country?*, Boston: Beacon Press.

Part VI

RIGHTS AND EQUALITY

36
SOME QUESTIONS ABOUT RIGHTS

Christopher Morris

Rights are everywhere. We have rights to vote, to free speech, to our property, to operate a car, to marry, to attend public institutions of learning, to open a bank account, to make gifts or bequests, to bake cookies, to drink too much. In the American tradition we also have, in addition to rights to life and to liberty, a right to pursue happiness. And there are many more. Some are big (e.g., the right to liberty), others are small (e.g., the right to apply for a license to operate a particular piece of machinery). But there are many of them.

Rights like these are usually both constraining and enabling. Typically, the rights of others constrain what we can do, and our rights enable us to do certain things we might not otherwise be able to do securely or at all. Rights seem to be very important. They figure everywhere in law and in political and social life. Some kinds of rights are more prominent in some political cultures than others, but it is hard to imagine a legal or political system with none. They certainly are important and of interest to us, readers of this volume.

Why are rights important? Presumably because they constrain and enable. How is this done? That is a matter of some controversy. We might at the outset say that rights constrain and enable roughly by requiring that something be done or not done. In effect, they settle in some ways what is to be done. If one has a right to be served in a restaurant or to run for office or to apply for a license, then, barring some further consideration, that is what ought to happen—one ought to be served or allowed to run or to apply. If I owe you a certain sum of money, and you have a right to that money, then should you demand to be repaid, that is what I must do (barring other considerations). Rights can settle what is to be done.

How do rights do this? This is a difficult question, and there is considerable disagreement about the answer. There seem to be different kinds of rights, some legal, others moral, some stringent, others less so, and this may make it more difficult to understand what rights are. How do rights come to be? The answer to this question is also a matter of some controversy. We shall explore these and other questions with the aim of illuminating the nature and function of rights in legal and political systems and of uncovering some of the underlying philosophical questions revealed by controversies about rights.

What Are Rights and How Do They Work?

I said that rights constrain and enable roughly by requiring that something be done or not done. This is not quite right; it's roughly true of one familiar and important kind of right. So we need to offer an analysis of rights. Virtually every account today starts with the analysis developed by the American jurist Wesley Newcomb Hohfeld (1879–1918). He distinguished several different elements, any one or combination of which can be a right in one sense or another, and his distinctions serve as the building blocks for virtually all contemporary accounts (see Hohfeld 1919).

We typically have rights to do things such as to pick up a bill we find lying on the ground or to sit on an unoccupied bench in the park. We have a right to do so in the sense that we are *at liberty* to do so; that is, we have no duty not to do these things. Hohfeld's term was "privilege," and theorists commonly talk of "a liberty" or "a Hohfeldian liberty" or sometimes "a liberty right." When we assert a right to do something such as sit on a bench, we often are expressing a Hohfeldian privilege, the first of four "elements" that he introduced to our vocabulary.

One can have privileges or liberties, it is important to note, in the absence of any duties. Indeed, in a world with no duties, everyone would have a liberty or liberty right to do anything. As Thomas Hobbes argued, such a world would be quite awful. (This is Hobbes's "state of nature," the natural condition of humankind, prior to the development of a state. See Hobbes 1991/1651, ch. 13.) Some other rights, however, are connected to duties, and it is especially these that "enable and constrain" in the way indicated earlier. These rights are usually called "claim rights" and entail a correlative duty on the part of others. They are standardly understood thus: one person has a claim right against another if and only if the second has a duty or obligation to the first. For example, a lender has a claim right against another that he repay his loan at an indicated time, or we all have a right that others not injure us in certain ways. In both cases the right is correlated with a duty on the part of the other individual (to repay the loan, not to injure). More completely: person A has a claim right to ___ against person B if and only if B has a duty to A regarding ___ (A has a liberty to do ___ if and only if A has no duty *not* to do ___).

Someone with a claim right to do something is "enabled" in some way or "protected," and the corresponding person(s) with a duty are constrained. Having bought a ticket to see the movie, one has a claim right to see it, and others have a duty to make this possible. Unlike the unoccupied park bench that I have a liberty to use, I may not sit on the chair on your front porch without your permission.

In a world with no duties, there are no claim rights. In such a world we would lack important protections, as others would have liberties to do whatever they wished to us. The introduction of claim rights and duties would be a significant change, enabling us to do many things we could not otherwise do, protecting our interests and liberties.

We may sit on the chair on your porch if invited, that is, with your permission. Similarly, if I have promised a friend to repay a loan tomorrow, I may postpone my repayment if my friend so indicates; my friend may even forgive my debt. The holder of a claim right is often able to permit another to do something he otherwise has a duty not to do, by waiving the duty or by annulling it altogether. These additional "rights" are *powers*, capacities to alter the liberties and claim rights of agents. If I may release you from your duty to repay your debt to me, then I have a power which I can exercise and thereby change our jural relations; I extinguish my claim right and your correlative duty to me. Many claim rights will include a power to modify or transfer or extinguish the claim right—for instance, ownership rights usually include such powers. But some rights may lack such powers. The American rights to life and liberty were thought by Thomas Jefferson to be inalienable. This means they cannot be extinguished or abandoned by their bearers; this had the implication that King George III could consequently not rightly claim that British Americans had alienated these rights when they became his subjects. The legal right to vote is typically inalienable in some respects; citizens cannot transfer it or lend it to others. (The right can, of course, be taken away or forfeited. "Inalienable," it is important to note, only means that the bearer lacks certain powers).

This notion of a power is crucial for understanding many legal and political relations, especially authority. A person's or a body's authority to create law is a power, one that changes what subjects may do or claim. It is impossible to understand political or legal authority without this notion of a power. The right to rule, claimed by monarchs, parliaments and peoples, is in large part a power to create or to modify the claim rights, liberties and duties of those subject to its rule. The "the right to marry," for instance, is also in large part a power, one that enables two people to enter into a complex relationship with various claim rights, duties and responsibilities. To deny some—e.g., homosexuals—the right to marry is to deny them a power accorded to heterosexuals; more precisely, it is to construe the right to marry as the power to marry a person of the opposite sex only.

Technically, a power is to be characterized as follows: a person has a power if and only if he or she has the capacity to alter the claim rights or duties of others, including his or her own. A power is a second-order capacity. It is a capacity to alter other jural relations. The point is easily grasped by thinking of rules or norms that give people claim rights and duties. These are what the important British jurist H. L. A. Hart called "primary rules." These rules may be changed in accordance with "secondary rules," those that indicate how changes may be made. According to Hart, a developed legal system will consist of both primary and secondary rules (Hart 1994/1961, ch. V). Agents who are enabled by the secondary rules to alter the primary ones have a power, and this power is a second-order capacity to change the first-order rules. Powers can, of course, be third order as well; for instance, in a hierarchical organization or system such as a corporation or the military, superiors may alter the powers of subordinates.

If someone may not have his claim rights or duties altered by others, then he possesses an "immunity," the fourth of Hohfeld's elements. One way of "protecting" a right within a political or legal system is by giving bearers immunities with regard to it. Our right to free speech may be in part an immunity; the legislature lacks the power to alter it.

These are the elements of the analysis that Hohfeld originally developed and which many have adopted and expanded. (Many sources offer further explanation of Hohfeld's categories. A good place to start is Wenar 2011.) They are the main elements we need in order to clarify the different kinds of rights that we have and to raise the questions we need to consider if we are interested in understanding the nature and functions of rights in political and legal systems. I said earlier that rights constrain and enable. How do they do this? In a number of ways. The first and simplest way of constraining someone is by imposing a duty. Such a duty, correlated with a claim right, enables the bearer of the latter to do things. My right to be paid by my employer enables me to obtain goods and services, to plan and the like. We might say that claim rights offer *protection*. A claim right to liberty, for instance, may protect the bearer's *choices*; others have duties not to interfere with them. Or it may protect the bearer's *interests*; others have duties to safeguard and to preserve the bearer's liberty. (Many contemporary theorists distinguish between choice- and interest-protecting *accounts* of rights. But it is not clear why rights could not protect both interests and liberty.)

It is relatively obvious why we should want to protect choices and interests. They are both valuable and vulnerable. The acts of others—malicious or innocent—can threaten our choices or set back our interests. Bullies, defrauders, trespassers and the clumsy can make our lives go less well. And the world is filled with predators and parasites. Protection is clearly desirable.

How do rights protect? As I said, they constrain. How do they do this? In the first instance by imposing duties. (They can also protect by imposing liabilities, which I have not discussed.) Duties that require action or forbearance constrain people. Suppose I have borrowed a sum and am obligated to repay it on a certain date. Then, at that time, I may not use that money for other purposes and must turn it over to its owner. Suppose I need a car and that you have one that I covet. If you will not lend or give it to me, I may not use it. People tempted to take the lives of others may not do so, barring the normal excusing or justifying circumstances (e.g., self-defense).

How exactly do duties constrain? They forbid or require action; that much is clear. But how do they compel those subject to duties to comply? This is an important question, one that is central to the other questions we are raising. A duty is a requirement, an instruction one must follow. But the modal terms here are not causal. It is hard to refrain from "complying" with the laws of gravity after falling off of a ladder. This way of putting the point is humorous, as there is no question of voluntary compliance. The laws of falling bodies are not normative laws like those of a legal system or of morality; they are causal regularities that apply to material bodies like ours, independently of our wills. When the rule of a moral or legal system applies to us, we usually *can* disregard or disobey it; we are normally able to do so, but we choose not to. These laws are normative and *can* be violated. Causal laws *cannot* be disregarded or violated.

So how do duties constrain? A popular answer is through consequences. Children confronting a directive will sometimes say, "Who's going to make me?" or "Says who?" The last question raises questions about *authority* and the source of the directive, as we shall see later. The first raises questions about *compliance*. Specifically, this question supposes that compliance is assured typically by force of some kind; people are made to comply. Suppose this is right. Then rights protect when duties are enforced.

There is some truth to this claim; duties do often have to be enforced. Legal systems typically attach sanctions to duty-imposing laws, and people are often cognizant of these. One need only think of parking or speeding laws to appreciate the importance of sanctions; many people are quite casual about compliance when they do not fear penalties. But sanctions and force cannot be the whole story. There are, for one, other consequences of failing to comply with duties. An important one, emphasized in much recent social science, is that people are less likely to cooperate with those who fail to comply with rules and norms imposed by law and society. A person or business that fails to pay its bills or honor its agreements will have a harder time buying needed goods and services. Someone who frequently fails to uphold commitments will cease to be trusted. This will be more or less true depending on circumstances (for instance, whether the violators are easily identified). But it seems clear that many considerations regarding the likely consequence of this violation will often ensure considerable compliance with many duties.

Do duties constrain *solely* through consequences? An important feature of what we might call *consequential* considerations is that they are "forward looking." The fact that my noncompliance with a duty today will affect the willingness of people to cooperate with me tomorrow is a fact about what is likely to happen in the future. Interestingly, many influential conceptions of rational choice presuppose that the *only* considerations that can be reasons for action are forward looking in this way. This is interesting and important because, on the face of it, the way that norms and rules *seem* to work is different. The fact that you made a promise to me yesterday is a reason for you to do something now; the fact that you injured me yesterday is a reason for you to compensate or apologize to me today. Noncompliance with rights and duties seems to raise considerations that are "backward looking." On the surface, duties seem to constrain nonconsequentially. This suggests that consequences cannot be the whole story. You ought to repay the loan because of some facts in the past (e.g., your assumption of certain commitments); you ought not to injure this person even if the consequences are likely to be positive. We are familiar with these sorts of thoughts. The question is what to make of them.

Claim rights and their correlative duties are supposed to constrain by *settling* what is to be done, barring other considerations overriding them. My promise to meet you for lunch tomorrow settles what I am to do, even though something much more interesting has come up. The way the commitment is supposed to work is to settle what I am to do tomorrow, unless of course an emergency or something of the sort occurs. The commitment is one made in the past. And this is the source of some puzzlement.

The Puzzle

Suppose you have a duty to someone to whom you are indebted. The duty requires repayment of a debt today. When you made this commitment, it made sense. What should you do now?

Suppose that repaying the debt is the best thing you could do today; the overall consequences are better than other alternatives. Then clearly this is what you should do. Suppose now that repaying the debt is not the best thing you could do today. Your prospects are considerably better if you invest that money in the stock market or contribute it to a charity (other alternatives can be substituted). Then you should not repay the debt and instead should do the best alternative available.

In the first case you should comply with the duty because in so doing you do the best thing. In the second case you should not comply with the duty because there are better alternatives. In both cases the duty is irrelevant to your choice. It consequently does not constrain your action. The duty does nothing (see Shapiro 2001 and 2005).

I have formulated the puzzle focusing on duties to someone, correlated with claim rights. But it is a quite general puzzle about rights, duties, norms, rules and all members of the family of what we might call "deontic constraints" (see Heath 2008). This is of some significance, as we shall see, as some are skeptical about rights without realizing that their skepticism is in fact much more far reaching. The puzzle challenges the picture we have of the way in which all of these constraints are supposed to work.

These constraints are supposed to work by settling what we are to do (subject to some conditions). They are to do this by changing our reasons for action. The argument I have just stated offers a challenge. What are we to think? We need to consider more carefully the way we are to reason when faced with a duty or another deontic constraint. The argument implicitly supposes that we ought to reason by determining what our best alternatives are and opting for these. We may factor in our commitments and other constraints, *but only as these affect how things go from now.* As Bernard Williams said, "The correct perspective on one's life is *from now*" (Williams 1981). This conception of rational choice, like those dominant in the social sciences, assumes a forward-looking perspective. Such a perspective is perhaps not far from the truth—many of the considerations governing rational choice are future oriented—but it's not clear that it is the whole truth. When one accepts a backward-looking consideration such as a commitment, one is assuming that not all considerations must be forward looking. One normally assumes, for instance, that a commitment made in the past can affect how one should act now and do so independently of how abiding by past commitments affects future prospects.

Suppose this is right. Then how are we to reason when considering deontic constraints like rights? If these are genuine reasons, they should be taken into account and should be weighed along with other considerations. This also sounds right, but it may be wrong. There are different kinds of reasons. Some, perhaps most, reasons are rightly thrown into the balance and are weighed one against another; one chooses according to the balance of reasons. But others are not. If rights and their correlative duties are, within limits, to settle what is done, they cannot merely be thrown into the balance— they must outweigh other considerations. But this is not the right way to think about this either. For some duties surely are trivial or minor—for instance, my promise to stop by your office to talk about something. Such a promise could not have much weight. Nevertheless, it is supposed to settle what is to be done, even if it could be overridden by a variety of other considerations (e.g., I felt ill). Joseph Raz has argued that the reasons offered by duties are complex; they consist of a first-order duty to ____, and a second-order reason to disregard other reasons favoring not to ____. And an account like his seems to be on the right track, at least with regard to how we very often reason about duties and commitments (see Raz 1999. See also McClennen 2004, and the references therein to the works of Bratman, Gauthier, McClennen and Shapiro).

We need not settle here the details of the account. The thought is that rights and their correlative duties constrain what we are to do by affecting the way we should reason practically. We are to recognize that backward-looking considerations are reasons, and that these reasons have a complex structure which would have us reason nonconsequentially or against the balance of reasons. Once we understand deontic constraints in this way, we can begin to resolve the puzzle presented earlier. We are not to abandon a commitment or act against a duty solely because there are better things we could do, considering only forward-looking considerations. Commitments and duties are the sources of backward-looking considerations.

Sources of Rights

We think we have many rights, but where do they come from? We have not said anything about their sources. We might pause and ask what exactly the question means. But we should first consider the answer that immediately comes to mind: rights come from many places. We seem to have legal rights, moral rights and perhaps other kinds too. Some legal rights are more basic or fundamental than others, some are procedural and so on. Some legal rights seem to replicate our moral rights (e.g., rights to liberty or life). And baseball players have certain rights, as do members of a chess club. There seem to be many sources of rights. Let us consider this possibility.

First let us clarify what we understand when we say that there is a right, one which comes from somewhere. We are thinking mostly of claim rights, entailing duties on the part of others. So if someone has a right, then someone else will have a duty or obligation to the right-holder. We might add, further, that a duty or obligation is a reason for action. More controversially, we might also say that it is, or at least is supposed to be, a reason of the right sort, one that settles what is to be done (subject to certain conditions). So what are some of the sources of rights?

Consider first the law. We have legal rights. They "come from" the law. How does that work? Consider a particular state. It claims the right to rule its territory; that is, it claims the right to make, to adjudicate and to enforce laws that obligate everyone residing or passing through its territory, as well as citizens abroad. Suppose the state is legitimate; that is, it has a certain status, satisfying certain standards, which accords it the right to rule. Then the laws it makes have a certain authority over these people. The laws obligate them, and they have reason to obey the laws except when permitted to do otherwise. Many of these laws will create rights and duties.

This is a simple, widely accepted picture that supposes that the authority of a law is conditioned by the legitimacy of the state. An illegitimate state, we may assume, might lack that authority, and a different story would have to be provided for the law's authority, if it has any. This simple account is not uncontroversial. Much ink has been spilled trying to determine the conditions for legitimacy: for instance, consent (what kinds?), the people's will, their welfare, consensus. Let us suppose that this account is right, that if a state is legitimate, then it will possess a right to rule and that this right will give it the power to make laws determining the rights of subjects of the laws. If this supposition is correct, then one source for our rights will be the authority of the state, what flows from its legitimacy. If a state is legitimate, then the rights it creates for its subjects, subject to certain conditions, will obligate others and be reasons for action. One of the answers to the "Says who?" question mentioned earlier is this: the state or the law says so (or "the People assembled").

It has proved very difficult to establish that reasonably just states have the legitimacy that would give them the powers described above. Genuine consent might do this, but only a small number of the subjects of any state have consented in the ways required to have this effect (see Simmons 2001a, 2001b and 2005; Green 1988). Some have argued that it is doubtful that even reasonably just and decent states possess the full powers attributed to them (see Morris 1998 and 2008). Suppose this is the case and that no state is fully legitimate. Might a state nevertheless create rights?

Consider a state that establishes or secures a norm. As a consequence, most people, most of the time, conform with the norm, and a smaller number of people comply with it because it has a certain authority. Then we might say that the practice, secured by the state, creates some rights. They are genuine rights, with genuine obligations, which are reasons for action. (It may be, however, on this weaker account that they are not reasons of the requisite sort. The matter of reasons for action complicates these questions considerably.)

Now what about moral rights? We seem to have rights that have a moral source, in particular, justice. The virtue of justice is that part of morality that deals with what is owed to others, that to which they have a right ("Justice, as it is treated here, as one of the cardinal virtues, covers all those things owed to other people: it is under injustice that murder, theft and lying come" (Foot 2002/1958–1959: 125)). Surely there are moral rights, for instance, the right not to be killed or not to be defrauded. There are three main kinds of accounts of how we might come to have moral rights. The first is simply a version of the story we have just considered, a conventionalist account: the establishment of certain practices, under certain conditions, creates rights.

The second is an instrumental account and represents a widely accepted way of attempting to ground rights. On this view, rights exist and are to be respected because they serve good ends. This is a position famously defended by John Stuart Mill in the last chapter of *Utilitarianism* (Mill 1985/1861). He argues that "When we call anything a person's right, we mean that he has a valid claim on society to protect him in the possession of it, either by the force of law, or by that of education and opinion. . . . To have a right, then, is, I conceive, to have something which society ought to defend me in the possession of" (ibid., ch. v).

It is thought by many that we hold some rights by virtue of being human or beings of a certain kind. This thought is ambiguous. A practice or convention could give rights to all beings of a certain kind, just as a legal system gives certain rights to all (and only) citizens. But when someone asserts that some rights are held by humans by virtue of their humanity they often mean something else. The source of the right, it is thought, is a natural property held by the possessor—e.g., humanity, reason, free will. Trivially, everyone with that property will possess the right, but they will do so by *virtue* of their possession of the property. This kind of view is usually called a status view of the source of rights as it focuses on the kind of thing the possessor is said to be. Obviously, some of our rights have other sources, for instance, in convention. But defenders of human and natural rights usually want to claim that these rights are not based in convention and are independent of and prior to law; they are rights that people have by virtue of their possession of certain natural properties. This thought is commonplace in the natural-law and natural-rights traditions, but it is also associated with the Kantian tradition that holds that rational beings have a certain status and are owed respect by virtue of being beings of a certain kind. But it also comes naturally to someone trying to express the source of the injustice of slavery or horrific killings ("they are humans!"). This understanding of the source of some rights has undergone a revival in the last several decades (see Nozick 1974: 48–51). (As these traditions are usually associated with a form of moral realism or rationalism, it is common to think that status accounts of rights may presuppose a position of this kind. This may be a mistake, as a variety of positions in ethics, including metaethical expressivism, can accommodate this thought. See Hurka 1989. But this question is beyond the scope of this chapter.)

There seem to be legal and moral sources to rights. And there may be other sources as well. The reference to conventions and practices—e.g., the law—makes one realize that there may well be rights that are neither legal nor moral. Participants in a game of baseball or chess may have certain rights that come from the practices establishing these games. And manners and etiquette and customs of all kinds may create rights. Our blindness to a wide range of phenomena may lead us to think that all rights are only moral or legal.

Worries About Rights

Rights, that is, claim rights and liberties, have figured prominently in the political discourse of modern defenders of liberty and critics of state power. Rights take center stage in the revolutions of the late eighteenth century. These movements, especially the French Revolution, provoked conservative criticisms of different kinds. One such criticism was that the appeal to natural rights characteristic of these rebellions contributed to anarchy and disorder. Jeremy Bentham—who was no conservative—made this criticism specifically of the French Declaration of the Rights of Man and of the Citizen of 1789. He argued, "in justifying past insurrections, [the authors of the Declaration] plant and cultivate a propensity to perpetual insurrection in time future; they sow the seeds of anarchy broadcast; in justifying the demolition of existing authorities, they undermine all future ones" (Bentham 1838–1843).

Bentham's worry concerned *natural* rights, rights which are possessed "anterior to the establishment of government," prior to and independently of the state or legal system. He worried that such rights are often thought of as *imprescriptible*, "that these rights *can not* be abrogated by government." The second clause of the French Declaration announces that "The aim of all political association is the preservation of the natural and imprescriptible rights of man." But even if they were prescriptible and could be lost or taken away, Bentham worried about the anarchist implications of such doctrines. His concerns are warranted, and one can find confirmation of them in contemporary writings. Natural-rights theorists often have difficulty justifying states and find themselves on "the edge of anarchy," to borrow the title of a book on the political thinking of John Locke (Simmons 1993). Nozick famously asserted that "Individuals have rights, and there are things no person or group may do to them (without violating their rights). So strong and far reaching are these rights that they raise the question of what, if anything, the state and its officials may do" (Nozick 1974: ix). The assumption of natural rights offers a challenge to much of contemporary political and legal philosophy: "The fundamental question of political philosophy, one that precedes questions about how the state should be organized, is whether there should be any state at all. Why not have anarchy?" (ibid.: 4).

Natural rights are not merely rights that exist prior to and independently of government or state (this was Bentham's characterization). They are rights that people have by virtue of being human or persons. They are a species of what we might call *prior rights*, rights that are held prior to and independently of state and law. Bentham was concerned about natural and imprescriptible rights—"nonsense on stilts," he called them. But *non*-natural prior rights also present most of the same challenges to state authority. If humans, prior to and independently of states, possess certain basic *conventional* rights, then these may be standards for action that have the same independence and similar authority as natural rights. They may seem to be less of a threat to state authority than conventional prior rights, but it is not clear that this is the case. It is possible, for instance, that first occupancy often establishes ownership and may justify rebellion against a regime that violates property rights.

Prior rights challenge state authority just as much as natural rights do. In fact, any standard of justice—rights, duties, principles—that is prior to and independent of the state may challenge the latter's authority. What is essential to such challenges is that the norm in question be such that one is led to reject the state's claim to be the ultimate judge of the limits of its power. Thomas Hobbes rightly worried about the subversive effects of any moral standard believed to have authority prior to and independently of the state.

Suppose that Bentham is right to think that natural rights are a threat to the state. The problem seems to be largely *practical*. Suppose that there are natural rights to life and liberty and to one's property. And, importantly, suppose that most residents of a particular state do not recognize its right to be the ultimate determiner of what people have a right to do. A state can recognize that subjects have natural rights while retaining the right to be the ultimate interpreter of their meaning and implications. The American constitutional system, for instance, seems to recognize the prior rights of its citizens (cf. the Ninth Amendment to the U.S. Constitution—"The enumeration in the Constitution of certain rights shall not be construed to deny or disparage others retained by the people." See Barnett 2006). Suppose, then, that such a condition exists. What kind of threat does the belief in natural rights pose to this state? That depends entirely on the number of people who choose to disobey. Suppose that most people most of the time comply with most laws, especially the most important laws. Then the belief that there are important prior rights does not *per se* threaten that state. Suppose in addition that this particular state chooses to enforce all and only laws that most people think to be just (as turn-of-the-century humorist Finley Peter Dunne put it, "No matter whether the country follows the flag or not, the Supreme Court follows the election returns"). Then its stability should not be threatened.

Bentham was quite confident that there are no natural rights. "We know what it is for men to live without government—and living without government, to live without rights" (Bentham 1838–1843). An examination of social groups with no government tells us what to expect, he said: "no habit of obedience, and thence no government—no government, and thence no laws—no laws, and thence no such things as rights" (ibid.). The story here is a variant of that told by Thomas Hobbes. The important seventeenth-century philosopher distinguished between a genuine commonwealth or state and "a state of nature"; the two categories for him exhausted all the possibilities. In the latter there is no government, no law, no rights (and duties), and life is miserable for all. Hobbes's theory of law is different from both Bentham and his disciple John Austin. Hobbes thought that states—that is, sovereigns and their laws—possessed authority (see his definition of law and of command, Hobbes 1991/1651, chs. 25–26). But he also thought that states needed to monopolize power in order to be stable and effective, humans being such that without effective enforcement, laws would cease to motivate ("Covenants, without the Sword, are but Words, and of no strength to secure a man at all." Hobbes 1991/1651, ch. 27).

Hobbes thought, like Bentham and Austin, that in the absence of a state, there are no rights or duties. Hobbes's thesis is more radical and his skepticism deeper than Bentham's, who was a moral utilitarian. Hobbes thought that in the absence of a state and system of law, there are no rights or duties, only liberties to do whatever one thought necessary to one's self-preservation. In Hobbes's account there are only states of nature (with no law or claim rights) and commonwealths. Only in the latter do we find law and rights. On Hobbes's view, law and rights require a political society with complex institutions; in the absence of the requisite institutions, there is no law or rights. This means that, outside of a state with a system of law, there can be no conventional rights or duties, no practices that give rise to norms. This is a bold thesis, one that denies the claim made at the outset of this essay that conventions and practices could be sources of rights. So conventions or manners or games such as baseball or even the English common law would not, in Hobbes's view, be sources of rights outside of or independently of an established, stable state. The questions raised here are too complicated to be settled in a short space, but Hobbes's view seems implausible. Consider only that states develop historically quite slowly, and the legal systems we know and live under are the product of centuries of change. Depending on how we characterize a state, it is not clear that states existed in the early centuries of the development of English common law. But what we call England was not a Hobbist state of nature at this time either. This is important. For the Hobbist account, adopted with some changes by Bentham, has room only for states and states of nature. And in the latter there can be no rights. But this picture is historically unrealistic. Medieval Europe, for instance, was organized politically in quite complex ways, none of which is adequately characterized as a state or state of nature (see Morris 1998 and 2011).

Hobbes and Bentham thought that there are no natural claim rights. If we think of natural rights as nonconventional rights that we possess by virtue of certain natural attributes, then the nonexistence of such rights does not entail that there are no rights whatsoever in a state of nature. There could still be *conventional* rights prior to and independently of states and developed legal systems. (Hume's well-known conventionalist account of justice and property can be generalized into an account of rights. See Hume 1978/1739–1740, bk. III, part II, sects. I–II.) Or at least it is not implausible to think so. Hobbes and Bentham conflated natural rights with noninstitutional or nonconventional ones, and this seems to be a serious mistake. Not only may there be natural rights, but there may also be conventional rights which are prior to and independent of states.

We have raised a number of questions about rights, having to do with their nature and the manner in which they are supposed to work, the sources of rights, and a variety of important worries and concern about them. There is much more to be said, and much of it is said in the excellent works listed below.

References

Barnett, R. E. (2006) "The Ninth Amendment: It Means What It Says," *Texas Law Review* 85 (1).

Bentham, J. (1838–1843) "Anarchical Fallacies: Being an Examination of the Declarations of Rights Issued During the French Revolution," in J. Bowring, ed., *The Works of Jeremy Bentham, Volume 2*, Edinburgh: William Tait.

Foot, P. (2002/1958–1959) "Moral Beliefs," in *Virtues and Vices and Other Essays in Moral Philosophy*, Oxford: Clarendon Press, pp. 110–31.

Green, L. (1988) *The Authority of the State*, Oxford: Clarendon Press.

Hart, H. L. A. (1994/1961) *The Concept of Law*, 2nd edition, Oxford: Clarendon Press.

Heath, J. (2008) *Following the Rules: Practical Reasoning and Deontic Constraint*, New York: Oxford University Press.

Hobbes, T. (1991/1651) *Leviathan*, R. Tuck, ed., Cambridge: Cambridge University Press.

Hohfeld, W. N. (1919) *Fundamental Legal Conceptions as Applied in Judicial Reasoning and Other Legal Essays*, New Haven, CT: Yale University Press.

Hume, D. (1978/1739–1740) *A Treatise of Human Nature*, 2nd edition, Oxford: Clarendon Press.

Hurka, T. (1989) "Sumner on Natural Rights," *Dialogue* 28: 117–30.

McClennen, E. F. (2004) "The Rationality of Being Guided by Rules," in A. R. Mele and P. Rawlings, eds., *The Oxford Handbook of Rationality*, Oxford: Oxford University Press, pp. 222–39.

Mill, J. S. (1985/1861) *Utilitarianism*, in J. M. Robson, ed., *The Collected Works of John Stuart Mill, Volume X*, London: Routledge and Kegan Paul.

Morris, C. W. (1998) *An Essay on the Modern State*, Cambridge: Cambridge University Press.

—— (2008) "State Legitimacy and Social Order," in J. Kühnelt, ed., *Political Legitimization Without Morality*, Heidelberg: Springer, pp. 15–32.

—— (2011) "The State," in G. Klosko, ed., *The Oxford Handbook of the History of Political Philosophy*, Oxford: Oxford University Press, pp. 544–60.

Nozick, R. (1974) *Anarchy, State, and Utopia*, New York: Basic Books.

Raz, J. (1999) *Practical Reason and Norms*, New York: Oxford University Press.

Shapiro, S. J. (2001) "Judicial Can't," *Nous* 35: 530–57.

—— (2005) "The Rationality of Rule-Guided Behavior: A Statement of the Problem," Yale Faculty Scholarship Series, paper 1337, http://digitalcommons.law.yale.edu/fss_papers/1337.

Simmons, A. J. (1993) *On the Edge of Anarchy: Locke, Consent, and the Limits of Society*, Princeton: Princeton University Press.

—— (2001a) "Philosophical Anarchism," in A. J. Simmons, *Justification and Legitimacy: Essays on Rights and Obligations*, Cambridge: Cambridge University Press, pp. 102–21.

—— (2001b) "Legitimacy," in L. C. Becker and C. B. Becker, *Encyclopedia of Ethics, Volume 2*, 2nd edition, New York and London: Routledge, pp. 960–63.

—— (2005) "The Duty to Obey and Our Natural Moral Duties," in C. H. Wellman and A. J. Simmons, *Is There a Duty to Obey the Law?*, Cambridge: Cambridge University Press, pp. 93–196.

Wenar, L. (2011) "Rights," in E. N. Zalta, ed., *The Stanford Encyclopedia of Philosophy*, http://plato.stanford. edu/entries/rights.

Williams, B. (1981) "Persons, Character, and Morality," in B. Williams, *Moral Luck*, Cambridge: Cambridge University Press.

Further Reading

For further reading, see: R. G. Frey, ed. (1984) *Utility and Rights*, Minneapolis: University of Minnesota Press; G. W. Rainbolt (2006) *The Concept of Rights*, Dordrecht: Springer; A. J. Simmons (1992) *The Lockean Theory of Rights*, Princeton: Princeton University Press; H. Steiner (1994) *An Essay on Rights*, Oxford and Cambridge, Mass.: Basil Blackwell; L. W. Sumner (1987) *The Moral Foundation of Rights*, Oxford: Clarendon Press; J. J. Thomson (1990) *The Realm of Rights*, Cambridge, Mass.: Harvard University Press; J. Waldron, ed. (1987) *Nonsense Upon Stilts: Bentham, Burke, and Marx on the Rights of Man*, London: Methuen; C. Wellman (1997) *An Approach to Rights*, Dordrecht: Kluwer; and L. Wenar (2005) "The Nature of Rights," *Philosophy and Public Affairs* 33: 223–53.

37
DISCRIMINATION AND EQUALITY

Kasper Lippert-Rasmussen

Introduction

Anti-discrimination law is often referred to as "equality law" (Holmes 2005: 185). This is not coincidental. Conceptually, discrimination is tied to inequality. It is impossible to discriminate against someone unless there is some dimension in which the discriminator treats the discriminatee worse than those against whom she does not discriminate (Alexander 1992: 191; Fiss 1976: 109; Gardner 1996: 355; Heinrich 2007: 109). To be sure, for any given conduct that qualifies as discrimination due to adverse treatment in one dimension, there may be other dimensions in which the discriminator treats the discriminatee equally with others. A charity organization that serves pork chops to Muslim and Christian homeless alike treats them unequally in the dimension "serving food not prohibited by the recipient's religion." Yet, it also treats homeless people equally in the dimension "type of food, gastronomically speaking, served to recipients." The latter does not show that the charity does not discriminate. It simply reflects that any action admits of an endless number of true descriptions.

Morally, it is natural to assume that discrimination is wrong, at least in part, in virtue of the inequality it involves. Moreover, if discrimination is necessarily pro tanto wrong, it must be wrong in virtue of its essential properties and unequal treatment is one such property. Yet, clearly it is not wrong per se to treat some worse than others in some dimensions, e.g., a judge who releases the innocent and convicts the guilty does not act wrongly. Hence, friends of an equality-based account of the wrongness of discrimination must specify the specific kind of unequal treatment that wrongful discrimination involves.

Equality-based accounts of the wrongness of discrimination differ from non-equality-based ones. One such account says that discrimination is wrong, when it is, because of the harmful effects it typically involves, where harm is determined relative to how well off the discriminatee would have been in the absence of discrimination (and not relative to, say, how well off the discriminatee would have been had everyone been treated equally. The subset of harm-based accounts that identifies harm through such an equality-fixed baseline—i.e., someone is harmed if she is worse off than she would have been had she been treated equally, e.g., by not having been subjected to discrimination, nepotism, etc.—is a species of equality-based accounts.) Since it is not a necessary property of discrimination that it harms anyone, harm-based accounts imply the possibility of non-wrongful discrimination. Unless, of course, they build into the very definition of discrimination that it is *wrongful*, harmful differential treatment. I favor a harm-based account of the wrongness of discrimination (Lippert-Rasmussen 2006). This account has problems of its own, but these are not my concern here.

A given token of discrimination may be wrong for equality as well as non-equality-related reasons. My focus is exclusively on the former. There are two ways, at least, in which the wrongness of discrimination could be explained on egalitarian grounds. Derek Parfit distinguishes between telic and deontic egalitarianism. According to the former view, "it is in itself bad if some people are worse off" than others through no choice or fault of their own (Parfit 1998: 3). According to the latter, "it is not in itself bad if some people are worse off than others" (Parfit 1998: 6). While it is often unjust that some are worse off than others, deontic egalitarians do not object to the inequality itself: "What is unjust, and therefore bad, is not strictly the state of affairs, but the way in which it was produced" (Parfit 1998: 7). It is not necessary for the inequality-producing process being unjust that it led to outcome inequality (Lippert-Rasmussen 2007a). Hence, deontic egalitarians may find discriminatory acts unjust even if, ironically, they result in discriminators and discriminatees being equally well off. Telic egalitarians may have no complaints in such a case.

Parfit says little about which features of the production of an outcome make it unjust. I assume that deontic egalitarians think that it is the feature of some people treating others unequally in a way that is morally wrongful. This needs elaboration and I return to it shortly. Suffice here to say that subscribing to the formal principle of equality that people who are not relevantly different should be treated equally does not make one a deontic egalitarian.

Telic egalitarianism implies that discrimination is not morally bad or wrong as such. Undoubtedly, when institutionalized and widely practiced discrimination results in large groups of people ending up worse off than others through no choice and fault of their own, telic egalitarianism condemns this outcome. However, discrimination *may* not result in anyone's ending up worse off through no choice or fault of their own (cf. Holmes 2005: 193). First, discrimination against a certain group may counterbalance non-choice advantages that it enjoys such that discrimination restores equality, in which case telic egalitarianism deems discrimination instrumentally good in one respect, e.g., ethnic prejudice against a certain wealthy group of immigrants may counterbalance inequalities in educational opportunities resulting from this immigrant group's superior financial situation.

Second, suppose people are only discriminated against on the basis of properties they have through their own choice (or fault); suppose that, due to pharmaceutical inventions one can choose one's sexuality through drugs; and suppose that people who are discriminated against end up worse off than others. If discrimination on the basis of sexuality is wrong in such a case, telic egalitarianism may fail to explain it.

It might be suggested that telic egalitarians should be concerned not with outcomes, but with opportunities. However, as the case of wrongful age discrimination reminds us, wrongful discrimination can coexist with equality of opportunities where this is cashed out in terms of the Rawlsian requirement that "any two persons with the same native talent and the same ambition should have the same prospects of success in the competition for positions of advantage that distribute primary social goods" (Arneson 1999: 73; cf. Rawls 1971: 66, 72). Equality of opportunity so understood fails to assess negatively wrongful discriminatory patterns of socialization that cause, say, gender differences in ambitions. Also, like with equality of outcome, wrongful discrimination against a certain group could in principle counterbalance its better opportunities in nondiscrimination dimensions.

Some have argued that telic egalitarians misconstrue the point of equality (Anderson 1999; Miller 1998; Scheffler 2003). It is not that everyone has equal amounts of some good but that individuals relate to one another as equals. This is incompatible with various forms of domination, servility and oppression, but it does not require distributive equality, i.e., in an egalitarian, democratic society not so well-off people need not see themselves as socially inferior to well-off people despite the latter people's superior income and fortune. In response, Fleurbaey (2008: 245) has argued that on a suitably permissive understanding of the relevant good, this view is a species of telic egalitarianism, say, one that deems inequality of social standing to be bad. Whatever the merits of this response, it is important here that while, historically, discrimination has often generated social hierarchies, it may subsist together with their absence and yet seem morally objectionable. Suppose we live in a multiethnic society in which there are ten equally powerful ethnic groups. Members of each group discriminate against members of all other groups such that everyone is equally subjected to ethnic discrimination and no ethnic group dominates the others. Here discrimination does not translate into "highly visible and morally irrelevant differences into systematic social disadvantage" (Sunstein 1994: 2411), thereby violating any anti-caste considerations: no group is disadvantaged relative to any other and no citizen is a second-class citizen. If discrimination in this scenario is morally wrong, a concern for the absence of social hierarchy cannot explain it. So let us turn to the other of Parfit's two main egalitarian categories, deontic egalitarians.

Deontic egalitarians hold that discrimination is unjust to the extent that it involves treating others unequally in a way that is morally wrongful. There are a number of ways in which discrimination may be thought to do so. First, some egalitarians have held a mental state-focused position according to which a discriminator acts unjustly if her differential treatment of others reflects what I will call an inegalitarian mental state, e.g., a belief to the effect that people do not have equal moral status. Second, others share with mental accounts the focus on the lesser moral status expressed through the discriminatory act but think that what matters morally is that the unequal treatment is objectively, i.e., independently of the discriminator's mental states, demeaning and, thus, clashes with equality of moral status. Third, some believe that discrimination involves unfairness in that it treats the claims of different individuals unequally and that this is what makes discrimination wrong (cf. Broome 1994: 37; Halldenius 2005: 456). These accounts do not exhaust the logical space of possible deontic egalitarian accounts, but they all explain the wrongness of discrimination in a way that involves an essential reference to the ideal of equality.

I focus on the first two deontic accounts: in part because they have been most fully developed in the literature on discrimination; in part because they seem well placed to explain the wrongness of some of the most repugnant forms of discrimination. More specifically, I focus on Larry Alexander's and Deborah Hellman's deontic egalitarian accounts of the wrongness of certain forms of discrimination. My aim is to show why, despite their ingenuity and insightfulness, neither is satisfactory. More generally, I am skeptical of egalitarian mental state- and objective meaning-based accounts of wrongness. Some of my objections to Alexander's and Hellman's accounts apply to these accounts in general.

One caveat: whether Alexander's or Hellman's accounts are correct bears indirectly only on how discrimination should be regulated legally. First, there is no direct inference from the immorality of certain actions to what legal status they, morally speaking, ought to have and, second, while their accounts have implications for which kinds of differential treatment constitute wrongful discrimination, their primary focus lies on what makes differential treatment wrongful discrimination. In many contexts, the fact that an action is morally wrong is one, albeit by no means a decisive, reason for making it illegal. However, nothing below hinges on this assumption.

Discrimination Based on Beliefs About Inferior Moral Worth

Mental-state accounts contend that discrimination is wrong, when it is, because it reflects a certain morally objectionable mental state on behalf of the discriminator. The idea that mental states determine the wrongness of an action is well known outside the context of discrimination. For instance, the doctrine of double effect holds that actions involving some bad effect may be permissible when this effect is merely foreseen but not when it is intended. The doctrine is often invoked to explain why terrorism differs morally from conventional warfare involving a similar number of innocent casualties (McMahan 2009: 346). More generally, Anderson and Pildes have defended the view that "what makes an action morally right depends on whether it expresses the appropriate valuations of . . . persons" where "'Expression' refers to the ways that an action or a statement (or any other vehicle of expression) manifests a state of mind" (Anderson and Pildes 2000: 1504, 1506).

There is a wide range of objectionable mental states which an account of the wrongness of discrimination may invoke. For instance, mental-state accounts may ground the wrongness of discrimination in noncognitive states such as hostility or in cognitive states such as the belief that members of a certain group are inferior. More generally, mental-state accounts vary in terms of which propositional attitudes—e.g., believing, expecting, hoping, doubting—and in terms of which contents—i.e., object, say, "I will win the lottery"—believed, expected, hoped for or doubted, etc.—they contend are the loci of the wrongness of discrimination. Also, they may vary in terms of how they flesh out the relation of reflection that obtains between the mental state and the relevant discriminatory action.

Not all mental-state accounts are concerned with equality. For instance, Richard Arneson proposes that: "Discrimination that is intrinsically morally wrong occurs when an agent treats a person identified as being of a certain type differently than she otherwise would have done because of unwarranted animus or prejudice against persons of that type" (Arneson 2006: 779). A person who treats Copts differently than Muslims because of unwarranted animus or prejudice against Copts responds differently to members of those two groups. But she might have no mental states to the effect that Copts have lesser worth than Muslims, e.g., because she is an unreflective person who does not bother to rationalize her aversions. Similarly, Matt Cavanagh (2002: 166) believes that discrimination which involves treating people "with unwarranted contempt" is wrong. Being contemptuous need not clash with equality of moral status. I can feel contempt for someone, say, whom I consider a superior person, on account of how she has squandered her talents. Similarly, I may think of an animal as having a lower moral status and yet harbor no contempt for it. With this broader picture as background, I turn to Alexander's account.

In an article which deservedly has become a standard reference in the last two decades' writings on discrimination, Alexander observes that "discrimination is not one thing, but many" (Alexander 1992: 153). Most forms of discrimination are wrong, when they are, for contingent consequentialist reasons. However, in his view one species of discrimination is intrinsically wrong for a different and Kantian reason, namely discrimination "premised on the belief that some types of people are morally worthier than others" (Alexander 1992: 161), where for some to have greater moral worth than others is for them to merit "greater moral concern" than others (Alexander 1992: 160). Presumably, by "intrinsically wrong" Alexander does not rule out the possibility that, all things considered, some such actions may be morally permissible, e.g., because they minimize the overall number of such intrinsically wrongful acts.

One attractive feature of this suggestion is that some paradigm forms of racist discrimination have involved this belief, e.g., the belief held by the Nazis that Jews are sub-human. It is unclear, however, that all paradigm forms of discrimination involve beliefs about unequal moral status. Paternalistic sexism holds that men and women have different functions, but *in principle* this is compatible with the view that they have equal moral worth. Similarly, discrimination against disabled persons often involves various forms of condescending treatment, but those who engage in it hardly believe that disabled people merit less moral concern than the able-bodied.

Alexander suggests three reasons why this kind of discrimination is intrinsically morally wrong. First, he submits that the underlying biases "are intrinsically morally wrong because they reflect incorrect moral judgments" (Alexander 1992: 161). However, it is not in general true that, because one acts on the basis of false beliefs, one's action is intrinsically morally wrong. If I hold the false but justified belief that people like myself are less inclined to act altruistically, and treat people who are different from me better than myself for this reason, my act is ill informed but it is not intrinsically morally wrong.

Second, commenting on Nazi biases, Alexander writes: "Their biases were intrinsically morally wrong because Jews are clearly not of lesser moral worth than Aryans" (Alexander 1992: 158–59). This suggests an explanation that is more specific than the previous one. Discrimination is not intrinsically morally wrong simply because it involves a bias based on a false belief, but because it involves a bias that is based on a belief that is *clearly* (presumably, even to the discriminator) false. But again: acting on the basis of beliefs that are clearly false is not wrong in general. Suppose I believe that I deserve less than others. Suppose, moreover, that this belief is clearly false and yet I act on it. Setting aside controversial moral duties to self, here my act is based on a clearly false belief without being morally wrong. One might suspect that there is some aspect of the mind of the mental states of the Nazi bias holder that explains why she fails to grasp the easily accessible truth of equal moral worth, but then it is this mental state that renders her discriminatory act morally wrong, not her failing to believe a clearly true proposition.

Third, one might emphasize a different aspect of the previous citation, namely that the relevant falsehood concerns relative moral worth. Such false beliefs might plausibly be held to constitute "a failure to show the moral respect due to the recipient" (Alexander 1992: 159). The underlying thought seems to be the Kantian one that persons have a duty to respect one another's moral worth and that in holding a person to have less moral worth than others, one violates this duty. This is the most promising interpretation of Alexander's view and one I explore below. Specifically, I focus on three important questions that it raises. First, why is the content of the belief that renders discrimination intrinsically morally wrong one that concerns unequal moral worth and that only? Second, why is the only relevant propositional attitude to this content the attitude of believing? Third, how must the relevant belief relate to the relevant discriminatory act for it to be intrinsically wrong? I address these questions in the order just listed.

Moral worth is a very Kantian notion. Roughly, the idea is that in virtue of being a rational, self-conscious, self-legislating individual one should be treated as an end in oneself and not merely as a means (Kant 1987/1785: 91). Non-personal animals like mice are not rational beings and, thus, do not have moral worth. Accordingly, they can be treated very differently from persons. Rational beings may vary in terms of how rational they are, but variations do not affect their moral worth. Nor does what they do affect their level of moral worth (but see Alexander 1992: 200).

Judging someone to have moral worth is one species of assessment of someone's moral status. Alternatively, one might assess people's Aristotelian virtuousness or deem persons morally more or less deserving. One has moral worth regardless of what one does, but this is true of neither virtue nor moral deservingness. Suppose a discriminator rejects the notion of moral worth, but assesses people in terms of moral desert and discriminates against Swedes on the basis of the clearly false belief that Swedes are less morally deserving than Danes. On Alexander's account, unlike discrimination based on a clearly false judgment about moral worth this does not amount to an intrinsically wrongful type of discrimination. Yet, this difference needs to be explained. Given that discrimination manifesting biases based on clearly false beliefs about unequal *moral worth* renders discrimination intrinsically wrong, why is discrimination that manifests biases based on clearly false beliefs about unequal *moral status in general* not intrinsically morally wrong?

Alexander does not address this question. He mentions the case of a bias in favor of the "morally virtuous" over the "morally vicious" and suggests that this bias may be "morally required" (Alexander 1992: 159). If so, discrimination manifesting such a justified bias could hardly be intrinsically wrong. But this does not speak to the question of discrimination manifesting unjustified biases rooted in clearly false assessments of the relative moral virtue of different socially salient groups.

Second, turning to the issue of propositional attitudes, suppose Alexander's discriminator does not *believe* but *assumes* that Jews have less moral worth than non-Jews and acts on this basis. Provided that it can be disrespectful to make such an assumption, as indeed it can, it is unclear why this agent's discriminatory act may not be intrinsically wrong in the same way as that of the agent who actually holds the relevant belief about unequal moral worth. Moreover, suppose the agent believes that Jews have the same worth as non-Jews, but wishes that this will be different in the future, say, through a reduction of the cognitive powers of all Jews to a level below the threshold necessary for personhood. If Alexander is right, it is difficult to see why actions motivated by such desires are not disrespectful too, although, in a perverse way, they manifest recognition that the discriminatees *have* equal moral worth. Is it not disrespectful to want to reduce a rational being to a nonrational being? Indeed, if, as some claim, acts can be disrespectful irrespective of their being manifestations of disrespectful mental states (Glasgow 2009: 83–84), Alexander's account should be developed in a way that makes it cross the boundaries of mental-state accounts to allow for disrespectful, intrinsically wrongful acts of discrimination that reflect no disrespectful mental state, e.g., carelessly using a gesture that, by convention, signals disrespect.

Third, let me finally address the issue of how the relevant false belief must be related to discrimination for it to make the latter intrinsically morally wrong. My critique here will be different from the two previous ones. Their general thrust was that Alexander's account should be broadened to include other disrespectful contents and propositional attitudes. Now my critique will question the focus on mental states in the first place.

One can hold a clearly false belief about unequal moral status and yet disregard this belief in one's deliberations about how to act. A neo-Nazi bureaucrat may treat a Jewish citizen no differently from an impartial, nonprejudiced bureaucrat. Indeed she may treat her better than non-Jewish citizens for fear of complaints of discrimination and consequent dismissal. Yet, in both cases the agent acts with no less disrespect than in the case where she actually discriminates against those whom she believes to have lesser moral worth. Hence, if what renders discriminatory acts intrinsically morally wrong is the disrespect these involve, there could be nondiscriminatory acts, or even acts of discrimination *in favor of*, that are just as intrinsically wrong as discriminatory acts.

Moreover, there could be discriminatory acts that are not based on the relevant belief about unequal moral worth. Suppose the neo-Nazi bureaucrat manages to set aside her belief about unequal status when dealing with citizens, but that her conduct is influenced by an unconscious bias triggered by some property other than being Jewish where, however, this property is one many Jews have and which is causally unconnected to the bureaucrat's belief about unequal moral worth. The question is: is the bureaucrat's discriminatory act intrinsically wrong in the way it would have been had it been based on her belief about unequal moral worth? It is hard to believe that the mere fact that an agent believes that a discriminatee has a lower moral status should render her discriminatory action more wrongful compared to that of an agent who performs exactly the same action and for the same reason, but has no inert belief of the relevant sort. In support of this claim, note that to hold a certain belief it is not required that it is present to the agent's mind at the time of acting. Everything that the former agent thought of, responded to, perceived, felt, etc., at the moment of performing the discriminatory action may be identical to what the latter agent thought of, etc. It is just that if you had asked the former agent if she thought that Jews have a lesser moral worth, she would have said "Yes." This comparison strongly suggests that if a judgment of unequal worth has no causal influence on the agent's action, it does not render it wrong.

So suppose this is correct. We should now compare two agents, both of whom have the relevant beliefs about unequal moral status—we can even imagine that the belief comes to the mind of both agents at the time of acting; one acts partly on the basis of this belief whereas the other one, like the neo-Nazi bureaucrat a few paragraphs ago, does not. Apart from that their actions are identical in all other respects. Clearly, we would want to hold both agents accountable for their disrespectful beliefs of unequal worth and for whatever flaws in their deliberation these beliefs result in, but it is unclear that we might ever want to say that one of them acted wrongly, whereas the other did not (cf. Scanlon 2008: 22). If so, beliefs about unequal moral worth are irrelevant to permissibility (which is not to say that it is not relevant to other types of assessment or other objects of assessment, e.g., the discriminatee's moral character or the quality of the agent's deliberations).

As further support for this conclusion, consider a Nietzschean case of discrimination against the strong by the weak and resentful. Suppose a Norwegian official believes idiosyncratically that Danes merit greater moral concern than Norwegians and resents them for it, which manifests itself in her treating Danes disadvantageously compared to Norwegians. Compare this to a case of a Norwegian treating Danes in exactly the same adverse way because she believes Danes have a lower moral status. To prevent perceived victimhood from influencing our intuitions here, suppose both Norwegian discriminators live equally bad lives on account of their ethnic prejudice. To eliminate any pollution of our intuitions about how the discriminating act might carry different messages depending on the underlying thought, suppose that the official anonymously makes a decision about whether to admit the relevant Danish applicant to a university and identical letters of rejection are sent out in both cases. If Alexander's account is correct, these two cases should differ in terms of wrongness. But it seems they do not. More generally, arguments analogous to the one offered here can be offered against a wider range of mental-state accounts.

My discussion of Alexander's position can be summed up in two conclusions. First, insofar as we accept that discrimination based on beliefs about unequal moral worth is intrinsically wrong, we should allow that discrimination based on other inequality involving mental states, e.g., clearly false beliefs about unequal moral deservingness or desires about unequal moral worth, is intrinsically wrong. Second, it is unclear, however, that the fact that discrimination is rooted in beliefs about unequal moral worth renders it intrinsically wrong. This is neither to deny that it is unjust to discriminate, nor to claim that there is nothing wrong with the character or deliberations of an agent who discriminates on the basis of such a belief. Such claims are open to a friend of the harm-based account.

Discrimination and Demeaning Treatment

I now turn to Hellman's (2008) version of the objective-meaning account. In her view, the mental state of the discriminator is irrelevant to the distinctive wrongfulness of discrimination as is the kind of harm to the discriminatee that it may involve. Objective-meaning accounts hold that this results from the fact that discriminatory acts have a certain morally objectionable, mental state-independent meaning. If, as a dean, I introduce male professors by their title and family name and female professors simply by their first name, this is discriminatory and objectively demeaning to women and, hence, morally wrong. This is so, whatever mental state my actions reflect and however my way of introducing them affects anyone's interests. These factors may add to the wrongness of the discriminatory act, but they do not form the distinctive wrong-making feature of discrimination (Hellman 2008: 17).

Objective-meaning accounts form a large family whose members differ in terms of which objectionable meaning the wrongfulness of discrimination derives from. Here my interest is in accounts according to which the wrongfulness is tied to the relevant discriminatory action's objectively meaning that some kind of inequality between the discriminatee and the discriminator obtains. Moreover, just as the idea that mental states affect wrongfulness is not limited in its scope to acts of discrimination, the idea that the objective meaning of an act determines wrongfulness is not so restricted. Jean Hampton (1988: 52) defends the view that to wrong someone in general is to treat her in a way "that is objectively demeaning."

On Hellman's account, wrongful discrimination is differential treatment that is demeaning to the discriminatee, where an act or omission demeans someone if, and only if, the following two conditions are satisfied. First, the relevant individual is treated as "not fully human" or "not of equal moral worth" (Hellman 2008: 35), debased or degraded (Hellman 2008: 35), and she is not merely insulted but also "put down," diminished and denigrated (Hellman 2008: 29). To demean is to "treat another as a lesser" (Hellman 2008: 29). A demeaning act "expresses that the other is less worthy of concern or respect" (Hellman 2008: 35). Second, the agent who does the demeaning must be in a position of power or have a superior status (Hellman 2008: 35, 57). A boss might demean an employee, but an employee cannot demean her boss, unless she has some employment-unrelated power or status.

Whether these two conditions are satisfied depends on context: "Whether classification demeans depends on the social or conventional meaning of drawing a particular distinction in a particular context" (Hellman 2008: 29, 7). Having a sign on restroom doors saying "Men Only" is not demeaning, whereas a sign saying "White Men Only" would be. This need not be so in all contexts, but in a cultural context where the memory of Jim Crow lingers on, the latter is demeaning even if there is another equally suitable facility with a "Black Men Only" sign on the door. Intentions of the discriminator and the perceptions of the discriminatee are not decisive, if relevant at all, for whether discriminatory acts demean. Similarly, whether the second condition is satisfied depends on "history and the current social status" (Hellman 2008: 14) of the relevant groups of people.

In Hellman's view, discrimination that satisfies these two conditions is demeaning and for that reason wrong, because it clashes with the bedrock principle of equal moral worth. One implication is that it does not even appear to be part of the definition of discrimination that it involves disadvantageous treatment besides carrying a demeaning message. One might treat a discriminatee advantageously—e.g., use more resources in a way that signals one's belief that they have more difficulties learning than others—all things considered and in all respects other than the message that one's treatment of them carries.

Another implication of Hellman's view is this: because the distinctive wrongness of discrimination consists in its objective meaning, in principle, whenever we are faced with wrongful discrimination we may either eliminate the differential treatment or change its objective meaning. Changing social meanings may be unfeasible, e.g., because social meaning is determined by history and even if historical consciousness can change, history cannot. Suppose, however, that we change the social meanings of a society blighted by racist and sexist discrimination such that the relevant differential treatment persisted unchanged to the highest degree compatible with rendering it non-demeaning. On Hellman's account such a society would have eliminated wrongful discrimination.

A third implication of Hellman's account is that demeaning acts of discrimination against people who no longer exist—e.g., members of a certain extinct religious group—may be wrongful in the distinctive way that demeaning acts of discrimination against people who do exist are. A shopkeeper who falsely believes that there are still people around who belong to the persecuted and suppressed religious minority and puts up a sign saying that these people are not welcome in her shop demeans these (now deceased) people. Arguably, no one is harmed (or perhaps even offended), but since (neither) harm (nor offense) plays no role in Hellman's account, she cannot deny that this case involves wrongful discrimination on this ground. Also, it is surely possible to demean people after they have ceased to exist, e.g., many thought that Ward Churchill demeaned those victims of 9/11 working in the twin towers by referring to them as "little Eichmanns."

Before proceeding to my criticisms of Hellman's account, I want to make a friendly amendment. As noted above, she offers many, nonequivalent phrasings of the first condition. For instance, to debase or degrade someone is different from not treating them as fully human. To say of someone that he is not very intelligent may degrade him, but it is not to suggest that he is not fully human. Also, by treating someone as not fully human a deep ecologist may not debase or degrade as in her view there is nothing debased or degraded about not being fully human.

Some of Hellman's phrasings imply that discrimination is not tied to unequal treatment. For instance, she says that demeaning discrimination involves the relevant individual being treated as "not fully human." While this may be demeaning, it need not be discriminatory as is shown by the possibility that one treats all human beings—oneself included—as if they are not fully human. Yet, she writes that "demeaning is an inherently comparative concept" (Hellman 2008: 33). Also, it is unclear what it means to treat someone as not "fully human." Does it mean not treating them as if they belong to the human species? Or does it mean treating them as if they are not persons? Probably only the most extreme forms of discrimination involve treating discriminatees as if either is the case. Accordingly, I shall understand "treating someone as not fully human" in Hellman's sense as treating someone as if she is not of equal moral worth, i.e., X treats Y as not fully human because, given how X treats Z, treating Y in the way X treats Y would be permissible only if Y had lesser equal moral worth than Z. Pedantically, I would add that by the complaint about treating someone as if she is "not of *equal* [my emphasis] worth," strictly speaking, Hellman means the complaint of treating someone as if she is of "*lesser* worth than other people" (and not "higher"). So construed, and if we set aside the hierarchy condition, we have an account that is related to Alexander's in its focus, i.e., lesser moral status. The difference lies in the fact that Alexander concentrates on the beliefs of the discriminator, whereas Hellman focuses on the objective meaning of the differential treatment. Presumably, these two can come apart. An agent can perform an act that has no demeaning objective meaning despite her objectionable mental state, and an agent can perform an act that has an objectionable objective meaning despite her innocent underlying mental state.

Is the objective-meaning account with this friendly amendment satisfactory? No doubt, it is relevant to the wrongfulness of discrimination that it is objectively demeaning. This often results in stigmatic harms (Brest 1976) and for that reason, friends of a harm-based account might accept many of the insights in Hellman's account. However, the issue is whether discriminatory acts are wrongful *simply* because they are demeaning, i.e., independently of any stigmatic harm. I am skeptical of this view and offer five challenges below.

The first is a challenge to the rationale she offers for her account. As noted, Hellman offers various nonequivalent phrasings of the first condition of demeaning discrimination. This reflects a dilemma for Hellman's account. She wants to tie the wrongfulness of demeaning someone to the "bedrock principle of equal moral worth of persons" (Hellman 2008: 30). The advantage is that if the claim that discrimination that demeans is wrong per se follows from a bedrock principle, presumably we can be very confident about the implied principle as well. But if, on the one hand, we interpret this principle in such a way that it has a plausible claim to be a bedrock principle, not many wrongful demeaning acts of discrimination will violate it. If, on the other hand, we interpret it broadly such that any demeaning, discriminatory wrongful acts will violate it, it becomes a very implausible candidate for a bedrock principle.

To illustrate this dilemma, consider the notion of demeaning acts. Acts can be more or less demeaning. For instance, there is a difference between simply ignoring what adolescents say in discussions about politics at family gatherings and in paying slightly less attention to it than what adults say. Both dispositions are demeaning to adolescents and wrongful, but clearly the latter disposition is less demeaning and it would seem shrill to complain that in paying slightly less (or even no) attention to their views, you fail to treat them as having the same worth as other persons. In responding to such a complaint, you might reasonably say that you hold no such view and that many of the other features normally associated with the principle of equal moral worth of persons are features that you think apply to them. So, for instance, you would not consider it less wrong to kill an adolescent than an adult and, in general, you are not less inclined to give deliberative weight to the interests of adolescents than to the interests of adults. While this might show that you do not violate the principle of equal moral worth of persons, it does not get you off the hook with regard to the charge of demeaning adolescents. Hence, you can demean someone without denying their equal moral worth. It follows that if discrimination is differential treatment that is wrong because it demeans, wrongful discrimination need not involve denying the equal moral worth of discriminatees. But this flatly contradicts Hellman's account.

To avoid this challenge we might expand our notion of equal moral worth such that paying slightly less attention to the expressed political views of teenagers does involve a failure to respect the principle of equal moral worth. This habit is morally wrong, but I doubt that any moral principle which implies this can have the status of a "bedrock principle."

Further support for this skeptical claim about the status of Hellman's basic principle comes from the fact that there are many ways, other than Hellman's, in which one can cash out the equal moral worth of persons. For instance, it might be held to imply that everyone's interests count equally or that everyone should end up unequally well off unless they are responsible for ending up worse off. If, counterfactually and unrealistically (Hellman 2008: 49) but conceptually possible, we were to imagine a scenario in which no one is demeaned but many are much worse off than others in non-demeaning ways through no responsibility of their own, it is hard to see that this conforms better to the principle of equal moral worth of persons than one in which many are objectively demeaned, but in ways they simply do not care about and, let us suppose, are not harmful to them, and no one is worse off than others through no responsibility of their own (cf. Adler 2000, 1462–93; Thomsen forthcoming). And if Hellman makes this claim, the equal moral worth of a person cannot be the relatively uncontroversial "bedrock" moral principle that it is often thought to be.

One might respond that Hellman leaves open the possibility that there are other ways of offending against "the equal moral worth of persons" than through demeaning others (Hellman 2008: 31). Hence, she might agree that the former scenario clashes with the principle of equal moral worth. She might even concede that it does so to a higher degree than the latter scenario. But if so, she cannot claim to identify wrongful discrimination on the basis of which kinds of differential treatment are demeaning (Hellman 2008: 29), because she would have conceded that differential treatment may clash with the principle of equal moral worth, even if it is not demeaning.

To sum up: Hellman's account faces a dilemma. Either we understand the principle of equal moral worth in a rather narrow way that makes it plausible to assert it as a basic moral principle, or we understand it in a very broad way. If we do the former, to the extent possible, it becomes doubtful that it justifies a prohibition on non-harmful acts that, conventionally speaking, are demeaning. Many demeaning acts do not involve denying the equal moral worth of the persons one demeans. If we do the latter, such that all demeaning acts involve denying the equal moral worth of persons, the principle is very controversial and any account of the wrongfulness of discrimination that builds upon it will be correspondingly controversial.

Second, independently of the problem of whether the equal moral worth principle explains the prohibition on demeaning discrimination, there is the problem of epiphenomenality, i.e., while any wrongful act of discrimination is demeaning, some underlying factor explains both the fact that they are wrongful and that they are demeaning— the fact that discriminatory acts are demeaning does no explanatory work in relation to the wrongfulness of these acts (Moreau 2010: 177–78). In effect, Hellman's account says that it is impermissible to discriminate because discrimination involves demeaning the discriminatee where this amounts to treating the discriminatee in a way that would be permissible only if she had a lower moral worth than other people, which she does not. But then, presumably, there are facts about her in virtue of which the discriminatory action is impermissible and these facts are those in virtue of which the discriminatory action is impermissible. So, for instance, when South Africa under apartheid treated blacks impermissibly by denying them access to higher education, it treated them in a way that would be permissible only if they had a lower moral status, i.e., they were not persons. Yet, this is not what makes the discriminatory policy wrong. What does make it wrong is, say, that they are persons like other South Africans and that if the latter have access to higher education than so should the former.

Third, if discriminatory actions are wrong in virtue of being demeaning, the question arises of whether all wrongful forms of discrimination carry a demeaning message. If not, at best Hellman's account provides a partial account of the wrongness of discrimination. In fact, many forms of discrimination do not per se seem to involve any objective meaning of lesser moral worth. Forms of indirect discrimination involving job-relevant language tests used for nonsuspect reasons, for instance, might disadvantage immigrants in unjust, but non-demeaning, ways. Here Hellman might concede that this involves wrongful differential treatment because "(s)ometimes institutions or actors have special obligations that derive from their mandates or their roles that require them to employ particular criteria in differentiating among people. Failing to comply with these norms is wrong, but is not the wrong of wrongful discrimination" (Hellman 2008: 137). In Hellman's view, the wrong of wrongful discrimination is that it demeans the discriminatees.

In part, I agree with Hellman's view here, but it involves the concession on her part that different cases of wrongful discrimination are wrongful for different reasons and some cases of wrongful discrimination are not wrongful because they demean. Hence, her account should not be seen as a general account of the wrongfulness of wrongful discrimination, but as a partial account that explains the wrongfulness of an important subclass of cases of wrongful explanation. The aim to provide such an account is perfectly legitimate, but it is less ambitious than that of explaining the wrongfulness of discrimination in general. More importantly for our purposes, it implies that not all forms of wrongful discrimination clash with the equal moral worth of persons.

Fourth, it is problematic to tie discrimination to a failure to "treat those affected as persons of equal moral worth" (Hellman 2008: 7), if we want to allow for wrongful discrimination of nonpersons. Assuming that small children are not yet persons, treating boys and girls differently cannot be accounted for in terms of a failure to respect equal worth deriving from personhood. We might, of course, say that sex discrimination of babies, unlike sex discrimination of persons, is wrong only for indirect reasons, i.e., it amounts to a failure to respect the "inherent dignity and worth" (Hellman 2008: 6) of, say, female persons. But, first, sex discrimination of babies seems wrong independently of a moral concern for existing persons. Second, it is unclear that discrimination against female babies need involve disrespect for female persons. After all, it might conceivably be performed by persons who think female persons have greater moral worth than male persons.

Finally, Hellman's hierarchy requirement is problematic. Take racist hate crimes, where the victim belongs to a group of people which historically has had and presently has a higher status than the group to which the perpetrators belong. One would suppose that if anyone is ever demeaned, a person who is beaten up or killed simply because her assailants believe members of her race have an inferior moral status is demeaned. Hellman seems compelled to say either that this is not so, because it all depends on which race the victim has, or that what matters here is the local hierarchy which was established when the victim was overpowered by her assailants (cf. Blum 2002: 33–52). The former option is problematic on the assumption that it is not morally less wrong to beat up or kill whites simply because of their race than to kill blacks when all other things are equal except for the general facts about history and status. Suppose you hear about a racially motivated crime in some faraway country. Would you inquire whether the victim belonged to a dominant group before you formed a judgment about the wrongfulness of the act? The latter option is problematic but it implies that to demean is something that automatically follows from successfully performing certain discriminatory acts. In any case, it seems that this is not the option Hellman prefers, since she often stresses whether a group is subordinated "in our culture" (Hellman 2008: 37), which suggests that she disregards the local context. The basic problem here is that, offhand, there is no requirement attached to showing "lack of respect for another's equal moral worth" that the one who expresses this lack of respect is in a position of power or higher status. When Hellman writes that "[t]o demean, rather than merely to insult, requires a certain degree of power" (Hellman 2008: 36), she is employing a technical distinction between demeaning and insulting. Moreover, it is unclear that the distinction is morally relevant.

To sum up: Hellman's objective-meaning account of the wrongfulness of discrimination may not be the best one available, e.g., because its conditions of hierarchy and history may be unjustifiable; that the mere fact that an act of discrimination is demeaning is not what explains its wrongness; that the wrongness of demeaning discrimination cannot be based on the bedrock principle of equal worth; and that not all wrongful discriminatory acts are demeaning. I agree fully that in many contexts discrimination *is* demeaning and that it is often wrongful to demean others, because demeaning is often harmful. Indeed, systematically demeaning certain groups will often involve great harm to very many people. But these points are not matters of contention between harm-based accounts and Hellman's and, accordingly, not points that support her account (cf. Adler 2000: 1375, 1377).

Conclusion

One way to tie the wrongness of discrimination to equality is by contending that it derives from treating someone in a way that reflects a lesser moral status, either as a matter of the discriminator's beliefs about the status of the discriminatee or as a matter of the objective meaning of the discriminator's act. I have challenged the two most sophisticated versions of these views, arguing that neither provides a satisfactory account. However, there are other ways of tying the wrongness of discrimination to equality, e.g., by accounting for it in terms of the unequal treatment of the claims of different people. Alternatively, we might think that the wrongness is not to be explained in terms of unequal treatment or resulting inequality, but, say, in terms of the harm to discriminatees (or others) that discrimination involves. These are options to be explored elsewhere (Lippert-Rasmussen 2007b).

Acknowledgments

I thank Andrei Marmor, Søren Flinch Midtgaard, Rasmus Sommer Hansen, Frej KlemThomsen and Suzanne Uniacke for some very helpful comments on earlier drafts of this chapter.

References

Adler, M. (2000) "Expressive Theories of Law: A Skeptical Overview," *University of Pennsylvania Law Review* 148: 1363–1501.

Alexander, L. (1992) "What Makes Wrongful Discrimination Wrong? Biases, Preferences, Stereotypes, and Proxies," *University of Pennsylvania Law Review* 141: 149–219.

Anderson, E. S. (1999) "What Is the Point of Equality?" *Ethics* 109: 287–337.

—— and Pildes, R. H. (2000) "Expressive Theories of Law: A General Restatement," *University of Pennsylvania Law Review* 148: 1503–1575.

Arneson, R. (1999) "Against Rawlsian Equality of Opportunity," *Philosophical Studies* 93: 77–112.

—— (2006) "What Is Wrongful Discrimination?" *San Diego Law Review* 43: 775–807.

Blum, L. (2002)"I'm Not a Racist But . . .": The Moral Quandary of Race, Ithaca, NY: Cornell University Press.

Brest, P. (1976) "In Defense of the Antidiscrimination Principle," *Harvard Law Review* 90: 1–55.

Broome, J. (1994) "Fairness Versus Doing the Most Good," *The Hastings Center Report* 24: 36–39.

Cavanagh, M. (2002) *Against Equality of Opportunity*, Oxford: Clarendon Press.

Fiss, O. M. (1976) "Groups and the Equal Protection Clause," *Philosophy & Public Affairs* 5(2): 107–77.

Fleurbaey, M. (2008) *Fairness, Responsibility, and Welfare*, Oxford: Oxford University Press.

Gardner, J. (1996) "Discrimination as Injustice," *Oxford Journal of Legal Studies* 16(3): 353–67.

Glasgow, J. (2009) "Racism Is Disrespect," *Ethics* 120(1): 64–93.

Halldenius, L. (2005) "Dissecting 'Discrimination,'" *Cambridge Quarterly of Healthcare Ethics* 14: 455–63.

Hampton, J. (1988) "Forgiveness, Resentment and Hatred," in J. G. Murphy and J. Hampton, eds., *Forgiveness and Mercy*, New York: Cambridge University Press, pp. 35–87.

Heinrich, B. (2007) "What Is Discrimination and When Is It Morally Wrong?" *Jahrbuch für Wissenschaft und Ethik* 12: 97–114.

Hellman, D. (2008) *When Is Discrimination Wrong?*, Cambridge, Mass.: Harvard University Press.

Holmes, E. (2005) "Anti-Discrimination Rights Without Equality," *The Modern Law Review* 68(2): 175–94.

Kant, I. (1987/1785) *The Moral Law*, London: Hutchinson.

Lippert-Rasmussen, K. (2006) "The Badness of Discrimination," *Ethical Theory and Moral Practice* 9(2): 167–85.

—— (2007a) "The Insignificance of the Difference between Telic and Deontic Egalitarianism," in N. Holtug and K. Lippert-Rasmussen, eds., *Egalitarianism: New Essays on the Nature and Value of Equality*, Oxford: Oxford University Press, pp. 101–24.

—— (2007b) "Private Discrimination: A Prioritarian, Desert-Accommodating Account," *San Diego Law Review* 43: 817–56.

McMahan, J. (2009) "Intention, Permissibility, Terrorism, and War," *Philosophical Perspectives* 23: 345–72.

Miller, D. (1998) "Equality and Justice," in A. Mason, ed., *Ideals of Equality*, Oxford: Blackwell.

Moreau, S. (2010) "What Is Discrimination?" *Philosophy & Public Affairs* 38(2): 143–79.

Parfit, D. (1998) "Equality and Priority," in A. Mason, ed., *Ideals of Equality*, Oxford: Blackwell.

Rawls, J. (1971) *A Theory of Justice*, Cambridge, Mass.: Harvard University Press.

Scanlon, T. (2008) *Moral Dimensions: Permissibility, Meaning, and Blame*, Cambridge, Mass.: Belknap Press of Harvard University Press.

Scheffler, S. (2003) "What Is Egalitarianism?" *Philosophy and Public Affairs* 31(1): 5–39.

Sunstein, C. (1994) "The Anticaste Principle," *Michigan Law Review* 92(8): 2410–2455.

Thomsen, F. K. (forthcoming) "Discrimination and Disrespect."

Further Reading

For further reading, see: A. Altman (2011) "Discrimination," in E. N. Zalta, ed., *The Stanford Encyclopedia of Philosophy*, http://plato.stanford.edu/archives/spr2011/entries/discrimination (provides an excellent overview over the topic); R. Dworkin (1985) *A Matter of Principle*, Cambridge, Mass.: Harvard University Press (a very important discussion of discrimination and affirmative action); K. Lippert-Rasmussen (2010) "Reaction Qualifications Revisited," 35 *Social Philosophy and Practice* 3: 413–39 (explores discrimination in relation to so-called reaction qualifications); F. Schauer (2003) *Profiles, Probabilities, and Stereotypes*, Cambridge, Mass.: Harvard University Press (offers a comprehensive discussion of statistical discrimination); D. Wasserman (1998) "Discrimination, Concept of," in R. Chadwick, ed., *Encyclopedia of Applied Ethics, Volume 1*, San Diego: Academic Press, pp. 805–13 (a very useful entry); and R. Wasserstrom (1977) "Racism, Sexism, and Preferential Treatment: An Approach to the Topics," *University of California Law Review* 24: 581–615 (a classic).

38

PRIVACY

Judith Wagner DeCew

Much philosophical and legal discussion of the scope and value of privacy is quite recent, and until the past 120 years, privacy protection may have been taken for granted. Nevertheless, the concept of privacy is not new. Historical evidence that privacy has been discussed and valued for centuries is not difficult to find. Perhaps most famous is Aristotle's distinction in *The Politics* (1941) between the *polis*, or political realm, and the *oikos*, or domestic realm. The political realm of governing, open to men only, was deemed by Aristotle to be a public arena, whereas the domestic realm of home and family was viewed by him to be a private arena. This Aristotelian distinction between public and private spheres of life has continued to influence and dominate much of the scholarship on privacy. John Locke provides another well-known example of a historical reference to a public/private distinction. Locke invokes the distinction in the chapter on property in his *Second Treatise on Government* (1988/1690). In the state of nature, he argues, one owns one's own body and yet other property is held in common, or deemed public. When one mixes one's labor with property—harvesting grain or catching fish, for example—that which was held in common becomes one's private property. Although individuals are cautioned to leave "enough and as good" for others, private-property acquisition is heralded by Locke as an appropriate goal. These are two reminders that the concept of privacy has played a prominent role in major philosophical works since ancient times.

As Alan Westin has pointed out, while human beings like to think that their desire for privacy is distinctively human, studies have shown that virtually all animals share a need for privacy by seeking individual seclusion, territoriality or small-group intimacy (Westin 1967). Moreover, Westin argues persuasively that anthropological, sociological and biological literature demonstrates that most cultures around the world mirror these behaviors, and use distance-setting mechanisms to protect a private space to promote individual well-being and small-group intimacy, thereby exhibiting both the value of privacy and the need to preserve it. Although not all societies protect privacy in the same way, in virtually every society individuals engage in patterns of behavior and adopt avoidance rules in order to seek privacy. Cultures that rely on communal living often have religious or other ceremonies where privacy through isolation is provided. When privacy cannot be attained by individuals through physical isolation, people demonstrate ways of finding privacy by turning away or averting their eyes, or by finding psychological ways to protect their private thoughts and sentiments. Westin concludes that privacy is a cross-species and cross-cultural value, and that claims to individual privacy in some form are universal for virtually all societies.

The first serious discussions of the meaning of privacy in the United States developed in the law, as legal protection for privacy was granted and expanded. The initial legal protection of privacy was introduced in tort law. Warren and Brandeis (1890) argued that privacy protection should be established as a legal right to give individuals the right "to be let alone" to protect their "inviolate personality." They urged that protection of individual rights over the person and one's property were already established in common law, and that political, social and economic changes demanded recognition of new rights. Protection against actual bodily injury had been extended to protect against injury attempts, and protection from physical harm was expanded to protect human emotions through slander and libel. Similarly, they thought, new inventions and technology such as the printing press and camera called for a new step to curtail invasions of privacy by newspapers and photography, to protect a general right to the immunity of the person and the right to one's personality, and also to guarantee one's right to control information published in the media about oneself and one's family. Thus they argued that privacy protection was already implicitly protected, could fill gaps left by other remedies such as nuisance, trespass and intentional infliction of emotional distress, and thus should be explicitly recognized as a right to privacy. Arguing that this would not be the addition of a new right, or judicial legislation, they urged it was reasonable to explicitly acknowledge individual rights to keep publicity about oneself and one's likeness unavailable to others—as long as privacy protection did not prohibit publications of general interest protected by freedom of the press, or data on a "public figure" about whom the public might have a right to know some personal information. By 1905 this privacy right to control information about oneself was affirmed and expanded.

Legal theorists worked to articulate the meaning and scope of this tort privacy protection. William L. Prosser (1960) defended privacy but was troubled about the difficulty of such unresolved questions as whether one could have a reasonable expectation of privacy in public spaces, whether information that is part of the public record could still deserve privacy protection many years later and who should count as a "public figure" deserving a lesser expectation of privacy than normal citizens. Later cases and analysis suggest that answers to the first two questions are affirmative (Nissenbaum 2010; *Melvin v. Reid* (1931) 112 Cal. App. 283), and the last question remains a matter of debate. Edward J. Bloustein argued that all privacy wrongs were similar and conceptually linked as ways of protecting an individual's inviolate personality, including an individual's independence, human dignity, integrity and freedom from emotional distress (Bloustein 1964: 39ff). Privacy protection formed the essence required for an individual to be a unique and self-determined being and was the tool needed for protection against intrusions demeaning to individuality and affronts to personal human dignity that can occur in manifold ways.

Other commentators concurred that tort privacy protection could be meaningfully seen as a unitary right protecting one's ability to control information about oneself, yet they provided alternative accounts of the moral value of this type of privacy. Some argued that the right protected one's integrity as a person, as an essential context for the fundamental relations of respect, love, friendship and trust (Fried 1968). On this view, being able to control how much personal information one shares with others is necessary to define oneself and one's values free from undesired impingement by others, and gives one the ability to determine one's distance from others, namely with whom one remains a mere acquaintance, with whom one becomes a friend and with whom one becomes an intimate companion. Philosophers including Stanley I. Benn, Robert Gerstein, James Rachels, Jeffrey Reiman and Richard A. Wasserstrom generally agreed. Benn focused on the need for privacy to protect respect for persons, human dignity and

personal relations free from being the object of scrutiny, and autonomy from social pressures to conform—a sphere of privacy as a necessary condition for one's personality to
bloom and thrive (Benn 1971). Gerstein emphasized privacy as required for intimacy,
without uninvited intrusions that would lead to a chilling effect (Gerstein 1978). He
argued that one cannot "lose" oneself in an intimate relationship if one is constantly
worried about being overheard or put under surveillance. Rachels (1975) and Wasserstrom (1978) endorsed the view that privacy is necessary for the development of different relationships, and Reiman (1976) developed privacy as fundamental for intimacy
and personhood, as a social ritual by which an individual's moral title to existence is
confirmed.

Despite the well-established protection of tort privacy to control information about
oneself in the courts, and the almost universal acceptance of the value of informational privacy by the populace, it has been persuasively argued that the U.S. (and many
countries in Asia) has developed a limited system of privacy protection that focuses on
self-regulation within industry and government so that personal information is readily
available. In contrast, the European Union (EU) and others have adopted an alternative
vision highlighting consumer protection and individual privacy against the economic
interests of firms and public officials (Newman 2008). The EU's Data Protection Directive of 1995, now adopted in some form by all 27 EU nations, contains comprehensive
rules with privacy commissioners or agencies empowered to enhance individual privacy
protection, requiring that personal information not be collected or used for purposes
other than those initially intended without individual consent, etc., despite the challenges of the September 11, 2001 terrorist attacks. This contrasts sharply with the U.S.
approach allowing entities such as insurance companies and employers ample access to
personal information, given a lack of governmental support for privacy legislation and
a patchwork of privacy guidelines. The U.S. has generally stood behind efficiency and
laissez-faire arguments that business and government need unfettered access to personal
data to guarantee economic growth and national security. In contrast, the EU has sent
a coherent signal that privacy has critical value in a robust information society because
citizens will only participate in an online environment if they feel their privacy is guaranteed against ubiquitous business and government surveillance.

A second major way in which privacy protection has evolved in the United States
is through the Fourth Amendment: "The right of the people to be secure in their persons, houses, papers, and effects, against unreasonable searches and seizures, shall not
be violated . . ." This is clearly related to privacy in tort law, as an unreasonable search
or seizure is one way of gaining personal information. Initial privacy protection under
this amendment relied on the literal wording from the Bill of Rights. Thus information
gained from wiretaps outside of houses involved no search and no seizure, and the language of the amendment could not be extended to wiretaps (*Olmstead v. U.S.* (1928)
277 U.S. 438). This interpretation was overruled in *Katz v. U.S.* ((1967) 389 U.S. 347),
judging that evidence obtained through an electronic listening and recording device in
public was disallowed, even though there was no physical entrance into the area. The
judgment favored an expectation of privacy even in a public place; it argued that Fourth
Amendment privacy is not just about physical intrusion but protects people and not
places. Brandeis's famous privacy argument won the day: the Constitution recognizes
the significance of one's spiritual nature, feelings and intellect, and seeks to protect
Americans in their beliefs, thoughts, emotions and sensations, prohibiting unjustifiable governmental intrusion upon the privacy of the individual no matter what means

are employed. This second type of privacy protection from the Fourth Amendment has endured but may become controversial. Recent cases involving thermal-imaging devices challenged privacy, and other new technologies used intrusively will continue to test staunch Fourth Amendment privacy safeguards.

A third type of privacy protection has developed in constitutional law. In *Griswold v. Connecticut* ((1965) 381 U.S. 479), the majority opinion defended a married couple's right to get information and instruction about birth control, and in the process first announced that despite there being no word "privacy" in the Constitution, this concept could be defended as a constitutional right to privacy. The majority defended the right to privacy as being older than the Bill of Rights, defended marriage as an enduring, sacred and intimate relation and association and defended one's home as a special and private area. They cited famous cases they viewed as precedents—concerning personal decisions about one's home, family and marriage, including the right to association, rights to educate one's children as one chooses, rights to decide about a child's study in private school, protection against mandatory sterilization and more. One can recognize an insight in the reasoning. There is no right not to be assaulted articulated in the Constitution, for example, but it is surely protected and deemed to be a basic right. There is good reason to believe that the founding fathers took privacy within marriage and family to be so fundamental that they saw no reason to mention it explicitly.

Nevertheless, the constitutional right to privacy has been harshly criticized by Judge Robert Bork (1990), philosopher William Parent (1983a, 1983b) and others. Perhaps most seriously, this third type of constitutional privacy protection has been viewed by some as not being about privacy at all. On one hand, these critics reject defense of the right as having no justifiable legal grounds as a privacy right but only a defense of liberty or autonomy. On the other hand, the right has been characterized as being overly vague, so that it is unclear what exactly it protects and what it does not. Regarding the first complaint, it has been successfully argued in reply that while we have multiple individual liberties such as freedom of expression, many do not seem to be about anything particularly personal or related to the types of concerns we might be willing and able to see as privacy issues. If so, then liberty is a broader concept than privacy and privacy claims are a subset of claims to liberty. Many philosophical commentators have supported this view that privacy protects freedom or liberty, and that privacy protection gains for us freedom to define ourselves and our relations to others (Schoeman 1984, 1992; Fried 1968; Reiman 1976).

A moving account of understanding privacy as a necessary and an indispensable condition for freedom comes from a literary quotation from Milan Kundera:

> But one day in 1970 or 1971, with the intent to discredit Prochazka, the police began to broadcast these conversations [with Professor Vaclav Cerny, with whom he liked to drink and talk] as a radio serial. For the police it was an audacious, unprecedented act. And, surprisingly: it nearly succeeded; instantly Prochazka *was* discredited: because in private, a person says all sorts of things, slurs friends, uses coarse language, acts silly, tells dirty jokes, repeats himself, makes a companion laugh by shocking him with outrageous talk, floats heretical ideas he'd never admit in public, and so forth. Of course, we all act like Prochazka, in private we bad-mouth our friends and use coarse language; that we act different in private than in public is everyone's most conspicuous experience, it is the very ground of the life of the individual; curiously, this obvious

fact remains unconscious, unacknowledged, forever obscured by lyrical dreams of the transparent glass house, it is rarely understood to be the value one must defend beyond all others. Thus only gradually did people realize (though their rage was all the greater) that the real scandal was not Prochazka's daring talk but the rape of his life; they realized (as if by electric shock) that private and public are two essentially different worlds and that respect for that difference is the indispensable condition, the sine qua non, for a man to live free; that the curtain separating these two worlds is not to be tampered with, and that curtain-rippers are criminals. And because the curtain-rippers were serving a hated regime, they were unanimously held to be particularly contemptible criminals.

(Kundera 1984: 260–61)

The analogies between Kundera's scenario and electronic surveillance and street cameras common in society today are clear. There is further evidence that privacy and liberty are distinct concepts, that liberty is a broader notion and that privacy is essential for protecting liberty. We have many forms of liberty unrelated to what we might value as private and inappropriate for government intervention for personal reasons. The right to travel from state to state without a passport, for example, seems to be a freedom far different from the freedom to make choices about personal and intimate concerns about one's body—for example, the use of contraception. The U.S. Supreme Court has recognized this, calling the constitutional privacy cases those about an "individual interest in making certain kinds of important decisions" (*Whalen v. Roe* (1977) 429 U.S. 589).

However this philosophical reply about the relationship between privacy and liberty does not address the second critique about the vagueness of the right. The constitutional right to privacy has protected information and access to birth control, the right of couples to choose the marriage partner of their choice regardless of race, the right of an individual to view pornographic materials in the privacy of his or her home (as long as there is no production or distribution of the material), abortion rights and ultimately the right of individuals—gay or straight—to engage in consenting adult sexual intimacy in their own homes, striking down anti-sodomy statutes. While these sorts of decisions are admittedly somewhat varied, the question is, what "kinds of important decisions" are worthy of being protected? The Court at one point said that the constitutional right to privacy protects certain decisions about home, procreation, family and marriage, and has added that it covers certain personal decisions about one's lifestyle.

The problem is trying to articulate what exactly are the interests protected by privacy concerns and how they may relate to concerns about freedom, intimacy and self-development. Unfortunately this is a serious and intransigent difficulty. One approach has been to dismiss privacy as a philosophically important concept. Judith Jarvis Thomson's famous critique of privacy in this sense is a reductionist view that there is no need for a right to privacy because all talk of privacy can be reduced to talk of rights to property and to bodily security and perhaps other rights (Thomson 1975: 295ff). Thomson's account, however, has been widely and amply criticized by Thomas Scanlon (1975: 315), James Rachels, Jeffrey Reiman, Julie Inness (1992) and others who have argued that it is just as likely that the reverse is true, and rights to property and bodily security can be derived from a more fundamental right to privacy.

Yet it has not been easy for philosophers to provide clear guidelines on the positive side of understanding what privacy protects and why it is important. There has been consensus that the significance of privacy is almost always justified for the individual interests it protects, most importantly protections of freedom and autonomy in a liberal democratic society (Reiman 2004; Roessler 2005). Philosophers have argued that it does seem reasonable to view a subset of liberty cases as privacy cases, namely those which involve choices or decisions about one's body, marriage, intimate relationships and lifestyle (Schoeman 1992; DeCew 1997). Schoeman eloquently defended the importance of privacy for protection of self-expression and social freedom. More recent literature has extended this view and has focused on the value of privacy not merely for the individual interests it protects, but also for its irreducible social value. Concerns over the accessibility and retention of electronic communications and the expansion of camera surveillance have led commentators to focus attention on loss of individual privacy as well as privacy protection with respect to the state and society (Reiman 2004; Solove 2008; Nissenbaum 2010).

Priscilla Regan writes, for example:

> I argue that privacy is not only of value to the individual, but also to society in general. . . . Privacy is a *common value* in that all individuals value some degree of privacy and have some common perceptions about privacy. Privacy is also a *public value* in that it has value not just to the individual as an individual or to all individuals in common but also to the democratic political system. Privacy is rapidly becoming a *collective value* in that technology and market forces are making it hard for any one person to have privacy without all persons having a similar minimum level of privacy.
>
> (Regan 1995: 213, her italics)

According to Daniel Solove, "By understanding privacy as shaped by the norms of society, we can better see why privacy should not be understood solely as an individual right. . . . Instead, privacy protects the individual because of the benefits it confers on society." Moreover, "the value of privacy should be understood in terms of its contribution to society" (Solove 2008: 98, 171fn). Solove believes that privacy fosters and encourages the moral autonomy of citizens, a central requirement of governance in a democracy. One way of understanding these comments—that privacy not only has intrinsic and extrinsic value to individuals, but also has instrumental value to society— is to recognize that these views have been developed from earlier philosophical writings (Fried, Rachels, Schoeman) on the value of privacy, which have noted that privacy heightens respect for individual autonomy in decision-making for self-development and individual integrity and human dignity, and that privacy enhances the value of various social roles and relationships that contribute to a functioning society. According to this contemporary scholarship, privacy norms help regulate social relationships such as intimate relations, family relationships and professional relationships, including those between a physician and a patient, a teacher and a student, a lawyer and a client and so on. Thus privacy enhances social interaction on a variety of levels, and in this way enhances intimacy, self-development and the ability to present ourselves in public as we wish. According to Solove, a society without respect for privacy for oneself and others becomes a "suffocating society" (Solove 2008: 15; cf. Kundera, supra).

It may be messy and difficult to find adequate words to express just what privacy governs, and it is understandable that some still believe the term "privacy" is too vague and not well enough articulated. Consider, however, Ronald Dworkin's observation about another general concept: "Equality is a popular but mysterious political ideal.

People can become equal (or at least more equal) in one way with the consequence that they become unequal (or more unequal) in others. . . . It does not follow that equality is worthless as an ideal" (Dworkin 1981: 185). Similarly with the ambiguity and vagueness of liberty (positive vs. negative, freedom of expression, etc.): it may protect a range of different but related interests; it does not follow that it is worthless as an ideal. These concepts, like privacy, are crucial for understanding our role as social beings and for protecting values fundamental to living lives free from various unacceptable governmental and individual intrusions and surveillance.

Nevertheless, the concern about just what privacy protects, and an understanding of privacy's value for individuals as well as society, leads to additional difficulties about understanding the boundaries between the private and the public in problematic cases, and in particular the darker side of privacy raised by feminist critiques of privacy. Here, the lingering effects of Aristotle's distinction between the public political and private domestic spheres continue to be damaging. If privacy protects individual intimacy and family relationships, it is important to ask whether it is possible to defend privacy staunchly in the face of familiar objections to privacy protection based on feminist critiques that privacy has been used, and perhaps still is, to shield male dominance in family relations.

The feminist critique of privacy has been discussed by many, perhaps most famously by Catharine MacKinnon. Nevertheless, as Ruth Gavison and Carole Pateman have made clear, there is no single or privileged version of the feminist critique of privacy and it is difficult to clarify what the feminist critique really is (Gavison 1992; Pateman 1989). MacKinnon begins by pointing out that the state ensures a private sphere that secures "inviolable personality" and "autonomy of control over the intimacies of personal identity" by centering its self-restraint on the body and home, especially the bedroom. "By staying out of marriage and the family—essentially meaning sexuality, that is, heterosexuality—from contraception through pornography to the abortion decision, the law of privacy proposes to guarantee individual bodily integrity, personal exercise of moral intelligence, and freedom of intimacy" (MacKinnon 1989: 187). But, she continues, women's rights to access those values have not been guaranteed, because this privacy protection assumes that women, like men, are free and equal, an assumption MacKinnon finds patently false. Thus privacy protection is one more instance where the law fails to account for the preexisting oppression and inequality of women. She writes:

> For women the measure of the intimacy has been the measure of the oppression. This is why feminism has had to explode the private. This is why feminism has seen the personal as the political. The private is public for those for whom the personal is political. In this sense, for women there is no private, either normatively or empirically. Feminism confronts the fact that women have no privacy to lose or to guarantee. Women are not inviolable. Women's sexuality is not only violable, it is—hence, women are—seen in and as their violation. To confront the fact that women have no privacy is to confront the intimate degradation of women in the public order. The doctrinal choice of privacy in the abortion context reaffirms and reinforces what the feminist critique of sexuality criticizes: the public/private split.
>
> (MacKinnon 1989: 191)

MacKinnon's first claim here is that women have no privacy, and thus privacy protection provides no benefit to women. Her second claim is that feminism has demonstrated the importance of questioning the public/private split and has had to "explode the private." Susan Moller Okin has echoed this disturbing worry: "The protection of the privacy of a domestic sphere in which inequality exists is the protection of the right of the strong to exploit and abuse the weak" (Okin 1989: 174). Batterers and child molesters rely on the shroud of secrecy that surrounds abuse to maintain their power. One response is to remove privacy protection in the domestic arena. MacKinnon believes women have no privacy that can be taken away. However, the *descriptive* fact that women and children (and some men) are indeed violated in the family and in private contexts implies nothing whatsoever about the *normative* value of protecting a private zone within which they can have the power to limit intrusions and violations. With regard to MacKinnon's claim that we must "explode the private," she appears to imply that there is no public/private distinction and we have had to jettison the private realm. Her general feminist claim is probably that the legal and political conception of privacy has been used to shield and reinforce the patriarchal family structure with male domination and all. Thus this version of feminism objects to privacy as it has been legally and politically understood. But it is reasonable to ask whether there *should be* no public/private distinction. There is indeed a deeper question about whether some form of public/private distinction can be maintained without unrestricted male domination.

Jean Bethke Elshtain describes one form of the feminist critique as follows:

In its give-no-quarter form in radical feminist argument, any distinction between the personal and the political was disdained. . . . Rather, there was a collapse of one into the other. . . . Nothing personal was exempt from political definition, direction, and manipulation—not sexual intimacy, not love, not parenting. . . . The private sphere fell under a thoroughgoing politicized definition. Everything was grist for a voracious publicity mill; nothing was exempt, there was nowhere to hide.

(Elshtain 1995: 43)

Ruth Gavison has referred to a similar understanding of the feminist critique of privacy saying, "Usually, when the dichotomy between public and private is challenged, the argument is that all is (or should be) public" (Gavison 1992: 28). Here these scholars appear to echo MacKinnon's critique of privacy. Yet Gavison hastens to note feminist equivocations on the rejection of the public/private split:

But once we look at particular questions, it is rare to find feminists who argue consistently either that everything should be regulated by the state, or that family and all other forms of intimate relationships should disappear in favor of public communities that . . . police the different ways in which members interact. When pushed, feminists explicitly deny this is their ideal. . . . [I]t is hard to specify even one context or dimension of the distinction in which the claim is that the whole category of the private is useless.

(Gavison 1992: 28–29)

MacKinnon is absolutely correct that abusive relationships in traditionally private domains are pervasive—more pervasive than many are willing to acknowledge—and that when the private sphere is maintained as unavailable for public scrutiny the abuse, violation and degradation will continue to be unchecked. When the public/private distinction is used to cover and shield abuse, then it works to the detriment of women and children and others abused. This is the darker side of privacy. But what is the alternative? If we reject the public/private distinction and "explode the private," does it follow that nothing is or should be private? Although MacKinnon believes the public/private distinction perpetuates the subjection of women, it is important to consider whether we must conclude that there are *no* contexts in which women wish to keep the state out of their lives. Personal circumstances and family life are subject to some regulations on rape and sexuality, divorce, policies on child care, adoption and welfare. But should there be no limits on such regulations? Do women really want state regulations to be unlimited? Do women want the state to mandate how many children they may have, to mandate abortion or sterilization, to use family size to determine allowance or withdrawal of welfare benefits, and to allow the state to insinuate itself in all personal and intimate family affairs? I find that doubtful, and given that I am unconvinced that rights to personal autonomy and liberty can fully protect the right to determine what one does with one's body, I believe that privacy protection often continues to be an effective way to exclude unwarranted governmental intrusion. Governmental regulations may be insidious, or they may be more reasonable, allowing a woman to charge her husband with rape, for example. There is an important difference between a government that protects a woman's decision to accuse her husband of rape, and one that forces her to do so. Thus it is crucial to highlight the role of *individual* male power and domestic abuse, but it is also important not to underestimate the implications of *state-sponsored* expressions of control over women. The dilemma, then, is how to distinguish justified and unjustified state intervention in the private realm.

Others have taken the approach that the boundaries between public and private need to be redrawn. They would not jettison privacy but recognize that what happens in the family is not always beyond scrutiny. An alternative understanding of the feminist critique of privacy, therefore, is that feminists merely want to reject the public/private distinction *as it has been understood in the past*, from Aristotle on. Frances Olsen, for example, worries that rejection of the public/private split will lead to an alternative system in which "the state controls every aspect of human life; nothing is personal and private" (Olsen 1983: 83). On her view, "We cannot choose between the two sides of the dualism because we need both" (ibid.: 88). Carole Pateman agrees that feminists believe a proper understanding is that social life is possible only when "the two spheres, the domestic (private) and civil society (public) held to be separate and opposed, are inextricably interrelated" (Pateman 1989: 123). Feminists articulating this strand of the feminist critique are arguing that the public/private dichotomy is misleading when it fails to recognize the interconnections between public and private life.

The reality of domination and abuse in private needs to be aired more fully and addressed, but collapsing the public/private distinction and leaving everything public is an unacceptable and dangerous alternative. Absent domestic violence and coercion, there is great value for women and men in preserving privacy—and a sanctuary where they can live free from scrutiny, the pressure to conform, free to express their identities through relationships and choices about their bodies and lifestyles. No one has yet explained how to understand the public/private dichotomy in a way that intertwines the two. But it is possible that Mill's famous harm principle—despite its notorious ambiguities—can be invoked in important ways in some cases, often domestic ones, to help determine when government intervention can be justified in the private realm. Harm to others needs to be reported, not shrouded in private, and following Mill, we may want to believe that adult voluntary and consenting behavior is not the business of the state or the courts. Nevertheless, as for Mill, there are serious problems with drawing a clear line between cases leading to harm to others and those that are self-regarding or occur with the voluntary consent of others. Deeply entrenched cultural beliefs, in favor of female genital mutilation, for example, seem to lead to the conclusion that even with "consent" the state should not necessarily remain out of the affairs of individuals. Otherwise it would seem that a physician must honor a woman's rational yet culturally entrenched decision that the physician must perform genital mutilation surgery on her. Thus it seems there must be some constraints on what counts as significant and meaningful consent.

Nevertheless, the harm to others vs. harm to self distinction can perhaps help with other cases where the public/private boundary is blurred. For example, one may wonder whether parents should have the power to withhold cancer treatment or other medical treatments from children—for religious or other reasons—when such treatments are medically sound and have been shown to increase survival rates. While some may view this as a completely private family decision, it seems extremely difficult to justify in the face of clear harm to the children. As a family decision it may be viewed as presumptively private, but it is also a situation where privacy is and should be overridden by considerations of harm to others. Privacy claims are not absolute, and the privacy interests need to be taken seriously, but they can certainly be overridden by concerns about harm to others, threats of harm and at times even paternalism and more. Returning to a clearer case, we can understand why private consumption of pornography and ownership of pornography in the privacy of one's home is self-regarding in Mill's sense and not appropriate for state intervention and regulation, whereas production and distribution of pornography to others, where there are genuinely increased threats of violence against women and children, pose a serious enough threat of harm to justify either a ban or regulation, depending on the alternative which best controls the pornographic material in the face of a black-market value for such material. Determining and documenting the likelihood and extent of harm—and whether to consider not merely physical but also emotional harm and other considerations that may override privacy—will not be easy, but it may provide a rule of thumb that can be a starting guideline. Nevertheless, we have seen that it also leads to further complications, especially in cases where different cultures and religions endorse gender roles and other aspects in family circles that are oppressive to women (female genital mutilation, the Muslim burka controversy and such). If considerations of harm to others can override privacy, what other considerations can do so as well? It is typical for governmental agencies to cite national security concerns as adequate for overriding individual expectations of privacy, but clarifying which national security concerns are serious enough to justify privacy breaches can lead to an interminable tangle of arguments, as is clear from debates surrounding the Patriot Act.

Two relatively recent court cases on privacy help demonstrate the way in which thought about constitutional privacy, the public/private distinction and the role of government as a public enforcer against individual claims to privacy is evolving. In *Bowers v. Hardwick* ((1986) 478 U.S. 186) the U.S. Supreme Court refused to strike down Georgia's anti-sodomy statute and the privacy argument lost by a narrow margin. Some have argued that the Court failed to consider the privacy issue at all, but that is misleading. The majority did consider the privacy claim, even if summarily, and rejected it. They argued that no demonstration had ever been given that there was a connection between family, marriage or procreation on one hand, and homosexual sodomy on the other. An enraged dissent condemned the majority's refusal to take into account the intimacy of the issue at stake, retorting that only the most willful blindness could prevent one from recognizing the right of individuals to conduct intimate, consenting, adult relationships within the privacy of their own homes as being at the heart of the Constitution's protection of privacy.

The decision in *Lawrence v. Texas* ((2003) 539 U.S. 558) overturned *Bowers*. The Court was aided in *Lawrence* by the fact that the statute was worded as aimed solely at homosexuals and thus discriminatory. While the majority could have treated the issue merely as a liberty or autonomy case, it placed a major focus on privacy. Regarding the anti-sodomy statutes the majority argued that such restrictions were:

> . . . touching upon the most private human conduct, sexual behavior, and in the most private of places, the home. The statutes do seek to control a personal relationship that, whether or not entitled to formal recognition in the law, is within the liberty of persons to choose without being punished as criminals.
>
> This, as a general rule, should counsel against attempts by the State, or a court, to define the meaning of the relationship or to set its boundaries absent injury to a person or abuse of an institution the law protects. It suffices for us to acknowledge that adults may choose to enter upon this relationship in the confines of their homes and their own private lives and still retain their dignity as free persons. When sexuality finds overt expression in intimate conduct with another person, the conduct can be but one element in a personal bond that is more enduring.
>
> ((2003) 539 U.S. 558)

Noting that punishing consenting adults for private acts had not been discussed much in the legal literature, the majority referred to precedents which confirmed that our laws and traditions afford constitutional protections to personal decisions relating to marriage, procreation, contraception, family relationships, child rearing and education. The Court quoted at length from *Planned Parenthood of Southeastern Pa. v. Casey* ((1992) 505 U.S. 833) about the most intimate and personal choices a person may make in a lifetime, choices central to personal dignity and autonomy and the right to define one's own concept of existence, of meaning and so on. The majority concluded that the "petitioners are entitled to respect for their *private* lives. The State cannot demean their existence or control their destiny by making their *private* sexual conduct a crime" (emphasis mine). It is significant that, by using language continuing to support privacy as a grounding for the decision, the majority opinion makes clear that nothing can justify the statute's "intrusion into the personal and private life of the individual." This provides a strong general recognition and confirmation that with meaningful consent and the absence of harm to others or other overriding considerations, privacy must be protected.

Given that privacy protection has developed in three distinct areas of law—with separate introductions and historical developments in different decades for each—it is not surprising that both legal texts and many legal theorists (and a few philosophers) treat the privacy interests at stake as very different. The separate classifications of these three interests may be viewed by some as a historical coincidence or may provide some with a sense of order in the law. Let me close by emphasizing, to the contrary, that there are important historical, conceptual and philosophical reasons for understanding all three interests in privacy developed in the law—tort, Fourth Amendment and constitutional—as being closely related. First, note that the Court majority in *Lawrence* adopted, in this recent crucial case, an understanding of constitutional privacy that is remarkably close to early descriptions of the value of affording protection for informational privacy and privacy protection under the Fourth Amendment. The wording echoes early writings by legal theorists and philosophers, as well as Milan Kundera, on the value and meaning of privacy as being central to human dignity, one's personhood and at the heart of one's right to define one's own existence.

Second, historical uses of the term "privacy" are not solely focused on informational privacy. For Aristotle, the public and private spheres are realms of life, and the domestic or private sphere is located within the home and family, clearly distinct from the public realm of government. For Locke, one owns one's own body, and presumably thus has control over one's body, and then makes property one's own by mixing one's labor with it. Thus, historical references to privacy include references to a sphere surrounding one's body and family and personal property—echoing the current, ordinary-language use of "privacy" and the Supreme Court's invocation of the term "privacy" in the constitutional cases.

Third, it is noteworthy that the sweeping language from Warren and Brandeis's argument for protection of a right to privacy in tort law protecting information about oneself and one's reputation is echoed in the similar language in Brandeis's famous quote in the dissent of the *Olmstead* case:

> The makers of our Constitution undertook to secure conditions favorable to the pursuit of happiness. They recognized the significance of man's spiritual nature, of his feelings and his intellect. They knew that only a part of the pain, pleasure and satisfactions of life are to be found in material things. They sought to protect Americans in their beliefs, their thoughts, their emotions and their sensations. They conferred, as against the Government, the right to be let alone—the most comprehensive of rights and the right most valued by civilized men. To protect that right, every unjustifiable intrusion by the Government upon the privacy of the individual, whatever the means employed, must be deemed a violation of the Fourth Amendment.
>
> ((1928) 277 U.S. 478)

This language became part of the majority view in the Fourth Amendment *Katz* case later on, and it is reflected again in the groundbreaking 1965 *Griswold* decision. This dissent is also quoted at length in a 1969 constitutional privacy case where it is called well established and a fundamental right to be free from unwanted governmental intrusions into one's privacy. The wording makes it clear that in all these varied cases privacy protects both peace of mind and bodily integrity. It is, moreover, difficult to believe that it is a mere accident that Brandeis's quotation and language was used as a basis for all three types of privacy protection in the law.

Fourth, another way of seeing the close relationship and connections between the three types of privacy protected in law is to note the similarity of reasons appealed to in seeking privacy protection for tort and Fourth Amendment law as well as various interests now covered by constitutional privacy. There is a philosophical argument for connecting the three strands of privacy protection in the law, based on the range of similar reasons given in defense of their importance.

People have many different reasons for wanting to control information about themselves, and their motives range from freedom from libel and defamation to commercial gain. Often, however, freedom from scrutiny, embarrassment, judgment and even ridicule are at stake, as well as protection from pressure to conform, prejudice, emotional distress, and the losses in self-esteem, opportunities or finances arising from those harms. In such cases, we are more inclined to view the claim to control information as a privacy claim. A tort privacy action to control information about oneself, and Fourth Amendment claims about unreasonable searches and seizures, are two mechanisms that society and the law have created to accomplish such protection. By themselves they are not wholly adequate, however, because the interests that justify the screen on information include the interest in being free to decide and make choices about family, marriage and lifestyle absent the threat of the same problematic consequences that accompany an information leak. In other words, it is plausible to maintain that worries about what information others have about one are often *due* to worries about social control by government or others. What one can do to me, or what I can do free of the threat of scrutiny, judgment and pressure to conform, may often depend on what information (personal or not) an individual, the state or others have about me. Clearly my behavior is also affected by the extent to which I can make my own choices. Therefore, both the threat of an information leak and the threat of decreased control over decision-making can have a chilling effect on my behavior. If this is correct, then the desire to protect a sanctuary for ourselves, a refuge within which we can shape and carry on our lives and relationships with others—intimacies as well as other activities—without the threat of scrutiny, embarrassment and the deleterious consequences they might bring, is a major underlying reason for providing information control, protection from unreasonable search and seizure, and control over decision-making (cf. DeCew 1997: 63–64). Thus there are clear conceptual connections between privacy interests and the values they protect in tort, Fourth Amendment and constitutional law.

The point can be highlighted by noting cases where all the relevant privacy concerns seem importantly relevant and intertwined, as in recent cases about drug testing in public schools. Informational privacy was obviously relevant—in the Lindsay Earls case (*Board of Education et al. v. Earls et al.* (2002) 536 U.S. 822), the results of student drug tests were strewn about at least one teacher's desk where anyone passing by could see them, and clearly the drug tests, though targeted at drug use, could also detect prescription medications a student might be taking, and information about pregnancy, diabetes and other medical conditions. The Court clearly treated the *Earls* case and earlier ones as Fourth Amendment privacy cases—asking whether the drug tests were a violation of prohibitions against unreasonable search and seizure. Furthermore, issues that go to the heart of constitutional privacy were also involved: concerns about whether or not students were being watched while urinating, puncturing one's skin for blood samples, etc., especially if the drug tests were mandatory or random and not announced. In such cases the courts have been concerned about the role of public schools as guardians of students in attendance there. But the privacy issues are still significant, and the drug testing cases raise privacy questions about one's control over information about oneself, about whether drug tests are reasonable or not as a search and seizure, as well as concerns about the inviolability of the body.

I have argued that privacy interests protected in tort, Fourth Amendment and constitutional law can be seen as historically, conceptually and philosophically related, demonstrating that privacy may be considered a distinct and fairly coherent set of values and concerns. Privacy has been discussed since ancient times, appears to be a cross-species and cross-cultural value, and can be seen to be highly valuable despite important feminist concerns about its use to shield domination and abuse. While there are no clear guidelines for drawing boundaries between public and private domains, harm to others can be one of several considerations in differentiating borderline cases, particularly in domestic contexts. Privacy is not an absolute value, but can be viewed as the default, requiring government and others to justify their need to intrude. The digital age, and the scope of privacy post 9/11, far from leaving individuals caring less about their privacy, has increased interest in, and urgent pleas for, more careful and thoughtful privacy guidelines and controls, whether for the more extensive wiretapping of individuals and e-mail tracking justified using the Patriot Act, electronic medical records, airport scanners or biometric identification. Facebook's lack of genuine privacy protection, for example, is accepted by many, but has drawn outrage from others. Tracking of Internet use has led to increased demand for "do not track" options analogous to "do not call" legislation protecting citizens from unwanted solicitation. As technology advances, new privacy challenges will proliferate, and both the courts and philosophical dialogue are having a difficult time keeping up with these changes. The current literature on privacy is massive, and the worries about privacy protection are becoming tougher and more numerous. But for the public, the desire and value and demand for privacy protection remains unabated.

References

Aristotle (1941) *The Politics*, in R. McKeon, ed. and B. Jowett, trans., *The Basic Works of Aristotle*, New York: Random House, pp. 1127–1324.

Benn, S. I. (1984/1971) "Privacy, Freedom, and Respect for Persons," in F. D. Schoeman, ed., *Philosophical Dimensions of Privacy: An Anthology*, Cambridge: Cambridge University Press, pp. 223–44.

Bloustein, E. J. (1964) "Privacy as an Aspect of Human Dignity: An Answer to Dean Prosser," *New York University Law Review* 39: 962–1007.

Board of Education of Independent School District of Pottawatomie County et al. v. Earls et al. (2002) 536 U.S. 822.

Bork, R. (1990) *The Tempting of America*, New York: Free Press.

Bowers v. Hardwick (1986) 478 U.S. 186.

DeCew, J. W. (1997) *In Pursuit of Privacy: Law, Ethics and the Rise of Technology*, Ithaca, NY: Cornell University Press.

Dworkin, R. (1981) "What Is Equality? Part 1: Equality of Welfare," *Philosophy & Public Affairs* 10: 185–246.

Elshtain, J. B. (1995) *Democracy on Trial*, New York: Basic Books.

Fried, C. (1968) "Privacy," *Yale Law Journal* 77: 475–93.

Gavison, R. (1992) "Feminism and the Public/Private Distinction," 45 *Stanford Law Review* 1.

Gerstein, R. (1978) "Intimacy and Privacy," *Ethics* 89: 76–81.

Griswold v. Connecticut (1965) 381 U.S. 479.

Inness, J. (1992) *Privacy, Intimacy and Isolation*, Oxford: Oxford University Press.

Katz v. U.S. (1967) 389 U.S. 347.

Kundera, M. (1984) *The Unbearable Lightness of Being*, New York: Harper Collins.

Lawrence v. Texas (2003) 539 U.S. 558.

Locke, J. (1988/1690) *Second Treatise on Government*, T. P. Reardon, ed., New York: Macmillan, Library of Liberal Arts.

MacKinnon, C. (1989) *Toward a Feminist Theory of the State*, Cambridge, Mass.: Harvard University Press.

Melvin v. Reid (1931) 112 Cal. App. 283.

Newman, A. L. (2008) *Protectors of Privacy: Regulating Personal Data in the Global Economy*, Ithaca, NY and London: Cornell University Press.

Nissenbaum, H. (2010) *Privacy in Context: Technology, Policy, and the Integrity of Social Life*, Palo Alto, CA: Stanford University Press.

Okin, S. M. (1989) *Justice, Gender, and the Family*, New York: Basic Books.

Olmstead v. U.S. (1928) 277 U.S. 438.

Olsen, F. E. (1983) "The Family and the Market: A Study of Ideology and Legal Reform," *Harvard Law Review* 96: 1497–1578.

Parent, W. (1983a) "A New Definition of Privacy for the Law," *Law and Philosophy* 2: 305–38.

—— (1983b) "Privacy, Morality and the Law," *Philosophy & Public Affairs* 12: 269–88.

Pateman, C. (1989) "Feminist Critiques of the Public/Private Dichotomy," in C. Pateman, *The Disorder of Women: Democracy, Feminism, and Political Theory*, Stanford, CA: Stanford University Press, pp. 118–40.

Planned Parenthood of Southeastern Pa. v. Casey (1992) 505 U.S. 833.

Prosser, W. (1960) "Privacy," *California Law Review* 48: 383.

Rachels, J. (1975) "Why Privacy Is Important," *Philosophy & Public Affairs* 4: 323–33.

Regan, P. (1995) *Legislating Privacy*, Chapel Hill, NC: University of North Carolina Press.

Reiman, J. (1976) "Privacy, Intimacy, and Personhood," *Philosophy & Public Affairs* 6: 26–44.

—— (2004) "Driving to the Panopticon: A Philosophical Exploration of the Risks to Privacy Posed by the Information Technology of the Future," in B. Roessler, ed., *Privacies: Philosophical Evaluations*, Palo Alto, CA: Stanford University Press.

Roessler, B. (2005) *The Value of Privacy*, Cambridge, Mass.: Polity Press.

Scanlon, T. (1975) "Thomson on Privacy," *Philosophy & Public Affairs* 4: 315–22.

Schoeman, F. (1984) *Philosophical Dimensions of Privacy: An Anthology*, Cambridge: Cambridge University Press.

—— (1992) *Privacy and Social Freedom*, Cambridge: Cambridge University Press.

Solove, D. (2008) *Understanding Privacy*, Cambridge, Mass.: Harvard University Press.

Thomson, J. J. (1975) "The Right to Privacy," *Philosophy & Public Affairs* 4: 295–314.

Warren, S. and Brandeis, L. (1890) "The Right to Privacy," 4 *Harvard Law Review*.

Wasserstrom, R. A. (1984/1978) "Privacy: Some Arguments and Assumptions," in F. D. Schoeman, ed., *Philosophical Dimensions of Privacy: An Anthology*, Cambridge: Cambridge University Press, pp. 317–32.

Westin, A. (1984/1967) "The Origins of Modern Claims to Privacy," in F. D. Schoeman, ed., *Philosophical Dimensions of Privacy: An Anthology*, Cambridge: Cambridge University Press, pp. 56–74.

Whalen v. Roe (1977) 429 U.S. 589.

Further Reading

For further reading, see: A. L. Allen (1988) *Uneasy Access: Privacy for Women in a Free Society*, Totowa, NJ: Rowman & Littlefield; A. L. Allen-Castelitto (1999) "Coercing Privacy," *William and Mary Law Review* 40: 723–57; R. Arneson (2000) "Egalitarian Justice versus the Right to Privacy?" *Social Philosophy and Policy* 17: 91–119; C. J. Bennet (2008) *The Privacy Advocates: Resisting the Spread of Surveillance*, Cambridge, Mass.: MIT Press; J. L. Cohen (1992) "Redescribing Privacy: Identity, Difference and the Abortion Controversy," *Columbia Journal of Gender and Law* 3: 43–117; A. Etzioni (1999) *The Limits of Privacy*, New York: Basic Books; E. P. Foley (2006) *Liberty for All: Reclaiming Individual Privacy in a New Era of Public Morality*, New Haven, CT: Yale University Press; R. Gavison (1980) "Privacy and the Limits of Law," *Yale Law Journal* 89: 421–71; A. Moore (2010) *Privacy Rights: Moral and Legal Foundations*, University Park, PA: Penn State University Press; J. B. Rule (2007) *Privacy in Peril*, Oxford: Oxford University Press; W. G. Staples, ed. (2007) *Encyclopedia of Privacy*, Westport, CT: Greenwood Press; and R. Wacks (2010) *Privacy: A Very Short Introduction*, Oxford: Oxford University Press.

39

FREEDOM OF SPEECH

Alon Harel

Part I: Introduction

Freedom of speech is among the most cherished constitutional rights in liberal democracies. It is entrenched in most contemporary constitutions as well as in international human rights treaties. It is often classified as a "first generation right"—a right protecting individuals from interference by the state. It is understood to be foundational to liberal polities either in the sense that it is a precondition to the existence of a liberal polity and/or that it is tightly related to liberal values such as autonomy, dignity and liberty. At the same time, the scope of what constitutes speech, what speech ought to be protected, the weight or the value attributed to the protection of speech vis-à-vis other rights or policy concerns, and the reasons underlying its protection are highly controversial. These controversies have important political and legal implications and they are reflected in the differential protection granted to speech in different jurisdictions.

The primary philosophical challenge is to explain why (and whether) speech ought to be protected more (or differently) than non-speech activities. When we protect speech we privilege speech relative to non-speech activities. The normative debate concerning the justifications for protecting speech also sheds light on what counts as speech. Only communicative action that at least potentially promotes the values underlying the protection of speech counts as speech. Consequently, identifying the values underlying the protection of speech also influences what activities count as "speech." Thus, at least in legal discourse, the question of what counts as speech and what counts as protected speech are often interrelated. To address the normative question of why speech is protected, as well as to identify what counts as speech, we examine below in Part II four major theories purporting to justify the protection of speech: the marketplace of ideas, the autonomy-based theory, the self-realization justification and the democratic justification. We establish that none of these theories alone can justify the protection of speech as is currently practiced in contemporary liberal polities.

In recent years many feminists and ethnic or religious minorities have challenged the protection of certain forms of speech, e.g., racist speech or pornography. More particularly it was claimed that certain forms of speech either conflict with other rights, e.g., equality, or even may deprive minorities of the capacity or ability to exercise effectively their own right to free speech (the silencing argument). It is the task of Part III to explore some of the minoritarian challenges to what constitutes speech and what constitutes protected speech.

Some radical critics of liberalism challenge the importance and significance of freedom of speech as such. They maintain that freedom of speech masks large-scale silencing and repression. "Repressive tolerance," as it is sometimes labeled, is a radical position that rejects central, traditional, liberal political rights in the name of values such as autonomy and equality and regards the liberal protection of speech (independently of its content or merit) as a repressive mechanism designed to strangle rather than facilitate genuine public deliberation. These challenges will be examined in Part IV. We conclude by pointing out that the three positions described below (liberalism, minoritarian critics of liberalism and radical critics of liberalism) share similar assumptions and values. To the extent that minoritarian and radical critics of liberalism advocate restrictions of speech, they do so by invoking the very same values advocated by liberals: autonomy, dignity and equality.

Part II: Rationales for Protecting Speech

The scope of what the right to free speech includes is of course controversial. Often the scope of what constitutes "speech" is influenced by normative considerations. Yet, it is evident that the term "speech" is much too narrow to describe all the activities that are traditionally covered by the right to free speech. As Schauer noted: "What is 'speech' in ordinary usage is not necessarily what is 'speech' for purposes of the concept of free speech" (Schauer 1982: 13). Waving a flag, wearing a button with political symbols and producing a movie are also protected by the right to free speech. In contrast, there are activities that are clearly speech (in the ordinary sense of the word) that are not protected by the right to free speech, such as hiring somebody to commit murder. Often the right to free speech protects communicative activity—namely activity that conveys ideas, expresses emotions or sentiments, or conveys or evinces attitudes. Yet not all communicative activity is protected; physically attacking a person as an expression of hatred is not covered by the right to free speech even if it is a communicative activity.

The standard view is that free speech differs from a principle of general liberty. The protections granted to speech are far greater than the protection of activities that are not classified as speech (Schauer 1982: 7–8; Greenawalt 1989a: 120). This does not imply that the protection of speech is absolute; most advocates of protecting speech concede that urgent considerations often override the concern for protecting speech. Yet concerns which justify limitations on speech ought to be more urgent, more weighty or different in kind than concerns justifying the limitations of most other liberties. The question is, therefore, why speech should have greater protection compared with other types of activities that may be just as important and value enhancing as non-speech activities.

The special protection of speech is part of a more general phenomenon characterizing many rights; rights protect certain forms of behavior, e.g., speech, religion, equality, etc. They provide, therefore, differential protection to different activities. One of the great challenges of a theory of rights in general and a theory justifying the protection of any particular right is to explain the reasons underlying the differential protection of activities, all of which seem to produce similar benefits and generate similar harms. In the context of speech, we can ask why should speech and non-speech activities which are equally autonomy enhancing (or, more generally, equally value enhancing) be protected differentially (Harel 2005)? We shall address this question at the end of this section.

The rest of this section is devoted to explaining the rationales justifying the protection of speech. The traditional justifications for protecting speech fall into two categories. Under the first category, speech is protected in order to shield an individual from restrictions even when such restrictions would be conducive to welfare. Dignity-based and autonomy-based concerns fall into this category; their advocates often maintain that speech ought to be protected even when its protection is detrimental to important societal values. Under the second category, protecting speech is justified because in the long run it is conducive to social welfare. The claim that protecting speech is conducive to the discovery of truth is an influential example of a justification of the second category; it is founded on the conjecture that protection of speech is conducive to the society as a whole. Note that this difference in the type of justification has important ramifications. The first camp (the deontological camp) is typically less willing to conduct "balancing" of speech concerns with other non-speech concerns. In contrast, the second camp (the consequentialist camp) regards the protection of speech as a means to promote social welfare. It follows that speech, which is not conducive to social welfare, deserves no protection (Nagel 1995: 86–89).

Let us examine, therefore, four main justifications used in the literature: the marketplace of ideas, the autonomy-based argument, the self-realization argument and the democracy argument. Note that these justifications are only a subset of the potential justifications for rights-based protection of speech and that the categorization provided here is not the only categorization provided in the literature. Furthermore, like many classifications, there are arguments that can fall into more than one category.

The Marketplace of Ideas

Under the conventional marketplace of ideas argument, the protection of speech is conducive in the long run to the discovery of truth. It is evident that this argument is not an individualistic argument based on either the rights of the speaker to speak his mind or the right of the audience to benefit from the speech. Instead, it is based on long-term societal benefits resulting from the protection of speech. Speech has an instrumental value in promoting truth and promoting truth is socially valuable. One of the earliest attempts to justify the protection of speech dates back to the seventeenth century. John Milton argued that:

> [T]hough all the winds of doctrine were let loose to play upon the earth, so Truth be in the field, we do injuriously by licensing and prohibiting to misdoubt her strength. Let her and Falshood grapple; who ever knew Truth put to the worse, in a free and open encounter?
>
> (Milton 1644)

But why should truth and falsehood grapple with each other? Why should not we simply censor falsehood and thus guarantee the victory of truth? Why is the victory of truth guaranteed? A philosophically sophisticated version of the argument was developed by John Stuart Mill, who identified three distinct claims (Mill 1859). In Mill's view: 1) if a censored opinion contains truth, its silencing is damaging as it lessens the probability that truth be revealed. In his view: "complete liberty of contradicting and disproving our opinion, is the very condition which justifies us in assuming its truth"; 2) if conflicting opinions each contain some truth, the clash between them is the only method of discovering what the truth is; and 3) even if the opinion has no truth in it, challenging the accepted position contributes to its vitality and decreases the chances that it degenerates into a prejudice or dogma. Mill famously contrasted "dead dogma" with "living truth" and he maintained that: "Truth gains more even by the errors of one who, with due study and preparation, thinks for himself, than by the true opinions of those who only hold them because they do not suffer themselves to think" (Mill 1859).

Mill's view has been immensely influential; it has been endorsed by courts and by numerous legal theorists (Ingber 1984). In a dissenting opinion that later became orthodoxy in the United States, Justice Oliver Wendell Holmes Jr. argued that: "the best test of truth is the power of the thought to get itself accepted in the competition of the market" (*Abrams v. U.S.* (1919) 250 U.S. 616). The claim that robust discussion is conducive to the discovery of truth has a particular appeal in the Anglo-American world and it has been analogized to the traditional justification for the adversary system based on cross-examination (Schauer 1982: 16).

Ironically, the economists who first identified the virtues of the marketplace of commodities were quick to point out the paradoxical nature of this analogy. Ronald Coase asked the following question: if indeed the protection of freedom of speech is grounded in the marketplace of ideas, why is speech so much more protected than the marketplace of commodities? His answer was cynical: "The market for ideas is the market in which the intellectual conducts his trade. The explanation of the paradox is self-interest and self-esteem. Self-esteem leads the intellectuals to magnify the importance of their own market. . . . But self-interest combines with self-esteem to ensure that, while others are regulated, regulation should not apply to them" (Coase 1974: 386; Coase 1977: 1). Coase also pointed out that perhaps the real motive for protection of freedom of speech is not the keen interest in truth but the fact that "the public is commonly more interested in the struggle between truth and falsehood than it is in truth itself" (Coase 1974: 391).

Even if one ultimately rejects Coase's cynical explanation for the special protection of speech on grounds of self-interest and self-esteem of intellectuals, the differential treatment of speech on the one hand and commodities on the other hand is a challenge to the advocates of this argument. The marketplace of ideas clearly increases the chances of "true ideas" to appear in the market of ideas, but it also increases the spread of false ideas (Schauer 1982: 28; Ingber 1984: 7). The famous assertion that false speech should be countered by "more speech, not enforced silence" is based on an empirical generalization that truth has greater chances of winning in the marketplace of ideas. Mill himself concedes that truth does not prevail if persecuted and says that: "It is a piece of idle sentimentality that truth, merely as truth, has any inherent power denied to error of prevailing against the dungeon and the stake" (1859). Yet the same argument ought to be extended to the case in which truth is not persecuted; the premise that freedom of speech leads on the whole to the discovery of truth is not more than an unsubstantiated conjecture (Ingber 1984; Schauer 1982: 28; Barendt 2005: 9). It has also been argued correctly that the so-called marketplace of ideas is not open to everyone who wants to communicate her ideas (Barendt 2005: 12). Disparities of power and money may have destructive influence on the robustness of public discourse. Furthermore, even if protecting speech is conducive to truth, it is not clear that truth is always or even typically desirable. Often the regulation of speech is based on arguments of public policy that have nothing to do with truth or falsehood (Schauer 1982: 22–23). A true expression such as publication of a criminal record of a defendant may undermine her prospects for a fair trial. True expressions may violate privacy, undermine stability and lead to violence. Some theorists also have pointed out that the marketplace of ideas argument presupposes a process of rational thinking and, consequently, the less rational individuals are, the less forceful the theory of the marketplace is (Schauer 1982: 30; Ingber 1984: 15; Baker 1982: 14). Most skeptical of all have been those who have argued against the claim that truth is objective and maintain that truth is being created rather than discovered (Baker 1989: 13).

Yet despite these difficulties there are less ambitious arguments based on the marketplace of ideas that have merit. Mill was right that challenging even true ideas increases the vitality and potency of these ideas. Furthermore, as Mill himself noticed, challenging even true ideas is conducive to the very critical capacity to scrutinize ideas and, therefore, in the long run, may be as conducive to truth as it is conducive to the development of the critical deliberative tools necessary to evaluate truth and falsehood. Under this understanding, free speech is conducive to truth because it is conducive to the development of intellectual virtues that, in turn, are instrumental to truth. Furthermore, the claim that free speech is conducive to intellectual virtues may support the protection of speech even if the development of such virtues is not conducive to truth, as it seems that the perfection of intellectual virtues is valuable independently of whether such perfection is conducive to truth.

The Autonomy-Based Argument

The autonomy-based argument is only one of several characteristically liberal arguments made in favor of protecting speech. These arguments include arguments from dignity, diversity and autonomy (Schauer 1982: 60–72). It is to be emphasized that the autonomy-based argument is in effect a family of arguments. One theorist identified six distinctive meanings of autonomy that are used in defending the right to free speech (Briston 1998). We will examine here only two distinct autonomy-based justifications: one based on a negative conception of autonomy and another based on a positive conception of autonomy. Under the negative concept of autonomy, autonomy is designed to protect individuals from outside control of the state and to maintain a personal space for the individuals; in contrast the positive conception is designed to guarantee the actual exercise of autonomy. It is not merely the protection from outside or external interference which counts as autonomy enhancing but the actual, active exercise of one's deliberative powers.

Under the justification based on a negative conception of autonomy, speech is a private domain—an area that is under the exclusive control of the individual. Often this argument is based on the view that protection of rights has intrinsic rather than instrumental value (Nagel 1995: 86). The right to free speech is, under this view, a fundamental and nonderivative element of morality. Thomas Scanlon developed the most sophisticated version of this argument. In Scanlon's view: "To regard himself as autonomous a person must see himself as sovereign in deciding what to believe and in weighing competing reasons for action. . . . An autonomous person cannot accept without independent consideration the judgment of others as to what he should believe or what he should do" (Scanlon 1972: 215–16). A similar reference to sovereignty of the person is made by Nagel, who argues that: "The sovereignty of each person's reason over his own beliefs and values requires that he be permitted to express them. . . it also requires that he not be protected against exposure to views or arguments that might influence him in ways others deem pernicious" (Nagel 1995: 96). In both cases what is at stake is the view of persons as autonomous agents, and autonomy is identified with what can be labeled sovereignty—immunity from certain forms of external control. An individual is sovereign if she does not accept without questioning the judgments of others. Scanlon rejects the instrumental arguments for protecting speech (based on societal well-being) and adopts instead a noninstrumental, non-consequentialist, highly individualistic approach. If speech is to be protected solely on the basis of controversial, empirical claims about its long-term positive effects or the negative effects of restrictions, then the free speech principle is vulnerable to empirical challenges and subject to contingent factors concerning its expected societal effects (Scanlon 1972: 205).

Scanlon starts his discussion with a very important and seemingly paradoxical observation. The right to free speech does not target restrictions on speech as such but only, or primarily, restrictions that are grounded in certain justifications for these restrictions. Particularly pernicious are restrictions that are based on the risk that the views communicated were to be believed or acted upon (Scanlon 1972: 209). Compare for instance restricting the dissemination of information as to how to make nerve gas in the kitchen to a restriction of a particularly effective piece of political propaganda that may lead to schism and bloody civil war. Both restrictions are designed to promote the public good and the harms resulting from the speech in both cases could be similar. Yet it is the second restriction that seems problematic. This is because the speech restricted in the second case is one that promulgates what the speaker takes to be good reasons for action, while in the first case it merely provides individuals with the means to do what they want to do anyhow (Scanlon 1972: 211–12). Similarly, if someone urges me to commit violence the choice to commit violence is ultimately mine: "The contribution to the genesis of [the] action made by the act of expression is, so to speak, superseded by the agent's own judgment" (Scanlon 1972: 212).

These observations led Scanlon to articulate what he labels the Millian principle that consists of two sub-principles. Restrictions of speech could not be justified on the grounds that a) the speech harms those who come, as a result of it, to have false beliefs; or b) the speech harms people as a result of harmful acts committed as a result of the fact that the act of expression leads agents to believe (or increased their tendency to believe) these acts are worth performing. Scanlon also shows that his analysis can account for famous exceptions to the protection of speech, e.g., shouting "fire" in a crowded theater.

Scanlon himself recognized some of the limitations of the Millian principle. First, the Millian principle is under-inclusive; restricting all speech for the sake of saving resources necessary for protecting speakers is consistent with the Millian principle as the restriction is justified on grounds that are not recognized by the Millian principle as justifying protection of speech. Second, the Millian principle is over-restrictive as there are clearly justified restrictions that violate the Millian principle, such as restrictions on speech that create "clear and present danger" (*Schenck v. United States* (1919) 249 U.S. 47). For instance, a speaker who urges his audience to condemn all homosexuals as they are morally depraved may under certain circumstances create clear and present danger (because the audience may act upon the belief that homosexuals are evil). Hence, such speech may fall within the scope of the second part of the Millian principle: the speech harms people as a result of harmful acts (of violence) committed as a result of the fact that the act of expression leads agents to form beliefs (concerning the moral depravity of homosexuals). As to the problem of under-inclusiveness, Scanlon maintains that the protection of speech may be grounded in different justifications; he does not argue therefore that the Millian principle is the exclusive justification for the protection of speech. As to the problem of over-inclusiveness, Scanlon concedes that the Millian principle is not an absolute principle; it may be defeated by conflicting considerations.

Yet opponents of the Millian principle exposed additional theoretical weaknesses. For example, why could not autonomous persons agree "to foreclose some inputs for them which they would ideally like to have in some situations" (Greenawalt 1989a: 115)? If people are autonomous should not they also be free to bar the dissemination of ideas that they know (or judge) are dangerous (Barendt 2005: 17; Briston 1998: 329)? Under this view, our moral dignity dictates to respect not only our judgments concerning what is right or wrong but also our judgments concerning what the best circumstances for deliberating about right and wrong are. Why should our second-order judgments (concerning what the best preconditions for deliberation on right and wrong are) deserve less protection than our first-order judgments (concerning what is right and wrong)?

Scanlon himself later developed an effective critique of the negative view of autonomy based on a positive conception of autonomy (Scanlon 1979). Scanlon distinguishes sharply between autonomy as a constraint on justifications for authority (based on the moral agency of persons) and moral autonomy understood as the actual ability to exercise independent rational judgments (Scanlon 1979: 533). The exercise of such judgments hinges on an environment that is conducive to the making of such judgments. Under this view, the protection of autonomy may even justify restrictions on speech as the exercise of the right to free speech presupposes an environment which is conducive to deliberation and some forms of speech are detrimental to the exercise of such a right. What really counts is the fostering of an environment that is conducive to rational deliberation (Barendt 2005: 17). While this view is clearly more open to abuse, it takes seriously the realities of deliberation in the society and, in particular, the fact that autonomy is not a natural pre-given product; it develops in societies which maintain certain practices and are guided by certain values (Taylor 1985). Hence, ironically, as we show below in Part III, restrictions on speech could be grounded in the need to foster autonomy and even to facilitate and perpetuate the capacity to exercise the right to free speech. As certain forms of speech, e.g., pornography and racist speech hinder, exclude and silence women and minorities, restricting such forms of speech may be conducive to the very protection of the right to free speech.

Some advocates of a positive conception of autonomy emphasize the fact that diversity of speech is a public rather than an individual good which is designed to facilitate "public portrayal and expression of forms of life" which "validates the styles of life portrayed" (Raz 1995: 153). The existence of "forms of life" is under this view a precondition for individual autonomy. Being Christian, Jewish or atheist has social meanings and such meanings are essential for these forms of life to promote individual autonomy. Freedom of speech is designed to "familiarize the public at large with ways of life"; to "reassure those whose ways of life are being portrayed that they are not alone, that their problems are common problems, that their experiences known to others"; and they serve as validation of the relevant ways of life. . ." and "give them the stamp of public acceptability" (Raz 1995: 155). Raz further maintains that it is often essential to validate one's own form of life by rejecting other forms of life. Hence he believes that even if religious condemnation of homosexuality may be wrong, it is part of a form of life that ought to be tolerated. This is because "disagreement, condemnation and even hostility to certain aspects of rival ways of life is an essential element of each way of life" (Raz 1995: 166).

This compelling justification suffers however from the difficulties pointed out above. Negative portrayals of rival forms of life may indeed be constitutive to one's own form of life, but they may also be destructive to those whose forms of life are negatively portrayed. This is true in particular when those whose forms of life are negatively portrayed are vulnerable and, consequently, cannot lead their lives without the approval or cooperation of those who condemn their way of life. Gays belonging to a religious community or women in a traditional Islamic or Jewish community are dependent upon their community psychologically and economically and yet they may find that their preferred way of life is being marginalized.

The positive understanding of autonomy deviates sharply in its recommendations from the negative understanding of autonomy. Yet its implementation in practice raises grave difficulties, as it is open to manipulation and abuse. What a fertile environment for autonomy should consist of is notoriously vague and such determinations have to be based on empirical generalizations that are highly controversial. Most significantly, the positive conception of autonomy is sometimes closer to the instrumental consequentialist justifications; its advocates often regard the protection of speech as well as its regulation as a means designed to bring about a more robust social and political discourse. Lastly, some theorists raised a general concern about autonomy (both negative and positive) and argued that autonomy cannot justify the right to free speech. Under their view, autonomy is a sectarian value (Cohen 1993: 222). It is a value that characterizes liberal forms of life but is not shared by others. The justification for protecting speech ought to appeal not only to liberals; it ought to address even those who reject autonomy as a central political value.

The Self-Realization/Self-Growth/Self-Fulfillment Argument

Positive autonomy is similar to another influential justification for free speech that takes many different forms. Under this view, the protection of speech is congenial to the self-development and self-perfection of individuals. This view is based on a certain vision of human beings as striving towards improvement and growth. It is understood by some theorists to be rooted in Aristotelian conceptions of good life (Schauer 1982: 49). Most significantly it maintains that by exercising the right to free speech, individuals "instantiate or reflect what it is to be human" (Barendt 2005: 13).

The self-growth/self-fulfillment argument could be interpreted either as an individualistic non-consequentialist argument or as a consequentialist argument. Under the first interpretation, a person has a right to self-growth/self-fulfillment even at the expense of other important societal values (including perhaps the value of maximizing the aggregate self-fulfillment of individuals in the society). Under the second interpretation, the protection of free speech is designed to facilitate, sustain or even maximize self-growth/self-fulfillment of individuals in the society.

Opponents of this argument have pointed out that it is difficult to see why free speech is more fundamental to self-growth and self-fulfillment than other liberties. After all, other non-speech activities are as essential to self-growth and self-fulfillment as much as speech (Barendt 2005: 13) My decision to walk naked in the city of Jerusalem may be as self-fulfilling and as essential to self-growth as verbal advocacy of nudism highlighting its spiritual and liberating significance. Yet the former decision is not protected while the latter decision is. In fact, it seems that this view gives too great an emphasis to some forms of self-fulfillment, namely intellectual self-fulfillment, at the expense of other forms of self-fulfillment. It therefore is subject to the concerns raised by Coase that the special privileging of speech in our society is biased towards the interests of intellectuals at the expense of the interests of other groups.

Furthermore, it is doubtful that all forms of speech, which are currently protected, are indeed congenial to self-development/self-fulfillment. One of the most famous and most celebrated cases of free speech is the decision to protect the Nazi march in Skokie, Illinois (a municipality populated by the Jewish victims of the Holocaust). It does not seem that this march is conducive to self-fulfillment of the victims; if anything these people are more likely to be intimidated by the march. It is also questionable whether the march contributes to the self-growth/self-fulfillment of the participants in the march. After all, self-growth is a normative concept which presupposes striving towards improvement and perfection. To the extent that self-growth and self-fulfillment differ from merely satisfying one's preferences, namely that it is a concept founded on a normative ideal, the speech of the Nazi protesters fails to contribute even to the Nazis' own self-growth.

The Democratic Defense of Free Speech

Among the classical justifications for free speech is the claim that free speech is a prerequisite for democracy. As the very concept of democracy is controversial, it is to be expected that there are several different democracy-based arguments for free speech. Is democracy valuable as a procedural method on grounds of fairness or equality? Or is it based on the greater likelihood of desirable decisions to emerge from a democratic process? If it is the former, the desirability of free speech need not hinge on its quality or its expected consequences. If it is the latter, then what counts is rational or deliberative participation (that is more likely to result in good or desirable decisions) and the scope of the protection of speech ought to reflect this concern.

A primary advocate of the democratic justification is Meiklejohn, who develops his position as a theory of interpretation of the United States Constitution (Meiklejohn 1948). In his view, the democratic defense of free speech is based on the necessity to make all information available to the sovereign electorate. As the people need to make decisions, they ought to be provided with the information necessary to make such decisions. Restricting speech is therefore detrimental to the democratic process, as it undermines the ability of individuals to reason politically. Furthermore, freedom of speech seems to rely on the perception that politicians are servants rather than masters. Freedom of speech is necessary to communicate the electorate's wishes to the government and thus to guarantee accountability on the part of the government (Schauer 1982: 37–39). It follows also that freedom of speech is essential to supervising and monitoring the politicians. Politicians who are subjected to the power of popular opinion are more likely to react to the pressure of public opinion and decide in accordance with the interests of the electorate. Amartya Sen has shown for instance that: "A free press and an active political opposition constitute the best early-warning system a country threatened by famines can have" (Sen 1999: 181).

The democratic justification as articulated by Meiklejohn was limited to political speech. It is not always easy to identify what political speech is. Arguably, it may be identified in two radically different ways. Under the first, political speech is defined on the basis of the intentions of the speakers while under the latter it is defined on the basis of its consequences (Scanlon 1979: 538). If political speech is defined on the basis of its consequences the scope of political speech may be much broader, as speech that is not aimed by the speaker to be political influences society and its politics by changing social values and social mores. Feminists, for instance, have emphasized the fact that pornography ought to be understood as political speech (even though it is not intended as such), as it influences and shapes the views and images of women and men in the society.

Despite these potential extensions, the democratic argument is limited as it is applicable only to political speech. Defending the protection of artistic or scientific speech requires, therefore, separate justifications (Barendt 2005: 18–19). Some may argue that differentiating between political speech and other categories of speech is undesirable in that it overemphasizes the significance of the political sphere at the expense of other spheres of activity. Furthermore, as Schauer points out, the use of such an argument is paradoxical, as a democracy could in fact justify restrictions of speech if these restrictions were supported by the public (Schauer 1982: 41).

Such an argument could be rebutted on the grounds that democracy is not a mere empty procedure. The will of the people is valuable only because it is based on information, as reasoned deliberation must be founded on such information. Yet it is not always true that providing more information is in fact congenial to the conducting of reasoned deliberation and the making of rational decisions. This naïve assumption ignores not only common sense and historical experience but also the vast contemporary literature of behavioral economics indicating that information often is detrimental to the making of reasoned decisions. It also ignores the huge disparities of power that often distort the political process. Would not some limitations on the power of the rich and powerful to speak bring about much better and more deliberative democratic discourse than the one that characterizes contemporary western democracies? To illustrate the great significance of this question it is sufficient to point out the heated controversy over campaign finance in the United States. Those who wish to restrict campaign finance point out the disproportional and distorting influence of large corporations on the political process.

These concerns are reminiscent of a familiar dilemma: either the democracy argument values the pure procedural aspects of democracy or it is grounded in other, nonprocedural considerations. If only procedure matters, one may justify the protection of the right to free speech, but it is unclear why such a procedure is so valuable. Alternatively it may be based on the conviction that reasoned deliberation has value either in itself or on the basis of the contribution of democratic procedures to the making of the right, correct or desirable decisions. In such a case, it is easier to justify the compelling appeal of the goal—the securing of institutions that are conducive to reasoned deliberation. It is, however, more difficult to establish why protecting speech is conducive to the realization of this goal. It is not necessarily the case that all forms of speech are conducive to reasoned deliberation.

An attempt to develop a new democratic justification for protecting speech can be found in the concept of "democratic culture" (Balkin 2004). Under this view, in the era of the Internet there is a practical opportunity to shift the meaning of democracy from the traditional understanding of democracy as concerned with the integrity of the democratic process to a broader and more diffused understanding of democracy as providing an equal opportunity to participate in the creation of culture. Freedom of speech "allows ordinary people to participate freely in the spread of ideas and in the creation of meanings that, in turn, help constitute them as persons" (Balkin 2004: 3). This understanding of the concept of democracy (equated with the equal opportunity to participate in culture creation) distances one from the more narrowly understood political meaning of the term "democracy"; it fits better the self-realization/self-growth/self-fulfillment argument analyzed above and is subject to the concerns raised there.

The Paradox of the Right to Free Speech: A Tentative Resolution

We have surveyed some of the most influential arguments favoring the protection of speech. While each one of the justifications has its strengths and weaknesses, they all are subject to a challenge that is quite familiar in the discourse of rights. Rights, it is often argued, are grounded in values, e.g., autonomy, self-realization, self-fulfillment. We have seen that most if not all justifications for free speech are grounded in such values. But if this is the case, why should we protect the rights rather than the values underlying the rights? For instance, if the protection of speech is grounded in autonomy, why do our constitutions and bills of rights protect speech rather than all autonomy-enhancing activities? Or if it is grounded in self-realization, why do we not protect all activities which are conducive to self-realization?

One natural answer is pragmatic. As the promotion of the values underlying rights is so manipulative and open to abuse, we need to make more particular rules that are designed to limit and constrain our institutions. In the context of free speech it is often argued that governments are untrustworthy and are particularly disposed to regulate speech for bad rather than good reasons (Barendt 2005: 21–23). Under this view, our rights (including the right to free speech) do not reflect an underlying moral reality, namely the particularly great value of the activities or goods protected by rights; they merely reflect institutional and pragmatic considerations. We protect the right to free speech (and not all autonomy-enhancing activities) because legislatures and executives are likely to restrict speech (but not other autonomy-enhancing activities) for the wrong reasons and in a wrong way.

Another suggestion to resolve the paradox is to identify values that can only be promoted by protecting the relevant right at stake. Thus, in the context of speech, Joshua Cohen tried to identify what he believes are distinctively expressive interests—interests which can be promoted only by protecting speech (Cohen 1993, 225–30). Yet the attempt to identify interests that are unique to expression is artificial. It seems that expression is tied up with values that can often be promoted not only by speech but also by other values. Thus for instance Cohen identifies the interest of addressing "a matter of political justice." But addressing such a matter can be achieved in ways other than speech, e.g., by participating in what one regards as one's civic duties.

The two attempts described above to resolve the paradox—the pragmatic defense and the claim that there are distinctively expressive values—fail. Fortunately there is an alternative view, under which the primary justification for protecting the right to free speech (rather than all autonomy-enhancing activities) is that the enhancement of autonomy depends on societal conventions of protecting certain practices for the sake of enhancing autonomy. In societies in which speech is protected for the sake of autonomy, people use speech in autonomy-enhancing ways. There is thus a close dependence between the values underlying rights and the activities protected by rights, such that protecting a defined set of activities for the sake of enhancing autonomy facilitates the exercise of autonomy. Promoting and reinforcing autonomy must take concrete form, i.e., it must be grounded in identifying and protecting activities that are autonomy enhancing. The values cannot be protected in abstract without delineating the activities whose protection is necessary for their realization. Identifying what the autonomy-enhancing activities are has an educational and constitutive role in facilitating the exercise of autonomy. Rights, including the right to free speech, are not redundant and the value of their protection is not reducible to the values underlying these rights (Harel

2005). Autonomy cannot even in principle be promoted without protecting certain well-defined autonomy-enhancing activities, e.g., speech.

Part III: Minoritarian Challenges

In recent years, the most effective theoretical challenges to the protection of speech have been minoritarian challenges based on the claim that pornography and hate speech directed against minority groups (such as racial minorities, sexual minorities) are detrimental to the vital interests of minorities. The challenges can be divided into two types: extrinsic concerns and intrinsic concerns. The former minoritarian concerns point out that protection of speech is often detrimental to (non-speech) vital conflicting interests or rights of minorities and that protecting effectively those interests or rights requires the censoring of some forms of speech. Thus it has been argued that protecting racist speech is detrimental to equality and that sometimes equality should override the free-speech concerns. The intrinsic concerns are based on a more nuanced understanding of what speech consists of; they are based on the view that a genuine protection of freedom of speech sometimes requires the imposition of limitations on speech as certain forms of speech silence minorities and prevent them from either being able to exercise their own right to free speech or prevent their speech from being heard. The forceful metaphor of "silencing" is often used to convey these claims and the conclusion is that freedom of speech itself is enhanced rather than curtailed by imposing some restrictions on speech.

Many of the minoritarian challenges were designed explicitly as practical challenges aimed at transforming the law and, in particular, the stringent protection granted to speech under the First Amendment of the U.S. Constitution. This practical concern is often detrimental to the philosophical concerns as minoritarian challenges are grounded in the need to address the doctrinal nuances of American constitutional law. Hence, they are not always congenial for the purposes of theoretical investigation. Yet some of the minoritarian challenges are philosophically important, as they expose some of the ambiguities concerning the scope and the meaning of the right to free speech as well as rights in general. What is the scope of speech and what forms of speech are also acts? Should the right to free speech be designed such that it maximizes the exercise of the right, i.e., protects and promotes an environment that is conducive to the exercise of such a right? Should it take into account distributive justice considerations, namely give priority to the speech of vulnerable groups whose speech is less often heard, at the expense of less vulnerable groups? Should it guarantee not only the right to free speech but also provide opportunities for the speech to be heard? As much of the sophisticated work addressing these issues has been done in the context of pornography, our examination will focus on this work. Yet the arguments are applicable to other forms of speech, e.g., racist speech. The following sections examine the claims that pornography is not (only) speech but (also) an act, and that pornography silences and, consequently, that regulating it promotes rather than curtails the protection of speech.

Is Pornography Speech?

Feminists have long argued that pornography reinforces and perpetuates violence, sexual harassment and discrimination against women. Yet this view does not distinguish pornography from other forms of protected speech that may contribute to violence and discrimination. To address this objection, Catherine MacKinnon and Andrea Dworkin maintain that pornography ought not to be classified (exclusively) as speech but (also or primarily) as an act (MacKinnon 1987: 148, 154; A. Dworkin 1991). Pornography does not simply depict subordination of women; it is an act of subordination! In their famous anti-pornography ordinance that was passed by the Indianapolis City Council in 1984 (but later overturned on appeal on the grounds that it violated the right to free speech of pornographers), pornography was defined as: "the graphic sexually explicit *subordination* of women in pictures or words." Sexually explicit materials need not necessarily subordinate and in fact they may even be congenial to gender equality. This definition differs from the traditional definition under which pornography is identified with sexually explicit materials or, more narrowly, as sexually explicit materials that are designed to produce sexual arousal. In fact, some feminists want to extend the definition of pornography even to materials that are not sexually explicit. These claims may raise the suspicion that the debate about pornography is merely semantic; the two camps simply use the term "pornography" to denote different things.

This suspicion is misleading. Some theorists maintain that sexually explicit materials (including materials that depict subordination of women) do not and in fact cannot subordinate. Under this view one ought to distinguish sharply between depictions of subordination (which may also perpetuate subordination) and acts of subordination, between fiction and reality. In his famous judgment striking down the Indianapolis ordinance, Judge Frank H. Easterbrook acknowledged that pornography depicts subordination of women and, furthermore, that such depictions "tend to perpetuate subordination" (*American Booksellers v. Hudnut* (1985) 771 F.2d 323 (7th Cir. 1985): 329). Yet it does not follow that pornography subordinates. The feminist challenge is to establish what it is in pornography that turns it from speech that simply depicts subordination and perpetuates it into speech that subordinates.

Feminist philosophers defended the claim that pornography is an act of subordination (and not merely depiction of subordination) by using the famous J. L. Austin speech act theory. Under this theory, words are often used not to depict (truly or falsely) some states of affairs but rather to perform acts in the world including warning, promising and marrying (Hornsby 1995: 223–25; Langton 2009: 27–28). Austin famously distinguished between three types of acts that can be performed by speech (speech acts): locutionary acts, perlocutionary acts and illocutionary acts. Locutionary acts are indeed mere descriptions. Perlocutionary acts are speech acts that change or affect the world, e.g., in the case of pornography it is claimed that pornography *causes* the perpetuation of subordination or discrimination. Illocutionary speech acts can do things in the world. Thus, for instance, the utterance "I promise to meet you for lunch" may under the proper circumstances constitute a promise and the declaration "I hereby pronounce you husband and wife" may under the proper circumstances constitute marriage.

Hornsby and Langton suggest that pornography is an illocutionary act of subordination. Precisely as the words "I promise" do not merely depict a promise but also (under the proper "felicity conditions") constitute the act of promising, so pornography is not merely a depiction of subordination but also an act that subordinates women. To support the claim, Langton (following MacKinnon) provides a list of other speech acts that subordinate, such as the utterance "whites only" uttered by an official in South Africa during the apartheid. Langton suggests that speech acts that subordinate fall into two categories of illocutionary acts labeled by Austin as verdictives and excertives. Verdictives include actions of ranking, valuing and placing, such as the utterance "You are the winner of the race" when uttered by an umpire in a race. Close relatives to verdictives are excertives, namely speech acts that order, permit, prohibit, authorize, etc. Pornography is an excertive because it is used to "rank women as sex objects." It is also a verdictive as it "sexualize[s] rape, battery, sexual harassment . . . and it thereby celebrates, promotes, authorizes and legitimizes sexual violence" (MacKinnon 1987: 173; Langton 2009: 40). MacKinnon further argues that: "Pornography *participates* in its audience's eroticism through creating an accessible sexual object, the possession and consumption of which *is* male sexuality, as socially constructed; to be consumed and possessed as which, *is* female sexuality, as socially constructed; pornography is a process that constructs it that way" (MacKinnon 1987: 173).

Hornsby and Langton's reconstruction of MacKinnon's argument is aimed at establishing the distinctive illocutionary features of pornography. One difficulty in this claim is that the mere fact that speech has illocutionary effects has very little normative relevance. It is possible that a perlocutionary pornographic speech will have much greater effects on subordination than an illocutionary act of subordination. Neither Hornsby nor Langton establish that a speech act that subordinates (illocutionary act) is more deserving of regulation than a speech act that merely causes subordination (perlocutionary act) even when the subordination resulting from the latter type of speech is not less significant or less hideous than the subordination resulting from the former. Further, legal systems which regulate speech do not focus on the regulation of illocutionary acts of subordination. The existing definitions of most speech offenses rely heavily on the intention/meaning tests (a definition which rests on locutionary acts such as hate speech) or the materialization of harm test (a definition that rests on the perlocutionary act, such as speech, that is likely to cause violence or lead to discrimination) rather than on the illocutionary aspect of the speech (Harel 2000). Under this objection, it does not matter whether speech results in subordination because it subordinates (or because it is an act of subordination) or whether it results in subordination by causing or perpetuating subordination in some other way (Harel 2011).

Furthermore, Langton believes that for pornography to constitute an act (either verdictive or excertive) it ought to be authoritative. What makes the statement "whites only" a speech act with illocutionary force is the fact that the person who utters it has authority over others. She believes that in many cases pornography has such authority as "the authors of pornographic speech are not mere bystanders to the game; they are speakers whose verdict counts" (Langton 2009: 44).

Yet it is hard to defend this position. First, even if pornography is authoritative it is unclear that it is authoritative *to the relevant audience*, namely women (Green 1998: 292–97). Furthermore, in order to maintain that pornography is authoritative, it is not sufficient that pornography causes men to believe that women consent to sex (or that women ought to consent). Instead it is necessary to establish that they believe women consent because they believe that pornography dictates or at least provides accurate information as to what is right and wrong, normal or deviant in sex. If this were true, the man for whom pornography is authoritative would say to the reluctant woman: "You ought to have sex with me *as I have learned from pornography* that it is deviant or abnormal for real women not to have sex with studs like me." Yet while pornography may trigger or cause such convictions among men, it is most unlikely that men would justify their beliefs or behavior by pointing out that this is the way sex is depicted in pornographic materials (Harel 2011). Pornography does not seem to have an authoritative force, as consumers of pornography do not perceive it as a manual instructing them what good or normal sex is. Perhaps one exception to this claim is the case of minors who may be led to believe that pornography provides information as to what "normal sex" is or how sex ought to be performed.

Does Pornography Silence?

MacKinnon also says that pornography "silences women." Hence, under her view, the anti-pornography legislation is grounded in the same values as the values underlying the protection of speech itself. Regulation of pornography is necessary to protect women's speech (MacKinnon 1987: 164).

There are different possible interpretations of this claim. First, the claim can be understood as suggesting that women are less likely to exercise their right to free speech as a result of pornography either because they are intimidated or because their inferior status in society (resulting from the prevalence of pornography) undermines their confidence and results in passivity. Second, the claim can be understood as suggesting that while women may exercise their right to free speech they are unlikely to be heard; their speech is silenced not in the sense that women fail to exercise their right to free speech but in the sense that their speech fails to persuade. Women fail to be full-fledged participants in the marketplace of ideas because women speakers are perceived to be of lesser public importance or significance. Third, as Langton argues, women may be silenced because their speech "misfires"; it fails to achieve the effects one aims to achieve by speaking. Langton describes this form of silencing as illocutionary silencing (Langton 2009: 48).

To illustrate what illocutionary silencing is, Langton uses the utterance "no" uttered by a woman. The utterance "no" is used "typically to disagree, to refuse, or to prohibit." Yet when uttered by a woman it often "does not count as the act of refusal." Under this view the silencing of women results in depriving women of the possibility to use the word "no" and more generally deprives women of the ability to refuse sexual encounters. While some feminists have emphasized that pornography often sexualizes refusal, Langton wants to maintain that pornography precludes the very possibility of refusal.

In attacking the first and the second interpretations of this claim, Ronald Dworkin has argued that the right to free speech does not include "a right to circumstances that encourage one to speak, and a right that others grasp and respect what one means to say." Under this view the right to free speech is a negative right designed to remove any state-induced barriers to speech, but it is not designed to provide favorable circumstances for speech or to guarantee a favorable audience (R. Dworkin 1996: 232).

Yet, as has been shown persuasively by rights theorists, Dworkin's view has some major disadvantages (Taylor 1985). After all, at least part of the value of the right to free speech is grounded in the fact that many people of different persuasions exercise such a right. If some forms of speech intimidate and humiliate in ways which curtail the exercise of the right to free speech, why should we not limit the right in ways that in the long run reinforce the willingness to engage in speech, i.e., exercise the right? Similarly, should not the state reinforce the willingness of men to hear what women have to say? And should not such considerations override the right of those who denigrate women and perhaps other minorities to exercise their right? If part of the value of protecting the right to free speech is grounded in the importance of exercising the right and also in the importance of having an opportunity to persuade and influence, then it does not seem that the scope of the right to free speech ought to ignore such considerations. Institutional concerns, in particular the concern of abuse, may limit our willingness to take such considerations into account. Yet in principle it seems that such considerations ought to influence the scope of the right to free speech. Furthermore, Ronald Dworkin fails to address the third silencing argument, namely illocutionary silencing. Depriving women of the capacity to refuse would, even under his view, constitute silencing, which justifies limitations on the free speech of pornographers (Langton 2009: 65–72).

While both the claim that pornography is an act and the claim that pornography silences are important contemporary challenges to the protection of speech, more radical challenges can be found in Marxist or neo-Marxist theories. We turn now to examine one such challenge.

Part IV: Repressive Tolerance

In a famous essay (which has overall been ignored by liberal theorists), Herbert Marcuse describes liberal tolerance as a repressive tool. In his view, tolerance is a tool for reinforcing passivity and legitimating a false consensus founded on ignorance of progressive alternatives and on systematic indoctrination. Furthermore, Marcuse argued:

> The tolerance which enlarged the range and content of freedom was always partisan—intolerant towards the protagonists of the repressive status quo. . . . In the firmly established liberal society of England and the United States, freedom of speech and assembly was granted even to the radical enemies of society, provided that they did not make the transition from word to deed, from speech to action.
>
> (Marcuse 1965)

Marcuse continues:

> The realization of liberty necessitates tolerance, but this tolerance cannot be indiscriminate and equal with respect to the contents of the expression, neither in word nor in deed; it cannot protect false words and wrong deeds which demonstrate that they contradict and counteract the possibilities of liberation. . . . Society cannot be indiscriminate where the pacification of existence, where freedom and happiness themselves are at stake: here certain things cannot be said, certain ideas cannot be expressed, certain policies cannot be proposed, certain behavior cannot be permitted without making tolerance an instrument for the continuation of servitude.
>
> (Marcuse 1965)

Being a political activist, Marcuse often resorts to political rhetoric and, yet, his concerns are real. First, Marcuse is concerned that neutral tolerance blurs the fact that there is an objective truth to be discovered. The authentic liberal rationale for protection of speech—the search for truth—is lost when the idea that there is truth is eroded as a result of blurring the difference between truth and falsehood. Second, the liberal freedoms give a false sense that society is free and that any change would develop gradually and normally. Yet if the sense of freedom is indoctrinated it serves to repress the search for real alternatives and pacifies resistance. The freedoms are used to manipulate and indoctrinate individuals "for whom heteronomy has become autonomy." Third, the language of public discourse has degenerated such that it forecloses real public deliberation. For instance, the leveling of all news, e.g., the fact that a "newscaster reports the torture and murder of civil rights workers in the same unemotional tone with which he says his commercials" blurs the distinctions between what is significant and insignificant; between important and unimportant. Fourth, to free individuals from current indoctrination "the trend would have to be reversed; they would have to get information slanted in the opposite direction." As truth is never given in a non-mediated way—it is always mediated by those who present it—it is necessary to undo the appearances which in our society are marked as truth (rather than truisms). Marcuse does not hesitate to suggest limiting the freedoms of "groups and movements which promote aggressive policies, armament, chauvinism, discrimination on the grounds of race and religion, or which oppose the extension of public services." Liberal tolerance will mean, therefore, regulating speech that is regressive and promoting and privileging speech that is liberating. This is necessary as current liberal democracies are repressive and the continuing repression, although subtle, constitutes a "clear and present danger" (Marcuse 1965).

The radicalism of Marcuse's view is echoed in more contemporary radical critics of current liberal regimes (Chomsky 1994, ch. 9). Yet one need not be a radical to see the significance of the observations made by Marcuse. The more concrete and specific (and therefore more politically efficacious) minoritarian critiques of the protection of speech can all be regarded as applied efforts to implement Marcuse's more radical recommendations. In fact, the seeds of Marcuse's critique can already be found in the liberal tradition itself. As Marcuse rightly pointed out, Mill advocated the protection of speech on the grounds that such a protection is liberating, and he acknowledged that the conditions for liberation do not apply everywhere. Perhaps the difference between the radicalism of Marcuse and the moderation of contemporary liberals is not in their readiness to promote genuine liberation (by whatever means) but merely in disagreement as to whether our society has indeed arrived at the stage in which protection of speech and tolerance is genuinely liberating. For tolerance and freedom of speech to be liberating, individuals ought to reach a degree of deliberative-critical powers; they ought to be capable of resisting the seductive powers of an overly commercial public sphere and to acquire powers of reasoning. It is debatable whether our society has ever reached this stage, or, if it had reached it, whether it has been lost.

Part V: Summary

We have completed a full circle. We started by analyzing the traditional rationales for free speech: marketplace of ideas, autonomy, self-realization and the democracy argument. We pointed out a paradox in the discourse of rights—the paradox of the differential treatment of activities. If what underlies the protection of speech is autonomy or self-realization, why should we protect speech rather than protect these values? Do we not fetishize speech by protecting it rather than protecting the values underlying it? We suggested that perhaps the protection of autonomy depends on societal conventions of protecting certain practices for the sake of enhancing autonomy. There is thus a close dependence between the values underlying rights and the activities protected by rights, such that protecting a defined set of activities for the sake of enhancing autonomy facilitates the identification and realization of autonomy. We turned to explore the contemporary minoritarian critiques of the free-speech protection. We have shown the complexity of the right to free speech by establishing that it is unclear what the boundary between speech and act is and it is unclear what forms of speech are truly liberating and what forms silence. Last, we turned to Marcuse's radical critique of repressive tolerance. We found that while in some respects this is indeed a radical critique, it is founded on the very same values and sensitivities of traditional liberals: autonomy, liberation, self-realization, etc. The great task of liberal democracies is not to protect speech as such in a mechanical manner but to create and sustain the preconditions for speech to be genuinely autonomy enhancing and liberating. This ideal is shared by liberals, their minoritarian critics and their most radical critics.

References

Abrams v. United States (1919) 250 U.S. 616.
American Booksellers v. Hudnut (1985) 771 F.2d 323 (7th Cir. 1985).
Baker, C. E. (1982) *Human Liberty and Freedom of Speech*, New York: Oxford University Press.
Balkin, J. (2004) "Digital Speech and Democratic Culture: A Theory of Freedom of Expression for the Information Society," 79 *New York University Law Review*: 1–55.
Barendt, E. (2005) *Freedom of Speech*, 2nd edition, Oxford: Oxford University Press.
Briston, S. (1998) "The Autonomy Defense of Free Speech," 108 *Ethics*: 312–39.
Chomsky, N. (1994) *Secrets, Lies and Democracy*, Tucson, AZ: Odonian Press.
Coase, R. H. (1974) "The Market for Goods and the Market for Ideas," 64 *The American Economic Review*: 384–91.
____ (1977) "Advertising and Free Speech," 6 *The Journal of Legal Studies*: 1–34.
Cohen, J. (1993) "Freedom of Expression," *Philosophy and Public Affairs*: 207–63.
Dworkin, A. (1991) *Pornography: Men Possessing Women*, New York: Plume.
Dworkin, R. (1996) "MacKinnon's Words," in *Freedom's Law: The Moral Reading of the American Constitution*, Cambridge, Mass: Harvard University Press, p. 214.
Green, L. (1998) "Pornographizing, Subordination, and Silencing," in R. Post, ed., *Censorship and Silencing: Practices of Cultural Regulation*, Los Angeles: Getty Research Institute, pp. 285–311.
Greenawalt, K. (1989a) *Speech, Crime, and the Uses of Language*, New York: Oxford University Press.
____ (1989b) "Free Speech Justifications," 89 *Columbia Law Review*: 119–55.
Harel, A. (2000) "The Regulation of Speech: A Normative Investigation of Criminal Law Prohibitions of Speech," in D. Kretzmer and F. Kershman Hazan, eds., *Freedom of Speech and Incitement Against Democracy*, The Hague, Netherlands: Kluwer Law International, pp. 247–74.
____ (2005) "Theories of Rights," in M. P. Golding and W. A. Edmundson, eds., *The Blackwell Guide to Philosophy of Law and Legal Theory*, Malden, Mass.: Blackwell Publishing, pp. 191–206.
____ (2011) "Is Pornography a Speech Act and Does It Matter?" *Jerusalem Review of Legal Studies* 3(5).
Hornsby, J. (1995) "Speech Acts and Pornography," in S. Dwyer, ed., *The Problem of Pornography*, Belmont, CA: Wadsworth Publishing, pp. 220–32.
Ingber, S. (1984) "The Marketplace of Ideas: A Legitimizing Myth," *Duke Law Journal*: 1–91.
Langton, R. (2009) "Speech Acts and Unspeakable Acts," in R. Langton, *Sexual Solipsism: Philosophical Essays on Pornography and Objectification*, Oxford: Oxford University Press, pp. 25–63.
MacKinnon, C. (1987) *Feminism Unmodified: Discourses on Life and Law*, Cambridge, Mass.: Harvard University Press.
Marcuse, H. (1965) "Repressive Tolerance," in R. P. Wolff, B. Moore, Jr. and H. Marcuse, *A Critique of Pure Tolerance*, Boston: Beacon Press, pp. 95–137.
Meiklejohn, A. (1948) *Free Speech and Its Relation to Self-Government*, New York: Harper & Brothers Publishers.
Mill, J. S. (1859) *On Liberty*, London: Parker and Son.
Milton, J. (1644) *Areopagitica: A Speech of Mr. John Milton for the Liberty of Unlicensed Printing to the Parliament of England*.
Nagel, T. (1995) "Personal Rights and Public Space," 24 *Philosophy and Public Affairs*: 83–107.
Raz, J. (1995) "Free Expression and Personal Identification," in J. Raz, *Ethics in the Public Domain: Essays in the Morality of Law and Politics*, Oxford: Clarendon Press, pp. 146–69.
Scanlon, T. (1972) "A Theory of Freedom of Expression," 1 *Philosophy and Public Affairs*: 204–26.
____ (1979) "Freedom of Expression and Categories of Expression," 40 *University of Pittsburgh Law Review*: 519–50.
Schauer, F. (1982) *Free Speech: A Philosophical Enquiry*, Cambridge: Cambridge University Press.
Schenck v. United States (1919) 249 U.S. 47.
Sen, A. (1999) *Development as Freedom*, New York: Knopf.

Taylor, C. (1985) "Atomism," in C. Taylor, *Philosophical Papers Volume II: Philosophy and the Human Sciences*, Cambridge: Cambridge University Press, pp. 187–209.

Further Reading

For further reading, see: L. Alexander (2005) *Is There a Right to Freedom of Expression?*, Cambridge: Cambridge University Press; S. Dwyer, ed. (1995) *The Problem of Pornography*, Belmont, CA: Wadsworth Publishing; C. MacKinnon (1987) *Feminism Unmodified: Discourses on Life and Law*, Cambridge, Mass.: Harvard University Press, part III; H. Marcuse (1965) "Repressive Tolerance," in R. P. Wolff, B. Moore, Jr. and H. Marcuse, *A Critique of Pure Tolerance*, Boston: Beacon Press, pp. 95–137; J. S. Mill (1859) *On Liberty*, ch. II; T. Nagel (1995) "Personal Rights and Public Space," 24 *Philosophy and Public Affairs*: 83–107; J. Raz (1995) "Free Expression and Personal Identification," in J. Raz, *Ethics in the Public Domain: Essays in the Morality of Law and Politics*, Oxford: Clarendon Press, pp. 146–69; T. Scanlon (1972) "A Theory of Freedom of Expression," 1 *Philosophy and Public Affairs*: 204–26; and F. Schauer (1982) *Free Speech: A Philosophical Enquiry*, Cambridge: Cambridge University Press.

INDEX

INDEX

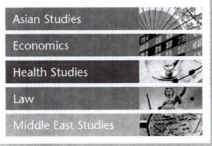